collections

Houghton
Mifflin
Harcourt

collections

GRADE 9

Program Consultants:

Kylene Beers

Martha Hougen

Carol Jago

William L. McBride

Erik Palmer

Lydia Stack

About Our
Program Consultants

Kylene Beers Nationally known lecturer and author on reading and literacy; 2011 recipient of the Conference on English Leadership Exemplary Leader Award; coauthor of *Notice and Note: Strategies for Close Reading*; former president of the National Council of Teachers of English. Dr. Beers is the nationally known author of *When Kids Can't Read: What Teachers Can Do* and coeditor of *Adolescent Literacy: Turning Promise into Practice*, as well as articles in the *Journal of Adolescent and Adult Literacy*. Former editor of *Voices from the Middle*, she is the 2001 recipient of NCTE's Richard W. Halley Award, given for outstanding contributions to middle-school literacy. She recently served as Senior Reading Researcher at the Comer School Development Program at Yale University as well as Senior Reading Advisor to Secondary Schools for the Reading and Writing Project at Teachers College.

Martha Hougen National consultant, presenter, researcher, and author. Areas of expertise include differentiating instruction for students with learning difficulties, including those with learning disabilities and dyslexia; and teacher and leader preparation improvement. Dr. Hougen has taught at the middle school through graduate levels. Recently her focus has been on working with teacher educators to enhance teacher and leader preparation to better meet the needs of all students. Currently she is working with the University of Florida at the Collaboration for Effective Educator Development, Accountability, and Reform Center (CEEDAR Center) to improve the achievement of students with disabilities by reforming teacher and leader licensure, evaluation, and preparation. She has led similar efforts in Texas with the Higher Education Collaborative and the College & Career Readiness Initiative Faculty Collaboratives. In addition to peer-reviewed articles, curricular documents, and presentations, Dr. Hougen has published two college textbooks: *The Fundamentals of Literacy Assessment and Instruction Pre-K–6* (2012) and *The Fundamentals of Literacy Assessment and Instruction 6–12* (2014).

Carol Jago Teacher of English with 32 years of experience at Santa Monica High School in California; author and nationally known lecturer; and former president of the National Council of Teachers of English. Currently serves as Associate Director of the California Reading and Literature Project at UCLA. With expertise in standards assessment and secondary education, Ms. Jago is the author of numerous books on education, including *With Rigor for All* and *Papers, Papers, Papers*, and is active with the California Association of Teachers of English, editing its scholarly journal *California English* since 1996. Ms. Jago also served on the planning committee for the 2009 NAEP Framework and the 2011 NAEP Writing Framework.

William L. McBride Curriculum specialist. Dr. McBride is a nationally known speaker, educator, and author who now trains teachers in instructional methodologies. He is coauthor of *What's Happening?*, an innovative, high-interest text for middle-grade readers, and author of *If They Can Argue Well, They Can Write Well*. A former reading specialist, English teacher, and social studies teacher, he holds a master's degree in reading and a doctorate in curriculum and instruction from the University of North Carolina at Chapel Hill. Dr. McBride has contributed to the development of textbook series in language arts, social studies, science, and vocabulary. He is also known for his novel *Entertaining an Elephant*, which tells the story of a veteran teacher who becomes reinspired with both his profession and his life.

Erik Palmer Veteran teacher and education consultant based in Denver, Colorado. Author of *Well Spoken: Teaching Speaking to All Students* and *Digitally Speaking: How to Improve Student Presentations*. His areas of focus include improving oral communication, promoting technology in classroom presentations, and updating instruction through the use of digital tools. He holds a bachelor's degree from Oberlin College and a master's degree in curriculum and instruction from the University of Colorado.

Lydia Stack Internationally known teacher educator and author. She is involved in a Stanford University project to support English Language Learners, *Understanding Language*. The goal of this project is to enrich academic content and language instruction for English Language Learners (ELLs) in grades K-12 by making explicit the language and literacy skills necessary to meet state standards and Next Generation Science Standards. Her teaching experience includes twenty-five years as an elementary and high school ESL teacher, and she is a past president of Teachers of English to Speakers of Other Languages (TESOL). Her awards include the TESOL James E. Alatis Award and the San Francisco STAR Teacher Award. Her publications include *On Our Way to English, Visions: Language, Literature, Content,* and *American Themes*, a literature anthology for high school students in the ACCESS program of the U.S. State Department's Office of English Language Programs.

Additional thanks to the following Program Reviewers

Rosemary Asquino
Sylvia B. Bennett
Yvonne Bradley
Leslie Brown
Haley Carroll
Caitlin Chalmers
Emily Colley-King
Stacy Collins
Denise DeBonis
Courtney Dickerson
Sarah Easley
Phyllis J. Everette
Peter J. Foy Sr.

Carol M. Gibby
Angie Gill
Mary K. Goff
Saira Haas
Lisa M. Janeway
Robert V. Kidd Jr.
Kim Lilley
John C. Lowe
Taryn Curtis MacGee
Meredith S. Maddox
Cynthia Martin
Kelli M. McDonough
Megan Pankiewicz

Linda Beck Pieplow
Molly Pieplow
Mary-Sarah Proctor
Jessica A. Stith
Peter Swartley
Pamela Thomas
Linda A. Tobias
Rachel Ukleja
Lauren Vint
Heather Lynn York
Leigh Ann Zerr

Finding Common Ground

KEY LEARNING OBJECTIVES

Cite text evidence.
Support inferences about theme.
Analyze author's choices about structure.
Analyze representations in different mediums.
Determine central idea.

Analyze and evaluate author's claim.
Analyze author's purpose and rhetoric.
Delineate and evaluate an argument.
Analyze seminal U.S. documents.

Close Reader

eBook *Explore It!*

 Video Links | **eBook** *Read On!* Novel list and additional selections | **Visit hmhfyi.com** for current articles and informational texts.

The Struggle for Freedom

KEY
LEARNING
OBJECTIVES

Analyze author's choices about style and
   structure.
Analyze author's point of view and cultural
   background.
Analyze how an author unfolds events.
Analyze connections between ideas and events.

Analyze impact of word choice on tone.
Determine author's point of view.
Analyze author's use of rhetoric.
Analyze accounts in different mediums.
Analyze seminal U.S. documents.

Close Reader

SPEECH
A Eulogy for Dr. Martin Luther King Jr.   Robert F. Kennedy

SHORT STORY
The Prisoner Who Wore Glasses   Bessie Head

eBook *Explore It!*

 Video Links   **eBook** *Read On!* Novel list and additional selections   **Visit hmhfyi.com** for current articles and informational texts.

The Bonds Between Us

KEY LEARNING OBJECTIVES

Cite text evidence.
Support inferences about theme.
Analyze character and theme.
Interpret figurative language.
Analyze the impact of word choice on tone.
Analyze author's point of view and cultural background.

Analyze ideas in informational text.
Analyze the purpose and development of ideas in media.
Determine technical meanings of words.
Analyze and evaluate author's claims.

Close Reader

eBook *Explore It!*

▶ **Video Links**   **eBook** *Read On!*
Novel list and additional selections

 Visit hmhfyi.com for current articles and informational texts.

Image Credits: ©Carlos Sanchez Pereyra/Alamy Images

COLLECTION 4
Sweet Sorrow

KEY LEARNING OBJECTIVES	Analyze character motivations.	Analyze interpretations of Shakespeare.
	Analyze parallel plots.	Determine word meanings.
	Analyze point of view.	Analyze ideas presented in an essay.
	Analyze source material.	

Close Reader

DRAMA

from The Tragedy of Romeo and Juliet:
   Prologue
   Act II. Scene 2

William Shakespeare

eBook *Explore It!*

 Video Links

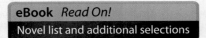 **eBook** *Read On!*
Novel list and additional selections

 Visit hmhfyi.com
for current articles and
informational texts.

COLLECTION 5

A Matter of Life or Death

KEY LEARNING OBJECTIVES

Support inferences about theme.
Determine figurative meanings and tone.
Analyze effects of author's choices about structure.
Determine central idea of a text.

Summarize the text.
Analyze ideas and events presented in a text.
Analyze impact of word choice on tone.
Analyze author's purpose and use of rhetoric.
Delineate and evaluate an argument.

Close Reader

eBook *Explore It!*

 Video Links

eBook *Read On!*
Novel list and additional selections

 Visit hmhfyi.com for current articles and informational texts.

Image Credits: ©The Asahi Shimbun/Getty Images

Heroes and Quests

KEY LEARNING OBJECTIVES	
Analyze character.	Cite text evidence.
Analyze epic poems.	Determine central idea of a text.
Analyze figurative meanings.	Analyze ideas and events presented in a text.
Interpret figurative language.	Delineate and evaluate an argument.

Close Reader

EPIC POEM
from the Odyssey:
   from The Cyclops   Homer, *translated by* Robert Fitzgerald

NONFICTION
from The Good Soldiers   David Finkel

Image Credits: ©Oliver Burston/Ikon Images/Getty Images

eBook *Explore It!*

 Video Links   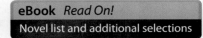 **eBook** *Read On!* Novel list and additional selections   **Visit hmhfyi.com** for current articles and informational texts.

Student Resources

Connecting to Your World

Every time you read something, view something, write to someone, or react to what you've read or seen, you're participating in a world of ideas. You do this every day, inside the classroom and out. These skills will serve you not only at home and at school, but eventually (if you can think that far ahead!), in your career.

The digital tools in this program will tap into the skills you already use and help you sharpen those skills for the future.

Start your exploration at my.hrw.com

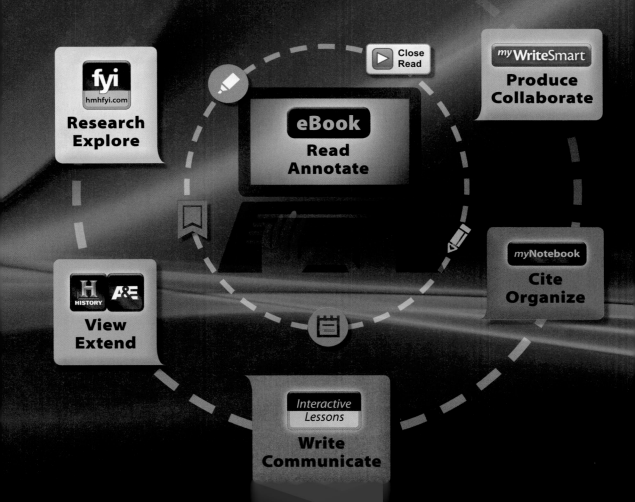

Writing and Speaking & Listening

Communication in today's world requires quite a variety of skills. To express yourself and win people over, you have to be able to write for print, for online media, and for spoken presentations. To collaborate, you have to work with people who might be sitting right next to you or at the other end of an Internet connection.

Available Only in Your eBook

Interactive Lessons

The interactive lessons in these collections will help you master the skills needed to become an expert communicator.

What Does a Strong Argument Look Like?

Read this argument and answer the questions about how the writer states and supports his position.

Tip

Pitching Perfect Pitch
by José Alvarez

Did you know that when you are listening to your favorite vocalist, you might be hearing a computer-generated pitch? Many record companies use pitch-correction software to ensure that their performers are pitch-perfect. While perfectionism is an admirable goal, there is a fine line between using technology to enhance music and using it to make performers into something they're not. Whether recording in the studio or playing a live performance, musicians should not use pitch-correction software. ●

Music production has become a digital experience. Producers use software to cut and paste pieces of music together, just like you cut and paste words together in your word-processing software. ○ When editing these different things together digitally, slight imperfections can occur where the pieces are joined. Enter the correction software. What began as a method to streamline the digital editing process has turned into an almost industry-wide standard of altering a musician"s work. "Think of it like plastic surgery," says a Grammy-winning recording engineer.

What is the writer's position, or **claim**, on the use of pitch-correction software?

- [ ] Musicians should learn to live with their imperfections.
- [✓] Musicians should never use the software.
- [ ] Musicians should use the software to enhance live performances only.

Writing Arguments

Master the art of proving your point.

Interactive Lessons

1. Introduction
2. What Is a Claim?
3. Support: Reasons and Evidence
4. Building Effective Support
5. Creating a Coherent Argument
6. Persuasive Techniques
7. Formal Style
8. Concluding Your Argument

Writing Informative Texts

Shed light on complex ideas and topics.

Interactive Lessons

1. Introduction
2. Developing a Topic
3. Organizing Ideas
4. Introductions and Conclusions
5. Elaboration
6. Using Graphics and Multimedia
7. Precise Language and Vocabulary
8. Formal Style

Writing Narratives

A good storyteller can always capture an audience.

Interactive Lessons

1. Introduction
2. Narrative Context
3. Point of View and Characters
4. Narrative Structure
5. Narrative Techniques
6. The Language of Narrative

Writing as a Process

Get from the first twinkle of an idea to a sparkling final draft.

Interactive Lessons	1. Introduction	4. Revising and Editing
	2. Task, Purpose, and Audience	5. Trying a New Approach
	3. Planning and Drafting	

Producing and Publishing with Technology

Learn how to write for an online audience.

Interactive Lessons	1. Introduction	3. Interacting with Your Online Audience
	2. Writing for the Internet	4. Using Technology to Collaborate

Conducting Research

There's a world of information out there. How do you find it?

Interactive Lessons	1. Introduction	5. Conducting Field Research
	2. Starting Your Research	6. Using the Internet for Research
	3. Types of Sources	7. Taking Notes
	4. Using the Library for Research	8. Refocusing Your Inquiry

Evaluating Sources

Approach all sources with a critical eye.

Using Textual Evidence

Put your research into writing.

Participating in Collaborative Discussions

There's power in putting your heads together.

Analyzing and Evaluating Presentations

**Is there substance
behind the style?**

Giving a Presentation

**Learn how to talk to a roomful
of people.**

Using Media in a Presentation

**If a picture is worth a thousand words,
just think what you can do with a video.**

Supporting
Close Reading,
Research, and Writing

Understanding complex texts is hard work, even for experienced readers. It often takes multiple close readings to understand and write about an author's choices and meanings. The dynamic digital tools in this program will give you opportunities to learn and practice this critical skill of close reading—and help you integrate the text evidence you find into your writing.

Learn How to Do a Close Read

An effective close read is all about the details; you have to examine the language and ideas a writer includes. See how it's done by accessing the **Close Read Screencasts** in your eBook. Hear modeled conversations about anchor texts.

of the birds, how they soared and glided overhead. He pointed out the slow, graceful sweep of their wings as they beat the air steadily, without fluttering. Soon Icarus was sure that he, too, could fly and, raising his arms up and down, skirted over the white sand and even out over the waves, letting his feet touch the snowy foam as the water thundered and broke over the sharp rocks. Daedalus watched him proudly but

Soon Icarus was sure that he, too, could fly and, raising his arms up and down, skirted over the white sand and even out over the waves, letting his feet touch the snowy foam as the water thundered and broke over the sharp rocks.

There might be a sense of danger here.

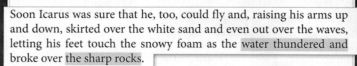

Daedalus watched him proudly but with misgivings. He called Icarus to his side and, putting his arm round the boy's shoulders, said, 'Icarus, my son, we are about to make our flight. No human being has ever traveled through the air before, and I want you to listen carefully to my instructions.

Annotate the Texts

Practice close reading by utilizing the powerful annotation tools in your eBook. Mark up key ideas and observations using highlighters and sticky notes.

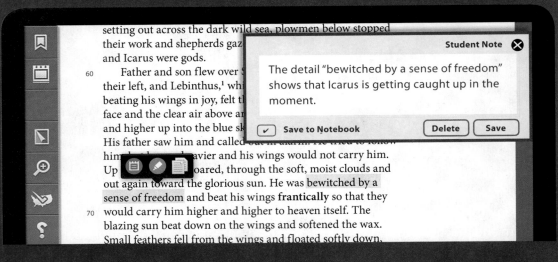

setting out across the dark wild sea, plowmen below stopped
their work and shepherds gaz
and Icarus were gods.

60   Father and son flew over
their left, and Lebinthus,¹ whi
beating his wings in joy, felt t
face and the clear air above ar
and higher up into the blue sk
His father saw him and called
him
Up   oared, through the soft, moist clouds and
out again toward the glorious sun. He was bewitched by a
sense of freedom and beat his wings **frantically** so that they
70   would carry him higher and higher to heaven itself. The
blazing sun beat down on the wings and softened the wax.
Small feathers fell from the wings and floated softly down.

Student Note

The detail "bewitched by a sense of freedom" shows that Icarus is getting caught up in the moment.

☑ Save to Notebook   Delete   Save

Collect Text Evidence

*my*Notebook

Save your annotations to your notebook. Gathering and organizing this text evidence will help you complete performance tasks and other writing assignments.

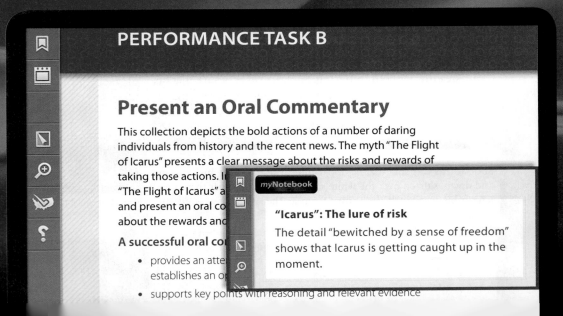

PERFORMANCE TASK B

Present an Oral Commentary

This collection depicts the bold actions of a number of daring individuals from history and the recent news. The myth "The Flight of Icarus" presents a clear message about the risks and rewards of taking those actions. I
"The Flight of Icarus" a
and present an oral co
about the rewards and

A successful oral co

• provides an atte
  establishes an o

• supports key points with reasoning and relevant evidence

*my*Notebook

"Icarus": The lure of risk

The detail "bewitched by a sense of freedom" shows that Icarus is getting caught up in the moment.

Find More Text Evidence on the Web

Tap into the *FYI* website for links to high-interest informational texts about collection topics. Capture text evidence from any Web source by including it in your notebook.

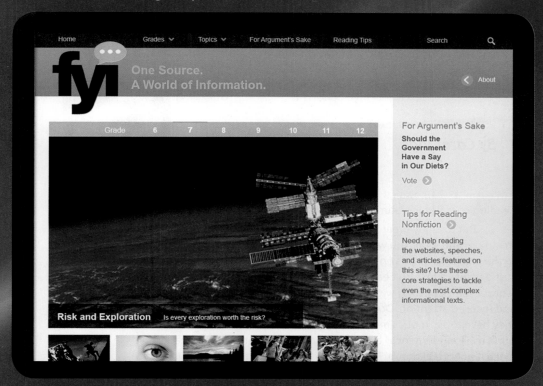

Integrate Text Evidence into Your Writing

Use the evidence you've gathered to formulate interpretations, draw conclusions, and offer insights. Integrate the best of your text evidence into your writing.

Navigating Complex Texts

By Carol Jago

Reading complex literature and nonfiction doesn't need to be painful.

But to enjoy great poetry and prose you are going to have to do more than skim and scan. You will need to develop the habit of paying attention to the particular words on the page closely, systematically, even lovingly. Just because a text isn't easy doesn't mean there is something wrong with it or something wrong with you. Understanding complex text takes effort and focused attention. Do you sometimes wish writers would just say what they have to say more simply or with fewer words? I assure you that writers don't use long sentences and unfamiliar words to annoy their readers or make readers feel dumb. They employ complex syntax and rich language because they have complex ideas about complex issues that they want to communicate. Simple language and structures just aren't up to the task.

Excellent literature and nonfiction—the kind you will be reading over the course of the year—challenge readers in many ways. Sometimes the background of a story or the content of an essay is so unfamiliar that it can be difficult to understand why characters are behaving as they do or to follow the argument a writer is making. By persevering—reading like a detective and following clues in the text—you will find that your store of background knowledge grows. As a result, the next time you read about this subject, the text won't seem nearly as hard. Navigating a terrain you have been over once before never seems quite as rugged the second time through. The more you read, the better reader you become.

Good readers aren't scared off by challenging text. When the going gets rough, they know what to do. Let's take vocabulary, a common measure of text complexity, as an example. Learning new words is the business of a lifetime. Rather than shutting down when you meet a word you don't know, take a moment to think about the word. Is any part of the word familiar to you? Is there something in the context of the sentence or paragraph that can help you figure out its meaning? Is there someone or something that can provide you with a definition? When we read literature or nonfiction from a time period other than our own, the text is often full of words we don't know.

Each time you meet those words in succeeding readings you will be adding to your understanding of the word and its use. Your brain is a natural word-learning machine. The more you feed it complex text, the larger vocabulary you'll have and as a result, the easier navigating the next book will be.

Have you ever been reading a long, complicated sentence and discovered that by the time you reached the end you had forgotten the beginning? Unlike the sentences we speak or dash off in a note to a friend, complex text is often full of sentences that are not only lengthy but also constructed in intricate ways. Such sentences require readers to slow down and figure out how phrases relate to one another as well as who is doing what to whom. Remember, rereading isn't cheating. It is exactly what experienced readers know to do when they meet dense text on the page. On the pages that follow you will find stories and articles that challenge you at a sentence level. Don't be intimidated. By paying careful attention to how those sentences are constructed, you will see their meanings unfold before your eyes.

Another way text can be complex is in terms of the density of ideas. Sometimes a writer piles on so much information that you find even if your eyes continue to move down the page, your brain has stopped taking in anything. At times like this, turning to a peer and discussing particular lines or concepts can help you pay closer attention and begin to unpack the text. Sharing questions and ideas, exploring a difficult passage together, makes it possible to tease out the meaning of even the most difficult text.

> **"Your brain is a natural word-learning machine. The more you feed it complex text, the larger vocabulary you'll have."**

Poetry is by its nature particularly dense and for that reason poses particular challenges for casual readers. Don't ever assume that once through a poem is enough. Often, a seemingly simple poem in terms of word choice and length—for example an Emily Dickinson, Mary Oliver, or W.H. Auden poem—expresses extremely complex feelings and insights. Poets also often make reference to mythological and Biblical allusions which contemporary readers are not always familiar with. Skipping over such references robs your reading of the richness the poet intended. Look up that bird. Check out the note on the page. Ask your teacher.

You will notice a range of complexity within each collection of readings. This spectrum reflects the range of texts that surround us: some easy, some hard, some seemingly easy but hard, some seemingly hard but easy. Navigating this sea of texts should stretch you as a reader and a thinker. How could it be otherwise when your journey is in the realms of gold? Please accept this invitation to an intellectual voyage I think you will enjoy.

Finding Common Ground

❝ We may have different religions, different languages, different colored skin, but we all belong to one human race. ❞

—Kofi Annan

Finding Common Ground

The focus of this collection is the individual and society—from the individual's struggle to be a part of a society to a nation's struggle to unite for a common cause.

hmhfyi.com

COLLECTION

PERFORMANCE TASK Preview

At the end of this collection, you will have the opportunity to complete two tasks:

• Plan and deliver a speech about how people can learn to live together.

• Write an essay discussing how symbols or images can convey ideas about the individual's role in society.

ACADEMIC VOCABULARY

Study the words and their definitions in the chart below. You will use these words as you discuss and write about the texts in this collection.

Word	Definition	Related Forms
enforce (ĕn-fôrs´) *tr v.*	to compel observance of or obedience to	enforceable, enforcer, enforcement
entity (ĕn´ tĭ-tē) *n.*	a thing that exists as a unit	entities
internal (ĭn-tûr´nəl) *adj.*	inner; located within something or someone	internality, internally
presume (prĭ-zoōm´) *v.*	to take for granted as being true; to assume something is true	presumably, presumption, presumed
resolve (rĭ-zŏlv´) *v.*	to decide or become determined	resolution, resolvable

Background *Author* **Anna Quindlen** *(b. 1953) was born in Philadelphia. She is a columnist and author who has been described as having a "common touch" because so many people relate to her writings about politics and gender-specific issues. In 1992, she became the third woman to win a Pulitzer Prize for commentary. "A Quilt of a Country" was published after the World Trade Center attacks of September 11, 2001. The argument was written at a time when many people were thinking about what it means to be an American.*

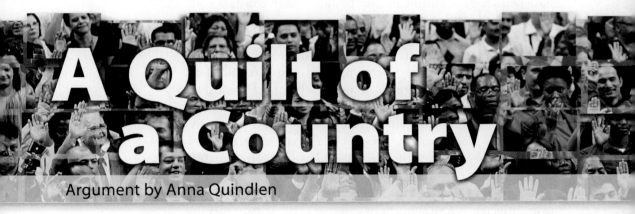

A Quilt of a Country

Argument by Anna Quindlen

AS YOU READ Pay attention to how the details in the text support the idea of America as "an improbable idea." Write down any questions you generate during reading.

America is an improbable idea. A mongrel[1] nation built of ever-changing disparate[2] parts, it is held together by a notion, the notion that all men are created equal, though everyone knows that most men consider themselves better than someone. "Of all the nations in the world, the United States was built in nobody's image," the historian Daniel Boorstin wrote. That's because it was built of bits and pieces that seem **discordant,** like the crazy quilts that have been one of its great folk-art forms, velvet and calico and checks and brocades. Out of many, one. That is the ideal.

10   The reality is often quite different, a great national striving consisting frequently of failure. Many of the oft-told stories of the most **pluralistic** nation on earth are stories not of tolerance, but of bigotry. Slavery and sweatshops, the burning of crosses

discordant
(dĭ-skôr´dnt) *adj.*
conflicting or not harmonious.

pluralistic
(plŏŏr´ə-lĭs´tĭc) *adj.*
consisting of many ethnic and cultural groups.

---

[1] **mongrel:** something produced by mixing different breeds.
[2] **disparate:** distinct or not alike.

and the ostracism[3] of the other. Children learn in social-studies class and in the news of the lynching of blacks, the denial of rights to women, the murders of gay men. It is difficult to know how to convince them that this amounts to "crown thy good with brotherhood," that amid all the failures is something spectacularly successful. Perhaps they understand it at this

20 moment, when enormous tragedy, as it so often does, demands a time of reflection on enormous blessings.

This is a nation founded on a conundrum,[4] what Mario Cuomo[5] has characterized as "community added to individualism." These two are our defining ideals; they are also in constant conflict. Historians today bemoan the ascendancy of a kind of prideful apartheid[6] in America, saying that the clinging to ethnicity, in background and custom, has undermined the concept of unity. These historians must have forgotten the past, or have gilded it. The New York of my children is no more Balkanized,[7] probably

30 less so, than the Philadelphia of my father, in which Jewish boys would walk several blocks out of their way to avoid the Irish divide of Chester Avenue. (I was the product of a mixed marriage, across barely bridgeable lines: an Italian girl, an Irish boy. How quaint it seems now, how incendiary then.) The Brooklyn of Francie Nolan's famous tree, the Newark of which Portnoy complained, even the uninflected WASP suburbs of Cheever's characters:[8] they are ghettos, pure and simple. Do the Cambodians and the Mexicans in California coexist less easily today than did the Irish and Italians of Massachusetts a century ago? You know the answer.

40 What is the point of this splintered whole? What is the point of a nation in which Arab cabbies chauffeur Jewish passengers through the streets of New York—and in which Jewish cabbies chauffeur Arab passengers, too, and yet speak in theory of hatred, one for the other? What is the point of a nation in which one part seems to be always on the verge of fisticuffs with another, blacks and whites, gays and straights, left and right, Pole and Chinese and Puerto Rican and Slovenian? Other countries with such divisions have in fact divided into new nations with new names, but not this one, impossibly **interwoven** even in its hostilities.

interwoven
(ĭn′tər-wō′vən) *adj.*
 blended or laced together.

---

[3] **ostracism:** exclusion or separation from society.

[4] **conundrum:** a riddle or a puzzle.

[5] **Mario Cuomo:** Governor of New York from 1983 until 1994.

[6] **apartheid:** a political system of racial or ethnic separation and discrimination.

[7] **Balkanized:** divided into small, uncooperative groups like countries on the Balkan Peninsula in the early 20th century.

[8] **Francie Nolan's . . . WASP suburbs of Cheever's characters:** characters in the novels *A Tree Grows in Brooklyn* and *Portnoy's Complaint;* John Cheever's characters were generally White Anglo-Saxon Protestants, or WASPs.

"What is the point of this splintered whole?"

50   Once these disparate parts were held together by a common
enemy, by the fault lines of world wars and the electrified fence of
communism. With the end of the cold war[9] there was the creeping
concern that without a focus for hatred and distrust, a sense of
national identity would evaporate, that the left side of the hyphen—
African-American, Mexican-American, Irish-American—would
overwhelm the right. And slow-growing domestic traumas like
economic unrest and increasing crime seemed more likely to
emphasize division than community. Today the citizens of the United
States have come together once more because of armed conflict and
60   enemy attack. Terrorism has led to devastation—and unity.

Yet even in 1994, the overwhelming majority of those surveyed
by the National Opinion Research Center agreed with this
statement: "The U.S. is a unique country that stands for something
special in the world." One of the things that it stands for is this
vexing notion that a great nation can consist entirely of refugees
from other nations, that people of different, even warring religions
and cultures can live, if not side by side, then on either side of the
country's Chester Avenues. Faced with this **diversity** there is little
point in trying to isolate anything remotely resembling a national
70   character, but there are two strains of behavior that, however
tenuously, abet the concept of unity.

diversity
(dĭ-vûr´sĭ-tē) n.
having varied
social and/or ethnic
backgrounds.

---

[9] **cold war:** diplomatic and economic hostility between the United States and the
Soviet Union and their respective allies in the decades following World War II.

There is that Calvinist undercurrent[10] in the American psyche that loves the difficult, the demanding, that sees mastering the impossible, whether it be prairie or subway, as a test of character, and so glories in the struggle of this fractured coalescing. And there is a grudging fairness among the citizens of the United States that eventually leads most to admit that, no matter what the English-only advocates try to suggest, the new immigrants are not so different from our own parents or grandparents. Leonel Castillo, former director of the Immigration and Naturalization Service and himself the grandson of Mexican immigrants, once told the writer Studs Terkel proudly, "The old neighborhood Ma-Pa stores are still around. They are not Italian or Jewish or Eastern European any more. Ma and Pa are now Korean, Vietnamese, Iraqi, Jordanian, Latin American. They live in the store. They work seven days a week. Their kids are doing well in school. They're making it. Sound familiar?"

Tolerance is the word used most often when this kind of coexistence succeeds, but tolerance is a vanilla-pudding word, standing for little more than the allowance of letting others live unremarked and unmolested. Pride seems excessive, given the American willingness to endlessly complain about them, them being whoever is new, different, unknown, or currently under suspicion. But patriotism is partly taking pride in this unlikely ability to throw all of us together in a country that across its length and breadth is as different as a dozen countries, and still be able to call it by one name. When photographs of the faces of all those who died in the World Trade Center destruction are assembled in one place, it will be possible to trace in the skin color, the shape of the eyes and the noses, the texture of the hair, a map of the world. These are the representatives of a mongrel nation that somehow, at times like this, has one spirit. Like many improbable ideas, when it actually works, it's a wonder.

COLLABORATIVE DISCUSSION Why does Anna Quindlen consider America to be "an improbable idea"? Discuss Quindlen's argument with a partner.

---

[10]**Calvinist undercurrent:** the social influence of Calvinism, a Christian religion with a strict moral code and a belief in God as absolutely sovereign.

Delineate and Evaluate an Argument

In "A Quilt of a Country," Anna Quindlen presents an **argument** about how America works as a country. An argument presents a claim, or position, on an issue and supports it with reasons and evidence. To evaluate the strength of Quindlen's argument, you must **delineate,** or describe in detail, these elements:

- Identify the **claim,** or Quindlen's position, on the issue.
- Look for the **reasons** Quindlen uses to support her claim. Reasons should be valid and logical.
- Evaluate whether the **evidence** Quindlen cites for each reason is credible, or believable, and relevant to the claim. Evidence can include facts, statistics, examples, anecdotes, or quotations.
- Look for **counterarguments,** which are statements that address opposing viewpoints. Does Quindlen anticipate opposing viewpoints and provide counterarguments to disprove them?

Analyze and Evaluate Author's Claim

To support a **claim,** authors develop and refine their ideas throughout the text. An author may use a particular sentence to develop a claim, or use an entire paragraph or larger section of the text to develop a claim with reasons and evidence.

Use a chart to help you analyze and evaluate how Anna Quindlen develops her claim in "A Quilt of a Country." First, identify the claim. Then, list specific reasons or evidence from the text. Finally, evaluate if the reason or evidence supports the claim. Read this example from a student newspaper editorial.

CLAIM *More time should be given to students to transition between classes.*

Reasons/Evidence from Text	How the Reasons/Evidence Support the Claim
"Students have told me how rushed they are to gather materials from their lockers for their next classes."	The evidence is a quotation from the school counselor, an objective observer who hears from many students. Her statement is logical support for the claim because it would be easier to gather materials if students had more time.

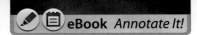
Analyzing the Text

Cite Text Evidence Support your responses with evidence from the selection.

1. **Summarize** What is Anna Quindlen's claim in "A Quilt of a Country"? Summarize her claim in your own words.

2. **Interpret** In lines 7–8, what does Quindlen mean when she describes America as being "like the crazy quilts that have been one of its great folk-art forms"? How does this description support her claim?

3. **Evaluate** What opposing viewpoint does Quindlen respond to in paragraph 3? What counterargument does she offer to it? List the reasons and evidence she includes in her counterargument and evaluate if it is relevant and sufficient.

4. **Analyze** In paragraph 4, Quindlen uses **repetition** and **parallelism**— expressing related ideas using similar grammatical constructions. What sentence structure and words does she repeat? What is the effect of this repetition?

5. **Analyze** Reread Quindlen's conclusion. What specific words and phrases does she use to link the conclusion to her introduction? How do these words and phrases support her argument?

6. **Evaluate** Quindlen uses many different types of evidence throughout the argument to support her claim, for example, facts, statistics, and quotations. Identity at least three examples of evidence and evaluate how she uses each one to support her claim.

PERFORMANCE TASK

Writing Activity: Argument Using what you have learned about how to develop an argument, write and support a claim about a positive aspect of your school or community.

1. Think about something you feel is an important, positive feature of your school or community. Write a claim about it.

2. Make notes about the reasons that support your claim. Then collect evidence that supports your reasons. Consider an opposing claim and list valid counterarguments.

3. Write the draft of your argument. Work carefully to present your reasons and evidence in a logical order.

4. Revise your draft to eliminate unrelated or illogical evidence. Finally, check your work to make sure you have used the conventions of standard English.

Critical Vocabulary

Practice and Apply Answer the following questions and explain your ideas.

discordant	pluralistic	interwoven	diversity

1. If a piece of music is **discordant**, do you want to continue listening or not? Why?

2. Is a society made up of one cultural group a **pluralistic** society, or not? Why?

3. Is an all-school assembly an example of an **interwoven** school community? Explain.

4. What is one way that **diversity** strengthens a community? Explain your idea.

Vocabulary Strategy: Patterns of Word Changes

Words can have different meanings or be different parts of speech. Many words have several different meanings listed in the dictionary. For example, the word *equal*, as used in "A Quilt of a Country," means "having the same privileges or rights." However, it also means "being the same or identical." Knowing the different meanings of words can help you become an effective reader.

Words also change depending on the part of speech to which they belong. The Critical Vocabulary words *discordant* and *pluralistic* change spelling and meaning when the part of speech changes. Knowing how a word functions in a sentence will help you gain a complete understanding of the word's meaning.

Practice and Apply Complete the sentences with the correct word from the chart.

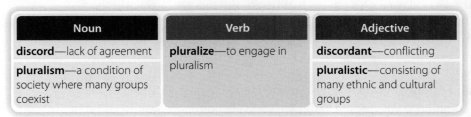

Noun	Verb	Adjective
discord—lack of agreement	**pluralize**—to engage in pluralism	**discordant**—conflicting
pluralism—a condition of society where many groups coexist		**pluralistic**—consisting of many ethnic and cultural groups

1. The people shouting indicated the level of _____ during the meeting.

2. Some governmental entities claim to be _____ because people of different ethnic groups work together.

3. The _____ parts of the book made it difficult to understand.

4. Even when a country tries to have _____, there can be unfairness and resentment.

Language and Style: Noun Clauses

A subordinate clause contains a subject and a verb, but it cannot stand alone in a sentence. A **noun clause** is a subordinate clause that takes the place of a noun in a sentence. It usually begins with *that, what, whatever, why, whether, how, who, whom, whoever,* or *whomever.*

A noun clause may function in a sentence as the subject, the direct object, the predicate nominative, or the object of a preposition.

Examples of Noun Clauses	
subject	**What Anna Quindlen wrote** was very thoughtful.
direct object	Many people don't appreciate **that America is made up of many diverse cultures.**
predicate nominative	My suggestion is **that we learn how to live together peacefully.**
object of a preposition	I will share my ideas with **whoever will listen.**

Writers use noun clauses to convey precise meanings and to add variety and interest to their writing. Read this sentence from the text in which Anna Quindlen strings together multiple noun clauses:

> It is difficult to know <u>how to convince them that this amounts to "crown thy good with brotherhood," that amid all the failures is something spectacularly successful.</u>

In this sentence, the first noun clause, *how to convince,* is the direct object of *know.* The second two noun clauses that begin with *that* are direct objects of *convince.* This sentence has a different structure from surrounding sentences in the paragraph. By using noun clauses to vary sentence structures, Quindlen keeps her readers engaged and interested.

Practice and Apply Look back at the argument about a positive aspect of your school or community you created in this selection's Performance Task. Revise your argument to include at least one noun clause for each of the four functions listed in the chart above. Then, discuss with a partner how the noun clauses add variety and interest to your writing.

Nadine Gordimer (b. 1923) *was born in South Africa. Her family was privileged and white in a country that practiced apartheid—an official policy of segregation of nonwhite South Africans enforced by the government. Nadine Gordimer became politically opposed to the policy. Her early works, such as* The Soft Voice of the Serpent *and* The Lying Days, *explore themes of exile and the effects of apartheid on internal life in South Africa. Before apartheid ended in 1994, some of Gordimer's writings were banned by the South African government; however, these texts were appreciated in other parts of the world. She has been awarded many literary prizes, including the Nobel Prize for Literature in 1991.*

Once Upon a Time

Short Story by Nadine Gordimer

AS YOU READ Pay attention to the relationship of the characters to the community in which they live. What steps do the parents take to ensure their family's safety?

Someone has written to ask me to contribute to an anthology of stories for children. I reply that I don't write children's stories; and he writes back that at a recent congress/book fair/seminar a certain novelist said every writer ought to write at least one story for children. I think of sending a postcard saying I don't accept that I "ought" to write anything.

And then last night I woke up—or rather was wakened without knowing what had roused me.

A voice in the echo chamber of the subconscious?

A sound.

A creaking of the kind made by the weight carried by one foot after another along a wooden floor. I listened. I felt the apertures of my ears **distend** with concentration. Again: the creaking. I was waiting for it; waiting to hear if it indicated that feet were moving from room to room, coming up the passage—to my door. I have no burglar bars, no gun under the pillow, but I have the same fears as people who do take these precautions, and my windowpanes

distend
(dĭ-stĕnd´) *v.*
to bulge or expand.

10

are thin as rime,[1] could shatter like a wineglass. A woman was murdered (how do they put it) in broad daylight in a house two blocks away, last year, and the fierce dogs who guarded an old widower and his collection of antique clocks were strangled before he was knifed by a casual laborer he had dismissed without pay.

I was staring at the door, making it out in my mind rather than seeing it, in the dark. I lay quite still—a victim already—but the arrhythmia[2] of my heart was fleeing, knocking this way and that against its body-cage. How finely tuned the senses are, just out of rest, sleep! I could never listen intently as that in the distractions of the day; I was reading every faintest sound, identifying and classifying its possible threat.

But I learned that I was to be neither threatened nor spared. There was no human weight pressing on the boards, the creaking was a buckling, an epicenter[3] of stress. I was in it. The house that surrounds me while I sleep is built on undermined ground; far beneath my bed, the floor, the house's foundations, the stopes[4] and passages of gold mines have hollowed the rock, and when some face trembles, detaches, and falls, three thousand feet below, the whole house shifts slightly, bringing uneasy strain to the balance and counterbalance of brick, cement, wood, and glass that hold it as a structure around me. The misbeats of my heart tailed off like the last muffled flourishes on one of the wooden xylophones made by the Chopi and Tsonga[5] migrant miners who might have been down there, under me in the earth at that moment. The stope where the fall was could have been disused, dripping water from its ruptured veins; or men might now be interred there in the most profound of tombs.

I couldn't find a position in which my mind would let go of my body—release me to sleep again. So I began to tell myself a story; a bedtime story.

In a house, in a suburb, in a city, there were a man and his wife who loved each other very much and were living happily ever after. They had a little boy, and they loved him very much. They had a cat and a dog that the little boy loved very much. They had a car and a caravan trailer for holidays, and a swimming pool which was fenced so that the little boy and his playmates would not fall in and drown. They had a housemaid who was absolutely trustworthy

---

[1] **rime:** a coating of frost.
[2] **arrhythmia:** an irregular heartbeat.
[3] **epicenter:** the focal point.
[4] **stopes:** step-like holes or trenches made by miners.
[5] **Chopi and Tsonga:** (chō′pē and tsôn′ga) ethnic groups that live in Mozambique.

and an itinerant[6] gardener who was highly recommended by the neighbors. For when they began to live happily ever after they were warned, by that wise old witch, the husband's mother, not to take on anyone off the street. They were inscribed in a medical benefit society, their pet dog was licensed, they were insured against fire, flood damage, and theft, and subscribed to the local Neighborhood Watch, which supplied them with a plaque for their gates lettered YOU HAVE BEEN WARNED over the silhouette of a would-be intruder. He was masked; it could not be said if he was black or white, and therefore proved the property owner was no racist.

It was not possible to insure the house, the swimming pool, or the car against riot damage. There were riots, but these were outside the city, where people of another color were quartered. These people were not allowed into the suburb except as reliable housemaids and gardeners, so there was nothing to fear, the husband told the wife. Yet she was afraid that some day such people might come up the street and tear off the plaque YOU HAVE BEEN WARNED and open the gates and stream in. . . . Nonsense, my dear, said the husband, there are police and soldiers and tear gas and guns to keep them away. But to please her—for he loved her very much and buses were being burned, cars stoned, and schoolchildren shot by the police in those quarters out of sight and hearing of the suburb—he had electronically controlled gates fitted. Anyone who pulled off the sign YOU HAVE BEEN WARNED and tried to open the gates would have to announce his **intentions** by pressing a button and speaking into a receiver relayed to the house. The little boy was fascinated by the device and used it as a walkie-talkie in cops and robbers play with his small friends.

The riots were suppressed, but there were many burglaries in the suburb and somebody's trusted housemaid was tied up and shut in a cupboard by thieves while she was in charge of her employers' house. The trusted housemaid of the man and wife and little boy was so upset by this misfortune befalling a friend left, as she herself often was, with responsibility for the possessions of the man and his wife and the little boy that she implored her employers to have burglar bars attached to the doors and windows of the house, and an alarm system installed. The wife said, She is right, let us take heed of her advice. So from every window and door in the house where they were living happily ever after they now saw the trees and sky through bars, and when the little boy's pet cat tried to climb in by the fanlight[7] to keep him company in his little bed

intention
(ĭn-tĕn′shən) *n.*
purpose or plan.

---

[6] **itinerant:** frequently traveling to different places.
[7] **fanlight:** an arched window, usually over a door.

at night, as it customarily had done, it set off the alarm keening[8] through the house.

The alarm was often answered—it seemed—by other burglar alarms, in other houses, that had been triggered by pet cats or nibbling mice. The alarms called to one another across the gardens in shrills and bleats and wails that everyone soon became accustomed to, so that the din roused the inhabitants of the suburb no more than the croak of frogs and musical grating of cicadas'[9] legs. Under cover of the electronic harpies'[10] discourse intruders sawed the iron bars and broke into homes, taking away hi-fi equipment, television sets, cassette players, cameras and radios, jewelry and clothing, and sometimes were hungry enough to devour everything in the refrigerator or paused **audaciously** to drink the whiskey in the cabinets or patio bars. Insurance companies paid no compensation for single malt, a loss made keener by the property owner's knowledge that the thieves wouldn't even have been able to appreciate what it was they were drinking.

Then the time came when many of the people who were not trusted housemaids and gardeners hung about the suburb because they were unemployed. Some importuned for a job: weeding or painting a roof; anything, *baas*,[11] madam. But the man and his wife remembered the warning about taking on anyone off the street. Some drank liquor and fouled the street with discarded bottles. Some begged, waiting for the man or his wife to drive the car out of the electronically operated gates. They sat about with their feet in the gutters, under the jacaranda trees that made a green tunnel of the street—for it was a beautiful suburb, spoiled only by their presence—and sometimes they fell asleep lying right before the gates in the midday sun. The wife could never see anyone go hungry. She sent the trusted housemaid out with bread and tea, but the trusted housemaid said these were loafers and *tsotsis*,[12] who would come and tie her up and shut her in a cupboard. The husband said, She's right. Take heed of her advice. You only encourage them with your bread and tea. They are looking for their chance. . . . And he brought the little boy's tricycle from the garden into the house every night, because if the house was surely secure, once locked and with the alarm set, someone might still be able to climb over the wall or the electronically closed gates into the garden.

You are right, said the wife, then the wall should be higher. And the wise old witch, the husband's mother, paid for the extra bricks

audacious
(ô-dā´shəs) *n.*
bold, rebellious.

---

[8] **keening:** wailing or crying.
[9] **cicadas:** large, loud insects.
[10]**harpies:** mythological creatures who were part woman and part bird.
[11]*baas:* (bäs) a white person in a position of authority in relation to nonwhites.
[12]*tsotsis:* (tsō´tsēs) dishonest, untrustworthy people.

as her Christmas present to her son and his wife—the little boy got a Space Man outfit and a book of fairy tales.

But every week there were more reports of **intrusion**: in broad daylight and the dead of night, in the early hours of the morning, and even in the lovely summer twilight—a certain family was at dinner while the bedrooms were being ransacked upstairs. The man and his wife, talking of the latest armed robbery in the suburb, were distracted by the sight of the little boy's pet cat effortlessly arriving over the seven-foot wall, descending first with a rapid bracing of extended forepaws down on the sheer vertical surface, and then a graceful launch, landing with swishing tail within the property. The whitewashed wall was marked with the cat's comings and goings; and on the street side of the wall there were larger red-earth smudges that could have been made by the kind of broken running shoes, seen on the feet of unemployed loiterers, that had no innocent destination.

When the man and wife and little boy took the pet dog for its walk round the neighborhood streets they no longer paused to admire this show of roses or that perfect lawn; these were hidden behind an array of different varieties of security fences, walls, and devices. The man, wife, little boy, and dog passed a remarkable choice: there was the low-cost option of pieces of broken glass embedded in cement along the top of walls, there were iron grilles ending in lance points, there were attempts at reconciling the aesthetics of prison architecture with the Spanish Villa style (spikes painted pink) and with the plastic urns of neoclassical façades (twelve-inch pikes finned like zigzags of lightning and painted pure white). Some walls had a small board affixed, giving the name and telephone number of the firm responsible for the installation of the devices. While the little boy and the pet dog raced ahead, the husband and wife found themselves comparing the possible effectiveness of each style against its appearance; and after several weeks when they paused before this barricade or that without

intrusion
(ĭn-trōo´ shən) *n.*
act of trespass or invasion.

needing to speak, both came out with the conclusion that only one
was worth considering. It was the ugliest but the most honest in its
suggestion of the pure concentration-camp style, no frills, all evident
efficacy. Placed the length of walls, it consisted of a continuous coil
of stiff and shining metal **serrated** into jagged blades, so that there
would be no way of climbing over it and no way through its tunnel
without getting entangled in its fangs. There would be no way out,
only a struggle getting bloodier and bloodier, a deeper and sharper
hooking and tearing of flesh. The wife shuddered to look at it. You're
right, said the husband, anyone would think twice. . . . And they
took heed of the advice on a small board fixed to the wall: Consult
DRAGON'S TEETH The People For Total Security.

    Next day a gang of workmen came and stretched the razor-
bladed coils all round the walls of the house where the husband
and wife and little boy and pet dog and cat were living happily
ever after. The sunlight flashed and slashed, off the serrations, the
cornice of razor thorns encircled the home, shining. The husband
said, Never mind. It will weather. The wife said, You're wrong. They
guarantee it's rustproof. And she waited until the little boy had run
off to play before she said, I hope the cat will take heed. . . . The
husband said, Don't worry, my dear, cats always look before they
leap. And it was true that from that day on the cat slept in the little
boy's bed and kept to the garden, never risking a try at breaching
security.

    One evening, the mother read the little boy to sleep with a fairy
story from the book the wise old witch had given him at Christmas.
Next day he pretended to be the Prince who braves the terrible
thicket of thorns to enter the palace and kiss the Sleeping Beauty
back to life: he dragged a ladder to the wall, the shining coiled
tunnel was just wide enough for his little body to creep in, and
with the first fixing of its razor teeth in his knees and hands and
head he screamed and struggled deeper into its tangle. The trusted
housemaid and the itinerant gardener, whose "day" it was, came
running, the first to see and to scream with him, and the itinerant
gardener tore his hands trying to get at the little boy. Then the man
and his wife burst wildly into the garden and for some reason (the
cat, probably) the alarm set up wailing against the screams while
the bleeding mass of the little boy was hacked out of the security
coil with saws, wire cutters, choppers, and they carried it—the
man, the wife, the hysterical trusted housemaid, and the weeping
gardener—into the house.

serrate
(sĕr´āt´) *adj.*
having a jagged,
saw-toothed edge.

COLLABORATIVE DISCUSSION Was the boy safer because of the
precautions his parents took to protect the family? Discuss your thoughts
with a partner using details from the story to support your ideas.

Analyze Author's Choices: Text Structure

Nadine Gordimer's "Once Upon a Time" was originally published in 1989. The late 1980s were a period of internal unrest in South Africa and this story reflects the fear and isolation that people felt as the policy of apartheid continued to be enforced. To convey her ideas, Gordimer structured her story using some of the traditional elements of fairy tales. For example, the title "Once Upon a Time" and the fact that the family is "living happily ever after" are both traditional elements of fairy tales. This **structure**, or arrangement of the parts of the story, holds together the elements of the story. The choices that Gordimer made about the structure of her story help create effects such as tension and surprise, as in a fairy tale. As you analyze the structure, look for other fairy tale elements as shown in the chart and think about how this story is similar to and different from other fairy tales you have read.

Elements of a Fairy Tale
• The main characters are opposed by an evil force.
• Animals have special abilities.
• The story is used to teach a lesson.
• Good characters have bad things happen to them.
• The setting does not seem quite real.
• Details in the story foreshadow that the problem, or conflict, will be resolved in a "happily ever after" ending.

Support Inferences About Theme

Gordimer develops the **theme,** or the underlying message, through the details and symbols she includes in the story. An author can use all the elements of a story to develop a theme, including the characters, plot, and setting. For example, to convey a theme about the rewards of working hard, an author might relate a story about a hockey team that finally wins a championship. As the story develops, the players discover each other's strengths and weaknesses and learn that working together brings success to everyone.

An author might also develop the theme through the use of a **symbol**—a person, a place, or an object that stands for something beyond itself. In the hockey team story, the author might use the symbol of a trophy to represent the team's success.

As you analyze "Once Upon a Time," make **inferences,** or logical guesses, about the theme by considering the details and symbols Gordimer includes. Pay particular attention to the characters' actions and motivations, as well as the setting— including the historical background—to help you infer the theme.

Analyzing the Text

Cite Text Evidence   Support your responses with evidence from the selection.

1. **Identify Patterns** How is the structure of this story similar to a fairy tale? What elements do they share? Cite details from the text to support your analysis.

2. **Connect** Nadine Gordimer wrote many stories about the injustices of apartheid. She was also active in bringing change to the political entities of South Africa. Even though her books were banned in South Africa for a time, she resolved to stay instead of living in exile. What do you learn about Gordimer's political point of view by reading this story? Explain your ideas using evidence from the story.

3. **Infer** Authors often leave things unstated in a story, leaving the reader with questions about the outcome. What can you infer about what Gordimer leaves unstated at the end of her story? How does it relate to her statements about the family living "happily ever after"?

4. **Evaluate** In lines 58, 136, and 194, the phrase "wise old witch" is used to describe the husband's mother. Explain how the wise old witch can be interpreted to symbolize the government of South Africa.

5. **Draw Conclusions** How does the cat symbolize and support the theme of this story? Explain.

6. **Infer** What is the theme of this story? Explain how Gordimer develops this theme through the story's elements, such as structure and symbols.

PERFORMANCE TASK

Speaking Activity: Fairy Tale Nadine Gordimer uses her writing to convey ideas about the society and country she lives in. Explore this idea by developing a modern fairy tale that you can perform with a partner.

1. Identify a community or school event that has happened or that you have observed. Then make notes about the two characters and plot of your fairy tale.

2. Think about a theme for your fairy tale. For example, you might consider the themes of fairness, justice, or equality. What important symbols can you include to convey your theme?

3. Combine your ideas to write a short fairy tale that conveys a message. Refer back to "Once Upon a Time" to examine how Nadine Gordimer wrote a powerful political commentary using a fairy tale structure.

4. Perform your fairy tale with your partner. Ask your audience to evaluate if you were successful in conveying your underlying message.

Critical Vocabulary

distend   intention   audacious   intrusion   serrate

Practice and Apply Choose which of the two situations best fits the word's meaning.

1. **distend**
   a. The bicyclist will inflate the tires on her bike.
   b. The wheel rim bent when the bicyclist hit a pothole.

2. **intention**
   a. The soccer player showed his determination to shoot for the goal.
   b. The soccer player's purpose was to play better in the next game.

3. **audacious**
   a. The daring boy brought gum to the computer lab.
   b. The mischievous boy was caught by his teacher.

4. **intrusion**
   a. The newspaper talked about the girl's wrongful entrance into the clubhouse.
   b. The girl's interruption of the conversation made the club members unhappy.

5. **serrate**
   a. The edge of the paper was cut into a decorative pattern.
   b. The toothed edge of the paper looked like a set of teeth.

Vocabulary Strategy: Words from Latin

Word and Dictionary Definition	Etymology	Latin Definition
surround (line 33) "to enclose on all sides"	from the Latin *super-* + *unda*	*unda* means "wave"

Etymologies show the origin and historical development of a word. For example, the Critical Vocabulary word *distend* comes from the Latin word *distendere*, which means "to stretch." Exploring the etymology of words can help you clarify their precise meanings. It can also help you expand your vocabulary.

Practice and Apply Follow these steps for each Critical Vocabulary word:

- Look up the word in a dictionary.

- Find the etymology of each word. If you are not sure how to read the etymology, look at the front or the back of your dictionary. There will be a section that explains how the etymology is noted and what the abbreviations mean.

- Compare the Latin definition of each word with the English definition. Are they the same? How does the English definition relate to the Latin meaning?

Language and Style: Prepositional Phrases

Authors use various types of phrases to convey specific meanings and to add variety and interest to their writing. **Prepositional phrases** are phrases consisting of a preposition and an object of the preposition, usually a noun or a pronoun. Here are some common prepositions and phrases that can be created with them.

Preposition	Object of Preposition	Prepositional Phrase
from	the street	from the street
before	the rain	before the rain
during	the game	during the game
until	her test	until her test
outside	the gate	outside the gate

Read the following sentence from the story.

<u>In a house, in a suburb, in a city,</u> there were a man and his wife who loved each other very much and were living happily ever after.

Nadine Gordimer might have written the sentence this way:

In a suburban house, there were a man and his wife who loved each other very much and were living happily ever after.

While this sentence conveys the same meaning, it doesn't have the same interest as the original sentence. The prepositional phrases used one after another, *in a house, in a suburb, in a city,* help the author change gears from a story about something that happened to her to a story about another family. The phrases mimic the way a storyteller might use a steady beat or rhythm to start a story.

Examine another sentence from "Once Upon a Time":

One evening, the mother read the little boy to sleep <u>with a fairy tale from the book</u> the wise old witch had given him at Christmas.

Although Gordimer could have written several shorter sentences, this sentence with a series of prepositional phrases conveys the sense of a fairy tale.

Practice and Apply Review the modern fairy tale that you created about a current event for this selection's Performance Task. Working independently, revise your fairy tale to include prepositional phrases that clarify your ideas and that add variety and interest to your sentences. Compare your revisions to those of your partner.

Kimberly M. Blaeser (b. 1955), *of German and Anishinaabe ancestry, is a member of the Minnesota Chippewa tribe. Blaeser began her career as a journalist but is now a professor at the University of Wisconsin-Milwaukee. Blaeser is also a writer whose work includes poetry, personal essays, short stories, and reviews. Her first collection of poems,* Trailing You, *won the First Book Award in Poetry from the Native Writer's Circle of Americas in 1993. In her work, Blaeser often alludes to her dual heritage and to the collective nature of the human experience.*

Rituals of Memory

Essay by Kimberly M. Blaeser

AS YOU READ Look for evidence about how Blaeser's mixed ancestry shapes her experiences and her ideas on memories. Write down any questions you generate during reading.

Memory begins with various wonders. For my friend Mary, it began with hair. Her hair grew tightly curled, so strong the spirals defied taming. Brushing and combing brought tears. When Mary tried to run her fingers through her hair as she saw others do, her fingers became hopelessly captured by the curls. Hair, she deduced, must grow in loops, out of our head at one point, back into it at another. Because her locks had never been cut, the loops never broken, her fingers became entangled in the loops.

Perhaps that story delights me because it stands as a wonderful example of our always innocent attempts to explain the world. Or perhaps because it seems a fine metaphor for the looped relationships of family, place, and community, the **innate** patterns of ourselves that always keep us returning. No matter how long our lives, no matter how far our experience takes us from our origins, our lives remain connected, always loop back to that center of our identity, our spirit.

10

innate
(ĭ-nāt´) *adj.* inborn; existing at birth.

"*My memories entangle themselves oddly among the roots of several cultures.*"

I believe we belong to the circle and, for our survival, we will return in one way or another to renew those rhythms of life out of which our sense of self has emerged. Some of us have a physical
20 place and a people we return to. We also have what Gerald Vizenor calls the "interior landscapes" of our imaginative and spiritual lives. Perhaps our strongest link to the sacred center, the pulsing core of being, is memory and the storytelling and ceremonies that feed it— our own rituals of memory.

My memories entangle themselves oddly among the roots of several cultures: Native American, perhaps **foremost** in my mind, but also a German Catholic background, the culture of rural America, the close looping of small towns in the Midwest, and what I guess could be called Minnesota wilderness culture. But these
30 several cultures did not always exist in opposition or in isolation from one another. I remember Memorial Day celebrations when my father joined the Legionnaires[1] in their visits to all the graveyards in Mahnomen and Nay-Tah-Waush.[2] Uniformed, sometimes sweating in the early summer heat, they marched to the sites, stood at attention as taps was played, and then, as a gesture of salute to the fallen veterans, they shot over the graves. Each year, through late morning and early afternoon, we followed the men on these tours. We stood, moved to goose bumps by the lonely trumpet tune, scrambling with all the other children for spent casings when each
40 ceremony was concluded.

The last site on their schedule was the Indian burial grounds close to the BAB landing. As a child I saw nothing unusual about a dozen American Legionnaires marching back on the little wooded

foremost
(fôr´mōst´) *adv.* most importantly.

---

[1] **Legionnaires:** members of the American Legion, a social, service-based organization of American veterans.
[2] **Mahnomen and Nay-Tah-Waush:** cities in northwestern Minnesota.

path and paying solemn respect to those Indian warriors who I would later realize were really of another nation. On this march through the tall grasses and hazelnut bushes that crowded the path, my older brother and I often fell in step. Several times I marched beside Sig Tveit and his trumpet, his arm linked through mine. We stood, all of us—those descended from settlers of Norwegian,

50 German, or other European origins, and those descended from Anishinaabe or other Indian people. Together in a moment out of ordinary time, we paused in the little opening at the wooden grave houses, oblivious to the wood ticks, which must later be picked carefully from our clothes and our flesh, oblivious to the buzzing of mosquitoes or sand flies, oblivious as well to the more trivial tensions of contemporary politics. We stood together in a great ceremonial loop of our humanity, in our need to remember our ancestors and the lives they lived, together in our desire to **immerse** ourselves in their honor, to always carry those memories forward

60 with us, to be ourselves somehow made holy by the ritual of those memories. We emerged quiet from those little woods, from that darker place of memory, into the too bright sunshine of a late May day in the twentieth century.

    And then we arrived back at the sandy beach. The men brought out drinks from the trunks of their cars, laughter and talk sprang up, picnic foods came out, and people would disperse again—to their own families.

    I don't know if the Legionnaires still march back into the woods each year. I like to believe they do. For that kind of experience has

70 helped me keep balance when the strands of my mixed heritage seem to pull one against another. However unconscious, it was a moment of crossover, a moment when the borders of culture were **nullified** by the greater instincts of humanity to remember and to give honor.

    Perhaps the Memorial Days of those early years have become one of the watermarks[3] of my life because they brought to ceremonial focus the many tellings of the past that filled up the hours and days of my childhood. As children, we were never so much taught as storied. All work and play had memories attached.

80 "Indians," Ed Castillo says, "can hold more than one thing sacred." With school began my double life. I went to Catholic grade school, where I earned a reputation for being quiet, obedient, pious, and bright. I learned my Baltimore Catechism[4]—*"Who made you?"*

immerse
(ĭ-mûrs´) *v.* to absorb or involve deeply.

nullify
(nŭl´ə-fī´) *v.* to make of no value or consequence.

---

[3] **watermarks:** marks impressed in paper that can be viewed when the paper is held up to the light.
[4] **Baltimore Catechism:** a summary of Christian beliefs in a question-and-answer format that was taught in Catholic schools until the late 1960s.

"God made me." "Why did God make you?" "God made me because he loves me."—learned my singsong phonics—*ba be bi ba bu, ca ce ci ca cu, da de di da du*—studied my spelling—*i before e, except after c, or when it sounds like a as in neighbor and weigh*. In between school days, we gathered hazelnuts, went partridge hunting, fished, had long deer-hunting weekends, went to powwows,[5] went spearing and ice fishing, played canasta and whist, learned the daisy chain, beaded on looms, made fish house candles, sausage, and quilts. No one then questioned the necessity or value of our school education, but somehow I grew up knowing it wasn't the only—maybe not even the most important— education I would need, and sometimes we stole time from that education for the other one. My parents might keep us home from school or come and get us midday for some more lovely adventure on a lake or in the woods. I'm still thankful for those stolen moments, because now I know by heart not only the Hail Mary, the Our Father, and the National Anthem, but the misty prayers water gives off at dawn and the ancient song of the loon; I recognize not only the alphabet and the parts of the English sentence, but the silhouetted form of the shipoke and the intricate language of a beaver's teeth and tail.

My life at school and in the Catholic Church is officially recorded and documented—dates of baptism, First Communion and confirmation, quarterly grade reports, attendance records— just as my academic life is later documented at universities in Minnesota, Indiana, and Wisconsin. But for my other education, practical and spiritual, I have no grades or degrees, no certificates to commemorate the annual rituals. I have some **tangibles** of those processes—a jingle dress, fans of feathers, sometimes photos—but mostly I have stories, dreams, and memories.

tangible
(tăn´jə-bəl) *n.*
something that can be touched.

COLLABORATIVE DISCUSSION With a partner, discuss Blaeser's views on how memories are formed. What does she believe influences her memories? In your discussion, cite evidence from the text.

---

[5] **powwows:** a celebration of Native American culture in which diverse nations gather for the purpose of singing, dancing, and honoring their ancestors.

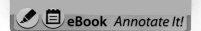
Determine Central Idea

The **central idea** of an essay is the most important point conveyed in the essay. Sometimes the central idea is stated in the first paragraph, but more often, you will need to infer the central idea that is implied by specific details. As you analyze "Rituals of Memory," keep notes using these strategies to help you understand how Blaeser develops the central idea over the course of the text:

- Identify the topic of each paragraph.
- Examine the specific details the author includes in the paragraph.
- Ask what idea or message the details convey about the topic.
- Write a sentence that states the idea or message in your own words.

Analyzing the Text

Cite Text Evidence   Support your responses with evidence from the selection.

1. **Analyze** An extended metaphor compares two unlike things at length and in a number of different ways. In the first four paragraphs, Blaeser provides an extended metaphor for rituals. To what does she compare rituals? Explain how the comparisons relate to the idea that rituals are connected and repeated.

2. **Identify Patterns** In lines 51–56, Blaeser uses repetition, or phrases that repeat the same pattern, to describe the annoyances she and the others ignored during their tribute. What is the purpose of this repetition?

3. **Connect** In line 81, Blaeser says, "With school began my double life." Explain how Blaeser has two lives. How do her two lives relate to her previous statement, "My memories entangle themselves oddly among the roots of several cultures"?

4. **Infer** What is the central idea that Blaeser develops in "Rituals of Memory"? Cite details from the text that helped you determine the central idea.

PERFORMANCE TASK

Speaking Activity: Discussion In her essay, Blaeser lists a few mementoes that are linked to memorable events in her life. What connections can you make between objects and memories? Share your reflections in a group discussion.

1. Collect two keepsakes or souvenirs that represent meaningful events from your life, events that you are willing to discuss. Make notes on how these objects serve as reminders and why the events are important to you.

2. Bring your notes to a group discussion along with your mementoes, if you can. If not, take a photograph or video recording of the objects to show. Share your objects, describe your events, and explain their significance.

Critical Vocabulary

innate	foremost	immerse	nullify	tangible

Practice and Apply Complete each phrase with your ideas about the Critical Vocabulary word. Share your work with a partner.

1. Weather conditions should be a **foremost** consideration when . . .

2. Her improved report card was **tangible** evidence that her extra study hours . . .

3. The sisters' bickering will **nullify** the efforts of their parents to . . .

4. Her **innate** creativity is revealed through . . .

5. 3D movies **immerse** the audience in the action by . . .

Vocabulary Strategy: Denotations and Connotations

A word may have different meanings. The literal definition of a word found in a dictionary is called the **denotation**. A **connotation** is what a word implies or suggests in addition to its literal meaning. This means that words with the same or similar denotations may have different connotations, or shades of meaning. A connotation may be positive or negative.

Kimberly Blaeser uses specific words to convey certain meanings. For example, the Critical Vocabulary word *immerse* (line 58) has a positive connotation and suggests that Blaeser's family and friends engaged themselves deeply in their tribute to their ancestors. However, notice how the connotation changes if you replace the word *immerse* with the word *involve*. The connotation of the word *involve* is also positive, but it suggests something less dedicated than *immerse*.

Practice and Apply Read each example from the text. Write an explanation of the connotation of the underlined word. Then, replace the underlined word with the word in parentheses, which has a similar denotation. Explain how the connotation of the new word changes the meaning of the sentence.

1. Line 9: "Perhaps the story <u>delights</u> me because it stands as a wonderful example of our always innocent attempts to explain the world." (intrigues)

2. Line 25: "My memories entangle themselves <u>oddly</u> among the roots of several cultures . . . ." (ridiculously)

3. Line 38: "We stood, moved to goose bumps by the lonely trumpet tune, <u>scrambling</u> with all the other children for spent casings when each ceremony was concluded." (pushing)

4. Line 91: "No one then <u>questioned</u> the necessity or value of our school education . . . ." (challenged)

Background *President **Abraham Lincoln** (1809–1865) is considered an American hero for preserving the Union and emancipating the slaves. He was a skillful politician, leader, and orator. One of his most famous speeches was delivered at the dedication of the National Cemetery at Gettysburg, Pennsylvania, in 1863, site of one of the most deadly battles of the Civil War. The victory for the Union forces marked a turning point in the Civil War, but losses on both sides at Gettysburg were staggering: 28,000 Confederate soldiers and 23,000 Union soldiers were killed or wounded. Lincoln was assassinated by John Wilkes Booth in 1865. Lincoln's dedication to the ideals of freedom and equality continue to inspire people around the world.*

The Gettysburg Address

Speech by Abraham Lincoln

AS YOU READ Pay attention to how Lincoln's speech emphasizes the importance of ending the Civil War and reuniting the country.

Four score and seven[1] years ago our fathers brought forth on this continent, a new nation, **conceived** in liberty, and dedicated to the proposition that all men are created equal.

    Now we are engaged in a great civil war, testing whether that nation, or any nation so conceived and so dedicated, can long endure. We are met on a great battle field of that war. We have come to dedicate a portion of that field, as a final resting place for those who here gave their lives that that nation might live. It is altogether fitting and proper that we should do this.

10   But, in a larger sense, we cannot dedicate—we cannot consecrate[2]—we cannot hallow[3]—this ground. The brave men, living and dead, who struggled here have consecrated it, far above our poor power to add or **detract**. The world will little note, nor long remember what we say here, but it can never forget what they did here. It is for us, the living, rather, to be dedicated here to the

conceive
(kən-sēv´) *v.*
to form or develop in the mind; devise.

detract
(dĭ-trăkt´) *v.*
to take away from.

---

[1] **four score and seven:** eighty-seven.

[2] **consecrate:** to dedicate as sacred.

[3] **hallow:** define as holy.

unfinished work which they who fought here have thus far so nobly advanced. It is rather for us to be here dedicated to the great task remaining before us—that from these honored dead we take increased devotion to that cause for which they gave the last full

20 measure of devotion—that we here highly **resolve** that these dead shall not have died in vain—that this nation, under God, shall have a new birth of freedom—and that government of the people, by the people, for the people, shall not **perish** from the earth.

resolve
(rĭ-zŏlv´) *v.*
to decide or become determined.

perish
(pĕr´ĭsh) *v.*
to die or come to an end.

IN THIS TEMPLE
AS IN THE HEARTS OF THE PEOPLE
FOR WHOM HE SAVED THE UNION
THE MEMORY OF ABRAHAM LINCOLN
IS ENSHRINED FOREVER

COLLABORATIVE DISCUSSION With a partner, discuss Lincoln's beliefs about the importance of reuniting the country. Cite specific evidence from the speech to support your ideas.

Analyze Seminal U.S. Documents

Speeches, essays, and other texts that have great historical and literary significance are called **seminal documents.** In the United States, the Gettysburg Address is a seminal document, as are George Washington's Farewell Address, Franklin D. Roosevelt's Four Freedoms Speech, and Martin Luther King Jr.'s "Letter from Birmingham Jail." As you analyze the speech, look for these characteristics that can help you recognize and analyze seminal documents:

Strong themes such as freedom, equality, strength, democracy

Concepts such as fairness, justice, respect, honor

Seminal Documents

Engaging ideas presented in an original way

Themes and concepts that encourage the audience to take action

Analyze Author's Purpose and Rhetoric

An author may write a speech for one or more reasons. These reasons are called the **author's purpose.** An author's purpose might be to inform or explain, to persuade, to express thoughts or feelings, or to entertain.

To help advance a purpose, an author will often use **rhetoric,** or the art of using specific words and language structures to make the message memorable. In the Gettysburg Address, Lincoln makes effective use of two rhetorical devices:

- **Repetition** is the use of the same word or words more than once. Repetition is used to emphasize key ideas.
- **Parallelism** is a form of repetition in which a grammatical pattern is repeated. Parallelism is used to create rhythm and evoke emotions.

Look at this example from President Ronald Reagan's Remarks at Moscow State University. Notice how he repeats the word *freedom* and uses parallelism to emphasize a key idea:

"The key is freedom—freedom of thought, freedom of information, freedom of communication."

As you analyze the Gettysburg Address, notice the repeated words and parallel clauses and phrases, such as *we are engaged, we are met, we have come*. Think about how Lincoln uses both repetition and parallelism to advance his purpose.

Analyzing the Text

Cite Text Evidence Support your responses with evidence from the selection.

1. **Analyze** Why did Lincoln write and deliver the Gettysburg Address? What were his two main purposes? Explain using evidence from the speech.

2. **Infer** What is "the unfinished work" of those who died (line 16)?

3. **Infer** What does Lincoln mean when he refers to "a new birth of freedom" (line 22)? Explain your response with evidence from the text.

4. **Identify Patterns** The word *dedicate* is repeated several times in the speech. What does *dedicate* mean? What idea does Lincoln emphasize with the repetition of this word?

5. **Identify Patterns** Identify two examples of parallelism in the speech. How does Lincoln use parallel structure to persuade the audience to accept his message?

6. **Draw Conclusions** Seminal U.S. documents often refer to themes and ideals that are important to the audience they address. What is the **theme,** or underlying message, of the Gettysburg Address? Are those themes still important today? Explain the underlying message and the American ideals that the speech upholds.

PERFORMANCE TASK

Speaking Activity: Presentation The Gettysburg Address is one of the most famous speeches in U. S. history. Work in a small group to prepare an oral presentation of the speech. Follow these steps:

1. Reread the speech silently to yourself, making notes about pacing and emphasis. Pay particular attention to the effects of punctuation on your presentation.

2. In a small group, have a volunteer read the speech aloud. Discuss any questions about the meaning of the speech and the best way to present it. Summarize in writing points of agreement and disagreement,

acknowledging that different people may want to emphasize different words or phrases in the speech.

3. Practice your speech with a partner. After each partner has delivered the speech, discuss what was effective in the performance. Use your summary to help guide your constructive criticism.

4. Use the feedback from your partner to deliver the speech to your class.

Critical Vocabulary

conceive   detract   resolve   perish

Practice and Apply Choose which Critical Vocabulary word is most closely associated with the underlined word or phrase in each sentence.

1. Additional details in a speech sometimes <u>take away from</u> the whole message.

2. A special election can be used to <u>decide</u> a tie in the vote for the student body president.

3. It takes a creative person <u>to form an idea</u> in his or her mind about an important issue and then convey that message to an audience.

4. Sometimes organizations such as clubs <u>come to an end</u> when the members are no longer interested.

Vocabulary Strategy: Multiple-Meaning Words

Words that have more than one definition are considered **multiple-meaning words.** To determine a word's appropriate meaning within a text, you need to look for context clues in the words, sentences, and paragraphs that surround it. Look at the word *fitting* in this sentence from the Gettysburg Address:

It is altogether <u>fitting</u> and proper that we should do this. (lines 8–9)

The word *fitting* can mean "the act of trying on clothes" or "a small part for a machine." However, the word *proper* is a context clue that the tells you the correct meaning of *fitting* in this sentence is "appropriate."

Practice and Apply Find these multiple-meaning words in the speech: *engaged* (line 4), *testing* (line 4), *poor* (line 13), *measure* (line 20). Working with a partner, use context clues to determine each word's meaning as it is used in the speech.

1. Determine how the word functions in the sentence. Is it a noun, an adjective, a verb, or an adverb?

2. If the sentence does not provide enough information, read the paragraph in which the word appears and consider the larger context of the speech.

3. Write down your definition and the clues you used to determine the correct meaning of each word.

Language and Style: Parallel Structure

One grammatical feature that makes Abraham Lincoln's rhetoric so effective is his use of **parallel structure**, or the repetition of grammatical forms within a sentence. The repetition can occur at the word, phrase, or clause level. Lincoln uses parallel structure to express and connect ideas that are related or equal in importance and to create rhythm and evoke emotions. Consider these examples from the Gettysburg Address:

Type of Structure	Example from the Gettysburg Address
parallel words	living and dead (line 12)

Type of Structure	Example from the Gettysburg Address
parallel phrases	of the people, by the people, for the people (lines 22–23)

Type of Structure	Example from the Gettysburg Address
parallel clauses	we cannot dedicate—we cannot consecrate—we cannot hallow (lines 10–11)

Practice and Apply With a partner, look back at the Gettysburg Address and identify additional examples of parallel structure. Then imagine you were at Gettysburg on the day President Lincoln delivered his speech. Write a brief letter to Lincoln explaining how you were affected by his remarks. Use at least two examples of parallel structure in your letter. Exchange letters with a partner and discuss how effectively you each used parallel structure to communicate your message to Lincoln.

Background *The Vietnam Veterans Memorial was dedicated in 1982 to commemorate the 2.7 million military men and women who served in the conflict. There are approximately 58, 272 names inscribed on the wall in chronological order from the first death, injury, or missing-in-action date to the last. The polished black granite V-shaped wall was designed by Maya Lin and was intended to be a place of reflection and harmony without any political message.*

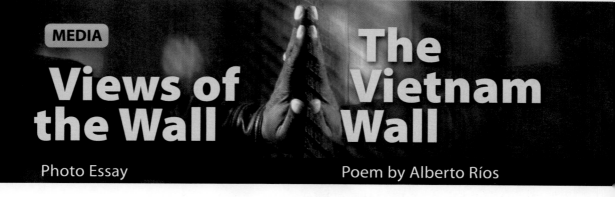

MEDIA

Views of the Wall
The Vietnam Wall

Photo Essay   Poem by Alberto Ríos

AS YOU VIEW AND READ Consider how both the photographs and the poem express the reactions of visitors to the Vietnam Veterans Memorial. Write down any questions you generate.

Views of the Wall
Photo Essay

The Vietnam Wall
Poem by Alberto Ríos

I
Have seen it
And I like it: The magic,
The way like cutting onions
5 It brings water out of nowhere.
Invisible from one side, a scar
Into the skin of the ground
From the other, a black winding
Appendix line.
10   A dig.
            An archaeologist can explain.
The walk is slow at first
Easy, a little black marble wall
Of a dollhouse,
15 A smoothness, a shine
The boys in the street want to give.
One name. And then more
Names, long lines, lines of names until
They are the shape of the U.N. building[1]
20 Taller than I am: I have walked
Into a grave.
And everything I expect has been taken away, like that, quick:
            The names are not alphabetized.
            They are in the order of dying.
25   An alphabet of—somewhere—screaming.
I start to walk out. I almost leave
But stop to look up names of friends,
My own name. There is somebody
Severiano Ríos.
30 Little kids do not make the same noise
Here, junior high school boys don't run
Or hold each other in headlocks.
No rules, something just persists
Like pinching on St. Patrick's Day
35 Every year for no green.
            No one knows why.

---

[1] **U. N. Building:** headquarters of the United Nations in New York City.

Flowers are forced
Into the cracks
Between sections.
40 Men have cried
At this wall.
I have
Seen them.

COLLABORATIVE DISCUSSION In a small group, discuss how the photographs and the poem depict visitors' reactions to the Vietnam Veterans Memorial. What details are emphasized in each? Use details from the photo essay and the poem to support your discussion.

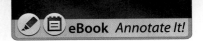

Analyze Representations in Different Mediums

A subject, such as the Vietnam Veterans Memorial, can be represented in different **artistic mediums,** such as poems, stories, paintings, or photographs. Each artistic medium can emphasize certain aspects of the subject. For example, an author might emphasize an emotion evoked by the subject and give a personal, internal reaction. A visual artist, on the other hand, may show intricate, physical details of the subject that a writer might not be able to express. Rather than using words to describe people's emotions, an artist shows them using visual images. Analyzing how different mediums express the same or similar ideas can help you become a more critical reader and viewer.

Analyzing Text and Media

Cite Text Evidence Support your responses with evidence from the selections.

1. **Draw Conclusions** What is the central idea of both the photo essay and the poem? How is the subject matter related to the central idea that the photographs and the poem convey?

2. **Analyze** A **simile** makes a comparison between two unlike things, using the words *like* or *as*. Explain the simile Ríos uses in lines 3–4. Are the photographs in the photo essay able to show this kind comparison? Explain.

3. **Compare** What are the similarities and differences between presenting ideas in photographs versus a poem? What does each emphasize or leave out?

PERFORMANCE TASK

Media Activity: Reflection Choose between two mediums (Activity A or B) to express ideas about the value of war memorials.

A. Think about the ideas expressed in the poem and the photo essay. Draw a picture or paint a scene to express similar ideas. Then write a short description of the difference between what a painting or drawing can express as compared to photographs or a poem.

B. Work with a partner to produce a short video interviewing classmates and teachers about the memorial. Include a final scene in which you and your partner discuss the advantages and disadvantages of using film to capture emotions about the memorial.

Present a Speech

This collection focuses on the conflict and the tension between individuals and society—from the individual's struggle to be a part of a society to a nation's struggle to unite for a common cause. Look back at the anchor text, "A Quilt of a Country," and at the other texts you have read in this collection. Synthesize your ideas about them by preparing and presenting a speech.

An effective speech

- has a clear, logical, and well-defended claim
- provides evidence from the texts to support a claim
- includes an introduction, a logically structured body including transitions, and a conclusion
- demonstrates appropriate and clear use of language
- engages listeners with appropriate emphasis, volume, and gestures

PLAN

Analyze the Text Think back to the quotation from Kofi Annan that opened this collection: "We may have different religions, different languages, different colored skin, but we all belong to one human race."

- Now choose three texts from this collection, including "A Quilt of a Country," and identify what each author suggests about how individuals can live together as members of "one human race."
- Make notes from each text about how the authors convey their ideas relating to the individual's role in society.
- Note specific examples and quotations in the texts that provide strong evidence for each author's ideas.

Evaluate Your Own View Which author shares your own view about the role of individuals in living together as members of "one human race"?

- Make notes on your view about the role of individuals in society.
- Provide evidence from your experience that supports your view.
- Explain why you agree or disagree with the authors of your three chosen texts.

myNotebook

Use the notebook in your eBook to record examples and quotations that address each author's ideas about the individual's role in society.

ACADEMIC VOCABULARY

As you share your ideas about the role of individuals in society, be sure to use these words.

enforce
entity
internal
presume
resolve

Make a Claim Based on these texts and your own experience, write a claim about the individual's role in society. This will be the central idea of your speech. Remember that you will need to provide sufficient evidence to support your claim.

Get Organized Organize your notes in an outline. You will need to present your ideas clearly so that your audience—your classmates—can follow the reasoning and evidence for your claim.

- Write your claim about the role of individuals in society in the introduction section of your outline.
- In the body section, list the main reasons that support your claim.
- For each reason, cite evidence from the three texts and from your own experience that support the reason.
- Reiterate your claim in the concluding section.

PRODUCE

Write Your Speech Use your notes to write a clearly organized speech with an introduction, a body, and a conclusion. Share your ideas about the individual's role in society, providing support for your claim with evidence from the texts. Keep in mind the purpose of your speech and your audience. Remember to include

- transitions between the main sections of your speech
- quotations and examples from the texts and your own experience to support your claim
- formal language and sentence structures appropriate for an oral presentation
- a variety of grammatical structures that will keep your audience engaged and interested in your speech

Plan Your Presentation When you deliver your speech to an audience, you will need to make it come alive with appropriate expression, volume, and gestures. Read over your draft and mark places in the text where you might want to

- emphasize a word or phrase
- pause to give the audience time to consider an important idea
- use gestures to convey meaning or emotion

*my***WriteSmart**

Write your rough draft in *my*WriteSmart. Focus on getting your ideas down, rather than perfecting your choice of language.

Make Sense of Things

It is now time to revise your draft to make sure your audience will understand it. Your goal is to clearly and concisely present your ideas about the individual's role as a member of "one human race." Use the chart on the following page to review the characteristics of an effective speech. Then read the rough draft of your speech, ensuring that your listeners will be able to

- follow your reasoning, organization, and development of ideas
- understand specific meanings conveyed by your words and sentences
- correctly interpret emphasis and gestures

*my*WriteSmart

Have your partner or a group of peers review your draft in *my*WriteSmart. Ask your reviewers to note places where you should add emphasis or gestures.

Practice Your Delivery

Before presenting to the class, practice with a partner.

- Mark your text to show where you will use your voice or a gesture to emphasize a point.
- Speak at an appropriate volume so that your audience can hear you clearly.
- Practice your pace so that you can finish on time. Have your partner time you while you practice.
- Allow your partner to give you feedback, and then make any changes to your speech before presenting to the whole class.

	Ideas and Evidence	Organization	Language
ADVANCED	• The introduction immediately engages the audience; the claim clearly states the speaker's position. • Valid reasons and relevant evidence from the texts and from the speaker's experience strongly support the speaker's claim. • The concluding section effectively summarizes the claim.	• The reasons and evidence are organized consistently and logically throughout the speech. • Varied transitions logically connect reasons and evidence to the speaker's claim.	• The speech reflects a formal style and an objective, or controlled, tone. • Sentence beginnings, lengths, and structures vary and have a rhythmic flow. • Grammar, usage, and mechanics are correct.
COMPETENT	• The introduction could do more to capture the audience's attention; the speaker's claim states a position. • Most reasons and evidence from the texts and from the speaker's experience support the speaker's claim, but they could be more substantial. • The concluding section restates the claim.	• The organization of reasons and evidence is confusing in a few places. • A few more transitions are needed to connect reasons and evidence to the speaker's claim.	• The style is informal in a few places, and the tone is defensive at times. • Sentence beginnings, lengths, and structures vary somewhat. • Some grammatical and usage errors are repeated in the speech.
LIMITED	• The introduction is ordinary; the speaker's claim identifies an issue, but the position is not clearly stated. • The reasons and evidence from the texts and from the speaker's experience are not always logical or relevant. • The concluding section includes an incomplete summary of the claim.	• The organization of reasons and evidence is logical in some places, but it often doesn't follow a pattern. • Many more transitions are needed to connect reasons and evidence to the speaker's position.	• The style becomes informal in many places, and the tone is often dismissive of other viewpoints. • Sentence structures barely vary, and some fragments or run-on sentences are evident. • Grammar and usage are incorrect in many places, but the speaker's ideas are still clear.
EMERGING	• The introduction is confusing. • Significant supporting reasons and evidence from the texts and from the speaker's experience are missing. • The concluding section is missing.	• A logical organization is not used; reasons and evidence are presented randomly. • Transitions are not used, making the speech difficult to understand.	• The style is inappropriate, and the tone is disrespectful. • Repetitive sentence structure, fragments, and run-on sentences make the speech monotonous and hard to follow. • Many grammatical and usage errors change the meaning of the speaker's ideas.

Write an Analytical Essay

This collection focuses on the conflict and the tension between individuals and society—from the individual's struggle to be a part of a society to a nation's struggle to unite for a common cause. Look back at the anchor text, "Once Upon a Time," and at the other texts you have read in this collection. Synthesize your ideas about them by writing an analytical essay.

An effective analytical essay

- clearly and accurately analyzes the content of the texts
- provides quotations or examples from the texts to illustrate main points
- has an introduction, a logically structured body including transitions, and a conclusion
- follows the conventions of written English

PLAN

my Notebook

Use the annotation tools in your eBook to locate evidence that supports your controlling idea. Save each piece of evidence to your notebook.

Analyze the Text Choose three texts from this collection, including "Once Upon a Time," and identify a powerful symbol or image used in each text to convey an idea about the individual's role in society.

- Make notes about the symbol or image used in each text.
- Think about how each writer uses the symbol or image to develop the theme or central idea of the text.
- Compare and contrast the authors' views. Do the authors share a common view about the individual's role in society, or do they differ? Explain.

ACADEMIC VOCABULARY

As you share your ideas about the role of individuals in society, be sure to use these words.

> enforce
> entity
> internal
> presume
> resolve

Get Organized Organize your notes in an outline.

Your introduction should

- begin with an engaging question or comment to help the audience connect to the topic
- identify the authors and titles of each text
- include a controlling idea that identifies the symbols or images each author uses to develop the theme or central idea

The body of the essay should

- present and support a main idea about the individual's role in society as presented in each of the texts
- show important connections between your chosen symbol or image and the theme or central idea of each text
- provide evidence from each text to illustrate the main idea
- explain how the quotations or examples support the main idea

Your conclusion should

- make a concluding statement that follows from or supports your main ideas
- state a more general or universal conclusion about the role of the individual in society

PRODUCE

Write a Draft Use your outline to write an analytical essay explaining how the authors use symbols or images to develop themes or central ideas in their work. Remember to

- provide a clear and cohesive introduction, body, and conclusion
- support your main points with evidence from the text
- explain how the evidence supports your ideas
- use language that is appropriate for your audience
- include transitions to link the major sections of the text

As you draft your analytical essay, remember that this kind of writing requires formal language and a respectful tone. Essays that analyze texts are expected to be appropriate for an academic context.

my WriteSmart

Write your rough draft in *my*WriteSmart. Focus on getting your ideas down, rather than perfecting your choice of language.

REVISE

Make Sense of Things You should now have a rough draft that explores the authors' use of symbols and images to develop their ideas about the individual's role in society. Revise your draft so that your readers will easily understand your analytical essay and the claim you are making. It is your goal to produce a clear and coherent text.

my WriteSmart

Have your partner or a group of peers review your draft in *my*WriteSmart. Ask your reviewers to note any main points that are not adequately supported with text evidence.

Refer to the chart on the following page to review the characteristics of a well-written analytical essay. Ensure that your first draft

- makes important connections between each symbol or image and the theme or central idea of the text
- has sufficient evidence to support these connections
- has a clearly developed introduction, body, and conclusion
- uses language and tone appropriate for an essay
- follows the conventions of standard English

Then write a new draft of your essay, incorporating any changes.

PRESENT

Exchange Essays When your new draft is completed, exchange your essay with a partner. Read your partner's essay and provide feedback. Reread the criteria for an effective analytical essay and ask the following questions:

- What did your partner do well in the essay?
- How could your partner's essay be improved?

	Ideas and Evidence	Organization	Language
ADVANCED	• An eloquent introduction includes the titles and authors of the works; the controlling idea presents a unique idea about the symbolism or images in the texts. • Specific, relevant evidence from the texts supports the key points. • A satisfying concluding section synthesizes the ideas, summarizes the analysis, and offers a unique insight into the texts.	• Key points and supporting details are organized effectively and logically throughout the analysis. • Varied transitions successfully show the relationships between ideas.	• The analysis has an appropriately formal style and a knowledgeable, objective tone. • Language is precise and captures the writer's thoughts with originality. • Sentence beginnings, lengths, and structures vary and have a rhythmic flow. • Spelling, capitalization, and punctuation are correct. If handwritten, the analysis is legible. • Grammar and usage are correct.
COMPETENT	• The introduction identifies the titles and authors of the works but could be more engaging; the controlling idea sets up symbolism or images for analysis. • One or two key points need more support. • The concluding section synthesizes most of the ideas and summarizes most of the analysis, but it doesn't provide an original insight.	• The organization of key points and supporting details is confusing in a few places. • A few more transitions are needed to clarify the relationships between ideas.	• The style becomes informal in a few places, and the tone does not always communicate confidence. • Most language is precise. • Sentence beginnings, lengths, and structures vary somewhat. • Several spelling, capitalization, and punctuation mistakes occur. If handwritten, the analysis is mostly legible. • Some grammatical and usage errors are repeated in the literary analysis.
LIMITED	• The introduction identifies the titles and the authors of the works; the controlling idea only hints at the main idea of the analysis. • Details support some key points but are often too general. • The concluding section gives an incomplete summary of the analysis and restates the controlling idea.	• Most key points are organized logically, but many supporting details are out of place. • More transitions are needed throughout the analysis to connect ideas.	• The style is informal in many places, and the tone reflects a superficial understanding of the works. • Language is repetitive or vague at times. • Sentence structures barely vary, with some fragments or run-on sentences. • Spelling, capitalization, and punctuation are often incorrect but do not make reading the analysis difficult. If handwritten, the analysis may be partially illegible. • Grammar and usage are incorrect in many places, but the writer's ideas are still clear.
EMERGING	• The appropriate elements of an introduction are missing. • Details and evidence are irrelevant or missing. • The analysis lacks a concluding section.	• A logical organization is not used; ideas are presented randomly. • Transitions are not used, making the analysis difficult to understand.	• The style and tone are inappropriate for the analysis. • Language is inaccurate, repetitive, and vague. • Repetitive sentence structure, fragments, and run-on sentences make the writing monotonous and difficult to follow. • Spelling, capitalization, and punctuation are incorrect throughout. If handwritten, the analysis may be partially or mostly illegible. • Many grammatical and usage errors change the meaning of the writer's ideas.

The Struggle for Freedom

❝If there is no struggle, there is no progress.**❞**

—Frederick Douglass

The Struggle for Freedom

From the American civil rights movement to the Middle East and Latin America, this collection explores the universal desire for freedom.

hmhfyi.com

COLLECTION

PERFORMANCE TASK Preview

At the end of this collection, you will have the opportunity to complete a task:

• Write an argumentative essay about whether freedom should be given or must be demanded.

ACADEMIC VOCABULARY

Study the words and their definitions in the chart below. You will use these words as you discuss and write about the texts in this collection.

Word	Definition	Related Forms
decline (dĭ-klīn´) *v.*	to fall apart or deteriorate slowly	declinable, decliner
enable (ĕ-nā´bəl) *tr.v.*	to give the means or opportunity	enabler
impose (ĭm-pōz´) *v.*	to bring about by force	imposer, imposition
integrate (ĭn´tĭ-grāt´) *v.*	to pull together into a whole; unify	integration, disintegrate
reveal (rĭ-vēl´) *tr.v.*	to show or make known	revealable, revealment

The March on Washington

I Have a Dream
Speech by Martin Luther King Jr.

from Nobody Turn Me Around: A History of the 1963 March on Washington
History Writing by Charles Euchner

MEDIA
AMERICA The Story of Us: March on Washington
Video by HISTORY®

Background *On August 28, 1963, thousands of Americans marched on Washington, D.C., to urge Congress to pass a civil rights bill. Martin Luther King Jr. delivered his "I Have a Dream" speech on the steps of the Lincoln Memorial before more than 250,000 people. After you read and analyze the speech, you will read an excerpt from a history text which describes the historic speech in detail and includes first-hand accounts from people who were on the National Mall that day. Then you will watch a short video about the march and compare the two accounts.*

Martin Luther King Jr. *(1929–1968) became a catalyst for social change in the 1950s and 1960s. Preaching a philosophy of nonviolence, he galvanized people of all races to participate in boycotts, marches, and demonstrations against racial injustice. His moral leadership stirred the conscience of the nation and helped bring about the passage of the Civil Rights Act of 1964. In that same year, he was awarded the Nobel Peace Prize. King continued his work for justice and equality until he was assassinated in 1968.*

I Have a Dream
Speech by Martin Luther King Jr.

AS YOU READ Note ways in which Dr. King uses words and phrases to inspire his audience. Write down any questions you have.

I am happy to join with you today in what will go down in history as the greatest demonstration for freedom in the history of our nation.

Five score[1] years ago, a great American, in whose symbolic shadow we stand today, signed the Emancipation Proclamation.[2] This momentous decree came as a great beacon light of hope to millions of Negro slaves who had been seared in the flames of withering injustice. It came as a joyous daybreak to end the long night of their captivity.

10 But one hundred years later, the Negro still is not free; one hundred years later, the life of the Negro is still sadly crippled by the manacles of segregation and the chains of discrimination; one hundred years later, the Negro lives on a lonely island of poverty in the midst of a vast ocean of material prosperity; one hundred years later, the Negro is still languishing in the corners of American society and finds himself in exile in his own land.

So we've come here today to dramatize a shameful condition. In a sense we've come to our nation's capital to cash a check. When the architects of our republic wrote the magnificent words of the 20 Constitution and the Declaration of Independence, they were signing a promissory note[3] to which every American was to fall heir. This note was the promise that all men, yes, black men as well as white men, would be guaranteed the unalienable rights of life, liberty, and the pursuit of happiness.

It is obvious today that America has **defaulted** on this promissory note insofar as her citizens of color are concerned. Instead of honoring this sacred obligation, America has given the Negro people a bad check, a check which has come back marked "insufficient funds." But we refuse to believe that the bank of justice 30 is bankrupt. We refuse to believe that there are insufficient funds in the great vaults of opportunity of this nation. And so we've come to

default
(dĭ-fôlt´) v.
to fail to keep a promise to repay a loan.

---

[1] **five score:** 100; *score* means "twenty." (This phrasing recalls the beginning of Abraham Lincoln's Gettysburg Address: "Four score and seven years ago . . .")

[2] **Emancipation Proclamation:** a document signed by President Lincoln in 1863, during the Civil War, declaring that all slaves in states still at war with the Union were free.

[3] **promissory note:** a written promise to repay a loan.

cash this check, a check that will give us upon demand the riches of freedom and the security of justice.

We have also come to this hallowed spot to remind America of the fierce urgency of now. This is no time to engage in the luxury of cooling off or to take the tranquilizing drug of gradualism. Now is the time to make real the promises of democracy; now is the time to rise from the dark and **desolate** valley of segregation to the sunlit path of racial justice; now is the time to lift our nation from
40 the quicksands of racial injustice to the solid rock of brotherhood; now is the time to make justice a reality for all of God's children. It would be fatal for the nation to overlook the urgency of the moment. This sweltering summer of the Negro's legitimate discontent will not pass until there is an invigorating autumn of freedom and equality.

Nineteen sixty-three is not an end, but a beginning. And those who hope that the Negro needed to blow off steam and will now be content will have a rude awakening if the nation returns to business as usual. There will be neither rest nor tranquility in America until
50 the Negro is granted his citizenship rights. The whirlwinds of revolt will continue to shake the foundations of our nation until the bright day of justice emerges.

But there is something that I must say to my people, who stand on the worn threshold which leads into the palace of justice. In the process of gaining our rightful place, we must not be guilty of wrongful deeds. Let us not seek to satisfy our thirst for freedom by drinking from the cup of bitterness and hatred. We must forever conduct our struggle on the high plain of dignity and discipline. We must not allow our creative protests to **degenerate** into physical
60 violence. Again and again we must rise to the majestic heights of meeting physical force with soul force. The marvelous new militancy, which has engulfed the Negro community, must not lead us to a distrust of all white people. For many of our white brothers, as evidenced by their presence here today, have come to realize that their destiny is tied up with our destiny. And they have come to realize that their freedom is **inextricably** bound to our freedom. We cannot walk alone. And as we walk, we must make the pledge that we shall always march ahead. We cannot turn back.

There are those who are asking the devotees of civil rights,
70 "When will you be satisfied?" We can never be satisfied as long as the Negro is the victim of the unspeakable horrors of police brutality; we can never be satisfied as long as our bodies, heavy with the fatigue of travel, cannot gain lodging in the motels of the highways and the hotels of the cities; we cannot be satisfied as long as the Negro's basic mobility is from a smaller ghetto to a larger one; we can never be satisfied as long as our children are

desolate
(dĕsʹə-lĭt) *adj.*
unhappy; lonely.

degenerate
(dĭ-jĕnʹər-āt) *v.*
to decline morally.

inextricably
(ĭn-ĕkʹstrĭ-kə-blē)
adv. in a way
impossible to
untangle.

stripped of their selfhood and robbed of their dignity by signs
stating For Whites Only; we cannot be satisfied as long as the
Negro in Mississippi cannot vote and a Negro in New York believes
80   he has nothing for which to vote. No! No, we are not satisfied, and
we will not be satisfied until "justice rolls down like waters and
righteousness like a mighty stream."

     I am not unmindful that some of you have come here out of
great trials and tribulations. Some of you have come fresh from
narrow jail cells. Some of you have come from areas where your
quest for freedom left you battered by the storms of persecution
and staggered by the winds of police brutality. You have been the
veterans of creative suffering. Continue to work with the faith
that unearned suffering is **redemptive**. Go back to Mississippi. Go
90   back to Alabama. Go back to South Carolina. Go back to Georgia.
Go back to Louisiana. Go back to the slums and ghettos of our
Northern cities, knowing that somehow this situation can and will
be changed. Let us not wallow in the valley of despair.

     I say to you today, my friends, even though we face the
difficulties of today and tomorrow, I still have a dream. It is a
dream deeply rooted in the American dream. I have a dream that
one day this nation will rise up and live out the true meaning of
its creed, "We hold these truths to be self-evident; that all men
are created equal." I have a dream that one day on the red hills of
100   Georgia, sons of former slaves and the sons of former slave owners
will be able to sit down together at the table of brotherhood. I have
a dream that one day even the state of Mississippi, a state sweltering
with the heat of injustice, sweltering with the heat of oppression,
will be transformed into an oasis of freedom and justice. I have
a dream that my four little children will one day live in a nation
where they will not be judged by the color of their skin, but by the
content of their character.

     I have a dream today!

     I have a dream that one day down in Alabama—with its vicious
110   racists, with its Governor having his lips dripping with the words of
interposition and nullification[4]—one day right there in Alabama,
little black boys and black girls will be able to join hands with little
white boys and white girls as sisters and brothers.

     I have a dream today!

     I have a dream that one day every valley shall be exalted, and
every hill and mountain shall be made low. The rough places
will be plain and the crooked places will be made straight, "and

redemptive
(rĭ-dĕmp´tĭv) *adj.*
causing freedom or
salvation.

---

[4] **Governor . . . nullification:** Rejecting a federal order to desegregate the
University of Alabama, Governor George Wallace claimed that the principle of
nullification (a state's alleged right to refuse a federal law) allowed him to resist
federal "interposition," or interference, in state affairs.

the glory of the Lord shall be revealed, and all flesh shall see it together."

120   This is our hope. This is the faith that I go back to the South with. With this faith we will be able to hew out of the mountain of despair a stone of hope. With this faith we will be able to transform the jangling discords of our nation into a beautiful symphony of brotherhood. With this faith we will be able to work together, to pray together, to struggle together, to go to jail together, to stand up for freedom together, knowing that we will be free one day. And this will be the day. This will be the day when all of God's children will be able to sing with new meaning, "My country 'tis of thee, sweet land of liberty, of thee I sing. Land where my fathers died, 130   land of the pilgrims' pride, from every mountainside, let freedom ring." And if America is to be a great nation, this must become true.

        So let freedom ring from the prodigious hilltops of New Hampshire; let freedom ring from the mighty mountains of New York; let freedom ring from the heightening Alleghenies of Pennsylvania; let freedom ring from the snowcapped Rockies of Colorado; let freedom ring from the curvaceous slopes of California. But not only that. Let freedom ring from Stone Mountain of Georgia; let freedom ring from Lookout Mountain of Tennessee; let freedom ring from every hill and molehill of 140   Mississippi. "From every mountainside, let freedom ring."

        And when this happens, and when we allow freedom to ring, when we let it ring from every village and every hamlet, from every state and every city, we will be able to speed up that day when all of God's children—black men and white men, Jews and Gentiles, Protestants and Catholics—will be able to join hands and sing in the words of the old Negro spiritual, "Free at last. Free at last. Thank God Almighty, we are free at last."

COLLABORATIVE DISCUSSION Which parts of the speech did you find the most inspiring? With a partner, discuss how King uses words and phrases to support his argument. Cite specific textual evidence from the speech in your discussion.

Analyze Author's Use of Rhetoric

To establish a point of view or purpose, authors and speakers like Martin Luther King Jr. use **rhetorical devices** to shape the structure of sentences and paragraphs within a work. Rhetorical devices can evoke an emotional response in an audience and make the message memorable. Here are some examples.

Repetition	Parallelism	Extended Metaphor
Uses the same word or words more than once for emphasis	Uses similar grammatical constructions to express ideas that are related or equal in importance. It often creates a rhythm.	Makes a comparison between two unlike things that continues at some length
"Let there be justice for all. Let there be peace for all. Let there be work, bread, water, and salt for all."	"We cannot, we must not, refuse to protect the right of every American to vote in every election. . . . And we ought not, and we cannot, and we must not wait another eight months before we get a bill."	"'A house divided against itself cannot stand.' I believe this government cannot endure permanently half slave and half free. I do not expect the Union to be dissolved; I do not expect the house to fall; but I do expect it will cease to be divided. It will become all one thing, or all the other."
—*from* "Glory and Hope" by Nelson Mandela	—*from* "We Shall Overcome" by Lyndon Baines Johnson	— *from* "A House Divided" by Abraham Lincoln

Analyze Seminal U. S. Documents

A **seminal U. S. document** is a document or speech from which a change in our nation's laws, society, or ideas about itself grew. Reading and analyzing important speeches like "I Have a Dream" is one of the best ways to understand our history and our national experience. To understand a speech's importance, you need to know something about its background, or **historical context.** Asking questions will help you understand its context better. To answer some of these questions, you may need to research information about the speaker and the events and attitudes of the day.

- Who is the speaker?
- Who was the audience?
- When and where was the speech presented?
- What was the purpose of the speech?
- How did the speech contribute to our national experience?

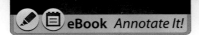

Analyzing the Text

Cite Text Evidence   Support your responses with evidence from the selection.

1. **Infer** The central point of an **argument** is the **claim,** or proposition. What is King's claim in this speech? What evidence does he cite to support his claim?

2. **Analyze** How does King structure, or organize, his speech? Explain how each section integrates his ideas and advances his argument.

3. **Interpret** An **allusion** is an indirect reference to something that the audience is expected to know. In his speech, King makes more than one allusion to the Declaration of Independence. Identify the allusions and explain how they advance King's argument.

4. **Interpret** King uses an extended metaphor to compare a familiar object—a bad check—to an abstract idea. How does King develop the metaphor? What does he believe was promised to African Americans? How has America given African Americans a "bad check?"

5. **Analyze** Find examples of parallelism in lines 36–41. What effect does the parallel structure create? What point is King emphasizing?

6. **Analyze** Identify two examples of repetition in the speech. Explain why these words or phrases are important and how they advance King's argument.

7. **Evaluate** Why do you think King's "I Have a Dream" speech is remembered as one of the most significant speeches in American history? Explain what makes the speech memorable and how it contributes to the ideal of an American society.

PERFORMANCE TASK

Writing Activity: Analysis In Collection 1, you read another seminal United States speech, Abraham Lincoln's Gettysburg Address. Compare the ideas in Lincoln's speech to "I Have a Dream." Write a one- to two-page analytical essay in which you compare how Lincoln and King address the theme of freedom.

1. Identify each speaker's purpose.

2. Evaluate how the idea of freedom is articulated in each speech.

3. Give examples of how each speaker uses rhetorical devices to achieve his purpose.

4. Use the conventions of standard English.

Critical Vocabulary

default   desolate   degenerate   inextricably   redemptive

Practice and Apply Answer the following questions in complete sentences, incorporating the Critical Vocabulary words and their meanings.

1. Look back at line 25. Why does King say that America has **defaulted,** and what makes this word choice especially effective?

2. Look back at line 38. In what ways is segregation **desolate**? How might referring to segregation as **desolate** help persuade listeners?

3. Look back at line 59. How is physical violence a good example of how protests might **degenerate**? How does this reflect King's views?

4. Look back at line 66. How is the freedom of white people **inextricably** bound to that of black people?

5. Look back at line 89. How and why does King use the word **redemptive** to link the concepts of freedom and religious faith?

Language and Style: Repetition and Parallelism

One grammatical feature that makes King's rhetoric so effective is his use of **repetition** and **parallelism**—expressing related ideas using similar grammatical constructions. By creating a pattern through repeated phrases and structures, King both creates a strong rhythm in his speech and links his ideas in listeners' minds. Here are some examples from "I Have a Dream":

Repetition

> We can <u>never be satisfied</u> as long as the Negro is the victim of the unspeakable horrors of police brutality; <u>we can never be satisfied</u> as long as our bodies, heavy with the fatigue of travel, cannot gain lodging in the motels of the highways and the hotels of the cities; . . .

Parallelism

> ". . . we will be able <u>to work together</u>, <u>to pray together</u>, <u>to struggle together</u>, <u>to go to jail together</u>, <u>to stand up for freedom together</u> . . ."

Practice and Apply Look back at the essay you wrote for this selection's Performance Task. Find two places where you can revise your wording to make it parallel. Then, locate two places where you can use repetition for effect. Finally, write two sentences explaining how repetition and parallel structure helped you communicate your ideas to readers.

Background *This excerpt from* Nobody Turn Me Around: A People's History of the 1963 March on Washington *provides a detailed account of one of the most iconic days in American history.*

from Nobody Turn Me Around: A People's History of the 1963 March on Washington
History Writing by Charles Euchner

AS YOU READ Note how the author structures the text to help you visualize the event. Write down any questions you generate.

Always, he begins slowly, like thunder rolling from a distance before a great storm.

Martin Luther King speaks deliberately, like a 45 rpm record being played at 33⅓ rpm speed.[1] His long, thick, baritone words stretch out to establish a new mood. In a low drawl, he emphasizes syllables to create his own **cadence,** to bring his audience into the flow of emotions.

"I am *hap*py to *join* with you to*day*," he says, sounding mournful, "in what will go *down* in *his*tory as the *great*est
10 *demon*stration for *free*dom in the *his*tory of our *nat*ion."

Martin Luther King invokes Abraham Lincoln and tells the long, hard story of the subjection of American blacks.

"Five score years ago, a great American, in whose symbolic shadow we stand today, signed the Emancipation Proclamation. This momentous decree came as a great beacon light of hope to millions of Negro slaves who had been seared in the flames of withering injustice. It came as a joyous daybreak to end the long night of their captivity."

King's Southern accent, softened by time spent in his family's
20 bourgeois circles[2] and tempered by years in the North, put a special emphasis on his words: "in the *his-tor-eh* of our *ow-a* nation" . . . "a *gret* American" . . . "symbolic *shadda*" . . . "*gret beckon* light."

Long night of captivity. King's brooding voice tells two **parallel** stories of exile and return. For hundreds of years, Jews were held in captivity, as slaves, in Egypt—like blacks in America. They struggled to maintain their own identity—like blacks in America. They endured because of their faith in God—like blacks in

cadence
(kād´ns) *n.* lyrical rhythm.

parallel
(păr´ə-lĕl´) *adj.* related; corresponding.

---

[1] **45 rpm record . . . 33 ½ speed:** a recorded disc, designed to spin on a turntable at 45 revolutions per minute, playing at a slower speed (33 ½ rpm), which produces a deeper, drawn-out sound.
[2] **bourgeois circles (bŏŏr-zhwä´):** middle-class group of friends.

America. And then one day, they freed themselves from bondage—
like blacks will, one day, as well.

30   His voice is steady, but King wants to find his pacing. If he
moves slowly, he will not falter, and he will find a way to bring the
crowd with him.

Right away, King uses anaphora, the repetition of key words
and phrases at the beginning of successive statements. Repetition
brings the listener back to a familiar place, then connects to a
new thought or image. Repetition keeps the audience involved.
Repetition makes it easy to remember the words and to get into a
rhythm, as they become familiar. Repetition invites the call and
response in black churches across the South. *Yeah! Uh-huh! Amen!*
40 *That's right!*

After recalling the story of Lincoln freeing the slaves, with the
simple stroke of a pen in the middle of a bloody war, King laments
the inferior position of blacks a century later. Each mournful
repetition deepens the pain, raises the dramatic tension. Each
repetition condemns the oppressor. The oration becomes poetry:

> But one hundred years later, the Negro still is not free.
> One hundred years later, the life of the Negro is still
>   sadly crippled by the manacles of segregation and
>   the chains of discrimination.
50 One hundred years later, the Negro lives on a lonely
>   island of poverty in the midst of a vast ocean of
>   material prosperity.
> One hundred years later, the Negro is still languished
>   in the corners of American society and finds
>   himself in exile in his own country.

King looks down at his text, shakes his head as he speaks. He
rocks back and forth on the balls of his feet as he finds his rhythm.

Every **invocation** of "one hundred years" emphasizes the
horrors of the black's position in American life. *Not free. Crippled.*
60 *Manacles. Chains. Lonely island of poverty. Languished in the
corners. Exile in his own country.*

And then King introduces Clarence Jones's[3] metaphor of the
bad check, so simple and so basic. A bad check represents bad faith,
failed promises, broken contracts.

> In a sense we have come to our nation's capital to cash
>   a check. When the architects of our republic wrote
>   the magnificent words of the Constitution and the

invocation
(ĭn′və-kā′shən) *n.* a
formal appeal, often
used in prayer.

---

[3] **Clarence Jones:** (b. 1931) King's attorney and advisor, who helped prepare many
speeches.

Declaration of Independence, they were signing a
promissory note to which every American was to
fall heir. This note was a promise that all men—
yes, black men as well as white men—would be
guaranteed the unalienable rights of life, liberty, and
the pursuit of happiness.

It is obvious today that America has defaulted on this
promissory note insofar as her citizens of color
are concerned. Instead of honoring this sacred
obligation, America has given the Negro people a
bad check, a check which has come back marked
"insufficient funds."

The first burst of applauses rises up from the crowd.
"But we *refuse* to believe that the bank of justice is bankrupt.
We *refuse* to believe that there are insufficient funds in the great
vaults of opportunity of this nation."

Laughter from the crowd. Shouts: "Uh huh!" "Yeah!" "Sure enough!"

"So we have come to cash this check—a check that will give us upon demand the riches of freedom and the security of justice."

A second, greater burst of applause.

90 Now King honors his country, calling attention to the **civic** power of Lincoln's monument. He rejects calls to "go slow" and "cool off."

"We have also come to this hallowed spot to remind America of *the fierce urgency of now.* This is no time to engage in the luxury of cooling off or to take the tranquilizing drug of gradualism."

The crowd ripples with recognition, then knowing laughter. A thin black man sitting close to the stage hears the tranquilizer reference, looks down for a moment, thoughtfully, then looks up and explodes in laughter. King's line releases some toxin from the body.

100 For this one moment, the stubbornness of racism lifts and the people revel in a moment of integrated community.

> Now is the time to make real the promises of
>   democracy.
> Now is the time to rise from the dark and desolate
>   valley of segregation to the sunlit path of racial
>   justice.
> Now is the time to lift our nation from the quicksands
>   of racial injustice to the solid rock of brotherhood.
> Now is the time to make justice a reality for all of
110   God's children.

Each invocation pulls the audience into the future. And people in the crowd respond. *You got it! Yes it is! Yeah! Amen! Now is the time! Now! That's right!*

Across the Mall, people have quieted down. King's voice echoes, his baritone voice triumphing over the tinny sounds of the loudspeakers. Whispers can be heard in spots. A soft breeze, occasionally rippling over the crowd, is louder than the sounds of the masses below.

King now warns the Washington establishment—and the vast 120 middle class, what one politician would call the "forgotten middle class" and the "silent majority"—that gradual improvements will not satisfy blacks anymore. Conflict could turn into a bloodbath unless the American people redeem the promise of freedom.

> It would be fatal for the nation to overlook
>   the urgency of the moment.

This sweltering summer of the Negro's legitimate
discontent will not pass until there is an
invigorating autumn of freedom and equality.
Nineteen sixty-three is not an end, but a beginning.
130   Those who hope that the Negro needed to blow off
steam and will now be content will have a rude
awakening if the nation returns to business as usual.
There will be neither rest nor tranquility in America
until the Negro is granted his citizenship rights.
The whirlwinds of revolt will continue to shake the
foundations of our nation until the bright day of
justice emerges.

Subtly, King conjures images of apocalypse. The "whirlwinds
of revolt" echo the countless moments where the Bible talks about
140 staggering catastrophe, when evil brings forth flood, famine,
drought, a plague of locusts, and the chaos of the Tower of Babel.[4]
As Jeremiah (4:20) teaches: "Disaster on disaster is proclaimed /
For the whole land is devastated."

> **For this one moment, the stubbornness of racism lifts and the people revel in a moment of integrated community.**

King warns his people to maintain their own dignity, to avoid
the temptation to embrace bitterness or violence. He speaks to the
followers of Malcolm X, who offers a simpler, purer, solution—
fighting back, by any means necessary.[5]

---

[4] **Tower of Babel:** according to the bible, a tall structure built when people all
spoke the same language. God disrupted the work by so confusing the language
of the workers they could no longer work together.

[5] **Malcolm X…necessary:** (1925–1965) African American activist who believed
that people should demand and protect their human rights in any way they can.

"But there is something that I must say to my people who stand on the warm threshold which leads into the palace of justice. In the process of gaining our rightful place, we must not be guilty of wrongful deeds.

"Let us not seek to satisfy our thirst for freedom by drinking from the cup of bitterness and hatred."

O Lord! Amen! Yes! Sure enough!

"We must forever conduct our struggle on the high plane of dignity and discipline. We must not allow our creative protest to degenerate into physical violence. Again and again, we must rise to the majestic heights of meeting physical force with soul force.

"The marvelous new militancy which has engulfed the Negro community must not lead us to a distrust of all white people, for many of our white brothers, as evidenced by their presence here today, have come to realize"—his voice rises—"that their destiny is tied up with our destiny."

Marvelous militancy. All summer, critics of the civil rights movement have wondered why blacks cannot be more patient. The president, congressmen, newspaper publishers, TV commentators, professors, mayors, unions, corporate CEOs, churches, social organizations—everyone seemed to be saying to go slow. But the time for patience is over. Militancy—*marvelous militancy,* borne of great patience and suffering, expressed with love, and applied with the tools of nonviolence—is now the movement's watchword.

Cheers rise up, louder and more sustained than before. People smile.

"They have come to realize that their freedom is inextricably bound to our freedom. We cannot walk alone.

"As we walk, we must make the pledge that we shall always march ahead. We cannot turn back. There are those who are asking the devotees of civil rights, 'When will you be satisfied?'"

Not everyone could hear King's words. The sound system, the best available, still crackled and blanked out. Far from the Lincoln Memorial, people followed the words on transistor radios—and by watching the movement of bodies ahead. "Down near the front there were people jumping up, waving hands and flags and signs," Elsa Rael said. "We were a little out of it, so we had to make our own joy—so we were singing. We got small bursts of words from King and shut up."

> We can never be satisfied as long as the Negro is
> the victim of the unspeakable horrors of police
> brutality.

190   We can never be satisfied, as long as our bodies, heavy
           with the fatigue of travel, cannot gain lodging in the
           motels of the highways and the hotels of the cities.
       We cannot be satisfied as long as the Negro's basic
           mobility is from a smaller ghetto to a larger one.
       We can never be satisfied as long as our children
           are stripped of their selfhood and robbed of their
           dignity by signs stating "For Whites Only."
       We cannot be satisfied as long as a Negro in
           Mississippi cannot vote and a Negro in New York
200   believes he has nothing for which to vote.
       No, no, we are not satisfied, and we will not be
           satisfied until justice rolls down like waters and
           righteousness like a mighty stream.

With each line, King increases the stakes for his movement. He
begins with police brutality, the search for night lodging and food,
and life in the ghetto. He moves on to children's dignity and the
right to vote. He ends with the prophet Amos's great image of the
Kingdom of Heaven on earth.

Each round gets cheers. First scattered clapping and cheers and
210 calls. *Yes!* Then more. *That's right!* Finally, huge applause. *My Lord!*

Every good preacher—every good leader—connects with the
real circumstances of his audience's lives. *I know your pain. I have
shared in your pain. I have been beaten and jailed and **reviled**. I have
not forgotten how you have suffered. I know, so you can trust me.*
King has spent a decade learning about the problems of the people
assembled before him. He has worked, intimately, with people at
the highest and lowest levels of society.

revile
(rĭ-vīl´) *v.* to
condemn or insult.

       I am not unmindful that some of you have come here
           out of great trials and tribulations.
220   Some of you have come fresh from narrow jail cells.
       Some of you have come from areas where your quest
           for freedom left you battered by the storms of
           persecution and staggered by the winds of police
           brutality.
       You have been the veterans of creative suffering.
       Continue to work with the faith that unearned
           suffering is redemptive.

That brief phrase—*unearned suffering is redemptive*—strikes
Harold Bragg "like an electric shock."
230   Harold and his wife, Lynn, traveled all night from Kent, Ohio,
in their VW Beetle. Harold sits on a stool, holding an umbrella over

Lynn's head to block the sun. For the first part of King's speech, they listen to King "like it was a lesson from a great master."

Now the idea of suffering for redemption surges through Harold's body. He remembers his father telling him about his grandfather—one of the few black landowners in Alabama—sitting on a horse, getting shot by a white farmer who was jealous that a colored man could command such an **expanse**. His father, five years old when this happened back in 1917, saw his father fall dead off the horse.

240   The lesson his father and mother passed on when he told their children that story was: "You return hatred with love."

King's whole speech has told of the hard, violent, brutal, unfair, unjust life of blacks in America. The wrong people have suffered. So many people have been teargassed, beaten, kicked, burned, bombed, shot.

expanse
(ĭk-spăns´) *n.* a large area.

But that suffering—like Christ's suffering on the cross—can bring a better day. That suffering can change people's hearts. That suffering can clear poison from the system.

Then change can come.

250 *Unearned suffering is redemptive.* Believe it, and you will fight on—with Martin. Disbelieve it, and you will be gripped by despair—or the combative, uncompromising, separatist jingoism of Malcolm.[6]

For now, the crowd stands with King. Even the separatists stand with King, now.

For that redemption to happen—to change the world—people need to return to their homes to fight and suffer, still more, for the cause of justice. So:

> Go back to Mississippi,
> go back to Alabama,
260 > go back to South Carolina,
> go back to Georgia,
> go back to Louisiana,
> go back to the slums and ghettos of our northern
>   cities,
> knowing that somehow this situation can and will be
>   changed. Let us not wallow in the valley of despair,
> I say to you today, my friends.

Just feet from King, Mahalia Jackson[7] calls out. Mahalia is an old family friend of the Kings. She has been a guest in the Kings' 270 house. She was with King in Detroit about a month ago when King talked about a dream.

"Tell them about the dream, Martin!" she shouts. "*Please* . . . tell them about the dream!"

King does not hear her, but he doesn't need to hear her. He already knows he's going to talk about the dream. He shouted out his dream last night, in his hotel room, after everyone else went to bed.

Clarence Jones, sitting about fifteen feet away, sees King grab the podium, lean back, and turn over his prepared text. "These 280 people don't know it," Jones says, "but they are about to go to *church.*"

> So even though we face the difficulties of today and
>   tomorrow, I still have a dream.
> It is a dream deeply rooted in the American Dream . . . .

---

[6] **separatist jingoism of Malcolm:** Malcolm X's belief that African Americans should develop and support their own social institutions and communities.

[7] **Mahalia Jackson:** (1911–1972) a leading African American singer of gospel music who became very active in the civil-rights movement.

I have a dream that one day this nation will rise up
and live out the true meaning of its creed: "We
hold these truths to be self-evident: that all men are
created equal."
I have a dream that one day on the red hills of Georgia
290   the sons of former slaves and the sons of former
slave owners will be able to sit down together at the
table of brotherhood.
I have a dream that one day even the state of
Mississippi, a state sweltering with the heat of
injustice, sweltering with the heat of oppression, will
be transformed into an oasis of freedom and justice.

Richard Pritchard, a skinny white preacher from Wisconsin
who returned to the United States from Africa just last night, sits
by the reflecting pool. When his wife told him about the march, he
300 jumped into a car at his family's home in New Jersey. All day he's
been jet-lagged and weary from his early morning drive.

But now, lightning shoots through his body as he hears about
the dream. He remembers—*feels*—his own dream, which called
him to the ministry decades before.

Pritchard became a minister because he believed God saved
him as a small child, when he spent three years in the hospital

" Talk about the dream transforms time and space. "

with tuberculosis. And then, as a young priest, he saw racism in God's own flock. White priests wouldn't take assignments in black churches—and so he decided to become the pastor of a black parish in Kansas City. Later, at a different church, members of his own parish made racist statements. Didn't they understand that God loved blacks as much as whites?

"My dream was to make Christ more realistic," he says. "I used to talk about it—*my dream*. When I was a kid I used to hear how the English talked about the Welsh as savages in the hills, and that's what they were saying about blacks. I could feel how blacks would feel. In Christ there is no Jew or Greek, slave or free, male or female. We are all free in Christ."

So skinny you can see his bones, the Reverend Pritchard dangles his feet in the water. He is being baptized anew. King's dream is his dream. The image almost removes him from the throng, and at the same time connects him even more with the throng.

"It's funny, it hit me with such force."

> I have a dream that my four little children will one
>   day live in a nation where they will not be judged
>   by the color of their skin but by the content of their
>   character.
> I have a dream today.
> I have a dream that one day, down in Alabama, with
>   its vicious racists, with its governor having his
>   lips dripping with the words of interposition and
>   nullification; one day right there in Alabama, little
>   black boys and black girls will be able to join hands
>   with little white boys and white girls as sisters and
>   brothers.
> I have a dream today.
> I have a dream that one day every valley shall be
>   exalted, every hill and mountain shall be made
>   low, the rough places will be made plain, and the
>   crooked places, will be made straight, and the glory
>   of the Lord shall be revealed, and all flesh shall see
>   it together.

Talk about the dream transforms time and space. What might come to pass, later, seems at hand, *now*. With faith, ideals can be more real than the pain or poverty of the here and now.

Sitting on a patch of grass far from the Lincoln Memorial, sipping cold drinks from thermoses, Ruth bat Mordecai and some kids from a New York-based American Jewish Congress youth group listen to Martin Luther King's dream.

As King gives voice to his dream, Ruth watches some black boys nearby. The boys laugh as King's voice climbs the ladder, higher and higher. They laugh so freely that their bodies shake. Ruth knows the crowd includes cynics, and she resents having her experience of King's dream ruined by *these ones*. How can you openly mock *Dr. King*—at an event like *this?* And nobody seems to care!

"Suddenly," she recalls, "we understand. The black boys are laughing not in mockery but in joy—at the utter preposterousness of what Dr. King promises, and at its unutterable beauty."

Across the Mall, people call out the lines to each other.

"I have a dream," one says,

"That *one* day, little black boys and black girls . . ." says another. "I have a *dream!*" someone else says.

"*Dowwwn* in Ala*bama* . . ." comes the response.

Strangers shout out: "I have a *dream!*"

Tears fill Harold Bragg's eyes. "It's like being before the pearly gates, as though we had reached the Promised Land," he says, "even though King was laying out what was *to come.*"

With this dream, King brings his audience into a separate world, a distant, far-off place, but still so familiar. What is unreal is also very real.

Then King moves to sustain his people for the hard journey ahead. He reminds the crowd that they need faith—stronger than any troubles of the moment—to realize the dream.

> This is our hope. This is the faith that I go back to the
> South with.
> With this faith we will be able to hew out of the
> mountain of despair a stone of hope.
> With this faith we will be able to transform the
> jangling discords of our nation into a beautiful
> symphony of brotherhood.
> With this faith we will be able to work together, to pray
> together, to struggle together, to go to jail together,
> to stand up for freedom together, knowing that we
> will be free one day.

King connects simple statements, repeated again and again—"One hundred years later," "Now is the time," "We cannot be satisfied," "Go back," "I have a dream," "With this faith"—to
America's true national anthem.

"This will be the day," he says, "when all of God's children will be able to sing with a new meaning, 'My country, 'tis of thee, sweet land of *liberty,* of *thee* I sing. Land where my *fathers* died, land of the *pilgrim's* pride, from *every* mountainside, *let freedom ring.*' And if America is to be a great nation this *must* become true."

If . . .

Then, full of the passion of the words of that simple anthem, King imagines freedom ringing—a dreamlike image—and **exhorts** the crowd to make this vision happen. He sings out lines full of sounds and sights—postcards from the American Dream.

> So let freedom ring from the prodigious hilltops of
>   New Hampshire.
> Let freedom ring from the mighty mountains of New
>   York.
> Let freedom ring from the heightening Alleghenies of
>   Pennsylvania!
> Let freedom ring from the snowcapped Rockies of
>   Colorado!
> Let freedom ring from the curvaceous slopes of
>   California!

All of these are Northern places, and their images are ones of pure beauty. But that's not enough, King now **invokes** the sites of repression across the South.

> But not only that.
> Let freedom ring from Stone Mountain of Georgia!
> Let freedom ring from Lookout Mountain of
>   Tennessee!
> Let freedom ring from every hill and molehill of
>   Mississippi!
> From every mountainside,
> let freedom ring!

Those lines come from one of King's old friends, a preacher from Chicago named Archibald Carey. In a speech at the 1952 Republican Convention, Carey sang "My Country, 'Tis of Thee" and cried "Let freedom ring!" and issued some of those same postcards.

Finally, dizzy from the view of a nation teeming with freedom, King offers the moment of deliverance.

He sways now. He lifts his whole body with the speech. The people in the crowd follow their King. They sway, they smile, and they laugh with anticipation of every new image.

exhort
(ĭg-zôrt´) *v.* to strongly urge or encourage.

invoke
(ĭn-vōk´) *v.* to refer or call attention to.

400

410

420

430

And when this happens,
when we allow freedom to ring,
when we let it *ring* from every village and every
     hamlet,
from *every* state and *every* city,
we will be able to speed up that day when all of God's
     children,
black men and *white* men,
Jews and *Gentiles,*
Protestants and *Catholics*—

440

Martin Luther King turns to his right and raises his right arm high, his elbow bent slightly, blessing the congregation at this great mass.

"—will be able to join hands and sing in the *words* of the old Negro spiritual, "Free at *last*! Free at *last*! Thank God *Almighty,* we are *free at last*!"

COLLABORATIVE DISCUSSION With a partner, discuss how the writer structures his account of the March on Washington. Cite specific details and examples from the text.

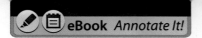

Analyze Ideas and Events

To show connections between ideas, authors structure a text so that each sentence and paragraph supports and develops a central idea. In recounting a historical event, authors usually provide readers with details and support for the central idea such as:

- a factual account of the event
- background information
- quotations and anecdotes, or personal stories, from eyewitnesses

Charles Euchner's approach is unusual because he goes beyond what we usually see in a history text to offer his own detailed analysis of the text of Martin Luther King Jr.'s "I Have a Dream" speech. For example, in lines 62–64, Euchner analyzes King's extended metaphor of the bad check.

> **And then King introduces Clarence Jones's metaphor of the bad check, so simple and so basic. A bad check represents bad faith, failed promises, broken contracts.**

Euchner then goes on to quote from King's speech and includes details of how the audience responds to the metaphor. This structure of support enables Euchner's readers to visualize the actual effect of the speech as it was delivered. This type of idea development throughout the history text shapes and refines the central idea. Think about the other kinds of support Euchner uses in his account. How do the details he includes relate to his analysis of the speech?

Analyzing the Text

Cite Text Evidence   Support your responses with evidence from the selection.

1. **Analyze** Briefly describe the text structure Euchner uses in his account. How does he organize the text so that each idea is connected and developed? Cite specific examples to support your response.

2. **Analyze** Notice that Euchner uses present-tense verbs in his account. In what verb tense is historical text usually written? What effect does using present-tense verbs create? Cite specific examples to support your response.

3. **Infer** Describe the eyewitness accounts and anecdotes Euchner includes. Why do you think he chose these witnesses? What inference about the crowd can you make based on the witnesses he includes?

4. **Evaluate** Euchner provides background information on historic events and biblical allusions included in "I Have a Dream." Identify one example and explain how it helped you better understand the speech.

Critical Vocabulary

cadence	parallel	invocation	civic
revile	expanse	exhort	invoke

Practice and Apply   Explain which Critical Vocabulary word is most closely associated with the underlined word.

1. Which word goes with <u>town</u>? Why?

2. Which word goes with <u>convince</u>? Why?

3. Which word goes with <u>similar</u>? Why?

4. Which word goes with <u>distance</u>? Why?

5. Which word goes with <u>dislike</u>? Why

6. Which word goes with <u>point out</u>? Why?

7. Which word goes with <u>prayer</u>? Why?

8. Which word goes with <u>music</u>? Why?

Vocabulary Strategy: Words from Greek and Latin

Studying the **etymology** of words means that you look at the historical development of words and determine their basic elements. Many words in the English language come from Greek and Latin roots. Knowing the meaning of **roots,** or basic word elements, can help you determine the meaning of unfamiliar words. For example, the Critical Vocabulary word *civic* contains the Latin root *civ-* that means "citizen." Another example is contained in the word *parallel*. This word contains the Greek root *par(a)* that means "beside, near." Knowing the meanings of *civ-* and *par(a)* can help you determine the meanings of other words with the same roots.

Practice and Apply   Look up these words from the selection in a dictionary. Write the meaning of the Latin or Greek root word, and then write a sentence using another word with that same root.

Word	Root	Word	Root
audience (line 6)	*audi-*	**liberty** (line 72)	*lib-*
symbolic (line 13)	*sym-*	**bankrupt** (line 81)	*rupt-*
capital (line 65)	*cap-*	**politician** (line 120)	*poli-*

AMERICA The Story of Us: March on Washington

Video by HISTORY®

AS YOU VIEW Identify similarities and differences between the history text and the video. Write down any questions you generate as you watch the video.

COLLABORATIVE DISCUSSION With a partner, discuss the similarities and differences in the history text and the video, supporting your ideas with evidence from both.

Analyze Accounts in Different Mediums

Factual information about historic events can be presented in a variety of ways, including written histories and short documentary videos. Each **medium** has particular strengths and weaknesses, and imposes different structures. For example, a short documentary video is under time limitations that require the producer to carefully consider what aspects of the event to include. On the other hand, a video includes images and audio that a written text cannot. To get the most complete picture of a historic event, choose a variety of media sources, and think about the kinds of information that are included, omitted, and emphasized in each account. You might ask yourself these questions about each medium:

- Who is narrating the account?
- What background information is included in the account?
- What details are emphasized in the account?
- What details are missing from the account?

Analyzing Text and Media

Cite Text Evidence   Support your responses with evidence from the selections.

1. **Compare** Describe how the video presents the March on Washington. How does it differ from the history text's account? Cite specific examples from the video and the text.

2. **Analyze** The history text includes eyewitness accounts of the day, while the video uses interviews with people commenting on the significance of the day. How does each type of account affect your understanding of the day?

3. **Evaluate** What ideas are emphasized in both the text and the video? Explain how the video and text together give you a more complete understanding of the March on Washington.

PERFORMANCE TASK

Writing Activity: Account Imagine that you were in the audience for King's speech, and write a one-page first-person account of your experience.

- Gather information and impressions about the event from both the history text and the video.

- Consider how you would respond in that situation, and write a one-page letter or diary entry.

- Be sure to include specific details that convey the atmosphere in the Mall.

- Use the conventions of standard written English.

Background *In 2010, the call for democratic reforms reverberated throughout the Middle East and North Africa in a movement known as the Arab Spring. In Egypt, the unrest forced Hosni Mubarak's long-ruling regime out of power. This excerpt from* **Ahdaf Soueif's** *personal account of the revolution describes the third day of mass protests in Cairo. Soueif (b. 1950) was born in Egypt and resides in both Cairo and London. Her novel* The Map of Love *was a finalist for the Booker Prize for Fiction, and she contributes to the* Guardian *and other English and Arabic news organizations.*

from
Cairo: My City, Our Revolution

Diary by Ahdaf Soueif

AS YOU READ Pay attention to details that reveal the author's feelings about Cairo and the revolution.

Friday 28 January, 5.00 p.m.

The river is a still, steely grey, a dull pewter. Small scattered fires burn and fizz in the water. We've pushed out from the shore below the Ramses Hilton and are heading into mid-stream. My two nieces, Salma and Mariam, are on either side of me in the small motor boat. As we get further from the shore our coughing and choking subsides. We can draw breath, even though the breath burns. And we can open our eyes—

To see an **opaque** dusk, heavy with tear gas. Up ahead, Qasr el-Nil Bridge is a mass of people, all in motion, but all in place.

10　We look back at where we were just minutes ago, on 6 October Bridge,[1] and see a Central Security Forces personnel carrier on fire, backing off, four young men chasing it, leaping at it, beating at its windscreen. The vehicle is reversing wildly, careering backwards east towards Downtown. Behind us, a ball of fire lands in the river;

opaque
(ō-pāk´) *adj.*
clouded, difficult to
see through.

---

[1] **Qasr el–Nil Bridge . . . 6 October Bridge:** two bridges, about two miles apart, that cross the Nile River in central Cairo.

a bright new pool of flame in the water. The sky too is grey—so different from the airy twilight you normally get on the river at this time of day. The Opera House looms dark on our right and we can barely make out the slender height of the Cairo Tower. We don't know it yet, but the lights of Cairo will not come on tonight.

20   A great shout goes up from Qasr el-Nil. I look at Salma and Mariam. 'Yes, let's,' they say. I tell the boatman we've changed our minds: we don't want to cross the river to Giza[2] and go home, we want to be dropped off under Qasr el-Nil Bridge.

And that is why we—myself and two beautiful young women—appeared suddenly in the Qasr el-Nil underpass among the Central Security vehicles racing to get out of town and all the men leaning over the parapet[3] above us with stones in their hands stopped in mid-throw and yelled 'Run! Run!' and held off with the stones so they wouldn't hit us as we skittered through the screeching vehicles

30   to a spot where we could scramble up the bank and join the people at the mouth of the bridge. . . .

---

[2] **Giza:** city southwest of Cairo and site of the great pyramids.

[3] **parapet:** a low protective wall along the edge of a raised structure.

So we ran through the underpass, scrambled up the bank and found ourselves within, inside, and part of the masses. When we'd seen the crowd from a distance it had seemed like one bulk, solid. Close up like this it was people, individual persons with spaces between them—spaces into which you could fit. We stood on the traffic island in the middle of the road. Behind us was Qasr el-Nil Bridge, in front of us was Tahrir,[4] and we were doing what we Egyptians do best, and what the regime ruling us had tried so hard to destroy: we had come together, as individuals, millions of us, in a great cooperative effort. And this time our project was to save and to **reclaim** our country. We stood on the island in the middle of the road and that was the moment I became part of the revolution. . . .

For twenty years I have shied away from writing about Cairo. It hurt too much. But the city was there, close to me, looking over my shoulder, holding up the **prism** through which I understood the world, inserting herself into everything I wrote. It hurt. And now, miraculously, it doesn't. Because my city is mine again.

'Masr' is Egypt, and 'Masr' is also what Egyptians call Cairo. On Tuesday 1 February, I watched a man surveying the scene in Tahrir with a big smile: the sun was shining and people were everywhere, old and young, rich and poor, they talked and walked and sang and played and joked and chanted. Then he said it out loud: 'Ya Masr, it's been a long time. We have missed you.' . . .

On the traffic island at the Qasr el-Nil entrance to Tahrir you turned 360 degrees and everywhere there were people. I could not tell how many thousands I could see. Close up, people were handing out tissues soaked in vinegar for your nose, Pepsi to bathe your eyes, water to drink. I stumbled and a hand under my elbow steadied me. The way ahead of us was invisible behind the smoke. From time to time there would be a burst of flame. The great hotels: the Semiramis Intercontinental, Shepheard's, the Ramses Hilton, had all darkened their lower floors and locked their doors. On the upper-floor balconies stick figures were watching us. At the other end of the Midan,[5] from the roof of the American University, the snipers were watching us, too. Silently. Everywhere there was a continuous thud of guns and from time to time a loud, **intermittent** rattling sound. We stood. That was our job, the people at the back: we stood and we chanted our declaration of peace: 'Selmeyya! Selmeyya!' while our comrades at the front, unarmed, fought with the security forces. From time to time a great cry would go up and

reclaim
(rĭ-klām´) v. to retake possession; reform.

prism
(prĭz´əm) n. a transparent, light-refracting object which figuratively refers to an individual's viewpoint.

intermittent
(ĭn´tər-mĭt´nt) adj. occurring at erratic or irregular intervals.

---

[4] **Tahrir (te-rər´):** Arabic word for "liberation." Tahrir Square is a large, open area in downtown Cairo.
[5] **Midan (mīdān):** Arabic word for "Square."

we would surge forward: our friends had won us another couple of metres and we followed them and held our ground. We sang the national anthem. Eight months ago some young protestors from the 6 April Group had been arrested in Alexandria for singing the national anthem; it was 'instigatory'[6] the prosecution said. We sang it. On 28 January, standing at that **momentous** crossroads, the Nile behind us, the Arab League building to our left, the old Ministry of Foreign Affairs to our right, seeing nothing up ahead except the gas

80 and smoke and fire that stood between us and our capital, we stood our ground and sang and chanted and placed our lives, with all trust and confidence, in each other's hands.

Some of us died.

momentous
(mō-měn′təs) *adj.*
very important;
fateful.

COLLABORATIVE DISCUSSION Why does Soueif change her mind about going home? With a partner, discuss how she feels about her decision to become part of the revolution. Cite specific textual evidence from the diary to support your ideas.

---

[6] **instigatory:** action that encourages people to rebel.

Analyze Ideas and Events

A **diary** is a form of **autobiographical narrative** that includes a daily record of an author's thoughts, experiences, or feelings. Diaries typically recount events in **chronological order;** however, authors often explore relationships between present and past events. For example, Ahdaf Soueif highlights the significance of the protesters singing the Egyptian national anthem by telling readers about protesters who had previously been arrested for doing so. In her diary, Soueif also alludes to events that occur after the entry date of January 28.

When you analyze how an author describes events in a diary, look closely at the order of events and the connections between them. If the author includes information about past and future events, consider how this connects to the current events, helps provide context, and contributes to the overall meaning. Think about why the author chooses to include certain events in a particular order and how this affects your understanding of the text.

Analyze Impact of Word Choice on Tone

Tone is an author's attitude toward his or her subject. To create a tone, authors choose words with specific **connotations,** or the attitudes or feelings associated with a word. The connotation of a word or phrase may be positive or negative. For example, the phrase *president's administration* has positive associations, while *president's regime* has negative ones. By noticing an author's choice of words, you can detect and analyze his or her tone.

In "Cairo: My City, Our Revolution," Ahdaf Soueif shifts or changes her tone to reflect the events she is describing. As you analyze the text, think about how specific words impact the tone of particular sentences or whole sections of the text. Use a chart to help you analyze specific words and details.

Word Choice	Tone
"The Opera House looms dark on our right"	*Looms* has a negative connotation and creates a threatening tone in the sentence.

Analyzing the Text

Cite Text Evidence   Support your responses with evidence from the selection.

1. **Analyze** Soueif first describes Cairo as viewed from the river at a distance, rather than from within the protest. How does this help the reader visualize the scene?

2. **Cite Evidence** Describe the tone of the first two paragraphs. How does Soueif's word choice in the first two paragraphs affect the tone? Give specific examples to support your analysis.

3. **Infer** At the end of the second paragraph Soueif tells readers that "the lights of Cairo will not come on tonight," referring to a government-imposed curfew and shutdown of Internet and phone communications. How does this glimpse into the future contribute to Soueif's description of the present?

4. **Cite Evidence** Once Soueif and her nieces join the protest, there is a distinct shift in the tone. Describe this change, citing specific examples of language that contribute to the tone.

5. **Interpret** Personification is a type of figurative language in which human qualities are given to nonliving things. In lines 45–47, how does Soueif **personify** the city of Cairo?

6. **Infer** In lines 49–54, Soueif provides a description of the scene in Tahrir on February 1. How does this scene help the reader understand how the events are unfolding?

7. **Analyze** Notice how Soueif ends this diary entry with the simple sentence, "Some of us died." How does this sentence contrast with the events she describes in lines 55–58? How does it change the tone of the text?

PERFORMANCE TASK

Research Activity: Oral Report In her diary, Ahdaf Soueif provides her own personal account of the Egyptian revolution of 2011. Explore the topic in greater depth through two brief tasks:

1. Conduct research about a specific event in the revolution. Gather information from multiple sources and remember to cite them following standard format.

2. Write a brief report of your findings and share it with the class. Be sure to include well-chosen, relevant, and sufficient facts in your report.

Critical Vocabulary

opaque   **reclaim**   **prism**   **intermittent**   **momentous**

Practice and Apply Use the Critical Vocabulary words to answer each question. Then, with a partner, take turns supporting your answers.

1. Which word is an antonym, or a word opposite in meaning, to the word **insignificant**?

2. Which word most closely relates to the word **irregular**?

3. Which word is an antonym to the word **transparent**?

4. Which word most closely relates to the word **reflection**?

5. Which word most closely relates to the word **restore**?

Vocabulary Strategy: Reference Sources

When you read an informational text, looking up words or terms in print and digital **reference sources** such as dictionaries, glossaries or thesauruses can help you better understand the central ideas of the text.

Read this sentence from Ahdaf Soueif's diary.

And this time our project was to save and to <u>reclaim</u> our country.

In this sentence, you can determine the general meaning of the Critical Vocabulary word *reclaim* by using the context clue "to save." However, if you also look up the word *reclaim* in a dictionary, you gain a further understanding that the people were working to reclaim, or bring back, their country from the ruling regime that had restricted their freedoms.

Practice and Apply The underlined words in these sentences are also used in "Cairo: My City, Our Revolution." Use context clues in each sentence to write a definition for the underlined word. Then look up the words in a dictionary, glossary, or thesaurus. Confirm or revise your definitions with additional information from the reference sources.

1. The protester avoided contact and <u>shied</u> away from the angry crowd.

2. The car went <u>careering</u> toward the barrier at full speed to break it down.

3. The people sent the government a message when they wrote their <u>declaration</u> of freedom.

4. The tall fences could not hold back the crowd as they slowly pushed and <u>surged</u> down the street.

Language and Style: Noun Phrases

A **noun phrase** includes a noun and its **modifiers,** or the words that affect the noun's meaning. In "Cairo: My City, Our Revolution," Ahdaf Soueif uses noun phrases to add vivid descriptions of the protests.

Read the following sentence from the diary:

> And we can open our eyes—
> To see <u>an opaque dusk, heavy with tear gas</u>.

By splitting the sentence between the first and second paragraphs, the author emphasizes the underlined noun phrase. The author could have provided the information in this sentence much more simply:

> The tear gas limits our visibility.

Instead, she uses the noun phrase to allow readers to see and feel what the air feels like. Later in the paragraph, the author uses another descriptive noun phrase to contrast this image from the usual appearance and feel of the sky:

> The sky too is grey—so different from the <u>airy twilight</u> you normally get at this time of day.

When you revise your own writing to add descriptive noun phrases, think about the specific meaning you want to convey to your audience. Ask yourself what details need more variety and interest. It may help to jot down ideas in a graphic organizer.

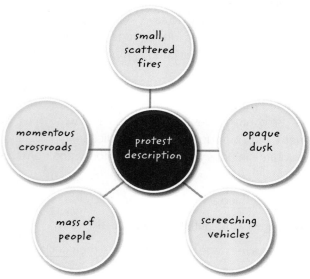

Practice and Apply Look back at the report you created for this selection's Performance Task. Revise the report to add more descriptive noun phrases. Remember to use the conventions of standard English grammar and usage. When you have finished revising, exchange reports with a partner and discuss how you strengthened your writing.

Background *The Iranian Revolution in the late 1970's resulted in the overthrow of the pro-western Shah of Iran. Iranians established a theocracy, or religious government, based on the rule of Islam. The new government passed laws that segregate men and women and that force women to adhere to an Islamic dress code. Iranian women are required to wear veils that cover their hair and neck and coats that cover their arms and legs. The "morality police" ensure that people comply with the laws. People who do not comply may be taken to the morality police headquarters (called the Committee in Persepolis 2) to be questioned, beaten, or jailed.*

from
Reading Lolita in Tehran

Memoir by Azar Nafisi

from **Persepolis 2**

Graphic Novel by Marjane Satrapi
Translated by Anjali Singh

Azar Nafisi (b. 1947), *an Iranian, taught English literature in Tehran from 1979 until 1995. The laws passed after the revolution made Nafisi's job difficult. University faculty scrutinized novels that Nafisi taught, and Nafisi was chastised for not wearing a veil. In 1995, Nafisi left the university and began teaching a small group of women in her home, where they were free to discuss books, like* Lolita, *that were considered unacceptable by Iranian authorities. In 1997, she left Iran for the United States, where she now teaches.*

Marjane Satrapi (b. 1969) *was born in Iran. After the revolution, Satrapi's parents sent her to Europe to attend school. Later, she studied illustration and learned to create comics.* Persepolis 1 *tells the story of her childhool in Iran, and* Persepolis 2 *tells the story of her adolescence in Europe and Iran and of her struggle to fit in. Both books were made into the animated movie ,* Persepolis, *which won many awards. Satrapi has written other graphic novels, including* Chicken with Plums. *She lives in Paris with her husband.*

AS YOU READ Identify points of comparison between the memoir and the graphic novel. Write down any questions you generate as you read.

from **Reading Lolita in Tehran**
Memoir by Azar Nafisi

How can I create this other world outside the room? I have no choice but to appeal once again to your imagination. Let's imagine one of the girls, say Sanaz, leaving my house and let us follow her from there to her final destination. She says her good-byes and puts on her black robe and scarf over her orange shirt and jeans, coiling her scarf around her neck to cover her huge gold earrings. She directs wayward strands of hair under the scarf, puts her notes into her large bag, straps it on over her shoulder and walks out into the hall. She pauses a moment on top of the stairs to put on thin lacy black gloves to hide her nail polish.

We follow Sanaz down the stairs, out the door and into the street. You might notice that her gait[1] and her gestures have changed. It is in her best interest not to be seen, not be heard or noticed. She doesn't walk upright, but bends her head towards the ground and doesn't look at passersby. She walks quickly and with a sense of determination. The streets of Tehran and other Iranian cities are patrolled by militia, who ride in white Toyota patrols, four gun-carrying men and women, sometimes followed by a minibus. They are called the Blood of God. They patrol the streets to make sure that women like Sanaz wear their veils properly, do not wear makeup, do not walk in public with men who are not their fathers, brothers or husbands. She will pass slogans on the walls, quotations from Khomeini[2] and a group called the Party of God: MEN WHO WEAR TIES ARE U.S. LACKEYS.[3] VEILING IS A WOMAN'S PROTECTION. Beside the slogan is a charcoal drawing of a woman: her face is featureless and framed by a dark chador.[4] MY SISTER, GUARD YOUR VEIL. MY BROTHER, GUARD YOUR EYES.

If she gets on a bus, the seating is **segregated**. She must enter through the rear door and sit in the back seats, **allocated** to women. Yet in taxis, which accept as many as five passengers, men and women are squeezed together like sardines, as the saying goes, and the same goes with minibuses, where so many of my students complain of being harassed by bearded and God-fearing men.

You might well ask, What is Sanaz thinking as she walks the streets of Tehran? How much does this experience affect her? Most

segregate
(sĕg′rĭ-gāt′) *v.* to cause people to be separated based on gender, race, or other factors.

allocate
(ăl′ə-kāt′) *v.* to assign or designate for.

---

[1] **gait:** manner of walking.
[2] **Khomeini (kō-mā′ nē):** Ruhollah Khomeini (1902–1989), religious and political leader of Iran after the 1979 revolution.
[3] **U.S. lackeys:** people who serve United States policies. The Iranian government is hostile to the U.S. because it supported the former Shah of Iran.
[4] **chador:** a long scarf that covers a Muslim woman's hair, neck, and shoulders.

probably, she tries to distance her mind as much as possible from her surroundings. Perhaps she is thinking of her brother, or of her distant boyfriend and the time when she will meet him in Turkey. Does she compare her own situation with her mother's when she was the same age? Is she angry that women of her mother's generation could walk the streets freely, enjoy the company of the opposite sex, join the police force, become pilots, live under laws that were among the most progressive in the world regarding women? Does she feel humiliated by the new laws, by the fact that after the revolution, the age of marriage was lowered from eighteen to nine, that stoning became once more the punishment for adultery and prostitution?

In the course of nearly two decades, the streets have been turned into a war zone, where young women who disobey the rules are hurled into patrol cars, taken to jail, flogged, fined, forced to wash the toilets and humiliated, and as soon as they leave, they go back and do the same thing. Is she aware, Sanaz, of her own power? Does she realize how dangerous she can be when her every stray gesture is a disturbance to public safety? Does she think how vulnerable the Revolutionary Guards are who for over eighteen years have patrolled the streets of Tehran and have had to endure young women like herself, and those of other generations, walking, talking, showing a strand of hair just to remind them that they have not **converted**?

We have reached Sanaz's house, where we will leave her on her doorstep, perhaps to confront her brother on the other side and to think in her heart of her boyfriend.

These girls, my girls, had both a real history and a fabricated one. Although they came from very different backgrounds, the regime that ruled them had tried to make their personal identities and histories **irrelevant**. They were never free of the regime's definition of them as Muslim women.

convert
(kən-vûrt´) *v.* to change one's system of beliefs.

irrelevant
(ĭ-rĕl´ə-vənt) *adj.* insignificant, unimportant.

from **Persepolis 2: The Story of a Return**

Graphic Novel by Marjane Satrapi

COLLABORATIVE DISCUSSION With a partner, discuss common elements in the memoir and graphic novel. How is the way the authors communicate with readers similar and different in the texts? Support your ideas with evidence from both.

Determine Author's Point of View

Point of view refers to how an author thinks or feels about a subject. In a memoir, an author uses rhetoric, choosing words carefully to advance a point of view. Graphic novelists, however, use both graphics and rhetoric to advance their points of view.

- Azar Nafisi wrote *Reading Lolita in Tehran* after she left Iran to live abroad. Her **perspective** as a woman and a scholar living under an oppressive regime is reflected in the rhetoric she uses. In the excerpt, Nafisi reproduces slogans that scream in uppercase letters: MY SISTER, GUARD YOUR VEIL. MY BROTHER, GUARD YOUR EYES. She constructs phrases such as, "flogged, fined, forced to wash toilets and humiliated," and "when her every stray gesture is a disturbance to public safety" to communicate her point of view.
- Unlike the memoir, *Persepolis 2* tells Marjane Satrapi's story through words and stark black and white images. In this excerpt, the author's perspective as a young woman out of place in a rigid and uncompromising society is reflected in the way the main character's face is drawn. It is also shown in the juxtaposition of panels next to each other. Careful readers must study details in the drawings, as well as read captions and thought bubbles, to understand the author's point of view.

Analyze Accounts in Different Mediums

A personal story can be told using different **mediums,** or ways of communicating. Mediums may include memoirs, graphic novels, plays, or films. Each format allows the author to emphasize details that help to tell his or her story. The challenge for the author is determining which medium tells the story in the most compelling way. The challenge for readers or viewers is to determine which details are emphasized and how those details convey the author's message.

Read this sentence from *Reading Lolita in Tehran*:

> **They patrol the streets to make sure that women like Sanaz wear their veils properly, do not wear makeup, do not walk in public with men who are not their fathers, brothers or husbands.**

Notice how this memoir is a personal account written from memory or first-hand knowledge. The writer uses concrete details and sensory words to help the reader visualize events and people.

In contrast, the middle panel in the second row of *Persepolis 2* provides visuals for the reader to understand a similar situation. Graphic novels show action through images and use words sparingly, through speech bubbles and captions. Readers must pay attention to the visual details in the drawings and to the sequence of the panels to understand the author's message.

Analyzing Text and Media

Cite Text Evidence   Support your responses with evidence from the selections.

1. **Interpret** Identify details the author of *Reading Lolita in Tehran* uses to describe Sanaz. Why might the author have included these details?

2. **Critique** How is the rhetoric that both authors use effective in conveying their points of view? Explain with evidence from the texts.

3. **Infer** The author of *Reading Lolita in Tehran* wonders aloud if Sanaz is aware of her own power. What power is the author referring to? Does the main character in *Persepolis* feel that she has a similar power? Explain.

4. **Analyze** Look at the second and third panels in *Persepolis 2*. How does the author use both words and graphics to make a point about how the people's struggle had changed?

5. **Infer** The narrator of *Persepolis 2* says that she spent an entire day at the Committee because of a pair of red socks. What might red socks have **symbolized,** or represented, to the Committee?

6. **Interpret** In *Persepolis 2*, the narrator's facial expression remains the same in each of the panels. How would you describe the narrator's facial expression? How does this consistency help reveal the author's point of view?

7. **Synthesize** What ideas are emphasized in both the text and the graphic novel? Explain how the graphic novel and text together enable readers to have a more complete understanding of the problems women face in Iran.

PERFORMANCE TASK

Media Activity: Graphic Novel Imagine that Nafisi had written her memoir in the form of a graphic novel. How would she have integrated graphics and rhetoric?

- Using a computer or poster board and a pencil, create a series of graphic novel panels that follow Sanaz as she leaves the author's home.

- Add captions and speech and thought bubbles, including details from the memoir that you think advance the story.

- In a small group, compare your graphic representations of Nafisi's memoir. Discuss whether you were able to convey the same ideas and point of view through graphics as Nafisi was able to convey in her memoir. Was your use of rhetoric in your graphic representation as effective as Nafisi's in her memoir?

Critical Vocabulary

segregate   allocate   irrelevant   convert

Practice and Apply Use your understanding of the vocabulary words to answer the questions.

1. Are your friends' opinions ever **irrelevant**? Explain.

2. If you were in charge of **allocating** money to each of the clubs or sports teams in school, how would you do it?

3. Why might you **segregate** children according to age?

4. Is someone who believes fiercely in something likely to **convert**? Explain.

Vocabulary Strategy: Denotations and Connotations

A word's **denotation** is its strict dictionary definition. But many words have slight nuances or differences in meaning. These nuances, or **connotations,** have associated meanings and emotions.

Nafisi explains that in Iran, the buses are segregated. The Critical Vocabulary word *segregate* has a similar denotation to the word *separate*. They both mean "to set apart." But the word *segregate* has an altogether different connotation. To segregate suggests separating people or things forcefully, often in an unfair way.

Practice and Apply For each Critical Vocabulary word below, write the word's denotation. Then write the connotation of the word as it appears in the story.

Vocabulary Word	Denotation	Connotation
allocate		
irrelevant		
convert		

Language and Style: Rhetorical Questions

Authors strive to make effective choices for meaning or style. In her memoir *Reading Lolita in Tehran,* Azar Nafisi makes repeated use of rhetorical questions to engage the audience and to make a point. **Rhetorical questions** are questions that do not require or expect an answer. Depending on the context, they are often posed for dramatic effect.

Read the following sentence from the memoir.

Does she realize how dangerous she can be when her every stray gesture is a disturbance to public safety?

Nafisi could instead have written the sentence this way:

She is dangerous because her every stray gesture is a disturbance to public safety.

By using a rhetorical question instead of a statement, Nafisi invites the reader to think carefully about the scene described and to agree with her viewpoint. The question does not expect an answer. Instead, it makes a dramatic statement about the way the Iranian regime views women.

Here are some other examples of rhetorical questions in the excerpt from *Reading Lolita in Tehran.*

Rhetorical Question	Meaning
"How can I create this other world outside the room?"	Nafisi uses the rhetorical question as an opener to explain why she creates an imaginary scene involving Sanaz.
"Does she compare her own situation with her mother's when she was the same age?"	The question engages readers and invites them to consider any background knowledge they have about Iran's history.
"Is she aware, Sanaz, of her own power?"	Nafisi uses the rhetorical question to provide dramatic effect and to give the questions that follow meaning.

Practice and Apply Think of an injustice that you have observed or read about. Write a brief paragraph describing and reflecting on the injustice. Use rhetorical questions, as Nafisi does, to convey meaning and for dramatic effect. Remember to check your work for standard English grammar and usage.

Background *Born in Argentina,* **Luisa Valenzuela** *(b. 1938) published her first story at the age of seventeen. After graduating from the University of Buenos Aires, she moved to Paris and traveled abroad for several years. She returned home in 1974 to find political turmoil and oppression: a fascist dictatorship, a system of government in which a leader suppresses opposition through violent means, now ruled Argentina. Despite threats of censorship and physical harm, she began using her writing to document the horrors of life under a dictator.*

The Censors

Short Story by Luisa Valenzuela   Translated by David Unger

AS YOU READ Pay attention to the clues that reveal how Juan's feelings about his work change during the story.

Poor Juan! One day they caught him with his guard down before he could even realize that what he had taken as a stroke of luck was really one of fate's dirty tricks. These things happen the minute you're careless and you let down your guard, as one often does. Juancito let happiness—a feeling you can't trust—get the better of him when he received from a confidential source Mariana's new address in Paris and he knew that she hadn't forgotten him. Without thinking twice, he sat down at his table and wrote her a letter. *The* letter that keeps his mind off his job during the day and won't let him sleep at night (what had he scrawled, what had he put on that sheet of paper he sent to Mariana?).

Juan knows there won't be a problem with the letter's contents, that it's irreproachable, harmless. But what about the rest? He knows that they examine, sniff, feel, and read between the lines of each and every letter, and check its tiniest comma and most accidental stain. He knows that all letters pass from hand to hand and go through all sorts of tests in the huge censorship offices and that, in the end, very few continue on their way. Usually it

takes months, even years, if there aren't any snags; all this time
20 the freedom, maybe even the life, of both sender and receiver is in
jeopardy. And that's why Juan's so down in the dumps: thinking
that something might happen to Mariana because of his letters.
Of all people, Mariana, who must finally feel safe there where she
always dreamed she'd live. But he knows that the *Censor's Secret
Command* operates all over the world and cashes in on the discount
in air rates; there's nothing to stop them from going as far as that
hidden Paris neighborhood, kidnapping Mariana, and returning to
their cozy homes, certain of having fulfilled their noble mission.

Well, you've got to beat them to the punch, do what everyone
30 tries to do: sabotage the machinery, throw sand in its gears, get to
the bottom of the problem so as to stop it.

This was Juan's sound plan when he, like many others, applied
for a censor's job—not because he had a calling or needed a job:
no, he applied simply to intercept his own letter, a consoling but
unoriginal idea. He was hired immediately, for each day more and
more censors are needed and no one would bother to check on his
references.

Ulterior motives couldn't be overlooked by the *Censorship
Division*, but they needn't be too strict with those who applied.
40 They knew how hard it would be for those poor guys to find the
letter they wanted and even if they did, what's a letter or two when
the new censor would snap up so many others? That's how Juan
managed to join the *Post Office's Censorship Division*, with a certain
goal in mind.

The building had a festive air on the outside which contrasted
with its inner **staidness**. Little by little, Juan was absorbed by his
job and he felt at peace since he was doing everything he could to
get his letter for Mariana. He didn't even worry when, in his first
month, he was sent to *Section K* where envelopes are very carefully
50 screened for explosives.

It's true that on the third day, a fellow worker had his right
hand blown off by a letter, but the division chief claimed it was
sheer **negligence** on the victim's part. Juan and the other employees
were allowed to go back to their work, albeit feeling less secure.
After work, one of them tried to organize a strike to demand higher
wages for unhealthy work, but Juan didn't join in; after thinking it
over, he reported him to his superiors and thus got promoted.

You don't form a habit by doing something once, he told
himself as he left his boss's office. And when he was transferred to
60 *Section J*, where letters are carefully checked for poison dust, he felt
he had climbed a rung in the ladder.

By working hard, he quickly reached *Section E* where the job
was more interesting, for he could now read and analyze the letters'

staidness
(stād´nĭs) *n.* the
quality of being
steady, calm, and
serious.

negligence
(nĕg´lĭ-jəns) *n.*
carelessness or
failure to take normal
precautions.

> ## Soon his work became so absorbing to him that his noble mission blurred in his mind.

contents. Here he could even hope to get hold of his letter which, judging by the time that had elapsed, had gone through the other sections and was probably floating around in this one.

Soon his work became so absorbing that his noble mission blurred in his mind. Day after day he crossed out whole paragraphs in red ink, pitilessly chucking many letters into the censored basket.
70 These were horrible days when he was shocked by the subtle and conniving ways employed by people to pass on **subversive** messages; his instincts were so sharp that he found behind a simple 'the weather's unsettled' or 'prices continue to soar' the wavering hand of someone secretly scheming to overthrow the Government.

His zeal brought him swift promotion. We don't know if this made him happy. Very few letters reached him in *Section B*—only a handful passed the other hurdles—so he read them over and over again, passed them under a magnifying glass, searched for microprint with an electronic microscope, and tuned his sense
80 of smell so that he was beat by the time he made it home. He'd barely manage to warm up his soup, eat some fruit, and fall into bed, satisfied with having done his duty. Only his darling mother worried, but she couldn't get him back on the right road. She'd say, though it wasn't always true: Lola called, she's at the bar with the girls, they miss you, they're waiting for you. Or else she'd leave a bottle of red wine on the table. But Juan wouldn't overdo it: any distraction could make him lose his edge and the perfect censor

subversive
(səb-vûr′sĭv) *adj.*
intended to undermine or overthrow those in power.

had to be alert, keen, attentive, and sharp to nab cheats. He had a truly patriotic task, both self-denying and uplifting.

90   His basket for censored letters became the best fed as well as the most cunning basket in the whole *Censorship Division*. He was about to congratulate himself for having finally discovered his true mission, when his letter to Mariana reached his hands. Naturally, he censored it without regret. And just as naturally, he couldn't stop them from executing him the following morning, another victim of his devotion to his work.

COLLABORATIVE DISCUSSION Were you surprised by Juan's change of heart? With a partner, discuss what hints the author provided to make the story's ending plausible. Cite specific evidence from the text to support your ideas.

Analyze Point of View: Cultural Background

Luisa Valenzuela's cultural experience as an Argentine writer is reflected in both the content and style of this short story. Valenzuela wrote it upon returning to her native country in 1974 after spending several years abroad. The mood in Buenos Aires, the capital, was one of fear and oppression. Valenzuela once wrote, "Upon returning to my city after a long absence… it wasn't mine any longer. Buenos Aires belonged then to violence and state terrorism." Argentina was rapidly falling under the control of a fascist dictatorship. Working under the threat of censorship, suppression, and violence, Valenzuela believed it was her responsibility as a writer to witness and record the atrocities of the day. Her works, including this short story, explore such difficult topics as censorship, extreme violence, and political repression.

Analyze Author's Choices

To communicate their experiences and ideas, writers make specific stylistic and structural choices. You can analyze Valenzuela's choices in this short story by looking at these elements.

Pacing	Foreshadowing	Irony
Pacing is the way in which an author manipulates time. Authors may use techniques to slow the action, thereby creating a mood of tension or mystery. For example, Valenzuela builds tension by devoting the first part of the story to Juan's fear that his letter to Mariana will be found. Conversely, authors may accelerate a story's pace by presenting a series of plot events in rapid succession.	**Foreshadowing** is a writer's use of clues to hint at events that will occur later in the story. Foreshadowing creates suspense, mystery, and surprise, and makes readers eager to find out what will happen next. In this story, the description of a fellow worker's gruesome injury is an example of foreshadowing.	Irony takes place when something happens that is the opposite of what readers would expect. One type is **verbal irony,** when what is said is the opposite of what is meant. The narrator's description of the Censorship Bureau as having "a festive air" is an example of verbal irony. Another type is **situational irony,** in which a character or the reader expects one thing to happen but something else happens instead. Juan's increasing dedication to his job as a censor is an example of situational irony.

Analyzing the Text

Cite Text Evidence   Support your responses with evidence from the selection.

1. **Infer** The narrator uses many **idioms,** commonly-used expressions that mean something other than the literal meaning of their words. For example, when Juan is "caught . . . with his guard down," the author means that he wasn't being cautious, not that he physically protected himself most of the time. What tone, or attitude toward the character and the audience, do the idioms create?

2. **Analyze** In his career as a censor, Juan moves from *Section K* to *Section B*. Describe the pacing or progression of his advancement. Besides the Section letters, what devices and word choices does the author use to speed up or slow down the pace of the story?

3. **Cite Evidence** How does the author foreshadow, or hint at, the changes that will occur in Juan's personality and his life? Provide examples of foreshadowing from the text, and explain their connection to the story's outcome.

4. **Compare** Compare Juan's work goal or motivation near the beginning of the story with his goal or motivation near the end. How does the author communicate the way this change occurs?

5. **Infer** The narrator calls Juan's basket of letters "the best fed as well as the most cunning basket in the whole *Censorship Division.*" What does this statement reveal about the way Juan performs his job?

6. **Interpret** Why does Juan censor his own letter "without regret"? How is his final action as a censor an example of irony? How does this ending illustrate Valenzuela's point of view about the political situation in Argentina?

PERFORMANCE TASK

Writing Activity: Letter Juan's letter to Mariana is central to this story's plot. Explore that letter through two brief writing tasks. In both pieces of writing, include evidence from the text and use the conventions of standard English.

1. In the character of Juan, write the one-page letter you imagine he wrote to Mariana at the beginning of the story. Then annotate a copy of the letter to identify evidence of anti-government ideas that a censor might find.

2. Write a one-page report in the character of Juan as a *Censorship Division* employee explaining why the letter shows that Juan is a traitor to his country.

Critical Vocabulary

staidness   **negligence**   **subversive**

Practice and Apply Create a semantic map like the one that follows for each Critical Vocabulary word. Use a dictionary or thesaurus as needed. This example is for a word appearing in line 30 of the story.

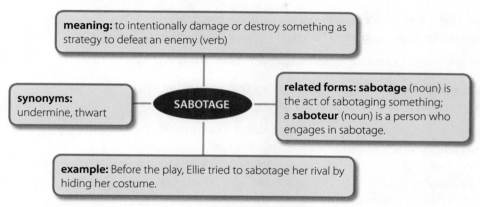

Vocabulary Strategy: Suffixes That Form Nouns

The Critical Vocabulary words *staidness* and *negligence* are formed by adding a noun suffix to an adjective, or describing word. Something that is *staid* shows *staidness*; someone who is *negligent* reveals his *negligence*. Noticing word patterns will help you more quickly develop an accurate definition for any unfamiliar words you encounter in your reading. Here are some common noun suffixes you will see in English words:

Suffixes	Meanings	Examples
–ance, –ence	act or condition of	radiance, excellence
–cy	state or condition of	sufficiency, redundancy
–dom	state, rank, or condition	officialdom, martyrdom
–hood	state or condition of	likelihood, childhood

Practice and Apply For each row of the chart, identify an additional example that uses a suffix shown. With each word you choose, follow these steps:

1. Identify the base—that is, the main word part without the suffix. Note the part of speech (adjective, verb, noun) and meaning of each base word.

2. Write a definition for each word you chose that incorporates the base word meaning and the suffix meaning.

3. Finally, use each word you chose in a sample sentence.

Language and Style: Colons and Semicolons

An author's use of punctuation not only can help readers understand the message but also can help create meaning and tone. In "The Censors," Luisa Valenzuela uses colons and semicolons to great effect.

Read the following sentence from the story.

And that's why Juan's so down in the dumps: thinking that something might happen to Mariana because of his letter.

The author could instead have written the sentence this way:

Juan's down in the dumps from thinking that something might happen to Mariana because of his letter.

By setting up the sentence as she does, the author involves readers in making meaning. The two-part sentence provides readers with a question (What's bothering Juan?) followed by its answer (Thinking that he's endangered Mariana). Readers naturally pause at the colon to prepare for what comes after it. Here are some other common uses of colons:

Uses of Colons	
Purpose	Example
illustrate or provide an example of what was just stated	Argentina has seen much political turmoil: since World War II the nation has endured numerous military coups and dictatorships.
introduce a quotation	Valenzuela is no stranger to censorship: "I wrote . . . thinking that I should write in illegible handwriting so that no one could read over my shoulder."
introduce a list	Valenzuela has lived in many places: Paris, New York, Barcelona, and Buenos Aires.

Now read this sentence from "The Censors":

Usually it takes months, even years, if there aren't any snags; all this time the freedom, maybe even the life, of both sender and receiver is in jeopardy.

Valenzuela could have chosen to create two separate sentences; her use of the semicolon shows that the second idea results from the first.

Practice and Apply Look back at the letter and report you created in response to this selection's Performance Task. Revise each to add at least one colon and one semicolon. Then discuss with a partner how each punctuation mark you added improves your meaning or tone.

Write an Argument

The texts in this collection focus on the universal desire for freedom and the ongoing struggle around the world to win political, social, and sometimes even personal freedom. Some people argue that freedom is never given; it must be demanded. Do you agree with this belief? Choose three texts from this collection, including the anchor text, "I Have a Dream," and identify how each writer addresses the struggle for freedom in his or her society. Then, write an argument in which you cite evidence from all three texts to support your claim.

An effective argument should:

- make a claim and develop the claim with valid reasons and relevant evidence from the texts
- anticipate opposing claims and counter them with well-supported reasons and relevant evidence
- establish clear, logical relationships among claims, counterclaims, reasons, and evidence
- include an introduction, a logically structured body linked with transitions, and a conclusion
- follow the conventions of standard written English

PLAN

Analyze the Texts Reread "I Have a Dream" and take notes about how Martin Luther King Jr. addresses the struggle for freedom in American society. Does he believe that freedom is given or that it must be demanded by the people? Pay attention to specific details as you gather evidence from the text. Then review your two other texts, and make notes on how the authors address the struggle for freedom.

Debate Your Claim Writing an argument is similar to having a debate, only it's written on paper. You must be prepared to make counterclaims, or arguments, to answer an opposing claim. In a mini-debate with a partner, present your claim and the evidence you have gathered from the texts to support your claim. Your partner will then make an argument against your claim. You will respond to the opposing claim with reasons and evidence that support your position. Once you have completed your debate, it is your partner's turn to present his or her argument, and you will make an opposing claim.

*my*Notebook

Use the annotation tools in your eBook to locate evidence that supports your argument. Save each piece of evidence to your notebook.

ACADEMIC VOCABULARY

As you share your ideas about freedom, be sure to use these words.

> decline
> enable
> impose
> integrate
> reveal

This activity will enable both you and your partner to more easily anticipate any counterarguments to your claim.

Before the debate:

- Write a clear statement of your claim.
- Outline the main reasons that support your claim. Match each piece of evidence you collected in your analysis of the three texts with the reason it most clearly supports.
- Make note of potential opposing claims your partner might make. Plan your responses, or counterclaims.
- Write a closing statement that supports your position.

During the debate:

- Take turns speaking. Begin by presenting your claim and giving two or three reasons to support your claim.
- Allow your partner to respond with an opposing claim.
- Follow up with a response, using more detailed evidence from the texts.
- Listen carefully to your partner, and be prepared to modify your statement to respond to new ideas.
- Make notes about your partner's claims.

After the debate:

- Discuss each other's reasoning and use of evidence and how you can improve your argument.
- Note both the strengths and weaknesses of your argument.

Get Organized Organize your notes in an outline. Be sure to integrate any new information gathered from the debate. Did the debate reveal any weaknesses in your argument? What can you do to strengthen your argument?

- Decide what organizational pattern you will use for your essay. Will you present your claim along with all the reasons and evidence to support it, and then write about potential opposing claims? Or, will you present one reason to support your claim followed by an opposing claim, and then continue with the next reason and opposing claim?
- Use your organizational pattern to sort the textual evidence you have gathered into a logical order. Will you discuss evidence from each text one by one in different sections of your essay, or will you present evidence from multiple texts in the same section?
- Choose an engaging quotation or detail to introduce your essay.
- Use or revise your closing statement from the debate. Make sure that it is appropriate for an essay format.

Draft Your Essay Write a draft of your essay, following your outline.

- Introduce your claim. Present your argument in an interesting way that will grab the attention of your readers.

- Present your reasons, evidence, and opposing claims in logically ordered paragraphs.

- Explain how the evidence from the texts supports your ideas about the struggle for freedom in a society.

- Use transitions to clarify the relationships between claims and reasons, between reasons and evidence, and between claims and counterclaims.

- Write a conclusion that follows from and supports your argument.

my **Write**Smart

Write your rough draft in *my*WriteSmart. Focus on getting your ideas down, rather than perfecting your choice of language.

Improve Your Draft Refer to the chart on the following page to review the characteristics of a well-written argument. Ask yourself these questions as you revise:

- Is my introduction strong and confident? Will my readers be interested in finding out the reasons for my position?

- Have I presented both a claim and relevant evidence to support it?

- Have I acknowledged opposing claims and countered them with reasons and evidence?

- Is my essay cohesive? Do I need additional transitions to make connections clear?

- Does my conclusion follow logically from the body of my essay and provide a solid ending?

- Have I used formal English, avoiding slang and nonstandard English?

my **Write**Smart

Have your partner or a group of peers review your draft in *my*WriteSmart. Ask your reviewers to note any reasons that do not support your claim.

Exchange Essays When your final draft is completed, exchange essays with a partner. Read your partner's essay and provide feedback. Be sure to point out aspects of the essay that are particularly strong, as well as areas that could be improved.

COLLECTION **2** **TASK**
ARGUMENT

	Ideas and Evidence	**Organization**	**Language**
ADVANCED	• The introduction is memorable and persuasive; the claim clearly states a position on a substantive topic. • Valid reasons and relevant evidence from the texts convincingly support the writer's claim. • Opposing claims are anticipated and effectively addressed with counterclaims. • The concluding section effectively summarizes the claim.	• The reasons and textual evidence are organized consistently and logically throughout the argument. • Varied transitions logically connect reasons and textual evidence to the writer's claim.	• The writing reflects a formal style and an objective, or controlled, tone. • Sentence beginnings, lengths, and structures vary and have a rhythmic flow. • Spelling, capitalization, and punctuation are correct. If handwritten, the argument is legible. • Grammar and usage are correct.
COMPETENT	• The introduction could do more to capture the reader's attention; the claim states a position on an issue. • Most reasons and evidence from the texts support the writer's claim, but they could be more convincing. • Opposing claims are anticipated, but the counterclaims need to be developed more. • The concluding section restates the claim.	• The organization of reasons and textual evidence is confusing in a few places. • A few more transitions are needed to connect reasons and textual evidence to the writer's claim.	• The style is informal in a few places, and the tone is defensive at times. • Sentence beginnings, lengths, and structures vary somewhat. • Several spelling and capitalization mistakes occur, and punctuation is inconsistent. If handwritten, the argument is mostly legible. • Some grammatical and usage errors are repeated in the argument.
LIMITED	• The introduction is ordinary; the claim identifies an issue, but the writer's position is not clearly stated. • The reasons and evidence from the texts are not always logical or relevant. • Opposing claims are anticipated but not addressed logically. • The concluding section includes an incomplete summary of the claim.	• The organization of reasons and textual evidence is logical in some places, but it often doesn't follow a pattern. • Many more transitions are needed to connect reasons and textual evidence to the writer's position.	• The style becomes informal in many places, and the tone is often dismissive of other viewpoints. • Sentence structures barely vary, and some fragments or run-on sentences are present. • Spelling, capitalization, and punctuation are often incorrect but do not make reading the argument difficult. If handwritten, the argument may be partially illegible. • Grammar and usage are incorrect in many places, but the writer's ideas are still clear.
EMERGING	• The introduction is missing. • Significant supporting reasons and evidence from the texts are missing. • Opposing claims are neither anticipated nor addressed. • The concluding section is missing.	• An organizational strategy is not used; reasons and textual evidence are presented randomly. • Transitions are not used, making the argument difficult to understand.	• The style is inappropriate, and the tone is disrespectful. • Repetitive sentence structure, fragments, and run-on sentences make the writing monotonous and hard to follow. • Spelling and capitalization are often incorrect, and punctuation is missing. If handwritten, the argument may be partially or mostly illegible. • Many grammatical and usage errors change the meaning of the writer's ideas.

The Bonds Between Us

" The welfare of each of us is dependent fundamentally
upon the welfare of all of us. "

—Theodore Roosevelt

The Bonds Between Us

In this collection, you will explore what links us to family, friends, pets, and community.

hmhfyi.com

COLLECTION

PERFORMANCE TASK Preview

At the end of this collection, you will have the opportunity to complete two tasks:

• Write a narrative about interpersonal connections that employs narrative techniques.

• Develop a group multimedia presentation that explores the bonds that people form.

ACADEMIC VOCABULARY

Study the words and their definitions in the chart below. You will use these words as you discuss and write about the texts in this collection.

Word	Definition	Related Forms
capacity (kə-păs´ĭ-tē) *n.*	the ability to contain, hold, produce, or understand something	capacities, incapacitate
confer (kən-fûr´) *v.*	to grant or give to	conferral, conferrable
emerge (ĭ-mûrj´) *v.*	to come forth , out of, or away from	emergence, emergent
generate (jĕn´ə-rāt´) *v.*	to produce or cause something to happen or exist	generative, degenerate
trace (trās) *v.*	to discover or determine the origins or developmental stages of something	traceability, traceable, retrace

Background *In 2000,* **Jhumpa Lahiri** *(b. 1967) was awarded the Pulitzer Prize for her debut work of fiction, the short-story collection* The Interpreter of Maladies. *This story from the collection is set in 1971, the year in which civil war erupted in Pakistan. At the time, Pakistan had two distinct parts, West Pakistan and East Pakistan. India invaded the region in support of the eastern Pakistani people. The Pakistani army surrendered in the city of Dhaka (Dacca), and East Pakistan became a new nation, Bangladesh.*

When Mr. Pirzada Came to Dine

Short Story by Jhumpa Lahiri

AS YOU READ Pay attention to details that reveal the conflicts faced by the characters during the story. Note any questions as you read.

In the autumn of 1971 a man used to come to our house, bearing confections in his pocket and hopes of ascertaining the life or death of his family. His name was Mr. Pirzada, and he came from Dacca, now the capital of Bangladesh, but then a part of Pakistan. That year Pakistan was engaged in civil war. The eastern frontier, where Dacca was located, was fighting for **autonomy** from the ruling regime in the west. In March, Dacca had been invaded, torched, and shelled by the Pakistani army. . . . By the end of the summer, three hundred thousand people were said to have died. In
10 Dacca Mr. Pirzada had a three-story home, a lectureship in botany[1] at the university, a wife of twenty years, and seven daughters between the ages of six and sixteen whose names all began with the letter A. "Their mother's idea," he explained one day, producing from his wallet a black-and-white picture of seven girls at a picnic, their braids tied with ribbons, sitting cross-legged in a row, eating

autonomy
(ô-tŏn´ə-mē) *n.* independent self-governance.

---

[1] **botany** (bŏt´n-ē): the science or study of plants.

chicken curry off of banana leaves. "How am I to distinguish?
Ayesha, Amira, Amina, Aziza, you see the difficulty."

Each week Mr. Pirzada wrote letters to his wife, and sent comic
books to each of his seven daughters, but the postal system, along
20 with most everything else in Dacca, had collapsed, and he had not
heard a word of them in over six months. Mr. Pirzada, meanwhile,
was in America for the year, for he had been awarded a grant from
the government of Pakistan to study the foliage of New England. In
spring and summer he had gathered data in Vermont and Maine,
and in autumn he moved to a university north of Boston, where we
lived, to write a short book about his discoveries. The grant was a
great honor, but when converted into dollars it was not generous.
As a result, Mr. Pirzada lived in a room in a graduate dormitory,
and did not own a proper stove or a television set. And so he came
30 to our house to eat dinner and watch the evening news.

At first I knew nothing of the reason for his visits. I was ten
years old, and was not surprised that my parents, who were from
India, and had a number of Indian acquaintances at the university,
should ask Mr. Pirzada to share our meals. It was a small campus,
with narrow brick walkways and white pillared buildings, located
on the fringes of what seemed to be an even smaller town. The
supermarket did not carry mustard oil, doctors did not make house
calls, neighbors never dropped by without an invitation, and of
these things, every so often, my parents complained. In search of
40 **compatriots**, they used to trail their fingers, at the start of each new
semester, through the columns of the university directory, circling
surnames familiar to their part of the world. It was in this manner
that they discovered Mr. Pirzada, and phoned him, and invited him
to our home.

I have no memory of his first visit, or of his second or his
third, but by the end of September I had grown so accustomed to
Mr. Pirzada's presence in our living room that one evening as I was
dropping ice cubes into the water pitcher, I asked my mother to
hand me a fourth glass from a cupboard still out of my reach. She
50 was busy at the stove, presiding over a skillet of fried spinach with
radishes, and could not hear me because of the drone of the exhaust
fan and the fierce scrapes of her spatula. I turned to my father, who
was leaning against the refrigerator, eating spiced cashews from a
cupped fist.

"What is it, Lilia?"

"A glass for the Indian man."

"Mr. Pirzada won't be coming today. More importantly,
Mr. Pirzada is no longer considered Indian," my father announced,

compatriot
(kəm-pā′trē-ət) *n.*
a fellow citizen or
person from same
country.

brushing salt from the cashews out of his trim black beard. "Not
60   since Partition.² Our country was divided. 1947."

When I said I thought that was the date of India's independence
from Britain, my father said, "That too. One moment we were free
and then we were sliced up," he explained, drawing an X with his
finger on the countertop, "like a pie. Hindus here, Muslims there.
Dacca no longer belongs to us." He told me that during Partition
Hindus and Muslims had set fire to each other's homes. For many,
the idea of eating in the other's company was still unthinkable.

It made no sense to me. Mr. Pirzada and my parents spoke the
same language, laughed at the same jokes, looked more or less the
70   same. They ate pickled mangoes with their meals, ate rice every
night for supper with their hands. Like my parents, Mr. Pirzada
took off his shoes before entering a room, chewed fennel seeds after
meals as a digestive, drank no alcohol, for dessert dipped austere
biscuits³ into successive cups of tea. Nevertheless my father insisted
that I understand the difference, and he led me to a map of the
world taped to the wall over his desk. He seemed concerned that
Mr. Pirzada might take offense if I accidentally referred to him as
an Indian, though I could not really imagine Mr. Pirzada being
offended by much of anything. "Mr. Pirzada is Bengali, but he is
80   a Muslim," my father informed me. "Therefore he lives in East
Pakistan, not India." His finger trailed across the Atlantic, through
Europe, the Mediterranean, the Middle East, and finally to the
sprawling orange diamond that my mother once told me resembled
a woman wearing a sari⁴ with her left arm extended. Various
cities had been circled with lines drawn between them to indicate
my parents' travels, and the place of their birth, Calcutta, was
signified by a small silver star. I had been there only once and had
no memory of the trip. "As you see, Lilia, it is a different country,
a different color," my father said. Pakistan was yellow, not orange.
90   I noticed that there were two distinct parts to it, one much larger
than the other, separated by an expanse of Indian territory; it was
as if California and Connecticut **constituted** a nation apart from
the U.S.

My father rapped his knuckles on top of my head. "You are,
of course, aware of the current situation? Aware of East Pakistan's
fight for sovereignty?"⁵ I nodded, unaware of the situation.

constitute
(kŏn′stĭ-to͞ot′) v.
to form or comprise.

---

² **Partition:** the division in 1947 of the Indian subcontinent into two
independent countries, India and Pakistan, after British withdrawal.

³ **biscuits:** a British term for cookies or crackers.

⁴ **sari (sä′rē):** a garment worn mostly by women of Pakistan and India, consisting
of a length of fabric with one end wrapped around the waist to form a skirt and
the other end draped over the shoulder or covering the head.

⁵ **sovereignty:** complete independence and self-goverance.

We returned to the kitchen, where my mother was draining a
pot of boiled rice into a colander. My father opened up the can on
the counter and eyed me sharply over the frames of his glasses as he
100 ate some more cashews. "What exactly do they teach you at school?
Do you study history? Geography?"

"Lilia has plenty to learn at school," my mother said. "We live
here now, she was born here." She seemed genuinely proud of the
fact, as if it were a reflection of my character. In her estimation, I
knew, I was assured a safe life, an easy life, a fine education, every
opportunity. I would never have to eat rationed food, or obey
curfews, or watch riots from my rooftop, or hide neighbors in
water tanks to prevent them from being shot, as she and my father
had. "Imagine having to place her in a decent school. Imagine her
110 having to read during power failures by the light of kerosene lamps.
Imagine the pressures, the tutors, the constant exams." She ran a
hand through her hair, bobbed to a suitable length for her part-
time job as a bank teller. "How can you possibly expect her to know
about Partition? Put those nuts away."

"But what does she learn about the world?" My father rattled
the cashew can in his hand. "What is she learning?"

We learned American history, of course, and American
geography. That year, and every year, it seemed, we began by
studying the Revolutionary War. We were taken in school buses
120 on field trips to visit Plymouth Rock,[6] and to walk the Freedom
Trail, and to climb to the top of the Bunker Hill Monument.[7] We
made dioramas out of colored construction paper depicting George
Washington crossing the choppy waters of the Delaware River,
and we made puppets of King George wearing white tights and a
black bow in his hair. During tests we were given blank maps of the
thirteen colonies, and asked to fill in names, dates, capitals. I could
do it with my eyes closed.

The next evening Mr. Pirzada arrived, as usual, at six o'clock.
Though they were no longer strangers, upon first greeting each
130 other, he and my father maintained the habit of shaking hands.

"Come in, sir. Lilia, Mr. Pirzada's coat, please."

He stepped into the foyer, **impeccably** suited and scarved,
with a silk tie knotted at his collar. Each evening he appeared
in ensembles of plums, olives, and chocolate browns. He was a
compact man, and though his feet were perpetually splayed, and his

impeccably
(ĭm-pĕk´ə-blē) *adv.*
perfectly.

---

[6] **Plymouth Rock:** a boulder in Plymouth, Massachusetts, said to be the site
where the Pilgrims disembarked from the *Mayflower*.
[7] **Freedom Trail . . . Bunker Hill Monument:** historic sites in Boston, which
commemorate critical events in the American struggle for independence from
Great Britain.

belly slightly wide, he nevertheless maintained an efficient posture, as if balancing in either hand two suitcases of equal weight. His ears were insulated by tufts of graying hair that seemed to block out the unpleasant traffic of life. He had thickly lashed eyes shaded with a trace of camphor,[8] a generous mustache that turned up playfully at the ends, and a mole shaped like a flattened raisin in the very center of his left cheek. On his head he wore a black fez[9] made from the wool of Persian lambs, secured by bobby pins, without which I was never to see him. Though my father always offered to fetch him in our car, Mr. Pirzada preferred to walk from his dormitory to our neighborhood, a distance of about twenty minutes on foot, studying trees and shrubs on his way, and when he entered our house his knuckles were pink with the effects of the crisp autumn air.

"Another refugee, I am afraid, on Indian territory."

"They are estimating nine million at the last count," my father said.

Mr. Pirzada handed me his coat, for it was my job to hang it on the rack at the bottom of the stairs. It was made of finely checkered gray-and-blue wool, with a striped lining and horn buttons, and carried in its weave the faint smell of limes. There were no recognizable tags inside, only a hand-stitched label with the phrase "Z. Sayeed, Suitors" embroidered on it in cursive with glossy black thread. On certain days a birch or maple leaf was tucked into a pocket. He unlaced his shoes and lined them against the baseboard; a golden paste clung to the toes and heels, the result of walking through our damp, unraked lawn. Relieved of his trappings, he grazed my throat with his short, restless fingers, the way a person feels for solidity behind a wall before driving in a nail. Then he followed my father to the living room, where the television was tuned to the local news. As soon as they were seated my mother appeared from the kitchen with a plate of mincemeat kebabs with coriander chutney. Mr. Pirzada popped one into his mouth.

"One can only hope," he said, reaching for another, "that Dacca's refugees are as heartily fed. Which reminds me." He reached into his suit pocket and gave me a small plastic egg filled with cinnamon hearts. "For the lady of the house," he said with an almost **imperceptible** splay-footed bow.

"Really, Mr. Pirzada," my mother protested. "Night after night. You spoil her."

"I only spoil children who are incapable of spoiling."

imperceptible
(ĭm´pər-sĕp´tə-bəl)
adj. unnoticeable.

---

[8] **camphor (kăm´fər):** a fragrant compound from an Asian evergreen tree, used in skin-care products.

[9] **fez (fĕz):** a man's felt hat in the shape of a flat-topped cone, worn mainly in the eastern Mediterranean region.

It was an awkward moment for me, one which I awaited in part with dread, in part with delight. I was charmed by the presence of Mr. Pirzada's rotund elegance, and flattered by the faint theatricality of his attentions, yet unsettled by the superb ease of his gestures, which made me feel, for an instant, like a stranger in my own home. It had become our ritual, and for several weeks, before we grew more comfortable with one another, it was the only time he spoke to me directly. I had no response, offered no comment, betrayed no visible reaction to the steady stream of honey-filled lozenges, the raspberry truffles, the slender rolls of sour pastilles. I could not even thank him, for once, when I did, for an especially spectacular peppermint lollipop wrapped in a spray of purple cellophane, he had demanded, "What is this thank-you? The lady at the bank thanks me, the cashier at the shop thanks me, the librarian thanks me when I return an overdue book, the overseas operator thanks me as she tries to connect me to Dacca and fails. If I am buried in this country I will be thanked, no doubt, at my funeral."

It was inappropriate, in my opinion, to consume the candy Mr. Pirzada gave me in a casual manner. I coveted each evening's treasure as I would a jewel, or a coin from a buried kingdom, and I would place it in a small keepsake box made of carved sandalwood beside my bed, in which, long ago in India, my father's mother used to store the ground areca nuts[10] she ate after her morning bath. It was my only memento of a grandmother I had never known, and until Mr. Pirzada came to our lives I could find nothing to put inside it. Every so often before brushing my teeth and laying out my clothes for school the next day, I opened the lid of the box and ate one of his treats.

That night, like every night, we did not eat at the dining table, because it did not provide an unobstructed view of the television set. Instead we huddled around the coffee table, without conversing, our plates perched on the edges of our knees. From the kitchen my mother brought forth the **succession** of dishes: lentils with fried onions, green beans with coconut, fish cooked with raisins in a yogurt sauce. I followed with the water glasses, and the plate of lemon wedges, and the chili peppers, purchased on monthly trips to Chinatown and stored by the pound in the freezer, which they liked to snap open and crush into their food.

Before eating Mr. Pirzada always did a curious thing. He took out a plain silver watch without a band, which he kept in his breast pocket, held it briefly to one of his tufted ears, and wound it with three swift flicks of his thumb and forefinger. Unlike the watch on

succession
(sək-sĕsh´ən) *n.*
sequence; ordered
arrangement.

---

[10]**areca (ə-rē´kə) nuts:** seeds of the betel palm, chewed as a stimulant.

his wrist, the pocket watch, he had explained to me, was set to the
220 local time in Dacca, eleven hours ahead. For the duration of the
meal the watch rested on his folded napkin on the coffee table. He
never seemed to consult it.

Now that I had learned Mr. Pirzada was not an Indian, I began
to study him with extra care, to try to figure out what made him
different. I decided that the pocket watch was one of those things.
When I saw it that night, as he wound it and arranged it on the
coffee table, an uneasiness possessed me; life, I realized, was being
lived in Dacca first. I imagined Mr. Pirzada's daughters rising from
sleep, tying ribbons in their hair, anticipating breakfast, preparing
230 for school. Our meals, our actions, were only a shadow of what had
already happened there, a lagging ghost of where Mr. Pirzada really
belonged.

At six-thirty, which was when the national news began, my
father raised the volume and adjusted the antennas. Usually I
occupied myself with a book, but that night my father insisted
that I pay attention. On the screen I saw tanks rolling through
dusty streets, and fallen buildings, and forests of unfamiliar trees
into which East Pakistani refugees had fled, seeking safety over

Image Credits: (b) ©Loungepark/The Image Bank/Getty Images; (inset) ©Tomas Skopal/Shutterstock

the Indian border. I saw boats with fan-shaped sails floating on
wide coffee-colored rivers, a barricaded university, newspaper
offices burnt to the ground. I turned to look at Mr. Pirzada; the
images flashed in miniature across his eyes. As he watched he had
an immovable expression on his face, composed but alert, as if
someone were giving him directions to an unknown destination.

During the commercial my mother went to the kitchen to get
more rice, and my father and Mr. Pirzada deplored the policies
of a general named Yahyah Khan. They discussed intrigues I did
not know, a catastrophe I could not comprehend. "See, children
your age, what they do to survive," my father said as he served me
another piece of fish. But I could no longer eat. I could only steal
glances at Mr. Pirzada, sitting beside me in his olive green jacket,
calmly creating a well in his rice to make room for a second helping
of lentils. He was not my notion of a man burdened by such grave
concerns. I wondered if the reason he was always so smartly dressed
was in preparation to endure with dignity whatever news **assailed**
him, perhaps even to attend a funeral at a moment's notice. I
wondered, too, what would happen if suddenly his seven daughters
were to appear on television, smiling and waving and blowing
kisses to Mr. Pirzada from a balcony. I imagined how relieved he
would be. But this never happened.

That night when I placed the plastic egg filled with cinnamon
hearts in the box beside my bed, I did not feel the ceremonious
satisfaction I normally did. I tried not to think about Mr. Pirzada,
in his lime-scented overcoat, connected to the unruly, sweltering
world we had viewed a few hours ago in our bright, carpeted living
room. And yet for several moments that was all I could think about.
My stomach tightened as I worried whether his wife and seven
daughters were now members of the drifting, clamoring crowd that
had flashed at intervals on the screen. In an effort to banish the
image I looked around my room, at the yellow canopied bed with
matching flounced curtains, at framed class pictures mounted on
white and violet papered walls, at the penciled inscriptions by the
closet door where my father had recorded my height on each of my
birthdays. But the more I tried to distract myself, the more I began
to convince myself that Mr. Pirzada's family was in all likelihood
dead. Eventually I took a square of white chocolate out of the box,
and unwrapped it, and then I did something I had never done
before. I put the chocolate in my mouth, letting it soften until the
last possible moment, and then as I chewed it slowly, I prayed that
Mr. Pirzada's family was safe and sound. I had never prayed for
anything before, had never been taught or told to, but I decided,
given the circumstances, that it was something I should do. That
night when I went to the bathroom I only pretended to brush my

assail
(ə-sāl´) v.
attack, disturb.

teeth, for I feared that I would somehow rinse the prayer out as well. I wet the brush and rearranged the tube of paste to prevent my parents from asking any questions, and fell asleep with sugar on my tongue.

No one at school talked about the war followed so faithfully in my living room. We continued to study the American Revolution, and learned about the injustices of taxation without representation, and memorized passages from the Declaration of Independence. During recess the boys would divide in two groups, chasing each other wildly around the swings and seesaws, Redcoats against the colonies. In the classroom our teacher, Mrs. Kenyon, pointed frequently to a map that emerged like a movie screen from the top of the chalkboard, charting the route of the *Mayflower*, or showing us the location of the Liberty Bell. Each week two members of the class gave a report on a particular aspect of the Revolution, and so one day I was sent to the school library with my friend Dora to learn about the surrender at Yorktown. Mrs. Kenyon handed us a slip of paper with the names of three books to look up in the card catalogue. We found them right away, and sat down at a low round table to read and take notes. But I could not concentrate. I returned to the blond-wood shelves, to a section I had noticed labeled "Asia." I saw books about China, India, Indonesia, Korea. Eventually I found a book titled *Pakistan: A Land and Its People*. I sat on a footstool and opened the book. The laminated jacket crackled in my grip. I began turning the pages, filled with photos of rivers and rice fields and men in military uniforms. There was a chapter about Dacca, and I began to read about its rainfall, and its jute[11] production. I was studying a population chart when Dora appeared in the aisle.

"What are you doing back here? Mrs. Kenyon's in the library. She came to check up on us."

I slammed the book shut, too loudly. Mrs. Kenyon emerged, the aroma of her perfume filling up the tiny aisle, and lifted the book by the tip of its spine as if it were a hair clinging to my sweater. She glanced at the cover, then at me.

"Is this book a part of your report, Lilia?"

"No, Mrs. Kenyon."

"Then I see no reason to consult it," she said, replacing it in the slim gap on the shelf. "Do you?"

As weeks passed it grew more and more rare to see any footage from Dacca on the news. The report came after the first

---

[11] **jute:** the fiber from an Asian plant, used for sacking and cording.

set of commercials, sometimes the second. The press had been censored, removed, restricted, rerouted. Some days, many days, only a death toll was announced, prefaced by a **reiteration** of the general situation. . . . More villages set ablaze. In spite of it all, night after night, my parents and Mr. Pirzada enjoyed long, leisurely
330 meals. After the television was shut off, and the dishes washed and dried, they joked, and told stories, and dipped biscuits in their tea. When they tired of discussing political matters they discussed, instead, the progress of Mr. Pirzada's book about the deciduous trees[12] of New England, and my father's nomination for tenure, and the peculiar eating habits of my mother's American coworkers at the bank. Eventually I was sent upstairs to do my homework, but through the carpet I heard them as they drank more tea, and listened to cassettes of Kishore Kumar, and played Scrabble on the coffee table, laughing and arguing long into the night about the
340 spellings of English words. I wanted to join them, wanted, above all, to console Mr. Pirzada somehow. But apart from eating a piece of candy for the sake of his family and praying for their safety, there was nothing I could do. They played Scrabble until the eleven o'clock news, and then, sometime around midnight, Mr. Pirzada walked back to his dormitory. For this reason I never saw him leave, but each night as I drifted off to sleep I would hear them, anticipating the birth of a nation on the other side of the world.

   One day in October Mr. Pirzada asked upon arrival, "What are these large orange vegetables on people's doorsteps? A type of
350 squash?"
   "Pumpkins," my mother replied. "Lilia, remind me to pick one up at the supermarket."
   "And the purpose? It indicates what?"
   "You make a jack-o'-lantern," I said, grinning ferociously. "Like this. To scare people away."
   "I see," Mr. Pirzada said, grinning back. "Very useful."
   The next day my mother bought a ten-pound pumpkin, fat and round, and placed it on the dining table. Before supper, while my father and Mr. Pirzada were watching the local news, she told me
360 to decorate it with markers, but I wanted to carve it properly like others I had noticed in the neighborhood.
   "Yes, let's carve it," Mr. Pirzada agreed, and rose from the sofa. "Hang the news tonight." Asking no questions, he walked into the kitchen, opened a drawer, and returned, bearing a long serrated knife. He glanced at me for approval. "Shall I?"

reiteration (rē-ĭt´ə-rā´shən) *n.* restatement or repetition.

---

[12]**deciduous** (də-sĭj´ōōəs) **trees:** trees that shed or lose leaves at the end of the growing season.

I nodded. For the first time we all gathered around the dining table, my mother, my father, Mr. Pirzada, and I. While the television aired unattended we covered the tabletop with newspapers. Mr. Pirzada draped his jacket over the chair behind him, removed a pair of opal cuff links, and rolled up the starched sleeves of his shirt.

"First go around the top, like this," I instructed, demonstrating with my index finger.

He made an initial incision and drew the knife around. When he had come full circle he lifted the cap by the stem; it loosened effortlessly, and Mr. Pirzada leaned over the pumpkin for a moment to inspect and inhale its contents. My mother gave him a long metal spoon with which he gutted the interior until the last bits of string and seeds were gone. My father, meanwhile, separated the seeds from the pulp and set them out to dry on a cookie sheet, so that we could roast them later on. I drew two triangles against the ridged surface for the eyes, which Mr. Pirzada dutifully carved, and crescents for eyebrows, and another triangle for the nose. The mouth was all that remained, and the teeth posed a challenge. I hesitated.

"Smile or frown?" I asked.

"You choose," Mr Pirzada said.

As a compromise I drew a kind of grimace, straight across, neither mournful nor friendly. Mr. Pirzada began carving, without the least bit of intimidation, as if he had been carving jack-o'-lanterns his whole life. He had nearly finished when the national news began. The reporter mentioned Dacca, and we all turned to listen: An Indian official announced that unless the world helped to relieve the burden of East Pakistani refugees, India would have to go to war against Pakistan. The reporter's face dripped with sweat as he relayed the information. He did not wear a tie or jacket, dressed instead as if he himself were about to take part in the battle. He shielded his scorched face as he hollered things to the cameraman. The knife slipped from Mr. Pirzada's hand and made a gash dipping toward the base of the pumpkin.

"Please forgive me." He raised a hand to one side of his face, as if someone had slapped him there. "I am—it is terrible. I will buy another. We will try again."

"Not at all, not at all," my father said. He took the knife from Mr. Pirzada, and carved around the gash, evening it out, dispensing altogether with the teeth I had drawn. What resulted was a disproportionately large hole the size of a lemon, so that our jack-o'-lantern wore an expression of placid astonishment, the eyebrows no longer fierce, floating in frozen surprise above a vacant, geometric gaze.

For Halloween I was a witch. Dora, my trick-or-treating partner, was a witch too. We wore black capes fashioned from dyed pillowcases and conical hats with wide cardboard brims. We shaded our faces green with a broken eye shadow that belonged to Dora's mother, and my mother gave us two burlap sacks that had once contained basmati rice, for collecting candy. That year our parents decided that we were old enough to roam the neighborhood unattended. Our plan was to walk from my house to Dora's, from where I was to call to say I had arrived safely, and then

420 Dora's mother would drive me home. My father equipped us with flashlights, and I had to wear my watch and synchronize it with his. We were to return no later than nine o'clock.

When Mr. Pirzada arrived that evening he presented me with a box of chocolate-covered mints.

"In here," I told him, and opened up the burlap sack. "Trick or treat!"

"I understand that you don't really need my contribution this evening," he said, depositing the box. He gazed at my green face, and the hat secured by a string under my chin. Gingerly he lifted

430 the hem of the cape, under which I was wearing a sweater and zipped fleece jacket. "Will you be warm enough?"

I nodded, causing the hat to tip to one side.

He set it right. "Perhaps it is best to stand still."

The bottom of our staircase was lined with baskets of miniature candy, and when Mr. Pirzada removed his shoes he did not place them there as he normally did, but inside the closet instead. He began to unbutton his coat, and I waited to take it from him, but Dora called me from the bathroom to say that she needed my help drawing a mole on her chin. When we were finally ready my mother took a
440 picture of us in front of the fireplace, and then I opened the front door to leave. Mr. Pirzada and my father, who had not gone into the living room yet, hovered in the foyer. Outside it was already dark. The air smelled of wet leaves, and our carved jack-o'-lantern flickered impressively against the shrubbery by the door. In the distance came the sounds of scampering feet, and the howls of the older boys who wore no costume at all other than a rubber mask, and the rustling apparel of the youngest children, some so young that they were carried from door to door in the arms of their parents.

"Don't go into any of the houses you don't know," my father
450 warned.

Mr. Pirzada knit his brows together. "Is there any danger?"

"No, no," my mother assured him. "All the children will be out. It's a tradition."

"Perhaps I should accompany them?" Mr. Pirzada suggested. He looked suddenly tired and small, standing there in his splayed, stockinged feet, and his eyes contained a panic I had never seen before. In spite of the cold I began to sweat inside my pillowcase.

"Really, Mr. Pirzada," my mother said, "Lilia will be perfectly safe with her friend."
460 "But if it rains? If they lose their way?"

"Don't worry," I said. It was the first time I had uttered those words to Mr. Pirzada, two simple words I had tried but failed to tell him for weeks, had said only in my prayers. It shamed me now that I had said them for my own sake.

He placed one of his stocky fingers on my cheek, then pressed it to the back of his own hand, leaving a faint green smear. "If the lady insists," he **conceded**, and offered a small bow.

We left, stumbling slightly in our black pointy thrift-store shoes, and when we turned at the end of the driveway to wave
470 good-bye, Mr. Pirzada was standing in the frame of the doorway, a short figure between my parents, waving back.

"Why did that man want to come with us?" Dora asked.

"His daughters are missing." As soon as I said it, I wished I had not. I felt that my saying it made it true, that Mr. Pirzada's daughters really were missing, and that he would never see them again.

concede
(kən-sēd´) v.
to surrender or
acknowledge defeat.

"You mean they were kidnapped?" Dora continued. "From a park or something?"

"I didn't mean they were missing. I meant, he misses them.
480　They live in a different country, and he hasn't seen them in a while, that's all."

We went from house to house, walking along pathways and pressing doorbells. Some people had switched off all their lights for effect, or strung rubber bats in their windows. At the McIntyres' a coffin was placed in front of the door, and Mr. McIntyre rose from it in silence, his face covered with chalk, and deposited a fistful of candy corns into our sacks. Several people told me that they had never seen an Indian witch before. Others performed the transaction without comment. As we paved our way with the
490　parallel beams of our flashlights we saw eggs cracked in the middle of the road, and cars covered with shaving cream, and toilet paper garlanding the branches of trees. By the time we reached Dora's house our hands were chapped from carrying our bulging burlap bags, and our feet were sore and swollen. Her mother gave us bandages for our blisters and served us warm cider and caramel popcorn. She reminded me to call my parents to tell them I had arrived safely and when I did I could hear the television in the background. My mother did not seem particularly relieved to hear from me. When I replaced the phone on the receiver it occurred to
500　me that the television wasn't on at Dora's house at all. Her father was lying on the couch, reading a magazine, with a glass of wine on the coffee table, and there was saxophone music playing on the stereo.

After Dora and I had sorted through our plunder, and counted and sampled and traded until we were satisfied, her mother drove me back to my house. I thanked her for the ride, and she waited in the driveway until I made it to the door. In the glare of her headlights I saw that our pumpkin had been shattered, its thick shell strewn in chunks across the grass. I felt the sting of tears in
510　my eyes, and a sudden pain in my throat, as if it had been stuffed with the sharp tiny pebbles that crunched with each step under my aching feet. I opened the door, expecting the three of them to be standing in the foyer, waiting to receive me, and to grieve for our ruined pumpkin, but there was no one. In the living room Mr. Pirzada, my father, and mother were sitting side by side on the sofa. The television was turned off, and Mr. Pirzada had his head in his hands.

What they heard that evening, and for many evenings after that, was that India and Pakistan were drawing closer and closer
520　to war. Troops from both sides lined the border, and Dacca was insisting on nothing short of independence. The war was soon to

"Just as I have no memory of his first visit, I have no memory of his last."

be waged on East Pakistani soil. The United States was siding with West Pakistan, the Soviet Union with India and what was soon to be Bangladesh. War was declared officially on December 4, and twelve days later, the Pakistani army, weakened by having to fight three thousand miles from their source of supplies, surrendered in Dacca. All of these facts I know only now, for they are available to me in any history book, in any library. But then it remained, for the most part, a remote mystery with haphazard clues. What

530   I remember during those twelve days of the war was that my father no longer asked me to watch the news with them, and that Mr. Pirzada stopped bringing me candy, and that my mother refused to serve anything other than boiled eggs with rice for dinner. I remember some nights helping my mother spread a sheet and blankets on the couch so that Mr. Pirzada could sleep there, and high-pitched voices hollering in the middle of the night when my parents called our relatives in Calcutta to learn more details about the situation. Most of all I remember the three of them operating during that time as if they were a single person, sharing a

540   single meal, a single body, a single silence, and a single fear.

In January, Mr. Pirzada flew back to his three-story home in Dacca, to discover what was left of it. We did not see much of him in those final weeks of the year; he was busy finishing his manuscript, and we went to Philadelphia to spend Christmas with friends of my parents. Just as I have no memory of his first visit, I have no memory of his last. My father drove him to the airport one afternoon while I was at school. For a long time we did not hear

from him. Our evenings went on as usual, with dinners in front of the news. The only difference was that Mr. Pirzada and his extra
550 watch were not there to accompany us. According to reports Dacca was repairing itself slowly, with a newly formed parliamentary government. The new leader, Sheikh Mujib Rahman, recently released from prison, asked countries for building materials to replace more than one million houses that had been destroyed in the war. Countless refugees returned from India, greeted, we learned, by unemployment and the threat of famine. Every now and then I studied the map above my father's desk and pictured Mr. Pirzada on that small patch of yellow, perspiring heavily, I imagined, in one of his suits, searching for his family. Of course,
560 the map was outdated by then.

Finally, several months later, we received a card from Mr. Pirzada **commemorating** the Muslim New Year, along with a short letter. He was reunited, he wrote, with his wife and children. All were well, having survived the events of the past year at an estate belonging to his wife's grandparents in the mountains of Shillong. His seven daughters were a bit taller, he wrote, but otherwise they were the same, and he still could not keep their names in order. At the end of the letter he thanked us for our hospitality, adding that although he now understood the meaning
570 of the words "thank you" they still were not adequate to express his gratitude. To celebrate the good news my mother prepared a special dinner that evening, and when we sat down to eat at the coffee table we toasted our water glasses, but I did not feel like celebrating. Though I had not seen him for months, it was only then that I felt Mr. Pirzada's absence. It was only then, raising my water glass in his name, that I knew what it meant to miss someone who was so many miles and hours away, just as he had missed his wife and daughters for so many months. He had no reason to return to us, and my parents predicted, correctly, that we would never see him again.
580 Since January, each night before bed, I had continued to eat, for the sake of Mr. Pirzada's family, a piece of candy I had saved from Halloween. That night there was no need to. Eventually, I threw them away.

commemorate
(kə-mĕm´ə-rāt´) v.
to celebrate or honor.

COLLABORATIVE DISCUSSION What conflicts does Mr. Pirzada experience in the story? What conflicts does Lilia face? Who is changed more at the end of the story? Cite textual evidence from the story to support your ideas.

Support Inferences About Theme

A **theme,** or central idea, is an underlying message about life or human nature that emerges from specific details in a story. Authors do not usually state the theme directly; instead, they convey themes with descriptive details, by repeating specific words and images, and through the words and actions of the story's characters. As a reader, you must look for important details and make **inferences,** or logical guesses, about the theme.

In "When Mr. Pirzada Came to Dine," look for clues about theme in the interactions between Mr. Pirzada and Lilia, the 10-year-old narrator of the story. What does Lilia focus on when she describes Mr. Pirzada, his family, and his life in eastern Pakistan? What does Lilia share about her own life? Focus on these key details to make inferences about the theme of the story.

Analyze Character and Theme

An author develops **characters** by describing what they do and say, how they interact with other characters, and how they change during the story. Details about the characters often develop the story's themes. The chart provides examples of how to use text evidence to analyze characters and make inferences about theme.

Text Evidence	Examples	Inferences and Questions
Descriptive details about a character's appearance	"He stepped into the foyer, impeccably suited and scarved, with a silk tie knotted at his collar. . . . On his head he wore a black fez made from the wool of Persian lambs, secured by bobby pins. . . ."	This description of Mr. Pirzada shows that he cares about his appearance. What can you infer from his choice of a suit and tie paired with the fez of his homeland?
Character's words and actions	"He reached into his suit pocket and gave me a small plastic egg filled with cinnamon hearts. 'For the lady of the house,' he said . . ."	Mr. Pirzada presents Lilia with gifts throughout the story. What is the meaning behind this special attention?
Character's thoughts and observations	"I began to study him with extra care, to try to figure out what made him different. I decided that the pocket watch was one of those things."	Lilia thinks about Mr. Pirzada's pocket watch. What does she realize about him as she watches him care for his watch?

Analyzing the Text

Cite Text Evidence Support your responses with evidence from the selection.

1. **Infer** Describe the gifts that Mr. Pirzada gives Lilia and how Lilia cares for these gifts. Why might she feel she should not eat the candy "in a casual manner"?

2. **Interpret** How is Mr. Pirzada's pocket watch different from the watch he wears on his wrist? What does the pocket watch help Lilia understand about Mr. Pirzada and his situation?

3. **Infer** How does Mr. Pirzada react to the idea of Lilia going out trick-or-treating? What does Lilia mean when she tries to explain it to her friend by saying, "His daughters are missing"?

4. **Analyze** Throughout the story, Lilia listens as her parents and Mr. Pirzada discuss the war between India and Pakistan. Why does she become more interested in the war? What deeper change does this interest represent in Lilia?

5. **Interpret** A **symbol** is something that stands for or represents both itself and something else. The objects associated with characters in a story are often symbols that provide clues about who they are and what they are experiencing. What are at least three objects associated with Mr. Pirzada, and what do they symbolize?

6. **Cite Evidence** What theme about growing up does the story convey? Think about Lilia's experiences and the way she changes during the story.

7. **Draw Conclusions** At the end of the story, why does Lilia feel she can finally throw away her remaining candies from Mr. Pirzada?

PERFORMANCE TASK

Writing Activity: Letters "When Mr. Pirzada Came to Dine" is told from the point of view of 10-year-old Lilia. What might we learn if we could know Mr. Pirzada's point of view? Write two letters from Mr. Pirzada to his family in Dacca. Be sure to base the details in your letters on insights we gain through Lilia's observations in the story.

- In the first letter, have Mr. Pirzada describe Lilia and her family. Have him explain why he enjoys giving Lilia candy and what she does with it.

- In the second letter, have him describe Halloween. Include details about the pumpkin carving and Lilia's trick-or-treating.

Critical Vocabulary

autonomy	compatriot	constitute	impeccably	imperceptible
succession	assail	reiteration	concede	commemorate

Practice and Apply With a partner, describe what is similar and different about the words in each pair.

1. autonomy/freedom
2. compatriot/friend
3. constitute/assemble
4. impeccably/neatly
5. imperceptible/slight

6. succession/parade
7. assail/trouble
8. reiteration/emphasis
9. concede/quit
10. commemorate/remember

Vocabulary Strategy: Patterns of Word Changes

Suffixes change a word's meaning and part of speech. For example, the Critical Vocabulary word *succession* is formed by adding the noun suffix *-ion* to a verb, or action word. The verb *succeed*, which means "to follow," becomes the noun *succession*, which means "a series or sequence." Identifying patterns of word changes will help you define unfamiliar words you encounter in your reading. Here are some common English suffixes:

Suffix	Part of Speech	Meaning	Examples
-tion, -ion	noun	act or condition of	revolution, explosion
-fiy, -fy	verb	make or become	terrify, specify
-able, -ible	adjective	ability	understandable, approachable

Practice and Apply For each row of the chart, identify another example that uses one of the suffixes shown. With each word you choose, follow these steps:

1. Identify the base, the main word part without the suffix. Note the part of speech (noun, verb, adjective) and meaning of each base word.
2. Write a definition for each word.
3. Use each word in a sample sentence.

Language and Style: Adverbial Clauses

A **subordinate clause** has a subject and verb but cannot stand alone as a sentence. It is introduced by a subordinating conjunction, such as *how, when, where, why, because,* or *whether.*

An **adverbial clause** is a subordinate clause that functions as an adverb—that is, it modifies a verb, an adjective, or an adverb in a sentence. Authors use adverbial clauses to convey specific meaning and to add variety to their writing.

In the following example from "When Mr. Pirzada Came to Dine," an adverbial clause beginning with the subordinating conjunction *when* modifies the verb *said*:

> **When I said I thought that was the date of India's independence from Britain,** my father said, "That too."

The adverbial clause makes the connection between the two ideas—what Lilia said and what her father said—clear to readers. Remove the adverbial clause, and the writing becomes choppier and slightly less clear:

> I said I thought that was the date of India's independence from Britain. My father said, "That too."

Now read this sentence:

> He seemed concerned **that Mr. Pirzada might take offense if I accidentally referred to him as an Indian,** though I could not really imagine Mr. Pirzada being offended by much of anything.

This sentence contains two adverbial clauses. The clause *that Mr. Pirzada might take offense* modifies the verb *concerned,* and the clause *if I accidentally referred to him as an Indian* modifies the verb *take.* These clauses pack a great deal of detail into one complex sentence. Without them, it would not be clear exactly why Lilia's father is concerned:

> He seemed concerned, though I could not really imagine Mr. Pirzada being offended by much of anything.

Practice and Apply Review the letters you created in response to this selection's Performance Task. In both letters, find two places where you can incorporate adverbial clauses into your writing. Have a partner review your work.

Frans B.M. de Waal (b. 1948) *was born in the Netherlands. Trained in biology, de Waal analyzes the behaviors and social interactions of primates, an order of mammals that includes monkeys, chimpanzees, gorillas, lemurs, and* homo sapiens, *or humans. He is the director of The Living Links Center at the Yerkes National Primate Research Center in Lawrenceville, Georgia, and the author of numerous books including* Chimpanzee Politics.

Monkey See, Monkey Do, Monkey Connect

Science Writing by Frans de Waal

AS YOU READ Trace and consider the examples de Waal provides about human and primate behavior. Write down any questions.

What intrigues me most about laughter is how it spreads. It's almost impossible not to laugh when everybody else is. There have been laughing epidemics, in which no one could stop and some even died in a prolonged fit. There are laughing churches and laugh therapies based on the healing power of laughter. The must-have toy of 1996—Tickle Me Elmo—laughed hysterically after being squeezed three times in a row. All of this because we love to laugh and can't resist joining laughing around us. This is why comedy shows on television have laugh tracks and why theater audiences are sometimes sprinkled with "laugh plants": people paid to produce raucous laughing at any joke that comes along.

The infectiousness of laughter even works across species. Below my office window at the Yerkes Primate Center, I often hear my chimps laugh during rough-and-tumble games, and I cannot suppress a chuckle myself. It's such a happy sound. Tickling and wrestling are the typical laugh triggers for apes, and probably the original ones for humans. The fact that tickling oneself is notoriously ineffective attests to its social significance. And when

10

young apes put on their play face, their friends join in with the
20 same expression as rapidly and easily as humans do with laughter.

Shared laughter is just one example of our primate sensitivity
to others. Instead of being Robinson Crusoes sitting on separate
islands,[1] we're all interconnected, both bodily and emotionally.
This may be an odd thing to say in the West, with its tradition of
individual freedom and liberty, but *Homo sapiens*[2] is remarkably
easily swayed in one emotional direction or another by its fellows.

This is precisely where **empathy** and sympathy start—not in
the higher regions of imagination, or the ability to consciously
reconstruct how we would feel if we were in someone else's
30 situation. It began much more simply, with the **synchronization**
of bodies: running when others run, laughing when others laugh,
crying when others cry, or yawning when others yawn. Most of us
have reached the incredibly advanced stage at which we yawn even
at the mere mention of yawning—as you may be doing right now!—
but this is only after lots of face-to-face experience.

Yawn **contagion**, too, works across species. Virtually all animals
show the peculiar "paroxystic respiratory cycle characterized by a
standard cascade of movements over a five- to ten-second period,"
which is the way the yawn has been defined. I once attended
40 a lecture on involuntary pandiculation (the medical term for
stretching and yawning) with slides of horses, lions, and monkeys—
and soon the entire audience was pandiculating. Since it so easily
triggers a chain reaction, the yawn reflex opens a window onto
mood transmission, an essential part of empathy. This makes it all
the more intriguing that chimpanzees yawn when they see others
do so.

Yawn contagion reflects the power of unconscious synchrony,
which is as deeply ingrained in us as in many other animals.
Synchrony may be expressed in the copying of small body
50 movements, such as a yawn, but also occurs on a larger scale,
involving travel or movement. It is not hard to see its survival value.
You're in a flock of birds and one bird suddenly takes off. You have
no time to figure out what's going on: You take off at the same
instant. Otherwise, you may be lunch.

Or your entire group becomes sleepy and settles down, so you
too become sleepy. Mood contagion serves to coordinate activities,
which is crucial for any traveling species (as most primates are). If
my companions are feeding, I'd better do the same, because once
they move off, my chance to forage will be gone. The individual
60 who doesn't stay in tune with what everyone else is doing will lose

empathy
(ĕmʹpə-thē) *n.* the
ability to understand
and identify with
another's feelings.

synchronization
(sĭngʹkrə-nĭ-zāʹshən)
n. coordinated,
simultaneous action.

contagion
(kən-tāʹjən) *n.* the
spreading from one
to another.

---

[1] **Robinson Crusoes . . . islands:** Crusoe, the title character of Daniel Defoe's
1719 novel, was stranded alone on a tropical island.

[2] *Homo sapiens* (hōʹmō sāʹpē-ənz): the species of primates that includes humans.

out like the traveler who doesn't go to the restroom when the bus has stopped.

The herd instinct produces weird phenomena. At one zoo, an entire baboon troop gathered on top of their rock, all staring in exactly the same direction. For an entire week they forgot to eat, mate, and groom. They just kept staring at something in the distance that no one could identify. Local newspapers were carrying pictures of the monkey rock, speculating that perhaps the animals had been frightened by a UFO. But even though this explanation had the unique advantage of combining an account of primate behavior with proof of UFOs, the truth is that no one knew the cause except that the baboons clearly were all of the same mind.

Finding himself in front of the cameras next to his pal President George W. Bush, former British prime minister Tony Blair—known to walk normally at home—would suddenly metamorphose into a distinctly un-English cowboy. He'd swagger with arms hanging loose and chest puffed out. Bush, of course, strutted like this all the time and once explained how, back home in Texas, this is known as "walking." Identification is the hook that draws us in and makes us adopt the situation, emotions, and behavior of those we're close to. They become role models: We empathize with them and emulate[3] them. Thus children often walk like the same-sex parent or mimic their tone of voice when they pick up the phone.

How does one chimp imitate another? Does he identify with the other and absorb its body movements? Or could it be that he doesn't need the other and instead focuses on the problem faced by the other? This can be tested by having a chimpanzee show another how to open a puzzle box with goodies inside. Maybe all that the watching ape needs to understand is how the thing works. He may notice that the door slides to the side or that something needs to be lifted up. The first kind of imitation involves reenactment of observed manipulations; the second merely requires technical know-how.

Thanks to ingenious studies in which chimps were presented with a so-called ghost box, we know which of these two explanations is correct. A ghost box derives its name from the fact that it magically opens and closes by itself so that no actor is needed. If technical know-how were all that mattered, such a box should suffice. But in fact, letting chimps watch a ghost box until they're bored to death—with its various parts moving and producing rewards hundreds of times—doesn't teach them anything.

---

[3] **emulate:** to imitate or behave like.

To learn from others, apes need to see actual fellow apes: Imitation requires identification with a body of flesh and blood. We're beginning to realize how much human and animal cognition runs via the body. Instead of our brain being like a little computer that orders the body around, the body-brain relation is a two-way street. The body produces internal sensations and communicates with other bodies, out of which we construct social connections and an appreciation of the surrounding reality. Bodies insert themselves into everything we perceive or think. Did you know, for example, that physical condition colors perception? The same hill is assessed as steeper, just from looking at it, by a tired person than by a well-rested one. An outdoor target is judged as farther away than it really is by a person burdened with a heavy backpack than by one without it.

Or ask a pianist to pick out his own performance from among others he's listening to. Even if this is a new piece that the pianist has performed only once, in silence (on an electronic piano and without headphones on), he will be able to recognize his own play. While listening, he probably re-creates in his head the sort of bodily sensations that accompany an actual performance. He feels the closest match listening to himself, thus recognizing himself through his body as much as through his ears.

The field of "embodied" **cognition** is still very much in its infancy but has profound **implications** for how we look at human relations. We involuntarily enter the bodies of those around us so that their movements and emotions echo within us as if they're our own. This is what allows us, or other primates, to re-create what we have seen others do. Body mapping is mostly hidden and unconscious, but sometimes it "slips out," such as when parents make chewing mouth movements while spoon-feeding their baby. They can't help but act the way they feel their baby ought to. Similarly, parents watching a singing performance of their child often get completely into it, mouthing every word. I myself still remember as a boy standing on the sidelines of soccer games and involuntarily making kicking or jumping moves each time someone I was cheering for got the ball.

The same can be seen in animals, as illustrated in an old black-and-white photograph from Wolfgang Köhler's classic tool-use studies on chimpanzees. One ape, Grande, stands on boxes that she has stacked up to reach bananas hung from the ceiling, while Sultan watches intently. Even though Sultan sits at a distance, he raises his arm in precise synchrony with Grande's grasping movement. Another example comes from a chimpanzee filmed while using a heavy rock as a hammer to crack nuts. The actor is being observed by a younger ape, who swings his own (empty) hand

cognition
(kŏg-nĭsh´ən) *n.* the process or pattern of gaining knowledge.

implication
(ĭm´plĭ-kā´shən) *n.* consequence or effect.

down in sync every time the first one strikes the nut. Body mapping provides a great shortcut to imitation.

150   When I see synchrony and mimicry—whether it concerns yawning, laughing, dancing, or aping—I see social connection and bonding. I see an old herd instinct that has been taken up a notch. It goes beyond the tendency of a mass of individuals galloping in the same direction, crossing the river at the same time. The new level requires that one pay better attention to what others do and absorb how they do it. For example, I knew an old monkey matriarch with a curious drinking style. Instead of the typical slurping with her lips from the surface, she'd dip her entire underarm in the water, then lick the hair on her arm. Her children started doing the same, and then her grandchildren. The entire
160 family was easy to recognize.

    There is also the case of a male chimpanzee who had injured his fingers in a fight and hobbled around leaning on a bent wrist instead of his knuckles. Soon all of the young chimpanzees in the colony were walking the same way in single file behind the unlucky male. Like chameleons changing their color to match the environment, primates automatically copy their surroundings.

When I was a boy, my friends in the south of the Netherlands always ridiculed me when I came home from vacations in the north, where I played with boys from Amsterdam. They told me that I talked funny. Unconsciously, I'd return speaking a poor imitation of the harsh northern accent.

The way our bodies—including voice, mood, posture, and so on—are influenced by surrounding bodies is one of the mysteries of human existence, but one that provides the glue that holds entire societies together. It's also one of the most underestimated phenomena, especially in disciplines that view humans as rational decisionmakers. Instead of each individual independently weighing the pros and cons of his or her own actions, we occupy nodes within a tight network that connects all of us in both body and mind.

COLLABORATIVE DISCUSSION What is de Waals's claim about how humans are connected? With a partner, discuss the examples he provides in support of his ideas.

Analyze and Evaluate Author's Claims

A **claim** is the author's position on a topic or issue. The science article "Monkey See, Monkey Do, Monkey Connect" is an informational text that states a specific claim about the behavior of human beings. Although Frans de Waal is an expert on the topic, it is not enough for him to simply state his claim and expect readers to accept what he is saying. He must **support** his claim throughout the essay with **reasons,** or declarations made to justify an action, decision, or belief, and **evidence** such as facts, details, and examples.

To evaluate de Waal's support for his claim, it is important to delineate, or outline, the reasons and evidence he provides. This will help you evaluate whether he has presented valid reasons and enough support for his claim.

Determine Technical Meanings

"Monkey See, Monkey Do, Monkey Connect" contains **technical vocabulary** that may be unfamiliar to you. When you encounter an unfamiliar word, you can use context clues to determine its meaning. The context of a word is made up of the punctuation marks, words, sentences, and paragraphs that surround the word. The chart below shows how a reader might use context clues to define the technical terms *empathy* and *synchronization*.

Technical Words	Context	Meaning of Words
empathy synchronization	"This is precisely where **empathy** and sympathy start—not in the higher regions of imagination, or the ability to consciously reconstruct how we would feel if we were in someone else's situation. It began much more simply, with the **synchronization** of bodies: running when others run, laughing when others laugh, crying when others cry, or yawning when others yawn."	• The word *sympathy* and the phrase "how we would feel if we were in someone else's situation" explains the meaning of *empathy*. • The image of bodies "running when others run, laughing when others laugh, crying when others cry, or yawning when others yawn" helps readers visualize *synchronization*.

Analyzing the Text

Cite Text Evidence   Support your responses with evidence from the selection.

1. **Analyze** An author carefully chooses words and phrases to establish **tone**, or a particular attitude toward his or her subject. For example, some articles use formal language to convey a serious tone while others have a more conversational style. What tone does de Waal establish in the opening paragraphs of his essay? What words and phrases create this tone?

2. **Cite Evidence** What is the primary claim that emerges in this essay? Provide evidence from the text to support your idea.

3. **Interpret** In what ways are the laughing humans described in the first paragraph like the playful chimps de Waal observes? How does this information support his claim?

4. **Identify** In lines 25-26, what does de Waal say developed because ". . . *Homo sapiens* is remarkably easily swayed in one emotional direction or another by its fellows"? Cite evidence from the text in your explanation.

5. **Infer** What is the "herd instinct"? According to de Waal, what is the positive side of people watching and imitating one another? What might be a potential downside to this part of human nature?

6. **Interpret** Explain the significance of the "ghost box." Trace what researchers learned from the ghost box experiment, and how might it relate to the ways in which people learn.

7. **Draw Conclusions** What, according to de Waal, is the "glue that holds entire societies together"? What are the strongest pieces of evidence in the text to support this claim?

PERFORMANCE TASK

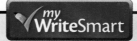

Speaking Activity: Debate The author of "Monkey See, Monkey Do, Monkey Connect" presents one view of the ways in which humans relate to one another. Do you agree with his view, or do you believe that people are, or should be, "Robinson Crusoes sitting on separate islands"?

- Form teams of two to three students each, with half arguing the points of the article and half taking the position that humans are, or should be, more "rational decisionmakers."
- Each team should gather evidence to support its position.

- Follow the rules for debating found in the Handbook at the end of this book. Afterward, write a brief evaluation of which side presented a stronger case.

Critical Vocabulary

empathy   synchonization   contagion   cognition   implication

Practice and Apply Explain which Critical Vcabulary word listed above is most closely associated with the familiar word shown below.

1. Which vocabulary word is associated with *thinking*?

2. Which vocabulary word is associated with *suggestion*?

3. Which vocabulary word is associated with *sympathy*?

4. Which vocabulary word is associated with *disease*?

5. Which vocabulary word is associated with *coordination*?

Vocabulary Strategy: Words from Greek

A **root** is a word part that contains the core meaning of a word. Many English words contain roots that come from Greek. The Critical Vocabulary word *synchronization* contains the prefix *syn-*, meaning "with or together," combined with the Greek root *chrono*, meaning "time." *Chrono* is the basis of many other words in our everyday vocabulary.

The Greek Root *Chrono*		
chronic	anachronistic	chronometer
chronicle	synchronicity	chronograph

Understanding the meaning of the root chrono and using the context clues in the sentences below can help you determine the meaning of the words in the chart.

1. My sister has a *chronic* cough that keeps her awake every night.

2. The book will *chronicle* the history of our town.

3. A computer is *anachronistic* on the set of a play about colonial life.

4. It was *synchronicity* that we bumped into each other without planning to meet.

5. The *chronometer* accurately calculated when it would arrive.

6. We timed ourselves with a *chronograph*.

Practice and Apply The Critical Vocabulary word *empathy* also contains a Greek root, *pathos*. Work with a partner to define the Greek root *pathos*. Then, write about how the meaning of this root,combined with the word's other parts, relates to the meaning of the word *empathy*. Work together to create a chart of other words containing the root *pathos*. Write sentences with the words you identify.

Language and Style: Colons

Authors use colons to add clarity to their writing. They also use colons for emphasis in order to draw attention to key ideas. In an essay, colons are commonly used to introduce a list, quotation, or independent clause.

Read this sentence from the essay.

> **This is why comedy shows on television have laugh tracks and why theater audiences are sometimes sprinkled with "laugh plants": people paid to produce raucous laughing at any joke that comes along.**

Notice how de Waal uses the colon to lead into a definition of the term "laugh plants."

In this section of the essay, the colon has a different purpose. It introduces a list.

> **It began much more simply, with the synchronization of bodies: running when others run, laughing when others laugh, crying when others cry, or yawning when others yawn.**

Now read the same sentence without the colon. Consider how the sentence loses clarity without the colon to introduce the list.

> **It began much more simply, with the synchronization of bodies running when others run, laughing when others laugh, crying when others cry, or yawning when others yawn.**

You can also use a colon to introduce a long quotation or a related independent clause.

> **They become role models: We empathize with them and emulate them.**

When an independent clause follows a colon, the clause usually begins with a capital letter.

Practice and Apply   Write two paragraphs summarizing key points in the article, "Monkey See, Monkey Do, Monkey Connect." Use colons in at least three places. At least one should introduce a list and one should introduce a quotation or independent clause.

Yasunari Kawabata (1899–1972) *was born in Osaka, Japan, and became an orphan when he was quite young. This experience may have led to the themes of loneliness and death in much of his writing. He published his first story "Izu Dancer" in 1926, and he became a major author in Japan after his novel* Snow Country *was published in 1948. In 1968, he was awarded the Nobel Prize in Literature "for his narrative mastery, which with great sensibility expresses the essences of the Japanese mind."*

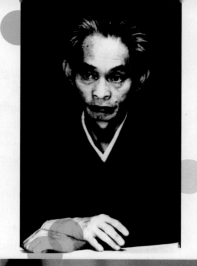

The Grasshopper and the Bell Cricket

Short Story by Yasunari Kawabata   Translated by Lane Dunlop and J. Martin Holman

AS YOU READ Consider the details that show the narrator's feelings throughout the story.

Walking along the tile-roofed wall of the university, I turned aside and approached the upper school. Behind the white board fence of the school playground, from a dusky clump of bushes under the black cherry trees, an insect's voice could be heard. Walking more slowly and listening to that voice, and feeling reluctant to part with it, I turned right so as not to leave the playground behind. When I turned to the left, the fence gave way to an embankment[1] planted with orange trees. At the corner, I exclaimed with surprise. My eyes gleaming at what they saw up
10 ahead, I hurried forward with short steps.

At the base of the embankment was a bobbing cluster of beautiful varicolored lanterns, such as one might see at a festival in a remote country village. Without going any farther, I knew that it was a group of children on an insect chase among the bushes of the embankment. There were about twenty lanterns. Not only were

---
[1] **embankment:** a man-made elevated area of land used to prevent flooding or to raise a roadway.

there crimson, pink, indigo, green, purple, and yellow lanterns, but one lantern glowed with five colors at once. There were even some little red store-bought lanterns. But most of the lanterns were beautiful square ones that the children had made themselves with love and care. The bobbing lanterns, the coming together of children on this lonely slope—surely it was a scene from a fairy tale?

One of the neighborhood children had heard an insect sing on this slope one night. Buying a red lantern, he had come back the next night to find the insect. The night after that, there was another child. This new child could not buy a lantern. Cutting out the back and front of a small carton and papering it, he placed a candle on the bottom and fastened a string to the top. The number of children grew to five, and then to seven. They learned how to color the paper that they stretched over the windows of the cutout cartons, and to draw pictures on it. Then these wise child-artists, cutting out round, three-cornered, and **lozenge** leaf shapes in the cartons, coloring each little window a different color, with circles and diamonds, red and green, made a single and whole decorative pattern. The child with the red lantern discarded it as a tasteless object that could be bought at a store. The child who had made his own lantern threw it away because the design was too simple. The pattern of light that one had had in hand the night before was unsatisfying the morning after. Each day, with cardboard, paper, brush, scissors, penknife, and glue, the children made new lanterns out of their hearts and minds. Look at my lantern! Be the most unusually beautiful! And each night, they had gone out on their insect hunts. These were the twenty children and their beautiful lanterns that I now saw before me.

Wide-eyed, I **loitered** near them. Not only did the square lanterns have old-fashioned patterns and flower shapes, but the names of the children who had made them were cut in squared letters of the syllabary.[2] Different from the painted-over red lanterns, others (made of thick cutout cardboard) had their designs drawn onto the paper windows, so that the candle's light seemed to **emanate** from the form and color of the design itself. The lanterns brought out the shadows of the bushes like dark light. The children crouched eagerly on the slope wherever they heard an insect's voice.

"Does anyone want a grasshopper?" A boy, who had been peering into a bush about thirty feet away from the other children, suddenly straightened up and shouted.

"Yes! Give it to me!" Six or seven children came running up. Crowding behind the boy who had found the grasshopper, they peered into the bush. Brushing away their outstretched hands and

lozenge
(lŏz´ĭnj) *n.* a diamond-shaped object.

loiter
(loi´tər) *v.* to stand or wait idly.

emanate
(ĕm´ə-nāt´) *v.* to emit or radiate from.

---

[2] **syllabary:** A set of written characters for a lanuage, with each character representing a syllable.

spreading out his arms, the boy stood as if guarding the bush where
60 the insect was. Waving the lantern in his right hand, he called again
to the other children.

"Does anyone want a grasshopper? A grasshopper!"

"I do! I do!" Four or five more children came running up.
It seemed you could not catch a more precious insect than a
grasshopper. The boy called out a third time.

"Doesn't anyone want a grasshopper?"

Two or three more children came over.

"Yes. I want it."

It was a girl, who just now had come up behind the boy who'd
70 discovered the insect. Lightly turning his body, the boy gracefully
bent forward. Shifting the lantern to his left hand, he reached his
right hand into the bush.

"It's a grasshopper."

"Yes. I'd like to have it."

The boy quickly stood up. As if to say "Here!" he thrust out his
fist that held the insect at the girl. She, slipping her left wrist under
the string of her lantern, enclosed the boy's fist with both hands.
The boy quietly opened his fist. The insect was transferred to
between the girl's thumb and index finger.

80 "Oh! It's not a grasshopper. It's a bell cricket." The girl's eyes
shone as she looked at the small brown insect.

"It's a bell cricket! It's a bell cricket!" The children echoed in an
envious chorus.

"It's a bell cricket. It's a bell cricket."

Glancing with her bright intelligent eyes at the boy who had
given her the cricket, the girl opened the little insect cage hanging
at her side and released the cricket in it.

"It's a bell cricket."

"Oh, it's a bell cricket," the boy who'd captured it muttered.
90 Holding up the insect cage close to his eyes, he looked inside it. By
the light of his beautiful many-colored lantern, also held up at eye
level, he glanced at the girl's face.

Oh, I thought. I felt slightly jealous of the boy, and **sheepish**.
How silly of me not to have understood his actions until now! Then
I caught my breath in surprise. Look! It was something on the girl's
breast that neither the boy who had given her the cricket, nor she
who had accepted it, nor the children who were looking at them
noticed.

In the faint greenish light that fell on the girl's breast, wasn't the
100 name "Fujio" clearly **discernible**? The boy's lantern, which he held
up alongside the girl's insect cage, inscribed his name, cut out in the
green papered aperture, onto her white cotton kimono. The girl's
lantern, which dangled loosely from her wrist, did not project its

sheepish
(shē′pĭsh) *adj.*
showing
embarrassment.

discernible
(dĭ-sûr′nə-bəl) *adj.*
recognizable or
noticeable.

pattern so clearly, but still one could make out, in a trembling patch of red on the boy's waist, the name "Kiyoko." This chance interplay of red and green—if it was chance or play—neither Fujio nor Kiyoko knew about.

Even if they remembered forever that Fujio had given her the cricket and that Kiyoko had accepted it, not even in dreams would Fujio ever know that his name had been written in green on Kiyoko's breast or that Kiyoko's name had been inscribed in red on his waist, nor would Kiyoko ever know that Fujio's name had been inscribed in green on her breast or that her own name had been written in red on Fujio's waist.

Fujio! Even when you have become a young man, laugh with pleasure at a girl's delight when, told that it's a grasshopper, she is given a bell cricket; laugh with affection at a girl's chagrin when, told that it's a bell cricket, she is given a grasshopper.

Even if you have the wit to look by yourself in a bush away from the other children, there are not many bell crickets in the world. Probably you will find a girl like a grasshopper whom you think is a bell cricket.

And finally, to your clouded, wounded heart, even a true bell cricket will seem like a grasshopper. Should that day come, when it seems to you that the world is only full of grasshoppers, I will think it a pity that you have no way to remember tonight's play of light, when your name was written in green by your beautiful lantern on a girl's breast.

COLLABORATIVE DISCUSSION How does the narrator react to the scene on the hill? What does he feel as he watches? With a partner, discuss what details the author provides to show varied emotions. Cite textual evidence to support your ideas.

Analyze Point of View: Cultural Background

Point of view involves the perspective from which a story is told. An author's cultural background and experience are part of this perspective, and are often reflected in works of literature. You may need some additional information about the author's cultural background in order to understand what the author is trying to express. "The Grasshopper and the Bell Cricket" was written in the early twentieth century by a Japanese author. Knowing some facts about Japanese culture will help you understand the author's point of view and, as a result, enrich your analysis of this story.

- Traditionally nature is quite important in Japanese culture. The roots of this reverence for nature come from the Shinto religion, which honors all aspects of the natural world: water, rocks, trees, sun, birds, insects.
- Instead of hoping to tame or conquer nature, Japanese aim to live in harmony with it. Japanese culture shows both respect and gratitude for nature.
- In Japan, as in other cultures, crickets are symbols of good luck. The bell cricket is an insect appreciated for its song, not its beauty.

Analyze Impact of Word Choice: Tone

Tone is the writer's attitude toward the subject and characters in a literary work. Authors create tone through the word choices they make. One way to classify tone is as **formal** or **informal**. The chart shows some examples of elements authors use to create a specific tone. You can use this information to help you analyze Kawabata's word choice and evaluate the tone that is created in this short story.

Colloquialisms	Abbreviations and Contractions	Sentence Structure
Colloquialisms are words or phrases used in informal conversation. Consider for example these phrases: *bunch of kids* and *group of children*. The first one is more colloquial and creates a more informal tone.	The use of **abbreviations** and **contractions** tends to make writing more informal. In this story, Kawabata uses some contractions in dialogue, but mostly avoids them.	In addition to word choice, **sentence structure** can contribute to tone. Longer, more complex sentences tend to create a more formal tone, while simpler sentences often create a more informal tone.

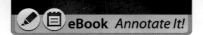

Analyzing the Text

Cite Text Evidence   Support your responses with evidence from the selection.

1. **Interpret** Examine the first two paragraphs of the story. What is the tone of these paragraphs? Cite words and phrases that contribute to the tone.

2. **Cite Evidence** Remember that nature is important in Japanese culture. What point of view about nature emerges in this selection? Cite details from the story to support your answer.

3. **Analyze** In lines 80–92, what point of view does the narrator express about people? Why is it important to understand the role of bell crickets in Japanese culture in order to understand the narrator's point of view? Explain using details from the story.

4. **Infer** Determine the **theme**, or underlying message, that the narrator expresses in lines 119–122 when he writes, "Even if you have the wit to look by yourself in a bush away from the other children, there are not many bell crickets in the world. Probably you will find a girl like a grasshopper whom you think is a bell cricket".

5. **Draw Conclusions** Think about the narrator's perspective as an older person. What point of view about life is the narrator trying to express in the advice given to Fujio in lines 115–118?

6. **Compare** Is the tone of this story the same at the beginning and at the end? Explain.

PERFORMANCE TASK

Writing Activity: Journal Entry or Letter Think about how specific words can create either an informal or formal tone. In both responses, use key details from the text and standard English.

1. In the character of the girl who receives the bell cricket, use informal language to describe the insect hunts and what happened on this night, as you would in a journal entry.

2. Look at the last three paragraphs. In the character of the narrator, write a personal letter to Fujio. Use a formal tone as you give him your advice.

Critical Vocabulary

lozenge   **loiter**   **emanate**   **sheepish**   **discernible**

Practice and Apply Answer the questions to show your understanding of the Critical Vocabulary words. Use a dictionary or thesaurus as needed.

1. Which would you be more likely to do if you are feeling **sheepish:** blush and grin or scowl and shout? Why?

2. If a container **emanates** light, can you see the light or not? Why?

3. Which would be more **discernible,** something written in crayon or in invisible ink? Why?

4. If I **loiter,** do I run away or do I hang around? Why?

5. Which item has a **lozenge** shape: kite or egg? Why?

Vocabulary Strategy: Context Clues

When you read, you can use **context clues** to understand unfamiliar words. **Context** is how a word relates to the overall meaning of a sentence, paragraph, or piece of writing.

Here are some types of context clues you may find in texts:

Synonyms or Definition	Contrast	Examples
The text may provide a definition or synonym.	The text may give an antonym, or contrasting information.	The text may list examples of the word.

Look at this example from the story.

> Then these wise child-artists, cutting out round, three-cornered, and *lozenge* leaf shapes in the cartons . . .

You read that *lozenge* is part of a list of shapes, an example of a shape. You also know from contrasting information that a *lozenge* is not round or three-cornered.

Practice and Apply Locate these words in the story: *discarded* (line 35), *crouched* (line 52), *inscribed* (line 101). Then, use context clues to write definitions for each word. Check your definitions in a dictionary.

Language and Style: Using Verb Phrases

Verb phrases are a combination of one or more helping verbs and a main verb. In "The Grasshopper and the Bell Cricket," Yasunari Kawabata uses many verb phrases to express shifts in time.

Read this sentence from the story.

> **At the base of the embankment was a bobbing cluster of beautiful varicolored lanterns such as one <u>might see</u> at a festival in a remote country village.**

By using the verb phrase *might see,* the author creates a possibility for a comparison—lanterns on the embankment and lanterns at a festival.

Now, read this sentence from the story.

> **But most of the lanterns were beautiful square ones which the children <u>had made</u> themselves with love and care.**

Here the author uses the verb phrase *had made* to show that the children's action of making the laterns took place in the past prior to the narrator seeing them.

Note that words might come between the parts of the verb phrase. In this example from the story, *does* and *want* create the verb phrase, and the phrase is interrupted by the subject, a common occurrence in a question.

> **<u>Does</u> anyone <u>want</u> a grasshopper?**

The table shows some common helping verbs. You can use these helping verbs in their different forms in verb phrases.

Common Helping Verbs in Verb Phrases		
be	can	am
do	have	may
might	shall	should
will	would	could

Practice and Apply With a partner, review your journal entries or letters you created in response to this selection's Performance Task. Note the use of verb phrases in your works. Help each other revise verb phrases to make your writing more effective in showing shifts in time, or work together to create sentences that contain verb phrases. Remember to consider the tense of the verbs when you are revising.

With Friends Like These…

Informational Text by Dorothy Rowe

AS YOU READ Pay attention to the author's ideas about what makes friendship possible between two people. Write down any questions.

We value friends, but the path of friendship, like love, rarely runs smooth. We may feel jealous of a friend's achievements when we want to feel happy for her. We might find it hard to give friends objective advice, unrelated to the person we want them to be. We can be reluctant to allow each other to change, sometimes falling out in a way that is painful for all involved. And yet, friendships are vitally important; central to our enjoyment of life.

More fundamentally, friendships are essential to our sense of who we are. Neuroscientists have shown that our brain does not reveal to us the world as it is, but rather as possible interpretations of what is going on around us, drawn from our past experience. Since no two people ever have exactly the same experience, no two people ever see anything in exactly the same way.

Most of our brain's constructions are unconscious. Early in our life our stream of conscious and unconscious constructions create, like a real stream, a kind of whirlpool that quickly becomes our most precious possession, that is, our sense of being a person, what we call "I," "me," "myself." Like a whirlpool, our sense of being a person cannot exist separately from the stream that created it.

Because we cannot see reality directly, all our ideas are guesses about what is going on. Thus our sense of being a person is made up of these guesses. All the time we are creating ideas about who we are, what is happening now, what has happened in our world, and what our future will be. When these ideas are shown by events to be reasonably accurate, that is, our ideas are **validated,** we feel secure in ourselves, but when they are proved wrong, we feel that we are falling apart.

Friends are central to this all-important sense of validation. When a friend confirms to us that the world is as we see it, we feel

validate
(văl´ĭ-dāt´) *v.* to establish the value, truth, or legitimacy of.

30　safer, reassured. On the other hand, when we say, "I'm shattered," or "I'm losing my grip," we might not be using clichés to describe a bad day but talking about something quite terrifying that we are experiencing: our sense of who we are is being challenged. So terrifying is this experience that we develop many different tactics aimed at warding off invalidation and defending ourselves against being annihilated as a person.

Emotional support

We are constantly **assessing** how safe our sense of being a person is. Our assessments are those interpretations we call emotions. All our emotions relate to the degree of safety or danger our sense of being
40　a person is experiencing. So important are these interpretations to our survival that we do not need to put them into words, although of course we can. Our positive emotions are interpretations to do with safety, while the multitude of negative emotions define the particular kind of danger and its degree. Joy is: "Everything is the way I want it to be"; jealousy is: "How dare that person have something that is rightly mine."

　　We can be invalidated by events such as the bankruptcy of the firm that employs us, but most frequently we are invalidated by other people.
50　　A friend told me how her husband had used her password and pin to drain her bank account and fund his secret gambling habit. Losing her savings was a terrible blow, but far worse was her loss of trust in the person she saw as her best friend.

　　When she described herself as falling apart, I assured her that what was falling apart were some of her ideas. All she had to do was to endure a period of uncertainty until she could construct ideas that better reflected her situation.

　　Friendship can be rewarding but, like all relationships, it can also be risky. Other people can let us down, insult or humiliate
60　us, leading us to feel diminished and in danger. Yet we need other people to tell us when we have got our guesses right, and, when we get things wrong, to help us make more accurate assessments. Live completely on your own and your guesses will get further and further away from reality.

　　The degree of risk we perceive from our friends relates directly to the degree of self-confidence we feel. When confident of ourselves, we feel that we can deal with being invalidated; when lacking self-confidence, we often see danger where no danger need exist. Take jealousy, for example. Feeling self-confident, we can
70　rejoice in our friend's success at a new job; feeling inferior, we see danger and try to defend ourselves with: "It's not fair." We can fail

assess
(ə-sĕs´) v. to evaluate.

to see that our friendship should be more important to us than our injured pride.

Our levels of confidence also relate to how ready we are to accept change, and how able we are to allow our friends to change. To feel secure in ourselves, we need to be able to predict events reasonably accurately. We think we know our friends well, and so can predict what they will do. We create a mental image of our friends, and we want to keep them within the bounds of that image. Our need to do this can override our ability to see our friends in the way they see themselves. We do not want them to change because then we would have to change our image of them. Change creates uncertainty, and uncertainty can be frightening.

Falling out

However, an inability to allow change can lead to the end of a friendship. Falling out with a friend shows us that our image of them, from which we **derive** our predictions about that friend, is wrong; and if that is the case, our sense of being a person is threatened.

derive
(dĭ-rīv´) *v.* to obtain or extract from.

If we lose a friend, we have to change how we see ourselves and our life. Each of us lives in our own individual world of meaning. We need to find friends whose individual world is somewhat similar to our own so that we are able to communicate with one another.

The people who can validate us best are those we can see as equals, and with whom there can be mutual affection, trust, loyalty and acceptance. Such people give us the kind of validation that builds a lasting self-confidence despite the difficulties we encounter.

These are our true friends.

COLLABORATIVE DISCUSSION Why do certain people become friends while others do not? With a partner, discuss the factors that allow two people to become friends, and the factors that prevent it in other cases. Cite specific textual evidence to support your ideas.

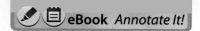

Analyze Ideas

An informational text presents a series of facts and ideas on a particular topic. The author's challenge is to present his or her ideas in a way that will make sense to readers. An effective informational text

- introduces each idea clearly and in a way that engages readers' interest
- presents ideas in a logical order
- develops ideas with examples and supporting facts
- shows readers the connections between ideas

"With Friends Like These . . ." presents facts and ideas about the important role of friendship in human life. To analyze this text, identify the central idea that the author introduces in each paragraph or section. Think about how the author develops and supports each idea, and how it relates to the ideas presented before and after. Trace the order in which ideas are presented, and consider why the author chose that order. Finally, ask yourself what the author does to engage readers and make them interested in her topic.

Analyzing the Text

Cite Text Evidence   Support your responses with evidence from the selection.

1. **Infer** Reread the first paragraph. What **tone**, or attitude, is created by the author's use of the first-person pronouns *we* and *our*? Why do you think she chose to introduce her topic to readers in this way?

2. **Connect** In lines 9–27, the author develops her ideas with information from the fields of neuroscience and psychology. How does she connect this information back to the idea that "friendships are essential to our sense of who we are"?

3. **Analyze** In lines 74–83, the author discusses people's capacity to accept change. Why does she introduce these ideas immediately before the section "Falling out"?

PERFORMANCE TASK

Speaking Activity: Discussion Reread lines 94–99 at the end of the selection. Then confer with a partner on the ideas about friendship expressed in these lines.

- Analyze the passage closely by making a list of the specific aspects of true friendship it mentions.
- Discuss each aspect and decide whether you agree that it is essential for a lasting friendship.
- List other things you believe are essential to friendship and discuss why.
- Generate a brief written summary of your discussion, including the conclusions you reached and your reasons for them.

Critical Vocabulary

validate   **assess**   **derive**

Practice and Apply Working with a partner, develop a brief scene that depicts the meaning of each Critical Vocabulary word but does not include the word. Swap your scenes with another pair. Pairs will then analyze each other's scenes and identify the Critical Vocabulary word that is being conveyed in each one.

- an experience that makes a character feel **validated**
- a character **assessing** a situation or another character
- a character who **derives** an idea from something he or she observes

Vocabulary Strategy: Patterns of Word Changes

You have probably noticed that many words can change form to become new words with related meanings. When you learn the common **patterns of word changes,** you can recognize different forms of familiar words and figure out what they mean. Knowing the patterns will also help you spell different forms of a word correctly.

The Critical Vocabulary word *validate* is a verb. By adding affixes, you can change the part of speech and meaning of the word. Adding the suffix *-ion* creates the noun *validation*, which means "the act of establishing the truth or legitimacy of something." Removing *-ate* creates the adjective *valid*, which means "true or legitimate." Adding the prefix *in-* creates the verb *invalidate*, which means "establish that something is not true or legitimate."

This chart shows more words from the selection and their various forms. Note the patterns of spelling changes that occur between verb, noun, and adjective forms.

Verb	Noun	Adjective
relate	relation, relationship	relative
describe	description	descriptive
defend	defense	defensive, indefensible
perceive	perception	perceptive

Practice and Apply For each verb in the chart, identify one new verb that has the same ending (*-ate, -ibe, -end, -ceive*). Then, follow these steps:

1. Create a chart with your words in the first column. Complete the chart with noun and adjective forms of each word.

2. Use a dictionary to check your spelling of the new words.

3. Choose one word from each row of your chart and use it in a sentence.

Language and Style:
Adjective and Adverb Phrases

A **prepositional phrase** is a phrase that consists of a preposition, its object, and any modifiers of the object. Prepositional phrases that modify nouns or pronouns are called **adjective phrases**. Prepositional phrases that modify verbs, adjectives, or adverbs are called **adverb phrases**.

"With Friends Like These . . ." opens with these sentences:

> We value friends, but the path <u>of friendship</u>, like love, rarely runs smooth. We may feel jealous <u>of a friend's achievements</u> when we want to feel happy <u>for her</u>.

The prepositional phrase *of friendship* functions as an adjective modifying *path*. The phrases *of a friend's achievements* and *for her* act as adverbs modifying *jealous* and *happy*. Notice how removing the adverb phrases makes the second sentence much less specific:

> We may feel jealous when we want to feel happy.

This chart shows sentences from the selection that use prepositional phrases as either adjectives or adverbs. Read each sentence carefully and note the relationship between the phrase and the word it modifies. There may be other words between the phrase and the word it modifies.

Adjective Phrase	Adverb Phrase
Each of us lives in our own individual world *of meaning.* (modifies the noun *world*)	More fundamentally, friendships are essential *to our sense of who we are.* (modifies the adjective *essential*)

Practice and Apply Write a summary of the author's ideas about how friendships validate our sense of who we are. Then, revise your paragraph to include at least one of each kind of phrase shown in the chart—a prepositional phrase that functions as an adjective and a prespositional phrase that functions as an adverb.

At Dusk

Poem by Natasha Trethewey

Natasha Trethewey (b. 1966) *was named United States Poet Laureate in 2012. She views her responsibility in this role as being someone who has "really got to do the work of bringing poetry to the widest audience possible." A native of Gulfport, Mississippi, Trethewey has published several collections of poetry and is a professor of English and creative writing at Emory University. Her first collection,* Domestic Work (2000), *earned her the Cave Canem Poetry Prize, awarded each year to the best first book by an African American poet. Trethewey has since won many other honors, including the Pulitzer Prize for poetry in 2007 for her book* Native Guard.

AS YOU READ Think about the decision faced by the cat in the poem, and the advantages and disadvantages of each possible course of action. Write down any questions you generate as you read the poem.

At Dusk

At first I think she is calling a child,
my neighbor, leaning through her doorway
at dusk, street lamps just starting to hum
the backdrop of evening. Then I hear
5   the high-pitched wheedling we send out
to animals who know only sound, not
the meanings of our words—*here here*—
nor how they sometimes fall short.
In another yard, beyond my neighbor's
10   sight, the cat lifts her ears, turns first
toward the voice, then back
to the constellation of fireflies flickering
near her head. It's as if she can't decide
whether to leap over the low hedge,
15   the neat row of flowers, and bound
onto the porch, into the steady circle
of light, or stay where she is: luminous
possibility—all that would keep her
away from home—flitting before her.
20   I listen as my neighbor's voice trails off.
She's given up calling for now, left me
to imagine her inside the house waiting,
perhaps in a chair in front of the TV,
or walking around, doing small tasks;
25   left me to wonder that I too might lift
my voice, sure of someone out there,
send it over the lines stitching here
to there, certain the sounds I make
are enough to call someone home.

COLLABORATIVE DISCUSSION Confer with a partner to discuss how the cat's situation is similar to one that a person might face. Generate a list of advantages and disadvantages to returning home versus exploring new possibilities.

Interpret Figurative Language

A poem captures a moment and often tells a story using compact language. Poets use **imagery,** or descriptive words and phrases that re-create sensory experiences for the reader. They also choose words and phrases carefully to convey a certain **tone**—the attitude an author takes toward a subject; and **mood**—the feeling or atmosphere an author creates for the reader. A poem's tone might be formal or informal, serious or sarcastic. The mood might be dark and brooding,or light and energetic.

Analyzing the word choices Natasha Trethewey makes throughout "At Dusk" will help you see the overall impact that her choices have on the poem's tone, mood, and meaning. This chart can help guide your interpretation of the poem's imagery.

Lines from Poem	Interpretation
"street lamps just starting to hum / the backdrop of evening"	This image establishes the scene. • What does the poet want readers to see and hear? • What mood is created by the darkening sky?
"the cat lifts her ears, turns first / toward the voice, then back / to the constellation of fireflies flickering / near her head. It's as if she can't decide/ whether to leap over the low hedge, / . . .or stay where she is"	The speaker imagines what the cat might be thinking or feeling. • Why might the cat have trouble deciding what to do? • What do you learn about the speaker by the thoughts and feelings she assigns to the cat?
"She's given up calling for now, left me / to imagine her inside the house waiting, / perhaps in a chair in front of the TV"	The speaker watches the neighbor's reaction. • What feeling does the image of someone giving up and settling in front of the TV convey?
"certain the sounds I make / are enough to call someone home"	The poem ends with the speaker's thoughts about what he or she has observed. • What is the mood of the last line of the poem? • Whom might the speaker want to call home?

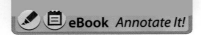

Analyzing the Text

Cite Text Evidence Support your responses with evidence from the selection.

1. **Interpret** The speaker talks about the cat not hearing meanings of our words "nor how they sometimes fall short" (line 8). What might this mean?

2. **Interpret** What might keep the cat from returning home? What might the image of a "constellation of fireflies flickering" represent to the speaker?

3. **Infer** Judging from the speaker's observations, is he or she alone or with people? Support your inference with details from the poem.

4. **Analyze** What connection does the speaker have to the neighbor at this moment? How does the speaker feel when the neighbor gives up on calling the cat?

5. **Analyze** What is the tone of this poem? What words and phrases convey the tone?

6. **Draw Conclusions** Explain the significance of the title "At Dusk."

PERFORMANCE TASK

Speaking Activity: Poetry Reading The language of poetry is meant to be heard as well as read. Get together with a partner or small group to read "At Dusk" aloud.

- Sit across from one another; or, if you are in a small group, sit in a circle facing one another.
- Take turns reading the poem aloud. Practice reading with feeling, emphasizing key words and phrases.

- After your reading, discuss what words and phrase stand out to you when you hear them read aloud.
- Write a brief summary of what you learned by reading the poem aloud.

Background *A public service announcement (PSA) is a message usually produced for television or radio about a topic or issue of interest to the public. The purpose of a PSA is to raise public awareness and encourage the audience to take action. Media and news organizations distribute public service announcements at no charge. This particular announcement is for the* Corporation for National and Community Service, *a federal agency that provides support to volunteer organizations and to individual volunteers around the country.*

MEDIA ANALYSIS

Count On Us

Public Service Announcement from the Corporation for National and Community Service

AS YOU VIEW Pay attention to how the visuals, music, and text work together to send a message. Write down any questions you generate during viewing.

COLLABORATIVE DISCUSSION In a small group, discuss how this public service announcement compares to others you have seen or heard. What are some common topics or issues that PSA's try to bring to public attention? What kinds of visuals are used to convey ideas?

Image Credits: (c) ©Jerry McCrea/Star Ledger/Corbis

Analyze Purpose and Development of Ideas

A **public service announcement** (PSA) is a type of advertisement. Advertisements are structured to achieve a purpose. A television commercial, for example, is usually created to encourage people to buy something. A PSA's purpose is to encourage the audience to take action, such as by donating goods and services to victims of a natural disaster. PSA's have these common elements:

clear and concise message	message or central idea is clear even without the audio
logical presentation	visuals, text, and music are arranged logically to support each other in conveying the central idea
emotional hook	visuals and music evoke, or bring forth, particular emotions to engage the audience
critical information	important information is included, such as the name of the organization or important statistics
call to action	viewers understand what the announcement wants them to do

Analyzing the Media

Cite Text Evidence   Support your responses with evidence from the selection.

1. **Draw Conclusions** How is this public service announcement structured to "hook" the viewer emotionally?

2. **Analyze** Is this PSA organized logically? Do the visuals, text, and music work together to send a coherent message? Cite specific scenes to support your answer.

3. **Identify** Explain the central idea and purpose of this announcement. What "call to action" does it express to viewers?

PERFORMANCE TASK

Media Activity: Public Service Announcement Explore using media to send a message and call for action.

- Create a PSA to raise awareness of a school issue. Generate a list of possible issues.
- Use video, audio, or a poster format to produce your PSA.

- Remember to give your audience specific details and organize your visuals so that the message and call to action is clear.
- Share your PSA with your class.

PERFORMANCE TASK A

Write a Fictional Narrative

The texts in this collection focus on our connections to family, friends, pets, and community. Look back at the anchor text, "When Mr. Pirzada Came to Dine," and at the other fiction and poetry you have read in this collection. How do these texts use narrative techniques to explore interpersonal connections? Synthesize your ideas about the texts by writing a narrative that shows how a character or characters connect with others.

An effective fictional narrative

- begins by introducing a setting, a narrator, and a main character
- has an engaging plot with a central conflict that the characters try to resolve
- provides a clear sequence of events
- uses a variety of narrative techniques to develop characters, plot, and a theme about personal connections
- includes sensory language and descriptive details
- ends with a logical and satisfying resolution to the conflict

PLAN

*my*Notebook

Use the notebook in your eBook to record examples of narrative techniques in the selections, such as dialogue, pacing, description, and plot lines.

Identify Narrative Techniques Reread "When Mr. Pirzada Came to Dine" and your other chosen texts, taking notes on narrative techniques. Ask yourself the following questions:

- What point of view does each author use to tell the story? Identify the narrator as first person or third person.
- How does the author reveal characters' personalities? Find examples of dialogue or descriptive details.
- How does the author allow important ideas to emerge through the text without stating them directly? For example, Mr. Pirzada does not say that he misses his daughters. What details does the author use to show readers how he feels?
- How does the author control pacing? Look for passages with descriptive detail that makes readers slow down. Contrast them with passages in which events take place very quickly.
- How does the author convey themes through the story?

ACADEMIC VOCABULARY

As you discuss narrative techniques with your group, try to use these words.

capacity
confer
emerge
generate
trace

Have a Group Discussion Discuss your analysis of narrative techniques in a group with two other classmates. Each classmate will present his or her reflections on one text.

- Take turns presenting your analyses.
- Take notes on the points your classmates raise and questions you would like to ask.
- After all three texts have been presented, evaluate the narrative techniques used in each text. Were any techniques more effective than others? Why?
- Decide which narrative techniques will be most useful when it is time to draft your own story.

Brainstorm Use a web diagram or other graphic organizer to generate ideas for your narrative.

- Think about what connects you or someone you know to family, friends, pets, or a community. Consider interests and hobbies, goals and dreams, ethnicity or nationality, neighborhood or school.
- Building on one of these connections, write down ideas for characters, setting, plot, conflict, and theme.
- Remember that this is a fictional account and that you are using ideas from real life to help you get started.

Get Organized Organize your notes, using an outline or a graphic organizer. Create an outline or use a story map to clarify the structure of your narrative. Look back at the chosen texts from this collection to help you. Ask yourself:

- How does the story begin? What can I do to engage readers and make them want to keep reading?
- What is the story's plot? What is the central conflict? Are there any other conflicts related to the central one?
- What is the sequence of events? How do they lead to a climax—a turning point or moment of greatest intensity?
- How does the story end? Is the conflict resolved? How?
- Select which point of view you will use in your narrative. Take notes on other narrative techniques you plan to use.
- Flesh out your setting and characters. What will your readers want to know? Give details about the setting. Describe your characters' appearance, personality, and anything else that makes them stand out.
- Think about the details you will use to convey a theme about personal connections.

Draft Your Narrative Write a draft of your narrative, following your notes, outline, and graphic organizers.

*my*WriteSmart

Write your rough draft in *my*WriteSmart. Focus on getting your ideas down, rather than perfecting your choice of language.

- Begin by introducing the setting, the main character(s), and an experience or conflict that will be central to the plot.
- Describe a sequence of events surrounding the conflict. If you include a flashback that is outside the main sequence of events, make the shift clear for readers.
- Use descriptive details, sensory language, and narrative techniques such as dialogue.
- Provide a satisfying ending that resolves the central conflict.

Improve Your Draft Exchange drafts with a partner. When reading your partner's draft, ask yourself these questions. Then use feedback from your partner and the chart of the following page to revise your draft.

*my*WriteSmart

Have your partner or a group of peers review your draft in *my*WriteSmart. Ask your reviewers to note any places where the plot could be better developed.

- Does the story begin in an engaging way? What could make the beginning be more interesting or exciting?
- Is there anything confusing about the sequence of events?
- Are the characters fully developed—that is, are there enough details to make them seem real?
- Does the dialogue sound natural?
- Is the conflict resolved in a logical way?

Gather Round When your final draft is completed, read your narrative to a small group. Use your voice and gestures to present a lively reading. Be prepared to answer questions or respond to comments from your group members.

Ideas and Evidence	Organization	Language
ADVANCED • The story begins memorably; the exposition clearly introduces the setting and a main character and establishes the conflict in a unique way. • The writer uses precise description and realistic dialogue to develop characters and events. • The plot is thoroughly developed; the story reveals a significant theme. • The story ends by resolving the conflict and tying up loose ends.	• The sequence of events is effective, clear, and logical. • The pace and organization keep the reader curious about the next plot event.	• The point of view is effective and consistent throughout the story. • Vivid sensory details reveal the setting and characters. • Sentence beginnings, lengths, and structures vary and have a rhythmic flow. • Spelling, capitalization, and punctuation are correct. If handwritten, the narrative is legible. • Grammar and usage are correct.
COMPETENT • The exposition introduces the setting, a main character, and a conflict, but it could be more engaging. • The writer often uses description and dialogue to develop characters and events. • The plot is adequately developed; the story suggests a theme. • The story resolves the conflict, but more details are needed to bring the plot to a satisfying conclusion.	• The sequence of events is mostly clear and logical. • The pace could move along more quickly to hold the reader's interest.	• The point of view is mostly consistent. • A few more sensory details are needed to describe the setting and characters. • Sentence beginnings, lengths, and structures mostly vary. • Several spelling, capitalization, and punctuation mistakes occur. If handwritten, the narrative is mostly legible. • Some grammatical and usage errors are repeated in the story.
LIMITED • The story opening is uneventful; the exposition identifies a setting and a main character but only hints at a conflict. • The writer occasionally uses description and dialogue to develop characters and events. • The plot development is uneven in a few places; a theme is only hinted at. • The story resolves some parts of the conflict.	• The sequence of events is confusing in a few places. • The pace often lags.	• The point of view shifts in a few places. • The sensory details are ordinary or not used regularly enough. • Sentence structures vary somewhat. • Spelling, capitalization, and punctuation are often incorrect but do not make comprehending the story difficult. If handwritten, the narrative may be partially illegible. • Grammar and usage are incorrect in many places, but the writer's ideas are still clear.
EMERGING • The exposition is missing critical information about the setting and main character and does not set up a conflict. • The writer does not use description and dialogue to develop characters and events. • The plot is barely developed, and lacks a theme. • The story lacks a clear resolution.	• There is no clear sequence of events, making it easy for the reader to lose interest in the plot. • The pace is ineffective.	• The story lacks a clear point of view. • Sensory details are rarely or never used to describe the setting and characters. • A repetitive sentence structure makes the writing monotonous. • Spelling, capitalization, and punctuation are incorrect throughout. If handwritten, the narrative may be partially or mostly illegible. • Many grammatical and usage errors change the meaning of the writer's ideas.

Create a Group Multimedia Presentation

This collection focuses on our links to family, friends, pets, and community. Look back at the anchor text, "Monkey See, Monkey Do, Monkey Connect," and at the other texts you have read in the collection. Consider the various kinds of connections explored in each text. Then synthesize your ideas by collaborating on a multimedia presentation about the bonds people form with others.

An effective multimedia presentation	Participants in an effective collaboration
• uses technology to share information through text, graphics, images, and sound • integrates information from a variety of sources and media • presents information and supporting evidence from the texts clearly, concisely, and logically • uses language and structures appropriate for an oral presentation	• prepare in advance by reading and analyzing the chosen texts • work with group members to decide on the goals and deadlines of the project and to assign individual roles • encourage participation from all group members • allow for different perspectives and seek to achieve consensus

PLAN

Analyze the Texts Reread "Monkey See, Monkey Do, Monkey Connect." Take notes on how mimicking behavior acts as a form of bonding between animals or humans. Then choose two other texts from the collection and review them for ideas about bonds and how they are formed. Identify specific examples, details, and quotations.

Get Organized Join a small group to prepare for the presentation.

- Select an effective leader and a reliable recorder.
- Confer with your group members on rules for discussions, including how participants will take turns, make decisions, and resolve disagreements.

*my*Notebook

Use the annotation tools in your eBook to locate evidence that supports your main points. Save each piece of evidence to your notebook.

ACADEMIC VOCABULARY

As you share ideas for your multimedia presentation, try to use these words.

capacity

confer

emerge

generate

trace

- Remind all participants that their role is to contribute relevant information, listen attentively, ask pertinent questions, and clarify ideas.

Assign Parts of the Presentation Select an element of the presentation for each group member to produce.

- Discuss your analysis of the texts, and generate ideas about what the main points of your presentation will be. The recorder should write down final decisions.
- Find out what types of software and technology are available to you. Your school may have an authoring program that will allow you to combine word processing with different types of media.
- Decide which type of media (video, audio, slide show, and so on) you will use to present each main point.
- Assign a group member to write and produce each part of the presentation.

PRODUCE

my WriteSmart

Produce a rough draft of your presentation using the authoring software of your choice. Then upload your draft to myWriteSmart for a peer and teacher review.

Write and Produce Your Part Use your notes and the available technology to create your part of the presentation.

- Write down a clear statement of the main point you will convey in your part.
- Use the type of media your group selected to illustrate your main idea. Try to use the technology to its full capacity. For example, don't use a video clip to show a still image; instead, use it to show a scene with action and movement.
- Present your information clearly and concisely, tracing all main points back to supporting evidence from the texts.

Storyboard the Parts Join your group and combine individual parts of the presentation to form a logically ordered, cohesive whole.

- Have each group member share his or her part.
- Discuss the order in which you will present the parts. Decide on the order that is most logical and effective.
- Craft an opening to your presentation that will grab the audience's attention. For example, you might start by posing an intriguing question or by showing an interesting video clip.
- Create a storyboard to show exactly what your audience will see and hear in each part of the presentation.

*my*WriteSmart

Have your group of peers review your draft in *my*WriteSmart. Ask your reviewers to note any main points that are not adequately supported with evidence.

Practice Your Presentation Your group should now have a rough version of your final presentation. Following your storyboard, practice delivering the presentation. As you observe how it unfolds, keep these questions in mind:

- Are there any problems with the technology that need to be solved? For example, will the audience have trouble seeing or hearing anything? Is it possible to start audio and video clips at exactly the right time?

- Are the transitions between ideas and between types of media smooth? If not, can pieces of the presentation be rearranged or reworked?

Make Sense of Things Now that you've had a chance to practice, it's time to revise your presentation. Refer to the chart on the following page for the characteristics of a well-planned multimedia presentation. With your group, make any adjustments necessary to ensure that

- your presentation begins in a way that will engage and interest the audience

- your audience will easily understand your main points and the evidence you present for each point

- the presentation integrates a variety of media in an effective way

- each part of the presentation takes full advantage of the type of technology used

- the presentation ends with a satisfying conclusion

- the entire presentation demonstrates an appropriate use of standard English

Share Your Presentation Discuss with your group how to deliver your presentation to the rest of your classmates. The way you present will depend on the types of technology used. You may be able to have small groups explore your project independently, or you may need to present to the whole class. In either situation, allow your audience to comment, ask questions, and provide feedback.

- Find out what aspects of your presentation were particularly strong.

- Ask how your presentation could be improved.

COLLECTION 3 TASK B
MULTIMEDIA PRESENTATION

	Ideas and Evidence	Organization	Language
ADVANCED	• The presentation begins memorably and engages the audience's attention. • Information and supporting evidence are presented clearly, concisely, and logically . • The presentation uses digital media strategically to enhance the audience's understanding and to add interest.	• The topic is clearly introduced at the start of the presentation. • The presentation maintains a consistent focus on the topic. • The presentation ends with a satisfying and thought-provoking conclusion.	• The presentation maintains a consistent and appropriately formal tone through the use of standard English. • The presentation uses specialized and technical vocabulary as appropriate, clearly defining these terms for the audience. • Narration flows smoothly with the use of transitions and varied sentence structures.
COMPETENT	• The presentation starts in a way that engages the audience. • Information and supporting evidence are presented clearly and logically, although some unnecessary information is included. • The presentation uses digital media in a way that helps the audience understand the topic.	• The topic is introduced at the start of the presentation. • The presentation stays focused on the topic, with a few minor lapses. • The presentation ends with an appropriate conclusion.	• The presentation mostly maintains a formal tone through the use of standard English. • The presentation uses some specialized and technical vocabulary and defines these terms for the audience. • Narration mostly flows smoothly with the use of transitions and varied sentence structures.
LIMITED	• The presentation has a somewhat bland opening that may not engage the audience. • Most information and supporting evidence are presented clearly, but there is some unnecessary information and some gaps in logic. • The use of digital media does not work to enhance the audience's understanding.	• The topic is hinted at but not made clear at the start of the presentation. • The presentation strays from the topic in several places. • The presentation ends with a brief concluding statement but leaves some ideas unresolved.	• The presentation has an inconsistent tone, sometimes using nonstandard or very informal English. • The presentation uses few specialized and technical vocabulary and fails to define these terms for the audience. • Narration needs more transitions to clarify links between ideas and uses monotonous sentence structures.
EMERGING	• The presentation opens in a way that does not engage the audience. • Information is not presented clearly and logically, and supporting evidence is lacking. • The presentation uses digital media ineffectively, causing confusion for the audience.	• No clear topic is introduced at the start of the presentation. • The presentation lacks focus throughout. • The presentation ends abruptly.	• The presentation has an overly informal tone, using nonstandard English and/or slang. • The presentation uses vague language and no specialized terms. • Narration lacks transitions to clarify links between ideas and uses choppy simple sentences.

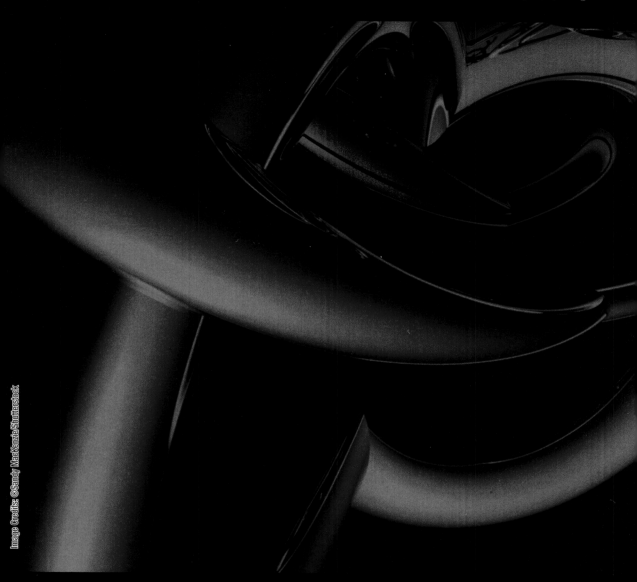

Image Credits: ©Sandy MacKenzie/Shutterstock

Sweet Sorrow

" Love is the great intangible. "

—Diane Ackerman

Sweet Sorrow

This collection explores the nature of love and the conflicts surrounding it.

fyi
hmhfyi.com

COLLECTION
PERFORMANCE TASK Preview

At the end of this collection, you will have the opportunity to complete a task:

• Write an analytical essay exploring an aspect of love.

ACADEMIC VOCABULARY

Study the words and their definitions in the chart below. You will use these words as you discuss and write about the texts in this collection.

Word	Definition	Related Forms
attribute (ăt´rə-byōōt´) *n.*	a characteristic, quality, or trait	attributable, attributed
commit (kə-mĭt´) *v.*	to carry out, engage in, or perform	commitment, recommit
expose (ĭk-spōz´) *v.*	to make visible or reveal	exposure, exposition
initiate (ĭ-nĭsh´ē-āt´) *v.*	to start or cause to begin	initiative, initiator
underlie (ŭn´dər-lī´) *v.*	to be the cause or support of	underlying, underlay

Diane Ackerman (b. 1948), *author of* A Natural History of the Senses, An Alchemy of Mind, *and* The Zookeeper's Wife, *weaves her love of science and natural history into her poetry, fiction, and nonfiction. Her memoir,* One Hundred Names for Love, *chronicles her husband's struggle to reclaim language after a stroke. In describing that time, Ackerman said, "I've always transcended best by pretending that I'm Margaret Mead viewing a scene for the first time or an alien from another planet regarding the spectacle of life on Earth and discovering how spectacular, unexpected, and beautiful it is."*

from
Love's Vocabulary

Essay by Diane Ackerman

AS YOU READ Pay attention to the many creative descriptions of love throughout the essay. Write down any questions you generate during reading.

Love is the great **intangible**. In our nightmares, we can create beasts out of pure emotion. Hate stalks the streets with dripping fangs, fear flies down narrow alleyways on leather wings, and jealousy spins sticky webs across the sky. In daydreams, we can maneuver with poise, foiling an opponent, scoring high on fields of glory while crowds cheer, cutting fast to the heart of an adventure. But what dream state is love? Frantic and serene, vigilant and calm, wrung-out and fortified, explosive and sedate—love commands a vast army of moods. Hoping for victory, limping from the latest
10 skirmish, lovers enter the arena once again. Sitting still, we are as daring as gladiators.

When I set a glass prism on a windowsill and allow the sun to flood through it, a spectrum of colors dances on the floor. What we call "white" is a rainbow of colored rays packed into a small space. The prism sets them free. Love is the white light of emotion. It includes many feelings which, out of laziness and confusion, we crowd into one simple word. Art is the prism that sets them free,

intangible
(ĭn-tăn′jə-bəl) *n.* something that is difficult to grasp or explain.

then follows the gyrations[1] of one or a few. When art separates this thick tangle of feelings, love bares its bones. But it cannot be measured or mapped. Everyone admits that love is wonderful and necessary, yet no one can agree on what it is. I once heard a sportscaster say of a basketball player, "He does all the intangibles. Just watch him do his dance." As lofty as the idea of love can be, no image is too profane to help explain it. Years ago, I fell in love with someone who was both a sport and a pastime. At the end, he made fade-away jump shots in my life. But, for a while, love did all the intangibles. It lets us do our finest dance.

Love. What a small word we use for an idea so immense and powerful it has altered the flow of history, calmed monsters, kindled works of art, cheered the forlorn, turned tough guys to mush, consoled the enslaved, driven strong women mad, glorified the humble, fueled national scandals, bankrupted robber barons, and made mincemeat of kings. How can love's spaciousness be conveyed in the narrow confines of one syllable? If we search for the source of the word, we find a history vague and confusing, stretching back to the Sanskrit *lubhyati* ("he desires"). I'm sure the etymology rambles back much farther than that, to a one-syllable word heavy as a heartbeat. Love is an ancient delirium, a desire older than civilization, with taproots[2] stretching deep into dark and mysterious days.

We use the word *love* in such a sloppy way that it can mean almost nothing or absolutely everything. It is the first conjugation[3] students of Latin learn. It is a universally understood motive for crime. "Ah, he was in love," we sigh, "well, that explains it." In fact, in some European and South American countries, even murder is forgivable if it was "a crime of passion." Love, like truth, is the unassailable defense. Whoever first said "love makes the world go round" (it was an anonymous Frenchman) probably was not thinking about celestial mechanics, but the way love seeps into the machinery of life to keep generation after generation in motion. We think of love as a positive force that somehow ennobles the one feeling it. When a friend confesses that he's in love, we congratulate him.

In folk stories, unsuspecting lads and lasses ingest a love potion and quickly lose their hearts. As with all intoxicants, love comes in many **guises** and strengths. It has a mixed bouquet, and may include some piquant ingredients.[4] One's taste in love will have a

guise
(gīz) *n.* form or outward appearance; outfit.

---

[1] **gyrations:** spiral or circular movements.

[2] **taproots:** the main roots of a tree or plant from which other roots grow.

[3] **conjugation:** in grammar, the various forms of a verb.

[4] **piquant (pē´kənt) ingredients:** components that make something pleasantly spicy.

"We use the word love in such a sloppy way that it can mean almost nothing or absolutely everything."

lot to do with one's culture, upbringing, generation, religion, era, gender, and so on. Ironically, although we sometimes think of it as the ultimate Oneness, love isn't monotone or uniform. Like a batik[5] created from many emotional colors, it is a fabric whose pattern and brightness may vary. What is my goddaughter to think when she hears her mother say: "I love Ben & Jerry's Cherry Garcia ice cream"; "I really loved my high school boyfriend"; "Don't you just love this sweater?" "I'd love to go to the lake for a week this summer"; "Mommy loves you." Since all we have is one word, we talk about love in **increments** or unwieldy ratios. "How much do you love me?" a child asks. Because the parent can't answer *I* (verb that means unconditional parental love) *you,* she may fling her arms wide, as if welcoming the sun and sky, stretching her body to its limit, spreading her fingers to encompass all of Creation, and say: "This much!" Or: "Think of the biggest thing you can imagine. Now double it. I love you a hundred times that much!"

When Elizabeth Barrett Browning wrote her famous sonnet "How do I love thee?" she didn't "count the ways" because she had an arithmetical turn of mind, but because English poets have always had to search hard for personal signals of their love. As a society, we are embarrassed by love. We treat it as if it were an obscenity. We reluctantly admit to it. Even saying the word makes us stumble and blush. Why should we be ashamed of an emotion so beautiful and natural? In teaching writing students, I've sometimes given them the assignment of writing a love poem. "Be precise, be

increment
(ĭn´krə-mənt) *n.* an addition or increase by a standard measure of growth.

---

[5] **batik (bə-tēk´):** colorful design created by applying different dyes and wax to fabric.

individual, and be descriptive. But don't use any clichés," I caution them, "or any curse words." Part of the reason for this assignment is that it helps them understand how inhibited we are about love. Love is the most important thing in our lives, a passion for which we would fight or die, and yet we're reluctant to linger over its name. Without a **supple** vocabulary, we can't even talk or think about it directly. On the other hand, we have many sharp verbs for the ways in which human beings can hurt one another, dozens of verbs for the subtle **gradations** of hate. But there are pitifully few synonyms for love. Our vocabulary of love and lovemaking is so paltry that a poet has to choose among clichés, profanities, or euphemisms. Fortunately, this has led to some richly imagined works of art. It has inspired poets to create their own private vocabularies. Mrs. Browning sent her husband a poetic abacus[6] of love, which in a roundabout way expressed the sum of her feelings. Other lovers have tried to calibrate their love in equally ingenious ways. In "The Flea," John Donne watches a flea suck blood from his arm and his beloved's, and rejoices that their blood marries in the flea's stomach.

Yes, lovers are most often reduced to comparatives and quantities. "Do you love me more than her?" we ask. "Will you love me less if I don't do what you say?" We are afraid to face love head-on. We think of it as a sort of traffic accident of the heart. It is an emotion that scares us more than cruelty, more than violence, more than hatred. We allow ourselves to be foiled by the vagueness of the word. After all, love requires the utmost vulnerability. We equip someone with freshly sharpened knives; strip naked; then invite him to stand close. What could be scarier?

If you took a woman from ancient Egypt and put her in an automobile factory in Detroit, she would be understandably disoriented. Everything would be new, especially her ability to stroke the wall and make light flood the room, touch the wall elsewhere and fill the room with summer's warm breezes or winter's blast. She'd be astonished by telephones, computers, fashions, language, and customs. But if she saw a man and woman stealing a kiss in a quiet corner, she would smile. People everywhere and everywhen understand the phenomenon of love, just as they understand the appeal of music, finding it deeply meaningful even if they cannot explain exactly what that meaning is, or why they respond viscerally to one composer and not another. Our Egyptian woman, who prefers the birdlike twittering of a sistrum,[7] and a twentieth-century man, who prefers the clashing jaws of heavy

supple
(sŭp´əl) *adj.* flexible or easily adaptable.

gradation
(grā-dā´shən) *n.* a slight, successive change in color, degree or tone.

---

[6] **abacus:** a device for performing calculations by manipulating beads strung on wires in a rectangular frame.

[7] **sistrum:** an ancient percussion instrument that sounds like a metal rattle.

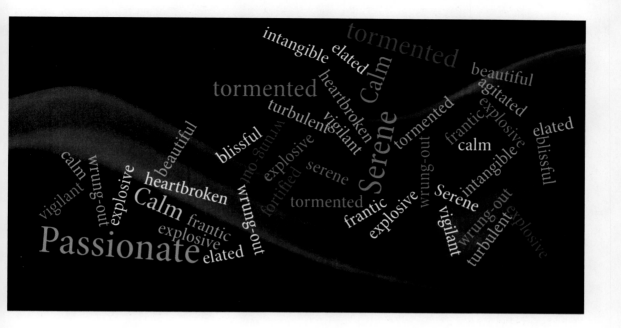

metal, share a passion for music that both would understand. So it is with love. Values, customs, and protocols may vary from ancient days to the present, but not the majesty of love. People are unique in the way they walk, dress, and gesture, yet we're able to look at two people—one wearing a business suit, the other a sarong[8]—
130 and recognize that both of them are clothed. Love also has many fashions, some bizarre and (to our taste) shocking, others more familiar, but all are part of a phantasmagoria[9] we know. In the Serengeti[10] of the heart, time and nation are irrelevant. On that plain, all fires are the same fire.

Remember the feeling of an elevator falling in your chest when you said good-bye to a loved one? Parting is more than sweet sorrow, it pulls you apart when you are glued together. It feels like hunger pains, and we use the same word, *pang*. Perhaps this is why Cupid is depicted with a quiver of arrows, because at times love feels like
140 being pierced in the chest. It is a wholesome violence. Common as child birth, love seems rare nonetheless, always catches one by surprise, and cannot be taught. Each child rediscovers it, each couple redefines it, each parent reinvents it. People search for love as if it were a city lost beneath the desert dunes, where pleasure is the law, the streets are lined with brocade cushions, and the sun never sets.

---

[8] **sarong:** a traditional Southeast Asian women's garment made from a long piece of fabric that is wrapped around the body.

[9] **phantasmagoria (făn-tăz´mə-gôr´ē-ə):** a dreamlike sequence of surreal images or events.

[10] **Serengeti:** a vast plain in Tanzania known for its migratory animals.

If it's so obvious and popular, then what is love? I began researching this book because I had many questions, not because I knew at the outset what answers I might find. Like most people, I believed what I had been told: that the idea of love was invented by the Greeks, and romantic love began in the Middle Ages. I know now how misguided such hearsay is. We can find romantic love in the earliest writings of our kind. Much of the vocabulary of love, and the imagery lovers use, has not changed for thousands of years. Why do the same images come to mind when people describe their romantic feelings? Custom, culture, and tastes vary, but not love itself, not the essence of the emotion.

COLLABORATIVE DISCUSSION Does the author answer the question "What is love?" With a partner, discuss how love is described in the essay. Select the description you think is best and support your choice with evidence from the text.

Analyze Ideas

In her essay, Diane Ackerman explores the concept of love in all of its mystery and complexity. Calling love "the great intangible" that no one can adequately define, she unfolds a series of ideas about love, from across time and place, and she supports each idea by providing facts, details, and examples. Throughout the essay, Ackerman makes connections to her central point about the language we use to describe love.

In analyzing the ideas presented in the essay, consider these questions:
- What is the significance of the order in which Ackerman introduces her ideas or makes her points?
- How does the author introduce, develop, and support each idea?
- How does the author make connections between her many ideas on love? Does she repeat any of these ideas?

Determine Word Meanings

Nonfiction writers often use literary techniques and elements such as figures of speech and allusions to convey ideas and to set a tone. Analyze Ackerman's use of literary techniques in this essay by looking at the elements in the chart.

Figurative Language	Connotation	Tone
Authors use **figurative language**—such as similes, metaphors, and personification—to help readers make connections to their own experiences. **Personification,** for example, attributes human qualities or abilities to an object, animal, or idea. In the first paragraph, how does the author personify the emotions of hate, fear, and jealousy? What does this personification imply about the power of emotions?	To influence how readers respond to their ideas, authors choose words and phrases that have **connotations,** or shades of associated meaning. For example, consider the underlying message the author conveys by using words and phrases such as "fields of glory," "love commands," "victory," and "daring as gladiators." What is the cumulative effect of employing so many figurative words?	**Tone** is the writer's attitude toward the subject or toward the reader of a work. To analyze tone, consider the writer's word choices. Are the connotations mostly positive or mostly negative? What kind of images do figures of speech present? How does Ackerman's use of an invented word ("People everywhere and *everywhen* . . .") convey her tone?

Analyzing the Text

Cite Text Evidence Support your responses with evidence from the selection.

1. **Infer** Ackerman begins by stating that "Love is the great intangible." What does she mean by this statement? What details and examples in the first two paragraphs help to support this idea?

2. **Evaluate** In lines 28–33, what human qualities does Ackerman attribute to love? Describe the tone she creates by this use of personification.

3. **Cite Evidence** In lines 60–62, how does Ackerman use figurative language to support her idea that love "isn't monotone or uniform"? What additional evidence does she provide to support this point?

4. **Analyze** Why does Ackerman include references to Elizabeth Barrett Browning's poem "How Do I Love Thee?" and John Donne's poem "The Flea"? What point is she trying to make by citing these literary works?

5. **Infer** In line 105, Ackerman calls love "a sort of traffic accident of the heart." What idea about love is she conveying?

6. **Interpret** In lines 126–127, Ackerman writes, "Values, customs, and protocols may vary from ancient days to the present, but not the majesty of love." What does she mean by this statement? What example does she use to develop this idea?

7. **Evaluate** What is Ackerman's tone throughout the essay? Cite specific words and phrases she uses to create the tone.

PERFORMANCE TASK

Speaking Activity: Discussion Does Ackerman provide convincing evidence that, as a nation, "we are embarrassed by love"?

1. Form groups of four to five students and discuss these questions:

- Why does Ackerman say we are embarrassed by love or inhibited about it? What evidence does she cite?
- Does Ackerman herself find love embarrassing? Cite examples from the text.

2. As a group, write a one-page summary of your discussion. Be sure to include specific examples from the text and revise the summary to use the conventions of standard English.

Critical Vocabulary

intangible   **guise**   **increment**   **supple**   **gradation**

Practice and Apply Create a semantic map like the one shown for the remaining Critical Vocabulary words. Use a dictionary or thesaurus as needed.

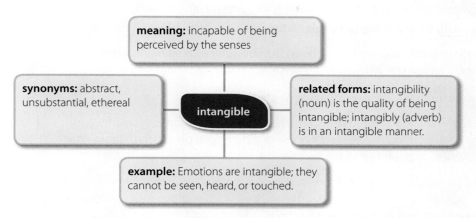

meaning: incapable of being perceived by the senses

synonyms: abstract, unsubstantial, ethereal

intangible

related forms: intangibility (noun) is the quality of being intangible; intangibly (adverb) is in an intangible manner.

example: Emotions are intangible; they cannot be seen, heard, or touched.

Vocabulary Strategy: Synonyms

When you encounter an unfamiliar word in an essay, you can often determine its meaning by substituting a **synonym**—a word with a similar meaning—for the unfamiliar word. For example, in the first line of the essay, Ackerman uses the Critical Vocabulary word *intangible*. The context clue "dream state" later in the paragraph indicates something unsubstantial. The synonym *unsubstantial* makes sense in the sentence.

Practice and Apply Work with a partner to locate these words in the essay: *immense* (line 28), *ennobles* (line 51), *monotone* (line 60), *inhibited* (line 85). Follow these steps:

1. Look for a synonym in the sentence or paragraph where the unfamiliar word occurs.

2. Use context clues to determine meaning and think of a synonym that fits.

3. Substitute your synonym for the unfamiliar word to see if it makes sense.

4. Consult a dictionary or a thesaurus to confirm the meaning.

Language and Style: Participial Phrases

A **participle** is a verb form that functions as an adjective. Like adjectives, they modify nouns and pronouns. Most participles are present-participle forms, ending in *–ing*, or past-participle forms, ending in *–ed* or *–en*. A **participial phrase** is a group of words that consists of either the present or past participle form of a verb and its modifiers. For example, the participial phrase in this sentence from "Love's Vocabulary" consists of a present participle (sitting) and an adverb (still):

<u>Sitting still</u>, we are as daring as gladiators.

The phrase *sitting still* modifies the pronoun *we*. The author could have conveyed the same information this way:

We are sitting still. We are as daring as gladiators.

However, the rhythm of these two sentences is choppy and uninteresting. Reread Ackerman's sentence and notice how her use of a participial phrase to combine the ideas adds variety and interest to her writing.

Several participial phrases may be used in one sentence to show different actions. Ackerman creates a sense of drama and builds interest by using participial phrases in combination to show several actions:

<u>Hoping for victory</u>, <u>limping from the latest skirmish</u>, lovers enter the arena once again.

Here, two participial phrases, separated by commas, modify the noun *lovers*. Ackerman could have written simply, "Lovers enter the arena once again." However, she includes participial phrases to tell us more about the lovers. She adds meaning by describing the lovers' states of mind and by presenting a dramatic visual image.

Participial phrases may be placed at the beginning, the middle, or the end of a sentence. When using participial phrases in your own writing, it is important to place them carefully and to use punctuation correctly for clarity.

- A participial phrase should be placed close to the word it modifies, to avoid confusing the reader.
- A participial phrase that begins a sentence is followed by a comma.
- A participial phrase that is at the end of a sentence is preceded by a comma.
- A participial phrase that occurs in the middle of a sentence is set off by two commas, unless it is essential to the meaning of the sentence. If the sentence would not make sense without the phrase, omit the commas.

Practice and Apply Look back at the summary of the discussion about love and embarrassment you created in this selection's Performance Task. In your same group, revise the summary to add at least three participial phrases. Then discuss how the participial phrases improve the meaning or tone of the summary.

Background Kate Tempest *is a London-born poet, playwright, and rapper. She began performing at age 16 and has performed all over the world, winning acclaim and awards at music festivals and poetry slams. Her first collection of poetry,* Everything Speaks in its Own Way, *was published in 2012 and includes a CD and a DVD along with the text. The Royal Shakespeare Company commissioned Kate to write and perform "My Shakespeare" for the World Shakespeare Festival in 2012. Thousands of artists from around the world participated in this festival throughout Britain as well as online.*

MEDIA ANALYSIS

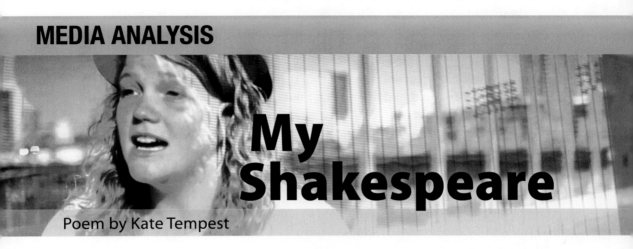

My Shakespeare

Poem by Kate Tempest

AS YOU VIEW AND READ Think about what Kate Tempest's delivery—her voice and gestures—add to the poem. Write down any questions you generate during both viewing and reading.

My Shakespeare

Performance by Kate Tempest

He's in every lover who ever stood alone beneath a window,
In every jealous whispered word,
in every ghost that will not rest.
He's in every father with a favorite,
5 Every eye that stops to linger
On what someone else has got, and feels the tightening in their
      chest.

He's in every young man growing boastful,
Every worn out elder, drunk all day;
muttering false prophecies and squandering their lot.
10 He's there—in every mix-up that spirals far out of control—and
      never seems to end,
even when its beginnings are forgot.

He's in every girl who ever used her wits. Who ever did her best.
In every vain admirer,
Every passionate, ambitious social climber,
15 And in every misheard word that ever led to tempers fraying,
Every pawn that moves exactly as the player wants it to,
And still remains convinced that it's not playing.

He's in every star crossed lover, in every thought that ever set your
teeth on edge, in every breathless hero, stepping closer to the ledge,
20 his is the method in our madness, as pure as the driven snow—his is
the hair standing on end, he saw that all that glittered was not gold.
He knew we hadn't slept a wink, and that our hearts were upon our
sleeves, and that the beast with two backs had us all upon our knees
as we fought fire with fire, he knew that too much of a good thing,
25 can leave you up in arms, the pen is mightier than the sword, still
his words seem to sing our names as they strike, and his is the milk
of human kindness, warm enough to break the ice—his, the green
eyed monster, in a pickle, still, discretion is the better part of valor,
his letters with their arms around each others shoulders, swagger
30 towards the ends of their sentences, pleased with what they've done,
his words are the setting for our stories—he has become a poet who
poetics have embedded themselves deep within the fabric of our
language, he's in our mouths, his words have tangled round our own
and given rise to expressions so effective in expressing how we feel,
35 we can't imagine how we'd feel without them.

See—he's less the tights and garters—more the sons demanding
    answers from the absence of their fathers.
The hot darkness of your last embrace.
He's in the laughter of the night before, the tightened jaw of the
    morning after,
He's in us. Part and parcel of our Royals and our rascals.
40 He's more than something taught in classrooms, in language that's
    hard to understand,
he's more than a feeling of inadequacy when we sit for our exams,
He's in every wise woman, every pitiful villain,
Every great king, every sore loser, every fake tear.
His legacy exists in the life that lives in everything he's written,
45 And me, I see him everywhere, he's my Shakespeare.

COLLABORATIVE DISCUSSION With a partner, discuss the overall effect
of the video. Cite words and phrases in the video that depart from the
text of the poem and consider whether these variations affect your
response.

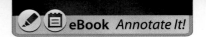

Analyze Source Material: Interpretations of Shakespeare

Kate Tempest's passionate performance of her poem demonstrates the great appeal Shakespeare has for today's youth. Shakespeare's work has been translated into more than 80 languages; it has been adapted, televised, filmed, recorded, and digitized. Shakespeare's significant presence on the Internet attests to the fact that his work has inspired—and is still inspiring—the work of countless artists.

Authors often draw on historical, literary, and cultural sources for themes or topics, using their own imagination to transform the source material into their own original works of art. Just as Shakespeare drew inspiration from earlier sources, Kate Tempest attributes her inspiration for "My Shakespeare" to the works of Shakespeare himself. In the first three stanzas, she makes allusions to the characters, themes, and scenarios exposed in Shakespeare's well-known plays. The fourth stanza comprises phrases coined by Shakespeare that are still in use today. In the last stanza, Tempest gets at the heart of Shakespeare's continued relevance.

Analyzing Text and Video

Cite Text Evidence   Support your responses with evidence from the selection.

1. **Infer** "He's in every lover . . . beneath a window" is an allusion to Romeo that is recognizable even to readers who have not read *Romeo and Juliet*. What does the repetition of the words "in every" throughout the poem signal to readers? What message does Tempest convey through these words?

2. **Cite Evidence** Explain the statement that Shakespeare is "in our mouths, his words have tangled round our own." What evidence does the author provide to support this idea?

3. **Analyze** In the last stanza, Tempest acknowledges the negative ideas that today's young people might have about Shakespeare. How do the text and the video work together to refute these ideas?

PERFORMANCE TASK

Media Activity: Reflection   Can Kate Tempest's Shakespeare be *your* Shakespeare?

- Create a blog that features Kate Tempest's performance of "My Shakespeare."
- Write an introduction or make your own video to introduce Kate Tempest's performance.
- Explain how you responded to the poem, citing specific examples from the text and the video.
- Use conventions of standard written English.

Shakespearean Drama

*Shakespeare's 38 plays may be more popular today than they were in Elizabethan times. While Shakespeare's comedies and histories remain crowd-pleasing classics, his tragedies are perhaps his most powerful works. One of the most famous, **The Tragedy of Romeo and Juliet,** relates the tale of two love-struck teens caught between the tension of their feuding families.*

Characteristics of Shakespearean Tragedy

A **tragedy** is a drama that results in a catastrophe—most often death—for the main characters. Shakespearean tragedies, however, offer us more than just despair; they provide comic moments that counter the underlying tension of the serious plot. Before you begin *The Tragedy of Romeo and Juliet,* familiarize yourself with some of the character types and dramatic conventions of Shakespearean tragedy.

Characters	Dramatic Conventions
Tragic Hero • the protagonist, or central character • usually fails or dies because of a character flaw or a cruel twist of fate	**Soliloquy** • a speech given by a character alone • exposes a character's thoughts and feelings to the audience
Antagonist • the adversary or hostile force opposing the protagonist • can be a character, a group of characters, or a nonhuman entity	**Aside** • a character's remark that others on stage do not hear • reveals the character's private thoughts
Foil • a character whose personality and attitude contrast sharply with those of another character • emphasizes another character's attributes and traits, such as a timid, introverted character making a talkative one seem even chattier	**Dramatic Irony** • when the audience knows more than the characters • helps build suspense
	Comic Relief • a humorous scene or speech intended to relieve tension • heightens the seriousness of the main action by contrast

The Language of Shakespeare

Blank Verse Shakespeare wrote his plays primarily in blank verse, unrhymed lines of **iambic pentameter,** a meter that contains five unstressed syllables (˘), each followed by a stressed syllable (´). Read the following lines aloud, making sure to emphasize each stressed syllable:

> ˘   ´   ˘ ´   ˘   ´   ˘   ´   ˘   ´
> *Here's much to do with hate but more with love.*

While this pattern forms the general rule, variations in the rhythm prevent the play from sounding monotonous. As you read, pay close attention to places where characters speak in rhyming poetry instead of unrhymed verse.

Allusion and Word Play An **allusion** is a reference to a literary or historical person or event that the audience is expected to know. Shakespeare's audience was familiar with Greek and Roman mythology and the Bible, so his plays include many references to these works.

Shakespeare also includes many **puns,** humor resulting from words with similar sounds and different meanings. For example, a depressed Romeo utters a pun using the word *light* when he offers to carry a torch: "Being but heavy, I will bear the light."

Elizabethan Words to Know

'a: he.

an, and: if.

anon: soon; right away.

aught: anything.

coz: short for cousin; used to refer to relatives or close friends.

ere: before.

e'er: ever.

god-den: good evening.

God gi' go-den: God give you a good evening.

hence: from here.

hie: hurry.

hither: here.

marry: a short form of "by the Virgin Mary" and so a mild exclamation.

morrow: morning.

naught: nothing.

o'er: over.

prithee: pray thee, or please.

sirrah: a term used to address a servant.

soft: be still; quiet; wait a minute.

thither: there.

whence: where.

wherefore: why.

wot: know.

yond, yonder: over there.

Reading Shakespearean Drama

Use the following tips to help you better understand *Romeo and Juliet*:

Reading Drama

- Study the opening cast of characters to see who's in the play.

- Read the stage directions to find out where a scene takes place as well as who's on stage and what they're doing. Stage directions in *Romeo and Juliet* are minimal, so you'll sometimes have to infer what's happening from the dialogue.

- Visualize the setting and the action by noting key details in the stage directions.

Reading Shakespearean Tragedy

- Keep track of the relationships between characters—are they friends, relatives, or enemies? Also, consider a character's dramatic function— tragic hero, antagonist, foil, or comic relief—which will help you interpret his or her words and actions.

- Note important character traits revealed through dialogue, soliloquies, and asides, as well as the through the action. Do the characters exhibit any flaws or weaknesses?

- Look for cause-and-effect relationships between events, especially those events that lead to the tragic outcome. You can keep track of them by using a graphic like this flowchart.

Cause
To cheer up Romeo, Benvolio and some other Montagues lead him to a party that the Capulets are giving.

Effect
At the party, Romeo sees Juliet for the first time, and he falls madly in love with her.

Reading Shakespeare's Language

- Use the marginal notes to figure out word meanings and unusual sentence structures. Record difficult lines and then rephrase them in modern speech.

- Paraphrase passages to help clarify their meaning and to summarize events, ideas, and themes. Use your own words without including your own opinions.

- Just as when you read poetry, don't automatically stop reading when you come to the end of a line. Look carefully at each line's punctuation and consider the meaning of the complete sentence or phrase.

Elizabethan Theater

A Wide Audience

Though acting companies toured throughout England, London was the center of the Elizabethan stage. One reason that London's theaters did so well was that they attracted an avid audience of rich and poor alike. In fact, Elizabethan theaters were among the few forms of entertainment available to working-class people, and one of the only places where people of all classes could mix. Shakespeare appealed to English audience members of all classes because he always included variety in his plays. He presented poetic speeches, exciting action scenes, fast-paced humor, and wise observations about human nature. His characters performed acts of bravery and kindness and committed heinous crimes. As a result, his work was respected by the educated and powerful people of the day, and the common people loved him too.

The Globe

In 1599, Shakespeare and other shareholders of The Lord Chamberlain's Men built the Globe Theater, a three-story wooden structure with an open courtyard at its center where the actors performed on an elevated platform. The theater held 3,000 people, with most of them standing near the courtyard stage in an area known as the pit. The pit audience paid the lowest admission fee—usually just one penny. Theatergoers willing and able to pay more sat in the covered inner balconies that surrounded the courtyard.

The audiences became emotionally involved in the performances and openly displayed their pleasure or disapproval. They cheered, booed and hissed, and even threw rotten vegetables. They roared their approval at battle scenes and swordfights, the cheers competing with such dramatic sound effects as trumpet blares, drum rolls, and thunder claps.

Staging

Elizabethan theater relied heavily on an audience's imagination. Most theaters had no curtains, no lighting, and very little scenery. Instead, props, sound effects, and certain lines of dialogue defined the setting of a scene. While the staging was simple, the scenes were hardly dull. Flashing swords, brightly colored banners, and elegant costumes contributed to the spectacle.

The costumes also helped audience members imagine that women appeared in the female roles, which were actually performed by young men. In Shakespeare's time, women could not belong to theater companies in England—Elizabethan society considered it highly improper for a woman to appear on stage. As a result, boys underwent a rigorous initiation into the dramatic techniques, dance routines, and vocal qualities necessary to perform the female parts.

The Tragedy of Romeo and Juliet

Drama by William Shakespeare

William Shakespeare *has long been considered the greatest writer in the English language—and perhaps the greatest playwright of all time. Four hundred years after their premier performances, his plays remain more popular than ever, and they have been produced more often and in more countries than those of any other author. However, despite Shakespeare's renown we have relatively few details about his life and career as an actor, poet, and playwright.*

Shakespeare came from Stratford-upon-Avon, a small village about 90 miles northwest of London, and was probably born in 1564. Though no records exist, we assume that he attended the local grammar school. In 1582 he married Anne Hathaway, daughter of a farmer. The couple's first child arrived in 1583, and twins, a boy and a girl, followed two years later.

We know nothing about the next seven years of Shakespeare's life, but he likely left his family behind and joined a traveling theater troupe. His trail resurfaces in London, where he had become a successful poet and playwright. He wrote for and acted with The Lord Chamberlain's Men, a popular theater troupe. By 1597, the year that The Tragedy of Romeo and Juliet *was published, he had become a shareholder of the theater company. As his popularity grew, Shakespeare also became part owner of London's Globe Theater. In 1603 King James I became a patron of the Globe Theater, and the theater troupe became known as The King's Men.*

In 1609 Shakespeare published his sonnets, a series of poems that received wide popular acclaim. Shakespeare then began to take advantage of his wealth and fame, spending more time in Stratford-upon-Avon and retiring there permanently around 1612. He would write no more plays after that year. No records confirm the cause or date of his death; a monument marking his gravesite indicates that he passed away on April 23, 1616. Although we have little data documenting his life, more pages have been written about Shakespeare than about any author in the history of Western civilization.

THE TIME: The 14th century

THE PLACE: Verona (və-rō´nə) and Mantua (măn´chōō-ə) in northern Italy

CAST

The Montagues

Lord Montague (mŏn´tə-gyōō´)
Lady Montague
Romeo, son of Montague
Benvolio (bĕn-vō´lē-ō), nephew of Montague and friend of Romeo
Balthasar (băl´thə-sär´), servant to Romeo
Abram, servant to Montague

The Capulets

Lord Capulet (kăp´yōō-lĕt´)
Lady Capulet
Juliet, daughter of Capulet
Tybalt (tĭb´əlt), nephew of Lady Capulet
Nurse to Juliet
Peter, servant to Juliet's nurse
Sampson, servant to Capulet
Gregory, servant to Capulet
An Old Man of the Capulet family

Others

Prince Escalus (ĕs´kə-ləs), ruler of Verona
Mercutio (mĕr-kyōō´shē-ō), kinsman of the prince and friend of Romeo
Friar Laurence, a Franciscan priest
Friar John, another Franciscan priest
Count Paris, a young nobleman, kinsman of the prince
Apothecary (ə-pŏth´ĭ-kĕr´ē)
Page to Paris
Chief Watchman
Three Musicians
An Officer
Chorus
Citizens of Verona, **Gentlemen** and **Gentlewomen** of both houses, **Maskers, Torchbearers, Pages, Guards, Watchmen, Servants,** and **Attendants**

AS YOU READ Look for clues that reveal the personalities of Romeo and Juliet. Write down any questions you generate during reading.

Prologue

[*Enter* Chorus.]

Chorus. Two households, both alike in dignity,
In fair Verona, where we lay our scene,
From ancient grudge break to new mutiny,
Where civil blood makes civil hands unclean.
5 From forth the fatal loins of these two foes,
A pair of star-crossed lovers take their life,
Whose misadventured piteous overthrows
Doth with their death bury their parents' strife.
The fearful passage of their death-marked love,
10 And the continuance of their parents' rage,
Which, but their children's end, naught could remove,
Is now the two hours' traffic of our stage,
The which if you with patient ears attend,
What here shall miss, our toil shall strive to mend.

[*Exit.*]

ACT I

Scene 1 *A public square in Verona.*

[*Enter* Sampson *and* Gregory, *servants of the house of Capulet, armed with swords and bucklers (shields).*]

Sampson. Gregory, on my word, we'll not carry coals.

Gregory. No, for then we should be colliers.

Sampson. I mean, an we be in choler, we'll draw.

Gregory. Ay, while you live, draw your neck out of collar.

5 **Sampson.** I strike quickly, being moved.

Gregory. But thou art not quickly moved to strike.

Sampson. A dog of that house of Montague moves me.

Gregory. To move is to stir, and to be valiant is to stand. Therefore, if thou art moved, thou runnest away.

10 **Sampson.** A dog of that house shall move me to stand. I will take the wall of any man or maid of Montague's.

Gregory. That shows thee a weak slave, for the weakest goes to the wall.

3–4 ancient ... unclean: A new outbreak of fighting (**mutiny**) between families has caused the citizens of Verona to have one another's blood on their hands.

6 star-crossed: doomed. The position of the stars when the lovers were born was not favorable. In Shakespeare's day, people took astrology very seriously.

7 misadventured: unlucky.

11 but: except for; **naught:** nothing.

14 what ... mend: The play will fill in the details not mentioned in the prologue.

1–2 we'll not carry coals: we won't stand to be insulted; **colliers:** those involved in the dirty work of hauling coal, who were often the butt of jokes.

3–4 in choler: angry; **collar:** a hangman's noose.

11 take the wall: walk. People of higher rank had the privilege of walking closer to the wall, to avoid any water or garbage in the street.

Sampson. 'Tis true; and therefore women, being the weaker
15   vessels, are ever thrust to the wall. Therefore push I will
Montague's men from the wall and thrust his maids to the wall.

Gregory. The quarrel is between our masters and us their men.

Sampson. 'Tis all one. I will show myself a tyrant. When I have
fought with the men, I will be cruel with the maids: I will cut
20   off their heads.

Gregory. The heads of the maids?

Sampson. Ay, the heads of the maids, or their maidenheads.
Take it in what sense thou wilt.

Gregory. They must take it in sense that feel it.

25   **Sampson.** Me they shall feel while I am able to stand;
and 'tis known I am a pretty piece of flesh.

Gregory. 'Tis well thou art not fish; if thou hadst, thou hadst
been poor-John. Draw thy tool! Here comes two of the house
of Montagues.

[*Enter* Abram *and* Balthasar, *servants to the Montagues.*]

30   **Sampson.** My naked weapon is out. Quarrel! I will back thee.

Gregory. How? turn thy back and run?

Sampson. Fear me not.

Gregory. No, marry. I fear thee!

Sampson. Let us take the law of our sides; let them begin.

35   **Gregory.** I will frown as I pass by, and let them take it as they list.

Sampson. Nay, as they dare. I will bite my thumb at them;
which is disgrace to them, if they bear it.

Abram. Do you bite your thumb at us, sir?

Sampson. I do bite my thumb, sir.

40   **Abram.** Do you bite your thumb at us, sir?

Sampson [*aside to* Gregory]. Is the law of our side if I say ay?

Gregory [*aside to* Sampson]. No.

Sampson. No, sir, I do not bite my thumb at you, sir; but I bite
my thumb, sir.

45   **Gregory.** Do you quarrel, sir?

Abram. Quarrel, sir? No, sir.

Sampson. But if you do, sir, I am for you. I serve as good a man
as you.

14–24 Sampson's tough talk includes boasts about his ability to overpower women.

28 poor-John: a salted fish, considered fit only for poor people to eat.

33 marry: a short form of "by the Virgin Mary" and so a mild exclamation.

34–44 Gregory and Sampson decide to pick a fight by insulting the Montague servants with a rude gesture (**bite my thumb**).

Abram. No better.

50 **Sampson.** Well, sir.

[*Enter* Benvolio, *nephew of Montague and first cousin of Romeo.*]

Gregory [*aside to* Sampson]. Say "better." Here comes one of my master's kinsmen.

Sampson. Yes, better, sir.

Abram. You lie.

55 **Sampson.** Draw, if you be men. Gregory, remember thy swashing blow.

[*They fight.*]

Benvolio. Part, fools!   [*beats down their swords*]
Put up your swords. You know not what you do.

[*Enter* Tybalt, *hot-headed nephew of Lady Capulet and first cousin of Juliet.*]

Tybalt. What, art thou drawn among these heartless hinds?   **59 heartless hinds:** cowardly servants.
60 Turn thee, Benvolio! look upon thy death.

Benvolio. I do but keep the peace. Put up thy sword,
Or manage it to part these men with me.

Tybalt. What, drawn, and talk of peace? I hate the word   **63 drawn:** with your sword out.
As I hate hell, all Montagues, and thee.
65 Have at thee, coward!   **65 Have at thee:** Defend yourself.

[*They fight.*]

[*Enter several of both houses, who join the fray; then enter* Citizens *and* Peace Officers, *with clubs.*]

Officer. Clubs, bills, and partisans! Strike! beat them down!   **66 bills, and partisans:** spears.

Citizens. Down with the Capulets! Down with the Montagues!

[*Enter old* Capulet *and* Lady Capulet.]

Capulet. What noise is this? Give me my long sword, ho!

Lady Capulet. A crutch, a crutch! Why call you for a sword?   **69 A crutch . . . sword:** You need a crutch more than a sword.

70 **Capulet.** My sword, I say! Old Montague is come
And flourishes his blade in spite of me.

[*Enter old* Montague *and* Lady Montague.]

Montague. Thou villain Capulet!—Hold me not, let me go.

Lady Montague. Thou shalt not stir one foot to seek a foe.

[*Enter* Prince Escalus, *with attendants. At first no one hears him.*]

Prince. Rebellious subjects, enemies to peace,
75 Profaners of this neighbor-stained steel—
Will they not hear? What, ho! you men, you beasts,
That quench the fire of your pernicious rage
With purple fountains issuing from your veins!
On pain of torture, from those bloody hands
80 Throw your mistempered weapons to the ground
And hear the sentence of your moved prince.
Three civil brawls, bred of an airy word
By thee, old Capulet, and Montague,
Have thrice disturbed the quiet of our streets
85 And made Verona's ancient citizens
Cast by their grave beseeming ornaments
To wield old partisans, in hands as old,
Cankered with peace, to part your cankered hate.
If ever you disturb our streets again,
90 Your lives shall pay the forfeit of the peace.
For this time all the rest depart away.
You, Capulet, shall go along with me;
And, Montague, come you this afternoon,
To know our farther pleasure in this case,
95 To old Freetown, our common judgment place.
Once more, on pain of death, all men depart.

[*Exeunt all but* Montague, Lady Montague, *and* Benvolio.]

Montague. Who set this ancient quarrel new abroach?
Speak, nephew, were you by when it began?

Benvolio. Here were the servants of your adversary
100 And yours, close fighting ere I did approach.
I drew to part them. In the instant came
The fiery Tybalt, with his sword prepared;
Which, as he breathed defiance to my ears,
He swung about his head and cut the winds,
105 Who, nothing hurt withal, hissed him in scorn.
While we were interchanging thrusts and blows,
Came more and more, and fought on part and part,
Till the Prince came, who parted either part.

Lady Montague. O, where is Romeo? Saw you him today?
110 Right glad I am he was not at this fray.

Benvolio. Madam, an hour before the worshiped sun
Peered forth the golden window of the East,
A troubled mind drave me to walk abroad,
Where, underneath the grove of sycamore
115 That westward rooteth from the city's side,
So early walking did I see your son.

74–81 The prince is furious about the street fighting caused by the feud. He orders the men to drop their weapons and pay attention.

77 pernicious: destructive.

82–90 Three . . . peace: The prince holds Capulet and Montague responsible for three recent street fights, each probably started by an offhand remark or insult (**airy word**). He warns that they will be put to death if any more fights occur.

Exeunt: the plural form of *exit*, indicating that more than one person is leaving the stage.

97 Who . . . abroach: Who reopened this old argument?

99 adversary: enemy.

100 ere: before.

107 on part and part: some on one side, some on the other.

110 fray: fight.

113 drave: drove.

115 rooteth: grows.

Towards him I made, but he was ware of me
And stole into the covert of the wood.
I—measuring his affections by my own,
120 Which then most sought where most might not be found,
Being one too many by my weary self—
Pursued my humor, not pursuing his,
And gladly shunned who gladly fled from me.

Montague. Many a morning hath he there been seen,
125 With tears augmenting the fresh morning's dew,
Adding to clouds more clouds with his deep sighs;
But all so soon as the all-cheering sun
Should in the farthest East begin to draw
The shady curtains from Aurora's bed,
130 Away from light steals home my heavy son
And private in his chamber pens himself,
Shuts up his windows, locks fair daylight out,
And makes himself an artificial night.
Black and portentous must this humor prove
135 Unless good counsel may the cause remove.

Benvolio. My noble uncle, do you know the cause?

Montague. I neither know it nor can learn of him.

Benvolio. Have you importuned him by any means?

Montague. Both by myself and many other friends;
140 But he, his own affections' counselor,
Is to himself—I will not say how true—
But to himself so secret and so close,
So far from sounding and discovery,
As is the bud bit with an envious worm
145 Ere he can spread his sweet leaves to the air
Or dedicate his beauty to the sun.
Could we but learn from whence his sorrows grow,
We would as willingly give cure as know.

[*Enter* Romeo *lost in thought.*]

Benvolio. See, where he comes. So please you step aside,
150 I'll know his grievance, or be much denied.

Montague. I would thou wert so happy by thy stay
To hear true shrift. Come, madam, let's away.

[*Exeunt* Montague *and* Lady.]

Benvolio. Good morrow, cousin.

Romeo.   Is the day so young?

Benvolio. But new struck nine.

117–123 made: moved; **covert:** covering. Romeo saw Benvolio coming and hid in the woods. Benvolio himself was seeking solitude and did not go after him.

124–135 Romeo has been seen wandering through the woods at night, crying. At dawn he returns home and locks himself in his room. Montague feels that his son needs guidance.

129 Aurora's bed: Aurora was the goddess of the dawn.

134 portentous: indicating evil to come; threatening.

138 importuned: asked in an urgent way.

140 his own affections' counselor: Romeo keeps to himself.

143–148 so far from . . . know: Finding out what Romeo is thinking is almost impossible. Montague compares his son to a young bud destroyed by the bite of a worm before it has a chance to open its leaves. Montague wants to find out what is bothering Romeo so he can help him.

152 shrift: confession.

153 cousin: any relative or close friend. The informal version is *coz.*

Romeo. Ay me! sad hours seem long.

155 Was that my father that went hence so fast?

Benvolio. It was. What sadness lengthens Romeo's hours?

Romeo. Not having that which having makes them short.

Benvolio. In love?

Romeo. Out—

160 **Benvolio.** Of love?

Romeo. Out of her favor where I am in love.

Benvolio. Alas that love, so gentle in his view,
Should be so tyrannous and rough in proof!

Romeo. Alas that love, whose view is muffled still,
165 Should without eyes see pathways to his will!
Where shall we dine?—O me! What fray was here?—
Yet tell me not, for I have heard it all.

162–165 love:
references to Cupid, the
god of love, typically
pictured as a blind boy
with wings and a bow
and arrow. Anyone hit
by one of his arrows falls
in love instantly.

Here's much to do with hate, but more with love.
Why then, O brawling love! O loving hate!
170 O anything, of nothing first create!
O heavy lightness! serious vanity!
Misshapen chaos of well-seeming forms!
Feather of lead, bright smoke, cold fire, sick health!
Still-waking sleep, that is not what it is!
175 This love feel I, that feel no love in this.
Dost thou not laugh?

Benvolio.　　　　No, coz, I rather weep.

Romeo. Good heart, at what?

Benvolio.　　　　　　At thy good heart's oppression.

Romeo. Why, such is love's transgression.
Griefs of mine own lie heavy in my breast,
180 Which thou wilt propagate, to have it prest
With more of thine. This love that thou hast shown
Doth add more grief to too much of mine own.
Love is a smoke raised with the fume of sighs;
Being purged, a fire sparkling in lovers' eyes;
185 Being vexed, a sea nourished with lovers' tears.
What is it else? A madness most discreet,
A choking gall, and a preserving sweet.
Farewell, my coz.

Benvolio.　　Soft! I will go along.
An if you leave me so, you do me wrong.

190 **Romeo.** Tut! I have lost myself; I am not here:
This is not Romeo, he's some other where.

Benvolio. Tell me in sadness, who is that you love?

Romeo. What, shall I groan and tell thee?

Benvolio.　　　　　　　　　Groan? Why, no;
But sadly tell me who.

195 **Romeo.** Bid a sick man in sadness make his will.
Ah, word ill urged to one that is so ill!
In sadness, cousin, I do love a woman.

Benvolio. I aimed so near when I supposed you loved.

Romeo. A right good markman! And she's fair I love.

200 **Benvolio.** A right fair mark, fair coz, is soonest hit.

Romeo. Well, in that hit you miss. She'll not be hit
With Cupid's arrow. She hath Dian's wit,
And, in strong proof of chastity well armed,

168–176 Romeo, confused and upset, tries to describe his feelings about love. He uses phrases like "loving hate" and other contradictory expressions.

176–182 Benvolio expresses his sympathy for Romeo. Romeo replies that this is one more problem caused by love. He now feels worse than before because he must carry the weight of Benvolio's sympathy along with his own grief.

184 purged: cleansed (of the smoke).

185 vexed: troubled.

187 gall: something causing bitterness or hate.

188 Soft: Wait a minute.

192 sadness: seriousness.

201–204 She'll . . . unharmed: The girl isn't interested in falling in love. She is like Diana, the goddess of chastity.

From Love's weak childish bow she lives unharmed.
205 She will not stay the siege of loving terms,
Nor bide the encounter of assailing eyes,
Nor ope her lap to saint-seducing gold.
O, she is rich in beauty; only poor
That, when she dies, with beauty dies her store.

210 **Benvolio.** Then she hath sworn that she will still live chaste?

Romeo. She hath, and in that sparing makes huge waste;
For beauty, starved with her severity,
Cuts beauty off from all posterity.
She is too fair, too wise, wisely too fair,
215 To merit bliss by making me despair.
She hath forsworn to love, and in that vow
Do I live dead that live to tell it now.

Benvolio. Be ruled by me: forget to think of her.

Romeo. O, teach me how I should forget to think!

220 **Benvolio.** By giving liberty unto thine eyes:
Examine other beauties.

Romeo.   'Tis the way
To call hers (exquisite) in question more.
These happy masks that kiss fair ladies' brows,
Being black, puts us in mind they hide the fair.
225 He that is strucken blind cannot forget
The precious treasure of his eyesight lost.
Show me a mistress that is passing fair,
What doth her beauty serve but as a note
Where I may read who passed that passing fair?
230 Farewell. Thou canst not teach me to forget.

Benvolio. I'll pay that doctrine, or else die in debt.

[*Exeunt.*]

Scene 2 *A street near the Capulet house.*

[*Enter* Capulet *with* Paris, *a kinsman of the Prince, and* Servant.]

Capulet. But Montague is bound as well as I,
In penalty alike; and 'tis not hard, I think,
For men so old as we to keep the peace.

Paris. Of honorable reckoning are you both,
5 And pity 'tis you lived at odds so long.
But now, my lord, what say you to my suit?

Capulet. But saying o'er what I have said before:
My child is yet a stranger in the world,

205–207 She will not . . . gold: She is not swayed by Romeo's love or his wealth.

212–213 For beauty . . . posterity: She wastes her beauty, which will not be passed on to future generations.

215–216 To merit . . . despair: The girl will reach heaven (**bliss**) by being so virtuous, which causes Romeo to feel despair; **forsworn to:** sworn not to.

221–222 'Tis . . . more: That would only make me appreciate my own love's beauty more.

223 Masks were worn by Elizabethan women to protect their faces from the sun.

227–229 Show me . . . fair: A woman who is exceedingly (**passing**) beautiful will only remind me of my love, who is even prettier.

231 I'll pay . . . debt: I'll convince you you're wrong, or die trying.

1 bound: obligated.

4 reckoning: reputation.

6 what say . . . suit: Paris is asking for Capulet's response to his proposal to marry Juliet.

She hath not seen the change of fourteen years;
10 Let two more summers wither in their pride
Ere we may think her ripe to be a bride.

Paris. Younger than she are happy mothers made.

Capulet. And too soon marred are those so early made.
The earth hath swallowed all my hopes but she;
15 She is the hopeful lady of my earth.
But woo her, gentle Paris, get her heart;
My will to her consent is but a part.
An she agree, within her scope of choice
Lies my consent and fair according voice.
20 This night I hold an old accustomed feast,
Whereto I have invited many a guest,
Such as I love, and you among the store,
One more, most welcome, makes my number more.
At my poor house look to behold this night
25 Earth-treading stars that make dark heaven light.
Such comfort as do lusty young men feel
When well-appareled April on the heel
Of limping Winter treads, even such delight
Among fresh female buds shall you this night
30 Inherit at my house. Hear all, all see,
And like her most whose merit most shall be;
Which, on more view of many, mine, being one,
May stand in number, though in reck'ning none.
Come, go with me.   [*to* Servant, *giving him a paper*]
                    Go, sirrah, trudge about
35 Through fair Verona; find those persons out
Whose names are written there, and to them say,
My house and welcome on their pleasure stay.

[*Exeunt* Capulet *and* Paris.]

Servant. Find them out whose names are written here! It is
written that the shoemaker should meddle with his yard and the
40 tailor with his last, the fisher with his pencil and the painter
with his nets; but I am sent to find those persons whose names
are here writ, and can never find what names the writing person
hath here writ. I must to the learned. In good time!

[*Enter* Benvolio *and* Romeo.]

Benvolio. Tut, man, one fire burns out another's burning;
45 One pain is lessened by another's anguish;
Turn giddy, and be holp by backward turning;
One desperate grief cures with another's languish.

---

10 Let two more summers . . . pride: let two more years pass.

14 The earth . . . she: All my children are dead except Juliet.

16 woo her: try to win her heart.

18–19 An . . . voice: I will give my approval to the one she chooses.

20 old accustomed feast: a traditional or annual party.

29–33 Among . . . none: Tonight at the party you will see the loveliest girls in Verona, including Juliet. When you see all of them together, your opinion of Juliet may change.

34 sirrah: a term used to address a servant.

38–43 The servant cannot read. He confuses the craftsmen and their tools, tapping a typical source of humor for Elizabethan comic characters.

44–49 Tut, man . . . die: Benvolio says Romeo should find a new love— that a "new infection" will cure the old one.

Take thou some new infection to thy eye,
And the rank poison of the old will die.

50 **Romeo.** Your plantain leaf is excellent for that.

Benvolio. For what, I pray thee?

Romeo.   For your broken shin.

Benvolio. Why, Romeo, art thou mad?

Romeo. Not mad, but bound more than a madman is;
Shut up in prison, kept without my food,
55 Whipped and tormented and—God-den, good fellow.

Servant. God gi' go-den. I pray, sir, can you read?

Romeo. Ay, mine own fortune in my misery.

Servant. Perhaps you have learned it without book. But
I pray, can you read anything you see?

60 **Romeo.** Ay, if I know the letters and the language.

Servant. Ye say honestly. Rest you merry!

[*Romeo's joking goes over the clown's head. He concludes that
Romeo cannot read and prepares to seek someone who can.*]

Romeo. Stay, fellow; I can read.   [*He reads.*]
"Signior Martino and his wife and daughters;
County Anselmo and his beauteous sisters;
65 The lady widow of Vitruvio;
Signior Placentio and his lovely nieces;
Mercutio and his brother Valentine;
Mine uncle Capulet, his wife, and daughters;
My fair niece Rosaline and Livia;
70 Signior Valentio and his cousin Tybalt;
Lucio and the lively Helena."
[*gives back the paper*]
A fair assembly. Whither should they come?

Servant. Up.

Romeo. Whither?

75 **Servant.** To supper, to our house.

Romeo. Whose house?

Servant. My master's.

Romeo. Indeed I should have asked you that before.

Servant. Now I'll tell you without asking. My master is the great
80 rich Capulet; and if you be not of the house of Montagues, I
pray come and crush a cup of wine. Rest you merry!

55 God-den: good evening. Romeo interrupts his lament to talk to the servant.

56 God gi' go-den: God give you a good evening.

69 Rosaline: This is the woman that Romeo is in love with. Mercutio, a friend of both Romeo and the Capulets, is also invited to the party.

72 whither: where.

81 crush a cup of wine: slang for "drink some wine."

[*Exit.*]

Benvolio. At this same ancient feast of Capulet's
Sups the fair Rosaline whom thou so lovest,
With all the admired beauties of Verona.
85 Go thither, and with unattainted eye
Compare her face with some that I shall show,
And I will make thee think thy swan a crow.

85 **unattainted:** unbiased; unprejudiced.

Romeo. When the devout religion of mine eye
Maintains such falsehood, then turn tears to fires;
90 And these, who, often drowned, could never die,
Transparent heretics, be burnt for liars!
One fairer than my love? The all-seeing sun
Ne'er saw her match since first the world begun.

88–91 **When . . . liars:** If the love I have for Rosaline, which is like a religion, changes because of such a lie (that others may be more beautiful), let my tears be turned to fire and my eyes be burned.

Benvolio. Tut! you saw her fair, none else being by,
95 Herself poised with herself in either eye;
But in that crystal scales let there be weighed
Your lady's love against some other maid
That I will show you shining at this feast,
And she shall scant show well that now shows best.

94–99 **Tut . . . best:** You've seen Rosaline alone; now compare her with some other women.

100 **Romeo.** I'll go along, no such sight to be shown,
But to rejoice in splendor of mine own.

100–101 Romeo agrees to go to the party, but only to see Rosaline.

[*Exeunt.*]

Scene 3 *Capulet's house.*

[*Enter* Lady Capulet *and* Nurse.]

Lady Capulet. Nurse, where's my daughter? Call her forth to me.

Nurse. Now, by my maidenhead at twelve year old,
I bade her come. What, lamb! what, ladybird!
God forbid! Where's this girl? What, Juliet!

[*Enter* Juliet.]

5 **Juliet.** How now? Who calls?

Nurse. Your mother.

Juliet. Madam, I am here. What is your will?

Lady Capulet. This is the matter—Nurse, give leave awhile,
We must talk in secret. Nurse, come back again;
10 I have remembered me, thou's hear our counsel.
Thou knowest my daughter's of a pretty age.

8–11 **give leave . . . counsel:** Lady Capulet seems nervous, not sure whether she wants the nurse to stay or leave; **of a pretty age:** of an attractive age, ready for marriage.

Nurse. Faith, I can tell her age unto an hour.

Lady Capulet. She's not fourteen.

Nurse.   I'll lay fourteen of my teeth—
And yet, to my teen be it spoken, I have but four—
15 She's not fourteen. How long is it now
To Lammastide?

Lady Capulet. A fortnight and odd days.

Nurse. Even or odd, of all days in the year,
Come Lammas Eve at night shall she be fourteen.
Susan and she (God rest all Christian souls!)
20 Were of an age. Well, Susan is with God;
She was too good for me. But, as I said,
On Lammas Eve at night shall she be fourteen;
That shall she, marry; I remember it well.
'Tis since the earthquake now eleven years;
25 And she was weaned (I never shall forget it),
Of all the days of the year, upon that day.
For I had then laid wormwood to my dug,
Sitting in the sun under the dovehouse wall.
My lord and you were then at Mantua—
30 Nay, I do bear a brain—But, as I said,
When it did taste the wormwood on the nipple
Of my dug and felt it bitter, pretty fool,
To see it tetchy and fall out with the dug!
Shake, quoth the dovehouse! 'Twas no need, I trow,
35 To bid me trudge.
And since that time it is eleven years,
For then she could stand alone; nay, by the rood,
She could have run and waddled all about;
For even the day before, she broke her brow;
40 And then my husband (God be with his soul!
'A was a merry man) took up the child.
"Yea," quoth he, "dost thou fall upon thy face?
Thou wilt fall backward when thou has more wit,
Wilt thou not, Jule?" And, by my holidam,
45 The pretty wretch left crying, and said "Ay."
To see now how a jest shall come about!
I warrant, an I should live a thousand years,
I never should forget it. "Wilt thou not, Jule?" quoth he,
And, pretty fool, it stinted, and said "Ay."

50 **Lady Capulet.** Enough of this. I pray thee hold thy peace.

Nurse. Yes, madam. Yet I cannot choose but laugh
To think it should leave crying and say "Ay."
And yet, I warrant, it had upon its brow
A bump as big as a young cock'rel's stone;
55 A perilous knock; and it cried bitterly.

14 teen: sorrow.

16 Lammastide:
August 1, a religious
feast day. It is two weeks
(**a fortnight**) away.

17–49 The nurse
babbles about Juliet's
childhood. Her own
daughter, Susan, was
the same age as Juliet,
and died in infancy,
leaving the nurse
available to become a
wet nurse to (that is,
breastfeed) Juliet. An
earthquake happened
on the day she stopped
breastfeeding Juliet (**she
was weaned**).

**27 laid wormwood
to my dug:** applied
a plant with a bitter
taste to her breast to
discourage the child
from breastfeeding.

33 tetchy: cranky.

**34–35 Shake . . .
trudge:** When the dove
house shook, I knew
enough to leave.

37 by the rood: by the
cross of Christ (a mild
oath).

39 broke her brow: cut
her forehead.

42–49 "Yea," . . . "Ay":
The nurse's husband
made a crude joke,
asking the baby whether
she'd fall the other way
(on her back) when she
was older. Although
Juliet didn't understand
the question, she
stopped crying (**stinted**)
and answered "Yes." The
nurse finds the story so
funny that she can't stop
retelling it.

"Yea," quoth my husband, "fallst upon thy face?
Thou wilt fall backward when thou comest to age,
Wilt thou not, Jule?" It stinted, and said "Ay."

Juliet. And stint thou too, I pray thee, nurse, say I.

60 **Nurse.** Peace, I have done. God mark thee to his grace!
Thou wast the prettiest babe that e'er I nursed.
An I might live to see thee married once,
I have my wish.

Lady Capulet. Marry, that "marry" is the very theme
65 I came to talk of. Tell me, daughter Juliet,
How stands your disposition to be married?

Juliet. It is an honor that I dream not of.

Nurse. An honor? Were not I thine only nurse,
I would say thou hadst sucked wisdom from thy teat.

70 **Lady Capulet.** Well, think of marriage now. Younger than you,
Here in Verona, ladies of esteem,
Are made already mothers. By my count,
I was your mother much upon these years
That you are now a maid. Thus then in brief:
75 The valiant Paris seeks you for his love.

Nurse. A man, young lady! lady, such a man
As all the world—why he's a man of wax.

Lady Capulet. Verona's summer hath not such a flower.

64 Marry . . . "marry": two different usages of the same word—the first meaning "by the Virgin Mary" and the second meaning "to wed."

73–74 I was . . . maid: I was your mother at about your age, yet you are still unmarried.

77 a man of wax: a man so perfect he could be a wax statue, of the type sculptors once used as models for their works.

Nurse. Nay, he's a flower, in faith—a very flower.

80 **Lady Capulet.** What say you? Can you love the gentleman?
This night you shall behold him at our feast.
Read o'er the volume of young Paris' face,
And find delight writ there with beauty's pen;
Examine every several lineament,
85 And see how one another lends content;
And what obscured in this fair volume lies
Find written in the margent of his eyes.
This precious book of love, this unbound lover,
To beautify him only lacks a cover.
90 The fish lives in the sea, and 'tis much pride
For fair without the fair within to hide.
That book in many's eyes doth share the glory,
That in gold clasps locks in the golden story;
So shall you share all that he doth possess,
95 By having him making yourself no less.

Nurse. No less? Nay, bigger! Women grow by men.

Lady Capulet. Speak briefly, can you like of Paris' love?

Juliet. I'll look to like, if looking liking move;
But no more deep will I endart mine eye
100 Than your consent gives strength to make it fly.

[*Enter a* Servingman.]

Servingman. Madam, the guests are come, supper served up, you called, my young lady asked for, the nurse cursed in the pantry, and everything in extremity. I must hence to wait. I beseech you follow straight.

105 **Lady Capulet.** We follow thee. [*Exit* Servingman.] Juliet, the
County stays.

Nurse. Go, girl, seek happy nights to happy days.

[*Exeunt.*]

Scene 4 *A street near the Capulet house.*

[*Enter* Romeo, Mercutio, Benvolio, *with five or six other* Maskers;
Torchbearers.]

Romeo. What, shall this speech be spoke for our excuse?
Or shall we on without apology?

Benvolio. The date is out of such prolixity.
We'll have no Cupid hoodwinked with a scarf,
5 Bearing a Tartar's painted bow of lath,
Scaring the ladies like a crowkeeper;
Nor no without-book prologue, faintly spoke

82–89 Read . . . cover:
Lady Capulet uses an extended metaphor that compares Paris to a book that Juliet should read.

84 every several lineament: each separate feature (of Paris' face).

87 margent . . . eyes: She compares Paris' eyes to the margin of a page, where notes are written to explain the content.

88–91 This . . . hide: This beautiful book (Paris) needs only a cover (wife) to become even better. He may be hiding even more wonderful qualities inside.

96 Women get bigger (pregnant) when they marry.

98–100 I'll look . . . fly: I'll look at him with the intention of liking him, if simply looking can make me like him; **endart:** look deeply, as if penetrating with a dart.

103–104 extremity: great confusion; **straight:** immediately.

105 the County stays: Count Paris is waiting for you.

1–10 What, shall this . . . be gone: Romeo asks whether they should send a messenger announcing their arrival at the party. Benvolio says that they'll dance one dance (**measure them a measure**) and then leave.

After the prompter, for our entrance;
But let them measure us by what they will,
10 We'll measure them a measure, and be gone.

Romeo. Give me a torch. I am not for this ambling;
Being but heavy, I will bear the light.

Mercutio. Nay, gentle Romeo, we must have you dance.

Romeo. Not I, believe me. You have dancing shoes
15 With nimble soles; I have a soul of lead
So stakes me to the ground I cannot move.

Mercutio. You are a lover. Borrow Cupid's wings
And soar with them above a common bound.

Romeo. I am too sore enpiercèd with his shaft
20 To soar with his light feathers, and so bound
I cannot bound a pitch above dull woe.
Under love's heavy burden do I sink.

Mercutio. And, to sink in it, should you burden love—
Too great oppression for a tender thing.

25 **Romeo.** Is love a tender thing? It is too rough,
Too rude, too boist'rous, and it pricks like thorn.

Mercutio. If love be rough with you, be rough with love.
Prick love for pricking, and you beat love down.
Give me a case to put my visage in.
30 A visor for a visor! What care I
What curious eye doth quote deformities?
Here are the beetle brows shall blush for me.

Benvolio. Come, knock and enter, and no sooner in
But every man betake him to his legs.

35 **Romeo.** A torch for me! Let wantons light of heart
Tickle the senseless rushes with their heels;
For I am proverbed with a grandsire phrase,
I'll be a candle-holder and look on;
The game was ne'er so fair, and I am done.

40 **Mercutio.** Tut, dun's the mouse, the constable's own word!
If thou art Dun, we'll draw thee from the mire
Of, save your reverence, love, wherein thou stickst
Up to the ears. Come, we burn daylight, ho!

Romeo. Nay, that's not so.

Mercutio.   I mean, sir, in delay
45 We waste our lights in vain, like lamps by day.

12 heavy: sad. Romeo makes a joke based on the meanings of *heavy* and *light*.

14–32 Romeo continues to talk about his sadness, while Mercutio jokingly makes fun of him to try to cheer him up.

29–32 Give . . . for me: Give me a mask for an ugly face. I don't care if people notice my appearance. Here, look at my bushy eyebrows.

34 betake . . . legs: dance.

35–38 Let . . . look on: Let playful people tickle the grass (**rushes**) on the floor with their dancing. I'll follow the old saying (**grandsire phrase**) and just be a spectator.

40–43 Tut . . . daylight: Mercutio jokes, using various meanings of the word *dun*, which sounds like Romeo's last word, *done*. He concludes by saying they should not waste time (**burn daylight**).

Take our good meaning, for our judgment sits
Five times in that ere once in our five wits.

Romeo. And we mean well in going to this masque;
But 'tis no wit to go.

Mercutio.   Why, may one ask?

50 **Romeo.** I dreamt a dream tonight.

Mercutio.   And so did I.

Romeo. Well, what was yours?

Mercutio.   That dreamers often lie.

Romeo. In bed asleep, while they do dream things true.

Mercutio. O, then I see Queen Mab hath been with you.
She is the fairies' midwife, and she comes

55 In shape no bigger than an agate stone
On the forefinger of an alderman,

53–95 Mercutio talks of Mab, queen of the fairies, a folktale character well-known to Shakespeare's audience. His language includes vivid descriptions, puns, and satires of people; and ultimately he gets caught up in his own wild imaginings.

55 agate stone: jewel for a ring.

Drawn with a team of little atomies
Athwart men's noses as they lie asleep;
Her wagon spokes made of long spinners' legs,
60 The cover, of the wings of grasshoppers;
Her traces, of the smallest spider's web;
Her collars, of the moonshine's wat'ry beams;
Her whip, of cricket's bone; the lash, of film;
Her wagoner, a small grey-coated gnat,
65 Not half so big as a round little worm
Pricked from the lazy finger of a maid;
Her chariot is an empty hazelnut,
Made by the joiner squirrel or old grub,
Time out o' mind the fairies' coachmakers.
70 And in this state she gallops night by night
Through lovers' brains, and then they dream of love;
O'er courtiers' knees, that dream on curtsies straight;
O'er lawyers' fingers, who straight dream on fees;
O'er ladies' lips, who straight on kisses dream,
75 Which oft the angry Mab with blisters plagues,
Because their breaths with sweetmeats tainted are.
Sometime she gallops o'er a courtier's nose,
And then dreams he of smelling out a suit,
And sometime comes she with a tithe-pig's tail
80 Tickling a parson's nose as 'a lies asleep,
Then dreams he of another benefice.
Sometime she driveth o'er a soldier's neck,
And then dreams he of cutting foreign throats,
Of breaches, ambuscadoes, Spanish blades,
85 Of healths five fathom deep; and then anon
Drums in his ear, at which he starts and wakes,
And being thus frighted, swears a prayer or two
And sleeps again. This is that very Mab
That plaits the manes of horses in the night
90 And bakes the elflocks in foul sluttish hairs,
Which once untangled much misfortune bodes.
This is the hag, when maids lie on their backs,
That presses them and learns them first to bear,
Making them women of good carriage.
95 This is she—

Romeo.   Peace, peace, Mercutio, peace!
Thou talkst of nothing.

Mercutio.   True, I talk of dreams;
Which are the children of an idle brain,
Begot of nothing but vain fantasy;
Which is as thin of substance as the air,

---

57 atomies: tiny creatures.

59 spinners' legs: spiders' legs.

61 traces: harness.

68 joiner: carpenter.

77–78 Sometimes she . . . suit: Sometimes Mab makes a member of the king's court dream of receiving special favors.
81 benefice: a well-paying position for a clergyman.

84 ambuscadoes: ambushes; **Spanish blades:** high-quality Spanish swords.

89 plaits: braids.

96–103 True . . . South: Mercutio is trying to keep Romeo from taking his dreams too seriously.

100 And more inconstant than the wind, who woos
Even now the frozen bosom of the North
And, being angered, puffs away from thence,
Turning his face to the dew-dropping South.

Benvolio. This wind you talk of blows us from ourselves.
105 Supper is done, and we shall come too late.

Romeo. I fear, too early; for my mind misgives
Some consequence, yet hanging in the stars,
Shall bitterly begin his fearful date
With this night's revels and expire the term
110 Of a despised life, closed in my breast,
By some vile forfeit of untimely death.
But he that hath the steerage of my course
Direct my sail! On, lusty gentlemen!

Benvolio. Strike, drum.

[*Exeunt.*]

Scene 5 *A hall in Capulet's house; the scene of the party.*

[Servingmen *come forth with napkins.*]

First Servingman. Where's Potpan, that he helps not to take
away? He shift a trencher! he scrape a trencher!

Second Servingman. When good manners shall lie all in one or
two men's hands, and they unwashed too, 'tis a foul thing.

5 **First Servingman.** Away with the joint-stools, remove the court-
cupboard, look to the plate. Good thou, save me a piece of
marchpane and, as thou lovest me, let the porter let in Susan
Grindstone and Nell. Anthony, and Potpan!

Second Servingman. Ay, boy, ready.

10 **First Servingman.** You are looked for and called for, asked for
and sought for, in the great chamber.

Third Servingman. We cannot be here and there too. Cheerly,
boys! Be brisk awhile, and the longer liver take all.

[*Exeunt.*]

[Maskers *appear with* Capulet, Lady Capulet, Juliet, *all the*
Guests, *and* Servants.]

Capulet. Welcome, gentlemen! Ladies that have their toes
15 Unplagued with corns will have a bout with you.
Ah ha, my mistresses! which of you all
Will now deny to dance? She that makes dainty,
She I'll swear hath corns. Am I come near ye now?
Welcome, gentlemen! I have seen the day

106–111 Romeo, still depressed, fears that some terrible event caused by the stars will begin at the party. Remember the phrase "star-crossed lovers" from the prologue.

1–13 These opening lines are a comic conversation among three servants as they work.

2 trencher: wooden plate.

6–7 plate: silverware and silver plates; **marchpane:** marzipan, a sweet made from almond paste.

14–27 Capulet welcomes his guests and invites them all to dance. He alternates talking with his guests and telling the servants what to do.

17–18 She that . . . corns: Any woman too shy to dance will be assumed to have corns, ugly and painful growths on the toes.

20 That I have worn a visor and could tell
    A whispering tale in a fair lady's ear,
    Such as would please. 'Tis gone, 'tis gone, 'tis gone!
    You are welcome, gentlemen! Come, musicians, play.
    A hall, a hall! give room! and foot it, girls.

    [*Music plays and they dance.*]

25 More light, you knaves! and turn the tables up,
    And quench the fire, the room is grown too hot.
    Ah, sirrah, this unlooked-for sport comes well.
    Nay, sit, nay, sit, good cousin Capulet,
    For you and I are past our dancing days.
30 How long is't now since last yourself and I
    Were in a mask?

    Second Capulet. By'r Lady, thirty years.

    Capulet. What, man? 'Tis not so much, 'tis not so much!
    'Tis since the nuptial of Lucentio,
    Come Pentecost as quickly as it will,
35 Some five-and-twenty years, and then we masked.

    Second Capulet. 'Tis more, 'tis more! His son is elder, sir;
    His son is thirty.

    Capulet.   Will you tell me that?
    His son was but a ward two years ago.

    Romeo [*to a* Servingman]. What lady's that, which doth enrich
        the hand
40 Of yonder knight?

    Servant. I know not, sir.

    Romeo. O, she doth teach the torches to burn bright!
    It seems she hangs upon the cheek of night
    Like a rich jewel in an Ethiop's ear—
45 Beauty too rich for use, for earth too dear!
    So shows a snowy dove trooping with crows
    As yonder lady o'er her fellows shows.
    The measure done, I'll watch her place of stand
    And, touching hers, make blessed my rude hand.
50 Did my heart love till now? Forswear it, sight!
    For I ne'er saw true beauty till this night.

    Tybalt. This, by his voice, should be a Montague.
    Fetch me my rapier, boy. What, dares the slave
    Come hither, covered with an antic face,
55 To fleer and scorn at our solemnity?
    Now, by the stock and honor of my kin,
    To strike him dead I hold it not a sin.

20 visor: mask.

28–38 Capulet and his relative watch the dancing as they talk of days gone by.

33 nuptial: marriage.

44–45 Ethiop's ear: the ear of an Ethiopian (African); **for earth too dear:** too precious for this world.

52–57 Tybalt recognizes Romeo's voice and tells his servant to get his sword (**rapier**). He thinks Romeo has come to make fun of (**fleer**) their party.

Capulet. Why, how now, kinsman? Wherefore storm you so?

Tybalt. Uncle, this is a Montague, our foe;
60 A villain, that is hither come in spite
To scorn at our solemnity this night.

Capulet. Young Romeo is it?

Tybalt. 'Tis he, that villain Romeo.

Capulet. Content thee, gentle coz, let him alone.
'A bears him like a portly gentleman,
65 And, to say truth, Verona brags of him
To be a virtuous and well-governed youth.
I would not for the wealth of all this town
Here in my house do him disparagement.
Therefore be patient, take no note of him.
70 It is my will; the which if thou respect,
Show a fair presence and put off these frowns,
An ill-beseeming semblance for a feast.

64 portly: dignified.

68 do him disparagement: speak critically or insultingly to him.

72 semblance: outward appearance.

Tybalt. It fits when such a villain is a guest.
I'll not endure him.

Capulet.   He shall be endured.
75 What, goodman boy? I say he shall. Go to!
Am I the master here, or you? Go to!
You'll not endure him? God shall mend my soul!
You'll make a mutiny among my guests!
You will set cock-a-hoop! You'll be the man.

80 **Tybalt.** Why, uncle, 'tis a shame.

Capulet.   Go to, go to!
You are a saucy boy. Is't so, indeed?
This trick may chance to scathe you. I know what.
You must contrary me! Marry, 'tis time.—
Well said, my hearts!—You are a princox—go!
85 Be quiet, or—More light, more light!—For shame!
I'll make you quiet; what!—Cheerly, my hearts!

Tybalt. Patience perforce with willful choler meeting
Makes my flesh tremble in their different greeting.
I will withdraw; but this intrusion shall,
90 Now seeming sweet, convert to bitter gall.

[*Exit.*]

Romeo. If I profane with my unworthiest hand
This holy shrine, the gentle fine is this:
My lips, two blushing pilgrims, ready stand
To smooth that rough touch with a tender kiss.

95 **Juliet.** Good pilgrim, you do wrong your hand too much,
Which mannerly devotion shows in this;
For saints have hands that pilgrims' hands do touch,
And palm to palm is holy palmers' kiss.

Romeo. Have not saints lips, and holy palmers too?

100 **Juliet.** Ay, pilgrim, lips that they must use in prayer.

Romeo. O, then, dear saint, let lips do what hands do!
They pray; grant thou, lest faith turn to despair.

Juliet. Saints do not move, though grant for prayers' sake.

Romeo. Then move not while my prayer's effect I take.
105 Thus from my lips, by thine my sin is purged.

[*kisses her*]

Juliet. Then have my lips the sin that they have took.

Romeo. Sin from my lips? O trespass sweetly urged!
Give me my sin again.

75 goodman boy: a term used to address an inferior; **Go to:** Stop, that's enough!

79 set cock-a-hoop: cause everything to be upset.

82–83 scathe: harm; **I know . . . contrary me:** I know what I'm doing! Don't you dare challenge my authority.

84–86 Capulet intersperses his angry speech to Tybalt with comments to his guests and servants.

87–90 Patience . . . gall: Tybalt says he will restrain himself, but his suppressed anger (**choler**) makes his body shake.

91–108 Romeo and Juliet are in the middle of the dance floor, with eyes only for each other. They touch the palms of their hands. Their conversation revolves around Romeo's comparison of his lips to pilgrims who have traveled to a holy shrine. Juliet goes along with the comparison.

105 purged: washed away.

[kisses her]

Juliet. You kiss by the book.

Nurse. Madam, your mother craves a word with you.

110 **Romeo.** What is her mother?

Nurse. Marry, bachelor,
Her mother is the lady of the house.
And a good lady, and a wise and virtuous.
I nursed her daughter that you talked withal.
I tell you, he that can lay hold of her
115 Shall have the chinks.

Romeo. Is she a Capulet?
O dear account! my life is my foe's debt.

Benvolio. Away, be gone, the sport is at the best.

Romeo. Ay, so I fear; the more is my unrest.

Capulet. Nay, gentlemen, prepare not to be gone;
120 We have a trifling foolish banquet towards.

[They whisper in his ear.]
Is it e'en so? Why then, I thank you all.
I thank you, honest gentlemen. Good night.
More torches here! *[Exeunt* Maskers.*]* Come on then, let's to bed.
Ah, sirrah, by my fay, it waxes late;
125 I'll to my rest.

[Exeunt all but Juliet *and* Nurse.*]*

Juliet. Come hither, nurse. What is yond gentleman?

Nurse. The son and heir of old Tiberio.

Juliet. What's he that now is going out of door?

Nurse. Marry, that, I think, be young Petruchio.

130 **Juliet.** What's he that follows there, that would not dance?

Nurse. I know not.

Juliet. Go ask his name.—If he be married,
My grave is like to be my wedding bed.

Nurse. His name is Romeo, and a Montague,
135 The only son of your great enemy.

Juliet. My only love, sprung from my only hate!
Too early seen unknown, and known too late!
Prodigious birth of love it is to me
That I must love a loathed enemy.

140 **Nurse.** What's this? what's this?

108 kiss by the book: Juliet could mean "You kiss like someone who has practiced." Or she could be teasing Romeo, meaning "You kiss coldly, as though you had learned how by reading a book."

109 At the nurse's message, Juliet walks to her mother.

115 shall have the chinks: shall become rich.

116 my life . . . debt: my life belongs to my enemy.

120 towards: coming up.

137–138 Too early . . . too late: I fell in love with him before I learned who he is; **prodigious:** abnormal; unlucky.

Juliet.   A rhyme I learnt even now
Of one I danced withal.

[*One calls within, "Juliet."*]

Nurse.   Anon, anon!
Come, let's away; the strangers all are gone.

[*Exeunt.*]

COLLABORATIVE DISCUSSION With a partner, discuss your first
impressions of Romeo and Juliet. What are they like? What actions or
lines of dialogue reveal their personalities?

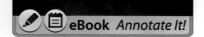

Analyzing the Text

> Cite Text Evidence   Support your responses with evidence from the selection.

1. **Interpret** An important **theme,** or message, in *Romeo and Juliet* is the struggle against fate, or forces that determine how a person's life will turn out. Explain how Act I's Prologue establishes the fate of the main characters and introduces the struggles they will face.

2. **Infer** In Scene 1, Tybalt says, "What, drawn, and talk of peace? I hate the word / As I hate hell, all Montagues, and thee. / Have at thee, coward!" (lines 63–65). What can you infer about Tybalt's personality and his role in the play, based on these words?

3. **Analyze** A **foil** is a character who highlights, through sharp contrast, the qualities of another character. Which two sets of characters in Act I are foils for each other? What do you learn about the characters by seeing them in contrast to one another?

4. **Identify** *Romeo and Juliet* is a play that deals with serious and tragic events, yet Shakespeare does weave jokes and comical situations into Act I. One example is the conversation among the servants at the beginning of Scene 5. Identify other examples of humor in the first act.

5. **Interpret** Foreshadowing is the use of hints or clues to suggest events that will happen later in the story. Explain the **foreshadowing** in these lines from Act I:

   - Scene 4, lines 106–111
   - Scene 5, line 133

6. **Predict** Which events in Act I seem key to setting up the conflicts that will move the action of the rest of the play forward? Explain your response.

PERFORMANCE TASK

Speaking Activity: Discussion In *Romeo and Juliet*, characters are motivated by passion and strong emotions.

- Notice that throughout Act I, Shakespeare contrasts themes of love and hate through characters' words and actions.
- Work with a partner to identify passages that express love or hate. Read the passages aloud with your partner. Read with feeling to express the emotions that underlie the words.

- Discuss what dramatic effect Shakespeare creates by pairing these two emotions in the first act of the play.
- Write a summary that outlines the main points of your discussion.

AS YOU READ Look for words and phrases that reveal the developing relationship between Romeo and Juliet and the intensity of their feelings for each other. Write down any questions you generate during reading.

Prologue

[*Enter* Chorus.]

Chorus. Now old desire doth in his deathbed lie,
And young affection gapes to be his heir.
That fair for which love groaned for and would die,
With tender Juliet matched, is now not fair.
5 Now Romeo is beloved, and loves again,
Alike bewitched by the charm of looks;
But to his foe supposed he must complain,
And she steal love's sweet bait from fearful hooks.
Being held a foe, he may not have access
10 To breathe such vows as lovers use to swear,
And she as much in love, her means much less
To meet her new beloved anywhere;
But passion lends them power, time means, to meet,
Temp'ring extremities with extreme sweet.

[*Exit.*]

1–4 Now ... fair: Romeo's love for Rosaline (**old desire**) is now dead. His new love for Juliet (**young affection**) replaces the old.

7 but ... complain: Juliet, a Capulet, is Romeo's supposed enemy, yet she is the one to whom he must plead (**complain**) his love.

14 Temp'ring ... sweet: moderating great difficulties with extreme delights.

ACT II

Scene 1 *A lane by the wall of Capulet's orchard.*

[*Enter* Romeo *alone.*]

Romeo. Can I go forward when my heart is here?
Turn back, dull earth, and find thy center out.

[*climbs the wall and leaps down within it*]

[*Enter* Benvolio *with* Mercutio.]

Benvolio. Romeo! my cousin Romeo! Romeo!

Mercutio.   He is wise,
And, on my life, hath stol'n him home to bed.

5 **Benvolio.** He ran this way, and leapt this orchard wall.
Call, good Mercutio.

Mercutio.   Nay, I'll conjure too.
Romeo! humors! madman! passion! lover!
Appear thou in the likeness of a sigh;
Speak but one rhyme, and I am satisfied!
10 Cry but "Ay me!" pronounce but "love" and "dove";
Speak to my gossip Venus one fair word,
One nickname for her purblind son and heir,
Young Adam Cupid, he that shot so trim

1–2 Can ... out: How can I leave when Juliet is still here? My body (**dull earth**) has to find its heart (**center**).

6 conjure: use magic to call him.

8–21 Appear ... us: Mercutio jokes about Romeo's lovesickness.

When King Cophetua loved the beggar maid!
15 He heareth not, he stirreth not, he moveth not;
The ape is dead, and I must conjure him.
I conjure thee by Rosaline's bright eyes,
By her high forehead and her scarlet lip,
By her fine foot, straight leg, and quivering thigh,
20 And the demesnes that there adjacent lie,
That in thy likeness thou appear to us!

Benvolio. An if he hear thee, thou wilt anger him.

Mercutio. This cannot anger him. 'Twould anger him
To raise a spirit in his mistress' circle
25 Of some strange nature, letting it there stand
Till she had laid it and conjured it down.
That were some spite; my invocation
Is fair and honest and in his mistress' name
I conjure only but to raise up him.

30 **Benvolio.** Come, he hath hid himself among these trees
To be consorted with the humorous night.
Blind is his love, and best befits the dark.

Mercutio. If love be blind, love cannot hit the mark.
Now will he sit under a medlar tree
35 And wish his mistress were that kind of fruit
As maids call medlars when they laugh alone.
Oh, Romeo, that she were, O, that she were
An open et cetera, thou a pop'rin pear!
Romeo, good night. I'll to my truckle bed;
40 This field-bed is too cold for me to sleep.
Come, shall we go?

Benvolio.   Go then, for 'tis in vain
To seek him here that means not to be found.

[*Exeunt.*]

Scene 2 *Capulet's orchard.*

[*Enter* Romeo.]

Romeo. He jests at scars that never felt a wound.

[*Enter* Juliet *above at a window.*]

But soft! What light through yonder window breaks?
It is the East, and Juliet is the sun!
Arise, fair sun, and kill the envious moon,
5 Who is already sick and pale with grief
That thou her maid art far more fair than she.
Be not her maid, since she is envious;

20 demesnes: areas; **adjacent:** next to.

23–29 'Twould ... raise up him: It would anger him if I called a stranger to join his beloved (**mistress**), but I'm only calling Romeo to join her.

31 To be ... night: to keep company with the night, which is as gloomy as Romeo is.

34 medlar: a fruit that looks like a small brown apple.

39 truckle bed: trundle bed, a small bed that fits in beneath a bigger one.

1 He jests ... wound: Romeo has overheard Mercutio and comments that Mercutio makes fun of love because he has never been wounded by it.

Her vestal livery is but sick and green,
And none but fools do wear it; cast it off.
10 It is my lady; O, it is my love!
O that she knew she were!
She speaks, yet she says nothing. What of that?
Her eye discourses; I will answer it.
I am too bold; 'tis not to me she speaks.
15 Two of the fairest stars in all the heaven,
Having some business, do entreat her eyes
To twinkle in their spheres till they return.
What if her eyes were there, they in her head?
The brightness of her cheek would shame those stars
20 As daylight doth a lamp; her eyes in heaven
Would through the airy region stream so bright
That birds would sing and think it were not night.
See how she leans her cheek upon her hand!
O that I were a glove upon that hand,
25 That I might touch that cheek!

Juliet.   Ay me!

Romeo.   She speaks.
O, speak again, bright angel! for thou art
As glorious to this night, being o'er my head,

13–14 Her eye . . . speaks: Romeo shifts back and forth between wanting to speak to Juliet and being afraid.

15–22 Two of . . . not night: Romeo compares Juliet's eyes to stars in the sky.

25 Juliet begins to speak, not knowing that Romeo is nearby.

26–32 thou art . . . of the air: He compares Juliet to an angel (**winged messenger of heaven**) who stands on (**bestrides**) the clouds.

As is a winged messenger of heaven
Unto the white-upturned wond'ring eyes
30 Of mortals that fall back to gaze on him
When he bestrides the lazy-pacing clouds
And sails upon the bosom of the air.

Juliet. O Romeo, Romeo! wherefore art thou Romeo?
Deny thy father and refuse thy name!
35 Or, if thou wilt not, be but sworn my love,
And I'll no longer be a Capulet.

Romeo [*aside*]. Shall I hear more, or shall I speak at this?

Juliet. 'Tis but thy name that is my enemy.
Thou art thyself, though not a Montague.
40 What's Montague? It is nor hand, nor foot,
Nor arm, nor face, nor any other part
Belonging to a man. O, be some other name!
What's in a name? That which we call a rose
By any other name would smell as sweet.
45 So Romeo would, were he not Romeo called,
Retain that dear perfection which he owes
Without that title. Romeo, doff thy name;
And for that name, which is no part of thee,
Take all myself.

Romeo.   I take thee at thy word.
50 Call me but love, and I'll be new baptized;
Henceforth I never will be Romeo.

Juliet. What man art thou that, thus bescreened in night,
So stumblest on my counsel?

Romeo.   By a name
I know not how to tell thee who I am.
55 My name, dear saint, is hateful to myself,
Because it is an enemy to thee.
Had I it written, I would tear the word.

Juliet. My ears have yet not drunk a hundred words
Of that tongue's utterance, yet I know the sound.
60 Art thou not Romeo, and a Montague?

Romeo. Neither, fair saint, if either thee dislike.

Juliet. How camest thou hither, tell me, and wherefore?
The orchard walls are high and hard to climb,
And the place death, considering who thou art,
65 If any of my kinsmen find thee here.

Romeo. With love's light wings did I o'erperch these walls;
For stony limits cannot hold love out,

33 wherefore: why. Juliet asks why Romeo is who he is—someone from her enemy's family.

43–47 Juliet tries to convince herself that a name is just a meaningless word that has nothing to do with the person. She asks Romeo to get rid of (**doff**) his name.

52–53 Juliet is startled that someone hiding (**bescreened**) nearby hears her private thoughts (**counsel**).

66–69 With . . . me: Love helped me climb (**o'erperch**) the walls. Neither walls nor your relatives are a hindrance (**let**) to me.

And what love can do, that dares love attempt.
Therefore thy kinsmen are no let to me.

70 **Juliet.** If they do see thee, they will murder thee.

Romeo. Alack, there lies more peril in thine eye
Than twenty of their swords! Look thou but sweet,
And I am proof against their enmity.

Juliet. I would not for the world they saw thee here.

75 **Romeo.** I have night's cloak to hide me from their sight;
And but thou love me, let them find me here.
My life were better ended by their hate
Than death prorogued, wanting of thy love.

Juliet. By whose direction foundst thou out this place?

80 **Romeo.** By love, that first did prompt me to enquire.
He lent me counsel, and I lent him eyes.
I am no pilot, yet, wert thou as far
As that vast shore washed with the farthest sea,
I would adventure for such merchandise.

85 **Juliet.** Thou knowest the mask of night is on my face;
Else would a maiden blush bepaint my cheek
For that which thou hast heard me speak tonight.
Fain would I dwell on form—fain, fain deny
What I have spoke; but farewell compliment!

90 Dost thou love me? I know thou wilt say "Ay";
And I will take thy word. Yet, if thou swearst,
Thou mayst prove false. At lovers' perjuries,
They say Jove laughs. O gentle Romeo,
If thou dost love, pronounce it faithfully.

95 Or if thou thinkst I am too quickly won,
I'll frown, and be perverse, and say thee nay,
So thou wilt woo; but else, not for the world.
In truth, fair Montague, I am too fond,
And therefore thou mayst think my 'havior light;

100 But trust me, gentleman, I'll prove more true
Than those that have more cunning to be strange.
I should have been more strange, I must confess,
But that thou overheardst, ere I was ware,
My true love's passion. Therefore pardon me,

105 And not impute this yielding to light love,
Which the dark night hath so discovered.

Romeo. Lady, by yonder blessed moon I swear,
That tips with silver all these fruit-tree tops—

72–73 Look ... enmity:
Smile on me, and I will
be defended against
my enemies' hatred
(**enmity**).

78 than death ...
love: than my death
postponed (**prorogued**)
if you don't love me.

85–89 Thou ...
compliment: Had
I known you were
listening, I would have
gladly (**fain**) behaved
more properly, but now
it's too late for good
manners (**farewell**
compliment).

92–93 At ... laughs:
Jove, the king of the
gods, laughs at lovers
who lie to each other.

95–101 Or if ...
strange: You might think
I've fallen in love too
easily and that I'm too
outspoken. But I'll be
truer to you than those
who play games to hide
their real feelings (**be**
strange).

Juliet. O, swear not by the moon, the inconstant moon,
110 That monthly changes in her circled orb,
Lest that thy love prove likewise variable.

Romeo. What shall I swear by?

Juliet.   Do not swear at all;
Or if thou wilt, swear by thy gracious self,
Which is the god of my idolatry,
115 And I'll believe thee.

Romeo.   If my heart's dear love—

Juliet. Well, do not swear. Although I joy in thee,
I have no joy of this contract tonight.
It is too rash, too unadvised, too sudden;
Too like the lightning, which doth cease to be
120 Ere one can say "It lightens." Sweet, good night!
This bud of love, by summer's ripening breath,
May prove a beauteous flow'r when next we meet.
Good night, good night! As sweet repose and rest
Come to thy heart as that within my breast!

125 **Romeo.** O, wilt thou leave me so unsatisfied?

Juliet. What satisfaction canst thou have tonight?

Romeo. The exchange of thy love's faithful vow for mine.

Juliet. I gave thee mine before thou didst request it;
And yet I would it were to give again.

130 **Romeo.** Wouldst thou withdraw it? For what purpose, love?

Juliet. But to be frank and give it thee again.
And yet I wish but for the thing I have.
My bounty is as boundless as the sea,
My love as deep; the more I give to thee,
135 The more I have, for both are infinite.
I hear some noise within. Dear love, adieu!

[Nurse *calls within.*]

Anon, good nurse! Sweet Montague, be true.
Stay but a little, I will come again.

[*Exit.*]

Romeo. O blessed, blessed night! I am afeard,
140 Being in night, all this is but a dream,
Too flattering-sweet to be substantial.

[*Re-enter* Juliet, *above.*]

Juliet. Three words, dear Romeo, and good night indeed.
If that thy bent of love be honorable,

117 I have ... contract:
I am concerned about
this declaration of love
(**contract**).

Thy purpose marriage, send me word tomorrow,
145 By one that I'll procure to come to thee,
Where and what time thou wilt perform the rite;
And all my fortunes at thy foot I'll lay
And follow thee my lord throughout the world.

Nurse [*within*]. Madam!

150 **Juliet.** I come, anon.—But if thou meanst not well,
I do beseech thee—

Nurse [*within*].   Madam!

Juliet.   By-and-by I come.—
To cease thy suit and leave me to my grief.
Tomorrow will I send.

Romeo.   So thrive my soul—

Juliet. A thousand times good night! [*Exit.*]

155 **Romeo.** A thousand times the worse, to want thy light!
Love goes toward love as schoolboys from their books;
But love from love, towards school with heavy looks.

[*Enter* Juliet *again, above.*]

Juliet. Hist! Romeo, hist! O for a falc'ner's voice
To lure this tassel-gentle back again!
160 Bondage is hoarse and may not speak aloud;
Else would I tear the cave where Echo lies,
And make her airy tongue more hoarse than mine
With repetition of my Romeo's name.
Romeo!

165 **Romeo.** It is my soul that calls upon my name.
How silver-sweet sound lovers' tongues by night,
Like softest music to attending ears!

Juliet. Romeo!

Romeo.   My sweet?

Juliet.   What o'clock tomorrow
Shall I send to thee?

Romeo.   By the hour of nine.

170 **Juliet.** I will not fail. 'Tis twenty years till then.
I have forgot why I did call thee back.

Romeo. Let me stand here till thou remember it.

Juliet. I shall forget, to have thee still stand there,
Rememb'ring how I love thy company.

150–151 But if . . . thee:
Juliet is still worried that
Romeo is not serious.

**156–157 Love . . .
looks:** The simile means
that lovers meet as
eagerly as schoolboys
leave their books;
lovers separate with the
sadness of boys going to
school.

158–163 Hist . . . name:
I wish I could speak
your name as loudly
as a falconer calls his
falcon (**tassel-gentle**),
but because of my
parents I must whisper.
Echo was a nymph in
Greek mythology whose
unreturned love for
Narcissus caused her to
waste away till only her
voice was left.

175   **Romeo.** And I'll still stay, to have thee still forget,
Forgetting any other home but this.

  Juliet. 'Tis almost morning. I would have thee gone—
And yet no farther than a wanton's bird,
That lets it hop a little from her hand,

180   Like a poor prisoner in his twisted gyves,
And with a silk thread plucks it back again,
So loving-jealous of his liberty.

  Romeo. I would I were thy bird.

  Juliet.   Sweet, so would I.
Yet I should kill thee with much cherishing.

185   Good night, good night! Parting is such sweet sorrow,
That I shall say good night till it be morrow.

  [*Exit.*]

  Romeo. Sleep dwell upon thine eyes, peace in thy breast!
Would I were sleep and peace, so sweet to rest!
Hence will I to my ghostly father's cell,

190   His help to crave and my dear hap to tell.

  [*Exit.*]

Scene 3   *Friar Laurence's cell in the monastery.*

[*Enter* Friar Laurence *alone, with a basket.*]

  Friar Laurence. The grey-eyed morn smiles on the frowning
     night,
Chequ'ring the Eastern clouds with streaks of light;
And flecked darkness like a drunkard reels
From forth day's path and Titan's fiery wheels.

5   Now, ere the sun advance his burning eye
The day to cheer and night's dank dew to dry,
I must upfill this osier cage of ours
With baleful weeds and precious-juiced flowers.
The earth that's nature's mother is her tomb,

10   What is her burying grave, that is her womb;
And from her womb children of divers kind
We sucking on her natural bosom find;
Many for many virtues excellent,
None but for some, and yet all different.

15   O, mickle is the powerful grace that lies
In plants, herbs, stones, and their true qualities;
For naught so vile that on the earth doth live
But to the earth some special good doth give;
Nor aught so good but, strained from that fair use,

20   Revolts from true birth, stumbling on abuse.

177–182 I would … liberty: I know you must go, but I want you close to me like a pet bird that a thoughtless child (**wanton**) keeps on a string.

189–190 ghostly father: spiritual adviser or priest; **dear hap:** good fortune.

4 Titan is the god whose chariot pulls the sun into the sky each morning.

7 osier cage: willow basket.

9–12 The earth … find: The same earth that acts as a tomb is also the womb, or birthplace, of various useful plants that people can harvest.

15–18 mickle: great. The friar says that nothing from the earth is so evil that it doesn't do some good.

Virtue itself turns vice, being misapplied,
And vice sometime's by action dignified.
Within the infant rind of this small flower
Poison hath residence, and medicine power;
25 For this, being smelt, with that part cheers each part;
Being tasted, slays all senses with the heart.
Two such opposed kings encamp them still
In man as well as herbs—grace and rude will;
And where the worser is predominant,
30 Full soon the canker death eats up that plant.

[*Enter* Romeo.]

Romeo. Good morrow, father.

Friar Laurence.   Benedicite!
What early tongue so sweet saluteth me?
Young son, it argues a distempered head
So soon to bid good morrow to thy bed.
35 Care keeps his watch in every old man's eye,
And where care lodges sleep will never lie;
But where unbruised youth with unstuffed brain
Doth couch his limbs, there golden sleep doth reign.
Therefore thy earliness doth me assure
40 Thou art uproused with some distemp'rature;

28 **grace and rude will:**
good and evil. Both exist
in people as well as in
plants.

31 **Benedicite**
(bĕ´nĕ-dī´sĭ-tē´): God
bless you.

33–42 **it argues
. . . tonight:**
Only a disturbed
(**distempered**) mind
could make you get up
so early. Old people may
have trouble sleeping,
but it is not normal for
someone as young as
you. Or were you up all
night?

Or if not so, then here I hit it right—
Our Romeo hath not been in bed tonight.

Romeo. That last is true, the sweeter rest was mine.

Friar Laurence. God pardon sin! Wast thou with Rosaline?

45 **Romeo.** With Rosaline, my ghostly father? No.
I have forgot that name, and that name's woe.

Friar Laurence. That's my good son! But where hast thou been
   then?

Romeo. I'll tell thee ere thou ask it me again.
I have been feasting with mine enemy,
50 Where on a sudden one hath wounded me
That's by me wounded. Both our remedies
Within thy help and holy physic lies.
I bear no hatred, blessed man, for, lo,
My intercession likewise steads my foe.

49–56 Romeo tries to explain the situation, asking for help both for himself and his "foe" (Juliet). The friar does not understand Romeo's convoluted language and asks him to speak clearly so that he can help.

55 **Friar Laurence.** Be plain, good son, and homely in thy drift.
Riddling confession finds but riddling shrift.

Romeo. Then plainly know my heart's dear love is set
On the fair daughter of rich Capulet;
As mine on hers, so hers is set on mine,
60 And all combined, save what thou must combine
By holy marriage. When, and where, and how
We met, we wooed, and made exchange of vow,
I'll tell thee as we pass; but this I pray,
That thou consent to marry us today.

65 **Friar Laurence.** Holy Saint Francis! What a change is here!
Is Rosaline, that thou didst love so dear,
So soon forsaken? Young men's love then lies
Not truly in their hearts, but in their eyes.
Jesu Maria! What a deal of brine
70 Hath washed thy sallow cheeks for Rosaline!
How much salt water thrown away in waste,
To season love, that of it doth not taste!
The sun not yet thy sighs from heaven clears,
Thy old groans ring yet in mine ancient ears.
75 Lo, here upon thy cheek the stain doth sit
Of an old tear that is not washed off yet.
If e'er thou wast thyself, and these woes thine,
Thou and these woes were all for Rosaline.
And art thou changed? Pronounce this sentence then:
80 Women may fall when there's no strength in men.

69 brine: salt water—that is, the tears that Romeo has been shedding for Rosaline.

80 Women . . . men: If men are so weak, women may be forgiven for sinning.

81–82 chidst: scolded. The friar replies that he scolded Romeo for being lovesick, not for loving.

Romeo. Thou chidst me oft for loving Rosaline.

Friar Laurence. For doting, not for loving, pupil mine.

Romeo. And badest me bury love.

Friar Laurence.   Not in a grave
To lay one in, another ought to have.

85 **Romeo.** I pray thee chide not. She whom I love now
Doth grace for grace and love for love allow.
The other did not so.

Friar Laurence.   O, she knew well
Thy love did read by rote, that could not spell.
But come, young waverer, come go with me.
90 In one respect I'll thy assistant be;
For this alliance may so happy prove
To turn your households' rancor to pure love.

Romeo. O, let us hence! I stand on sudden haste.

Friar Laurence. Wisely, and slow. They stumble that run fast.

[*Exeunt.*]

Scene 4 *A street.*

[*Enter* Benvolio *and* Mercutio.]

Mercutio. Where the devil should this Romeo be?
Came he not home tonight?

Benvolio. Not to his father's. I spoke with his man.

Mercutio. Why, that same pale hard-hearted wench, that
    Rosaline,
5 Torments him so that he will sure run mad.

Benvolio. Tybalt, the kinsman to old Capulet,
Hath sent a letter to his father's house.

Mercutio. A challenge, on my life.

Benvolio. Romeo will answer it.

10 **Mercutio.** Any man that can write may answer a letter.

Benvolio. Nay, he will answer the letter's master, how he dares,
being dared.

Mercutio. Alas, poor Romeo, he is already dead! stabbed with a
white wench's black eye; shot through the ear with a love song;
15 the very pin of his heart cleft with the blind bow-boy's butt-shaft;
and is he a man to encounter Tybalt?

Benvolio. Why, what is Tybalt?

85–88 She whom ... spell: Romeo says that the woman he loves feels the same way about him. That wasn't true of Rosaline. The friar replies that Rosaline knew that he didn't know what real love is.

91–92 For this ... prove: this marriage may work out so well; **rancor:** bitter hate.

3 man: servant.

6–12 Tybalt ... dared: Tybalt, still angry with Romeo, has sent a letter challenging Romeo to a duel. Benvolio says that Romeo will accept Tybalt's challenge and fight him.

15 blind bow-boy's butt-shaft: Cupid's dull practice arrow. Mercutio suggests that Romeo fell in love with very little work on Cupid's part.

Mercutio. More than Prince of Cats, I can tell you. O, he's the courageous captain of compliments. He fights as you sing
20 pricksong—keeps time, distance, and proportion; rests me his minim rest, one, two, and the third in your bosom! the very butcher of a silk button, a duelist, a duelist! a gentleman of the very first house, of the first and second cause. Ah, the immortal *passado!* the *punto reverso!* the *hay!*

25 **Benvolio.** The what?

Mercutio. The pox of such antic, lisping, affecting fantasticoes— these new tuners of accent! "By Jesu, a very good blade! a very tall man! a very good whore!" Why, is not this a lamentable thing, grandsire, that we should be thus afflicted with these strange flies,
30 these fashion-mongers, these perdona-mi's, who stand so much on the new form that they cannot sit at ease on the old bench? O, their bones, their bones!

[*Enter* Romeo, *no longer moody.*]

Benvolio. Here comes Romeo! here comes Romeo!

Mercutio. Without his roe, like a dried herring. O, flesh, flesh,
35 how art thou fishified! Now is he for the numbers that Petrarch flowed in. Laura, to his lady, was but a kitchen wench (marry, she had a better love to berhyme her), Dido a dowdy, Cleopatra a gypsy, Helen and Hero hildings and harlots, Thisbe a grey eye or so, but not to the purpose. Signior Romeo, *bon jour!* There's
40 a French salutation to your French slop. You gave us the counterfeit fairly last night.

Romeo. Good morrow to you both. What counterfeit did I give you?

Mercutio. The slip, sir, the slip. Can you not conceive?

45 **Romeo.** Pardon, good Mercutio. My business was great, and in such a case as mine a man may strain courtesy.

Mercutio. That's as much as to say, such a case as yours constrains a man to bow in the hams.

Romeo. Meaning, to curtsy.

50 **Mercutio.** Thou hast most kindly hit it.

Romeo. A most courteous exposition.

Mercutio. Nay, I am the very pink of courtesy.

Romeo. Pink for flower.

Mercutio. Right.

55 **Romeo.** Why, then is my pump well-flowered.

18–24 More than . . . hay: Prince of Cats refers to a cat in a fable, named Tybalt. Mercutio makes fun of Tybalt's new style of dueling, comparing it to singing (**pricksong**). *Passado, punto reverso,* and *hay* were terms used in the new dueling style.

26–32 The pox . . . their bones: Mercutio continues to make fun of people who embrace new styles and new manners of speaking.

34–39 without his roe: only part of himself (Mercutio makes fun of Romeo's name and his lovesickness; **numbers:** verses. Petrarch wrote sonnets to his love, Laura. According to Mercutio, Romeo's feelings for Rosaline are so intense that great loves in literature could never measure up.

39–44 *bon jour:* "Good day" in French; **There's . . . last night:** Here's a greeting to match your fancy French trousers (**slop**). You did a good job of getting away from us last night. (A piece of counterfeit money was called a **slip.**)

55 pump: shoe; **well-flowered:** Shoes with flowerlike designs.

Mercutio. Well said! Follow me this jest now till thou hast worn out thy pump, that, when the single sole of it is worn, the jest may remain, after the wearing, solely singular.

Romeo. Oh, single-soled jest, solely singular for the singleness!

60 **Mercutio.** Come between us, good Benvolio! My wits faint.

Romeo. Switch and spurs, switch and spurs! or I'll cry a match.

61 Switch . . . match: Keep going, or I'll claim victory.

Mercutio. Nay, if our wits run the wild-goose chase, I am done; for thou hast more of the wild goose in one of thy wits than, I am sure, I have in my whole five. Was I with you there for the 65 goose?

64–65 Was . . . goose: Have I proved that you are a foolish person?

Romeo. Thou wast never with me for anything when thou wast not there for the goose.

Mercutio. I will bite thee by the ear for that jest.

Romeo. Nay, good goose, bite not!

70 **Mercutio.** Thy wit is a very bitter sweeting; it is a most sharp sauce.

Romeo. And is it not, then, well served in to a sweet goose?

Mercutio. O, here's a wit of cheveril, that stretches from an inch narrow to an ell broad!

75 **Romeo.** I stretch it out for that word "broad," which, added to the goose, proves thee far and wide a broad goose.

Mercutio. Why, is not this better now than groaning for love? Now art thou sociable, now art thou Romeo; now art thou what thou art, by art as well as by nature. For this driveling love is like

80 a great natural that runs lolling up and down to hide his bauble in a hole.

Benvolio. Stop there, stop there!

Mercutio. Thou desirest me to stop in my tale against the hair.

Benvolio. Thou wouldst else have made thy tale large.

85 **Mercutio.** O, thou art deceived! I would have made it short; for I was come to the whole depth of my tale, and meant indeed to occupy the argument no longer.

[*Enter* Nurse *and* Peter, *her servant. He is carrying a large fan.*]

Romeo. Here's goodly gear!

Mercutio. A sail, a sail!

90 **Benvolio.** Two, two! a shirt and a smock.

Nurse. Peter!

Peter. Anon.

Nurse. My fan, Peter.

Mercutio. Good Peter, to hide her face; for her fan's the fairer of

95 the two.

Nurse. God ye good morrow, gentlemen.

Mercutio. God ye good-den, fair gentlewoman.

Nurse. Is it good-den?

Mercutio. 'Tis no less, I tell ye, for the bawdy hand of the dial is

100 now upon the prick of noon.

Nurse. Out upon you! What a man are you!

Romeo. One, gentlewoman, that God hath made himself to mar.

Nurse. By my troth, it is well said. "For himself to mar," quoth'a? Gentlemen, can any of you tell me where I may find the young

105 Romeo?

Romeo. I can tell you; but young Romeo will be older when you have found him than he was when you sought him. I am the youngest of that name, for fault of a worse.

73 cheveril: kidskin, which is flexible. Mercutio means that a little wit stretches a long way.

80–81 great natural: an idiot, like a jester or clown who carries a fool's stick (**bauble**).

88–89 goodly gear: something fine to joke about; **a sail:** Mercutio likens the nurse in all her petticoats to a huge ship coming toward them.

93 Fans were usually carried only by fine ladies. The nurse is trying to pretend that she is more than a servant.

Nurse. You say well.

110 **Mercutio.** Yea, is the worst well? Very well took, i' faith! wisely, wisely.

Nurse. If you be he, sir, I desire some confidence with you.

Benvolio. She will endite him to some supper.

Mercutio. A bawd, a bawd, a bawd! So ho!

115 **Romeo.** What hast thou found?

Mercutio. No hare, sir; unless a hare, sir, in a lenten pie, that is something stale and hoar ere it be spent.

[*sings*]

"An old hare hoar,
And an old hare hoar,
120 Is very good meat in Lent.
But a hare that is hoar,
Is too much for a score
When it hoars ere it be spent."

Romeo, will you come to your father's? We'll to dinner thither.

125 **Romeo.** I will follow you.

Mercutio. Farewell, ancient lady. Farewell, [*sings*] lady, lady, lady.

[*Exeunt* Mercutio *and* Benvolio.]

Nurse. Marry, farewell! I pray you, sir, what saucy merchant was this that was so full of his ropery?

Romeo. A gentleman, nurse, that loves to hear himself talk and
130 will speak more in a minute than he will stand to in a month.

Nurse. An 'a speak anything against me, I'll take him down, an 'a were lustier than he is, and twenty such Jacks; and if I cannot, I'll find those that shall. Scurvy knave! I am none of his flirt-gills; I am none of his skainsmates. [*turning to* Peter] And thou must
135 stand by too, and suffer every knave to use me at his pleasure?

Peter. I saw no man use you at his pleasure. If I had, my weapon should quickly have been out, I warrant you. I dare draw as soon as another man, if I see occasion in a good quarrel, and the law on my side.

140 **Nurse.** Now, afore God, I am so vexed that every part about me quivers. Scurvy knave! Pray you, sir, a word; and as I told you, my young lady bade me enquire you out. What she bid me say, I will keep to myself; but first let me tell ye, if ye should lead her into a fool's paradise, as they say, it were a very gross kind of
145 behavior, as they say; for the gentlewoman is young; and

112–113 confidence: The nurse means *conference*; she uses big words without understanding their meaning; **endite:** Benvolio makes fun of the nurse by using this word rather than *invite*.

114–124 Mercutio calls the nurse a **bawd,** or woman who runs a house of prostitution. His song uses the insulting puns **hare,** a rabbit or prostitute, and **hoar,** old.

128 ropery: roguery, or jokes.

133–134 The nurse is angry that Mercutio treated her like one of his loose women (**flirt-gills**) or his gangsterlike friends (**skainsmates**).

142–147 The nurse warns Romeo that he'd better mean what he said about marrying Juliet.

therefore, if you should deal double with her, truly it were an ill thing to be offered to any gentlewoman, and very weak dealing.

Romeo. Nurse, commend me to thy lady and mistress. I protest unto thee—

148 **commend me:** give my respectful greetings.

150 **Nurse.** Good heart, and i' faith I will tell her as much. Lord, Lord! she will be a joyful woman.

Romeo. What wilt thou tell her, nurse? Thou dost not mark me.

Nurse. I will tell her, sir, that you do protest, which, as I take it, is a gentlemanlike offer.

155–159 Romeo tells the nurse to have Juliet come to Friar Laurence's cell this afternoon, using the excuse that she is going to confess her sins (**shrift**). There she will receive forgiveness for her sins (**be shrived**) and be married.

155 **Romeo.** Bid her devise
Some means to come to shrift this afternoon;
And there she shall at Friar Laurence' cell
Be shrived and married. Here is for thy pains.

Nurse. No, truly, sir; not a penny.

160 **Romeo.** Go to! I say you shall.

Nurse. This afternoon, sir? Well, she shall be there.

Romeo. And stay, good nurse, behind the abbey wall.
Within this hour my man shall be with thee
And bring thee cords made like a tackled stair,
165 Which to the high topgallant of my joy
Must be my convoy in the secret night.
Farewell. Be trusty, and I'll quit thy pains.
Farewell. Commend me to thy mistress.

164–165 **tackled stair:** rope ladder; **topgallant:** highest point.

167 **quit thy pains:** reward you.

Nurse. Now God in heaven bless thee! Hark you, sir.

170 **Romeo.** What sayst thou, my dear nurse?

Nurse. Is your man secret? Did you ne'er hear say,
Two may keep counsel, putting one away?

Romeo. I warrant thee my man's as true as steel.

174–177 The nurse begins to babble about Paris' proposal but says that Juliet would rather look at a toad than at Paris.

Nurse. Well, sir, my mistress is the sweetest lady. Lord, Lord!
175 when 'twas a little prating thing—O, there is a nobleman in town, one Paris, that would fain lay knife aboard; but she, good soul, had as lief see a toad, a very toad, as see him. I anger her sometimes, and tell her that Paris is the properer man; but I'll warrant you, when I say so, she looks as pale as any clout in the
180 versal world. Doth not rosemary and Romeo begin both with a letter?

Romeo. Ay, nurse, what of that? Both with an R.

Nurse. Ah, mocker! that's the dog's name. R is for the—No; I know it begins with some other letter; and she hath the prettiest

179–186 **clout:** old cloth; **the versal world:** the entire world; **Doth not . . . hear it:** The nurse tries to recall a clever saying that Juliet made up about Romeo and rosemary, the herb, but cannot remember it. She is sure that the two words couldn't begin with *R* because this letter sounds like a snarling dog; **sententious:** The nurse means *sentences*.

185 sententious of it, of you and rosemary, that it would do you good
to hear it.

Romeo. Commend me to thy lady.

Nurse. Ay, a thousand times. [*Exit* Romeo.] Peter!

Peter. Anon.

190 **Nurse.** Peter, take my fan, and go before, and apace.

[*Exeunt.*]

Scene 5 *Capulet's orchard.*

[*Enter* Juliet.]

Juliet. The clock struck nine when I did send the nurse;
In half an hour she promised to return.
Perchance she cannot meet him. That's not so.
O, she is lame! Love's heralds should be thoughts,
5   Which ten times faster glide than the sun's beams
Driving back shadows over lowering hills.
Therefore do nimble-pinioned doves draw Love,
And therefore hath the wind-swift Cupid wings.
Now is the sun upon the highmost hill
10   Of this day's journey, and from nine till twelve
Is three long hours; yet she is not come.
Had she affections and warm youthful blood,
She would be as swift in motion as a ball;
My words would bandy her to my sweet love,
15   And his to me.
But old folks, many feign as they were dead—
Unwieldy, slow, heavy, and pale as lead.
[*Enter* Nurse *and* Peter.] O God, she comes! O honey nurse,
    what news?
Hast thou met with him? Send thy man away.

20 **Nurse.** Peter, stay at the gate.

[*Exit* Peter.]

Juliet. Now, good sweet nurse—O Lord, why lookst thou sad?
Though news be sad, yet tell them merrily;
If good, thou shamest the music of sweet news
By playing it to me with so sour a face.

25 **Nurse.** I am aweary, give me leave awhile.
Fie, how my bones ache! What a jaunce have I had!

Juliet. I would thou hadst my bones, and I thy news.
Nay, come, I pray thee speak. Good, good nurse, speak.

190 **apace:** quickly.

4–6 **Love's . . . hills:** Love's messengers should be thoughts, which travel ten times faster than sunbeams.

7 **nimble-pinioned . . . Love:** Swift-winged doves pull the chariot of Venus, goddess of love.

14 **bandy:** toss.

16 **feign as:** act as if.

21–22 The nurse teases Juliet by putting on a sad face as if the news were bad.

25–26 **give me . . . I had:** Leave me alone for a while. I ache all over because of the running back and forth I've been doing.

Nurse. Jesu, what haste! Can you not stay awhile?
30 Do you not see that I am out of breath?

Juliet. How art thou out of breath when thou hast breath
To say to me that thou art out of breath?
The excuse that thou dost make in this delay
Is longer than the tale thou dost excuse.
35 Is thy news good or bad? Answer to that.
Say either, and I'll stay the circumstance.
Let me be satisfied, is't good or bad?

Nurse. Well, you have made a simple choice; you know not how
to choose a man. Romeo? No, not he. Though his face be better
40 than any man's, yet his leg excels all men's; and for a hand and a
foot, and a body, though they be not to be talked on, yet they are
past compare. He is not the flower of courtesy, but, I'll warrant
him, as gentle as a lamb. Go thy ways, wench; serve God. What,
have you dined at home?

45 **Juliet.** No, no. But all this did I know before.
What say he of our marriage? What of that?

Nurse. Lord, how my head aches! What a head have I!
It beats as it would fall in twenty pieces.
My back o' t'other side—ah, my back, my back!
50 Beshrew your heart for sending me about
To catch my death with jauncing up and down!

Juliet. I' faith, I am sorry that thou art not well.
Sweet, sweet, sweet nurse, tell me, what says my love?

Nurse. Your love says, like an honest gentleman, and a
courteous,
55 and a kind, and a handsome, and, I warrant, a virtuous—Where
is your mother?

Juliet. Where is my mother? Why, she is within.
Where should she be? How oddly thou repliest!
"Your love says, like an honest gentleman,
60 'Where is your mother?'"

Nurse.   O God's Lady dear!
Are you so hot? Marry come up, I trow.
Is this the poultice for my aching bones?
Hence forward do your messages yourself.

Juliet. Here's such a coil! Come, what says Romeo?

65 **Nurse.** Have you got leave to go to shrift today?

Juliet. I have.

36 I'll ... circumstance: I'll wait for the details.

38 simple: foolish.

50–51 Beshrew ... down: Curse you for making me endanger my health by running around.

61–62 Marry ... bones: Control yourself! Is this the treatment I get for my pain?

64 coil: fuss.

Nurse. Then hie you hence to Friar Laurence' cell;
There stays a husband to make you a wife.
Now comes the wanton blood up in your cheeks:
70 They'll be in scarlet straight at any news.
Hie you to church; I must another way,
To fetch a ladder, by the which your love
Must climb a bird's nest soon when it is dark.
I am the drudge, and toil in your delight;
75 But you shall bear the burden soon at night.
Go; I'll to dinner; hie you to the cell.

Juliet. Hie to high fortune! Honest nurse, farewell.

[*Exeunt.*]

Scene 6 *Friar Laurence's cell.*

[*Enter* Friar Laurence *and* Romeo.]

Friar Laurence. So smile the heavens upon this holy act
That after-hours with sorrow chide us not!

Romeo. Amen, amen! But come what sorrow can,
It cannot countervail the exchange of joy
5 That one short minute gives me in her sight.

71–73 The nurse will get the ladder that Romeo will use to climb to Juliet's room after they are married.

1–2 So smile . . . us not: May heaven so bless this act that we won't regret it in the future (**after-hours**).

4 countervail: outweigh.

Do thou but close our hands with holy words,
Then love-devouring death do what he dare—
It is enough I may but call her mine.

Friar Laurence. These violent delights have violent ends
10 And in their triumph die, like fire and powder,
Which, as they kiss, consume. The sweetest honey
Is loathsome in his own deliciousness
And in the taste confounds the appetite.
Therefore love moderately: long love doth so;
15 Too swift arrives as tardy as too slow.

[*Enter* Juliet.]

Here comes the lady. O, so light a foot
Will ne'er wear out the everlasting flint.
A lover may bestride the gossamer
That idles in the wanton summer air,
20 And yet not fall; so light is vanity.

Juliet. Good even to my ghostly confessor.

Friar Laurence. Romeo shall thank thee, daughter, for us both.

Juliet. As much to him, else is his thanks too much.

Romeo. Ah, Juliet, if the measure of thy joy
25 Be heaped like mine, and that thy skill be more
To blazon it, then sweeten with thy breath
This neighbor air, and let rich music's tongue
Unfold the imagined happiness that both
Receive in either by this dear encounter.

30 **Juliet.** Conceit, more rich in matter than in words,
Brags of his substance, not of ornament.
They are but beggars that can count their worth;
But my true love is grown to such excess
I cannot sum up sum of half my wealth.

35 **Friar Laurence.** Come, come with me, and we will make short work;
For, by your leaves, you shall not stay alone
Till Holy Church incorporate two in one.

[*Exeunt.*]

9–15 These . . . slow: The friar compares Romeo's passion to gunpowder and the fire that ignites it—both are destroyed—then to honey, whose sweetness can destroy the appetite. He reminds Romeo to practice moderation in love.

23 as much to him: I give the same greeting to Romeo that he offers to me.

24–29 if the measure . . . encounter: If you are as happy as I am and have more skill to proclaim it, then sweeten the air by singing of our happiness to the world.

30–31 Conceit . . . ornament: True understanding (**conceit**) needs no words.

COLLABORATIVE DISCUSSION Romeo and Juliet fall in love and make life-changing decisions in a matter of days. Meet with a partner to discuss how this speed and intensity creates tension for the audience and affects the characters' actions.

Analyzing the Text

Cite Text Evidence Support your responses with evidence from the selection.

1. **Interpret** In literature, a **motif** is a repeated image, idea, or theme. Explain the light/dark or day/night motif in Romeo's speech at the beginning of Act II, Scene 2. What does he mean when he refers to Juliet as "the sun"? Where else in Act II does this motif appear?

2. **Analyze** In Act II, Scene 2, Juliet says, "What's in a name? That which we call a rose / By any other name would smell as sweet" (lines 43–44). What does she mean? How does this comparison relate to one of the conflicts in her life?

3. **Infer** After declaring their love for one another, why do Romeo and Juliet want to commit themselves right away to marriage? Support your inference with evidence from the text.

4. **Cite Evidence** In Scene 3, why is Friar Laurence suspicious of Romeo's declaration of love for Juliet? What is his motivation for agreeing to marry Romeo and Juliet, despite his reservations?

5. **Analyze** Explain Juliet's relationship with her nurse. What is the Nurse's primary motivation in helping Juliet to be with Romeo?

6. **Predict** In Scene 6, Friar Laurence urges Romeo to be cautious. Given what you know about Romeo, and about the fates guiding the "star-crossed lovers," do you think Romeo will take his advice? Explain.

PERFORMANCE TASK

Speaking Activity: Debate Both Friar Laurence and Mercutio have personal attributes that put them at odds with Romeo's passion. Analyze their differences and hold a debate in which each character presents his point of view.

- Working with two other students, discuss the characteristics and motivations of Friar Laurence, Mercutio, and Romeo. What differences do these three demonstrate in Act II?

- With each person in your group taking the point of view of one of these characters, debate Romeo's plan to marry Juliet.
- Work together to write a summary of your debate.

AS YOU READ Notice how events begin to shift in a more ominous or dangerous direction in this act. Write down any questions you generate during reading.

ACT III

Scene 1 *A public place.*

[*Enter* Mercutio, Benvolio, Page, *and* Servants.]

Benvolio. I pray thee, good Mercutio, let's retire.
The day is hot, the Capulets abroad,
And if we meet, we shall not scape a brawl,
For now, these hot days, is the mad blood stirring.

5 **Mercutio.** Thou art like one of those fellows that, when he enters the confines of a tavern, claps me his sword upon the table and says "God send me no need of thee!" and by the operation of the second cup draws him on the drawer, when indeed there is no need.

10 **Benvolio.** Am I like such a fellow?

Mercutio. Come, come, thou art as hot a Jack in thy mood as any in Italy; and as soon moved to be moody, and as soon moody to be moved.

Benvolio. And what to?

15 **Mercutio.** Nay an there were two such, we should have none shortly, for one would kill the other. Thou! why, thou wilt quarrel with a man that hath a hair more or a hair less in his beard than thou hast. Thou wilt quarrel with a man for cracking nuts, having no other reason but because thou hast hazel eyes.
20 What eye but such an eye would spy out such a quarrel? Thy head is as full of quarrels as an egg is full of meat; and yet thy head hath been beaten as addle as an egg for quarreling. Thou hast quarreled with a man for coughing in the street, because he hath wakened thy dog that hath lain asleep in the sun. Didst
25 thou not fall out with a tailor for wearing his new doublet before Easter? with another for tying his new shoes with old riband? And yet thou wilt tutor me from quarreling!

Benvolio. An I were so apt to quarrel as thou art, any man should buy the fee simple of my life for an hour and a quarter.

30 **Mercutio.** The fee simple? O simple!

[*Enter* Tybalt *and others.*]

Benvolio. By my head, here come the Capulets.

Mercutio. By my heel, I care not.

3–4 we shall . . . stirring: We shall not avoid a fight, since the heat makes people ill-tempered.

7–8 by the . . . drawer: feeling the effects of a second drink, is ready to fight (**draw on**) the waiter who's pouring the drinks (**drawer**).

12–13 as soon moved . . . to be moved: as likely to get angry and start a fight.

15–27 Mercutio teases his friend by insisting that Benvolio is quick to pick a fight, though everyone knows that Benvolio is gentle and peace loving.

25 doublet: jacket.

26 riband: ribbon or laces.

28–29 An I . . . quarter: If I picked fights as quickly as you do, anybody could own me for the smallest amount of money.

Tybalt. Follow me close, for I will speak to them. Gentlemen, good den. A word with one of you.

35 **Mercutio.** And but one word with one of us? Couple it with something; make it a word and a blow.

Tybalt. You shall find me apt enough to that, sir, an you will give me occasion.

Mercutio. Could you not take some occasion without giving?

40 **Tybalt.** Mercutio, thou consortest with Romeo.

Mercutio. Consort? What, dost thou make us minstrels? An thou make minstrels of us, look to hear nothing but discords. Here's my fiddlestick; here's that shall make you dance. Zounds, consort!

45 **Benvolio.** We talk here in the public haunt of men.
Either withdraw unto some private place
And reason coldly of your grievances,
Or else depart. Here all eyes gaze on us.

Mercutio. Men's eyes were made to look, and let them gaze.
50 I will not budge for no man's pleasure, I.

[*Enter* Romeo.]

Tybalt. Well, peace be with you, sir. Here comes my man.

Mercutio. But I'll be hanged, sir, if he wear your livery.
Marry, go before to field, he'll be your follower!
Your worship in that sense may call him man.

55 **Tybalt.** Romeo, the love I bear thee can afford
No better term than this: thou art a villain.

Romeo. Tybalt, the reason that I have to love thee
Doth much excuse the appertaining rage
To such a greeting. Villain am I none.
60 Therefore farewell. I see thou knowst me not.

Tybalt. Boy, this shall not excuse the injuries
That thou hast done me; therefore turn and draw.

Romeo. I do protest I never injured thee,
But love thee better than thou canst devise
65 Till thou shalt know the reason of my love;
And so, good Capulet, which name I tender
As dearly as mine own, be satisfied.

Mercutio. O calm, dishonorable, vile submission!
Alla stoccata carries it away.

40–44 consortest: friends with; Mercutio pretends to misunderstand him, assuming that Tybalt is insulting him by calling Romeo and him a **consort,** a group of traveling musicians. He then refers to his sword as his **fiddlestick,** the bow for a fiddle.

51–54 Mercutio again pretends to misunderstand Tybalt. By **my man,** Tybalt means "the man I'm looking for." Mercutio takes it to mean "my servant." (**Livery** is a servant's uniform.)

57–59 I forgive your anger because I have reason to love you.

61 Boy: an insulting term of address.

66 tender: cherish.

68–70 Mercutio assumes that Romeo is afraid to fight. ***Alla stoccata*** is a move used in sword fighting.

[*draws*]

70 Tybalt, you ratcatcher, will you walk?

Tybalt. What wouldst thou have with me?

Mercutio. Good King of Cats, nothing but one of your nine lives. That I mean to make bold withal, and, as you shall use me hereafter, dry-beat the rest of the eight. Will you pluck your
75 sword out of his pilcher by the ears? Make haste, lest mine be about your ears ere it be out.

72–74 nothing but . . . eight: I intend to take one of your nine lives (as a cat supposedly has) and give a beating to the other eight.

Tybalt. I am for you.

[*draws*]

Romeo. Gentle Mercutio, put thy rapier up.

Mercutio. Come, sir, your *passado!*

79 *passado:* a sword-fighting maneuver.

[*They fight.*]

80 **Romeo.** Draw, Benvolio; beat down their weapons.
Gentlemen, for shame! forbear this outrage!
Tybalt, Mercutio, the Prince expressly hath

80–84 Romeo wants Benvolio to help him stop the fight. They are able to hold back Mercutio.

Forbid this bandying in Verona streets.
Hold, Tybalt! Good Mercutio!

[Tybalt, *under* Romeo's *arm, thrusts* Mercutio *in, and flies with his* Men.]

Mercutio.   I am hurt.
85   A plague o' both your houses! I am sped.
Is he gone and hath nothing?

Benvolio.   What, art thou hurt?

Mercutio. Ay, ay, a scratch, a scratch. Marry, 'tis enough.
Where is my page? Go, villain, fetch a surgeon.

[*Exit* Page.]

Romeo. Courage, man. The hurt cannot be much.

90   **Mercutio.** No, 'tis not so deep as a well, nor so wide as a church
door; but 'tis enough, 'twill serve. Ask for me tomorrow, and you
shall find me a grave man. I am peppered, I warrant, for this
world. A plague o' both your houses! Zounds, a dog, a rat, a
mouse, a cat, to scratch a man to death! A braggart, a rogue, a
95   villain, that fights by the book of arithmetic! Why the devil
came you between us? I was hurt under your arm.

Romeo. I thought all for the best.

Mercutio. Help me into some house, Benvolio,
Or I shall faint. A plague o' both your houses!
100 They have made worms' meat of me. I have it,
And soundly too. Your houses!

[*Exit, supported by* Benvolio.]

Romeo. This gentleman, the Prince's near ally,
My very friend, hath got this mortal hurt
In my behalf—my reputation stained
105 With Tybalt's slander—Tybalt, that an hour
Hath been my kinsman, O sweet Juliet,
Thy beauty hath made me effeminate
And in my temper softened valor's steel!

[*Reenter* Benvolio.]

Benvolio. O Romeo, Romeo, brave Mercutio's dead!
110 That gallant spirit hath aspired the clouds,
Which too untimely here did scorn the earth.

Romeo. This day's black fate on mo days doth depend;
This but begins the woe others must end.

[*Reenter* Tybalt.]

83 bandying: fighting.

**85 A plague . . .
sped:** I curse both the
Montagues and the
Capulets. I am destroyed.

**102–108 This
gentleman . . . valor's
steel:** My friend has
died protecting my
reputation against a
man who has been my
relative for only an hour.
My love for Juliet has
made me less manly and
brave.

110 aspired: soared to.

**112–113 This day's . . .
must end:** This awful day
will be followed by more
of the same.

Benvolio. Here comes the furious Tybalt back again.

115 **Romeo.** Alive in triumph, and Mercutio slain?
Away to heaven respective lenity,
And fire-eyed fury be my conduct now!
Now, Tybalt, take the "villain" back again
That late thou gavest me, for Mercutio's soul
120 Is but a little way above our heads,
Staying for thine to keep him company.
Either thou or I, or both, must go with him.

Tybalt. Thou, wretched boy, that didst consort him here,
Shalt with him hence.

Romeo. This shall determine that.

[*They fight*. Tybalt *falls*.]

125 **Benvolio.** Romeo, away, be gone!
The citizens are up, and Tybalt slain.
Stand not amazed. The Prince will doom thee death
If thou art taken. Hence, be gone, away!

Romeo. O, I am fortune's fool!

Benvolio. Why dost thou stay?

[*Exit* Romeo.]

[*Enter* Citizens.]

130 **Citizen.** Which way ran he that killed Mercutio?
Tybalt, that murderer, which way ran he?

Benvolio. There lies that Tybalt.

Citizen. Up, sir, go with me.
I charge thee in the Prince's name obey.

[*Enter* Prince *with his* Attendants, Montague, Capulet, *their* Wives, *and others.*]

Prince. Where are the vile beginners of this fray?

135 **Benvolio.** O noble Prince, I can discover all
The unlucky manage of this fatal brawl.
There lies the man, slain by young Romeo,
That slew thy kinsman, brave Mercutio.

Lady Capulet. Tybalt, my cousin! O my brother's child!
140 O Prince! O cousin! O husband! O, the blood is spilled
Of my dear kinsman! Prince, as thou art true,
For blood of ours shed blood of Montague.
O cousin, cousin!

Prince. Benvolio, who began this bloody fray?

116 **respective lenity:** considerate mildness.

124 The sword fight probably goes on for several minutes, till Romeo runs his sword through Tybalt.

129 **I am fortune's fool:** Fate has made a fool of me.

135–136 Benvolio says he can tell (**discover**) what happened.

141–142 **as thou . . . Montague:** If your word is good, you will sentence Romeo to death for killing a Capulet.

Benvolio. Tybalt, here slain, whom Romeo's hand did slay.
Romeo, that spoke him fair, bid him bethink
How nice the quarrel was, and urged withal
Your high displeasure. All this—uttered
With gentle breath, calm look, knees humbly bowed—
Could not take truce with the unruly spleen
Of Tybalt deaf to peace, but that he tilts
With piercing steel at bold Mercutio's breast;
Who, all as hot, turns deadly point to point,
And, with a martial scorn, with one hand beats
Cold death aside and with the other sends
It back to Tybalt, whose dexterity
Retorts it. Romeo he cries aloud,
"Hold, friends! friends, part!" and swifter than his tongue,
His agile arm beats down their fatal points,
And 'twixt them rushes; underneath whose arm
An envious thrust from Tybalt hit the life
Of stout Mercutio, and then Tybalt fled,
But by-and-by comes back to Romeo,
Who had but newly entertained revenge,
And to't they go like lightning; for, ere I
Could draw to part them, was stout Tybalt slain;
And, as he fell, did Romeo turn and fly.
This is the truth, or let Benvolio die.

Lady Capulet. He is a kinsman to the Montague;
Affection makes him false, he speaks not true.
Some twenty of them fought in this black strife,
And all those twenty could but kill one life.
I beg for justice, which thou, Prince, must give.
Romeo slew Tybalt; Romeo must not live.

Prince. Romeo slew him; he slew Mercutio.
Who now the price of his dear blood doth owe?

Montague. Not Romeo, Prince; he was Mercutio's friend;
His fault concludes but what the law should end,
The life of Tybalt.

Prince.   And for that offense
Immediately we do exile him hence.
I have an interest in your hate's proceeding,
My blood for your rude brawls doth lie a-bleeding;
But I'll amerce you with so strong a fine
That you shall all repent the loss of mine.
I will be deaf to pleading and excuses;
Nor tears nor prayers shall purchase out abuses.
Therefore use none. Let Romeo hence in haste,

146–147 Romeo, that . . . was: Romeo talked calmly (**fair**) and told Tybalt to think how trivial (**nice**) the argument was.

150–151 could . . . peace: could not quiet the anger of Tybalt, who would not listen to pleas for peace.

156–157 whose dexterity retorts it: whose skill returns it.

159–160 his agile . . . rushes: He rushed between them and pushed down their swords.

164 entertained: thought of.

178–179 Romeo is guilty only of avenging Mercutio's death, which the law would have done anyway.

179–190 The prince banishes Romeo from Verona. He angrily points out that one of his own relatives is dead because of the feud and declares that Romeo will be put to death unless he flees immediately.

Else, when he is found, that hour is his last.
Bear hence this body, and attend our will.
190 Mercy but murders, pardoning those that kill.

[*Exeunt.*]

Scene 2 *Capulet's orchard.*

[*Enter* Juliet *alone.*]

Juliet. Gallop apace, you fiery-footed steeds,
Toward Phoebus' lodging! Such a wagoner
As Phaëton would whip you to the West,
And bring in cloudy night immediately.
5   Spread thy close curtain, love-performing night,
That runaways' eyes may wink, and Romeo
Leap to these arms, untalked of and unseen.
Lovers can see to do their amorous rites
By their own beauties; or, if love be blind,
10   It best agrees with night. Come, civil night,
Thou sober-suited matron, all in black,
And learn me how to lose a winning match,
Played for a pair of stainless maidenhoods.
Hood my unmanned blood bating in my cheeks
15   With thy black mantle; till strange love, grown bold,
Think true love acted simple modesty.
Come, night; come, Romeo, come; thou day in night;
For thou wilt lie upon the wings of night
Whiter than new snow on a raven's back.
20   Come, gentle night; come, loving, black-browed night;
Give me my Romeo; and, when he shall die,
Take him and cut him out in little stars,
And he will make the face of heaven so fine
That all the world will be in love with night
25   And pay no worship to the garish sun.
O, I have bought the mansion of a love,
But not possessed it; and though I am sold,
Not yet enjoyed. So tedious is this day
As is the night before some festival
30   To an impatient child that hath new robes
And may not wear them. Oh, here comes my nurse,

[*Enter* Nurse, *wringing her hands, with the ladder of cords in her lap.*]

And she brings news; and every tongue that speaks
But Romeo's name speaks heavenly eloquence.
Now, nurse, what news? What hast thou there? the cords
35   That Romeo bid thee fetch?

2–3 Phoebus: Apollo, the god of the sun; **Phaëton:** a mortal who lost control of the sun's chariot when he drove it too fast.

14–16 Hood . . . modesty: Juliet asks that the darkness hide her blushing cheeks on her wedding night.

26–27 I have . . . possessed it: Juliet protests that she has gone through the wedding ceremony (**bought the mansion**) but is still waiting to enjoy the rewards of marriage.

34 the cords: the rope ladder.

Nurse.   Ay, ay, the cords.

Juliet. Ay me! what news? Why dost thou wring thy hands?

Nurse. Ah, well-a-day! he's dead, he's dead, he's dead!
We are undone, lady, we are undone!
Alack the day! he's gone, he's killed, he's dead!

40   **Juliet.** Can heaven be so envious?

Nurse.   Romeo can,
Though heaven cannot. O Romeo, Romeo!
Who ever would have thought it? Romeo!

Juliet. What devil art thou that dost torment me thus?
This torture should be roared in dismal hell.
45   Hath Romeo slain himself? Say thou but "I,"
And that bare vowel "I" shall poison more
Than the death-darting eye of a cockatrice.
I am not I, if there be such an "I,"
Or those eyes shut, that make thee answer "I."
50   If he be slain, say "I," or if not, "no."
Brief sounds determine of my weal or woe.

Nurse. I saw the wound, I saw it with mine eyes,
(God save the mark!) here on his manly breast.
A piteous corse, a bloody piteous corse;
55   Pale, pale as ashes, all bedaubed in blood,
All in gore blood. I swounded at the sight.

Juliet. O, break, my heart! poor bankrout, break at once!
To prison, eyes; ne'er look on liberty!
Vile earth, to earth resign; end motion here,
60   And thou and Romeo press one heavy bier!

Nurse. O Tybalt, Tybalt, the best friend I had!
O courteous Tybalt! honest gentleman!
That ever I should live to see thee dead!

Juliet. What storm is this that blows so contrary?
65   Is Romeo slaughtered, and is Tybalt dead?
My dear-loved cousin, and my dearer lord?
Then, dreadful trumpet, sound the general doom!
For who is living, if those two are gone?

Nurse. Tybalt is gone, and Romeo banished;
70   Romeo that killed him, he is banished.

Juliet. O God! Did Romeo's hand shed Tybalt's blood?

Nurse. It did! it did! alas the day, it did!

37–42 well-a-day: an expression used when someone has bad news. The nurse wails and moans without clearly explaining what has happened, leading Juliet to assume that Romeo is dead.

45–50 Juliet's "I" means "aye," or "yes." A **cockatrice** is a mythological beast whose glance kills its victims.

51 my weal or woe: my happiness or sorrow.

53–56 God . . . mark: an expression meant to scare off evil powers, similar to "Knock on wood"; **corse:** corpse; **swounded:** fainted.

57–60 Juliet say her heart is broken and bankrupt (**bankrout**). She wants to be buried with Romeo, sharing his burial platform (**bier**).

Juliet. O serpent heart, hid with a flow'ring face!
Did ever dragon keep so fair a cave?
75 Beautiful tyrant! fiend angelical!
Dove-feathered raven! wolvish-ravening lamb!
Despised substance of divinest show!
Just opposite to what thou justly seemst,
A damned saint, an honorable villain!
80 O nature, what hadst thou to do in hell
When thou didst bower the spirit of a fiend
In mortal paradise of such sweet flesh?
Was ever book containing such vile matter
So fairly bound? O, that deceit should dwell
85 In such a gorgeous palace!

Nurse.   There's no trust,
No faith, no honesty in men; all perjured,
All forsworn, all naught, all dissemblers.
Ah, where's my man? Give me some aqua vitae.
These griefs, these woes, these sorrows make me old.
90 Shame come to Romeo!

Juliet.   Blistered be thy tongue
For such a wish! He was not born to shame.
Upon his brow shame is ashamed to sit;
For 'tis a throne where honor may be crowned
Sole monarch of the universal earth.
95 O, what a beast was I to chide at him!

Nurse. Will you speak well of him that killed your cousin?

Juliet. Shall I speak ill of him that is my husband?
Ah, poor my lord, what tongue shall smooth thy name
When I, thy three-hours' wife, have mangled it?
100 But wherefore, villain, didst thou kill my cousin?
That villain cousin would have killed my husband.
Back, foolish tears, back to your native spring!
Your tributary drops belong to woe,
Which you, mistaking, offer up to joy.
105 My husband lives, that Tybalt would have slain;
And Tybalt's dead, that would have slain my husband.
All this is comfort; wherefore weep I then?
Some word there was, worser than Tybalt's death,
That murdered me. I would forget it fain;
110 But O, it presses to my memory
Like damned guilty deeds to sinners' minds!
"Tybalt is dead, and Romeo—banished."
That "banished," that one word "banished,"
Hath slain ten thousand Tybalts. Tybalt's death

81 bower . . . fiend: give a home to the spirit of a demon.

87 all . . . dissemblers: All are liars and pretenders.

88 aqua vitae: brandy.

102–106 Juliet is uncertain whether her tears should be of joy or of sorrow.

115 Was woe enough, if it had ended there;
     Or, if sour woe delights in fellowship
     And needly will be ranked with other griefs,
     Why followed not, when she said "Tybalt's dead,"
     Thy father, or thy mother, nay, or both,
120 Which modern lamentation might have moved?
     But with a rearward following Tybalt's death,
     "Romeo is banished"—to speak that word
     Is father, mother, Tybalt, Romeo, Juliet,
     All slain, all dead. "Romeo is banished"—
125 There is no end, no limit, measure, bound,
     In that word's death; no words can that woe sound.
     Where is my father and my mother, nurse?

     Nurse. Weeping and wailing over Tybalt's corse.
     Will you go to them? I will bring you thither.

130 **Juliet.** Wash they his wounds with tears? Mine shall be spent,
     When theirs are dry, for Romeo's banishment.
     Take up those cords. Poor ropes, you are beguiled,
     Both you and I, for Romeo is exiled.
     He made you for a highway to my bed;
135 But I, a maid, die maiden-widowed.
     Come, cords; come, nurse. I'll to my wedding bed;
     And death, not Romeo, take my maidenhead!

114–127 If the news of Tybalt's death had been followed by the news of her parents' deaths, Juliet would have felt grief. To follow the story of Tybalt's death with the news of Romeo's banishment creates a sorrow so deep it cannot be expressed in words.

132 beguiled: cheated.

135–137 I... maidenhead: I will die a widow without ever really having been a wife. Death, not Romeo, will be my husband.

Nurse. Hie to your chamber. I'll find Romeo
To comfort you. I wot well where he is.

139 **wot:** know.

140 Hark ye, your Romeo will be here at night.
I'll to him; he is hid at Laurence' cell.

Juliet. O, find him! give this ring to my true knight
And bid him come to take his last farewell.

[*Exeunt.*]

Scene 3 *Friar Laurence's cell.*

[*Enter* Friar Laurence.]

Friar Laurence. Romeo, come forth; come forth, thou fearful man.
Affliction is enamored of thy parts,
And thou art wedded to calamity.

2 **affliction . . . parts:**
Trouble loves you.

[*Enter* Romeo.]

Romeo. Father, what news? What is the Prince's doom?

4 **doom:** sentence.

5 What sorrow craves acquaintance at my hand
That I yet know not?

Friar Laurence.　　Too familiar
Is my dear son with such sour company.
I bring thee tidings of the Prince's doom.

Romeo. What less than doomsday is the Prince's doom?

9 **doomsday:** death.

10 **Friar Laurence.** A gentler judgment vanished from his lips—
Not body's death, but body's banishment.

10 **vanished:** came.

Romeo. Ha, banishment? Be merciful, say "death";
For exile hath more terror in his look,
Much more than death. Do not say "banishment."

15 **Friar Laurence.** Hence from Verona art thou banished.
Be patient, for the world is broad and wide.

Romeo. There is no world without Verona walls,
But purgatory, torture, hell itself.
Hence banished is banish'd from the world,

17–23 **There is . . .
murders me:** Being
exiled outside Verona's
walls is as bad as being
dead. And yet you smile
at my misfortune.

20 And world's exile is death. Then "banishment,"
Is death misterm'd. Calling death "banishment,"
Thou cuttst my head off with a golden axe
And smilest upon the stroke that murders me.

Friar Laurence. O deadly sin! O rude unthankfulness!
25 Thy fault our law calls death; but the kind Prince,
Taking thy part, hath rushed aside the law,
And turned that black word death to banishment.
This is dear mercy, and thou seest it not.

Romeo. 'Tis torture, and not mercy. Heaven is here,
30 Where Juliet lives; and every cat and dog
And little mouse, every unworthy thing,
Live here in heaven and may look on her;
But Romeo may not. More validity,
More honorable state, more courtship lives
35 In carrion flies than Romeo. They may seize
On the white wonder of dear Juliet's hand
And steal immortal blessing from her lips,
Who, even in pure and vestal modesty,
Still blush, as thinking their own kisses sin;
40 But Romeo may not—he is banished.
This may flies do, when I from this must fly;
They are free men, but I am banished.
And sayst thou yet that exile is not death?
Hadst thou no poison mixed, no sharp-ground knife,
45 No sudden mean of death, though ne'er so mean,
But "banished" to kill me—"banished"?
O friar, the damned use that word in hell;
Howling attends it! How hast thou the heart,
Being a divine, a ghostly confessor,
50 A sin-absolver, and my friend professed,
To mangle me with that word "banished"?

Friar Laurence. Thou fond mad man, hear me a little speak.

Romeo. O, thou wilt speak again of banishment.

Friar Laurence. I'll give thee armor to keep off that word;
55 Adversity's sweet milk, philosophy,
To comfort thee, though thou art banished.

Romeo. Yet "banished"? Hang up philosophy!
Unless philosophy can make a Juliet,
Displant a town, reverse a prince's doom,
60 It helps not, it prevails not. Talk no more.

Friar Laurence. O, then I see that madmen have no ears.

Romeo. How should they, when that wise men have no eyes?

Friar Laurence. Let me dispute with thee of thy estate.

Romeo. Thou canst not speak of that thou dost not feel.
65 Wert thou as young as I, Juliet thy love,
An hour but married, Tybalt murdered,
Doting like me, and like me banished,
Then mightst thou speak, then mightst thou tear thy hair,
And fall upon the ground, as I do now,
70 Taking the measure of an unmade grave.

33–35 More validity . . . than Romeo: Even flies that live off the dead (**carrion**) will be able to get closer to Juliet than Romeo will.

44–46 Hadst . . . to kill me: Couldn't you have killed me with poison or a knife instead of with that awful word *banished*?

52 fond: foolish.

54–56 The friar offers philosophical comfort and counseling (**adversity's sweet milk**) as a way to overcome hardship.

63 dispute: discuss; **estate:** situation.

[Nurse *knocks within.*]

Friar Laurence. Arise; one knocks. Good Romeo, hide thyself.

Romeo. Not I; unless the breath of heartsick groans
Mist-like infold me from the search of eyes.

[knock]

Friar Laurence. Hark, how they knock! Who's there? Romeo,
    arise;
75 Thou wilt be taken.—Stay awhile!—Stand up;

[knock]

Run to my study.—By-and-by!—God's will,
What simpleness is this.—I come, I come!

[knock]

Who knocks so hard? Whence come you? What's your will?

Nurse [*within*]. Let me come in, and you shall know my errand.
80 I come from Lady Juliet.

Friar Laurence.   Welcome then.

[*Enter* Nurse.]

Nurse. O holy friar, O, tell me, holy friar,
Where is my lady's lord, where's Romeo?

Friar Laurence. There on the ground, with his own tears made
    drunk.

Nurse. O, he is even in my mistress' case,
85 Just in her case! O woeful sympathy!
Piteous predicament! Even so lies she,
Blubb'ring and weeping, weeping and blubbering.
Stand up, stand up! Stand, an you be a man.
For Juliet's sake, for her sake, rise and stand!
90 Why should you fall into so deep an O?

Romeo [*rises*]. Nurse—

Nurse. Ah sir! ah sir! Well, death's the end of all.

Romeo. Spakest thou of Juliet? How is it with her?
Doth not she think me an old murderer,
95 Now I have stained the childhood of our joy
With blood removed but little from her own?
Where is she? and how doth she? and what says
My concealed lady to our canceled love?

Nurse. O, she says nothing, sir, but weeps and weeps;
100 And now falls on her bed, and then starts up,
And Tybalt calls; and then on Romeo cries,
And then down falls again.

72–73 Romeo will hide only if his sighs create a mist and shield him from sight.

84–85 he is even . . . her case: He is acting the same way that Juliet is.

90 into so deep an O: into such deep grief.

96 blood . . . from her own: the blood of a close relative of hers.

98 concealed lady: secret bride.

Romeo.   As if that name,
Shot from the deadly level of a gun,
Did murder her; as that name's cursed hand
105 Murdered her kinsman. O tell me, friar, tell me,
In what vile part of this anatomy
Doth my name lodge? Tell me, that I may sack
The hateful mansion.

[*draws his dagger*]

Friar Laurence.   Hold thy desperate hand.
Art thou a man? Thy form cries out thou art;
110 Thy tears are womanish, thy wild acts denote
The unreasonable fury of a beast.
Unseemly woman in a seeming man!
Or ill-beseeming beast in seeming both!
Thou hast amazed me. By my holy order,
115 I thought thy disposition better tempered.
Hast thou slain Tybalt? Wilt thou slay thyself?
And slay thy lady too that lives in thee,
By doing damned hate upon thyself?
Why railst thou on thy birth, the heaven, and earth?
120 Since birth and heaven and earth, all three do meet
In thee at once; which thou at once wouldst lose.
Fie, fie, thou shamest thy shape, thy love, thy wit,
Which, like a usurer, aboundst in all,
And usest none in that true use indeed
125 Which should bedeck thy shape, thy love, thy wit.
Thy noble shape is but a form of wax,
Digressing from the valor of a man;
Thy dear love sworn but hollow perjury,
Killing that love which thou hast vowed to cherish;
130 Thy wit, that ornament to shape and love,
Misshapen in the conduct of them both,
Like powder in a skilless soldier's flask,
Is set afire by thine own ignorance,
And thou dismembered with thine own defense.
135 What, rouse thee, man! Thy Juliet is alive,
For whose dear sake thou wast but lately dead.
There art thou happy. Tybalt would kill thee,
But thou slewest Tybalt. There art thou happy.
The law, that threatened death, becomes thy friend
140 And turns it to exile. There art thou happy.
A pack of blessings light upon thy back;
Happiness courts thee in her best array;
But, like a misbehaved and sullen wench,
Thou poutst upon thy fortune and thy love.

102 that name: the name Romeo.

106–108 in what vile part . . . mansion: Romeo asks where in his body (**anatomy**) his name can be found so that he can cut the name out.

108–125 Hold thy . . . bedeck thy shape, thy love, thy wit: You're not acting like a man. Would you send your soul to hell by committing suicide (**doing damned hate upon thyself**)? Why do you curse your birth, heaven, and earth? You are refusing to make good use of your advantages, just as a miser refuses to spend his money.

126–134 The friar explains how by acting as he is, Romeo is misusing his shape (his outer form or body), his love, and his wit (his mind or intellect).

145 Take heed, take heed, for such die miserable.
Go get thee to thy love, as was decreed,
Ascend her chamber, hence and comfort her.
But look thou stay not till the watch be set,
For then thou canst not pass to Mantua,
150 Where thou shalt live till we can find a time
To blaze your marriage, reconcile your friends,
Beg pardon of the Prince, and call thee back
With twenty hundred thousand times more joy
Than thou wentst forth in lamentation.
155 Go before, nurse. Commend me to thy lady,
And bid her hasten all the house to bed,
Which heavy sorrow makes them apt unto.
Romeo is coming.

Nurse. O Lord, I could have stayed here all the night
160 To hear good counsel. O, what learning is!
My lord, I'll tell my lady you will come.

Romeo. Do so, and bid my sweet prepare to chide.

[Nurse *offers to go and turns again*.]

Nurse. Here is a ring she bid me give you, sir.
Hie you, make haste, for it grows very late.

[*Exit*.]

165 **Romeo.** How well my comfort is revived by this!

Friar Laurence. Go hence; good night; and here stands all your
    state:
Either be gone before the watch be set,
Or by the break of day disguised from hence.
Sojourn in Mantua. I'll find out your man,
170 And he shall signify from time to time
Every good hap to you that chances here.
Give me thy hand. 'Tis late. Farewell; good night.

Romeo. But that a joy past joy calls out on me,
It were a grief so brief to part with thee.
175 Farewell.

[*Exeunt*.]

Scene 4 *Capulet's house.*

[*Enter* Capulet, Lady Capulet, *and* Paris.]

Capulet. Things have fall'n out, sir, so unluckily
That we have had no time to move our daughter.
Look you, she loved her kinsman Tybalt dearly,
And so did I. Well, we were born to die.

148–149 look . . . Mantua: Leave before the guards take their places at the city gates; otherwise you will not be able to escape.

151 blaze . . . friends: announce your marriage and get the families (**friends**) to stop feuding.

162 bid . . . chide: Tell Juliet to get ready to scold me for the way I've behaved.

166–171 and here . . . here: Either leave before the night watchmen go on duty, or get out at dawn in a disguise. Stay awhile in Mantua. I'll find your servant and send messages to you about what good things are happening here.

1–2 Things have . . . our daughter: Such terrible things have happened that we haven't had time to persuade (**move**) Juliet to think about your marriage proposal.

5 'Tis very late; she'll not come down tonight.
I promise you, but for your company,
I would have been abed an hour ago.

Paris. These times of woe afford no time to woo.
Madam, good night. Commend me to your daughter.

8 Sad times are not good times for talking of marriage.

10 **Lady Capulet.** I will, and know her mind early tomorrow;
Tonight she's mewed up to her heaviness.

11 Tonight she is locked up with her sorrow.

[Paris *offers to go and* Capulet *calls him again.*]

Capulet. Sir Paris, I will make a desperate tender
Of my child's love. I think she will be ruled
In all respects by me; nay more, I doubt it not.

12 desperate tender: bold offer.

15 Wife, go you to her ere you go to bed;
Acquaint her here of my son Paris' love
And bid her (mark you me?) on Wednesday next—
But, soft! what day is this?

Paris. Monday, my lord.

Capulet. Monday! ha, ha! Well, Wednesday is too soon.
20 A Thursday let it be—a Thursday, tell her,
She shall be married to this noble earl.

Will you be ready? Do you like this haste?
We'll keep no great ado—a friend or two;
For hark you, Tybalt being slain so late,
25 It may be thought we held him carelessly,
Being our kinsman, if we revel much.
Therefore we'll have some half a dozen friends,
And there an end. But what say you to Thursday?

Paris. My lord, I would that Thursday were tomorrow.

30 **Capulet.** Well, get you gone. A Thursday be it then.
Go you to Juliet ere you go to bed;
Prepare her, wife, against this wedding day.
Farewell, my lord.—Light to my chamber, ho!
Afore me, it is so very very late
35 That we may call it early by-and-by.
Good night.

[*Exeunt.*]

Scene 5 *Capulet's orchard.*

[*Enter* Romeo *and* Juliet *above, at the window.*]

Juliet. Wilt thou be gone? It is not yet near day.
It was the nightingale, and not the lark,
That pierced the fearful hollow of thine ear.
Nightly she sings on yond pomegranate tree.
5 Believe me, love, it was the nightingale.

Romeo. It was the lark, the herald of the morn;
No nightingale. Look, love, what envious streaks
Do lace the severing clouds in yonder East.
Night's candles are burnt out, and jocund day
10 Stands tiptoe on the misty mountain tops.
I must be gone and live, or stay and die.

Juliet. Yond light is not daylight; I know it, I.
It is some meteor that the sun exhales
To be to thee this night a torchbearer
15 And light thee on thy way to Mantua.
Therefore stay yet; thou needst not to be gone.

Romeo. Let me be ta'en, let me be put to death.
I am content, so thou wilt have it so.
I'll say yon grey is not the morning's eye,
20 'Tis but the pale reflex of Cynthia's brow;
Nor that is not the lark whose notes do beat
The vaulty heaven so high above our heads.
I have more care to stay than will to go.

23 no great ado: no big festivity.

34–35 it is . . . by-and-by: It's so late at night that soon we'll be calling it early in the morning.

2 It was . . . lark: The nightingale sings at night; the lark sings in the morning.

9 Night's candles: stars.

12–25 Juliet continues to pretend it is night to keep Romeo from leaving. Romeo says he'll stay if Juliet wishes it, even if it means death.

20 Cynthia's brow: Cynthia is another name for Diana, the Roman goddess of the moon. She was often pictured with a crescent moon on her forehead.

Come, death, and welcome! Juliet wills it so.
25 How is't, my soul? Let's talk; it is not day.

Juliet. It is, it is! Hie hence, be gone, away!
It is the lark that sings so out of tune,
Straining harsh discords and unpleasing sharps.
Some say the lark makes sweet division;
30 This doth not so, for she divideth us.
Some say the lark and loathed toad changed eyes;
O, now I would they had changed voices too,
Since arm from arm that voice doth us affray,
Hunting thee hence with hunt's-up to the day!
35 O, now be gone! More light and light it grows.

Romeo. More light and light—more dark and dark our woes!

[*Enter* Nurse, *hastily.*]

Nurse. Madam!

Juliet. Nurse?

Nurse. Your lady mother is coming to your chamber.
40 The day is broke; be wary, look about.

[*Exit.*]

Juliet. Then, window, let day in, and let life out.

Romeo. Farewell, farewell! One kiss, and I'll descend.

[*He starts down the ladder.*]

26 Romeo's mention of death frightens Juliet, and she urges him to leave quickly.

29 division: melody.

31–34 I wish the lark had the voice of the hated (**loathed**) toad, since its voice is frightening us apart and acting as a morning song for hunters (**hunt's-up**).

Juliet. Art thou gone so, my lord, my love, my friend?
I must hear from thee every day in the hour,
45 For in a minute there are many days.
O, by this count I shall be much in years
Ere I again behold my Romeo!

Romeo. Farewell!
I will omit no opportunity
50 That may convey my greetings, love, to thee.

Juliet. O, thinkst thou we shall ever meet again?

Romeo. I doubt it not; and all these woes shall serve
For sweet discourses in our time to come.

Juliet. O God, I have an ill-divining soul!
55 Methinks I see thee, now thou art below,
As one dead in the bottom of a tomb.
Either my eyesight fails, or thou lookst pale.

Romeo. And trust me, love, in my eye so do you.
Dry sorrow drinks our blood. Adieu! adieu!

[*Exit.*]

60 **Juliet.** O Fortune, Fortune! all men call thee fickle.
If thou art fickle, what dost thou with him
That is renowned for faith? Be fickle, Fortune,
For then I hope thou wilt not keep him long
But send him back.

Lady Capulet [*within*]. Ho, daughter! are you up?

65 **Juliet.** Who is't that calls? It is my lady mother.
Is she not down so late, or up so early?
What unaccustomed cause procures her hither?

[*Enter* Lady Capulet.]

Lady Capulet. Why, how now, Juliet?

Juliet.   Madam, I am not well.

Lady Capulet. Evermore weeping for your cousin's death?
70 What, wilt thou wash him from his grave with tears?
An if thou couldst, thou couldst not make him live.
Therefore have done. Some grief shows much of love;
But much of grief shows still some want of wit.

Juliet. Yet let me weep for such a feeling loss.

75 **Lady Capulet.** So shall you feel the loss, but not the friend
Which you weep for.

Juliet.   Feeling so the loss,
I cannot choose but ever weep the friend.

46 much in years: very old.

54–56 I have . . . tomb: Juliet sees an evil vision of the future.

59 Dry . . . blood: People believed that sorrow drained the blood from the heart, causing a sad person to look pale.

60–62 fickle: changeable in loyalty or affection. Juliet asks fickle Fortune why it has anything to do with Romeo, who is the opposite of fickle.

67 What . . . hither: What unusual reason brings her here?

72–73 have . . . wit: Stop crying (**have done**). A little grief is evidence of love, while too much grief shows a lack of good sense (**want of wit**).

Lady Capulet. Well, girl, thou weepst not so much for his death
As that the villain lives which slaughtered him.

80 **Juliet.** What villain, madam?

Lady Capulet. That same villain Romeo.

Juliet [*aside*]. Villain and he be many miles asunder.—
God pardon him! I do, with all my heart;
And yet no man like he doth grieve my heart.

Lady Capulet. That is because the traitor murderer lives.

85 **Juliet.** Ay, madam, from the reach of these my hands.
Would none but I might venge my cousin's death!

Lady Capulet. We will have vengeance for it, fear thou not.
Then weep no more. I'll send to one in Mantua,
Where that same banished runagate doth live,
90 Shall give him such an unaccustomed dram
That he shall soon keep Tybalt company;
And then I hope thou wilt be satisfied.

Juliet. Indeed I never shall be satisfied
With Romeo till I behold him—dead—
95 Is my poor heart so for a kinsman vexed.
Madam, if you could find out but a man
To bear a poison, I would temper it;
That Romeo should, upon receipt thereof,
Soon sleep in quiet. O, how my heart abhors
100 To hear him named and cannot come to him,
To wreak the love I bore my cousin Tybalt
Upon his body that hath slaughtered him!

Lady Capulet. Find thou the means, and I'll find such a man.
But now I'll tell thee joyful tidings, girl.

105 **Juliet.** And joy comes well in such a needy time.
What are they, I beseech your ladyship?

Lady Capulet. Well, well, thou hast a careful father, child;
One who, to put thee from thy heaviness,
Hath sorted out a sudden day of joy
110 That thou expects not nor I looked not for.

Juliet. Madam, in happy time! What day is that?

Lady Capulet. Marry, my child, early next Thursday morn
The gallant, young, and noble gentleman,
The County Paris, at Saint Peter's Church,
115 Shall happily make thee there a joyful bride.

81–102 In these lines Juliet's words have double meanings. To avoid lying to her mother, she chooses her words carefully. They can mean what her mother wants to hear—or what Juliet really has on her mind.

89 runagate: runaway.

90 unaccustomed dram: poison.

93–102 Dead could refer either to Romeo or to Juliet's heart. Juliet says that if her mother could find someone to carry a poison to Romeo, she would mix (**temper**) it herself.

Juliet. Now by Saint Peter's Church, and Peter too,
He shall not make me there a joyful bride!
I wonder at this haste, that I must wed
Ere he that should be husband comes to woo.
120 I pray you tell my lord and father, madam,
I will not marry yet; and when I do, I swear
It shall be Romeo, whom you know I hate,
Rather than Paris. These are news indeed!

Lady Capulet. Here comes your father. Tell him so yourself,
125 And see how he will take it at your hands.

[*Enter* Capulet *and* Nurse.]

Capulet. When the sun sets the air doth drizzle dew,
But for the sunset of my brother's son
It rains downright.
How now? a conduit, girl? What, still in tears?
130 Evermore show'ring? In one little body
Thou counterfeitst a bark, a sea, a wind:
For still thy eyes, which I may call the sea,
Do ebb and flow with tears; the bark thy body is,
Sailing in this salt flood; the winds, thy sighs,
135 Who, raging with thy tears and they with them,
Without a sudden calm will overset
Thy tempest-tossed body. How now, wife?
Have you delivered to her our decree?

Lady Capulet. Ay, sir; but she will none, she gives you thanks.
140 I would the fool were married to her grave!

Capulet. Soft! take me with you, take me with you, wife.
How? Will she none? Doth she not give us thanks?
Is she not proud? Doth she not count her blest,
Unworthy as she is, that we have wrought
145 So worthy a gentleman to be her bridegroom?

Juliet. Not proud you have, but thankful that you have.
Proud can I never be of what I hate,
But thankful even for hate that is meant love.

Capulet. How, how, how, how, choplogic? What is this?
150 "Proud"—and "I thank you"—and "I thank you not"—
And yet "not proud"? Mistress minion you,
Thank me no thankings, nor proud me no prouds,
But fettle your fine joints 'gainst Thursday next
To go with Paris to Saint Peter's Church,
155 Or I will drag thee on a hurdle thither.
Out, you green-sickness carrion! out, you baggage!
You tallow-face!

127 the sunset . . . son: the death of Tybalt.

129–137 conduit: fountain. Capulet compares Juliet to a boat (**bark**), an ocean, and the wind because of her excessive crying.

141 take me with you: let me understand you.

146–148 Not proud . . . meant love: I'm not pleased, but I am grateful for your intentions.

149–157 Capulet calls Juliet a person who argues over fine points (**choplogic**) and a spoiled child (**minion**). He tells her to prepare herself (**fettle your fine joints**) for the wedding or he'll haul her there in a cart for criminals (**hurdle**). He calls her a piece of dead flesh (**green-sickness carrion**) and a coward (**tallow-face**).

Lady Capulet. Fie, fie; what, are you mad?

Juliet. Good father, I beseech you on my knees,

[*She kneels down.*]

Hear me with patience but to speak a word.

160 **Capulet.** Hang thee, young baggage! disobedient wretch!
I tell thee what—get thee to church a Thursday
Or never after look me in the face.
Speak not, reply not, do not answer me!
My fingers itch. Wife, we scarce thought us blest

165 That God had lent us but this only child;
But now I see this one is one too much,
And that we have a curse in having her.
Out on her, hilding!

Nurse.   God in heaven bless her!
You are to blame, my lord, to rate her so.

170 **Capulet.** And why, my Lady Wisdom? Hold your tongue,
Good Prudence. Smatter with your gossips, go!

Nurse. I speak no treason.

Capulet.   O, God-i-god-en!

Nurse. May not one speak?

Capulet.   Peace, you mumbling fool!
Utter your gravity o'er a gossip's bowl,

175 For here we need it not.

Lady Capulet.   You are too hot.

Capulet. God's bread! it makes me mad. Day, night, late, early,
At home, abroad, alone, in company,
Waking or sleeping, still my care hath been
To have her matched; and having now provided

180 A gentleman of princely parentage,
Of fair demesnes, youthful, and nobly trained,
Stuffed, as they say, with honorable parts,
Proportioned as one's thought would wish a man—
And then to have a wretched puling fool,

185 A whining mammet, in her fortunes tender,
To answer "I'll not wed, I cannot love;
I am too young, I pray you pardon me"!
But, an you will not wed, I'll pardon you.
Graze where you will, you shall not house with me.

190 Look to't, think on't; I do not use to jest.
Thursday is near; lay hand on heart, advise:
An you be mine, I'll give you to my friend;

164 My fingers itch: I feel like hitting you.

168 hilding: a good-for-nothing person.

171 smatter: chatter.

174 Utter … bowl: Save your words of wisdom for a gathering of gossips.

179 matched: married.

184 puling: crying.
185 mammet: doll.

189–195 Capulet swears that he'll kick Juliet out and cut her off financially if she refuses to marry.

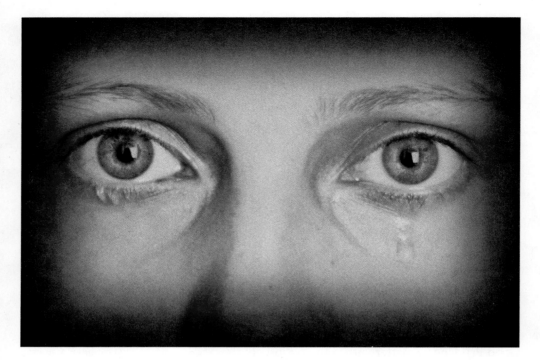

An you be not, hang, beg, starve, die in the streets,
For, by my soul, I'll ne'er acknowledge thee,
195 Nor what is mine shall never do thee good.
Trust to't. Bethink you. I'll not be forsworn.

[*Exit.*]

Juliet. Is there no pity sitting in the clouds
That sees into the bottom of my grief?
O sweet my mother, cast me not away!
200 Delay this marriage for a month, a week;
Or if you do not, make the bridal bed
In that dim monument where Tybalt lies.

Lady Capulet. Talk not to me, for I'll not speak a word.
Do as thou wilt, for I have done with thee.

[*Exit.*]

205 **Juliet.** O God!—O nurse, how shall this be prevented?
My husband is on earth, my faith in heaven.
How shall that faith return again to earth
Unless that husband send it me from heaven
By leaving earth? Comfort me, counsel me.
210 Alack, alack, that heaven should practice stratagems
Upon so soft a subject as myself!
What sayst thou? Hast thou not a word of joy?
Some comfort, nurse.

196 I'll not be forsworn: I will not break my promise to Paris.

207–211 Juliet is worried about the sin of being married to two men. She asks how heaven can play such tricks (**practice stratagems**) on her.

Image Credits: ©Flickr Select/foxline.com.ua/Getty Images

Nurse. Faith, here it is.
Romeo is banish'd; and all the world to nothing
215 That he dares ne'er come back to challenge you;
Or if he do, it needs must be by stealth.
Then, since the case so stands as now it doth,
I think it best you married with the County.
O, he's a lovely gentleman!
220 Romeo's a dishclout to him. An eagle, madam,
Hath not so green, so quick, so fair an eye
As Paris hath. Beshrew my very heart,
I think you are happy in this second match,
For it excels your first; or if it did not,
225 Your first is dead—or 'twere as good he were
As living here and you no use of him.

Juliet. Speakst thou this from thy heart?

Nurse. And from my soul too; else beshrew them both.

Juliet. Amen!

230 **Nurse.** What?

Juliet. Well, thou hast comforted me marvelous much.
Go in; and tell my lady I am gone,
Having displeased my father, to Laurence' cell,
To make confession and to be absolved.

235 **Nurse.** Marry, I will; and this is wisely done.

[*Exit.*]

Juliet. Ancient damnation! O most wicked fiend!
Is it more sin to wish me thus forsworn,
Or to dispraise my lord with that same tongue
Which she hath praised him with above compare
240 So many thousand times? Go, counselor!
Thou and my bosom henceforth shall be twain.
I'll to the friar to know his remedy.
If all else fail, myself have power to die.

[*Exit.*]

222 beshrew: curse.

223–225 This new marriage will be better than the first, which is as good as over.

229 Amen: I agree— that is, curse your heart and soul.

236–238 Ancient damnation: old devil; **dispraise:** criticize.

241 Thou . . . twain: I'll no longer tell you my secrets.

COLLABORATIVE DISCUSSION Discuss with a partner the chain of events that begins to turn the story of Romeo and Juliet into a tragedy. Do you believe the main characters are making mistakes that will lead them down a tragic path? Cite textual evidence to support your ideas.

Analyzing the Text

Cite Text Evidence   Support your responses with evidence from the selection.

1. **Interpret** What is the meaning of Mercutio's repeated curse, "A plague o' both your houses!" (Scene 1, lines 85, 93)? What might this curse foreshadow?

2. **Evaluate** What is Romeo's motivation for killing Tybalt? Is his action justified or a mistake? Explain your response.

3. **Cite Evidence** In what ways do Romeo and Juliet need the help of Friar Laurence and the Nurse in order to save their love and move forward? Support your response with evidence from the text.

4. **Analyze** In Scene 5, Lord Capulet becomes enraged when Juliet says she will not marry Paris. In what way are his words and actions in this scene like those of Romeo and Juliet? What are the likely consequences of his actions?

5. **Interpret** Explore how Shakespeare continues to use the light/dark or day/night motif in Scene 5, lines 1–35. Why does Juliet want the darkness to continue?

6. **Analyze** How and why does Juliet's relationship with her nurse change? Do you believe Juliet is justified in her feelings toward the nurse? Explain, citing details from the text.

PERFORMANCE TASK

Writing Activity: Journal Entries Use two brief writing tasks to explore the parallel feelings of despair Romeo and Juliet feel in Act III.

1. Write a one-page journal entry from the point of view of Juliet when she learns of the death of Tybalt.

2. Write a one-page journal entry from the point of view of Romeo when he is at the Friar's cell awaiting exile.

Base both pieces of writing on evidence from the text.

AS YOU READ Note the details of the plan Juliet and Friar Laurence initiate in this act. Pay attention to the reactions of other characters as the plan unfolds. Write down any questions you generate during reading.

ACT IV

Scene 1 *Friar Laurence's cell.*

[*Enter* Friar Laurence *and* Paris.]

Friar Laurence. On Thursday, sir? The time is very short.

Paris. My father Capulet will have it so,
And I am nothing slow to slack his haste.

Friar Laurence. You say you do not know the lady's mind.
5   Uneven is the course; I like it not.

Paris. Immoderately she weeps for Tybalt's death,
And therefore have I little talked of love;
For Venus smiles not in a house of tears.
Now, sir, her father counts it dangerous
10   That she do give her sorrow so much sway,
And in his wisdom hastes our marriage
To stop the inundation of her tears,
Which, too much minded by herself alone,
May be put from her by society.
15   Now do you know the reason of this haste.

Friar Laurence [*aside*]. I would I knew not why it should be
         slowed.—
Look, sir, here comes the lady toward my cell.

[*Enter* Juliet.]

Paris. Happily met, my lady and my wife!

Juliet. That may be, sir, when I may be a wife.

20   **Paris.** That may be must be, love, on Thursday next.

Juliet. What must be shall be.

Friar Laurence.   That's a certain text.

Paris. Come you to make confession to this father?

Juliet. To answer that, I should confess to you.

Paris. Do not deny to him that you love me.

25   **Juliet.** I will confess to you that I love him.

Paris. So will ye, I am sure, that you love me.

Juliet. If I do so, it will be of more price,
Being spoke behind your back, than to your face.

2–3 My . . . haste: Capulet is eager to have the wedding on Thursday and so am I.

4–5 You . . . course: You don't know how Juliet feels about this. It's a very uncertain (**uneven**) plan.

13–14 Which . . . society: which, thought about too much by her in privacy, may be put from her mind if she is forced to be with others.

Paris. Poor soul, thy face is much abused with tears.

30 **Juliet.** The tears have got small victory by that,
For it was bad enough before their spite.

Paris. Thou wrongst it more than tears with that report.

Juliet. That is no slander, sir, which is a truth;
And what I spake, I spake it to my face.

35 **Paris.** Thy face is mine, and thou hast slandered it.

Juliet. It may be so, for it is not mine own.
Are you at leisure, holy father, now,
Or shall I come to you at evening mass?

Friar Laurence. My leisure serves me, pensive daughter, now.
40 My lord, we must entreat the time alone.

Paris. God shield I should disturb devotion!
Juliet, on Thursday early will I rouse ye.
Till then, adieu, and keep this holy kiss.

[*Exit.*]

Juliet. O, shut the door! and when thou hast done so,
45 Come weep with me—past hope, past cure, past help!

Friar Laurence. Ah, Juliet, I already know thy grief;
It strains me past the compass of my wits.
I hear thou must, and nothing may prorogue it,
On Thursday next be married to this County.

50 **Juliet.** Tell me not, friar, that thou hearst of this,
Unless thou tell me how I may prevent it.
If in thy wisdom thou canst give no help,
Do thou but call my resolution wise
And with this knife I'll help it presently.
55 God joined my heart and Romeo's, thou our hands;
And ere this hand, by thee to Romeo's sealed,
Shall be the label to another deed,
Or my true heart with treacherous revolt
Turn to another, this shall slay them both.
60 Therefore, out of thy long-experienced time,
Give me some present counsel; or, behold,
'Twixt my extremes and me this bloody knife
Shall play the umpire, arbitrating that
Which the commission of thy years and art
65 Could to no issue of true honor bring.
Be not so long to speak. I long to die
If what thou speakst speak not of remedy.

Friar Laurence. Hold, daughter, I do spy a kind of hope,
Which craves as desperate an execution

30–31 The tears ... spite: The tears haven't ruined my face; it wasn't all that beautiful before they did their damage.

35 Paris says he owns Juliet's face (since she will soon marry him). Insulting her face, he says, insults him, its owner.

47–48 compass: limit; **prorogue:** postpone.

52–53 If in ... wise: If you can't find a way to help me, at least agree that my plan is wise.

56–67 And ere this hand ... of remedy: Before I sign another wedding agreement (**deed**), I will use this knife to kill myself. If you, with your years of experience (**long-experienced time**), can't help me, I'll end my sufferings (**extremes**) and solve the problem myself.

70 As that is desperate which we would prevent.
    If, rather than to marry County Paris,
    Thou hast the strength of will to slay thyself,
    Then is it likely thou wilt undertake
    A thing like death to chide away this shame,
75 That copest with death himself to scape from it;
    And, if thou darest, I'll give thee remedy.

Juliet. O, bid me leap, rather than marry Paris,
    From off the battlements of yonder tower,
    Or walk in thievish ways, or bid me lurk
80 Where serpents are; chain me with roaring bears,
    Or shut me nightly in a charnel house,
    O'ercovered quite with dead men's rattling bones,
    With reeky shanks and yellow chapless skulls;
    Or bid me go into a new-made grave
85 And hide me with a dead man in his shroud—
    Things that, to hear them told, have made me tremble—
    And I will do it without fear or doubt,
    To live an unstained wife to my sweet love.

Friar Laurence. Hold, then. Go home, be merry, give consent
90 To marry Paris. Wednesday is tomorrow.
    Tomorrow night look that thou lie alone:
    Let not the nurse lie with thee in thy chamber.
    Take thou this vial, being then in bed,
    And this distilled liquor drink thou off;
95 When presently through all thy veins shall run
    A cold and drowsy humor; for no pulse
    Shall keep his native progress, but surcease;
    No warmth, no breath, shall testify thou livest;
    The roses in thy lips and cheeks shall fade
100 To paly ashes, thy eyes' windows fall
    Like death when he shuts up the day of life;
    Each part, deprived of supple government,
    Shall, stiff and stark and cold, appear like death;
    And in this borrowed likeness of shrunk death
105 Thou shalt continue two-and-forty hours,
    And then awake as from a pleasant sleep.
    Now, when the bridegroom in the morning comes
    To rouse thee from thy bed, there art thou dead.
    Then, as the manner of our country is,
110 In thy best robes uncovered on the bier
    Thou shalt be borne to that same ancient vault
    Where all the kindred of the Capulets lie.
    In the meantime, against thou shalt awake,
    Shall Romeo by my letters know our drift;

115 And hither shall he come; and he and I
Will watch thy waking, and that very night
Shall Romeo bear thee hence to Mantua.
And this shall free thee from this present shame,
If no inconstant toy nor womanish fear
120 Abate thy valor in the acting it.

Juliet. Give me, give me! O, tell me not of fear!

Friar Laurence. Hold! Get you gone, be strong and prosperous
In this resolve. I'll send a friar with speed
To Mantua, with my letters to thy lord.

125 **Juliet.** Love give me strength! and strength shall help afford.
Farewell, dear father.

[*Exeunt.*]

Scene 2 *Capulet's house.*

[*Enter* Capulet, Lady Capulet, Nurse, *and* Servingmen.]

Capulet. So many guests invite as here are writ.

[*Exit a* Servingman.]

Sirrah, go hire me twenty cunning cooks.

Servingman. You shall have none ill, sir; for I'll try if they can
lick their fingers.

5 **Capulet.** How canst thou try them so?

Servingman. Marry, sir, 'tis an ill cook that cannot lick his own
fingers. Therefore he that cannot lick his fingers goes not with
me.

Capulet. Go, begone.

[*Exit* Servingman.]

10 We shall be much unfurnished for this time.
What, is my daughter gone to Friar Laurence?

Nurse. Ay, forsooth.

Capulet. Well, he may chance to do some good on her.
A peevish self-willed harlotry it is.

[*Enter* Juliet.]

15 **Nurse.** See where she comes from shrift with merry look.

Capulet. How now, my headstrong? Where have you been
gadding?

Juliet. Where I have learnt me to repent the sin
Of disobedient opposition
To you and your behests, and am enjoined

119–120 inconstant toy: foolish whim; **abate thy valor:** weaken your courage.

1–8 Capulet is having a cheerful conversation with his servants about the wedding preparations. One servant assures him that he will test (**try**) the cooks he hires by making them taste their own food (**lick their fingers**).

10 unfurnished: unprepared.

14 A silly, stubborn girl she is.

19 behests: orders; **enjoined:** commanded.

20   By holy Laurence to fall prostrate here
      To beg your pardon. Pardon, I beseech you!
      Henceforward I am ever ruled by you.

      Capulet. Send for the County. Go tell him of this.
      I'll have this knot knit up tomorrow morning.

24 I'll have this wedding scheduled for tomorrow morning.

25   **Juliet.** I met the youthful lord at Laurence' cell
      And gave him what becomed love I might,
      Not stepping o'er the bounds of modesty.

      Capulet. Why, I am glad on't. This is well. Stand up.
      This is as't should be. Let me see the County.
30   Ay, marry, go, I say, and fetch him hither.
      Now, afore God, this reverend holy friar,
      All our whole city is much bound to him.

      Juliet. Nurse, will you go with me into my closet
      To help me sort such needful ornaments
35   As you think fit to furnish me tomorrow?

      Lady Capulet. No, not till Thursday. There is time enough.

      Capulet. Go, nurse, go with her. We'll to church tomorrow.

      [*Exeunt* Juliet *and* Nurse.]

      Lady Capulet. We shall be short in our provision.
      'Tis now near night.

36–39 Lady Capulet urges her husband to wait until Thursday as originally planned. She needs time to get food (**provision**) ready for the wedding party.

      Capulet.   Tush, I will stir about,
40   And all things shall be well, I warrant thee, wife.
      Go thou to Juliet, help to deck up her.
      I'll not to bed tonight; let me alone.
      I'll play the housewife for this once. What, ho!
      They are all forth; well, I will walk myself
45   To County Paris, to prepare him up
      Against tomorrow. My heart is wondrous light,
      Since this same wayward girl is so reclaimed.

39–46 Capulet is so set on Wednesday that he promises to make the arrangements himself.

      [*Exeunt.*]

      Scene 3 *Juliet's bedroom.*

      [*Enter* Juliet *and* Nurse.]

      Juliet. Ay, those attires are best; but, gentle nurse,
      I pray thee leave me to myself tonight;
      For I have need of many orisons
      To move the heavens to smile upon my state,
5   Which, well thou knowest, is cross and full of sin.

3 orisons: prayers.

      [*Enter* Lady Capulet.]

      Lady Capulet. What, are you busy, ho? Need you my help?

Juliet. No madam; we have culled such necessaries
As are behooveful for our state tomorrow.
So please you, let me now be left alone,
10 And let the nurse this night sit up with you;
For I am sure you have your hands full all
In this so sudden business.

Lady Capulet.   Good night.
Get thee to bed and rest, for thou hast need.

[*Exeunt* Lady Capulet *and* Nurse.]

Juliet. Farewell! God knows when we shall meet again.
15 I have a faint cold fear thrills through my veins
That almost freezes up the heat of life.
I'll call them back again to comfort me.
Nurse!—What should she do here?
My dismal scene I needs must act alone.
20 Come, vial.
What if this mixture do not work at all?
Shall I be married then tomorrow morning?
No, no! This shall forbid it. Lie thou there.

[*lays down a dagger*]

What if it be a poison which the friar
25 Subtly hath ministered to have me dead,
Lest in this marriage he should be dishonored
Because he married me before to Romeo?
I fear it is; and yet methinks it should not,
For he hath still been tried a holy man.

7–8 we have . . . tomorrow: We have picked out (**culled**) everything appropriate for the wedding tomorrow.

23 This shall forbid it: A dagger will be her alternative means of keeping from marrying Paris.

24–58 Juliet lists her various doubts and fears about what she is about to do.

30 How if, when I am laid into the tomb,
    I wake before the time that Romeo
    Come to redeem me? There's a fearful point!
    Shall I not then be stifled in the vault,
    To whose foul mouth no healthsome air breathes in,
35 And there die strangled ere my Romeo comes?
    Or, if I live, is it not very like
    The horrible conceit of death and night,
    Together with the terror of the place—
    As in a vault, an ancient receptacle
40 Where for this many hundred years the bones
    Of all my buried ancestors are packed;
    Where bloody Tybalt, yet but green in earth,
    Lies fest'ring in his shroud; where, as they say,
    At some hours in the night spirits resort—
45 Alack, alack, is it not like that I,
    So early waking—what with loathsome smells,
    And shrieks like mandrakes torn out of the earth,
    That living mortals, hearing them, run mad—
    O, if I wake, shall I not be distraught,
50 Environed with all these hideous fears,
    And madly play with my forefathers' joints,
    And pluck the mangled Tybalt from his shroud,
    And, in this rage, with some great kinsman's bone
    As with a club dash out my desp'rate brains?
55 O, look! methinks I see my cousin's ghost
    Seeking out Romeo, that did spit his body
    Upon a rapier's point. Stay, Tybalt, stay!
    Romeo, I come! this do I drink to thee.

    [*She drinks and falls upon her bed within the curtains.*]

Scene 4 *Capulet's house.*

[*Enter* Lady Capulet *and* Nurse.]

Lady Capulet. Hold, take these keys and fetch more spices, nurse.

Nurse. They call for dates and quinces in the pastry.

[*Enter* Capulet.]

Capulet. Come, stir, stir, stir! The second cock hath crowed,
    The curfew bell hath rung, 'tis three o'clock.
5   Look to the baked meats, good Angelica;
    Spare not for cost.

    Nurse.   Go, you cot-quean, go,
    Get you to bed! Faith, you'll be sick tomorrow
    For this night's watching.

36–43 Juliet fears the vision (**conceit**) she might have on waking in the family tomb and seeing the rotting body of Tybalt.

45–54 She fears that the smells together with the sounds of ghosts screaming might make her lose her mind and commit bizarre acts. Mandrake root was thought to look like the human form and to scream when pulled from the ground.

57 stay: stop.

2 pastry: the room where baking is done.

5 Angelica: In his happy mood, Capulet calls the nurse by her name.

6 cot-quean: a "cottage quean," or housewife. This is a joke about Capulet doing women's work (arranging the party).

Capulet. No, not a whit. What, I have watched ere now
10   All night for lesser cause, and ne'er been sick.

Lady Capulet. Ay, you have been a mouse-hunt in your time;
But I will watch you from such watching now.

[*Exeunt* Lady Capulet *and* Nurse.]

Capulet. A jealous hood, a jealous hood!

[*Enter three or four* Servants, *with spits and logs and baskets*.]

                                 Now, fellow,
What is there?

15   **First Servant.** Things for the cook, sir; but I know not what.

Capulet. Make haste, make haste. [*Exit* Servant.] Sirrah, fetch
   drier logs.
Call Peter; he will show thee where they are.

Second Servant. I have a head, sir, that will find out logs
And never trouble Peter for the matter.

20   **Capulet.** Mass, and well said, merry whoreson, ha!
Thou shalt be loggerhead. [*Exit* Servant.] Good faith, 'tis day.
The County will be here with music straight,
For so he said he would. [*music within*] I hear him near.
Nurse! Wife! What, ho! What, nurse, I say!

[*Reenter* Nurse.]

25   Go waken Juliet; go and trim her up.
I'll go and chat with Paris. Hie, make haste,
Make haste! The bridegroom he is come already:
Make haste, I say.

[*Exeunt.*]

Scene 5   *Juliet's bedroom.*

[*Enter* Nurse.]

Nurse. Mistress! what, mistress! Juliet! Fast, I warrant her, she.
Why, lamb! why, lady! Fie, you slugabed!
Why, love, I say! madam! sweetheart! Why, bride!
What, not a word? You take your pennyworths now,
5   Sleep for a week; for the next night, I warrant,
The County Paris hath set up his rest
That you shall rest but little. God forgive me,
Marry and amen, how sound is she asleep!
I needs must wake her. Madam, madam, madam!
10   Aye, let the County take you in your bed,
He'll fright you up, i' faith. Will it not be?

[*opens the curtains*]

11–13 Lord and Lady Capulet joke about his being a woman chaser (**mouse-hunt**) as a young man. He makes fun of her jealousy (**jealous hood**).

20–23 The joking between Capulet and his servants includes the mild oath **Mass,** short for "by the Mass," and **loggerhead,** a word for a stupid person as well as a pun, since the servant is searching for drier logs. **straight:** right away.

1–11 The nurse chatters as she bustles around the room. She calls Juliet a **slugabed,** or sleepyhead, who is trying to get her **pennyworths,** or small portions, of rest now, since after the wedding Paris won't let her get much sleep.

What, dressed and in your clothes and down again?
I must needs wake you. Lady! lady! lady!
Alas, alas! Help, help! my lady's dead!
15 O well-a-day that ever I was born!
Some aqua vitae, ho! My lord! my lady!

[*Enter* Lady Capulet.]

Lady Capulet. What noise is here?

Nurse.   O lamentable day!

17 lamentable: filled with grief.

Lady Capulet. What is the matter?

Nurse.   Look, look! O heavy day!

Lady Capulet. O me, O me! My child, my only life!
20 Revive, look up, or I will die with thee!
Help! help! Call help.

[*Enter* Capulet.]

Capulet. For shame, bring Juliet forth; her lord is come.

Nurse. She's dead, deceased; she's dead! Alack the day!

Lady Capulet. Alack the day, she's dead, she's dead, she's dead!

25 **Capulet.** Ha! let me see her. Out alas! she's cold,
Her blood is settled, and her joints are stiff;
Life and these lips have long been separated.
Death lies on her like an untimely frost
Upon the sweetest flower of all the field.

30 **Nurse.** O lamentable day!

Lady Capulet.   O woeful time!

Capulet. Death, that hath ta'en her hence to make me wail,
Ties up my tongue and will not let me speak.

[*Enter* Friar Laurence *and* Paris, *with* Musicians.]

Friar Laurence. Come, is the bride ready to go to church?

Capulet. Ready to go, but never to return.
35 O son, the night before thy wedding day
Hath death lain with thy wife. See, there she lies,
Flower as she was, deflowered by him.
Death is my son-in-law, Death is my heir;
My daughter he hath wedded. I will die
40 And leave him all. Life, living, all is Death's.

40 Life . . . Death's: My life, my possessions, and everything else of mine belongs to Death.

Paris. Have I thought long to see this morning's face,
And doth it give me such a sight as this?

Lady Capulet. Accursed, unhappy, wretched, hateful day!
Most miserable hour that e'er time saw

45 In lasting labor of his pilgrimage!
But one, poor one, one poor and loving child,
But one thing to rejoice and solace in,
And cruel Death hath catched it from my sight!

Nurse. O woe! O woeful, woeful, woeful day!
50 Most lamentable day, most woeful day
That ever, ever I did yet behold!
O day! O day! O day! O hateful day!
Never was seen so black a day as this.
O woeful day! O woeful day!

55 **Paris.** Beguiled, divorced, wronged, spited, slain!
Most detestable Death, by thee beguiled,
By cruel, cruel thee quite overthrown!
O love! O life! not life, but love in death!

Capulet. Despised, distressed, hated, martyred, killed!
60 Uncomfortable time, why camest thou now
To murder, murder our solemnity?
O child! O child! my soul, and not my child!
Dead art thou, dead! alack, my child is dead,
And with my child my joys are buried!

65 **Friar Laurence.** Peace, ho, for shame! Confusion's cure lives not
In these confusions. Heaven and yourself
Had part in this fair maid! now heaven hath all,
And all the better is it for the maid.
Your part in her you could not keep from death,
70 But heaven keeps his part in eternal life.
The most you sought was her promotion,
For 'twas your heaven she should be advanced;
And weep ye now, seeing she is advanced
Above the clouds, as high as heaven itself?
75 O, in this love, you love your child so ill
That you run mad, seeing that she is well.
She's not well married that lives married long,
But she's best married that dies married young.
Dry up your tears and stick your rosemary
80 On this fair corse, and, as the custom is,
In all her best array bear her to church;
For though fond nature bids us all lament,
Yet nature's tears are reason's merriment.

Capulet. All things that we ordained festival
85 Turn from their office to black funeral—
Our instruments to melancholy bells,
Our wedding cheer to a sad burial feast;

46–48 But one . . . my sight: I had only one child to make me happy, and Death has taken (**catched**) her from me.

55 Beguiled: tricked

60–61 why . . . solemnity: Why did Death have to come to murder our celebration?

65–78 The friar says that the cure for disaster (**confusion**) cannot be found in cries of grief. Juliet's family and heaven once shared her; now heaven has all of her. All the family ever wanted was the best for her; now she's in heaven—what could be better than that? It is best to die young, when the soul is still pure, without sin.

79–80 stick . . . corse: Put rosemary, an herb, on her corpse.

82–83 though . . . merriment: Though it's natural to cry, common sense tells us we should rejoice for the dead.

84 ordained festival: intended for the wedding.

Our solemn hymns to sullen dirges change;
Our bridal flowers serve for a buried corse;
90 And all things change them to the contrary.

Friar Laurence. Sir, go you in; and, madam, go with him;
And go, Sir Paris. Every one prepare
To follow this fair corse unto her grave.
The heavens do lower upon you for some ill;
95 Move them no more by crossing their high will.

[*Exeunt* Capulet, Lady Capulet, Paris, *and* Friar.]

First Musician. Faith, we may put up our pipes, and be gone.

Nurse. Honest good fellows, ah, put up, put up,
For well you know this is a pitiful case.

[*Exit.*]

Second Musician. Aye, by my troth, the case may be amended.

[*Enter* Peter.]

100 **Peter.** Musicians, oh, musicians, "Heart's ease, heart's ease." Oh,
an you will have me live, play "Heart's ease."

First Musician. Why "Heart's ease"?

Peter. Oh, musicians, because my heart itself plays "My heart is
full of woe." Oh, play me some merry dump, to comfort me.

105 **First Musician.** Not a dump we, 'tis no time to play now.

Peter. You will not, then?

First Musician. No.

Peter. I will then give it you soundly.

First Musician. What will you give us?

88 sullen dirges: sad, mournful tunes.

94–95 The heavens . . . will: The fates (**heavens**) frown on you for some wrong you have done. Don't tempt them by refusing to accept their will (Juliet's death).

Image Credits: (t) ©Artem Furman/Shutterstock; (tl) ©AKaiser/Shutterstock

Peter. No money, on my faith, but the gleek. I will give you the minstrel.

First Musician. Then will I give you the serving creature.

Peter. Then will I lay the serving creature's dagger on your pate. I will carry no crotchets. I'll re you, I'll fa you, do you note me?

First Musician. An you re us and fa us, you note us.

Second Musician. Pray you put up your dagger, and put out your wit.

Peter. Then have at you with my wit! I will drybeat you with an iron wit, and put up my iron dagger. Answer me like men:
     "When griping grief the heart doth wound
     And doleful dumps the mind oppress,
     Then music with her " "He ask—"
Why "silver sound"? Why "music with her silver sound"?—What say you, Simon Catling?

First Musician. Marry, sir, because silver hath a sweet sound.

Peter. Pretty! What say you, Hugh Rebeck?

Second Musician. I say "silver sound" because musicians sound for silver.

Peter. Pretty too! What say you, James Soundpost?

Third Musician. Faith, I know not what to say.

Peter. Oh, I cry you mercy, you are the singer. I will say for you. It is "music with her silver sound" because musicians have no gold for sounding.
     "Then music with her silver sound
     With speedy help doth lend redress."

[*Exit.*]

First Musician. What a pestilent knave is this same!

Second Musician. Hang him, Jack! Come, we'll in here. Tarry for the mourners, and stay dinner.

[*Exeunt.*]

COLLABORATIVE DISCUSSION With a partner, discuss the measures taken by Juliet and Friar Laurence to fool Juliet's family. Do you agree with their plan and think there were no other options, or do you think the plan was selfish or unwise? Support your ideas with details from the play.

Analyzing the Text

Cite Text Evidence Support your responses with evidence from the selection.

1. **Analyze** Review Juliet's dialogue with Paris in Scene 1. If Juliet had never met Romeo, might she have fallen in love with Paris? Explain your response.

2. **Identify** Shakespeare often employs a literary technique known as dramatic irony. **Dramatic irony** exists when the reader or viewer knows something that one or more of the characters do not. For example, when Paris asks Juliet to confess to Friar Laurence that she loves him, she carefully avoids denying it. We know that Juliet loves Romeo, not Paris. Identify two other examples of dramatic irony in Act IV. Explain how these ironic moments contribute to the building tension in the play.

3. **Analyze** In Scene 2, how does Shakespeare increase the pace of the plot even further? What effect is this likely to have on the audience?

4. **Interpret** What fears does Juliet have before going through with Friar Laurence's plan? What do her fears reveal about her state of mind?

5. **Compare** Juliet drinks the sleeping potion, despite her fears. What does this reveal about her character? Has she changed from the beginning of the play, before she met Romeo? Explain your response.

6. **Analyze** Shakespeare includes a humorous exchange between Peter and the musicians at the end of Act IV, right after Juliet's family discovers her body. What is the impact of this choice on the audience? What message is conveyed by having a humorous scene immediately follow a tragic one?

PERFORMANCE TASK

Speaking and Writing Activity: Dramatic Reading and Letter Explore through reading and writing the plan devised by Friar Laurence to fool Juliet's family.

1. In a small group, read aloud Scene 4 and Scene 5 (lines 1–21) of Act IV.

2. Listen for the excitement expressed by the characters in Scene 4. Contrast this with their grief in Scene 5.

3. Then think about what Juliet might say to her family to explain her actions. Work together to write a letter from Juliet in which she explains why she felt she had no other options.

In your dramatic reading, try to capture the emotion of the words on the page as Shakespeare wrote them. Your letter from Juliet should be based on details in the play.

AS YOU READ Notice the unexpected events, misunderstandings, and examples of poor timing that finally bring the play to its tragic end. Write down any questions you generate during reading.

ACT V

Scene 1 *A street in Mantua.*

[*Enter* Romeo.]

Romeo. If I may trust the flattering truth of sleep,
My dreams presage some joyful news at hand.
My bosom's lord sits lightly in his throne,
And all this day an unaccustomed spirit
5 Lifts me above the ground with cheerful thoughts.
I dreamt my lady came and found me dead
(Strange dream that gives a dead man leave to think!)
And breathed such life with kisses in my lips
That I revived and was an emperor.
10 Ah me! how sweet is love itself possessed,
When but love's shadows are so rich in joy!

[*Enter Romeo's servant,* Balthasar, *booted.*]

News from Verona! How now, Balthasar?
Dost thou not bring me letters from the friar?
How doth my lady? Is my father well?
15 How fares my Juliet? That I ask again,
For nothing can be ill if she be well.

Balthasar. Then she is well, and nothing can be ill.
Her body sleeps in Capels' monument,
And her immortal part with angels lives.
20 I saw her laid low in her kindred's vault
And presently took post to tell it you.
O, pardon me for bringing these ill news,
Since you did leave it for my office, sir.

Romeo. Is it e'en so? Then I defy you, stars!
25 Thou knowst my lodging. Get me ink and paper
And hire posthorses. I will hence tonight.

Balthasar. I do beseech you, sir, have patience.
Your looks are pale and wild and do import
Some misadventure.

Romeo.   Tush, thou art deceived.
30 Leave me and do the thing I bid thee do.
Hast thou no letters to me from the friar?

Balthasar. No, my good lord.

17–19 Balthasar replies that Juliet is well, since although her body lies in the Capulets' (**Capels'**) burial vault, her soul (**her immortal part**) is with the angels.

21 presently took post: immediately rode (to Mantua).

23 you did . . . office: you gave me the duty of reporting important news to you.

24 I . . . stars: Romeo angrily challenges fate, which has caused him so much grief.

28–29 import some misadventure: suggest that something bad will happen.

Romeo.   No matter. Get thee gone
And hire those horses. I'll be with thee straight.

[*Exit* Balthasar.]

Well, Juliet, I will lie with thee tonight.
35 Let's see for means. O mischief, thou art swift
To enter in the thoughts of desperate men!
I do remember an apothecary,
And hereabouts he dwells, which late I noted
In tattered weeds, with overwhelming brows,
40 Culling of simples. Meager were his looks,
Sharp misery had worn him to the bones;
And in his needy shop a tortoise hung,
An alligator stuffed, and other skins
Of ill-shaped fishes; and about his shelves
45 A beggarly account of empty boxes,
Green earthen pots, bladders, and musty seeds,
Remnants of packthread, and old cakes of roses
Were thinly scattered, to make up a show.
Noting this penury, to myself I said,
50 "An if a man did need a poison now
Whose sale is present death in Mantua,
Here lives a caitiff wretch would sell it him."
O, this same thought did but forerun my need,
And this same needy man must sell it me.
55 As I remember, this should be the house.
Being holiday, the beggar's shop is shut.
What, ho! apothecary!

[*Enter* Apothecary.]

Apothecary.   Who calls so loud?

Romeo. Come hither, man. I see that thou art poor.
Hold, there is forty ducats. Let me have
60 A dram of poison, such soon-speeding gear
As will disperse itself through all the veins
That the life-weary taker may fall dead,
And that the trunk may be discharged of breath
As violently as hasty powder fired
65 Doth hurry from the fatal cannon's womb.

Apothecary. Such mortal drugs I have; but Mantua's law
Is death to any he that utters them.

Romeo. Art thou so bare and full of wretchedness
And fearest to die? Famine is in thy cheeks,
70 Need and oppression starveth in thine eyes,
Contempt and beggary hangs upon thy back:

35–40 Let's ... means: Let me find a way (to join Juliet in death); **apothecary:** pharmacist; **tattered weeds:** ragged clothes; **culling of simples:** selecting herbs.

47 cakes of roses: rose petals pressed together to create a perfume.

49 penury: poverty.

50–52 "An if a man ... sell it him": Though it is a crime to sell poison in Mantua, the apothecary is such a miserable (**caitiff**) wretch that he would probably do it for the money.

59 ducats: gold coins.

60–65 Romeo wants fast-acting (**soon-speeding**) poison that will work as quickly as gunpowder exploding in a cannon.

67 any ... them: any person who dispenses or sells them.

The world is not thy friend, nor the world's law;
The world affords no law to make thee rich;
Then be not poor, but break it and take this.

75 **Apothecary.** My poverty but not my will consents.

Romeo. I pay thy poverty and not thy will.

Apothecary. Put this in any liquid thing you will
And drink it off, and if you had the strength
Of twenty men, it would dispatch you straight.

80 **Romeo.** There is thy gold—worse poison to men's souls,
Doing more murder in this loathsome world,
Than these poor compounds that thou mayst not sell.
I sell thee poison; thou hast sold me none.
Farewell. Buy food and get thyself in flesh.

85 Come, cordial and not poison, go with me
To Juliet's grave; for there must I use thee.

[*Exeunt.*]

Scene 2 *Friar Laurence's cell in Verona.*

[*Enter* Friar John.]

Friar John. Holy Franciscan friar, brother, ho!

[*Enter* Friar Laurence.]

Friar Laurence. This same should be the voice of Friar John.
Welcome from Mantua. What says Romeo?
Or, if his mind be writ, give me his letter.

5 **Friar John.** Going to find a barefoot brother out,
One of our order to associate me,
Here in this city visiting the sick,
And finding him, the searchers of the town,
Suspecting that we both were in a house

10 Where the infectious pestilence did reign,
Sealed up the doors, and would not let us forth,
So that my speed to Mantua there was stayed.

Friar Laurence. Who bare my letter, then, to Romeo?

Friar John. I could not send it—here it is again—

15 Nor get a messenger to bring it thee,
So fearful were they of infection.

Friar Laurence. Unhappy fortune! By my brotherhood,
The letter was not nice, but full of charge,
Of dear import, and the neglecting it

20 May do much danger. Friar John, go hence,

72–74 Romeo urges the apothecary to improve his situation by breaking the law and selling him the poison.

75 I'm doing this for the money, not because I think it's right.

79 dispatch you straight: kill you instantly.

85 Romeo refers to the poison as a **cordial,** a drink believed to be good for the heart.

5–12 Friar John asked another friar (**barefoot brother**) to go with him to Mantua. The health officials of the town, believing that the friars had come into contact with a deadly plague (**infectious pestilence**), locked them up to keep them from infecting others.

13 bare: carried (bore).

18–20 The letter wasn't trivial (**nice**) but contained a message of great importance (**dear import**). The fact that it wasn't sent (**neglecting it**) may cause great harm.

Get me an iron crow and bring it straight
Unto my cell.

Friar John.   Brother, I'll go and bring it thee.

[*Exit.*]

Friar Laurence. Now must I to the monument alone.
Within this three hours will fair Juliet wake.
25 She will beshrew me much that Romeo
Hath had no notice of these accidents;
But I will write again to Mantua,
And keep her at my cell till Romeo come—
Poor living corse, closed in a dead man's tomb!

[*Exit.*]

Scene 3 *The cemetery that contains the Capulets' tomb.*

[*Enter* Paris *and his* Page *with flowers and a torch.*]

Paris. Give me thy torch, boy. Hence, and stand aloof.
Yet put it out, for I would not be seen.
Under yond yew tree lay thee all along,
Holding thine ear close to the hollow ground.
5 So shall no foot upon the churchyard tread
(Being loose, unfirm, with digging up of graves)
But thou shalt hear it. Whistle then to me,
As signal that thou hearst something approach.
Give me those flowers. Do as I bid thee, go.

10 **Page** [*aside*]. I am almost afraid to stand alone
Here in the churchyard; yet I will adventure.

[*withdraws*]

21 **iron crow:** crowbar.

25–26 **She . . .
accidents:** She will be
furious with me when
she learns that Romeo
doesn't know what has
happened.

1 **aloof:** some distance
away.

Paris. Sweet flower, with flowers thy bridal bed I strew

[*He strews the tomb with flowers.*]

(O woe! thy canopy is dust and stones)
Which with sweet water nightly I will dew;
15 Or, wanting that, with tears distilled by moans.
The obsequies that I for thee will keep
Nightly shall be to strew thy grave and weep.

[*The* Page *whistles.*]

The boy gives warning something doth approach.
What cursed foot wanders this way tonight
20 To cross my obsequies and true love's rite?
What, with a torch? Muffle me, night, awhile.

[*withdraws*]

[*Enter* Romeo *and* Balthasar *with a torch, a mattock, and a crow of iron.*]

Romeo. Give me that mattock and the wrenching iron.
Hold, take this letter. Early in the morning
See thou deliver it to my lord and father.
25 Give me the light. Upon thy life I charge thee,
Whate'er thou hearest or seest, stand all aloof
And do not interrupt me in my course.
Why I descend into this bed of death
Is partly to behold my lady's face,
30 But chiefly to take thence from her dead finger
A precious ring—a ring that I must use
In dear employment. Therefore hence, be gone.
But if thou, jealous, dost return to pry
In what I farther shall intend to do,
35 By heaven, I will tear thee joint by joint
And strew this hungry churchyard with thy limbs.
The time and my intents are savage-wild,
More fierce and more inexorable far
Than empty tigers or the roaring sea.

40 **Balthasar.** I will be gone, sir, and not trouble you.

Romeo. So shalt thou show me friendship. Take thou that.
Live, and be prosperous; and farewell, good fellow.

Balthasar [*aside*]. For all this same, I'll hide me hereabout.
His looks I fear, and his intents I doubt.

[*withdraws*]

45 **Romeo.** Thou detestable maw, thou womb of death,
Gorged with the dearest morsel of the earth,

12–17 Paris promises to decorate Juliet's grave with flowers and sprinkle it with either perfume (**sweet water**) or his tears. He will perform these honoring rites (**obsequies**) every night.

20 cross: interfere with.

21 muffle: hide.

mattock . . . iron: an ax and a crowbar.

32 in dear employment: for an important purpose.

33 jealous: curious.

37–39 Romeo's intention is more unstoppable (**inexorable**) than hungry (**empty**) tigers or the waves of an ocean.

45–48 Romeo addresses the tomb as though it were devouring people. He calls it a hateful stomach (**detestable maw**) that is filled (**gorged**) with Juliet, the **dearest morsel of the earth**.

Thus I enforce thy rotten jaws to open,
And in despite I'll cram thee with more food.

[Romeo *opens the tomb.*]

Paris. This is that banish'd haughty Montague
50 That murdered my love's cousin—with which grief
It is supposed the fair creature died—
And here is come to do some villainous shame
To the dead bodies. I will apprehend him.
Stop thy unhallowed toil, vile Montague!
55 Can vengeance be pursued further than death?
Condemned villain, I do apprehend thee.
Obey, and go with me; for thou must die.

Romeo. I must indeed; and therefore came I hither.
Good gentle youth, tempt not a desp'rate man.
60 Fly hence and leave me. Think upon these gone;
Let them affright thee. I beseech thee, youth,
Put not another sin upon my head
By urging me to fury. O, be gone!
By heaven, I love thee better than myself.
65 For I come hither armed against myself.
Stay not, be gone. Live, and hereafter say
A madman's mercy bid thee run away.

Paris. I do defy thy conjuration
And apprehend thee for a felon here.

70 **Romeo.** Wilt thou provoke me? Then have at thee, boy!

[*They fight.*]

Page. O Lord, they fight! I will go call the watch.

[*Exit.*]

Paris. O, I am slain! [*falls*] If thou be merciful,
Open the tomb, lay me with Juliet.

[*dies*]

Romeo. In faith, I will. Let me peruse this face.
75 Mercutio's kinsman, noble County Paris!
What said my man when my betossed soul
Did not attend him as we rode? I think
He told me Paris should have married Juliet.
Said he not so? or did I dream it so?
80 Or am I mad, hearing him talk of Juliet,
To think it was so? O, give me thy hand,
One writ with me in sour misfortune's book!
I'll bury thee in a triumphant grave.
A grave? O, no, a lantern, slaughtered youth,

49–53 Recognizing Romeo, Paris speaks these first few lines to himself. He is angry with Romeo, believing that Romeo's killing Tybalt caused Juliet to die of grief.

68 I reject your appeal.

82 Romeo notes that, like himself, Paris has been a victim of bad luck.

84–87 Romeo will bury Paris with Juliet, whose beauty fills the tomb with light. Paris' corpse (**Death**) is being buried (**interred**) by a dead man in that Romeo expects to be dead soon.

85 For here lies Juliet, and her beauty makes
This vault a feasting presence full of light.
Death, lie thou there, by a dead man interred.

[*lays* Paris *in the tomb*]

How oft when men are at the point of death
Have they been merry! which their keepers call
90 A lightning before death. O, how may I
Call this a lightning? O my love! my wife!
Death, that hath sucked the honey of thy breath,
Hath had no power yet upon thy beauty.
Thou art not conquered. Beauty's ensign yet

94 ensign: sign.

95 Is crimson in thy lips and in thy cheeks,
And death's pale flag is not advanced there.
Tybalt, liest thou there in thy bloody sheet?
O, what more favor can I do to thee
Than with that hand that cut thy youth in twain

98–100 O, what . . . enemy: I can best repay you (Tybalt) by killing your enemy (myself) with the same hand that cut your youth in two (**twain**).

100 To sunder his that was thine enemy?
Forgive me, cousin! Ah, dear Juliet,
Why art thou yet so fair? Shall I believe
That unsubstantial Death is amorous,
And that the lean abhorred monster keeps

102–105 Romeo can't get over how beautiful Juliet still looks. He asks whether Death is loving (**amorous**) and whether it has taken Juliet as its lover (**paramour**).

105 Thee here in dark to be his paramour?
For fear of that I still will stay with thee
And never from this palace of dim night
Depart again. Here, here will I remain
With worms that are thy chambermaids. O, here
110 Will I set up my everlasting rest
And shake the yoke of inauspicious stars

111–112 shake . . . flesh: rid myself of the burden of an unhappy fate (**inauspicious stars**).

From this world-wearied flesh. Eyes, look your last!
Arms, take your last embrace! and, lips, O you
The doors of breath, seal with a righteous kiss
115 A dateless bargain to engrossing death!

115 dateless: eternal; never-ending. Romeo means that what he is about to do can never be undone.

Come, bitter conduct; come, unsavory guide!
Thou desperate pilot, now at once run on
The dashing rocks thy seasick weary bark!
Here's to my love! [*drinks*] O true apothecary!
120 Thy drugs are quick. Thus with a kiss I die.

117–118 Romeo compares himself to the pilot of a ship (**bark**) who is going to crash on the rocks because he is so weary and sick.

[*falls*]

[*Enter* Friar Laurence, *with lantern, crow, and spade.*]

Friar Laurence. Saint Francis be my speed! how oft tonight
Have my old feet stumbled at graves! Who's there?

Balthasar. Here's one, a friend, and one that knows you well.

Friar Laurence. Bliss be upon you! Tell me, good my friend,
125 What torch is yond that vainly lends his light
To grubs and eyeless skulls? As I discern,
It burneth in the Capels' monument.

Balthasar. It doth so, holy sir; and there's my master,
One that you love.

Friar Laurence.   Who is it?

Balthasar.   Romeo.

130 **Friar Laurence.** How long hath he been there?

Balthasar.   Full half an hour.

Friar Laurence. Go with me to the vault.

Balthasar.   I dare not, sir.
My master knows not but I am gone hence,
And fearfully did menace me with death
If I did stay to look on his intents.

135 **Friar Laurence.** Stay then; I'll go alone. Fear comes upon me.
O, much I fear some ill unthrifty thing.

Balthasar. As I did sleep under this yew tree here,
I dreamt my master and another fought,
And that my master slew him.

Friar Laurence.   Romeo!

[*stoops and looks on the blood and weapons*]

140 Alack, alack, what blood is this which stains
The stony entrance of this sepulcher?
What mean these masterless and gory swords
To lie discolored by this place of peace?

[*enters the tomb*]

Romeo! O, pale! Who else? What, Paris too?
145 And steeped in blood? Ah, what an unkind hour
Is guilty of this lamentable chance!
The lady stirs.

[Juliet *rises*.]

Juliet. O comfortable friar! where is my lord?
I do remember well where I should be,
150 And there I am. Where is my Romeo?

Friar Laurence. I hear some noise. Lady, come from that nest
Of death, contagion, and unnatural sleep.
A greater power than we can contradict
Hath thwarted our intents. Come, come away.

132–134 My master ... intents: My master told me to go away and threatened me with death if I watched what he did.

136 unthrifty: unlucky.

140–143 Alack ... place of peace? Why are these bloody swords lying here at the tomb (**sepulcher**), a place that should be peaceful? (The swords are also **masterless,** or without their owners.)

148 comfortable: comforting.

153–154 A greater ... intents: A greater force than we can fight (**contradict**) has ruined our plans (**thwarted our intents**).

155 Thy husband in thy bosom there lies dead;
And Paris too. Come, I'll dispose of thee
Among a sisterhood of holy nuns.
Stay not to question, for the watch is coming.
Come, go, good Juliet. I dare no longer stay.

160 **Juliet.** Go, get thee hence, for I will not away.

[*Exit* Friar Laurence.]

What's here? A cup, closed in my true love's hand?
Poison, I see, hath been his timeless end.
O churl! drunk all, and left no friendly drop
To help me after? I will kiss thy lips.
165 Haply some poison yet doth hang on them
To make me die with a restorative.

[*kisses him*]

Thy lips are warm!

Chief Watchman [*within*]. Lead, boy. Which way?

Juliet. Yea, noise? Then I'll be brief. O happy dagger!

[*snatches Romeo's dagger*]

170 This is thy sheath; there rust, and let me die.

[*She stabs herself and falls.*]

[*Enter* Watchmen *with the* Page *of Paris.*]

Page. This is the place. There, where the torch doth burn.

Chief Watchman. The ground is bloody. Search about the
churchyard.
Go, some of you; whoe'er you find attach.

156–157 I'll dispose . . . nuns: I'll find a place for you in a convent of nuns.

162 timeless: happening before its proper time.

163 churl: miser.

165 Haply: perhaps.

173 attach: arrest.

Image Credits: (t) ©Everett Collection, Inc.; (tr) ©AKaiser/Shutterstock

[*Exeunt some of the* Watch.]

Pitiful sight! here lies the County slain;
175 And Juliet bleeding, warm, and newly dead,
Who here hath lain this two days buried.
Go, tell the Prince; run to the Capulets;
Raise up the Montagues; some others search.

[*Exeunt others of the* Watch.]

We see the ground whereon these woes do lie,
180 But the true ground of all these piteous woes
We cannot without circumstance descry.

[*Reenter some of the* Watch, *with* Balthasar.]

Second Watchman. Here's Romeo's man. We found him in the
churchyard.

Chief Watchman. Hold him in safety till the Prince come hither.

[*Reenter* Friar Laurence *and another* Watchman.]

Third Watchman. Here is a friar that trembles, sighs, and weeps.
185 We took this mattock and this spade from him
As he was coming from this churchyard side.

Chief Watchman. A great suspicion! Stay the friar too.

[*Enter the* Prince *and* Attendants.]

Prince. What misadventure is so early up,
That calls our person from our morning rest?

[*Enter* Capulet, Lady Capulet, *and others.*]

190 **Capulet.** What should it be, that they so shriek abroad?

Lady Capulet. The people in the street cry "Romeo,"
Some "Juliet," and some "Paris"; and all run,
With open outcry, toward our monument.

Prince. What fear is this which startles in our ears?

195 **Chief Watchman.** Sovereign, here lies the County Paris slain;
And Romeo dead, and Juliet, dead before,
Warm and new killed.

Prince. Search, seek, and know how this foul murder comes.

Chief Watchman. Here is a friar, and slaughtered Romeo's man,
200 With instruments upon them fit to open
These dead men's tombs.

Capulet. O heavens! O wife, look how our daughter bleeds!
This dagger hath mista'en, for, lo, his house
Is empty on the back of Montague,
205 And it missheathed in my daughter's bosom!

178 Raise up: awaken.

**179–181 We see . . .
descry:** We see the earth
(**ground**) these bodies
lie on. But the real cause
(**true ground**) of these
deaths is yet for us to
discover (**descry**).

182–187 The guards
arrest Balthasar and Friar
Laurence as suspicious
characters.

194 startles: causes
alarm.

**203–205 This dagger
. . . in my daughter's
bosom:** This dagger
has missed its target. It
should rest in the sheath
(**house**) that Romeo
wears. Instead it is in
Juliet's chest.

Lady Capulet. O me! this sight of death is as a bell
That warns my old age to a sepulcher.

[*Enter* Montague *and others.*]

Prince. Come, Montague; for thou art early up
To see thy son and heir now early down.

210 **Montague.** Alas, my liege, my wife is dead tonight!
Grief of my son's exile hath stopped her breath.
What further woe conspires against mine age?

Prince. Look, and thou shalt see.

Montague. O thou untaught! what manners is in this,
215 To press before thy father to a grave?

Prince. Seal up the mouth of outrage for a while,
Till we can clear these ambiguities
And know their spring, their head, their true descent;
And then will I be general of your woes
220 And lead you even to death. Meantime forbear,
And let mischance be slave to patience.
Bring forth the parties of suspicion.

Friar Laurence. I am the greatest, able to do least,
Yet most suspected, as the time and place
225 Doth make against me, of this direful murder;
And here I stand, both to impeach and purge
Myself condemned and myself excused.

Prince. Then say at once what thou dost know in this.

Friar Laurence. I will be brief, for my short date of breath
230 Is not so long as is a tedious tale.
Romeo, there dead, was husband to that Juliet;
And she, there dead, that Romeo's faithful wife.
I married them; and their stol'n marriage day
Was Tybalt's doomsday, whose untimely death
235 Banish'd the new-made bridegroom from this city;
For whom, and not for Tybalt, Juliet pined.
You, to remove that siege of grief from her,
Betrothed and would have married her perforce
To County Paris. Then comes she to me
240 And with wild looks bid me devise some mean
To rid her from this second marriage,
Or in my cell there would she kill herself.
Then gave I her (so tutored by my art)
A sleeping potion; which so took effect
245 As I intended, for it wrought on her
The form of death. Meantime I writ to Romeo

210 liege: lord.

214–215 what manners . . . grave: What kind of behavior is this, for a son to die before his father?

216–221 Seal . . . patience: Stop your emotional outbursts until we can find out the source (**spring**) of these confusing events (**ambiguities**). Wait (**forbear**) and be patient, and let's find out what happened.

223–227 Friar Laurence confesses that he is most responsible for these events. He will both accuse (**impeach**) himself and clear (**purge**) himself of guilt.

236 It was Romeo's banishment, not Tybalt's death, that made Juliet so sad.

That he should hither come as this dire night
To help to take her from her borrowed grave,
Being the time the potion's force should cease.

248 **borrowed:** temporary.

250 But he which bore my letter, Friar John,
Was stayed by accident, and yesternight
Returned my letter back. Then all alone
At the prefixed hour of her waking
Came I to take her from her kindred's vault;

254 **kindred's:** family's.

255 Meaning to keep her closely at my cell
Till I conveniently could send to Romeo.
But when I came, some minute ere the time
Of her awaking, here untimely lay
The noble Paris and true Romeo dead.

260 She wakes; and I entreated her come forth
And bear this work of heaven with patience;
But then a noise did scare me from the tomb,
And she, too desperate, would not go with me,
But, as it seems, did violence on herself.

265 All this I know, and to the marriage
Her nurse is privy; and if aught in this
Miscarried by my fault, let my old life
Be sacrificed, some hour before his time,
Unto the rigor of severest law.

265–269 **and to ...law:** Her nurse can bear witness to this secret marriage. If I am responsible for any of this, let the law punish me with death.

270 **Prince.** We still have known thee for a holy man.
Where's Romeo's man? What can he say in this?

Balthasar. I brought my master news of Juliet's death;
And then in post he came from Mantua
To this same place, to this same monument.

273 **in post:** at full speed.

275 This letter he early bid me give his father,
And threatened me with death, going in the vault,
If I departed not and left him there.

Prince. Give me the letter. I will look on it.
Where is the County's page that raised the watch?
280 Sirrah, what made your master in this place?

279–280 The Prince asks for Paris' servant, who notified the guards (**raised the watch**). Then he asks the servant why Paris was at the cemetery.

Page. He came with flowers to strew his lady's grave;
And bid me stand aloof, and so I did.
Anon comes one with light to ope the tomb;
And by-and-by my master drew on him;
285 And then I ran away to call the watch.

283–285 **Anon ... call the watch:** Soon (**anon**) someone with a light came and opened the tomb. Paris drew his sword, and I ran to call the guards.

Prince. This letter doth make good the friar's words,
Their course of love, the tidings of her death;
And here he writes that he did buy a poison
Of a poor 'pothecary, and therewithal

290   Came to this vault to die and lie with Juliet.
Where be these enemies? Capulet, Montague,
See what a scourge is laid upon your hate,
That heaven finds means to kill your joys with love!
And I, for winking at your discords too,
295   Have lost a brace of kinsmen. All are punished.

Capulet. O brother Montague, give me thy hand.
This is my daughter's jointure, for no more
Can I demand.

Montague.   But I can give thee more;
For I will raise her statue in pure gold,
300   That whiles Verona by that name is known,
There shall no figure at such rate be set
As that of true and faithful Juliet.

Capulet. As rich shall Romeo's by his lady's lie—
Poor sacrifices of our enmity!

305   **Prince.** A glooming peace this morning with it brings.
The sun for sorrow will not show his head.
Go hence, to have more talk of these sad things;
Some shall be pardoned, and some punished;
For never was a story of more woe
310   Than this of Juliet and her Romeo.

[*Exeunt.*]

292–295 See what . . . punished: Look at the punishment your hatred has brought on you. Heaven has killed your children (**joys**) with love. For shutting my eyes to your arguments (**discords**), I have lost two relatives. We have all been punished.

297–298 jointure: dowry, the payment a bride's father traditionally made to the groom. Capulet means that no one could demand more of a bride's father than he has already paid.

301 at such rate be set: be valued so highly.

303–304 Capulet promises to do for Romeo what Montague will do for Juliet. Their children have become sacrifices to their hatred (**enmity**).

COLLABORATIVE DISCUSSION Working in a small group, review the events that lead to the tragic ending. Then discuss what makes *The Tragedy of Romeo and Juliet* still popular with today's audiences.

Analyze Character: Motivations

Characters in a literary work, like real people, have **motivations,** or reasons. for their actions. A character can be motivated by a variety of factors: by a goal, by loyalty to a group or cause, or by an emotion such as love, anger, or jealousy. A **complex character** is one who is driven by multiple, and sometimes conflicting, motivations at the same time.

In *Romeo and Juliet*, the character of Tybalt is an example of a character who is not particularly complex. What is Tybalt's single motivation before he meets his demise? The characters of Romeo and Juliet, on the other hand, are complex characters tormented throughout the play by conflicting motivations. Their struggles form the basis of the action in the play—and time after time prevent them from being able to live happily ever after. Think about the following factors:

- **Family obligation** In what ways do their families create conflict in their lives?
- **Love and passion** How does their love motivate them to meet new challenges?
- **Fear** How does fear shape their actions and prevent them from living and loving each other freely?
- **Misunderstanding** What twists and turns in the plot, as well as miscommunication, create conflict and drive them to make bad choices?
- **Despair** What actions by Romeo and Juliet are driven by extreme feelings of hopelessness?

Analyze Author's Choices: Parallel Plots

Romeo and Juliet is not a simple love story. It is a complex drama featuring **parallel plots**—separate story lines happening at the same time and linked by common characters and themes. The chart can help you identify and understand parallel plots in the play.

Plot	Purpose
The feud between the Capulets and the Montagues	How does this plot contribute to the drama of the play?
Romeo's unrequited love for Rosaline	What do we learn about Romeo through this experience?
Juliet's marriage proposal from Paris	What do we learn about Juliet and her relationship with her family?

Shakespeare also carefully structures his drama in a meaningful way. Recall that Acts I and II are comedic, featuring jokes and young love, while Act III leads to the final tragedy. What is the effect of this contrast?

Analyzing the Text

Cite Text Evidence Support your responses with evidence from the selection.

1. **Interpret** What dream does Romeo describe at the beginning of Act V, Scene 1? What part of his dream foreshadows events to come?

2. **Analyze** What plan does Romeo immediately formulate when he learns of Juliet's death? What does his response to her death expose about his character?

3. **Infer** In Scene 2, why is Friar Laurence in a panic when he finds out that his letter was not delivered to Romeo? Why is this a key turning point in the plot?

4. **Analyze** Reread Friar Laurence's speech in Scene 3, lines 223–269. What various and possibly conflicting motivations does he have for making these remarks?

5. **Interpret** Whom does Prince Escalus blame for the tragic events? Support your answer with details from his words in the last scene of the play.

6. **Connect** Recall Juliet's response when her mother suggests the idea of marrying Paris (Act I, Scene 3, lines 98–100). What does this reveal about Juliet's character before she meets Romeo? How does this contrast with Romeo's character in the parallel plot involving Rosaline? By Act V, how has Juliet changed?

7. **Analyze** Fate, or forces over which people have no control, is an important theme in this tragedy. Many events are blamed upon fate, starting with Shakespeare's description of Romeo and Juliet as "star-crossed lovers" in the Prologue. However, many events can also be blamed on the actions of characters. Do you believe fate or free will caused this tragic ending? Explain.

8. **Analyze** In a tragedy, a hero or heroine's character flaw is usually the cause of his or her downfall. Do you believe Romeo or Juliet had a character flaw that led to his or her death? Support your idea with evidence from the play.

PERFORMANCE TASK

Writing Activity: Eulogy Use your knowledge of Romeo and Juliet to write a eulogy, a tribute to someone who has died, for both of them.

1. With a partner, brainstorm important details about their lives and their relationship. Think about their motivations, how they fell in love, the challenges they faced, and how they changed each other.

2. With your partner, craft your eulogy, highlighting key details about the characters of the two young people. Be sure your ideas are grounded in details from the play.

In both pieces of writing, include evidence from the text and use the conventions of standard English.

Vocabulary Strategy: Puns

Shakespeare was a master of clever word play, including the use of puns. A **pun** is a joke built upon multiple meanings of a word or upon two words that sound similar but have different meanings. Near the end of Act IV, Peter challenges the musicians to help him develop a pun based on a verse.

> **Peter.** "When griping grief the heart doth wound
> And doleful dumps the mind oppress,
> Then music with her silver sound—"
>
> Why "silver sound"? Why "music with her silver sound"?—What say you, Simon Catling?
>
> **First Musician.** Marry, sir, because silver hath a sweet sound.
>
> **Peter.** Pretty! What say you, Hugh Rebeck?
>
> **Second Musician.** I say "silver sound" because musicians sound for silver.
>
> **Peter.** Pretty too! What say you, James Soundpost?
>
> **Third Musician.** Faith, I know not what to say.
>
> **Peter.** Oh, I cry you mercy, you are the singer. I will say for you. It is "music with her silver sound" because musicians have no gold for sounding.

Notice the multiple meanings for the phrase *silver sound*. The first musician uses *sound* as a noun. The adjective *silver* has a pleasant connotation, making the phrase mean "a sweet or beautiful sound." The second musician and Peter use *sound* as a verb. They use the word *silver* as a reference to money and to a metal that has a lesser value than gold. To the second musician and Peter, the phrase *silver sound* means "to make music for money, silver money, though, not gold."

Practice and Apply With a partner, locate and explain these puns from the play. Then brainstorm a few multiple-meaning words and words that sound similar but have different meanings that you could use in original puns. Write a brief dialogue like the one between Peter and the musicians that uses your puns.

1. "You have dancing shoes / With nimble soles; I have a soul of lead / So stakes me to the ground I cannot move." (Act I, Scene 4, lines 14–16)

2. "Ask for me tomorrow, and you shall find me a grave man." (Act III, Scene 1, lines 91–92)

Language and Style: Parallel Structure

Parallel structure is the repetition of words, phrases, or grammatical structures in order to add emphasis or to improve the sound and rhythm of a piece of writing. Shakespeare regularly makes use of parallel structure to create cadence, or a balanced, rhythmic flow of words. Here is an example from Act II, Scene 1, lines 8–11:

> Appear thou in the likeness of a sigh;
> Speak but one rhyme, and I am satisfied!
> Cry but "Ay me!" pronounce but "love" and "dove";
> Speak to my gossip Venus one fair word . . .

Shakespeare repeats the phrasing of a verb followed by *but*: "Speak but . . . Cry but . . . pronounce but. . . ." The parallel grammatical structures give equal weight to each phrase. Any one of these three tiny gestures from Rosaline, Mercutio jokes, would cause lovesick Romeo to rejoice. Read the passage aloud and you will hear the cadence that the parallel structures lend to the verse.

This example from Act I, Scene 5, lines 10–11 contains a series of four past-tense verbs, each followed by the word *for*:

> You are looked for and called for, asked for and sought for, in
> the great chamber.

In this case, the speaker (a servant) sounds rather ridiculous, as if he is trying to use flowery language to deliver a simple message.

In the next example, from Act IV Scene 1, lines 102–103, Shakespeare repeats three parallel adjectives:

> Each part, deprived of supple government,
> Shall, stiff and stark and cold, appear like death;

Friar Laurence uses these grim adjectives to describe what Juliet's body will be like once she drinks the potion. The repetition gives his speech a somber rhythm, like a funeral march.

Practice and Apply Revise the eulogy you wrote in this selection's Performance Task to include at least two examples of parallel structures. Share your revised work with a partner and discuss how the parallel structures increase the power and clarity of your language.

Publius Ovidius Naso (Ovid) (43 BC–AD 17) *is considered one of the greatest Roman poets. His family expected him to become a government official. However, his overriding interest in writing poetry initiated a change in career. His first published work,* Amores (The Loves), *a series of short poems about a love affair, was a success. After becoming popular through his early poems about love and intrigue, he started an ambitious narrative poem called* Metamorphoses. *This work retells important myths from ancient Greece and Rome, including "Pyramus and Thisbe."*

Pyramus and Thisbe

Myth Retold by Ovid   Translated by Allen Mandelbaum

AS YOU READ Pay attention to the similarities between the plot of this myth and other stories you have read or movies that you have seen. Write down any questions you generate during reading.

The house of Pyramus[1] and that of Thisbe[2]
stood side by side within the mighty city
ringed by the tall brick walls Semíramis
had built[3]—so we are told. If you searched all
5   the East, you'd find no girl with greater charm
than Thisbe; and no boy in Babylon
was handsomer than Pyramus. They owed
their first encounters to their living close
beside each other—but with time, love grows.
10 Theirs did—indeed they wanted to be wed,
but marriage was forbidden by their parents:
yet there's one thing that parents can't prevent:

---

[1] **Pyramus** (pĭr´ə-məs).
[2] **Thisbe** (thĭz´be).
[3] **the mighty city . . . had built:** the walled city of Babylon (băb´ə-lən), the ruins of which are south of Baghdad, Iraq. In Greek mythology, it was founded by Semíramis (sə-mĭr´ə-məs), a powerful Assyrian queen.

the flame of love that burned in both of them.
They had no confidant—and so used signs:
15 with these each lover read the other's mind:
when covered, fire acquires still more force.

The wall their houses shared had one thin crack,
which formed when they were built and then was left;
in all these years, no one had seen that cleft;
20 but lovers will discover every thing:
you were the first to find it, and you made
that cleft a passageway which speech could take.
For there the least of whispers was kept safe:
it crossed that cleft with words of tenderness.
25 And Pyramus and Thisbe often stood,
he on this side and she on that; and when
each heard the other sigh, the lovers said:
"O jealous wall, why do you block our path?
Oh wouldn't it be better if you let
30 our bodies join each other fully or,
if that is asking for too much, just stretched
your fissure wide enough to let us kiss!
And we are not ungrateful: we admit
our words reach loving ears." And having talked
35 in vain, the lovers still remained apart.
Just so, one night, they wished each other well,
and each delivered kisses to the wall—
although those kisses could not reach their goal.
But on the morning after, when firstlight
40 had banished night's bright star-fires from the sky
and sun had left the brine-soaked[4] meadows dry,
again they took their places at the cleft.
Then, in low whispers—after their laments—
those two devised this plan: they'd circumvent
45 their guardians' watchful eyes[5] and, cloaked by night,
in silence, slip out from their homes and reach
a site outside the city. Lest each lose
the other as they wandered separately
across the open fields, they were to meet
50 at Ninus' tomb[6] and hide beneath a tree
in darkness; for beside that tomb there stood

---

[4] **brine-soaked:** dew-covered.

[5] **they'd circumvent . . . eyes:** They would sneak past their parents.

[6] **Ninus' (nī´nəs) tomb:** According to Greek legend, King Ninus was Semíramis'
husband. When he died, she marked his burial place with a tall monument
outside the walls of Babylon.

a tall mulberry[7] close to a cool spring,
a tree well weighted down with snow-white berries.
Delighted with their plan—impatiently—
55 they waited for the close of day. At last
the sun plunged down into the waves, and night
emerged from those same waves.

                    Now Thisbe takes
great care, that none detect her as she makes
her way out from the house amid the dark;
60 her face is veiled; she finds the tomb; she sits
beneath the tree they'd chosen for their tryst.
Love made her bold. But now a lioness
just done with killing oxen—blood dripped down
her jaws, her mouth was frothing—comes to slake
65 her thirst at a cool spring close to the tree.
By moonlight, Thisbe sees the savage beast;
with trembling feet, the girl is quick to seek
a shadowed cave; but even as she flees,
her shawl slips from her shoulders. Thirst appeased,
70 the lioness is heading for the woods
when she, by chance, spies the abandoned shawl
upon the ground and, with her bloodstained jaws,
tears it to tatters.

              Pyramus had left
a little later than his Thisbe had,
75 and he could see what surely were the tracks
of a wild beast left clearly on deep dust.
His face grew ashen. And when he had found
the bloodstained shawl, he cried: "Now this same night
will see two lovers lose their lives: she was
80 the one more worthy of long life: it's I
who bear the guilt for this. O my poor girl,
it's I who led you to your death; I said
you were to reach this fearful place by night;
I let you be the first who would arrive.
85 O all you lions with your lairs beneath
this cliff, come now, and with your fierce jaws feast
upon my wretched guts! But cowards talk
as I do—longing for their death but not
prepared to act." At this he gathered up
90 the bloody tatters of his Thisbe's shawl

_____

[7] **mulberry:** a type of tree that produces small, sweet berries, which are usually
deep red or purple in color.

and set them underneath the shady tree
where he and she had planned to meet. He wept
and cried out as he held that dear shawl fast:
"Now drink from my blood, too!" And then he drew
95 his dagger from his belt and thrust it hard
into his guts. And as he died, he wrenched
the dagger from his gushing wound. He fell,
supine, along the ground. The blood leaped high;
it spouted like a broken leaden pipe
100 that, through a slender hole where it is worn,
sends out a long and hissing stream as jets
of water cleave the air. And that tree's fruits,
snow-white before, are bloodstained now; the roots
are also drenched with Pyramus' dark blood,
105 and from those roots the hanging berries draw
a darker, purple color.

Now the girl
again seeks out the tree: though trembling still,
she would not fail his tryst;[8] with eyes and soul
she looks for Pyramus; she wants to tell
110 her lover how she had escaped such perils.
She finds the place—the tree's familiar shape;
but seeing all the berries' color changed,
she is not sure. And as she hesitates,
she sights the writhing body on the ground—
115 the bloody limbs—and, paler than boxwood,[9]
retreats; she trembles—even as the sea
when light wind stirs its surface. She is quick
to recognize her lover; with loud blows
she beats her arms—though they do not deserve
120 such punishment. She tears her hair, enfolds
her love's dear form; she fills his wounds with tears
that mingle with his blood; and while she plants
her kisses on his cold face, she laments:
"What struck you, Pyramus? Why have I lost
125 my love? It is your Thisbe—I—who call
your name! Respond! Lift up your fallen head!"
He heard her name; and lifting up his eyes
weighed down by death, he saw her face—and then
he closed his eyes again.

---

[8] **fail his tryst:** neglect to meet him.
[9] **boxwood:** a white or light yellow type of wood.

                        She recognized
130   her own shawl and his dagger's ivory sheath.
      She cried: "Dear boy, you died by your own hand:
      your love has killed you. But I, too, command
      the force to face at least this task: I can
      claim love, and it will give me strength enough
135   to strike myself. I'll follow you in death;
      and men will say that I—unfortunate—
      was both the cause and comrade of your fate.
      Nothing but death could sever you from me;
      but now death has no power to prevent
140   my joining you. I call upon his parents
      and mine; I plead for him and me—do not
      deny to us—united by true love,
      who share this fatal moment—one same tomb.
      And may you, mulberry, whose boughs now shade
145   one wretched body and will soon shade two,
      forever bear these darkly colored fruits
      as signs of our sad end, that men remember
      the death we met together." With these words,
      she placed the dagger's point beneath her breast,
150   then leaned against the blade still warm with her
      dear lover's blood. The gods and parents heard
      her prayer, and they were stirred. Her wish was granted.

COLLABORATIVE DISCUSSION With a partner, discuss the underlying
story of this myth. How is it similar to other stories you have read or
movies you have seen? Cite details from the myth as you compare it with
other stories.

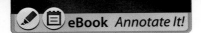

Analyze Source Material

Authors often gain inspiration from the works of other writers. For example, in his retelling of "Pyramus and Thisbe," Ovid was influenced by an ancient myth, passed down orally and in writing for generations. Ovid transformed the story of the unlucky Pyramus and Thisbe into a narrative poem by approaching the themes and topic from a fresh perspective, adjusting the character development, and strengthening the structure of the earlier myth. In the same manner, Shakespeare was influenced by and drew upon the works of Ovid as he wrote *The Tragedy of Romeo and Juliet*. Consider these points as you analyze how an author draws upon and transforms ideas from a specific text.

- What elements does the writer borrow from the source text?
- Do the texts share a topic or theme—that is, an enduring message?
- How does the writer transform elements from the original text?

Analyzing the Text

Cite Text Evidence   Support your responses with evidence from the selection.

1. **Connect** In the Prologue to *Romeo and Juliet*, the play is summarized in this manner, "A pair of star-crossed lovers take their life, / Whose misadventured piteous overthrows / Doth with their death bury their parents' strife." What changes did Shakespeare make to the central ideas of "Pyramus and Thisbe"?

2. **Compare** Reread lines 107–152 in the poem. How does this scene compare to Act V, Scene 3, lines 74–120, of *Romeo and Juliet*?

3. **Connect** What common **theme,** or message, can be attributed to both "Pyramus and Thisbe" and *Romeo and Juliet*? Is this theme still relevant to audiences today? Cite evidence from both sources.

PERFORMANCE TASK

Writing Activity: Essay Write a comparison of "Pyramus and Thisbe" and *Romeo and Juliet*.

- Consider the fact that *Romeo and Juliet* is a play, while "Pyramus and Thisbe" is a narrative poem.
- Compare and contrast the play and the narrative poem in terms of plot, conflict, and characters.
- In your essay, consider how the genre of each text affects these elements.
- Review your essay with a partner and revise for standard English grammar and usage.

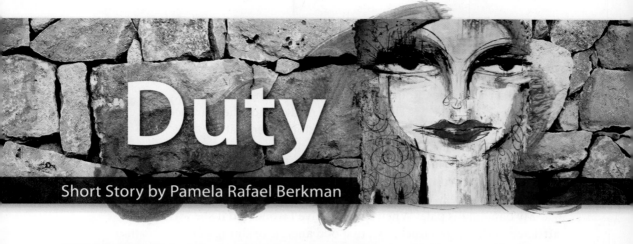

Duty

Short Story by Pamela Rafael Berkman

AS YOU READ Notice who is telling the story and think about what you already know about the play *The Tragedy of Romeo and Juliet.* Write down any questions you generate during reading.

We heard the running in the streets, we heard the name "Romeo!" called out, but not "Juliet." We had no reason to think Juliet. We knew nothing of what had happened, we thought our daughter already dead. But then we found ourselves summoned, not by servants but by armed men, come from the prince. We were sent for, my husband and I, to come to the opening of our tomb, the tomb of our family, the great yawning maw[1] of death. It had been newly fed.

When we came we found the stone rolled away, like that which covered Our Savior's grave.[2] Now I stand over the bodies of my girl and my enemy's boy, here in the dusty crypt. They are coiled like pale snakes, young serpents of death, he contorted more awfully, by cause of the poison. She stabbed herself instead, made a dagger's sheath of her breasts. And her earlier death was a pretense, to get her to this place and away from us.

The chamber is lined with gloomy stones, the skeletons are faded, gray, common in the sickly light of day that feebly shines—if "shine" is the word could be used for it—through the opening. My nephew Tybalt is over there, a few feet off, green and stinking on his bier,[3] dead three days ago. Crumpled beside him is that fool Paris, who no less than Romeo died for love of my daughter. And I stand and look across the children, across all these pallets of the dead, adorned with jewels, flowers still fresh around Juliet, kept so in

---

[1] **yawning maw:** jaws opened wide.

[2] **the stone . . . Our Savior's grave:** three women who visited the burial site of Jesus discovered that the stone sealing the tomb had been moved and that his body was gone.

[3] **bier (bîr):** a platform that holds a body or a coffin before it is buried.

the cool of this underground place. I stare across them at Romeo's father, Montague.

'Tis not only ourselves, the **bereaved** parents, my husband and I and *his* father and mother, about the tomb now. The county Paris's page, the wretched boy Romeo's attendant Balthasar, the old friar, the prince, Nurse—all are clustered here. And outside the entrance, so short a time ago closed off by the great stone, there gather peasants, working men, merchants, beggars in rags, courtesans, and prostitutes, all the city. The day will not be bright, we feel that even now, the dawn so gray and stale, not fresh and cool as a dawn should be. No breezy wind and yet no heat. A still, dead dawn.

My daughter is pale. When she was alive I wondered if she was **afflicted** with the greensickness, that odd anemic draining of the blood from the face that makes girls her age often so white, with no roses in their skins. I was not so afflicted myself, though many of my sisters and cousins were so. I was, I fear, not sympathetic to their weakness, flushed and strong as I always was, their faces white as tallow.[4]

Now I know she could not have been ill in that kind. I had not seen pale until I saw this face before me; in life she was a red rose compared with this creature drained of blood, all the blood of her body warm on these disgusting stones, running in rivulets[5] between them, dyeing the mortar, the source of the river the sharp little dagger still in her left breast. *He* does not bleed, though he is twisted about horribly, his face an ugly contortion of death, one side of his mouth high in a kind of crooked smile, his fingers held up, bent backward and stiff before his eyes, as though he wished to obscure those orbs[6] from our sight but could not succeed before the last convulsion seized him.

Mistress Montague—I do beg pardon, *Lady* Montague—is about to faint. Not I. I do not **succumb** to the female weakness of fear of blood, or of the dead. But she cries out to her husband, who stands, it seems, amazed, without comprehension or action. Clouds pass over the faint sun outside, and the light is for a moment yet more gray.

And it is very strange, to be watching so closely the clouds and the light outside the tomb at this moment, and I am sure if I were more foolish I would wonder if I were heartless. Perhaps I do wonder yet. How strange, to watch myself watch the clouds and the light, to feel so very much abroad from here where I am, so removed that I watch myself *watching myself* watch the clouds and the light

bereaved
(bĭ-rēvd´) *adj.* having suffered the loss of a loved one; grieving.

afflict
(ə-flĭkt´) *v.* to cause pain to; to trouble.

succumb
(sə-kŭm´) *v.* to surrender or fall victim to.

---

[4] **tallow:** hard fat derived from animals, used to make candles and soap.
[5] **rivulets:** small streams.
[6] **orbs:** globes or spheres; here it is referring to Romeo's eyes.

this morning, while my own girl, my own little poppet,[7] my bean, as she once was within me, lies here curled at my feet, curled around *him*, for *that*, that boy. Oh, she was too young to know there is little more useless than a boy! I did not so succumb to such foolishness, I did *not*; when my turn came, I held my head high, I gathered my

---

[7] **poppet:** a cute, darling child.

70 strength, I performed the duty required of me, the duty that was best for all, for me, even now. I know this.

How was the stone at the door of the tomb rolled away? I suppose that boy wrenched it aside with the strength of his doomed love. Boys. No boy ever did any such thing for me, despite my beauty. I am still beautiful. I am twenty-seven. I was only a year older than she is—was—now when my old husband, Capulet, and I conceived her. The boy's father, Montague, is yet only thirty. He may have another son, if he has none already. He is not old. Not gray and cantankerous,[8] like my husband. Who smells of decay.

80 Like this tomb.

She has no age now, I suppose, my daughter. My bean.

We have been waiting for the prince to speak first. He carries in his hand a letter, the red seal of which he breaks, and then begins.

"Here he writes that he did buy poison of a poor apothecary, and therewithal came to this vault to die and lie with Juliet."

We know it all. We heard it shouted among the crowd in the streets as we came, despite the rhythmic metal steps of our escorts. "Romeo is dead!" "Juliet did love him!" "They lie now in each other's arms in the tomb in the churchyard!" "She was not truly

90 dead yesterday! Did you hear?" "They were married and none knew!" How do such things creep so quickly, like the plague, into the common knowledge of the city?

Yet the prince would have none but himself give the story authority. He would officiate at it. He further reads the note, the confession of the mortal sin of suicide, left by that boy to his father confessor, Friar Lawrence. The friar nods sagely, as though he knows something, as though he can build for us from this fleshy, deadly crypt some sense and order. But he cannot. Who could build such things, with three boys and a girl slimy with death arranged

100 about us? Order? Cause? Effect? He **deludes** himself with his own importance.

The friar speaks. "Romeo, there, was husband to that Juliet, and she, there dead, that Romeo's faithful wife. I married them."

Why? How dare he marry children against what he knew would be the wishes of their parents! He's to blame, *I* know, however history may hold it, however gently the prince looks on him now.

"How came your master here?" His Grace requests of poor Paris's page. "To duel with Romeo Montague and die, before this pair then took their own lives?"

110 The servant stutters, a simpleton, addressed by so great a personage, then manages, "He came with flowers to strew his lady's grave, and bid me stand aloof, and so I did."

delude
(dĭ-lōōd´) *v.* to deceive or instill a false belief in.

---

[8] **cantankerous:** grouchy.

Oh, Paris. Milksop.[9] Even as she rejected him in death, he was slave to my daughter's beauty, which was not fine or perfect but simply youthful. Paris, you tadpole, you eunuch.[10]

Nurse is babbling, telling all, hysterical. "You were too hot!" she screams at my husband, as I did when Juliet refused to marry the county Paris, only the day before yesterday—though I was enraged with my daughter, no less than my husband was. How was I to know the fool had already surrendered the prize to this callow boy, this stepped-upon worm at my feet? Yet my lord threatened to turn her from the house, and that I would have no woman suffer. Now with Nurse and all the company, I turn accusing upon my husband, old Lord Capulet. His nose so long, his hair so thin and falling about his ears. He had no time to dress, his doublet is on over his nightshirt, his legs are scrawny and goatlike, though his stomach bulges. Tears quiver over the end of his nose. Regret. Can it be that my hot-blooded lord and master feels regret? I have no mercy on him. There, do you see? I say with my accusing eyes. 'Twas his doing, all his and his men's fancies and prides.

But Nurse turns on me. She nursed me, too, when she was a girl and I but three weeks old, and yet she turns on me. "God in heaven bless her!" she cries, spittle on her purple face, waving her arms above my blood-drained daughter. Her own daughter dead, she poured all herself into mine. What a creature. "You were to blame, my lady, to rate her so!" Well.

She turns to the prince. "I tried, Your Grace, to defend her from the second marriage, unholy as it was." Liar. "And my lady told her, 'Talk not to me, for I'll not speak a word. Do as thou wilt, for I have done with thee.' Oh, how could a mother?"

I see the **repulsed** stares turn toward me. Simperers. It is unexpected in a mother? But yet not in a father? I did what must be done. What else was I to do? 'Twas her father's word was law, not mine.

Yet Nurse babbles on. "Cold, cold mother. My lamb, she was a faithful wife!" she screams, and throws herself upon her. The prince's men drag her away as she screams, and there is an awkward moment as they push her through the narrow opening, out into the street and the crowd. We hear her screams continue, though they fade, and are finally drowned by the steps, the clinks, of her guardians.

Friar Lawrence, now, must have his say. He whirls upon me and my husband. "You!"

repulsed
(rĭ-pŭlsd´) *adj.*
disgusted.

---

[9] **Milksop:** a weak, cowardly man.
[10] **eunuch:** a person who lacks "masculinity"; one who has been castrated.

"Are you content, bloodthirsty woman? *Are* you a woman? Unnatural creature!"

"Good Father?" I answer. I am calm. I answer with dignity.

"You betrothed and would have married her perforce to county Paris! Then she comes to me." He gulps air and turns to the little group about us, his hand outstretched to point me out. "And you called for the death of Romeo when he killed your hot-blooded kinsman! Are you content, bloodthirsty woman? *Are* you a woman? Unnatural creature!"

A man, a *eunuch,* to judge a mother! How dare he! When in old Sparta a prisoner of war was to be executed, was it not to their women that he was handed? Was it not their women who tore him to bits? "Unnatural creature," indeed!

And cold, am I? "Do as thou wilt, for I have done with thee." So I did say. And had her father not already spoken? I was merciful, quick, as I hear are the mothers in that far-off savage land of

160

legend, Tchin, where they must by law break their daughter's feet, to keep them small as a child's forever. Best for young Juliet to close her eyes and get it done with, the thing accomplished, go to the wedding as though one were a guest, get to the church, only go, no need to think, allow yourself to be dressed by your maids beforehand as though only for a feast, as I did when I was married to this old man. It is like saying one's rosary; simply making the mouth and body move, no need to hold the thoughts in your mind as you do what you do. The things you need do are most often simple enough. So I would have told her on her wedding morning, had I been given the chance. I knew that in the end such a course would be easiest for her.

I did not know, of course, about *his* son. Montague's. I confess I see why my daughter had a preference. Paris is—was—milk toast, certainly. Here he lies now, dead at our feet, not even a good hand with a rapier. He is smaller and paler than, and defeated by, that son of the handsome, broad-chested Montague, Montague who is so close to me now that if I put out my hand I could lay it upon his round arm. He meets my eyes across the bodies of the dead children. All here do look on me now, but he does not appear to hear the friar's insults. He thinks, perhaps, on something else. His own white nightshirt only partially covers his shoulders, hard and firm as they are, and sharp and yet youthful. His jewels are about his neck, his dressing gown shimmering red and green and gold— he was perhaps on his way to bed, not freshly roused out of it. Yet he breaks his look from mine to whisper to the stained red stones we tread upon, where lies his son. He whispers, "What manners is in this, to press before thy father to a grave?" Any might take him for a loving family man, not one who is less in his own bed than a courtesan's, which is what he is. He who left his son to wander the city unchecked and encounter my daughter.

I make no sound. I am the highest-ranking woman in Verona, the highest-ranking personage after the prince and my husband, and though the friar may rant, none other dare do me any open disrespect. My neck is straight. My eyes are level.

Juliet, child, wretched fool! Paris would have been grateful to her for being beautiful, would have petted and worshiped her. I said I would she were wedded to her grave when she refused him, and so she is. Why under heaven would she believe she might marry where she would, an unsuitable boy? Who told her such a thing? Not I. I was far too mindful a mother. How could she? Well, she has found her deserved punishment. May she revel in it. She has paid for her one night with her love, a thing I never had, a thing I was denied, denied *myself*, and what harm would it have done me? None might ever have known.

I stare at Montague. He feels it, brings his eyes back to mine. My heart softens, only a moment, as I see the anguish. Only a moment.

"Do you remember?" I say. That is all, but he knows what I mean. All those about us think I am merely cruelly taunting him, reminding him of when his son yet lived, and sharpen their sneers at me. My husband reaches across bodies to him, they grip each other's right arms, they kiss, they embrace. They vow statues of these children raised in pure gold, peace evermore. None consult *me*. None ask if I want peace evermore. I watch Montague's white shirt falling over the soft, curling dark hair of his chest.

He knows that I ask if he remembers the night fourteen years ago of my father's Christmas revels. The night I pushed him away, pushed away his warm kisses in the cold, silent garden, his hands hot on me. The night long ago when I knew nothing. I thought my worth was in my worth to my family. Soiled, I had no price.

Him I loved. Him I did not marry.

COLLABORATIVE DISCUSSION What did you notice about the narrator of the story? With a partner, discuss how *The Tragedy of Romeo and Juliet* influenced Berkman's "Duty." Cite specific textual evidence to support your ideas.

Analyze Source Material: Interpretations of Shakespeare

The brilliant works of William Shakespeare have inspired writers and other artists for hundreds of years. In his play *The Tragedy of Romeo and Juliet*, Shakespeare explores the ideas of youthful love, family rivalry, a woman's duty to her family, and the role of fate in one's life. It is one of Shakespeare's best-known and most-beloved plays, especially among young people. In "Duty," contemporary author Pamela Rafael Berkman transforms Shakespeare's familiar tale of "star-crossed lovers" by exploring the story from an unexpected angle.

When authors interpret the work of other artists, they often choose to highlight a particular aspect of the original work. For example, they may borrow the setting or plot of the original work and use it to introduce new characters and situations. Or they may focus on a theme or character from the original and use that as a springboard to initiate a new story. Such new interpretations may deepen the reader's understanding and appreciation of the original work.

Author's Choices: Point of View

An author's choice of **point of view,** or the perspective from which a story is told, has an enormous impact on how readers experience and interpret the story's events. In "Duty," Berkman retells the last scene from *The Tragedy of Romeo and Juliet* through Lady Capulet's eyes. The chart shows how a shift in perspective can affect a reader's interpretation of a story.

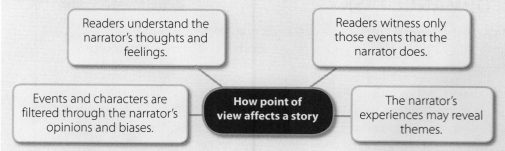

Readers understand the narrator's thoughts and feelings.

Readers witness only those events that the narrator does.

Events and characters are filtered through the narrator's opinions and biases.

How point of view affects a story

The narrator's experiences may reveal themes.

By presenting events from Lady Capulet's powerful, first-person point of view, the author invites readers to develop new opinions about Shakespeare's story of young love. As you analyze "Duty," keep these questions in mind:

- How does the point of view expose readers to additional facts about Lady Capulet?
- What is surprising about Lady Capulet's perspective on events and on other characters in the story?
- Does retelling the story from Lady Capulet's point of view affect your interpretation of the source material, *Romeo and Juliet*?

Analyzing the Text

> **Cite Text Evidence**   Support your responses with evidence from the selection.

1. **Infer** "Duty" is told from Lady Capulet's point of view. What is her opinion of Juliet and Romeo?

2. **Identify** Identify several specific details from Shakespeare's play that Berkman incorporates in her story. How does she transform each one?

3. **Identify** What surprising facts do readers learn about the characters from the play when Lady Capulet tells the story? What hints about the surprise ending does Berkman provide throughout the story?

4. **Analyze** How does the author reveal the narrator's views on duty? Describe the importance of these views to the story.

5. **Analyze** In what ways does the narrator's point of view influence the reader's opinions of the characters of Romeo and Juliet?

6. **Interpret** Lady Capulet observes that Juliet "was too young to know that there is little more useless than a boy." What themes about love and duty are revealed through her point of view?

7. **Analyze** How does the author's use of first-person point of view affect the **mood,** or emotional atmosphere, of the story? In what way is this mood surprising?

8. **Compare** Whose story is more tragic, Juliet's or Lady Capulet's? Explain.

PERFORMANCE TASK

Writing Activity: Journal Entries Use characters from *Romeo and Juliet*, as presented in "Duty," to explore how point of view can be used to transform source material.

1. In the character of Lady Capulet, create a journal entry in which she delivers her opinions on the responsibilities of children to their parents and their families.

2. In the character of Juliet's nurse, create another journal entry in which the nurse delivers her opinion on how Lady Capulet raised her daughter, Juliet.

In both pieces of writing, include evidence from the text and use the conventions of standard English.

Critical Vocabulary

bereaved	afflict	succumb	delude	repulse

Practice and Apply Choose which of the two sentences best fits the meaning of each Critical Vocabulary word. Then write a sentence to explain your answer.

bereaved:
1. A boy sobs over the death of his favorite dog.
2. A boy demands a new dog when his old dog dies.

afflict:
1. A girl quickly brushes an insect off of her arm.
2. A girl scratches at the bug bites covering her arms and legs.

succumb:
1. The boy stared at the bowl of candy, then licked his lips.
2. The boy stared at the bowl of candy, then grabbed a handful.

delude:
1. A student thinks he made the best science project in the school's history.
2. A student thinks he could have worked harder on his science project.

repulse:
1. A shopkeeper refuses to wait on a poorly dressed customer.
2. A shopkeeper hangs a sign on the door that reads CLOSED.

Vocabulary Strategy: Context Clues

The meaning of unfamiliar words can often be determined based on **context,** or how words are used within a text. Ask yourself the following questions:

- What is the overall meaning of the sentence, paragraph, or text?
- How does the unfamiliar word function in the sentence?
- Does my guess match the word's dictionary meaning?

For example, the word *bereaved* in this story is used as an adjective to modify *parents*, and the "bereaved parents" are in a tomb. Later in the paragraph, the narrator describes a day that is a "still, dead dawn." The mood evoked is one of intense sadness. Therefore, you may guess that *bereaved* means "saddened." To verify if a guess is correct, check a dictionary.

Practice and Apply Determine the meanings of these four words from the story: *crypt* (line 11), *pallets* (line 22), *contortion* (line 48), *apothecary* (line 84).

1. Identify the function of the word in the sentence: Is it a noun, a verb, or an adjective?

2. Infer the word's meaning based on the context.

3. Look up the word in a dictionary to check your inference.

Language and Style:
Independent and Dependent Clauses

A **clause** is a group of words with a subject and a verb. There are two types of clauses: **independent clauses** can stand alone as a sentence; **dependent clauses** cannot. Instead, dependent clauses act as modifiers by adding meaning to independent clauses. Dependent clauses often begin with these words: *as if, as, since, than, that, though, until, whenever, where, while, who,* and *why*. These words are conjunctions that clarify the connection between clauses.

Read the following sentence from the story.

> **When we came we found the stone rolled away, <u>like that which</u> <u>covered Our Savior's grave.</u>**

This sentence contains one independent clause and two dependent clauses. Notice how the independent clause *we found the stone rolled away* forms a complete thought and can stand alone as a sentence. The two dependent clauses, which are underlined, provide additional information about the independent clause, but they cannot stand alone.

The two types of clauses function together effectively to convey the author's meaning. Without the clauses, the author's ideas might be presented this way:

> **We came. We found the stone rolled away. It resembled Our Savior's grave.**

These simple sentences are choppy and less interesting to read. Here are more examples of effective independent and dependent clauses from "Duty." The dependent clauses are underlined.

> **Crumpled beside him is that fool Paris, <u>who no less than Romeo</u> <u>died for love of my daughter.</u>**

> **I was not so afflicted myself, <u>though many of my cousins and sisters</u> <u>were so.</u>**

Practice and Apply Return to the journal entries you created for this selection's Performance Task. Revise each entry to include two sentences that are independent clauses and two sentences that contain dependent clauses. Share your work with a partner and discuss how the clauses help show connections between ideas and events and add variety to your writing.

COLLECTION **4**

PERFORMANCE TASK

Interactive Lessons

If you need help...
- **Writing an Informative Text**
- **Using Textual Evidence**

Write an Analytical Essay

This collection explores the many facets of love—joy, pain, passion, and conflict, to name just a few. Look back at the anchor text, *The Tragedy of Romeo and Juliet,* and at the other texts in the collection. As you review the selections, consider the attributes or characteristics of love that are represented in each text. Synthesize your ideas by writing an analytical essay.

An effective analytical essay

- includes a clear thesis statement
- develops a comparison using examples from the texts
- organizes central ideas in a logically structured body
- uses transitions to create cohesion between sections of the essay
- has a concluding section that relates back to the introduction and leaves the reader with a thought-provoking statement about love

PLAN

*my*Notebook

Use the annotation tools in your eBook to find evidence to support your ideas about the characteristics of love. Save each piece of evidence to your notebook.

Analyze the Texts Review *The Tragedy of Romeo and Juliet* to identify several aspects of love that Shakespeare explores in the play. Then look for connections between the play and other texts.

- What aspect of love is explored in both Shakespeare's play and two other texts? Choose three texts, including *Romeo and Juliet,* that explore the same characteristic of love.
- Examine all three texts and take notes on how the portrayal of love is similar and different in each. In your notes, list details, examples, and quotations that support your conclusions.

ACADEMIC VOCABULARY

As you share your ideas about how love is portrayed, be sure to use these words.

attribute

commit

expose

initiate

underlie

Get Organized Organize your details and evidence in an outline.

- Write a clear thesis statement about how a particular aspect of love is depicted in *Romeo and Juliet* and in your two other chosen texts.

- Decide which organizational pattern you will use for your essay. For example, you might present all your ideas about *Romeo and Juliet* first, then write about the second text, and finally write about the third text. Another approach would be to discuss the similar ideas about love in all three texts, followed by a discussion of differences between the texts.

- Use your organizational pattern to sort the evidence you have gathered from the selections into a logical order.

- Search for an interesting quotation or detail to complement your thesis statement.

- Write down some ideas for your concluding section.

PRODUCE

my **WriteSmart**

Write your rough draft in *my*WriteSmart. Focus on getting your ideas down, rather than perfecting your choice of language.

Draft Your Essay Write a draft of your essay, following your outline.

- Introduce your thesis statement, the underlying idea on which your essay will be based. Be as explicit and clear as possible so that readers will immediately understand your point of view on the topic.

- Present your details, quotations, and examples from the texts in logically ordered paragraphs. Each paragraph should have a central idea related to your thesis with evidence to support it. Explain how each piece of evidence supports the central idea.

- Use transitions to link sections of the text and to clarify the relationships among your ideas. Some transitions that are commonly used to compare and contrast ideas are *similarly, however, even though, on the one hand, on the other hand,* and *in the same way.*

- Write a concluding section that follows logically from the body of the essay. Leave your readers with an interesting statement about love that will give them something to think about after they have finished reading.

Improve Your Draft Revise your draft to make sure it is clear, coherent, and engaging. Refer to the chart on the following page to review the characteristics of a well-written analytical essay. Ask yourself these questions as you revise:

- Does my introduction present my thesis statement clearly? Will my readers want to continue reading?

- Are the titles and authors of the selections accurately identified in my introduction?

- Have I discussed both similarities and differences about the portrayal of love in *Romeo and Juliet* and the two other texts?

- Have I provided sufficient and relevant textual evidence to support my central ideas?

- Do my ideas evolve in a logical order? Are transitions smooth and coherent?

- Have I maintained a formal style of English appropriate for an analytical essay? Does my choice of words convey a knowledgeable and confident tone, or attitude, toward the topic?

- Does my concluding section relate back to the introduction and provide a final statement about love that is interesting to my audience?

PRESENT

Exchange Essays When your final draft is completed, exchange essays in a small group. Read your group members' essays. Be prepared to initiate a response from your readers. For example, write a few questions that you would like your group members to consider as they read your essay. Finally, use the questions below to provide feedback to your group members.

- Which aspects of the essay are particularly strong?

- Did any sections of the essay leave you feeling confused? How could they be clarified?

- Do you agree with your group members' analyses of how love is portrayed in the texts? Was there sufficient textual evidence to support his or her views?

	Ideas and Evidence	Organization	Language
ADVANCED	• The introduction is appealing; the thesis statement clearly identifies the subjects and sets up points for comparison and contrast. • Concrete, relevant details and examples from the texts skillfully support each key point. • The concluding section summarizes the points of comparison and contrast, and leaves the reader with a thought-provoking idea.	• Key points and supporting textual evidence are organized logically, effectively, and consistently throughout the essay. • Transitions are well crafted and successfully connect related ideas.	• The writing reflects a formal style and an objective, knowledgeable tone. • Language is vivid and precise. • Sentence beginnings, lengths, and structures vary and have a rhythmic flow. • Spelling, capitalization, and punctuation are correct. If handwritten, the analysis is legible. • Grammar and usage are correct.
COMPETENT	• The introduction could be more engaging; the thesis statement identifies the subjects and sets up one or two points for comparison and contrast. • One or two key points need more textual support. • The concluding section synthesizes most of the ideas and summarizes most points of comparison and contrast, but offers no new insight.	• The organization of key points and supporting textual evidence is confusing in a few places. • A few more transitions are needed to connect ideas.	• The style is inconsistent in a few places, and the tone is subjective at times. • Vague language is used in a few places. • Sentence beginnings, lengths, and structures vary somewhat. • Some spelling, capitalization, and punctuation mistakes occur. If handwritten, the analysis is mostly legible. • Some grammatical and usage errors are repeated in the essay.
LIMITED	• The thesis statement identifies the subjects and only hints at the points of comparison and contrast. • Evidence from the texts supports some key points but is often too general. • The concluding section gives an incomplete summary of the points of comparison and contrast and restates the controlling idea.	• Some key points are organized logically, but many supporting details from the texts are out of place. • More transitions are needed throughout the comparison to connect ideas.	• The style is too informal; the tone conveys subjectivity and a lack of understanding of the topic. • Vague, general language is used in many places. • Sentence structures barely vary, and some fragments or run-on sentences are present. • Spelling, capitalization, and punctuation are often incorrect but do not make comprehending the essay difficult. If handwritten, the analysis may be partially illegible. • Grammar and usage are incorrect in many places, but the writer's ideas are still clear.
EMERGING	• The appropriate elements of an introduction are missing. • Evidence from the texts is irrelevant or missing. • An identifiable concluding section is missing.	• A logical organization is not used; ideas are presented randomly. • Transitions are not used, making the comparison-contrast essay difficult to understand.	• The style and tone are inappropriate for the essay. • Language is too vague or general to convey the information. • Repetitive sentence structure, fragments, and run-on sentences make the writing monotonous and difficult to follow. • Spelling, capitalization, and punctuation are incorrect throughout. If handwritten, the analysis may be partially or mostly illegible. • Many grammatical and usage errors change the meaning of the writer's ideas.

A Matter of Life or Death

"To endure what is unendurable is true endurance."

—Japanese proverb

A Matter of Life or Death

This collection provides a wide-ranging look at how humans endure in the face of adversity.

hmhfyi.com

PERFORMANCE TASK Preview

At the end of this collection, you will have the opportunity to complete two tasks:

- Write an argument about the personal qualities necessary for survival.
- Participate in a panel discussion about how people adapt in order to survive.

ACADEMIC VOCABULARY

Study the words and their definitions in the chart below. You will use these words as you discuss and write about the texts in this collection.

Word	Definition	Related Forms
dimension (dĭ-měn´shən) *n.*	a feature, scale, or measurement of something	dimensional, dimensionality
external (ĭk-stûr´nəl) *adj.*	related to, part of, or from the outside	externalize, externally
statistic (stə-tĭs´tĭk) *n.*	a piece of numerical data	statistical, statistician
sustain (sə-stān´) *v.*	to support or cause to continue	sustainable, unsustainable
utilize (yōōt´l-īz´) *v.*	to make use of	utility, utilization

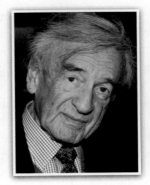

Elie Wiesel (b. 1928) *is a teacher, writer, and Nobel Peace Prize winner. Born in Romania, Wiesel, along with his family, was among millions of European Jews deported to concentration camps during the Holocaust. In 1944, the Nazis sent the family to Auschwitz, where Wiesel's mother and sister perished. Months later, when Wiesel and his father were moved to Buchenwald concentration camp, his father also died. Buchenwald was eventually liberated, and Wiesel went on to write about his experience. His many works include* Dawn *and* The Accident, *both sequels to* Night.

from Night

Memoir by Elie Wiesel

AS YOU READ Pay attention to how the descriptions of life in the concentration camp compare to what you already know about the topic. Write down any questions you generate during reading.

The SS[1] offered us a beautiful present for the new year. We had just returned from work. As soon as we passed the camp's entrance, we sensed something out of the ordinary in the air. The roll call was shorter than usual. The evening soup was distributed at great speed, swallowed as quickly. We were anxious.

I was no longer in the same block as my father. They had transferred me to another Kommando,[2] the construction one, where twelve hours a day I hauled heavy slabs of stone. The head of my new block was a German Jew, small with piercing eyes. That evening he announced to us that henceforth no one was allowed to leave the block after the evening soup. A terrible word began to circulate soon thereafter: selection.

10

---

[1] **SS:** abbreviation of *Schutzstaffel*, German for "defense force"; an armed unit of the Nazi Party that controlled concentration camps.

[2] **Kommando (kə-măn´dō):** German for "command," a small-group organization for laborers in the camps.

Image Credits: (bc) ©Beau Lark/Corbis; (c) ©Julian Kumar/Godong/Corbis; (tr) ©Paul Zimmerman/Getty Images

We knew what it meant. An SS would examine us. Whenever he found someone extremely frail—a "Muselman" was what we called those inmates—he would write down his number: good for the crematorium.

After the soup, we gathered between the bunks. The veterans told us: "You're lucky to have been brought here so late. Today, this is paradise compared to what the camp was two years ago. Back then, Buna³ was a veritable hell. No water, no blankets, less soup and bread. At night, we slept almost naked and the temperature was thirty below. We were collecting corpses by the hundreds every day. Work was very hard. Today, this is a little paradise. The Kapos⁴ back then had orders to kill a certain number of prisoners every day. And every week, selection. A merciless selection . . . Yes, you are lucky."

"Enough! Be quiet!" I begged them. "Tell your stories tomorrow, or some other day."

They burst out laughing. They were not veterans for nothing.

"Are you scared? We too were scared. And, at that time, for good reason."

The old men stayed in their corner, silent, motionless, hunted-down creatures. Some were praying.

One more hour. Then we would know the verdict: death or **reprieve.**

And my father? I first thought of him now. How would he pass selection? He had aged so much. . . .

Our *Blockälteste*⁵ had not been outside a concentration camp since 1933. He had already been through all the slaughterhouses, all the factories of death. Around nine o'clock, he came to stand in our midst:

"*Achtung!*"⁶

There was instant silence.

"Listen carefully to what I am about to tell you." For the first time, his voice quivered. "In a few moments, selection will take place. You will have to undress completely. Then you will go, one by one, before the SS doctors. I hope you will all pass. But you must try to increase your chances. Before you go into the next room, try to move your limbs, give yourself some color. Don't walk slowly, run! Run as if you had the devil at your heels! Don't look at the SS. Run, straight in front of you!"

He paused and then added:

> **reprieve**
> (rĭ-prēv´) *n.* The cancellation or postponement of punishment.

---

³ **Buna (bōō´nə):** a section of the concentration camp at Auschwitz.
⁴ **Kapos (kä´pōs):** prisoners who performed certain duties for the guards.
⁵ **Blockälteste (blök´ĕl´təs-tə):** a rank of Kapos; a prisoner designated by the Nazis to be the leader or representative of a block, or group of barracks.
⁶ **Achtung! (ăk´tōōng):** German command for "Attention!"

Image Credits: ©Scott Barbour/Getty Images

"And most important, don't be afraid!"

That was a piece of advice we would have loved to be able to follow.

I undressed, leaving my clothes on my cot. Tonight, there was no danger that they would be stolen.

Tibi and Yossi, who had changed Kommandos at the same time I did, came to urge me:

60   "Let's stay together. It will make us stronger."

Yossi was mumbling something. He probably was praying. I had never suspected that Yossi was religious. In fact, I had always believed the opposite. Tibi was silent and very pale. All the block inmates stood naked between the rows of bunks. This must be how one stands for the Last Judgment.

"They are coming!"

Three SS officers surrounded the notorious Dr. Mengele,[7] the very same who had received us in Birkenau. The *Blockälteste* attempted a smile. He asked us:

70   "Ready?"

Yes, we were ready. So were the SS doctors. Dr. Mengele was holding a list: our numbers. He nodded to the *Blockälteste*: we can begin! As if this were a game.

---

[7] **Dr. Mengele (mĕn-gə´lə):** Josef Mengele (1911–1979), Nazi physician at Auschwitz known for conducting cruel experiments on prisoners.

The first to go were the "notables" of the block, the *Stubenälteste*,[8] the Kapos, the foremen, all of whom were in perfect physical condition, of course! Then came the ordinary prisoners' turns. Dr. Mengele looked them over from head to toe. From time to time, he noted a number. I had but one thought: not to have my number taken down and not to show my left arm.

80   In front of me, there were only Tibi and Yossi. They passed. I had time to notice that Mengele had not written down their numbers. Someone pushed me. It was my turn. I ran without looking back. My head was spinning: you are too skinny . . . you are too weak . . . you are too skinny, you are good for the ovens . . . The race seemed endless; I felt as though I had been running for years . . . You are too skinny, you are too weak . . . At last I arrived. Exhausted. When I had caught my breath, I asked Yossi and Tibi:

"Did they write me down?"

"No," said Yossi. Smiling, he added, "Anyway, they couldn't
90   have. You were running too fast . . ."

I began to laugh. I was happy. I felt like kissing him. At that moment, the others did not matter! They had not written me down.

Those whose numbers had been noted were standing apart, abandoned by the whole world. Some were silently weeping.

THE SS OFFICERS left. The *Blockälteste* appeared, his face reflecting our collective weariness.

"It all went well. Don't worry. Nothing will happen to anyone. Not to anyone . . ."

He was still trying to smile. A poor **emaciated** Jew questioned
100 him anxiously, his voice trembling:

"But . . . sir. They *did* write me down!"

At that, the *Blockälteste* vented his anger: What! Someone refused to take his word?

"What is it now? Perhaps you think I'm lying? I'm telling you, once and for all: nothing will happen to you! Nothing! You just like to wallow in your despair, you fools!"

The bell rang, signaling that the selection had ended in the entire camp.

With all my strength I began to race toward Block 36; midway,
110 I met my father. He came toward me:

"So? Did you pass?"

"Yes. And you?"

"Also."

emaciated
(ĭ-mā´shē-āt´id) *adj.* made extremely thin and weak.

---

[8] **Stubenälteste (shtyōō´bə-nĭl-tŭs´-tə):** a rank of Kapos; prisoners designated by the Nazis to be the leaders of their barracks, or rooms.

We were able to breathe again. My father had a present for me: a half ration of bread, bartered for something he had found at the depot, a piece of rubber that could be used to repair a shoe.

The bell. It was already time to part, to go to bed. The bell regulated everything. It gave me orders and I **executed** them blindly. I hated that bell. Whenever I happened to dream of a better world, I imagined a universe without a bell.

120

execute
(ĕk´sĭ-kyōōt´) v.
to carry out, or
accomplish.

A FEW DAYS passed. We were no longer thinking about the selection. We went to work as usual and loaded the heavy stones onto the freight cars. The rations had grown smaller; that was the only change.

We had risen at dawn, as we did every day. We had received our black coffee, our ration of bread. We were about to head to the work yard as always. The *Blockälteste* came running:

"Let's have a moment of quiet. I have here a list of numbers. I shall read them to you. All those called will not go to work this morning; they will stay in camp."

130

Softly, he read some ten numbers. We understood. These were the numbers from the selection. Dr. Mengele had not forgotten.

The *Blockälteste* turned to go to his room. The ten prisoners surrounded him, clinging to his clothes:

"Save us! You promised . . . We want to go to the depot, we are strong enough to work. We are good workers. We can . . .we want . . ."

He tried to calm them, to reassure them about their fate, to explain to them that staying in the camp did not mean much, had no tragic significance: "After all, I stay here every day . . ."

140

The argument was more than flimsy. He realized it and, without another word, locked himself in his room.

The bell had just rung.

"Form ranks!"

Now, it no longer mattered that the work was hard. All that mattered was to be far from the block, far from the crucible[9] of death, from the center of hell.

I saw my father running in my direction. Suddenly, I was afraid.

"What is happening?"

150

He was out of breath, hardly able to open his mouth.

"Me too, me too . . . They told me too to stay in the camp."

They had recorded his number without his noticing.

"What are we going to do?" I said anxiously.

But it was he who tried to reassure me:

---

[9] **crucible:** a vessel used for melting materials at high temperatures.

"It's not certain yet. There's still a chance. Today, they will do another selection . . . a **decisive** one . . ."

I said nothing.

He felt time was running out. He was speaking rapidly, he wanted to tell me so many things. His speech became confused, his
160 voice was choked. He knew that I had to leave in a few moments. He was going to remain alone, so alone . . .

"Here, take this knife," he said. "I won't need it anymore. You may find it useful. Also take this spoon. Don't sell it. Quickly! Go ahead, take what I'm giving you!"

My inheritance . . .

"Don't talk like that, Father." I was on the verge of breaking into sobs. "I don't want you to say such things. Keep the spoon and knife. You will need them as much as I. We'll see each other tonight, after work."

170 He looked at me with his tired eyes, veiled by despair. He insisted:

"I am asking you . . . Take it, do as I ask you, my son. Time is running out. Do as your father asks you . . ."

Our Kapo shouted the order to march.

The Kommando headed toward the camp gate. Left, right! I was biting my lips. My father had remained near the block, leaning against the wall. Then he began to run, to try to catch up with us. Perhaps he had forgotten to tell me something… But we were marching too fast . . . Left, right!

180 We were at the gate. We were being counted. Around us, the **din** of military music. Then we were outside.

ALL DAY, I PLODDED AROUND like a sleepwalker. Tibi and Yossi would call out to me, from time to time, trying to reassure me. As did the Kapo who had given me easier tasks that day. I felt sick at heart. How kindly they treated me. Like an orphan. I thought: Even now, my father is helping me.

I myself didn't know whether I wanted the day to go by quickly or not. I was afraid of finding myself alone that evening. How good it would be to die right here!

190 At last, we began the return journey. How I longed for an order to run! The military march. The gate. The camp. I ran toward Block 36.

Were there still miracles on this earth? He was alive. He had passed the second selection. He had still proved his usefulness . . . I gave him back his knife and spoon.

COLLABORATIVE DISCUSSION With a partner, discuss two unexpected details from Wiesel's description of life in the concentration camp. Explain why they were surprising, citing specific passages in your discussion.

Analyze Author's Purpose and Rhetoric

Purpose is an author's reason for writing a text. Authors may write to persuade, to inform, or to entertain. They may even write for more than one purpose, but their purpose is rarely stated directly. Instead, readers infer, or draw conclusions about, the purpose based on the author's **rhetoric,** or style, and other clues in the text.

To advance their purpose, authors must engage the reader with a compelling style that includes thoughtful ideas and interesting details. Elie Wiesel chose to write in the form of a **memoir**—an autobiographical account of his personal experiences and observations of a significant event. Use these questions to help you think about Wiesel's reason for writing *Night*.

- What is the historical context for this memoir? About what significant event and people is Wiesel sharing memories?
- What perspective do you understand from reading this first-person account?
- Think about other nonfiction books or articles that you have read about Wiesel's topic. How does Wiesel's first-person account differ from these?
- What insight do you gain into the effect this historical event had on people?

Analyze Impact of Word Choice on Tone

The **tone** of a work is the author's attitude toward the subject and audience. A writer's tone might be formal and serious, angry, or lighthearted. There could even be several tones reflected in a single work. Writers shape tone through **word choices.** Words with particular connotations subtly change the meaning of a sentence and help to create the tone of a passage. Look at the examples from the selection. Which words help create the tone?

Tone	Example from *Night*
Fear and dread	"One more hour. Then we would know the verdict: death or reprieve."
Despair	"He felt time was running out. He was speaking rapidly, he wanted to tell me so many things. His speech became confused, his voice was choked."
Upbeat and encouraging	"Were there still miracles on this earth? He was alive. He had passed the second selection. He had still proved his usefulness."

Analyzing the Text

Cite Text Evidence Support your responses with evidence from the selection.

1. **Infer** In lines 32–33, Wiesel writes, "The old men stayed in their corner, silent, motionless, hunted-down creatures. Some were praying." Which words in this quotation have strong connotations? How do these words convey the tone of Wiesel's narrative?

2. **Cite Evidence** What evidence does Wiesel provide to support the idea that though beaten down, the prisoners had creative ways of coping with their confinement and of sustaining themselves?

3. **Analyze** Look back at the scene in which Wiesel must run before the SS doctors during selection (lines 83–86). Why does Wiesel repeat his thoughts, "you are too skinny, you are too weak"? How does the repetition help readers understand his experience?

4. **Interpret** Wiesel sometimes uses punctuation and sentence structure to convey meaning. Reread the second to last paragraph in the text. Why does he use short, incomplete sentences? How does this stylistic approach affect meaning?

5. **Analyze** Wiesel includes statements and reactions from other prisoners, the head of the block, and the veterans of the camp that reveal different perspectives about life in the concentration camp. Identify examples of these different perspectives and explain what they reveal about the prisoners' ordeal.

6. **Draw Conclusions** Why do you think Wiesel chose to call his memoir *Night*? What might be the significance of that title?

PERFORMANCE TASK

Writing Activity: Analysis Elie Wiesel's account of the concentration camp is deeply personal. Think about what he wrote and what he may have wanted to achieve with his account. Then write a brief analysis in which you answer the following questions:

- Why did Wiesel write *Night*? What did he hope to accomplish? Did he succeed?
- Did his descriptions of life in the camp connect with you, the reader? How?

- Elie Wiesel's account of the Holocaust was written years after the events took place. How might *Night* be different if it had been written as a diary, a first-person account of events immediately after they happened?
- Would you recommend this memoir to others? Why?

In your writing, include evidence from the text to support your analysis and use the conventions of standard English.

Critical Vocabulary

reprieve	emaciated	execute	decisive	din

Practice and Apply Use your knowledge of the Critical Vocabulary words to respond to each question.

1. Wiesel describes one of the prisoners as **emaciated.** What did the prisoner look like?

2. When Wiesel's father passed the second **decisive** selection, Wiesel was relieved. Explain why.

3. While a prisoner, Wiesel would **execute** his orders in the camp. Did the guards likely have a complaint about his work? Explain.

4. The narrator could hear the **din** of military music in the background. What did the music sound like?

5. The prisoners at the concentration camp hoped for a **reprieve** from death. What were they hoping for?

Vocabulary Strategy: Multiple-Meaning Words

The Critical Vocabulary word *execute* means "to accomplish or carry out fully." *Execute* has another definition, "to put to death." Like *execute*, many words have **multiple meanings.** Use the strategies below to determine or clarify the meaning of multiple-meaning words.

- Use context, or the way the word is used in a sentence or paragraph, to determine meaning. This strategy requires looking at the words and sentences around the unknown word to clarify meaning. For example, look at the following sentence: *Mountain climbing was her passion, and she wanted to scale every peak.* The context tells you that *scale* refers to climbing.
- Consult general and specialized reference materials, particularly glossaries and dictionaries, to determine or clarify a word's precise meaning. Dictionary entries provide all the definitions of a word, as well as its part of speech, so select the definition that makes sense.

Practice and Apply Work in a group to locate these words in the selection: *present* (line 1), *block* (line 6), *bunks* (line 17), *reflecting* (line 96). Use context clues or reference materials to determine the precise meaning for each word.

Language and Style: Tone

An author's attitude toward a subject or an audience helps create the overall feeling that a selection conveys. Authors establish **tone** by making effective word choices for meaning and style.

Read the following sentences from the selection:

Those whose numbers had been noted were standing apart, abandoned by the whole world. Some were silently weeping.

Wiesel might have written the sentence like this:

The prisoners whose numbers had been called were standing by themselves crying.

How is the second sentence different from the first? Look again at the first sentence. Notice that Wiesel uses words with strong connotations. Words like *apart, abandoned, silently,* and *weeping* create strong imagery for the reader, which in turn shapes a tone of tragedy and despair. Wiesel's use of formal language also adds to the weight and seriousness of the memoir's tone. Note the difference in the use of formal versus informal language in these passages.

Formal	Informal
"Listen carefully to what I am about to tell you." For the first time, his voice quivered. "In a few moments, selection will take place. You will have to undress completely. Then you will go, one by one, before the SS doctors. I hope you will all pass."	"Listen, everyone," he said as his voice shook. "Selection's going to start soon. You'll have to take your clothes off, then walk by the SS doctors one at a time. I hope everyone passes."
"What is it now? Perhaps you think I'm lying? I'm telling you, once and for all: nothing will happen to you! Nothing! You just like to wallow in your despair, you fools!"	"What? Do you think I'm lying? Nothing's going to happen to you! You're just feeling sorry for yourselves!"

Practice and Apply Look back at the analysis you wrote in response to this selection's Performance Task. Revise it to include formal, rather than informal, language and at least two sentences that contain strong imagery. Then discuss with a partner how formal language and strong imagery improve the meaning and tone of your work.

Is Survival Selfish?

Argument by Lane Wallace

AS YOU READ Think about whether you would use the word *selfish* to describe someone who survives a disaster. Write down any questions you generate during reading.

When the ocean liner *Titanic* sank in April of 1912, one of the few men to survive the tragedy was J. Bruce Ismay, the chairman and managing director of the company that owned the ship. After the disaster, however, Ismay was savaged by the media and the general public for climbing into a lifeboat and saving himself when there were other women and children still on board. Ismay said he'd already helped many women and children into lifeboats and had only climbed in one himself when there were no other women or children in the area and the boat was ready to release. But it didn't matter. His reputation was ruined. He was labeled an uncivilized coward and, a year after the disaster, he resigned his position at White Star.

The "women and children first" protocol of the *Titanic* may not be as strong a social stricture[1] as it was a century ago. But we still tend to **laud** those who risk or sacrifice themselves to save others in moments of danger or crisis and look less kindly on those who focus on saving themselves, instead.

But is survival really selfish and uncivilized? Or is it smart? And is going in to rescue others always heroic? Or is it sometimes just stupid? It's a complex question, because there are so many factors involved, and every survival situation is different.

Self-preservation is supposedly an instinct. So one would think that in life-and-death situations, we'd all be very focused on whatever was necessary to survive. But that's not always true. In July

laud
(lôd) *v.* to praise.

_____
[1] **social stricture:** behavioral restriction placed on society.

2007, I was having a drink with a friend in Grand Central Station[2] when an underground steam pipe exploded just outside. From where we sat, we heard a dull "boom!" and then suddenly, people were running, streaming out of the tunnels and out the doors.

My friend and I walked quickly and calmly outside, but to get any further, we had to push our way through a crowd of people who were staring, **transfixed**, at the column of smoke rising from the front of the station. Some people were crying, others were screaming, others were on their cell phones . . . but the crowd, for the most part, was *not* doing the one thing that would increase everyone's chances of survival, if in fact a terrorist bomb with god knows what inside it had just gone off—namely, moving away from the area.

We may have an instinct for survival, but it clearly doesn't always kick in the way it should. A guy who provides survival training for pilots told me once that the number one determining factor for survival is simply whether people hold it together in a crisis or fall apart. And, he said, it's impossible to predict ahead of time who's going to hold it together, and who's going to fall apart.

So what is the responsibility of those who hold it together? I remember reading the account of one woman who was in an airliner that crashed on landing. People were frozen or screaming, but nobody was moving toward the emergency exits, even as smoke began to fill the cabin. After realizing that the people around her were too paralyzed to react, she took direct action, crawling over several rows of people to get to the exit. She got out of the plane and survived. Very few others in the plane, which was soon **consumed** by smoke and fire, did. And afterward, I remember she said she battled a lot of guilt for saving herself instead of trying to save the others.

Could she really have saved the others? Probably not, and certainly not from the back of the plane. If she'd tried, she probably would have perished with them. So why do survivors **berate** themselves for not adding to the loss by attempting the impossible? Perhaps it's because we get very mixed messages about survival ethics.

On the one hand, we're told to put our own oxygen masks on first, and not to jump in the water with a drowning victim. But then the people who ignore those **edicts** and survive to tell the tale are lauded as heroes. And people who do the "smart" thing are sometimes criticized quite heavily after the fact.

In a famous mountain-climbing accident chronicled in the book and documentary *Touching the Void*, climber Simon Yates was

transfix
(trăns-fĭks´) *v.* to captivate or make motionless with awe.

consume
(kən-so͞om´) *v.* to completely destroy or eradicate.

berate
(bĭ-rāt´) *v.* to criticize or scold.

edict
(ē´dĭkt´) *n.* an official rule or proclamation.

---

[2] **Grand Central Station:** a large commuter-rail and subway terminal in New York City.

> **"It's impossible to predict ahead of time who's going to hold it together, and who's going to fall apart."**

attempting to rope his already-injured friend Joe Simpson down a mountain in bad weather when the belay[3] went awry. Simpson ended up hanging off a cliff, unable to climb up, and Yates, unable to lift him up and losing his own grip on the mountain, ended up cutting the rope to Simpson to save himself. Miraculously, Simpson survived the 100 foot fall and eventually made his way down the mountain. But Yates was criticized by some for his survival decision, even though the alternative would have almost certainly led to both of their deaths.

In Yates' case, he had time to think hard about the odds, and the possibilities he was facing, and to realize that he couldn't save anyone but himself. But what about people who have to make more instantaneous decisions? If, in fact, survivors are driven by instinct not civilization, how do you explain all those who choose otherwise? Who would dive into icy waters or onto subway tracks or disobey orders to make repeat trips onto a minefield to bring wounded to safety? Are they more civilized than the rest of us? More brave? More noble?

It sounds nice, but oddly enough, most of the people who perform such impulsive rescues say that they didn't really think before acting. Which means they weren't "choosing" civilization

---

[3] **belay:** the securing of a rope to a cleat or another object.

over instinct. If survival is an instinct, it seems to me that there must be something equally instinctive that drives us, sometimes, to run into danger instead of away from it.

Perhaps it comes down to the ancient "fight or flight" impulse. Animals confronted with danger will choose to attack it, or run from it, and it's hard to say which one they'll choose, or when. Or maybe humans are such social herd animals, dependent on the herd for survival, that we feel a pull toward others even as we feel a contrary pull toward our own preservation, and the two impulses battle it out within us . . . leading to the mixed messages we send each other on which impulse to follow.

Some people hold it together in a crisis and some people fall apart. Some people might run away from danger one day, and toward it the next. We pick up a thousand cues in an instant of crisis and respond in ways that even surprise ourselves, sometimes.

But while we laud those who sacrifice themselves in an attempt to save another, there is a fine line between brave and foolish. There can also be a fine line between smart and selfish. And as a friend who's served in the military for 27 years says, the truth is, sometimes there's no line at all between the two.

COLLABORATIVE DISCUSSION With a partner, review the various stories of survivors and discuss whether you would describe each person's actions as *selfish*. Is being selfish always bad? Cite textual evidence as well as your own reasoning in your discussion.

Delineate and Evaluate an Argument

In an **argument,** the author expresses a position on an issue and then attempts to support that position. A successful argument persuades readers to agree with the author's position. To **evaluate** whether an argument is successful, you must first **delineate,** or outline, its basic parts. The diagram shows a simplified outline.

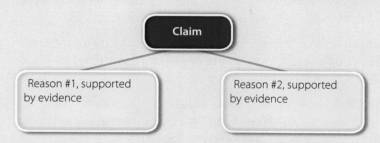

- The **claim** is the author's position on the topic or issue. It is the central idea around which the argument is structured.
- **Reasons** are explanations that support the claim by answering the question *Why does the author hold that opinion?* An author's reasoning must be clear and logical to create a valid argument.
- **Evidence** includes facts, statistics, personal experiences, statements by experts, and other information. The evidence supports the reasons and, ultimately, the author's claim.

Most arguments begin by stating a claim and then present reasons and evidence for the claim. To be convincing, an argument must include evidence that is valid, relevant, and sufficient. Use this checklist to evaluate evidence presented in "Is Survival Selfish?"

Evaluating Evidence Checklist
Evidence is valid if
• it is well known or common knowledge
• the author identifies the source
• the source appears to be trustworthy
• research shows the source to be reliable
Evidence is relevant if
• it is closely related to the topic or issue
• it supports the claim
Evidence is sufficient if
• there is enough of it
• it comes from a variety of sources

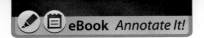
Analyzing the Text

Cite Text Evidence   Support your responses with evidence from the selection.

1. **Summarize** Lane Wallace begins her argument with a series of questions to get her readers thinking about what is selfish and what is heroic. In your own words, state the claim that she expresses in lines 18–21. Take into account the information she presents in the rest of her argument, including her conclusions at the end.

2. **Analyze** Wallace writes that "the number one determining factor for survival is simply whether people hold it together in a crisis or fall apart" (lines 40–42). Is this an example of a claim, a reason, or evidence? Explain.

3. **Critique** In lines 24–37 what evidence does Wallace offer to support her idea that people are not always focused on doing "whatever [is] necessary to survive" in a crisis? Is the evidence relevant and sufficient? Explain.

4. **Evaluate** In lines 44–60, Wallace notes that survivors often suffer from feelings of guilt. Does she think these feelings are justified? Does she support her reasoning with relevant and sufficient evidence? Explain your response.

5. **Evaluate** Reread lines 86–91. As evidence for Wallace's claim, is this paragraph valid and relevant? Explain.

6. **Interpret** In the final paragraph, Wallace writes that there is "a fine line between smart and selfish," and that "sometimes there's no line at all." What does she mean by this, and how does her conclusion restate her claim?

PERFORMANCE TASK

Speaking Activity: Debate In the selection, Lane Wallace explores whether survivors are selfish for trying to save their own lives while rescuers are heroic for trying to save others. Review the author's argument before completing this activity.

1. Divide the class into two teams. One team should take the position that survivors are selfish and uncivilized and that rescuers are heroic; the other team should take the position that survivors are smart and that rescuers are foolish.

2. Work with your team to gather evidence and use it to build a well-reasoned argument.

3. Hold a debate in which members from each team take turns stating the reasons and evidence for their claim, as well as responding to the other team's argument.

4. After the debate, write a brief evaluation of each team's argument and explain which argument was more convincing.

Critical Vocabulary

laud   **transfix**   **consume**   **berate**   **edict**

Practice and Apply Each of these word pairs contains one Critical Vocabulary word. Describe what is different and alike about the words in each pair. Use a dictionary or thesaurus as needed.

1. laud/welcome

2. transfix/stare

3. consume/fill

4. berate/battle

5. edict/tale

Vocabulary Strategy: Synonyms

Words that share the same or nearly the same meaning are called **synonyms.** Authors sometimes use synonyms to vary word choice and make their writing more interesting. For example, in line 49 of "Is Survival Selfish?" the author uses the word *paralyzed*. The synonym *transfixed* might also have worked, but the author had already used it in line 31.

If you come across an unfamiliar word in a text, try to think of another word that would make sense in the context of the sentence. Then check a dictionary or a thesaurus to see if your word is truly a synonym for the unfamiliar word. Note any subtle differences between the synonyms and try to understand why the author chose that precise word. Ask yourself whether the context sentence has the same or a slightly different meaning with your synonym as with the author's original word.

Practice and Apply Use a print or online thesaurus to complete this activity.

1. Create a two-column chart. In the first column, write the Critical Vocabulary words. In the second column, write at least two synonyms for each word.

2. Write a sentence using each Critical Vocabulary word.

3. For each sentence you write, exchange the Critical Vocabulary word for one of its synonyms. Work together with a partner to choose the best synonym for each sentence. Discuss whether using a synonym changes the meaning of each original sentence.

Language and Style: Indefinite Pronouns

When authors want to refer to a specific person, they use personal pronouns, such as *he, she,* or *I* ("She got out of the plane and survived"). To refer to one or more people or things that are not specifically mentioned, authors use **indefinite pronouns,** such as *anyone, all,* or *some.* In "Is Survival Selfish?" Lane Wallace uses a variety of indefinite pronouns.

Read this sentence from the selection:

But Yates was criticized by <u>some</u> for his survival decision . . . .

The indefinite pronoun *some* refers to the people who criticized Yates. It would be awkward—and probably impossible—to mention by name all of those who criticized the climber, so the author's use of *some* makes sense.

This chart lists other indefinite pronouns found in "Is Survival Selfish?"

Indefinite Pronoun	Example
others	". . . sacrifice themselves to save others . . ."
one	". . . one would think that in life-and-death situations . . ."
whatever	". . . whatever was necessary to survive."
nobody	". . . nobody was moving toward the emergency exits . . ."
another	". . . in an attempt to save another . . ."

Some words that can function as indefinite pronouns can also function as adjectives. For example, read this sentence from the selection:

<u>Some</u> people hold it together in a crisis and <u>some</u> people fall apart.

Here, *some* is used as an adjective because it describes the plural noun *people.*

Indefinite pronouns are sometimes used in pairs. Consider the following examples from the selection:

. . . the mixed messages we send <u>each other</u> . . .

Very <u>few others</u> in the plane . . .

In these examples, *each other* and *few others* may be considered compound indefinite pronouns because the words in each pair act together as a pronoun.

Practice and Apply Using the topic of survival ethics, write one sentence for each of the indefinite pronouns listed in the chart above. When you are finished, discuss your sentences with a partner.

from
Deep
Survival

Science Writing by Laurence Gonzales

AS YOU READ Think about the title of the selection and consider what the term *deep survival* means to the author. Write down any questions you generate during reading.

Juliane Koepcke was flying with her mother and ninety other passengers on Christmas Eve, 1971, when lightning struck, causing an extensive structural failure of the Lockheed Electra. Juliane fell out of the broken airplane into the Peruvian jungle. She was seventeen years old, wearing her Catholic confirmation dress and white high heels. Miraculously, she suffered only cuts and a broken collarbone from the crash. Later, she reported feeling "a hefty concussion." Then she was falling toward the jungle.

10   As she recalled, "I remember thinking that the jungle trees below looked just like cauliflowers." To someone who knows about survival, that statement is telling. She wasn't screaming; she wasn't in a panic. She was in wonder at the world in which she found herself. She was taking it all in, touching her new reality. Checking out her environment while falling. Amazing cool.

Amazing and also characteristic of a true survivor. Bill Garleb, an American GI who survived the Bataan Death March[1] in the Philippines, found his senses increasingly sharp as he experienced a deep wonder at the birds and colors and smells of the jungle.

A dozen other passengers survived the midair **disintegration**
20   of Juliane's plane, and their attitude, and hence their behavior and fate, were quite different from hers.

Juliane awoke alone on the floor of the jungle, still strapped into her seat. There was no sign of her mother, who'd been beside her in the plane. She spent the night trying to keep out of the rain

disintegration
(dĭs-ĭn´tĭ-grā´shən) *n.*
the process of a whole coming apart in pieces.

---

[1] **Bataan Death March:** the forced transfer of captured American and Filipino soldiers by the Japanese after the World War II Battle of Bataan. Thousands died during the ordeal in April 1942.

under her seat. The next day, she **deduced** that even the helicopters and airplanes she could hear wouldn't be able to see her through the jungle canopy.[2] She'd have to get herself out. It was another important moment: She didn't spend time bemoaning her fate. She looked to herself, took responsibility, made a plan.

30   Her parents were researchers who worked in the jungle, and she was familiar with that environment. But Juliane had had no survival training. She didn't know where she was or which way she ought to go, but her father had told her that if she went downhill, she'd find water. He'd said that rivers usually led to civilization. And while that strategy can just as easily lead into a swamp, at least she had a plan that she believed in. She had a task.

Meanwhile, the others who had lived through the fall decided to await rescue, which is not necessarily a bad idea either. But expecting someone else to take responsibility for your well-being

40   can be fatal. In *Alive*, Piers Paul Read tells the story of the survivors of another airplane crash, this one in the Andes.[3] Everyone who survived the crash stayed put, assuming that they'd be rescued. Many died; the others wound up eating each other to keep from starving before someone finally walked out and found help.

Juliane had nothing except a few pieces of candy and some small cakes. She had no survival equipment, no tools, no compass or map—none of the things I'd been taught to use in survival school. But she very deliberately set up a program for herself. She set off, resting through the heat of the day and traveling during the

50   cooler periods. She walked for eleven days through dense jungle while being literally eaten alive by leeches and strange tropical insects, which bored into her, laid their eggs, and produced worms that hatched and tunneled out through her skin.

Eventually, she came to a hut along the banks of the river she'd been following. She staggered and collapsed inside. There is always a lot of chance involved in a survival situation, both good luck and bad. It was Juliane's good fortune that three hunters turned up the next day and delivered her to a local doctor. But, as Louis Pasteur[4] said, "Luck favors the prepared mind."

60   Tough and clearheaded, this teenage girl, who had lost her shoes (not to mention her mother) on the first day, saved herself; the other survivors took the same eleven days to sit down and die.

The forces that put them there were beyond their control. But the course of events for those who found themselves alive on the

deduce
(dĭ-do͞os´) *v.* to know through reason or logical conclusion.

---

[2] **jungle canopy:** the dense layer formed by the leaves and branches of the tallest trees.

[3] **Andes:** a mountain range in western South America running from Venezuela to Argentina.

[4] **Louis Pasteur:** (1822–1895) French chemist and biologist.

ground were the result of deep and personal individual reactions to a new environment.

The knottiest mystery of survival is how one unequipped, ill-prepared seventeen-year-old girl gets out alive and a dozen adults in similar circumstances, better equipped, do not. But the deeper I've gone into the study of survival, the more sense such outcomes make. Making fire, building shelter, finding food, signaling, navigation— none of that mattered to Juliane's survival. Although we cannot know what the others who survived the fall were thinking and deciding, it's possible that they knew they were supposed to stay put and await rescue. They were rule followers, and it killed them.

In the World Trade Center disaster,[5] many people who were used to following the rules died because they did what they were told by authority figures. An employee of the Aon Insurance Company on the ninety-third floor of the south tower had begun his escape but returned to his office after the security guards made a general announcement that the building was safe and that people should stay inside until they were told to leave. Before he died, he spoke to his father on the phone: "Why did I listen to them—I shouldn't have." Another man, an employee of Fuji Bank, actually reached the ground-floor lobby, only to be sent back in by a security guard. A third worker called a family member and recorded a final message on the answering machine: "I can't go anywhere because they told us not to move. I have to wait for the firefighters."

In thinking for herself, Juliane wasn't even particularly brave. Survival is not about bravery and heroics. Heroes can be perfect heroes and wind up dead. By definition, survivors must live. Juliane was afraid most of the time (of everything from piranhas when she had to wade in the water to the worms that were crawling around under her skin to the real or imagined creatures of the forest). Survivors aren't fearless. They *use* fear: they turn it into anger and focus.

Conversely, searchers are always amazed to find people who have died while in possession of everything they needed to survive. John Leach writes that "Victims have been recovered from life rafts with a survival box (containing flares, rations, first-aid kit and so on) unopened and the necessary contents unused."

"Some people just give up," Ken Hill told me, referring to his search and rescue operations in Nova Scotia. "Fifteen years I've been studying this, and I can't figure out why."

What saved Juliane was an inner resource, a state of mind. She certainly didn't have any physical equipment. But she'd been

conversely
(kən-vûrs′lē) *adv.* in a way that contradicts or reverses something.

---

[5] **World Trade Center disaster:** the destruction of New York office buildings by hijacked airplanes on September 11, 2001.

prepared mentally, somehow. A lifetime of experience shapes us
to meet or be crushed by such challenges as a bad divorce, the
110 shattering of a career, a terrible illness or accident, a collapsing
economy, a war, prison camp, the death of a loved one, or being
stranded in the jungle. I went to survival school to try to understand
that mystery and see if I could master my own journey. . . .

We took off from Pittsfield, Massachusetts, sharing the flying
duties, and landed in Lynchburg, Virginia. As I climbed out of
the cockpit and onto the wing, I caught my first glimpse of our
instructor. Byron Kerns runs the Mountain Shepherd Survival
School. He swaggered across the fueling ramp toward us wearing
an 18-inch Panamanian machete on his belt, a big, macho-looking
120 guy with twelve years of military experience, including a stint with
the Marines. He had worked at the famous Air Force Survival
School in Washington State. When I saw him, I thought, We're in
for it now.

That night, Byron explained that we were going to head off into
the Virginia woods the next morning, early, and we'd be drilling for
several days on such matters as map and compass work, firecraft,
shelter, and signaling. We'd learn to find water or **distill** it from the
air. We would not think about food, because it wasn't necessary.
The Air Force plan was that you'd be found within three days.
130 "Your job," he said, "is to stay alive for seventy-two hours." When
he left, Jonas[6] said, "This guy's going to whip you like a redheaded
stepchild."[7]

Early the next morning, as we moved up a rocky river drainage
through the mountains, I noticed that Kerns would stop frequently
to point out something of beauty or interest. He spoke softly, as if
we were in a church. He laughed a lot. He liked to be still and just
think or smoke a cigarette. I saw no sign of the drill sergeant I'd
expected. In our first exercise, Kerns asked me and Jonas to make a
fire, and in a matter of minutes we had a roaring blaze going. Kerns
140 had turned away to get something from his pack. When he turned
back, the flames were leaping several feet off the ground. "Whoa,"
he said, laughing, "easy, easy. I just wanted to know if you could
start a fire. Some people can't." Then he gently separated the pile of
wood and put it out.

Byron Kerns turned out to be soft-spoken, polite, cheerfully
earnest, and gentle to a fault. He moved slowly, never hurried,
and was always carefully assessing himself and his environment.
He wasn't prone to high emotional states. He carried with him a

distill
(dĭ-stĭl´) v. to
transform vapor into
liquid.

---

[6] **Jonas Dovydenas:** (b. 1939) Lithuanian-born photographer.
[7] **a redheaded stepchild:** a person who is mistreated because he or she is
unwanted.

Image Credits: ©John Slater/Getty Images

contagious air of calm. He reminded me of my father, actually.
150 Like so many retired pilots, my father wore soft shoes, talked softly, and walked slowly. (As a pilot, you want to wear soft shoes so that you can feel the rudder pedals. You don't want to make sudden, unplanned motions in a combat aircraft cockpit, where the controls are sensitive and lots of things can explode.) That **demeanor**, once learned under penalty of death, is carried through the rest of your life. Kerns also had that quiet, dark, and private humor.

Even after a lifetime in the wilderness, Kerns entered the woods with a deep sense of respect and humility, like a man approaching a magnificent, dangerous, and unpredictable creature. It's the same
160 way a good pilot approaches his aircraft.

As we worked in the wilderness, learning technical skills, Kerns kept talking about Positive Mental Attitude. It was the number one item on the checklist he'd given us, and that checklist was from the Big Daddy of all checklist writers, the U.S. Air Force. Positive Mental Attitude.

"It must be important," I told Jonas.

"Yeah, but what is it?" he asked.

"Think good thoughts and you'll be saved?"

"I'd rather have a chain saw and a cheeseburger," Jonas said. "A
170 cell phone and a GPS would be nice, too."

demeanor
(dǐ-mē´nər) *n.*
attitude or perceived behavior.

As we slogged through the woods, practicing firecraft, shelter making, knots, and navigation . . . I kept asking Kerns, but he couldn't explain it. Nobody could. It meant the difference between life and death; he could tell me that. He had an adult portion of it; he assured me of that. "It's not what's in your pack," he'd say. "It's what's in here." He'd tap his chest. No wonder Tom Wolfe had called it *The Right Stuff*.[8] You couldn't exactly title a book *Positive Mental Attitude*, now, could you?

Kerns didn't always have it, though. He'd had to acquire it.
180 Early on in his Air Force days, he took a group of pilots into the mountains near Spokane for survival training maneuvers. "I was a greenhorn and just misjudged our situation," he told us. Back then, he was pretending to be the macho drill instructor I'd expected: Go, go, go, push, push, push. He was not yet cool. He was acting cool.

His class had been crossing a vast field of slushy snow, which made the going rough. The pilots began to suffer from fatigue, but Kerns kept driving them. "I now realize that was a mistake," he said. As the temperature dropped, darkness came down like a curtain. "Suddenly everybody wanted to give up. They just sat
190 down and lost all their will." Apathy is a typical reaction to any sort of disaster, and if you're exhausted in a field of snow at sundown in the mountains, you're pretty much about to witness the simple disaster of nature separating you permanently from everything you know and love in this world. That apathy can rapidly lead to complete psychological deterioration. Then you sit down and hypothermia[9] sets in, which produces more apathy, a more profound psychological deterioration, and ultimately, death.

Fatigue almost always comes as a surprise. It is as much a psychological condition as a physical one, and scientists have
200 struggled without success to understand it. It's like the difficulty of studying sand in order to understand the Sand Pile Effect. There's nothing in the muscles or nerves or even the biochemistry of the body that would seem to predict or explain fatigue. Once fatigue sets in, though, it is almost impossible to recover from it under survival conditions. It is not just a matter of being tired. It's more like a spiritual collapse, and recovery requires more than food and rest.

Following the explosive burst of activity that is sometimes required for survival, or in the panic stage when you're running
210 or climbing or swimming, you're like a woman who's just given birth to a baby. You're depleted and wide open to fatigue. It may take weeks to recover; and if you're not taking care of yourself, that

---

[8] **Tom Wolfe . . . The Right Stuff:** the title of Wolfe's 1979 book about the Mercury space program refers to the personal qualities required in astronauts.

[9] **hypothermia:** abnormally low body temperature.

fatigue can lead to an inability to sleep, which in turn can result in a sudden psychological collapse. The physical and psychological factors rapidly erode each other, which is why it is so important to pace yourself, rest frequently, and stay hydrated. That's why Kerns's pushing the pilots so hard had been a mistake.

A survival situation is a ticking clock: You have only so much stored energy (and water), and every time you exert yourself, you're using it up. The trick is to become extremely stingy with your scarce resources, balancing risk and reward, investing only in efforts that offer the biggest return.

In survival situations, people greatly underestimate the need for rest. While Kerns, Jonas, and I were doing map and compass exercises, he would frequently stop and look around at the woods, chatting with us. I'd be thinking: *Let's go, let's go, I know the way.* And he'd just stand there. Now I understand why. You should operate at about 60 percent of your normal level of activity, he explained, and rest and rehydrate frequently. If the weather is cool and you're sweating, you're working too hard. . . .

When Kerns at last realized how serious his situation was with his fatigued Air Force pilots, he recounted, "I fell to my knees and I prayed. Faith is a very important thing in your will to survive."

As Peter Leschak put it, "Whether a deity is actually listening or not, there is value in formally announcing your needs, desires, worries, sins, and goals in a focused, prayerful attitude. Only when you are aware can you take action." Survival psychologists have observed the same thing.

Kerns added, "All at once, it hit me that I might actually lose them. Those million-dollar pilots could die."

By chance, he found a fence and used the cedar post to start a fire. (Chance is nothing more than opportunity, and it is all around at every turn; the trick lies in recognizing it.) "It's amazing to see what fire can do. You're out in the woods, you're cold, you're lost, you're lonely. But the minute you light that fire, you're home, the lights are on, and supper's cooking. It made a world of difference going from complete darkness to light and warmth. It just turned everybody around."

Kerns learned many lessons that night. His mastery and confidence turned the pilots around even more than the fire. It showed them the way, and it made Kerns more able to save himself. That lesson was driven home again and again: Helping someone else is the best way to ensure your own survival. It takes you out of yourself. It helps you to rise above your fears. Now you're a rescuer, not a victim. And seeing how your leadership and skill buoy others up gives you more focus and energy to persevere. The cycle reinforces itself: You buoy them up, and their response buoys you

"Plan the flight and fly the plan. But don't fall in love with the plan."

up. Many people who survive alone report that they were doing it for someone else (a wife, boyfriend, mother, son) back home. When
260 Antoine de Saint-Exupéry was lost in the Lybian Desert, it was the thought of his wife's suffering that kept him going. . . .

In the 84th-floor offices of the World Trade Center's south tower, and an hour before the collapse, Ronald DiFrancesco was one of the people who met Brian Clark, the fire warden with the flashlight who was asking people: "Up or down?" DiFrancesco went up, hoping to find air. But after ten or so floors, he encountered people who were succumbing to fatigue and smoke. The people, all of whom would die, were just giving up and falling asleep. DiFrancesco, too, was collapsing, but then he said to himself, "I've
270 got to see my wife and kids again." And with that, he got up and bolted down the stairs to safety.

Doctors and nurses often survive better than others because they have someone to help. They have a well-defined purpose. Purpose is a big part of survival, but it must be accompanied by work. Grace without good works is not salvation. The survivor plans by setting small, manageable goals and then systematically achieving them. Hence the Air Force checklist and the notion, which my father drilled into me: Plan the flight and fly the plan. But don't fall in love with the plan. Be open to a changing world
280 and let go of the plan when necessary so that you can make a new

plan. Then, as the world and the plan both go through their book of changes, you will always be ready to do the next right thing.

People are animals with animal instincts, but they lack many of the other survival mechanisms animals possess, such as fur to keep them warm, fangs and claws, and flight or speed. Culture creates a collective survival mechanism for the species. People survive better in numbers. They survive because they use cognition to organize, say, for a hunt, and to make things, even as cognition inhibits their animalness, including strength. That's why, when cognition is turned off, people are amazed by their own strength: because cognition continuously inhibits it. That is the whole secret to cognition: It is a mechanism for modulating emotional (physical) responses.

Every culture evolves survival rituals. Some, especially nontechnical ones, are devoted to not much more than survival. In Native American cultures, one ritual is the vision quest, in which a young person goes into the wild and fasts in search of a vision. It can be seen as a type of survival training, for if there is no food, no water, no way, a person has already practiced sitting still and making the best of the situation. He'll have confidence in his ability to survive it.

The survival lessons that apply today are ancient. The *Tao Te Ching* is broken into two parts, "Integrity," and "The Way," which can be thought of as the two halves of surviving anything. Lao-tzu's[10] book is a handbook for a ruler, but it is also a handbook for the brain. An imbalance of the brain's functions leads us into trouble, and a triumph of balance gets us out. I've found similar lessons in Epictetus, Herodotus, Thucydides, the Bible, the Bhagavad Gītā.[11] "Is there any thing whereof it may be said, See, this is new?" says Ecclesiastes. But there are always new people who haven't heard that there's nothing new under the sun. And there's always someone who doesn't get the word.

I had always wondered where our American survival rituals were. I think now that they're everywhere around us. The Boy Scouts in its original conception was a survival school. Sports are survival training in that they teach strength, agility, strategy, and the endurance of pain. But our culture is filled with survival stories as well. Cool is the ultimate American conception of the survival model. James Stockdale, a fighter pilot who was shot down over Vietnam in 1965, spoke many times about how he survived seven

[10] *Tao Te Ching . . .* **Lao-tzu's (dao dé jīng . . . lou´dzŭ´):** a classic sixth-century B.C. Chinese text describing the way of seeing and behaving that forms the basis of the Taoist religion.

[11] **Epictetus, Herodotus, Thucydides, the Bible, the Bhagavad Gītā:** an ancient Greek philosopher, two ancient Greek historians, the Christian book of scripture, and a section of the Mahabharata, or Hindu scripture.

and a half years in prison camp. "One should include a course of familiarization with pain," he said.

Stockdale observed, "You have to practice hurting. There is no question about it. . . . You have to practice being hazed. You have to learn to take a bunch of junk and accept it with a sense of humor."

He's talking about being cool, just as he was when his F-8 fighter-bomber was hit with 57-millimeter fire. He had been on a relaxed bomb run at the time. He'd even taken off his uncomfortable oxygen mask. "I could barely keep that plane from
330 flying into the ground while I got that damned oxygen mask to my mouth so I could tell my wingman that I was about to eject. What rotten luck. And on a milk run! My mind was clear, and I said to myself, 'five years.' I knew we were making a mess of the war in Southeast Asia, but I didn't think it would last longer than that." The Spartan practice of enduring the bite of the fox is "a course of familiarization with pain." Then there are the schools like Kerns's, which attempt to teach wilderness survival by directly meeting the problem head-on with Yankee ingenuity.

Like being lost, survival is a transformation; being a leader can
340 ensure that, when you reach the final stage of that metamorphosis, it is with an attitude of commitment, not resignation. The transformation of survival is permanent. People who have had the experience often go on to become the best search and rescue professionals. They have come to understand, perhaps unconsciously, that they can only live fully by helping others through that same transformation. All the survivors I've talked to have told me how horrible the experience was. But they have also told me, often with deep puzzlement, how beautiful it was. They wouldn't trade the experience for anything in the world.

350 It gradually dawned on me that only by researching and dissecting the mysterious quality the Air Force so dully called Positive Mental Attitude would I ever understand survival.

And I thought: Wait a minute. My father was in the Army Air Corps. Maybe that's what he had that allowed him to live.[12] If so, he'd certainly never talked about it. But what pilot would? I felt as if I'd stepped to the edge of the very thing I'd been after all my life. Here, concealed in the most unimaginative phrase possible, was the deep mystery I'd been trying to unravel.

COLLABORATIVE DISCUSSION With a partner, discuss whether the title *Deep Survival* is a good fit for the selection. Cite specific evidence from the text to support your answer.

---

[12]**My father . . . allowed him to live:** During World War II, the author's father fell from a plane without a parachute and miraculously survived.

Determine Central Idea and Summarize the Text

When you **summarize** a text, you give a brief, objective account of the central idea the author presents in the work. The **central idea** is the main point that the author wants you to understand. To keep your summary **objective,** include only the author's ideas; do not include your responses or ideas about the text. Follow these steps to determine the central idea of the excerpt from *Deep Survival* and create an objective summary of the text:

1. Read the complete text without taking any notes.

2. Reread the text, focusing on the main ideas and the most important details. This time take notes, listing key words, main ideas with their supporting details, and quotations that make strong points.

3. Make an inference, or logical assumption, about the central idea of the text. Ask yourself: What do most of the ideas and details have in common? What does Gonzales want his readers to know?

4. In your own words, write a brief, objective summary of the text, focusing on the author's central idea only and omitting the supporting details.

Analyze Ideas and Events

Laurence Gonzales introduces and develops his ideas on the topic of survival through the use of **anecdotes,** or brief stories. He alternates the anecdotes with his own ideas and observations, as well as with information from experts. As you analyze the text, consider how the author utilizes particular sentences and paragraphs to communicate his ideas and how they build on one another. Consider this example:

Portion of Text	Type	Questions for Analysis
Lines 1–59	Anecdote (Juliane Koepcke's plane crash)	In lines 15–18, the author steps outside of the anecdote to present information from another survivor. How does this information clarify the point the author is making in the anecdote about Juliane?

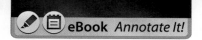

Analyzing the Text

Cite Text Evidence   Support your responses with evidence from the selection.

1. **Cite Evidence**   In lines 1–14, what detail does Gonzales focus on when he describes Juliane's fall from the airplane? How can you tell that he finds this detail interesting?

2. **Analyze**   What comparison does Gonzales make in lines 60–76? How does this comparison support one of his main points?

3. **Connect**   Reread lines 67–89. What connection does Gonzales make between the experience of passengers in the plane and the anecdote about the World Trade Center disaster?

4. **Cite Evidence**   What evidence does Gonzales cite to prove the point that survival is not always a matter of luck or preparation?

5. **Interpret**   Gonzales relates an anecdote about pilots who undergo survival training and get stranded in the snow (lines 179–190, 231–261). What important truths about survival are revealed by the anecdote?

6. **Connect**   Gonzales provides information on survival rituals in different cultures (lines 294–312). How does this relate to Kerns's ideas about Positive Mental Attitude? How does it relate to Gonzales's statement that "Cool is the ultimate American conception of the survival model"?

7. **Draw Conclusions**   What does Gonzales's analysis of survival lead him to conclude about why some people seem to have an amazing ability to survive life-threatening situations against all odds, while others seem to just give up? In other words, what is his central idea?

PERFORMANCE TASK

Writing Activity: Argument   What quotation from the text best supports Laurence Gonzales's central idea—his most important message about survival? Write an argument explaining why you agree or disagree with Gonzales's ideas about survival.

1. Sum up what the author wants you to know about survival. Then, write a claim stating your position about what it takes to survive a life-threatening event.

2. Make notes about reasons that support your claim. Then, collect evidence that supports your reasons. Consider an opposing claim and list valid counterarguments.

3. Write a draft of your argument. Be sure to present your reasons and evidence in a logical order.

4. Revise your draft to eliminate unrelated or illogical evidence. Finally, check your work to make sure you have used the conventions of standard English.

Critical Vocabulary

disintegration   **deduce**   **conversely**   **distill**   **demeanor**

Practice and Apply Complete the sentences to demonstrate your comprehension of each Critical Vocabulary word.

1. The **disintegration** of an airplane in flight would cause . . .

2. Juliane **deduced** that rescue planes would not find her because . . .

3. Some people who have no survival equipment can survive life-threatening situations through wits alone; **conversely**, some people who have survival equipment . . .

4. In survival school, people learn how to **distill** water from air so that . . .

5. A calm **demeanor** is an important asset in a military pilot because . . .

Vocabulary Strategy: Context Clues

If you are uncertain of the meaning of a word, you can often figure out its meaning by using **context clues,** or information in the surrounding sentences or paragraphs. For example, the Critical Vocabulary word *disintegration* (line 19) is used in the description of a plane crash. The context includes the phrases "extensive structural failure" and "broken airplane." These clues tell you that *disintegration* means "breaking up into pieces."

Practice and Apply Find each of these words in the selection: *canopy* (line 27), *apathy* (line 190), *buoy* (line 255), *bolted* (line 271), *metamorphosis* (line 340). With a partner, discuss the context clues that can help you figure out each word's meaning. Follow these steps:

1. Determine the word's function in the sentence. For example, is it a noun that names a person, place, or thing, or is it a verb that describes an action?

2. Read the sentence in which the word appears. Does the overall meaning of the sentence allow you to guess the word's meaning?

3. If the sentence does not provide enough information, read the paragraph in which the word appears. If necessary, reread the previous paragraph and the one that follows to look for clues.

4. If you still do not have enough clues, think about the larger context of the selection. How does the word fit with what you know about the subject?

Language and Style: Colons and Semicolons

When used correctly, punctuation helps clarify meaning for readers by linking ideas and by showing places to pause. In the excerpt from *Deep Survival*, Laurence Gonzales uses both **colons** and **semicolons** to add clarity and interest to the text.

A colon is used to introduce a sentence, a quotation, or a list. A complete sentence that follows a colon usually begins with a capital letter.

Uses of Colons	
Purpose	**Example**
illustrate or provide an example of what was just stated	It was another important moment: She didn't spend time bemoaning her fate. (lines 27–28)
introduce a quotation	Before he died, he spoke to his father on the phone: "Why did I listen to them—I shouldn't have." (lines 83–85)
introduce a list	The Survival School provides training in the following skills: using maps and compasses, building and tending a fire, and signaling.

A semicolon is used to connect closely related ideas. It is stronger than a comma but less abrupt than a period. It indicates that the statement that follows will add explanation.

Uses of Semicolons	
Purpose	**Example**
separate independent clauses and add explanation	She wasn't screaming; she wasn't in a panic. (lines 11–12)
precede a conjunctive adverb that joins two clauses	Juliane had no survival training; nevertheless, she managed to survive a dangerous jungle journey without external help.
separate parallel phrases that contain commas	A survival box should contain flares, for signaling rescuers; rations, for keeping up strength; and a first-aid kit, for medical emergencies.

Practice and Apply Look back at the argument you wrote for this selection's Performance Task. Revise your argument to include at least one colon and one semicolon. Then discuss with a partner how each punctuation mark you added improved or clarified your meaning.

Louise Erdrich (b. 1954) *is best known for exploring the Native American experience in her novels, poetry, and children's books. Born in Little Falls, Minnesota, she grew up in North Dakota. Of German American and Ojibwa (Chippewa) descent, her writing reflects a fascination with the influence of family and heritage on individuals and community. She lives in Minneapolis, Minnesota, where she owns a bookstore and continues to write. Her best-known works include the novels* Love Medicine, The Beet Queen, *and* The Round House.

The Leap

Short Story by Louise Erdrich

AS YOU READ Pay attention to how the narrator conveys her feelings about her mother as the story unfolds. Write down any questions you generate during reading.

My mother is the surviving half of a blindfold trapeze act, not a fact I think about much even now that she is sightless, the result of **encroaching** and stubborn cataracts. She walks slowly through her house here in New Hampshire, lightly touching her way along walls and running her hands over knickknacks, books, the drift of a grown child's belongings and castoffs. She has never upset an object or as much as brushed a magazine onto the floor. She has never lost her balance or bumped into a closet door left carelessly open.

10   It has occurred to me that the catlike precision of her movements in old age might be the result of her early training, but she shows so little of the drama or flair one might expect from a performer that I tend to forget the Flying Avalons. She has kept no sequined costume, no photographs, no fliers or posters from that part of her youth. I would, in fact, tend to think that all memory of double somersaults and heartstopping catches had left her arms and legs were it not for the fact that sometimes, as I sit sewing in

Image Credits: (c) ©H. Armstrong Roberts/Retrofile/Getty Images; (tr) ©Ulf Andersen/Getty Images

> **encroach**
> (ĕn-krōch´) *v.* to gradually intrude upon or invade.

the room of the rebuilt house in which I slept as a child, I hear
the crackle, catch a whiff of smoke from the stove downstairs and
suddenly the room goes dark, the stitches burn beneath my fingers,
and I am sewing with a needle of hot silver, a thread of fire.

I owe her my existence three times. The first was when she
saved herself. In the town square a replica tent pole, cracked and
splintered, now stands cast in concrete. It commemorates the
disaster that put our town smack on the front page of the Boston
and New York tabloids. It is from those old newspapers, now
historical records, that I get my information. Not from my mother,
Anna of the Flying Avalons, nor from any of her in-laws, nor
certainly from the other half of her particular act, Harold Avalon,
her first husband. In one news account it says, "The day was mildly
overcast, but nothing in the air or temperature gave any hint of the
sudden force with which the deadly gale would strike."

I have lived in the West, where you can see the weather
coming for miles, and it is true that out here we are at something
of a disadvantage. When extremes of temperature collide, a hot
and cold front, winds generate instantaneously behind a hill and
crash upon you without warning. That, I think, was the likely
situation on that day in June. People probably commented on the
pleasant air, grateful that no hot sun beat upon the striped tent
that stretched over the entire center green. They bought their
tickets and surrendered them in anticipation. They sat. They ate
caramelized popcorn and roasted peanuts. There was time, before
the storm, for three acts. The White Arabians of Ali-Khazar rose on
their hind legs and waltzed. The Mysterious Bernie folded himself
into a painted cracker tin, and the Lady of the Mists made herself
appear and disappear in surprising places. As the clouds gathered
outside, unnoticed, the ringmaster cracked his whip, shouted his
introduction, and pointed to the ceiling of the tent, where the
Flying Avalons were perched.

They loved to drop gracefully from nowhere, like two sparkling
birds, and blow kisses as they threw off their plumed helmets and
high-collared capes. They laughed and flirted openly as they beat
their way up again on the trapeze bars. In the final vignette[1] of their
act, they actually would kiss in midair, pausing, almost hovering
as they swooped past one another. On the ground, between bows,
Harry Avalon would skip quickly to the front rows and point out
the smear of my mother's lipstick, just off the edge of his mouth.
They made a romantic pair all right, especially in the blindfold
sequence.

---

[1] **vignette:** a brief scene.

"I owe her my existence three times."

60   That afternoon, as the anticipation increased, as Mr. and Mrs. Avalon tied sparkling strips of cloth onto each other's face and as they puckered their lips in mock kisses, lips destined "never again to meet," as one long breathless article put it, the wind rose, miles off, wrapped itself into a cone, and howled. There came a rumble of electrical energy, drowned out by the sudden roll of drums. One detail not mentioned by the press, perhaps unknown—Anna was pregnant at the time, seven months and hardly showing, her stomach muscles were that strong. It seems incredible that she would work high above the ground when any fall could be so 70 dangerous, but the explanation—I know from watching her go blind—is that my mother lives comfortably in extreme elements. She is one with the constant dark now, just as the air was her home, familiar to her, safe, before the storm that afternoon.

     From opposite ends of the tent they waved, blind and smiling, to the crowd below. The ringmaster removed his hat and called for silence, so that the two above could concentrate. They rubbed their hands in chalky powder, then Harry launched himself and swung once, twice, in huge calibrated[2] beats across space. He hung from his knees and on the third swing stretched wide his

---

[2] **calibrated:** checked or determined by comparison with a standard.

80 arms, held his hand out to receive his pregnant wife as she dove from her shining bar.

It was while the two were in midair, their hands about to meet, that lightning struck the main pole and sizzled down the guy wires, filling the air with a blue radiance that Harry Avalon must certainly have seen through the cloth of his blindfold as the tent buckled and the edifice toppled him forward, the swing continuing and not returning in its sweep, and Harry going down, down into the crowd with his last thought, perhaps, just a prickle of surprise at his empty hands.

90 My mother once said that I'd be amazed at how many things a person can do within the act of falling. Perhaps, at the time, she was teaching me to dive off a board at the town pool, for I associated the idea with midair somersaults. But I also think she meant that even in that awful doomed second one could think, for she certainly did. When her hands did not meet her husband's, my mother tore her blindfold away. As he swept past her on the wrong side, she could have grasped his ankle, the toe-end of his tights, and gone down clutching him. Instead, she changed direction. Her body twisted toward a heavy wire and she managed to hang on to the braided 100 metal, still hot from the lightning strike. Her palms were burned so terribly that once healed they bore no lines, only the blank scar tissue of a quieter future. She was lowered, gently, to the sawdust ring just underneath the dome of the canvas roof, which did not entirely settle but was held up on one end and jabbed through, torn, and still on fire in places from the giant spark, though rain and men's jackets soon put that out.

Three people died, but except for her hands my mother was not seriously harmed until an overeager rescuer broke her arm in **extricating** her and also, in the process, collapsed a portion of the 110 tent bearing a huge buckle that knocked her unconscious. She was taken to the town hospital, and there she must have hemorrhaged,[3] for they kept her, confined to her bed, a month and a half before her baby was born without life.

Harry Avalon had wanted to be buried in the circus cemetery next to the original Avalon, his uncle, so she sent him back with his brothers. The child, however, is buried around the corner, beyond this house and just down the highway. Sometimes I used to walk there just to sit. She was a girl, but I rarely thought of her as a sister or even as a separate person really. I suppose you could call it the 120 egocentrism[4] of a child, of all young children, but I considered her a less finished version of myself.

extricate
(ĕk´strĭ-kāt´) v. to release or disentangle from.

---

[3] **hemorrhaged:** bled heavily.
[4] **egocentrism:** belief in the primary or sole importance of the self.

When the snow falls, throwing shadows among the stones, I can easily pick hers out from the road, for it is bigger than the others and in the shape of a lamb at rest, its legs curled beneath. The carved lamb looms larger as the years pass, though it is probably only my eyes, the visions shifting, as what is close to me blurs and distances sharpen. In odd moments, I think it is the edge drawing near, the edge of everything, the unseen horizon we do not really speak of in the eastern woods. And it also seems to me,
130 although this is probably an idle fantasy, that the statue is growing more sharply etched, as if, instead of weathering itself into a porous mass, it is hardening on the hillside with each snowfall, perfecting itself.

It was during her confinement in the hospital that my mother met my father. He was called in to look at the set of her arm, which was complicated. He stayed, sitting at her bedside, for he was something of an armchair traveler and had spent his war quietly, at an air force training grounds, where he became a specialist in arms and legs broken during parachute training exercises. Anna
140 Avalon had been to many of the places he longed to visit—Venice, Rome, Mexico, all through France and Spain. She had no family of her own and was taken in by the Avalons, trained to perform from a very young age. They toured Europe before the war, then based themselves in New York. She was illiterate.

It was in the hospital that she finally learned to read and write, as a way of overcoming the boredom and depression of those weeks, and it was my father who insisted on teaching her. In return for stories of her adventures, he graded her first exercises. He bought her her first book, and over her bold letters, which the pale guides
150 of the penmanship pads could not contain, they fell in love.

I wonder if my father calculated the exchange he offered: one form of flight for another. For after that, and for as long as I can remember, my mother has never been without a book. Until now, that is, and it remains the greatest difficulty of her blindness. Since my father's recent death, there is no one to read to her, which is why I returned, in fact, from my failed life where the land is flat. I came home to read to my mother, to read out loud, to read long into the dark if I must, to read all night.

Once my father and mother married, they moved onto the old
160 farm he had inherited but didn't care much for. Though he'd been thinking of moving to a larger city, he settled down and broadened his practice in this valley. It still seems odd to me, when they could have gone anywhere else, that they chose to stay in the town where the disaster had occurred, and which my father in the first place had found so **constricting**. It was my mother who insisted upon it,

constrict
(kən-strĭkt´) *v.* to limit or impede growth.

after her child did not survive. And then, too, she loved the sagging farmhouse with its scrap of what was left of a vast acreage of woods and hidden hay fields that stretched to the game park.

170   I owe my existence, the second time then, to the two of them and the hospital that brought them together. That is the debt we take for granted since none of us asks for life. It is only once we have it that we hang on so dearly.

I was seven the year the house caught fire, probably from standing ash. It can rekindle, and my father, forgetful around the house and perpetually exhausted from night hours on call, often emptied what he thought were ashes from cold stoves into wooden or cardboard containers. The fire could have started from a flaming box, or perhaps a buildup of creosote[5] inside the chimney was the culprit. It started right around the stove, and the heart of the house

180   was gutted. The baby-sitter, fallen asleep in my father's den on the first floor, woke to find the stairway to my upstairs room cut off by flames. She used the phone, then ran outside to stand beneath my window.

When my parents arrived, the town volunteers had drawn water from the fire pond and were spraying the outside of the

---

[5] **creosote:** a flammable, oily byproduct of burning carbon-based fuels like coal, peat, and wood.

house, preparing to go inside after me, not knowing at the time that there was only one staircase and that it was lost. On the other side of the house, the superannuated[6] extension ladder broke in half. Perhaps the clatter of it falling against the walls woke me, for I'd been asleep up to that point.

As soon as I awakened, in the small room that I now use for sewing, I smelled the smoke. I followed things by the letter then, was good at memorizing instructions, and so I did exactly what was taught in the second-grade home fire drill. I got up, I touched the back of my door before opening it. Finding it hot, I left it closed and stuffed my rolled-up rug beneath the crack. I did not hide under my bed or crawl into my closet. I put on my flannel robe, and then I sat down to wait.

Outside, my mother stood below my dark window and saw clearly that there was no rescue. Flames had pierced one side wall, and the glare of the fire lighted the massive limbs and trunk of the vigorous old elm that had probably been planted the year the house was built, a hundred years ago at least. No leaf touched the wall, and just one thin branch scraped the roof. From below, it looked as though even a squirrel would have had trouble jumping from the tree onto the house, for the breadth of that small branch was no bigger than my mother's wrist.

Standing there, beside Father, who was preparing to rush back around to the front of the house, my mother asked him to unzip her dress. When he wouldn't be bothered, she made him understand. He couldn't make his hands work, so she finally tore it off and stood there in her pearls and stockings. She directed one of the men to lean the broken half of the extension ladder up against the trunk of the tree. In surprise, he **complied**. She ascended. She vanished. Then she could be seen among the leafless branches of late November as she made her way up and, along her stomach, inched the length of a bough that curved above the branch that brushed the roof.

Once there, swaying, she stood and balanced. There were plenty of people in the crowd and many who still remember, or think they do, my mother's leap through the ice-dark air toward that thinnest extension, and how she broke the branch falling so that it cracked in her hands, cracked louder than the flames as she vaulted with it toward the edge of the roof, and how it hurtled down end over end without her, and their eyes went up, again, to see where she had flown.

I didn't see her leap through air, only heard the sudden thump and looked out my window. She was hanging by the backs of her

comply
(kəm-plī´) *v.* to obey an instruction or command.

---

[6] **superannuated:** obsolete; ready for retirement.

heels from the new gutter we had put in that year, and she was
230 smiling. I was not surprised to see her, she was so matter-of-fact.
She tapped on the window. I remember how she did it, too. It
was the friendliest tap, a bit **tentative**, as if she was afraid she had
arrived too early at a friend's house. Then she gestured at the latch,
and when I opened the window she told me to raise it wider and
prop it up with the stick so it wouldn't crush her fingers. She swung
down, caught the ledge, and crawled through the opening. Once
she was in my room, I realized she had on only underclothing, a
bra of the heavy stitched cotton women used to wear and step-in,
lace-trimmed drawers. I remember feeling light-headed, of course,
240 terribly relieved, and then embarrassed for her to be seen by the
crowd undressed.

    I was still embarrassed as we flew out the window, toward
earth, me in her lap, her toes pointed as we skimmed toward the
painted target of the fire fighter's net.

    I know that she's right. I knew it even then. As you fall, there
is time to think. Curled as I was, against her stomach, I was not
startled by the cries of the crowd or the looming faces. The wind
roared and beat its hot breath at our back, the flames whistled.
I slowly wondered what would happen if we missed the circle or
250 bounced out of it. Then I wrapped my hands around my mother's
hands. I felt the brush of her lips and heard the beat of her heart in
my ears, loud as thunder, long as the roll of drums.

tentative
(tĕn′tə-tĭv) *adj.* with
caution and without
confidence.

COLLABORATIVE DISCUSSION How does the narrator feel about her
mother? With a partner, discuss how the author reveals the character of
the mother through the narrator. Cite specific evidence from the text to
support your ideas.

Analyze Author's Choices: Flashback and Tension

The ability to create **tension,** or suspense, is central to the author's craft. Tension propels a story forward and keeps the reader wondering what will happen next. One effective technique for creating tension is the **flashback**—a literary device used to manipulate time by inserting an earlier event into the present action, often by having a character recall something that happened in the past. As a flashback is introduced, the verb tense will shift from the present to the past or past perfect tense. Signal words, such as *once* (as in, *once upon a time*) and *remember* (as in, *I remember when*) might be used to alert the reader that a shift in time is about to occur. They also remind the reader that a flashback is still in effect.

The chart tracks some shifts in time and tension in "The Leap." By following the action, you can see how shifts in the story's **chronology,** or order, help to sustain or build tension. Complete your own chart as you analyze the story.

Tension Tracker		
Example	**Flashback Clues** (verb tense; signal words)	**Action Summary**
"I owe her my existence three times. The first was when..."	shift from present to past tense	narrator begins to explain her debt to her mother
"I have lived in the West ..."	shift to past perfect tense	narrator provides information about her own adult life

Support Inferences About Theme

In a short story, the **theme,** or the underlying message, usually develops and emerges through **inference.** An inference is a logical conclusion based on clues in the text as well as on your own experience. To uncover the theme, begin by analyzing the story's title. Then, look for clues in the text that indicate what the title might mean. Be aware of the possibility that the title may have multiple meanings. By keeping a list of clues, you can create a summary of supporting inferences that will help you to determine the story's theme. For example, you might note that the word *leap* is in the title, and because the narrator's mother was a trapeze artist, she was probably able to make dangerous leaps. Ask yourself, what might be the figurative meaning of a *leap*? Look for these kinds of clues to determine the theme the author wants to convey.

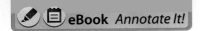

Analyzing the Text

Cite Text Evidence   Support your responses with evidence from the selection.

1. **Interpret** How do lines 15–21 act as a flashback? What clues do they give about the rest of the story? Provide specific evidence in your response.

2. **Infer** In lines 98–100, Anna decides to reach for the hot braided metal rather than for her husband as he falls. What does this reveal about her character? What inferences can you make about the story's title in this passage?

3. **Interpret** Identify the leaps in the story. Which leaps are literal? Which are figurative?

4. **Analyze** The narrator speaks of the three ways that she owes her existence to her mother. Identify the three ways and the literary techniques used to reveal them. How does each revelation affect the story's tension?

5. **Compare** What do these scenes reveal about the mother's character?

   - Anna saves herself during the trapeze accident.
   - Anna saves her daughter from the house fire.

6. **Draw Conclusions** Based upon what the narrator reveals, draw conclusions about the mother and her relationship with her daughter. Cite evidence from the text to support your response.

7. **Infer** Reread lines 227–252. What does the narrator learn? What inferences can you make about the story's theme?

PERFORMANCE TASK

Speaking Activity: Discussion Imagery about circuses occurs throughout "The Leap." Explore the author's use of circus imagery in a writing exercise and in discussion groups.

1. Reread the story, jotting down notes on specific references to the circus. Beside each reference, note whether each image contributes to character, theme, setting, or any other aspect of the story.

2. In small discussion groups, use your notes to respond to this question: In what ways does circus imagery contribute to the story? Write a brief summary of your discussion.

Critical Vocabulary

encroach   extricate   constrict   comply   tentative

Practice and Apply Answer these questions, using a dictionary or thesaurus as needed. Make sure your answers reflect your understanding of each Critical Vocabulary word's meaning.

1. Should rescue crews provide a **tentative** response to **encroaching** forest fires? Why or why not?

2. Would it feel **constricting** if one always **complied** with the wishes of others? Explain.

3. Why would you **extricate** yourself from a planned road trip upon learning of an **encroaching** blizzard?

Vocabulary Strategy: Prefixes

The Critical Vocabulary words *encroach*, *extricate*, *constrict,* and *comply* all contain **prefixes,** an affix added to the beginning of a base word. Knowing the meaning of common prefixes, such as *en-*, *ex-*, *con-*, and *com-*, will help you clarify the meaning of unknown words. Here are the meanings of some common prefixes and examples of other words that contain the prefixes:

Prefixes	Meanings	Examples
en-	to go into or onto	energy, entire
ex-	out of or away from	exchange, extend
com-, con-	together, with, jointly	comfort, contain, condition

If a base word is unfamiliar, use your knowledge of the word's prefix and how the word is used in context to clarify its meaning. If necessary, consult a dictionary to determine the precise meaning of a word.

Practice and Apply Identify a new word, either from the selection or on your own, that contains each of the prefixes in the chart. For each word you choose, follow these steps:

1. Identify the base word, the main word part. For example, the base word for *exchange* is *change.*

2. Write a definition for each word that incorporates the prefix meaning and the base word meaning. Use a dictionary to check your definition. Make changes if needed.

3. Finally, write a sample sentence for each word you chose.

Language and Style: Relative Clauses

A **clause** is a group of words that contains a subject and a predicate. **Relative clauses** describe nouns and function as adjectives. Here are the characteristics of a relative clause:

- It begins with a signal word: a relative pronoun (*that, which, who, whom, whose*) or a relative adverb (*when, where,* or *why*).
- It follows a noun or a noun phrase.
- It provides extra information about a noun or a noun phrase, or it answers the questions *What kind? How many?* or *Which one?*

Authors use relative clauses not only to convey specific meanings but also to add interest and variety to their work. Read this sentence from "The Leap":

> **It commemorates the disaster <u>that put our town smack on the front page of the Boston and New York tabloids.</u>**

The clause fulfills all the elements of a relative clause: it begins with a relative pronoun—*that*; it follows a noun—*disaster*; it answers the question *Which one?*—the disaster that put the town in the tabloids.

Erdrich could have expressed the same ideas this way:

> **It commemorates the disaster. The disaster put our town smack on the front page of the Boston and New York tabloids.**

Notice how the sentence with the relative clause is smoother and easier to read. Here are some other examples of relative clauses from the "The Leap":

Relative Clauses		
Signal Word	**Relative Clause**	**Words Modified**
which	He was called in to look at the set of her arm, <u>which was complicated.</u>	"the set of her arm"
who	. . . and it was my father <u>who insisted on teaching her.</u>	"father"
where	. . . they chose to stay in the town <u>where the disaster had occurred</u> . . .	"town"

Practice and Apply Look back at the summary you created in response to this selection's Performance Task. Revise the summary to include at least three relative clauses. With a partner, discuss your revised summaries. Then work together to identify at least five more relative clauses in "The Leap" that are not included as examples in this lesson.

Wisława Szymborska (1923–2012) *was born in western Poland and spent most of her life in Krakow, Poland. Her first two published volumes of poetry, written in post–World War II Communist-dominated Poland, were written in the style of Socialist Realism. Szymborska later disowned these works. Her disillusionment with communism was reflected in* Calling Out to Yeti, *published in 1957. Her poems, noted for their unique, ironic tone, have been translated into many languages. Szymborska was awarded the Nobel Prize in Literature in 1996.*

The End and the Beginning

Poem by Wisława Szymborska   translated by Joanna Trzeciak

AS YOU READ Think about all the aspects of daily life that are disrupted by war. Write down any questions you generate during reading.

After every war
someone has to clean up.
Things won't
straighten themselves up, after all.

5 Someone has to push the rubble
to the side of the road,
so the corpse-filled wagons
can pass.

Someone has to get mired
10 in scum and ashes,
sofa springs,
splintered glass,
and bloody rags.

Someone has to drag in a girder
15 to prop up a wall.
Someone has to glaze a window,
rehang a door.

Photogenic it's not,
and takes years.
20 All the cameras have left
for another war.

We'll need the bridges back,
and new railway stations.
Sleeves will go ragged
25 from rolling them up.

Someone, broom in hand,
still recalls the way it was.
Someone else listens
and nods with unsevered[1] head.
30 But already there are those nearby
starting to mill about[2]
who will find it dull.

From out of the bushes
sometimes someone still unearths
35 rusted-out arguments
and carries them to the garbage pile.

Those who knew
what was going on here
must make way for
40 those who know little.
And less than little.
And finally as little as nothing.

In the grass that has overgrown
causes and effects,
45 someone must be stretched out
blade of grass in his mouth
gazing at the clouds.

COLLABORATIVE DISCUSSION What part of cleaning up after a war is
the most difficult? With a partner, discuss the speaker's observations
about this. Cite specific evidence from the text to support your answer.

---

[1] **unsevered:** not cut off; not separated.
[2] **mill about:** move idly or aimlessly.

Determine Figurative Meanings and Tone

In poetry, an author's word choices, and the images that those words create, help convey the speaker's meaning and set the **tone,** or attitude toward the subject. Analyzing the precise meanings of words and phrases that a poet uses can deepen your understanding of the poem. You can analyze the significance of Wisława Szymborska's word choices in "The End and the Beginning" by looking at the elements outlined in this chart.

Imagery	Connotation	Tone
Poets often use **imagery,** or descriptive words and phrases that re-create sensory experiences for the reader. Imagery usually appeals to one or more of the five senses—sight, hearing, smell, taste, and touch—to help readers imagine exactly what is being described. For example, the striking image of "corpse-filled wagons" passing through rubble-lined roads calls to mind photographs that most readers will have seen of war-torn, bombed out cities. The image helps the reader identify with what the speaker is observing. Look for other images in the poem that engage your senses and evoke a strong emotional response.	Poets choose words and expressions not only for their **denotative,** or dictionary, meanings, but also for their **connotative,** or subjective, meanings. Connotative meanings suggest feelings or ideas that go beyond the dictionary definitions. For example, look at these three possible word choices: • "someone has to clean up" • "someone has to tidy up" • "someone has to reorganize" In line 2, Szymborska chose to use *clean up*. This phrase suggests dirtiness and also casts blame on those who made the mess. The words *tidy up* and *reorganize* would not have conveyed the same precise meaning.	A poet's choice of language conveys his or her **tone,** or attitude. Elements to consider when evaluating tone include • words with positive or negative connotations • use of informal language such as idioms or colloquial expressions • repetition of significant words or ideas Szymborska repeats the word *someone* throughout this poem. The use of this indefinite pronoun adds an impersonal quality to the poem, yet the effect of war is intensely personal.

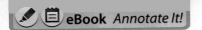

Analyzing the Text

Cite Text Evidence Support your responses with evidence from the selection.

1. **Infer** Notice how the speaker repeats the word "someone" throughout the poem. What statement about war is she making by using an indefinite pronoun rather than referring to a specific person?

2. **Analyze** Answer these questions to explore how Szymborska creates the tone of the poem. Cite words and phrases from the poem to support your answers.

   - Does the speaker use formal or informal language? What is the effect of this choice?
   - What is the speaker's attitude toward the situation he or she is describing?
   - How does the tone of the poem change beginning with line 30?

3. **Interpret** In line 18, the speaker says the aftermath of war is not "photogenic." What images in the poem reinforce this idea about war? How does she show the dimensions of the devastation?

4. **Interpret** Reread the last stanza of the poem. What does the grass **symbolize,** or represent? What does the speaker mean when she describes someone as being "stretched out / blade of grass in his mouth / gazing at the clouds"?

5. **Draw Conclusions** Consider why Szymborska titled her poem "The End and the Beginning" rather than using the more common order "The Beginning and the End." How does the title reflect the message of the poem? Reread stanzas 5 and 10 and explain how they reflect this message.

6. **Connect** Poland experienced great political unrest and upheaval during Szymborska's lifetime: Nazi and Soviet occupations during World War II, postwar repressive Communist control, decades-long resistance of workers against the Communist regime, and, in 1989, the election of a new, non-Communist government. How does Poland's political situation inform Szymborska's choice of subject and her tone in "The End and the Beginning"?

PERFORMANCE TASK

Writing Activity: Reflection Szymborska uses vivid images that, on a literal level, describe the physical activity of recovering from a war. Think about how the images also have a figurative meaning, related to the work of rebuilding a government and a society that have been destroyed by war.

1. Select two examples of imagery from the poem and analyze the meaning of the images as they relate to rebuilding a government or a society.

2. Write a brief explanation of the figurative meaning of each image that you chose.

3. Share and discuss your findings with a partner.

COLLECTION **5**

PERFORMANCE TASK A

Interactive Lessons

If you need help . . .
- **Writing an Argument**
- **Writing as a Process**
- **Using Textual Evidence**

Write an Argument

This collection explores how people cope with situations of extreme hardship and danger—who survives, who doesn't, and why. Look back at the anchor text, *Night,* and at the other texts in the collection. Based on the evidence from at least three selections, would you say that survival requires selfishness? Synthesize your ideas by writing an argument in support of your position.

An effective argument

- makes a persuasive claim and develops the claim with valid reasons and relevant evidence from the texts

- anticipates counterclaims and addresses them with well-supported counterarguments

- establishes clear, logical relationships among claims, counterclaims, reasons, and evidence

- includes a logically structured body, including transitions

- has a satisfying conclusion that effectively summarizes the claim

- maintains a formal tone through the use of appropriate language and the conventions of standard English

---

PLAN

Analyze the Texts Reread *Night,* taking notes about survival. Consider who passes the selection and why. Is it necessary to be selfish in order to survive a selection? Then choose two other texts from the collection and make notes about survival in those texts, too. Pay attention to specific details and gather evidence to support your ideas.

Make a Claim Based on the ideas conveyed in the texts, write a claim that clearly and concisely states your position on whether or not survival requires selfishness. Your claim is effective if

- it makes your position on the issue clear to readers

- you have reasons that will persuade your readers to agree with the claim

- you can support the claim with sufficient evidence from the texts

***my* Notebook**

Use the annotation tools in your eBook to find evidence that supports your ideas about survival. Save each piece of evidence to your notebook.

ACADEMIC VOCABULARY

As you build your argument about survival, be sure to use these words.

dimension

external

statistic

sustain

utilize

Build Your Argument Create a graphic organizer that states your claim, shows several reasons that support your claim, and outlines textual evidence such as details, examples, and quotations for each reason.

Develop Counterarguments Think about your audience. What might your readers say to oppose your claim? How would you try to persuade them to agree with you? Develop counterarguments to address any potential counterclaims.

- Think of at least two counterclaims that a reader who disagrees with your claim might make.
- Decide how you would respond to each counterclaim. You may need to conduct further research to collect relevant facts, details, or statistics.
- Outline the reasons and evidence for your counterarguments.

Get Organized Organize your ideas in an outline, using the notes from your analysis and your graphic organizer. Be sure to include

- a clearly stated claim
- sufficient reasons and evidence to support your claim
- clearly presented counterclaims
- counterarguments supported by additional evidence to refute the counterclaims and further persuade your readers

PRODUCE

Draft Your Essay Write a well-organized draft of your argument. Think about your purpose and audience as you write.

- Introduce your argument in a memorable way that will grab the attention of your readers, perhaps with an interesting detail or quotation from one of the texts. Clearly state your claim.
- Present your reasons, evidence, and counterarguments in logically ordered paragraphs.
- Explain how the evidence from the texts supports your ideas about whether survival requires selfishness.
- Include transitions to connect your reasons and evidence to your claim.
- Use formal language and a respectful tone appropriate for an academic context.
- Write a persuasive conclusion that summarizes your position.

my **WriteSmart**

Write your rough draft in *my*WriteSmart. Focus on getting your ideas down, rather than perfecting your choice of language.

*my*WriteSmart

Have your partner
or a group of peers
review your draft in
*my*WriteSmart. Ask
your reviewers to note
any reasons that do
not support the claim
or that lack sufficient
evidence.

Exchange Essays Share your essay with a partner. Peer editing can be an effective method of revision to help you identify any areas of your argument that lack evidence or that cause confusion for the reader. Constructive feedback should include specific information based on the chart on the next page. As you read your partner's essay, consider these questions:

- In the introduction, does the claim sound strong, confident, and persuasive?
- Has my partner provided relevant evidence to support claims and refute counterclaims?
- Is my partner's essay cohesive? Are additional transitions needed to make connections clear?
- Has my partner sustained a formal style of English and an objective tone?
- Does the conclusion follow logically from the body of the essay and provide an effective summary of the argument?

When you are finished, have a discussion about your essays. Ask your partner for feedback on how you can improve your argument. Talk about the reasoning and evidence used to support your claim, and whether or not you have successfully anticipated and addressed counterclaims. Take notes on your partner's feedback and then revise your essay, incorporating any changes that will improve your draft.

Share with a Group When your final draft is completed, read your essay to a small group. Your classmates should listen and take notes as you present your argument. Do your classmates understand your position? Have you successfully persuaded your audience to agree with your argument? Be prepared to respond to any comments or questions from your group.

	Ideas and Evidence	Organization	Language
ADVANCED	• The introduction is memorable and persuasive; the claim clearly states a position on a substantive topic. • Valid reasons and relevant evidence from the texts convincingly support the writer's claim. • Counterclaims are anticipated and effectively addressed with counterarguments. • The concluding section effectively summarizes the claim.	• The reasons and textual evidence are organized consistently and logically throughout the argument. • Varied transitions logically connect reasons and textual evidence to the writer's claim.	• The writing reflects a formal style and an objective, or controlled, tone. • Sentence beginnings, lengths, and structures vary and have a rhythmic flow. • Spelling, capitalization, and punctuation are correct. If handwritten, the argument is legible. • Grammar and usage are correct.
COMPETENT	• The introduction could do more to capture the reader's attention; the claim states a position on an issue. • Most reasons and evidence from the texts support the writer's claim, but they could be more convincing. • Counterclaims are anticipated, but the counterarguments need to be developed more. • The concluding section restates the claim.	• The organization of reasons and textual evidence is confusing in a few places. • A few more transitions are needed to connect reasons and textual evidence to the writer's claim.	• The style is informal in a few places, and the tone is defensive at times. • Sentence beginnings, lengths, and structures vary somewhat. • Several spelling and capitalization mistakes occur, and punctuation is inconsistent. If handwritten, the argument is mostly legible. • Some grammatical and usage errors are repeated in the argument.
LIMITED	• The introduction is ordinary; the claim identifies an issue, but the writer's position is not clearly stated. • The reasons and evidence from the texts are not always logical or relevant. • Counterclaims are anticipated but not addressed logically. • The concluding section includes an incomplete summary of the claim.	• The organization of reasons and textual evidence is logical in some places, but it often doesn't follow a pattern. • Many more transitions are needed to connect reasons and textual evidence to the writer's position.	• The style becomes informal in many places, and the tone is often dismissive of other viewpoints. • Sentence structures barely vary, and some fragments or run-on sentences are present. • Spelling, capitalization, and punctuation are often incorrect but do not make comprehending the argument difficult. If handwritten, the essay may be partially illegible. • Grammar and usage are incorrect in many places, but the writer's ideas are still clear.
EMERGING	• The introduction is missing. • Significant supporting reasons and evidence from the texts are missing. • Counterclaims are neither anticipated nor addressed. • The concluding section is missing.	• An organizational strategy is not used; reasons and textual evidence are presented randomly. • Transitions are not used, making the argument difficult to understand.	• The style is inappropriate, and the tone is disrespectful. • Repetitive sentence structure, fragments, and run-on sentences make the writing monotonous and hard to follow. • Spelling and capitalization are often incorrect, and punctuation is missing. If handwritten, the argument may be partially or mostly illegible. • Many grammatical and usage errors change the meaning of the writer's ideas.

Participate in a Panel Discussion

This collection focuses on the ways people endure through devastating experiences. Look back at the anchor text, "The End and the Beginning," and at the other texts in the collection. How do individuals and communities adapt to radically different situations in order to survive? Synthesize your ideas by holding a panel discussion about how each selection shows people adapting for survival.

An effective participant in a panel discussion

- makes a clear, logical, and well-defended generalization about the ways people adapt for survival in one of the selections
- uses quotations and specific examples from the selections to illustrate ideas
- responds thoughtfully and politely to the ideas of the moderator and other panel members
- evaluates other panel members' contributions, including the use of valid reasoning and sound evidence
- summarizes the discussion by synthesizing ideas about adapting for survival from all the texts

PLAN

Get Organized Work with your classmates to prepare for the discussion.

- Join a group of four classmates and select one student to be the moderator for your discussion.
- Choose three collection texts, including "The End and the Beginning," for your group to discuss. Each student who is not the moderator will be the expert on one of these texts. Decide which student will focus on each text.
- Create a format for your discussion—a schedule that shows the order in which members of the panel will speak and for how long. It will be the moderator's job to keep the discussion moving along on schedule.
- Set rules regarding the appropriate times for either the moderator or the audience (your classmates) to ask the panel members questions.

*my*Notebook

Use the annotation tools in your eBook to find evidence that supports your ideas about how people adapt for survival. Save each piece of evidence to your notebook.

ACADEMIC VOCABULARY

As you participate in your panel discussion, try to use these words.

> dimension
> external
> statistic
> sustain
> utilize

Gather Evidence Work with your group to analyze your three chosen texts. Gather evidence that you will use to discuss adaptation and survival. Note specific details, examples, and quotations. Ask yourself these questions as you take notes:

- How do the people in each text adapt to their situation in order to survive?

- What aspects of a person's character allow some people to adapt more easily to devastating situations?

- What kinds of external forces affect a person's ability to adapt to a devastating experience?

- What generalization, or broad conclusion, can you make about how people adapt to devastating events in order to survive?

During this time, the moderator should make a list of relevant questions to be asked during the discussion.

PRODUCE

my **Write**Smart

Write your outline in *my*WriteSmart. Focus on getting your ideas down, rather than perfecting your choice of language.

Write and Practice Work individually to outline your ideas about your assigned text. Then practice with your group.

- State a clear generalization about the ways people adapt to devastating experiences.

- Write several central ideas that support your generalization. Each idea should relate your generalization to the text.

- Sort through the evidence you have collected and match each piece of evidence with the central idea it most clearly supports. Provide clear examples.

- Present your ideas to your group. The moderator will ask questions about your ideas and examples, preparing you to "think on your feet" during the real discussion.

- If you are the moderator, use this time to decide how you will introduce and conclude the panel discussion. Write a statement that tells the audience the topic of the discussion and its format. Write notes for a concluding statement. Be prepared to modify your remarks based on new ideas that emerge from the discussion.

*my*WriteSmart

Have your partner or a group of peers review your outline in *my*WriteSmart. Ask your reviewers to note any evidence that does not support your generalization about how people adapt for survival.

Reinforce Your Ideas Based on the practice session and the chart on the following page, make changes to your outline. Consider the following questions:

- Were you able to defend your generalization? If not, revise your statement so that it better reflects your textual evidence and your central ideas.

- Were you able to answer the moderator's questions clearly and without hesitation? If not, you may need to reorganize your outline so that you can find the information you need more quickly and easily.

- Did the moderator's questions help you see your text in a new light? If so, add new evidence to your outline that you can share during the real discussion.

PRESENT

Have the Discussion Now it's time to present your panel discussion before the rest of the class. Have your outline at hand for reference during the discussion.

- Begin by having the moderator introduce the topic, the panelists, and the basic format for the discussion. The moderator will then ask the first question and continue to facilitate the discussion in the agreed-upon format.

- Utilize your outline to remind you of your main points, but try to speak directly to the panel and to the audience. Don't just read from your paper.

- Listen closely to what all speakers say so that you can respond appropriately.

- Sustain a respectful tone toward your fellow panel members, even when you disagree with their ideas.

- When all the panelists have made their statements and discussed ideas amongst themselves, the moderator should invite audience members to ask questions.

- Conclude by having the moderator summarize the discussion and thank the panelists for their participation.

Summarize Write a summary of the main points from the discussion. Then explain whether the discussion made you rethink your generalization, and why.

	Ideas and Evidence	Organization	Language
ADVANCED	• The panelist clearly states a valid generalization and supports it with strong, relevant ideas and well-chosen evidence from the texts. • The panel member carefully evaluates others' evidence and reasoning and responds with insightful comments and questions. • The panelist synthesizes the analysis of the texts to help listeners understand the generalization.	• The panelist's remarks are based on a well-organized outline that clearly identifies the generalization and the supporting ideas and evidence. • The panelist concludes with a statement that reinforces the generalization and includes the ideas that have emerged from the discussion.	• The panelist adapts speech to the context of the discussion, using appropriately formal English to discuss the texts and ideas. • The panelist consistently quotes accurately from the texts to support ideas. • The panel member consistently maintains a polite and thoughtful tone throughout the discussion.
COMPETENT	• The panelist states a generalization and supports it with relevant ideas and evidence from the texts. • The panel member evaluates others' evidence and reasoning and responds with appropriate comments and questions. • The panelist synthesizes some ideas and links to the generalization.	• The panelist's remarks are based on an outline that identifies the generalization, supporting ideas, and evidence. • The panelist concludes with a statement that reinforces the generalization.	• The panelist mostly uses formal English to discuss literature and ideas. • The panelist mostly quotes accurately from the texts to support ideas. • The panel member maintains a polite and thoughtful tone throughout most of the discussion.
LIMITED	• The panelist states a reasonably clear generalization and supports it with some ideas and evidence. • The panel member's response to others' comments shows limited evaluation of the evidence and reasoning. • The panelist does not synthesize ideas but simply repeats the generalization in a vague way.	• The panelist's remarks reflect an outline that may identify the generalization but does not organize ideas and evidence very effectively. • The panelist makes a weak concluding statement that does little to reinforce the generalization.	• The panelist uses some formal and some informal English to discuss the texts and ideas. • The panelist's quotations and examples sometimes do not accurately reflect the texts. • The panel member occasionally forgets to maintain a polite tone when responding to others' comments and questions.
EMERGING	• The panelist's generalization is unclear; ideas and evidence are not coherent. • The panel member does not evaluate others' evidence and reasoning. • The panelist does not synthesize ideas.	• The panelist does not follow an outline that organizes ideas and evidence. • The panelist's remarks lack any kind of conclusion or summary.	• The panelist uses informal English and/or slang, resulting in a lack of clarity. • The panelist's quotations and examples do not accurately reflect the texts. • The panel member does not maintain a polite tone when responding to others' comments and questions.

Heroes and Quests

"If a journey doesn't have something to teach you about yourself, then what kind of journey is it?"

—Kira Salak

Heroes and Quests

The hero's journey takes many forms, from traveling through forbidding places to exploring the mind.

hmhfyi.com

COLLECTION
PERFORMANCE TASK Preview

At the end of this collection, you will have the opportunity to complete a task:

- Write an analytical essay about the factors that motivate people to undertake arduous journeys.

ACADEMIC VOCABULARY

Study the words and their definitions in the chart below. You will use these words as you discuss and write about the texts in this collection.

Word	Definition	Related Forms
motivate (mō´tə-vāt´) v.	to provide a cause for doing something	motivation, motivational
objective (əb-jĕk´tĭv) n.	an intention, purpose, or goal	objectively, subjective
pursuit (pər-sōot´) n.	the action of chasing or following something	pursue, pursuer
subsequent (sŭb´sĭ-kwĕnt´) adj.	coming after or following	subsequently, sequential
undertake (ŭn´dər-tāk´) v.	to assume responsibility for or take on a job or course of action	undertaking, undertook

The Epic

Extraordinary heroes in pursuit of hideous monsters. Brutal battles fought and perilous quests undertaken. Spectacular triumphs and crushing defeats. The epic, still very much alive in today's novels and movies, began thousands of years ago in the oral tradition of ancient Greece. There, listeners gathered around poet-storytellers to hear the daring exploits of the hero Odysseus. Across storm-tossed seas, through wild forests, amid countless dangers and subsequent narrow escapes, the hero, motivated by a singular focus on his objective, prevails against all odds. It's no wonder that Homer's **Odyssey** *remains one of the most beloved epics in Western literature. It captivates us and carries us off into a time and place quite different from—yet somehow similar to—our own.*

Characteristics of the Epic

An **epic** is a long narrative poem. It recounts the adventures of an epic hero, a larger-than-life figure who undertakes great journeys and performs deeds requiring remarkable bravery and cunning. As you begin your own journey through Homer's epic, you can expect to encounter the following elements.

Elements of the Epic	
Epic Hero • Possesses superhuman strength, craftiness, and confidence • Helped or harmed by gods or fate • Embodies qualities valued by the culture • Overcomes perilous situations	**Archetypes** Characters and situations recognizable across times and cultures • brave hero • evil temptress • sea monster • loyal servant • suitors' contest • buried treasure
Epic Plot Depicts a long, strange journey filled with such complications as • strange creatures • divine intervention • treacherous weather • large-scale events	**Epic Themes** Reflect universal concerns, such as • courage • the fate of a nation • loyalty • life and death • beauty • a homecoming
Epic Setting • Includes fantastic or exotic lands • Involves more than one nation or culture	

The Language of Homer

Since Homer's work originated as ancient Greek verse, you will read an English translation. Many translations of the *Odyssey* have appeared over the years, and each translator has interpreted it differently. Consider, for example, these two passages from Book 2. The first adopts a formal tone that is much closer to the original. The second version employs a more conversational voice.

Translation 1	Translation 2
When Primal Dawn spread on the eastern sky her fingers of pink light, Odysseus's true son stood up, drew on his tunic and mantle, slung on a sword-belt and a new-edged sword, tied his smooth feet into good rawhide sandals, and left his room, a god's brilliance upon him. —translated by Robert Fitzgerald (1961)	Dawn came, showing her rosy fingers through the early mists, and Telemachus leapt out of bed. He dressed himself, slung a sharp sword over his shoulder, strapt a stout pair of boots on his lissom feet, and came forth from his chamber like a young god. —translated by W.H.D. Rouse (1937)

The people of ancient Greece who first experienced the *Odyssey* heard it sung in a live performance. The poet, or another performer, used epic similes, epithets, and allusions to help keep the audience enthralled.

- A **simile** is a comparison between two unlike things, using the word *like* or *as*. Homer often employs the **epic simile**, a comparison developed at great length over several lines. For example, the epic simile in the following passage compares an angry Odysseus to a roasting sausage.

> His rage
> held hard in leash, submitted to his mind,
> while he himself rocked, rolling from side to side,
> as a cook turns a sausage, big with blood
> and fat, at a scorching blaze, without a pause,
> to broil it quick: so he rolled left and right, . . .

- An **epithet** renames a person or thing with a descriptive phrase. To maintain the meter of the poem or complete a line of verse, the poet would often use an epithet containing the necessary number of syllables. For example, Homer often refers to Odysseus by such epithets as "son of Laertes" and "raider of cities."
- An **allusion** is a reference to a literary or historical person, place, event, or composition. For example, when Telemachus, Odysseus' son, beholds the palace of Menelaus, he exclaims, "This is the way the court of Zeus must be." Every listener in Greece immediately understood the allusion to Zeus, the ruler of the gods.

Reading the Epic

Any journey through the *Odyssey* offers the reader a complex experience. On one level, Homer provides an action-packed narrative that makes us eagerly anticipate each thrilling step in the adventure. On another level, readers can analyze and appreciate the poem as a work of art. The following strategies can help you navigate your own voyage.

Reading the Epic as Narrative

- Pay close attention to the changing narrators. Who is telling the story at a given point? Consider the ways in which different narrators deepen your understanding of characters and events.
- Visualize the setting and the action by observing key details in the text.
- Note major events and conflicts and try to predict their outcomes. Use a chart like the one shown to track characters, including gods and goddesses. Categorize characters as friends or foes, and explain how they help or hinder Odysseus's efforts.

Characters Who Help	Characters Who Hinder
Goddess Athena pleads with Zeus to help Odysseus escape from Calypso's island.	The god Poseidon stirs up powerful storms that cause problems for Odysseus and his crew.

Reading the Epic as Poetry

- Read the epic aloud. Listen for sound devices, such as **alliteration, meter,** and **rhyme,** and notice how they reflect and enhance meaning.
- Follow punctuation closely, and remember that the end of a line does not indicate the end of a thought.
- Consider how imagery and figurative language, including epic similes, reveal characters and events. Note allusions and epithets.

Reading the Epic within the Context of Its Time

- Look closely at how Odysseus behaves. What character traits does he display? What do these traits tell you about the values of the time?
- Draw upon your own prior knowledge of ancient Greek civilization and history. What events and customs would have influenced Homer?
- Remember that the Greeks of Homer's time believed the gods took an active interest in human affairs. (In fact, the gods themselves behaved very much like humans.) How do such religious beliefs influence the epic?

Examining the Homeric Epics

Considered the greatest masterpieces of the epic form, the *Iliad* and the *Odyssey* present high drama and intense emotions. In both books, important plot elements include the interference of gods in human affairs, the epic heroism of the central characters, and the saga of the Trojan War and its aftermath.

The Trojan War

The legendary conflict between Greece (or Achaea) and Troy began around 1200 B.C. Paris, a Trojan prince, kidnapped Helen, the wife of Menelaus, king of Sparta. Menelaus recruited the armies of allied kingdoms to attack Troy and recover his wife. For ten years the Greek forces held Troy under siege, but they could not penetrate the walls of the city.

Finally, Odysseus, king of Ithaca, came up with a plan to break the stalemate. He ordered his men to build a giant wooden horse. One morning the people of Troy awoke to find that horse outside the city gates—and no Greeks in sight. Assuming the Greeks had retreated and had left the horse as a peace offering, they brought the horse inside the gates. They soon discovered, too late, that the horse was filled with Greek soldiers and that their city was doomed.

Heroism

Great heroes play key roles in Homer's epics. The *Iliad* tells the story of Achilles, the mightiest Greek warrior, and of his bitter quarrel with Agamemnon, brother of Menelaus and commander of the Greek forces at Troy. The tale climaxes in a fierce battle between Achilles and Hector, Paris's brother, and Hector's subsequent funeral.

The *Odyssey* recounts Odysseus' adventures as he struggles to make his way home from post-war Troy, along with the conflicts that arise in Ithaca just before and after his return. He prevails against gruesome monsters, enchanting women, and greedy rivals intent on preventing him from reaching his objective. Although Odysseus lacks the superhuman martial abilities of Achilles, he employs great cleverness and guile to get out of difficult situations.

The Intervention of Gods

Adding to the heroes' struggles are the residents of Mount Olympus, bickering gods who like nothing better than influencing and manipulating human affairs. For example, Athena, goddess of wisdom, supports the Greeks in the Trojan War; Aphrodite, goddess of love, sides with Troy. Further, the heroes often displease other gods who place additional obstacles in their paths. The Olympians display human shortcomings and petty jealousies, and people become pawns as the gods pursue advantages in their internal quarrels.

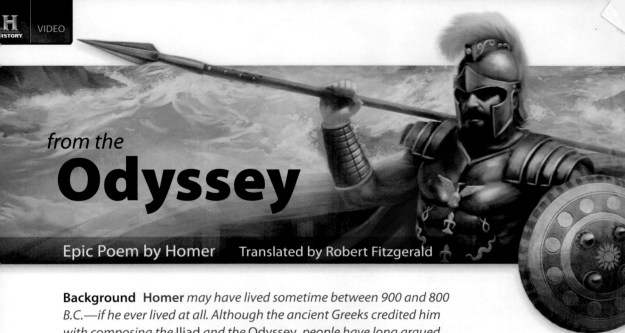

from the
Odyssey

Epic Poem by Homer   Translated by Robert Fitzgerald

Background Homer *may have lived sometime between 900 and 800 B.C.—if he ever lived at all. Although the ancient Greeks credited him with composing the* Iliad *and the* Odyssey, *people have long argued about whether or not he really existed. Many theories speculate on who Homer may have been and where he may have lived. Details in the stories suggest that he was born and lived in the eastern Aegean Sea, either on the islands of Chios or Smyrna, and that he was blind.*

Whatever position modern scholars take on the debate, most believe that one or two exceptionally talented individuals created the Homeric epics. The Iliad *and the* Odyssey *each contain 24 books of verse, but they probably predate the development of writing in Greece. The verses, which were originally sung, gradually became part of an important oral tradition. Generations of professional reciters memorized and performed the poems at festivals throughout Greece. By 300 B.C., several versions of the books existed, and scholars undertook the job of standardizing the texts.*

Homer's poems profoundly influenced Greek culture and, as a result, contributed to the subsequent development of Western literature, ideas, and values. The Roman poet Virgil wrote a related poem, the Aeneid, *in Latin, and Odysseus appears in Dante's* Inferno. *Poets throughout English literature, from Geoffrey Chaucer in the Middle Ages to William Shakespeare in the Renaissance to John Keats in the Romantic era, have found inspiration in Homer. James Joyce's 1922 novel* Ulysses *(the Latin form of Odysseus' name) transforms one ordinary Dublin day into an Odyssean journey. Dozens of movies have retold the saga of the Trojan War and the long journey home, both directly and symbolically. For thousands of years people have taken the tales of a wandering Greek bard and made them their own.*

Important Characters in the *Odyssey (in order of mention)*

Book 1

Helios (hē′lē-ŏs′)—the sun god, who raises his cattle on the island of Thrinacia (thrĭ-nā′shə)

Zeus (zo͞os)—the ruler of the Greek gods and goddesses; father of Athena and Apollo

Telemachus (tə-lĕm′ə-kəs)—Odysseus' son

Penelope (pə-nĕl′ə-pē)—Odysseus' wife

Book 9

Alcinous (ăl-sĭn′ō-əs)—the king of the Phaeacians (fē-ā′shənz)

Circe (sûr′sē)—a goddess and enchantress who lives on the island of Aeaea (ē-ē′ə)

Cicones (sĭ-kō′nēz)—allies of the Trojans, who live at Ismarus (ĭs-măr′əs)

Lotus Eaters—inhabitants of a land Odysseus visits

Cyclopes (sī-klō′pēz)—a race of one-eyed giants; an individual member of the race is a Cyclops (sī′klŏps)

Apollo (ə-pŏl′ō)—the god of music, poetry, prophecy, and medicine

Poseidon (pō-sīd′n)—the god of the seas, earthquakes, and horses; father of the Cyclops who battles Odysseus

Athena (ə-thē′nə)—the goddess of war, wisdom, and cleverness; goddess of crafts

Book 10

Aeolus (ē′ə-ləs)—the guardian of the winds

Laestrygones (lĕs′trĭ-gō′nēz)—cannibal inhabitants of a distant land

Eurylochus (yo͝o-rĭl′ə-kəs)—a trusted officer of Odysseus

Persephone (pər-sĕf′ə-nē)—the wife of Hades, ruler of the underworld

Tiresias (tī-rē′sē-əs) of Thebes (thēbz)—a blind prophet whose spirit Odysseus visits in the underworld

Book 11

Elpenor (ĕl-pē′nôr)—one of Odysseus' crew, killed in an accident

Book 12

Sirens (sī′rənz)—creatures, part woman and part bird, whose songs lure sailors to their death

Scylla (sĭl′ə)—a six-headed sea monster who devours sailors

Charybdis (kə-rĭb′dĭs)—a dangerous whirlpool personified as a female sea monster

Book 17

Argos (är′gŏs)—Odysseus' dog

Eumaeus (yo͞o-mē′əs)—a servant in Odysseus' household

Books 21–23

Antinous (ăn-tĭn′ō-əs)—a suitor of Penelope's

Eurymachus (yo͝o-rĭm′ə-kəs)—a suitor of Penelope's

Philoetius (fĭ-lē′shəs)—a servant in Odysseus' household

Amphinomus (ăm-fĭn′ə-məs)—a suitor of Penelope's

Eurynome (yo͝o-rĭn′ə-mē)—a female servant in Odysseus' household

Eurycleia (yo͝or′ĭ-klē′ə)—an old female servant, still loyal to Odysseus

PART ONE: THE WANDERINGS OF ODYSSEUS

AS YOU READ Pay attention to details that tell how Odysseus confronts the various challenges of his journey. Write down any questions you generate during reading.

BOOK 1:

A Goddess Intervenes

Sing in me, Muse, and through me tell the story
of that man skilled in all ways of contending,
the wanderer, **harried** for years on end,
after he plundered the stronghold
5   on the proud height of Troy.

                              He saw the townlands
and learned the minds of many distant men,
and weathered many bitter nights and days
in his deep heart at sea, while he fought only
to save his life, to bring his shipmates home.
10   But not by will nor valor could he save them,
for their own recklessness destroyed them all—
children and fools, they killed and feasted on
the cattle of Lord Helios, the Sun,
and he who moves all day through heaven
15   took from their eyes the dawn of their return.

Of these adventures, Muse, daughter of Zeus,
tell us in our time, lift the great song again. . . .

*The story of Odysseus begins with the goddess Athena's appealing to
Zeus to help Odysseus, who has been wandering for ten years on the
seas, to find his way home to his family on Ithaca. While Odysseus
has been gone, his son, Telemachus, has grown to manhood and his
wife, Penelope, has been besieged by suitors wishing to marry her and
gain Odysseus' wealth. The suitors have taken up residence in her
home and are constantly feasting on the family's cattle, sheep, and
goats. They dishonor Odysseus and his family. Taking Athena's
advice, Telemachus travels to Pylos for word of his father. Meanwhile,
on Ithaca, the evil suitors plot to kill Telemachus when he returns.*

1 Muse: a daughter of Zeus, credited with divine inspiration.

harried (hăr´ēd) *adj.* tormented; harassed **harry** *v.*

11–13 their own recklessness . . . the Sun: a reference to an event occurring later in the poem—an event that causes the death of Odysseus' entire crew.

BOOK 9:

New Coasts and Poseidon's Son

For seven of the ten years Odysseus has spent wandering the
Mediterranean Sea, he has been held captive by the goddess Calypso
on her island. In Book 5, Zeus sends the god Hermes to tell Calypso
to release Odysseus; she helps him build a raft on which he can sail to
his next destination. He must sail for 20 days before landing on the
island of Scheria, where he will be helped in his effort to return home.
In Books 6–8, Odysseus is welcomed by King Alcinous, who gives a
banquet in his honor. That night the king begs Odysseus to tell who
he is and what has happened to him. In Books 9–12, Odysseus relates
to the king his adventures.

"I AM LAERTES' SON"

           "What shall I
say first? What shall I keep until the end?
The gods have tried me in a thousand ways.
But first my name: let that be known to you,
5 and if I pull away from pitiless death,
friendship will bind us, though my land lies far.

I am Laertes' son, Odysseus.

                      Men hold me
formidable for guile in peace and war:
this fame has gone abroad to the sky's rim.
10 My home is on the peaked sea-mark of Ithaca
under Mount Neion's wind-blown robe of leaves,
in sight of other islands—Dulichium,
Same, wooded Zacynthus—Ithaca
being most lofty in that coastal sea,
15 and northwest, while the rest lie east and south.
A rocky isle, but good for a boy's training;
I shall not see on earth a place more dear,
though I have been detained long by Calypso,
loveliest among goddesses, who held me
20 in her smooth caves, to be her heart's delight,
as Circe of Aeaea, the enchantress,
desired me, and detained me in her hall.
But in my heart I never gave consent.
Where shall a man find sweetness to surpass
25 his own home and his parents? In far lands

**7–8 hold me
formidable for guile:**
consider me impressive
for my cunning and
craftiness.

11–13 Mount Neion's
(nē´ŏnz´); **Dulichium**
(do͞o-lĭk´ē-əm); **Same**
(sā´mē); **Zacynthus**
(zə-sĭn´thəs).

18–26 Odysseus
refers to two beautiful
goddesses, Calypso and
Circe, who have delayed
him on their islands.
(Details about Circe
appear in Book 10.)

he shall not, though he find a house of gold.
What of my sailing, then, from Troy?

What of those years
of rough adventure, weathered under Zeus? . . ."

Odysseus explains that soon after leaving Troy, he and his crew land
near Ismarus, the city of the Cicones. The Cicones are allies of the
Trojans and therefore enemies of Odysseus. Odysseus and his crew
raid the Cicones, robbing and killing them, until the Ciconian army
kills 72 of Odysseus' men and drives the rest out to sea. Delayed by a
storm for two days, Odysseus and his remaining companions then
continue their journey.

THE LOTUS EATERS

"I might have made it safely home, that time,
30   but as I came round Malea the current
took me out to sea, and from the north
a fresh gale drove me on, past Cythera.
Nine days I drifted on the teeming sea
before dangerous high winds. Upon the tenth
35   we came to the coastline of the Lotus Eaters,
who live upon that flower. We landed there
to take on water. All ships' companies
mustered alongside for the mid-day meal.
Then I sent out two picked men and a runner
40   to learn what race of men that land sustained.
They fell in, soon enough, with Lotus Eaters,
who showed no will to do us harm, only
offering the sweet Lotus to our friends—
but those who ate this honeyed plant, the Lotus,
45   never cared to report, nor to return:
they longed to stay forever, browsing on
that native bloom, forgetful of their homeland.
I drove them, all three wailing, to the ships,
tied them down under their rowing benches,
50   and called the rest: 'All hands aboard;
come, clear the beach and no one taste
the Lotus, or you lose your hope of home.'
Filing in to their places by the rowlocks
my oarsmen dipped their long oars in the surf,
55   and we moved out again on our sea faring.

30 Malea (mä-lē′ä).

32 Cythera (sĭ-thîr′ə).

38 mustered:
assembled; gathered.

THE CYCLOPS

In the next land we found were Cyclopes,
giants, louts, without a law to bless them.
In ignorance leaving the fruitage of the earth in mystery
to the immortal gods, they neither plow
60 nor sow by hand, nor till the ground, though grain—
wild wheat and barley—grows untended, and
wine-grapes, in clusters, ripen in heaven's rain.
Cyclopes have no muster and no meeting,
no consultation or old tribal ways,
65 but each one dwells in his own mountain cave
dealing out rough justice to wife and child,
indifferent to what the others do. . . ."

56 Cyclopes (sī-klō′pēz): refers to the creatures in plural; *Cyclops* is singular.

*Across the bay from the land of the Cyclopes is a lush, deserted
island. Odysseus and his crew land on the island in a dense fog
and spend days feasting on wine and wild goats and observing the
mainland, where the Cyclopes live. On the third day, Odysseus
and his company of men set out to learn if the Cyclopes are friends
or foes.*

"When the young Dawn with finger tips of rose
came in the east, I called my men together
70 and made a speech to them:

                              'Old shipmates, friends,
the rest of you stand by; I'll make the crossing
in my own ship, with my own company,
and find out what the mainland natives are—
for they may be wild savages, and lawless,
75 or hospitable and god fearing men.'

At this I went aboard, and gave the word
to cast off by the stern. My oarsmen followed,
filing in to their benches by the rowlocks,
and all in line dipped oars in the gray sea.

77 stern: the rear end of a ship.

80 As we rowed on, and nearer to the mainland,
at one end of the bay, we saw a cavern
yawning above the water, screened with laurel,
and many rams and goats about the place
inside a sheepfold—made from slabs of stone
85 earthfast between tall trunks of pine and rugged
towering oak trees.

82 screened with laurel: partially hidden by laurel trees.

A prodigious man
slept in this cave alone, and took his flocks
to graze afield—remote from all companions,
knowing none but savage ways, a brute
90 so huge, he seemed no man at all of those
who eat good wheaten bread; but he seemed rather
a shaggy mountain reared in solitude.
We beached there, and I told the crew
to stand by and keep watch over the ship;
95 as for myself I took my twelve best fighters
and went ahead. I had a goatskin full
of that sweet liquor that Euanthes' son,
Maron, had given me. He kept Apollo's
holy grove at Ismarus; for kindness
100 we showed him there, and showed his wife and child,
he gave me seven shining golden talents
perfectly formed, a solid silver winebowl,
and then this liquor—twelve two-handled jars
of brandy, pure and fiery. Not a slave
105 in Maron's household knew this drink; only
he, his wife and the storeroom mistress knew;
and they would put one cupful—ruby-colored,
honey-smooth—in twenty more of water,
but still the sweet scent hovered like a fume
110 over the winebowl. No man turned away
when cups of this came round.

97–98 Euanthes
(yōō-ăn´thēz); **Maron**
(măr´ŏn´).

101 talents: bars
of gold or silver of a
specified weight, used
as money in ancient
Greece.

A wineskin full

I brought along, and victuals in a bag,
for in my bones I knew some towering brute
would be upon us soon—all outward power,
115 a wild man, ignorant of civility.

We climbed, then, briskly to the cave. But Cyclops
had gone afield, to pasture his fat sheep,
so we looked round at everything inside:
a drying rack that sagged with cheeses, pens
120 crowded with lambs and kids, each in its class:
firstlings apart from middlings, and the 'dewdrops,'
or newborn lambkins, penned apart from both.
And vessels full of whey were brimming there—
bowls of earthenware and pails for milking.
125 My men came pressing round me, pleading:

'Why not

take these cheeses, get them stowed, come back,
throw open all the pens, and make a run for it?
We'll drive the kids and lambs aboard. We say
put out again on good salt water!'

Ah,

130 how sound that was! Yet I refused. I wished
to see the caveman, what he had to offer—
no pretty sight, it turned out, for my friends.
We lit a fire, burnt an offering,
and took some cheese to eat; then sat in silence
135 around the embers, waiting. When he came
he had a load of dry boughs on his shoulder
to stoke his fire at suppertime. He dumped it
with a great crash into that hollow cave,
and we all scattered fast to the far wall.
140 Then over the broad cavern floor he ushered
the ewes he meant to milk. He left his rams
and he-goats in the yard outside, and swung
high overhead a slab of solid rock
to close the cave. Two dozen four-wheeled wagons,
145 with heaving wagon teams, could not have stirred
the tonnage of that rock from where he wedged it
over the doorsill. Next he took his seat
and milked his bleating ewes. A practiced job
he made of it, giving each ewe her suckling;
150 thickened his milk, then, into curds and whey,
sieved out the curds to drip in withy baskets,
and poured the whey to stand in bowls

112 victuals (vĭt´lz): food.

121–122 The Cyclops has separated his lambs into three age groups.

123 whey: the watery part of milk, which separates from the curds, or solid part, during the making of cheese.

129 good salt water: the open sea.

133 burnt an offering: burned a portion of the food as an offering to secure the gods' goodwill. (Such offerings were frequently performed by Greek sailors during difficult journeys.)

151 withy baskets: baskets made from twigs.

cooling until he drank it for his supper.
When all these chores were done, he poked the fire,
155 heaping on brushwood. In the glare he saw us.

'Strangers,' he said, 'who are you? And where from?
What brings you here by sea ways—a fair traffic?
Or are you wandering rogues, who cast your lives
like dice, and ravage other folk by sea?'

157 fair traffic: honest
trading.

160 We felt a pressure on our hearts, in dread
of that deep rumble and that mighty man.
But all the same I spoke up in reply:

'We are from Troy, Achaeans, blown off course
by shifting gales on the Great South Sea;
165 homeward bound, but taking routes and ways
uncommon; so the will of Zeus would have it.
We served under Agamemnon, son of Atreus—
the whole world knows what city
he laid waste, what armies he destroyed.
170 It was our luck to come here; here we stand,
beholden for your help, or any gifts
you give—as custom is to honor strangers.
We would entreat you, great Sir, have a care
for the gods' courtesy; Zeus will avenge
175 the unoffending guest.'

172–175 It was a
sacred Greek custom to
honor strangers with
food and gifts. Odysseus
is reminding the Cyclops
that Zeus will punish
anyone who mistreats
a guest.

He answered this
from his brute chest, unmoved:

'You are a ninny,
or else you come from the other end of nowhere,
telling me, mind the gods! We Cyclopes
care not a whistle for your thundering Zeus
180 or all the gods in bliss; we have more force by far.
I would not let you go for fear of Zeus—
you or your friends—unless I had a whim to.
Tell me, where was it, now, you left your ship—
around the point, or down the shore, I wonder?'

185 He thought he'd find out, but I saw through this,
and answered with a ready lie:

'My ship?
Poseidon Lord, who sets the earth a-tremble,
broke it up on the rocks at your land's end.
A wind from seaward served him, drove us there.
190 We are survivors, these good men and I.'

Neither reply nor pity came from him,
but in one stride he clutched at my companions
and caught two in his hands like squirming puppies
to beat their brains out, spattering the floor.
195 Then he dismembered them and made his meal,
gaping and crunching like a mountain lion—
everything: innards, flesh, and marrow bones.
We cried aloud, lifting our hands to Zeus,
powerless, looking on at this, appalled;
200 but Cyclops went on filling up his belly
with manflesh and great gulps of whey,
then lay down like a mast among his sheep.
My heart beat high now at the chance of action,
and drawing the sharp sword from my hip I went
205 along his flank to stab him where the midriff
holds the liver. I had touched the spot
when sudden fear stayed me: if I killed him
we perished there as well, for we could never
move his **ponderous** doorway slab aside.
210 So we were left to groan and wait for morning.

When the young Dawn with fingertips of rose
lit up the world, the Cyclops built a fire
and milked his handsome ewes, all in due order,
putting the sucklings to the mothers. Then,
215 his chores being all dispatched, he caught
another brace of men to make his breakfast,
and whisked away his great door slab
to let his sheep go through—but he, behind,
reset the stone as one would cap a quiver.
220 There was a din of whistling as the Cyclops
rounded his flock to higher ground, then stillness.
And now I pondered how to hurt him worst,
if but Athena granted what I prayed for.
Here are the means I thought would serve my turn:

225 a club, or staff, lay there along the fold—
an olive tree, felled green and left to season
for Cyclops' hand. And it was like a mast
a lugger of twenty oars, broad in the beam—
a deep-sea-going craft—might carry:
230 so long, so big around, it seemed. Now I
chopped out a six foot section of this pole
and set it down before my men, who scraped it;
and when they had it smooth, I hewed again
to make a stake with pointed end. I held this

ponderous (pŏn′dər-əs)
adj. heavy in a clumsy
way; bulky.

216 brace: pair.

218–219 The Cyclops
reseals the cave with the
massive rock as easily
as an ordinary human
places the cap on a
container of arrows.

226 left to season: left
to dry out and harden.

228 lugger: a small,
wide sailing ship.

235 in the fire's heart and turned it, toughening it,
    then hid it, well back in the cavern, under
    one of the dung piles in **profusion** there.
    Now came the time to toss for it: who ventured
    along with me? whose hand could bear to thrust
240 and grind that spike in Cyclops' eye, when mild
    sleep had mastered him? As luck would have it,
    the men I would have chosen won the toss—
    four strong men, and I made five as captain.

    At evening came the shepherd with his flock,
245 his woolly flock. The rams as well, this time,
    entered the cave: by some sheep-herding whim—
    or a god's bidding—none were left outside.
    He hefted his great boulder into place
    and sat him down to milk the bleating ewes
250 in proper order, put the lambs to suck,
    and swiftly ran through all his evening chores.
    Then he caught two more men and feasted on them.
    My moment was at hand, and I went forward
    holding an ivy bowl of my dark drink,
255 looking up, saying:
                            'Cyclops, try some wine.
    Here's liquor to wash down your scraps of men.
    Taste it, and see the kind of drink we carried
    under our planks. I meant it for an offering
    if you would help us home. But you are mad,
260 unbearable, a bloody monster! After this,
    will any other traveller come to see you?'

    He seized and drained the bowl, and it went down
    so fiery and smooth he called for more:

    'Give me another, thank you kindly. Tell me,
265 how are you called? I'll make a gift will please you.
    Even Cyclopes know the wine-grapes grow
    out of grassland and loam in heaven's rain,
    but here's a bit of nectar and ambrosia!'

    Three bowls I brought him, and he poured them down.
270 I saw the fuddle and flush come over him,
    then I sang out in cordial tones:

                                    'Cyclops,
    you ask my honorable name? Remember
    the gift you promised me, and I shall tell you.

profusion
(prə-fyo͞o′zhən) *n.*
abundance.

268 nectar (nĕk′tər) **and
ambrosia** (ăm-brō′zhə):
the drink and food of the
gods.

270 fuddle and flush:
the state of confusion
and redness of the face
caused by drinking
alcohol.

My name is Nohbdy: mother, father, and friends,
275 everyone calls me Nohbdy.'

And he said:

'Nohbdy's my meat, then, after I eat his friends.
Others come first. There's a noble gift, now.'

Even as he spoke, he reeled and tumbled backward,
his great head lolling to one side: and sleep
280 took him like any creature. Drunk, hiccupping,
he dribbled streams of liquor and bits of men.

Now, by the gods, I drove my big hand spike
deep in the embers, charring it again,
and cheered my men along with battle talk
285 to keep their courage up: no quitting now.
The pike of olive, green though it had been,
reddened and glowed as if about to catch.
I drew it from the coals and my four fellows
gave me a hand, lugging it near the Cyclops
290 as more than natural force nerved them; straight
forward they sprinted, lifted it, and rammed it
deep in his crater eye, and I leaned on it
turning it as a shipwright turns a drill
in planking, having men below to swing
295 the two-handled strap that spins it in the groove.
So with our brand we bored that great eye socket
while blood ran out around the red hot bar.
Eyelid and lash were seared; the pierced ball
hissed broiling, and the roots popped.

In a smithy
300 one sees a white-hot axehead or an adze
plunged and wrung in a cold tub, screeching steam—
the way they make soft iron hale and hard—:
just so that eyeball hissed around the spike.
The Cyclops bellowed and the rock roared round him,
305 and we fell back in fear. Clawing his face
he tugged the bloody spike out of his eye,
threw it away, and his wild hands went groping;
then he set up a howl for Cyclopes
who lived in caves on windy peaks nearby.
310 Some heard him; and they came by divers ways
to clump around outside and call:

286 the pike: the pointed stake.

299 smithy: blacksmith's shop.

300 adze (ădz): an axlike tool with a curved blade.

310 divers: various.

'What ails you,
Polyphemus? Why do you cry so sore
in the starry night? You will not let us sleep.
Sure no man's driving off your flock? No man
315　has tricked you, ruined you?'

312 **Polyphemus**
(pŏl´ə-fē´məs): the name
of the Cyclops.

Out of the cave
the mammoth Polyphemus roared in answer:

'Nohbdy, Nohbdy's tricked me, Nohbdy's ruined me!'

To this rough shout they made a sage reply:

318 sage: wise.

'Ah well, if nobody has played you foul
320　there in your lonely bed, we are no use in pain
given by great Zeus. Let it be your father,
Poseidon Lord, to whom you pray.'

319–322 Odysseus'
lie about his name has
paid off.

So saying
they trailed away. And I was filled with laughter
to see how like a charm the name deceived them.
325　Now Cyclops, wheezing as the pain came on him,
fumbled to wrench away the great doorstone
and squatted in the breach with arms thrown wide

327 breach: opening.

for any silly beast or man who bolted—
hoping somehow I might be such a fool.
330　But I kept thinking how to win the game:
death sat there huge; how could we slip away?
I drew on all my wits, and ran through tactics,
reasoning as a man will for dear life,
until a trick came—and it pleased me well.
335　The Cyclops' rams were handsome, fat, with heavy
fleeces, a dark violet.

Three abreast
I tied them silently together, twining
cords of willow from the ogre's bed;
then slung a man under each middle one
340　to ride there safely, shielded left and right.
So three sheep could convey each man. I took
the woolliest ram, the choicest of the flock,
and hung myself under his kinky belly,
pulled up tight, with fingers twisted deep
345　in sheepskin ringlets for an iron grip.
So, breathing hard, we waited until morning.

When Dawn spread out her finger tips of rose
the rams began to stir, moving for pasture,
and peals of bleating echoed round the pens
350 where dams with udders full called for a milking.
Blinded, and sick with pain from his head wound,
the master stroked each ram, then let it pass,
but my men riding on the pectoral fleece
the giant's blind hands blundering never found.
355 Last of them all my ram, the leader, came,
weighted by wool and me with my meditations.
The Cyclops patted him, and then he said:

'Sweet cousin ram, why lag behind the rest
in the night cave? You never linger so,
360 but graze before them all, and go afar
to crop sweet grass, and take your stately way
leading along the streams, until at evening
you run to be the first one in the fold.
Why, now, so far behind? Can you be grieving
365 over your Master's eye? That carrion rogue
and his accurst companions burnt it out
when he had conquered all my wits with wine.
Nohbdy will not get out alive, I swear.
Oh, had you brain and voice to tell
370 where he may be now, dodging all my fury!
Bashed by this hand and bashed on this rock wall
his brains would strew the floor, and I should have
rest from the outrage Nohbdy worked upon me.'

He sent us into the open, then. Close by,
375 I dropped and rolled clear of the ram's belly,
going this way and that to untie the men.
With many glances back, we rounded up
his fat, stiff-legged sheep to take aboard,
and drove them down to where the good ship lay.
380 We saw, as we came near, our fellows' faces
shining; then we saw them turn to grief
tallying those who had not fled from death.
I hushed them, jerking head and eyebrows up,
and in a low voice told them: 'Load this herd;
385 move fast, and put the ship's head toward the breakers.'
They all pitched in at loading, then embarked
and struck their oars into the sea. Far out,
as far off shore as shouted words would carry,
I sent a few back to the **adversary**:

353 pectoral fleece: the wool covering a sheep's chest.

385 put . . . the breakers: turn the ship around so that it is heading toward the open sea.

adversary (ăd´vər-sĕr´ē) *n.* an opponent; enemy.

390 'O Cyclops! Would you feast on my companions?
Puny, am I, in a Caveman's hands?
How do you like the beating that we gave you,
you damned cannibal? Eater of guests
under your roof! Zeus and the gods have paid you!'

390–394 Odysseus
assumes that the gods
are on his side.

395 The blind thing in his doubled fury broke
a hilltop in his hands and heaved it after us.
Ahead of our black prow it struck and sank
whelmed in a spuming geyser, a giant wave
that washed the ship stern foremost back to shore.
400 I got the longest boathook out and stood
fending us off, with furious nods to all
to put their backs into a racing stroke—
row, row, or perish. So the long oars bent
kicking the foam sternward, making head
405 until we drew away, and twice as far.
Now when I cupped my hands I heard the crew
in low voices protesting:

395–403 The hilltop
thrown by Polyphemus
lands in front of the ship,
causing a huge wave
that carries the ship back
to the shore. Odysseus
uses a long pole to push
the boat away from the
land.

                               'Godsake, Captain!

406 cupped my hands:
put his hands on either
side of his mouth in
order to magnify his
voice.

Why bait the beast again? Let him alone!'
'That tidal wave he made on the first throw
410 all but beached us.'

'All but stove us in!'

'Give him our bearing with your trumpeting,
he'll get the range and lob a boulder.'

'Aye

He'll smash our timbers and our heads together!'

I would not heed them in my glorying spirit,
415   but let my anger flare and yelled:

'Cyclops,

if ever mortal man inquire
how you were put to shame and blinded, tell him
Odysseus, raider of cities, took your eye:
Laertes' son, whose home's on Ithaca!'

420   At this he gave a mighty sob and rumbled:

'Now comes the weird upon me, spoken of old.
A wizard, grand and wondrous, lived here—Telemus,
a son of Eurymus; great length of days
he had in wizardry among the Cyclopes,
425   and these things he foretold for time to come:
my great eye lost, and at Odysseus' hands.
Always I had in mind some giant, armed
in giant force, would come against me here.
But this, but you—small, pitiful and twiggy—
430   you put me down with wine, you blinded me.
Come back, Odysseus, and I'll treat you well,
praying the god of earthquake to befriend you—
his son I am, for he by his avowal
fathered me, and, if he will, he may
435   heal me of this black wound—he and no other
of all the happy gods or mortal men.'

Few words I shouted in reply to him:
'If I could take your life I would and take
your time away, and hurl you down to hell!
440   The god of earthquake could not heal you there!'

At this he stretched his hands out in his darkness
toward the sky of stars, and prayed Poseidon:
'O hear me, lord, blue girdler of the islands,
if I am thine indeed, and thou art father:
445   grant that Odysseus, raider of cities, never
see his home: Laertes' son, I mean,

**421 Now comes . . .
of old:** Now I recall the
destiny predicted long
ago.

**421–430 Now comes
. . . you blinded me:**
Polyphemus tells of a
prophecy made long
ago by Telemus, a
prophet who predicted
that Polyphemus would
lose his eye at the hands
of Odysseus.

**432 the god of
earthquake:** Poseidon.

433 avowal: honest
admission.

who kept his hall on Ithaca. Should destiny
intend that he shall see his roof again
among his family in his father land,
450 far be that day, and dark the years between.
Let him lose all companions, and return
under strange sail to bitter days at home.'

In these words he prayed, and the god heard him.
Now he laid hands upon a bigger stone
455 and wheeled around, titanic for the cast,
to let it fly in the black-prowed vessel's track.
But it fell short, just aft the steering oar,
and whelming seas rose giant above the stone
to bear us onward toward the island.

                                             There
460 as we ran in we saw the squadron waiting,
the trim ships drawn up side by side, and all
our troubled friends who waited, looking seaward.
We beached her, grinding keel in the soft sand,
and waded in, ourselves, on the sandy beach.
465 Then we unloaded all the Cyclops' flock
to make division, share and share alike,
only my fighters voted that my ram,
the prize of all, should go to me. I slew him
by the sea side and burnt his long thighbones
470 to Zeus beyond the stormcloud, Cronus' son,
who rules the world. But Zeus disdained my offering;
destruction for my ships he had in store
and death for those who sailed them, my companions.

Now all day long until the sun went down
475 we made our feast on mutton and sweet wine,
till after sunset in the gathering dark
we went to sleep above the wash of ripples.

When the young Dawn with finger tips of rose
touched the world, I roused the men, gave orders
480 to man the ships, cast off the mooring lines;
and filing in to sit beside the rowlocks
oarsmen in line dipped oars in the gray sea.
So we moved out, sad in the vast offing,
having our precious lives, but not our friends."

455 titanic for the cast: drawing on all his enormous strength in preparing to throw.

457 aft: behind.

459 the island: the deserted island where most of Odysseus' men had stayed behind.

470 Cronus' son: Zeus' father, Cronus, was a Titan, one of an earlier race of gods.

483 offing: the part of the deep sea visible from the shore.

BOOK 10:

Circe, the Grace of the Witch

Odysseus and his men next land on the island of Aeolus, the wind king, and stay with him a month. To extend his hospitality, Aeolus gives Odysseus two parting gifts: a fair west wind that will blow the fleet of ships toward Ithaca, and a great bag holding all the unfavorable, stormy winds. Within sight of home, and while Odysseus is sleeping, the men open the bag, thinking it contains gold and silver. The bad winds thus escape and blow the ships back to Aeolus' island. The king refuses to help them again, believing now that their voyage has been cursed by the gods.

The discouraged mariners next stop briefly in the land of the Laestrygones, fierce cannibals who bombard the fleet of ships with boulders. Only Odysseus, his ship, and its crew of 45 survive the shower of boulders. The lone ship then sails to Aeaea, home of the goddess Circe, who is considered by many to be a witch. There, Odysseus divides his men into two groups. Eurylochus leads one platoon to explore the island, while Odysseus stays behind on the ship with the remaining crew.

"In the wild wood they found an open glade,
around a smooth stone house—the hall of Circe—
and wolves and mountain lions lay there, mild
in her soft spell, fed on her drug of evil.
5 None would attack—oh, it was strange, I tell you—
but switching their long tails they faced our men
like hounds, who look up when their master comes
with tidbits for them—as he will—from table.
Humbly those wolves and lions with mighty paws
10 fawned on our men—who met their yellow eyes
and feared them.

                    In the entrance way they stayed
to listen there: inside her quiet house
they heard the goddess Circe.

                               Low she sang
in her beguiling voice, while on her loom
15 she wove ambrosial fabric sheer and bright,
by that craft known to the goddesses of heaven.
No one would speak, until Polites—most
faithful and likable of my officers, said:

10 fawned on: showed affection for.

15 ambrosial: fit for the gods.

17 Polites (pə-lī′tēz).

'Dear friends, no need for stealth: here's a young weaver
20 singing a pretty song to set the air
a-tingle on these lawns and paven courts.
Goddess she is, or lady. Shall we greet her?'

So reassured, they all cried out together,
and she came swiftly to the shining doors
25 to call them in. All but Eurylochus—
who feared a snare—the innocents went after her.
On thrones she seated them, and lounging chairs,
while she prepared a meal of cheese and barley
and amber honey mixed with Pramnian wine,
30 adding her own vile pinch, to make them lose
desire or thought of our dear father land.
Scarce had they drunk when she flew after them
with her long stick and shut them in a pigsty—
bodies, voices, heads, and bristles, all
35 swinish now, though minds were still unchanged.
So, squealing, in they went. And Circe tossed them
acorns, mast, and cornel berries—fodder
for hogs who rut and slumber on the earth.

Down to the ship Eurylochus came running
40 to cry alarm, foul magic doomed his men!
But working with dry lips to speak a word
he could not, being so shaken; blinding tears
welled in his eyes; **foreboding** filled his heart.
When we were frantic questioning him, at last
45 we heard the tale: our friends were gone. . . ."

Eurylochus tells Odysseus what has happened and begs him to sail
away from Circe's island. Against this advice, however, Odysseus
rushes to save his men from the enchantress. On the way, he meets
the god Hermes, who gives him a magical plant called moly to protect
him from Circe's power. Still, Hermes warns Odysseus that he must
make the goddess swear she will play no "witches' tricks." Armed with
the moly and Hermes' warning, Odysseus arrives at Circe's palace.

Circe gives Odysseus a magic drink, but it does not affect
him and he threatens to kill her with his sword. Circe turns the pigs
back into men but puts them all into a trance. They stay for one year,
until Odysseus finally begs her to let them go home. She replies that
they must first visit the land of the dead and hear a prophecy from
the ghost of Tiresias.

foreboding
(fôr-bō′dĭng) *n.* a sense
of approaching evil.

BOOK 11:

The Land of the Dead

Odysseus and his crew set out for the land of the dead. They arrive
and find the place to which Circe has directed them.

"Then I addressed the blurred and breathless dead,
vowing to slaughter my best heifer for them
before she calved, at home in Ithaca,
and burn the choice bits on the altar fire;

5 as for Tiresias, I swore to sacrifice
a black lamb, handsomest of all our flock.
Thus to **assuage** the nations of the dead
I pledged these rites, then slashed the lamb and ewe,
letting their black blood stream into the wellpit.

10 Now the souls gathered, stirring out of Erebus,
brides and young men, and men grown old in pain,
and tender girls whose hearts were new to grief;
many were there, too, torn by brazen lanceheads,
battle-slain, bearing still their bloody gear.

15 From every side they came and sought the pit
with rustling cries; and I grew sick with fear.
But presently I gave command to my officers
to flay those sheep the bronze cut down, and make
burnt offerings of flesh to the gods below—

20 to sovereign Death, to pale Persephone.
Meanwhile I crouched with my drawn sword to keep
the surging phantoms from the bloody pit
till I should know the presence of Tiresias.

One shade came first—Elpenor, of our company,
25 who lay unburied still on the wide earth
as we had left him—dead in Circe's hall,
untouched, unmourned, when other cares compelled us.
Now when I saw him there I wept for pity
and called out to him:

                'How is this, Elpenor,
30 how could you journey to the western gloom
swifter afoot than I in the black lugger?'

He sighed, and answered:

                'Son of great Laertes,
Odysseus, master mariner and soldier,
bad luck shadowed me, and no kindly power;

assuage (ə-swāj´) *v.* to calm or pacify

10 Erebus (ĕr´ə-bəs): a region of the land of the dead, also known as the underworld or Hades. Hades is also the name of the god of the underworld.

18 flay: to strip off the outer skin of.

> # "Do not abandon me unwept, unburied, to tempt the gods' wrath, while you sail for home."

35 ignoble death I drank with so much wine.
    I slept on Circe's roof, then could not see
    the long steep backward ladder, coming down,
    and fell that height. My neck bone, buckled under,
    snapped, and my spirit found this well of dark.
40 Now hear the grace I pray for, in the name
    of those back in the world, not here—your wife
    and father, he who gave you bread in childhood,
    and your own child, your only son, Telemachus,
    long ago left at home.

                                When you make sail
45 and put these lodgings of dim Death behind,
    you will moor ship, I know, upon Aeaea Island;
    there, O my lord, remember me, I pray,
    do not abandon me unwept, unburied,
    to tempt the gods' wrath, while you sail for home;
50 but fire my corpse, and all the gear I had,
    and build a cairn for me above the breakers—
    an unknown sailor's mark for men to come.
    Heap up the mound there, and implant upon it
    the oar I pulled in life with my companions.'

**50–51 fire my corpse
. . . cairn:** Elpenor wants
Odysseus to hold a
funeral for him.

55 He ceased, and I replied:

'Unhappy spirit,
I promise you the barrow and the burial.'

So we conversed, and grimly, at a distance,
with my long sword between, guarding the blood,
while the faint image of the lad spoke on.
60 Now came the soul of Anticlea, dead,
my mother, daughter of Autolycus,
dead now, though living still when I took ship
for holy Troy. Seeing this ghost I grieved,
but held her off, through pang on pang of tears,
65 till I should know the presence of Tiresias.
Soon from the dark that prince of Thebes came forward
bearing a golden staff; and he addressed me:

'Son of Laertes and the gods of old,
Odysseus, master of land ways and sea ways,
70 why leave the blazing sun, O man of woe,
to see the cold dead and the joyless region?
Stand clear, put up your sword;
let me but taste of blood, I shall speak true.'

At this I stepped aside, and in the scabbard
75 let my long sword ring home to the pommel silver,
as he bent down to the sombre blood. Then spoke
the prince of those with gift of speech:

'Great captain,
a fair wind and the honey lights of home
are all you seek. But anguish lies ahead;
80 the god who thunders on the land prepares it,
not to be shaken from your track, implacable,
in rancor for the son whose eye you blinded.
One narrow strait may take you through his blows:
denial of yourself, restraint of shipmates.
85 When you make landfall on Thrinacia first
and quit the violet sea, dark on the land
you'll find the grazing herds of Helios
by whom all things are seen, all speech is known.
Avoid those kine, hold fast to your intent,
90 and hard seafaring brings you all to Ithaca.
But if you raid the beeves, I see destruction
for ship and crew. Though you survive alone,
bereft of all companions, lost for years,
under strange sail shall you come home, to find

**58 with my long sword
...blood:** the ghosts are
attracted to the blood of
the sacrifice; Odysseus
must hold them at bay
with his sword.

66 prince of Thebes:
Tiresias, the blind seer,
comes from the city of
Thebes (thēbz).

89–91 kine; beeves:
two words for cattle.

95   your own house filled with trouble: insolent men
     eating your livestock as they court your lady.
     Aye, you shall make those men atone in blood!
     But after you have dealt out death—in open
     combat or by stealth—to all the suitors,
100   go overland on foot, and take an oar,
     until one day you come where men have lived
     with meat unsalted, never known the sea,
     nor seen seagoing ships, with crimson bows
     and oars that fledge light hulls for dipping flight.
105   The spot will soon be plain to you, and I
     can tell you how: some passerby will say,
     "What winnowing fan is that upon your shoulder?"
     Halt, and implant your smooth oar in the turf
     and make fair sacrifice to Lord Poseidon:
110   a ram, a bull, a great buck boar; turn back,
     and carry out pure hekatombs at home
     to all wide heaven's lords, the undying gods,
     to each in order. Then a seaborne death
     soft as this hand of mist will come upon you
115   when you are wearied out with rich old age,
     your country folk in blessed peace around you.
     And all this shall be just as I foretell.' . . ."

> **101–102** where men have lived with meat unsalted: refers to an inland location where men do not eat salted (preserved) meat as sailors do aboard a ship.

Odysseus speaks to the shade of his mother. She tells him that
Penelope and Telemachus are still grieving for him and that his
father, Laertes, has moved to the country, where he, too, mourns his
son. Odysseus' mother explains that she died from a broken heart.
Odysseus also speaks with the spirits of many great ladies and men
who died, as well as those who were being punished for their earthly
sins. Filled with horror, Odysseus and his crew set sail.

BOOK 12:

The Sirens; Scylla and Charybdis

Odysseus and his men return to Circe's island. While the men sleep,
Circe takes Odysseus aside to hear about the underworld and to offer
advice.

"Then said the Lady Circe:
'So: all those trials are over.

Listen with care

to this, now, and a god will arm your mind.
Square in your ship's path are Sirens, crying
5 beauty to bewitch men coasting by;
woe to the innocent who hears that sound!
He will not see his lady nor his children
in joy, crowding about him, home from sea;
the Sirens will sing his mind away
10 on their sweet meadow lolling. There are bones
of dead men rotting in a pile beside them
and flayed skins shrivel around the spot.

Steer wide;

keep well to seaward; plug your oarsmen's ears
with beeswax kneaded soft; none of the rest
15 should hear that song.

But if you wish to listen,

let the men tie you in the lugger, hand
and foot, back to the mast, lashed to the mast,
so you may hear those harpies' thrilling voices;
shout as you will, begging to be untied,
20 your crew must only twist more line around you
and keep their stroke up, till the singers fade.
What then? One of two courses you may take,
and you yourself must weigh them. I shall not
plan the whole action for you now, but only
25 tell you of both.

Ahead are beetling rocks

and dark blue glancing Amphitrite, surging,
roars around them. Prowling Rocks, or Drifters,
the gods in bliss have named them—named them well.
Not even birds can pass them by. . . .

30 A second course

lies between headlands. One is a sharp mountain
piercing the sky, with stormcloud round the peak
dissolving never, not in the brightest summer,

2–3 In Circe, Odysseus has found a valuable ally. In the next hundred lines, she describes in detail each danger that he and his men will meet on their way home.

14 kneaded (nē´dĭd): squeezed and pressed.

18 those harpies' thrilling voices: the delightful voices of those horrible female creatures.

25 beetling: jutting or overhanging.

26 glancing Amphitrite (ăm´fĭ-trī´tē): sparkling seawater. (Amphitrite is the goddess of the sea and the wife of Poseidon. Here, Circe uses the name to refer to the sea itself.)

31 headlands: points of land jutting out into the sea; promontories.

to show heaven's azure there, nor in the fall.

34 **heaven's azure**
(ăzh´ər): the blue sky.

35 No mortal man could scale it, nor so much
as land there, not with twenty hands and feet,
so sheer the cliffs are—as of polished stone.
Midway that height, a cavern full of mist
opens toward Erebus and evening. Skirting
40 this in the lugger, great Odysseus,
your master bowman, shooting from the deck,
would come short of the cavemouth with his shaft;
but that is the den of Scylla, where she yaps
abominably, a newborn whelp's cry,

abominably
(ə-bŏm´ə-nə-blē) *adv.* in a
hateful way; horribly.

45 though she is huge and monstrous. God or man,
no one could look on her in joy. Her legs—
and there are twelve—are like great tentacles,
unjointed, and upon her serpent necks
are borne six heads like nightmares of ferocity,
50 with triple serried rows of fangs and deep
gullets of black death. Half her length, she sways
her heads in air, outside her horrid cleft,
hunting the sea around that promontory
for dolphins, dogfish, or what bigger game
55 thundering Amphitrite feeds in thousands.
And no ship's company can claim
to have passed her without loss and grief; she takes,
from every ship, one man for every gullet.

The opposite point seems more a tongue of land
60 you'd touch with a good bowshot, at the narrows.
A great wild fig, a shaggy mass of leaves,
grows on it, and Charybdis lurks below
to swallow down the dark sea tide. Three times
from dawn to dusk she spews it up
65 and sucks it down again three times, a whirling
maelstrom; if you come upon her then
the god who makes earth tremble could not save you.
No, hug the cliff of Scylla, take your ship
through on a racing stroke. Better to mourn
70 six men than lose them all, and the ship, too.'

66 **maelstrom**
(māl´strəm): a large,
violent whirlpool.

So her advice ran; but I faced her, saying:

'Only instruct me, goddess, if you will,
how, if possible, can I pass Charybdis,
or fight off Scylla when she raids my crew?'

75 Swiftly that loveliest goddess answered me:

'Must you have battle in your heart forever?
The bloody toil of combat? Old contender,
will you not yield to the immortal gods?
That nightmare cannot die, being eternal
80 evil itself—horror, and pain, and chaos;
there is no fighting her, no power can fight her,
all that avails is flight.

82 all ... flight: all you can do is flee.

               Lose headway there
along that rockface while you break out arms,
and she'll swoop over you, I fear, once more,
85 taking one man again for every gullet.
No, no, put all your backs into it, row on;
invoke Blind Force, that bore this scourge of men,
to keep her from a second strike against you.

87 invoke ... men: pray to the goddess Blind Force, who gave birth to Scylla.

Then you will coast Thrinacia, the island
90 where Helios' cattle graze, fine herds, and flocks
of goodly sheep. The herds and flocks are seven,
with fifty beasts in each.

89 coast: sail along the coast of.

                    No lambs are dropped,
or calves, and these fat cattle never die.
Immortal, too, their cowherds are—their shepherds—
95 Phaethusa and Lampetia, sweetly braided
nymphs that divine Neaera bore
to the overlord of high noon, Helios.
These nymphs their gentle mother bred and placed
upon Thrinacia, the distant land,
100 in care of flocks and cattle for their father.

95–96 Phaethusa (fā´ə-thoō´sə); **Lampetia** (lăm-pē´shə); **Neaera** (nē-ē´rə).

Now give those kine a wide berth, keep your thoughts
intent upon your course for home,
and hard seafaring brings you all to Ithaca.
But if you raid the beeves, I see destruction
105 for ship and crew.

101–105 Circe warns Odysseus not to steal Helios' fine cattle because Helios will take revenge.

                Rough years then lie between
you and your homecoming, alone and old,
the one survivor, all companions lost.' . . ."

At dawn, Odysseus and his men continue their journey. Odysseus
decides to tell the men only of Circe's warnings about the Sirens,
whom they will soon encounter. He is fairly sure that they can survive
this peril if he keeps their spirits up. Suddenly, the wind stops.

               "The crew were on their feet
briskly, to furl the sail, and stow it; then,

110 each in place, they poised the smooth oar blades
and sent the white foam scudding by. I carved
a massive cake of beeswax into bits
and rolled them in my hands until they softened—
no long task, for a burning heat came down
115 from Helios, lord of high noon. Going forward
I carried wax along the line, and laid it
thick on their ears. They tied me up, then, plumb
amidships, back to the mast, lashed to the mast,
and took themselves again to rowing. Soon,
120 as we came smartly within hailing distance,
the two Sirens, noting our fast ship
off their point, made ready, and they sang. . . .

The lovely voices in ardor appealing over the water
made me crave to listen, and I tried to say
125 'Untie me!' to the crew, jerking my brows;
but they bent steady to the oars. Then Perimedes
got to his feet, he and Eurylochus,
and passed more line about, to hold me still.
So all rowed on, until the Sirens
130 dropped under the sea rim, and their singing
dwindled away.

                        My faithful company

rested on their oars now, peeling off
the wax that I had laid thick on their ears;
then set me free.

                        But scarcely had that island
135 faded in blue air than I saw smoke
and white water, with sound of waves in tumult—
a sound the men heard, and it terrified them.
Oars flew from their hands; the blades went knocking
wild alongside till the ship lost way,
140 with no oarblades to drive her through the water.
Well, I walked up and down from bow to stern,
trying to put heart into them, standing over
every oarsman, saying gently,

                                                'Friends,
have we never been in danger before this?
145 More fearsome, is it now, than when the Cyclops
penned us in his cave? What power he had!
Did I not keep my nerve, and use my wits
to find a way out for us?

117–118 plumb amidships: exactly in the center of the ship.

126 Perimedes (pĕr´ĭ-mē´dēz).

134–139 The men panic when they hear the thundering surf.

                                                      Now I say

    by hook or crook this peril too shall be
150   something that we remember.

                                               Heads up, lads!

    We must obey the orders as I give them.
    Get the oarshafts in your hands, and lay back
    hard on your benches; hit these breaking seas.
    Zeus help us pull away before we founder.
155   You at the tiller, listen, and take in
    all that I say—the rudders are your duty;
    keep her out of the combers and the smoke;
    steer for that headland; watch the drift, or we
    fetch up in the smother, and you drown us.'

160   That was all, and it brought them round to action.
    But as I sent them on toward Scylla, I
    told them nothing, as they could do nothing.
    They would have dropped their oars again, in panic,
    to roll for cover under the decking. Circe's
165   bidding against arms had slipped my mind,
    so I tied on my cuirass and took up
    two heavy spears, then made my way along
    to the foredeck—thinking to see her first from there,
    the monster of the gray rock, harboring
170   torment for my friends. I strained my eyes
    upon that cliffside veiled in cloud, but nowhere
    could I catch sight of her.

                                     And all this time,

    in **travail,** sobbing, gaining on the current,
    we rowed into the strait—Scylla to port
175   and on our starboard beam Charybdis, dire
    gorge of the salt sea tide. By heaven! when she
    vomited, all the sea was like a cauldron
    seething over intense fire, when the mixture
    suddenly heaves and rises.

                               The shot spume
180   soared to the landside heights, and fell like rain.

    But when she swallowed the sea water down
    we saw the funnel of the maelstrom, heard
    the rock bellowing all around, and dark
    sand raged on the bottom far below.
185   My men all blanched against the gloom, our eyes
    were fixed upon that yawning mouth in fear
    of being devoured.

154 founder: sink.

157 combers: breaking waves.

158–159 watch . . . smother: keep the ship on course, or it will be crushed in the rough water.

travail (trə-vāl´) *n.* painful effort.

176 gorge: throat; gullet.

179 shot spume: flying foam.

185 blanched: became pale.

Then Scylla made her strike,
whisking six of my best men from the ship.
I happened to glance aft at ship and oarsmen

190 and caught sight of their arms and legs, dangling
high overhead. Voices came down to me
in anguish, calling my name for the last time.

A man surfcasting on a point of rock
for bass or mackerel, whipping his long rod

195 to drop the sinker and the bait far out,
will hook a fish and rip it from the surface
to dangle wriggling through the air:

so these

were borne aloft in spasms toward the cliff.

She ate them as they shrieked there, in her den,

200 in the dire grapple, reaching still for me—
and deathly pity ran me through
at that sight—far the worst I ever suffered,
questing the passes of the strange sea.

We rowed on.

The Rocks were now behind; Charybdis, too,

205 and Scylla dropped astern. . . ."

189 aft: toward the rear
of the ship.

**198 borne aloft in
spasms:** lifted high while
struggling violently.

200 grapple: grasp.

Odysseus tries to persuade his men to bypass Thrinacia, the island of the sun god, Helios, but they insist on landing. Driven by hunger, they ignore Odysseus' warning not to feast on Helios' cattle. This disobedience angers the sun god, who threatens to stop shining if payment is not made for the loss of his cattle. To appease Helios, Zeus sends down a thunderbolt to sink Odysseus' ship. Odysseus alone survives. He eventually drifts to Ogygia, the home of Calypso, who keeps him on her island for seven years. With this episode, Odysseus ends the telling of his tale to King Alcinous.

COLLABORATIVE DISCUSSION In what instances does Odysseus demonstrate his greatest acts of heroism? Discuss your ideas with a partner. Cite specific textual evidence to support your ideas.

Analyze Character: Epic Hero

Odysseus is an **epic hero**—a larger-than-life character who embodies the ideals of a nation or race. Epic heroes take part in long, dangerous adventures and accomplish great deeds. They are considered **archetypes** because they can be found in many works from different cultures throughout the ages.

Although epic heroes may have superhuman abilities, they still have human flaws. These flaws make them more complex and appealing. For example, Odysseus demonstrates extraordinary strength and courage, but his overconfidence results in a tendency to dismiss warnings. His imperfections help make him more likable than a perfect character, and the audience can relate to his mistakes. These questions can help you analyze how the complex character of Odysseus develops over the course of the epic:

- What do you learn about Odysseus' character through how he faces various conflicts?
- What traits, or qualities, does Odysseus show through his interactions with other characters?
- What do Odysseus' character traits tell you about what the ancient Greeks found admirable?

Analyzing the Text

Cite Text Evidence   Support your responses with evidence from the selection.

1. **Infer** What do you learn about the character of Odysseus through the poet's introduction in Book 1 (lines 1–17)?

2. **Summarize** How does Odysseus regard the Cyclopes, based on the description in lines 56–67 of Book 9? What does this description reveal about Odysseus' values as well as the values of the ancient Greeks?

3. **Interpret** As Odysseus recalls his men's pleas to flee the Cyclops' cave, he remarks, "Ah, / how sound that was! Yet I refused. I wished / to see the caveman, what he had to offer." What qualities of an epic hero does Odysseus reveal in this comment?

4. **Analyze** What strengths does Odysseus demonstrate in his encounter with the Cyclops? Explain.

5. **Summarize** Why does Odysseus continue to taunt the Cyclops as he pulls away from the shore? What traits does he demonstrate through this behavior, and what are the consequences?

6. **Analyze** A **foil** is a character who contrasts with another character. How does the character of Eurylochus serve as a foil to Odysseus in Book 10?

7. **Infer** What does the audience learn about Odysseus from his encounters with his shipmate Elpenor and his mother Anticlea in Book 11?

Critical Vocabulary

harried	ponderous	profusion	adversary
foreboding	assuage	abominably	travail

Practice and Apply   Use the Critical Vocabulary words to answer the questions. Then, with a partner, take turns providing evidence to support your answers.

1. Which word is an antonym, or a word with the opposite meaning, of *friend*?

2. Which word most closely relates to *prediction*?

3. Which word is an antonym of *calm*?

4. Which word most closely relates to *atrociously*?

5. Which word is an antonym of *shortage*?

6. Which word most closely relates to *soothe*?

7. Which word most closely relates to *struggle*?

8. Which word most closely relates to *awkward*?

Vocabulary Strategy: Prefixes

Recognizing **prefixes** can help you understand the meanings of unfamiliar words. For example, in the Critical Vocabulary word *foreboding*, the prefix *fore-*, meaning "beforehand," combines with the verb *bode*, meaning "to give signs of something." This can help you understand the definition "a sense of impending doom." Here are some more examples.

Prefixes	Meanings	Examples
ad-, as-	to, toward, before	adversary, assuage
pro-	in place of, in favor of, forward	profusion, proceed
ab-	away from	abominably, abject
sub-	below, almost, close after	subsequent, subordinate
ob-	before, toward, inversely	objective, obligate

Practice and Apply   Consult a dictionary to determine the meaning of each example word in the chart. Then, discuss with a partner how each word's prefix relates to its meaning. Finally, identify another example word for each prefix, and use the word in a sentence.

PART TWO: THE HOMECOMING

AS YOU READ Pay attention to how the events in the epic build toward a resolution. Write down any questions you generate during reading.

BOOK 17:

The Beggar at the Manor

In Books 13–15, King Alcinous and his friends send Odysseus on his way home. Odysseus sleeps while the rowers bring him to Ithaca. When he awakens, he fails to recognize his homeland until Athena appears and tells him that he is indeed home. She disguises him as an old man, so that he can surprise the suitors, and then urges him to visit his faithful swineherd, Eumaeus. Athena goes to Telemachus and tells him to return home. She warns him of the suitors' plot to kill him and advises him to stay with the swineherd for a night. Telemachus does as she bids.

In Book 16, Odysseus reveals his identity to Telemachus, and a tearful reunion ensues. Telemachus lets Odysseus know that they face more than 100 suitors. Odysseus tells Telemachus to return home. He will follow, and Telemachus must pretend not to know him. He must also lock away Odysseus' weapons and armor. Telemachus returns home, and Odysseus and the swineherd soon follow. Odysseus is still diguised as a beggar.

While he spoke

an old hound, lying near, pricked up his ears
and lifted up his muzzle. This was Argos,
trained as a puppy by Odysseus,
5 but never taken on a hunt before
his master sailed for Troy. The young men, afterward,
hunted wild goats with him, and hare, and deer,
but he had grown old in his master's absence.
Treated as rubbish now, he lay at last
10 upon a mass of dung before the gates—
manure of mules and cows, piled there until
fieldhands could spread it on the king's estate.
Abandoned there, and half destroyed with flies,
old Argos lay.

But when he knew he heard
15 Odysseus' voice nearby, he did his best
to wag his tail, nose down, with flattened ears,
having no strength to move nearer his master.
And the man looked away,
wiping a salt tear from his cheek; but he
20 hid this from Eumaeus. Then he said:

"I marvel that they leave this hound to lie
here on the dung pile;
he would have been a fine dog, from the look of him,
though I can't say as to his power and speed
25 when he was young. You find the same good build
in house dogs, table dogs landowners keep
all for style."
                                And you replied, Eumaeus:

"A hunter owned him—but the man is dead
in some far place. If this old hound could show
30 the form he had when Lord Odysseus left him,
going to Troy, you'd see him swift and strong.
He never shrank from any savage thing
he'd brought to bay in the deep woods; on the scent
no other dog kept up with him. Now misery
35 has him in leash. His owner died abroad,
and here the women slaves will take no care of him.
You know how servants are: without a master
they have no will to labor, or excel.
For Zeus who views the wide world takes away
40 half the manhood of a man, that day
he goes into captivity and slavery."

Eumaeus crossed the court and went straight forward
into the mégaron among the suitors;
but death and darkness in that instant closed
45 the eyes of Argos, who had seen his master,
Odysseus, after twenty years. . . .

Odysseus enters his home as a beggar, and the suitors mock and
abuse him. Penelope asks to speak with the beggar, but Odysseus puts
her off until nightfall.

43 mégaron: the main
hall of a palace or house

BOOK 21:

The Test of the Bow

In Books 18–20, Odysseus observes the suitors and finds that two in particular, Antinous and Eurymachus, are rude and demanding. Penelope asks Odysseus the beggar for news of her husband. He says he has heard that Odysseus is on his way home. Penelope, however, has given up hope for Odysseus' return. She proposes an archery contest to the suitors, with marriage to her as the prize. She enters the storeroom and takes down the heavy bow that Odysseus left behind.

Now the queen reached the storeroom door and halted.
Here was an oaken sill, cut long ago
and sanded clean and bedded true. Foursquare
the doorjambs and the shining doors were set
5 by the careful builder. Penelope untied the strap
around the curving handle, pushed her hook
into the slit, aimed at the bolts inside
and shot them back. Then came a rasping sound
as those bright doors the key had sprung gave way—
10 a bellow like a bull's vaunt in a meadow—
followed by her light footfall entering
over the plank floor. Herb-scented robes
lay there in chests, but the lady's milkwhite arms
went up to lift the bow down from a peg
15 in its own polished bowcase.

Now Penelope

sank down, holding the weapon on her knees,
and drew her husband's great bow out, and sobbed
and bit her lip and let the salt tears flow.
Then back she went to face the crowded hall,
20 tremendous bow in hand, and on her shoulder hung
the quiver spiked with coughing death. Behind her
maids bore a basket full of axeheads, bronze
and iron implements for the master's game.
Thus in her beauty she approached the suitors,
25 and near a pillar of the solid roof
she paused, her shining veil across her cheeks,
her maids on either hand and still,
then spoke to the banqueters:

15–18 Notice that Penelope still grieves for Odysseus, even after 20 years.

21 quiver (kwĭv´ər): a case in which arrows are carried.

22–23 axeheads ... game: metal heads of axes (without handles) that Odysseus employs in a display of archery skill.

"My lords, hear me:

30 suitors indeed, you **commandeered** this house
to feast and drink in, day and night, my husband
being long gone, long out of mind. You found
no justification for yourselves—none
except your lust to marry me. Stand up, then:
we now declare a contest for that prize.

35 Here is my lord Odysseus' hunting bow.
Bend and string it if you can. Who sends an arrow
through iron axe-helve sockets, twelve in line?
I join my life with his, and leave this place, my home,
my rich and beautiful bridal house, forever
40 to be remembered, though I dream it only.". . .

*Despite heating and greasing the bow, the lesser suitors prove unable
to string it. The most able suitors, Antinous and Eurymachus, hold
off. While the suitors are busy with the bow, Odysseus—still disguised
as an old beggar—goes to enlist the aid of two of his trusted servants,
Eumaeus, the swineherd, and Philoetius, the cowherd.*

Two men had meanwhile left the hall:
swineherd and cowherd, in companionship,
one downcast as the other. But Odysseus
followed them outdoors, outside the court,
45 and coming up said gently:

"You, herdsman,
and you, too, swineherd, I could say a thing to you,
or should I keep it dark?
No, no; speak,
my heart tells me. Would you be men enough
to stand by Odysseus if he came back?
50 Suppose he dropped out of a clear sky, as I did?
Suppose some god should bring him?
Would you bear arms for him, or for the suitors?"

The cowherd said:

"Ah, let the master come!
Father Zeus, grant our old wish! Some courier
55 guide him back! Then judge what stuff is in me
and how I manage arms!"
Likewise Eumaeus
fell to praying all heaven for his return,
so that Odysseus, sure at least of these,
told them:

---

commandeer
(kŏm´ən-dîr´) *v.* to take
control of by force.

35–37 Note that the
contest has two parts:
first the suitor must
bend the heavy bow
and string it—a task
that requires immense
strength and skill—and
then he must shoot an
arrow straight through
the holes in 12 axe
heads set up in a row.

"I am at home, for I am he.

60 I bore **adversities**, but in the twentieth year
I am ashore in my own land. I find
the two of you, alone among my people,
longed for my coming. Prayers I never heard
except your own that I might come again.

65 So now what is in store for you I'll tell you:
If Zeus brings down the suitors by my hand
I promise marriages to both, and cattle,
and houses built near mine. And you shall be
brothers-in-arms of my Telemachus.

70 Here, let me show you something else, a sign
that I am he, that you can trust me, look:
this old scar from the tusk wound that I got
boar hunting on Parnassus. . . ."

Shifting his rags

75 he bared the long gash. Both men looked, and knew,
and threw their arms around the old soldier, weeping,
kissing his head and shoulders. He as well
took each man's head and hands to kiss, then said—
to cut it short, else they might weep till dark—

80 "Break off, no more of this.
Anyone at the door could see and tell them.
Drift back in, but separately at intervals
after me.

Now listen to your orders:
when the time comes, those gentlemen, to a man,
85 will be dead against giving me bow or quiver.
Defy them. Eumaeus, bring the bow
and put it in my hands there at the door.
Tell the women to lock their own door tight.
Tell them if someone hears the shock of arms
90 or groans of men, in hall or court, not one
must show her face, but keep still at her weaving.
Philoetius, run to the outer gate and lock it.
Throw the cross bar and lash it.". . .

Odysseus the beggar asks the suitors if he might try the bow. Worried that the old man may show them up, they refuse, but Penelope urges them to let Odysseus try. At Telemachus' request, Penelope leaves the men to settle the question of the bow among themselves. Two trusted servants lock the doors of the room, and Telemachus orders the bow be given to Odysseus.

adversity
(ăd-vûr´sĭ-tē) *n.* hardship; misfortune.

73 Parnassus
(pär-năs´əs): a mountain in central Greece.

And Odysseus took his time,
95   turning the bow, tapping it, every inch,
    for borings that termites might have made
    while the master of the weapon was abroad.
    The suitors were now watching him, and some
    jested among themselves:

                    "A bow lover!"

100   "Dealer in old bows!"

                    "Maybe he has one like it
    at home!"

          "Or has an itch to make one for himself."

    "See how he handles it, the sly old buzzard!"

And one disdainful suitor added this:

"May his fortune grow an inch for every inch he bends it!"
105 But the man skilled in all ways of contending,
satisfied by the great bow's look and heft,
like a musician, like a harper, when
with quiet hand upon his instrument
he draws between his thumb and forefinger
110 a sweet new string upon a peg: so effortlessly
Odysseus in one motion strung the bow.
Then slid his right hand down the cord and plucked it,
so the taut gut vibrating hummed and sang
a swallow's note.

In the hushed hall it smote the suitors
115 and all their faces changed. Then Zeus thundered
overhead, one loud crack for a sign.
And Odysseus laughed within him that the son
of crooked-minded Cronus had flung that omen down.
He picked one ready arrow from his table
120 where it lay bare: the rest were waiting still
in the quiver for the young men's turn to come.
He nocked it, let it rest across the handgrip,
and drew the string and grooved butt of the arrow,
aiming from where he sat upon the stool.

Now flashed
125 arrow from twanging bow clean as a whistle
through every socket ring, and grazed not one,
to thud with heavy brazen head beyond.

Then quietly
Odysseus said:

"Telemachus, the stranger
you welcomed in your hall has not disgraced you.
130 I did not miss, neither did I take all day
stringing the bow. My hand and eye are sound,
not so **contemptible** as the young men say.
The hour has come to cook their lordships' mutton—
supper by daylight. Other amusements later,
135 with song and harping that adorn a feast."

He dropped his eyes and nodded, and the prince
Telemachus, true son of King Odysseus,
belted his sword on, clapped hand to his spear,
and with a clink and glitter of keen bronze
140 stood by his chair, in the forefront near his father.

106 heft: weight.

114 smote: struck; affected sharply.

115–116 The thunder, a sign from Zeus, indicates that the gods are on Odysseus' side.

118 Cronus (krō´nəs): Zeus' father.

122 nocked it: placed the arrow's feathered end against the bowstring.

127 brazen: made of brass.

contemptible (kən-tĕmp´tə-bəl) *adj.* deserving of scorn; despicable.

BOOK 22:

Death in the Great Hall

Now shrugging off his rags the wiliest fighter of the islands
leapt and stood on the broad door sill, his own bow in his hand.
He poured out at his feet a rain of arrows from the quiver
and spoke to the crowd:

> "So much for that. Your clean-cut game is over.
5 Now watch me hit a target that no man has hit before,
> if I can make this shot. Help me, Apollo."

He drew to his fist the cruel head of an arrow for Antinous
just as the young man leaned to lift his beautiful drinking cup,
embossed, two-handled, golden: the cup was in his fingers:
10 the wine was even at his lips: and did he dream of death?
How could he? In that **revelry** amid his throng of friends
who would imagine a single foe—though a strong foe indeed—
could dare to bring death's pain on him and darkness on his
    eyes?
Odysseus' arrow hit him under the chin
15 and punched up to the feathers through his throat.

Backward and down he went, letting the winecup fall
from his shocked hand. Like pipes his nostrils jetted
crimson runnels, a river of mortal red,
and one last kick upset his table
20 knocking the bread and meat to soak in dusty blood.

Now as they craned to see their champion where he lay
the suitors jostled in uproar down the hall,
everyone on his feet. Wildly they turned and scanned
the walls in the long room for arms; but not a shield,
25 not a good ashen spear was there for a man to take and throw.
All they could do was yell in outrage at Odysseus:

"Foul! to shoot at a man! That was your last shot!"

"Your own throat will be slit for this!"

> "Our finest lad is down!

You killed the best on Ithaca."

> "Buzzards will tear your eyes out!"

revelry (rĕv´əl-rē) *n.*
noisy merrymaking;
festivity.

18 runnels: streams.

23–25 Earlier, in
preparation for this
confrontation, Odysseus
and Telemachus
removed all the
weapons and shields
that were hanging on
the walls.

30 For they imagined as they wished—that it was a wild shot,
an unintended killing—fools, not to comprehend
they were already in the grip of death.
But glaring under his brows Odysseus answered:

"You yellow dogs, you thought I'd never make it
35 home from the land of Troy. You took my house to plunder,
twisted my maids to serve your beds. You dared
bid for my wife while I was still alive.
Contempt was all you had for the gods who rule wide heaven,
contempt for what men say of you hereafter.
40 Your last hour has come. You die in blood."

As they all took this in, sickly green fear
pulled at their entrails, and their eyes flickered   **42 entrails:** internal
looking for some hatch or hideaway from death.   organs.
Eurymachus alone could speak. He said:

45 "If you are Odysseus of Ithaca come back,
all that you say these men have done is true.
Rash actions, many here, more in the countryside.   **47 rash:** foolish;
But here he lies, the man who caused them all.   thoughtless.
Antinous was the ringleader; he whipped us on
50 to do these things. He cared less for a marriage
than for the power Cronion has denied him   **51 Cronion**
as king of Ithaca. For that   (krō´nē-ŏn´): Zeus, the
he tried to trap your son and would have killed him.   son of Cronus.
He is dead now and has his portion. Spare
55 your own people. As for ourselves, we'll make
restitution of wine and meat consumed,   **restitution**
and add, each one, a tithe of twenty oxen   (rĕs´tĭ-tōō´shən) *n.* a
with gifts of bronze and gold to warm your heart.   making good for loss or
Meanwhile we cannot blame you for your anger."   damage; repayment.

                                                           57 tithe: payment.
60 Odysseus glowered under his black brows
and said:
                    "Not for the whole treasure of your fathers,
all you enjoy, lands, flocks, or any gold
put up by others, would I hold my hand.
There will be killing till the score is paid.
65 You forced yourselves upon this house. Fight your way out,
or run for it, if you think you'll escape death.
I doubt one man of you skins by."   **67 skins by:** sneaks
                                                           away.
They felt their knees fail, and their hearts—but heard
Eurymachus for the last time rallying them.

70 "Friends," he said, "the man is **implacable**.
Now that he's got his hands on bow and quiver
he'll shoot from the big door stone there
until he kills us to the last man.

                                    Fight, I say,

let's remember the joy of it. Swords out!
75 Hold up your tables to deflect his arrows.
After me, everyone: rush him where he stands.
If we can budge him from the door, if we can pass
into the town, we'll call out men to chase him.
This fellow with his bow will shoot no more."

80 He drew his own sword as he spoke, a broadsword of fine
        bronze,
honed like a razor on either edge. Then crying hoarse and loud
he hurled himself at Odysseus. But the kingly man let fly
an arrow at that instant, and the quivering feathered butt
sprang to the nipple of his breast as the barb stuck in his liver.
85 The bright broadsword clanged down. He lurched and fell
        aside,
pitching across his table. His cup, his bread and meat,
were spilt and scattered far and wide, and his head slammed
        on the ground.
Revulsion, anguish in his heart, with both feet kicking out,
he downed his chair, while the shrouding wave of mist closed
        on his eyes.

90 Amphinomus now came running at Odysseus,
broadsword naked in his hand. He thought to make
the great soldier give way at the door.
But with a spear throw from behind Telemachus hit him
between the shoulders, and the lancehead drove
95 clear through his chest. He left his feet and fell
forward, thudding, forehead against the ground.

Telemachus swerved around him, leaving the long dark spear
planted in Amphinomus. If he paused to yank it out
someone might jump him from behind or cut him down with
        a sword
100 at the moment he bent over. So he ran—ran from the tables
to his father's side and halted, panting, saying:

"Father let me bring you a shield and spear,
a pair of spears, a helmet.
I can arm on the run myself; I'll give
105 outfits to Eumaeus and this cowherd.
Better to have equipment."

implacable
(ĭm-plăk´ə-bəl) *adj.*
impossible to soothe;
unforgiving.

88–89 Eurymachus'
death is physically
painful, but he also has
"revulsion, anguish in his
heart."

90 Amphinomus
(ăm-fĭn´ə-məs): one of
the suitors.

"Run then, while I hold them off with arrows as long as the arrows last."

Said Odysseus:

"Run then, while I hold them off with arrows
as long as the arrows last. When all are gone
if I'm alone they can dislodge me."

                                               Quick

110   upon his father's word Telemachus
ran to the room where spears and armor lay.
He caught up four light shields, four pairs of spears,
four helms of war high-plumed with flowing manes,
and ran back, loaded down, to his father's side.

115   He was the first to pull a helmet on
and slide his bare arm in a buckler strap.
The servants armed themselves, and all three took their stand
beside the master of battle.

                                      While he had arrows
he aimed and shot, and every shot brought down

120   one of his huddling enemies.
But when all barbs had flown from the bowman's fist,
he leaned his bow in the bright entry way
beside the door, and armed: a four-ply shield
hard on his shoulder, and a crested helm,

125   horsetailed, nodding stormy upon his head,
then took his tough and bronze-shod spears. . . .

113 helms: helmets.

The suitors make various unsuccessful attempts to expel Odysseus from his post at the door. Athena urges Odysseus on to battle, yet holds back her fullest aid, waiting for Odysseus and Telemachus to prove themselves. Six of the suitors attempt an attack on Odysseus, but Athena deflects their arrows. Odysseus and his men seize this opportunity to launch their own attack, and the suitors begin to fall. At last Athena's presence becomes known to all, as the shape of her shield becomes visible above the hall. The suitors, recognizing the intervention of the gods on Odysseus' behalf, are frantic to escape but to no avail. Odysseus and his men are compared to falcons who show no mercy to the flocks of birds they pursue and capture. Soon the room is reeking with blood. Thus the battle with the suitors comes to an end, and Odysseus prepares himself to meet Penelope.

BOOK 23:

The Trunk of the Olive Tree

Greathearted Odysseus, home at last,
was being bathed now by Eurynome
and rubbed with golden oil, and clothed again
in a fresh tunic and a cloak. Athena
5   lent him beauty, head to foot. She made him
taller, and massive, too, with crisping hair
in curls like petals of wild hyacinth
but all red-golden. Think of gold infused
on silver by a craftsman, whose fine art
10 Hephaestus taught him, or Athena: one
whose work moves to delight: just so she lavished
beauty over Odysseus' head and shoulders.
He sat then in the same chair by the pillar,
facing his silent wife, and said:

                        "Strange woman,
15 the immortals of Olympus made you hard,
harder than any. Who else in the world
would keep aloof as you do from her husband
if he returned to her from years of trouble,
cast on his own land in the twentieth year?

20 Nurse, make up a bed for me to sleep on.
Her heart is iron in her breast."

                           Penelope

spoke to Odysseus now. She said:

                        "Strange man,
if man you are . . . This is no pride on my part
nor scorn for you—not even wonder, merely.
25 I know so well how you—how he—appeared
boarding the ship for Troy. But all the same . . .
Make up his bed for him, Eurycleia.
Place it outside the bedchamber my lord
built with his own hands. Pile the big bed
30 with fleeces, rugs, and sheets of purest linen."

With this she tried him to the breaking point,
and he turned on her in a flash raging:

"Woman, by heaven you've stung me now!
Who dared to move my bed?

---

2 Eurynome
(yŏŏ-rĭn´ə-mē): a female
servant.

10 Hephaestus
(hĭ-fĕs´təs): the god of
metalworking.

11 lavished: showered.

**15 immortals of
Olympus:** the gods, who
live on Mount Olympus.

27–30 The bed, built
from the trunk of an
olive tree still rooted in
the ground, is actually
unmovable.

35 No builder had the skill for that—unless
a god came down to turn the trick. No mortal
in his best days could budge it with a crowbar.
There is our pact and pledge, our secret sign,
built into that bed—my handiwork
40 and no one else's!

An old trunk of olive
grew like a pillar on the building plot,
and I laid out our bedroom round that tree,
lined up the stone walls, built the walls and roof,
gave it a doorway and smooth-fitting doors.
45 Then I lopped off the silvery leaves and branches,
hewed and shaped that stump from the roots up
into a bedpost, drilled it, let it serve
as model for the rest. I planed them all,
inlaid them all with silver, gold and ivory,
50 and stretched a bed between—a pliant web
of oxhide thongs dyed crimson.

There's our sign!
I know no more. Could someone else's hand
have sawn that trunk and dragged the frame away?"

Their secret! as she heard it told, her knees
55 grew **tremulous** and weak, her heart failed her.
With eyes brimming tears she ran to him,
throwing her arms around his neck, and kissed him,
murmuring:

"Do not rage at me, Odysseus!
No one ever matched your caution! Think
60 what difficulty the gods gave: they denied us
life together in our prime and flowering years,
kept us from crossing into age together.
Forgive me, don't be angry. I could not
welcome you with love on sight! I armed myself
65 long ago against the frauds of men,
impostors who might come—and all those many
whose underhanded ways bring evil on!
Helen of Argos, daughter of Zeus and Leda,
would she have joined the stranger, lain with him,
70 if she had known her destiny? known the Achaeans
in arms would bring her back to her own country?
Surely a goddess moved her to adultery,
her blood unchilled by war and evil coming,
the years, the **desolation**; ours, too.

**50–51 a pliant web...
crimson:** a network of
ox-hide straps, dyed red,
stretched between the
sides of the bed to form
a springy base for the
bedding.

tremulous
(trĕm´yə-ləs) *adj.* marked
by trembling or shaking.

68 Argos (är´gŏs); **Leda**
(lē´də).

desolation
(dĕs´ə-lā´shən) *n.* lonely
grief; misery.

75 But here and now, what sign could be so clear
as this of our own bed?
No other man has ever laid eyes on it—
only my own slave, Actoris, that my father
sent with me as a gift—she kept our door.
80 You make my stiff heart know that I am yours."

78 Actoris (ăk-tôrʹĭs).

Now from his breast into his eyes the ache
of longing mounted, and he wept at last,
his dear wife, clear and faithful, in his arms,
longed for
                    as the sunwarmed earth is longed for by a swimmer
85 spent in rough water where his ship went down
under Poseidon's blows, gale winds and tons of sea.
Few men can keep alive through a big surf

to crawl, clotted with brine, on kindly beaches
in joy, in joy, knowing the abyss behind:
90 and so she too rejoiced, her gaze upon her husband,
her white arms round him pressed as though forever. . . .

Odysseus and Penelope tell each other about all that happened to them while Odysseus was away. Then Odysseus visits his father, Laertes, to give him the good news of his safe return. Meanwhile, the townspeople, angry about the deaths of the young suitors, gather to fight Odysseus. In the end, Athena steps in and makes peace among them all.

COLLABORATIVE DISCUSSION What are the moments of greatest tension in Part 2? With a partner, discuss what details in the text help build tension. Cite specific textual evidence to support your ideas.

Analyze Author's Choices: Epic Poem

In the simplest terms, an epic is a long adventure story. An **epic** plot spans many years and involves a long journey. Often, the fate of an entire nation is at stake. An epic **setting** spans great distances and foreign lands. Epic **themes** reflect timeless concerns, such as courage, honor, life, and death.

Consider these questions as you analyze how the author's choices about the structure of the *Odyssey* help create a compelling narrative:

- How are the characteristics of an epic reflected in the plot, setting, characters, and themes?
- In what ways does the *Odyssey* embody the qualities and ideals of ancient Greek culture?
- What themes are still applicable today?

Analyze Figurative Meanings

Epics are often rich with **figurative language,** or words used to symbolize ideas and evoke emotions rather than to convey literal meanings. As you analyze the figurative meanings in the *Odyssey*, consider the cumulative impact that this language has on the reader's ability to imagine the settings, characters, and events.

Figurative Language	Example
An **epic simile** (also called a Homeric simile) is a long, elaborate comparison that often continues for a number of lines.	Odysseus compares gouging out the Cyclops's eye to turning a huge drill: "I leaned on it / turning it as a shipwright turns a drill / in planking, having men below to swing / the two-handled strap that spins it in the groove. / So with our brand we bored that great eye socket. . . ."
An **epithet** is a brief phrase that reflects traits associated with a particular person or thing.	Odysseus is referred to as "son of Laertes," "raider of cities," and "that man skilled in all ways of contending".
An **allusion** is an indirect reference to a famous person, place, event, or literary work.	The poet calls upon a daughter of Zeus, often credited with inspiration: "Sing in me, Muse, and through me tell the story".
A **metaphor** directly compares two things by saying that one thing *is* another.	Odysseus comments on Penelope's aloofness: "Her heart is iron in her breast".

Analyzing the Text

Cite Text Evidence   Support your responses with evidence from the selection.

1. **Summarize** In what ways does the role of the gods in Part Two reflect the characteristics of an epic?

2. **Identify** What universal themes does Homer explore in the *Odyssey*? Choose two events from either Part One or Part Two, and explain how Homer conveys a **theme,** or central message, in each.

3. **Analyze** What motivates Penelope to test Odysseus' identity? What does this reveal about her character and how she has been affected by her husband's absence?

4. **Interpret** How does the order in which Odysseus reveals himself to his friends and loved ones build suspense? Explain.

5. **Compare** In what ways are Penelope's struggles similar to and different from those of Odysseus? What ideal traits do both characters possess?

6. **Analyze** The epithet "that man skilled in all ways of contending" first appears in Book 1 and subsequently in Book 21 as Odysseus strings his bow in front of the suitors. How does this epithet have greater impact and meaning in Book 21 in the epic?

7. **Interpret** Determine the meaning of the figurative language in this line: "He poured out at his feet a rain of arrows from the quiver" (Book 22, line 3). What impact does this metaphor have on the description of Odysseus as a warrior?

PERFORMANCE TASK

Writing Activity: Narrative The point of view in the *Odyssey* rarely wavers from Odysseus' perspective. Nevertheless, other characters' words and actions hint at what they are thinking. Explore the epic from another point of view through this brief writing task:

- Narrate an event from the *Odyssey* from the point of view one of the following characters: Polyphemus, Circe, Eurylochus, Tiresias, Scylla, Athena, Eumaeus, Telemachus, Eurymachus, or Penelope.

- Engage and orient the reader using techniques such as dialogue and description to set up the situation and create a smooth progression of events.
- Use precise words and phrases, telling details, and sensory language to convey a vivid picture of the events.

Critical Vocabulary

commandeer	adversity	contemptible	revelry
restitution	implacable	tremulous	desolation

Practice and Apply Use your knowledge of the Critical Vocabulary words to answer each question. Then, take turns explaining your answers to a partner.

1. Would it be effective for a person trying to **commandeer** a situation to speak in a **tremulous** voice? Why?

2. Why might people who have survived some kind of **adversity** engage in **revelry?**

3. Is it always possible to make **restitution** after doing something **contemptible?** Why?

4. How might an **implacable** assault on a city lead to **desolation?**

Vocabulary Strategy: Words from Latin

Recognizing **word roots** can help you determine the meanings of unfamiliar words. For example, the Critical Vocabulary word *desolation*, meaning "a feeling of loneliness," contains the Latin root *sol*, which means "alone." This root is found in numerous other English words. Study the Latin roots and their meanings in the chart, along with example words that contain each root.

Latin Root	Meaning	Examples
sol-	alone	soliloquy, solo
trem-	tremble	tremor, tremulous
plac-	calm	implacable, placate
vers-	turn	adversity, versatile

Practice and Apply For each Latin root in the chart, follow these steps:

1. Look online or in print resources for one additional example of a word that uses the Latin root.

2. Use your knowledge of the root's meaning to write a definition for each example word.

3. Consult a dictionary to confirm each example word's meaning.

4. Use each example word in a sentence.

Language and Style: Absolute Phrases

An **absolute phrase** consists of a noun and a participle, a verb form ending in -ed or -ing that acts as an adjective. Absolute phrases must be set off with commas and may also contain objects of the participle and any modifiers. Rather than modifying a specific word in a sentence, absolute phrases describe the main clause of a sentence. Absolute phrases are a helpful way to add information to a sentence.

Look at this example of an absolute phrase from the *Odyssey*.

**I drove them, <u>all three wailing</u>, to the ships,
tied them down under their rowing benches,
and called the rest.**

In this sentence, the absolute phrase *all three wailing* is also an example of imagery. The phrase adds information and helps evoke a sense of what it was like for Odysseus to drag his men from the land of the Lotus Eaters.

This chart shows two other examples of absolute phrases.

Absolute Phrase	What It Modifies
<u>Arrows soaring past them</u>, the suitors scanned the room looking for weapons and shields.	The noun *arrows* is modified by the participle *soaring* and the additional modifiers *past them*. The absolute phrase modifies, or describes, the rest of the sentence, *the suitors scanned the room looking for weapons and shields*.
Odysseus dreamed only of his return to Ithaca, <u>his mind focused on his reunion with Penelope</u>.	The noun *mind* is modified by the participle *focused* and the additional modifiers *his* and *on his reunion with Penelope*. The absolute phrase modifies the rest of the sentence, *Odysseus dreamed only of his return to Ithaca*.

Practice and Apply Look back at the narrative you wrote in response to this selection's Performance Task. Revise your narrative to include at least two absolute phrases. Share your revised narrative with a partner and discuss how your revisions add variety and interest.

Kira Salak (b. 1971) *wrote* The Cruelest Journey *to document her 600-mile solo kayak trip on the Niger River. The first person to ever achieve this feat, she traveled through a remote and dangerous region in Africa. Salak is an adventurer, an explorer, and a journalist. She has covered the civil war in the Democratic Republic of Congo, traveled across Papua New Guinea, and biked across Alaska. In 2005, she received a National Geographic Emerging Explorer Award, which recognizes people who are helping build world knowledge through exploration.*

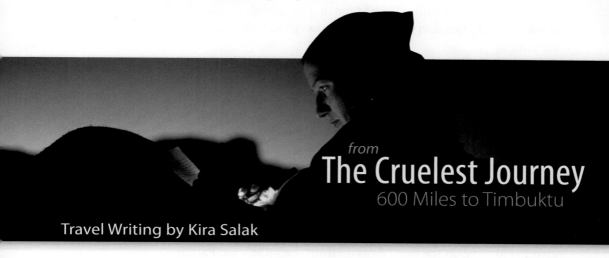

from
The Cruelest Journey
600 Miles to Timbuktu

Travel Writing by Kira Salak

AS YOU READ What does Salak think and feel about her journey? Make note of her thoughts, comments, and any telling details you notice. Write down any questions you generate during reading.

from Chapter One

In the beginning, my journeys feel at best ludicrous, at worst insane. This one is no exception. The idea is to paddle nearly 600 miles on the Niger River in a kayak, alone, from the Malian town of Old Ségou to Timbuktu. And now, at the very hour when I have decided to leave, a thunderstorm bursts open the skies, sending down apocalyptic rain, washing away the very ground beneath my feet. It is the rainy season in Mali, for which there can be no comparison in the world. Lightning pierces trees, slices across houses. Thunder racks the skies and pounds the earth like mortar
10 fire, and every living thing huddles in tenuous shelter, expecting the world to end. Which it doesn't. At least not this time. So that we all give a collective sigh to the salvation of the passing storm as it rumbles its way east, and I survey the river I'm to leave on this morning. Rain or no rain, today is the day for the journey to begin.

And no one, not even the oldest in the village, can say for certain whether I'll get to the end.

"Let's do it," I say, leaving the shelter of an adobe hut. My guide from town, Modibo, points to the north, to further storms. He says he will pray for me. It's the best he can do. To his knowledge, no man has ever completed such a trip, though a few have tried. And certainly no woman has done such a thing. This morning he took me aside and told me he thinks I'm crazy, which I understood as concern and thanked him. He told me that the people of Old Ségou think I'm crazy too, and that only uncanny[1] good luck will keep me safe.

Still, when a person tells me I can't do something, I'll want to do it all the more. It may be a failing of mine. I carry my inflatable kayak through the narrow passageways of Old Ségou, past the small adobe huts melting in the rains, past the huddling goats and smoke of cooking fires, people peering out at me from the dark entranceways. It is a labyrinth[2] of ancient homes, built and rebuilt after each storm, plastered with the very earth people walk upon. Old Ségou must look much the same as it did in Scottish explorer Mungo Park's time when, exactly 206 years ago to the day, he left on the first of his two river journeys down the Niger to Timbuktu, the first such attempt by a Westerner. It is no coincidence that I've planned to leave on the same day and from the same spot. Park is my benefactor of sorts, my guarantee. If he could travel down the Niger, then so can I. And it is all the guarantee I have for this trip— that an obsessed 19th-century adventurer did what I would like to do. Of course Park also died on this river, but I've so far managed to overlook that.

I gaze at the Niger through the adobe passageways, staring at waters that began in the mountainous rain forests of Guinea and traveled all this way to central Mali—waters that will journey northeast with me to Timbuktu before cutting a great circular swath through the Sahara and retreating south, through Niger, on to Nigeria, passing **circuitously** through mangrove swamps and jungle, resting at last in the Atlantic in the Bight of Benin.[3] But the Niger is more than a river; it is a kind of faith. Bent and plied by Saharan sands, it perseveres more than 2,600 miles from beginning to end through one of the hottest, most desolate regions of the world. And when the rains come each year, it finds new strength of purpose, surging through the sunbaked lands, giving people the boons of crops and livestock and fish, taking nothing, asking nothing. It humbles all who see it.

circuitously
(sər-kyōo´ĭ-təs-lē) *adv.*
in an indirect and lengthy manner.

---

[1] **uncanny:** mysterious or impossible to explain.
[2] **labyrinth:** a complex collection of paths, such as a maze.
[3] **Bight of Benin:** a gulf on Africa's west coast between Ghana and Nigeria.

If I were to try to explain why I'm here, why I chose Mali and the Niger for this journey—now that is a different matter. I can already feel the resistance in my gut, the familiar clutch of fear.

I used to avoid stripping myself down in search of motivation, scared of what I might uncover, scared of anything that might suggest a taint of the pathological.[4] And would it be enough to say that I admire Park's own trip on the river and want to try a similar challenge? That answer carries a whiff of the **disingenuous**; it sounds too easy to me. Human motivation, itself, is a complicated thing. If only it was simple enough to say, "Here is the Niger, and I want to paddle it." But I'm not that kind of traveler, and this isn't that kind of trip. If a journey doesn't have something to teach you about yourself, then what kind of journey is it? There is one thing I'm already certain of: Though we may think we choose our journeys, they choose us.

Hobbled donkeys cower under a new onslaught of rain, ears back, necks craned. Little children dare each other to touch me, and I make it easy for them, stopping and holding out my arm. They stroke my white skin as if it were velvet, using only the pads of their fingers, then stare at their hands to check for wet paint.

Thunder again. More rain falls. I stop on the shore, near a centuries-old kapok tree under which I imagine Park once took shade. I open my bag, spread out my little red kayak, and start to pump it up. I'm doing this trip under the sponsorship of *National Geographic Adventure,* which hopes to run a magazine story about it. This means that they need photos, lots of photos, and so a French photographer named Rémi Bénali feverishly snaps pictures of me. I don't know what I hate more—river storms or photo shoots. I value the privacy and **integrity** of my trips, and I don't want my journey turning into a circus. The magazine presented the best compromise it could: Rémi, renting a motor-driven pirogue,[5] was given instructions to find me on the river every few days to do his thing.

My kayak is nearly inflated. A couple of women nearby, with colorful cloth wraps called *pagnes* tied tightly about their breasts, gaze at me cryptically, as if to ask: *Who are you and what do you think you're doing?* The Niger churns and slaps the shore, in a surly mood. I don't pretend to know what I'm doing. Just one thing at a time now, kayak inflated, kayak loaded with my gear. Paddles fitted together and ready. Modibo is standing on the shore, watching me.

"I'll pray for you," he reminds me.

I balance my gear, adjust the straps, get in. And, finally, irrevocably, I paddle away. . . .

disingenuous
(dĭs´ĭn-jĕn´yoo-əs)
adj. insincere, deceitful.

integrity
(ĭn-tĕg´rĭ-tē) *n.*
consistency and strength of purpose.

---

[4] **taint of the pathological:** trace of mental illness.
[5] **pirogue (pĭ-rōg´):** a canoe made from a hallowed tree trunk.

100   The storm erupts into a new overture. Torrential rains. Waves
higher than my kayak, trying to capsize me. But my boat is self-
bailing[6] and I stay afloat. The wind drives the current in reverse,
tearing and ripping at the shores, sending spray into my face.
I paddle madly, crashing and driving forward. I travel inch by
inch, or so it seems, arm muscles smarting and rebelling against
this journey. I crawl past New Ségou, fighting the Niger for more
distance. Large river steamers rest in jumbled rows before cement
docks, the town itself looking dark and deserted in the downpour.
No one is out in their boats. The people know something I don't:
110   that the river dictates all travel.

A popping feeling now and a screech of pain. My right arm
lurches from a ripped muscle. But this is no time and place for such
an injury, and I won't tolerate it, stuck as I am in a storm. I try to
get used to the pulses of pain as I fight the river. There is only one
direction to go: forward. Stopping has become anathema.[7]

I wonder what we look for when we **embark** on these kinds of trips.
There is the pat answer that you tell the people you don't know:
that you're interested in seeing a place, learning about its people.
But then the trip begins and the hardship comes, and hardship is

embark
(ĕm-bärk´) *v.* to set
out on a course or a
journey (often aboard
a boat).

---

[6] **self-bailing:** the boat has holes, or scuppers, that allow water to drain from the cockpit.
[7] **anathema:** something hated or despised.

120 more honest: it tells us that we don't have enough patience yet, nor humility, nor gratitude. And we thought that we did. Hardship brings us closer to truth, and thus is more difficult to bear, but from it alone comes compassion. And so I've told the world that it can do what it wants with me during this trip if only, by the end, I have learned something more. A bargain, then. The journey, my teacher.

And where is the river of just this morning, with its whitecaps that would have liked to drown me, with its current flowing backward against the wind? Gone to this: a river of smoothest glass, a placidity unbroken by wave or eddy, with islands of lush greenery
130 awaiting me like distant Xanadus.[8] The Niger is like a mercurial god, meting out punishment and benediction on a whim. And perhaps the god of the river sleeps now, returning matters to the mortals who ply its waters? The Bozo and Somono[9] fishermen in their pointy canoes. The long passenger pirogues, overloaded with people and merchandise, rumbling past, leaving diesel fumes in their wake. And now, inexplicably, the white woman in a little red boat, paddling through waters that flawlessly mirror the cumulus clouds above. We all belong here, in our way. It is as if I've entered a very lucid dream, continually surprised to find myself here on
140 this river—I've become a hapless actor in a mysterious play, not yet knowing what my part is, left to gape at the wonder of what I have set in motion. Somehow: I'm in a kayak, on the Niger River, paddling very slowly but very surely to Timbuktu.

As Salak continues on her journey, she encounters raging storms, dangerous hippos, and unrelenting heat. Because she is traveling in a small kayak and unable to carry many supplies, she comes ashore each night, seeking shelter and food from the locals, who live along the banks of the river. The locals are very curious about a woman undertaking such a dangerous journey alone. Some of them greet her warmly and generously; others with hostility. Finally, weak from dysentery, she approaches her final destination—Timbuktu.

from Chapter Thirteen

"This river will never end," I say out loud, over and over again, like a mantra. My map shows an obvious change to the northeast, but that turn hasn't come for hours, may never come at all. To be so close to Timbuktu, and yet so immeasurably far away. All I know is that I must keep paddling. I *have* to be close. Determined still to get

---

[8] **Xanadus (zăn´ə-do͞oz´):** Xanadu, the summer palace of Kublai Khan; connotes an elaborate, ideal paradise.
[9] **Bozo and Somono:** ethnic groups native to Mali and the Niger River delta.

to Timbuktu's port of Korioumé by nightfall, I shed the protection
of my long-sleeved shirt, pull the kayak's thigh straps in tight, and
prepare for the hardest bout of paddling yet.

I paddle like a person possessed. I paddle the hours away, the
sun falling aside to the west but still keeping its heat on me. I keep
up a cadence in my head, keep my breaths regular and deep, in
synch with my arm movements. The shore passes by slowly, but it
passes. As the sun gets ominously low, burning a flaming orange,
the river turns almost due north and I can see a distant, square-
shaped building made of cement: the harbinger of what can only
be Korioumé. Hardly a tower of gold, hardly an El Dorado, but I'll
take it. I paddle straight toward it, ignoring the pains in my body,
my raging headache. *Timbuktu, Timbuktu!* Bozo fishermen ply
the river out here, and they stare at me as I pass. They don't ask for
money or cadeaux[10]—can they see the determination in my face,
sense my fatigue? All they say is, *"Ça va, madame?"*[11] with obvious
concern. One man actually stands and raises his hands in a cheer,
urging me on. I take his kindness with me into the final stretch,
rounding the river's sharp curve to the port of Korioumé.

I see Rémi's boat up ahead; he waits for me by the port, telephoto
lens in hand. It's the first time during this trip that I'm not fazed by
being photographed. I barely notice him. I barely notice anything
except the port ahead of me. All I can think about is stopping. Here
is the ending I've promised myself for weeks. Here I am, 600 miles of
river covered, with the port of Timbuktu straight ahead.

Something tugs at my kayak. I'm yanked back: fishnets,
caught in my rudder. To be this close, within sight of my goal, and
thwarted by yet one more thing. The universe surely has a sense of
humor. I jump into the water, fumbling at the nylon netting tangled
around the screws holding the rudder to the inflatable rubber. It's
shallow here, and my bare feet sink into river mud full of sharp
pieces of rock that cut instantly into my soles. I try to ignore the
pain, working fast, pulling the netting off until I free my kayak.
When I get inside, the blood from my feet mixes with gray river
water like a final offering to the Niger. I maneuver around the nets,
adjust my course for the dock of Korioumé, and paddle hard.

Just as the last rays of the sun color the Niger, I pull up beside
a great white river steamer, named, appropriately, the *Tombouctou*.
Rémi's boat is directly behind me, the flash from his camera
lighting up the throng of people gathering on shore. There is no
more paddling to be done. I've made it. I can stop now. I stare up
at the familiar crowd waiting in the darkness. West African pop
music blares from a party on the *Tombouctou*.

---

[10] **cadeaux (kə-dō´):** French word meaning "gifts."
[11] **Ça va, madame? (sävä, mä-däm´):** French for "How are you, madam?"

Slowly, I undo my thigh straps and get out of my kayak, hauling it from the river and dropping it onshore for the last time. A huge crowd has gathered around me, children squeezing in to stroke my kayak. People ask where I have come from and I tell them, "Old Ségou." They can't seem to believe it.

"Ségou?" one man asks. He points down the Niger. His hand waves and curves as he follows the course of the river in his mind.

"Oui," I say.

"Ehh!" he exclaims.

"Ségou, Ségou, Ségou?" a woman asks.

I nod. She runs off to tell other people, and I can see passersby rushing over to take a look at me. What does a person look like who has come all the way from Ségou? They stare down at me in my sweat-stained tank top, my clay-smeared skirt, my sandals both held together with plastic ties.

I unload my things to the clamor of their questions, but even speaking seems to pain me now. Such a long time getting here. And was the journey worth it? Or is it blasphemy to ask that now? I can barely walk, have a high fever. I haven't eaten anything for more than a day. How do you know if the journey is worth it? I would give a great deal right now for silence. For stillness.

My exhaustion and sickness begin to alter this arrival, numbing the sense of finish and self-congratulation and replacing it with only the most important of questions. I've found that illness does this to me, quiets the busy thoughts of the mind, gives me a rare clarity that I don't usually have. I see the weeks on the river, the changing tribal groups, the lush shores down by Old Ségou metamorphosing[12] slowly into the treeless, sandy spread near Timbuktu. I'm wishing I could explain it to people—the subtle yet certain way the world has altered over these past few weeks. The inevitability of it. The grace of it. Grace, because in my life back home every day had appeared the same as the one before. Nothing seemed to change; nothing took on new variety. It had felt like a **stagnant** life.

I know now, with the utter conviction of my heart, that I want to avoid that stagnant life. I want the world to always be offering me the new, the grace of the unfamiliar. Which means—and I pause with the thought—a path that will only lead through my fears. Where there are certainty and guarantees, I will never be able to meet that unknown world.

Night settles on the shore, and Rémi pulls his boat up alongside the cement dock. I deflate my kayak for the last time and pack it up, carrying it and my things onto the boat. Heather[13] and Rémi

stagnant
(stăg´nənt) *adj.*
unchanging; without activity or development.

---

[12] **metamorphosing:** completely changing into another form.
[13] **Heather:** photographer Rémi Bénali's girlfriend, who is traveling with him.

both give me a hug of congratulation, but I'm still too numb to really comprehend that I've done it yet. To celebrate, Rémi offers me my choice of their onboard selection of soft drinks. I take an Orange Fanta. Outside, barely discernible in the darkness, the crowd of onlookers continues to discuss what I've done. I can hear them exchanging the word "Ségou" and I wonder if they believe that I've paddled this far. But it doesn't matter. I lie down on one of the benches. My head feels hot, and it aches to the metronome-like beating[14] of my heart.

Rémi has gone onshore and tries valiantly to get us a taxi into Timbuktu, but the driver of the only car available at this late hour demands an exorbitant sum of more than $150 to drive 30 kilometers. It is the first time I've seen Rémi get so blustering and assertive, and he argues passionately for a lower sum. We are all hoping for what we've promised ourselves tonight—a hotel room in Timbuktu with blessed air-conditioning—but the driver won't budge his price, thinking he has us. As we're all nearly out of our magazine expense money, I suggest we camp and go to Timbuktu the next morning, when there are sure to be plenty of taxis to take us there at a reasonable price. For the first time, I see this disappointment as just another uncontrollable part of life, like the storms that arose on the Niger. Nothing personal.

I point to the opposite shore as a place to camp away from the crowds. Rémi and Heather agree, and so the great boat is started up and we speed over the Niger beneath a sky dazed with stars. We ground the boat on the opposite shore, and I go about setting up my tent. I'm too sick to fully acknowledge the end of my trip. Rémi offers me a drink to celebrate, but I know I wouldn't be able to keep it down. I do manage to swallow some antibiotics and antinausea pills, which quiet my stomach enough to allow me to eat a mango and some of the noodles Rémi's cook has made for us. As I sit to eat, I'm swaying back and forth in my mind, as if I were still careering over the waves of the Niger. I've heard that this happens to sailors, that they get so attached to being tossed by the waves that they have trouble readjusting to solid ground. For me, it is as if the Niger still keeps a part of me, as if to tell me that I finally belong to it.

COLLABORATIVE DISCUSSION Were you surprised by how Salak felt at the end of her trip? With a partner, discuss Salak's thoughts on beginning the trip and details that may have led to her feelings at the end of the trip. Cite specific evidence from the text to support your ideas.

---

[14] **metronome-like beating:** steady, rhythmic pulsing.

Analyze Ideas and Events

A **travel narrative** is a type of nonfiction that records an author's experiences exploring new places. Travel writers don't just present a series of facts; they tell a story that includes characters, a conflict to be resolved, and themes about life. In this excerpt, Kira Salak uses narrative techniques to reveal her own reflections on her journey. She doesn't just tell you what she sees, she shows you how she feels. By including vivid details and imagery to describe people, places, and events, Salak builds tension and gets readers involved in her adventure. In addition to description and imagery, Salak uses other techniques in her narrative:

- The **mood** of a work is the emotional response it creates in readers. What details does Salak include to create the mood of her narrative?
- **Pacing** refers to the passage of time in a written work. Short, choppy sentences can speed up a narrative, while longer sentences slow it down. The use of the present tense adds immediacy, giving readers the sense that events are unfolding right now. How does Salak vary the pacing in her narrative?
- Writers of nonfiction may use **dialogue** to show what people are like and to advance the action of the story. How does Salak use dialogue in her narrative?

Determine Central Idea and Cite Evidence

The author of a travel narrative aims to tell a good story full of interesting people, places, and events. In most cases, the author also wants to communicate a **central idea** about life and people. To determine the central idea, ask yourself what purpose the author has for sharing certain details—including descriptions of the journey as well as the author's reflections on what happens.

As you think about the central idea of this selection, consider how Salak feels at the beginning of her journey and what she has learned about herself by the end. Look for specific evidence in the text to support your analysis. Two methods you can use to **cite textual evidence** are quoting the text and paraphrasing the text.

Quoting	Paraphrasing
Quoting the text means using the author's exact words to support an analysis of the text. Use a quotation when the author's specific words are critical to making your point. Always use quotation marks to show that you are using the author's words rather than your own. *Kira Salak begins her narrative by writing, "In the beginning, my journeys feel at best ludicrous, at worst insane."*	**Paraphrasing** the text is restating something in your own words. Paraphrasing helps you clarify the author's meaning, because you must understand it before you can rephrase it. For example, the first sentence of the selection could be paraphrased this way: *The author says that early on, her journeys always feel foolish or crazy.*

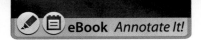

Analyzing the Text

Cite Text Evidence   Support your responses with evidence from the selection.

1. **Identify Patterns** Many travel narratives follow an arc similar to the plot of a story—a conflict is introduced, intensifies, comes to a climax, and is resolved. Outline the arc of the story told in this travel narrative.

2. **Analyze** The mood at the beginning of Chapter One is ominous. What is the mood as the excerpt from Chapter Thirteen begins? What details create this mood?

3. **Interpret**   Reread lines 57–71. What reasons does Salak give for making this trip? Why does she really undertake this journey? What does she expect to learn from this experience?

4. **Compare** Compare the pacing in lines 100–115 to that in lines 116–143. Which section seems to move faster, and why? How does the pacing help convey what the author is saying in each passage?

5. **Evaluate** Salak writes, "In the beginning, my journeys feel at best ludicrous, at worst insane." Do you think Salak's journey to Timbuktu was either of these things? Use quotations and paraphrases of the text to support your response.

6. **Analyze** What does the dialogue in lines 197–201 add to the narrative? How does the dialogue contribute to the central idea of the selection?

7. **Summarize**   Briefly describe the author. What seems to motivate Salak to undertake these journeys? Support your description with details about her actions, words, and thoughts.

PERFORMANCE TASK

Writing Activity: Analysis At first glance, you might think this selection is about travel on the Niger River, an adventure in Mali, or a long journey. What central idea gives meaning to all the details about Salak's adventure?

- Write a brief essay that analyzes the central idea of this selection. State the central idea and then use quotations and paraphrases to support your analysis.
- Remember to follow the conventions of standard English in your writing.

- Exchange essays with a partner and give each other feedback. Did you both use quotation marks to indicate the author's words? Are your paraphrases accurate? Does your evidence support the central idea you identified?

Critical Vocabulary

circuitously   disingenuous   integrity   embark   stagnant

Practice and Apply Answer each question in a way that demonstrates your comprehension of the Critical Vocabulary word.

1. What might be the benefits of traveling **circuitously** to an unfamiliar destination?

2. Have you ever given a **disingenuous** answer? Explain.

3. When have you acted with **integrity?** Explain.

4. What would you do to get ready to **embark** on a trip around the world?

5. What would you do if you felt your life was **stagnant?**

Vocabulary Strategy: Denotation and Connotation

The **denotation,** or dictionary meaning, of the Critical Vocabulary word *embark* is "to start something." *Embark* also has certain **connotations,** or associations that are suggested by the word but that go beyond the literal meaning of the word.

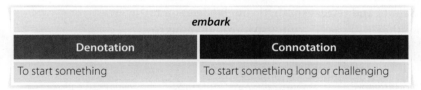

embark	
Denotation	**Connotation**
To start something	To start something long or challenging

You wouldn't *embark* on a quick errand, but you would *embark* on a long voyage.

Practice and Apply The words in each pair have similar denotations. Write sentences that demonstrate differences in the connotations of the words in each pair.

1. *still* and *stagnant*

2. *leave* and *embark*

3. *purity* and *integrity*

4. *dishonest* and *disingenuous*

5. *indirectly* and *circuitously*

Language and Style: Sentence Length

Authors vary **sentence length** and style to keep a piece from becoming monotonous. Authors also use sentence length to achieve a specific effect. For example, long sentences tend to slow readers down, while short sentences are read more quickly. A series of short, choppy sentences can also add tension.

Read this sentence from the selection:

> I gaze at the Niger through the adobe passageways, staring at waters that began in the mountainous rain forests of Guinea and traveled all this way to central Mali—waters that will journey northeast with me to Timbuktu before cutting a great circular swath through the Sahara and retreating south, through Niger, on to Nigeria, passing circuitously through mangrove swamps and jungle, resting at last in the Atlantic in the Bight of Benin.

Salak could have written the passage this way:

> I gaze at the Niger through the adobe passageways. I stare at waters that began in the mountainous rain forests of Guinea and traveled all this way to central Mali. These waters will journey northeast with me to Timbuktu. Then they will cut a great circular swath through the Sahara and retreat south, through Niger, on to Nigeria. Along the way, they will pass circuitously through mangrove swamps and jungle. They will rest at last in the Atlantic in the Bight of Benin.

By using a long, winding sentence, the author mirrors the flow of the river she is describing.

Later, Salak changes her sentence style as shown in this example:

> Just one thing at a time now, kayak inflated, kayak loaded with my gear. Paddles fitted together and ready.

Here, Salak uses shorter phrases and sentences to mirror the sequence of quick actions she is performing.

Authors also use breaks in sentences for effect. Consider this sentence:

> Which means—and I pause with the thought—a path that will only lead through my fears.

The use of dashes to offset Salak's side comment causes readers to pause with her and think carefully about the insight she is sharing.

Practice and Apply Go back to the analysis you wrote in response to this selection's Performance Task. Find at least three places where you can enhance your essay by using different sentence lengths.

Background **Michael Griffin** *served as the administrator of the National Aeronautics and Space Administration (NASA) from 2005 to 2009. President Eisenhower founded NASA in 1958 soon after the Soviet Union launched the first artificial satellite. NASA has sent Americans into space, created the space shuttle as a reusable spacecraft, worked on the International Space Station, and landed rovers to learn about the conditions on Mars. NASA works to learn more about space, find ways to get to and explore space, and determine how our knowledge of space affects us on Earth.*

The Real Reasons We Explore Space

Argument by Michael Griffin

AS YOU READ Notice which reasons Griffin examines before he outlines the real reason he thinks we explore space. Write down any questions you generate during reading.

I am convinced that if NASA were to disappear tomorrow, if we never put up another Hubble Space Telescope, never put another human being in space, people in this country would be profoundly distraught. Americans would feel that we had lost something that matters, that our best days were behind us, and they would feel themselves somehow diminished. Yet I think most would be unable to say why.

There are many good reasons to continue to explore space, which most Americans have undoubtedly heard. Some have been
10   debated in public policy circles and evaluated on the basis of financial investment. . . .

But these are not reasons that would make Americans miss our space program. They are merely the reasons we are most comfortable discussing. I think of them as "acceptable reasons" because they can be logically defended. When we **contemplate** committing large sums of money to a project, we tend to dismiss reasons that are emotional or value-driven or can't be captured on a

contemplate
(kŏn′təm-plāt′) *v.*
think carefully about.

spreadsheet.[1] But in space exploration those are the reasons—what I think of as "real reasons"—that are the most important.

When Charles Lindbergh[2] was asked why he crossed the Atlantic, he never once answered that he wanted to win the $25,000 that New York City hotel owner Raymond Orteig offered for the first nonstop aircraft flight between New York and Paris. Burt Rutan and his backer, Paul Allen, certainly didn't develop a private spacecraft to win the Ansari X-Prize for the $10 million in prize money. They spent twice as much as they made. Sergei Korolev and the team that launched Sputnik[3] were not tasked by their government to be the first to launch an artificial satellite; they had to fight for the honor and the resources to do it.

I think we all know why people strive to accomplish such things. They do so for reasons that are **intuitive** and compelling to all of us but that are not necessarily logical. They're exactly the opposite of acceptable reasons, which are eminently logical but neither intuitive nor emotionally compelling.

First, most of us want to be, both as individuals and as societies, the first or the best in some activity. We want to stand out. This behavior is rooted in our genes. We are today the descendants of people who survived by outperforming others. Without question that drive can be carried to an unhealthy extreme; we've all seen more wars than we like. But just because the trait can be taken too far doesn't mean that we can do without it completely.

A second reason is curiosity. Who among us has not had the urge to know what's over the next hill? What child has not been drawn to explore beyond the familiar streets of the neighborhood?

Finally, we humans have, since the earliest civilizations, built monuments. We want to leave something behind to show the next generation, or the generations after that, what we did with our time here. This is the impulse behind cathedrals and pyramids, art galleries and museums.

Cathedral builders would understand what I mean by real reasons. The monuments they erected to the awe and mystery of their God required a far greater percentage of their gross domestic product[4] than we will ever put into the space business, but we look back across 600 or 800 years of time, and we are still awed by what

intuitive
(ĭn-tōō´ĭ-tĭv) *adj.*
known or understood without reasoning; instinctive.

---

[1] **spreadsheet:** a computer program, often used in accounting, that calculates data entered into its rows and columns.

[2] **Charles Lindbergh:** (1902–1974) an American pilot who in 1927 became the first person to successfully fly alone across the Atlantic.

[3] **Sergei Korolev . . . Sputnik (sûr´gā kô-rô´lĕv . . . spŏot´nĭk):** Korolev (1907–1966), a Russian engineer, designed the rocket that carried the first satellite (*Sputnik*) into space in 1957.

[4] **gross domestic product:** the monetary value of all the goods and services that a country produces during a certain time period.

the builders accomplished. Those buildings, therefore, also stand as monuments to the builders.

The return the cathedral builders made on their investment could not have been summarized in a cost/benefit analysis. They began to develop civil engineering, the core discipline for 60   any society if it wishes to have anything more than thatched huts. They gained societal advantages that were probably even more important than learning how to build walls and roofs. For example, they learned to embrace deferred gratification, not just on an individual level, where it is a crucial element of maturity, but on a societal level, where it is equally vital. The people who started the cathedrals didn't live to finish them. The society as a whole had to be dedicated to the completion of those projects. We owe Western civilization as we know it today to that kind of thinking: the ability to have a constancy of purpose across years and decades.

70   It is my **contention** that the products of our space program are today's cathedrals. The space program satisfies the desire to compete, but in a safe and productive manner, rather than in a harmful one. It speaks abundantly to our sense of human curiosity, of wonder and awe at the unknown. Who can watch people assembling the greatest engineering project in the history of mankind—the International Space Station—and not wonder at the ability of people to conceive and to execute the project? And it also addresses our need for leaving something for future generations.

Of course the space program also addresses the acceptable 80   reasons, and in the end this is **imperative**. Societies will not succeed in the long run if they place their resources and their efforts in enterprises that, for whatever reason, don't provide concrete value. But I believe that projects done for the real reasons that motivate humans also serve the acceptable reasons. In that sense, the value of space exploration really is in its spinoffs, as many have argued. But it's not in spinoffs like Teflon and Tang and Velcro, as the public is so often told—and which in fact did not come from the space program. And it's not in spinoffs in the form of better heart monitors or cheaper prices for liquid oxygen for hospitals, although 90   the space program's huge demand for liquid oxygen spurred fundamental improvements in the production and handling of this volatile substance. The real spinoffs are, just as they were for cathedral builders, more fundamental.

Anyone who wants to build spacecraft, who wants to be a subcontractor, or who even wants to supply bolts and screws to the space industry must work to a higher level of precision than human beings had to do before the space industry came along. And that standard has influenced our entire industrial base, and therefore our economy.

contention
(kən-tĕn´shən) *n.* argued assertion.

imperative
(ĭm-pĕr´ə-tĭv) *adj.* crucial, necessary.

100   As for national security, what is the value to the United States of being involved in enterprises which lift up human hearts everywhere? What is the value to the United States of being a leader in such efforts, in projects in which every technologically capable nation wants to take part? The greatest strategy for national security, more effective than having better guns and bombs than everyone else, is being a nation that does the kinds of things that make others want to do them with us.

What do you have to do, how do you have to behave, to do space projects? You have to value hard work. You have to live
110   by excellence, or die from the lack of it. You have to understand and practice both leadership and followership. You have to build partnerships; leaders need partners and allies, as well as followers.

You have to accept the challenge of the unknown, knowing that you might fail, and to do so not without fear but with mastery of fear and a determination to go anyway. You have to defer gratification because we work on things that not all of us will live to see—and we know it.

We now believe that 95 percent of the universe consists of dark energy or dark matter, terms for things that we as yet know nothing
120   about. Is it even conceivable that one day we won't learn to harness them? As cavemen learned to harness fire, as people two centuries ago learned to harness electricity, we will learn to harness these new things. It was just a few years ago that we confirmed the existence of dark matter, and we would not have done so without the space program. What is the value of knowledge like that? I cannot begin to guess. A thousand years from now there will be human beings who don't have to guess; they will know, and they will know we gave this to them.

COLLABORATIVE DISCUSSION With a partner, discuss the various reasons Griffin cites for exploring space. Are they good reasons? Cite specific textual evidence to support your ideas.

Delineate and Evaluate an Argument

To **delineate,** or outline, an **argument,** first identify the author's claim. Look at the introduction, where the author often states the claim, and at the conclusion, where the author often restates the claim, sums up key points, or suggests actions based on conclusions. Then identify the specific reasons and evidence the author uses to support that position.

Consider whether the tone of the argument is objective or biased. Is the author supporting the claim with evidence including facts, statistics, personal experiences, statements by experts, and other information? Can the facts be verified? Are the author's sources reliable? Then assess whether the author's reasoning is valid. Look for false statements and fallacious reasoning, such as the examples in the chart.

Technique	Example	Explanation
False Cause and Effect	I ate shrimp last night and feel sick today. The shrimp must have been bad.	A connection between two ideas doesn't always mean that one causes the other.
Circular Reasoning	Ms. Vasquez is a great teacher because she does a great job teaching.	Circular reasoning restates the argument as a reason to support it.
Overgeneralization	I saw three shooting stars this past winter. Shooting stars appear in winter.	Generalizations based on limited data may not be accurate. Stereotypes are a form of generalization.

Evaluate whether the author plays on readers' emotions with words and phrases. While authors often appeal to emotions, they should also offer evidence and logical thinking. As a reader, be aware of ways authors may try to manipulate your emotions:

- **Bandwagon** (everyone is doing it)
- **Personal attack** (discrediting an idea by attacking the person who expressed it)
- **Transfer** (connecting feelings about one thing to something else)
- **Loaded language** (choosing words that elicit strong feelings)

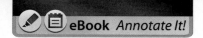
Analyzing the Text

Cite Text Evidence Support your responses with evidence from the selection.

1. **Summarize** Identify Griffin's claim, or central idea, and delineate the key ideas of his argument.

2. **Evaluate** Griffin makes a distinction between "acceptable" reasons and "real" reasons for exploring space. Explain what he means by each type of reason. Which type of reason does he use to support his claim?

3. **Analyze** Does Griffin appeal to logic, emotion, or both in this piece? Cite examples that support your response.

4. **Interpret** In what part of the argument does Griffin make use of a bandwagon approach to convince readers of the validity of his claim? Explain.

5. **Analyze** Why does Griffin include Charles Lindbergh, Burt Rutan and Paul Allen, and Sergei Korolev in this selection? How does their motivation provide supporting evidence for Griffin's claim?

6. **Interpret** How does the analogy in Griffin's statement, "It is my contention that the products of our space program are today's cathedrals," connect to his claim?

7. **Evaluate** What purpose might Griffin have had for writing this piece? Given that purpose, how effective is Griffin's argument? Why?

PERFORMANCE TASK

Writing Activity: Editorial Michael Griffin argues that exploring space is important and provides both "acceptable" and "real" value. However, space exploration comes with a large price tag. Is that price tag worth it? Should exploring space be part of our national budget?

Write an editorial for or against continuing the space program. In your editorial,

- state a clear claim for your argument and present at least three supporting reasons
- use evidence consisting of examples, questions, and facts

- avoid faulty logic
- include a conclusion restating your claim
- use the conventions of standard English

Critical Vocabulary

contemplate   intuitive   contention   imperative

Practice and Apply Choose which of the two situations best fits each vocabulary word's meaning.

1. **Contemplate**
   a. You carefully consider the options before making a decision.
   b. You choose carelessly without considering the consequences.

2. **Intuitive**
   a. You weigh the advantages and disadvantages of a situation.
   b. You follow your instincts when making an important decision.

3. **Contention**
   a. You come to a decision after evaluating evidence.
   b. You assert an opinion about a specific issue.

4. **Imperative**
   a. You take a class that is required for graduation.
   b. You fill your schedule with electives.

Vocabulary Strategy: Synonyms and Antonyms

Synonyms are words that have the same or similar meanings. **Antonyms** are words with opposite meanings. As a reader, recognizing synonyms and antonyms can help you understand new vocabulary words. For example, the word *necessary* is a synonym for the Critical Vocabulary word *imperative*, while *optional* is an antonym. You can use an online or print thesaurus to find synonyms and antonyms.

Practice and Apply Use a thesaurus to find a synonym and antonym for the remaining Critical Vocabulary words. Then write sentences using the synonym and the antonym as shown in this example:

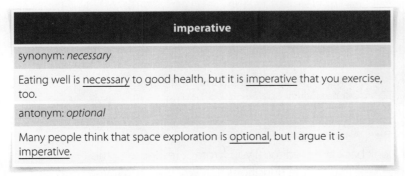

imperative
synonym: *necessary*
Eating well is <u>necessary</u> to good health, but it is <u>imperative</u> that you exercise, too.
antonym: *optional*
Many people think that space exploration is <u>optional</u>, but I argue it is <u>imperative</u>.

Language and Style: Transitions

Transitions are words or phrases that help connect ideas in a piece of writing. Read the following sentence from the selection:

> <u>But</u> these are not reasons that would make Americans miss our space program.

The word *but* lets the reader know that the author is shifting ideas. This statement as a whole leads the reader from the reasons Americans have heard to what the author thinks are the real reasons to explore space.

Later, the author identifies three reasons people strive to accomplish things. In the paragraphs that follow, he begins with these words and phrases: *First*, *A second reason*, and *Finally*. These transitions make it clear that the author is moving from one idea to another and then another. They also show that these three ideas are examples of the intuitive reasons the author wants to explain.

Given these examples, you can see that transitions are able to create a contrast between ideas, or they can link ideas. However, transitions can also

- introduce a sequence
- help orient readers in time or space
- identify examples, causes, or effects
- indicate conclusions

The chart below contains examples of transitional words and phrases related to a specific purpose.

Common Transitional Words and Phrases	
Purpose	**Examples**
Contrast ideas	but, however, although, on the other hand, while
Connect ideas	also, in addition, furthermore, too, first, second, finally
Introduce sequence	first, second, finally, initially, next, then, later
Orient readers in time or space	while, before, after, then, so far, meanwhile, here, nearby, above, below, next to
Identify examples, causes, or effects	for example, for instance, as a result, therefore, consequently
Indicate a conclusion	in conclusion, in summary

Practice and Apply Look back at the editorial you wrote in response to this selection's Performance Task. Identify the transitions that you used and revise your essay to add appropriate or stronger transitions. Then discuss with a partner how these transitions affect the flow of your essay and the connections between ideas.

The Journey

Poem by Mary Oliver

Mary Oliver (b.1935) *is known for observing the natural world in a way that is both romantic and unflinchingly honest. Oliver's poems often draw attention to small details—a bird calling, a still pond, a grasshopper. Her vivid imagery of the natural world opens a window for her to explore larger issues, such as love, loss, wonder, and grief.*

Oliver published her first book of poetry, No Voyage and Other Poems, *in 1963. She has published numerous other collections, including* American Primitive, *which won the Pulitzer Prize for Poetry in 1984. She has also won the National Book Award. But Oliver is not just an award-winning poet; she is also a popular poet whose work appeals to many readers.*

Besides writing poetry, Oliver has taught at colleges and universities including Bennington College in Vermont. She has also written many essays, as well as two books about the craft of writing poetry. Her long-time residence is in Provincetown, Massachusetts, a place that has inspired much of her writing with its natural beauty.

AS YOU READ Pay attention to details that describe barriers to the journey in the poem. Write down any questions you generate during reading.

The Journey

One day you finally knew
what you had to do, and began,
though the voices around you
kept shouting
5 their bad advice—
though the whole house
began to tremble
and you felt the old tug
at your ankles.
10 "Mend my life!"
each voice cried.
But you didn't stop.
You knew what you had to do,
though the wind pried
15 with its stiff fingers
at the very foundations—
though their melancholy
was terrible.
It was already late
20 enough, and a wild night,
and the road full of fallen
branches and stones.
But little by little,
as you left their voices behind,
25 the stars began to burn
through the sheets of clouds,
and there was a new voice,
which was slowly
recognized as your own,
30 that kept you company
as you strode deeper and deeper
into the world,
determined to do
the only thing you could do—
35 determined to save
the only life you could save.

COLLABORATIVE DISCUSSION What kind of journey do *you* take in
this poem? With a partner, discuss what obstacles need to be overcome
to complete this journey. Is the journey worth the effort? Cite specific
textual evidence to support your ideas.

Interpret Figurative Language

Figurative language is language that communicates meanings beyond the literal meanings of words. In figurative language, words are often used to represent ideas and concepts they would not otherwise be associated with. Poets use figurative language to make interesting comparisons and to help readers see subjects in a new light.

In "The Journey," Mary Oliver uses two types of figurative language—personification and metaphor.

Personification	Metaphor
Authors use **personification** to give human qualities to an object, animal, or idea. For example, an author might describe what a beach looks like during a storm by giving the sea human qualities: "*The angry sea took hungry bites from the shore.*"	Authors use **metaphors** to compare two things that are basically unlike but have something in common. Unlike similes, metaphors do not use the words *like* or *as*. The author describing the storm might instead use a metaphor: "*The sea was a wild animal attacking the shore.*" An **extended metaphor** is a longer metaphor that continues the comparison at length, even throughout an entire poem or literary work.

You probably noticed some examples of figurative language and imagery during your first reading of "The Journey." In subsequent readings, analyze Oliver's use of these devices more closely. Ask yourself how the devices make her poem more vivid and powerful.

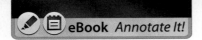
Analyzing the Text

Cite Text Evidence Support your responses with evidence from the selection.

1. **Interpret** In line 3, who are "the voices around you"? What might the voices represent?

2. **Analyze** How does Oliver personify the wind? What is the figurative meaning of this strong wind outside the home of a person who is undertaking a journey?

3. **Interpret** Notice that the poem is written in one long stanza, not broken into smaller stanzas. How does Oliver use this structure to develop an extended metaphor?

4. **Analyze** Trace the nature images that occur throughout the poem. How does Oliver use each image to develop the extended metaphor in the poem?

5. **Interpret** What do the branches and stones on the road **symbolize,** or represent?

6. **Infer** What is the **theme,** or underlying message, of the poem? How do the title and structure of the poem help convey the theme?

PERFORMANCE TASK

Speaking Activity: Discussion Think about the journey portrayed in this poem and the journey Kira Salak undertakes in *The Cruelest Journey: 600 Miles to Timbuktu* (also in this collection). What similarities and differences are there between the journeys?

- Meet with a small group to discuss your responses to the question.
- Cite evidence from both selections to support your ideas.

- When you are done, write a summary of the key points of your discussion. Conclude by making a generalization about the nature of journeys.

Research and Write an Analytical Essay

This collection explores the concept of the journey as an act of traveling as well as a personal passage or transformation. Recall the collection quotation by Kira Salak: "If a journey doesn't have something to teach you about yourself, then what kind of journey is it?" Review three texts in this collection, including the anchor text, the *Odyssey*, and consider Salak's perspective on travel. What compels characters or real people to set off on a journey—physical, mental, or spiritual—and what do they learn from their experiences? Synthesize your ideas in an analytical essay. Use evidence from the texts and from additional sources to support your conclusions.

An effective analytical essay

- includes a clear controlling idea about how and why people gain personal insights from their travel experiences or their mental/spiritual journeys
- engages the reader in the introduction with an interesting observation, quotation, or detail from one of the selections
- organizes central ideas in a logically structured body that clearly develops the controlling idea
- smoothly integrates source information that avoids plagiarism, with correctly cited sources
- uses transitions to show how ideas are related
- includes quotations or examples from the texts to illustrate central ideas
- has a concluding section that sums up the central ideas of the analysis

PLAN

my **Notebook**

Use the annotation tools in your eBook to find evidence that supports your ideas about journeys. Save each piece of evidence to your notebook.

Analyze the Texts Review and take notes on the *Odyssey* and two other texts in the collection. Write down important details, examples, and relevant quotations from all three texts that support your central idea about journeys. Consider the type of journey, the reason for the journey, and what the characters or people learn about themselves along the way.

Conduct Further Research What other stories, memoirs, poems, or essays might enrich your discussion of journeys? Search for additional evidence in print and digital sources to support your controlling idea. Note any relevant facts, quotations, or examples. Be sure to include source information so that you can accurately cite your sources.

Get Organized Prioritize your ideas in a graphic organizer.

- Write a controlling idea about the journeys people take and subsequent effects on the traveler.

- Decide what organizational pattern you will use to develop your essay. In what order will you present the central reasons that support your controlling idea? Will you begin your essay with your strongest reason or save it for last?

- Use your organizational pattern to sort the evidence you have gathered. A hierarchy diagram like this can help you organize your reasons and evidence for each section in the body of your essay.

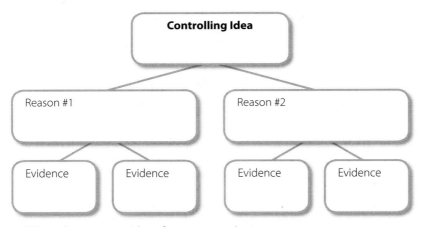

- Write down some ideas for your conclusion.

As you share your ideas about journeys, be sure to use these words.

> motivate
> objective
> pursuit
> subsequent
> undertake

PRODUCE

*my*WriteSmart

Draft Your Essay Write a draft of your essay, following your graphic organizer. Consider your purpose and audience and remember that essay writing requires formal language and a respectful tone. Essays that analyze texts are expected to be appropriate for an academic context.

Write your rough draft in *my*WriteSmart. Focus on getting your ideas down, rather than perfecting your choice of language.

- Introduce a clear and concise controlling idea.

- Present your details, quotations, and examples from the selections and additional sources in logically ordered paragraphs.

- Each paragraph should have a central idea related to your controlling idea with evidence to support it. Explain how each piece of evidence supports the central idea.

- Use transitions to connect the main sections of your essay and to clarify the relationships among your ideas.

- Write a conclusion that summarizes your analysis and presents a final synthesis of your central ideas.

REVISE

my **WriteSmart**

Have your partner or a group of peers review your draft in *my*WriteSmart. Ask your reviewers to note any ideas or evidence that does not support your controlling idea.

Exchange Essays Share your essay with a partner. Peer editing can be an effective method of revision to help you identify any confusing areas of your analysis. Constructive feedback should include specific information, as shown in the chart on the following page. As you read your partner's essay, consider these questions:

- Does the introduction correctly identify titles and authors of the works being discussed?

- Does your partner's controlling idea include a perspective that applies to all the texts?

- Are the ideas in the essay developed in a logical order, using appropriate transitions to connect them?

- Has your partner provided sufficient and relevant textual evidence from the collection and additional sources?

- Does your partner accurately cite other print and digital sources?

- Does your partner maintain a formal style and objective tone?

- Is the conclusion an accurate summary of the analysis? Does it eloquently synthesize the central ideas of the essay?

Discuss your essay with your partner. Use the information from your feedback session to improve your draft. Make sure it is clear, coherent, and engaging.

PRESENT

Share Your Essay When your final draft is completed, read your essay aloud to a small group. Your audience should listen, take notes, and be prepared to comment or ask questions.

Publish Online Create a class blog about journeys. Upload your essays to allow your classmates and other readers to comment on the ideas expressed in your analyses. You may also want to share your own travel experiences and what you learned about yourself.

	Ideas and Evidence	Organization	Language
ADVANCED	• An eloquent introduction includes the titles and authors of the selections; the controlling idea describes the view of journeys presented in the selections. • Specific, relevant details support the central ideas. • A satisfying concluding section synthesizes the ideas and summarizes the analysis.	• Central ideas and supporting evidence are organized effectively and logically throughout the essay. • Varied transitions successfully show the relationships between ideas.	• The analysis has an appropriately formal style and a knowledgeable, objective tone. • Language is precise and captures the writer's thoughts with originality. • Sentence beginnings, lengths, and structures vary and have a rhythmic flow. • Spelling, capitalization, and punctuation are correct. If handwritten, the analysis is legible. • Grammar and usage are correct.
COMPETENT	• The introduction identifies the titles and authors of the selections but could be more engaging; the controlling idea encompasses the view of journeys in at least two selections. • One or two central ideas need more support. • The concluding section synthesizes most of the ideas and summarizes most of the analysis.	• The organization of central ideas and supporting evidence is confusing in a few places. • A few more transitions are needed to clarify the relationships between ideas.	• The style becomes informal in a few places, and the tone does not always communicate confidence. • Most language is precise. • Sentence beginnings, lengths, and structures vary somewhat. • Several spelling, capitalization, and punctuation mistakes occur. If handwritten, the analysis is mostly legible. • Some grammatical and usage errors are repeated in the essay.
LIMITED	• The introduction identifies the titles and the authors of the selections; the controlling idea only hints at the main idea of the analysis. • Details support some central ideas but are often too general. • The concluding section gives an incomplete summary of the analysis and merely restates the controlling idea.	• Most central ideas are organized logically, but many supporting details are out of place. • More transitions are needed throughout the essay to connect ideas.	• The style is informal in many places, and the tone reflects a superficial understanding of the selections. • Language is repetitive or vague at times. • Sentence structures barely vary, and some fragments or run-on sentences are present. • Spelling, capitalization, and punctuation are often incorrect but do not make comprehending the essay difficult. If handwritten, the analysis may be partially illegible. • Grammar and usage are incorrect in many places, but the writer's ideas are still clear.
EMERGING	• The appropriate elements of an introduction are missing. • Details and evidence are irrelevant or missing. • The analysis lacks a concluding section.	• A logical organization is not used; ideas are presented randomly. • Transitions are not used, making the essay difficult to understand.	• The style and tone are inappropriate. • Language is inaccurate, repetitive, and vague. • Repetitive sentence structure, fragments, and run-on sentences make the writing monotonous and difficult to follow. • Spelling, capitalization, and punctuation are incorrect throughout. If handwritten, the analysis may be partially or mostly illegible. • Many grammatical and usage errors change the meaning of the writer's ideas.

Writing Arguments

Many of the Performance Tasks in this book ask you to craft an argument in which you support your ideas with text evidence. Any argument you write should include the following sections and characteristics.

Introduce Your Claim

Clearly state your **claim**—the point your argument makes. As needed, provide context or background information to help readers understand your position. Note the most common opposing views as a way to distinguish and clarify your ideas. From the very beginning, make it clear for readers why your claim is strong; consider providing an overview of your reasons or a quotation that emphasizes your view in your introduction.

EXAMPLES

Vague claim: We need more recreational facilities.	**Precise claim:** The city should build a new skate park downtown.
Not distinguished from opposing view: There are plenty of people who consider skate parks unsafe.	**Distinguished from opposing view:** While some people consider skate parks unsafe, the facts say differently.
Confusing relationship of ideas: Teens need more to do. Skate parks are enjoyed by people of all ages.	**Clear relationship of ideas:** By providing a safe activity not only for teens but for people of all ages, a skate park would benefit the entire community.

Develop Your Claim

The body of your argument must provide strong, logical reasons for your claim and must support those reasons with relevant evidence. A **reason** tells why your claim is valid; **evidence** provides specific examples that illustrate a reason. In the process of developing your claim, you should also refute **counterclaims,** or opposing views, with equally strong reasons and evidence. To demonstrate that you have thoroughly considered your view, provide a well-rounded look at both the strengths and limitations of your claim and opposing claims. The goal is not to undercut your argument but rather to answer your readers' potential objections to it. Be sure, too, to consider how much your audience may already know about your topic in order to avoid boring or confusing your readers.

EXAMPLES

Claim lacking reasons: A skate park would be a good thing.	**Claim developed by reasons:** Among the benefits of a skate park are a potential reduction in petty crimes committed by bored teens and improved physical fitness across the community.
Omission of limitations: The people opposed to this idea wouldn't use a skate park.	**Fair discussion of limitations:** We should not dismiss safety concerns. Planning for the park should include safe ramp designs, first aid facilities, and ongoing maintenance.
Inattention to audience's knowledge: A kick-flip ollie can be executed just about anywhere, but with a half-pipe more advanced tricks are possible.	**Awareness of audience's knowledge:** Readers unfamiliar with skateboarding may be surprised to learn that most injuries happen to beginners in their driveways, not in well-planned skate parks.

Link Ideas

Even the strongest reasons and evidence will fail to sway readers if it is unclear how the reasons relate to the central claim of an argument. Make the connections clear for your readers, using not only transitional words and phrases, but also clauses and even entire sentences as bridges between ideas you have already discussed and ideas you are introducing.

EXAMPLES

Transitional word linking claim and reason: The entire community will benefit from a skate park downtown. First, health care and law enforcement costs may be reduced if bored or sedentary teens spend their free time there instead of in less productive activities.

Transitional phrase linking reason and evidence: Skating in a planned park would actually reduce injuries. In fact, the American Academy of Pediatrics states that "communities should be encouraged to develop safe skateboarding areas away from pedestrian and motor vehicle traffic."

Transitional clause linking claim and counterclaim: The health benefits of the park are clear. Those opposed to the park plan, though, would say otherwise: They feel that there is too much potential for injuries from falls.

Use Appropriate Style and Tone

An effective argument is most often written in a direct and formal style. The style and tone you choose in an argument should not be an afterthought—the way you express your argument can either drive home your ideas or detract from them. Even as you argue in favor of your viewpoint, take care to remain objective in tone—avoid using loaded language when discussing opposing claims.

EXAMPLES

Informal style: The park will help out the whole city, so they should be the ones to fork out for it.	**Formal style:** Because the benefits of the park include everyone in the city, it is logical for the city to provide the funding for the project.

continued

Biased tone: It doesn't make any sense to be against this plan.	**Objective tone:** Arguments opposing this plan have been refuted by statistics from many sources.
Inattention to conventions: We need to make this dream a reality!	**Attention to conventions:** This proposal, which will greatly benefit the community at little cost, deserves City Council attention.

Conclude Your Argument

Your conclusion may range from a sentence to a full paragraph, but it must wrap up your argument in a satisfying way; a conclusion that sounds tacked-on helps your argument no more than providing no conclusion at all. A strong conclusion is a logical extension of the argument you have presented. It carries forth your ideas through an inference, question, quotation, or challenge.

EXAMPLES

Inference: Support for a safe and enjoyable city begins with our youth.

Question: Who doesn't want to live in an active city with engaged young people?

Quotation: As the First Lady's Let's Move campaign points out, "community leaders can promote physical fitness by . . . revitalizing parks, playgrounds, and community centers; and by providing fun and affordable sports and fitness programs."

Challenge: Facilities of this type make the difference between an average city and a truly great one.

Writing
Informative Essays

Most of the Performance Tasks in this book ask you to write informational or explanatory essays in which you present a topic and examine it thoughtfully, through a well-organized analysis of relevant content. Any informative or explanatory essay that you create should include the following parts and features.

Introduce Your Topic

Develop a strong **thesis statement.** That is, clearly state your **topic** and the **organizational framework** through which you will connect or distinguish elements of your topic. For example, you might state that your essay will compare ideas, examine causes and effects, or explore a problem and its solutions.

EXAMPLES

Topic: animal shelters
Sample Thesis Statements
Compare-contrast: To decide whether to adopt a pet from a shelter or buy one from a breeder, consider the costs and then benefits of each source.
Cause-effect: While the causes of overcrowding in community animal shelters aren't difficult to guess at, the results are often hidden from the public eye.
Problem-solution: Our town's animal shelter faces a growing problem with overcrowding, but through community action we can manage the issue.

Clarifying the organizational framework up front will help you organize the body of your essay, suggest **headings** you can use to guide your readers, and help you identify **graphics** that you may need to clarify information. For example, if you compare and contrast the costs and benefits of adopting versus buying a pet, you might create a chart like the one shown to guide your writing. You could include the same chart in your essay as a graphic for readers. The row or column headings serve as natural paragraph headings.

	Animal Shelter	Reputable Breeding Facility
Costs	Minimal fee to cover spay/neuter and immunization costs	Usually several hundred dollars
Benefits	Knowledge that you have rescued a pet from a crowded kennel and probably euthanasia	Getting a specific pedigree with predictable traits

Develop Your Topic

In the body of your essay, flesh out the organizational framework you established in your introduction with strong supporting paragraphs. Include only support directly relevant to your topic. Don't rely on a single source, and make sure the sources you do use are reputable and current. The following table illustrates types of support you might use to develop aspects of your topic. It also shows how transitions link text sections, create cohesion, and clarify the relationships among ideas.

Types of Support in Informative Essays	Uses of Transitions in Informative Essays
Facts and examples: One cause of overcrowding is economic hardship; for example, when home foreclosures increase, the population of animal shelters also rises.	*One cause* signals the shift from the introduction to the body text in a cause-and-effect essay. *For example* introduces the support for the cause being cited.

continued

Types of Support in Explanatory/ Informative Essays	Uses of Transitions in Explanatory/ Informative Essays
Concrete details: On the other hand, if you want to choose from among a wide variety of dogs, visit your local shelter. Our shelter currently lists German shepherds, a labradoodle, a Pomeranian, and dozens more on its Website.	*On the other hand* transitions the reader from one point of comparison to another in a compare-contrast essay.
Statistics: Turn to the Humane Society of the United States if you doubt the scope of the problem. The HSUS estimates that shelters euthanize 3 to 4 million cats and dogs annually.	The entire transitional sentence introduces the part of a problem-solution essay that demonstrates the existence of a problem.

You can't always include all of the information you'd like to in a short essay, but you can plan to point readers directly to useful **multimedia links** either in the body of or at the end of your essay.

Use Appropriate Style and Tone

Use **formal English** to establish your credibility as a source of information. To project authority, use the language of the domain, or field, that you are writing about. However, be sure to define unfamiliar terms to avoid using jargon your audience may not know. Provide extended definitions when your audience is likely to have limited knowledge of the topic. Using quotations from reputable sources can also give your text authority; be sure to credit the source of quoted material. In general, keep the tone objective, avoiding using slang or biased expressions.

Informal, jargon-filled, biased language: Puppy mill owners should be forced to live as horribly as the animals they raise. They have no feelings for the pooches they proliferate except maybe greed for the coin these cash cows create.

Extended definition in formal style and objective tone: A "puppy mill" refers to a large-scale dog breeding operation that places profit before the well-being of its dogs, often housing them in tight quarters, forcing them to breed continuously, and neglecting their emotional, physical, and genetic health. According to Melanie Kahn, an HSUS spokesperson, "Many people don't realize that when they buy a puppy from a pet store or online they are likely supporting a puppy mill."

Conclusion

Wrap up your essay with a concluding statement or section that sums up or extends the information in your essay.

EXAMPLES

Articulate implications: Twenty-five percent of dogs in shelters are purebred. If we can encourage people who would normally seek a purebred dog from a breeder to adopt a shelter pet instead, we can significantly reduce the number of animals euthanized each year.

Emphasize significance: The number of pets languishing in shelters each year is small compared to the number of pets owned by U.S. households; a fractional increase in household pet ownership could save these animals from euthanasia.

Writing Narratives

When you are writing a fictional tale, an autobiographical incident, or a firsthand biography, you write in the narrative mode. That means telling a story with a beginning, a climax, and a conclusion. Though there are important differences between fictional and nonfiction narratives, you use similar processes to develop them.

Identify a Problem, Situation, or Observation

For a nonfiction **narrative,** dig into your memory bank for a problem you dealt with or an observation you've made about your life. For fiction, try to invent a problem or situation that can unfold in interesting ways.

EXAMPLES

Problem (nonfiction)	Last year I wanted to raise money to participate in a class trip to Washington, D.C.
Situation (fiction)	A social media website user periodically notices mysterious changes to his "status."

Establish a Point of View

Decide who will tell your story. If you are writing a reflective essay about an important experience or person in your own life, you will be the **narrator** of the events you relate. If you are writing a work of fiction, you can choose to create a first person narrator or tell the story from the third-person point of view. In that case, the narrator can focus on one character or reveal the thoughts and feelings of all the characters. These examples show the differences between a first- and third-person narrator.

EXAMPLES

First-person narrator (nonfiction)	Seven hundred fifty dollars: That's what it would cost me to go on the class trip to Washington D.C., but it might as well have been a million dollars.
Third-person narrator (fiction)	Peter's fingers froze over the "What's new with you" prompt of his status page. The box was already filled out, waiting for him to press the Update key. "My mom found a new job!" said the box. Peter hadn't written those words. And, as far as he knew, his mother had stopped looking for work months ago.

Gather Details

To make real or imaginary experiences come alive on the page, you will need to use **narrative techniques** like description and dialogue. Use the questions in the left column of the following chart to help you search your memory or imagination for the details that will form the basis of your narrative. You don't have to respond in full sentences, but try to capture the sights, sounds, and feelings that bring your narrative to life.

Who, What, When, Where?	Narrative Techniques
People: Who are the people or characters involved in the experience? What did they look like? What did they do? What did they say?	**Description:** Mr. Maguire, social studies teacher. Wears funny ties and cracks jokes but doesn't get to know students personally, in my opinion. **Dialogue:** He once said, "The families in this town are completely removed from the problems of two-thirds of the world." I said under my breath, "You don't know my family."

continued

Who, What, When, Where?	Narrative Techniques
Experience: What led up to or caused the event? What is the main event in the experience? What happened as a result of the event?	**Description:** A big deposit for the class trip—$200—would be due by Thanksgiving; I knew my family didn't have the cash. I would have to figure out a way to raise it myself. 　　When schools were closed after a blizzard, I got my chance. After stoking up the courage to knock on doors, I shoveled until my blistered hands were numb, my back ached, and my clothes were wet with freezing perspiration.
Places: When and where did the events take place? What were the sights, sounds, and smells of this place?	**Description:** Fall of eighth grade—it was the last year of middle school and we felt special—top of the heap. The smell of autumn filled the air—decaying leaves, wood-burning stoves. Local farmers were predicting an early and rough winter.

Sequence Events

Before you begin writing, list the key events of the experience or story in **chronological,** or time, order. Place a star next to the point of highest tension—for example, the point at which a key decision determines the outcome of events. In fiction, this point is called the **climax,** but a gripping nonfiction narrative will also have a climactic event.

To build **suspense**—the uncertainty a reader feels about what will happen next—you'll want to think about the **pacing** or rhythm of your narrative. Consider disrupting the chronological order of events by beginning at the end and then starting over. Or interrupt the forward progression or flow of events with a **flashback,** which takes the reader to an earlier point in the narrative.

Another way to build suspense is with **multiple plot lines.** For example, the personal narrative about the class trip involves a second plot line in which a snowstorm is bearing down on the narrator's hometown. Both plot lines intersect when the narrator shovels snow for a week and as a result raises money for the class trip.

First Draft	Revision
My father, who is an incurable optimist, said the storm could be the break I needed.	Wiggling his eyebrows, my father said, "When life gives you a snowstorm, invest in a snow shovel!" [telling details]
Piles of snow were everywhere, and people couldn't get out of their driveways.	Snow banks three feet high lined the streets, and neighbors batted kitchen brooms at the snow around their cars. [precise words and phrases]
Peter felt weirded out by the mysterious post on his "What's new with you" page.	As Peter read the mysterious post, the tiny hairs at the base of his scalp rose and his palms sweated. [sensory details]

Conclude Your Narrative

At the conclusion of the narrative, you or your narrator will reflect on the meaning of the events. The conclusion should follow logically from the climactic moment of the narrative. The narrator of a personal narrative usually reflects on the significance of the experience—the lessons learned or the legacy left.

EXAMPLE

The school steps were piled with luggage that balmy Friday as excited students waited to board the buses. I stood by, remembering the tingle of frostbite in my fingertips and the ache in my back from that marathon week of shoveling snow. This scene, the one before me now, is what had kept me going. Straightening my back and flexing my fingers, I reached down and picked up my bag. With a satisfied smile, I joined my friends on the bus.

Conducting Research

The Performance Tasks in this book will require you to complete research projects related to the texts you've read in the collections. Whether the topic is stated in a Performance Task or is one you generate, the following information will guide you through your research project.

Focus Your Research and Formulate a Question

Some topics for a research project can be effectively covered in three pages; others require an entire book for a thorough treatment. Begin by developing a topic that is neither too narrow nor too broad for the time frame of the assignment. Also check your school and local libraries and databases to help you determine how to choose your topic. If there's too little information, you'll need to broaden your focus; if there's too much, you'll need to limit it.

With a topic in hand, formulate a **research question;** it will keep you on track as you conduct your research. A good research question cannot be answered in a single word and should be open-ended. It should require investigation. You can also develop related research questions to explore your topic in more depth.

EXAMPLES

Possible topics for the *Odyssey*	The hero Odysseus—too broad The monster the Cyclops—too narrow Settings and events—fact or fiction?
Possible research question	To what degree are settings and events in the *Odyssey* based on fact?
Related questions	If any of the events are real, where did they take place? To what extent do historians agree or disagree on which aspects of the *Odyssey* are real?

Locate and Evaluate Sources

To find answers to your research question, you'll need to investigate primary and secondary sources, whether in print or digital formats. **Primary sources** contain original, firsthand information, such as diaries, autobiographies, interviews, speeches, and eyewitness accounts. **Secondary sources** provide other people's versions of primary sources in encyclopedias, newspaper and magazine articles, biographies, and documentaries.

Your search for sources begins at the library and on the Internet. Use advanced search features to help you find things quickly. Add a minus sign (-) before a word that should not appear in your results. Use an asterisk (*) in place of unknown words. List the name of and location of each possible source, adding comments about its potential usefulness. Assessing, or evaluating, your sources is an important step in the research process. Your goal is to use sources that are **credible,** or reliable and trustworthy.

Criteria for Assessing Sources	
Relevance: It covers the target aspect of my topic.	• How will the source be useful in answering my research question?
Accuracy: It includes information that can be verified by more than one authoritative source.	• Is the information up-to-date? Are the facts accurate? How can I verify them? • What qualifies the author to write about this topic? Is he or she an authority?
Objectivity: It presents multiple viewpoints on the topic.	• What, if any, biases can I detect? Does the writer favor one view of the topic?

Incorporate and Cite Sources

When you draft your research project, you'll need to include material from your sources. This material can be **direct quotations, summaries,** or **paraphrases** of the original source material. Two well-known **style manuals** provide information on how to cite a range of print and digital sources: the *MLA Handbook for Writers of Research Papers* (published by the Modern Language Association) and Kate L. Turabian's *A Manual for Writers of Research Papers, Theses, and Dissertations* (published by The University of Chicago Press). Both style manuals provide a wealth of information about conducting, formatting, drafting, and presenting your research, including guidelines for citing sources within the text (called parenthetical citations) and preparing the list of Works Cited, as well as correct use of the mechanics of writing. Your teacher will indicate which style manual you should use. The following examples use the format in the *MLA Handbook*.

Any material from sources must be completely documented, or you will commit **plagiarism,** the unauthorized use of someone else's words or ideas. Plagiarism is not honest. As you take notes for your research project, be sure to keep complete information about your sources so that you can cite them correctly in the body of your paper. This applies to all sources, whether print or digital. Having complete information will also enable you to prepare the list of Works Cited. The list of Works Cited, which concludes your research project, provides author, title, and publication information for both print and digital sources. The following pages show the *MLA Handbook's* Works Cited citation formats for a variety of sources.

EXAMPLES

Direct quotation [The writer is citing the poet Homer's word in the *Odyssey*, page 74.]	In Book Four of the *Odyssey,* Menelaus describes the island of Pharos as "as far out as the distance a hollow ship can make in a whole day's sailing" (Homer 74).
Summary [The writer is summarizing the conclusion of Tim Severin on page 75 of *The Ulysses Voyage: Sea Search for the Odyssey.*]	Severin was unable to trace Odysseus' journey exactly and found many parts of Homer's tale puzzling. He concluded that the geographies of folklore and navigation overlapped (245).
Paraphrase [The writer is paraphrasing, or stating in her own words, material from page 25 of Bernard Knox's book and from the *Brittanica Student Encyclopedia* on the Homeric Legend.]	The third-century-B.C. geographer Eratosthenes, for example, thought that Homer's story was completely imaginary (Knox 25; "Homeric Legend").

MLA Citation Guidelines

Today, you can find free websites that generate ready-made citations for research papers, using the information you provide. Such sites have some time-saving advantages when you're developing a Works Cited list. However, you should always check your citations carefully before you turn in your final paper. If you are following MLA style, use these guidelines to evaluate and finalize your work.

Books

One author

Severin, Tim. *The Ulysses Voyage: Sea Search for the Odyssey.* London: Hutchinson, 1987. Print.

Two authors or editors

Steiner, George, and Robert Fagles, eds. *Homer: A Collection of Critical Essays.* Englewood Cliffs: Prentice, 1962. Print.

Three authors

Heubeck, Alfred, Stephanie West, and J. B. Hainsworth. *A Commentary on Homer's Odyssey.* New York: Oxford UP, 1988. Print.

Four or more authors

The abbreviation et al. means "and others." Use et al. instead of listing all the authors.

Melick, Peter, et al. *The Odyssey Explained.* New York: Garden UP, 1997. Print.

No author given

Greek Literature: An Overview. New York: Sunrise, 1993. Print.

An author and a translator

Homer. *The Odyssey of Homer: A Modern Translation.* Trans. Richmond Lattimore. New York: Harper, 1967. Print.

An author, a translator, and an editor

La Fontaine, Jean de. *Selected Fables.* Trans. Christopher Wood. Ed. Maya Slater. New York: Oxford UP, 1995. Print.

Parts of Books

An introduction, a preface, a foreword, or an afterword written by someone other than the author(s) of a work

Knox, Bernard. Introduction. *The Odyssey of Homer.* Trans. Robert Fagles. New York: Penguin, 1996. 3–64. Print.

A poem, a short story, an essay, or a chapter in a collection of works by one author

Sappho. "He Is More Than a Hero." *The Works of Sappho.* Trans. Edward Osmond. New York: Garden UP, 1990. 53. Print.

A poem, a short story, an essay, or a chapter in an anthology of works by several authors

Solonos, Costa. "Journeys." Trans. Carl Foreman. *Greek Voices.* Ed. Katharine Greene and Gerald Spencer. London: Greenwood, 1985. 83–85. Print.

A novel or a play in a collection

Sophocles. *Antigone. The Three Theban Plays.* Trans. Robert Fagles. New York: Penguin, 1984. Print.

Magazines, Newspapers, and Encyclopedias

An article in a newspaper

Wilford, John Noble. "Was Troy a Metropolis? Homer Isn't Talking." *New York Times* 22 Oct. 2002: D1+. Print.

An article in a magazine

Severin, Tim. "The Quest for Ulysses." *National Geographic* Aug. 1986: 194–225. Print.

An article in an encyclopedia

"Homer." *The World Book Encyclopedia.* 2000 ed. Print.

Miscellaneous Nonprint Sources

An interview

Baldwin, Richard. Personal interview. 13 Mar. 2011.

A video recording

The Odyssey of Troy. A&E Home Video, 1994. DVD.

Electronic Publications

A CD-ROM

"Homeric Legend." *Britannica Student Encyclopedia.* 2004 ed. Chicago: Encyclopaedia Britannica, 2004. CD-ROM.

A document from an Internet site

Entries for online sources should contain as much of the information shown as available.

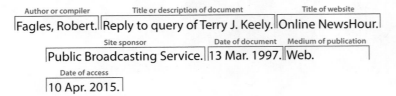

Struck, Peter. "Map of Odysseus' Journey." Mythology. Course pages. Dept. of Classical Studies, U of Pennsylvania. 2004. Web. 9 Mar. 2011.

Participating in a Collaborative Discussion

Often, class activities, including the Performance Tasks in this book, will require you to work collaboratively with classmates. Whether your group will analyze a work of literature or try to solve a community problem, use the following guidelines to ensure a productive discussion.

Prepare for the Discussion

A productive discussion is one in which all the participants bring useful information and ideas to share. If your group will discuss a short story the class read, first re-read and annotate a copy of the story. Your annotations will help you quickly locate evidence to support your points.

Participants in a discussion about an important issue should first research the issue and bring notes or information sources that will help guide the group. If you disagree with a point made by another group member, your case will be stronger if you back it up with specific evidence from your sources.

EXAMPLES

> **Disagreeing without evidence:** It doesn't make sense to be concerned about the school's environmental footprint.
>
> **Providing evidence for disagreement:** I disagree about the relevance of environmental concerns to our school community. Several national environmental organizations point out that schools can play an important role in reducing the community's environmental footprint.

Set Ground Rules

The rules your group needs will depend on what your group is expected to accomplish. A discussion of themes in a poem will be unlikely to produce a single consensus; however, a discussion aimed at developing a solution to a problem should result in one strong proposal that all group members support. Answer the following questions to set ground rules that fit your group's purpose:

- What will this group produce? A range of ideas, a single decision, a plan of action, or something else?
- How much time is available? How much of that time should be allotted to each part of our discussion (presenting ideas, summarizing or voting on final ideas, creating a product such as a written analysis or a speech)?
- What roles need to be assigned within the group? Do we need a leader, a note-taker, a timekeeper, or other specific roles?
- What is the best way to synthesize our group's ideas? Should we take a vote, list group members as "for" or "against" in a chart, or use some other method to reach consensus or sum up the results of the discussion?

Move the Discussion Forward

Everyone in the group should be actively involved in synthesizing ideas. To make sure this happens, ask questions that draw out ideas, especially from less-talkative members of the group. If an idea or statement is confusing, try to paraphrase it or ask the speaker to explain more about it. If you disagree with a statement, say so politely and explain in detail why you disagree.

SAMPLE DISCUSSION

EFFECTIVE BEHAVIOR	WHAT IT LOOKS LIKE
Support others' contributions. In this example, Raul realizes that Kenisha's views are different from his. Instead of interrupting, he listens carefully to make sure he understands her evidence and what she thinks it means.	Raul listens to Kenisha while she presents her research and views on how to calculate their school's environmental footprint. "I read that article, too," Raul thinks to himself. "Then I read a more recent article that included a much longer list of considerations than those that were in the first article. I'll make a note about it and let Kenisha finish."
State your own views thoughtfully. As the discussion continues, Raul explains how his research turned up different results. He shows that he has used a reliable source.	"I read the same article Kenisha did," Raul begins, "but I found a more recent and I think more useful article on sustainable building in the journal *Architectural Engineering and Construction*. It describes how one high school calculated its environmental footprint before building a new addition."

Respond to Ideas

In a diverse group, everyone may have a different perspective on the topic of discussion, and that's a good thing. Consider what everyone has to say, and don't resist changing your view if other group members provide convincing evidence for theirs. If, instead, you feel more strongly than ever about your view, don't hesitate to say so and provide reasons related to what those with opposing views have said. Before wrapping up the discussion, try to sum up the points on which your group agrees and disagrees.

SAMPLE DISCUSSION

EFFECTIVE BEHAVIOR	WHAT IT LOOKS LIKE
Summarize agreements and disagreements. Cecilia compares the key points. She notices that Raul and Kenisha agree except for one point.	Cecilia is going to speak next, but rather than silently rehearsing her views, she compares Raul's views with Kenisha's. "Raul listed the same five considerations that Kenisha did. The only difference between them is how water consumption is calculated."
Justify your views or consider new ones. Considering Cecilia's comments, Raul sees that he and Kenisha differ on one point. He can justify his view but is willing to combine his approach with Kenisha's and Cecilia's.	Cecilia points out that Kenisha's and Raul's views differ in only one important respect. As Raul listens to Cecilia's summary, he thinks, "Cecilia is right. Kenisha's view and mine are almost the same except for one issue." He makes a mental note of this and continues to listen to Cecilia for more information and insight.

Debating an Issue

The selection and collection Performance Tasks in this text will direct you to engage in debates about issues relating to the selections you've read. Use the guidelines that follow to have a productive and balanced argument about both sides of an issue.

The Structure of a Formal Debate

In a debate, two teams compete to win the support of the audience about an issue. In a **formal debate,** two teams, each with three members, present their arguments on a given **proposition** or **policy statement.** One team argues for the proposition or statement and the other team argues against it. Each debater must consider the proposition closely and must research both sides of it. To argue convincingly either for or against a proposition, a debater must be familiar with both sides of the issue.

Plan the Debate

The purpose of a debate is to allow participants and audience members to consider both sides of an issue. Use these planning suggestions to hold a balanced and productive debate:

- **Identify Debate Teams** Form groups of six members based on the issue presented in the Performance Task. Three members of the team will argue for the **affirmative side** of the issue—that is, they support the issue. The other three members will argue for the **negative side** of the issue—that is, they do not support the issue.
- **Appoint a Moderator** The moderator will present the topic and goals of the debate, keep track of the time, and introduce and thank the participants.
- **Research and Prepare Notes** Search the texts you've read as well as print and online sources for **valid reasons** and **evidence** to support your team's claim. As with argument, be sure to anticipate possible opposing claims and compile evidence to counter those claims. You will use notes from your research during the debate.

- **Assign Debate Roles** One team member will introduce the team's **claim** and supporting evidence. Another team member will respond to questions and **opposing claims** in an exchange with a member of the opposing team. The last member will present a strong closing argument.

Hold the Debate

A formal debate is not a shouting match—rather, a well-run debate is an excellent forum for participants to express their viewpoints, build on others' ideas, and have a thoughtful, well-reasoned exchange of ideas. The moderator will begin by stating the topic or issue and introducing the participants. Participants should follow the moderator's instructions concerning whose turn it is to speak and how much time each speaker has.

FORMAL DEBATE FORMAT

SPEAKER	ROLE	TIME
Affirmative Speaker 1	Present the claim and supporting evidence for the affirmative ("pro") side of the argument.	5 minutes
Negative Speaker 1	Ask probing questions that will prompt the other team to address flaws in the argument.	3 minutes
Affirmative Speaker 2	Respond to the questions posed by the opposing team and counter any concerns.	3 minutes

continued

SPEAKER	ROLE	TIME
Negative Speaker 2	Respond to any questions posed by the opposing team, and counter any concerns.	5 minutes
Affirmative Speaker 3	Summarize the claim and evidence for the affirmative side, and explain why your reasoning is more valid.	3 minutes
Negative Speaker 3	Summarize the claim and evidence for the negative side, and explain why your reasoning is more valid.	3 minutes

Evaluate the Debate

Use the following guidelines to evaluate a team in a debate:

- Did the team prove that the issue is significant? How thorough was the analysis?
- How did the team effectively argue that you should support their affirmative or negative side of the proposition or issue?
- How effectively did the team present reasons and evidence, including evidence from the texts, to support the proposition?
- How effectively did the team rebut, or respond to, arguments made by the opposing team?
- Did the speakers maintain eye contact and speak at an appropriate rate and volume?
- Did the speakers observe proper debate etiquette—that is, did they follow the moderator's instructions, stay within their allotted time limits, and treat their opponents respectfully?

Reading Arguments

An **argument** expresses a position on an issue or problem and supports it with reasons and evidence. Being able to analyze and evaluate arguments will help you distinguish between claims you should accept and those you should not.

Analyzing an Argument

A sound argument should appeal strictly to reason. An argument includes the following elements:

- A **claim** (or **thesis** or **controlling idea**) is the writer's position on an issue or problem.
- **Support** is any material that serves to prove a claim. In an argument, support usually consists of reasons and evidence.
- **Reasons** are declarations made to justify an action, decision, or belief.
- **Evidence** is the specific references, quotations, facts, examples, and opinions that support a claim. Evidence may also consist of statistics, reports of personal experience, or the views of experts.
- **Counterarguments** and **counterclaims** are arguments made to oppose other arguments. A good argument anticipates opposing counterclaims by providing counterarguments to answer them.

Claim	My curfew should be extended from 11 P.M. to midnight on Saturday night.

Reason	I don't have enough time to spend with my friends on weekdays because of homework and my job.

Evidence	On weekends I spend four hours doing homework and four hours at my job.

Counter-argument	I know that it's difficult for you to sleep when I'm out late, but you need to trust that I'll be home by midnight and give me a chance to prove it.

Practice and Apply

Identify the claim, reason, evidence, and counterargument used in this argument.

On the second Monday in October, Americans celebrate Columbus Day. We honor the Italian explorer who has been credited with discovering the Americas in 1492. Some people, however, think that we need to look more closely at what Christopher Columbus actually did and at his place in our history. I am one of those people.

First of all, although we honor Columbus as the first European to set foot in the Americas, he may not have been the first. Archaeologists have found Norse ruins in Greenland and what is now Newfoundland, dating from around A.D. 1000. This evidence seems to prove that Vikings actually reached the North American continent nearly 500 years before Columbus ever left the shores of Spain.

Second, although Columbus did reach the Americas, he did not discover them. Millions of people were already living here when he arrived.

Defenders of Columbus argue that, in a way, he did discover the Americas. Even if he wasn't the first European to set foot on the land, his voyages made the rest of the world aware of the Americas. In the years following Columbus' voyages, Europeans came to establish colonies and to explore the land.

I argue that this spread of culture brought great harm as well as great good to the Americas. The Europeans who came to the Americas brought deadly diseases with them. The native people had no immunity to such diseases as mumps, measles, smallpox, and typhus. As a result, hundreds of thousands of people died.

In conclusion, I don't suggest that people should boycott their local Columbus Day parades. I do think, though, that we should create a more balanced picture of the man we're honoring.

Recognizing Persuasive Techniques

Argumentative texts typically rely on more than just the logical appeal of an argument to be convincing. They also rely on **persuasive techniques**—devices that can sway you to adopt a position or take an action. Persuasive techniques are used in advertising, political speeches, films, and fundraisers. The chart shown here explains several ways a writer may attempt to sway you to adopt his or her position. Learn to recognize these techniques, and you will be less likely to be influenced by them.

Persuasive Technique	Example
Appeals by Association	
Bandwagon appeal Uses the argument that a person should believe or do something because "everyone else" does	More and more people are making the switch to Discountline long-distance service.
Testimonial Relies on endorsements from well-known people or satisfied customers	Pierre DuPont, world-class rock climber, would be left hanging without DuraTwine rope.
Snob appeal Taps into people's desire to be special or part of an elite group	Treat yourself to Tropical Paradise because, after all, you deserve the best under the sun.
Transfer Connects a product, candidate, or cause with a positive emotion or idea	Freedom . . . you can feel it the instant you put your hands on the wheel of a Farnsworth 4 × 4 SL.
Appeal to loyalty Relies on people's affiliation with a particular group	This car is made in America by Americans.
Emotional Appeals	
Appeals to pity, fear, or vanity Use strong feelings, rather than facts, to persuade	Without more police, we'll be at the mercy of thieves.

Word Choice

Glittering generality Makes a generalization that includes a word or phrase with positive connotations, such as freedom and honor, to promote a product or idea.	A vote for Evan Smith is a vote for democracy.

Practice and Apply

Identify the persuasive techniques used in the model.

Indiana and Issun Boshi— Building Another Great Team

Indiana is basketball country. Names like Bobby Knight, Larry Bird, and Isaiah Thomas have added greatness to the game for over a quarter century.

That's why Issun Boshi, Japan's leading automobile company, chose Indiana as its U.S. teammate. The new plant will produce 150,000 new vehicles a year, built by 25,000 hard-working Hoosiers just like you. In addition, many of those workers will be driving the cars they make at a special discount—that's only fair; that's the American way. It's how we play the game.

Just ask Indiana sportscaster Wally Elliot, who says, "Issun Boshi and Hoosier pride— now that's what I call an expansion team."

Analyzing Logic and Reasoning

When you evaluate an argument, you need to look closely at the writer's logic and reasoning. To do this, it is helpful to identify the type of reasoning the writer is using.

The Inductive Mode of Reasoning

When a writer leads from specific evidence to a general principle or generalization, that writer is using **inductive reasoning.** Here is an example of inductive reasoning.

Specific Facts

Fact 1 The American Society of Composers, Authors, and Publishers (ASCAP) was formed on Friday, February 13, 1914, to collect royalties on copyrighted music.

continued

Specific Facts

Fact 2 The licensing of the first female flight instructor took place on Friday, October 13, 1939.

Fact 3 On Friday, February 13, 1948, Orville Wright announced that he was giving the famous flying machine *Kitty Hawk* to the Smithsonian Institution.

Generalization

Good things can happen on Friday the 13th.

Strategies for Evaluating Inductive Arguments

Ask yourself the following questions to evaluate an inductive argument:

- **Is the evidence valid and sufficient support for the conclusion?** Inaccurate facts lead to inaccurate conclusions.
- **Does the conclusion follow logically from the evidence?** From the facts listed in the previous example, the conclusion that good things happen only on Friday the 13th would be too broad a generalization.
- **Is the evidence drawn from a large enough sample?** Even though there are only three facts listed above, the sample is large enough to support the claim. If you wanted to support the conclusion that only good things happen on Friday the 13th, the sample is not large enough.

The Deductive Mode of Reasoning

When a writer arrives at a conclusion by applying a general principle to a specific situation, the writer is using **deductive reasoning.** Here's an example.

Journalism that stretches the truth is deceptive.	General principle or premise
▼	
Hollywood Snoop Magazine stretches the truth.	Specific situation
▼	
Hollywood Snoop Magazine practices deceptive journalism.	Specific conclusion

Strategies for Evaluating Deductive Arguments

Ask yourself the following questions to evaluate a deductive argument:

- **Is the general principle actually stated, or is it implied?** Note that writers often use deductive reasoning in an argument without stating the general principle. They just assume that readers will recognize and agree with the principle. So you may want to identify the general principle for yourself.
- **Is the general principle sound?** Don't just assume the general principle is sound. Ask yourself whether it is really true.
- **Is the conclusion valid?** To be valid, a conclusion in a deductive argument must follow logically from the general principle and the specific situation.

The following chart shows two conclusions drawn from the same general principle.

All team members wore school colors on Friday.	
Accurate Deduction	**Inaccurate Deduction**
Mara is on the volleyball team; therefore, Mara wore school colors on Friday.	Jaime wore school colors on Friday; therefore, Jaime is on a school team.

Jaime could have worn school colors in support of a team without being a member.

Practice and Apply

Identify the mode of reasoning used in the following paragraph.

   Preteens and teenagers have access to a range of technology that their parents didn't have. Information that was once hard to find can now be obtained easily on the Internet. Smart phones provide many ways to communicate—text messages, social media sites, and decreasingly, old-fashioned phone calls. The effect is a childhood different than that experienced in the past.

Identifying Faulty Reasoning

Sometimes an argument at first appears to make sense but isn't valid because it is based on a fallacy. A fallacy is an error in logic. Learn to recognize these common **rhetorical** and **logical fallacies.**

Type of Fallacy	Definition	Example
Circular reasoning	Supporting a statement by simply repeating it in different words	Teenagers should avoid fad diets, because it is important for **adolescents to stay away from popular weight-loss plans.**
Either/or fallacy	A statement that suggests that there are only two choices available in a situation that really offers more than two options	**Either** students should be allowed to leave school to have lunch at nearby fast-food restaurants, **or** they should be allowed to choose the cafeteria menu.
Oversimplification	An explanation of a complex situation or problem as if it were much simpler than it is	Making the team depends on **whether the coach likes you.**
Overgeneralization	A generalization that is too broad. You can often recognize overgeneralizations by the use of words such as *all, everyone, every time, anything, no one,* and *none.*	**No one** cares that there is not **enough parking downtown.**
Stereotyping	A dangerous type of overgeneralization. Stereotypes are broad statements about people on the basis of their gender, ethnicity, race, or political, social, professional, or religious group.	The only thing **the members of that political party care about is big business.**
Attacking the person or name-calling	An attempt to discredit an idea by attacking the person or group associated with it. Candidates often engage in name-calling during political campaigns.	**My opponent is not smart enough** to be mayor.
Evading the issue	Refuting an objection with arguments and evidence that do not address its central point	Yes, I broke my campaign promise not to raise taxes, **but higher taxes have led to increases in police patrols, paved highways, and smaller class size in schools.**
Non sequitur	A statement that uses irrelevant "proof" to support a claim. A non sequitur is sometimes used to win an argument by diverting the reader's attention to proof that can't be challenged.	I know I'll pass math. **Mr. Gray is my math teacher and my football coach.**
False cause	The mistake of assuming that because one event occurred after another event in time, the first event caused the second one to occur	The mayor declared a get-tough crime policy, and sure enough, **crime rates dropped.**

Type of Fallacy	Definition	Example
False analogy	A comparison that doesn't hold up because of a critical difference between the two subjects	She walks to the store and back every day, **so surely she can walk in the 10K race**.
Hasty generalization	A conclusion drawn from too little evidence or from evidence that is biased	That corner must be dangerous. **There were two car accidents there last week**.

Practice and Apply

Look for examples of logical fallacies in the following argument. Identify each one and explain why you identified it as such.

Watching television causes a child's grades to drop. What other conclusion can be drawn? Money-hungry media moguls produce horrible programming just to sell advertising time. These programs interfere with children's thinking. If you say television isn't bad for children, you would probably say the earth is flat. Parents who care should at least limit their children's viewing. The most responsible parents should turn off the TV—permanently. They can either unplug the TV or expect their children to become uneducated slugs.

Evaluating Arguments

Learning how to evaluate a text's arguments and identify bias will help you become more selective when doing research and also help you improve your own reasoning and arguing skills. **Bias** is an inclination for or against a particular opinion or viewpoint. A writer may reveal a strongly positive or negative opinion on an issue by presenting only one way of looking at it or by heavily weighting the evidence on one side of the argument. Additionally, the presence of either of the following is often a sign that a writer is biased:

Loaded language consists of words with strongly positive or negative connotations that are intended to influence a reader's attitude.

EXAMPLE

The safety of our children depends on our driving the savage criminals out of this horrible neighborhood. (*Savage* and *horrible* have very negative connotations.)

Propaganda is any form of communication that is so distorted that it conveys false or misleading information. Some politicians create and distribute propaganda. Logical fallacies are often used in propaganda. For instance, the following example shows an oversimplification. The writer uses one fact to support a particular point of view but does not reveal another fact that does not support that viewpoint.

EXAMPLE

Since the new park opened, vandalism in the area has increased by 10 percent. Clearly, the park has had a negative impact on the area. (The writer does not include the fact that the vandalism was caused by people who were not drawn into the area by the park.)

Strategies for Evaluating Evidence

It is important to have a set of standards by which you can evaluate arguments. Use the questions below to help you critically assess an argument.

- **Are the facts presented credible and thus verifiable?** Facts can be proved by eyewitness accounts, authoritative sources such as encyclopedias and almanacs, experts, or research.

- **Are the opinions presented well substantiated?** Any opinions offered should be supported by facts, be based on research or eyewitness accounts, or be the opinions of experts on the topic.

- **Is the evidence relevant and sufficient?** Relevant evidence applies to the conclusion, and sufficient evidence leaves no reasonable questions unanswered. If a choice is offered, background for making the choice should be provided. If taking a side is called for, all sides of the issue should be presented.

- **Is the evidence biased?** Be alert to evidence that contains loaded language or other signs of bias.
- **Is the evidence authoritative?** The people, groups, or organizations that provided the evidence should have credentials that support their authority.
- **Is it important that the evidence be current?** Where timeliness is crucial, as in the areas of medicine and technology, the evidence should reflect the latest developments in the areas.

Practice and Apply

Read the argument below. Identify the facts, opinion, and elements of bias.

Why are students who show up late for tests, fill in answers randomly, and then snooze for the rest of the period allowed to jeopardize school test scores and reduce the quality of instruction for motivated kids? The answer is simple—compulsory attendance laws. These laws say that kids must be in school. But a study by economists William Landes and Lewis Solomon found little evidence that such laws increase attendance rates at all. Why not tell poor attenders, who are almost always failing too, "You're done. You don't belong here." Private schools do it, and the ability to expel students contributes to a positive climate.

Strategies for Determining a Strong Argument

Make sure that all or most of the following statements are true:

- The argument presents a claim or controlling idea.
- The claim is connected to its support by a general principle that most readers would readily agree with. Valid general principle: *It is the job of a school to provide a well-rounded physical education program.* Invalid general principle: *It is the job of a school to produce healthy, physically fit people.*
- The reasons make sense.
- The reasons are presented in a logical and effective order.
- The claim and all reasons are adequately supported by sound evidence.
- The evidence is sufficient, credible, and relevant.

- The logic is sound. There are no instances of faulty reasoning.
- The argument adequately anticipates and addresses reader concerns and counterclaims with counterarguments.

Practice and Apply

Use the preceding criteria to evaluate the strength of the following editorial.

According to veterinarian and animal-rights advocate Dr. Michael W. Fox, more than 100 million animals are used each year in laboratory tests. These animals are used to study such things as the causes and effects of illnesses and to test drugs. This unnecessary and cruel animal testing must be stopped.

The most important reason to stop this testing is that it's wrong to make living creatures suffer. Even though they can't talk or use tools as people do, animals have feelings. Zoologist Ann Speirs says that animals may suffer even more than people do, because they can't understand what's happening to them.

People who favor animal research argue that the medical advances gained justify animal experimentation. They also say that the suffering experienced by the animals is minor. People like that are dumber than any guinea pig or rat.

Another important reason to stop this testing is that everybody knows it isn't reliable. Many drugs that help animals are harmful to people. One example is the drug thalidomide. After it was tested in animals in the 1950s and early 1960s, it was given to pregnant women. More than 10,000 of these women gave birth to handicapped babies. The process works the other way, too. Many drugs that help people kill animals. Two common examples are penicillin and aspirin.

Animal testing also affects the environment. The Animal Protection Service says that a quarter of a million chimpanzees, monkeys, and baboons are taken from their natural homes and used in laboratory experiments every year. Those animals will never be able to reproduce, and whole species may become extinct.

A final reason for not using animals in experiments is that there are other research methods available. Two examples are using bits of animal tissue and cells and using computer models.

In conclusion, animal testing has to stop because it just can't go on.

Grammar

Writing that is full of mistakes can confuse or even annoy a reader. A business letter with a punctuation error might lead to a miscommunication and delay a reply. Or a sentence fragment might lower your grade on an essay. Paying attention to grammar, punctuation, and capitalization rules can make your writing clearer and easier to read.

Quick Reference: Parts of Speech

Part of Speech	Function	Examples
Noun	names a person, a place, a thing, an idea, a quality, or an action	
Common	serves as a general name, or a name common to an entire group	poet, novel, love, journey
Proper	names a specific, one-of-a-kind person, place, or thing	Lewis, Jackson, Pleasant Street, Stanley Cup
Singular	refers to a single person, place, thing, or idea	child, park, flower, truth
Plural	refers to more than one person, place, thing, or idea	children, parks, flowers, truths
Concrete	names something that can be perceived by the senses	roof, flash, Dublin, battle
Abstract	names something that cannot be perceived by the senses	intelligence, fear, joy, loneliness
Compound	expresses a single idea through a combination of two or more words	haircut, father-in-law, Christmas Eve
Collective	refers to a group of people or things	army, flock, class, species
Possessive	shows who or what owns something	Strafford's, Bess's, children's, witnesses'
Pronoun	takes the place of a noun or another pronoun	
Personal	refers to the person making a statement, the person(s) being addressed, or the person(s) or thing(s) the statement is about	I, me, my, mine, we, us, our, ours, you, your, yours, she, he, it, her, him, hers, his, its, they, them, their, theirs
Reflexive	follows a verb or preposition and refers to a preceding noun or pronoun	myself, yourself, herself, himself, itself, ourselves, yourselves, themselves
Intensive	emphasizes a noun or another pronoun	(same as reflexives)
Demonstrative	points to one or more specific persons or things	this, that, these, those

continued

Part of Speech	Function	Examples
Interrogative	signals a question	who, whom, whose, which, what
Indefinite	refers to one or more persons or things not specifically mentioned	both, all, most, many, anyone, everybody, several, none, some
Relative	introduces an adjective clause by relating it to a word in the clause	who, whom, whose, which, that
Reciprocal	refers to individual parts of a plural antecedent	each other, one another
Verb	expresses an action, a condition, or a state of being	
Action	tells what the subject does or did, physically or mentally	run, reaches, listened, consider, decides, dreamed
Linking	connects the subject to something that identifies or describes it	am, is, are, was, were, sound, taste, appear, feel, become, remain, seem
Auxiliary	precedes the main verb in a verb phrase	be, have, do, can, could, will, would, may, might
Transitive	directs the action toward someone or something; always has an object	The storm **sank** the ship.
Intransitive	does not direct the action toward someone or something; does not have an object	The ship **sank**.
Adjective	modifies a noun or pronoun	**strong** women, **two** epics, **enough** time
Adverb	modifies a verb, an adjective, or another adverb	walked **out, really** funny, **far** away
Preposition	relates one word to another word	at, by, for, from, in, of, on, to, with
Conjunction	joins words or word groups	
Coordinating	joins words or word groups used the same way	and, but, or, for, so, yet, nor
Correlative	used as a pair to join words or word groups used the same way	both . . . and, either . . . or, neither . . . nor
Subordinating	introduces a clause that cannot stand by itself as a complete sentence	although, after, as, before, because, when, if, unless
Interjection	expresses emotion	wow, ouch, hurrah

Quick Reference: The Sentence and Its Parts

The diagrams that follow will give you a brief review of the essentials of a sentence and some of its parts.

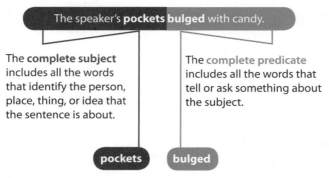

The speaker's **pockets bulged** with candy.

The **complete subject** includes all the words that identify the person, place, thing, or idea that the sentence is about.

The complete predicate includes all the words that tell or ask something about the subject.

pockets

bulged

The **simple subject** tells exactly whom or what the sentence is about. It may be one word or a group of words, but it does not include modifiers.

The simple predicate, or verb, tells what the subject does or is. It may be one word or several, but it does not include modifiers.

Every word in a sentence is part of a complete subject or a complete predicate.

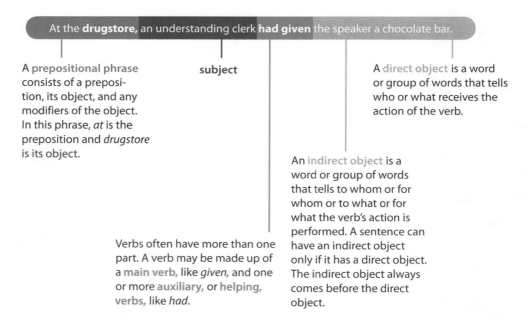

At the **drugstore,** an understanding clerk **had given** the speaker a chocolate bar.

A prepositional phrase consists of a preposition, its object, and any modifiers of the object. In this phrase, *at* is the preposition and *drugstore* is its object.

subject

A direct object is a word or group of words that tells who or what receives the action of the verb.

An indirect object is a word or group of words that tells to whom or for whom or to what or for what the verb's action is performed. A sentence can have an indirect object only if it has a direct object. The indirect object always comes before the direct object.

Verbs often have more than one part. A verb may be made up of a main verb, like *given,* and one or more auxiliary, or helping, verbs, like *had.*

Quick Reference: Punctuation

Mark	Function	Examples
End Marks period, question mark, exclamation point	ends a sentence	We can start now. When would you like to leave? What a fantastic hit!
period	follows an initial or abbreviation **Exception:** postal abbreviations of states	Mrs. Dorothy Parker, C. P. Cavafy, p.m., lb., oz., Blvd., Dr., NE (Nebraska), NV (Nevada)

period	follows a number or letter in an outline	I. Volcanoes
		   A. Central-vent
		     1. Shield

Comma	separates part of a compound sentence	I had never liked poetry, but now I really love it.
	separates items in a series	She is brave, loyal, and kind.
	separates adjectives of equal rank that modify the same noun	The slow, easy route is best.
	sets off a term of address	Maria, how can I help you? You must do something, soldier.
	sets off a parenthetical expression	Hard workers, as you know, don't quit. I'm not a quitter, believe me.
	sets off an introductory word, phrase, or dependent clause	Yes, I forgot my key. At the beginning of the day, I feel fresh. While she was out, I was here. Having finished my chores, I went out.
	sets off a nonrestrictive, or nonessential, phrase or clause	Ed Pawn, the captain of the chess team, won. Ed Pawn, who is the captain, won. The two leading runners, sprinting toward the finish line, finished in a tie.
	sets off parts of dates and addresses	Mail it by May 14, 2015, to the Hauptman Company, 321 Market Street, Memphis, Tennessee.
	follows the salutation and closing of a letter	Dear Jim, Sincerely yours,
	separates words to avoid confusion	By noon, time had run out. What the minister does, does matter. While cooking, Jim burned his hand.

continued

Mark	Function	Examples
Semicolon	separates items that contain commas in a series	We spent the first week of summer vacation in Chicago, Illinois; the second week in St. Louis, Missouri; and the third week in Albany, New York.
	separates parts of a compound sentence that are not joined by a coordinating conjunction	The last shall be first; the first shall be last. I read the Bible; however, I have not memorized it.
	separates parts of a compound sentence when the parts contain commas	After I ran out of money, I called my parents; but only my sister was home, unfortunately.
Colon	introduces a list	Those we wrote were the following: Dana, John, and Will.
	introduces a long quotation	Abraham Lincoln wrote: "Four score and seven years ago, our fathers brought forth on this continent a new nation. . . ."
	follows the salutation of a business letter	To Whom It May Concern: Dear Leonard Atole:
	separates certain numbers	1:28 p.m., Genesis 2:5
Dash	emphasizes parenthetical information or indicates an abrupt break in thought	I was thinking of my mother—who is arriving tomorrow—just as you walked in.
Parentheses	enclose less-important material	It was so unlike him (John is always on time) that I began to worry. The last World Series game (did you see it?) was fun.
Hyphen	joins parts of a compound adjective before a noun	The not-so-rich taxpayer won't stand for this!
	joins part of a compound with *all-*, *ex-*, *self-*, or *-elect*	The ex-firefighter helped rescue him. Our president-elect is self-conscious.
	joins part of a compound number (to ninety-nine)	Today, I turned twenty-one.
	joins part of a fraction	My cup is one-third full.
	joins a prefix to a word beginning with a capital letter	Which Pre-Raphaelite painter do you like best? It snowed in mid-October.
	indicates that a word is divided at the end of a line	How could you have any reason-able expectations of getting a new computer?
Apostrophe	used with *s* to form the possessive of a noun or an indefinite pronoun	my friend's book, my friends' books, anyone's guess, somebody else's problem

continued

Mark	Function	Examples
	replaces one or more omitted letters in a contraction or numbers in a date	don't (omitted *o*), he'd (omitted *woul*), the class of '99 (omitted *19*)
	used with *s* to form the plural of a letter	I had two A's on my report card.
Quotation Marks	set off a speaker's exact words	Sara said, "I'm finally ready." "I'm ready," Sara said, "finally." Did Sara say, "I'm ready"? Sara said, "I'm ready!"
	set off the title of a story, article, short poem, essay, song, or chapter	I liked McLean's "Marine Corps Issue" and Oliver's "The Journey." I like Joplin's "Me and Bobby McGee."
	indicate sarcasm or irony	Chris is a real "friend." He always shows up when he needs help but never when I do.
Ellipses	replace material omitted from a quotation	"When in the course of human events . . . and to assume among the powers of the earth. . . ."
Italics	indicate the title of a book, play, magazine, long poem, opera, film or TV series, or the name of a ship	*The Hunger Games, Hamlet, People,* the *Odyssey, Madama Butterfly, Gone with the Wind, The Big Bang Theory, USS Constitution*

Quick Reference: Capitalization

Category	Examples
People and Titles	
Names and initials of people	Amy Tan, W. H. Auden
Titles used before names	Professor Holmes, Senator Long
Deities and members of religious groups	Jesus, Allah, Buddha, Zeus, Baptists, Roman Catholics
Names of ethnic and national groups	Hispanics, Jews, African Americans
Geographical Names	
Cities, states, countries, continents	Philadelphia, Kansas, Japan, Europe
Regions, bodies of water, mountains	the South, Lake Baikal, Mount Everest
Geographic features, parks	Great Basin, Yellowstone National Park
Streets and roads, planets	318 East Sutton Drive, Charles Court, Jupiter, Pluto
Organizations, Events, Etc.	
Companies, organizations, teams	Ford Motor Company, Boy Scouts of America, St. Louis Cardinals

continued

Category	Examples
Buildings, bridges, monuments	Empire State Building, Eads Bridge, Washington Monument
Documents, awards	Declaration of Independence, Stanley Cup
Special named events	Mardi Gras, World Series
Government bodies, historical periods and events	U.S. Senate, House of Representatives, Middle Ages, Vietnam War
Days and months, holidays	Thursday, March, Thanksgiving, Labor Day
Specific cars, boats, trains, planes	Porsche, *Mississippi Queen, Stourbridge Lion, Concorde*
Proper Adjectives	
Adjectives formed from proper nouns	French cooking, Freudian psychology, Edwardian age, Midwestern university
First Words and the Pronoun *I*	
First word in a sentence or quotation	This is it. He said, "Let's go."
First word of sentence in parentheses that is not within another sentence	The spelling rules are covered in another section. (Consult that section for more information.)
First words in the salutation and closing of a letter	Dear Madam, Very truly yours,
First word in each line of most poetry Personal pronoun *I*	Then am I A happy fly If I live Or if I die.
First word, last word, and certain parts of speech in a title	*A Tale of Two Cities,* "The World Is Too Much with Us"

Grammar Handbook

1 Nouns

A **noun** is a word used to name a person, a place, a thing, an idea, a quality, or an action. Nouns can be classified in several ways.

1.1 COMMON NOUNS

Common nouns are general names, common to entire groups.

1.2 PROPER NOUNS

Proper nouns name specific, one-of-a-kind people, places, and things.

Common	Proper
guitarist, museum, lake, month	B.B. King, Rock and Roll Hall of Fame, Lake Pontchartrain, February

1.3 SINGULAR AND PLURAL NOUNS

A noun may take a **singular form** *(city, foot)* or a **plural form** *(cities, feet)*, depending on whether it names a single person, place, thing, or idea or more than one. Be sure to spell plural forms correctly.

For more information, see **Forming Plural Nouns**, page R54.

1.4 POSSESSIVE NOUNS

A **possessive noun** shows who or what owns something.

2 Pronouns

A **pronoun** is a word that is used in place of a noun or another pronoun. The word or word group to which the pronoun refers is called its **antecedent.**

2.1 PERSONAL PRONOUNS

Personal pronouns change their form to express person, number, gender, and case. The forms of these pronouns are shown in the following chart.

	Nominative	Objective	Possessive
Singular			
First person	I	me	my, mine
Second person	you	you	your, yours
Third person	she, he, it	her, him, it	her, hers, his, its
Plural			
First person	we	us	our, ours
Second person	you	you	your, yours
Third person	they	them	their, theirs

2.2 AGREEMENT WITH ANTECEDENT

Pronouns should agree with their antecedents in number, gender, and person.

If an antecedent is singular, use a singular pronoun.

> EXAMPLE: *I lost my new **cell phone**. I may have left it on the bus.*

If an antecedent is plural, use a plural pronoun.

> EXAMPLES: *Take the **snacks** out of the grocery bag, and put them in the pantry. **Delores and Arnetta** rode their bikes to the park.*

The gender of a pronoun must be the same as the gender of its antecedent.

> EXAMPLE: *The **man** thought he left his hat in the **room**. He ran back to it to look for the hat.*

The person (first, etc.) of the pronoun must be the same as the person of its antecedent.

> EXAMPLE: *You folks will have to go to the stadium to buy your tickets for the concert.*

2.3 PRONOUN CASE

Personal pronouns change form to show how they function in sentences. Different functions are shown by different **cases: nominative, objective,** and **possessive.** For examples, see Section 2.1.

A **nominative pronoun** is used as a subject or a predicate nominative in a sentence.

An **objective pronoun** is used as a direct object, an indirect object, or the object of a preposition.

SUBJECT   OBJECT   OBJECT OF PREPOSITION

He will lead them to us.

A **possessive pronoun** shows ownership. The pronouns *mine, yours, hers, his, its, ours,* and *theirs* can be used in place of nouns.

   EXAMPLE: *This horse is* mine.

The pronouns *my, your, her, his, its, our,* and *their* are used before nouns.

   EXAMPLE: *This is* my *horse.*

WATCH OUT! Many spelling errors can be avoided if you watch out for *its* and *their.* Don't confuse the possessive pronouns *its* and *their* with the contractions *it's* and *they're.*

TIP To decide which pronoun to use in a comparison, such as "She works harder than (I or me)," fill in the missing word(s): *She works harder than I work.*

2.4 REFLEXIVE AND INTENSIVE PRONOUNS

These pronouns are formed by adding *-self* or *-selves* to certain personal pronouns. Their forms are the same, and they differ only in how they are used.

A **reflexive pronoun** follows a verb or preposition and reflects back on an earlier noun or pronoun.

   EXAMPLES: *He likes* himself *too much. She is now* herself *again.*

Intensive pronouns intensify or emphasize the nouns or pronouns to which they refer.

   EXAMPLES: *They* themselves *will educate their children. You did it* yourself.

WATCH OUT! Avoid using *hisself* or *theirselves.* Standard English does not include these forms.

   NONSTANDARD: *The sniper kept* hisself *hidden behind a chimney.*

   STANDARD: *The sniper kept* himself *hidden behind a chimney.*

2.5 RECIPROCAL PRONOUNS

The **reciprocal pronouns** *each other* and *one another* refer to the individual members of a plural antecedent. These pronouns express mutual actions or relationships between the members they represent. Reciprocal pronouns can also take the possessive forms *each other's* and *one another's.*

EXAMPLES: *The ducks on the pond quacked at* one another.
John and Pedro borrowed each other's *favorite* book.

TIP Some authorities hold that *each other* should be used in reference to two things or people and that *one another* should be used in reference to more than two. Following traditional usage guidelines such as this can give your writing a more formal tone.

2.6 DEMONSTRATIVE PRONOUNS

Demonstrative pronouns point out things and persons near and far.

	Singular	Plural
Near	this	these
Far	that	those

2.7 INDEFINITE PRONOUNS

Indefinite pronouns do not refer to specific persons or things and usually have no antecedents. The chart shows some commonly used indefinite pronouns.

Singular	Plural	Singular or Plural	
another	both	all	most
anybody	few	any	none
no one	many	more	some
neither	several		

TIP Indefinite pronouns that end in *one, body,* or *thing* are always singular.

INCORRECT: *Did* everybody *play* their *part well?*

CORRECT: *Did* everybody *play* his or her *part well?*

If the indefinite pronoun might denote either a male or a female, *his or her* may be used to refer to it, or the sentence may be recast.

EXAMPLES: *Did everybody play his or her part well?*
Did all the students play their parts well?

2.8 INTERROGATIVE PRONOUNS

An **interrogative pronoun** tells a reader or listener that a question is coming. The interrogative pronouns are *who, whom, whose, which,* and *what.*

EXAMPLES: Who *is going to rehearse with you?*
From whom *did you receive the script?*

TIP *Who* is used as a subject; *whom,* as an object. To find out which pronoun you need to use in a question, change the question to a statement.

QUESTION: *(Who/Whom) did you meet there?*

STATEMENT: *You met (?) there.*

Since the verb has a subject (you), the needed word must be the object form, whom.

EXAMPLE: *Whom did you meet there?*

WATCH OUT! A special problem arises when you use an interrupter, such as *do you think,* within a question.

EXAMPLE: *(Who/Whom) do you think will win?*

If you eliminate the interrupter, it is clear that the word you need is *who.*

2.9 RELATIVE PRONOUNS

Relative pronouns relate, or connect, adjective clauses to the words they modify in sentences. The noun or pronoun that a relative clause modifies is the antecedent of the relative pronoun. Here are the relative pronouns and their uses.

	Subject	Object	Possessive
Person	who	whom	whose
Thing	which	which	whose
Thing/ Person	that	that	whose

Often short sentences with related ideas can be combined by using a relative pronoun to create a more effective sentence.

SHORT SENTENCE: *Poe wrote "The Raven."*

RELATED SENTENCE: *"The Raven" is one of the most famous poems in American literature.*

COMBINED SENTENCE: *Poe wrote "The Raven," which is one of the most famous poems in American literature.*

Practice and Apply

Write the correct form of each incorrect pronoun.

1. Whom has read "The Gift of the Magi"?
2. Jim needs money for a present for Della, so he takes his watch to the pawnshop hisself.
3. Would anybody else sell their watch to buy a Christmas present?
4. He chooses a beautiful pair of them jeweled combs for Della's hair.
5. Della sells her long hair to buy a watch chain for himself.

2.10 PRONOUN REFERENCE PROBLEMS

The referent of a pronoun should always be clear. Avoid problems by rewriting sentences.

An **indefinite reference** occurs when the pronoun *it, you,* or *they* does not clearly refer to a specific antecedent.

UNCLEAR: *In the new production of Romeo and Juliet, you have more experienced actors.*

CLEAR: *The new production of Romeo and Juliet has more experienced actors.*

A **general reference** occurs when the pronoun *it, this, that, which,* or *such* is used to refer to a general idea rather than a specific antecedent.

UNCLEAR: *Jenna takes acting lessons. This has improved her chances of getting a part in the school play.*

CLEAR: *Jenna takes acting lessons. The lessons have improved her chances of getting a part in the school play.*

Ambiguous means "having more than one possible meaning." An **ambiguous reference** occurs when a pronoun could refer to two or more antecedents.

UNCLEAR: *Odysseus escaped from Cyclops, and he blinded him.*

CLEAR: *Odysseus escaped from Cyclops, and he blinded Cyclops.*

Practice and Apply

Rewrite the following sentences to correct indefinite, ambiguous, and general pronoun references.

1. In Miss Lottie's yard you don't have any grass.
2. Miss Lottie plants marigolds. This makes her barren yard look strange.
3. Lizabeth and her brother throw stones at the marigolds, which ends Miss Lottie's planting.
4. Miss Lottie stares at Lizabeth as if she is strange.

3 Verbs

A **verb** is a word that expresses an action, a condition, or a state of being.

3.1 ACTION VERBS

Action verbs express mental or physical activity.

EXAMPLE: *Mr. Cho slept with the window open.*

3.2 LINKING VERBS

Linking verbs join subjects with words or phrases that rename or describe them.

EXAMPLE: *When he awoke the next morning, his bed was wet from the rain.*

3.3 PRINCIPAL PARTS

Action and linking verbs typically have four principal parts, which are used to form verb tenses. The principal parts are the **present,** the **present participle,** the **past,** and the **past participle.**

Action verbs and some linking verbs also fall into two categories: regular and irregular. A **regular verb** is a verb that forms its past and past participle by adding *-ed* or *-d* to the present form.

Present	Present Participle	Past	Past Participle
risk	(is) risking	risked	(has) risked
solve	(is) solving	solved	(has) solved
drop	(is) dropping	dropped	(has) dropped
carry	(is) carrying	carried	(has) carried

An **irregular verb** is a verb that forms its past and past participle in some other way than by adding *-ed* or *-d* to the present form.

Present	Present Participle	Past	Past Participle
begin	(is) beginning	began	(has) begun
break	(is) breaking	broke	(has) broken
go	(is) going	went	(has) gone

3.4 VERB TENSE

The **tense** of a verb indicates the time of the action or state of being. An action or state of being can occur in the present, the past, or the future. There are six tenses, each expressing a different range of time.

The **present tense** expresses an action or state that is happening at the present time, occurs regularly, or is constant or generally true. Use the present part.

> NOW: *That snow looks deep.*
>
> REGULAR: *It snows every day.*
>
> GENERAL: *Snow falls.*

The **past tense** expresses an action that began and ended in the past. Use the past part.

> EXAMPLE: *The storyteller finished his tale.*

The **future tense** expresses an action or state that will occur. Use *shall* or *will* with the present part.

> EXAMPLE: *They will attend the next festival.*

The **present perfect tense** expresses an action or state that (1) was completed at an indefinite time in the past or (2) began in the past and continues into the present. Use *have* or *has* with the past participle.

> EXAMPLE: *Poetry has inspired many readers.*

The **past perfect tense** expresses an action in the past that came before another action in the past. Use *had* with the past participle.

> EXAMPLE: *He had built a fire before the dog ran away.*

The **future perfect tense** expresses an action in the future that will be completed before another action in the future. Use *shall have* or *will have* with the past participle.

> EXAMPLE: *They will have read the novel before they see the movie version of the tale.*

An auxiliary verb is not used with a past-tense irregular verb, but it is always used with a past-participle irregular verb.

> INCORRECT: *I have saw her before.* (*Saw* is the past tense form and shouldn't be used with *have*.)
>
> CORRECT: *I have seen her somewhere before.*
>
> INCORRECT: *I seen her before.* (*Seen* is the past participle form of an irregular verb and shouldn't be used without an auxiliary verb.)

3.5 PROGRESSIVE FORMS

The progressive forms of the six tenses show ongoing actions. Use forms of *be* with the present participles of verbs.

> PRESENT PROGRESSIVE: *She is rehearsing her lines.*
>
> PAST PROGRESSIVE: *She was rehearsing her lines.*
>
> FUTURE PROGRESSIVE: *She will be rehearsing her lines.*
>
> PRESENT PERFECT PROGRESSIVE: *She has been rehearsing her lines.*
>
> PAST PERFECT PROGRESSIVE: *She had been rehearsing her lines.*

FUTURE PERFECT PROGRESSIVE: *She will have been rehearsing her lines.*

WATCH OUT! Do not shift from tense to tense needlessly. Watch out for these special cases.

- In most compound sentences and in sentences with compound predicates, keep the tenses the same.

  INCORRECT: *His boots freeze, and he shook with cold.*

  CORRECT: *His boots freeze, and he shakes with cold.*

- If one past action happens before another, do shift tenses.

  INCORRECT: *They wished they started earlier.*

  CORRECT: *They wished they had started earlier.*

Practice and Apply

Rewrite each sentence, using a form of the verb in parentheses. Identify each form that you use.

1. Many people (benefit) from the civil rights movement.
2. Martin Luther King Jr. (remain) a towering figure in the history of nonviolent protest.
3. King (become) the leader of the Montgomery bus boycott.
4. When he (speak) to the crowds in Washington, D.C., more than 200,000 people heard his words.
5. Our class (read) his speech "I Have a Dream."

Rewrite each sentence to correct an error in tense.

6. It is a chilly morning as Rosa Parks went to work.
7. She leaves her job early and was preparing to go out of town.
8. She boarded the bus and is taking a seat in the "colored" section.
9. After several more stops, there are no more seats in the front of the bus.
10. Rosa Parks refused to give up her seat and is arrested.

3.6 ACTIVE AND PASSIVE VOICE

The voice of a verb tells whether its subject performs or receives the action expressed by the verb. When the subject performs the action, the verb is in the **active voice.** When the subject is the receiver of the action, the verb is in the **passive voice.**

Compare these two sentences:

ACTIVE: *Richard Wilbur wrote "The Writer."*

PASSIVE: *"The Writer" was written by Richard Wilbur.*

To form the passive voice, use a form of *be* with the past participle of the verb.

WATCH OUT! Use the passive voice sparingly. It can make writing awkward and less direct.

AWKWARD: *"The Writer" is a poem that was written by Richard Wilbur.*

BETTER: *Richard Wilbur wrote the poem "The Writer."*

There are occasions when you will choose to use the passive voice because

- you want to emphasize the receiver: *The king was shot.*
- the doer is unknown: *My books were stolen.*
- the doer is unimportant: *French is spoken here.*

4 Modifiers

Modifiers are words or groups of words that change or limit the meanings of other words. Adjectives and adverbs are common modifiers.

4.1 ADJECTIVES

Adjectives modify nouns and pronouns by telling which one, what kind, how many, or how much.

WHICH ONE: *this, that, these, those*

EXAMPLE: *That bird is a scarlet ibis.*

WHAT KIND: *small, sick, courageous, black*

EXAMPLE: *The sick bird sways on the branch.*

HOW MANY: *some, few, ten, none, both, each*

EXAMPLE: *Both brothers stared at the bird.*

HOW MUCH: *more, less, enough, fast*

EXAMPLE: *The bird did not have enough strength to remain perched.*

4.2 PREDICATE ADJECTIVES

Most adjectives come before the nouns they modify, as in the examples above. A **predicate adjective,** however, follows a linking verb and describes the subject.

EXAMPLE: *My friends are very intelligent.*

Be especially careful to use adjectives (not adverbs) after such linking verbs as *look, feel, grow, taste,* and *smell.*

EXAMPLE: *The bread smells wonderful.*

4.3 ADVERBS

Adverbs modify verbs, adjectives, and other adverbs by telling where, when, how, or to what extent.

WHERE: *The children played outside.*

WHEN: *The author spoke yesterday.*

HOW: *We walked slowly behind the leader.*

TO WHAT EXTENT: *He worked very hard.*

Adverbs may occur in many places in sentences, both before and after the words they modify.

EXAMPLES: *Suddenly the wind shifted.*

The wind suddenly shifted.

The wind shifted suddenly.

4.4 ADJECTIVE OR ADVERB?

Many adverbs are formed by adding *-ly* to adjectives.

EXAMPLES: *sweet, sweetly; gentle, gently*

However, *-ly* added to a noun will usually yield an adjective.

EXAMPLES: *friend, friendly; woman, womanly*

4.5 COMPARISON OF MODIFIERS

Modifiers can be used to compare two or more things. The form of a modifier shows the degree of comparison. Both adjectives

and adverbs have **comparative** and **superlative** forms.

The **comparative form** is used to compare two things, groups, or actions.

EXAMPLES: *His father's hands were stronger than his own.*

His father was more courageous than the other man.

The **superlative form** is used to compare more than two things, groups, or actions.

EXAMPLES: *His father's hands were the strongest in the family.*

His father was the most courageous of them all.

4.6 REGULAR COMPARISONS

Most one-syllable and some two-syllable adjectives and adverbs have comparatives and superlatives formed by adding *-er* and *-est*. All three-syllable and most two-syllable modifiers have comparatives and superlatives formed with *more* or *most*.

Modifier	Comparative	Superlative
small	smaller	smallest
thin	thinner	thinnest
sleepy	sleepier	sleepiest
useless	more useless	most useless
precisely	more precisely	most precisely

WATCH OUT! Note that spelling changes must sometimes be made to form the comparatives and superlatives of modifiers.

EXAMPLES: *friendly, friendlier* (Change *y* to *i*, and add the ending.)

sad, sadder (Double the final consonant, and add the ending.)

4.7 IRREGULAR COMPARISONS

Some commonly used modifiers have irregular comparative and superlative forms. They are listed in the following chart. You may wish to memorize them.

Modifier	Comparative	Superlative
good	better	best
bad	worse	worst
far	farther *or* further	farthest *or* furthest
little	less *or* lesser	least
many	more	most
well	better	best
much	more	most

4.8 PROBLEMS WITH MODIFIERS

Study the tips that follow to avoid common mistakes:

Farther and Further Use *farther* for distances; use *further* for everything else.

Double Comparisons Make a comparison by using -er/-est or by using *more/most*. Using -er with *more* or using -est with *most* is incorrect.

INCORRECT: *I like her more better than she likes me.*

CORRECT: *I like her better than she likes me.*

Illogical Comparisons An illogical or confusing comparison results when two unrelated things are compared or when something is compared with itself. The word *other* or the word *else* should be used when comparing an individual member to the rest of a group.

ILLOGICAL: *The narrator was more curious about the war than any student in his class.* (implies that the narrator isn't a student in the class)

LOGICAL: *The narrator was more curious about the war than any other student in his class.* (identifies that the narrator is a student)

Bad vs. Badly *Bad*, as an adjective, is used before a noun or after a linking verb. *Badly*, always an adverb, never modifies a noun. Be sure to use the right form after a linking verb.

INCORRECT: *Ed felt badly after his team lost.*

CORRECT: *Ed felt bad after his team lost.*

Good vs. Well *Good*, as an adjective, is used before a noun or after a linking verb. *Well* is often an adverb meaning "expertly" or "properly." *Well* can also be used as an adjective after a linking verb when it means "in good health."

INCORRECT: *Helen writes very good.*

CORRECT: *Helen writes very well.*

CORRECT: *Yesterday I felt bad; today I feel well.*

Double Negatives If you add a negative word to a sentence that is already negative, the result will be an error known as a double negative. When using *not* or *-n't* with a verb, use *any-* words, such as *anybody* or *anything,* rather than *no-* words, such as *nobody* or *nothing,* later in the sentence.

INCORRECT: *We haven't seen nobody.*

CORRECT: *We haven't seen anybody.*

Using *hardly, barely,* or *scarcely* after a negative word is also incorrect.

INCORRECT: *They couldn't barely see two feet ahead.*

CORRECT: *They could barely see two feet ahead.*

Misplaced Modifiers Sometimes a modifier is placed so far away from the word it modifies that the intended meaning of the sentence is unclear. Place modifiers as close as possible to the words they modify.

MISPLACED: *We found the child in the park who was missing.* (The child was missing, not the park.)

CLEARER: *We found the missing child in the park.*

Dangling Modifiers Sometimes a modifier doesn't appear to modify any word in a sentence. Most dangling modifiers are participial phrases or infinitive phrases.

DANGLING: *Looking out the window, his brother was seen driving by.*

CLEARER: *Looking out the window, Josh saw his brother driving by.*

continued

Type	Definition	Example
Interrogative	asks a question	Did you read "Pancakes"?
Imperative	gives a command or direction	Read the story.
Exclamatory	expresses strong feeling or excitement	The story is funny!

Practice and Apply

Choose the correct word or words from each pair in parentheses.

1. *The House on Mango Street* gives (better, more better) insight into Mexican-American culture than any other book I've read.
2. Sandra Cisneros's family moved so often that she hardly had (any, no) friends.
3. She felt (bad, badly) that she didn't live in a perfect house like the ones she saw on TV.
4. At one time Cisneros didn't think (nothing, anything) was positive about belonging to a different culture.

Practice and Apply

Rewrite each sentence that contains a misplaced or dangling modifier. Write "correct" if the sentence is written correctly.

1. The house on Loomis Street belongs to Esperanza's family with the broken water pipes.
2. Esperanza has to carry water from the house in empty milk jugs.
3. A nun asks Esperanza from the convent where she lives.
4. Feeling bad about the nun's reaction, the house is no longer good enough for Esperanza.

5 The Sentence and Its Parts

A **sentence** is a group of words used to express a complete thought. A complete sentence has a subject and a predicate.

5.1 KINDS OF SENTENCES

There are four basic types of sentences.

Type	Definition	Example
Declarative	states a fact, a wish, an intent, or a feeling	Joan Bauer understands youths.

5.2 COMPOUND SUBJECTS AND PREDICATES

A compound subject consists of two or more subjects that share the same verb. They are typically joined by the coordinating conjunction *and* or *or*.

EXAMPLE: *A short story or novel will keep you engaged.*

A compound predicate consists of two or more predicates that share the same subject. They too are typically joined by a coordinating conjunction, usually *and, but,* or *or.*

EXAMPLE: *The class finished all the poetry but did not read the short stories.*

5.3 COMPLEMENTS

A **complement** is a word or group of words that completes the meaning of the sentence. Some sentences contain only a subject and a verb. Most sentences, however, require additional words placed after the verb to complete the meaning of the sentence. There are three kinds of complements: direct objects, indirect objects, and subject complements.

Direct objects are words or word groups that receive the action of action verbs. A direct object answers the question *what* or *whom*.

EXAMPLES: *The students asked many questions.* (Asked what?)

The teacher quickly answered the students. (Answered whom?)

Indirect objects tell to whom or what or for whom or what the actions of verbs are performed. Indirect objects come before direct objects. In the examples that follow, the indirect objects are highlighted.

> EXAMPLES: *My sister usually gave her friends good advice.* (Gave to whom?)
>
> *Her brother sent the store a heavy package.* (Sent to what?)

Subject complements come after linking verbs and identify or describe the subjects. A subject complement that names or identifies a subject is called a **predicate nominative.** Predicate nominatives include **predicate nouns** and **predicate pronouns.**

> EXAMPLES: *My friends are very hard workers.*
>
> *The best writer in the class is she.*

A subject complement that describes a subject is called a predicate adjective.

> EXAMPLE: *The pianist appeared very energetic.*

6 Phrases

A **phrase** is a group of related words that does not contain a subject and a predicate but functions in a sentence as a single part of speech.

6.1 NOUN PHRASES

A **noun phrase** includes a noun and the modifiers that distinguish it. Modifiers might come before or after the noun.

> EXAMPLES: *The record-breaking quarterback led his team to the state championship game.*
>
> *The quarterback who threw four interceptions in one game was traded to another team.*

In these examples, the noun *quarterback* is modified by *record-breaking* and *who threw four interceptions in one game.* The noun and its modifiers form the noun phrase.

Add a modifier to at least one noun in each of the following sentences to create a noun phrase.

1. The man hit another car on his drive to work.
2. The gumbo set my mouth on fire.
3. A noise awakened her in the middle of the night.
4. My cousin borrowed my aunt's car without asking for permission to use it.
5. Before he left for Europe, my friend called me from the airport.

6.2 VERB PHRASES

A **verb phrase** consists of at least one main verb and one or more helping verbs. A helping verb (also called an auxiliary verb) helps the main verb express action or state of being.

Besides all forms of the verb *be,* some common helping verbs are *can, could, did, do, does, had, have, may, might, must, shall, should, will,* and *would.*

> EXAMPLE: *She should think about her future.*

Sometimes the parts of a verb phrase are interrupted by other parts of speech.

> EXAMPLE: *She had always been thinking about her future.*

In this example, the adverb *always* interrupts the verb phrase *had been thinking.*

The word *not* is an adverb. It is never part of a verb phrase, even when it is joined to a verb as the contraction *–n't.*

> EXAMPLES: *She should not have lifted that rock.*
>
> *She shouldn't have lifted that rock.*

Rewrite each sentence to include a helping verb.

1. His physical therapist designed an exercise program for him.
2. Before exercising he spends at least five minutes warming up.
3. When lifting heavy objects, he wears a back brace.
4. The doctor reminds him of proper lifting techniques at every check-up.
5. Without physical therapy, healing is often difficult.

6.3 PREPOSITIONAL PHRASES

A **prepositional phrase** is a phrase that consists of a preposition, its object, and any modifiers of the object. Prepositional phrases that modify nouns or pronouns are called **adjective phrases.** Prepositional phrases that modify verbs, adjectives, or adverbs are **adverb phrases.**

> ADJECTIVE PHRASE: *The central character of the story is a villain.*
>
> ADVERB PHRASE: *He reveals his nature in the first scene.*

Remember that adjectives modify nouns by telling which one, what kind, how much, or how many. Adverbs modify verbs, adjectives, and other adverbs by telling where, when, how, or to what extent. The same is true of prepositional phrases that act as adjective phrases or adverb phrases.

Identify the prepositional phrases and the words they modify in the following sentences. State whether the prepositional phrase is an adjective phrase or an adverb phrase.

1. A daily newspaper has something for almost everyone.
2. Our entire family reads the newspaper in the morning.
3. Dad always begins with the sports page; Mom prefers the national news.

continued

4. My sister's favorite part of the newspaper is the lifestyle section.
5. She enjoys features like "How-to Hints."

6.4 APPOSITIVES AND APPOSITIVE PHRASES

An **appositive** is a noun or pronoun that identifies or renames another noun or pronoun. An **appositive phrase** includes an appositive and modifiers of it.

An appositive can be either **essential** or **nonessential.** An **essential appositive** provides information that is needed to identify what is referred to by the preceding noun or pronoun.

> EXAMPLE: *The book is about the author Richard Wright.*

A **nonessential appositive** adds extra information about a noun or pronoun whose meaning is already clear. Nonessential appositives and appositive phrases are set off with commas.

> EXAMPLE: *The book, an autobiography, tells how he began writing.*

7 Verbals and Verbal Phrases

A **verbal** is a verb form that is used as a noun, an adjective, or an adverb. A **verbal phrase** consists of a verbal along with its modifiers and complements. There are three kinds of verbals: **infinitives, participles,** and **gerunds.**

7.1 INFINITIVES AND INFINITIVE PHRASES

An **infinitive** is a verb form that usually begins with *to* and functions as a noun, an adjective, or an adverb. An **infinitive phrase** consists of an infinitive plus its modifiers and complements. The examples that follow show several uses of infinitive phrases.

> NOUN: *To know her is my only desire.* (subject)
>
> I'm *planning to walk with you.* (direct object)

ADJECTIVE: *We saw his need to be loved.*
(adjective modifying need)

ADVERB: *She wrote to voice her opinions.*
(adverb modifying wrote)

Because *to,* the sign of the infinitive, precedes infinitives, it is usually easy to recognize them. However, sometimes *to* may be omitted.

EXAMPLE: *Let no one dare [to] enter this shrine.*

7.2 PARTICIPLES AND PARTICIPIAL PHRASES

A **participle** is a verb form that functions as an adjective. Like adjectives, participles modify nouns and pronouns. Most participles are present-participle forms, ending in *-ing,* or past-participle forms ending in *-ed* or *-en.* In the examples below, the participles are highlighted.

MODIFYING A NOUN: *The dying man had a smile on his face.*

MODIFYING A PRONOUN: *Frustrated, everyone abandoned the cause.*

Participial phrases are participles with all their modifiers and complements.

MODIFYING A NOUN: *The dogs searching for survivors are well trained.*

MODIFYING A PRONOUN: *Having approved your proposal, we are ready to act.*

Practice and Apply

Identify the participial phrases in the following sentences, and indicate which word each phrase modifies.

1. How are skyscrapers created, and what keeps them standing tall?
2. From this foundation rises a steel skeleton, supporting the walls and floors.
3. Chicago, nearly destroyed by fire in 1871, was later rebuilt with innovative designs.
4. The first skyscraper constructed on a metal frame was built there during this period.
5. Architects, using the latest materials, were glad to design in new ways.

7.3 DANGLING AND MISPLACED PARTICIPLES

A participle or participial phrase should be placed as close as possible to the word that it modifies. Otherwise the meaning of the sentence may not be clear.

MISPLACED: *The boys were looking for squirrels searching the trees.*

CLEARER: *The boys searching the trees were looking for squirrels.*

A participle or participial phrase that does not clearly modify anything in a sentence is called a dangling participle. A **dangling participle** causes confusion because it appears to modify a word that it cannot sensibly modify. Correct a dangling participle by providing a word for the participle to modify.

DANGLING: *Running like the wind, my hat fell off.* (The hat wasn't running.)

CLEARER: *Running like the wind, I lost my hat.*

7.4 GERUNDS AND GERUND PHRASES

A gerund is a verb form ending in *-ing* that functions as a noun. Gerunds may perform any function nouns perform.

SUBJECT: *Running is my favorite pastime.*

DIRECT OBJECT: *I truly love running.*

INDIRECT OBJECT: *You should give running a try.*

SUBJECT COMPLEMENT: *My deepest passion is running.*

OBJECT OF PREPOSITION: *Her love of running keeps her strong.*

Gerund phrases are gerunds with all their modifiers and complements.

SUBJECT: *Wishing on a star never got me far.*

OBJECT OF PREPOSITION: *I will finish before leaving the office.*

APPOSITIVE: *Her avocation, flying airplanes, finally led to full-time employment.*

Practice and Apply

Rewrite each sentence, adding the phrase shown in parentheses.

1. "Daughter of Invention" was written by Julia Alvarez. (a short story)
2. The narrator loves writing. (to record her experiences)
3. She will appear at an assembly. (to give a speech)
4. She finally finishes her speech. (working feverishly for hours)
5. She reads her speech to her parents. (feeling proud)

7.5 ABSOLUTE PHRASES

An **absolute phrase** is a noun or pronoun, its participle, and any modifiers. It modifies an entire sentence, or independent clause, rather than just one word.

> EXAMPLE: *The theater buzzing with excitement, the crowd waited for the band to take the stage.*

In this example, *The theater buzzing with excitement* is an absolute phrase that modifies the sentence *the crowd waited for the band to take the stage*. The noun *theater* is modified by the participle *buzzing* and by the prepositional phrase *with excitement*. Notice that a comma separates the absolute phrase from the sentence, or independent clause.

Practice and Apply

Add an absolute phrase to modify each sentence. With a partner, discuss how the additions improve the original sentences.

1. The kids ate the entire bowl of oranges.
2. The sun set beyond the sparkling lake.
3. The board of directors rejected her proposal.
4. He decided to join the drama club.
5. We ran through the field of tall grass.

8 Clauses

A **clause** is a group of words that contains a subject and a predicate. There are two kinds of clauses: independent clauses and subordinate clauses.

8.1 INDEPENDENT AND SUBORDINATE CLAUSES

An **independent clause** can stand alone as a sentence, as the word *independent* suggests.

> INDEPENDENT CLAUSE: *Taos is famous for its Great Bank Robbery.*

A sentence may contain more than one independent clause.

> EXAMPLE: *Many people remember the robbery, and they will tell you all about it.*

In the preceding example, the coordinating conjunction *and* joins two independent clauses.

Two independent clauses can also be joined with a **conjunctive adverb,** such as *consequently, finally, furthermore, however, moreover,* or *nevertheless.* To separate the two independent clauses, a semicolon is used before the conjunctive adverb.

> EXAMPLE: *The painter decided to take up sculpture; however, his studio was not big enough for large projects using granite.*

A **subordinate clause,** or dependent clause, cannot stand alone as a sentence. It is subordinate to, or dependent on, an independent clause.

> EXAMPLE: *Although the two men needed cash,* they didn't get it from the bank.

The highlighted clause cannot stand by itself.

Practice and Apply

Identify each italicized clause in the following sentences as independent or subordinate (dependent). Then explain your answers.

1. The fire started *because someone did not smother a campfire.*
2. *The family that bought our house* is moving next week.
3. *Since she had practiced diligently,* she won the golf match.
4. Wherever Maggie goes, *her golden retriever Hopper follows her.*
5. According to our math teacher, *the binary system is important to know.*

8.2 ADJECTIVE CLAUSES

An **adjective clause,** or relative clause, is a subordinate clause used as an adjective. It usually follows the noun or pronoun it modifies.

> EXAMPLE: *Tony Hillerman is someone whom millions know as a mystery writer.*

Adjective clauses are typically introduced by the relative pronoun *who, whom, whose, which,* or *that.*

For more information, see **Relative Pronouns**, page R31.

> EXAMPLES: *A person who needs money should get a job.*
>
> *The robbers, whose names were Gomez and Smith, entered the bank.*

An adjective clause can be either essential or nonessential. An **essential adjective clause** provides information that is necessary to identify the preceding noun or pronoun.

> EXAMPLE: *One robber wore a disguise that was meant to fool Taos's residents.*

A **nonessential adjective clause** adds additional information about a noun or pronoun whose meaning is already clear. Nonessential clauses are set off with commas.

> EXAMPLE: *The suspects, who drove away in a pickup truck, sideswiped a car driven by a minister.*

TIP The relative pronouns *whom, which,* and *that* may sometimes be omitted when they are objects in adjective clauses.

> EXAMPLE: *Hillerman is a writer [whom] millions enjoy.*

Practice and Apply

Revise the following sentences by substituting an adjective clause (relative clause) for each italicized adjective. Add specific details to make the sentences more interesting.

1. As I entered the building, a *colorful* painting caught my eye.
2. The *patient* photographer sat on a small ledge all day.

continued

Practice and Apply

3. The two attorneys argued over the *important* contract.
4. At the assembly, Ms. Bailey made two *surprising* announcements.
5. Saburo and his friends cautiously entered the *dark* cave.

8.3 ADVERB CLAUSES

An **adverb clause** is a subordinate clause that is used to modify a verb, an adjective, or an adverb. It is introduced by a subordinating conjunction.

Adverb clauses typically occur at the beginning or end of sentences.

> MODIFYING A VERB: *When we need you, we will call.*
>
> MODIFYING AN ADVERB: *I'll stay here where there is shelter from the rain.*
>
> MODIFYING AN ADJECTIVE: *Roman felt as good as he had ever felt.*

Practice and Apply

Identify each adverb clause in the following sentences. Then write what the clause tells: *when, where, why, how, to what extent,* or *under what condition.*

1. If you look through the newspapers from the first half of the twentieth century, you will see many pictures of Mohandas K. Gandhi.
2. This man led India to independence from Britain, and he took his spinning wheel wherever he went.
3. He did so because he viewed spinning as a symbol of the peaceful, traditional Indian lifestyle.
4. He also hoped to encourage the Indian people to make their own clothes so that they would not have to depend on British industries.
5. As a form of protest, Gandhi led marches or fasted until the government met his demands.

8.4 NOUN CLAUSES

A **noun clause** is a subordinate clause that is used as a noun. A noun clause may be used as a subject, a direct object, an indirect object, a predicate nominative, or the object of a preposition. Noun clauses are introduced either by pronouns, such as *that, what, who, whoever, which,* and *whose,* or by subordinating conjunctions, such as *how, when, where, why,* and *whether.*

TIP Because the same words may introduce adjective and noun clauses, you need to consider how a clause functions within its sentence. To determine if a clause is a noun clause, try substituting *something* or *someone* for the clause. If you can do it, it is probably a noun clause.

EXAMPLE: *I know whose woods these are.* ("I know *something*." The clause is a noun clause, direct object of the verb *know.*)

Practice and Apply

Identify the noun clause in each sentence. Then tell how the clause is used: as a subject, a predicate nominative, a direct object, an indirect object, or an object of a preposition.

1. We moved to Massachusetts and did not know what we would find there.
2. What surprised me first were the yellowish green fire engines.
3. Our neighbors explained that this color keeps the fire engines from being confused with other large red trucks.
4. Write your research paper about whomever you admire most.
5. The small grapefruit-sized bowling balls with no finger holes were not what she usually used.

Practice and Apply

Add descriptive details to each sentence by writing the type of clause indicated in parentheses.

1. My aunt has an interesting hobby. (adjective clause)
2. She works on her craft at night. (adverb clause)

continued

Practice and Apply

3. She writes. (noun clause)
4. She has written several books. (adjective clause)
5. I asked her to write a story about me. (adverb clause)

9 The Structure of Sentences

When classified by their structure, there are four kinds of sentences: simple, compound, complex, and compound-complex.

9.1 SIMPLE SENTENCES

A **simple sentence** is a sentence that has one independent clause and no subordinate clauses. The fact that such a sentence is called simple does not mean that it is uncomplicated. Various parts of simple sentences may be compound, and simple sentences may contain grammatical structures such as appositive and verbal phrases.

EXAMPLES: *Ray Bradbury, a science fiction writer, has written short stories and novels.* (appositive and compound direct object)

The narrator, recalling the years of his childhood, tells his story. (participial phrase)

9.2 COMPOUND SENTENCES

A **compound sentence** consists of two or more independent clauses. The clauses in compound sentences are joined with commas and coordinating conjunctions (*and, but, or, nor, yet, for, so*) or with semicolons. Like simple sentences, compound sentences do not contain any subordinate clauses.

EXAMPLES: *I enjoyed Bradbury's story "The Utterly Perfect Murder," and I want to read more of his stories.*

The narrator has lived a normal, complete life; however, he decides to kill his childhood playmate.

WATCH OUT! Do not confuse compound sentences with simple sentences that have compound parts.

EXAMPLE: *A subcommittee drafted a document and immediately presented it to the entire group.* (Here *and* joins parts of a compound predicate, not a compound sentence.)

9.3 COMPLEX SENTENCES

A **complex sentence** consists of one independent clause and one or more subordinate clauses. Each subordinate clause can be used as a noun or as a modifier. If it is used as a modifier, a subordinate clause usually modifies a word in the independent clause, and the independent clause can stand alone. However, when a subordinate clause is a noun clause, it is a part of the independent clause; the two cannot be separated.

MODIFIER: *One should not complain unless one has a better solution.*

NOUN CLAUSE: *We sketched pictures of whomever we wished.* (The noun clause is the object of the preposition *of* and cannot be separated from the rest of the sentence.)

9.4 COMPOUND-COMPLEX SENTENCES

A **compound-complex sentence** contains two or more independent clauses and one or more subordinate clauses. Compound-complex sentences are, simply, both compound and complex. If you start with a compound sentence, all you need to do to form a compound-complex sentence is add a subordinate clause.

COMPOUND: *All the students knew the answer, yet they were too shy to volunteer.*

COMPOUND-COMPLEX: *All the students knew the answer that their teacher expected, yet they were too shy to volunteer.*

9.5 PARALLEL STRUCTURE

When you write sentences, make sure that coordinate parts are equivalent, or **parallel,** in structure.

NOT PARALLEL: *Erin loved basketball and to play hockey.* (*Basketball* is a noun; *to play hockey* is a phrase.)

PARALLEL: *Erin loved basketball and hockey.* (*Basketball* and *hockey* are both nouns.)

NOT PARALLEL: *He wanted to rent an apartment, a new car, and traveling around the country.* (*To rent* is an infinitive, *car* is a noun, and *traveling* is a gerund.)

PARALLEL: *He wanted to rent an apartment, to drive a new car, and to travel around the country.* (*To rent, to drive,* and *to travel* are all infinitives.)

10 Writing Complete Sentences

Remember, a sentence is a group of words that expresses a complete thought. In writing that you wish to share with a reader, try to avoid both sentence fragments and run-on sentences.

10.1 CORRECTING FRAGMENTS

A **sentence fragment** is a group of words that is only part of a sentence. It does not express a complete thought and may be confusing to a reader or listener. A sentence fragment may be lacking a subject, a predicate, or both.

FRAGMENT: *Waited for the boat to arrive.* (no subject)

CORRECTED: *We waited for the boat to arrive.*

FRAGMENT: *People of various races, ages, and creeds.* (no predicate)

CORRECTED: *People of various races, ages, and creeds gathered together.*

FRAGMENT: *Near the old cottage.* (neither subject nor predicate)

CORRECTED: *The burial ground is near the old cottage.*

In your writing, fragments may be a result of haste or incorrect punctuation. Sometimes fixing a fragment will be a matter of attaching it to a preceding or following sentence.

FRAGMENT: *We saw the two girls. Waiting for the bus to arrive.*

CORRECTED: *We saw the two girls waiting for the bus to arrive.*

10.2 CORRECTING RUN-ON SENTENCES

A **run-on sentence** is made up of two or more sentences written as though they were one. Some run-ons have no punctuation within them. Others may have only commas where conjunctions or stronger punctuation marks are necessary. Use your judgment in correcting run-on sentences, as you have choices. You can make a run-on two sentences if the thoughts are not closely connected. If the thoughts are closely related, you can keep the run-on as one sentence by adding a semicolon or a conjunction.

RUN-ON: *We found a place for the picnic by a small pond it was three miles from the village.*

MAKE TWO SENTENCES: *We found a place for the picnic by a small pond. It was three miles from the village.*

RUN-ON: *We found a place for the picnic by a small pond it was perfect.*

USE A SEMICOLON: *We found a place for the picnic by a small pond; it was perfect.*

ADD A CONJUNCTION: *We found a place for the picnic by a small pond, and it was perfect.*

WATCH OUT! When you form compound sentences, make sure you use appropriate punctuation: a comma before a coordinating conjunction, a semicolon when there is no coordinating conjunction. A very common mistake is to use a comma alone instead of a comma and a conjunction. This error is called a **comma splice.**

INCORRECT: *He finished the apprenticeship, he left the village.*

CORRECT: *He finished the apprenticeship, and he left the village.*

11 Subject-Verb Agreement

The subject and verb in a clause must agree in number. Agreement means that if the subject is singular, the verb is also singular, and if the subject is plural, the verb is also plural.

11.1 BASIC AGREEMENT

Fortunately, agreement between subjects and verbs in English is simple. Most verbs show the difference between singular and plural only in the third person of the present tense. In the present tense, the third-person singular form ends in *-s*.

Present-Tense Verb Forms	
Singular	**Plural**
I sleep	we sleep
you sleep	you sleep
she, he, it sleeps	they sleep

11.2 AGREEMENT WITH *BE*

The verb *be* presents special problems in agreement, because this verb does not follow the usual verb patterns.

Forms of *Be*			
Present Tense		**Past Tense**	
Singular	**Plural**	**Singular**	**Plural**
I am	we are	I was	we were
you are	you are	you were	you were
she, he, it is	they are	she, he, it was	they were

11.3 WORDS BETWEEN SUBJECT AND VERB

A verb agrees only with its subject. When words come between a subject and a verb, ignore them when considering proper agreement. Identify the subject, and make sure the verb agrees with it.

EXAMPLES: *A story in the newspapers tells about the 1890s.*

Dad as well as Mom reads the paper daily.

11.4 AGREEMENT WITH COMPOUND SUBJECTS

Use plural verbs with most compound subjects joined by the word *and*.

EXAMPLE: *My father and his friends read the paper daily.*

To confirm that you need a plural verb, you could substitute the plural pronoun *they* for *my father and his friends*.

If a compound subject is thought of as a unit, use a singular verb. Test this by substituting the singular pronoun *it*.

EXAMPLE: *Peanut butter and jelly [it] is my brother's favorite sandwich.*

Use a singular verb with a compound subject that is preceded by *each, every,* or *many a*.

EXAMPLE: *Each novel and short story seems grounded in personal experience.*

When the parts of a compound subject are joined by *or, nor,* or the correlative conjunctions *either . . . or* or *neither . . . nor,* make the verb agree with the noun or pronoun nearest the verb.

EXAMPLES: *Cookies or ice cream is my favorite dessert.*

Either Cheryl or her friends are being invited. Neither ice storms nor snow is predicted today.

11.5 PERSONAL PRONOUNS AS SUBJECTS

When using a personal pronoun as a subject, make sure to match it with the correct form of the verb **be**. (See the chart in Section 11.2.) Note especially that the pronoun *you* takes the forms *are* and *were,* regardless of whether it is singular or plural.

WATCH OUT! *You is* and *you was* are nonstandard forms and should be avoided in writing and speaking. *We was* and *they was* are also forms to be avoided.

INCORRECT: *You was a good student.*

CORRECT: *You were a good student.*

INCORRECT: *They was starting a new school.*

CORRECT: *They were starting a new school.*

11.6 INDEFINITE PRONOUNS AS SUBJECTS

Some indefinite pronouns are always singular; some are always plural.

Singular Indefinite Pronouns			
another	either	neither	one
anybody	everbody	nobody	some-body
anyone	everyone	no one	some-one
anything	every-thing	nothing	some-thing
each	much		

EXAMPLES: *Each of the writers was given an award. Somebody in the room upstairs is sleeping.*

Plural Indefinite Pronouns			
both	few	many	several

EXAMPLES: *Many of the books in our library are not in circulation.*

Few have been returned recently.

Still other indefinite pronouns may be either singular or plural.

Singular or Plural Indefinite Pronouns		
all	more	none
any	most	some

The number of the indefinite pronoun *any* or *none* often depends on the intended meaning.

EXAMPLES: *Any of these topics has potential for a good article.* (any one topic)

Any of these topics have potential for good articles. (all of the many topics)

The indefinite pronouns *all, some, more, most,* and *none* are singular when they refer to quantities or parts of things. They are plural when they refer to numbers of individual things. Context will usually give a clue.

EXAMPLES: *All of the flour is gone.* (referring to a quantity)

All of the flowers are gone. (referring to individual items)

11.7 INVERTED SENTENCES

Problems in agreement often occur in inverted sentences beginning with *here* or *there;* in questions beginning with *how, when, why, where,* or *what;* and in inverted sentences beginning with phrases. Identify the subject—wherever it is—before deciding on the verb.

EXAMPLES: *There clearly are far too many cooks in this kitchen.*

Far from the embroiled cooks stands the master chef.

Practice and Apply

Locate the subject of each verb in parentheses in the sentences below. Then choose the correct verb form.

1. Many Greeks sail home from Troy, but few (struggles, struggle) as hard as Odysseus to get there.
2. Neither Odysseus nor his men (know, knows) what dangers lie ahead.
3. There (is, are) more dangers awaiting him than there (is, are) gods to save him.
4. Everybody who has read about Odysseus' trials (knows, know) what he endured.
5. There (is, are) few friends who can help him during his ten-year odyssey.

11.8 SENTENCES WITH PREDICATE NOMINATIVES

When a predicate nominative serves as a complement in a sentence, use a verb that agrees with the subject, not the complement.

EXAMPLES: *The speeches of Martin Luther King Jr. are a landmark in American civil rights history.* (*Speeches* is the subject and it takes the plural verb *are.*)

One landmark in American civil rights history is the speeches of Martin Luther King Jr. (The subject is *landmark* and it takes the singular verb *is.*)

11.9 *DON'T* AND *DOESN'T* AS AUXILIARY VERBS

The auxiliary verb *doesn't* is used with singular subjects and with the personal pronouns *she, he,* and *it.* The auxiliary verb *don't* is used with plural subjects and with the personal pronouns *I, we, you,* and *they.*

SINGULAR: *She doesn't know Martin Luther King's famous "I Have a Dream" speech.*

Doesn't the young woman read very much?

PLURAL: *We don't have the speech memorized. Don't speakers usually memorize their speeches?*

11.10 COLLECTIVE NOUNS AS SUBJECTS

Collective nouns are singular nouns that name groups of persons or things. *Team,* for example, is the collective name of a group of individuals. A collective noun takes a singular verb when the group acts as a single unit. It takes a plural verb when the members of the group act separately.

EXAMPLES: *Our team usually wins.* (The team as a whole wins.)

Our team vote differently on most issues. (The individual members vote.)

11.11 RELATIVE PRONOUNS AS SUBJECTS

When the relative pronoun *who, which,* or *that* is used as a subject in an adjective clause, the verb in the clause must agree in number with the antecedent of the pronoun.

SINGULAR: *I didn't read the* **poem** *about fireworks that was assigned.*

The antecedent of the relative pronoun *that* is the singular **poem;** therefore, *that* is singular and must take the singular verb *was.*

PLURAL: ***William Blake and Amy Lowell,** who are very different from each other, are both outstanding poets.*

The antecedent of the relative pronoun *who* is the plural compound subject *William Blake and Amy Lowell.* Therefore *who* is plural, and it takes the plural verb *are.*

Vocabulary and Spelling

The key to becoming an independent reader is to develop a toolkit of vocabulary strategies. By learning and practicing the strategies, you'll know what to do when you encounter unfamiliar words while reading. You'll also know how to refine the words you use for different situations—personal, school, and work.

Being a good speller is important when communicating your ideas in writing. Learning basic spelling rules and checking your spelling in a dictionary will help you spell words that you may not use frequently.

1 Using Context Clues

The context of a word is made up of the punctuation marks, words, sentences, and paragraphs that surround it. A word's context can give you important clues about its meaning, including both its denotation and connotation.

1.1 GENERAL CONTEXT

Sometimes you need to infer the meaning of a word by reading all the information in a passage.

After twelve hours without food, I was so ravenous that I ate seven slices of pizza.

You can figure out from the context that *ravenous* means "extremely hungry."

1.2 SPECIFIC CONTEXT CLUES

Sometimes writers help you understand the meanings of words by providing specific clues such as those shown in the chart.

Specific Context Clues		
Type of Clue	**Key Words/Phrases**	**Example**
Definition or restatement of the meaning of the word	or, which is, that is, in other words, also known as, also called	His first conjecture, **or guess,** was correct.
Example following an unfamiliar word	such as, like, as if, for example, especially, including	She loved macabre stories, **such as those by Edgar Allan Poe and Stephen King.**
Comparison with a more familiar word or concept	as, like, also, similar to, in the same way, likewise	Despite his physical suffering, his mind was as **lucid** as any **rational** person's.
Contrast with a familiar word or experience	unlike, but, however, although, on the other hand, on the contrary	Unlike her **clumsy** partner, she was an **agile** dancer.
Cause-and-effect relationship in which one term is familiar	because, since, when, consequently, as a result, therefore	Because this perfume has such a **sharp** scent, I will buy the one with a **subtle** fragrance.

1.3 IDIOMS, SLANG, AND FIGURATIVE LANGUAGE

An **idiom** is an expression whose overall meaning is different from the meaning of the individual words. **Slang** is informal language in which made-up words and ordinary words are used to mean something different from their meanings in formal English. **Figurative language** is language that communicates meaning beyond the literal meaning of the words. Use context clues to figure out the meanings of idioms, slang, and figurative language.

> *The mosquitoes drove us crazy on our hike through the woods.* (idiom; means "bothered")
> *That's a really cool backpack that you're wearing.* (slang; means "excellent" or "first-rate")
> *I was angry. Heat rose under my skin until I felt as if searing flames were threatening to engulf my whole body.* (figurative language; hot skin and flames symbolize anger)

2 Analyzing Word Structure

Many words can be broken into smaller parts. These word parts include base words, roots, prefixes, and suffixes.

2.1 BASE WORDS

A **base word** is a word part that by itself is also a word. Other words or word parts can be added to base words to form new words.

2.2 ROOTS

A **root** is a word part that contains the core meaning of the word. Many English words contain roots that come from older languages such as Greek, Latin, Old English (Anglo-Saxon), and Norse. Knowing the meaning of the word's root can help you determine the word's meaning.

Root	Meaning	Examples
bi (Greek)	life	biography
gramm (Greek)	letter, something written	grammar
grad (Latin)	step, degree	graduate
man (Latin)	hand	manual
hēadfod (Old English)	head, top	headfirst

2.3 PREFIXES

A **prefix** is a word part attached to the beginning of a word. Most prefixes come from Greek, Latin, or Old English.

Prefix	Meaning	Examples
pre-	before	**pre**school
ex-	out, from	**ex**tend
re-	again, back	**re**turn

2.4 SUFFIXES

A **suffix** is a word part that appears at the end of a root or base word to form a new word. Some suffixes do not change word meaning. These suffixes are

- added to nouns to change the number of persons or objects
- added to verbs to change the tense
- added to modifiers to change the degree of comparison

Suffix	Meaning	Examples
-s, -es	to change the number of a noun	snack + s = snacks
-d, -ed, -ing	to change verb tense	walk + ed = walked
-er, -est	to change the degree of comparison in modifiers	wild + er = wilder fast + est = fastest

Other suffixes can be added to a root or base to change the word's meaning. These suffixes can also determine a word's part of speech.

Suffix	Meaning	Examples
-age	action or process	pilgrimage
-able	ability	enjoyable
-ize	to make	criticize

Strategies for Understanding Unfamiliar Words

- Look for any prefixes or suffixes. Remove them to isolate the base word or the root.
- See if you recognize any elements— prefix, suffix, root, or base—of the word. You may be able to guess its meaning by analyzing one or two elements.
- Consider the way the word is used in the sentence. Use the context and the word parts to make a logical guess about the word's meaning.
- Consult a dictionary to see whether you are correct.

3 Understanding Word Origins

3.1 ETYMOLOGIES

Etymologies show the origin and historical development of a word. When you study a word's history and origin, you can find out when, where, and how the word came to be.

dra·ma (drä′mə) *n.* **1.** A work that is meant to be performed by actors. **2.** Theatrical works of a certain type or period in history. [Late Latin *drāma, drāmat-*, from Greek *drān,* to do or perform.]

for·mi·car·y (fôr′mĭ-kĕr´ē) *n., pl.* **-ies** A nest of ants; an anthill. [Medieval Latin *formīcārium,* from Latin *formīca,* ant.]

lock² (lŏk) *n.* **1a.** A length or curl of hair; a tress. **b.** The hair of the head. Often used in the plural. **2.** A small wisp or tuft, as of wool or cotton. [Middle English *lok* from Old English *loc, locc.*]

3.2 WORD FAMILIES

Words that have the same root make up a word family and have related meanings. The chart shows a common Greek and a common Latin root. Notice how the meanings of the example words are related to the meanings of their roots.

Latin Root	*vid, vis:* "see"
English	**vision** eyesight **video** visual portion of a televised broadcast **visible** possible to see

Greek Root	*phonē:* "sound"
English	**homophone** word that sounds like another word **phonetics** the study of speech sounds **telephone** a device that converts voice into a form that can be transmitted as sound waves

3.3 WORDS FROM CLASSICAL MYTHOLOGY

The English language includes many words from classical mythology. You can use your knowledge of Greek, Roman, and Norse myths to understand the origins and meanings of these words. For example, *herculean task* refers to the strongman Hercules. Thus *herculean task* probably means "a job that is large or difficult." The chart shows a few common words from mythology.

Greek	Roman	Norse
Achilles' heel	cereal	Thursday
aegis	volcano	berserk
muse	cupid	rune
Midas touch	floral	valkyrie

3.4 FOREIGN WORDS

The English language has grown to include words from diverse languages such as French, Dutch, Spanish, Italian, Portuguese, and Chinese. Many of these words stayed the way they were in their original languages.

French	Dutch	Spanish	Italian
ballet	boss	canyon	diva
beret	caboose	rodeo	carnival
mirage	dock	salsa	spaghetti

4 Synonyms and Antonyms

4.1 SYNONYMS

A **synonym** is a word with a meaning similar to that of another word. You can find synonyms in a thesaurus or a dictionary. In a dictionary, synonyms are often given as part of the definition of the word. The following word pairs are synonyms:

happy/joyful   sad/unhappy

angry/mad   beautiful/lovely

4.2 ANTONYMS

An **antonym** is a word with a meaning opposite that of another word. The following word pairs are antonyms:

best/worst   well/ill

light/dark   happy/sad

5 Denotation and Connotation

5.1 DENOTATION

A word's dictionary meaning is called its **denotation.** For example, the denotation of the word *rascal* is "an unethical, dishonest person."

5.2 CONNOTATION

The images or feelings you connect to a word add a finer shade of meaning, called **connotation.** The connotation of a word goes beyond its basic dictionary definition. Writers use connotations of words to communicate positive or negative feelings.

Positive	Neutral	Negative
gaze	look	glare
slender	thin	scrawny
playful	active	rowdy

Make sure you understand the denotation and connotation of a word when you read it or use it in your writing.

6 Analogies

An analogy is a comparison between two things that are similar in some way. Analogies are sometimes used in writing when unfamiliar objects or ideas are described or explained in terms of familiar ones. Analogies often appear on tests as well, usually in a format like this:

bird : fly ::   A) boat : water

B) bear : cave

C) fish : scales

D) fish : swim

E) sparrow : wings

Follow these steps to determine the correct answer:

- Read the first half of the analogy as "*bird* is to *fly* as. . . ."
- Read the answer choices as "*boat* is to *water*," "*bear* is to *cave*," and so on.
- Ask yourself how the words *bird* and *fly* are related. (A bird can fly.)
- Ask yourself which of the choices shows the same relationship. (A boat can't water and a bear can't cave, but a fish can swim. Therefore, the answer is D.)

7 Homonyms and Homophones

7.1 HOMONYMS

Homonyms are words that have the same spelling and sound but have different meanings.

The girl had to stoop to find her ball under the stoop.

Stoop can mean "a small porch," but an identically spelled word means "to bend down." Because the words have different meanings, each word has its own dictionary entry.

The lawyer argued the case of the missing jewelry case.

Case can mean "evidence in support of a claim." However, another identically spelled word means "container." Each word has a different meaning and its own dictionary entry.

Sometimes only one of the meanings of a homonym may be familiar to you. Use context clues to help you figure out the meaning of an unfamiliar word.

7.2 HOMOPHONES

Homophones are words that sound alike but have different meanings and spellings. The following homophones are frequently misused:

it's/its	they're/their/there
to/too/two	stationary/stationery

Many misused homophones are pronouns and contractions. Whenever you are unsure whether to write *your* or *you're* and *who's* or *whose*, ask yourself if you mean *you are* or *who is/has*. If you do, write the contraction. For other homophones, such as *fair* and *fare*, use the meaning of the word to help you decide which one to use.

8 Words with Multiple Meanings

Some words have acquired additional meanings over time that are based on the original meaning.

Thinking of the horror movie made my skin creep. I saw my little brother creep around the corner.

These two uses of *creep* have different meanings, but both of them have the same origin. You will find all the meanings of *creep* listed in one entry in the dictionary.

9 Specialized Vocabulary

Specialized vocabulary is special terms suited to a particular field, or domain, of study or work. For example, science, mathematics, and history all have their own domain-specific technical or specialized vocabularies. To figure out specialized terms, you can use context clues; your knowledge of Latin, Greek, and Old English roots and affixes; and reference sources, such as dictionaries on specific subjects, atlases, or manuals.

10 Using Reference Sources

10.1 DICTIONARIES

A **general dictionary** will tell you not only a word's definitions but also its pronunciation, parts of speech, and history and origin. A **specialized dictionary** focuses on terms related to a particular field of study or work. Use a dictionary to check the spelling of any word you are unsure of in your English class and for other subjects as well.

10.2 THESAURI

A **thesaurus** (plural, thesauri) is a dictionary of synonyms. A thesaurus can be especially helpful when you find yourself using the same modifiers over and over again.

10.3 SYNONYM FINDERS

A **synonym finder** is often included in word processing software. It enables you to highlight a word and be shown a display of its synonyms.

10.4 GLOSSARIES

A **glossary** is a list of specialized terms and their definitions. It is often found in the back of a book and sometimes includes pronunciations. Many textbooks contain glossaries. In fact, this textbook has three glossaries: the **Glossary of Literary and Informational Terms**, the **Glossary of Academic Vocabulary** and the **Glossary of Critical Vocabulary**. Use these glossaries to help you understand how terms are used in this textbook.

11 Spelling Rules

11.1 WORDS ENDING IN A SILENT *E*

Before adding a suffix beginning with a vowel or *y* to a word ending in a silent *e*, drop the *e* (with some exceptions).

amaze + -ing = amazing

love + -able = lovable

create + -ed = created

nerve + -ous = nervous

Exceptions: *change + -able = changeable; courage + -ous = courageous*

When adding a suffix beginning with a consonant to a word ending in a silent *e,* keep the *e* (with some exceptions).

late + -ly = lately

spite + -ful = spiteful

noise + -less = noiseless

state + -ment = statement

Exceptions: *truly, argument, ninth, wholly, awful,* and others.

When a suffix beginning with *a* or *o* is added to a word with a final silent *e,* the final *e* is usually retained if it is preceded by a soft *c* or a soft *g*.

bridge + -able = bridgeable

peace + -able = peaceable

outrage + -ous = outrageous

advantage + -ous = advantageous

When a suffix beginning with a vowel is added to words ending in *ee* or *oe,* the final silent *e* is retained.

agree + -ing = agreeing   free + -ing = freeing

hoe + -ing = hoeing   see + -ing = seeing

11.2 WORDS ENDING IN *Y*

Before adding most suffixes to a word that ends in *y* preceded by a consonant, change the *y* to *i*.

easy + -est = easiest

crazy + -est = craziest

silly + -ness = silliness

marry + -age = marriage

Exceptions: *dryness, shyness,* and *slyness.* However, when you add *-ing,* the *y* does not change.

empty + -ed = emptied but

empty + -ing = emptying

When adding a suffix to a word that ends in *y* preceded by a vowel, the *y* usually does not change.

play + -er = player

employ + -ed = employed

coy + -ness = coyness

pay + -able = payable

11.3 WORDS ENDING IN A CONSONANT

In one-syllable words that end in one consonant preceded by one short vowel, double the final consonant before adding a suffix beginning with a vowel, such as *-ed* or *-ing*. These are sometimes called 1+1+1 words.

dip + -ed = dipped   set + -ing = setting

slim + -est = slimmest   fit + -er = fitter

The rule does not apply to words of one syllable that end in a consonant preceded by two vowels.

feel + -ing = feeling   peel + -ed = peeled

reap + -ed = reaped   loot + -ed = looted

In words of more than one syllable, double the final consonant when (1) the word ends with one consonant preceded by one vowel and (2) the word is accented on the last syllable.

be·gin´   per·mit´   re·fer´

In the following examples, note that in the new words formed with suffixes, the accent remains on the same syllable:

be·gin´ + -ing = be·gin´ning = beginning

per·mit´ + -ed = per·mit´ted = permitted

In some words with more than one syllable, though the accent remains on the same syllable when a suffix is added, the final consonant is nevertheless not doubled, as in the following examples:

tra´vel + er = tra´vel·er = traveler

mar´ket + er = mar´ket·er = marketer

In the following examples, the accent does not remain on the same syllable; thus, the final consonant is not doubled:

re·fer´ + -ence = ref´er·ence = reference
con·fer´ + -ence = con´fer·ence = conference

11.4 PREFIXES AND SUFFIXES

When adding a prefix to a word, do not change the spelling of the base word. When a prefix creates a double letter, keep both letters.

dis- + approve = disapprove
re- + build = rebuild
ir- + regular = irregular
mis- + spell = misspell
anti- + trust = antitrust
il- + logical = illogical

When adding -ly to a word ending in l, keep both l's. When adding -ness to a word ending in n, keep both n's.

careful + -ly = carefully
sudden + -ness = suddenness
final + -ly = finally
thin + -ness = thinness

11.5 FORMING PLURAL NOUNS

To form the plural of most nouns, just add -s.

prizes   dreams   circles   stations

For most singular nouns ending in o, add -s.

solos   halos   studios   photos   pianos

For a few nouns ending in o, add -es.

heroes   tomatoes   potatoes   echoes

When the singular noun ends in s, sh, ch, x, or z, add -es.

waitresses   brushes   ditches
axes   buzzes

When a singular noun ends in y with a consonant before it, change the y to i and add -es.

army—armies   candy—candies
baby—babies   diary—diaries
ferry—ferries   conspiracy—conspiracies

When a vowel (a, e, i, o, u) comes before the y, just add -s.

boy—boys   **way—ways**
array—arrays   **alloy—alloys**
weekday—weekdays   **jockey—jockeys**

For most nouns ending in f or fe, change the f to v and add -es or -s.

life—lives   calf—calves   knife—knives
thief—thieves   shelf—shelves   loaf—loaves

For some nouns ending in f, add -s to make the plural.

roofs   chiefs   reefs   beliefs

Some nouns have the same form for both singular and plural.

deer   sheep   moose   salmon   trout

For some nouns, the plural is formed in a special way.

man—men   **goose—geese**
ox—oxen   **woman—women**
mouse—mice   **child—children**

For a compound noun written as one word, form the plural by changing the last word in the compound to its plural form.

stepchild—stepchildren   firefly—fireflies

If a compound noun is written as a hyphenated word or as two separate words, change the most important word to the plural form.

brother-in-law—brothers-in-law
life jacket—life jackets

11.6 FORMING POSSESSIVES

If a noun is singular, add 's.

mother—my mother's car Ross—Ross's desk

Exception: The s after the apostrophe is dropped after *Jesus', Moses',* and certain names in classical mythology (*Zeus'*). These possessive forms can thus be pronounced easily.

If a noun is plural and ends with s, just add an apostrophe.

parents—my parents' car
the Santinis—the Santinis' house

If a noun is plural but does not end in s, add 's.

people—the people's choice
women—the women's coats

11.7 SPECIAL SPELLING PROBLEMS

Only one English word ends in -*sede*: *supersede*. Three words end in -*ceed*: *exceed*, *proceed*, and *succeed*. All other verbs ending in the sound "seed" (except for the verb *seed*) are spelled with -*cede*.

concede	precede	recede	secede

In words with *ie* or *ei,* when the sound is long *e* (as in *she*), the word is spelled *ie* except after *c* (with some exceptions).

i before *e*	thief	relieve	field
	piece	grieve	pier
except after *c*	conceit	perceive	ceiling
	receive	receipt	
Exceptions:	either	neither	weird
	leisure	seize	

12 Commonly Confused Words

words	definitions	examples
accept/except	The verb *accept* means "to receive or believe"; *except* is usually a preposition meaning "excluding."	**Except** for some of the more extraordinary events, I can **accept** that the *Odyssey* recounts a real journey.
advice/advise	*Advise* is a verb; *advice* is a noun naming that which an *adviser* gives.	I **advise** you to take that job. Whom should I ask for **advice**?
affect/effect	As a verb, *affect* means "to influence." *Effect* as a verb means "to cause." If you want a noun, you will almost always want *effect*.	Did Circe's wine **affect** Odysseus' mind? It did **effect** a change in Odysseus' men. In fact, it had an **effect** on everyone else who drank it.
all ready/already	*All ready* is an adjective meaning "fully ready." *Already* is an adverb meaning "before or by this time."	He was **all ready** to go at noon. I have **already** seen that movie.
allusion/illusion	An *allusion* is an indirect reference to something. An *illusion* is a false picture or idea.	There are many **allusions** to the works of Homer in English literature. The world's apparent flatness is an **illusion**.
among/between	*Between* is used when you are speaking of only two things. *Among* is used for three or more.	**Between** *Hamlet* and *King Lear*, I prefer the latter. Emily Dickinson is **among** my favorite poets.
bring/take	*Bring* is used to denote motion toward a speaker or place. *Take* is used to denote motion away from such a person or place.	**Bring** the books over here, and I will **take** them to the library.

words	definitions	examples
fewer/less	*Fewer* refers to the number of separate, countable units. *Less* refers to bulk quantity.	We have **less** literature and **fewer** selections in this year's curriculum.
leave/let	*Leave* means "to allow something to remain behind." *Let* means "to permit."	The librarian will **leave** some books on display but will not **let** us borrow any.
lie/lay	To *lie* is "to rest or recline." It does not take an object. *Lay* always takes an object.	Rover loves to **lie** in the sun. We always **lay** some bones next to him.
loose/lose	*Loose* (lo͞os) means "free, not restrained"; *lose* (lo͞oz) means "to misplace or fail to find."	Who turned the horses **loose**? I hope we won't **lose** any of them.
precede/proceed	*Precede* means "to go or come before." Use *proceed* for other meanings.	Emily Dickinson's poetry **precedes** that of Alice Walker. You may **proceed** to the next section of the test.
than/then	Use *than* in making comparisons; use *then* on all other occasions.	Who can say whether Amy Lowell is a better poet **than** Denise Levertov? I will read Lowell first, and **then** I will read Levertov.
their/there/they're	*Their* means "belonging to them." *There* means "in that place." *They're* is the contraction for "they are."	**There** is a movie playing at 9 p.m. **They're** going to see it with me. Sakara and Erin drove away in **their** car after the movie.
two/too/to	*Two* is the number. *Too* is an adverb meaning "also" or "very." Use *to* before a verb or as a preposition.	Meg had **to** go **to** town, **too**. We had **too** much reading **to** do. **Two** chapters is **too** many.

Glossary of Literary and Informational Terms

Act An act is a major division within a play, similar to a chapter in a book. Each act may be further divided into smaller sections, called scenes. Plays can have as many as five acts, or as few as one.

Allegory An allegory is a work with two levels of meaning—a literal one and a symbolic one. In such a work, most of the characters, objects, settings, and events represent abstract qualities. Personification is often used in traditional allegories. As in a fable or a parable, the purpose of an allegory may be to convey truths about life, to teach religious or moral lessons, or to criticize social institutions.

Alliteration Alliteration is the repetition of consonant sounds at the beginning of words. Note the repetition of the *d* sound in these lines: The dare devil dove into the deep sea.

See also Consonance.

Allusion An allusion is an indirect reference to a famous person, place, event, or literary work.

Almanac *See* Reference Works.

Analogy An analogy is a point-by-point comparison between two things that are alike in some respect. Often, writers use analogies in nonfiction to explain unfamiliar subjects or ideas in terms of familiar ones.

See also Extended Metaphor; Metaphor; Simile.

Antagonist An antagonist is a principal character or force in opposition to a **protagonist,** or main character. The antagonist is usually another character but sometimes can be a force of nature, a set of circumstances, some aspect of society, or a force within the protagonist.

Archetype An archetype is a pattern in literature that is found in a variety of works from different cultures throughout the ages. An archetype can be a plot, a character, an image, or a setting. For example, the association of death and rebirth with winter and spring is an archetype common to many cultures.

Argument An argument is speech or writing that presents a claim about an issue or problem and supports it with reasons and evidence. An argument often takes into account other points of view, anticipating and answering objections that opponents of the position might raise.

See also Claim; Counterargument; Evidence.

Argumentative Essay *See* Essay.

Aside In drama, an aside is a short speech directed to the audience, or another character, that is not heard by the other characters on stage.

See also Soliloquy.

Assonance Assonance is the repetition of vowel sounds within nonrhyming words. An example of assonance is the repetition of the *u* sound in the following line: I made my usual maneuver on my snowboard.

Assumption An assumption is an opinion or belief that is taken for granted. It can be about a specific situation, a person, or the world in general. Assumptions are often unstated.

Author's Message An author's message is the main idea or theme of a particular work.

See also Main Idea; Theme.

Author's Perspective An author's perspective, or point of view, is a unique combination of ideas, values, feelings, and beliefs that influences the way the writer looks at a topic. **Tone,** or attitude, often reveals an author's perspective.

See also Author's Purpose; Tone.

Author's Position An author's position is his or her opinion on an issue or topic.

See also Claim.

Author's Purpose A writer usually writes for one or more of these purposes: to express thoughts or feelings, to inform or explain, to persuade, to entertain.

See also Author's Perspective.

Autobiography An autobiography is a writer's account of his or her own life. In almost every case, it is told from the first-person point of view. Generally, an autobiography focuses on the most significant events and people in the writer's life over a period of time. Shorter autobiographical narratives include **journals, diaries,** and **letters.** An **autobiographical essay,** another type of short autobiographical work, focuses on a single person or event in the writer's life.

See also Memoir.

Ballad   A ballad is a type of narrative poem that tells a story and was originally meant to be sung or recited. Because it tells a story, a ballad has a setting, a plot, and characters. **Traditional ballads** are written in four-line stanzas with regular rhythm and rhyme. **Folk ballads** were composed orally and handed down by word of mouth. These ballads usually tell about ordinary people who have unusual adventures or perform daring deeds. A **literary ballad** is a poem written by a poet in imitation of the form and content of a folk ballad.

Bias   Bias is an inclination toward a particular judgment on a topic or issue. A writer often reveals a strongly positive or strongly negative opinion by presenting only one way of looking at an issue or by heavily weighting the evidence. Words with intensely positive or negative connotations are often a signal of a writer's bias.

Bibliography   A bibliography is a list of books and other materials related to the topic of a text. Bibliographies can be good sources of works for further study on a subject.

See also Works Consulted.

Biography   A biography is the true account of a person's life, written by another person. As such, a biography is usually told from a third-person point of view. The writer of a biography usually researches his or her subject in order to present accurate information. The best biographers strive for honesty and balance in their accounts of their subjects' lives.

Blank Verse   Blank verse is unrhymed poetry written in **iambic pentameter.** That is, each line of blank verse has five pairs of syllables. In most pairs, an unstressed syllable is followed by a stressed syllable. The most versatile of poetic forms, blank verse imitates the natural rhythms of English speech. Much of Shakespeare's drama is in blank verse.

See also Iambic Pentameter.

Business Correspondence   Business correspondence includes all written business communications, such as business letters, e-mails, and memos. In general, business correspondence is brief, to the point, clear, courteous, and professional.

Cast of Characters   In the script of a play, a cast of characters is a list of all the characters in the play, usually in order of appearance. It may include a brief description of each character.

Cause and Effect   A **cause** is an event or action that directly results in another event or action. An **effect** is the direct or logical outcome of an event or action. Basic **cause-and-effect relationships** include a single cause with a single effect, one cause with multiple effects, multiple causes with a single effect, and a chain of causes and effects. The concept of cause and effect also provides a way of organizing a piece of writing. It helps a writer show the relationships between events or ideas.

Central Idea   *See* Main Idea; Theme.

Character   Characters are the individuals who participate in the action of a literary work. Like real people, characters display certain qualities, or **character traits;** they develop and change over time; and they usually have **motivations,** or reasons, for their behaviors. Complex characters can have multiple or conflicting motivations.

> **Main characters:** Main characters are the most important characters in literary works. Generally, the plot of a short story focuses on one main character, but a novel may have several main characters.
>
> **Minor characters:** The less prominent characters in a literary work are known as minor characters. Minor characters support the plot. The story is not centered on them, but they help carry out the action of the story and help the reader learn more about the main character.
>
> **Dynamic character:** A dynamic character is one who undergoes important changes as a plot unfolds. The changes occur because of his or her actions and experiences in the story. The change is usually internal and may be good or bad. Main characters are usually, though not always, dynamic.

Static character: A static character is one who remains the same throughout a story. The character may experience events and have interactions with other characters, but he or she is not changed because of them.

Round character: A round character is one who is complex and highly developed, having a variety of traits and different sides to his or her personality. Some of the traits may create conflict in the character. Round characters tend to display strengths, weaknesses, and a full range of emotions. The writer provides enough detail for the reader to understand their feelings and emotions.

Flat character: A flat character is one who is not highly developed. A flat character is one-sided: he or she usually has one outstanding trait, characteristic, or role. Flat characters exist mainly to advance the plot, and they display only the traits needed for their limited roles. Minor characters are usually flat characters.

See also Characterization.

Characterization The way a writer creates and develops characters' personalities is known as characterization. There are four basic methods of characterization:

- The writer may make direct comments about a character's personality or nature through the voice of the narrator.
- The writer may describe the character's physical appearance.
- The writer may present the character's own thoughts, speech, and actions.
- The writer may present thoughts, speech, and actions of other characters in response to a character.

See also Character.

Chorus In early Greek tragedy, the chorus commented on the actions of the characters in a drama. In some Elizabethan plays, such as Shakespeare's *Romeo and Juliet,* the role of the chorus is taken by a single actor who serves as a narrator and speaks the lines in the **prologue** (and sometimes in an **epilogue**). The chorus serves to foreshadow or summarize events.

Chronological Order Chronological order is the arrangement of events in their order of occurrence. This type of organization is used in both fictional narratives and in historical writing, biography, and autobiography.

Claim In an argument, a claim is the writer's position on an issue or problem. Although an argument focuses on supporting one claim, a writer may make more than one claim in a work.
See also Argument; Thesis Statement.

Clarify Clarifying is a reading strategy that helps a reader to understand or make clear what he or she is reading. Readers usually clarify by rereading, reading aloud, or discussing.

Classification Classification is a pattern of organization in which objects, ideas, or information is presented in groups, or classes, based on common characteristics.

Cliché A cliché is an overused expression. "Better late than never" and "hard as nails" are common examples. Good writers generally avoid clichés unless they are using them in dialogue to indicate something about characters' personalities.

Climax In a plot, the climax is the point of maximum interest or tension. Usually the climax is a turning point in the story, which occurs after the reader has understood the **conflict** and become emotionally involved with the characters. The climax sometimes, but not always, points to the **resolution** of the conflict.
See also Plot.

Comedy A comedy is a dramatic work that is light and often humorous in tone, usually ending happily with a peaceful resolution of the main conflict. A comedy differs from a farce by having a more believable plot, more realistic characters, and less boisterous behavior.

Comic Relief Comic relief consists of humorous scenes, incidents, or speeches that are included in a serious drama to provide a reduction in emotional intensity. Because comic relief breaks the tension, it allows an audience to prepare emotionally for events to come. Shakespeare often uses this device in his tragedies.

Compare and Contrast To compare and contrast is to identify similarities and differences in two or more subjects. Compare-and-contrast organization can be used to structure a piece of writing, serving as a framework for analyzing the similarities and differences in two or more subjects.

Complex Character *See* Character.

Complication A complication is an additional factor or problem introduced into the rising action of a story to make the conflict more difficult. Often, a plot complication makes it seem as though the main character is getting farther away from the thing he or she wants.

Conclusion A conclusion is a statement of belief based on evidence, experience, and reasoning. A **valid conclusion** is a conclusion that logically follows from the facts or statements upon which it is based. A **deductive conclusion** is one that follows from a particular generalization or premise. An **inductive conclusion** is a broad conclusion or generalization that is reached by arguing from specific facts and examples.

Conflict A conflict is a struggle between opposing forces. Almost every story has a main conflict—a conflict that is the story's focus. An **external conflict** involves a character pitted against an outside force, such as nature, a physical obstacle, or another character. An **internal conflict** is one that occurs within a character.

See also Plot.

Connect Connecting is a reader's process of relating the content of a text to his or her own knowledge and experience.

Connotation A connotation is an attitude or a feeling associated with a word, in contrast to the word's **denotation,** which is its literal, or dictionary, meaning. The connotations of a word may be positive or negative. For example, *enthusiastic* has positive associations, while *rowdy* has negative ones. Connotations of words can have an important influence on style and meaning and are particularly important in poetry.

Consonance Consonance is the repetition of consonant sounds within and at the end of words, as in "lonely afternoon." Consonance is unlike rhyme in that the vowel sounds preceding or following the repeated consonant sounds differ. Consonance is often used together with **alliteration, assonance,** and **rhyme** to create a musical quality, to emphasize certain words, or to unify a poem.

See also Alliteration.

Consumer Documents Consumer documents are printed materials that accompany products and services. They are intended for the buyers or users of the products or services and usually provide information about use, care, operation, or assembly. Some common consumer documents are applications, contracts, warranties, manuals, instructions, package inserts, labels, brochures, and schedules.

Context Clues When you encounter an unfamiliar word, you can often use context clues as aids for understanding. Context clues are the words and phrases surrounding the word that provide hints about the word's meaning.

Controlling Idea *See* Main Idea.

Counterargument A counterargument is an argument made to answer an opposing argument, or **counterclaim.** A good argument anticipates opposing viewpoints and provides counterarguments to refute (disprove) or answer them.

Counterclaim *See* Counterargument.

Couplet A couplet is a rhymed pair of lines. A couplet may be written in any rhythmic pattern, for example:

> Follow your heart's desire
> And good things may transpire.

See also Stanza.

Credibility Credibility refers to the believability or trustworthiness of a source and the information it contains.

Critical Essay *See* Essay.

Critical Review A critical review is an evaluation or critique by a reviewer or critic. Different types of reviews include film reviews, book reviews, music reviews, and art show reviews.

Critique *See* Critical Review.

Database A database is a collection of information that can be quickly and easily accessed and searched and from which information can be easily retrieved. It is frequently presented in an electronic format.

Debate A debate is basically an argument—but a very structured one that requires a good deal of preparation. In academic settings, debate usually refers to a formal argumentation contest in which two opposing teams defend and attack a proposition.

See also Argument.

Deductive Reasoning Deductive reasoning is a way of thinking that begins with a generalization, presents a specific situation, and then advances with facts and evidence to a logical conclusion. The following passage has a deductive argument embedded in it: "All students in the drama class must attend the play on Thursday. Since Ava is in the class, she had better show up." This deductive argument can be broken down as follows: generalization—all students in the drama class must attend the play on Thursday; specific situation—Ava is a student in the drama class; conclusion—Ava must attend the play.

Denotation *See* Connotation.

Dénouement *See* Falling Action.

Dialect A dialect is a form of language that is spoken in a particular geographic area or by a particular social or ethnic group. A group's dialect is reflected in its pronunciations, vocabulary, expressions, and grammatical structures. Writers use dialects to capture the flavors of locales and to bring characters to life, re-creating the way they actually speak.

Dialogue Dialogue is written conversation between two or more characters. Writers use dialogue to bring characters to life and to give readers insights into the characters' qualities, traits, and reactions to other characters. Realistic, well-paced dialogue also advances the plot of a narrative. In fiction, dialogue is usually set off with quotation marks. In drama, stories are told primarily through dialogue. Playwrights use stage directions to indicate how they intend the dialogue to be interpreted by actors.

Diary A diary is a daily record of a writer's thoughts, experiences, and feelings. As such, it is a type of autobiographical writing. The terms *diary* and *journal* are often used synonymously.

Diction A writer's or speaker's choice of words and way of arranging the words in sentences is called diction. Diction can be broadly characterized as formal or informal. It can also be described as technical or common, abstract or concrete, and literal or figurative. A writer for a science journal would use a more formal, more technical, and possibly more abstract diction than would a writer for the science section of a local newspaper.

See also Style.

Dictionary *See* Reference Works.

Drama Drama is literature in which plots and characters are developed through dialogue and action; in other words, it is literature in play form. Drama is meant to be performed. Stage plays, radio plays, movies, and television programs are types of drama. Most plays are divided into acts, with each act having an emotional peak, or climax. Certain modern plays have only one act. Most plays contain stage directions, which describe settings, lighting, sound effects, the movements and emotions of actors, and the ways in which dialogue should be spoken.

Dramatic Irony *See* Irony.

Dramatic Monologue A dramatic monologue is a lyric poem in which a speaker addresses a silent or absent listener in a moment of high intensity or deep emotion, as if engaged in private conversation. The speaker proceeds without interruption or argument, and the effect on the reader is that of hearing just one side of a conversation. This technique allows the poet to focus on the feelings, personality, and motivations of the speaker.

See also Lyric Poetry; Soliloquy.

Draw Conclusions To draw a conclusion is to make a judgment or arrive at a belief based on evidence, experience, and reasoning.

Dynamic Character *See* Character.

Editorial An editorial is an opinion piece that usually appears on the editorial page of a newspaper or as part of a news broadcast. The editorial section of a newspaper presents opinions rather than objective news reports.

See also Op-Ed Piece.

Either/Or Fallacy An either/or fallacy is a statement that suggests that there are only two possible ways to view a situation or only two options to choose from. In other words, it is a statement that falsely frames a dilemma, giving the impression that no options exist but the two presented —for example, "Either we stop the construction of a new airport, or the surrounding suburbs will become ghost towns."

Elegy An elegy is an extended meditative poem in which the speaker reflects on death— often in tribute to a person who has died recently—or on an equally serious subject. Most elegies are written in formal, dignified language and are serious in tone.

Emotional Appeals Emotional appeals are messages that evoke strong feelings—such as fear, pity, or vanity—in order to persuade instead of using facts and evidence to make a point. An **appeal to fear** is a message that taps into people's fear of losing their safety or security. An **appeal to pity** is a message that taps into people's sympathy and compassion for others to build support for an idea, a cause, or a proposed action. An **appeal to vanity** is a message that attempts to persuade by tapping into people's desire to feel good about themselves.

Encyclopedia *See* Reference Works.

Epic An epic is a long narrative poem on a serious subject, presented in an elevated or formal style. It traces the adventures of a great hero whose actions reflect the ideals and values of a nation or race. Epics address universal concerns, such as good and evil, life and death, and sin and redemption. The *Odyssey* is an epic.

Epic Hero An epic hero is a larger-than-life figure who embodies the ideals of a nation or race. Epic heroes take part in dangerous adventures and accomplish great deeds. Many

undertake long, difficult journeys and display great courage and superhuman strength.

Epic Simile An epic simile (also called a Homeric simile) is a long, elaborate comparison that often continues for a number of lines. Homer uses epic similes in the *Odyssey.*

See also Simile.

Epilogue An epilogue is a short addition at the end of a literary work, often dealing with the future of the characters. The concluding speech by Prince Escalus in *Romeo and Juliet* serves as an epilogue.

Epithet An epithet is a brief phrase that points out traits associated with a particular person or thing. In the *Odyssey,* Odysseus is often called "the master strategist."

Essay An essay is a short work of nonfiction that deals with a single subject. Some essays are **formal**—that is, tightly structured and written in an impersonal style. Others are **informal,** with a looser structure and a more personal style. Generally, an **informative** or **expository essay** presents or explains information and ideas. A **personal essay** is typically an informal essay in which the writer expresses his or her thoughts and feelings about a subject, focusing on the meaning of events and issues in his or her own life. In a **reflective essay,** the author makes a connection between a personal observation or experience and a universal idea, such as love, courage, or freedom. A **critical essay** evaluates a situation, a course of action, or a work of art. In an **argumentative** or **persuasive essay,** the author attempts to convince readers to adopt a certain viewpoint or to take a particular stand.

Evaluate To evaluate is to examine something carefully and judge its value or worth. Evaluating is an important skill for gaining insight into what you read. A reader can evaluate the actions of a particular character, for example, or can form an opinion about the value of an entire work.

Evidence Evidence is the specific pieces of information that support a claim. Evidence can take the form of facts, quotations, examples, statistics, or personal experiences, among others.

Exposition Exposition is the first stage of a plot in a typical story. The exposition provides important background information and introduces the setting and the important characters. The conflict the characters face may also be introduced in the exposition, or it may be introduced later, in the rising action.

See also Plot.

Expository Essay *See* Essay.

Extended Metaphor An extended metaphor is a figure of speech that compares two essentially unlike things at some length and in several ways. It does not contain the words *like* or *as*.

See also Metaphor.

External Conflict *See* Conflict.

Fable A fable is a brief tale told to illustrate a moral or teach a lesson. Often the moral of a fable appears in a distinct and memorable statement near the tale's beginning or end.

See also Moral.

Fact versus Opinion A fact is a statement that can be proved or verified. An opinion, on the other hand, is a statement that cannot be proved because it expresses a person's beliefs, feelings, or thoughts.

See also Inference; Generalization.

Fallacy A fallacy is an error in reasoning. Typically, a fallacy is based on an incorrect inference or a misuse of evidence. Some common logical fallacies are **circular reasoning, either/or fallacy, oversimplification, overgeneralization,** and **stereotyping.**

See also Either/Or Fallacy, Logical Appeal, Overgeneralization.

Falling Action In a plot, the falling action follows the climax and shows the results of the important action that happened at the climax. Tension eases as the falling action begins; however, the final outcome of the story is not yet fully worked out at this stage. Events in the falling action lead to the **resolution,** or **dénouement,** of the plot.

See also Climax; Plot.

Fantasy Fantasy is a type of fiction that is highly imaginative and portrays events, settings, or characters that are unrealistic. The setting might be a nonexistent world, the plot might involve magic or the supernatural, and the characters might employ superhuman powers.

Farce Farce is a type of exaggerated comedy that features an absurd plot, ridiculous situations, and humorous dialogue. The main purpose of a farce is to keep an audience laughing. The characters are usually stereotypes, or simplified examples of individual traits or qualities. Comic devices typically used in farces include mistaken identity, deception, physical comedy, wordplay—such as puns and double meanings—and exaggeration.

Faulty Reasoning *See* Fallacy.

Feature Article A feature article is a main article in a newspaper or a cover story in a magazine. A feature article is focused more on entertaining than informing. Features are lighter or more general than hard news and tend to be about human interest or lifestyles.

Fiction Fiction is prose writing that consists of imaginary elements. Although fiction can be inspired by actual events and real people, it usually springs from writers' imaginations. The basic elements of fiction are plot, character, setting, and theme. The novel and short story are forms of fiction.

See also Character; Novel; Plot; Setting; Short Story; Theme.

Figurative Language Figurative language is language that communicates meanings beyond the literal meanings of words. In figurative language, words are often used to symbolize ideas and concepts they would not otherwise be associated with. Writers use figurative language to create effects, to emphasize ideas, and to evoke emotions. Simile, metaphor, extended metaphor, hyperbole, and personification are examples of figurative language.

See also Hyperbole; Metaphor; Personification; Simile.

Figure of Speech *See* Figurative Language; Hyperbole; Metaphor; Personification; Simile; Understatement.

First-Person Point of View *See* Point of View.

Flashback A flashback is an account of a conversation, an episode, or an event that happened before the beginning of a story. Often, a flashback interrupts the chronological flow of a story to give the reader information needed to understand a character's present situation. Flashbacks also help create such effects as mystery, tension, or surprise.

Foil A foil is a character who provides a striking contrast to another character. By using a foil, a writer can call attention to certain traits possessed by a main character or simply enhance a character by contrast. In Shakespeare's *Romeo and Juliet,* Mercutio serves as a foil to Romeo.

Foreshadowing Foreshadowing is a writer's use of hints or clues to suggest events that will occur later in a story. The hints and clues might be included in a character's dialogue or behavior, or they might be included in details of description. Foreshadowing creates suspense, mystery, and surprise, and makes readers eager to find out what will happen.

Form Form refers to the principles of arrangement in a poem—the ways in which lines are organized. Form in poetry includes the following elements: the length of lines, the placement of lines, and the grouping of lines into stanzas.

See also Stanza.

Frame Story A frame story exists when a story is told within a narrative setting, or "frame"; it creates a story within a story. This storytelling technique has been used for over one thousand years and was employed in famous works such as *One Thousand and One Arabian Nights* and Geoffrey Chaucer's *The Canterbury Tales.*

Free Verse Free verse is poetry that does not contain regular patterns of rhythm or rhyme. The lines in free verse often flow more naturally than do rhymed, metrical lines and thus achieve a rhythm more like that of everyday speech.

Although free verse lacks conventional meter, it may contain various rhythmic and sound effects, such as repetitions of syllables or words. Free verse can be used for a variety of subjects.

See also Meter; Rhyme.

Functional Documents *See* Consumer Documents; Public Documents; Workplace Documents.

Generalization A generalization is a broad statement about a class or category of people, ideas, or things, based on a study of only some of its members.

See also Overgeneralization.

Genre The term *genre* refers to a category in which a work of literature is classified. The major genres in literature are fiction, nonfiction, poetry, and drama.

Government Publications Government publications are documents produced by government organizations. Pamphlets, brochures, and reports are just some of the many forms these publications may take. Government publications can be reliable resources for a wide variety of topics.

Graphic Aid A graphic aid is a visual tool that is printed, handwritten, or drawn. Charts, diagrams, graphs, photographs, and maps can all be graphic aids.

Graphic Organizer A graphic organizer is a "word picture"—that is, a visual illustration of a verbal statement—that helps a reader understand a text. Charts, tables, webs, and diagrams can all be graphic organizers. Graphic organizers and graphic aids can look the same. For example, a table in a science article will not be constructed differently from a table that is a graphic organizer. However, graphic organizers and graphic aids do differ in how they are used. Graphic aids are the visual representations that people encounter when they read informational texts. Graphic organizers are visuals that people construct to help them understand texts or organize information.

Haiku Haiku is a form of Japanese poetry in which 17 syllables are arranged in three lines of 5, 7, and 5 syllables each. The rules of haiku are strict. In addition to the syllabic count, the poet must create a clear picture that will evoke a strong emotional response in the reader. Nature is a particularly important source of inspiration for Japanese haiku poets, and details from nature are often the subjects of their poems.

Hero A hero is a main character or protagonist in a story. In older literary works, heroes tend to be better than ordinary humans. They are typically courageous, strong, honorable, and intelligent. They are protectors of society who hold back the forces of evil and fight to make the world a better place. In modern literature, a hero may simply be the most important character in a story. Such a hero is often an ordinary person with ordinary problems.

Historical Documents Historical documents are writings that have played a significant role in human events or are themselves records of such events. The Declaration of Independence, for example, is a historical document.

Historical Fiction A short story or novel can be classified as historical fiction when the settings and details of the plot include real places and real events of historical importance. Historical figures may appear as major or minor characters. In historical fiction, the setting generally influences the plot in important ways.

Horror Fiction Horror fiction contains strange, mysterious, violent, and often supernatural events that create suspense and terror in the reader. Edgar Allan Poe and Stephen King are famous authors of horror fiction.

How-To Writing A how-to book or article explains how to do something—usually an activity, a sport, or a household project.

Humor In literature, there are three basic types of humor, all of which may involve exaggeration or irony. **Humor of situation** arises out of the plot of a work. It usually involves exaggerated events or **situational irony,** which arises when something happens that is different from what was expected. **Humor of character** is often based on exaggerated personalities or on characters' failure to recognize their own flaws, a form of dramatic irony. **Humor of language** may include sarcasm, exaggeration, puns, or verbal irony, in which what is said is not what is meant.

See also Irony.

Hyperbole Hyperbole is a figure of speech in which the truth is exaggerated for emphasis or humorous effect.

Iambic Pentameter Iambic pentameter is a metrical pattern of five feet, or units, each of which is made up of two syllables, the first unstressed and the second stressed. Iambic pentameter is the most common meter used in English poetry; it is the meter used in blank verse and in the sonnet. Shakespeare used iambic pentameter in his plays.

See also Blank Verse; Sonnet.

Idiom An idiom is a common figure of speech whose meaning is different from the literal meaning of its words. For example, the phrase "raining cats and dogs" does not literally mean that cats and dogs are falling from the sky; the expression means "raining heavily."

Imagery Imagery consists of descriptive words and phrases that re-create sensory experiences for the reader. Imagery usually appeals to one or more of the five senses— sight, hearing, smell, taste, and touch—to help the reader imagine exactly what is being described.

Implied Controlling Idea An implied controlling idea is one that is suggested by details rather than stated explicitly.

See also Main Idea.

Implied Main Idea *See* Main Idea.

Index The index of a book is an alphabetized list of important topics and details covered in the book and the page numbers on which they can be found. An index can be used to quickly find specific information about a topic.

Inductive Reasoning Inductive reasoning is the process of logically reasoning from specific observations, examples, and facts to arrive at a general conclusion or principle.

Inference An inference is a logical assumption that is based on observed facts and one's own knowledge and experience.

Informational Nonfiction Informational nonfiction is writing that provides factual information. It often explains ideas or teaches processes. Examples include news reports, science textbooks, software instructions, and lab reports.

Informative Essay *See* Essay.

Internal Conflict *See* Conflict.

Internet The Internet is a global, interconnected system of computer networks that allows for communication through e-mail, listserves, and the World Wide Web. The Internet connects computers and computer users throughout the world.

Interview An interview is a conversation conducted by a writer or reporter, in which facts or statements are elicited from another person, recorded, and then broadcast or published.

Irony Irony is a special kind of contrast between appearance and reality—usually one in which reality is the opposite of what it seems. One type of irony is **situational irony,** a contrast between what a reader or character expects and what actually exists or happens. Another type of irony is **dramatic irony,** in which the reader or viewer knows something that a character does not know. **Verbal irony** exists when someone knowingly exaggerates or says one thing and means another.

Journal A journal is a periodical publication issued by a legal, medical, or other professional organization. Alternatively, the term may be used to refer to a diary or daily record.
See also Diary.

Legend A legend is a story handed down from the past, especially one that is popularly believed to be based on historical events. Though legends often incorporate supernatural or magical elements, they claim to be the story of a real human being and are often set in a particular time and place. These characteristics separate a legend from a myth.
See also Myth.

Limited Point of View *See* Point of View.

Line The line is the core unit of a poem. In poetry, line length is an essential element of the poem's meaning and rhythm. **Line breaks,** where a line of poetry ends, may coincide with grammatical units. However, a line break may also occur in the middle of a grammatical or syntactical unit, creating a meaningful pause or emphasis. Poets use a variety of line breaks to manipulate sense, grammar, and syntax and thereby create a wide range of effects.

Literary Criticism *See* Text Criticism.

Literary Nonfiction Literary nonfiction is nonfiction that is recognized as being of artistic value or that is about literature. Autobiographies, biographies, essays, and eloquent speeches typically fall into this category.

Loaded Language Loaded language consists of words with strongly positive or negative connotations intended to influence a reader's or listener's attitude.

Logical Appeal A logical appeal relies on logic and facts, appealing to people's reasoning or intellect rather than to their values or emotions. Flawed logical appeals—that is, errors in reasoning—are considered logical fallacies.
See also Fallacy.

Logical Argument A logical argument is an argument in which the logical relationship between the support and the claim is sound.

Lyric Poetry A lyric poem is a short poem in which a single speaker expresses personal thoughts and feelings. Most poems other than dramatic and narrative poems are lyric poems. In ancient Greece, lyric poetry was meant to be sung. Modern lyrics are usually not intended for singing, but they are characterized by strong melodic rhythms. Lyric poetry has a variety of forms and covers many subjects, from love and death to everyday experiences.

Magical Realism Magical realism is a literary genre that combines fantastic or magical events with realistic occurrences in a matter-of-fact way to delight or surprise the reader. A famous example of magical realism is Gabriel García Márquez's novel *One Hundred Years of Solitude.*

Main Idea A main idea, or controlling idea, is the most important idea or impression about a topic that a writer or speaker conveys. It can be the central idea of an entire work or of just a paragraph. Often, the main idea of a paragraph is expressed in a topic sentence. However, a main idea may just be implied, or suggested, by details. A main idea and supporting details can serve as a basic pattern of organization in a piece of writing, with the central idea about a topic being supported by details.

Make Inferences *See* Inference.

Memoir A memoir is a form of autobiographical writing in which a writer shares his or her personal experiences and observations of significant events or people. Often informal or even intimate in tone, memoirs usually give readers insight into the impact of historical events on people's lives.

See also Autobiography.

Metaphor A metaphor is a figure of speech that makes a comparison between two things that are basically unlike but have something in common. Unlike similes, metaphors do not contain the word *like* or *as*.

See also Extended Metaphor; Figurative Language; Simile.

Meter Meter is a regular pattern of stressed and unstressed syllables in a poem. The meter of a poem emphasizes the musical quality of the language. Each unit of meter, known as a **foot,** consists of one stressed syllable and one or two unstressed syllables. In representations of meter, a stressed syllable is indicated by the symbol ´; an unstressed syllable, by the symbol ˘. The four basic types of metrical feet are the **iamb,** an unstressed syllable followed by a stressed syllable (˘ ´); the **trochee,** a stressed syllable followed by an unstressed syllable (´ ˘); the **anapest,** two unstressed syllables followed by a stressed syllable (˘ ˘ ´); and the **dactyl,** a stressed syllable followed by two unstressed syllables (´ ˘ ˘).

See also Rhythm.

Mise en Scène *Mise en scène* is a term from the French that refers to the various physical aspects of a dramatic presentation, such as lighting, costumes, scenery, makeup, and props.

Monitor Monitoring is the strategy of checking your comprehension as you are reading and modifying the strategies you are using to suit your needs. Monitoring may include some or all of the following strategies: questioning,

clarifying, visualizing, predicting, connecting, and rereading.

Mood In a literary work, mood is the feeling or atmosphere that a writer creates for the reader. Descriptive words, imagery, and figurative language contribute to the mood of a work, as do the sound and rhythm of the language used.

See also Tone.

Moral A moral is a lesson taught in a literary work, such as a fable. For example, the moral "Do not count your chickens before they are hatched" teaches that one should not count on one's fortunes or blessings until they appear.

See also Fable.

Motivation *See* Character.

Myth A myth is a traditional story, usually concerning some superhuman being or unlikely event, that was once widely believed to be true. Frequently, myths were attempts to explain natural phenomena, such as solar and lunar eclipses or the cycle of the seasons. For some peoples, myths were both a kind of science and a religion. In addition, myths served as literature and entertainment, just as they do for modern-day audiences.

Greek mythology forms much of the background in Homer's *Odyssey*. For example, the myth of the judgment of Paris describes events that led to the Trojan War. The goddesses Athena, Hera, and Aphrodite asked a mortal— Paris—to decide which of them was the most beautiful. Paris chose Aphrodite and was rewarded by her with Helen, wife of the Greek king Menelaus.

Narrative Nonfiction Narrative nonfiction is writing that reads much like fiction, except that the characters, setting, and plot are real rather than imaginary. Its purpose is usually to entertain or to express opinions or feelings. Narrative nonfiction includes, but is not limited to, autobiographies, biographies, memoirs, diaries, and journals.

Narrative Poetry Narrative poetry tells a story or recounts events. Like a short story or a novel, a narrative poem has the following elements: plot, characters, setting, and theme.

Narrator The narrator of a story is the character or voice that relates the story's events to the reader.

See also Persona; Point of View.

News Article A news article is a piece of writing that reports on a recent event. In newspapers, news articles are usually written concisely and report the latest news, presenting the most important facts first and then more detailed information. In magazines, news articles are usually more elaborate than those in newspapers because they are written to provide both information and analysis. Also, news articles in magazines do not necessarily present the most important facts first.

Nonfiction Nonfiction is writing that tells about real people, places, and events. Unlike fiction, nonfiction is mainly written to convey factual information, although writers of nonfiction shape information in accordance with their own purposes and attitudes. Nonfiction can be a good source of information, but readers frequently have to examine it carefully in order to detect biases, notice gaps in the information provided, and identify errors in logic. Nonfiction includes a diverse range of writing—newspaper articles, letters, essays, biographies, movie reviews, speeches, true-life adventure stories, advertising, and more.

Novel A novel is an extended work of fiction. Like a short story, a novel is essentially the product of a writer's imagination. Because a novel is considerably longer than a short story, a novelist can develop a wider range of characters and a more complex plot.

Novella A novella is a work of fiction that is longer than a short story but shorter than a novel. A novella differs from a novel in that it concentrates on a limited cast of characters, a relatively short time span, and a single chain of events. The novella is an attempt to combine the compression of the short story with the development of the novel.

Ode An ode is a complex lyric poem that develops a serious and dignified theme. Odes appeal to both the imagination and the intellect, and many commemorate events or praise people or elements of nature.

Omniscient Point of View *See* Point of View.

Onomatopoeia Onomatopoeia is the use of words whose sounds echo their meanings, such as *buzz, whisper, gargle,* and *murmur.* Onomatopoeia as a literary technique goes beyond the use of simple echoic words, however. Skilled writers, especially poets, choose words whose sounds intensify images and suggest meanings.

Op-Ed Piece An op-ed piece is an opinion piece that usually appears opposite ("op") the editorial page of a newspaper. Unlike editorials, op-ed pieces are written and submitted by named writers.

Organization *See* Pattern of Organization.

Overgeneralization An overgeneralization is a generalization that is too broad. You can often recognize overgeneralizations by the appearance of words and phrases such as *all, everyone, every time, any, anything, no one,* and *none.* Consider, for example, this statement: "None of the sanitation workers in our city really care about keeping the environment clean." In all probability, there are many exceptions; the writer can't possibly know the feelings of every sanitation worker in the city.

Overview An overview is a short summary of a story, a speech, or an essay. It orients the reader by providing a preview of the text to come.

Oxymoron An oxymoron is a special kind of concise paradox that brings together two contradictory terms. "Deafening silence" and "original copy" are examples of oxymorons.

Paradox A paradox is a seemingly contradictory or absurd statement that may nonetheless suggest an important truth.

Parallelism Parallelism is the use of similar grammatical constructions to express ideas that are related or equal in importance. Martin Luther King Jr. uses parallelism in his "I Have a Dream" speech.

Parallel Plot A parallel plot is a particular type of plot in which two stories of equal importance are told simultaneously. The story moves back and forth between the two plots.

Paraphrase Paraphrasing is the restating of information in one's own words.

See also Summarize.

Parody A parody is an imitation of another work, a type of literature, or a writer's style, usually for the purpose of poking fun. It may serve as an element of a larger work or be a complete work in itself. The purpose of parody may be to ridicule through broad humor, deploying such techniques as exaggeration or the use of inappropriate subject matter. Such techniques may even provide insights into the original work.

Pastoral A pastoral is a poem presenting shepherds in rural settings, usually in an idealized manner. The language and form of a pastoral tends to be formal. English Renaissance poets were drawn to the pastoral as a means of conveying their own emotions and ideas, particularly about love.

Pattern of Organization A pattern of organization is a particular arrangement of ideas and information. Such a pattern may be used to organize an entire composition or a single paragraph within a longer work. The following are the most common patterns of organization: cause-and- effect, chronological order, compare-and-contrast, classification, deductive, inductive, order of importance, problem-solution, sequential, and spatial.

See also Cause and Effect; Chronological Order; Classification; Compare and Contrast; Problem-Solution Order; Sequential Order.

Periodical A periodical is a publication that is issued at regular intervals of more than one day. For example, a periodical may be a weekly, monthly, or quarterly journal or magazine. Newspapers and other daily publications generally are not classified as periodicals.

Persona A persona is a voice that a writer assumes in a particular work. A persona is like a mask worn by the writer, separating his or her identity from that of the speaker or the narrator. It is the persona's voice—not the writer's voice—that narrates a story or speaks in a poem.

See also Narrator; Speaker.

Personal Essay *See* Essay.

Personification Personification is a figure of speech in which human qualities are given to an object, animal, or idea, for example: The night wind sings an eerie song.

See also Figurative Language.

Persuasion Persuasion is the art of swaying others' feelings, beliefs, or actions. Persuasion normally appeals to both the intellect and the emotions of readers. **Persuasive techniques** are the methods used to influence others to adopt certain opinions or beliefs or to act in certain ways. Types of persuasive techniques include emotional appeals, logical appeals, and loaded language. When used properly, persuasive techniques can add depth to writing that's meant to persuade. Persuasive techniques can, however, be misused to cloud factual information, disguise poor reasoning, or unfairly exploit people's emotions in order to shape their opinions.

See also Emotional Appeals; Loaded Language; Logical Appeal.

Persuasive Essay *See* Essay.

Play *See* Drama.

Plot The sequence of events in a story is called the plot. A plot focuses on a central **conflict** or problem faced by the main character. The actions that the characters take to resolve the conflict build toward a climax. In general, it is not long after this point that the conflict is resolved and the story ends. A plot typically develops in five stages: exposition, rising action, climax, falling action, and resolution.

See also Climax; Exposition; Falling Action; Rising Action.

Poetry Poetry is a type of literature in which words are carefully chosen and arranged to create certain effects. Poets use a variety of sound devices, imagery, and figurative language to express emotions and ideas.

See also Alliteration; Assonance; Ballad; Free Verse; Imagery; Meter; Rhyme; Rhythm; Stanza.

Point of View Point of view refers to the method of narration used in a short story, novel, narrative poem, or work of nonfiction. In a work told from a **first-person** point of view, the narrator is a character in the story. In a work told from a **third-person** point of view, the narrative voice is outside the action, not one of the characters. If a story is told from a **third-person omniscient,** or all-knowing, point of view, the narrator sees into the minds of all the characters. If events are related from a **third-person limited** point of view, the narrator tells what only one character thinks, feels, and observes.

See also Narrator.

Predict Predicting is a reading strategy that involves using text clues to make a reasonable guess about what will happen next in a story.

Primary Source *See* Sources.

Prior Knowledge Prior knowledge is the knowledge a reader already possesses about a topic. This information might come from personal experiences, expert accounts, books, films, or other sources.

Problem-Solution Order Problem-solution order is a pattern of organization in which a problem is stated and analyzed and then one or more solutions are proposed and examined. Writers use words and phrases such as *propose, conclude, reason for, problem, answer,* and *solution* to connect ideas and details when writing about problems and solutions.

Procedural Texts Procedural texts are functional texts that were created to communicate instructions, rules, processes, or other detailed, step-by-step information.

See also Consumer Documents; Public Documents; Workplace Documents.

Prologue A prologue is an introductory scene in a drama. Some Elizabethan plays include prologues that comment on the theme or moral point that will be revealed in the play. The prologue is a feature of all Greek drama.

Prop The word *prop,* originally an abbreviation of the word *property,* refers to any physical object that is used in a drama.

Propaganda Propaganda is a form of communication that may use distorted, false, or misleading information. It usually refers to manipulative political discourse.

Prose Generally, prose refers to all forms of written or spoken expression that are not in verse. The term, therefore, may be used to describe very different forms of writing— short stories as well as essays, for example.

Protagonist A protagonist is the main character in a work of literature—the character who is involved in the central conflict of the story. Usually, the protagonist changes after the central conflict reaches a climax. He or she may be a hero and is usually the one with whom the audience tends to identify.

Public Documents Public documents are documents that were written for the public to provide information that is of public interest or concern. They include government documents, speeches, signs, and rules and regulations.

See also Government Publications.

Pun A pun is a joke that comes from a play on words. It can make use of a word's multiple meanings or of a word's sound.

Quatrain A quatrain is a four-line stanza, or group of lines, in poetry. The most common stanza in English poetry, the quatrain can have a variety of meters and rhyme schemes.

Realistic Fiction Realistic fiction is fiction that is a truthful imitation of ordinary life.

Recurring Theme *See* Theme.

Reference Works General reference works are sources that contain facts and background information on a wide range of subjects. More specific reference works contain in-depth information on a single subject. Most reference works are good sources of reliable information because they have been reviewed by experts. The following are some common reference works: encyclopedias, dictionaries, thesauri, almanacs, atlases, chronologies, biographical dictionaries, and directories.

Reflective Essay *See* Essay.

Refrain A refrain is one or more lines repeated in each stanza of a poem.

See also Stanza.

Repetition Repetition is a technique in which a sound, word, phrase, or line is repeated for emphasis or unity. Repetition often helps to reinforce meaning and create an appealing rhythm. The term includes specific devices associated with both prose and poetry, such as alliteration and parallelism.

See also Alliteration; Parallelism; Sound Devices.

Resolution *See* Falling Action.

Review *See* Critical Review.

Rhetorical Devices Rhetorical devices are techniques writers use to enhance their arguments and communicate more effectively. Rhetorical devices include analogy, parallelism, rhetorical questions, and repetition.

See also Analogy; Repetition; Rhetorical Questions.

Rhetorical Questions Rhetorical questions are those that do not require a reply. Writers use them to suggest that their arguments make the answer obvious or self-evident.

Rhyme Rhyme is the occurrence of similar or identical sounds at the end of two or more words, such as *suite, heat,* and *complete.* Rhyme that occurs within a single line of poetry is **internal rhyme.** Rhyme that occurs at the ends of lines of poetry is called **end rhyme.** End rhyme that is not exact but approximate is called **slant rhyme,** or **off rhyme.** Notice the following example of slant rhyme involving the words *care* and *dear:*

> You act like you don't care,
> But I know you do, my dear.

Rhyme Scheme A rhyme scheme is a pattern of end rhymes in a poem. A rhyme scheme is noted by assigning a letter of the alphabet, beginning with *a*, to each line. Lines that rhyme are given the same letter.

Rhythm Rhythm is a pattern of stressed and unstressed syllables in a line of poetry. Poets use rhythm to bring out the musical quality of language, to emphasize ideas, to create moods, and to heighten emotional responses. Devices such as alliteration, rhyme, assonance, consonance, and parallelism create rhythm.

See also Meter.

Rising Action Rising action is the stage in a plot in which the conflict develops and story events build toward a climax. During this stage, complications arise that make the conflict more intense. Tension grows as the characters struggle to resolve the conflict.

See also Plot.

Romance A romance refers to any imaginative story concerned with noble heroes, chivalric codes of honor, passionate love, daring deeds, and supernatural events. Writers of romances tend to idealize their heroes as well as the eras in which the heroes live. Medieval romances include stories of kings, knights, and ladies who are motivated by love, religious faith, or simply a desire for adventure.

Sarcasm Sarcasm is a kind of particularly cutting irony. Generally, sarcasm is the taunting use of praise to mean its opposite—that is, to insult someone or something.

Satire Satire is a literary technique in which ideas, customs, behaviors, or institutions are ridiculed for the purpose of improving society. Satire may be gently witty, mildly abrasive, or bitterly critical, and it often involves the use of irony and exaggeration to force readers to see something in a critical light.

Scanning Scanning is the process of searching through writing for a particular fact or piece of information. When you scan, your eyes sweep across a page, looking for key words that may lead you to the information you want.

Scansion Scansion is the notation of stressed and unstressed syllables in poetry. A stressed syllable is indicated by the symbol ´; an unstressed syllable, by the symbol ˘. Using scansion can help you determine the rhythm and meter of a poem.

See also Meter.

Scene In drama, the action is often divided into acts and scenes. Each scene presents an episode of the play's plot and typically occurs at a single place and time.

See also Act.

Scenery Scenery is a painted backdrop or other structures used to create the setting for a play.

Science Fiction Science fiction is fiction in which a writer explores unexpected possibilities of the past or the future, using known scientific data and theories as well as his or her creative imagination. Most science fiction writers create believable worlds, although some create fantasy worlds that have familiar elements.

See also Fantasy.

Screenplay A screenplay is a play written for film.

See also Teleplay.

Script The text of a play, film, or broadcast is called a script.

Secondary Source *See* Sources.

Sensory Details Sensory details are words and phrases that appeal to the reader's senses of sight, hearing, touch, smell, and taste. For example, the sensory detail "a fine film of rain" appeals to the senses of sight and touch. Sensory details stimulate the reader to create images in his or her mind.

See also Imagery.

Sequential Order A pattern of organization that shows the order in which events or actions occur is called sequential order. Writers typically use this pattern of organization to explain steps or stages in a process.

Setting Setting is the time and place of the action of a story.

See also Fiction.

Setting a Purpose The process of establishing specific reasons for reading a text is called setting a purpose.

Short Story A short story is a work of fiction that centers on a single idea and can be read in one sitting. Generally, a short story has one main conflict that involves the characters, keeps the story moving, and stimulates readers' interest.

See also Fiction.

Sidebar A sidebar is additional information set in a box alongside or within a news or feature article. Popular magazines often make use of sidebar information.

Signal Words Signal words are words and phrases that indicate what is to come in a text.

Readers can use signal words to discover a text's pattern of organization and to analyze the relationships among the ideas in the text.

Simile A simile is a figure of speech that makes a comparison between two unlike things, using the word *like* or *as,* for example: Her blue-eyed stare was like ice.

See also Epic Simile; Figurative Language; Metaphor.

Situational Irony *See* Irony.

Soliloquy In drama, a soliloquy is a speech in which a character speaks his or her thoughts aloud. Generally, the character is on the stage alone, not speaking to other characters and perhaps not even consciously addressing an audience. At the beginning of Act Two, Scene 3, of *Romeo and Juliet,* Friar Laurence has a long soliloquy. Shakespeare makes use of soliloquies in many of his plays.

See also Aside; Dramatic Monologue.

Sonnet A sonnet is a lyric poem of 14 lines, commonly written in **iambic pentameter.** Sonnets are often classified as Petrarchan or Shakespearean. The Shakespearean, or Elizabethan, sonnet consists of three quatrains, or four-line units, and a final couplet. The typical rhyme scheme is *abab cdcd efef gg*.

See also Iambic Pentameter; Rhyme Scheme.

Sound Devices Sound devices, or uses of words for their auditory effect, can convey meaning and mood or unify a work. Some common sound devices are alliteration, assonance, consonance, meter, onomatopoeia, repetition, rhyme, and rhythm.

See also Alliteration; Assonance; Consonance; Meter; Onomatopoeia; Repetition; Rhyme; Rhythm.

Sources A source is anything that supplies information. **Primary sources** are materials written by people who were present at events, either as participants or as observers. Letters, diaries, autobiographies, speeches, and photographs are primary sources. **Secondary sources** are records of events that were created sometime after the events occurred; the writers were not directly involved or were not present when the events took place. Encyclopedias, textbooks, biographies, most newspaper and magazine articles, and books and articles that interpret or review research are secondary sources.

Spatial Order Spatial order is a pattern of organization that highlights the physical positions or relationships of details or objects. This pattern of organization is typically found in descriptive writing. Writers use words and phrases such as *on the left, to the right, here, over there, above, below, beyond, nearby,* and *in the distance* to indicate the arrangement of details.

Speaker In poetry the speaker is the voice that "talks" to the reader, similar to the narrator in fiction. The speaker is not necessarily the poet.

See also Persona.

Speech A speech is a talk or public address. The purpose of a speech may be to entertain, to explain, to present a claim, to inspire, or any combination of these aims. "I Have a Dream" by Martin Luther King Jr. was written and delivered in order to inspire an audience.

Stage Directions A play typically includes instructions called stage directions, which are usually printed in italic type. They serve as a guide to directors, set and lighting designers, performers, and readers. When stage directions appear within passages of dialogue, parentheses are usually used to set them off from the words spoken by characters.

Stanza A stanza is a group of two or more lines that form a unit in a poem. A stanza is comparable to a paragraph in prose. Each stanza may have the same number of lines, or the number of lines may vary.

See also Couplet; Form; Poetry; Quatrain.

Static Character *See* Character.

Stereotype In literature, a simplified or stock character who conforms to a fixed pattern or is defined by a single trait is known as a stereotype. Such a character does not usually demonstrate the complexity of a real person. Familiar stereotypes in popular literature include the absentminded professor and the busybody.

Stereotyping Stereotyping is a type of overgeneralization. Stereotypes are broad statements made about people on the basis of their gender, ethnicity, race, or political, social, professional, or religious group.

Stream of Consciousness Stream of consciousness is a literary technique developed by modern writers, in which thoughts, feelings, moods, perceptions, and memories are presented as they randomly flow through a character's mind.

Structure Structure is the way in which the parts of a work of literature are put together. In poetry, structure involves the arrangement of words and lines to produce a desired effect. A common structural unit in poetry is the stanza, of which there are numerous types. In prose, structure is the arrangement of larger units or parts of a work. Paragraphs, for example, are basic units in prose, as are chapters in novels and acts in plays. The structure of a poem, short story, novel, play, or nonfictional work usually emphasizes certain important aspects of content.

See also Act; Stanza.

Style Style is the particular way in which a work of literature is written—not *what* is said but *how* it is said. It is the writer's unique way of communicating ideas. Many elements contribute to style, including word choice, sentence structure and length, tone, figurative language, and point of view. A literary style may be described in a variety of ways, such as formal, informal, journalistic, conversational, wordy, ornate, poetic, or dynamic.

Summarize To summarize is to briefly retell, or encapsulate, the main ideas of a piece of writing in one's own words.

See also Paraphrase.

Support Support is any material that serves to prove a claim. In an argument, support typically consists of reasons and evidence. In persuasive texts and speeches, however, support may include appeals to the needs and values of the audience.

Supporting Detail *See* Main Idea.

Surprise Ending A surprise ending is an unexpected plot twist at the end of a story. The surprise may be a sudden turn in the action or a piece of information that gives a different perspective to the entire story.

Suspense Suspense is the excitement or tension that readers feel as they wait to find out how a story ends or a conflict is resolved. Writers create suspense by raising questions in readers' minds about what might happen next. The use of **foreshadowing** and **flashback** are two ways in which writers create suspense.

See also Foreshadowing; Flashback.

Symbol A symbol is a person, a place, an object, or an activity that stands for something beyond itself. For example, a flag is a colored piece of cloth that stands for a country. A white dove is a bird that represents peace.

Synthesize To synthesize information is to take individual pieces of information and combine them with other pieces of information and with prior knowledge or experience to gain a better understanding of a subject or to create a new product or idea.

Tall Tale A tall tale is a humorously exaggerated story about impossible events, often involving the supernatural abilities of the main character. Stories about folk heroes such as Pecos Bill and Paul Bunyan are typical tall tales.

Teleplay A teleplay is a play written for television. In a teleplay, scenes can change quickly and dramatically. The camera can focus the viewer's attention on specific actions. The camera directions in teleplays are much like the stage directions in stage plays.

Text Criticism Text criticism is writing in which literary works, including their various elements, are analyzed, interpreted, evaluated, or compared.

Text Features Text features are design elements that indicate the organizational structure of a text and help make the key ideas and supporting information understandable. Text features include headings, boldface type, italic type, bulleted or numbered lists, sidebars, and graphic aids such as charts, tables, timelines, illustrations, and photographs.

Theme A theme, or central idea, is an underlying message about life or human nature that a writer wants the reader to understand.

It is a perception about life or human nature that the writer shares with the reader. In most cases, themes are not stated directly but must be inferred. A theme may imply how a person should live but should not be confused with a **moral.**

Recurring themes are themes found in a variety of works. For example, authors from varying backgrounds might convey similar themes having to do with the importance of family values. **Universal themes** are themes that are found throughout the literature of all time periods. For example, the *Odyssey* contains a universal theme relating to the hero's search for truth, goodness, and honor.

See also Moral.

Thesaurus *See* Reference Works.

Thesis Statement In an argument, a thesis statement is an expression of the claim that the writer or speaker is trying to support. In an essay, a thesis statement is an expression, in one or two sentences, of the main idea or purpose of the piece of writing.

See also Claim.

Third-Person Point of View *See* Point of View.

Tone Tone is the attitude a writer takes takes toward a subject. Unlike mood, which is intended to shape the reader's emotional response, tone reflects the feelings of the writer. A writer communicates tone through choice of words and details. Tone may often be described by a single word, such as *serious, humorous, formal, informal, somber, sarcastic, playful, ironic, bitter,* or *objective.*

See also Author's Perspective; Mood.

Topic Sentence The topic sentence of a paragraph states the paragraph's central idea. All other sentences in the paragraph provide supporting details.

Tragedy A tragedy is a dramatic work that presents the downfall of a dignified character (**tragic hero**) or characters who are involved in historically or socially significant events. The events in a tragic plot are set in motion by a decision that is often an error in judgment (**tragic flaw**) on the part of the hero. Succeeding events are linked in a cause-and-effect relationship and lead inevitably to a disastrous conclusion, usually death. Shakespeare's *Romeo and Juliet* is a tragedy.

Tragic Flaw *See* Tragedy.

Tragic Hero *See* Tragedy.

Traits *See* Character.

Turning Point *See* Climax.

Understatement Understatement is a technique of creating emphasis by saying less than is actually or literally true. It is the opposite of **hyperbole,** or exaggeration. One of the primary devices of irony, understatement can be used to develop a humorous effect, to create satire, or to achieve a restrained tone.

See also Hyperbole; Irony.

Universal Theme *See* Theme.

Verbal Irony *See* Irony.

Visualize Visualizing is the process of forming a mental picture based on written or spoken information.

Voice Voice is a writer's unique use of language that allows a reader to "hear" a human personality in the writer's work. Elements of style that contribute to a writer's voice include sentence structure, diction, and tone. Voice can reveal much about the author's personality, beliefs, and attitudes.

Website A website is a collection of "pages" on the World Wide Web that is usually devoted to one specific subject. Pages are linked together and are accessed by clicking hyperlinks or menus, which send the user from page to page within the site. Web sites are created by companies, organizations, educational institutions, branches of the government, the military, and individuals.

Word Choice *See* Diction.

Workplace Documents Workplace documents are materials that are produced or used within a work setting, usually to aid in the functioning of the workplace. They include job applications, office memos, training manuals, job descriptions, and sales reports.

Works Cited A list of works cited lists names of all the works a writer has referred to in his or her text. This list often includes not only books and articles but also nonprint sources.

Works Consulted A list of works consulted names all the works a writer consulted in order to create his or her text. It is not limited just to those works cited in the text.

See also Bibliography.

Using the Glossaries

The following glossaries list the Academic Vocabulary and Critical Vocabulary words found in this book in alphabetical order. Use these glossaries just as you would a dictionary—to determine the meanings, parts of speech, pronunciation, and syllabication of words. (Some technical, foreign, and more obscure words in this book are not listed here but are defined for you in the footnotes that accompany many of the selections.)

Many words in the English language have more than one meaning. These glossaries give the meanings that apply to the words as they are used in the selections in this book. Words closely related in form and meaning are listed together in one entry (for instance, *consumption* and *consume*), and the definition is given for the first form.

The following abbreviations are used to identify parts of speech of words:

adj. adjective   *adv.* adverb   *n.* noun   *v.* verb

Each word's pronunciation is given in parentheses. A guide to the pronunciation symbols appears in the Pronunciation Key below. The stress marks in the Pronunciation Key are used to indicate the force given to each syllable in a word. They can also help you determine where words are divided into syllables.

For more information about the words in these glossaries or for information about words not listed here, consult a dictionary.

Pronunciation Key

Symbol	Examples	Symbol	Examples	Symbol	Examples
ă	pat	m	mum	ûr	urge, term, firm, word, heard
ā	pay	n	no, sudden* (sud'n)		
ä	father	ng	thing	**Symbol**	**Examples**
âr	care	ŏ	pot	v	valve
b	bib	ō	toe	w	with
ch	church	ô	caught, paw	y	yes
d	deed, milled	ôr	core	z	zebra, xylem
ĕ	pet	oi	noise	zh	vision, pleasure, garage
ē	bee	ŏŏ	took		
f	fife, phase, rough	oor	lure	ə	about, item, edible, gallop, circus
g	gag	ōō	boot		
h	hat	ou	out	ər	butter
hw	which	p	pop		
ĭ	pit	r	roar	**Sounds in Foreign Words**	
ī	pie, by	s	sauce	KH	German ich, ach; Scottish loch
îr	pier	sh	ship, dish	N (bôn)	French, bon, fin
j	judge	t	tight, stopped	œ	French feu, oeuf; German schön
k	kick, cat, pique	th	thin		
l	lid, needle* (nēd'l)	*th*	this	ü	French tu; German über
		ŭ	cut		

* In English the consonants *l* and *n* often constitute complete syllables by themselves.

Stress Marks

The relevant emphasis with which the syllables of a word or phrase are spoken, called stress, is indicated in three different ways. The strongest, or primary, stress is marked with a bold mark (´). An intermediate, or secondary, level of stress is marked with a similar but lighter mark (´). The weakest stress is unmarked. Words of one syllable show no stress mark.

Glossary of Academic Vocabulary

attribute (ăt′rə-byo͞ot′) *n.* a characteristic, quality, or trait.

capacity (kə-păs′ĭ-tē) *n.* the ability to contain, hold, produce, or understand.

commit (kə-mĭt′) *v.* to carry out, engage in, or perform.

confer (kən-fûr′) *v.* to grant or give to.

decline (dĭ-klīn′) *v.* to fall apart or deteriorate slowly.

dimension (dĭ-měn′shən) *n.* a feature, scale, or measurement of something.

emerge (ĭ-mûrj′) *v.* to come forth, out of, or away from.

enable (ĕ-nā′bəl) *v.* to give the means or opportunity.

enforce (ĕn-fôrs′) *v.* to compel observance of or obedience to.

entity (ĕn′tĭ-tē) *n.* a thing that exists as a unit.

expose (ĭk-spōz′) *v.* to make visible or reveal.

external (ĭk-stûr′nəl) *adj.* related to, part of, or from the outside.

generate (jĕn′ə-rāt′) *v.* to produce or cause something to happen or exist.

impose (ĭm-pōz′) *v.* to bring about by force.

initiate (ĭ-nĭsh′ē-āt′) *v.* to start or cause to begin.

integrate (ĭn′tĭ-grāt′) *v.* to pull together into a whole; unify.

internal (ĭn-tûr′nəl) *adj.* inner; located within something or someone.

motivate (mō′tə-vāt′) *v.* to provide a cause for doing something.

objective (əb-jĕk′tĭv) *n.* an intention, purpose, or goal.

presume (prĭ-zo͞om′) *v.* to take for granted as being true; to assume something is true.

pursuit (pər-so͞ot′) *n.* the action of chasing or following something.

resolve (rĭ-zŏlv′) *v.* to decide or become determined.

reveal (rĭ-vēl′) *v.* to show or make known.

statistic (stə-tĭs′tĭk) *n.* a piece of numerical data.

subsequent (sŭb′sĭ-kwĕnt′) *adj.* coming after or following.

sustain (sə-stān′) *v.* to support or cause to continue.

trace (trās) *v.* to discover or determine the origins or developmental stages of something.

underlie (ŭn′ dər-lī′) *v.* to be the cause or support of.

undertake (ŭn′ dər-tāk′) *v.* to assume responsibility for or take on a job or course of action

utilize (yo͞ot′l-īz) *v.* to make use of.

Glossary of Critical Vocabulary

abominably (ə-bŏm´ə-nə-blē) *adv.* in a hateful way; horribly.

adversary (ăd´vər-sĕr´ē) *n.* an opponent; enemy.

adversity (ăd-vûr´sĭ-tē) *n.* hardship; misfortune.

afflict (ə-flĭkt´) *v.* to cause pain to; to trouble.

allocate (ăl´ə-kāt´) *v.* to assign or designate for.

assail (ə-sāl´) *v.* attack, disturb.

assess (ə-sĕs´) *v.* to evaluate.

assuage (ə-swāj´) *v.* to calm or pacify.

audacious (ô-dā´shəs) *n.* bold, rebellious.

autonomy (ô-tŏn´ə-mē) *n.* independent self-governance.

berate (bĭ-rāt´) *v.* to criticize or scold.

bereaved (bĭ-rēvd´) *adj.* having suffered the loss of a loved one; grieving.

cadence (kād´ns) *n.* lyrical rhythm.

circuitously (sər-kyōō´ĭ-təs-lē) *adv.* in an indirect and lengthy manner.

civic (sĭv´ĭk) *adj.* related to community and citizenship.

cognition (kŏg-nĭsh´ən) *n.* the process or pattern of gaining knowledge.

commandeer (kŏm´ən-dir´) *v.* to take control of by force.

commemorate (kŏ-mĕm´ə-rāt´) *v.* to celebrate or honor.

compatriot (kəm-pā´trē-ət) *n.* a fellow citizen or person from same country.

comply (kəm-plī´) *v.* to obey an instruction or command.

concede (kən-sēd´) *v.* to surrender or acknowledge defeat.

conceive (kən-sēv´) *v.* to form or develop in the mind; devise.

constitute (kŏn´stĭ-tōōt´) *v.* to form or comprise.

constrict (kən-strĭkt´) *v.* to limit or impede growth.

consume (kən-sōōm´) *v.* to completely destroy or eradicate.

contagion (kən-tā´jən) *n.* the spreading from one to another.

contemplate (kŏn´təm-plāt´) *v.* think carefully about.

contemptible (kən-təmp´tə-bəl) *adj.* deserving of scorn; despicable.

contention (kən-tĕn´shən) *n.* argued assertion.

conversely (kən-vûrs´lē) *adv.* in a way that contradicts or reverses something.

convert (kən-vûrt´) *v.* to change one's system of beliefs.

decisive (dĭ-sī´sĭv) *adj.* final or concluding.

deduce (dĭ-dōōs´) *v.* to know through reason or logical conclusion.

default (dĭ-fôlt´) *v.* to fail to keep a promise to repay a loan.

degenerate (dĭ-jĕn´ər-āt´) *v.* to decline morally.

delude (dĭ-lōōd´) *v.* to deceive or instill a false belief in.

demeanor (dĭ-mē´nər) *n.* attitude or perceived behavior.

derive (dĭ-rīv´) *v.* to obtain or extract from.

desolate (dĕs´ə-lĭt) *adj.* unhappy; lonely.

desolation (dĕs´ə-la´shən) *n.* lonely grief; misery.

detract (dĭ-trăkt´) *v.* to take away from.

din (dĭn) *n.* loud noise.

discernible (dĭ-sûr´nə-bəl) *adj.* recognizable or noticeable.

discordant (dĭ-skôr´dnt) *adj.* conflicting or not harmonious.

disingenuous (dĭs´ĭn-jĕn´yōō-əs) *adj.* insincere, deceitful.

disintegration (dĭs-ĭn´tĭ-grā´shən) *n.* the process of a whole coming apart in pieces.

distend (dĭ-stĕnd´) *v.* to bulge or expand.

distill (dĭ-stĭl´) *v.* to transform vapor into liquid.

diversity (dĭ-vûr´sĭ-tē) *n.* having varied social and/or ethnic backgrounds.

edict (ē´dĭkt´) *n.* an official rule or proclamation.

emaciated (ĭ-mā´shē-āt´id) *adj.* made extremely thin and weak.

emanate (ĕm´ə-nāt´) *v.* to emit or radiate from.

embark (ĕm-bärk´) *v.* to set out on a course or a journey (often aboard a boat).

empathy (ĕm´pə-thē) *n.* the ability to understand and identify with another's feelings.

encroach (ĕn-krōch´) *v.* to gradually intrude upon or invade.

execute (ĕk´sĭ-kyōōt´) *v.* to carry out or accomplish.

exhort (ĭg-zôrt´) *v.* to strongly urge or encourage.

expanse (ĭk-spăns´) *n.* a large area.

extricate (ĕk´strĭ-kāt´) *v.* to release or disentangle from.

foremost (fôr´mōst´) *adv.* most importantly.

foreboding (fôr-bō´dĭng) *n.* a sense of approaching evil.

gradation (grə-dā´shən) *n.* a slight, successive change in color, degree, or tone.

guise (gīz) *n.* form or outward appearance; outfit.

harried (hăr´ēd) *adj.* tormented; harassed.

immerse (ĭ-mûrs´) *v.* to absorb or involve deeply.

impeccably (ĭm-pĕk´ə-blē) *adv.* perfectly.

imperative (ĭm-pĕr´ə-tĭv) *adj.* crucial, necessary.

imperceptible (ĭm´pər-sĕp´tə-bəl) *adj.* unnoticeable.

implacable (ĭm´plăk´ə-bəl) *adj.* impossible to soothe; unforgiving.

implication (ĭm´plĭ-kā´shən) *n.* consequence or effect.

increment (ĭn´krə-mənt) *n.* an addition or increase by a standard measure of growth.

inextricably (ĭn-ĕk´strĭ-kə-blē) *adv.* in a way impossible to untangle.

innate (ĭ-nāt´) *adj.* inborn; existing at birth.

intangible (ĭn-tăn´jə-bəl) *n.* something that is difficult to grasp or explain.

integrity (ĭn-tĕg´rĭ-tē) *n.* consistency and strength of purpose.

intention (ĭn-tĕn´shən) *n.* purpose or plan.

intermittent (ĭn´tər-mĭt´nt) *adj.* occurring at erratic or irregular intervals.

interwoven (ĭn´tər-wō´vən) *adj.* blended or laced together.

intrusion (ĭn-trōō´zhən) *n.* act of trespass or invasion.

intuitive (ĭn-tōō´ĭ-tĭv) *adj.* known or understood without reasoning; instinctive.

invocation (ĭn´və-kā´shən) *n.* a formal appeal, often used in prayer.

invoke (ĭn-vōk´) *v.* to refer or call attention to.

irrelevant (ĭ-rĕl´ə-vənt) *adj.* insignificant, unimportant.

laud (lôd) *v.* to praise.

loiter (loi´tər) *v.* to stand or wait idly.

lozenge (lŏz´ĭnj) *n.* a diamond-shaped object.

momentous (mō-mĕn´təs) *adj.* very important; fateful.

negligence (nĕg´lĭ-jəns) *n.* carelessness or failure to take normal precautions.

nullify (nŭl´ə-fī´) *v.* to make of no value or consequence.

opaque (ō-pāk´) *adj.* clouded; difficult to see through.

parallel (păr´ə-lĕl´) *adj.* related; corresponding.

perish (pĕr´ĭsh) *v.* to die or come to an end.

pluralistic (ploŏr´ə-lĭs´tĭc) *adj.* consisting of many ethnic and cultural groups.

ponderous (pŏn´dər-əs) *adj.* heavy in a clumsy way; bulky.

prism (prĭz´əm) *n.* a transparent, light-refracting object which figuratively refers to an individual's viewpoint.

profusion (prə´fyoō´zhən) *n.* abundance.

reclaim (rĭ-klām´) *v.* to retake possession; reform.

redemptive (rĭ-dĕmp´tiv) *adj.* causing freedom or salvation.

reiteration (rē-ĭt´ə-rā´shən) *n.* restatement or repetition.

reprieve (rĭ-prēv´) *n.* the cancellation or postponement of punishment.

repulsed (rĭ-pŭlsd´) *adj.* disgusted.

resolve (rĭ-zŏlv´) *v.* to decide or become determined.

restitution (rĕs´tĭ-toō´shən) *n.* a making good for loss or damage; repayment.

revelry (rĕv´əl-rē) *n.* noisy merrymaking; festivity.

revile (rĭ-vīl´) *v.* to condemn or insult.

segregate (sĕg´rĭ-gāt´) *v.* to cause people to be separated based on gender, race, or other factors.

serrate (sĕr´āt´) *adj.* having a jagged, saw-toothed edge.

sheepish (shē´pĭsh) *adj.* showing embarrassment.

stagnant (stăg´nənt) *adj.* unchanging; without activity or development.

staidness (stād´nĭs) *n.* the quality of being steady, calm, and serious.

subversive (səb-vûr´sĭv) *adj.* intended to undermine or overthrow those in power.

succession (sək-sĕsh´ən) *n.* sequence; ordered arrangement.

succumb (sə-kŭm´) *v.* to surrender or fall victim to.

supple (sŭp´əl) *adj.* flexible or easily adaptable.

synchronization (sĭng´krə-nĭ-zā´shən) *n.* coordinated, simultaneous action.

tangible (tăn´jə-bəl) *n.* something that can be touched.

tentative (tĕn´tə-tĭv) *adj.* with caution and without confidence.

transfix (trăns-fĭks´) *v.* to captivate or make motionless with awe.

travail (trə-vāl´) *n.* painful effort.

tremulous (trĕm´yə-ləs) *adj.* marked by trembling or shaking.

validate (văl´ĭ-dāt´) *v.* to establish the value, truth, or legitimacy of.

Index of Skills

As You Read, 3, 11, 21, 27, 48, 55, 73, 81, 89, 103, 123, 133, 141, 147, 163, 183, 207, 228, 253, 266, 283, 289, 307, 317, 325, 339, 351, 371, 401, 421, 433, 441

As You View, 71, 151

As You View and Read, 33, 173

attacking the person (faulty reasoning), R19

audience, for Elizabethan theater, 180

author's choices
  analyzing, 17, 93, 279, 347, 417
  point of view, 85, 297

author's claim, R16
  analyzing and evaluating, 7, 129, 321, 322, 438
  identifying, 437

author's cultural background, 11, 73, 81, 89, 133

author's message, 25, 53, 335, 429, R57. *See also* central idea

author's perspective, R57

author's purpose, R57. *See also* author's perspective
  analyzing, 29, 152, 313
  definition of, 29
  determining, 429

autobiographical narratives, 77

autobiography, R57–R58

auxiliary verbs, R23, R24, R47

B

bad vs. *badly*, R36

ballads, R58

bandwagon appeals, 437, R17

base words, R49

between/among, R55

bias, R20, R58

biased tone, R3, R5

bibliography, R58. *See also* works cited

biography, R58

blank verse, 178, R58

blogs, 447

body, of essay, 42

book parts, citing, R10

books, citing, R10

brainstorming, 154

bring/take, R55

business correspondence, R58

C

calls to action, 152

capitalization
  first words, R28
  geographical names, R27
  I, R28
  organizations and events, R27–R28
  people and titles, R27
  proper adjectives, R28
  quick reference, R27–R28

cases
  nominative, R30
  objective, R30
  possessive, R30

cast of characters, R58

cause and effect, R48, R58

cause-and-effect relationships, 179, R4, R58

CD-ROMs, citing, R11

central idea, 335. *See also* main idea; theme
  determining, 25, 53, 335, 429
  supporting, 69

characterization, R59

characters, R58
  analyzing, 119, 279, 399
  antagonist, 177, R57
  asides by, 177
  complex, 279
  development of, 119
  dynamic, R58
  epic hero, 365, 368, 399, R62
  flat, R59
  foil, 177, 206, 399, R64
  main, R58
  minor, R58
  motivations of, 279, R58
  protagonist, R70
  round, R59
  Shakespearean, 177
  soliloquies by, 177
  static, R59
  tragic hero, 177, R74

character traits, R58

chorus, R59

chronological order, 77, R7, R59

chronology, 347

circular reasoning, 437, R19

citations, R9–R11

Cite Text Evidence, 8, 18, 25, 30, 36, 53, 69, 72, 78, 86, 94, 120, 130, 138, 144, 150, 152, 170, 176, 206, 227, 252, 265, 280, 288, 298, 314, 322, 336, 348, 354, 399, 418, 429, 430, 438, 444

claims. *See also* arguments; thesis statement
  analyzing, 7, 438
  author's, 129, 321, 437, R16
  counterclaims, 97, 356, R2, R16
  debating, 97–98, R14–R15
  definition of, 53, 129, R59
  developing, 97–98, 355–356, R2
  evaluating, 7, 438
  identifying, 7, 437
  introducing, 99, 356, R2
  linking ideas to, 99, 356, R3
  making, 38, 97, 355
  summarizing, 8
  supporting, 7, 321, R14, R16, R73

vague, R2
  writing activity, 8

clarify, reading strategy to, R59

classical mythology, words from, R50

classification, organizational pattern, R59

classroom discussions, R12–R13

clauses
  adjective, R42
  adverbial, 122, R42
  definition of, 300, 350, R41
  dependent, 300
  essential adjective, R42
  independent, 132, 300, 338, R41
  nonessential adjective, R42
  noun, 10, R43
  relative, 350
  subordinate, 10, 122, R41, R42
  transitional, R3

cliché, R59

climax, R7, R59

collaboration, group, 157

Collaborative Discussion, 6, 16, 24, 28, 35, 51, 68, 71, 76, 84, 92, 118, 128, 136, 143, 148, 151, 168, 175, 205, 226, 251, 264, 278, 287, 296, 312, 320, 334, 346, 352, 398, 416, 428, 436, 442

collaborative discussions, 359–362, R12–R13. *See also* panel discussions
  ground rules and goals for, 359, R12
  moving forward in, 360, R13
  posing and responding to questions in, 360–361
  preparing for, 359–360, R12
  responding to ideas in, 361, R13

collective nouns, R22, R47

colloquialisms, 137

colons, 96, 132, 338, R26

comedy, R59

comic relief, 177, R59

commas, R25

comma splices, R45

commonly confused words, R55–R56

common nouns, R22, R29

comparative form, R35–R36

compare and contrast, R4, R60

Compare Text and Media, 36, 47, 72, 81, 85

comparisons
  as context clues, R49
  double, R36
  illogical, R36
  irregular, R35–R36
  regular, R35

complements, R37–R38

complete predicate, R24

complete subject, R24

complex characters, 279

archetypes in, 365
characteristics of, 365
elements of, 365
epithets in, 366, 417
examining Homeric, 368
figurative language in, 367, 417
gods in, 368
heroes in, 365, 368, 399, R62
in historical context, 367
language of Homer, 366
metaphors in, 417
as narrative, 367
plot, 365, 417
as poems, 367
reading, 367
setting, 365, 417
themes, 365, 417
epic simile, 366, 417, R62
epilogue, R59, R62
epithets, 366, 417, R62
essays, R62
analytical, 41–44, 301–304,
445–448
argumentative, 97–100, 355–358,
R62. See also arguments
body of, 42, 99, 302, 357, 446–447
controlling idea of, 41, 302, 446
citing, R10
conclusion, 42, 99, 303, 357, 447, R5
critical, R62
draft of, 42, 99, 302, 356, 446–447
editorial, 438, R62
examples, 21–24, 163–168
exchanging with partner, 43, 99,
303, 357, 447
explanatory, 41–44, 301–304,
445–448
expository, 41–44, 301–304,
445–448, R62
formal, R62
informal, R62
informative, 41–44, 301–304,
445–448, R4–R5, R62
introduction, 41, 99, 302, 356, 446
personal, R62
persuasive, R62
photo essay, 33
presenting, 43, 303, 447
publishing online, 447
reflective, R62
revising, 42–43, 99, 303, 357, 447
writing activity, 288
essential adjective clauses, R42
essential appositives, R39
etymologies, 19, 70, R50
eulogy, 280
evading the issue, R19
evaluating, R62
arguments, 7, 8, 321, 437, R16–R21
author's claim, 7, 129, 322, 438
debates, R15

evidence, 321, R20–R21
speeches, 53, 54
text, 18, 69, 72, 170, 252, 430
video, 72
your own view, 37
events
analyzing, 69, 77, 335, 429
sequencing, in writing narratives,
154, R7
evidence, R62
evaluating, 321, R20–R21
gathering, 37, 41, 97, 157, 301, 355,
360, 445–446
to support claims, 7, 38, 98, 129,
321, 356, R2, R14, R16
from text, 8, 18, 25, 30, 53, 69, 72,
78, 86, 94, 119, 120, 130, 144,
150, 152, 170, 176, 206, 227,
252, 265, 280, 288, 298, 314,
322, 336, 348, 354, 399, 418,
429, 430, 438, 444
examples, as context clues, 139, R48
except/accept, R55
exclamation point, R25
exclamatory sentences, R37
explanatory essays, 41–44, 301–304,
445–448. See also analytical
essays
exposition, R63
expository essays, 41–44, 301–304,
445–448, R62
extended metaphors, 25, 52, 53, 443,
R63
external conflict, R60

F
fables, R63
fact versus opinion, 437, R63
fairy tales
elements of, 17
speaking activity, 18
fallacies, R19–R20, R63
fallacious reasoning, 437
falling action, R63
false analogy, R20
false cause, 437, R19
false statements, 437
fantasy, R63
farce, R63
farther/further, R36
faulty reasoning, 437, R19–R20. See
also fallacies
fear, appeals to, R17, R62
feature article, R63
fewer/less, R56
fiction, R63. See also drama; epics;
fictional narratives
fairy tales, 17, 18
fantasy, R63
historical, R65
novellas, R68

novels, R68
realistic, R70
romance, R71
science, R72
fictional narratives
building suspense, R7
conclusions of, R7
details for, 154, R6–R7
drafting, 155
elements of effective, 153
pacing, 93, 94, R7
Performance Task Evaluation
Chart, 156
planning, 153–154
point of view for, 154, R6
presenting, 155
revising, 155
sequencing of events in, 154, R7
writing, 153–156, R6–R7
figurative language, R48, R63
analyzing, 417
in epics, 367, 417
interpreting, 149, 353, 418, 443
metaphors, 417, 443
personification, 169, 443, R69
similes, 36, 366, 417
uses of, 169
figurative meanings, 353
first-person accounts, 72
first-person narrator, 297, R6
first-person point of view, 297, R70
flashbacks, 347, R7, R64
flat characters, R59
flowcharts, 179
foils, 177, 206, 399, R64
folk ballads, R58
foreign words, R51
foreshadowing, 93, 206, R64
form, R64
formal debates, R14–R15
formal essay, R62
formal language, 316
formal tone, 137, 138, 316, R3
fragments, sentence, R44–R45
frame story, R64
free verse, R64
further/farther, R36
future perfect progressive tense, R34
future perfect tense, R33
future progressive tense, R33
future tense, R33
fyi, 2, 46, 102, 162, 306, 364

G
general dictionary, R52
generalization, R17, R64
hasty, R20
overgeneralization, R19, R68
general references, R32
genre, R64
gerund phrases, R40

noun phrases, 80
parallel structure, 32, 282
participial phrases, 172
prepositional phrases, 20
relative clauses, 350
repetition and parallelism, 54
rhetorical questions, 88
semicolons, 96, 338
sentence length, 432
tone, 316
transitions, 440
verb phrases, 140
language conventions, R22–R47,
    R55–R56. *See also* Language
    and Style
Latin words, 19, 70, 419
lay/lie, R56
leave/let, R56
legend, R66. *See also* myths
less/fewer, R56
letters, writing activity, 94, 120, 138,
    265
lie/lay, R56
line, R66
line breaks, R66
linking verbs, R23, R32
lists, colons before, 96, 132, 338, R26
literary ballads, R58
literary nonfiction, R66
    examples, 3–6, 73–76, 81–84,
        141–143, 307–312, 421–428
literary techniques
    alliteration, 367, R57
    allusion, 53, 176, 178, 366, 417, R57
    assonance, R57
    to create tension, 93, 94, 347
    dramatic irony, 265
    foreshadowing, 93, 206, R64
    flashback, 347, 348
    hyperbole, R65, R75
    idioms, 94, R49, R65
    imagery, 149, 353, 367, 420, R65
    irony, 93, 177, 265, R66
    metaphors, 417, 443, R67
    onomatopoeia, R68
    oxymoron, R68
    paradox, R68
    personification, 169, 443, R69
    puns, 178, 281, R70
    rhetorical questions, 88, R71
    sarcasm, R71
    satire, R71
    similes, 36, 366, R72
    symbols, 17, 86, 120, 354, R74
literary text, 11–16, 34–35, 89–92,
    103–118, 133–136, 148, 174–175,
    183–278, 283–287, 289–296,
    339–346, 351–352, 371–416, 442
loaded language, 437, R20, R66
logic, analyzing, in arguments, 7, 321,
    437, R17–R18

logical appeals, R66
logical arguments, R66
logical fallacies, 437, R19–R20, R63
loose/lose, R56
loyalty, appeals to, R17
lyric poetry, R66

M

magazine articles, citing, R11
magical realism, R66
main characters, R58
main idea, R66–R67. *See also* central
    idea; theme
main verb, R24
*A Manual for Writers of Research
    Papers, Theses, and Dissertations*
    (Turabian), R9
media, 33, 71, 151, 173
    analyzing, 36, 72, 86, 152, 176
    compare text and, 36, 72, 81, 85
media activity, 36, 86, 152, 176
media analysis, 36, 72, 152, 176
mediums, analyzing different, 36,
    72, 85
memoirs, 81–83, 307–312, 313, R67
metaphors, 417, 443, R67
    extended, 25, 52, 53, 443, R63
meter, 178, 367, R67
    iambic pentameter, 178
minor characters, R58
mise en scène, R67
MLA citation guidelines, R10–R11
*MLA Handbook for Writers of
    Research Papers* (MLA), R9
moderators, debate, R14
Modern Language Association
    (MLA), R9
modifiers, 80, R34
    adjectives, R34–R35
    adverbs, R35
    comparisons, R35–R36
    dangling, R36–R37
    misplaced, R36
    problems with, R36–R37
monitor as reading strategy, R67
mood, 149, 429, R67
moral, R67, R74
motif, 227
motivations, 279, R58
multimedia links, R5
multimedia presentations
    creating group, 157–160
    elements of effective, 157
    Performance Task Evaluation
        Chart, 160
    practicing delivery of, 159
    presenting, 159
    producing, 158
    revising, 159
    storyboarding, 158
multiple-meaning words, 9, 31, 315, R52

multiple plot lines, R7
*my*Notebook, 37, 41, 97, 153, 157, 301,
    355, 359, 445
myths, 283–287, R67
*my*WriteSmart, 8 18, 25, 30, 36, 38,
    39, 42, 53, 72, 78, 86, 94, 99, 120,
    130, 138, 144, 150, 155, 158, 159,
    170, 176, 206, 227, 252, 265, 280,
    288, 298, 302, 303, 314, 322, 336,
    348, 354, 356, 357, 360, 361, 418,
    430, 438, 444, 446, 447

N

name-calling, as persuasive device,
    R19
narrative nonfiction, 73–76, 82–84,
    307–312, 421–428, R67
narrative poems, 283–288, 365, R67.
    See also epics
narratives
    autobiographical, 77
    conclusions of, 155, R7
    epics as, 367
    fictional, 153–156, R6–R7
    Performance Task Evaluation
        Chart, 156
    techniques, identifying, 153
    travel, 429
    writing, 418, R6–R7
narrative techniques, R6–R7
narrators, 367, R6, R68
negatives, double, R36
negative side, in debates, R14
newspaper articles, R68
    citing, R11
nominative pronouns, R30
nonessential adjective clauses, R42
nonessential appositives, R39
nonfiction, R68
    literary, R66
    narrative, R67
non sequitur, R19
noun clauses, 10, R43
noun form, 145
noun modifiers, 80
noun phrases, 80, R38
nouns, R22, R29
    abstract, R22
    collective, R22, R47
    common, R22, R29
    compound, R22
    concrete, R22
    plural, R22, R29, R54
    possessive, R22, R29, R54
    predicate, R38
    proper, R22, R29
    singular, R22, R29
    suffixes that form, 95
novellas, R68
novels, R68

possessive pronouns, R30
practicing, speech delivery, 39
precede/proceed, R56
predicate
    adjectives, R35
    complete, R24
    compound, R37
    nominatives, 10, R38, R47
    nouns, R38
    pronouns, R38
predict, R70
prefixes, 349, 400, R49, R54
prepositional phrases, 20, 146, R24, R39
prepositions, R23
    common, 20
    object of, 10, 20
presentations
    group multimedia presentation, 157–160
    informative speech, 37–40
    oral reports, 78
    planning, 38
    speaking activity, 30
present participles, 172, R32–R33
present perfect progressive tense, R33
present perfect tense, R33
present principal part, R32–R33
present progressive tense, R33
present tense, R33
primary sources, R8, R72
prior knowledge, R70
problems, identifying, in writing narratives, R6
problem-solution order, R4, R70
procedural texts, R70
prologue, R59, R70
pronouns, R22, R29
    antecedent agreement, R29–R30
    cases, R30
    demonstrative, R22, R31
    indefinite, 324, R23, R31, R46–R47
    intensive, R22, R30
    interrogative, R23, R31
    nominative, R30
    objective, R30
    personal, 324, R22, R29, R46
    possessive, R30
    predicate, R38
    reciprocal, R23, R30–R31
    reference problems, R32
    reflexive, R22, R30
    relative, R23, R31–R32, R42, R47
pronunciation key, R76
propaganda, R20, R70
proper adjectives, R28
proper nouns, R22, R29
propositions, R14
props in drama, R70
prose, R70
protagonists, 177, R70

public documents, R70
public service announcement (PSA), 151, 152
publishing online, 447
punctuation, 96
    apostrophe, R26–R27
    colons, 96, 132, 338, R26
    commas, R25
    dashes, 432, R26
    ellipses, R27
    in epics, 367
    exclamation point, R25
    hyphens, R26
    meaning making and, 96
    parentheses, R26
    period, R25
    question mark, R25
    quick reference, R25–R27
    quotation marks, R27
    semicolons, 96, 338, R26
puns, 178, 281, R70
purpose, analyzing, 29, 152, 313

Q

quatrain, R70
question mark, R25
questions
    research, R8
    rhetorical, 88, R71
quotation marks, R27
quotations
    colons before, 96, 132, 338, R26
    direct, R9
quoting, 429

R

reading
    arguments, R16–R21
    drama, 179
    epics, 367
    Shakespearean tragedy, 179
    Shakespeare's language, 179
realistic fiction, R70
reasoning
    circular, 437, R19
    deductive, R18, R61
    faulty, 437, R19–R20
    inductive, R17–R18, R65
reasons, to support claims, 7, 129, 321, R2
reciprocal pronouns, R23, R30–R31
recurring themes, R74
reference sources, 79
    bibliography, R58
    dictionaries, R52
    glossaries, R52–R53
    synonym finders, R52
    thesaurus, R52
    using, R52–R53
reference works, R70
reflection activity, 176, 354

reflective essays, R62
reflexive pronouns, R22, R30
refrain, R70
regular verbs, R32–R33
relative clauses, 350
relative pronouns, R23, R31–R32, R42, R47
repetition, 8, 25, 29, 32, 52, 54, R71
reread, 8, 30, 43, 97, 144, 153, 157, 172, 280, 288, 314, 322, 335, 336, 348, 354, 355
research
    activity, 78
    for analytical essay, 446
    conducting, R8–R9
    focus of, R8
    formulating question for, R8
resolution, R59, R63. *See also* falling action
restatement, as context clues, R48
rhetoric
    analyzing, 29, 52, 313
    point of view and, 85
rhetorical devices, 52, 53, 54, R71
rhetorical questions, 88, R71
rhyme, 367, R71
rhyme scheme, R71
rhythm, R71
rising action, R71
romance, R71
roots, 70, 131, 419, R49
rough drafts. *See* drafts
round characters, R59
rubric. *See* Performance Task Evaluation Chart
run-on sentences, R45

S

sarcasm, R71
satire, R71
scanning, R71
scansion, R71
scene, R71
scenery, R71
science fiction, R72
science writing, 123–128, 325–334
screenplay, R72
script, R72
secondary sources, R8, R72–R73
semantic maps, 95, 171
semicolons, 96, 338, R26
seminal documents, analyzing, 29, 52
sensory details, R72
sentence fragments, R44–R45
sentences, R37
    complements, R37–R38
    complete, writing, R44–R45
    complex, R44
    compound, R43–R44
    compound-complex, R44

technical vocabulary, 129
teleplay, R74
tense, verb, R33
tension, as a literary technique 93, 347
testimonials, R17
text
  analyzing, 8, 18, 25, 30, 41, 69, 78, 86, 94, 97, 120, 130, 138, 150, 157, 170, 176, 206, 227, 252, 265, 280, 288, 298, 301, 314, 322, 336, 348, 354, 355, 399, 418, 430, 438, 444, 445
  comparing media and, 36, 47, 72, 81, 85
  evaluating, 18, 69, 72
  evidence from, 8, 18, 25, 30, 53, 69, 72, 78, 86, 94, 119, 120, 130, 144, 150, 152, 170, 176, 206, 227, 252, 265, 280, 288, 298, 314, 322, 336, 348, 354, 399, 418, 430, 438, 444
  inferences, 18, 30, 69, 78, 94, 120, 130, 170, 314, 348
  informational, 79, 123–129, 141–144, 325–334
  paraphrasing, 429
  procedural, R70
  quoting, 429
  reading arguments, R16–R21
  summarizing, 335, 399, 418, 430, 438
text criticism, R74
text features, R74
text structure, 17, 18, 69, 347, 348
than/then, R56
theater, Elizabethan, 180
their/there/they're, R56
theme, R74. *See also* central idea; main idea
  analyzing, 119
  connecting common, 288
  definition, 17, 119
  developing, 17
  epic, 365, 417
  identifying, 418
  interpreting, 206
  making inferences about, 17, 18, 30, 119, 138, 347, 444
  recurring, R74
  universal, R74
thesaurus, R52
thesis statement, R4, R16, R74
third-person limited, R70
third-person narrator, R6
third-person omniscient, R70
third-person point of view, R70
tone, R74
  analyzing, 130, 144, 169, 313
  of argument, 437, R3

biased, R3, R5
  definition of, 77, 137, 149
  determining, 353
  formal, 137, 138, 316, R3
  informal, 137, 138, 316, R3
  for informative essay, R5
  objective, R3, R5
  poems, 149
  punctuation and, 96
  word choice and, 77, 130, 137, 169, 313, 316, 353
topic
  developing, R4–R5
  introducing, R4
  research, R8
topic sentence, R74
traditional ballads, R58
tragedy, R74–R75
  characteristics of Shakespearean, 177
  definition, 177
  reading, 179
tragic flaw, 177, R75
tragic heroes, 177, R74–R75
transfer technique, 437, R17
transitions, 302, 440, R3, R4, R5
transitive verbs, R23
travel narratives, 429
trochee, R67
Turabian, Kate L., R9
two/too/to, R56

U
understatement, R75
universal themes, R74

V
valid conclusion, R60
valid reasons, to support claims, R14
vanity, appeals to, R17, R62
verbal irony, 93, R66
verbal phrases, R39–R40
verbals, R39–R40
verb form, 145
verb phrases, R38–R39, 140
verbs, R23, R32
  action, R23, R32
  active voice, R34
  auxiliary, R23, R24, R47
  gerunds, R40
  helping, 140, R24
  intransitive, R23
  irregular, R33
  linking, R23, R32
  main, R24
  participles, 172, 420, R40
  passive voice, R34
  principal parts, R32–R33
  progressive forms, R33–R34

regular, R32–R33
  subject-verb agreement, R45–R47
  tenses, R33–R34
  transitive, R23
video, 71, 72, 176, 433
video recordings, citing, R11
visualizing, R75
vocabulary
  Academic Vocabulary, 2, 37, 41, 46, 97, 102, 153, 157, 162, 301, 306, 355, 359, 364, 446
  commonly confused words, R55–R56
  Critical Vocabulary, 9, 19, 26, 31, 54, 70, 79, 87, 95, 121, 131, 139, 145, 171, 299, 315, 323, 337, 349, 400, 419, 431, 439
  specialized, R52
  strategies for understanding, R48–R53
  technical, 129
Vocabulary Strategy
  antonyms, 439
  context clues, 139, 299, 337, R48–R49
  denotations and connotations, 26, 87, 431
  Greek words, 70, 131
  Latin words, 19, 70
  multiple-meaning words, 31, 315
  patterns of word changes, 9, 121, 145
  prefixes, 349, 400
  puns, 281
  reference sources, 79
  suffixes that form nouns, 95
  synonyms, 171, 323, 439
  words from Latin, 419
voice, R75

W
website, R75
well vs. *good*, R36
word changes, patterns of, 9, 95, 121, 145
word choice, 77, 130, 137, 149, 169, 313, 316, 353
word families, R50
word meanings
  determining, 129, 169, 171, 299, 337, 400, 419, 439
  figurative, 353
  and prefixes, 349
  and puns, 178, 281
word origins, R50–R51
word play, in Shakespearean drama, 178, 281
workplace documents, R75
works cited, R9, R10, R75
works consulted, R75

Index of Titles & Authors

Acknowledgments

Excerpt from *The Age of Empathy* by Frans de Waal. Text copyright © 2009 by Frans de Waal. Reprinted by permission of Harmony Books, a division of Random House, Inc. Any third party use of this material, outside of this publication, is prohibited. Interested parties must apply directly to Random House, Inc. for permission.

Excerpt from *The American Heritage Dictionary of the English Language, Fifth Edition*. Text copyright © 2011 by Houghton Mifflin Harcourt. Adapted and reprinted by permission of Houghton Mifflin Harcourt Publishing Company.

"At Dusk" from *Native Guard* by Natasha Trethewey. Text copyright © 2006 by Natasha Trethewey. Reprinted by permission of Houghton Mifflin Harcourt Publishing Company.

Excerpt from *Cairo: My City, Our Revolution* by Ahdaf Soueif. Text copyright © 2012 by Ahdaf Soueif. Reprinted by permission of Bloomsbury Publishing and Wylie Agency Inc.

"The Censors" by Luisa Valenzuela, translated by David Unger from *Short Shorts: An Anthology of the Shortest Stories* edited by Irving Howe. Text copyright © by Luisa Valenzuela. English translation copyright © 1982 by David Unger. First published in *Short Shorts* edited by David Godine Howe. Reprinted by permission of David Unger and Luisa Valenzuela.

Excerpt from *The Cruelest Journey: 600 Miles to Timbuktu* by Kira Salak. Text copyright © 2005 by Kira Salak. Adapted and reprinted by permission of the National Geographic Society and Kira Salak.

Excerpt from *Deep Survival: Who Lives, Who Dies, and Why* by Laurence Gonzales. Text copyright © 2003 by Laurence Gonzales. Reprinted by permission of W. W. Norton & Company, Inc.

"Duty" from *Her Infinite Variety: Stories of Shakespeare and the Women He Loved* by Pamela Rafael Berkman. Text copyright © 2001 by Pamela Rafael Berkman. Adapted and reprinted by permission of Simon & Schuster, Inc. and Harvey Klinger, Inc. on behalf of Pamela Rafael. All rights reserved.

"The End and the Beginning" from *Miracle Fair: Selected Poems of Wisława Szymborska*, translated by Joanne Trzeciak. Text copyright © 2001 by Joanna Trzeciak. Reprinted by permission of W. W. Norton & Company, Inc.

"The Grasshopper and the Bell Cricket" from *Palm in the Hand and Other Stories* by Yasunari Kawabata, translated by Lane Dunlop and J. Martin Holman. Translation copyright © 1988 by Lane Dunlop and J. Martin Holman. Reprinted by permission of North Point Press, a division of Farrar, Straus and Giroux, LLC.

"I Have a Dream" speech by Martin Luther King, Jr. Text copyright © 1963 by Martin Luther King, Jr. Text copyright renewed © 1991 by Coretta Scott King. Reprinted by permission of Writers House LLC on behalf of the Heirs of the Estate of Martin Luther King, Jr.

Excerpts from "I Have a Dream" by Martin Luther King, Jr., from *Nobody Turn Me Around: A People's History of the 1963 March on Washington* by Charles Euchner. Text copyright © 1963 by Martin Luther King, Jr. Text copyright renewed © 1991 by Coretta Scott King. Reprinted by permission of Writers House LLC on behalf of the Heirs of the Estate of Martin Luther King, Jr.

Excerpt from "Introduction: Love's Vocabulary" from *A Natural History of Love* by Diane Ackerman. Text copyright © 1994 by Diane Ackerman. Reprinted by permission of Random House, Inc. and Diane Ackerman care of Janklow & Nesbit Associates. Any third party use of this material, outside of this publication, is prohibited. Interested parties must apply directly to Random House, Inc. for permission.

"Is Survival Selfish?" by Lane Wallace from *The Atlantic*, www.theatlantic.com, January 29, 2010. Text copyright © 2010 by Lane Wallace (LaneWallace.com). Reprinted by permission of Lane Wallace.

"The Journey" from *Dream Work* by Mary Oliver. Text copyright © 1986 by Mary Oliver. Reprinted by permission of Grove/Atlantic Inc. and Charlotte Sheedy Literary Agency.

"The Leap" by Louise Erdrich from *Harper's Magazine*, March 1990. Text copyright © 1990 by Harper's Magazine. Reprinted by permission of Harper's Magazine. All rights reserved.

"My Shakespeare" by Kate Tempest. Text copyright © 2012 by Kate Tempest. Reprinted by permission of William Morris Endeavor Entertainment, LLC on behalf of Kate Tempest.

Excerpt from *Night* by Elie Wiesel, translated by Marion Wiesel. Text copyright © 2006 by Elie Wiesel, translation copyright © 2006 by Marion Wiesel. Reprinted by permission of Hill and Wang, a division of Farrar, Straus and Giroux, LLC, Recorded Books and George Borchardt, Inc.

Excerpt from *Nobody Turn Me Around: A People's History of the 1963 March on Washington* by Charles Euchner. Text copyright © 2010 by Charles Euchner. Reprinted by permission of Beacon Press and Trident Media, LLC. on behalf of Charles Euchner.

Excerpts from *The Odyssey* by Homer, translated by Robert Fitzgerald. Text copyright © 1961. Text copyright renewed ©1989 by Benedict R.C. Fitzgerald on behalf of the Fitzgerald children. Reprinted by permission of Farrar, Straus and Giroux, LLC and Benedict Fitzgerald.

"Once Upon a Time" from *Jump and Other Stories* by Nadine Gordimer. Text copyright © 1991 by Felix Licensing B.V. Adapted and reprinted by permission of Penguin Group (Canada), a Division of Pearson Canada, Inc., Farrar, Straus and Giroux, LLC, A.P. Watt at United Agents on behalf of Felix Licensing, B.V., and Russell & Volkening as agents of the author.

RESEARCH METHODS
A Tool For Life

THIRD EDITION

Research Methods is an introduction to the importance of scientific research in everyday life and uses familiar examples to keep students engaged. The text analyzes controversies in psychology to stimulate student interest while explaining crucial methodological concepts. It presents ethical issues related to research, as well as social and cultural factors that might affect it, and provides a comprehensive introduction to a wide variety of methodologies. Through this book, students will learn how to generate research questions and select appropriate methodology, as well as to write a successful research report.

Bernard C. Beins is Professor of psychology at Ithaca College. He has been President-elect of the New England Psychological Association and the Society for the Teaching of Psychology.

Research Methods

A Tool For Life

Third Edition

Bernard C. Beins

Ithaca College, New York

CAMBRIDGE
UNIVERSITY PRESS

University Printing House, Cambridge CB2 8BS, United Kingdom

One Liberty Plaza, 20th Floor, New York, NY 10006, USA

477 Williamstown Road, Port Melbourne, VIC 3207, Australia

4843/24, 2nd Floor, Ansari Road, Daryaganj, Delhi – 110002, India

79 Anson Road, #06–04/06, Singapore 079906

Cambridge University Press is part of the University of Cambridge.

It furthers the University's mission by disseminating knowledge in the pursuit of education, learning, and research at the highest international levels of excellence.

www.cambridge.org
Information on this title: www.cambridge.org/9781108436236
DOI: 10.1017/9781108399531

This book was previously published by Pearson Education, Inc. 2004, 2009, 2013.

Reissued by Cambridge University Press 2017

Printed in the United States of America by Sheridan Books, Inc

A catalogue record for this publication is available from the British Library.

ISBN 978-1-108-43623-6 Hardback

Once again, I dedicate this book to Simon, Agatha, and Linda who always provide me with inspiration and love.

CONTENTS

CHAPTER THREE

Planning Research: Generating a Question   58

CHAPTER FOUR

Practical Issues in Planning Your Research   92

CHAPTER FIVE

Measurement and Sampling   117

CHAPTER SEVEN

Experiments with One Independent Variable   166

CHAPTER EIGHT

Experiments with Multiple Independent Variables   190

CHAPTER NINE

Expanding on Experimental Designs: Repeated Measures and Quasi-Experiments   211

CHAPTER TEN

Principles of Survey Research   238

CHAPTER ELEVEN

Correlational Research   261

CHAPTER TWELVE

Studying Patterns in the Natural World: Observational Approaches   284

It would be tempting to think that research methods never change and that last year's model is perfectly good this year. In some ways that is true. Psychological research follows predictable paths, including predictable methodologies.

However, sometimes the emphasis and focus of research undergoes change, even as the basic principles remain the same. This edition of *Research Methods: A Tool for Life* reflects some changes that have emerged in our discipline. There is a chapter on cultural and individual differences in the research enterprise; it is an updated version of the chapter that has appeared in the two previous editions of the book.

Furthermore, in this edition, I have tried to embed more culturally focused research within each chapter, hoping that one focus of contemporary psychological research, cultural and cross-cultural issues, becomes more apparent in the discussions of different kinds of research. It is important to recognize that cultural issues in research do not belong only in a single chapter.

Rather, we need to attend to the importance of culture in our approaches to research and in the conclusions we draw. Thus, cultural and cross-cultural issues do not stand apart from the rest of psychology. They are in and of themselves an important aspect of our discipline. So, as you read each chapter, you will see descriptions of research that go beyond Guthrie's (2004) sentiment that "even the rat was white."

In addition, there is new material on ethics in research. Over the past several years, issues of ethics have surfaced that tell us that we still have to pay attention to the welfare of the people who volunteer for our studies and that ethical issues have an impact on us all.

In addition, there are other updates to the presentation, with research that reflects the current nature of scientific psychology. And as with the previous editions, I have tried to show how the sometimes abstract principles of research actually do have an effect on our lives outside the laboratory. In the long run, empirical research is the best basis for making decisions about our lives. That doesn't mean that we can be simplistic—no single laboratory study ever settles an argument. But, in the long run, the body of research on many topics has been shown to be a highly effective means of guiding our behaviors.

INSTRUCTOR AND STUDENT SUPPORT PACKAGE

MySearchLab with eText (http://www.mysearchlab.com) can be packaged with this text by ordering ISBN 0205903878, or purchased separately online. MySearchLab includes the full eText, glossary flashcards, chapter quizzes that report directly to an instructor gradebook, a full suite of writing and research tools, access to a variety of academic journals, census data, Associated Press newsfeeds, and discipline-specific readings. MySearchLab also includes a set of online experiment simulations to show students research in action.

Operation ARA (Acquiring Research Acumen), an online smart game that teaches critical thinking and research methods skills, is available within MySearchLab, as well as standalone (http://ara.pearsoncmg.com). This simulation features a "save the world" plot that requires students to learn and apply critical thinking skills and scientific principles to uncover and foil an extraterrestrial plot to colonize Earth. The game includes an embedded critical thinking assessment, provided in two forms so that it can be used as a pre- and a post-test, to assess critical thinking outcomes. Operation ARA was authored and developed by Keith Millis, Northern Illinois University; Art Graesser, University of Memphis; and Diane Halpern, Claremont McKenna College.

Research Methods Laboratory Manual (ISBN 0205741703), authored by Barney Beins and Jeffrey Holmes, both from Ithaca College, contains laboratory activities that are similar to a number of published psychological studies. The purpose of this book is to give students the opportunity to experience psychological research from the point of view of both the participant and the researcher. Each lab contains directions on collecting data, a summary of the research underlying the lab, instructions for performing various statistical analyses on the data, critical thinking questions, and questions to help students think about how they might extend the research into a research project. Ethical guidelines and a bibliography are also provided for each lab.

ACKNOWLEDGMENTS

My mentors throughout my educational years prepared me for a career that has allowed me to address interesting questions and to work with generations of motivated and very likable students. These mentors included the late Jim Kwiatkowski, John Jahnke, and Arthur Reber, all of whom had a role in my ability to mentor my own students.

I'd like to thank the reviewers of the second edition of this text for their input: Heather Hill, University of Texas at San Antonio; Merry Sleigh-Ritzer, Winthrop University; C. Mark Wessinger, University of Nevada; and Bonnie Wright, Gardner Webb University.

I am also grateful for the continued help that Stephen Frail and Maddy Schricker have provided throughout this project. In addition, I am thankful to Anand Natarajan for his excellent attention to detail in the editing phase of this project.

Finally, as always, I am eternally thankful for my wonderful family, Linda, Agatha, and Simon.

Reference

Guthrie, R. V. (2004). *Even the rat was white: A historical view of psychology* (2nd ed.). Upper Saddle River, NJ: Pearson Education.

PSYCHOLOGY, SCIENCE, AND LIFE

LEARNING OBJECTIVES

After going through this chapter, you will be able to:

- Identify and describe the four basic goals of science
- Explain why falsifiability is important in scientific research
- Define the five different ways of knowing
- Explain the advantages of using the scientific approach to knowing
- Describe the importance of culture on approaches to knowledge
- Describe the four characteristics of scientific research
- Explain how science is driven by government, culture, and society
- Explain how researchers try to generalize from laboratory research to the natural world
- Differentiate between science and pseudoscience
- Identify the general characteristics of pseudoscience

KEY TERMS

CHAPTER PREVIEW

You probably know a great deal about people and some interesting and important facts about psychology, but you probably know relatively little about psychological research. This book will show you how research helps you learn more about people from a psychological point of view. You can be certain of one thing: There are no simple explanations.

When you read through this chapter, you will learn that there are different ways of knowing about behavior. As a beginning psychologist, you will get a glimpse about why some types of knowledge are more useful than others. In addition, you will see that people can be resistant to changing what they believe. For instance, a lot of people believe in ESP or other paranormal phenomena, even though the scientific evidence for it just isn't there. One reason for such beliefs is that most people don't approach life the same way that scientists do, so the evidence they accept is sometimes pretty shaky.

Finally, this chapter will introduce you to some of the cautions you should be aware of when you read about psychological research in the popular media. Journalists are not scientists and scientists are not journalists, so there is a lot of potential for miscommunication between the two.

WHY ARE RESEARCH METHODS IMPORTANT TOOLS FOR LIFE?

The great thing about psychology is that people are both interesting and complicated, and we get to learn more about them. As you learn more, you will see that there can be a big difference between what we think we know about behavior and what is actually true. That is why you need this course—it will help you understand the world around you.

Your course on research begins the process of learning about how psychological knowledge emerges. This knowledge can be useful when applied to people's lives. For instance, even four years after a domestic terrorist destroyed a federal building in Oklahoma City, killing 168 people, about half the survivors were still suffering from some kind of psychiatric illness (North et al., 1999). This pattern mirrors the effects of the terrorist attacks in the United States in 2001, the devastation caused by a hurricane in Louisiana in 2005, and the experiences of many soldiers in combat in Iraq and Afghanistan, indicating the critical need to provide effective treatments (Humphreys, 2009).

We don't have to rely on such extreme examples of the use of psychological research. For example, scientists have suggested that some people suffer from addiction to indoor tanning (Zeller, Lazovich, Forster, & Widome, 2006), with some showing withdrawal symptoms when the researchers experimentally blocked the physiological effects of tanning (Kaur et al., 2006). In the Controversy box on tanning addiction, you can see a psychological approach to investigating whether people can become addicted to tanning.

Another complex question relating to everyday life has involved something as seemingly noncontroversial as the *Baby Einstein* DVDs that purport to enhance language learning. Researchers have found that with increasing exposure to the *Baby Einstein* videos, language development actually slows down (Zimmerman, Christakis, & Meltzoff, 2007). In fact, Christakis (2009) has claimed that there is no experimental evidence indicating any advantages for language development in young infants. The developer of the videos makes the opposite claim. So how should we respond?

The only way to address such issues is to do research, which means that we need to create knowledge where it does not already exist. It might sound strange to think of "creating" knowledge, but that is exactly what happens in research. You end up with information that didn't exist before. This is one of the exciting parts of doing research: When you complete a study, you know something that nobody else in the world knows.

■ ■ ■ ■ ■

CONTROVERSY:
On Tanning Addiction

Is it even reasonable to think that getting a tan might be an addiction? Isn't getting a tan just getting a tan? This is a question that we can address empirically. That is, we can collect data.

As noted before, Zeller et al. (2006) reported that adolescents find it difficult to stop their use of indoor tanning beds. What would you need to do to determine if tanning is an addiction? One approach is to see whether people engaging in this activity show the same orientation to it as do the people who are addicted to some substance, such as alcohol.

Clinicians diagnose addiction by asking whether alcohol users sometimes feel the need to reduce their alcohol consumption, whether people around them encourage them to quit drinking, whether they feel guilty about drinking, and whether they want to drink as soon as they awaken in the morning. When people respond yes to these questions, they could very well be addicted to alcohol.

What about asking related questions about tanning? Kourosh, Harrington, and Adinoff (2010) reported that investigators claim that up to 70 percent of frequent tanners respond that sometimes they think they should cut down on the frequency of tanning, that others annoy them about stopping, that they sometimes feel guilty about tanning, and that they want to do it when they get up in the morning. That is, frequent tanners respond to those questions in ways similar to alcoholics.

One mechanism for an addiction might be the physiological effect of exposure to ultraviolet light. Frequent tanners who had the choice between two tanning beds, one with UV exposure and one without, tended to select the one with UV exposure. Similarly, when the tanners received a drug that blocked the physiological effects of UV exposure, they showed withdrawal symptoms.

So tanning might become habitual not only because people think they look better with a tan but also because the UV light exerts a real biological effect with many of the characteristics associated with addiction to some drugs.

Question for Discussion: Researchers Martin and Petry (2005) have claimed that behaviors like excessive gambling or Internet use share clinical and biological elements with addiction to drugs and alcohol. Does it make sense to equate addictions to these behaviors to addictions to drugs?

Why Research Is Important

In reading textbooks or journal articles, we might get the impression that we can carry out a research project and an explanation jumps clearly out of the results. In reality, there is always uncertainty in research. When we plan our investigations, we make many decisions about our procedures; when we examine our results, we usually have to puzzle through them before we are confident that we understand what we are looking at. In textbooks and journals, we only see the end product of ideas that have worked out successfully, and we do not see the twists and turns that led to those successes.

This course in research methods will also help you prepare for a possible future in psychology. If you attend graduate school, you will see that nearly all programs in psychology require an introductory psychology course, statistics, and research methods or experimental psychology. Your graduate school professors want you to know how psychologists think; research-based courses provide you with this knowledge. Those professors will provide courses that will help you learn the skills appropriate for your career. As a psychologist, you also need to understand the research process so you can read scientific journals, make sense of the research reports, and keep abreast of current ideas. Even if you don't choose a career as a researcher, you can still benefit from understanding research. Many jobs require knowledge of statistics and research.

In addition, every day you will be bombarded by claims that scientists have made breakthroughs in understanding various phenomena. It will be useful for you to be able to evaluate whether to believe what you hear. A course in research will help you learn how to think critically about the things people tell you. Is their research sound? Is the conclusion they draw the best one? Do they have something to gain from getting certain results? This process of critical thinking is a hallmark of science, but it is also a useful tool in everyday life.

Answering Important Questions

There are many important scientific questions in need of answers. The journal *Science* (2005) listed what some scientists see as the top 25 questions that society needs to address. At least five of these are associated with issues that psychologists can help address:

- What is the biological basis of consciousness?
- How are memories stored and retrieved?
- How did cooperative behavior evolve?
- To what extent are genetic variation and personal health linked?
- Will the world's population outstrip the world's capability to accommodate 10 billion people?

These questions deal with behavior, either directly or indirectly. As such, psychologists will need to be involved in providing portions of the answers to each of these questions.

Of the next 100 important questions, 13 are psychological and behavioral, at least in part. These questions appear in Table 1.1, along with the areas of psychology to which they relate. As you can see, regardless of your specific interest in psychology, you will be able to find important questions to answer.

TABLE 1.1   Psychological Questions Listed Among the Top Unanswered Questions in *Science* (2005) Magazine and the Areas of Psychology Associated with Them

Area of Psychology	Question
Social psychology	What are the roots of human culture?
Cognitive psychology	What are the evolutionary roots of language and music?
Biological bases of behavior/Cognitive psychology	Why do we sleep?
Personality/Learning	Why do we dream?
Biological bases of behavior	What synchronizes an organism's circadian clocks?
Comparative psychology/Learning	How do migrating organisms find their way?
Social psychology/Biological bases of behavior	What is the biological root of sexual orientation?
Abnormal psychology	What causes schizophrenia?
Developmental psychology	Why are there critical periods for language learning?
Personality theory/Biological bases of behavior	How much of personality is genetic?
Biological bases of behavior	Do pheromones influence human behavior?
Developmental psychology/Biological bases of behavior	What causes autism?
Personality theory	Is morality hardwired into the brain?

Sometimes those questions hit very close to home. After Hurricane Katrina devastated New Orleans in 2005, people worked to reassemble their lives. Part of this task involved reopening businesses so that life could get back to normal. Researchers investigated some of the factors associated with businesses that resumed their work and discovered a notable psychological component. Family-owned businesses tended to open sooner than retail chains; in addition, if a business opened in a given location, neighboring businesses were likely to reopen as well (LeSage, 2011).

After you complete this course in research methods, you will be able to apply your new knowledge to areas outside of psychology. The research skills you pick up here will let you complete solid psychological research projects, and will also help you understand life better.

SCIENTIFIC AND NONSCIENTIFIC KNOWLEDGE

There are still occasional debates about the scientific status of psychology. But to address this issue logically, we first need to establish what constitutes science. According to the National Academy of Science, science is actually a process, not a body of knowledge:

Scientists gather information by observing the natural world and conducting experiments. They then propose how the systems being studied behave in general, basing their explanations on the data provided through their experiments and other observations. They test their explanations by conducting additional observations and experiments under different conditions. Other scientists confirm the observations independently and carry out additional studies that may lead to more sophisticated explanations and predictions about future observations and experiments. In these ways, scientists continually arrive at more accurate and more comprehensive explanations of particular aspects of nature. (National Academy of Sciences, 2008, p. 10)

If you take a look at any psychological research journal, you will clearly see that psychologists conduct experiments, generate explanations, confirm their findings, and strive to make their conclusions as comprehensive and as accurate as possible.

In addition, Boyack, Klavans, & Börner (2005) have identified so-called "hub sciences" around which other disciplines hover. They assessed a million articles from 7,121 natural and social science journals published in the year 2000 to see what areas influenced or were influenced by other areas. The authors found that there were seven hub sciences that were cited by the other sciences: mathematics, physics, chemistry, earth sciences, medicine, psychology, and the social sciences.

An important question about knowledge is how we acquire it. Obviously, scientific knowledge is one means, but it is not the only way that people deal with what they know. There are different paths to factual knowledge in our lives. We will see that not all roads to knowledge are equally useful. The nineteenth-century American philosopher Charles Sanders Peirce (1877) identified several ways of knowing, which he called **tenacity**, **authority**, the **a priori method**, and the **scientific approach**. He concluded that the best approach was the scientific approach.

Tenacity involves simply believing something because you don't want to give up your belief. People do this all the time; you have probably discovered that it can be difficult to convince people to change their minds. However, if two people hold mutually contradictory beliefs, both cannot be true. According to Peirce, in a "saner moment," we might recognize that others have valid points, which can shake our own beliefs.

An alternative to an individual's belief in what is true, Peirce thought, could reside in what authorities say is true. This approach removes the burden from any single person to make decisions; instead, one would rely on an expert of some kind. Peirce talked about authorities who would force beliefs under threat of some kind of penalty, but we can generalize to any acceptance of knowledge because somebody whom we trust says something is true. As Peirce noted, though, experts with different perspectives will hold different beliefs. How is one to know which expert is actually right?

He then suggested that people might fix their knowledge based on consensus and reasoned argument, the *a priori* approach. The problem here, he wrote, was that reasons for believing something may change over time, so what was seen as true in the past may change. Later thinkers have added **experience** as contributing to knowledge, but different people have different experiences, which can lead to different versions of "the truth". So experience is limited in its utility.

Tenacity—The mode of accepting knowledge because one is comfortable with it and simply wants to hold onto it.

Authority—The mode of accepting knowledge because a person in a position of authority claims that something is true or valid.

A Priori Method—The mode of accepting knowledge based on a premise that people have agreed on, followed by reasoned argument.

Scientific Approach—The mode of accepting knowledge based on empirically derived data.

Experience—A way of knowing that uses personal experience as the means of deciding what is true about behavior.

If we want to know universal truths, he reasoned, the most valid approach is through science, which is objective and self-correcting. Gradually, we can accumulate knowledge that is valid and discard ideas that prove to be wrong.

CHARACTERISTICS OF SCIENCE

Science Is Objective

What does it mean for our observations to be **objective**? One implication is that we define clearly the concepts we are dealing with. This is often easier said than done. Psychologists deal with complex and abstract concepts that are hard to measure. Nonetheless, we have to develop some way to measure these concepts in clear and systematic ways. For example, suppose we want to find out whether we respond more positively to attractive people than to others.

> **Objective—** Measurements that are not affected by personal bias and are well defined and specified are considered objective.

To answer our question, we first have to define what we mean by "attractive." The definition must be objective; that is, the definition has to be consistent, clear, and understandable, even though it may not be perfect.

Researchers have taken various routes to creating objective definitions of attractiveness. Wilson (1978) simply mentioned that "a female confederate...appearing either attractive or unattractive asked in a neutral manner for directions to a particular building on central campus at a large Midwestern University" (p. 313). This vague statement doesn't really tell us as much as we would like to know. We don't have a clear definition of what the researchers meant by attractiveness. Juhnke et al. (1987) varied the attire of people who seemed to be in need of help. The researchers defined attractiveness based on clothing. Unattractive people, that is, those wearing less desirable clothing, received help, even though they did not look very attractive. On the other hand, Bull and Stevens (1980) used helpers with either good or bad teeth in defining attractive and unattractive.

If the different research teams did not report how they created an unattractive appearance, we would have a harder time evaluating their research and repeating it exactly as they did it. It may be very important to know what manipulation the researchers used. Differences in attractiveness due to the kinds of clothes you are wearing may not lead to the same reactions as differences due to unsightly teeth.

> **Data Driven—** Interpretations of research that are based on objective results of a project are considered data driven.

Science Is Data Driven

Our conclusions as scientists must also be **data driven**. This simply means that our conclusions must follow logically from our data. There may be several equally good interpretations from a single set of data. Regardless of which interpretation we choose, it has to be based on the data we collect.

> **Empirical Approach—** The method of discovery that relies on systematic observation and data collection for guidance on drawing conclusions.

To say that science is based on data is to say that it is **empirical**. Empiricism refers to the method of discovery that relies on systematic observation and data for drawing conclusions. Psychology is an empirical discipline in that knowledge is based on the results of research, that is, on data.

The critical point here is that if we are to develop a more complete and accurate understanding of the world around us, scientific knowledge based on data will, in the long run, serve us better than intuition alone. Don't discount intuition entirely; quite a few scientific insights had their beginnings in intuitions that were scientifically studied and found to be true. We just can't rely entirely on intuition because it differs across people and may change over time.

Science Is Replicable and Verifiable

Our scientific knowledge has to be potentially **replicable** and **verifiable**. This means that others should have the opportunity to repeat a research project to see if the same results occur each time. Maybe the researchers who are trying to repeat the study will generate the same result; maybe they will not. We do not claim that *results* are scientific; rather, we claim that the *approach* is scientific. Any time somebody makes a claim but will not let others verify it as valid, we should be skeptical.

> **Replicable**—When scientists can recreate a previous research study, that study is replicable.

> **Verifiable**—When scientists can reproduce a previous research study and generate the same results, it is verifiable.

Why should one scientist repeat somebody else's research? As it turns out, there is a bias among journal editors to publish findings that show differences across groups and to reject studies showing no differences. So a relatively large number of research reports may describe differences that occurred accidentally. That is, groups may differ, but not for any systematic or reproducible reason. If the researcher were to repeat the study, a different result would occur.

Ioannidis (2005), referring to genetic and biomedical research, noted that "there is increasing concern that in modern research, false findings may be the majority or even the vast majority of published research claims" (p. 696)*. His conclusion comes, in part, from a recognition that journal editors and researchers are more impressed by findings that show that something interesting occurred but not by findings that do not reveal interesting patterns. Ioannidis's speculation may be true for psychological research, just as it is for biologically based studies.

> **Public**—Scientists make their research public, typically by making presentations at conferences or by publishing their work in journals or books.

Psychologists have recognized this problem for quite some time (e.g., Rosenthal, 1979). Fortunately, when a research project is repeated and the same outcome results, our confidence in the results increases markedly (Moonesinghe, Khoury, & Janssens, 2007). The reason that replication of research is such a good idea is that it helps us to weed out findings that turn out to be false and to strengthen our confidence in findings that are valid.

> **Peer Review**—A process in which researchers submit their research for publication in a journal or present their research at a conference to other experts in the field who evaluate the research.

Science Is Public

When we say that our research is *public*, we mean this literally. Scientists only recognize research as valid or useful when they can scrutinize it. Generally, we accept research as valid if it has undergone *peer review*. For instance, when a psychologist completes research, often the next step is to write the results in a scientific manuscript and submit it for publication in a research journal.

---

* Ioannidis JPA (2005) Why Most Published Research Findings Are False. *PLoS Med* 2(8): e124. doi:10.1371/journal.pmed.0020124

The editor of the journal will send the manuscript to experts in the field for their comments. If the editor and the reviewers agree that major problems have been taken care of, the article will appear in the journal. Otherwise, the article will be rejected. Among major journals in psychology, only about a quarter or fewer of all manuscripts that researchers submit are published.

Another approach to making our research public involves submitting a proposal to a research conference for a presentation. The process for acceptance to a conference resembles that for acceptance by a journal. In some cases, researchers may initially present their ideas at a conference, then follow up with a published article.

CULTURE AND DIFFERENT WAYS OF KNOWING

In the United States and Europe, we are used to thinking in certain ways. For instance, it is not unusual for people in the West to regard a fact as either true or false. That is, we create dichotomies. When we engage in research, we try to find the single correct answer to our question. Although we accept this approach as normal and appropriate, there are other approaches to knowledge that have as much validity to them as the Western approach.

For example, Eastern people are more willing to accept two contradictory statements as each having truth to them, whereas Western people prefer to accept a single truth when confronted with contradictions (Nisbett, Peng, Choi, & Norenzayan, 2001). In addition, the ways that people organize their world differ according to cultural orientation. For instance, when people in the West select two related words from triads like *monkey-panda-banana*, they tend to group the words functionally (i.e., *monkey-panda*), whereas people in the East use relational groupings (i.e., *monkey-banana*) (Ji, Zhang, & Nisbett, 2004).

These differences in approaches have distinct relevance regarding both the creation and the interpretation of research. In the past, Western researchers simply imported their methodologies to new cultures, asking research questions that might not have been particularly meaningful to people in those cultures. Fortunately, psychologists have become more aware that awareness of culture is a prerequisite to good research.

WHY WE DO RESEARCH

People are curious, social beings. As a result, most of us are interested in what others are up to and why. By the time you read this book, you have been observing others since childhood. You have probably become a sophisticated observer of others' behaviors and can predict pretty well how your friends will react if you act a certain way, at least some of the time. How did you gain this knowledge? Throughout your life, you have done things and then you observed the effect you had on others. Although you probably have not gone through life wearing the stereotypical white lab coat worn by some scientists, you have acted like a scientist when you discovered that "When I do this, they do that." One of the differences between scientific and nonscientific observation, though, is that scientists develop systematic plans, and we work to reduce bias in recording observations. In the end, though, curiosity and enjoyment in finding out about behavior underlies the reason why researchers do their work–they think it is fun.

As curious scientists, we generally work toward four goals based on our observations: description, explanation, prediction, and control of behavior.

Description

Our tendency to act and then to observe others' reactions fulfills what seems to be a basic need for us: describing the world around us. In fact, when you can **describe** events around you, you have taken the first step in scientific discovery. In research, description involves a systematic approach to observing behavior.

> **Description**—A goal of science in which behaviors are systematically and accurately characterized.

In your course on behavioral research, you will learn how, as scientists, we systematically begin to understand why people act as they do. The biggest difference between what you do in your everyday observations and what scientists do is that scientists pay attention to a lot of details that we normally think of as unimportant. Unlike most of us in everyday, casual observation, researchers develop a systematic plan for making objective observations so we can generate complete and accurate descriptions.

Explanation

This leads to another goal of science, **explanation**. When we truly understand the causes of behavior, we can explain them. This is where theory comes in. A **theory** helps us understand behavior in a general sense. In scientific use, a theory is a general, organizing principle. When we have enough relevant information about behavior, we can develop an explanatory framework that puts all of that information into a nice, neat package—that is, into a theory. Thus, to say that evolution is a theory means that it is the best set of ideas to explain biological phenomena. In everyday life, people often use the word *theory* when they mean *hypothesis* that scientists pose as expectations regarding the results of their research. So if a person says that evolution is only a theory, that person probably has a misunderstanding about what scientific theory really is.

> **Explanation**—A goal of science in which a researcher achieves awareness of why behaviors occur as they do.

> **Theory**—An set of interrelated concepts that scientists use to organize concepts and explain natural phenomena.

> **Hypothesis**—A testable prediction regarding the empirical outcome of research

In order to develop a theory, we look at the facts that we believe to be true and try to develop a coherent framework that links the facts to one another. The next step is to test the theory to see if it successfully predicts the results of new research. So we generate hypotheses, which are educated guesses, about behaviors, and we test those hypotheses with research. The research shows us whether our hypotheses are correct; if so, the theory receives further support.

If enough of our hypotheses support a theory, we regard it as more useful in understanding why people act in a certain way; if those hypotheses do not support the theory, we need to revise or abandon the theory. When we conduct research, we should have an open mind about an issue; we might have preconceived ideas of what to expect, but if we are wrong, we should be willing to change our beliefs.

When we test hypotheses, we make them objective and testable. This means that we define our terms clearly so others know exactly what we mean, and we specify how our

Falsifiability—A characteristic of science that any principle has to be amenable to testing to see if it is true or, more specifically, if it can be shown to be false.

research will assess whether a hypothesis is valid. One of the important elements of the scientific method is **falsifiability**. That is, we will test hypotheses to see if we can prove them wrong. Scientists do not believe that you can prove that an idea or theory is absolutely true. There may be a case that you have missed that would disprove the theory. But we can see when the theory breaks down, that is, when it is falsified. The best we can do is to try to falsify the theory through continual testing. Each time we try and fail to falsify the theory, our confidence in it increases.

For decades, people have used Freudian (psychodynamic) or behavioral theories to try to understand behavior. Both approaches have generated useful ideas about human behavior and have been accepted, at least in part, by the general public.

Many psychologists believe that a lot of Freud's ideas are not scientifically valid. In fact, when Freudian ideas have been subjected to experimentation, they often have not stood up well, although some psychologists maintain that Freudian ideas have received support from research (Westen, 1998).

Behavioral terms have also made their way into everyday language, as when people talk about positive or negative reinforcement. In the case of behaviorism, most psychologists affirm that it is a truly scientific approach. The ideas are objective and testable; in a wide variety of research programs, the utility of behavioral ideas has been well established.

In research, we use hypotheses to make predictions about behavior; theories are useful for helping us explain why our predictions are accurate. As psychologists, we use theory to explain behavior. Our explanations differ from the ones we generate in everyday life in that scientific explanations involve well-specified statements of when behaviors will or will not occur.

Prediction

Prediction—A goal of science in which a researcher can specify in advance those situations in which a particular behavior will occur.

Another goal is to expand your knowledge beyond simple description. So you can **predict** behavior. Suppose you tell a story. You are likely to make a prediction about how your friends will react to it. In considering whether to tell the story, you are making a prediction about their response. Every time you tell a story, you are engaging in a kind of experiment, making a prediction about the outcome. Naturally, you are sometimes wrong in your prediction because people are not easy to figure out.

Similarly, in behavioral research, we sometimes make poor predictions. When that happens, a scientist will try to figure out why the predictions were wrong and will attempt to make better ones next time. A big difference between casual and scientific predictions is that scientists generally specify in great detail what factors lead to a given outcome. For most of us in everyday life, we have a vague notion of what behaviors to expect from others and, as a result, will accept our predictions as true if somebody behaves in ways that are roughly approximate to what we expected. There is a lot of room for error.

In our relationships with others, we find it helpful to describe and to predict their behaviors because it gives us a sense of control; we know in advance what will happen. At the same time, most of us want to know even more. We want to know *why* people act as they do. This is a difficult process because people's behaviors arise for a lot of reasons.

Control of behavior

The final step in psychological research is **control of behavior**. Some people may ask whether it is right for us to try to control others' behaviors. Most psychologists would respond that we affect others' behaviors, just as they affect ours. It is not a matter of *should* we control behavior, but rather *how* does it happen. For example, parents try to raise children who show moral behavior. It would be reassuring to parents if they knew how to create such behavior in their children.

> **Control**—A goal of science in which a researcher can manipulate variables in order to produce specific behaviors.

In order to exert control of behavior effectively, we need to understand why the behavior occurs as it does. To understand the elements of control, we need to have well-formulated theories. At this point, we don't have a single theory of behavior that can capture the variety of human experience.

Psychologists with different theoretical orientations may use similar statements in describing behavior, but they will begin to diverge when making predictions, become even more different regarding explanation, and even more so with respect to control. Table 1.2 summarizes the four different goals of science and how psychologists have used them at various points in their research programs.

THE INTERACTION OF SCIENCE AND CULTURE

Many people undoubtedly think of science as happening in laboratories remote from the lives of real people. Nothing could be farther from the truth. Scientists live in communities and go to the same movies you do, coach their children's soccer teams, and worry about the same things that you do. Not surprisingly, culture shapes the research conducted by many scientists because our culture shapes the way we think. For example, after the terrorist attacks in the United States, some person or persons sent anthrax spores through the mail, infecting a number of people and killing some of them. This spurred increased scientific attention to anthrax.

In addition, in an energy crisis, researchers in psychology, biology, physics, and chemistry are motivated to study patterns of energy-using behavior, the development of biofuels, creation of efficient technologies, and conservation of energy. When environmental issues loom, such as the release of massive amounts of oil in the Gulf of Mexico in 2010, researchers in the natural sciences may be predisposed to focus on ecological issues, and behavioral researchers will study the impact of the crisis on people's lives and behaviors. Children will receive particular scrutiny because research has revealed their susceptibility to posttraumatic stress disorder in times of catastrophe (La Greca & Silverman, 2009; Osofsky, Osofsky, Kronenberg, Brennan, & Hansel, 2009). Psychologists are as much a part of the community as anyone, so it should come as no surprise that our research reflects the needs and concerns of our society.

Discussion of research ideas are also affected by social attitudes. After Thornhill and Palmer (2000) proposed evolutionary suggestions about the causes of rape in *The Sciences*, the consequent letters to the editor took an overwhelmingly negative tone (Jennings, 2000; Müller, 2000; Steinberg, Tooney, Sutton, & Denmark, 2000; Tang-Martínez & Mechanic, 2000).

TABLE 1.2 Example of the Goals of Research and How They Relate to the Development of Knowledge

Description	One evening in 1964, a woman named Kitty Genovese was attacked and murdered while walking home from work at 3 a.m. in Queens, New York. It was erroneously reported that 38 people saw what was happening from their apartment windows, but nobody helped; nobody even called the police (Manning, Levine, & Collins, 2007).
	Two psychologists (e.g., Latané & Darley, 1970) wondered why this might happen. Their first step in understanding this phenomenon was to describe what happened. Based on descriptions of the initial event, Latané and Darley (1970) investigated some of the implications of Genovese's murder as they relate to helping behavior.
	This event was so striking that it led to an enormous amount of research and analysis (e.g., Cunningham, 1984; Takooshian & O'Connor, 1984) and stands as a prime example of research that results from something that occurs outside the laboratory. (See Cialdini, 1980, for a discussion of using naturally occurring events as a basis for behavioral research.)
Explanation	Once we can document and predict events, we can try to explain why behaviors occur. Psychologists have identified some of the underlying factors that may help us understand why people do not help others. As Darley and Latané (1968) have noted, when there are more people around, we are less likely to notice that somebody needs help and, even when we notice, we are less likely to offer aid. Part of this failure to act involves what has been called diffusion of responsibility; that is, when others are around, we can pass blame for our inaction to them, assuming less (or none) for ourselves.
Prediction	We can try to determine those conditions where helping behavior is likely to occur. Helping occurs as people try to avoid feeling guilty (Katsev, Edelsack, Steinmetz, Walker, & Wright, 1978), and helping diminishes if people have been relieved of guilt (Cialdini, Darby, & Vincent, 1973). In addition, if people believe that another individual is similar to them, they will help (Batson, Duncan, Ackerman, Buckley, & Birch, 1981).
	Helping behavior involves complicated dynamics, so it will be difficult to identify precisely those conditions in which helping will occur, but we have identified some variables that allow us to make generally accurate predictions.
Control	Once we are confident of our predictions, we can ultimately control behavior. Behaviors in everyday life are seldom controlled by a single variable, but we can control behavior to a degree by manipulating the relevant variables.
	Programs to help poverty-stricken people often rely on guilt or empathic pleas. Depending on the particulars of the circumstances, we may help others if our mood is positive because we tend to generalize our good mood to everything around us (Clark & Teasdale, 1985); or we may help if our mood is negative, but we think that helping somebody will improve our mood (Manucia, Baumann, & Cialdini, 1984). Knowledge of these effects can help us control behaviors.

Can it be that not a single scientist, or even any reader of *The Sciences,* supported Thornhill and Palmer's ideas? It is more likely that people have refrained from writing letters in support of the evolutionary argument because they know that a great many people will take them to task for it. We can easily imagine that fear of reprisal might lead some people to avoid conducting research in the area. As such, research that might clarify the issue may never take place because nobody is willing to pursue it.

The Government's Role in Science

Societal issues often dictate scientific research, in part because of the way money is allocated for research. The federal government funds a great deal of the research that occurs in colleges and universities, where most scientific developments occur. As such, the government plays a large role in determining what kind of research takes place. How does the government decide which areas of research should have priority in funding? Ultimately, the decision-makers pay attention to issues of pressing importance to taxpayers.

In the United States, the federal government actively directs some scientific research. For instance, the highly secretive National Security Agency employs more mathematicians than any other organization in the world (Singh, 1999). These people work on finding ways to create and break secret codes that affect political, economic, and military activities. Many mathematicians who research the use of codes do so because the government encourages it.

Further, the U.S. government has affected social research indirectly, sometimes through questionable means. Harris (1980) noted that beginning in the 1930s, the Federal Bureau of Investigation (FBI) engaged in surveillance and kept files on the American Psychological Association (APA) and the Society for the Psychological Study of Social Issues, now a division of APA. The FBI used informants who reported on colleagues. One incident that Harris cited involved an individual who informed on a colleague who had spoken out against racism at the 1969 APA convention. The result of such activities by the government, according to Harris, may have been to lead psychologists to abandon some lines of research (e.g., on racial attitudes) because they were too controversial.

Cultural Values and Science

Even when governmental interference is not an issue, there are still cultural aspects to our research. For example, several decades ago, the number of children in daycare centers increased due to the need by single parents and two-income families. Initially there were concerns that this trend would hinder children's development. (Fortunately, research has revealed clear benefits to high-quality child care; Campbell, 2012.) Few behavioral scientists showed much interest in the question until fairly recently. The first PsycINFO citation with the term "childcare" in an abstract did not occur until 1927; for a long time, the use of that term was often associated with orphanages. In the early 1900s, work was more likely to center around the home, and the primary caregivers, the mothers, were less likely to work outside the home. Thus, the issue of the effects of childcare centers on the development of children was irrelevant to society.

In contemporary life, women's work has moved from inside the home to outside, and there are more single parents who must have paying jobs. The increase in research on the effects of childcare centers has become important to many people, including psychologists, spurring an increase in psychological research on the topic.

Another example of the effect of culture on research involves a commonly used technique to assess attitudes and opinions. Psychologists regularly ask people to rate something on a scale of one to seven. (Technically, this is called a Likert-type scale, named after the American psychologist Rensis Likert, who pioneered this popular technique.) The use of such a scale may not be appropriate for people in cultures different than ours because it calls for a certain mindset that others don't share with us (Carr, Munro, & Bishop, 1995). People in non-Western cultures may not think it makes sense to assess a complex concept on a simple rating scale. We tend to assume that others think as we do, but such an assumption may lead to research results that lack validity. Greater numbers of psychologists are addressing these concerns and focusing more systematically on cultural issues in research (see Matsumoto, 1994; Price & Crapo, 1999).

A person's culture determines not only what behaviors are of interest, but also how those behaviors are studied. Cultural perspective also influences how scientists interpret their data. An interesting example of the way that societal topics affect research occurred as Hugo Münsterberg (1914) decided to study whether women should be allowed to participate on juries. This topic is irrelevant now, but in the early 1900s, it was controversial. Some people thought that women wouldn't do as good a job on a jury as men did. Interestingly, nobody posed the question of whether men should serve on juries; it was just assumed that they would do it competently.

SCIENTIFIC LITERACY

Even if you don't engage in research yourself, it is important to be scientifically literate in our society. News about science abounds on the Internet, on television, and in newspapers and magazines. In addition, voters must decide about scientific issues, like whether the federal or state governments should fund stem cell research or should act to prevent possible global warming. In order to understand the issues, citizens need to understand the nature of scientific research.

Scientific literacy is a specialized form of critical thinking, which involves developing clear and specific questions, collecting and assessing relevant information, identifying important assumptions and perspectives, and generating effective solutions to problems (Defining Critical Thinking, 2004). These are all goals associated with conducting research.

Are people as scientifically literate as they should be? Unfortunately, research has suggested that only about 28 percent of Americans qualify as being scientifically literate (Miller, 2007a, b). This figure is low, but it actually represents progress. In the 1980s and early 1990s, only about 10 percent people were scientifically literate. Swami, Stieger, Pietschnig, Nader, and Voracek (2011) have reported that some people seem to be more resistant to scientific thinking than others are. In their research, they discovered that people categorize scientific myths as human related and nonhuman related. People who embraced the human myths (e.g., we use only 10 percent of our brains) scored high in measures of antiscientific orientation.

How can you develop scientific literacy? One way to foster such literacy is to learn about and to conduct research (Holmes, Beins, & Lynn, 2007). Knowledge of the process of doing research appears to facilitate an awareness of the scientific process. More specifically, training in psychological research prepares a person for the kind of thinking associated with scientific literacy and critical thinking as well as training in other scientific disciplines (Lehman, Lempert, & Nisbett, 1988). Similarly, taking psychology courses in general appears to be related to increased scientific literacy (Beins, 2010).

One issue that requires a high level of scientific literacy concerns the invalid claim that mercury in vaccines causes autism. This controversy involves the intersection of scientific knowledge, public policy, and the needs of people whose lives are affected by autism. The Controversy box on autism below provides a glimpse into these issues.

Science and Pseudoscience

Various people believe in phenomena that scientists reject as being invalid. For instance, many people believe that homeopathic medicine is effective in treating physical illness, a belief rejected by researchers and mainstream medical workers.

Homeopathic medicines contain ingredients that have been so diluted that a dose may not even have a single molecule of the substance associated with a supposed cure. Furthermore, controlled scientific studies have demonstrated a lack of effectiveness of homeopathic treatments. The few studies that show an effect generally reveal weak effects and may be methodologically flawed. Why do such people refuse to change their beliefs about this approach? There are many reasons, but one of them is that believers do not approach homeopathy through a scientific framework. Their belief in homeopathy stems more from a reliance on tenacity or authority.

Other nonscientific beliefs abound, involving paranormal phenomena like ESP, astrology, mental telepathy, and ghosts. Although scientists firmly reject the existence of such phenomena, surveys have revealed that nearly three quarters of all Americans believe in at least some of these things (Moore, 2005). If you look at Figure 1.1, you will

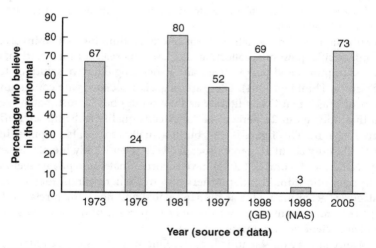

FIGURE 1.1   Percentage of respondents who claim to believe in some kind of paranormal phenomenon in different studies.

Sources:

[a] 1973 and 1998 (GB): Radford (1998), nonrandom samples from Great Britain.
[b] 1976 and 1997: Nisbet (1998) random samples from the United States.
[c] 1981: Singer and Benassi (1981), random samples from the United States.
[d] 1998 (NAS), sample of members of the National Academy of Sciences in the United States.
[e] 2005: Random sample from the United States.

see the disconnect between the general public and scientists. Why do so many people lend credibility to these ideas when the majority of scientists who have studied these things have found essentially no support for them? A number of years ago the magician James Randi (whose stage name is The Amazing Randi) issued a challenge that he would award $1,000,000 to anybody who could demonstrate paranormal phenomena that he could not successfully disprove through rigorous testing. To date, nobody has been able to do so, although some people have tried.

Most scientists reject the notion that paranormal phenomena exist. The most notable reason for scientific skepticism is that, under controlled conditions, the evidence for phenomena like ESP or mental telepathy remarkably disappear. Before we do the research, we should have an open mind about the issue, but we need to abandon such beliefs if research shows no evidence of their existence. Recently, Bem (2011) published some research suggesting the existence of paranormal phenomena, but there appear to be significant methodological flaws that lead to low levels of confidence in the research (e.g., Alcock, 2011; LeBel & Peters, 2011) and other researchers have not been able to replicate the results (Ritchie, Wiseman, & French, 2012).

Another basis for rejection of paranormal phenomena is that most of the explanations offered for such events are inconsistent with the physical laws that scientists recognize. If there is no way to explain a phenomenon, scientists are reluctant to accept it as valid. So sometimes researchers have failed to accept new ideas because they could not explain those ideas. Regarding paranormal phenomena, the well-established laws of physics that have led to our current marvels of technology cannot explain something like ESP. The failure to explain how the paranormal could occur and the inability to document these phenomena in the laboratory have made scientists reluctant to embrace them.

Pseudoscience—A domain of inquiry that has the superficial appearance of being scientific but which does not rely on the critical scientific principles of objectivity, verifiability, empiricism, and being public.

From the viewpoint of many psychologists, the term "parapsychology" is seen as unfortunate because it links our scientifically oriented discipline with **pseudoscience**. We regard a discipline as pseudoscientific when it claims that its knowledge derives from scientific research but fails to follow the basic principles of science.

Many scientists have worked to dispel pseudoscientific myths (e.g., Radner & Radner, 1982; Zusne & Jones, 1989), as have other critical thinkers, like James Randi. There are also publications that foster critical thinking about such issues, like *The Skeptical Inquirer*. This periodical exists to examine and debunk claims of paranormal phenomena. When scrutinized, claims in favor of paranormal phenomena don't hold up well. Table 1.3 reflects some of the major characteristics of pseudoscience.

In general, pseudosciences are characterized by a reliance on flimsy and questionable evidence, a resistance to change or further development of theory, a lack of ways to test the ideas, avoidance of contradictory information, and a lack of critical thought about ways to develop the theory.

Warning Signs of Bogus Science

As a consumer of research, you can spot some of the issues associated with claims that appear to be based on science but that are not. Even if you are not knowledgeable about the technical issues associated with a scientific topic, there are some warning signs that you should be dubious about facts that others claim are true, as noted by physicist Robert Park (2003).

TABLE 1.3   Characteristics of Pseudoscience

General Characteristics	Example
Pseudoscientists believe that there is no more to be learned; they fail to generate testable hypotheses or to conduct objective tests of theory. There tends to be no advancement of knowledge in the field, which is resistant to change. There are few tests of previous claims.	Homeopathic medicine makes claims about cures that are not based on research. The ideas never change and believers do not conduct systematic tests that would disconfirm their ideas.
Pseudoscience is based on dogma and uncritical belief; there may be hostility in the fact of counterevidence or disagreement.	Creationism is accepted by some as a matter of faith. There is no attempt to subject its tenets to scientific scrutiny. In addition, when disagreements arise, believers often show antagonism toward the individual without dealing with the evidence.
There is a suppression of or distortion of unfavorable data; selective use of data, including looking only for supportive information (confirmation bias).	People who believe that psychics can foretell the future will accept just about any statement that seems correct but will ignore errors in predictions.
Many ideas are not amenable to scientific evaluation; ideas are subjective and can't be tested objectively.	There have been claims that we have an undetectable aura surrounding us. If it is undetectable, there is no way to verify its presence.
There is an acceptance of proof with data of questionable validity; the lack of evidence is taken as support that a claim *could* be true.	Some people conclude that there is evidence for the existence of UFOs on the basis of anecdotal reports in the popular media or ancient myths. There is little or no independent evaluation of ideas, but more a reliance on questionable evidence that is not questioned.
Personal anecdotes and events that cannot be tested systematically are used to provide evidence; there is often a reliance on "experts" with no real expertise.	Anybody who claims an experience about foretelling the future or who relates a supposed experience with aliens becomes an expert whose statements are not to be questioned.
Pseudoscience involves terms that sound like scientific ideas, but the terms are not clearly defined. Often the ideas violate known scientific principles.	Varieties of extrasensory perception include phenomena like *telekinesis*, which sounds scientific. In reality, it is a poorly defined (and undocumented) notion. Paranormal phenomena do not conform to known physical laws, such as the fact that for all known forms of energy, the force exerted declines over distance, which is not the case for ESP, according to its adherents.
Pseudoscientific phenomena are "shy" or "fragile" in that they often disappear or weaken noticeably when subjected to well designed experiments, especially with nonbelievers.	The ability to identify stimuli that are not visible is sometimes striking when two believers conduct a study; when independent scientists conduct the study, the effect is often attenuated or eliminated.

(continued)

TABLE 1.3 Continued

General Characteristics	Example
Pseudoscience involves looking for mysteries that have occurred rather than trying to generate and test explanations for the phenomena.	Sometimes people solicit incidents from people that seem unusual. For instance, mystery hunters might look for instances when a person seems to have foretold the future in a dream, ignoring the fact that if you look at enough dreams, you can find coincidental patterns that resist normal explanations.
Pseudoscientists engage in explanation by scenario. They identify a phenomenon and provide an explanation that fits the facts after they are known, but doesn't provide a means for making predictions in advance.	Some years ago, Julian Jaynes suggested that, historically, the two hemispheres in the human brain were not connected as they are now. Thus, brain activity in the right hemisphere was perceived to be the voices of gods. Unfortunately for this explanation, there is no credible evidence that it is true. In fact, given what we know about evolution, there is no realistic way that our brains could have evolved as Jaynes suggested.

The first warning sign is when an investigator publicizes claims in the popular press rather than in a scientific journal. If an article appears in a journal, it will have undergone careful scrutiny by professionals in the field. Scientists are skeptical when a research claim first appears in the news because other scientists have probably not assessed its validity.

Second, when somebody claims that the scientific establishment is trying to suppress research findings, you should be careful. It may be difficult to publish radically new findings in a journal, so valid claims may need a higher standard of proof, but if the findings result from valid scientific approaches, journals will publish new work.

A third sign to be cautious is when a researcher's findings are difficult to detect, thus difficult to verify by an independent judge. A fourth problem appears when the only data for a discovery involve anecdotes, or stories, that other researchers cannot investigate more fully. One of the problems with anecdotes is that they can lead to powerful, emotional responses, so people are likely to accept claims about the stories as being valid. An unusual occurrence may take place, but scientists are unwilling to accept it as being real if they cannot investigate how general the phenomenon is.

A fifth warning sign is the claim by the investigator that a phenomenon is real because people have known about it for centuries. Simply because people have made claims for a long time does not indicate that their claims are correct. For hundreds of years, people thought that the earth was only a few thousand years old; we know now that this claim is not true.

The next sign that you should be wary of is that the investigator worked alone and discovered an important phenomenon that nobody else had happened upon. New findings are almost invariably the result of the accumulation of ideas. Contemporary science almost always involves a community of researchers or, at least, an awareness by a single researcher of the work of others.

Finally, if a researcher makes a bold claim of an entirely novel finding, the researcher must be able to propose a physical or scientific law that can account for the phenomenon. If a finding does not accord with the natural laws that scientists have established, the researcher must develop a coherent and believable explanation for the phenomenon.

Junk Science

Sometimes people, including scientists, use scientific research to promote their own causes. When they use science inappropriately, they may make claims that look good on the surface but that are really not valid. The term for such uses is called **junk science**. This term is as much a rhetorical term as a scientific one; that is, it is a term related to making arguments to support one's beliefs. A person using junk science is more interested in winning the argument than in presenting sound, valid scientific information.

> **Junk Science**—The use of scientific research for nonscientific goals, a term with negative connotations suggesting a problem with the way scientific research is used.

Sometimes people making arguments with junk science will call upon data and research results of questionable validity. For instance, according to the Union of Concerned Scientists, people may make use of data that have not gone through peer review, meaning that experts in the field have not had the opportunity to examine the research procedures or the data. Another hallmark of junk science is the use of simple data from complex research projects to generate a solution to a complicated problem. If the problem is complicated, it is not likely that a solution will emerge based on simple data.

In other instances, people appear to refer to scientific research, but they can't actually produce examples of research to support their claims. Some scientifically based organizations work to educate the public on these empty claims. For example, Sense about Science (http://www.senseaboutscience.org.uk) and the Committee for Skeptical Inquiry (http://www.csicop.org/) devote their energy to educate the public and the media about supposedly scientific claims that don't stand up under scrutiny.

■ ■ ■ ■ ■ ▬▬▬▬▬▬▬▬▬▬▬▬▬▬▬▬▬▬▬▬▬▬▬▬▬▬▬▬▬▬▬

CONTROVERSY:
What Causes Autism?

Children routinely receive vaccinations to prevent a variety of illnesses. So it would be ironic if vaccines were responsible for causing a disorder. Some nonscientists and physicians believe that the element mercury that manufacturers used to use as a preservative in vaccines actually cause autism (e.g., Olmstead, 2009; Tsouderos & Callahan, 2009). But when scientists have conducted research to see if there is a connection between vaccinations and autism, the results have revealed no systematic link between vaccines and autism (e.g., Baker, 2008;

Heron, Golding, & ALSPAC Study Team, 2004; Omer, Salmon, Orenstein, deHart, & Halsey, 2009; Schechter & Grether, 2008). In fact, the *British Medical Journal* retracted the original research article that supposedly showed a vaccine-autism link because the research was flawed. The researcher, Andrew Wakefield, lost his license to practice medicine and retracted some of his published research; he initiated a lawsuit in England for defamation against the journal, but dropped it and agreed to pay the legal costs associated with it. He later initiated a similar lawsuit in the United States (Sample, 2012; Zielinska, 2012).

So where did the controversy arise? And who should we believe? The issue arose because of a confluence of several different factors (Baker, 2008).

First, the U.S. Centers for Disease Control and Prevention (CDC) recommended in 1999 that the mercury-containing preservative thimerosal be removed from vaccinations because of the fear of mercury poisoning, which can cause developmental problems in fetuses and children. The CDC drew no connection between mercury and autism; in fact, no research had implicated thimerosal with any disease or health problems. The recommendation was purely preventive.

Second, around the same time, parents of children diagnosed with autism had become active in advocating for the children. These parents were reacting against hypotheses that parenting inadequacies were responsible for the onset of autism. One such hypothesis was Leo Kanner and Bruno Bettelheim's concept that autism arose because of "refrigerator mothers" who were emotionally cold with their children (Laidler, 2004). The parents were promoting a medical model to replace the psychoanalytically based hypothesis of Kanner and Bettelheim. It was among this community of advocates that the notion of an epidemic of autism took root. Experts (e.g., Fombonne, 2001) had predicted that the increased advocacy and greater awareness of autism would lead to more diagnoses of autism, which is exactly what happened.

A third factor was the conclusion by some people that mercury in vaccines was the culprit in the supposed epidemic of autism. (It is not entirely clear if the increase of autism is due to an actual increase in incidence or to more awareness and better diagnosis.)

Prior to the recommendation to remove mercury from vaccines, nobody had associated mercury with autism. However, some people concluded that because the CDC had recommended removal of mercury from vaccines and because there were some similarities in mercury poisoning and autistic behavior, mercury must be to blame.

A number of studies have investigated the potential mercury–autism link. What have researchers concluded? To date, there is no evidence of a causal connection between the two. In fact, the incidence of autism has increased even though mercury has disappeared from most vaccines (Schechter & Grether, 2008) and mercury levels in children with autism are no higher than those in children without autism (Hertz-Picciotto, Green, Delwiche, Hansen, Walker, & Pessah, 2009).

So why does the controversy persist? Part of the situation involves the desires of parents of children with autism to be able to place a cause for their children's problems and to prevent future occurrences. Part of the situation involves the coincidence of increased diagnoses of autism in the same time period that mercury disappeared from most vaccines. And part of the situation results from people's lack of scientific literacy in being able to evaluate scientific research and in their reliance on anecdotal information instead of systematically collected data.

Question for Discussion: How do people's hopes and desires influence their willingness to examine scientific data? If there is no connection between exposure to mercury and the appearance of autism, how could you convince people who accept such a link to change their minds?

There is no clear definition of what constitutes valid science versus junk science. Sometimes it is a matter of perspective by the person using it and the person hearing it. Nonetheless, by understanding the context in which the data were generated, whether the research followed the scientific method, and the relation between the data and the question at hand, you can begin to ask the right questions about whether you are on the receiving end of real science or junk science.

SUMMARY

Research exerts a large impact on our lives, so we are better off as citizens when we can examine research claims that people make. Knowing how to ask critical questions is also a useful skill in many other facets of our lives.

When psychologists engage in research, we do what other scientists do: We look for ways to describe behavior accurately, to establish a basis for predicting behavior, to explain why people act as they do, and ultimately to know how to control behavior. The best way to accomplish these goals is to study behavior scientifically.

Research is considered scientific when it conforms to certain game plans. Researchers strive to make objective measurements and to define precisely what they have done in their work. This allows others to evaluate the credibility of the research and to do further work to extend knowledge. After creating a research plan, psychologists collect data and draw conclusions from them. We hope that when scientists make a claim, they can support their arguments based on objective data, not on opinion.

Another critical component of scientific research is that it must be public. The knowledge we gain in research doesn't help us advance what we know unless researchers publicize their work, usually in the form of professional papers that appear in journals or in conference presentations attended by other scientists. Only by making clear statements about what research is all about and what discoveries the scientist has made can others verify the validity of the claims made by the investigator and attempt to reproduce those results in other research projects.

We rely on the scientific approach for the study of behavior because other ways of finding out about people's thoughts, feelings, and acts are not as reliable. Sometimes we can use intuition to understand the world around us, but too often intuition leads to poor judgments. Similarly, we can ask people who are authority figures; unfortunately, they are like the rest of us—sometimes they make mistakes. We can also use logic, but all of us know that people's behaviors often don't seem to follow any logic we can detect. Finally, all of us make judgments based on our own experiences. The problem with using our own experiences is that they may not reflect general principles. These other ways of understanding the world have their place, but the systematic and scientific study of behavior provides us with the best overall picture of the human condition.

As researchers investigate human behavior, they gather information and collect data. This is often the easy part. The complex part is trying to interpret what the information means. People do research for reasons that relate to their social and cultural outlook, and they interpret their results from within their own cultural framework. Sometimes people disagree vigorously on how to interpret research in all of the scientific disciplines; this reflects that science is just another type of human activity.

Finally, learning about research is one way to increase one's scientific literacy. Research promotes critical thinking about how to ask and answer questions systematically and objectively. Unfortunately, the majority of Americans show low levels of scientific literacy, which may account for acceptance by some people of certain types of pseudoscience that scientists firmly reject.

REVIEW QUESTIONS

Multiple Choice Questions

1. Researchers recently documented the fact that people who refused to think about the horrible events after a terrorist attach and isolated themselves were risk of developing posttraumatic stress disorder. This fact relates to which goal of science?
   a. control
   b. description
   c. explanation
   d. prediction

2. Researchers with different theoretical beliefs are likely to differ greatly with respect to their statements regarding the _____ of behavior.
   a. explanation
   b. testability
   c. falsifiability
   d. description

3. When colleges use high school grades and SAT or ACT scores to determine whether to admit a student, they are using the tests scores as a measure of the likelihood of student success in college. This is related to which goal of science?
   a. control
   b. description
   c. explanation
   d. prediction

4. After gaining an understanding of why behaviors occur as they do, a scientist interested in applying this knowledge would be interested in what goal of science?
   a. control
   b. description
   c. explanation
   d. prediction

5. Researchers test the strength of a theory by noting at what point it breaks down. This activity relates to
   a. control
   b. explanation
   c. falsifiability
   d. proof

6. If a person drew a conclusion about some topic based on opinion and prior beliefs, a researcher would claim that such a conclusion was not scientific because it was not
   a. objective
   b. intuitive
   c. data driven
   d. predicted

7. A scientist who decides to repeat an experiment to see if the results are the same; he or she is interested in what characteristic of scientific knowledge?
   a. objective
   b. data driven
   c. public
   d. verifiable

8. Beliefs based on intuition or on common knowledge that people hold firmly and are simply reluctant to abandon are based on what kind of knowledge?
    a. tenacity
    b. experience
    c. authority
    d. a priori method

9. When your professor informs you of fact and theory based on research, you develop a belief system that is consistent with that information. Your beliefs are based on
    a. authority
    b. experience
    c. a priori method
    d. science

10. One of the problems associated with knowledge based on experience is that
    a. our own experiences might not generalize to others.
    b. the use of logical deductions does not work in predicting behaviors.
    c. common knowledge might be erroneous, even if many people believe in it.
    d. experiential knowledge and scientific knowledge are usually very different from one another.

11. In planning scientific research, psychologists' choices of topics
    a. have generally been directed by theory, but seldom by cultural values.
    b. have not been influenced by the actions of the government.
    c. are most productive when they are removed from controversial topics.
    d. often reflect cultural values that they hold.

12. The effects of culture on research are reflected in the fact that
    a. the government tries to stay out of the personal choices of researchers.
    b. researchers may avoid controversial topics because of the reactions of others to their research.
    c. research methodologies in psychology tend to remain constant across virtually all societies.
    d. psychologists tend to study the same topics in the same ways across the decades.

13. A belief in parapsychology (e.g., ESP)
    a. is fairly uncommon in the general public, contrary to common belief.
    b. is typical of most scientists.
    c. has been documented in over half the general public in a number of surveys over several decades.
    d. is at the same level for scientists as it is for the general public.

14. Scientists become suspicious of scientific claims about new phenomena when the people raising the new ideas
    a. insist on publicizing their research in scientific journals instead of in the mainstream press where more people can view it.
    b. claim that the scientific establishment is actively working to suppress the their new ideas.
    c. are unable to provide solid anecdotal evidence and specific examples of the phenomenon in everyday life.
    d. do not want to be limited by existing scientific data and theory in providing explanations of the phenomena.

Essay Questions

15. Identify and describe the four goals of scientific research. Include in your description how the four goals build on one another.
16. Identify and describe the five ways of knowing described by the philosopher Charles Sander Peirce.
17. How do scientists and pseudoscientists differ with regard to the evidence that they will accept to support their ideas?

ANSWERS TO REVIEW QUESTIONS

Answers to Multiple Choice Questions

1.	b	6.	c	11.	d
2.	a	7.	d	12.	b
3.	d	8.	a	13.	c
4.	a	9.	a	14.	b
5.	c	10.	a		

Answers to Essay Questions

15. Identify and describe the four goals of scientific research. Include in your description how the four goals build on one another.
Suggested points:
  a. Description—the process of documenting the existence of behaviors of interest.
  b. Prediction—the ability to predict behaviors given knowledge of prior conditions.
  c. Explanation—identifying reasons for the occurrence of a behavior.
  d. Control—using knowledge of a phenomenon to predict when it will occur and being able to explain the reasons for the behavior in such a way as to control that behavior.

16. Identify and describe the five ways of knowing described by the philosopher Charles Sander Peirce and later thinkers.
  a. Tenacity (the obvious/intuition)—knowing something because "everybody knows it is true" or because "it is obvious" so that people are comfortable and simply refuse to abandon that knowledge.
  b. Authority—reliance on an expert or authority figure.
  c. A priori method—use of deductive logic or logical proof.
  d. Experience—use of one's own life as a measure of what is generally true.
  e. Scientific method—reliance on empirical methods that are objective, empirical, public, and replicable.

17. How do scientists and pseudoscientists differ with regard to the evidence that they will accept to support their ideas?
    Ideally, scientists continually revise their ideas based on empirically based evidence. In addition, they are willing to develop theories to accommodate new findings, to update their methods to improve on the quality of research, and to question new information critically.
    On the other hand, pseudoscientists rely on flimsy and questionable evidence; they are not willing to question information that supports their ideas. At the same time, they avoid contradictory information that fails to support their ideas. In addition, pseudoscientists show a resistance to change in their ideas and they are unlikely to seek further development of theory; in fact they tend to avoid testing their ideas critically.

■ ■ ■ ■ ■

CHAPTER TWO

ETHICS IN RESEARCH

CHAPTER OVERVIEW

LEARNING OBJECTIVES ■ **KEY TERMS** ■ **CHAPTER PREVIEW**

LEARNING OBJECTIVES

After going through this chapter, you will be able to:

- Describe unethical historical research in the United States and in Nazi Germany
- Describe behaviors of current researchers that violate ethics
- Define and give examples of behaviors that constitute plagiarism
- Identify the main reasons why researchers act unethically
- Describe and differentiate the aspirational goals versus the ethical standards created by the American Psychological Association (APA)
- Describe and give an example of the General Principles of ethics created by the APA
- Identify the General Principles of ethics created by the APA that are associated with conducting research

- Describe the reason for the creation of the Nuremburg Code for ethics in research
- Explain the role of the Institutional Review Board (IRB)
- Identify the situation in which researchers do not need approval from an Institutional Review Board
- Describe a situation in which the IRB can hinder effective research design
- Describe why a researcher could defend Stanley Milgram's obedience research when it took place but that defense would not be appropriate today
- Explain the concept of a cost-benefit analysis is assessing risk in research
- Identify the criticisms leveled against Milgram's obedience research and his response to those criticisms
- Identify criticisms associated with the use of deception in research
- Differentiate between the different types of deception
- Explain how researchers use debriefing, dehoaxing, and desensitization in research involving deception
- Explain whether the debriefing process is effective in research involving deception
- Describe the concept of ethical imperialism in research

KEY TERMS

Active deception, p. 45
Anonymity, p. 37
Aspirational goals, p. 33
Beneficence, p. 33
Coercion, p. 37
Confidentiality, p. 37
Cost-benefit analysis,
   p. 41

Cover story, p. 44
Debriefing, p. 45
Dehoaxing, p. 45
Desensitization, p. 45
Ethical standards, p. 33
Fidelity, p. 33
Institutional Review
   Board (IRB), p. 39

Integrity, p. 34
Justice, p. 34
Naturalistic
   observation, p. 43
Nonmaleficence, p. 33
Nuremberg Code, p. 37
Passive deception,
   p. 45

Plagiarism, p. 37
Respect for people's
   rights and dignity,
   p. 34
Responsibility,
   p. 33
Role playing, p. 43
Simulation, p. 43

CHAPTER PREVIEW

Most psychological research poses little physical or psychological risk to participants. Nonetheless, because some researchers in the past have conducted notorious and unethical projects, laws and guidelines have been developed for the protection of research participants. Another problem is that researchers made up data, invented entire experiments, and misrepresented their data in published journal articles.

Researchers generally become very interested and excited in their programs of research. Sometimes this means that they focus very narrowly in their work and forget to consider the implications of what they are doing. In this chapter, you will see that investigators may get so caught up in their research that they may endanger the people who participate in their studies.

The American Psychological Association (APA) has developed a set of guidelines that has evolved over the past half century. Many researchers in disciplines other than psychology rely on these guidelines. We must also follow legal requirements that federal and state governments have enacted for the protection of human participants in research.

Students sometimes mistakenly believe that the APA approves or vetoes research. It would be impossible for any single organization to oversee as much research as psychologists conduct. Ethical supervision occurs under the oversight of Institutional Review Boards (IRBs) that evaluate proposed projects; this takes place in the colleges and universities where the research is carried out.

In discussing ethics in the design of psychological studies, the famous research of Stanley Milgram (1963) and Philip Zimbardo (1973) comes to mind. Milgram's research participants thought they were delivering electrical shocks to another person, often to the extent that the other person might have died. Zimbardo created a prison simulation that led participants, all of them students, to treat one another very brutally. This type of research is very rare in psychology, which is why the most illustrative examples of ethically controversial research occurred over 30 years ago.

We can categorize research in two groups for our discussion. In the first category, involving clinically based research, the result of ignoring ethical dictates is potentially very serious. People approach clinical psychologists because of problems that need to be resolved. If clinical research involves ethical problems, those people could be seriously harmed.

The second category involves basic research in academic settings. Most psychological research has fairly minor risk-related implications for participants. Some psychological research can involve more than minimal risk, but most psychological research on topics like learning, motivation, social processes, and attitude change would virtually never lead to long-term, highly negative outcomes, no matter how incompetent or unethical the researcher. To decide whether a project is appropriate, we conduct a cost-benefit analysis; if the risk exceeds the benefit, we should not do the research; if the benefit exceeds the risk, the research may be acceptable. Before we conduct research, we need to assess the relative risk of the research compared to the benefits for two main reasons. First, it is the ethical and moral thing to do. Second, there are legal requirements that we do it. There has been an unfortunate history of abuse on the part of researchers; some of it is due to carelessness, some due to callousness, and some due to unconscionable social and governmental policies. We hope to avoid such problems in our research.

UNETHICAL RESEARCH PRACTICES—PAST AND PRESENT

Ethical Problems in the Early Years of the Twentieth Century

Through the past century, shameful episodes of unethical research practices have occurred, in many cases leading to extreme suffering and death. The troublesome decisions made by researchers have led to the Nuremburg Code and to the various federal laws designed to protect people. In this section, you will see examples of biomedical investigations that alerted society to the need for protection of people participating in research.

Among the most egregious examples include the investigations done by the Nazis during World War II. For example, according to Lifton (1986), the Nazi Carl Clauberg researched techniques for sterilizing women by injecting them with what was probably Formalin, which consists of formaldehyde and methanol (a kind of alcohol). Both substances are poisonous, and formaldehyde is an extreme irritant; survivors reported that the pain was excruciating. Clauberg injected this substance into the women's cervix, with the aim of destroying the fallopian tubes that are necessary for carrying an egg to the uterus for implantation.

This abuse by the Nazis is additionally horrible because, previously, Germany had an enlightened approach to research ethics prior to the Nazi takeover (López-Muñoz & Álamo, 2009). During the Nazi reign, the focus of research moved from the benefit of the patient to the benefit of the state.

As you will see, there have been violations in medical and psychiatric research that go beyond the bounds of good judgment and indicate a callous, sometimes horrific disregard for people. The Nazis did not corner the market on such research. Beginning in the 1930s and continuing until 1972, researchers at the Tuskegee Institute in the United States purposely withheld treatment from Black patients in order to study the progress of syphilis. When the study began, knowledge of the specific course of the disease and of effective treatment was minimal, but within a short period of time, it was evident that lack of treatment was devastating. Syphilis can lead to blindness, organically caused psychosis, and death. The negative effects on its patients were all too clear decades before the research ceased, and the research continued after treatment with penicillin was standard practice.

The ethical issues that arose are the ones that psychological researchers must consider in planning their research, even though most psychological research is ethically trouble-free and poses minimal or no risk to participants. In the Tuskegee study, the researchers engaged in behaviors that would not be legally permitted today; five major ethical problems and an example of each issue appear in Table 2.1. They withheld informed consent and failed to let the men know the physical and psychological

TABLE 2.1 Ethical Issues Associated with the Tuskegee Study

Ethical Problem	Example
Lack of informed consent	The men thought they were being treated for "bad blood," a common term at the time that referred to many possible diseases. They did not know they were participating in research, nor did they know of risks associated with their participation.
Physical and psychological harm	Lack of effective treatment led to problems caused by syphilis, including behavioral changes, blindness, psychosis, and death. They also underwent a painful spinal tap as part of the research. They agreed to be autopsied after death, which was atypical for this population. After the research became public, Black people often became suspicious of any government-sponsored health programs.
Excessive inducements	The men received free transportation to the clinic, a meal when they were at the clinic, and free medical treatment for minor problems.
Lack of voluntary participation	The excessive inducement may have been hard to refuse. In addition, the men were sharecroppers who were encouraged by landowners to participate, so they may have felt social pressure to participate.
Failure to debrief	At no point in the research did the men learn about the nature or the details of the study. Such information was available only after the existence of the research was leaked to the media.

risks of the research; they actively kept the men from receiving effective treatment when it was available; they offered inducements to participate that the men would find hard to resist; and the men may have felt pressured to participate, which meant that participation may not have been truly voluntary; and they did not debrief the men at any point. Researchers ended up studying these untreated men for 40 years, until a Public Health Service professional, Dr. Peter Buxtun, revealed the existence of the study to the *Washington Post* in 1972.

Beyond this, a report (Research Ethics and the Medical Profession, 1996) has documented a number of problematic studies that occurred during the 1950s and 1960s in the United States. In many cases, the guidelines that had existed regarding informed consent and voluntary participation were ignored.

Examples of harmful and unethical research included cases in which researchers at the University of Cincinnati, in conjunction with the U.S. military, subjected uninformed, terminally ill cancer patients to whole-body radiation to see how it affected those people (Rothman, 1994). Further, in separate projects in the decades after World War II, researchers at the Massachusetts Institute of Technology (funded by the National Institutes of Health, The Atomic Energy Commission, and the Quaker Oats Company), and investigators at Harvard Medical School, Massachusetts General Hospital, and Boston University School of Medicine administered radioactive substances to mentally retarded children living in facilities for the developmentally disabled (ACHRE Report, n.d., available at http://www.hss.energy.gov/healthsafety/ohre/roadmap/achre/chap7_5.html). Ethical breeches in medical research continued to occur in the 1960s and 1970s such that Congress created regulations to prevent physicians from abusing their relationships with patients.

Many of the episodes of notorious research come from the 1970s or earlier. Does this mean that we have solved the problems associated with unethical research practices? Or do ethical problems continue in research programs?

Unfortunately, questionable practices still exist. For example, dozens of experiments with human participants came to a halt at Duke University Medical Center in 1999 when the federal government discovered ethical lapses in the projects involving protection of research participants. One development occurred with a participant in a NASA-sponsored study who underwent testing in a chamber designed to simulate the pressure that you would feel at 30,000 feet above sea level. The man began to lose sensation in his limbs and, after treatment, became semiconscious. On the positive side of the ledger, as soon as this rare and unexpected problem occurred, the researchers terminated the study to protect a research participant; on the negative side, some ethicists questioned whether the project's risks had been adequately studied and whether the participant had received appropriate informed consent (Hilts & Stolberg, 1999).

Beyond this potentially harmful research from the past, recent investigators have engaged in potentially troublesome behaviors. In a recent survey, up to a third of respondents who had received grants from the National Institutes of Health reported engaging in some type of ethically questionable practices, including falsifying and fabricating data, plagiarism, having potentially inappropriate relationships with students or research participants, circumventing minor aspects of human-subject requirements, and others (Martinson, Anderson, & de Vries, 2005; Wadman, 2005). Sometimes researchers have even invented studies that they did not conduct (Charges of fake, 2005) or added their names to reference citations, making it appear that they co-authored published papers when they had not (Case summaries, 2004).

One of the few controversies involving psychology related to a paper whose authors failed to cite important research leading to the research in question (Liston & Kagan, 2002). Kagan and Liston did not plagiarize any earlier material, they just failed to cite it. Their article was brief, limited to just 500 words, they noted, so they had to leave out a lot of important material. Nonetheless, they received criticism regarding how appropriate their behavior was (Farley, 2003).

Ethics and Plagiarism

Scientists regard plagiarism as extremely unethical. Unfortunately, there are quite a few ways to fall prey to it (Avoid plagiarism, 2009). For example, using somebody else's words without attributing them to that person is unethical. Further, even if you take the ideas from somebody else's writing or speaking and translate those ideas into your own words, you must attribute those ideas to the person who originated them.

The issue is complicated, however. If you cite a well-known fact, you don't need to provide a citation. The tricky aspect involves deciding what constitutes a "well-known fact." In the end, you need to make a judgment about what your audience is likely to know.

One further issue involves self-plagiarism, which is the use of your own work multiple times. The issue of self-plagiarism is relevant to students because some sources (e.g., Avoid plagiarism, 2009) assert that students should not hand in the same paper for more than one course. Other sources, however, do not necessarily see a problem with it (What is plagiarism? 2010).

In the abstract, plagiarism is easy to identify. In practice, though, you have to make judgment calls. Fortunately, there are sources to which you can turn for guidance (e.g., Avoid plagiarism, 2009; Beins & Beins, 2012; What is plagiarism? 2010).

Current Examples of Ethical Lapses

Many, if not most, instances of ethical violations occur when researchers engage in inappropriate actions like plagiarism or falsifying data so that the results of a study conform to the researcher's expectations. Recently, however, a major breach of ethics in psychology involved a set of completely fabricated research reports spanning a decade or more: The Dutch psychologist Diederik Stapel admitted making up research results for studies that he never actually carried out (Kraut, 2012).

For example, Stapel reported in the prestigious journal *Science* that chaotic environments promote stereotyping and discrimination (Stapel & Lindenberg, 2011). The discovery of such consistent fraud ended up as major news stories in the popular press, such as *The New York Times* (Carey, 2011). The fraud was bad enough, but one implication is that the doctoral research of a dozen doctoral students has been called into question (Carey, 2011). They may have wasted years on research based on nonexistent data.

When this kind of problem arises, journals retract the publications, removing them from the record. Over the past two decades, the rate of retractions across all scientific disciplines has increased from about 40 a year in the 1990s to over 400 in 2011. Furthermore, the number of complaints of unethical behavior rose so much in the early 2000s that the U.S. Department of Health and Human Services could not keep up with the increase (Charges of fake, 2005). Some people believe that this dramatic increase may have resulted from greater vigilance on the part of the scientific community in detecting plagiarism and fraudulent data, but this issue is far from clear (Ghose, 2012).

In an attempt to monitor scientists' behaviors, the U.S. federal government's Office of Research Integrity (ORI) investigates claims of scientific misconduct in research associated with federal grants. In the period from 2001 and 2009, the office concluded that 101 researchers were guilty of misconduct related to data collection, analysis, and presentation. The number of cases identified by ORI is small and seldom involves behavioral research, but we don't know how often fraud goes undetected. According to several sources, one third of respondents on a survey reported engaging in unethical behavior and over two thirds said that they had observed others engaging in ethically questionable behavior (Fanelli, Innogen, & ISSTI, 2009; Martinson, Anderson, & de Vries, 2005; Wadman, 2005). Figure 2.1 shows how often the most common infractions investigated by ORI occurred from 2001 to 2009 (Handling misconduct, 2009; Office of Research Integrity Annual Report, 2001 to 2009). Most cases involved falsifying or fabricating data and plagiarism, but several other severe problems also occurred. The number of infractions is greater than the number of people involved because some people violated the ethical rules in multiple ways.

Most of the research associated with such problems has been biomedical in nature. The risks associated with it may involve life and death issues. Your research in psychology is likely to have less impact. However, the behavioral research you complete also has to conform to certain ethical principles and is bound by the same laws that professional researchers must follow.

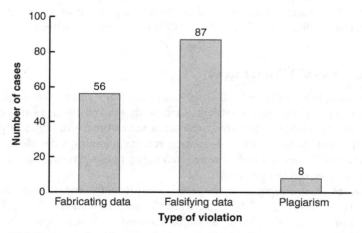

FIGURE 2.1   Incidence and types of ethical infractions investigated by the U.S. Office of Research Integrity from 2001 to 2009.

Source: © Copyright 2010. Bemerd C. Beins

Finally, you might ask why individuals engage in these unethical behaviors. Receipt of money is obviously one reason. In addition, according to a researcher who has investigated why scientists cheat, there are four other, basic reasons:

- Intense pressure to publish research and to obtain grants
- Inadequate mentoring
- Some sort of mental disorder
- Scientists from outside the United States who learned standards that differ from those in the United States (Charges of fake research, 2005).

ETHICAL GUIDELINES CREATED BY THE AMERICAN PSYCHOLOGICAL ASSOCIATION

Aspirational Goals— General set of ethical principles that guide psychologists in their research and other professional activities.

Ethical Standards—A set of enforceable rules created by the APA and by legal authorities that relate to moral values of right and wrong.

Beneficence and Nonmaleficence— Acting to promote the welfare of the people a psychologists deals with (beneficence) and avoidance of harm to them (Nonmaleficence).

Fidelity and Responsibility— Psychologists must act professionally in ways that support the discipline of psychology and benefit their community, especially regarding the well-being of the people with whom they interact professionally.

Researchers are not exempt from some of the same lapses in good judgment that beset the rest of us. In psychology, we are fortunate that serious breaches of ethics are rare.

Long before the general public learned of the excesses of some researchers, the APA had formulated a set of principles that would guide psychologists in their work. Some research disciplines have yet to develop such codes (Scientists should adopt, 2007). We will discuss primarily those guidelines that relate to research, although APA's guidelines pertain to all areas of psychological work, including therapy.

The first set of APA's ethical principles appeared in 1953, the most recent in 2002, with refinement in 2010. As stated in a recent version, psychologists should incorporate the rules as an integral part of their professional lives. "The development of a dynamic set of ethical standards for a psychologist's work-related conduct requires a personal commitment to a lifelong effort to act ethically" (American Psychological Association, 2002, p. 1062).

The General Principles espoused in the standards reflect "**aspirational goals** to guide psychologists toward the highest ideals of psychology" (p. 1061), whereas the **ethical standards** involve enforceable rules of conduct. When psychologists violate the ethical standards, they face possible loss of certification to work in their field of expertise. Such offenses are relatively rare and, when they occur, generally involve the areas of clinical and counseling psychology rather than research.

Aspirational Goals and Enforceable Rules

The five General Principles of the ethical guidelines appear in Table 2.2. As you look at them, you can see that the principles reflect the high moral character that we prize in people around us. In part, (a) **beneficence** and **nonmaleficence** relates to maximizing the positive outcomes of your work and minimizing the chances of harm. Psychologists must also act with (b) **fidelity** and **responsibility** in dealing with others. Psychologists

TABLE 2.2   General Ethical Principles and Examples of Violations

Beneficence and nonmaleficence	A psychologist would be in dangerous territory in conducting research in which he or she has a financial interest because that interest could cloud professional judgment to the detriment of the participant and others. Further, psychologists who are aware that they are experiencing mental health problems may be acting unethically with clients if their own mental health may lead to poor judgment.
Fidelity and responsibility	A psychologist would violate ethical principles by engaging in dual relationships with patients. One of the most notable transgressions occurs when a therapist engages in sexual relations with a person while providing therapy to that individual. Also a psychologist who knows that a colleague is engaging in unethical behavior would himself or herself be acting unethically by not taking steps to prevent further such behavior.
Integrity	Psychologists who intentionally misrepresent their research results or who falsify data are engaging in ethical misconduct because they are not striving to maximize gain to the scientific and professional community, but rather are simply trying for personal gain. In addition, psychologists who knowingly use their knowledge to mislead others, such as in courtroom testimony, are engaging in unethical conduct. In this case, they are not using their professional expertise responsibly or contributing to the welfare of society in general.
Justice	A psychologist who is not trained in the use of a test like the Minnesota Multiphasic Personality Inventory but who uses it in his or her research or with clients might be engaging in unethical behavior because the validity of test interpretations may be low.
Respect for people's rights and dignity	Psychologists who violate the confidentiality of their research participants act unethically. This means that if you are doing research, you may not discuss with others how a particular participant responded during a testing session. (Such a discussion could be appropriate, however, if you discuss a research session with a colleague who is also working on that project and you need to resolve a methodological problem.)

Integrity—Psychologists should promote the honest and truthful application of the discipline in science, teaching, and practice.

Justice—Psychologists must recognize the implications of their professional activity on others and strive to make the best professional judgments they can.

Respect for People's Rights and Dignity—Psychologists must recognize the dignity and value of all people and, to the fullest extent possible, eliminate biases in dealing with people.

should also strive for (c) **integrity** in promoting themselves and their work accurately. As psychologists, we should also aspire to (d) **justice**, recognizing our biases and the limitations to our expertise as they affect others. Finally, we need to show (e) **respect for people's rights and dignity**.

The enforceable ethical standards consist of 10 sections related to different aspects of professional, psychological work. These standards are listed in Table 2.3. Of these sections, the one that pertains most to us here involves research.

As the ethical guidelines pertain to research, psychologists have certain responsibilities to provide research participants with informed consent, to minimize the use of deception in research, to report research results accurately, and to correct any errors in reporting. One further mandate is that researchers must be willing to share their data with other researchers, provided it does not violate the confidentiality promised to research participants.

There are a few areas that are of special relevance to researchers. You will have to consider them when you plan your own research because you must present a proposal to your school's IRB or to delegated representatives of that committee before you can carry out your proposed research. The committee members may approve your research as proposed, but they may

TABLE 2.3   **General Standards of Ethical Behavior for Psychologists**

Section 1—Resolving Ethical Issues

Psychologists need to recognize problematic ethical situations and work to resolve them on an individual level when possible. Sometimes it may be necessary to seek formal remedies to perceived unethical conduct. When there are legal issues that pose a conflict between ethical guidelines of psychologists and the law, the psychologist should work to minimize the conflict. When a conflict cannot be resolved, it may be appropriate to defer to legal authorities.

Section 2—Boundaries of Competence

Researchers, including you, may conduct research only within the boundaries of their competence. You need to pay attention to this, although most research you are likely to carry out will not be problematic. In certain circumstances, though, such as if you planned on using psychodiagnostic tests, you might be in a gray area because many such instruments require specialized training for adequate administration and interpretation. One potential problem is that you would expose your research participants to risk if you interpreted test results in a way that changed their behaviors for the worse.

Section 3—Human Relations

Psychologists must strive to minimize discrimination or harassment of people with whom they have a professional relationship. Exploitation of another by use of power or authority is unethical. For example, if a psychologist has power over others (e.g., a professor over a teaching or lab assistant, a resident assistant, etc.), he or she should take care that not to coerce people when recruiting their participation for research. Psychologists should also avoid multiple relationships, one of the most egregious being sexual relationships with students or clients. Clients and research participants should also provide informed consent for research or therapy.

Section 4—Privacy and Confidentiality

You should not discuss the behavior or responses of research participants or clients with those outside your project or treatment setting if not seeking professional consultation. Your participants have a right to expect that their responses will be confidential and anonymous to the fullest extent possible.

Section 5—Advertising and Other Public Statements

Psychologists should not make fraudulent or misleading professional statements when presenting their work to the public. Nor should they misrepresent their professional expertise or credentials.

Section 6—Record Keeping and Fees

Psychologists must document their research and maintain their data so that they are available for legal or other reasons.

Section 7—Teaching, Training Supervision, Research, and Publishing

Psychologists are responsible for competent education and training of students and for accurate descriptions of education and training programs. Teachers must avoid exploiting those over whom they have authority.

(continued)

TABLE 2.3   Continued

Section 8—Research and Publication

With respect to research, it must be approved by an IRB. Participants should give informed consent and be debriefed (dehoaxed and desensitized). In informed consent, you have to provide them with the following information:

- the nature of the research
- their right to decline to participate and to withdraw at any time without penalty
- the foreseeable consequences of their participation, such as risks, discomfort, etc.

Some research projects involving anonymous questionnaires, naturalistic observation, and some archival research do not require informed consent. If you think this applies to you, you need to check with your local IRB or its representatives. Table 2.5 provides relevant information about this.

Deception in research is acceptable only if other alternatives are not available or appropriate. Presentation of results should accurately reflect the data.

Psychologists must give appropriate credit to those involved in research but should not give credit to an individual whose work on the research was minimal.

Sections 9 and 10—Assessment and Therapy

Psychologists must use contemporary assessment and therapeutic techniques and be adequately trained to use them. This complex realm is most relevant to doctoral level psychologists who provide service to clients.

---

require changes before you can begin. Depending on the nature of the regulations at your school, you may have to wait for a month or longer to receive permission. Your IRB will consider your research proposal based on the relevant state and federal regulations.

Ethical Standards as They Affect You

The General Principles and Standards developed by the APA cover a wide range of psychological activities (see Tables 2.2 and 2.3). At this point in your life, many of them will be completely irrelevant to you because you do not provide professional services. As a psychology student, however, you may carry out research projects, at which time the Principles might apply to you. In fact, the most recent version of the ethical guidelines specifically mention that they apply to student affiliates of APA (Ethical principles, 2002).

Your research activity may not be ethically troublesome, but you need to avoid crossing the line into the realm of unethical behavior. The major points appearing in Tables 2.2 and 2.3 do not exhaust the Principles; they merely highlight many of the points relevant to you. You should ultimately be aware of the APA's Code of Conduct (Ethical Principles, 1992), as well as the relevant legal considerations.

> **Informed Consent—**
> The requirement in research that specifies that researchers must notify participants about the nature of participation research and any risks involved.

Among the most important practical issues you will face when you conduct research are those associated with **informed consent**, that is, making sure that your participants know what they are going to do and understand the nature of the research. In addition, you must provide debriefing in which you inform participants of any deception involved in the research, called dehoaxing, and you make sure that you eliminate any potential sources

Anonymity—The practice of maintaining records so that nobody can identify which individual is associated with a certain set of data.

of negative feelings by the participants, called desensitization. If you think that there are likely to be any long-term consequences for your participants after they complete your research, you need to engage in compensatory follow-up, which means that you arrange for those problems to be remedied. So, for example, if you carried out a study in which you manipulated a person's self-esteem, you would be ethically bound to make sure that, at the end of the study, the participant was feeling good about himself or herself and understood the nature of the study and its manipulations.

Confidentiality—The practice of making sure that nobody outside a research project has access to data that can be identified with a specific individual.

An additional requirement when you conduct research is that you must protect the **anonymity** and **confidentiality** of your research participants. It is desirable that, after a study is over, you cannot link people's behaviors in a research project with them personally. If there are no identifying characteristics in the data that allow you to know whose data you are examining, the data are anonymous. In some cases, you will not be able to separate a person's identify from the data. For example, if you are tracking people over time, you have to be able to link their current data with their past data. In such a case, you need to make sure that nobody outside the research project has access to that information. When you do this, you are making sure that the data are confidential.

Coercion—Pressure that a potential participant feels in agreeing to take part in research.

Another ethical issue involved with interaction with participants involves **coercion**. If you were carrying out a study, you might want to solicit participation of your friends and classmates. They might not want to participate, but being your friends, they might feel social pressure. Their participation would not be truly voluntary.

Plagiarism—An ethical breach in which a person claims credit for another person's idea or research.

Finally, when you develop research ideas or when you write up a report of your project, you must avoid claiming credit that belongs to others. When an investigator asserts that he or she came up with an idea, but that idea was actually developed by another person, this is **plagiarism**. It is considered a very serious breach of ethics. If an investigator has received research money from the federal government, plagiarism can lead to severe sanctions.

LEGAL REQUIREMENTS AND ETHICS IN RESEARCH

Shortly after World War II, the international community recognized the need for laws concerning research with people. These laws are known as the **Nuremberg Code**, named for the German city where they were developed. The 10 points of the Code appear in Table 2.4.

Nuremberg Code— A set of legal principles adopted by the international community after the Nazi atrocities in World War II to insure fair and ethical treatment of research participants.

As you look at the Code, you might wonder why anybody had to enact such a code. All of the points seem to involve little but common sense. Unfortunately, the Nazis had victimized many people in research. The Nuremberg Code formalized a set of rules that could be used by researchers with integrity when they planned their studies that involve people.

In addition to the internationally recognized Nuremberg Code, the U.S. government has also passed laws to protect human subjects. These procedures were initially implemented in 1966 and have evolved over time (Reynolds, 1982).

TABLE 2.4 Ten Points of the Nuremburg Code

Point	Comment
1. Research on humans absolutely requires informed consent.	You cannot do research on people who are not able to give voluntary, informed consent. This requires that they be sufficiently aware of their rights to be able to make a choice that is good for them. You are also not allowed to use undue influence or power you have over a person. The individual must know what risks might be involved.
2. The experiment must have the possibility of contributing to our body of knowledge.	You should not perform research that has no chance of being useful to society. This does not mean that an investigation has to produce major results, but the outcome should add to the accumulation of knowledge about human and nonhuman behavior.
3. Researchers should be knowledgeable about the topic they investigate to maximize the likelihood that the results will be useful.	Especially for biomedical research, scientists should design their research based on previous work that has been conducted using animals. In addition, the scientist must be competent enough to design a study whose results will justify the experimentation.
4. The experiment should avoid unnecessary physical and mental suffering.	Sometimes research by its nature involves discomfort of some kind (e.g., a study of sleep deprivation). Researchers should design their work to minimize the extent of the discomfort should it be necessary. Embarrassment and frustration are examples of mental suffering that might be associated with psychological research.
5. No experiment should be conducted if there is good reason to believe that death or serious injury will occur.	When an investigation involves high levels of potential risk, this restriction can be relaxed if the researchers serve as participants in this research.
6. The degree of risk must be less than the potential gain from the research.	Scientists must perform a cost-benefit analysis. If the costs exceed the potential benefits, the research is inappropriate.
7. Prior arrangements must be in place for responding to an emergency that occurs during a research project.	The investigators must make provisions for emergencies that they can reasonably foresee. Sometimes a participant may suffer harm because of an entirely unforeseen circumstance. In such a case, the researcher might not be seen as acting unethically. Points 2 and 3 relate to this—a researcher should be sufficiently well informed to know what risks are likely.
8. The investigator must have appropriate training to conduct the research.	Researchers have to know what they are doing. If a researcher fails to anticipate dangers that an expert would recognize in advance, that researcher might be judged as acting unethically. Researchers must also ensure that workers subordinate to them are qualified to carry out the tasks assigned to them.
9. Research participants must be free to terminate their involvement at any time.	When an individual has reached the point that he or she no longer feels comfortable participating in research, the person has the right to leave without penalty.
10. The experimenter must terminate a research project if he or she believes that continuing the study will lead to injury or death.	The investigator has to be aware of the dynamics of the research situation. If he or she recognizes that there is an elevated level of risk, the investigator must end the study.

Institutional Review Boards

Changes in the regulations appear in the *Federal Register*, which reports on congressional activities of all kinds. One of the major provisions of the federal regulations mandates an **Institutional Review Board (IRB)**, a committee that consists of at least five people, including a member of the community who is not a researcher. The IRB reviews the potential risks associated with research and either approves or disapproves projects that investigators want to carry out.

Institutional Review Board (IRB)—A committee that reviews research projects to make sure that the projects are in compliance with accepted ethical guidelines. An IRB is required for every institution receiving federal funding in the United States.

Most research must receive approval from an IRB, but there are exceptions, as listed in Table 2.5. (Federal regulations stipulate that an IRB must document that a particular research does not require formal review.) These exceptions exist because the experts who work for the government recognize that not all research carries significant risk. For example, you are allowed to conduct some survey research and simple observational research in a public area without IRB approval. The reason is that those you survey or observe do not experience greater risk because you are studying them when compared to the risks of everyday life, although survey research that probes sensitive issues may require IRB approval.

TABLE 2.5 Types of Research Most Relevant to Psychology that Do Not Require Approval by an Institutional Review Board

In general, research activities in which the only involvement of human subjects will be in one or more of the four following categories are exempt from review by an IRB.

1. Research conducted in established or commonly accepted educational settings, involving normal educational practices, such as
   i. research on regular and special education instructional strategies, or
   ii. research on the effectiveness of or the comparison among instructional techniques, curricula, or classroom management methods.

2. Research involving the use of educational tests, survey procedures, interview procedures, or observation of public behavior. The exemption does not hold (and IRB approval is required) if
   i. information obtained is recorded in such a manner that human subjects can be identified, directly or through identifiers linked to the subjects; and
   ii. any disclosure of the human subjects' responses outside the research could reasonably place the subjects at risk of criminal or civil liability or be damaging to the subjects' financial standing, employability, or reputation.

3. Research involving the use of educational tests, survey procedures, interview procedures, or observation of public behavior is exempt as listed in paragraph (2) above; in addition, research is exempt from IRB approval if
   i. the human subjects are elected or appointed public officials or candidates for public office, or
   ii. Federal statute(s) require(s) without exception that the confidentiality of the personally identifiable information will be maintained throughout the research and thereafter.

4. Research involving the collection or study of existing, publicly available data, documents, records, pathological specimens, or diagnostic specimens; in addition, the research is exempt from IRB approval if the information is recorded by the investigator so that subjects cannot be identified, directly or through identifiers linked to the subjects.

One of the most important issues associated with research with people is that you need to inform them about the risks and benefits of the project. One way of recording the fact that you informed the participants and that they voluntarily agreed to take part in the study is through the informed-consent form. This form lays out the nature of the study, including potential risks for participating. Sometimes IRBs have specific formats that they want researchers to follow; in addition, institutions sponsoring research may use these forms as legal documents.

Investigators have found that research participants often cannot understand complicated informed-consent forms, even when the IRBs have created the forms. Likewise, the forms that some institutions use can be very legalistic and, to a typical reader, uninformative. According to one study, the prose in the average form was between the 10th- and 11th-grade reading level, but the half of the American public reads at the 8th-grade level or below (Paasche-Orlow, Taylor, & Barncati, 2003). This research involved medical informed consent, which is likely to be more complex and technical than behavioral research, but the important point is that research participants need to be able to understand what you are telling them in order for their consent to participate to be truly voluntary.

Ironically, Keith-Spiegel and Koocher (2005) have argued that when researchers believe that they have not received fair treatment from an IRB, they may engage in behaviors designed to deceive the IRB. The investigators may conclude that their research is truly ethical and that they need to identify ways to get around elements of the ethics review process on which the IRB treats them unfairly.

It is common to hear researchers complain about the difficulty in getting IRBs to approve their research projects, but many psychologists in one study (62 percent) responded that the turnaround time between submitting a proposal and receiving a decision is reasonable, a little over four weeks (Ashcraft and Krause, 2007).

There are some important questions associated with IRBs, however. For example, Sieber (2009) gave an example of student researchers who wanted to interview people living on the streets; the IRB mandated that the students tell those being interviewed that they didn't have to respond to any questions they didn't want to answer. The participants seemed to find that statement very funny because if they didn't want to answer, they weren't going to. The students believed that the street people did not take the interview seriously because of that.

Furthermore, sometimes IRBs make decisions that seem quite questionable. Ceci and Bruck (2009) reported that one of their research proposals was denied by their IRB as being potentially damaging to the children who would be participants even though the National Science Foundation (NSF) and the National Institutes of Health had reviewed the research proposal and found no problems. In fact, the NSF had even provided funding for the research.

THE IMPORTANCE OF SOCIAL CONTEXT IN DECIDING ON ETHICS IN RESEARCH

Consider this: A participant volunteers to help with research. He is told that he will be in the role of the teacher, delivering electrical shocks to another person, also a volunteer, every time that person makes a mistake in a learning task. With each mistake, the strength of the shock will increase, up to a level on a panel marked "Danger: Severe Shock," followed by a mysterious higher level of shock simply labeled "XXX." The learner remarks that he has a heart condition, but the experimenter replies that it won't matter. The learner is strapped into a chair in another room and connected to the apparatus that will deliver the electrical shocks.

After the learner makes several mistakes and receives shocks, he demands to quit, but the experimenter simply says the experiment must continue. Shortly thereafter, the learner (who mentioned a heart problem) becomes completely silent, but the researcher encourages the teacher to continue to deliver electrical shocks if the learner doesn't respond because a nonresponse is the same as a wrong answer.

Stanley Milgram's Research Project on Obedience

Suppose you were the participant. Would you continue shocking the learner? Or would you stop? If you were like the majority of people who took part in some of Stanley Milgram's (1963) experiments on conformity, you would have persisted in shocking the learner. How would you have felt afterward, knowing that you had delivered shocks to somebody with a heart condition, somebody who became utterly silent after a while, somebody you might have killed by shocking him?

(As you may already know, the victim did not receive shocks. Milgram employed deception to induce participants to feel personally involved in what they thought was a real set of conditions.)

Milgram (1974) described a variety of studies in his extensive research project that subjected his volunteers to this situation. Knowing what you know about the ethics of research, would you consider this research ethical? This experimentation has generated voluminous commentary. Some psychologists and ethicists believe that the studies were simply unethical (e.g., Baumrind, 1964). On the other hand, Milgram (1964) defended them as being within ethical boundaries. More recently, psychologists have revisited some of the issues associated with Milgram's research and its ethical dilemmas (e.g., Burger, 2009; Elms, 2009; Miller, 2009) without an extreme shock condition. The outcome was similar to Milgram's, suggesting that dynamics of obedience may not have changed greatly in the past half century.

The Ethical Issues

What are some of the important issues to consider here? If psychologists legitimately differ in their conclusions, it is pretty certain that we are in a gray area here. You might conclude that the research was acceptable, or you might condemn it. In the end, we need to make a judgment call using the best wisdom we can muster.

Cost-Benefit Analysis— An evaluation of the relative risks that research participants face in a study (the cost) relative to the potential benefit of the outcome of the research.

An IRB decides whether any given research project would subject people to undue risk relative to possible benefits from the research. Formally, the IRB is supposed to weigh the risks (physical and psychological harm) against the benefits (increased knowledge and applications) of the research. If the risks are greater than the benefits, the research should not be done; if the benefits exceed the risks, the research can be defended on ethical grounds. This type of assessment is often known as a **cost-benefit analysis**. The difficulty arises when the risks and the benefits are both high. A decision may not be easy to reach and different people may arrive at different, but legitimate, conclusions.

Unfortunately, before researchers carry out their studies, nobody knows for sure what harm may occur or what benefits will actually accrue. In advance, we are talking about possibilities, not actualities. Before a study takes place, we can guess at costs and benefits, but not until after investigators complete their work can we identify either the risk-associated problems that arose or the actual benefits of the research.

Criticisms of Milgram's Research.   With this uncertainty in mind, we can ask whether Milgram violated the rights of his participants. Among others, Baumrind (1964) asserted that Milgram's obedience research should not have been done. She said that the "dependent attitude" (p. 421) of the participants rendered them more susceptible to the manipulations of an authority figure, that is, the experimenter. She also named several ethical problems, asserting that Milgram did not show concern for participants' well-being, that the cost (i.e., degree of psychological distress and having been lied to) exceeded the benefits of having done the research, that the participants' long-term well-being was negatively affected, and that their attitudes toward authority figures would in the future be more negative. She also noted Milgram's statement that 14 of the 40 participants showed obvious distress and that three suffered seizures.

Baumrind (1964) did not accept Milgram's statement that the distress was momentary and that the gain in psychological knowledge outweighed the negatives: "I do regard the emotional disturbance described by Milgram as potentially harmful because it could easily effect an alteration in the subject's self-image or ability to trust adult authorities in the future" (p. 422). She also stated that Milgram's debriefing and dehoaxing processes would not have remedied the situation.

Milgram's Defense of His Research.   Not surprisingly, Milgram (1964) responded to Baumrind's criticisms. He disagreed with her assessments, saying that he tried to predict in advance how the participants would respond and had been confident that they would not engage in the shocking behavior very long. He went to great lengths, asking psychiatrists and others to estimate how often the participants were likely to engage in blind obedience. The experts thought that the overwhelming number of participants would not administer severe shocks. Thus, at the outset, Milgram firmly believed that virtually everybody would refuse to engage in extreme behavior. As a result, he felt that the risk to his participants would be minimal. As it turned out, the estimates that the experts gave were wrong— people did administer what they thought were severe electrical shocks. But it is important to note that Milgram tried to anticipate what would occur.

Milgram also noted that he debriefed and dehoaxed the participants, trying to ensure that they departed with no ill effects. Further, at his request, a psychiatrist interviewed 40 participants after a year. There seem to have been no problems at that time. In fact, Ring, Wallston, and Corey (1970) specifically examined participants' reactions to a Milgram-like study. These researchers reported that people may have felt distressed during participation, but the effects were short-lived. A large majority of the people responded that they were happy that they participated. Further, when Ring et al. debriefed their participants after using an approach like Milgram's, the level of tension by participants dropped relative to that of no debriefing.

Baumrind raised critically important points. According to the data we have, though, many or most of the problems she cited did not seem to materialize. Both Milgram's and

Baumrind's predictions were off the mark. This is another good example of how experts can be wrong, and why we should not simply rely on authority for the "truth."

The Social Context

We might want to consider the social context in which Milgram did his work. His studies took place from 1960 to 1963, which was not long after the end of World War II, when the Nazis had carried out numerous horrific experiments. In some very famous cases, the perpetrators of those acts claimed that they were merely following orders. Milgram, like many others, was greatly affected by the reports of these atrocities. In fact, when Milgram gave an overview of his research in his book *Obedience to Authority* (1974), he referred directly to the Nazi crimes in the very first paragraph of the book.

The United States, where Milgram did his research, was still in the process of recovering from the war. In addition, people were worried about the possibility that communists would try to conquer the world, turning people into blindly obedient automatons. It was reasonable that we would try to understand how seemingly normal people could commit the wartime acts of the Nazis, behaving with blind obedience. An experimental psychologist might try to reproduce the dynamics of obedience in the laboratory to find out how and why people defer to authorities. This is precisely what Stanley Milgram did.

As members of our society, we continually decide whether behaviors are acceptable. In the early years of the century, many people felt entirely comfortable discriminating against people of color in all aspects of life. Society has changed, and the number of people who agree that such discrimination is acceptable has diminished. In a similar vein, people in the post-war years may have been very comfortable with the idea of Milgram's research because the effects of blind obedience were still fresh in people's minds. Society has changed, and the number of people who would support such research has undoubtedly diminished. The question of blind obedience is no longer as relevant as it was in the aftermath of World War II. It is unlikely that an IRB would approve such research today. But in a different era, people might consider it acceptable or even desirable.

Incidentally, Milgram's application to become a member of APA was initially questioned on the basis of the ethics of his research. Ultimately, though, the organization accorded him membership, judging that he had not violated ethical guidelines in his work.

> **Role Playing**—An approach to research in which participants act as if they were participating in a study so the investigator can avoid using potentially unethical strategies that might lead to physical or psychological harm to the participants.

> **Naturalistic Observation**—A research technique in which the investigator studies behavior as it naturally occurs, without any manipulation of variables or intervention into the situation.

> **Simulation**—An approach to research in which the investigator creates an environment similar to one of interest in order to study behaviors in a realistic way. This approach is also known as the simulated environment.

WHAT YOU NEED TO DO IF YOUR RESEARCH INVOLVES DECEPTION

For decades, deception was very prevalent in social psychological research (Adair, Dushenko, & Lindsay, 1985). This means that many psychologists have accepted it as a reality of their research. As Figure 2.2 suggests, deception may have been more routine in the 1970s compared to today. Nonetheless, in spite of the criticisms leveled by opponents of deception, psychological researchers have not embraced alternate methodologies like **role playing**, **naturalistic observation**, or **simulation**.

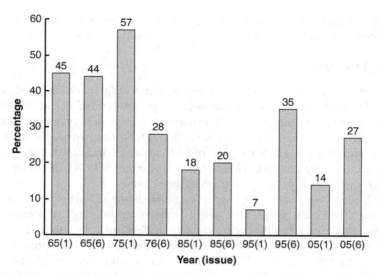

FIGURE 2.2   Percentage of studies using deception in a sample of articles from the *Journal of Personality and Social Psychology* from 1965 to 2005. The articles appeared in issues 1 and 6 of the journal from each year represented.

When many people argue against deception, they do so because they see it as immoral. In addition, a second area of concern involves the risk for participants who are deceived. In such a case, a person cannot give informed consent about his or her willingness to participate. We cannot ignore this important notion of informed consent. It is a critical component of national and international laws. Fortunately, there is good reason to believe that keeping participants ignorant of some aspects of the research has negligible effects on them in general (e.g., Bröder, 1995).

A very different type of criticism of the use of deception is that people will develop negative attitudes or suspicion toward psychology and psychological research (Orne, 1962). There is credible evidence, however, that people regard the science and practice of psychology very positively, even after learning that a researcher had deceived them (e.g., Soliday & Stanton, 1995). Christensen (1988) even reported that research participants believed that it would be undesirable if we failed to investigate important topics that might require the use of deception.

Some Research Projects Require Deception

Cover Story—The story a researcher creates to disguise the actual purpose of a study when deception is considered necessary to conduct a study.

The dilemma about using deception in research is that some research projects virtually require a level of deception. If you want participants to act naturally, you might have to create a **cover story** that keeps them from acting in a self-conscious manner during the study. If, after careful consideration, you conclude that you need to use deception, you must keep two points in mind.

First, you should minimize the amount deception involved. You need to make sure that you do not withhold critical information that would

Active Deception—The process of misinforming a research participant about some aspect of a study so that the individual is not aware of the investigator's intent in the project.

Passive Deception—The failure to provide complete information to a research participant about some aspect of a study so that the individual is not aware of the investigator's intent in the project.

Dehoaxing—The process of telling research participants of any deception or ruses used in a study.

Debriefing—Informing research participants at the conclusion of a research project of the purpose of the research, including disclosure of any deception and providing an opportunity for participants to ask questions about the research.

Desensitization—The process of eliminating any negative aftereffects that a participant might experience after taking part in a project.

make a difference in a person's decision about whether to participate in your research. Withholding too much information may mean that people cannot give appropriate informed consent about participation because they cannot assess the risks. As Fisher and Fyrberg (1994) noted, we can characterize different kinds of deception, depending on the degree to which we actually provide incorrect information to participants. For example, we can distinguish between active and passive deception.

In **active deception**, you would actively mislead the participants by providing them with information that is not true. In **passive deception**, you would not actually tell a lie. Instead, you would withhold information that might give clues to the participants about the purpose of the study. That is, you give them incomplete information.

All research involves telling our volunteers less than we know. Participants would probably not be terribly interested in all the details of our research. At the same time, with passive deception, you intend to keep the participants in the dark, so your intent is clearly to deceive.

With any use of deception, you need to debrief your participants adequately after the session ends. There are two components to **debriefing**. One element involves **dehoaxing**, which means that you tell the individuals what you did, how you deceived them, and why it was necessary. The second element involves **desensitization**, which means that you eliminate any potential sources of negative feelings by the participants.

The Effects of Debriefing on Research

Most psychologists debrief their participants immediately after a testing session concludes. Practically, this is the easiest approach. If a researcher decides to postpone the debriefing, it takes extra effort to contact the participants. One drawback to immediate debriefing is that participants might discuss the research with others. If you deceived them in order to make sure they acted naturally, there are obvious problems if your participants talk to others who later take part in your study.

How often will participants actually discuss the research with others? According to Marans (1988), of 50 participants in a debriefing-disclosure study, 10 (20 percent) reported discussing the experiment with other, potential participants. If 20 percent of participants disclose the nature of a study to others, this could pose a serious problem to the validity of research that relies on the naïveté of participants. On the other hand, Diener, Matthews, and Smith (1972) discovered that only 11 of 440 potential participants had learned about the deceptive elements of an experiment for which fellow students had volunteered. Diener et al. concluded that leakage of information is not a serious concern.

Further, Walsh (1976) reported that when researchers asked people not to disclose any information about the research, the participants refrained from discussing the study more than when such a request was not made. These results suggest that researchers must evaluate the potential problems of immediate debriefing on a study-by-study basis. If the investigator is worried that a participant might talk about the study and forewarn other potential participants of the nature of the study, the researcher might decide to defer debriefing until the end of the project. This would solve one problem: People remain naïve about the study. At the same time, this solution itself introduces a different problem, having to contact people later, which is not always easy.

Psychologists have asked the question of whether debriefing actually serves its purpose. That is, does it remove any negative responses of the participants? Although there is controversy (see Rubin, 1985), there seem to be few negative effects of deception when researchers take debriefing seriously. Gruder, Stumpfhauser, and Wyer (1977) studied the effects of feedback. These researchers provided participants with false feedback about poor performance after having taken an intelligence test. Gruder et al. wondered if there would be a difference in performance in a subsequent testing session depending on whether the participants learned about the false feedback in a debriefing session.

The results showed that when participants learned that the feedback was not accurate, their later performance on another test improved; there was no comparable trend among participants who were not debriefed. This suggests that false feedback about poor performance has a real effect on participants. On the other hand, debriefed participants were able to cast away the negative information readily. There are clear implications about the beneficial effects of debriefing and potential risks if it is not done or is not done well.

THE CONTROVERSY ABOUT DECEPTION

Do you like it when people lie to you? If you do, you are probably fairly unusual. Most people are upset when others lie to them. Over the years, psychologists have used deception in their research. Do people object to being lied to in these research settings? Or do you think that people are unconcerned? The answers to these questions are difficult because there are few absolute standards.

For instance, people in different cultures may show different responses to issues like deception in research. American students are more likely to be bothered by it than are Malaysian students because of a greater tendency on the part of Malaysians to defer to the judgments of respected authorities like a researcher, and to relinquish individual rights that Americans may deem more important (Bowman & Anthonysamy, 2006). So in determining the ethics of a research project, your decision should take cultural factors into account.

Related to cultural issues in research, the term *ethical imperialism* has appeared in the research literature. This concept refers to the idea that a researcher from one culture may try to apply his or her own ethical perspective on research participants in another culture. With the increase in cross-cultural research in psychology, this phenomenon may become much more prominent. For example, if Malaysian research participants were not bothered by some aspects of deception that Americans are bothered by, should an American researcher impose his or her ideals on the Malaysians? Or if a Malaysian researcher held views that differed from those of Americans, should he apply his or her standard to the Americans?

A further question involves whether a person from one culture truly understands the dynamics of people in another culture. Quraishi (2008) is a Muslim researcher who studied

Muslim prisoners. He concluded that because they could identify with one another, the research was more meaningful for all of them. In fact, with some Muslim populations, like Black Muslims, the cultural mismatch was notable. He used his experience with the Muslim prisoners to discuss how differences in race, ethnicity, and culture can affect the process of research.

If you were to search for published articles on ethics in psychological research, you would find that a great deal of it would relate to the use of deception. Some psychologists (e.g., Ortmann & Hertwig, 1997) have condemned the use of deception in research, calling for the outlawing of the practice, in part on purely moral grounds. In response, other psychologists have argued that moral philosophers do not agree that deception is unambiguously wrong (Korn, 1998), that the "social contract" between researchers and participants may permit behaviors that might elsewhere be considered unethical (Lawson, 1995), and that participants themselves do not condemn such an approach (Christensen, 1988).

Fisher and Fyrberg (1994) asked potential participants (i.e., college students) to evaluate research scenarios involving three types of deception: implicit deception, technical deception, and role deception. Implicit deception involves having participants complete their tasks for a purpose of which they are unaware; in this case, Fisher and Fyrberg used implicit deception to manipulate mood by means of an imagery task.

Technical deception involves misrepresentation of the use of equipment; Fisher and Fyrberg technically deceived participants by telling them that a particular equipment had broken down when it actually hadn't. Finally, role deception involves misrepresenting the role of another individual in the testing session; the researchers induced participants to believe that they had damaged another person's belongings.

The results suggested that people don't see much problem with implicit deception. Ninety percent of the students participating in Fisher and Fyrberg's study thought that the benefits of the research outweighed the costs. On the other hand, just over 70 percent of the students were comfortable with technical and role deception.

It might be informative to figure out why some research situations could lead to negative reactions. Psychologists who study embarrassment note that we feel embarrassed when we think somebody may evaluate us unfavorably (Miller, 1995). If we feel that we have been fooled in the presence of someone, we might be embarrassed because we feel that the person might think less of us. Thus, in a situation like technical deception or role deception, you might be annoyed at having been deceived. On the other hand, in implicit deception, the participants may determine that their lack of information should not be a cause of embarrassment.

Fisher (2005) has proposed that we consider deception on several dimensions. Her discussion related to research with children, but the three points discussed here have validity for any project involving deception:

- Will alternative methodologies produce data of equal validity to that involve deception?
- Does deception permit the research participant to make an informed consent, thereby minimizing potential harm?
- Will debriefing eliminate the potential for risk or could it cause problems in and of itself?

The question of using deception is complex. As Fisher and Fyrberg (1994) pointed out, participants are partners in research, not merely objects of study. As such, we have to balance the potential risks of psychological harm (e.g., embarrassment or anger at being deceived) with the potential benefits of research. We have to consider whether hiding the truth means that participants will not be able to make informed judgments about participation.

ETHICAL ISSUES IN SPECIAL CIRCUMSTANCES

Ethics in Cross-Cultural Research

One area of ethics that does not involve issues like deception or confidentiality focuses on the implications of culturally oriented research in and of itself. That is, researchers may have an impact on the people they study.

Medin (2012) has raised an important issue of being sensitive to people in different cultures. He has conducted research with American Indians and, at one point, one elder Menominee Indian said that they had been studied too much. The question that ultimately arose was the relative benefit that the researchers derived versus the benefit to those being studied. After considering the issue and discussing it with those involved, Medin decided that a fair exchange would include, among other things, an hour of volunteer time by research assistants to the community for each hour they spend conducting research with that community.

Further, there can be implications regarding conclusions drawn along cultural lines. For example, psychologists should consider whether research on cultural issues could lead to stereotyping of people in various groups. Iwamasa, Larrabee, and Merritt (2000) discovered that some behaviors stereotypically associated with different ethnic or racial groups were also associated with psychological disorders. Thus, one could naively conclude that when a person from a given group exhibits a certain behavior, that behavior reflects a disorder when, in reality, it might simply be a common way of behaving within that group.

In an opposite circumstance, a psychologist who is not familiar with the behaviors in a different cultural group could observe a behavior normal in the psychologist's culture and not recognize it as symptomatic of a problem within the other culture. For instance, among the Amish, symptoms of bipolar mood disorder include giving gifts during the wrong season of the year or excessive use of public telephones (Rogler, 1999). These examples illustrate APA's aspirational principle of justice.

Another aspirational principle that is relevant in cultural research involves respecting people's rights and dignity. That is, psychologists should appreciate individual differences associated with "age, gender, gender identity, race, ethnicity, culture, national origin, religion, sexual orientation, disability, language, and socioeconomic status" (Ethical principles of psychologists, 2002, p. 1063).

In this regard, ethics goes beyond the immediacy of the interaction between researcher and participant. For instance, Harrowing, Mill, Spiers, Kulig, and Kipp (2010) raised the issue of whether their conceptualization of what constituted ethical research made sense in the context of the culture of Uganda, where they conducted their research. You might think that if something is ethical in one culture, it would be ethical elsewhere. But ethicists have debated this issue.

In the research by Harrowing et al. (2010), they wondered whether "adherence to the standard pillars of autonomy, non-maleficence, beneficence and justice [was] appropriate and sufficient?" (p. 71). These researchers were engaged in biomedical research to prevent the spread of AIDS, so if their research did not help people in their quest to gain control of their environment, the research would not be ethical. By imposing the standards of people from another country and culture, the research might not have led to optimal outcomes for those involved because of the imposition of cultural barriers. For instance, if researchers concentrate on government regulations rather than inequities in health care, the research participants might ultimately suffer (Bhutta, 2002).

Another element is that investigators should not include people in the research if potential participants cannot provide informed consent and engage in the research voluntarily because of social class or customs. Problems might not be apparent to scientists from a different culture. In Western tradition, participants sign informed-consent forms to indicate that they know about any risks and that they are taking part voluntarily.

In some cultures, such as among Asian-American groups, informed consent is not an individual decision; rather, it is a decision made by the entire family (Miskimen, Marin, & Escobar, 2003). In other cultures, such as in Egypt, people sign forms only for major life decisions. To require a signature after verbal consent has been given is seen as evidence of a lack of trust between the people involved (Yick, 2007). And in the Dominican Republic, the provision on an informed-consent form that specifies that the individual can withdraw from the study at any time may be meaningless because in that country, the tradition is that signing a contract is binding, so the person will not feel free to leave the study (McIntosh et al., 2008).

Another point of departure from the tradition of obtaining informed consent is that providing information so a person can make a decision about participating can in itself be an issue. For example, among Navajo Indians in the United States, information shapes reality, so informed consent is very different with this population because the act of providing information leads to a different reality (Yick, 2007).

Finally, among APA's enforceable ethical standards, researchers need to attend to their competence in researching complex areas involving culture and whether they are really able to draw appropriate conclusions. Psychologists also have an ethical responsibility to provide adequate assessments and valid interpretation of results. Lack of cultural competence can lead to problems in interpreting data and implementing programs based on the research.

The ethical issues associated with research across cultures are very real. Your research may not have the implications of biomedical research, but the impact that you and your research have on participants with different cultural outlooks can be significant.

Ethics in Internet Research

A new challenge that we face as researchers involves ethical issues associated with using the Internet. We are in uncharted territory with Web research. The community of psychological researchers has had a century to figure out how to complete in-person research; we have had well over a quarter of a century to come up with legally sanctioned protections for participants. But with Web research, some very tricky questions arise about how to deal with the issues of confidentiality and anonymity (especially regarding sensitive topics), informed consent, protecting participants from unforeseen negative consequences, debriefing them, and how to arrange compensatory follow-up if it is needed (which we may never know).

There are two main advantages of remote, online data collection with respect to ethics, according to Barchard and Williams (2008). The first is that respondents feel a sense of anonymity that leads them to be more likely to respond to sensitive questions. And, second, respondents do not feel pressure to continue their participation if they become uncomfortable for some reason.

Countering these advantages, some disadvantages also exist. First, it is not possible to know whether participants understand the informed-consent process. Second, clarifying ambiguities and answering questions during debriefing are not possible. Third, the researcher does not know if a respondent is actually of a legal age to be able to participate (Barchard & Williams, 2008).

A sizeable amount of Web-based research in psychology involves questionnaires. These are generally regarded as being fairly benign, so the ethical risks associated with them are minimal. An added protection for the participants is that they can quit any time they want if they feel frustrated, overwhelmed, or otherwise uncomfortable. However, suppose a researcher wants to know about serious, private issues in a person's life. A notable concern appears here. Merely filling out a questionnaire may trigger an emotional response; if it happens in a laboratory, the researcher can try to deal with it immediately. The researcher can also arrange to contact the individual at a later point to make sure that there were no lasting problems. Nobody may ever know about the unfortunate consequences for remote people who participate online. It appears that this second issue may not lead to problems because respondents may feel less pressure to complete an uncomfortable task (Barchard & Williams, 2008). Further, the response rate to sensitive questions is higher in online surveys than in mail surveys, suggesting that participants do not regularly experience discomfort in answering sensitive questions (McCabe, 2004).

The research community recognizes these concerns and has begun to address them. Major, national organizations have entered the discussion. The Board of Scientific Affairs of the American Psychological Association, the American Association for the Advancement of Science, and the federal government's National Institutes of Health have been working to generate solutions to these ethical questions (Azar, 2000a).

Ethics in Animal Research

Psychologists have studied animal behavior for the past century. Much of the work has involved laboratory rats and pigeons that have learned to perform tasks in different conditions. Even though the study of animal behavior constituted one of the pillars of psychology, not all people have agreed on its value. Some have criticized animal research as being of limited applicability to human behavior and restricted mostly to one variant of one species, namely, the Norway rat (Beach, 1950). This is an important question: Can we learn about people by studying animals? The answer is definitely yes, although we cannot learn everything from animals.

A second group of people has condemned research with animals as being unethical. There are several aspects to their arguments. For instance, animal rights activists maintain that we do not have the right to keep animals in laboratory captivity. Some also believe that the animals are treated inhumanely. Over the past few decades, there has been growing sentiment against use of animals in research in society, although a majority of people still believe that if such research benefits humans, it is not unethical (see Plous, 1996a, for a discussion of these issues).

Researchers who work with animals have identified different elements of ethics in nonhuman animal research. Broadly speaking, the scientists have noted that investigators have to consider the ethics of fair treatment (e.g., housing and food) of the animals, the need for science to advance, and the benefit of human patients when knowledge is advanced by animal research (Ideland, 2009). In fact, the National Academies of Science in the United States has determined that the benefit of using chimpanzees in research does not outweigh the costs of keeping these intelligent, social animals in captivity for such purposes (Altevogt, Pankevich, Shelton-Davenport, & Kahn, 2011).

The use of animals in psychological research has diminished notably over the past several decades in the United States, Canada, and Western Europe. According to Plous (1996a), a quarter to a third of psychology departments have either closed their animal laboratories or are giving it serious consideration. Further, there is a remarkable decrease in the number of graduate students in psychology who conduct animal research (Thomas & Blackman, 1992, cited in Plous, 1996a).

Plous has found that psychologists, as a group, show overwhelming support (over 85 percent) for naturalistic observation, which does not involve animal confinement, somewhat less support for studies involving laboratory confinement (over 60 percent), and little support for research involving pain or death (17–34 percent). He has also discovered that undergraduate psychology majors are highly similar to their mentors in the attitudes they hold toward the use of animals in psychological research (Plous, 1996b). He also noted that among the general public, there is significant support for research involving rats (88 percent), but less for dogs (55 percent).

If a person's own moral principles imply that it is unethical to use animals in research, then no arguments about the benefit to people will persuade that individual to accept such research. That person has the right to hold his or her moral principles and others must recognize that right. At the same time, the majority of Americans accept animal research as being beneficial, as long as the investigations might be beneficial to human welfare and do not expose the animals to unreasonable distress. We must rely on knowledge and common sense to make the best decision.

Arguments and Counterarguments.   According to Coile and Miller (1984), some animal rights activists made claims about the plight of animals in psychological experiments that would make most of us wonder if the research is justified. The claims include the idea that animals receive intense electrical shocks that they cannot escape until they lose the ability to even scream in pain, that they are deprived of food and water, and suffer until they die.

Coile and Miller discussed six points raised by the activists (Mobilization for Animals, 1984, cited in Coile & Miller, 1984). Coile and Miller's arguments are three decades old but are probably still reasonably valid, especially given the changes in the nature of psychological research away from the animal model. Coile and Miller examined the previous five years of psychological journal articles that commonly report the use of research animals, like those in the *Journal of Experimental Psychology: Animal Behavior Processes* and the *Journal of Comparative Psychology.*

The claims of some activists were simply wrong regarding psychological research. The alleged, intense electric shocks, severe food and water deprivation, smashing of bones and mutilation of limbs, and pain designed to make animals psychotic never appeared in research reported in the most prestigious psychology journals.

The fact that the claims about the research are false does not mean that the animals do not experience pain or distress in some studies. In fact, various experiments clearly involve discomfort, some of it intense. Research on learned helplessness, for example, involved such an approach.

Coile and Miller argued that there can be good reason for engaging in this type of research, particularly in the biomedical realm. For example, experimental animals have been used to investigate treatments for such maladies as cancer and AIDS in people and distemper in animals and to study ways to relieve the chronic pain that some people live with. Researchers who seek to further our understanding of depression sometimes use electrical shock as a treatment; however, as Coile and Miller pointed out, depression can lead to suicide, which is the third leading cause of death in young adults.

Miller (1985) further amplified some of the benefits of animal research for people suffering from problems like scoliosis, enuresis (bed wetting), anorexia, loss of the use of limbs due to nerve damage, chronic pain, stress, and headaches. Many people would consider it justifiable to study animals in order to ease the plight of people suffering from such problems.

As Plous (1996a, b) has found, psychologists and psychology students hold quite similar attitudes about the use of animals in research. The general public also shows sympathy toward animal research; there is widespread support regarding the use of rats in biomedical research. People do not like to see animals exposed to intense suffering or distress, though.

Finally, what is important in dealing with issues of the ethics of animal research is to make sure that the information advanced by those on both sides of the issue is credible. Claims that are unfounded do not help people understand problems that actually need to be addressed, so appropriate action cannot be taken.

SUMMARY

Scientists who study people usually show consideration for the well-being of the individuals they study. After all, scientists are just like everybody else in most respects. Unfortunately, however, there have been cases in which researchers have shown a reprehensible lack of concern about the people who participate in their studies.

Probably the most notorious violators of ethics in research are the Nazi doctors who tortured people in the name of research. Unfortunately, they are not the only ones who have violated ethical standards. For instance, American researchers studying men with syphilis for several decades beginning in the 1920s withheld treatment to see the course of the disease. The men thought they were receiving appropriate levels of treatment.

In order to protect human participants, the American Psychological Association was one of the first organizations to promulgate ethical standards in research. APA has developed a set of aspirational goals and enforceable rules that its members must follow.

It is the responsibility of each researcher to be aware of these rules. Student researchers are just as responsible for ethical treatment of participants as professional researchers are.

Among psychologists, Stanley Milgram is undoubtedly the most famous person whose research was questioned on ethical grounds. He deceived his participants into thinking they were shocking another individual. The controversy over whether he should have conducted his projects persists. In the end, the decision about ethics involves complex issues that differ for each instance we consider.

After the Nazi atrocities, an international body created the Nuremburg Code that specifies the basic rights of human participants in research. It is an internationally recognized code. In the United States, the federal and state legislation similarly protects the welfare of participants. One of the newest areas that are receiving scrutiny is Web-based research. There are questions of informed consent and invasion of privacy that have yet to be addressed and resolved.

Another aspect of research ethics that has received considerable attention in the past few decades involves the treatment of animal subjects. Some people condemn any use of laboratory animals in research, regardless of the type of project. Other people feel that if such research will ultimately benefit people, some degree of discomfort or harm is acceptable. Medical researchers are more likely to inflict pain or distress in animals; psychological research is usually more benign and may involve little, if any, discomfort for the animals. The controversial issues associated with animal rights is still an evolving field.

REVIEW QUESTIONS

1. Researchers at the University of Cincinnati wanted to investigate how much radiation military personnel could be exposed to and still function. In order to study the effects of radiation, they
   a. gave food with radioactive substances to developmentally disabled children.
   b. withheld treatment from patients who had been accidentally exposed to radiation.
   c. exposed psychiatric patients to radiation without informed consent.
   d. subjected cancer patients to whole-body radiation without informed consent.

2. In recent psychological research that has received criticism on ethical grounds, authors Liston and Kagan (2002)
   a. failed to cite research by other psychologists that was important and relevant to the development of their ideas.
   b. claimed to have completed a study but they did not actually carry it out.
   c. subjected participants to high levels of pain without first obtaining informed consent.
   d. published a figure that originally came from the research of other psychologists that had appeared in a different journal.

3. According to research by the U.S. Office of Research Integrity, the single most frequently occurring ethical offenses involved
   a. not randomly assigning participants to groups.
   b. falsifying data.
   c. plagiarizing other researchers' ideas.
   d. fabricating data.

4. The enforceable rules of conduct associated with the ethical principles developed by the APA are
   a. aspirational goals.
   b. principles of responsibility.

    c. ethical standards.

    d. ethico-legal principles.

5. A psychologist who is providing therapy for a person should not develop a close friendship with the client because such dual relationships can compromise the success of the therapy. This problem relates to which General Ethical Principle of the APA?

    a. beneficence and nonmaleficence.

    b. respect for people's rights and dignity.

    c. justice.

    d. fidelity and responsibility.

6. In resolving ethical situations involving legal issues and confidentiality, a psychologist

    a. can never reveal what a client has revealed in a therapeutic session.

    b. may appropriately defer to legal authorities, even if it involves violating confidentiality.

    c. is obligated to keep information confidential if revealing it would cause embarrassment.

    d. is allowed to reveal confidential information only when a client gives written permission.

7. If you have deceived participants during the course of a study, you need to debrief them. When you tell them about the deception, you are engaging in

    a. dehoaxing.

    b. desensitization.

    c. ethical standards.

    d. informed consent.

8. When participants in Stanley Milgram's obedience studies left the research session, they were told that they had been deceived about the nature of the study. Because the participants might have experienced potentially serious distress after the study, Milgram arranged for visits with a psychiatrist. This process was called

    a. dehoaxing.

    b. desensitization.

    c. compensatory follow-up.

    d. informed consent.

9. The Nuremburg Code of ethics in human research arose because of the

    a. failure to provide medical treatment in the research on syphilis done at the Tuskegee Institute.

    b. addition of radioactive substances in children's food at a home for the developmentally disabled.

    c. Milgram's obedience studies.

    d. Nazi research in World War II.

10. Research may not require approval by an IRB if

    a. it occurs in a commonly accepted educational setting and assesses instructional strategies.

    b. it involves only passive deception.

    c. a similar study has already been done elsewhere with no ethical problems.

    d. it involves studies of children.

11. Research on how people respond to informed-consent forms has revealed that

    a. many Americans don't read well enough to understand what they are reading on the informed-consent forms.

    b. many people do not bother to read the informed-consent forms because they trust the researchers.

    c. the informed-consent forms often omit information important for people to understand the research.

    d. people are often upset after learning what they will have to undergo if they participate in the research.

12. The criticism of Milgram's obedience research by psychologist Diana Baumrind (1964) included the claim that the research
    a. did not include compensatory follow-up.
    b. should have been preceded by an attempt to estimate how many participants would be willing to give high levels of shock.
    c. did not include either dehoaxing or desensitization.
    d. the costs of the research in terms of participant distress were not outweighed by the benefits.
13. Milgram's obedience research was important at the time he conducted it because
    a. behavioral theories of the time predicted one outcome but Freudian theory predicted very different outcomes.
    b. the Nazi atrocities of World War II that were based on blind obedience was still fresh in people's memories.
    c. Milgram's studies were among the first to study the effect of obedience on racist behaviors.
    d. earlier studies of obedience had erroneously predicted how people would behave under stressful conditions.
14. Milgram defended his research by pointing out that he
    a. did not intend to harm anybody and could not foresee the problems that occurred.
    b. engaged both in debriefing and in dehoaxing of participants after the study ended.
    c. paid participants well enough to overcome any discomfort they had experienced.
    d. the research was so important that it was acceptable, even if a few people were harmed.
15. Studies about participants' reactions to being deceived in research have revealed that
    a. most participants are offended when they learn that they have been lied to.
    b. deception leads participants to be skeptical or suspicious about psychological research.
    c. participants regard the science and practice of psychology positively, even after learning that they have been deceived.
    d. they agree that ethical guidelines should prohibit deception in psychological research.
16. When you decide to tell participants something false about a research session in order to mislead them, you are using
    a. naturalistic observation.
    b. role playing.
    c. active deception.
    d. dehoaxing.
17. If volunteers complete an Internet-based survey on a sensitive and potentially distressing topic, one of the ethical considerations hard to deal with is
    a. debriefing the participants after they complete their responses.
    b. providing any necessary compensatory follow-up.
    c. reaching people who might not take distressing topics seriously.
    d. informing the participants that they can leave the study at any time.
18. Researchers have identified advantages of online research that include
    a. lessened ethical requirements because people complete online surveys on their own.
    b. a more diverse sample of participants.
    c. a reduced need to provide debriefing and clarification when people complete surveys.
    d. greater understanding by participants of informed-consent issues.
19. Some psychologists have criticized research with animals on ethical grounds. They have claimed that
    a. animal research cannot be used to understand or ultimately provide the basis for control of human behavior.
    b. psychological research with animals has doubled about every 10 years.

      c. keeping animals in captivity is unethical in and of itself.

      d. moral arguments are not a sufficient basis to justify ending animal research.

20. When psychology students evaluate research with animals, students

      a. usually have very negative attitudes about the use of cats, dogs, and rats.

      b. are very similar to their faculty mentors in their attitudes toward such research.

      c. support such research for their own studies, but not for the research of others.

      d. are very likely to agree that animals are necessary for their own research.

21. When participants complete a task for a purpose of which they are unaware, the researchers are using

      a. technical deception.

      b. implicit deception.

      c. role deception.

      d. naturalistic deception.

22. Participants are often uncomfortable when they learn that a research study has involved _____ deception.

      a. role.

      b. passive.

      c. implicit.

      d. active.

23. If researchers provide negative, false feedback to participants, the performance of those participants may worsen. According to research, subsequent debriefing

      a. leads to improved subsequent performance compared to participants who are not debriefed.

      b. often results in anger on the part of the deceived participants.

      c. makes no difference to the participants in subsequent behavior.

      d. leads to later frustration on the part of the participants.

24. When considering the ethics of survey research, an investigator should

      a. insure that all responses are anonymous and confidential.

      b. let respondents know from the very beginning that once they begin their participation, they need to continue with the project.

      c. remember that if the researcher makes a big point of assuring confidentiality and anonymity, it may needlessly arouse suspicions among respondents.

      d. avoid asking questions of a sensitive nature.

25. In their defense of research with animals, Coile and Miller argued that

      a. even though animals were often seriously harmed, the overall benefit to humans was high enough to justify the harm.

      b. animals do not really suffer pain as intensely as humans do, so the issue of pain in animal research is a minor issue.

      c. some day in the future, we will discover the benefits of research on animals, even if they have suffered.

      d. animal research is, in many cases, beneficial to animals because it gives people insight into behavioral issues in captive and wild animals.

Essay Questions

26. Identify the six general principles regarding ethical conduct and what behaviors they pertain to.

27. What types of research can be exempt from IRB consideration, according to U.S. federal law?

28. When people oppose the use of animal research, what arguments do they produce?

ANSWERS TO REVIEW QUESTIONS

1. d	10. a	19. c
2. a	11. a	20. b
3. d	12. d	21. b
4. c	13. b	22. a
5. d	14. b	23. a
6. b	15. c	24. c
7. a	16. c	25. d
8. c	17. b	
9. d	18. b	

Essay Questions

26. Identify the six general principles regarding ethical conduct and what behaviors they pertain to.

    Competence—Engaging in professional work for which one has adequate training and knowledge.

    Integrity—Refraining from engaging in inappropriate relationships with clients, colleagues, and research participants.

    Professional and Scientific Responsibility—Upholding ethical principles in one's own behavior and working to maximize it in colleagues.

    Respect for People's Rights and Dignity—Treating people with respect, obeying laws and regulations, and maintaining anonymity and confidentiality when appropriate.

    Concern for Others' Welfare—Acting in ways that minimize the possibility of physical or psychological harm to others.

    Social Responsibility—Using psychological knowledge for the benefit of people and animals.

27. What types of research can be exempt from IRB consideration, according to U.S. federal law?

    Research conducted in established or commonly accepted educational settings, involving normal educational practices can be exempt from approval, such as the effects of different instructional strategies.

    Research involving the use of educational tests, survey procedures, interview procedures, or observation of public behavior. (Surveys and interviews on sensitive or controversial topics may require IRB approval, though.)

    In addition, research involving public officials or political candidates can be exempt from IRB approval.

    Research involving the collection or study of existing, publicly available data, documents, records, pathological specimens, or diagnostic specimens is exempt if the personal identity of those providing the data is protected.

28. When people oppose the use of animal research, what arguments do they produce?

    Some people argue from a practical standpoint, saying that we don't learn very much about people from studying animals, so keeping animals confined to laboratories reduces the quality of the animals' lives and doesn't produce useful research results.

    Others argue from a moral standpoint, maintaining that we don't have the right to keep animals captive or to treat them inhumanely.

CHAPTER THREE

PLANNING RESEARCH
Generating a Question

CHAPTER OVERVIEW

LEARNING OBJECTIVES ■ KEY TERMS ■ CHAPTER PREVIEW

LEARNING OBJECTIVES

After going through this chapter, you will be able to:

- Describe more and less formal sources of research questions
- Explain how theory leads to testable hypotheses
- Describe different approaches to generating research ideas

- Describe the advantages and limitations of Internet-based research
- Explain the benefits of replication in research
- Conduct a basic literature search using PsycINFO®
- Identify the different sections of a journal article and their contents

KEY TERMS

Abstract, p. 84	Introduction, p. 84	Participants, p. 86	Replication, p. 77
Behaviorism, p. 63	Literature review, p. 78	Peer review, p. 79	Results section, p. 86
Construct validity, p. 77	Materials and apparatus,	Procedure, p. 86	Type I error, p. 77
Discussion section,	p. 86	Reference section,	Type II error, p. 77
p. 87	Method section, p. 86	p. 87	Validity, p. 76

CHAPTER PREVIEW

Research questions come from a variety of sources and motivations, most of them arising from the investigator's curiosity. At the same time, our ideas develop within a social context. The questions we consider important develop because of the combination of our personalities, our histories, what society values, and other factors that may have little to do with the scientific research question per se.

Ideas arise in different ways. Sometimes, researchers notice an event that captures their interest and they decide to create research to study it. At other times, researchers have a specific question to address or a problem to solve that leads to a research project. In some cases, researchers develop research ideas to test theories. No matter how the idea develops, researchers have to figure out the best way to investigate their questions.

To generate good research, investigators should be aware of the work of other scientists. This allows the investigator to advance our knowledge and to avoid simply repeating what others have done. Such background knowledge also helps a researcher generate new questions. Sources of information include scientific publications and presentations at research conferences. As your exposure to research expands, you will learn effective and efficient means of searching for prior work that relates to your own research question.

Electronic databases provide easy access to descriptions of research in psychology. By conducting a systematic literature review, psychologists can learn about the work of others, devise their own research questions, and ultimately publish research articles or make presentations at professional conferences.

WHERE RESEARCH IDEAS BEGIN: EVERYDAY OBSERVATIONS AND SYSTEMATIC RESEARCH

If we read journal articles or listen to psychologists give presentations of their research, we get a coherent picture of what led them to do their research, how they accomplished it, and what their results mean. The final product is a nice package whose ideas flow logically; we can see how the ideas developed and how they progressed. Researchers who communicate well can weave a good story. But where do the research ideas come from?

Why do researchers study topics ranging from thinking and problem solving to social relationships to personality development? The answer is fairly simple: The researchers are curious and doing the research is fun. Research involves solving puzzles and getting answers, so why shouldn't it be enjoyable?

Let's consider an example of a common part of daily life that is likely to lead to some very interesting psychological research: Facebook. Nadkarni and Hofmann (2012) have suggested that Facebook serves two fundamental needs: belonging and self-presentation. As they noted, "These needs can act independently and are influenced by a host of other factors, including the cultural background, sociodemographic variables, and personality traits, such as introversion, extraversion, shyness, narcissism, neuroticism, self-esteem, and self-worth" (p. 247).

This brief statement contains the seeds of a great number of research projects. What elements of personality are associated with a person's presence on Facebook? An interesting, complementary question might involve the characteristics of people who do not have a Facebook presence. Important variables might include personality, sociodemographic characteristics, cultural, or cognitive elements.

Nadkarni and Hofmann (2012) further investigated the role of Facebook in collectivistic versus individualistic groups. Such a project could include people from different cultures, given that it is quite feasible to use the Internet to reach people around the world. Or the project could focus on differences among people within the same culture on the individualistic–collectivistic continuum. The researchers also noted that it might be interesting to see how people differ in their self-presentation online versus offline.

In fact, other scientists have already begun addressing some of these issues. For example, DeAndrea, Shaw, and Levine (2010) have reported that African Americans use more first-person pronouns (e.g., *I, mine*) than European or Asian Americans and report more individual attributes. And other researchers (e.g., Vasalou, Joinson, & Courvoisier, 2010) have also reported differences in Facebook use across cultures. Ji et al's (2010) have shown that people from Korea and China use Facebook differently than people from the United States, and Vasalou, Joinson, and Courvoisier (2010) reported that commitment to others differs across countries.

As of early 2012, there were over 250 journal articles relating to Facebook. It is likely to grow into a very large and exciting body of research.

Informal and Formal Sources of Ideas

There are various ways that research ideas develop. We can characterize them on a continuum as being more or less formal. Figure 3.1 presents this continuum and the kind of question that leads to more research.

Informal			**Formal**
"This is interesting. I'd like to know more about it!"	"We have a problem to solve. Let's figure out the best way to do it."	"Our earlier project answered some of our questions, but there are still some unanswered questions."	"The theory says people should act this way. Let's test the theory."

FIGURE 3.1   Continuum representing the development of research ideas.

The Continuum of Research Ideas. Sometimes a research question will arise because a psychologist observes something in everyday life and decides that he or she would like to research it. The idea does not derive from theory or from previous research, but from curiosity about some behavior that takes place. This approach represents a very informal and idiosyncratic way of generating research ideas. If it weren't for the fact that the psychologist happens to notice something worth investigating in a particular situation, the research might not take place.

One step toward the more formal or systematic end of the continuum involves solving practical problems. That is, in a particular situation, you might look around and say, "We can do this better." The next step would be to design a program to test your ideas. Psychologists who work in organizations or in industry often specialize in solving such applied problems. Their approach is not based only on personal observation and curiosity but comes from a question that relates to the workplace. This strategy is somewhat more formal than deciding to study a behavior because it catches your eye. At the same time, it does not develop from other research or from a theory; it might be idiosyncratic to a particular time or place. The research takes place because the psychologist is in the position to solve practical problems as they arise in a particular setting.

A third point on the continuum involves researchers who evaluate the work of others or who are in the middle of a research program. Already-completed research has some loose ends, so the investigator takes the partial answers and tries to extend our knowledge. This is a more formal approach to research because the ideas that led to a particular project are embedded within a research context and help answer a question that others are also investigating.

At the most formal end of the continuum, a research idea can develop from a well-defined theory. That is, a theory predicts certain behaviors, so the psychologist tries to see whether the behaviors follow from theoretical predictions. This approach would represent the most formal approach because theoretical expectations may dictate the nature of the research. The questions to be answered are not the result of a single, unsystematic event, but rather unfold from a well-defined and systematic set of ideas. Most research ideas develop in the middle of the continuum. That is, old ideas lead to new ideas that we can test empirically.

According to Glueck and Jauch (1975), researchers in the natural and physical sciences tend to develop their projects based on a combination of their own insights and the results of previous research. Clark (cited in Glueck & Jauch, 1975) agreed that productive psychologists also tend to generate their research ideas based on earlier work. We see what others have done and we try to clear up the loose ends.

Table 3.1 presents how researchers say they develop their ideas. Investigators generate ideas on their own, from the research literature, and in conjunction with colleagues in their field at different institutions. Colleagues in their own institutions are seen as less helpful, probably because most departments have people with very different research interests.

Research ideas often arise from the personal interests of the investigators. For example, the noted psychologist Robert Sternberg became interested in issues of intelligence because of his own experience with taking tests. Sternberg, who was elected president of the American Psychological Association and has written or edited dozens of books and has authored hundreds of scientific journal articles, did not score very well on standardized intelligence tests.

TABLE 3.1   Different Sources of Ideas for Research in Order of Frequency of Occurrence, as Reported by Active Scientists. The more Frequent Sources Appear First in the Table (Glueck & Jauch, 1975).

Source of Research Ideas	Comment
Researcher's own ideas	People have more interest in their own ideas, so they are more likely to invest time and resources in studying those ideas.
Research literature	Reading others ideas can give you an idea for an extension to fill in the gaps in knowledge; it can also lead to an idea for trying to disprove a claim.
Distant colleagues	Researchers build up a network of contacts across the country or the world. Discussions with these colleagues provides stimulation to develop new ideas.
Departmental colleagues	In most science departments in colleges and universities, there may not be much overlap in specialized, professional interests among faculty in a department. It can be hard to develop joint research ideas because local colleagues very often have different interests.
Research team	In many laboratories, students carry out the research program of the director, who may develop most of the research ideas.
Local colleagues outside the department	It is rare that researchers can provide significant ideas to others outside their own area of expertise.

There is a clear discrepancy between the message given by this test scores ("he isn't very smart") and his remarkable achievements ("he is very smart"). Sternberg has spent a considerable part of his career studying the various forms intelligence can take. His research has investigated intelligence and knowledge, and how we can assess them.

The Effect of Theory

The dominant theoretical perspective affects the kind of research questions that investigators ask. We can see this pattern occurring in psychology now as it relates to animal research. From the early 1900s until well into the 1960s, psychologists studied animal behavior to help understand all behavior, including that of humans. This meant creating research questions that could be asked with nonhuman subjects.

Over the past few decades, though, there has been a notable change in the way psychologists do research. For example, in Great Britain, the amount of animal research has declined precipitously. The number of doctoral dissertations by young researchers in psychology that involve animals has declined by 62 percent over the past 25 years (Thomas & Blackman, 1992, cited in Plous, 1996a). We haven't exhausted the entire repertoire of research questions involving animals, we have just focused our attention differently.

As we have seen in the discussion of ethics in research, many people have noted that ethical concerns lead them away from research with animals. There are other significant factors as well. Social forces are complex, and major changes in the way people think reflect multiple underlying causes.

Reasons for Decreases in Animal Research.   Several reasons can help account for these changes. One reason is that, in general, students earning doctorates in psychology seem to be interested in different topics—those that don't involve animals.

A second possibility is that, as a society, we have become more sensitized to the ethical issues associated with animal research. Even though psychologists may support the use of animals in research, as we have seen in Chapter 2, these same psychologists may choose not to involve animals in their own professional work.

Behaviorism—A theoretical approach in psychology that focuses on studies of observable behaviors rather than internal, mental processes.

Another reason for the decline in animal research is that we have changed theoretical perspectives. For the first seven decades of the last century, the dominant paradigm was **behaviorism**. One of the fundamental tenets of behaviorism is that a few simple principles of learning and behavior can explain the behavior of virtually any organism of any species. Thus, it would not matter if you studied people or rats; the specific behaviors might differ, but the principles of learning, reinforcement, and punishment hold true across species, according to the behaviorists. Thus, what would be true for rat behavior should be true for human behavior.

Psychologists have expanded on this simple set of rules and have developed new ideas to explore more complex behavior and thought. Behaviorism has not been shown to be without value; indeed, its principles have led to some very useful outcomes. With the new cognitive orientation, psychologists began to ask different kinds of questions, although the new techniques available in neuroscientific approaches may signal a resurgence of animal research to address behavioral and psychological questions.

The Effect of the Cognitive Revolution.   What does this movement away from behaviorism and animal studies mean about the nature of the research we publish? According to Robins, Gosling, and Craik (1999), the so-called "cognitive revolution" in psychology is clear from the amount of research that is cognitive in nature. According to these researchers (1999), the percentage of articles using words related to cognition has risen dramatically since the early 1970s. As you can see in Figure 3.2, they reported

FIGURE 3.2 Percentage of articles by decade published in a small sample of psychology journals that include keywords associated with cognitive, behavioral, psychoanalytic, and neuroscience perspectives

Source: Robins, Gosling, and Craik (1999). Copyright American Psychological Association. Reprinted with permission.

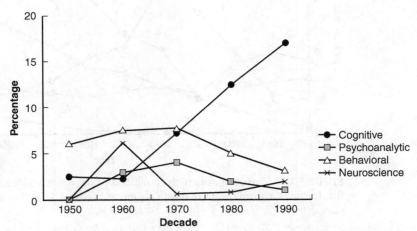

that according to a PsycINFO® search of keywords related to cognition, neuroscience, behaviorism, and psychoanalytic theory, the trend in psychology is toward the dominance of cognitive psychology, with the other approaches falling quite short of the level of research represented by cognitive psychology. This pattern was striking when you consider the inroads that neuroscience had made in psychology up to that point. Not surprisingly, their results created some controversy. A number of psychologists criticized the validity of their methodology and their conclusions (e.g., Friman, Allen, Kerwin, & Larzelere, 2000; Martin, 2000).

In fact, using a somewhat different method of searching for research associated with the four theoretical domains, Spear (2007) found a quite different pattern, one that revealed the importance of cognitive psychology, but also of neuroscience in psychology. According to Spear, the original research focused on psychology journals that were too narrow in scope. Spear rectified that by searching in a more diverse range of journals. When he did that, the effect of neuroscience became very prominent. Behaviorism and psychoanalytic theory still appear infrequently in the research literature, however. The frequency of occurrence of the varied perspectives in the wider search appears in Figure 3.3.

These two instances of research show how important methodology is in determining the results. With a narrow search of four psychology journals, Robins et al. (1999) found little presence of neuroscience; with a wider search of journals, Spear (2007) found that neuroscience is a large and growing area of psychological research.

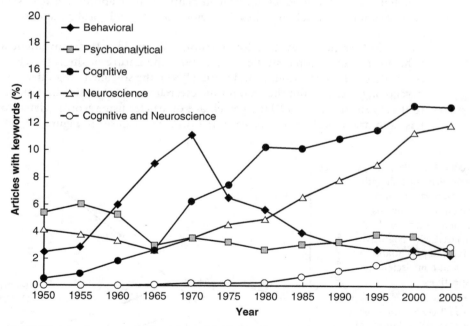

FIGURE 3.3   Percentage of articles published by decade in a wide range of psychology journals that include keywords associated with cognitive, behavioral, psychoanalytic, and neuroscience perspectives.

Source: Spear (2007). Copyright American Psychological Association. Reprinted with permission.

During the past three decades, the use of behavioral terms (e.g., reinforcement, punishment, discriminative stimulus) has declined. (Even though behavioral terms have decreased in use, the principles of behaviorism still account for some of the most generally useful principles of behavior.) These trends allow us to make predictions about the dominant patterns of psychological research in the future. It may be psychologically based and largely human, rather than biologically based and animal, although with the increase in neuroscientific approaches, animal models may return.

Rozin (2006, 2007) has described several different ways to think about developing research ideas. One approach he suggested focused on people's interests and passions rather than on negative psychological states. As he noted, important domains of most of our lives receive minimal attention from researchers. Much more attention has been paid to cognitive processes and learning than to the areas that excite our interest, like eating, sports, entertainment, and politics.

There are advantages of working in an area that has not received a lot of attention by researchers. For one thing, Rozin (2007) pointed out that much less background reading is required. In addition, pilot studies are more fun to do, and there is little danger that others are doing the same study you are doing. So your work will be novel. And perhaps most important, when you do have a finding, it is likely to represent a much bigger marginal increase in the state of knowledge. Studies 1 and 2 usually add more to knowledge than Studies 1,000 and 1,001 (p. 755).

There is much research on phobias but very little on what is almost certainly a more common positive opposite, passions. Passions are strong and enduring interests and engagements with something (Wrzesniewksi, Rozin, & Bennett, 2003). Passions are important to people in their everyday lives; in spite of their importance, however, we do not know how passions develop (e.g., Deci & Ryan, 1985). An undergraduate student named Amy Wrzesniewski stimulated Rozin (2007) to collaborate on creating a scale to measure people's intrinsic interest and passion in their work (Wrzesniewski, McCauley, Rozin, & Schwartz, 1997).

There are many interesting topics that student and professional researchers can investigate that have, so far, remained relatively untouched. Beginning with psychology's inception, it has focused on sensation, perception, learning, and other basic processes, not topics important to the quality of one's life (Rozin, 2006). Even social and personality psychologists have not devoted a lot of energy to these domains, although the emergence of positive psychology has changed that somewhat. Still a lot of interesting questions remain unasked and unanswered.

HOW CAN YOU DEVELOP RESEARCH IDEAS?

Professional researchers have an easier time developing a research project than a beginning student researcher because professionals have more knowledge and a greater sense of the field in which they work. In addition, once a person establishes a research program, new ideas often emerge easily.

How should you begin to select a problem for yourself? The first step is to acquire as much knowledge as you can about as many different areas as you can. The greater your scope of knowledge, the more likely you will be able to bring together different ideas into a unique project.

McGuire (1983) developed a set of useful techniques that you could use to generate research questions. His suggestions span the continuum from very informal to very formal. At the most personal and informal level, he suggested that you introspect about your own experiences and use your thoughts to generate research questions. At the more formal level, he proposed that you can look at research in a particular area and try to adapt some of those ideas to a new area. Table 3.2 presents a list of research

TABLE 3.2   Approaches to Generating Research Ideas and Some Examples of Ideas That Could Develop into Research Projects

Types of Phenomena	An Idea That You Could Develop
Studying spontaneously occurring events	
Intensive case studies	Study the behavior of a friend who consistently scores well on tests. Try to find out why and see if the technique works for others.
Extrapolate from similar problems already studied	Psychologists have investigated the credibility of expert witnesses. One question that remains to be answered, though, is whether jurors respond similarly to female and male expert witnesses.
Studying the validity of everyday beliefs and when these beliefs break down	
Reverse the direction of a commonsense hypothesis	Many common sayings, like "Opposites attract," suggest behavioral hypotheses. You could investigate whether opposites really do attract, by studying to see if similar people are more likely to date or form friendships.
Evaluating formal if–then statements	
Use the hypothetico-deductive method of saying that "if A is true, then B should be true"	If people are allowed to eat snacks in a situation where they can take the snacks from a single large bowl versus from multiple small bowls, they will eat less when the snack is in small bowls, consistent with the unit bias hypothesis (Geier, Rozin, & Doros, 2006).
Using previous research as a stepping stone	
Bring together areas of research that originally did not relate	Research on people with physical disabilities and research on sport and exercise psychology can come together for investigators who would like to apply knowledge on sport and exercise to a new population that has not been connected to this domain in the past (Crocker, 1993).
Tests of theory	Piagetian theory generally does not support the idea that children regress to previous levels of cognitive development; test children under difficult conditions (e.g., when they have a limited time to complete a long task) to see if they do regress.

Source: McGuire (1983).

possibilities that you could implement; the research questions may be relatively simple, but they can lead to productive ideas.

Generating Research Hypotheses

Table 3.2 illustrates that it isn't always difficult to generate research ideas. One suggestion is to evaluate commonsense ideas to see when they hold true and when they don't. You may hear that "opposites attract" as a principle of human behavior. This maxim leads to testable hypotheses. Once you define what you mean by "opposites" you can find out if we tend to select people opposite to us. You may find instead that "Birds of a feather flock together."

You could also combine previously unrelated topics. For instance, research on sports and physical disabilities don't usually fall together. You might be able to generate some interesting research projects by connecting them. It is important to remember that the more practice you get in developing ideas and the more knowledge you gain in a particular area, the easier it is to come up with new research projects.

Many of the ideas that you generate at first will probably have been studied already. The reason for this is that if the idea is obvious to you, it will probably be obvious to others. This can be a frustrating experience for students because you may not have enough background knowledge to be able to figure out how to proceed, so you feel that all the good ideas have been taken. This is where you can rely on professionals in the field (including your professor).

In making your plans, remember that you are not likely to make major breakthroughs. In reality, major changes in the way people think about an issue result from the results of many small studies that lead to a new synthesis of ideas.

Sometimes researchers make suggestions for future projects. For instance, Goodman-Delahunty (1998) provided a set of questions of particular relevance to psychologists interested in the interface between psychology and the law. And Nadkarni and Hofmann (2012) made suggestions about research involving Facebook. Reading the research of others can be useful in helping you develop your ideas.

Goodman-Delahunty reported that studies of sexual harassment typically involve college students as participants. Further, the research may not employ accurate legal definitions of sexual harassment. The mock trial transcripts are also not very complex, unlike real life. What would happen if you did a study with people from the working world? What about using more realistic scenarios? We don't know what would happen because researchers have not yet investigated these questions. Table 3.3 presents further topics for study. These examples involve psychology and the law, but you can use the same process for just about any other area of study.

Culture and Research

A vast amount of psychological research has involved participants from North America and Europe. Investigators have traditionally assumed that what held true for participants in such research was valid universally. Recently, however, psychologists have become more aware of the limitations to conclusions based on such culturally restricted samples.

TABLE 3.3 Examples of Potential Research Projects on Gender and Law That Are Based on Existing Research and Legal Questions

---

Current Situation: Sexual harassment creates a hostile working environment, but there are differences in people's conceptualizations of what constitutes harassment. Studies of gender differences in perception of sexual harassment are complex and inconsistent (Goodman-Delahunty, 1998).

Recommendations for Related Research:

- Do results differ when we use accurate, legal definitions of sexual harassment in research, which is not always done?
- Do simple, fictitious cases result in different outcomes than rich and complex scenarios that occur in actual legal cases?
- Do convenience samples consisting of college undergraduates produce results different from studies using other people?

Current Situation: Jurors have to evaluate the credibility and the evidence presented by expert witnesses. Are female and male experts regarded the same by different participants in trials related to battered women who kill their spouse (Schuller & Cripps, 1998)?

Recommendations for Related Research:

- What happens if we vary the sex of the expert witness as well as the nature of other testimony and evidence?
- Can we identify different mannerisms and characteristics of expert witnesses that may add or detract from their credibility and that may be confused with gender effects?
- Does gender of an expert witness make a difference in more versus less serious offenses?

Current Situation: Most sexual harassment claims are made by women against men, but on occasion, men are the victims of such harassment. Those inflicting the harassment may be either female or male, although men report fewer negative reactions to these experiences (Waldo, Berdahl, & Fitzgerald, 1998).

Recommendations for Related Research:

- Given that harassment might take different forms for female and male victims, do people show parallel criteria pertaining to women and to men?
- Can we identify whether male jurors will defer to female jurors during debate, or vice versa?
- Do juries take harassment of men as seriously as they do harassment of women? Gay men versus straight men?
- Will a jury deal with the questions of the severity of the harassment differently for men and women?

As a result, there is an exciting realm of possibilities of studying people with different cultural backgrounds. Such research could involve subgroups within typical samples, such as Americans or Europeans who are members of varied ethnic groups, people in different socioeconomic groups, people of different sexual orientations, and so forth. There is no guarantee that people who identify with different subpopulations respond the same way as people from the mainstream population.

In addition, cross-cultural research can reveal similarities and differences in thought, behavior, and attitude. Matsumoto and Yoo (2006) have identified several different approaches to cross-cultural research. At a basic level, it would be useful to know whether our research findings hold true across cultures or only within our own. More complex issues would be associated with finding out what facets of a culture are responsible for differences across groups.

Culturally relevant research is likely to constitute a significant part of future research in psychology. With diversification of populations in many different countries, many fruitful questions will arise. One critical aspect of this kind of research will involve making sure that our methodologies are meaningful for each group that we study.

THE VIRTUAL LABORATORY: RESEARCH ON THE INTERNET

Some psychological research requires specialized laboratory space and equipment. Whenever we want to measure specific behaviors or responses just as they occur, we must be in the presence of the people (or animals) we measure. It is hard to imagine that a behavioral researcher could study reinforcement or punishment without having direct contact with whomever is being observed. If developmental psychologists want to see whether an infant will cross a visual cliff, parents must bring the infant to the laboratory.

On the other hand, psychologists may be easily able to accomplish research at a distance that involves experimental manipulations or judgments of opinion and attitude. For such studies, it is common to bring participants to the laboratory for the research or to mail the materials. (Unfortunately, people often do not mail them back.) With the advent of easy access to the Internet, we no longer need to be in the physical presence of those who agree to participate in such research, and we don't need to go to the trouble and expense of mailing anything.

The concept of the laboratory is undergoing adjustment; it can be worldwide in scope. Table 3.4 presents some examples of actual Web-based research. Creative researchers should be able to use the Internet to good effect. An array of online research projects is available at http://psych.hanover.edu/Research/exponnet.html.

Internet Research

Some aspects of Internet research mirror those in traditional formats. For instance, changing fonts and text size, including a lot of bold and italic type, and lack of contrast between the text and the background reduce the usability of paper surveys; the pattern will likely hold true for Internet surveys. If researchers take care of these formatting considerations, computerized testing (including the Internet) may lead to comparability with other formats (Gosling, Vazire, Srivastava, & John, 2004; Vispoel, 2000).

The question is still ambiguous, however. For example, Shih and Fan (2008) found higher response rates for traditional, mailed surveys compared to Internet surveys. This finding was mitigated somewhat by the nature of the respondent. College students were more responsive to Internet surveys, whereas other groups (e.g., general consumers) were more responsive to mailed surveys (Yetter & Cappacioli, 2010). Furthermore, follow-up reminders were more useful in generating responses to mailed surveys than to Internet surveys.

Sometimes response rates are associated with the topic of the survey. For example, when Cranford et al. (2008) surveyed college students about alcohol use, response rates

TABLE 3.4   **A Very Abbreviated Listing of Samples of Web-Based Research Listed in 2012**

Social Psychology

- Attractiveness of faces
- Healing from the loss of a loved one
- In social: Personal judgments in social situations II
- In social: Personality judgments
- In Social: The communication game

Health Psychology

- Eating disorders and family relationships
- Predictors of self-medication with over-the-counter products
- Childbirth expectations survey
- Study on diabetes type I for French speaking people

Forensic Psychology

- Criminal justice survey
- Perceptions of a sexual assault
- Mock juror' perceptions
- Prostitution attitudes survey
- Eyewitness recognition study

Sexuality

- Gender related attitudes
- How's your love life?
- Sexual health of college students
- Gender and sexual orientation differences in scent preferences, attitudes, and behaviors
- Contact or same-sex attraction: What is causing the changing climate for gay and lesbian youth

Cognition

- How much do you know?
- Memories for songs
- Decision-making studies
- Sequential decision-making under uncertainty in a video game
- Who will win—it's all about logic

Source: John H. Krantz, Ph.D. Hanover College, http://psych.hanover.edu/Research/exponnet.html.

were higher among heavier drinkers. Not surprisingly, the demographics of the sample were also important in that White students were more likely to respond than minority students. The most common reason for not responding was that the person was too busy.

So you need to identify the population you want to sample and contact them in ways that are compatible with that group. It would be nice to know exactly who is likely to complete online surveys and experimental research. We do have a picture of who is connected to the Internet. Table 3.5 gives a breakdown of users. The incidence of Internet use in low-income households has risen in the past few years, but people in these households

TABLE 3.5   **Demographics of Internet Users**

Numbers reflect the percentage of adults in each group who used the Internet in 2007, 2009, and 2011, and teens in 2009.

	2007 (%)	2009 (%)	2011/2012 (%)	2009 Teens (%)
Total Adults	71	77	85	93
Women	70	78	85	94
Men	71	76	85	91
Age				
18–29	87	93	96	
30–49	83	83	93	
50–64	65	77	85	
65+	32	43	58	
Race/Ethnicity				
White, non-Hispanic	73	80	86	94
Black, non-Hispanic	62	72	86	87
English/Spanish-speaking Hispanic (Note: Language use varies by year)	78	61	80	95
Geography				
Urban	73	73	79	
Suburban	73	75	80	
Rural	60	71	72	
Household Income				
Less than $30,000/yr	55	62	75	88
$30,000–49,000	69	84	90	89
$50,000–74,999	82	93	93	96
$75,000+	93	95	99	97
Educational Attainment				
Less than high school	40	37	61	
High school	61	72	80	
Some college	81	87	94	
College +	91	94	97	

Sources: Demographics of Internet users (2007). Pew Internet & American Life Project, February 15–March 7, 2007. Tracking Survey Demographics of Internet Users (2007). http://www.pewinternet.org/trends/User_Demo_6.15.07.htm; Pew Internet & American Life Project, August 18–September 14, 2009 Tracking Survey. http://www.pewinternet.org/trends/Whos-Online.aspx. Reprinted with permission.

are connected at noticeably lower rates than people in higher-income homes. Accessibility to the Internet is also associated with age, race, where people live, and educational level (Demographics of Internet Users, 2009).

Furthermore, low-income people are much more likely to have access to the Internet away from home or work (e.g., at a library) than are higher-income people who are likely to have access to computers both at home and at work (http://pewinternet.org/Reports/2009/10-Home-Broadband-Adoption-2009.aspx. Retrieved August 30, 2012). These differences may have a significant impact on the nature of research samples and, perhaps, research results.

Teens use the Internet much more than older adults for social networking and entertainment; adults use e-mail, do research, and make purchases at comparable or higher levels than teens (Generational differences, 2009). Still, even among the heaviest users, young people, there may be a backlash regarding the degree to which people are willing to use their computers for less interesting (to them) applications (Vasquez, 2009).

These data have potential implications for your research. If you decide to conduct a study online, you want to maximize the return on your work and reach the people that you want to participate. What is the best way to get people to respond? This is not a question with an easy answer.

One study of Internet surveys led to minuscule response rates of 0.18 percent when notices of the survey appeared in a print magazine, requiring readers to switch to a computer to complete the survey. When a person was able to use a hyperlink to access a survey, the response rate was somewhat higher, 0.68 percent, but still extremely low. When a posting appeared in newsgroups, the response rate was estimated to be 1.68 percent. Finally, when respondents were e-mailed individually three times, the return rate was 31 percent, which is a respectable figure.

You can see the magnitude of the difference in Figure 3.4. Not surprisingly, persistence and a personal approach provide the best results (Schillewaert, Langerak, & Duhamel, 1998). Dillman et al. (2008) contacted potential respondents through telephone calls, the Internet, mail, or interactive voice response. For those who did not respond, the researchers used a different means of getting in touch (telephone or e-mail) a second time. They found that the additional contact improved response rates by over 30 percent in some cases, reflecting the importance of persistence in reaching your research sample.

An advantage of the e-mail technique is that responses arrive very quickly, much more so than laboratory and mail approaches. Further, the quality of the data (i.e., how complete the responses were) seems to be comparable, regardless of the means of notifying respondents (Schillewaert, Langerak, & Duhamel, 1998).

FIGURE 3.4   Response rates to online surveys for various means of contacting potential respondents.

Source: Schillewaert, Langerak, and Duhamel (1998).

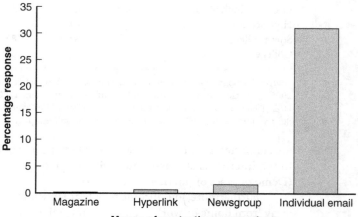

Online surveys aren't noticeably worse than other approaches and they have some practical advantages. It's not unreasonable to expect their frequency to increase as researchers become familiar with the characteristics of successful Internet surveys and the approaches that work best. Some important guidelines for Internet research appear in Table 3.6.

TABLE 3.6 Guidelines for Creating Internet-Based Research

---

1. **Become familiar with related research.** You can take cues from the work others have done and avoid simply repeating research that others have already done, perhaps with a better methodology than you would have developed on your own. The methodology of online research may differ from traditional forms, so it is a good idea to see what others have done.
2. **Keep your Web page simple and informative, but attractive.** The format and information on your Web page can affect whether people begin participation in your study and whether they will complete it. Reips (2010) has offered several helpful suggestions.
   - Try not to keep your potential participants waiting as they access lengthy Web pages.
   - Develop an attractive, professional-looking site.
   - Consider presenting only one question per Web page in an online survey.
   - Give progress indicators (e.g., "You are 25% finished with the survey") for short surveys, which seem to motivate people to continue.
   - Include demographic questions (age, sex, etc.) and any incentives for participating at the beginning of the study.
3. **Follow the regulations regarding ethics in research.** The same rules and regulations about ethics in research pertain to Internet-based research. Several important points stand out; you need to check out all aspects of the approval process, however.
   - Virtually every academic institution has an Institutional Review Board (IRB) to evaluate the degree of potential risk associated with participation in your research. All research, whether by students or by professional researchers requires approval by the IRB. Most schools have a specific form to complete.
   - You need to insure that participants understand the concept of informed consent. It will be crucial to let people know that participation is voluntary and that, by sending you their responses, they agree to let you include their responses in your analysis. You must tell them that they can terminate their participation at any time.
   - The law regards some people as unable to provide informed consent. That is, legally they are barred from volunteering to participate without approval of parents or guardians. For instance, people under the age of 18 may be legally unable to volunteer on their own. You should highlight this restriction.
   - Naturally, if there is any deception, you need to debrief your participants, but the best means of doing this is not clear at this point.
4. **Give an adequate description of your research.** It will also generate goodwill if you provide some means by which the participants can learn about the results of your research. You can gain cooperation from potential participants by educating them about the importance of your research. Tell them what questions you are addressing, how long their participation will take, and how you will protect their confidentiality. It would be ideal to keep their participation anonymous, so that nobody knows they took part.
5. **Check out your newly created Web site thoroughly.** If you create a Web site, you will be familiar with it, so some of the snags in using it may not be clear to you. It will help to get naive people to test your page. In addition, you can minimize problems if you check your Web page on as many different computers and web browsers as possible. Not all platforms display information identically; pretesting the Web pages can reduce the frustrations that your participants experience and can result in data that are more valid.
6. **Find out how to disseminate information about your study.** Several Web sites that list ongoing research, and various electronic discussion groups may allow you to post announcements about your research.

Respondent Motivation

It doesn't help a researcher if a potential respondent receives but ignores the information. For instance, over the past few decades, the response rate for surveys in general has decreased, and e-mail surveys have had lower response rates than have mail and telephone surveys (Cho & LaRose, 1999; Jin, 2011; Peytchev, Carley-Baxter, & Black, 2011; Yetter & Capaccioli, 2010). The lower response rate for Internet surveys compared to mail surveys seems to be general, holding true for such diverse groups as school professionals and turkey hunters.

You can try to motivate people to comply by using incentives. However, the motivating factors that work in mail surveys may not translate to the computer. Researchers have not yet determined the functional equivalents of mail incentives, which include money-in-mail surveys (Martinez-Ebers, 1997) and in face-to-face surveys (Willimack, Schuman, Pennell, & Lepkowski, 1995), and even tea bags (which don't work; Gendall, Hoek, & Brennan, 1998). In fact, Clark et al. (2011) studied mode of presentation (computer versus mail), incentives ($5 versus $30), and length of a survey (5 minutes versus 30 minutes) to see how response rates changed; none of these variables made a difference. Trying to find how to motivate people is a persistent problem. There is one bright spot, however: McCree, De La Cruz, and Montgomery (2010) found that, for college students, offering downloadable music from iTunes as a reward for participation can increase response rates.

Another potential problem is that there is so much research on the Internet that it is unlikely that any single researcher's work will stand out. Scientific investigators tend to be cautious in their approaches, which includes creating credible-looking, but not flashy, Web pages. Such Web sites have a hard time competing with the more glittering marketing or entertainment pages.

Advantages of Web-Based Research

We can see four clear advantages of Web research. The first involves the amount of time required to test a single participant. In traditional research it takes a lot of time for a researcher to test people individually; the investigator needs to arrive at the testing site in advance in order to set up the experimental apparatus and materials. Then the researcher waits for the participant to show up. People do not always honor their commitments, though; they may forget where to go or when to show up. If the participant appears, the session runs its course for perhaps 15 minutes up to an hour. Then the researcher needs to collect all the data forms, informed-consent forms, and put away any equipment.

For some projects, it would not be unreasonable to expect the time commitment to be an hour per person. Web-based research requires the initial time to create a Web page, but this time commitment probably would not exceed the time required to put together the in-the-lab, paper version of the study. Over time, a Web-based project could involve significantly less time per person than a laboratory-based project because there is no laboratory setup required for each new person. In fact, it can be remarkably easy to create an online survey through Web sites like SurveyMonkey (http://www.surveymonkey.com), which provides the ability to create surveys easily and to post them online with little technological knowledge.

A second advantage of Web-based research is that the investigator does not need to be available when a participant is interested in engaging in the task. The Web is open all day, every day. Data collection occurs at the convenience of the participant, not at the inconvenience of a researcher who has to set aside time from a busy schedule to be in the lab.

A third advantage of Web research is that data collection is automatic and accurate. In the traditional version of research, an investigator has to transfer information from an original data sheet to some other form so data analysis can take place. When the amount of data from a single person is large, it takes a long time to enter and record the data, and there are more chances for error. When research occurs on the Web, the investigator can create a means by which the data are automatically transferred to a file for data analysis. The chance for error diminishes drastically.

A fourth advantage is that we can generate a sample of participants that extends beyond college students; any interested person of any age who is living anywhere in the world can take part. The younger generation seems more attuned to Internet use, so researchers may be able to take advantage of this trend and increase research participation.

Potential Problems with Web-Based Research

As you will see throughout this book, any solution to potential problems in conducting research introduces its own problems. In the case of Web-based research, we eliminate the disadvantages of having to schedule participants to test in person, to code and transfer data, and so forth. At the same time, we introduce potential problems.

One concern is that, although the research can take place in the absence of the investigator, we lose the advantage of having a person who can help a participant who is uncertain of how to proceed, who might misunderstand directions, or who might have a question. Thus, although the investigator does not have to be present (an advantage), it is also true that the researcher cannot be there (a disadvantage). The question that we need to address is whether we gain or lose more through data collection in the laboratory versus on the Web.

Second, the gain in accuracy in data collection can be offset if remote participants provide poor data. If they do not take the research seriously or if they return to the Web site for repeated testing, the quality of the data will suffer. Once again, because of the remote nature of the procedure, the investigator may never know about the problem. Fortunately, research on the quality of data collected on the Web suggests that the quality is high (Azar, 2000b; Vadillo et al., 2006). For instance, Vadillo et al. presented their participants with a learning task that was either online or that used paper and pencil. The degree and pattern of learning were similar for both groups, leading to a sense of confidence that participants engage in the same types of behaviors and thought processes online as they do in a traditional laboratory setting.

In general, according to Krantz and Dalal (2000), the results of traditional laboratory studies with college students correspond quite closely to Web-based research, and the Internet samples are broader than the typical college student sample. This should provide some comfort to us as researchers because the behaviors of the larger group, computer users, resemble those of college students.

Third, there may be differences between computer users and the population as a whole. When we venture into the realm of online research, we can't be sure that the population of participants that we reach are always comparable to the usual samples we use.

Thus, for some tasks, like Vadillo et al.'s learning task, people may learn through the same processes, regardless of who they are. So an Internet sample would reflect a typical laboratory sample. But if a study involves some topics for which different types of people show different patterns, like health care issues, the online population may be different from the general population.

For instance, Couper, Kapteyn, Schonlau, and Winter (2007) studied an online population of older adults who provided information about their health, income, where they lived, their level of education, and so forth. These researchers discovered that less healthy, poor, and non-White populations were underrepresented in the online survey. As Table 3.5 suggests, this pattern should not be a surprise. If the researchers drew generalized conclusions about the health and well-being of the older population based on their online survey, those conclusions could be seriously inaccurate because of the nature of the people who have computer access and the inclination to participate in online surveys.

Unfortunately, even though the percentage of the population that is online is increasing, the extent to which disadvantaged groups are missing from Internet research seems to be holding constant. As you saw in Table 3.5, people who have low educational levels, those who live in rural areas, and those with low incomes are all noticeably underrepresented, although if the high level of Internet use by teens is any indication, the problem may diminish over time.

A fourth consideration involves the ethics of Internet research. As researchers, we need to act ethically, providing informed consent and debriefing, making sure that there is no immediate or long-term harm to participants, making sure that participants are of legal age, and so forth. When a participant is at a remote location, it may not be easy to guarantee ethical safeguards.

Finally, a fifth, fairly new concern relates to the fact that an increasing number of people access the Internet via cell phones (Mobile web audience, 2007). In fact, some segments of the population, most notably those under 35, expect advanced features like Internet access on their cell phones (Consumers in the 18–24 age segment, 2007). A survey on the small screen of a cell phone, combined with potentially slow access, might make a survey difficult to complete, leading to low-quality data.

CHECKING ON RESEARCH: THE ROLE OF REPLICATION

Validity—A property of data, concepts, or research findings whereby they are useful for measuring or understanding phenomena that they are of interest to a psychologist. Data, concepts, and research findings fall on a continuum of usefulness for a given application.

Behavior is complicated and multifaceted, so any single study cannot answer all of our questions about a topic definitively. In addition, no matter how well a researcher designs a study, problems can occur with the results. The participants might have been an unusual group or the assignment of those participants to different conditions may have led to nonequivalent groups. The wording of questions asked may have misled people. Or the selection of the variable to be measured might have been inappropriate. If any of these problems occurred, the **validity** of the results would suffer.

This may sound like a pessimistic view, but with enough systematic research on a topic, we can identify the problems and take them into account. Ideally, researchers will replicate their research, which means to

Replication—In research, the act of recreating or reproducing an earlier study to see if its results can be repeated. The replication can reproduce the original study exactly or with some modifications.

Type I Error—In statistics, erroneously deciding that there is a significant effect when the effect is due to measurement error.

Type II Error—In statistics, erroneously failing to decide that there is a significant effect when it is obscured by measurement error.

Construct Validity—The degree to which a measurement accurately measures the underlying concept that is supposed to be measured.

repeat the investigations to see if the same results emerge. **Replications** can take three basic different forms: exact replication, replication with extension, and conceptual replication. In exact replication, a researcher repeats an earlier investigation exactly. In replication with extension, the experimenter asks the same question, but adds something new. The advantage of the replication with extension is that you don't spend your time merely repeating what we think might be true and that we already know; you are advancing beyond the initial knowledge. In a conceptual replication, the researcher attacks the same basic question, but does it from a different approach.

Replication serves several important functions. First, it can check on the reliability of research results and help us avoid seeing things that aren't there (**Type I errors**) and failing to see things that are there (**Type II errors**). That is, if an initial project erroneously suggested that some behavioral pattern was real, replications could confirm or deny that claim. Or if research seemed to indicate erroneously that some behaviors were likely, replications could show that to be false.

Second, replication can provide additional support for theories. Each replication whose results confirm a theory's predictions increases our confidence in that theory. Or replications may fail to support the predictions, which can lead to new ideas that may be better than the old ones.

A third advantage of replication is that we can increase the **construct validity** of our concepts. This means that when we are dealing with complicated and abstract concepts, such as anxiety or depression, we develop more confidence in what they involve by making diverse measurements of the same concept.

A fourth effect of replications is to help protect against fraud. If researchers who might cheat know that their work will be put to the test, they may be less likely to engage in that fraud. If they have engaged in fraud, replications can call the earlier research into question. One of the stated functions of replication is to identify whether research can withstand close scrutiny.

Even with such clear positive aspects of replication, simple replications seldom occur; replications with extension are more prevalent, but they appear in research journals with considerably less frequency than original research reports.

We can identify several reasons as to why researchers advocate replication but do not do it. In the end, all the reasons come down to the relative payoff for the time and energy devoted to the replication. Scientists prefer to conduct original, novel research because it generates new knowledge, for which the rewards are greater. Familiar people in the history of psychology, like Sigmund Freud, have often worried a great deal that they would not get credit for their ideas.

The meager reward for replication dissuades most researchers from attempting them. Ross, Hall, and Heater (1998) have identified several specific reasons for the lack of published replications in nursing and occupational therapy research. The same principles hold for all behavioral research. First, they suggest, journals are reluctant to publish replications because the results are not new. Second, researchers may be reluctant to submit replications in the first place. Third, colleagues and professors encourage original research. Fourth, funding for replication research may be very limited. Fifth, in writing up the initial research, investigators may not provide enough detail for others who want to replicate. None of these barriers is insurmountable, but they certainly need to be overcome.

A good example of how a widely publicized research project led to subsequent attempts at replication and the correction of erroneous information involves the so-called Mozart effect (Rauscher, Shaw, & Ky, 1993, 1995). Other investigators repeated the research, but were unable to generate the same results. The Controversy box on music shows how our knowledge in this area increased as one set of research questions led to new ones.

DON'T REINVENT THE WHEEL: REVIEWING THE LITERATURE

All researchers recognize that replicating previous research is a good idea, but we also recognize that it is more useful to replicate with extension than simply to replicate. That is, it is important to develop and test new ideas as we verify the old ones. And it pays greater dividends if we can generate new knowledge in our research.

In order to maximize the gains in our research projects, it pays to know what researchers have already done. No matter what topic you choose for a research project, somebody has undoubtedly paved the way already. Researchers consider it completely legitimate to borrow ideas from others, as long as we give appropriate credit to them and don't pass the ideas off as our own.

You are allowed to borrow somebody else's methodology for your own purposes. If it worked for them, it might work for you, and it has the advantage of having been pretested. You can learn a lot about what to do (and what not do to) by reading the work of respected professionals.

What Is a Literature Review?

Literature Review—An overview of published journal articles, books, and other professional work on a given topic.

In order to find out what has been done in an area that interests you, you should conduct a **literature review**. Among researchers, the term "literature" refers to the body of work that is considered to be of high enough quality to appear in technical journals.

When researchers prepare a literature review for a journal article or for a conference presentation, they usually discuss relevant previous studies. Because many areas of research have generated a lot of studies, authors do not present an exhaustive listing of every study that has appeared in journals or books. The amount of information would be too great. Consequently, they write about the studies that have had greatest impact on the project currently underway and about research that psychologists consider very critical in the area. Most of the research in a literature review is fairly recent, although classic and important older articles generally receive attention as well.

The Effect of Peer Review on the Research Literature

Peer Review—A process in which scientific research and ideas are evaluated by experts in a field so that obvious errors or other problems can be spotted and corrected before a work is published or presented at a research conference.

As a researcher you need to differentiate among the various levels of writing that constitute our psychological literature. This is often a judgment call, but articles that appear in **peer-reviewed** journals have been taken seriously by experts. A peer-reviewed journal publishes articles that have undergone careful scrutiny and may have been revised by the authors several times until they have eliminated any major problems. This process is a stringent one. Among the best psychology journals, the rejection rate may be around 70 to 90 percent. Thus, the editor accepts only 30 percent or fewer of the articles that are submitted.

One of the reasons for such a low acceptance rate is that in psychology, our ideas are very complex and abstract. We often have to develop clever operational definitions of our concepts because we cannot observe and measure them directly. It takes considerable diligence to create and conduct a well-designed study that deals with the ideas successfully. There are many ways for ambiguities and uncertainties to creep in, so reviewers and editors frequently request an author to do additional work to take care of these problems.

In disciplines that are more descriptive, such as botany or other areas of biology, the acceptance rate for major journals is often much higher than in psychology. The ideas they work with are often more straightforward, so the research is easier to design. (The tools and techniques of the natural and physical sciences may be difficult to master, but so are those in the behavioral sciences. In any case, we shouldn't confuse the concepts of a science, which are the most important elements, with the tools, which are merely tools.) The differences between psychology and other disciplines in this regard do not imply that one domain is more or less important or useful; it simply means that different areas of research make different demands on researchers.

CONTROVERSY ON MUSIC MAKING YOU SMARTER: THE ROLE OF REPLICATION

Does music make you smarter? A number of years ago, the public became enthralled with the idea that listening to music by Mozart could increase intelligence. Rauscher et al. (1993, 1995) reported that listening to that music could increase scores on one component of an intelligence test; the researchers determined that scores on a standardized test increased significantly, about eight or nine points. The implications were remarkable. People envisioned a populace that was suddenly smarter.

Other researchers were immediately interested. First, there were practical implications. Could we do something to make our children smarter? One plan proposed by the governor of Georgia was to give a tape of this music to each family of a newborn baby in the state. The payoff could be great.

A second reason was that scientists were interested in finding out why intellectual functioning would improve. What was the actual cause? This is an interesting scientific question in its own right. Further, perhaps there were other, even more effective, means of enhancing thought processes.

Unfortunately, the first published report provided insufficient detail on the methodology, so it was difficult to replicate the study because the details were unavailable. The second report presented that information.

When details became available, Carstens, Haskins, and Hounshell (1995) found that listening to Mozart, compared to a silent period, had no effect on test performance. Then Newman, Rosenbach, Burns, Latimer, Matocha, and Vogt (1995) also reported a failure to replicate the original results. Surprisingly, they discovered that people with a preference for classical music actually showed lower test scores than others after listening to the music. As the puzzle grew, Rauscher, Shaw, and Gordon (1998) proposed more arguments to support their original conclusions.

Subsequently, Steele and his colleagues (1980) extended the methodology even further. They found no Mozart effect. Subsequently, Thompson, Schellenberg, and Husain (2001) varied the types of music to which participants listened, finding that arousal levels and mood accounted for the so-called Mozart effect. Higher arousal and positive mood were associated with better test scores, not specifically having listened to Mozart.

This sequence of studies illustrates how the scientific approach, with replication, can be self-correcting and can lead to more complete knowledge. Although it is exciting to think that we can get smart by listening to music, it is important to know the truth—that increases in test performance are more likely to result from high levels of motivation, perhaps from positive mood, and certainly through hard work.

Since the original research and replications appeared, many psychologists have concluded that the Mozart effect may be due to relaxation rather than to the music itself.

HOW TO CONDUCT A LITERATURE REVIEW

Researchers publish numerous articles each year. In fact, there are well over a thousand journals that publish psychology-related articles. Most libraries will have no more than a tiny fraction of them on hand, so even if you wanted to browse through each one of them, you would not be able to.

So how do you find out what has appeared in print? The easiest way is to use an electronic database that lists psychological research. The most useful database for psychologists is PsycINFO®, which is published by the American Psychological Association. It references over 1,300 journals published in 25 languages, and in its most complete version, PsycINFO® cites articles going back to 1887.

Electronic Databases

PsycINFO® is a modern successor to Psychological Abstracts (PA), which appeared in a paper version until 2006, when it was discontinued. PsycINFO® is extremely easy to use compared to PA. The basic strategy is to select a term of interest to you and to tell PsycINFO® to search for published articles related to that term. There are strategies that you can use to maximize the likelihood of finding what you are seeking without also generating a long string of less relevant material. On the flip side, there are ways to expand the number of citations you generate so you can get a more complete picture of the research in an area.

Using PsycINFO® is easy, but you need to learn how to do it if you want to maximize the return on your time. In the following sections, you will learn about useful strategies for searching databases. Keep in mind that we will be focusing on PsycINFO®. If you use other databases, the particulars of your search may differ somewhat, but once you learn PsycINFO®, you can adapt your search strategies to other databases.

Starting Your Search

A first step in searching for information is to decide on a relevant term that matches your interest. This is an important first step because it will determine the nature of the articles listed in your output.

The number of published articles listed in PsycINFO® continues to increase because researchers keep publishing their work. Thus, any specific examples that appear here will become outdated over time. Nonetheless, you can get an idea of how to generate worthwhile search strategies.

Suppose that you are interested in learning about the psychological aspects of adopting children. You could type the word *adoption* and begin the search. In 2012, entering the word *adoption* in the EBSCO Host database resulted in a list of 15,043 references. (Different platforms result in different numbers.) Obviously, it would be impossible to read every source, but you would not want to in any case because there are many citations that do not relate to your topic in the least. The reason that a search of *adoption* generates irrelevant references is that if you type in a word, PsycINFO® will search for the word, regardless of the way that word is used.

For example, among the results PsycINFO® lists in the search for the word *adoption,* only 6 of the first 40 listings dealt with adopting children. Many of the others related to the adoption of some kind of program or model. PsycINFO® does not know what meaning of the word *adoption* you intend without some help from you. If the article relates to adopting some strategy or plan, the database will include it, which is what happened with this search.

You can find ways to limit the search so that you don't have thousands of citations, many of which are irrelevant. One of the most useful steps is to specify that the database should list citations that include *adoption* as either keyword or Subject. In a keyword search, PsycINFO® looks for the word anywhere in the record except the references. A Subject search involves a search for a major topic of the entry. If you do not actively specify that you want keywords or descriptors (or in some other major field), PsycINFO® will look for the word *adoption* anywhere and everywhere.

The current search led to 12,586 hits.

You can further reduce the number of irrelevant citations. Table 3.7 illustrates the steps you can take to narrow your search to be more productive. One involves using the PsycINFO® thesaurus to identify a narrower term than you are using; another pertains to setting limits on the search process, like a restricted range of years in which articles were published, types of studies (theoretical versus empirical), and populations (adults, children, women, men, etc.). There are quite a few ways to set limits to restrict the scope of your search. The example in Table 3.7 goes from over 15,000 hits down to a much more manageable 158. Of course the final figure has some restrictions and would not

TABLE 3.7 **Examples of Strategies to Reduce the Number of Irrelevant Citations in a PsycINFO® Search**

Search for References to Adoption	Strategy to Narrow the Search	Number of References
Adoption anywhere in the citation		15,043
Adoption as Subject	Choose *Adoption* in Subject. (From this point on, change only the new search option and retain the earlier ones you selected.)	4,058
Adoption as Subject and including only work published since 1990	Choose *Publication Range From* 1990 to the current year (or whatever time span you want).	3,077
Adoption as Subject, including only work published since 1990 and only work published in the English language	Choose English only	2,941
Only work meeting the above criteria and published in peer-reviewed journals	Choose *Peer-reviewed journals.* This eliminates hard-to-access material like doctoral dissertations.	1,981
Only work meeting the above criteria and involving females in the adoption process	Choose *Population Group* = Female	809
Only work meeting the above criteria and involving children 12 years or younger	Choose *Age Range* as Childhood	268
Only work meeting the above criteria and linked to full text articles	Choose *Linked Full Tex*	158

include male adoptions, for example. Your narrowing of the search should meet your own particular needs.

If your search produces too few hits, there are ways of expanding it. One strategy is to insert a "wild card" in your search. For instance, in PsycINFO®, you can use an asterisk (*) to expand the search. When you enter the subject of your search as adopt*, PsycINFO® will look for any subject beginning with *adopt*, such as adopt, adoption, and adoptive. Using the wild card with *adopt* in the descriptors raises the number of hits from 2,202 to 3,695. This number is obviously more than you want to use, but using this wild card shows how the wild card can expand the number of hits.

You can also use the database's thesaurus, which tells you what terms to use when searching for a given concept. Table 3.8 gives a glimpse of the possibilities for expanding your search. By experimenting, you may be able to figure out alternate strategies for increasing the number of hits.

Different Sources of Information

There is a wealth of sources of information about psychological research. Some of that information is useful, some is suspect, and some is of unknown quality. When you read reports that the researchers themselves have written, you are dealing with primary sources. In general, if an article appears in a peer-reviewed research journal, you can have

TABLE 3.8   Strategies for Expanding the Number of Relevant Citations in PsycINFO®

Strategy to Expand the Search	Result
Use the *Thesaurus* option and enter "Adopt*"	You get a list of categories that PsycINFO® uses that are related to adoption.
Use the *Index* and enter "Adopt*" or "Adoption"	You get a dozen subject categories to search.
Example: Use the Thesaurus terms "Adopted-Children," "Adoptees," "Adoption-Child," "Interracial Adoption" and "Adoptive-Parents" connected by OR (i.e., Adopted-children OR adoptees OR adoption-child OR interracial-adoption OR adoptive-parents)	You get additional citations that relate to the Thesaurus terms and that still follow the previous limits you set. Using OR tells PsycINFO® to access any citation that uses any of your terms. If you connected them with AND, PsycINFO® would only access those citations that include all those terms at the same time, which would restrict the search greatly. In fact, a single journal article is unlikely to fall into all these categories.

confidence that there is merit to the information in the article. There may be limitations to the work, but it is probably generally valid.

Sometimes a writer will refer to the research by another psychologist, describing the methods, results, and interpretations. This type of work is a secondary source. The original research is likely to be valid if it appeared in a professional journal, but at this point, the new authors are giving their own interpretations of the original ideas. The secondary source is going to present a reduced version of the original, so there may be departures from what the original writers either wrote or intended. At times you may need to refer to a secondary source, as when you cannot get the original, but using primary sources is preferable when possible.

You may also see tertiary sources. These are descriptions of research based on somebody else's description of yet somebody else's original research. The farther you get from the original research, the more distortion you may find in the presentation of the information.

In addition to the different levels of information (primary, secondary, etc.), there are differences in the actual nature of the information you may encounter. Some sources (e.g., professional journals) are intended for a professional audience. But other sources are meant for the general public. As a rule, information in popular sources is less detailed and may be less useful for scientific purposes, although it may serve as a starting point for a review of the scientific literature.

One particularly contentious source is Wikipedia, the online encyclopedia that any person can edit (although there are some constraints on inserting new material). Many educators have a strong, negative impression of Wikipedia, suggesting that the information in it is not reliable. However, a study published in the journal *Nature* revealed that the quality of information in Wikipedia was essentially at the same level as in the highly respected *Encyclopedia Britannica*. (*Encyclopedia Britannica* disputed the findings.) It is probably safe to approach Wikipedia as a place to get some basic information, followed by the use of primary sources. The caveats associated with the use of different sources appear in various places (e.g., Beins & Beins, 2012).

HOW TO READ A JOURNAL ARTICLE

When you first begin reading scientific writing, it may seem like it has been written in another language, and the organization of the information can seem convoluted. After you get used to the style of research reports, your task of reading journal articles will be easier. There is a reason for the organization of journal articles, and there is a skill involved in understanding scientific writing. Most likely, for your psychology courses, you will be reading articles written in a format often called APA style. This means that the authors have followed the guidelines set forth in the *Publication Manual of the American Psychological Association* (American Psychological Association, 2010). This style differs from others that you may have encountered, like MLA (Modern Language Association, 1995) for the humanities, or various formats for each of the scientific disciplines. APA style may seem complicated, but the primary rules are fairly easy to learn. The *Publication Manual* is over 250 pages long, though, so you can expect that there is a lot of detail about specific formatting and writing issues.

Understanding the Format of a Research Paper

When you pick up a research article written in APA style, you will be able to figure out very quickly where to look to find the information you seek. Writers divide their manuscripts into six sections as a rule. The actual number of sections will differ, depending on the complexity of the research report. Regardless of the exact number of sections, there are specific reasons why information appears where it does. Table 3.9 presents an overview of the different sections of a research report written in APA style and some of the questions addressed in those sections. The table can serve as a worksheet to guide you in reading journal articles. If you write a brief answer to each of the questions in the table, you will have a pretty complete summary of the work that was done, why it was done, and what the authors think it means. Following are the sections into which authors divide their manuscripts:

Abstract—The part of a research report that summarizes the purpose of the research, the methodology, the results of the study, and the interpretations of the research.

Abstract.   In the **abstract**, the authors give an overview of the entire paper; this section is fairly short, usually 150–250 words. It presents a preview of the research question and hypotheses, the methodology, the results, and the discussion. The abstract is kept short so the reader can get a quick glimpse of the nature of the research.

Introduction—The part of a research report that gives an overview of the field to be investigated and the investigator's hypotheses about the outcome of the research.

Introduction.   After the abstract comes the **Introduction**, which provides background information so you can understand the purpose of the research. When the research involves specific tests of hypotheses, the authors will generally present these hypotheses here. This section also gives a general preview of how the researchers have conducted their project. The purpose of the introduction is to clarify the aim of the study and show how relevant ideas developed in previous research. You will virtually never see a journal article that does not refer to previous research on which the current article is based.

As you read through the introduction, you will see that the first ideas are relatively broad. These ideas relate to a more general depiction of the

TABLE 3.9   **Concepts That Are Clarified in the Different Sections of a Research Report**

Introduction
- What is the general topic of the research article?
- What do we know about this topic from previous research?
- What are the authors trying to demonstrate in their own research?
- What are their hypotheses?

Method

Participants—Who took part in the research?
- How many people (or animals) were studied?
- If there were nonhuman animals, what kind were they?
- If there were people, what were their characteristics (e.g., average and range of age, gender, race or ethnicity, were they volunteers or were they paid)?

Apparatus and Materials—What did the researchers need to carry out their study?
- What kind of stimuli, questions, etc. were used?
- How many different kinds of activities did participants complete?
- What instrumentation was used to present material to participants and to record their responses?

Procedure—What did the people actually do during the research session?
- After the participants arrived what did they do?
- What did the experimenters do as they interacted with participants?

Results
- What were patterns of behaviors among participants?
- Did behaviors differ when different groups were compared?
- What type of behaviors are predictable in the different testing conditions?
- What were the results of any statistical tests?

Discussion
- What do the results mean?
- What explanations can you develop for why the participants responded as they did?
- What psychological processes help you explain participants' responses?
- What questions have not been answered fully?
- How do your results relate to the research cited in the introduction?
- How do your results relate to other kinds of research?
- What new ideas emerge that you could evaluate in a subsequent experiment?

References
- What research was cited in the research report (e.g., work published in journals or other written sources, research presentations, personal communications)?

field of interest to the researchers. As the introduction progresses, the scope of the material narrows. The authors will describe and discuss in more detail the research that relates most closely to their own project. Finally, the authors will present their own ideas. By the time you finish reading the introduction, you will have a clear picture of the logic that led from the ideas of previous researchers to those of the authors.

Method—The part of a research report that provides information about those who participated in the study, how the research was actually carried out, and the materials and apparatus used for it.

Participants—A sub-section of the Method section that details the nature of the humans or nonhumans who took part in the research. Nonhuman animals are often referred to as *Subjects* whereas humans who took part are called *Participants*.

Materials and Apparatus—A subsection of the Method section that details what implements and stimuli were used to carry out the study. Sometimes the materials and apparatus appear in separate subsections.

Procedure—A subsection of the Method section that provides extensive detail about the actual process used to carry out the study.

Results—The part of a research report that details the quantitative and qualitative results of an investigation, including results of statistical analyses.

Method.   Following the introduction is the **Method section**. This section should allow an independent researcher to reproduce the project described in the article. The section contains an extreme amount of detail. Very often, students regard this section as not being very important. In some ways, you are right: even without it, you can understand why the researchers conducted the study and what results occurred. In another way, though, if you do not read this section, you might miss out on important details that affected the research outcome. This section is absolutely critical for those who want to replicate the original research.

Participants.   Writers subdivide the methods section into three or four sections. The first one, **Participants**, characterizes those who took part in the study. It describes how many participants were there, what were their ages, their racial and ethnic backgrounds, etc. This subsection provides the reader with enough information to understand if the nature of the participants may have influenced the outcome of the research in some way. If the research involved nonhuman animals, the type of animal (e.g., genus and species) are given.

Materials and Apparatus.   The next subsection, **Materials and Apparatus**, provides details about what you would need to carry out the study. Sometimes writers will create separate subsections for materials and apparatus if there is a need.

Procedure.   After the description of the implements of the study, the authors will describe the **Procedure**. In this subsection, they describe exactly what occurred during the research session. As a rule, the procedure subsection includes only what occurs during the data collection session. Based on the information in this section, an independent researcher could follow the steps that the original researchers took.

Results.   After the data collection is complete, scientists typically present the outcome in a **Results section** that usually includes statistical tests. Although choosing a statistical test seems to be a pretty straightforward task, there are actually controversies in some cases about the best approach to data analysis. If you chose one approach, you might end up with one conclusion; if you took an alternate approach, your conclusion might be different. This issue has such great implications that the American Psychological Association created a task force that issued guidelines about research methodology and statistics. The task force wrote an important article that highlights some of the controversies associated with statistics (Wilkinson & the Task Force on Statistical Inference, 1999).

The results section details the outcome of the study. For example, if a researcher compares two groups, this section tells whether they differed and by how much. The results section also presents the results of any statistical tests that the researchers conducted. This part of a research report can be very complicated because you have to translate technical materials and terminology into comprehensible English.

One way to make sure that you understand what you are reading is to keep track of the different research questions that the investigators have asked. You can do this by making note of them when you read the introduction. Then when they present the statistics, you can try to figure out the particular question that goes along with the statistic.

You will also encounter figures and tables in the results section. The purpose of these graphic elements is to provide an overview when the results are complicated. By creating a figure or chart, the authors can combine a large amount of information into a single picture.

Discussion.   The data do not mean anything until we, as researchers, decide what they mean. When we ask a research question, our task is to take complicated data about a question that we are the first to ask and see what the data tell us. Because nobody else has done what we have, we are the ones who have to figure out what it all means. A successful investigation generates new information that has to be interpreted and placed in the context of earlier research.

Discussion Section—The part of a research report that provides an interpretation of the results, going beyond a simple description of the results and statistical tests.

This final section involving treatment of the research ideas is the **Discussion section**, which provides closure to the project. That is, the investigators tell you what their results mean. Unlike the results section, which says what happened, the discussion tells you why it happened. Another way to characterize the distinction is that the results section provides fact, whereas the discussion section provides interpretation, explanation, and speculation. The results of a study are incontrovertible; they are what they are. What may be controversial, however, is the interpretation of the results.

Reference Section—The part of a research report that contains complete reference information about any work cited in the research report, that is, where the work was published or presented and the source of any work that has not been published or presented.

At the very end of the paper, the **Reference section** appears. This section simply gives information on where a reader can find the ideas that others generated and that you cited in your paper.

APA style dictates a specific format for virtually any kind of reference, including references from the World Wide Web. The details are quite specific. With practice, they are not hard to master.

Sometimes authors include material in one or more appendixes at the end of the paper. The function of an appendix is to provide information that may be important for replicating a study but may not be critical to understanding the research.

SUMMARY

Research ideas come from many different sources. Ultimately, it boils down to the fact that somebody has a question and wants to find an answer. Sometimes the source of a research project begins with an "I wonder what would happen if..." type of question. In other cases, there is a problem to be solved, and an investigator will use research skills to devise an answer that can be applied to the situation. In still other cases, a theory makes a prediction that a scientist can test through research.

Regardless of the source of ideas, the scientists who investigate them take their cues from the society around them. Scientists are members of their community and share the same attitudes and values as many others in our society. Thus, social issues are important in determining what a particular researcher will think important. This consideration is true for any scientific discipline, but it is especially true in the study of human behavior.

In our current social context, the Internet has become important in research. Psychologists are studying how to use the Internet as a research tool. A number of important issues need to be addressed before Web-based research can flourish, but scientists are working on the question.

Regardless of the topics of research or how the data are collected, we want to have confidence in the results. We want them to be meaningful. One way to ensure that scientific findings are useful is through replication, that is, repetition of the research by different investigators in different contexts. When the same results appear regularly, we can have greater confidence that our conclusions are warranted.

When you generate a research project, you can get guidance about how to conduct it by reading what others have done. This usually involves a literature review of published studies. Without such a review, you run the risk of simply repeating what others have already done. Such a replication may give you more confidence in the phenomenon you are studying, but most researchers want to include novel features in their research so they can advance the field with new knowledge. One way to increase what we know about the behaviors we study is through publication of the results in scientific journals and through presentations at research conferences.

Finally, if you conduct research, you may write it up in a formal report. You are likely to follow the style of presentation set forth in the *Publication Manual* of the American Psychological Association.

REVIEW QUESTIONS

Multiple Choice Questions

1. When researchers develop projects to test how well competing theories predict behaviors, their ideas
   a. tend to fall more toward the formal end of the continuum of ideas.
   b. usually end up testing ideas that arise from practical issues.
   c. rely on informal and idiosyncratic approaches.
   d. they seldom need to base their research on previous ideas and research.
2. When scientists develop their ideas for research projects, which of the following is most often the source of their ideas?
   a. Colleagues in different departments within their own institutions
   b. Colleagues in their own department
   c. The existing research literature
   d. Discussions within their research teams
3. When the dominant theory in psychology was behaviorism, researchers
   a. used behavioral observation to study cognitive processes.
   b. believed that you could learn just about anything regarding human behavior with animal models.
   c. neuroscientific approaches were used to understand brain processes that affect behavior.
   d. capitalized on the effects of the cognitive revolution to understand behaviors.

4. If you want to discover whether "Haste Makes Waste" or "He Who Hesitates Is Lost" is a better description of the effects of human behavior, you could make an experimental test. According to McGuire's (1983) description of the development of research ideas, such an approach would involve
    a. studying spontaneously occurring events.
    b. studying the validity of everyday beliefs and when they break down.
    c. evaluating formal if–then statements.
    d. using previous research as a stepping stone to new ideas.

5. Generating a research idea by finding an individual who acts in different or interesting ways would use which of McGuire's (1983) approaches to generating research ideas?
    a. studying spontaneously occurring events.
    b. studying the validity of everyday beliefs and when they break down.
    c. using an intensive case study.
    d. using previous research as a stepping stone to new ideas.

6. There are differences in the way we conduct laboratory and Internet-based research. The differences include the fact that
    a. actually carrying out the study on the Internet requires less time on the part of the experimenter than a laboratory study does.
    b. for Internet studies, the researcher has to be available more frequently because Internet users can access the research on the Internet just about any time of the day, so the researcher needs to be available to answer questions.
    c. laboratory research generally leads to more accurate recording of data because paper data sheets are right in front of the researcher who can enter them into a computerized database.
    d. because anybody can access the research on the Internet, an investigator can't be certain that the sample is representative of the population, whereas this isn't a problem with laboratory studies.

7. One of the problems with research on the Internet is that
    a. because many people can access the research, the samples differ from typical psychological research samples, so the results are often different.
    b. because of the remote nature of the research, the investigator might never know about problems that occur during the course of the study.
    c. the investigator usually has to commit more time for data collection than in laboratory studies.
    d. participants who have difficulty with the study are likely to contact the investigator at any time of the night or day to ask questions.

8. One practical issue in Internet-based research is that
    a. displays of the research Web page might be very different for people on different types of computers.
    b. sample sizes might become so large that the study becomes impractical to conduct.
    c. it is very difficult to create good descriptions of Internet based research because it reaches so many people.
    d. it is almost impossible to guarantee that participation in such research will be anonymous and confidential.

9. Research on how to conduct studies on the Internet has revealed that the lowest rate of return occurs when the investigator contacts potential respondents through which of the following?
    a. Hyperlinks on Web sites.
    b. Sending information to newsgroups.
    c. Individual e-mail messages.
    d. Announcements of the surveys in major magazines.

10. The technical differences among computers on which people complete Internet surveys
    a. are minimal with the standard Internet formatting of surveys.
    b. can lead to very different displays of the same survey.
    c. require that researchers avoid using colors that may not be the same on different computers.
    d. make constant response formats difficult to implement.
11. When a researcher repeats an earlier experiment but includes some novel elements, this process is called
    a. assessment of validity.
    b. replication with extension.
    c. conceptual replication.
    d. construct validity.
12. Replicating research so we can develop more confidence in our understanding of complex and abstract concepts helps us
    a. increase our construct validity.
    b. avoid both Type I and Type II errors.
    c. perform replication with extension.
    d. develop conceptual replication.
13. The process by which scientists try to guarantee that only high quality research results appear in journals involves getting experts to evaluate the work, this process is called
    a. construct validity.
    b. peer review.
    c. the literature review.
    d. conceptual review.
14. A literature review in a research article generally includes
    a. an exhaustive listing of just about every study published about the topic being reviewed.
    b. a discussion of what has been written by psychologists as well as by more popular authors.
    c. the ideas that are favorable to the researcher's theory.
    d. a discussion of research that is important but that has not yet been published.
15. If you wanted to understand the theoretical reasons that led researchers to conduct a project that appeared in an APA journal, you would read which section of their article?
    a. abstract
    b. introduction
    c. discussion
    d. references
16. The results section of an APA style report will contain
    a. information about the statistical tests used to analyze the data.
    b. a statement about the research hypotheses.
    c. the number and types of participants.
    d. an integration of the data with theory.

Essay Questions

17. Where on the continuum of formality of ideas is a beginning student's research likely to fall? Explain your answer.
18. Explain how changes in psychology and changes in society have affected psychologists' use of animals in research.
19. Why could it be more profitable for a beginning researcher to do an exact replication, while it would be more profitable for a seasoned researcher to do a conceptual replication?
20. What are the advantages of a literature review of research related to your own investigations?

ANSWERS TO REVIEW QUESTIONS

Answers to Multiple Choice Questions

1.	a	7.	b	13.	b
2.	c	8.	a	14.	a
3.	b	9.	d	15.	b
4.	b	10.	b	16.	a
5.	c	11.	b		
6.	a	12.	a		

Answers to Essay Questions

17. Where on the continuum of formality of ideas is a beginning student's research likely to fall? Explain your answer.

    Students are likely to pose research questions that arise from their own experiences, that is, from less formal points on the continuum. Students' levels of knowledge are going to be less than those of experienced researchers, so students will be less familiar with research to replicate, although after some preliminary study, they might be able to do so. Beginning students are unlikely to come up with significant tests of theory because they are just learning about the content of psychology.

18. Explain how changes in psychology and changes in society have affected psychologists' use of animals in research.

    Some psychologists have speculated that decrease in the amount of animal research has resulted, in part, from a change in theoretical perspectives, from behaviorism to cognitivism. Behaviorists were willing to generalize to people from animals, cognitive psychologists less so.

    A second reason is that psychologists have turned their attention to different research questions, ones that are less likely to be answered through animal research. Part of this may be due to the increasing number of women in psychology.

    A third reason is that people, including psychologists, are more sensitive to the ethical issues associated with animal research.

19. Why could it be more profitable for a beginning researcher to do an exact replication, while it would be more profitable for a seasoned researcher to do a conceptual replication?

    Beginning researchers can benefit from learning how to carry out research by following the well-specified procedures of earlier research. This will help them avoid overlooking important potential problems because most of these problems will have been ironed out by the original researchers. Seasoned researchers who can anticipate potential problems can be more confident that they will be able to create well-structured studies that go beyond the original studies.

20. What are the advantages of a literature review of research related to your own investigations?
    a. You can learn what experts in the area are interested in.
    b. You can get clues about how to conduct your own study, avoiding mistakes that might have beset earlier researchers.
    c. You can see how other researchers have defined their concepts and made their measurements.

CHAPTER FOUR

PRACTICAL ISSUES IN PLANNING YOUR RESEARCH

CHAPTER OVERVIEW

LEARNING OBJECTIVES

After going through this chapter, you will be able to:

- Describe differences in the nature of participants in different types of research
- Differentiate between basic (theoretical) research and applied research
- Identify advantages and disadvantages of laboratory versus field research
- Identify and describe the major research approaches
- Generate examples of research using the major research approaches
- Differentiate between populations and samples
- Describe the issues associated with determining how many participants to include in a study
- Identify why research with animals can help understand human behavior

KEY TERMS

CHAPTER PREVIEW

When most students are learning about research, they typically are not aware of how many decisions are made in putting a project together. You will find that when you read a journal article, you learn only what the researchers finally did, not what they tried that didn't work. The reason for this lack of information is that journal space is in short supply. There is always more to print than the journals have space for. As a result, authors omit just about everything not entirely germane to the topic they are studying. The authors report only what was successful. Another result is that as a reader, if you want to plan your own research project, you can use the information in published work, but you have to fill in a lot of details on your own.

The researchers leave out information on false starts, procedures that did not work out, and judgments that led to an unsatisfactory outcome. You can be sure that in virtually every research project ever conducted, the researchers made choices that caused them to stop and evaluate what they were doing and to make changes to improve the research design.

Some of the tasks associated with completing a study include describing in concrete terms the concepts you are interested in, figuring out how to measure them, identifying those you will test in your study, carrying out the project itself, looking at and understanding the results, then interpreting what you've discovered. If you make poor choices or conclusions at any step along the way, your research will be less meaningful than it could otherwise be.

In each case, the choices you make will each take you in a slightly different direction than some other choice. Each of these steps will involve making quite a few decisions that, you hope, will provide you with a clear answer to your original question.

PRACTICAL QUESTIONS IN PLANNING RESEARCH

When you read about successful research projects either in a scientific journal or in a popular magazine or when you see a report on television, the reporter makes the research sound as if it were put together perfectly and that there was only one reasonable way to have conducted it. In reality, if you were to follow a research project from beginning to end, you would see that the researchers had to make a great number of decisions about the study.

We investigate concepts that are very complex and abstract. This means that we need to simplify the complex ideas so our research doesn't become unmanageable. We also have to take abstract ideas and generate concrete ways to measure them. For example, love is an emotion that can help us understand why people act as they do. But what is it? It is a complex set of emotions that we don't have an easy way to measure.

If we consider the goals of science, we can see that we could try to describe what it means to love. To do so, we have to identify what behaviors reflect being in love. If we don't describe it well, we can't move to the more difficult goal of predicting when it will occur. How can you predict what you can't describe? Beyond that, we will not be able to understand when it occurs, or how to control it.

There are varied ways of measuring love. None of these ways is perfect, but each is useful in its own way. Researchers have measured love through skin conductance (Guerra et al., 2011), variations in the heart rate (Schneiderman, Zilberstein-Kra, Leckman, & Feldman, 2011), brain activity (Ortigue, Bianchi-Demicheli, Patel, Frum, & Lewis, 2010), a 13-item inventory (Rubin, 1970), and so on. Such variety is helpful because many of the existing self-report measures of love seem to measure the same thing and don't always do it terribly well (Graham, 2011).

In other areas of science, researchers frequently engage in descriptive research. They may count the number of plants that live in a particular type of field, or the number of animals born with deformities due to the presence of toxic substances. In this research, the concepts are fairly obvious and easy to measure. In some areas, the research may require complex tools to answer the scientists' questions, but although the tools are complex, the concepts are relatively simple. In psychology, we use tools that may be easy to develop (e.g., measuring behaviors on a scale of 1–10), but the concepts are complex.

Once you decide on a research question, you need to fill in the details about how you will carry out your project. This aspect of your task is not necessarily difficult, but you need to consider carefully myriad details. These details are the subject of the rest of this book. A research project can take many different paths; you have to decide how you want yours to proceed so that you arrive at the best answer to your question.

UNDERSTANDING YOUR RESEARCH

If your research is going to be data driven, you have to measure something. Because psychologists study complex ideas, the question of measurement sometimes poses difficulties. For instance, if you wanted to study depression, you could do so in any number of ways.

Social psychologists who study depression might investigate the extent to which a depressed person has social ties in the community. A researcher interested in family dynamics would focus on parents, siblings, and partners. Someone interested in psychological testing and assessment might try to identify tests that are most effective in identifying somebody who shows signs of depression. A neuroscientist could study the role of neurotransmitters in depression. All of these psychologists would tell you that they were studying depression, but each one would be doing it in a different way. Depending on how you approached the study of depression, you would define and measure that concept in different ways. In order to find out how to do that, your best first step would be to search the literature to see what others have already done.

You can see in Table 4.4 that investigators gather a lot of information from previously published research. The number of references cited in journal articles is considerable, providing some confidence that the investigators have a firm grasp of the issues they are dealing with and that they know how the major researchers in the area have done their work. In your own research projects, it is unlikely that you will have as many references as the typical published article. You are a beginning researcher without the background that professional researchers have gained in their work. It may be acceptable to include many fewer references as you develop a narrower focus in your first projects.

Carrying Out a Literature Search

Suppose you wanted to study stress levels and the effects they have on students. This is not an easy area to investigate because the concept of importance here, stress, is not directly observable. It is an internal, psychological state. You can observe only the behaviors and reactions associated with it. To understand it, you should find out what others have already learned. You do this by conducting an initial literature search.

A literature search serves several particularly important purposes. First, by learning about what other researchers have discovered, you can avoid merely repeating what they have done. It is always more exciting to create a study that generates knowledge that nobody knew before you did.

A second advantage of searching through the research literature is that you find the vast range of approaches that previous researchers have already used. With this knowledge, you can begin to identify the approach that might be most useful to you in answering your own question.

Third, you can see how others have defined their variables. This lets you see what worked for them. When planning research, there is absolutely nothing wrong with adopting the methods that others have used. If you think back on the concept that scientific knowledge is cumulative, you will recognize that researchers expect others to follow up on their work, just as they have followed up on the work of others. Table 4.1 gives a snapshot of the kind of information you can get from a review of the research literature. You see the results of the choices different investigators have made in creating their studies.

CONDUCTING YOUR STUDY

Experimental Research—
Investigation that involves manipulation and control of an independent or treatment variable with the intent of assessing whether the independent variable causes a change in the level of a dependent variable.

Another important choice in creating a research project concerns whether you intend to manipulate and control the situation or whether you will simply observe what occurs naturally. In **experimental research**, we actively manipulate what we expose the research participants to. In other types of research, we may not be able to manipulate variables for ethical or practical reasons.

Suppose you wanted to investigate the effects of stress on people. You could choose a descriptive approach in which you observed behaviors without interacting with the people you monitor. For example, you could look

TABLE 4.1 Differences in Research Methodologies in Psychology Journals Based on 20 Articles per Journal in 2011 and 2012

Journal	Average Number of Participants per Study	Percentage of Different Methodologies	Percentage of Studies in Different Settings	Percentage of Articles Using Different Statistical Tests	Number of References per Article
Journal of Applied Psychology (2011)	756	45% Survey 5% Experimental 5% Interview 25% Meta-analysis 20% Other	35% Workplace 10% Lab 25% Online 5% Homes 25% Meta-analysis	5% ANOVA 70% Correlation 10% Factor analysis 25% Meta-analysis	Mean = 95 Range = 57–219
Journal of Personality and Social Psychology	63,809 (278)*	80% Experimental 20% Survey	85% Laboratory 20% Online (one study used two methods)	70% ANOVA 80% Correlation 20% t-test 15% Chi-square 10% Other	Mean = 47 Range: 31–125
Journal of Experimental Psychology: General	64	95% Experimental 5% Theoretical	95% Laboratory 5% Online	95% ANOVA 15% Correlation 30% t-test 10% Chi-square 5% Other	Mean = 85 Range = 22–208

*Two studies had atypical sample sizes of 1.2 million and 3,972. When these data sets are removed, the mean is the lower value.

at behavior during stressful periods, like final exam week, compared to other less stressful times. This approach would enable you to describe stress-related behaviors that emerge during periods of differential stress.

A second method to study stress might involve administering a questionnaire that inquires about sources of stress and looks at their possible effects. If you used such an approach, you would not have to worry about the ethics of increasing stress levels in already stressed students. Holmes and Rahe (1967) and Miller and Rahe (1997) took the approach of developing a survey technique to study stress. They used a questionnaire to assess the amount of change in people's lives and the resultant changes in stress. These researchers found that apparently trivial events, even positive ones like going on vacation, contributed to overall stress levels that can have an effect on one's health. For reasons that we don't understand, the level of stress associated with specific events has increased across the decades, as you can see in Table 4.2.

A third strategy is to identify existing stress levels in your research participants, then see how they respond to some manipulation. Some investigators (e.g., Cohen et al., 2006; Cohen, Tyrrell, & Smith, 1991) did exactly this. They used nose drops to introduce either viruses or an inactive saline (i.e., saltwater) solution into the body and quarantined the people so they were not exposed to any other viral agents. These researchers found that people with higher levels of stress in their lives were more likely to come down with colds and, if they did, their colds were more severe. They also found that people with more positive emotional styles were less susceptible to colds.

TABLE 4.2   Change in Relative Amounts of Stress Associated with Different Events from 1967 to 1997

Event	Percentage Increase in Stress from 1967 to 1997	Presumed Valence for Most People (Positive/Negative)
Death of a spouse	19	Negative
Jail term	22	Negative
Marriage	0	Positive
Pregnancy	65	Positive
Sex difficulties	15	Negative
Death of a close friend	89	Negative
Change in work responsibilities	48	?
Change in schools	75	?
Change in recreation	53	?
Change in sleeping habits	62	?
Change in eating habits	80	?
Christmas	250	Positive

Source: Holmes & Rahe (1967); Miller & Rahe (1997).

Finally, you could bring research participants to a laboratory and induce stress, but as you have learned in Chapter 2, there would be ethical questions about that strategy (just as there would be if you exposed your participants to a virus). Few researchers actively induce stress in people; if they want to control stress levels directly, they often use laboratory animals. (For an example of a study on stress and learning using animals, see Kaneto, 1997.)

The important point here is that you could study stress and its effects in a number of different ways. Each approach involves asking slightly different questions about stress, resulting in a slightly different portrayal of its effects. All approaches are methodologically valid, and each has its own strengths and weaknesses.

When you decide how you want to conduct your study, you must consider ethical issues. When we consider research on stress, we have to pay attention to the effects it will have on research participants, both human and nonhuman, and balance those effects against the gains from doing the research. Studying the effects of stress on people's lives is certainly worthwhile. If we gain a more complete understanding of when stress reactions are likely to occur (i.e., description and prediction), why the stress builds up (i.e., explanation), and how we might avoid them (i.e., control), a lot of people will lead healthier lives. On the other hand, can we justify what we put our participants through in the research?

Determining the Research Setting

Once we decide on a research question and define our variables, we have to establish the location in which we will actually carry out the study. Some research almost by necessity requires a formal laboratory setting. If an investigation involves highly specialized equipment or a highly controlled environment, the researcher has few options other than the laboratory. For example, if you decided to study a behavior that is affected by variables that you don't intend to study, you could use a laboratory to eliminate or control those variables so you can pay attention to what interests you. This laboratory approach is typical in **basic research** in which some variables have large effects that can obscure a variable that has a small effect. To study the factor that has a small effect, you need a controlled environment to offset the effects of the unwanted variables. If the research question involves an application relating to a particular environment like a business, the investigator needs to conduct the study in a business setting.

Basic (Theoretical) Research—Research that tests or expands on theory, with no direct application intended.

Another decision is whether to test people one by one or in groups. If people are tested in groups rather than individually, they might perform differently on their tasks. Social psychologists have found that people perform differently when they think others are observing them. Zajonc (1965) reported that even rats and ants work differently when in groups. If you are conducting your own study, it could make a difference whether your participants are alone or in groups, but you often do not know whether their performance changes for the better, for the worse, or in ways that are irrelevant to what you are measuring.

Very often, applied research takes place in a natural environment where people are acting as they normally do. Basic (theoretical) research is more likely to occur in a laboratory

Quasi-Experiment—A research study set up to resemble a true experiment but that does not involve random assignment of participants to a group or manipulation and control of a true independent variable, instead relying on measuring groups based on preexisting characteristics.

Case Study—An intensive, in-depth study of a single individual or a few individuals, usually without manipulation of any variables to see how changes affect the person's behavior.

Longitudinal Study—A research project in which a group of participants is observed and measured over time, sometimes over many decades.

Archival Research—Investigation that relies on existing records like books or governmental statistics or other artifacts rather than on direct observation of participants.

or other controlled setting. The reason for choosing a natural environment for research is that it represents the actual question you want to answer: How do people behave in a particular situation? On the other hand, when psychologists conduct theoretical research, we often want to simplify the situation so we can identify the effect of a single variable that might get lost in a complex, real-world setting.

CHOOSING YOUR METHODOLOGY

After you have operationally defined your concepts and variables, you can establish your methodology. Psychologists have developed many techniques to study a wide variety of behaviors. Each approach has its own strengths and weaknesses and, no matter how hard you try, you can never eliminate all the weaknesses in any single study. You simply have to make choices that maximize the amount of useful information your study provides, while minimizing the number of problems you experience.

When we actively make changes in a situation to see how these changes affect behavior, we are likely to be using an experimental or quasi-experimental approach that looks at groups created specifically for comparison in a study. A **quasi-experiment** is like an experiment in some ways, but involves somewhat less control over some variables. If we are not to manipulate anything, we could adopt observational or survey techniques.

Sometimes we are interested in getting an extensive amount of information from our research participants. In using a detailed **case study** of one or a few individuals, we gain a rich and complex base of information. We can also study people repeatedly over time, using **longitudinal studies**.

If we are interested in a more holistic depiction of people, their attitudes, and their feelings rather than numerical information, we can use an approach known as qualitative research. Qualitative research typically does not rely on manipulating variables or measuring behavior quantitatively. Rather, a qualitative researcher observes behavior patterns and tries to interpret the behaviors without resorting to numerical analysis.

Finally, sometimes we can find out about behaviors and attitudes by studying existing records or other materials, which constitutes **archival research**. Ultimately, they all provide part of the picture of behavior that we can combine for fuller understanding.

Approaches to Psychological Research

Let's take a specific example. Suppose you wanted to see if stress level is associated with learning. Given that students report high stress levels, this could be a very important question. One decision you must make pertains to whether you would manipulate a person's stress level directly or whether you would simply measure the stress level as it naturally occurs.

Observational Research—Investigation that relies on studying behaviors as they naturally occur, without any intervention by the researcher.

Correlational Research—Investigation meant to discover whether variables covary—that is, whether there are predictable relationships among measurements of different variables.

If you decided not to actively manipulate a person's stress level for ethical or other reasons, you could make use of **observational research**, noting how people or animals behave in situations that are likely to lead to stress responses. By choosing simply to observe behaviors, psychologists engage in descriptive research. There are varied ways to conduct such studies. They all involve specifying particular behaviors and the behavioral and environmental contexts in which they occur.

An alternative strategy would be to measure a person's existing stress level and try to relate it to the amount of learning that takes place. This method involves **correlational research**. This strategy would avoid the ethical dilemma of elevating stress, but the downside is that you wouldn't know if changes in stress actually cause changes in the amount that a person learns.

Consider the situation of a student who is taking classes for which she is not prepared; she might have difficulty learning the material. When she recognizes that fact, it could lead to stress. There would be a relationship between stress and learning, but the causal factor is not the stress; in this example, the stress is the result.

On the other hand, people with naturally high stress levels may not learn well because they can't concentrate well. In this case there would still be a relationship between stress and learning, with the stress being the cause of poor learning.

The problem is that with a correlational design, there may be a predictable relationship between stress level and learning, but you do not know if stress affected learning, if learning affected the stress level, or if something else affected them both. If you don't actively manipulate stress levels experimentally (which could put people at risk), you can describe and maybe predict the connection between stress and learning, but you can't explain the causal mechanism.

If you actively manipulate stress to see how it affects behavior, you will be using experimental research. With an experiment, you control the research situation, which is clearly an advantage. In this approach, you would randomly assign participants to groups, expose them to different treatments, then see if the people in the groups behave differently from one another. In this example, you manipulate stress level to see what effect your manipulation has on some other behavior. The measured behavior that might change depending on stress level is the amount of learning that occurs.

Sometimes you might wish to compare groups to see if they differ in their learning as a result of different levels of stress, but you use preexisting groups such as women and men or people from different cultural groups. Such a design would resemble an experiment but, because people come to your experiment already belonging to a certain category, this variable isn't really manipulated. We refer to such a design as a quasi-experiment.

When researchers compare people from different cultural or ethnic groups, of necessity, they use quasi-experimental designs. As a result, it is impossible to identify the ultimate cause of any difference between the groups. It might be the variable of interest to the investigator, but it could be any number of any other variables. This uncertainty is a by-product of the fact that people in preexisting groups bring differences with them that may have nothing to do with the researcher's attempts at manipulation of variables.

You could also choose other approaches, such as a case study, in which you study a single individual's stress levels and the grades that person earns in classes. You can study the person in great depth over a long period of time. You end up with a lot of information about that person, which helps you put together a more complete picture of the behavior. Unfortunately, with such an approach, you do not know if this person's behavior is typical of other people. Case studies can be useful in formulating new research questions, but we have to consider whether it is prudent to use the behavior of a single individual as a model for people in general. Psychologists typically study groups rather than individuals, so case studies are relatively rare in the research literature.

The value of case studies (or case reports, as they are sometimes known) has been the subject of debate. One prestigious medical journal, the *Journal of the American Medical Association*, does not publish case studies. Other journals, like the *New England Journal of Medicine* and *Lancet*, appear to regard such reports as educational or as teaching tools.

Rare conditions may be of little use to practitioners and clinicians because of that rarity—most psychologists or medical personnel never see them. On the other hand, a report of unusual characteristics of a more frequent condition may be of greater use to practitioners.

Researchers do not cite case studies as frequently as they do other types of research. Nonetheless, a new journal, the *Journal of Medical Case Reports*, has begun publishing articles. It limits its articles to case studies (Gawrylewski, 2007a).

When we want to gather a lot of information about development over a period of time, we use longitudinal studies. Longitudinal research generally involves studying groups of people rather than individual people. This approach requires patience because observations can continue for months, years, and even decades. One of its advantages is that we could see the long-term effects of variables; long-range changes might be quite different than short-term effects.

It is even possible to study people's behaviors without ever being in contact with those people. Sometimes investigators engage in archival research in which they look at existing records to answer their questions. For instance, studying graduation rates during periods of social unrest may provide some insights into the link between stress due to social circumstances and educational attainment.

Recently, psychologists have increased the use of qualitative research. This approach doesn't rely on numerical information but often uses complex description to characterize the way people respond to a situation or experience it. Analyses of behavior in qualitative studies often involve discussions of how people experience and feel about events in their lives. So a study of stress and learning with qualitative research might focus on how people react to a situation when they are trying to learn and they feel stressed.

Table 4.3 presents some of the methodologies that psychologists use to study behavior. These do not exhaust all possibilities, but they represent the major strategies in our research.

Selecting Research Materials and Procedures

The details of your research include the materials and apparatus that you use to carry out your project. For example, if you are investigating the connection between stress and learning, you need to develop materials that people will try to learn; your choice of the

TABLE 4.3   Major Methodologies that Psychologists Use to Study Behavior

Methodology	Main Characteristics	Advantages	Disadvantages
Experiments	Variables are actively manipulated and the environment is as controlled as possible.	You can eliminate many extraneous factors that might influence behavior, so you can study those of interest. Consequently, you can draw conclusions about causes of behavior.	You may create an artificial environment, so people act in ways that differ from typical. Sometimes, there are ethical issues about manipulating variables.
Quasi-experiments (and ex post facto studies)	The design of the study resembles an experiment, but the variables are not manipulated. Instead the researcher creates categories based on preexisting characteristics of participants, like gender.	You can eliminate some of the extraneous factors that might influence behavior (but less so than in true experiments). You can also spot predictable relationships, even if you do not know the cause of behaviors.	Because you do not control potentially important variables, you cannot affirm cause-and-effect relationships.
Correlational studies	You measure variables as they already exist, without controlling them.	You can spot predictable behavior patterns. In addition, you do not strip away complicating variables, so you can see how behavior emerges in a natural situation.	You cannot assess what variables predictably cause behaviors to occur.
Surveys, tests, and questionnaires	You ask for self-reported attitudes, knowledge, statements of behavior from respondents.	You can collect a significant amount of diverse information easily. In some cases, you can compare your data with established response patterns from other groups who have been studied.	You do not know how accurately or truthfully your respondents report their behaviors and attitudes. You cannot spot cause-and-effect relationships.
Case studies	You study a single person or a few people in great depth, so you know a lot about them.	You can study people in their complexity and take their specific characteristics into account in trying to understand behavior.	You may not be able to generalize beyond the person or small group. They may not be representative of people in general.
Observational research	You study behaviors in their natural settings without intervening (in most cases).	You can study life and behavior in its complexity.	There are so many factors that influence behavior in the natural world that you cannot be sure why people act as they do.

TABLE 4.3   Continued

Methodology	Main Characteristics	Advantages	Disadvantages
Longitudinal research	You study people's behaviors over a long period of time.	You can see how behaviors change over time, particularly as an individual develops and matures.	This research may take weeks, months, or years to complete. In addition, people may change because society changes, not only because of their personal maturation.
Archival research	You use existing records and information to help you answer your research question, even though that information was gathered for other reasons.	You can trace information historically and use multiple sources to address your research question.	The information was gathered for purposes different than yours, so the focus may be different. You also do not know how accurate the records are or what information is missing.
Qualitative research	You study people in their natural environment and try to understand them holistically. There is reliance on descriptive rather than quantitative information.	You can gain useful insights into the complexity of people's behaviors. Very often the focus is on the meaning of text or conversation, rather than on its subcomponents.	This research often takes considerably longer than quantitative research and can involve painstaking analysis of the qualitative data. Some researchers do not like the fact that numerical analysis is not critical to this approach.

type of stimuli (complex or abstract ideas, classroom materials, nonsense syllables, words, pictures, foreign words, etc.) may affect your outcome. For example, researchers have known since your grandparents were children that more meaningful material is easier to remember than less meaningful information (Glaze, 1928).

In connection with stress, the choice of material to be learned could be critical. For example, Gadzella, Masten, and Stacks (1998) reported that when students were stressed, they didn't think very deeply about material to be learned. As such, if you wanted to see if stress affected learning, you might get a different result by using simple versus complex material. Similarly, Heuer, Spijkers, Kiesswetter, and Schmidtke (1998) found that stressors impaired the performance of more or less automatic, routine tasks, but not tasks that required more attention. Once again, your results might differ dramatically if you chose a learning task that required considerable attention.

Why Methodology Is Important

How you decide to test your participants is critical. For instance, psychologists have studied how easy it is to learn lists of frequently occurring words versus relatively rare words. Do you think it would be easier to remember common words or uncommon words?

Some creative, excellent psychological research has revealed that more common words are remembered better. Other just as creative and excellent psychological research has shown that less common words are easier to remember.

These conflicting results do not make much sense until you know about the details of the research. There are several ways to test a person's memory. One of them is to ask the person to recall as many words as possible from a list. When we do this, people tend to recall more common words better than less common words (Wallace, Sawyer, & Robertson, 1979).

On the other hand, we could give a test of recognition memory. In this case, we would present a large group of words and ask the individual to identify which words had occurred during the learning phase of the study. Thus, the learners do not need to search through memory; they simply have to identify the words they saw before. This methodology leads to better memory for less frequent words (Underwood & Freund, 1970).

Generations of students know about the relative ease of recognition compared to recall. "College students are aware of this fact and notoriously rely less on thorough preparation for objective (multiple choice) tests than for tests which demand recall. Recognition makes no demands upon availability of items," as Deese and Hulse (1967, p. 378) noted nearly half a century ago.

When you think about it, it makes sense that a recall task favors common words, whereas recognition favors less frequently occurring words. When you try to recall information, you have to search through memory for possibilities. Regarding your memory for words, you can recall more frequent words because they are easier to generate as possibilities in the first place. You have a harder time with infrequent words because you are less likely to generate them, so you don't consider them as possibilities.

As this example shows, your research methodology is important to the development of your ideas. The conclusions you draw from your research result from the way you do your research. No matter what kind of research project you plan, if you overlook the importance of your methodology, you will not have a full understanding of the question you want to answer.

CHOOSING YOUR PARTICIPANTS OR SUBJECTS

Population—The entire set of people or data that are of interest to a researcher.

Fifty years ago, psychologists studied the behaviors of rats as much as the behaviors of people. We are in a different era now and we ask different questions, so we mostly study human behavior (Plous, 1996a).

The group that we are interested in understanding constitutes our **population**. It varies in different research projects. If we are interested in stress and learning in college students, then college students constitute the population. If we are interested in how the "typical" person learns, our population consists of college students and many others. If we want to study animal behavior, then a type of animal may constitute our population.

Sample—A subset of the population that is studied in a research project.

Representative Sample—A subset of the population in a research project that resembles the entire population with respect to variables being measured.

Other than in a census, we seldom have access to the entire population, and it would be too costly to observe the entire group even if we could get to them all. So we use a subset of the population, our **sample**. When the sample is similar to the population, we say we have a **representative sample**.

The decisions we make about studying people involve such questions as who we will study, how we will recruit them for our research, how many people we will test, and in what conditions we will study them. We make some very practical choices. The decisions that we make depend in many cases on exactly what questions we want to ask.

The Nature of Your Participants

In general, psychologists do research with organisms that are easiest to study. Can you figure out some of the characteristics of these organisms? This question is important because it determines the type of research questions you can ask.

The typical research subject turns out to be a young, highly educated, cooperative, motivated, female psychology student. Wouldn't you want to work with people with those characteristics? Professional researchers are like you—they want to do their work with the greatest efficiency and the least inconvenience.

Rosenthal and Rosnow (1975) investigated volunteering rates for women and men; they discovered that women tend to volunteer more than men, although the nature of the research project affects this tendency. Rosenthal and Rosnow looked at research during an era in which men were likely to outnumber women in psychology classes; the reverse is true today, so the number of female volunteers will typically outnumber the number of males by a wide margin. For very practical reasons, having access to such a population of willing volunteers (i.e., students in psychology classes) means that psychologists are going to rely on that group of people.

The good news is that when students volunteer to participate in research, they will show up and do what you tell them. The bad news is that we don't always know whether such participants from psychology classes at a single college or university resemble the entire population. Do older people or younger people act the same way? Do less well-educated people act the same way? Do people from other parts of the country act the same way?

We don't know the answers to these questions. So why do we continue to rely on this very restricted population? The answer is because they are there. It would be more time consuming and difficult to locate a more diverse group who might not want to participate in a research study anyway.

Table 4.4 presents information about the number and the nature number of participants and statistical and typical of research in some journals. As you can see, experimental work typically features students, generally undergraduates. Articles in experimental journal like the *Journal of Experimental Psychology: General* (*JEP: General*) and the *Journal of Personality and Social Psychology* (*JPSP*) provide very little detail about the characteristics of the participants. Traditionally, experimental psychologists assumed that we could study any population in order to understand behavior in general; they reasoned that the details of particular groups might differ, but the patterns would be valid across all of them. We now recognize that this could be a problem if we want to know about generalizing results to different populations. As you can see from Table 4.4, psychology still relies heavily on convenience samples that are quite restricted in scope.

Such a pattern could obscure important differences in understanding behavior. For instance, psychologists have begun studying patterns of online friendships (Novotney, 2012). One question concerns whether online communications differ fundamentally from in-person relationships. Conclusions about this issue could differ depending on who participates in research. Ramírez-Esparza, Mehl, Álvarez-Bermúdez, and Pennebaker (2009)

TABLE 4.4   Examples of Descriptions of Participants in the First Issues of Three Major Psychological Journals in 2012 (Unless otherwise designated, students are from U.S. universities.)

Journal of Experimental Psychology: General

Title of Article	Participant Characteristics
Internal representations reveal cultural diversity in expectations of facial expressions of emotion	15 adults from the United Kingdom and North America with a mean age 27.3 years; 8 men and 7 women
	15 adults from Asian countries with a mean age 23.5 years; 5 men and 10 women
Washing away your (good or bad) luck: Physical cleansing affects risk-taking behavior	**Study 1:** 59 business students at a North American university
	Study 2: 147 students and staff from a university in Hong Kong
Culture, attention, and emotion	**Study 1:**
	64 students (30 women, 34 men) from a university in the United States; mean age 18.8 years
	69 students (48 women, 21 men) in a Russian university; mean age 19.0 years
	Study 2: 47 students (27 women, 20 men) from a Latvian university; mean age 20.5 years
Chess masters show a hallmark of face processing with chess	69 student chess players (27 experts, 22 recreational players, 20 novices); mean age 21.9, 24.6, and 23.1 years, respectively
Rocking to the beat: Effects of music and partner's movements on spontaneous interpersonal coordination	48 (23 women, 25 men) students; mean age 19.0 years
Sensorimotor coupling in music and the psychology of the groove	**Study 1:** 153 students (90 women, 63 men); mean age 20.8 years
	Study 2: 34 undergraduate students (25 women, 9 men); mean age 20.6 years
A frog in your throat or in your ear? Searching for the causes of poor singing	**Study 1:** Participants were 25 nonmusicians (15 women, 10 men) and 13 musicians (six women, seven men) from the Université de Montreal population; mean age 23.1 and 22.9 years, respectively
	Study 2 and 3: 31 participants (18 women, 13 men); mean age 22.7 years
	Study 4: 16 nonmusicians (12 women, 4 men); mean age 23.19 years
	Study 5: 28 nonmusicians (24 women, 4 men) and 15 musicians (12 women and three men); mean age 21.9 years
Aversive life events enhance human freezing responses	50 female, Dutch university students; mean age 20.6 years

TABLE 4.4   **Continued**

Journal of Personality and Social Psychology (Issue 1, 2012)

Title of Article	Participant Characteristics
Buyer's remorse or missed opportunity? Differential regrets for material and experiential purchases	**Study 1:** 56 Cornell undergraduates **Study 2:** 84 participants (46 women, 38 men); age span 18–61 years. Recruited through Amazon's Mechanical Turk **Study 3:** 75 Cornell undergraduates **Study 4:** 66 participants (38 women, 28 men,); mean age 34 years; recruited through Amazon's Mechanical Turk **Study 5:** 62 participants (33 men, 29 women) recruited through Amazon's Mechanical Turk
The infection of bad company: Stigma by association	**Study 1:** 98 undergraduates (30 men, 66 women, and 2 who chose not to disclose their gender) **Study 2:** 209 students (177 women, 30 men, and 2 people not identifying their gender); median age 19 years, 80% self-described as White/Non-Hispanic, and the rest were scattered across various racial/ethnic groups
Negative moods and the motivated remembering of past selves: The role of implicit theories of personal stability	**Study 1a:** 128 Simon Fraser University (SFU) undergraduates (23 male and 105 female); mean age 21.5 years **Study 1b:** 250 students (113 male and 137 female); mean age 20.8 years **Study 2a:** 89 undergraduates (25 male, 64 female); mean age 21.4 years **Study 2b:** 183 SFU and Wilfrid Laurier University (WLU) students (50 male, 133 female); mean age 20.5 years **Study 3a:** 103 students (34 male, 69 female); mean age 20.3 years **Study 4a:** 38 undergraduates (24 female, 14 male); mean age 21.0 years **Study 4b:** 346 undergraduates (75 male, 271 female) from SFU and WLU
On the perpetuation of ignorance: System dependence, system justification, and the motivated avoidance of sociopolitical information	**Study 1:** 48 students (27 men, 20 women, one unidentified) **Study 2:** 48 students (27 men, 20 women, one unidentified) **Study 3:** 163 Americans (70 men, 93 women); mean age 32.5, recruited using an online recruitment Web site **Study 4:** 197 American participants (86 men, 111 women); mean age 35.72 years; 97 employed, 18 freelance/self-employed, 7 retired, 18 homemaker, 25 unemployed, 30 student, and 2 unidentified; recruited through an online recruitment Web site **Study 5:** A Canadian public sample of 58 (20 men, 38 women); mean age 42.88; 35 employed, 8 retired, 6 disabled, 5 homemaker, 2 unemployed, and 2 not reported
Status conferral in intergroup social dilemmas: Behavioral antecedents and consequences of prestige and dominance	**Study 1:** 66 students (62.9% female, 37.1% men) mean age 21.2 years **Study 2:** 60 students (69% female, 31% male); mean age 21 years **Study 3:** 61 students (60% female, 40% male); mean age 22 years

(continued)

TABLE 4.4   Continued

Journal of Applied Psychology

Title of Article	Participant Characteristics
Bottom-line mentality as an antecedent of social undermining and the moderating roles of core self-evaluations and conscientiousness	Focal employee respondents ($N = 113$)
	■ 48.3% male and 50.3% female, and 1.4% did not indicate their sex
	■ 6.8% African American, 8.8% Asian American, 58.5% Caucasian, 15.6% Latino/a, 6.1% Hispanic, 1.4% Native American, 1.4% biracial, and 1.4% other
	■ 30.4% employed part-time, 69.6% employed full-time
	■ Mean age 25.37 years
	Coworker respondents ($N = 113$)
	■ 46.4% male and 53.6% female
	■ 5.8% African American, 5.1% Asian American, 64.5% Caucasian, 9.4% Latino/a, 8.0% Hispanic, 1.4% Native American, 3.6% biracial, and 2.2% other
	■ 30.4% employed part-time, 69.6% employed full-time
	■ Mean age 30.79 years
	Supervisor respondents ($N = 113$)
	■ 59.1% male and 40.9% female
	■ 7.3% African American, 5.8% Asian American, 65.0% Caucasian, 12.4% Latino/a, 4.4% Hispanic, 1.5% Native American, 0.7% biracial, and 2.9% other
	■ 2.9% employed part-time, 97.1% employed full-time
	Mean age 38.68 years
More than just the mean: Moving to a dynamic view of performance-based compensation	131 NBA players
	■ 29 franchises
	■ Mean age, 29 years
	Mean tenure in NB+A 6.9 years
Does power corrupt or enable? When and why power facilitates self-interested behavior	**Study 1**
	173 working adults
	■ 57.9% men and 42.1% women
	■ Mean age 41.45
	■ 79.9% White, 11.8%, Black, 5.6% Hispanic, 2.0% Asian, and 0.5% Native American; 0.2% no response
	■ Average tenure on the job 4.28 years
	Study 2
	102 undergraduates
	■ 37% men, 73% women
	Mean age 20.32 years

TABLE 4.4   Continued

Title of Article	Participant Characteristics
Testing the efficacy of a new procedure for reducing faking on personality tests within selection contexts	157 applicants ■ Competitors for 10 staff positions at a large Chinese university ■ 49 (31%) were male ■ Mean age 26 years old, all had at least a master's degree.
Choosing and using geospatial displays: Effects of design on performance and metacognition	**Study 1:** 38 students (20 women, 18 men); age range 18–22 **Study 2:** 26 undergraduate students (13 women, 13 men); age range 18–22

reported that people from Mexico and people from the United States differed in the sociability as a function of whether communications were natural or online. Mexicans were more sociable in person, whereas those in the United States were more sociable online. It would not be surprising to discover that within a given country, subgroups differed in their sociability because of cultural traditions.

Investigators studying more applied questions usually give greater detail about the people they study, including age, gender, and ethnicity. This makes sense if you consider the point of much **applied research**, which is to identify answers to questions related to specific situations or well-defined groups.

> **Applied Research—**
> Research that attempts to address practical questions rather than theoretical questions.

Deciding How Many Participants to Include

After we identify our participant population, we need to decide how many people we will study. The greater the sample size, the more time and effort it will take to complete the research. At the same time, if we test small samples, we diminish the chance of finding statistically significant results and increase the relative size of error in generalizing our results to our population. Berkowitz (1992) has commented that, in social psychology, research typically relies on sample sizes that are too small. Investigators may miss potentially important and interesting findings as a result. The larger your sample, the more likely you are to spot differences that are real, even if they are small. With smaller samples, we may detect large differences, but miss the small ones.

One of the other principles that should guide you in determining how many people to include in your research project involves variability. When you measure people, they will naturally produce different scores. Some of the discrepancy results from the fact that people differ due to intelligence, motivation, energy levels, and other personal characteristics. As a result, when you test them in a research setting, differences will emerge independent of any variables you are interested in. The greater the amount of variability among your participants to begin with, the harder it will be to spot changes in behavior due to different treatments. If you separated them into groups, they would show some differences regardless of whether you treated them differently. With groups of very different types of people, you might wind up with two groups that look very different only because the people start out different.

Consider this situation: Suppose you wanted to manipulate a variable and create a treatment group and a control group. You could assemble your sample and assign each person to one of the two conditions. Then you would expose one group to the treatment and leave the other group untreated. Finally, you would measure them to see if the two groups behaved differently.

If your participants were fairly similar to one another at the beginning, the effect of any treatment would be easier to spot because any differences in behavior would probably be due to that treatment. On the other hand, if the people were quite different before your manipulation, you might not know if any differences between groups were due to initial differences or to your manipulation.

The similarity among your participants is not the only factor influencing the sample size in your research. An additional consideration involves whether you think your manipulation will have a big or a small effect. The effect of your treatment might be real and consistent, but it might be small. For instance, if a teacher smiled at students in one class as they entered a classroom to take a test, it might relax them so their performance increased. The improvement would probably be fairly small, reflecting a small treatment effect. In order to be able to see a difference in scores because of a smiling teacher, you would need a large group of students.

On the other hand, if the teacher announced in advance that there would be particular questions on a test, this manipulation would have a big effect. You would not need such a large sample to see the effects of the information given to the students.

If your research manipulation is likely to have a large effect, you can get away with smaller samples, especially if your participants are relatively similar to begin with. If your manipulation has only a small effect, you will need larger samples to spot differences between groups, particularly if your participants differ from one another noticeably before the experiment begins. You cannot always know in advance how big your effect size will be, although the more you know about the research that others have done, the better your prediction will be. You also do not know how homogeneous your samples are, but on some campuses, the population is likely to be more homogeneous than the population as a whole; on other campuses, there is enough diversity that the campus may resemble the larger population. They are similar to one another, even if they differ from the vast array of people in general. The bottom line is to test as many people as possible so even small effects show up if they exist.

■ ■ ■ ■ ■

CONTROVERSY:
Can Animal Research Help Us Understand Human Stress?

Psychologists have had a long tradition of studying animals and then generalizing the animal behaviors to humans. Over the years, some people have objected to characterizing people as susceptible to the same factors that affect animals. So it is an important and interesting question as to whether studies of animals in a laboratory pertain to human behavior.

It would be helpful if we knew more about how to deal with stress responses so that, when tragedies occur, people can receive treatment. In order to devise maximally effective treatment, it is necessary to know how and why the responses develop.

Such researchers have found that mice who experience stressors that they cannot control (e.g., being forced to swim for 10 minutes) experience changes in the limbic system and affect the rate of extinction of fear responses conditioned to a tone. That is, they develop fear but cannot extinguish it. Additional research with animals has demonstrated that rats that experience chronic stress show less extinction of fear response than rats who are not stressed (Miracle et al., 2006; Schulz, Buddenberg, & Huston, 2007). In addition, in rats bred to show characteristics of learned helplessness, extinction of fear responses is retarded (Schulz et al., 2007).

On the other hand, investigators have also found that other substances can foster extinction of fear responses in mice (Cai et al., 2006; Varvel et al., 2007) and fish (Barreto, Volpato, & Pottinger, 2006).

All of the research just cited involves animals. Because it would be unethical to induce chronic stress in humans or to conduct experiments that might worsen symptoms of stress, psychologists have resorted to studying stress in animals. The big question is whether what is true for rats, mice, and fish also holds true for people.

There is evidence that the same patterns of failure or success in extinguishing fear responses that occur in trout (e.g., Barreto et al., 2006), in mice (e.g., Cai et al., 2006), and in rats (e.g., Miracle et al., 2006) may be at work in people (Felmingham et al., 2007). The same kinds of processes in the brain seem to be occurring in people and in animals who experience anxiety and stress (e.g., Rauch, Shin, & Phelps, 2006). Researchers appear to have reached consensus that animal models can provide the basis for the development treatment of anxiety and stress disorders in people (Anderson & Insel, 2006).

Thus, research with animals like rodents and fish have given us clues about the development and treatment of psychiatric disorders. Such developments are important because of the high levels of stress many people experience. For instance, after the terrorist attacks in the United States in 2001, many people had significant stress reactions, even if they were not directly affected by the attacks (Melnik et al., 2002). In addition, evidence suggests that students also experienced stress reactions (MacGeorge, Samter, Feng, Gillihan, & Graves, 2004). With constantly occurring stress events, we probably should not expect a reduction in psychological problems, particularly in light of data showing that stress and anxiety among college students at one institution increased by 73 percent between 1992 and 2001 (Benton et al., 2003).

It seems that we can use all the help we can get from the animals studied by researchers.

Question for Discussion: How can researchers gain confidence that their research results with animals pertain to people?

DIFFERING APPROACHES IN DIFFERENT AREAS OF PSYCHOLOGY

When psychologists plan research projects, we often use methods that others before us have developed. It is easier to use a strategy that somebody else has adopted successfully and reported in a journal article than to create your own.

The advantage of relying on the research procedures of others is that they have worked through the problems that arise in developing a new approach. In addition, the previous researchers have developed appropriate materials. As a result, we don't have to repeat the initial errors and false starts of other investigators.

Different Approaches in Different Journals

It is instructive to look at the published work of psychologists, that is, the literature of psychology, to see what decisions they have made in their work. If you look at Table 4.4, you will see that the articles that appear in different journals reflect different decisions by scientists as they develop their research projects. Because the American Psychological Association is the largest group of psychologists in the world, with about 150,000 members, and because APA publishes some of the most prestigious journals in psychology, you should expect that the articles in those journals reflect mainstream thinking in our field. As you can see in the table, journals have established different traditions.

In *JEP: General*, the research is almost entirely experimental. In contrast, in the *Journal of Applied Psychology* (*JAP*), the studies are correlational. The investigators simply make different decisions regarding how to answer their research questions.

The statistical approaches also reveal an interesting picture. Applied research often relies on correlational analysis, whereas experimental, laboratory research typically implies the use of analysis of variance (ANOVA) and *t*-tests that help us spot differences across groups.

Different Types of Participants in Different Journals

Another difference in the articles across journals involves the participants. Articles in the realm of applied psychology often employ more and diverse participants. Laboratory studies typically involve many more women than men, mostly students. Applied, workplace studies often have as many or more men than women, especially studies of managers.

Studies in the workplace are likely to be correlational rather than experimental; they are often survey studies. As a result, it is relatively inexpensive to get information from more people. As you can see in Table 4.4, the sample sizes are much larger for the *JAP* than for the *JEP: General* articles.

The greater the diversity among participants, the more confidence we have when we state that our research results will extend to different people. Especially for applied psychological research, we want our results to relate (i.e., to generalize) to others. Generalizability allows us to feel confident that our findings are not specific to a single group of people. Experimental approaches typically rely on undergraduate students, usually psychology students. We need to consider whether the results of such research would be the same if the investigators relied on a different sample. We often do not know the answer to these questions.

Making Choices in Your Research Design

As a researcher, you have limited time, energy, and money, so it is often not possible to conduct both a laboratory study and a field study. Consequently, you choose one and try to get the greatest amount of information from it.

At this point, it should be clear why it is important that scientific research be public. If you read about an experimental study done in a lab, you might question whether the same behaviors would occur in a more realistic setting. You could take the idea and develop a similar approach in the workplace. Most likely, the managers of the work setting are not going to let you disrupt their business with experimental manipulations, so you have to rely on correlational approaches. In the end, two projects relate to a common question, each with a different methodology.

We hope that both studies lead to similar conclusions. When they do, psychologists say that the research results have a type of validity called convergent validity. If not, we try to figure out why the two approaches led to different conclusions, which means doing more research. Because so many variables influence human behavior, we can be assured that each research project will provide only a small piece of the puzzle and that we will need many different projects and many different methodologies in order to assemble a complete picture of the behavior.

If you use a jigsaw puzzle as an analogy to research, you might say that we have a puzzle consisting of a great number of pieces and that occasionally we find that somebody has thrown pieces from another puzzle into our box. We often don't know that the odd piece has come from another puzzle until we spend a lot of time trying to make it fit. When we become aware that the stray piece belongs to a different puzzle, we toss it out. The good news is that we become aware of another interesting puzzle to work on later.

SUMMARY

Once you decide the general nature of your research question, you have to make a lot of practical decisions about how exactly to conduct your study. These practical decisions can make a big difference both in the shape your research takes and the conclusions you draw. Researchers studying similar questions often take very different paths to their answers.

A good place to begin any project is through a literature search. By investigating how others have approached research like yours, you can avoid having to reinvent techniques that have already worked for others. If you find useful ways of creating and measuring variables of interest to you, it only makes good sense for you to use them if they are appropriate. This is perfectly acceptable as long as you give credit to the researchers who developed the ideas initially. In some cases, however, you might want to create different ways of approaching the question because you might not be able to find anybody else who approached your question quite the way you would like. This is an example of the kind of practical decision you will make when setting up your project.

A different decision is to identify the group of people you will study. You will have to decide how you will contact them and how to convince them to participate. Psychologists very often solicit participation from students in beginning psychology classes who receive extra credit for their participation. It can be harder to get participants from other populations. The risk in using student samples is that you are not sure that your results generalize beyond that particular type of person.

Finally, it is important to remember that psychologists with different specialties will approach related questions very differently. Various areas of psychology have developed their own traditions regarding methodological approaches.

REVIEW QUESTIONS

Multiple Choice Questions

1. When you complete a literature search, you can
    a. avoid engaging in replication with extension.
    b. identify the different approaches used by various researchers to address the same question.
    c. ensure that you do not use a similar means to identify and create variables.
    d. make sure that you do not use measurements that everybody else has.
2. Because psychology involves trying to understand complex and abstract concepts, researchers need to develop _____ in order to make useful measurements of those concepts.
    a. operational definitions.
    b. hypothetical constructs.
    c. literature searches.
    d. independent variables.

3. When psychologists develop their experiments, they will decide what they want to manipulate as part of the experimental procedure. The variable controlled by the experimenter is the _____ variable.
   a. hypothetical.
   b. construct.
   c. extraneous.
   d. independent.

4. When you choose your operational definitions in the research you conduct, you have to remember that
   a. there is usually a single best way to deal with complex concepts.
   b. there is usually a great deal of controversy associated with selecting an operational definition.
   c. it is important to operationally define your variable so that it is meaningful across a wide range of cultures.
   d. different operational definitions of the same concept lead to different research questions and can generate different results.

5. If psychologists want to study the interactions among children on a playground, they are likely to choose
   a. experiments.
   b. quasi-experiments.
   c. observational research.
   d. correlational research.

6. If a journal article has a title like "The relation between political beliefs and activism in students," it is likely to be
   a. observational research.
   b. correlational research.
   c. experimental research.
   d. longitudinal research.

7. If an investigator wanted to study the differences in speed of problem solving in young versus old adults, the approach is likely to be
   a. observational research.
   b. correlational research.
   c. case study research.
   d. quasi-experimental research.

8. Researchers have studied the effects of traumatic events, like experiencing devastating hurricanes, on children over an extended period of time. Such research is
   a. observational research.
   b. qualitative research.
   c. experimental research.
   d. longitudinal research.

9. The systematic elimination of extraneous variables other than those you are interested in can be eliminated in what research design?
   a. qualitative research.
   b. correlational research.
   c. experimental research.
   d. longitudinal research.

10. Research involving a single person who is studied in great depth is characteristic of
    a. survey research.
    b. longitudinal research.

    c. case studies.

    d. qualitative research.

11. If a sample in a study is generally the same as the population, we say the sample is

    a. representative.

    b. reliable.

    c. constructed.

    d. dependent.

12. When an experiment makes use of a small number of participants, the results

    a. are easier to replicate than when there are many participants.

    b. may miss potentially important findings because research with small samples is not very sensitive.

    c. small differences between groups are easier to spot than with large numbers of participants.

    d. are seldom valid.

13. It is easier to spot differences among groups when research involves small samples if

    a. the investigator uses probability sampling.

    b. the participants are homogeneous regarding the behavior to be studied.

    c. the effect sizes for the behavior to be studied are also small.

    d. the hypothetical constructs are operationally defined.

14. Research articles that appear in the *Journal of Applied Psychology* are likely to be

    a. laboratory based.

    b. experimental.

    c. basic.

    d. correlational.

15. When research projects on a given topic lead to similar conclusions, the measurements show

    a. convergent validity.

    b. criterion validity.

    c. interrater validity.

    d. construct validity.

Essay Questions

16. Why is applied research often conducted outside a formal laboratory, whereas theoretical research generally takes place in a laboratory?

17. We hope to be able to generalize our research results to people other than those who actually participated in our research. For the typical psychology study, why is it hard to determine the people to whom our research will generalize?

ANSWERS TO REVIEW ANSWERS

Answers to Multiple Choice Questions

1. b	6. b	11. a
2. a	7. d	12. b
3. d	8. d	13. b
4. d	9. c	14. d
5. c	10. c	15. a

Answers to Essay Questions

16. Why is applied research often conducted outside a formal laboratory, whereas theoretical research generally takes place in a laboratory?

Suggested points:

Applied research very often answers a specific question about behaviors in a natural setting. As such, it may be important to study behaviors in the environments in which they typically occur, rather than in a restricted and somewhat artificial atmosphere of the lab.

On the other hand, in theoretical research, investigators are frequently interested in the effect of a variable that has a consistent, but small, effect on behavior. In such a situation, it makes sense to eliminate variables that have big effects on behavior that will obscure the effects of variables that have smaller effects. One way to get rid of the larger effects of variables you aren't interested in is to control the environment very carefully, which is easiest to do in a lab.

17. We hope to be able to generalize our research results to people other than those who actually participated in our research. For the typical psychology study, why is it hard to determine the people to whom our research will generalize?

Suggested points:

Most psychological research with people involves undergraduate psychology students, the majority of whom are female. So we are likely to be able to generalize to other young, educated women, although it isn't always clear if we can generalize to men or to people younger or older than the female college students. For some measurements, the participants we use may be representative of many other people, but for other measurements (e.g., attitudes), the participants may not be like older or younger people or men, or even female students at other schools or in different parts of the country or in other countries.

The issue is complicated because, for some measurements, our participants produce very similar results to many other groups (e.g., speed of learning one type of material versus another), whereas for other measurements (e.g., attitudes toward abortion), participants in a single location may not be like others.

CHAPTER FIVE

■ ■ ■ ■ ■

MEASUREMENT AND SAMPLING

CHAPTER OVERVIEW

LEARNING OBJECTIVES ■ **KEY TERMS** ■ **CHAPTER PREVIEW**

PSYCHOLOGICAL CONCEPTS
Measuring Complex Concepts
Operational Definitions

DEFINING AND MEASURING VARIABLES
The Importance of Culture and Context in
Defining Variables

MULTIPLE POSSIBLE OPERATIONAL DEFINITIONS

PROBABILITY SAMPLING
Simple Random Sampling
Systematic Sampling
Stratified Random Sampling
Cluster Sampling

NONPROBABILITY SAMPLING
Convenience Sampling
Quota Sampling
Purposive (Judgmental) Sampling
Chain-Referral Sampling

MAKING USEFUL MEASUREMENTS
Reliability
Validity

CONSIDERING VALIDITY IN RESEARCH
Construct Validity

CONTROVERSY: *INTELLIGENCE*
Internal and External Validity
Statistical Conclusion Validity
Convergent and Divergent Validity
The SAT: Questions of Reliability and Validity

CONTROVERSY: *THE HEAD START PROGRAM*

SCALES OF MEASUREMENT
Nominal Scales
Ordinal Scales
Ratio and Interval Scales

SUMMARY

REVIEW QUESTIONS
Multiple Choice Questions
Essay Questions

ANSWERS TO REVIEW QUESTIONS
Answers to Multiple Choice Questions
Answers to Essay Questions

LEARNING OBJECTIVES

After going through this chapter, you will be able to:

- Identify different ways to operationally define hypothetical constructs
- Describe the rationale for using operational definitions
- Highlight the importance of culture in the definitions of variables and constructs
- Differentiate probability sampling and nonprobability sampling
- Describe the different types of probability samples
- Describe the different types of nonprobability samples
- Explain the concept of measurement error

- Describe how issues of reliability and validity relate to psychological measurement
- Identify the different types of reliability
- Identify the different types of validity
- Describe the process and purpose of random assignment of participants to groups
- Describe the different scales of measurement in research

KEY TERMS

CHAPTER PREVIEW

Psychological concepts are often abstract and complex. As a result, researchers create operational definitions that make these difficult concepts easier to measure. The operational definitions provide a concrete set of definitions that different researchers can understand and, in most cases, agree on.

When creating operational definitions to use in research, the investigators have to keep culture and context in mind. People from different backgrounds may respond in different ways to the same stimulus. So concepts may take on different operational definitions in different cultural contexts.

In addition to specifying operational definitions, researchers must also decide who they are going to sample and how they are going to do it. One general classification is called probability sampling. This approach requires identification of the population of interest and a well-specified means of selecting individuals for the research. The simplest and most well-known type is simple random sampling, in which every person in the population has an equal chance to participate in the research. But there are also complicated designs involving probability sampling. The benefit of these approaches is that researchers can be confident that the sample represents the population.

A more common approach in psychology is to use nonprobability samples. The main nonprobability approach is to use convenient samples, often of college students. Although these samples are quite convenient, there is some concern that the results may not pertain to a wider population.

After researchers collect their data, they must face the question as to whether their measurements and their results are reliable. That is, if the investigators were to conduct another similar study, would they obtain the same results? If measurements and results are reliable, they may also be valid. That is, the measurements and results might help answer the researchers' questions. There are multiple forms of reliability and validity that are relevant in different circumstances.

Finally, when researchers collect their data, the results are sometimes qualitative, involving how many observations fall into a category. At other times, the results are quantitative, leading to various types of statistical analysis. Depending on the type of measurement, some researchers believe that certain statistical tests may be inappropriate, but this is a controversial issue that has spawned considerable disagreement.

PSYCHOLOGICAL CONCEPTS

In an experiment, a researcher manipulates and controls at least one variable. A variable is a construct whose measurement can result in different values, and it is typically contrasted with a constant, which is something that stays the same. A score on a test to measure the severity of depression would be a variable because the score can vary from one person or time to another.

Every discipline that deals with complex issues has its own set of hypothetical constructs. For instance, in physics, the concept of gravity is a hypothetical construct. We can see the effects of gravity, and knowing about it helps us function in everyday life, but we still don't really know what it is.

We measure overt behaviors, but we assume that the behaviors reflect mental and emotional processes that we can't observe. Even if we can't define exactly the cognitive or neural processes associated with depression, intelligence, motivation, or other constructs, our sometimes imprecise measurements have nonetheless led us to a better understanding of people.

Measuring Complex Concepts

Just about every realm of psychology deals with complex and abstract concepts. Think of the different domains that psychologists investigate. Forensic psychologists might deal with whether a person is competent to stand trial or has understood the nature of a crime of which he or she is suspected; they can only make a decision based on a person's external responses and behaviors. Similarly, psychologists interested in intelligence can only identify behaviors that they think are related to intelligence. If developmental psychologists want to know if a child understands the world, they may see if the child shows conservation (e.g., the ability to recognize that the amount of a substance doesn't change simply because its shape does). The researchers will observe the child's response but will have to make educated guesses about cognitive processes.

What we need in our research are reasonable ways to measure complex concepts like the mental competence that the forensic psychologists seek, the "intelligence" that the cognitive psychologists want to measure, or the sophistication of thought that the developmental psychologists hope to understand.

As you see, in order to measure an abstraction, we need something with which to make a measurement. That sounds simple, but in practice, it is often quite difficult. For instance, how do you know if somebody is depressed? How do you know the extent to which the person is depressed?

To work with depression, we need a measurement that is reliable. That is, we want a measurement that will produce about the same result every time we measure the depression level of an individual (assuming that the person's level of depression hasn't changed). We need more than reliability, though. We also need a measurement that is valid, that is, a measurement that will help us make accurate predictions about a depressed person's behavior.

Table 5.1 shows some examples of operational definitions that researchers have used. In some cases, the investigators used the operational definitions to record outcome variables or to measure a person's current psychological state. In other cases, the researchers manipulated the person's psychological state to see the effect that the manipulation had on some behavior.

TABLE 5.1   Examples of Operational Definitions of Hypothetical Constructs

Independent variables (IV) reflect manipulated variables used for creating groups to compare; dependent, or measured, variables (DV) reflect variables that are either preexisting or are the result of manipulation of the IV. Some variables are not amenable for use as true IVs, such as intelligence, which can't be manipulated by the experimenter.

Concept	Operational Definition and Research Topic	References
Depression	1. Score on Beck Depression Inventory (DV)–Relation between positive life events and depression	1. Dixon and Reid (2000)
	2. The mental state a person is in after reading negative or positive statements (IV)	2. Boettger, Schwier, and Bär (2011); Velten (1968)
Intelligence	1. Score on Kaufman Assessment Battery for Children (DV)–Cognitive Processing of Learning Disabled children	1. Teeter and Smith (1989)
	2. Score on Raven's Progressive Matrices Test (DV)–Cognitive functioning of immigrants	2. Kozulin (1999)
Happiness	1. Self-report score; amount of smiling and facial muscle activity (DV)–Happiness in people with severe depression	1. Gehrick and Shapiro (2000)
	2. Score on Depression–Happiness Scale (DV)–(a) Subjective well-being; (b) religiosity	2. (a) Lewis, McCollam, and Joseph (2000); (b) French and Stephen (1999)
	3. Behavioral observations of happiness (DV)–Happiness in people with profound multiple disabilities	3. Green and Reid (1999)
	4. Mental state of a person after listening to fearful, sad, happy, and neutral nonverbal vocalizations (IV)–Neural responses to emotional vocalizations	4. Morris, Scott, and Dolan (1999)

Operational Definitions

How would you go about measuring depression or any other hypothetical construct? You have to start with an operational definition. When we use an operational definition, we discuss an abstract concept in terms of how we measure it. For example, a clinical psychologist can't just look at an individual and know the degree of depression the person is experiencing. Some diagnostic measurement tool is necessary. The score on a test would be our operational definition. We would define a high score as reflecting greater depression and a low score as reflecting less.

Researchers regularly use the Beck Depression Inventory (BDI) to assess levels of depression. For example, Dixon and Reid (2000) used the BDI to assess the depression levels of college students having varying numbers of positive and negative life events; Sundblom, Haikonen, Niemi-Pynttaeri, and Tigerstedt (1994) used the BDI to examine the effects of spiritual healing on chronic pain, which can lead to depression.

A simple self-report test like the BDI is not perfect, but it provides valuable information. One important point to remember is that the score on the BDI is on a continuum and can be low or high. Although there can be a cutoff for "depressed" versus "not depressed," this criterion is arbitrary.

In a research project, using a BDI score to measure an existing level of depression is helpful. But suppose a researcher wants to manipulate an individual's mood, creating a temporary, mild state that resembles depression to see how it changes the person's behavior. The researcher could use the experimental paradigm to start with nearly identical groups, treat one of them in a certain way (like inducing depression in the participants), then measure their behaviors to see if there are any differences in behaviors across groups.

Variable—An element in a research project that, when measured, can take on more than one value.

Quite a few researchers have studied the effects of mild, induced depression on behavior by inducing a depressed mood. For instance, Velten (1997) asked participants to read a series of statements that would either elevate or depress their mood. In this research, he operationally defined being in a depressed condition as having been exposed to the depressing statements.

DEFINING AND MEASURING VARIABLES

Operational Definition—A working definition of a complex or abstract idea that is based on how it is measured in a research project.

Hypothetical Construct—An idea or concept that is useful for understanding behavior and thought but that is complex and not directly observable.

As you plan your project, you need to translate your general ideas into concrete terms. In considering research on stress, this involves creating an operational definition of stress, which is our variable of interest here. A **variable** is something of interest to us that can take on different values.

Operational definitions are important in psychology because we deal with concepts that are hard to define in concrete terms. For instance, most people would agree that stress is a real psychological state. Unfortunately, it is completely internal, a set of feelings and responses that are hard to measure. It is a **hypothetical construct** because we are hypothesizing that it is psychologically real. In just about every area of psychology, we deal with hypothetical constructs for which we need adequate measurements and operational definitions.

If you intend to study stress, you have to figure out what observable measurements can represent this concept meaningfully. As shown in Table 4.2, Holmes and Rahe (1967) measured stress through the amount of change a person experiences in his or her life. Think about what they had to do. They had to ask people how much change the people had experienced. This is not an easy issue. First of all, what does it mean to go through change? There are big changes and there are little changes. There are good changes and there are bad changes. What kind of change is worth mentioning? In addition, how far back should people go in their lives when they think of change? Holmes and Rahe had to answer these questions (and more) in deciding how to measure change.

Their Social Readjustment Rating Scale (SRRS) indicates the level of change in one's life ranging from severe, like the death of a spouse, to minor, like a change in sleeping habits. When Miller and Rahe (1997) updated the SRRS, they found somewhat different degrees of perceived stress in current society. For reasons we don't understand, people report that the same events today invariably generate higher levels of stress than they used to. The researchers also found gender differences in ratings of the degree of stress of various events, a finding that did not occur in the original scale. As Table 4.2 reveals, change can be for the better or for the worse, but it all contributes to stress. Further, it can vary depending on the cultural context.

Subsequent research has shown that SRRS scores constitute a useful predictor of negative outcomes, like an increased likelihood of brain lesions in people with multiple sclerosis (Mohr et al., 2000) and hair loss among women (York, Nicholson, Minors, & Duncan, 1998). On the other hand, SRRS scores do not predict frequency or intensity of headaches, which are more predictable from the severity of a person's daily hassles (Fernandez & Sheffield, 1996).

When psychologists create experiments, one kind of variable they define is the independent variable (IV). This is the variable that they manipulate in order to see if changes in this variable will affect behavior. Thus, if a researcher wants to see whether research participants give more help to a person with a tattoo or without a tattoo, the IV is presence or absence of the tattoo. In such a study, the researcher might measure how long the person provides help. This measurement, which may change depending on whether somebody who asks for help has a tattoo, is called the dependent variable (DV). When Strohmetz and Moore (2003) conducted such a study, they discovered that when the person with a tattoo was dressed in sweatshirt and jeans, that person received more help than when the person was dressed more formally.

The Importance of Culture and Context in Defining Variables

It is important to remember that not everybody reacts the same way to a given change; in fact, in different cultures, the same amount of change leads to quite different amounts of stress. In the United States, the death of a spouse leads to much greater relative adjustment than it does in Japan (Ornstein & Sobel, 1987).

Subsequently, Renner and Mackin (1998) created a scale more suitable for many college students. The original SRRS included items involving dealing with in-laws, having mortgages, and other aspects of life that do not pertain to all students. So Renner and Mackin created a list of 51 events of relevance to students. These include being raped or finding that you are HIV-positive, which have the greatest impact weight of any items on the scale; difficulty with a roommate; maintaining a steady dating relationship; getting straight As; and attending a football game. This new scale has not been evaluated for validity, but it contains items that students associate with stress.

If you were studying stress and people's responses to it, you could measure stress levels through either of these scales. Change in a person's life is not exactly the same as stress, but a score on the scale would serve as a reasonable operational definition of stress. Like any operational definition, it is not perfect, but it should work within the cultural context in which it was developed. When used with people from different backgrounds, however, it may be less useful.

People from different groups may show varied types and degrees of stress in their lives, so we have to use caution in the statements we make about the effects of stress. For example, Broman (2005) investigated the relation between stress and substance abuse among college students. He discovered that you have to factor in both race and gender to understand alcohol use as it relates to stress. Black men showed fewer alcohol problems in reaction to stress when compared to Black women and to White men and women. Furthermore, White women show a greater extent of problems with alcohol than White men and Blacks following traumatic stress. Traumatic experiences are associated with heavy episodic drinking for White women only.

Furthermore, stress among people in different countries shows different causes. For example, Seiffge-Krenke et al. (2010) investigated stress in over 8,000 adolescents across 17 countries. The investigators found that different dimensions of life were relevant to levels of stress across varied regions. The levels of stress associated with the future (e.g., employment), romantic stress, and stress associated with personal identity varied across regions. So a one-size-fits-all approach to measuring stress would not be useful in spotting degree of perceived stress across cultures because the nature of stress and the triggering factors for stress vary widely.

MULTIPLE POSSIBLE OPERATIONAL DEFINITIONS

You could measure stress in many ways. If you took a physiological approach, you might measure the amount of cortisol in a person's bloodstream because this chemical results when an individual experiences stress. The advantage of using this particular operational definition is that you can measure the substance very accurately and immediately. The disadvantage is that such an approach would cost a lot of time and money, and it would be invasive for the person who provided the blood. Luckily, we can measure cortisol more easily with modern technology. The chemical can be measured through the simple means of getting a sample of a person's saliva. It would still be costly, but less invasive. You could also measure stress through a questionnaire, as Miller and Rahe (1997) and Renner and Mackin (1998) did. This measurement of stress would be less precise than cortisol level, but it would be cheaper. A questionnaire can also measure long-term stress.

One fact to remember here is that cortisol level does not characterize a psychological response, only a biological response. It might help you understand about biological responses to stress, but not about the psychological experience of stress.

As a researcher, it is up to you to decide how you will define your concept. There is no perfect way; there are simply multiple ways that have their own strengths and weaknesses. Depending on the question you want to ask, you choose one over another. You could use Holmes and Rahe's scale or Renner and Mackin's, or you could find out how other researchers have decided to measure stress and adapt their strategies. In the end you have to select a method that you think will work for you.

PROBABILITY SAMPLING

Probability sampling is the gold standard of sampling. In its simplest definition, probability sampling means that everybody that you are interested in, your population, has an equal chance of participating in your study. Unfortunately, outside of some survey research, psychologists typically don't employ it because it would be very costly. If we were interested in how people in general behave, we would need to test people from every country, of all ages, with diverse backgrounds. For all of its desirability, researchers forego probability sampling in favor of less costly approaches, like the samples of college students that most research employs.

> **Probability Sampling—** A method used in research whereby any person in the population has a specified probability of being included in the sample.

We know that psychology students are not typical of people in general on a lot of dimensions; they are younger, more educated, more likely to be female, etc. A critical question is whether the differences are important in your research. If you are studying reaction times to the appearance of a visual stimulus on a screen, college students may be very similar to other people. On the other hand, if you want to study voting preferences, college students may be dissimilar to people not in college. In our research, we often do not know how well our sample mirrors the population of interest.

> **Generalization—**The property of research results such that they can be seen as valid beyond the sample involved in a study to a larger population.

When the sample is similar to the population, we can be confident in **generalization** of our results from the sample to the population. We hope that if our experimental and control groups consisting of students differ by some amount, then other groups will show a similar difference. We will be satisfied most of the time if we can establish patterns of behavior, even if we can't make precise predictions.

One of the difficulties regarding probability sampling is purely practical. We don't have enough resources to test people who are far away; we even miss out on nearby people whose schedules are such that they don't have time to take part in our research. So we don't bring them into the lab to test them or go out into the field to track them down.

Another difficulty associated with probability sampling is that, in order to use it, we have to be able to define our population of interest. In theory, we would have to be able to list every member of the population so we could pick our participants from the list. In much of our research, it is not really clear that we could do this, even in theory. We tend to use student samples not really knowing the population they represent. The general philosophy is that the patterns of behavior in student samples will resemble the patterns in other groups, so it may not matter that most samples involve students.

You can see how this pays out in research journals. As you saw in Table 4.4, authors of theoretical research articles provide relatively little information about their participants, mostly information about sex and average age of the participants. Even with such restricted samples, researchers are likely to discuss results in terms that apply to people in general, not simply to students.

You are most likely to encounter probability sampling in survey research like political polls. In this research, the investigators can identify their population (e.g., registered voters) pretty well and can contact a random subset of the entire population. The population is well defined and a random sample is reasonably easy to create.

There are four general strategies for probability sampling. They result in simple random samples, systematic samples, stratified random samples, and cluster samples.

Simple Random Sampling

Simple random sampling (SRS) involves identifying your population precisely, then identifying some probability that each person in it will appear in your sample. (We often refer to this approach just as random sampling.) In SRS, each person has an equal chance of being selected. In professionally conducted polls, the researchers use randomly selected telephone numbers, so each household with a phone has an equal chance of being called. The result is likely to be a sample that reflects the entire population.

> **Simple Random Sampling**—A process of sampling in research that specifies that each person in a population has the same chance of being included in a sample as every other person.

It is important to remember that even with a random sample, you may not have a truly representative sample; sometimes you get unlucky. For instance, if the voters they get in touch with are home because they are unemployed, the sample might show certain biases because such people hold different attitudes than those who are working. But the more people you call, the less likely you are to have a sample that is quite different from the whole population when you use random sampling.

Systematic Sampling

If you have a list of the entire population from which you will sample, you might decide to sample every 10th, 20th, 100th, etc. name after selecting a random position to start. This process will generate a **systematic sample**. Some (e.g., Judd, Smith, & Kidder, 1991) have argued that such a technique deviates from randomness because if you started with the fifth name, then went to the 15th, 25th, etc., then the 14th and 16th names (for example) have zero probability of being chosen. The counterargument is that empirical studies have shown the results of SRS and systematic sampling to be virtually identical, particularly if your list of people is in a random order to begin with; further, in many cases systematic sampling is simply easier to do (Babbie, 1995).

> **Systematic Sampling**—A process of sampling in which an apparently unbiased but nonrandom sample is created, such as by creating a list of every element in the population and selecting every nth member from the population.

Stratified Random Sampling

On occasion, you might decide that you want certain groups to be included in your sample in specific proportions. For instance, if you wanted to survey your college so that you could get responses from first-year students, sophomores, juniors, and seniors in equal proportions, you probably would not want to use SRS because you are likely to sample more first-year students because, in most schools, there are more of them; the less interested or able students have not yet dropped out, as they have with upper-level

> **Stratified Random Sampling**—A process of sampling in which groups of interest (e.g., male and female; young and old; Democratic, Republican, and Independent, etc.) are identified, then participants are selected at random from these groups.

students. As a result, you could employ **stratified random sampling**, in which you identify the proportion of your total sample that will have the characteristics you want.

Theoretically, stratification can be appropriate for virtually any variable you could think of. You can stratify by age, gender, socioeconomic status, education level, political affiliation, geographical location, height, weight, etc. In practice, though, some stratification is easier than others because you may not be able to identify in advance the members of your population according to some variables (e.g., height or weight) as easily as others (e.g., sex—by using the person's first name as a guide).

Cluster Sampling

Finally, sometimes a strategy like simple random sampling will be too cumbersome to be practical, especially if you have a sampling domain whose elements you cannot list. For instance, if you wanted to survey teachers' attitudes in elementary schools, you might have

> **Cluster Sampling**—A process of sampling in which a number of groups (or clusters) are identified in a population, then some clusters are randomly selected for participation in a research project.

so many schools in an area that it would be too time consuming to engage in simple random sampling. One alternative is **cluster sampling**.

In this approach, you would randomly select some number of schools, then sample from within each school chosen. In this method, large chunks of the population will be ruled out. You should still have a random sample, though, because your selection of schools was nonsystematic, that is, nonbiased, and the subsample is also nonsystematic. So in advance, there is no built-in bias in the sample, and you should have some confidence that your sample will represent the entire population.

In all of these probability sampling approaches, you have a good chance of ending up with samples that describe the population pretty well. As always, we should remember that we are dealing with probabilities, not certainties, so any given sample might not be useful for depicting the population. Still, this is the most certain of any strategy short of using the entire population. If you look at the results of surveys by professionals, it is clear that their techniques work very well.

NONPROBABILITY SAMPLING

> **Nonsampling Error**—A problem in sampling that leads to a nonrepresentative sample because some members of the population are systematically excluded from participation.

Most psychological research does not involve probability sampling. The implication is that we often do not know to whom our research results generalize. This means that we can say that a particular result applies to students like the ones we study, but we don't know if our results also pertain to people younger or older, less or more educated, poorer or richer, or any other characteristics.

Among the greatest problems with nonprobability samples is **nonsampling error**. This problem occurs when people who should be included in a sample are not. It results in a nonprobability sample that is not representative of the population as a whole. The end result is that a researcher doesn't know to whom the survey results apply.

To ignore nonsampling error is to jeopardize the validity of a research project's results. For instance, Wainer (1999) notes an interesting result from a historical set of data. In the mid-nineteenth century, the Swiss physician H. C. Lombard examined over 8,000 death certificates and tallied each individual's cause of death and each individual's profession. The profession generating greatest longevity was that of furriers at 70.0 years.

Surprisingly, the group with the shortest life expectancy was that of student, at 20.2 years. Has life changed so much in a century and a half? The problem, of course, is that students are typically fairly young, so if they die, their life span has been short. After they finish being students, they engage in various occupations, so they don't have the chance to die as students at age 70. This is a clear example of a nonsampling error: There is no opportunity to sample old students because they go into other categories before they die. The conclusion that being a student is dangerous clearly makes no sense, which Lombard recognized.

The problem is less obvious in some research because you don't always know who you are surveying and who is being left out. For instance, in research on bulimia, investigators often study people referred from medical doctors. It turns out that, compared to bulimics in the community in general, bulimics referred for treatment by a doctor show a greater incidence of self-induced vomiting, greater likelihood of misusing laxatives, and a more severe eating disorder in general (Fairburn et al., 1996). The difficulty here is with nonsampling error. Thus, conclusions about the characteristics and behavior of people suffering from bulimia will differ, depending on how a sample is drawn. If researchers rely on referrals from doctors, the sample will consist of people with more severe problems compared to a randomly drawn sample from the community.

The sampling approaches that psychologists use, particularly in laboratory studies, include convenience samples, quota samples, purposive (judgmental) samples, and respondent-driven (chain-referral) samples. Unfortunately, all of these approaches have limitations because of the people who do not participate in research.

Convenience Sampling

As you saw in Table 4.1, the journals of experimental psychology involve students almost exclusively. Fifty years ago, psychologists hoped to generalize about behavior from the activity of White rats in Skinner boxes. Rats were easy to obtain and were always there when the psychologists wanted to study them. Today, we have the same hope of generalizing from college students, who are also easy to obtain and generally pleasant to work with. As you learned before, when researchers rely on such a population because it is easy or available, we refer to **convenience sampling**.

Convenience Sampling—A nonrandom (nonprobability) sampling technique that involves using whatever participants can conveniently be studied, also known as an accidental sample and a haphazard sample.

Unfortunately, in many cases, we don't really know how well our research findings generalize from our samples. At the same time, when we create experimental groups and compare them, we may not be interested in precise measurements of differences between the groups, but rather patterns of differences. For instance, Recarte and Nunes (2000) investigated how students performed in a driving task when asked to complete verbal and spatial imagery tasks. Students are probably younger, on average, than the typical driver. Do you think this would matter when we discuss the effects of verbal versus spatial thought among drivers? Students may be better or worse in their driving than older people, but will the verbal–spatial comparison differ between older and younger groups? When researchers conduct this type of study, they hope not.

When psychologists test theories, they may not care about the specifics of the samples they work with. In fact, in experimental journals, the researchers report very little detailed information about the participants. The philosophy is that if the theory generates certain predictions, those predictions should come true, regardless of the population tested. If the psychologists are working to develop the details of the theory, they hope the characteristics of the sample are not all that important. On the other hand, if the researchers are hoping to be able to apply their findings to a particular population, characteristics of the sample are very important.

In the end, we have to use our best judgment when deciding how important the demographics of our samples are. Sometimes, using students is just fine; sometimes, it isn't. This is where judgment and experience become important.

Quota Sampling

Quota sampling is analogous to stratified sampling in that, in both, the researcher attempts to achieve a certain proportion of people of certain types in the final sample. Suppose an investigator wants to know if less able students differ from better students in their political beliefs.

| **Quota Sampling**—A nonrandom (nonprobability) sampling technique in which subgroups, usually convenience samples, are identified and a specified number of individuals from each group are included in the research. |

The researcher could recruit volunteers from a class, asking the students to indicate name, contact information, and grade point average. Then the researcher could make sure that the proportion of students with low averages in the final sample matches the proportion of students below a certain grade point average in the population, with the proportion of good students in the final sample matching the proportion of better students in the population. In this example, the researcher would need some way to establish the relevant grade point averages, like contacting the Registrar's Office on his or her campus.

This type of quota sampling is a variation on convenience sampling. The sample is not random, so the researcher does not know to whom the results generalize.

Purposive (Judgmental) Sampling

At times, a researcher may not feel the need to have a random sample. If the investigator is interested in a particular type of person, say somebody with special expertise, the investigator may try to find as many such people as possible and study them. The result is descriptive research that may say a lot about this group of experts.

For instance, if you were interested in how engineers develop products so that consumers can use them easily, you could get in touch with people who create consumer products. Then you could find out what factors they consider in making the products they create trouble-free when consumers get them home.

The problem with such a sample is the same as with any other nonprobability sample—you don't know who, beyond your sample, your results relate to. At the same time, you may wind up with a general sense of the important issues associated with the group of interest. This approach is sometimes called **purposive (judgmental) sampling** because it relies on the judgment of the researcher and a specific purpose for identifying participants.

Purposive (Judgmental) Sampling—A nonrandom (nonprobability) sampling technique in which participants are selected for a study because of some desirable characteristics, like expertise in some area.

Chain-Referral Sampling

Sometimes it is difficult to make contact with some populations because they might not want to be found (e.g., drug users, sex workers, illegal immigrants). They are not likely to be conveniently listed with their phone numbers. As a result, researchers have to use creative approaches to contact them. Investigators have developed several techniques to study such groups, which are sometimes called hidden populations; the broad term for these techniques is **chain-referral** methods. As a rule, these strategies are more likely to be practical for survey and interview research than for experimental studies.

Chain-Referral Sampling—Chain-referral sampling: A nonrandom (nonprobability) sampling technique in which a research participant is selected who then identifies further participants that he or she knows, often useful for finding hidden populations.

In these approaches, the researcher may use a contact in the group of interest to provide references to others who, in turn, provide other names. Another chain-referral technique involves finding where members of the group congregate, then sampling the individuals at that location. A third approach is to use a member of the group to recruit others; there may be an advantage to this technique because a known person of the group solicits participation, not an unknown and anonymous researcher. A final approach involves finding a key informant who knows the population of interest; rather than questioning members of the population, the researcher talks with a person knowledgeable about the group.

MAKING USEFUL MEASUREMENTS

Psychologists have spent a lot of time devising reliable and valid ways of measuring concepts that we cannot observe directly. So we may devise a test that gives good information about mental states that we cannot see. Difficulties arise when we try to measure something we can't see; we may make generally good, but imprecise, measurements that lead to **measurement error**.

Measurement Error—An error in data collection based on poor measuring instruments or human error that leads to invalid conclusions.

Measurement error does not mean that the investigator has made a mistake. The researcher may carry out his or her tasks flawlessly. The error arises because the measurement device is imperfect, and the participant may also be imperfect in providing data.

For example, if you were interested in knowing if good readers can identify individual words more quickly than poorer readers, you could present a single word and ask a participant to press a "Yes" button if the item is a word (e.g., crow) and a "No" button if the item is a nonword (e.g., corw). You are studying word recognition skill, which is a complex, internal process. For any given trial, the respondent may respond more slowly than usual because of fatigue. On another trial, the person may respond more quickly because he or she just saw the word before coming to the laboratory and it was fresh in memory. Both of these instances reflect measurement error.

In general, we say that measurement error occurs when something affects behavior other than the variable you are investigating. In the first example above, you would call slow responses due to fatigue measurement error because you are not studying fatigue—it has just gotten in the way. In the second example, we call the quick response due to familiarity with the word results in measurement error because the study is not focusing on word familiarity—it has just gotten in the way.

Every science faces measurement error. That is why the sciences use statistics; they help us understand the magnitude of the error that we can expect in our measurements.

Reliability

Reliability—A measure of the consistency or reproducibility of data collected using the same methodology on more than one occasion; across different, but related test items; or by different individuals.

Test–Retest Reliability—A measure of the consistency of data collected at different points in time.

Split-Half Reliability—A measure of the consistency of data across subgroups when the data from a test or other measuring instrument are broken down into smaller segments.

Interrater (Interobserver) Reliability—A measure of the consistency of observations of a single situation made by different people.

Because measurement error is a fact of life, psychologists have spent a lot of time developing the notion of **reliability**. If a measurement is reliable, then repeated measurements on the same person should result in similar outcomes each time. Reliability relates to consistency and repeatability in the results. If you completed an intelligence test, then repeated it later, you would probably get a different score each time, but they would likely be fairly similar. The similarity occurs because standardized intelligence tests are generally reliable. Just because an intelligence test is reliable, we shouldn't automatically assume that it shows validity, that is, that the test is useful. Tests can be reliable without giving us any useful information. For example, we could use your height as an estimate of your intelligence; the measurement would be reliable, but it wouldn't be valid. Similarly, standardized tests might be reliable, but we don't always know how valid they are.

When a measurement yields similar results with repeated testing, we say it shows **test–retest reliability**. There are other types of reliability as well. If questions from subcomponents of a test lead to similar results, the test may have **split-half reliability**.

Another aspect of reliability involves how consistently different investigators record behaviors that they observe independently of one another. If data from two observers tend to agree, their measurements show **interrater (interobserver) reliability**.

Reliability is not an all-or-none situation; different measuring instruments are more or less reliable. Regardless of the type of reliability in question, if measurements are to help us answer questions about behavior, they must show appropriate levels and types of reliability.

Validity

The concept of reliability differs from that of validity. Validity relates to the question of whether measurements provide information on what we really want to measure. Is the measurement really useful for what we want? In order for a measurement instrument to be valid, it must be reliable. You can get consistent (i.e., reliable) scores, but they may not give useful (i.e., valid) information. Even if scores are reliable, we don't know whether they are valid.

CONSIDERING VALIDITY IN RESEARCH

As researchers, we want our work to be meaningful. That means creating research designs that relate the independent variable (IV) meaningfully to the dependent variable (DV). Another, more technical way of saying that research results are meaningful is to say that they are valid.

> **Validity**—A property of data, concepts, or research findings whereby they are useful in varying degrees for measuring or understanding phenomena that are of interest to a psychologist.

There are several different types of **validity**; some are particularly relevant in experimental research. Some types involve the nature of variables; others relate to the structure of an experiment; yet another pertains to the statistics used to analyze the data. They are summarized in Table 5.2.

Validity is not an all-or-none situation. Rather, a measurement may show less or more validity, and its validity may legitimately and predictably change in different situations. Further, an experiment may show high levels of some types of validity, but lower levels of different types.

Construct Validity

When investigators develop an operational definition of a variable, they work to create a measurement that shows **construct validity**. This means that the abstract, underlying concept is being defined, or operationalized, in a way that is useful in understanding that concept.

> **Construct Validity**— The degree to which a measurement accurately measures the underlying concept that is supposed to be measured.

We can get a glimpse of how we can apply the concept of construct validity in the measurement of depression. Depression is complex, which is why psychologists need to study it extensively in order to begin to understand it. As you will see, doing research on depression well requires paying close attention to the details.

Psychologists generally accept the construct validity of the BDI because it is useful in dealing with depressed people. According to many research findings, the BDI has useful psychometric properties, which means that it can distinguish those with depression from those without, and it can document an individual's level of depression (Dozois, Dobson, & Ahnberg, 1998). Steer, Rissmiller, Ranieri, and Beck (1994) reported that the BDI can reliably differentiate patients with mood disorders from those with other kinds of psychological problems.

The BDI also appears to be useful cross-culturally when used with Mexican people in the United States (Dawes et al., 2010), with Portuguese (Campos & Gonçalves, 2011), with German speakers (Richter, Joachim, & Bastine, 1994), and with Arab college students in Kuwait (Al-Turkait & Ohaeri, 2010). It can also be useful with elderly people who are clinically depressed (Steer, Rissmiller, & Beck, 2000). Thus, we can conclude that for applications like these, the BDI's construct validity is just fine.

At the same time, the BDI may not be appropriate for all types of research on depression. Wagle, Ho, Wagle, and Berrios (2000) have provided evidence that it is not ideal for measuring depression in Alzheimer's patients, and it may perform less well than therapists'

TABLE 5.2   **Different Types of Validity and How They Affect Research**

Construct validity	How well do your operational definitions and procedures capture the hypothetical constructs you want to study?
	Example: If you want to study intelligence, you can administer an IQ test. It will be reasonably high in construct validity if you are interested in educational abilities, but lower in construct validity if you are interested in problem solving in daily activities.
Convergent and divergent (Discriminant) validity	Are there positive correlations between your variable and variables that are supposed to be positively correlated? If several different variables that are all related give you the same information, you have convergent validity.
	Are there negative correlations between your variable and others that are supposed to be unrelated?
	Example: Research on the topic of emotional intelligence has shown that measures of emotional intelligence and personality are related. This suggests that the measures of emotional intelligence overlap with personality traits and are not being measured separately from personality (Davies, Stankov, & Roberts, 1998). There is a lack of divergent validity here. The results do not remove the possibility that emotional intelligence reflects specific skills, it only means that we haven't figured out how to measure it if it does exist.
Internal and external validity	Is your research set up so that you can draw a firm conclusion from your data? Or are there other potential interpretations that arise because of limitations in your research design? If you have eliminated extraneous and confounding variables from your methodology, your study will have internal validity.
	Example: Mexican American students expressed preference for a Mexican American over a European American counselor. The researchers identified a social response bias, however, that led to the stated preference. When this confound was eliminated, the difference in preference disappeared (Abreu & Gabarain, 2000).
	Are your results meaningful beyond the setting and the participants involved in your research? If your findings will generalize to new people, new locations, and a different time, they show greater external validity. If your results pertain only to the context of your research project, they will have lower external validity.
	Example: In order to generalize his research results on obedience, Stanley Milgram studied nonstudents from an office building in downtown New Haven, CT. He obtained similar results as with college students, suggesting that his findings have external validity.
Statistical conclusion validity	Have you used the proper statistical approaches to analyzing your data? If you employ the wrong statistical model, your conclusions will be less valid. This is particularly relevant for complex approaches like complex analyses of variance, structural equation modeling, or other analyses involving multiple variables.

judgments in severely depressed people (Martinsen, Friis, & Hoffart, 1995). Furthermore, the component of the BDI associated with somatic (i.e., bodily) problems may be of limited utility with people dealing with chronic disease (e.g., Patterson, Morasco, Fuller, Indest, DLoftis, & Hauser, 2011). These results mean that the BDI is a highly valid instrument for many situations, but not for all.

In the research just mentioned, the investigators were interested in depression as an outcome or measured variable. Sometimes researchers use depression as a manipulated IV. They may induce a mildly depressed state in participants by using simple laboratory techniques, then observe the effect on some behavior. An important question is whether the lab techniques used to create depression are valid.

One widely known approach was developed by Emmet Velten, who asked his participants to read positive or negative statements in order to elevate or depress their mood. By doing this, he could actively manipulate mood state and see what effect it had on a subsequent behavior of interest.

Does Velten's induced depression resemble naturally occurring depression? That is, does depression as Velten operationalized it have construct validity? Researchers have questioned the validity of the Velten mood induction procedure because there is no guarantee that reading a series of statements induces a realistic version of depression. If the result of this manipulation does not lead to a state resembling depression, construct validity will be low or nonexistent.

There is reason to believe that Velten's version of depression shows adequate construct validity. For example, Bartolic and colleagues (1999) investigated whether brain activity differs depending on mood. They reasoned that positive (euphoric) and negative (dysphoric) emotional states produce different patterns of activity in the frontal lobes of the brain.

So they used Velten's mood induction procedure to change research participants' emotional states and found that the euphoric state leads to enhanced verbal performance, whereas dysphoric states lead to better figural processing. Their findings are consistent with previous studies of depression.

In further research, investigators have verified hypotheses related to depression and lowered mood states using the Velten procedure. For instance, Boettger, Schwier, and Bär (2011) induced a depressed mood in a sample of German participants and then exposed the participants to hot or cold stimuli. The participants reported greater pain and discomfort when in depressed mood compared to when in neutral mood. With a very different type of research question, Sinclair, Moore, Mark, Soldat, and Lavis (2010) noted that, normally, people in good moods do not process information as critically as those in depressed moods. These researchers demonstrated, however, that if you believe that thinking critically will keep you in a good mood, you will engage in that kind of thinking. In order to demonstrate this phenomenon, they used Velten's mood-induction technique with their Canadian participants, which again was shown to induce mood change in a valid way.

These results suggest that experimental participants are in an emotional state that resembles depression. That is, we see evidence of reasonable levels of construct validity.

On the other hand, sometimes people who are actually depressed behave differently from those whose depression has been induced by the Velten statements (Kwiatkowski &

Parkinson, 1994). Once again, when we deal with complex topics, we have to be careful that we are measuring what we think we are. Thinking about research you might do, you can often use the same operational definitions that others have used, but you also need to be aware that you can't adopt them blindly.

Issues with construct validity may not be apparent to researchers, but such validity is critical to understanding research results. For example, in understanding differences in behavior across ethnic groups, it is important to know how people have been categorized. Sometimes it is based on governmental records, sometimes on a person's self-report. Government categories are not scientifically based; they are political in nature. Self-reports of a person's ethnicity are also not scientific and may change depending on what kinds of questions are being asked. In either case, the construct validity of such classifications is suspect, so results may be misleading at best (Markus, 2008).

The Controversy box on intelligence illustrates how your approach to intelligence can lead to different conclusions. When it comes to intelligence, to issues of ethnicity, and to many other socially relevant concepts, if you don't measure or categorize people appropriately, your conclusions could be problematic.

CONTROVERSY:
Intelligence

One very widely used operational definition is the Intelligence Quotient, or IQ score. What is intelligence? We don't really know; we can only see the results of intelligence level as people function well or poorly in various aspects of their lives. Still, if we are going to predict behavior based on a person's intelligence level, we have to come up with an operational definition of this concept; that is, we have to measure it somehow. This is not easy to do well.

Traditionally, intelligence has meant an IQ score. In everyday life, many people do not recognize any difference between the concept of intelligence and the IQ score. In truth, though, an IQ score is a pale representation of intelligence. Standardized intelligence tests are fairly good at indicating how well a person is likely to perform in school. However, they don't necessarily say much about the individual's abilities in nonscholastic domains that are major components of Gardner's (1999; Gardner, Krechevsley, Sternberg, & Okagaki, 1994) and Sternberg's (1985, 1999) multi-component theories of intelligence. This means that when we consider a complex hypothetical construct like intelligence, different measurements will be useful in different situations.

IQ scores alone may be important and useful, but they can be even more important and useful when combined with other kinds of measurements. In fact, one growing focus of current research goes beyond simple measurements of IQ and includes measures of personality.

Heaven and Ciarrochi (2012) demonstrated the need to include personality characteristics in the discussion if we are going to get a good depiction of how intelligence relates to performance in school. They discovered that measurements of openness to experience and conscientiousness predict academic performance in combination with intelligence level. Similarly, Bartels et al. (2012) investigated the relation between IQ and personality in twins, finding that levels of openness, agreeableness, and neuroticism relate to intelligence.

Another potentially valuable measurement is that of emotional intelligence (Goleman, 1996). Basically, emotional intelligence (EI) is said to relate to a person's ability to be emotionally sensitive or attuned to others. In order for this construct to be useful for psychologists, we have to be able to measure it. There should be some test that generates scores that will differentiate people with different levels of such intelligence.

Mayer, Salovey, Caruso, and Sitarenios (2001) devised a measurement of EI, the Multi-Factor Emotional Intelligence Scale (MEIS) and provided some empirical support for it. (Some researchers are not convinced that EI is a separate type of intelligence; Davies, Stankov, & Roberts, 1998; Roberts, Zeidner, & Matthews, 2001).

Researchers have continued to develop measures of EI. For example, McCann (2010) has created two measures of EI, one based on cognitive processes and one on emotion, and Austin (2010) assessed EI based on work by Mayer, Salovey, Caruso, and Sinarenios (2001). In addition, Kun et al. (2012) and Fukuda, Saklofske, Tamaoka, & Lim (2012) have created tests for Hungarian and for Korean populations, respectively, so we are gaining a more diverse perspective on EI.

The combination of different measurements of personality, emotional ability, intellectual ability should ultimately create a robust and valid measurement of the complex construct of intelligence.

Internal and External Validity

The next types of validity we will consider are internal validity and external validity. When research shows **internal validity**, it means that you started your project with groups that were comparable with respect to the DV (or equated them using statistical procedures), eliminated confounds and extraneous variables, manipulated a variable that possessed construct validity, held everything but the IV treatments constant across your groups, and measured your participants' behaviors accurately on another variable that had construct validity.

Internal Validity—The degree to which an experiment is designed so that a causal relationship between the independent and dependent variable is demonstrated without interference by extraneous variables.

In order to have external validity, your experiment has to be meaningful in a context outside of your laboratory with people (or animals) other than the ones who took part in your study. In other words, would your findings be replicable in another setting with different participants and at a different time?

Internal Validity.   An example of a strategy of assigning people to groups that could very easily lead to bias is as follows. Suppose you were going to test two groups of participants with 10 participants in each group. You could assign the first 10 who showed up to Group 1 and the second 10 to Group 2. The first 10 people might be more eager, more motivated, more energetic, more cooperative, and so on. That's why they got there first. You could end up with two groups that consisted of very different types in each group. Any difference in behavior after your experimental manipulation could be due to their eagerness, motivation, energy, cooperation, or other factors, rather than to the manipulation. This strategy is easy but not advisable.

In contrast, the chief means that scientists use to create similar groups in an experiment is to use random assignment of participants to groups. Random assignment means that any single individual can end up in any group in the experiment and that the individual is placed in the group on the basis of some objective and unbiased strategy. No approach to assignment guarantees that in a single experiment, the groups to be compared would have equivalent scores on the DV at the start of the study. Sometimes an experimenter is

Random Assignment—
The process in which participants in a research study are nonsystematically placed in different treatment groups so those groups are equivalent at the start of an experiment.

simply beset by bad luck. But, in the long run, **random assignment** is an effective way to create equivalent groups.

You can randomly assign participants to groups by using a random number table. Figure 5.1 illustrates how you could assign 10 people to two groups on a random basis. In this case, if you took numbers from a random number table and used them to assign people to conditions, you could match the random numbers on the order in which people arrived at the lab, alphabetically, by height, by IQ score, by grade point average, or by any other means. As long as one of the lists is random, the grouping is random.

Across many experiments, this process is the most valuable in creating groups that don't differ systematically at the start. In any given experiment, you might be the victim of bad luck, so that all the smart, tall, nervous, friendly people are in

1. Go through a random number table and write down the numbers from 1 to N (your sample size) in the order in which they occur in the table. In this example, we will move down the columns, choosing the first two digits of the column in each block of numbers.
2. The critical numbers are shaded for this example.
3. Place your participants in order. (The actual order of listing of participants isn't critical here; any ordering will do–alphabetical, in order of arrival to the lab, etc.)
4. Pair each person with the random numbers as they occur.
5. Put each person paired with an odd number into Group 1 and each person paired with an even number into Group 2.

Example of Random Number Table

91477	29697	90242	59885	07839
09496	48263	55662	34601	56490
03549	90503	41995	06394	61978
19981	55031	34220	48623	53407
51444	89292	10273	90035	04758
66281	05254	35219	96901	38055
08461	61412	53378	13522	80778
36070	12377	52392	67053	49965
28751	01486	54443	01873	02586
64061	22061	10746	84070	71531

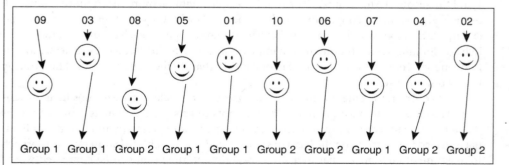

FIGURE 5.1   Steps to take to randomly assign participants to groups.

one group instead of being evenly distributed across conditions. Unfortunately, there is nothing you can do about it. You have to decide on a process of randomization (random number table, drawing names out of a hat, rolling dice, etc.) then follow it and live with the results. In the long run, random grouping of participants will lead to the most valid results.

As experimental procedures get more complicated and you add groups, you will have to adjust your randomization techniques. If you plan to create three groups with 10 participants randomly assigned to each group, you need to change your assignment strategy a little. Your first step would be to identify your participants and randomly order them.

Then using the random number table in Figure 5.1, you could identify two-digit numbers starting at the upper left of the list. If you have 30 participants, you will only need to pay attention to values in the table of 01 to 30. The first number in the table is 91, which you ignore because it is greater than 30. Moving down the column, we see the next number is 09; you would put the ninth person to show up in Group 1. The next number is 03; the third person would go in Group 2. The next number between 01 and 30 is 19; so the 19th person would go in Group 3. You would continue until each of the 30 participants would be assigned to one of the three groups. This approach would remove systematic bias in assigning participants to groups.

Random assignment of participants to groups keeps us from introducing systematic bias into the process of creating groups. Consequently, we can have confidence that any group differences after a treatment are due to the treatment. This produces a greater level of internal validity.

The internal validity of a research project is critical to the level of confidence you have in your conclusions. The greater the internal validity, the more you can have faith that you know what factors cause an individual to act in a certain way.

External Validity.   In addition to random assignment, there is another randomization process sometimes used in research. In some research, mostly surveys, investigators make use of random selection. When researchers use this technique, it means that everybody in the population has a specified probability of being included in the research.

The goal of random selection is to increase the representativeness of the sample. With random selection, a scientist can have confidence that the sample used in the research is generally similar to the population as a whole. If your sample is like the population, you can conclude that the results from your sample will be similar to what would happen if you measured the entire population. When you can generalize beyond your sample, your results show external validity.

External Validity—The property of data such that research results apply to people and situations beyond the particular sample of individuals observed in a single research setting.

In terms that you should be familiar with, random assignment relates to internal validity, the degree to which an experiment is structured so that its results can be interpreted unambiguously. On the other hand, random selection relates to **external validity**, the degree to which the experiment pertains to those other than the participants in the study. In experimental research, it is typical to have random assignment of participants to groups, but not to have random selection because it is easier to use convenience samples, usually college students.

In some cases, using college students will lead to low levels of external validity. On the other hand, college students are people, and you are interested in people. In many ways, they are going to be like other older and younger people who come from the same socioeconomic and ethnic groups. As such, their behaviors during experiments might very well reflect the behaviors of others from the same background.

If you use animals in your research, you are likely to use rats, mice, or pigeons. Traditionally, psychologists who studied learning processes have used rats or pigeons; researchers studying genetics have used mice. These creatures are very different from other animals; they have been bred for laboratories and are likely to be more docile than rats that you might see in the wild. Domesticated mice, for instance, are larger than wild mice and reach sexual maturity quicker. But domesticated mice are physically weaker and have poorer vision than their wild counterparts. Mice, like all domesticated animals, show more chromosomal breakage than wild animals (Austad, 2002).

Can you generalize from White lab rats, from pigeons, or from mice to other rats, pigeons, and mice? to other animals? to people? These are not questions that are always easily answered. You have to use good judgment and expert opinion, plus a lot of caution, when you generalize across species.

When psychologists discuss generalization, we are interested in whether our research results will pertain to other organisms, other settings, and other times. Given the success that psychologists have had in applying research results to contexts outside the laboratory, we can conclude that levels of external validity are often acceptable, even if not perfect.

In any case, Mook (1983) has suggested that asking about the generalizability of research results may not really be the best question to ask. He proposed that we may want to test a set of ideas or a theory in the lab. For purposes of testing a theory, internal validity is critical, but external validity (and generalization) isn't relevant.

To illustrate his point, Mook used Harry Harlow's classic studies of young monkeys that could turn in a time of distress to either a soft and cuddly, artificial "mother" or an uncomfortable, wire "mother" from which the monkey got its milk (from a baby bottle). Drive-reduction theory would lead to the prediction that the animal would turn to the wire mother. Harlow tested this assumption and found that, in times of distress, the monkey preferred warm and cuddly.

The experimental setup was very artificial. The monkeys were probably not representative of baby monkeys in general; after all, they had been raised in a laboratory. They were certainly not like people.

The important issue here is that Harlow's results further weakened a dying theory and helped replace it with a different theory. In some ways, it doesn't matter, Mook explained, whether the results would generalize to people. The critical issue in some cases is development of ideas to test a theory.

Statistical Conclusion Validity

After you complete your experimental procedure, it is typical to conduct a statistical analysis of the results. In an introductory statistics course, everything seems pretty straightforward with regard to the selection of an appropriate statistical procedure. As psychological methods become more complex, however, new statistical approaches are developed.

Psychologists also maintain that nominally and ordinally scaled variables do not lend themselves to tests like the Student's t-test or the analysis of variance (ANOVA). They assert that you should not use the *t*-test or ANOVA for such variables. Statisticians have never thought that scale of measurement was a particularly critical issue.

When the noted psychologist S. S. Stevens (1946) invented the concepts of nominal, ordinal, interval, and ratio schedules, he decided that different statistical tests were appropriate for different scales of measurement. It wasn't long before others spotted the flaws in Stevens's arguments. For instance, Lord (1953) showed that in some cases, it might be entirely appropriate to use a *t*-test with football numbers, which are on a nominal scale. Later, Gaito (1980) further argued that Stevens had confused the numbers and the concepts that they were supposed to represent. Even Stevens (1951) recognized that his earlier proclamations could keep researchers from answering important questions appropriately. More recently, Velleman and Wilkinson (1993) have articulated arguments about cases in which scales of measurement are or are not particularly meaningful. The traditional prohibitions against using parametric tests with ordinal data often don't really have a solid theoretical or mathematical basis.

The important thing to remember is that you should give adequate consideration to your statistical tests. If you are uncertain, ask somebody who knows. Researchers do this all the time, especially when they are engaged in research techniques that are new to them.

If you use the appropriate statistical test, and use it accurately, your results will have **statistical conclusion validity**.

Statistical Conclusion Validity—The characteristic of research results such that the conclusions drawn from the results are valid because the appropriate statistical analyses were used.

There have been recent discussions about what constitutes adequate statistical conclusion validity in research reports. The American Psychological Association constituted a task force to deliberate the issues. The final report noted that traditional tests of statistical significance were appropriate in many cases, but that they needed to be supplemented by other statistics, like measures of effect size and confidence intervals (Wilkinson et al., 1999). The task force also recommended using the simplest statistic that will answer the question the researcher poses.

Convergent and Divergent Validity

One way to have confidence in our findings is through **convergent validity**, which means achieving similar results with different methodologies. If two different approaches to a given question lead us to the same conclusion, our confidence in our methodology and results will increase. Similarly, we can gain confidence through **divergent validity**, which means that when two measurements that should be unrelated actually are unrelated. (Divergent validity is also called discriminant validity.)

Convergent Validity—The degree to which two measurements that attempt to measure the same hypothetical construct are consistent with one another.

Divergent Validity—The degree to which two measurements that should be assessing different constructs lead to different values.

The SAT: Questions of Reliability and Validity

The SAT is reasonably reliable, but the question is whether it is useful in predicting how well students will perform in college. If the SAT is useful for answering this question, we say it has predictive validity. We have a predictor variable, the SAT scores, that we use to predict the criterion variable, which is what we are really interested in. In a general sense, SAT scores do predict how well students perform in their first year in college, but it does not provide enough information by itself to make good predictions about college performance. Admissions offices must use SAT information in conjunction with other data if they are to make the best decisions about students who have applied to their institutions.

Another type of validity relates to the actual items that appear on a measurement instrument. For instance, a classroom test that has questions that assess how well students have learned a particular body of material will show content validity. If a measurement of an abstract concept (like academic strength, for example) really seems to assess that hypothetical construct, we say that the measurement shows construct validity. Depending on what we try to measure, we may be interested in different kinds of validity.

You can see the importance of validity in the Controversy box on head start. Depending on how researchers have measured the effectiveness of the program, they have arrived at opposite conclusions about how effective Head Start has been. The easy-to-measure variables suggested low effectiveness. Longer term, but more important (and valid) measurements reveal that Head Start has met many of its goals. Some research has not documented long-term academic gains, but enough studies have done so. Consequently, many educators believe that Head Start has lived up to its promise.

■ ■ ■ ■ ■

CONTROVERSY:
The Head Start Program

Researchers have to decide how they are going to complete their study. The choices reflect the way they define their concepts. This set of choices can be of paramount importance. To examine the effect of choices, let's consider the Head Start program, a federal program that provides educational opportunities for children deemed at risk for educational difficulty because of social and cultural factors. It would be nice to know whether it is effective because, as a country, we spend millions of dollars on it each year.

One of the choices a researcher would make in studying Head Start is how to define "effective." One way is to look at later IQ scores, which are easy to measure. Or you could look at students' grades during their elementary school years, which are also easy to measure. (One of the factors that arises repeatedly in research design is how easy it is for the investigator to carry out a project. If it is too costly or difficult, the researcher will most likely simplify or abandon it.)

Evaluation of the Head Start program reveals that the children in the program might initially show gains in IQ scores, but those gains are not permanent (Barnett, 1998). If you relied solely on IQ scores, you might conclude that Head Start and programs like it are not particularly useful. Fortunately, Barnett reviewed other measures of effectiveness, like graduation rates and school achievement. On both of these measures, children who experienced early childhood education programs showed success in the long term, into adulthood.

Thus, a conclusion based on IQ scores would be that the program was ineffective; one implication would be to discontinue the program. When you think about it, though, why are IQ scores so important? What do they tell us that is so important? Academic success and graduation lead to long-term benefits. Barnett concluded that the benefits significantly outweigh the costs of such programs.

Some studies suggest that the long-term improvements are small or nonexistent, even though most researchers have found support for the effectiveness of Head Start. When we deal with complex research, it isn't surprising to find contradictions in the research literature. Whenever we deal with complex issues, it often takes a lot of research to resolve discrepancies, especially when researchers study different samples and use different measurements in their studies. Each study that we do resolves some of the contradictions and provides another piece to the puzzle.

This example is important because it shows how important your decisions can be about your methodology. If "effective" is defined as IQ scores, the Head Start program seems ineffective. That is, the children are no better off afterward than they would have been without it. On the other hand, if you define "effective" as long-term benefit leading

to becoming a productive member of society, the program clearly meets its goals. In this research, it took a decade for the beneficial effects of Head Start to become apparent. Most of us don't want our research programs to last a decade, so we generally look at short-term effects. As we see in this situation, such decisions can lead to radically different conclusions.

Question for Discussion: How could planning differ depending on how effectiveness is defined in the research on Head Start?

SCALES OF MEASUREMENT

The highly respected psychophysicist S. S. Stevens (1951) argued that the numerical information provided by the data we collect depends on the type of measurements we make. Some data are relatively crude, providing information about categories in which observations fall. Other data are more mathematically sophisticated, permitting more complex algebraic manipulation.

As such, he reasoned, some data are appropriate for a given psychological test, but other data are not. His arguments have had significant impact on the way psychologists analyze data, even though there are compelling reasons to believe that Stevens overstated his case greatly (Gaito, 1980; Lord, 1953; Velleman & Wilkinson, 1993). Nonetheless, controversies and misunderstandings about the issues Stevens raised still persist.

Nominal Scales

Stevens labeled four different scales of measurement. At the simplest level, **nominal scales** involve simple categorization. People are generally recognized to come in two sexes, female and male (although there is some argument on that count, too, Fausto-Sterling, 1993). When we categorize people or things, we are engaging in the simplest form of measurement. As we conclude that one person is female and another is male, we are measuring them on a nominal scale.

Nominal Scale—
Measurements that involve putting observations into qualitatively different categories.

Usually, we talk about measurement in the context of "real" numbers, not categories, but assigning people to categories involves a simple variety of measurement. There isn't much arithmetic we can do with these numbers other than counting. We can tally the number of people who fall into categories of interest. With nominal data, though, we can differentiate among the categories themselves only descriptively.

Although we can tally different numbers of observations in each category, as when we say that there are more female psychology majors than male psychology majors, we can't compare any two measurements (e.g., one male, one female) and say that they differ quantitatively, that is, numerically. We can only say that the count of the observations differ, but we can't engage meaningfully in more complicated arithmetic operations.

Ordinal Scales

When our measurements do fall on a number line, we are dealing more quantitatively, not only descriptively and categorically. When we are able to compare two measurements and have the ability to decide that they differ (e.g., perhaps one is larger than the other), but we can't say how large the difference is, we are dealing with an **ordinal scale**.

> **Ordinal Scale**—Measurement that involves ordering data according to size.

In this case, we have some quantitative information, but only enough to say that one measurement falls above or below another on the number line. An absolute measure of the difference isn't possible on an ordinal scale. A typical example of measurements on an ordinal scale is ranks. Somebody who ranks first is ahead of somebody who ranks second; the second place person is, in turn, ahead of the third ranked person. But we don't know by how much they differ. First and second could be very close, with third very far away. On the other hand, first might be well ahead of second and third, who are close.

Ratio and Interval Scales

As we have seen, sometimes we use data that permit us to identify two people or things as being the same or different, which involves a nominal scale. These data may also allow us to identify which of two measurements is larger (or smaller) when they do differ; this involves an ordinal scale.

In many cases, we can go beyond ranking and assess an amount of difference between two measurements. When we are using such measurements and when the measurement system has an absolute zero (i.e., it will not permit negative numbers), we have a **ratio scale**. If the zero point on the scale is arbitrary (i.e., it will allow negative numbers), we have an **interval scale**. Practically speaking, we don't need to differentiate between interval and ratio scale numbers in our discussion here.

> **Ratio Scale**—Measurement that shows the characteristics of an interval scale but that has an absolute zero point.

In both of these scales, a fixed difference (e.g., 10 points) means the same thing regardless of where the number falls on the number line. The difference between 50 and 60 and the difference between 90 and 100 is 10 in both cases, and that difference means the same thing.

> **Interval Scale**—Measurement that involves data on a number line for which any two adjacent values are the same distance from one another as any other pair of adjacent values.

Remember that for ranks, the difference between finishing first and second, a difference of one place, doesn't reflect the same as the difference between last and next to last. If you have ever been to a track meet, you will have seen close battles between first and second in a race, but the time of the last and next to last runners might be considerable. The difference in ranking is the same, but the difference in their times is quite another matter.

There are arguments that some data we use in psychology look like interval or ratio data, but are really ordinal data. A common example in which there is disagreement about the scale of measurement involves intelligence as represented in IQ scores. The difference in behavior between somebody whose IQ score is 80 and somebody whose score is 90 may be quite noticeable, whereas the difference between people whose scores are 140 and 150 might be minimal. This pattern suggests that the difference of 10 points between members of each pair isn't really the same. This would be characteristic of an ordinal scale of measurement. That is, there are differences, but just as we don't know how big the differences are when people differ by a rank of one, we also don't know how big the real behavioral differences are when people differ in IQ scores by a fixed amount.

The importance of the issue, to the extent that it is important at all, is that some researchers identify one set of statistical tests that we can use when data are on an interval or ratio scale, and different sets of tests for each of nominal and ordinal scales.

Some researchers think that if IQ scores are really on an ordinal scale of measurement, the logical implication is that we should not be using certain statistical tests with them. Other researchers advance arguments to the contrary. In practice, psychologists may argue against using parametric tests with data like IQ scores, but most researchers use them anyway with no apparent problems.

SUMMARY

One of the first steps that researchers engage in while preparing to conduct a study is to make sure that their variables are well defined and measurable. The complex, abstract hypothetical constructs of interest to psychologists are often difficult to measure directly, so researchers rely on operational definitions that are clear and objective; these operational definitions are never perfect ways to measure concepts, but they are useful.

Once the concepts are defined, researchers have to decide whom they are going to sample. If the overall population of interest is well specified, researchers can use probability sampling that leads to groups of people that are likely to be representative of the entire population. Unfortunately, random sampling is virtually impossible for most psychological research, so investigators rely on convenience sampling. The people in these samples do not always behave in the same ways that the overall population does. In spite of this limitation, though, psychologists believe that research with convenience samples can often generalize to the population.

In the end, the usefulness of research will depend on whether measurements are reliable and valid. Reliability refers to whether the same results occur with repeated measurement or across different measurements. Validity refers to how well the measurements tap into the concepts that researchers are trying to measure. Measurements can be reliable but not valid. By definition, if measurements are valid, they must be reliable.

When we are able to control for outside factors that affect the behavior of research participants, we can maximize the internal validity of our studies. Sometimes we are more concerned with internal validity, that is, the structure of the experiment itself. At other times, though, we are more concerned with external validity, the extent to which our results make sense outside the confines of our own research setting.

There are other types of validity as well, including construct validity, which relates to how well we operationally define our hypothetical constructs. We also pay attention to convergent and divergent validity, the degree to which measurements are associated with related constructs or differ from unrelated constructs. Finally, statistical conclusion validity relates to whether a researcher uses statistical tests that lead to the most meaningful conclusions possible.

REVIEW QUESTIONS

Multiple Choice Questions

1. The complex, abstract concepts that we cannot observe directly but that we study in psychology are
   a. manipulations.
   b. variables.
   c. main effects.
   d. constructs.
2. When we discuss hypothetical constructs in terms of how we measure it, we are using
   a. quasi-experimental variables.
   b. operational definitions.
   c. task variables.
   d. factorial designs.
3. When psychologists develop their experiments, they will decide what they want to manipulate as part of the experimental procedure. The variable controlled by the experimenter is the _____ variable.
   a. hypothetical.
   b. extraneous.
   c. independent.
   d. construct.
4. If a research project is set up so everybody in the population of interest has an equal chance of being included, the research involves
   a. quota sampling.
   b. judgmental sampling.
   c. probability sampling.
   d. convenience sampling.
5. Suppose a researcher created a list of the names of everybody in a population of interest and selected every 10th name in order to get a list of participants. This means of sampling is
   a. simple random sampling.
   b. systematic sampling.
   c. quota sampling.
   d. cluster sampling.
6. You could create a stratified random sample by
   a. breaking the population into subgroups and randomly selecting participants from each subgroup.
   b. randomly selecting participants from the names of everybody in your population.
   c. creating clusters of people in the population and selecting everybody from randomly chosen clusters.
   d. using chain-referral sampling.

7. The research on bulimia often involves participants who are referred by doctors to the researchers. This means that those suffering from bulimia not requiring medical intervention are missed. This problems reflects
   a. measurement error.
   b. nonsampling error.
   c. a quasi-experimental design.
   d. participant sampling.

8. If you conducted research that relied on students from introductory psychology classes who volunteered to participate, you would be using a
   a. quota sample.
   b. stratified sample.
   c. systematic sample.
   d. convenience sample.

9. Purposive sampling involves
   a. using research participants from specifically identified subpopulations.
   b. making sure that critical subgroups are included in your research sample.
   c. identifying people with particular characteristics of interest to you and testing them.
   d. systematically sampling every nth person in the population.

10. Suppose a researcher measures a behavior in a research sample, then repeats data collection to see if the results are the same. If the data provided by each person is very similar on the two occasions, the measurement shows
    a. reliability.
    b. validity.
    c. generalizability.
    d. low nonsampling error.

11. A test shows split-half reliability if
    a. the test is split into small components and people respond similarly to each part.
    b. the test leads to similar results more than 50 percent of the time.
    c. the hypothetical constructs have adequate operational definitions.
    d. the predictor and criterion variables are related.

12. If a measurement of depression on a standardized depression inventory is useful in understanding an individual's depression, that measurement is said to
    a. show good reliability.
    b. eliminate nonsampling error.
    c. be representative.
    d. have validity.

13. Construct validity refers to how well
    a. your operational definitions relate to the underlying concepts you are trying to measure.
    b. your measurements agree with the measurements of others.
    c. your statistical tests help you answer your research questions.
    d. your measurements correlate with one another.

14. If you want to generalize the results of your research to a different population, your measurements should show
    a. convergent validity.
    b. construct validity.
    c. external validity.
    d. internal validity.

15. When laboratory research settings are created to resemble the real-life situations they are investigating, the effect is to lead to
   a. the Hawthorne effect.
   b. causal ambiguity.
   c. random selection.
   d. mundane realism.

Essay Questions

16. Describe how three different types of psychologists (e.g., social psychologist, developmental psychologist) could study a concept like happiness.
17. Identify two major reasons why psychological research typically does not involve probability samples.
18. If you have to sacrifice either internal validity or external validity, which would be better to sacrifice? Why?

ANSWERS TO REVIEW QUESTIONS

Answers to Multiple Choice Questions

1. d	6. a	11. a
2. b	7. b	12. d
3. c	8. d	13. a
4. c	9. c	14. c
5. b	10. a	15. d

Answers to Essay Questions

16. Describe how three different types of psychologists (e.g., social psychologist, developmental psychologist) could study a concept like happiness.

   Suggested points:

   a. A social psychologist could study how interactions with others influence happiness.
   b. A psychometrician would try to figure out ways to define and measure happiness.
   c. A neuroscientist could study what areas of the brain are involved in feelings of happiness.
   d. A developmental psychologist could monitor patterns of happiness through the lifespan.
   e. A clinical could investigate how people with emotional disturbances regain feelings of happiness.

17. Identify two major reasons why psychological research typically does not involve probability samples.

   Possible points:

   a. We generally don't have the resources necessary to sample randomly. It would take considerable time, money, and energy to collect information from diverse groups of people. So we take the easier route most of the time, using college students. It is an imperfect strategy but it does yield useful results.
   b. We may not be able to identify our population of interest specifically enough to be able to specify the population, so we cannot develop a sampling strategy that would generate a probability sample.
   c. When psychologists engage in theoretical research, the population may not be of great interest. The test of a theory should produce the expected results, regardless of the nature of either the sample or the population.

18. If you have to sacrifice either internal validity or external validity, which would be better to sacrifice? Why?

Suggested points:

Depending on your goals, one type of validity may be preferable if you have to sacrifice. If you are testing a theory, internal validity is more critical because you are assessing whether your theoretical ideas lead to good predictions about behavior and what causes it. If you are trying to find the effect of a single variable on behavior, internal validity will be critical.

If you are interested in applying results of research to a real-world setting, external validity might be more important. You might lose some confidence in your statements of causation, but you might have more confidence in your ability to make predictions accurately.

■ ■ ■ ■ ■

CHAPTER SIX

CONDUCTING AN EXPERIMENT
General Principles

CHAPTER OVERVIEW

LEARNING OBJECTIVES ■ **KEY TERMS** ■ **CHAPTER PREVIEW**

LEARNING OBJECTIVES

After going through this chapter, you will be able to:

- Outline the logic of experimental manipulations
- Identify the three criteria for establishing cause-and-effect relations
- Define the concept of causal ambiguity
- Differentiate experimental, control, and placebo groups
- Identify and explain the different types of reliability
- Identify and explain the different types of validity
- Explain the why validity implies reliability, but reliability does not imply validity
- Describe different kinds of experimenter effects
- Describe different kinds of participant effects
- Describe different kinds of interaction effects between experimenter and participant

KEY TERMS

Biosocial effect, p. 161
Blind study, p. 159
Causal ambiguity, p. 152
Confound, p. 154
Control group, p. 152
Covariance rule, p. 151
Cover story, p. 158
Demand characteristics,
    p. 159

Double blind study,
    p. 159
Evaluation
    apprehension, p. 160
Experiment, p. 149
Experimental realism,
    p. 162
Experimental group,
    p. 152

Experimenter bias,
    p. 158
Extraneous variable,
    p. 154
Hawthorne effect, p. 159
Internal validity rule,
    p. 151
Mundane realism,
    p. 162

Placebo group, p. 152
Psychosocial effect,
    p. 161
Single blind study,
    p. 159
Temporal precedence
    rule, p. 151

CHAPTER PREVIEW

If you want to study behavior, it is helpful to be able to describe and predict behavior, but it will be more satisfying to know why people act the way they do. It is relatively easy to observe different kinds of behavior and, from there, to make predictions about other behaviors. Most of us have a general sense of how people are going to act in certain circumstances (although we are fooled often enough). The real goal is to understand the causes of behavior.

In research, we choose experimental designs when we want to discover causation. Descriptive approaches can be quite useful for making predictions about behavior, but they do not inform us about the underlying reasons for those behaviors.

In the simplest experiment, the researcher creates a treatment group that will be compared to an untreated, or control, group. If the two groups start equal but end up different, we presume that the treatment made a difference. In practice, most studies employ more than two groups, but the logic is the same regardless of the number of groups.

Complications arise in any research project because small details of the research situation often have effects on participants' behaviors that we don't anticipate or even recognize. Further, because an experimental session involves an interaction between people—an experimenter and a participant—social effects can contribute to changes in behavior.

Nonetheless, we try to construct our research design to have maximal reliability and internal validity. We create an experimental approach that others can repeat and obtain the same pattern of results; we also put together a study whose results provide meaningful answers to our questions.

CHOOSING A METHODOLOGY: THE PRACTICALITIES OF RESEARCH

> **Experiment**—A research project in which the investigator creates initially equivalent groups, systematically manipulates an independent variable, and compares the groups to see if the independent variable affected the subsequent behavior.

In psychology, the word **experiment** has a specific meaning. It refers to a research design in which the investigator actively manipulates and controls variables. Scientists regard experimental methods of research as the gold standard against which we compare other approaches because experiments let us determine what causes behavior, which can lead to the ultimate scientific goal—control. In general, researchers often prefer experiments over other methods such as surveys, observational studies, or other descriptive and correlational approaches.

It is important to understand the difference between an experiment and other ways of carrying out a research project because in everyday language people often refer to any data collection project as an experiment. In fact, until the middle of the 1900s, psychologists, like other scientists, referred to any research project as an experiment. Since then, however, psychologists have used the term in a specific way.

An experiment is a methodology in which a researcher controls variables systematically. The researcher alters the level, intensity, frequency, or duration of a variable and examines any resulting change in behavior. As such, research is experimental only when the investigator has control over the variable that might affect a behavior. By controlling and manipulating variables systematically, we can determine which variables influence behaviors that we are studying.

Given that we recognize the advantage of the experimental approach, why would we bother to consider other types of research strategies? The answer is that ethical and practical considerations dictate the approaches we use. For example, suppose we wanted to know whether the amount of sleep a pregnant woman gets affects a baby's weight at birth. It would be unethical to force a woman to get a certain number of hours of sleep each night. It would also be impossible to do. You can't force people to sleep. In addition, in the course of living a life, people don't always stick to the same schedule every day. There are too many inconsistencies in people's lives to permit strict control over sleeping schedules.

An investigator who wanted to see the relation between amount of sleep women get and their newborn babies' weights would have two basic options: to experiment with non-human animals or to use a nonexperimental method.

In some areas of psychology, the experimental approach predominates. In other domains, researchers choose other methods. In the end, the choice of research strategies depends on the practicalities of the project. Sometimes experiments are possible and feasible; sometimes they are possible but not realistic. Sometimes they are simply impossible. Psychologists have to use good judgment and creativity in deciding what will work best in their research.

DETERMINING THE CAUSES OF BEHAVIOR

Describing behavior is fairly easy. Predicting behavior is usually more difficult. Understanding exactly why people act as they do and controlling behavior is fiendishly difficult, especially because our ideas of causation may be affected by our favored theory or our cultural perspective. Nonetheless, one of the ultimate goals of most sciences is to be able to exert control over events in our world.

Trying to Determine Causation in Research

Research psychologists who want to know what factors lead to a certain behavior follow a logical plan in the experiments they devise. The details of different studies vary widely, but the underlying concept is consistently very simple. In the simplest situation, we identify a factor that, when present, affects the way a person acts (or increases the probability of a certain behavior) but that, when absent, results in the person's acting differently.

For instance, we know that depressed people have typically experienced more stressful, negative life events than nondepressed people. Positive life events may lessen depression that already exists (Dixon & Reid, 2000). This fact may be quite relevant to you because college students seem particularly prone to stress and to symptoms of depression, being among the top 10 health concerns among college students (American College Health Association, 2009; Gloria, Castellanos, Kanagui-Muñoz, & Rico, 2012).

Could we find out if positive experiences would make a difference in level of depression? We might expose depressed students to different levels of positive feedback. If those who received the most feedback showed lower levels of depression, we could conclude that more positive feedback causes lower levels of depression.

Requirements for Cause–Effect Relationships

In simple terms, if three particular conditions are met, we conclude that a variable has a causal effect. The first condition for claiming causation involves the **covariance rule**. Two variables need to be correlated (i.e., to vary together in predictable ways—to covary) so you can predict the level of one variable given the level of the other. In the example of depression, you can predict the degree of depression from the number of positive life events. More positive life events are associated with lower depression (Dixon & Reid, 2000).

Covariance Rule—One of the criteria for assessing causation such that a causal variable must covary systematically with the variable it is assumed to cause.

Knowing that the two variables are correlated does not establish causation. As virtually all statistics students learn, correlation does not equal causation. But you need correlation if there is to be causation; correlation is one requirement for determining causation, even though it is not sufficient by itself. As Dixon and Reid pointed out, depression could be a causal variable, not the effect. People who were depressed might have sought out fewer positive situations.

Temporal Precedence Rule—One of the criteria for assessing causation such that the variable assumed to have a causal effect must precede the effect it is supposed to cause, that is, the cause must come before the effect.

In order to determine causation, we need to satisfy two other conditions. A second critical element is the **temporal precedence rule**; that is, the cause has to precede the effect. This makes sense based on our everyday experience. An effect occurs only after something else causes it to occur.

If covariance and temporal precedence hold, we need to meet one further criterion. We have to rule out other causal variables, satisfying the **internal validity rule**. Some unknown factor may be affecting the depression and also the number of positive life events. For instance, perhaps a person finds himself or herself socially isolated. This might cause depression; it might also cause a person to have fewer positive life events. Thus, it could be the social isolation that actually influences the degree of depression as well as the number of positive life events.

Internal Validity Rule—One of the criteria for assessing causation such that the variable assumed to be causal must be the most plausible cause, with other competing variables ruled out as the cause.

Establishing internal validity is extremely difficult because our behaviors are influenced by multiple factors. Even in a well-controlled experiment, it is not unusual for participants to be affected in ways the experimenter doesn't know. Later in the chapter, you will see how some of these extraneous variables affect our research.

Causal Ambiguity—The situation of uncertainty that results when a researcher cannot identify a single logical and plausible variable as being the cause of some behavior, ruling out other possible causal variables.

Experimental Group—The group (or groups) in an experiment that receives a treatment that might affect the behavior of the individuals in that group.

Control Group—The group in an experiment that receives either no treatment or a standard treatment with which new treatments are compared.

Placebo Group—In medical research, the comparison group in an experiment that receives what appears to be a treatment, but which actually has no effect, providing a comparison with an intervention that is being evaluated.

In summary, the only time we are safe in determining a causal relationship between two variables is when (a) two variables covary, (b) the causal variable precedes the effect, and (c) we can rule out any other variables that could affect the two variables in question. Unless these three criteria are met, we are in a state of **causal ambiguity**.

THE LOGIC OF EXPERIMENTAL MANIPULATION

The logic of an experiment is simple, even for complex studies. Most psychological experiments involve comparison of more than two groups, but describing research with two groups involves the same logic. So we'll start with a discussion of research with two sets of people (or other animals). If you understand the idea here, you will understand the structure of any experiment.

The basic idea of our simple, hypothetical experiment is this: You start with two groups that are the same, then you do something to one group that you don't do to the other. The group that experiences the manipulation is called the **experimental group**; the group that doesn't is called the **control group**. (In medical research, this approach is called a randomized clinical trial, or RCT, and may use a control group called the **placebo group** if it receives a sham, or fake, treatment.) If the two groups behave differently afterward, whatever you did to the experimental group must have caused the change. The scheme for the simplest experimental design appears in Figure 6.1.

If you understand the logic of this approach, you can comprehend more complex designs. Experimental designs usually involve multiple groups that receive different experimental manipulations; most of the time there is no control group as such. Rather, each group receives a different treatment. The simple questions that would allow us to create meaningful two-group studies have often been answered; we need to create more complex designs in order to advance our knowledge. In this chapter, you will learn about the principles and the practicalities of each component of the logic presented in Figure 6.1.

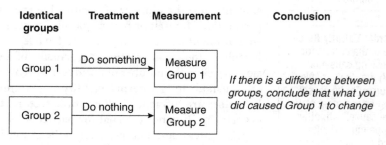

FIGURE 6.1   Logic of an experiment.

CONTROVERSY:
Withholding Treatment in Medical Research

One possible protocol for testing new medical treatments involves an experimental group that receives a new treatment and a placebo group that appears to be getting treatment but is not. For many maladies, people improve on their own, without any medical intervention. In the experimental/placebo design, the researchers are interested in the difference in rate of recovery or severity of symptoms between the two groups.

A critical question is whether people should be denied treatment for the sake of research that might benefit people later on, but not the patient now. Ethical guidelines prohibit sacrificing a person's health now for a future set of people. On the other hand, many current medical interventions have not been tested empirically to see if they actually work. Physicians often prescribe treatments because somebody taught them to, not because there has been research on the topic. For instance, for decades, physicians used lidocaine to prevent heart attacks even though there is evidence that it doesn't help (Olkin, 1992).

Further, many medical treatments in some specialties (up to 63 percent) have not been subjected to randomized clinical trials. (Many of these interventions are based on other kinds of evidence, though.) Still, the published research on the degree to which treatments have been empirically tested reveals that just under a quarter of them have not received scrutiny regarding their effectiveness (Imrie & Ramey, 2000).

We have a dilemma here. If we can't use a placebo group in research, we can never perform research to establish if a treatment works. This has troublesome implications. For example, in the 1950s, premature babies were given oxygen to help them breathe. This sounds reasonable, but the oxygen caused blindness in many of the babies. For ethical reasons it would have been unthinkable to withhold oxygen or even to lower the dosage in a research study.

As it turns out, though, premature babies of poor mothers were given lower levels of treatment, including less oxygen. These infants did not suffer the blindness that babies given standard treatment did.

It is interesting that we would not consider it ethical to withhold treatment for the babies in a research project, yet society as a whole does not think it is unethical to withhold treatment for poor babies due to economic factors. Ironically, in the case of the premature babies in the 1950s, this natural experiment showed the benefit of giving less oxygen or no oxygen; for once, those on the lower end of the economic continuum benefitted.

Currently, ethical guidelines in medical research on new treatments are such that the design typically involves comparing a new approach to a standard medical treatment, so there may not be a true placebo group.

Question for Discussion: If it is unethical to withhold treatment, how can researchers figure out if a given treatment actually works?

EXPERIMENTAL CONTROL

If you keep the basics of experimental research in mind, it becomes apparent why it is critical to control the research environment very carefully. The essence of good experimental research is the control that an investigator has over the situation and the people in it. When researchers create a solid experiment, they minimize the presence of factors other than the treatment variable that affect participants' behaviors, and they are able to measure a meaningful outcome.

It is easy to specify on paper that you are going to manipulate a variable and measure the effect on a person's behavior. But it is safe to say that most experiments involve problems and surprises that the researcher has not anticipated. People may stop paying attention to their task, they forget instructions, they fail to show up for a lab session that requires group participation, equipment breaks down, and so on.

The problem is that surprises can arise at many different points during an experiment. For one thing, try as we might to create comparable groups, we are not always able to do so. When we administer the experimental treatments, initial differences that we might not know about affect the participants' behaviors.

Further, researchers may inadvertently treat people differently, leading to changes in behavior that have nothing to do with the treatment variable. In addition, when we measure the outcome, we can make mistakes in recording the data or we might use a behavior that is not a very good measurement of what we are interested in. Finally, when we analyze the results of the research, we might use a statistical approach that is not the best one available, and we might interpret it incompletely or inaccurately.

Even though life tends to throw us curve balls, there are steps we can take to maximize the likelihood that research results will be meaningful and accurate.

LACK OF CONTROL IN EXPERIMENTAL RESEARCH: EXTRANEOUS VARIABLES AND CONFOUNDS

When you think of all the factors that can influence people's behaviors, you can appreciate how hard it can be to control all the variables that might influence the behavior you want to observe and measure. Factors other than your intended treatment that affect the outcome are called **extraneous variables**. They are variables that make unambiguous interpretation of your results impossible: You don't know if your results are due to the effect of an independent variable or to the extraneous variable.

Extraneous Variable— A variable that is not of interest to a researcher and that may not be known by the researcher that affects the dependent variable in an experiment, erroneously making it seem that the independent variable is having an effect on the dependent variable.

One particular type of extraneous variable is called a **confound** or a confounding variable. Such a variable systematically affects participants in one group differently than it affects those in other groups. As a result, when groups differ at the end of a study, it may be because a confounding variable, not the treatment variable, affected one group. If researchers aren't aware of the confound, they may attribute differences to the treatment.

A confound may also obscure real differences between groups by raising or lowering the scores in a group affected by that confound. A group that might ordinarily perform poorly on a task could, because of a confound, show high scores. So that group could have an average that is not much different from a group that is really more proficient. As a researcher, you would conclude that your treatment did not make a difference when it really did. The problem is that the confound helped the poorer group, obscuring a real effect of the treatment. Thus, extraneous variables can erase the difference between two groups that should differ. Or extraneous variables can make a difference appear where none should be.

Confound—A variable that is not controlled by an experimenter but that has a systematic effect on a behavior in at least one group in an experiment.

One example of published research illustrates how even experienced researchers rely on public scrutiny of their work in spotting extraneous variables. Such scrutiny leads to advances in knowledge that go beyond the original study. Quinn, Shin, Maguire, and Stone (1999) investigated whether using night lights for children under the age of two years will lead them to become nearsighted (myopic) later. Previously, scientists studying chickens noted that the birds developed visual problems if they did not experience a period of darkness each day. These researchers wondered whether nearsightedness in people might be related to the incidence of light throughout the day and night. The percentage of children who became nearsighted was higher for those who slept with night lights than those who didn't.

As you can see in the bars on the left side of Figure 6.2, the results are shocking. When children had slept with their rooms illuminated, the incidence of myopia was very high. The researchers knew that their findings were preliminary and, given the correlational nature of the data, not appropriate for cause–effect analysis (Quinn, Shin, Maguire, & Stone, 1999). Still, the findings were intriguing and Quinn et al. offered their results to the research community.

Subsequently, researchers have been able to identify some potential extraneous variables at work here. First, it may be that parents with myopia, which they can pass on to their children, prefer to have night lights so they themselves can see when they enter their infant's room at night. (Stone noted that their preliminary analysis of parental vision did not reveal problems for the research.)

Second, the study was done in an eye clinic, which makes it likely that the children who were studied did not reflect children in general. Characteristics of the sample other than whether they had night lights may have affected the results.

Third, the study relied on parental memory from an average of six years before the study. Such memories are notoriously unreliable. It could be that parents with poor vision simply remember about night lights, which help them see, whereas parents with normal vision might be less attuned to such memories.

Subsequent to the publication of the Quinn et al. research, other research provided reassurance that nighttime illumination would not cause myopia (Gwiazda, Ong, Held, & Thorn, 2000; Saw et al., 2001; Zadnik et al., 2000). As you can see in Figure 6.2, none of these researchers reported the same pattern that Quinn et al. (1999) did. So you can feel confident that night lights won't have negative effects on eyesight.

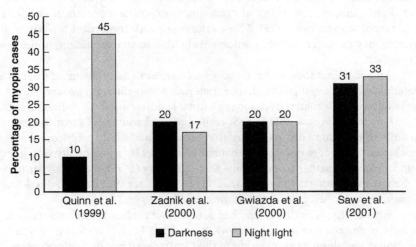

FIGURE 6.2 Incidence of Myopia as a function of presence or absence of night light.

In some studies, we may not be able to spot confounds and extraneous variables based on research reports. Fortunately, in the Quinn et al. work, because they provided enough detail about their methodology, others could continue to investigate their ideas.

Problems may also arise because research is a human enterprise. If there are two groups to be compared and if a researcher acts differently toward the people (or animals) in each group, the resulting behaviors may be different because of the way the participants were treated rather than because of the IV.

Rosenthal and Fode (1966) demonstrated that visual and verbal cues by an experimenter have an effect on participant behavior. Most researchers are aware that they may have an effect on the way experimental participants act. At the same time, the cues may be so subtle that the researchers (or their assistants) don't know what changes they are causing in participant behaviors.

Consider the effect of small wording changes on behavior. Elizabeth Loftus was among the first researchers to document the effect of "leading questions," that is, wording that may lead a respondent in a particular direction. Experimenters can unknowingly use leading questions or other wording that affects the way participants behave. Loftus (1975) showed her participants a film clip of an automobile accident, then asked them one of two questions:

1.   How fast was Car A going when it ran the stop sign? or
2.   How fast was Car A going when it turned right?

A final question asked, "Did you see a stop sign for Car A?" When participants had been asked Question 1, they were significantly more likely to respond that they had seen a stop sign. When the experimenter planted the seed of a memory, participants nourished that memory and began to believe in it. There actually was a stop sign in the film clip. Nonetheless, it was clear that the change in wording affected how people responded to later questions. There has subsequently been ample research demonstrating that false memories can be planted successfully (e.g., Mazzoni & Loftus, 1998; Loftus, 1997) and that slight changes in wording or even simply exposing a person to an idea can change later responses (Loftus, 2003). These effects are very important for you to understand because they can alter the way participants behave in an experiment, unbeknownst to the researcher.

An additional source of extraneous influences in an experiment can be the stimulus materials. When investigators change materials across different groups, subtle differences in the nature of the materials can make a notable difference in the outcome of the research.

Sometimes we are able to spot confounds and sources of error in research, but it is possible that we may not recognize that research has subtle problems that lead to poor conclusions. One area of research that has been beset by a potentially very important confound involves whether women show fear of success (FOS). Psychologists have identified FOS in women with a variety of tasks. Over two decades after the initial research appeared, though, some hidden problems became apparent.

Fortunately, scientific research is done so that problems can be corrected. As a result, we have overcome one stumbling block in studying FOS. It is clear now that FOS is not a function of sex alone, as you can see in the Controversy box on fear of success.

CONTROVERSY:
Do Women Fear Success?

Research over 40 years has suggested that women fear success. In a typical experimental participants read an essay and then wrote about it. Male participants read a story in which the main character was a man; female participants read about a woman. A critical sentence in the essay was "After first-term finals, John (Anne) finds himself (herself) at the top of his (her) medical school class." Horner (1968, cited in Kasof, 1993) reported that women wrote more negative essays, which he interpreted to indicate that women were more fearful of success than men. Subsequently, investigators studied such topics as sex discrimination, sex stereotypes, and fear of success by altering experimental stimuli for women and men by changing the name of the protagonist in a story.

We could debate Horner's original interpretation about women's fear of success, but there was a fundamental problem with the fear of success research that lay hidden for two decades. According to Kasof (1993), the names of the characters in the experimental stimuli were not comparable across sexes.

Researchers used male and female versions of a name, such as John and Joan or Christopher and Christine, and in as many as 96 percent of the studies, the female names were old-fashioned and associated with lower attractiveness, and they connoted lower intelligence than male names.

Recently, the attractiveness of the names seems to be more nearly equal. During this period, researchers learned that fear of success has little to do with sex per se and more to do with whether a woman holds a traditional view of sex roles (Basha & Ushasree, 1998; Krishnan & Sweeney, 1998; Kumari, 1995) and careers (Hay & Bakken, 1991), and whether she is gifted (Hay & Bakken, 1991).

Thus, psychologists have shown that the initial claims that fear of success was a female-oriented construct are misplaced. We also know now that fear of success is not limited to traditional, American samples. Investigators have documented it in Polish (Mandal, 2007), Indian (Sharma, Prabha, & Malhotra, 2009), and Chinese samples (Gao & Zhang, 2011).

Across cultures, additional factors include marital status in Chinese samples (Gao & Zhang, 2011), degree of self-actualization and anxiety in Western samples (Ryckman, Thornton, & Gold, 2009), and depression in Indian samples (Sharma et al., 2009).

Researchers have also studied fear of success in samples defined by their success: athletes. Among a group of elite French athletes, the reasons for fear of success differ across genders, with male athletes showing higher fear of success based on fear of losing motivation and heightened expectations of their performance. In contrast, female athletes were more concerned about social isolation as a result of their success (André, & Metzler, 2011). We still have unanswered questions that you could pursue, including those for a related concept: fear of failure.

Sometimes, apparently small changes in the way an experiment is set up (e.g., the stimulus names) introduce extraneous variables that can be more important than the IV. Now that we are aware of the effect of stimulus names, we may be able to identify more precisely who fears success.

Question for Discussion: How could replication with extension have helped overcome the problems with this research? Why do you think it took so long to discover the problem?

The problem with extraneous variables and confounds is that no experiment has complete control over what a participant experiences in the lab or over any of the participant's life experiences. If you set up an experiment as outlined in Figure 6.1, there are many variables other than the IV that could affect the outcome of your project. Conducting a sound study requires attention to detail and a good grasp of how researchers in the past have overcome the problems they faced.

EXPERIMENTER EFFECTS

> **Experimenter Bias**—The tendency of researchers to subtly and inadvertently affect the behaviors of participants in a study, obscuring the true effect (or lack thereof) of the independent variable.

One source of difficulty in research involves **experimenter bias**, the tendency for the researcher to influence a participant's behavior in a certain direction. If the experimenter thinks that one group will perform better on a task than another, the investigator may inadvertently lead the participants to act in the expected way.

How big a problem is such behavior on the part of the researcher? It is hard to tell, although when surveyors were studied to see how often they departed from the directions they were supposed to follow in administering questionnaires, the results showed that there were notable deviations from the standardized protocol (Kiecker & Nelson, 1996).

One of the most common departures involved rephrasing or rewording a question; the interviewers reported that, on average, they had done this about 18 percent of the times in their last hundred sessions. (The standard deviation was 27.2 percent, indicating that some interviewers may have changed the wording around half the time.)

These data suggest that, in an attempt to be helpful or to clarify a question, the surveyors regularly rephrased questionnaire items. Given the results of research like Loftus's (e.g., 2003), the changes in wording may very well have affected the survey results. We don't know how often comparable behaviors occur in experiments or how big the effects might be, but the survey results suggest that researchers deviate from their directions regularly.

Experimenter bias can also occur in the interpretation of data. For example, Medin, Bennis, and Chandler (2010) have noted that investigators studying people across cultural groups tend to view their own group as "typical," ignoring or being unaware of peculiarities of their in-group. By contrast, the out-group is seen as having more unusual characteristics. Thus, discussions of the two groups start out on an uneven footing, and comparisons are made on the basis of supposedly normal behavior (i.e., the behavior of one's own group) versus unusual behavior (i.e., the behavior of the out-group).

PARTICIPANT EFFECTS

The majority of psychological research with people involves college students. Students generally have some very desirable characteristics, three of which are a high degree of education, a willingness to cooperate, and a high level of motivation. These are helpful traits most of the time. Unfortunately, in the context of an experiment, they might pose some problems.

It isn't unusual for a student who participates in a study to try to figure out what the experimenter "wants." This can be a problem because the experimenter really wants the person to act naturally.

> **Cover Story**—A fictitious story developed by a researcher to disguise the true purpose of a study from the participants.

How might we keep participants from reliably picking up on clues? One means is to use automated operations whenever possible. If the participant reads the instructions, then carries out a task on a computer, there is less risk that the experimenter will influence the person's behavior.

A second strategy is to use a convincing **cover story**. This is a story about the study that hides the true nature of the research. Some people object

Blind Study—A research design in which the investigator, the participants, or both are not aware of the treatment that a participant is receiving.

Single Blind Study—A research design in which either the investigator or the participant is not aware of the treatment a participant is receiving.

Double Blind Study—A research design in which neither the investigator nor the participant is aware of the treatment being applied.

Hawthorne Effect—The tendency of participants to act differently from normal in a research study because they know they are being observed.

to deceptive cover stories, but others have argued that the nature and level of the deception is trivial. If you carry out your own research projects, you will have to decide on your own whether deception is warranted and appropriate.

Another solution is to use a **blind study**. In such an approach, the participants do not know the group to which they have been assigned, so it will be harder for participants to know what treatment they receive, so they are less likely to try to conform to expectations. When either the participants or the researchers do not know to which group the participants are assigned, we call it a **single blind study**. When the participants in different groups are blind, which is how single blind studies usually proceed, they don't have systematically different expectations that they might try to fulfill. When the investigators who actually conduct the study are blind to which group a person is in, it keeps a researcher from unintentionally giving clues to a participant. When neither the investigator nor the participant knows which group the participant has been assigned to, it is called a **double blind study**.

The Hawthorne Effect

When people change their behavior because they know they are in a scientific study, they can produce results that lack validity. This phenomenon is often referred to the **Hawthorne effect**.

The effect got its name because, nearly a century ago, researchers concluded that workers at Western Electric's Hawthorne plant near Chicago increased their output because they had been included in a research project. In reality, the studies were methodologically troublesome, including a number of confounding variables (Adair, 1984; Bramel & Friend, 1981). Nonetheless, the term *Hawthorne effect* remains in use to describe an individual's change in behavior while trying to be helpful to the researcher even though, according to at least one psychologist, it is so widely misunderstood that it is not even a useful concept (Lück, 2009).

Considerable discussion of the Hawthorne effect has been based on secondary sources. Writers typically pay little attention to the focus of the original work, which was on the effect of changes in illumination on workplace productivity. However, recent statistical re-analysis of the data of the original Hawthorne, including previously unpublished data, has shown the flaws in the research and reinforced the lack of an experimental effect of illumination (Izawa, French, & Hedge, 2011).

The Hawthorne effect is still a subject of research, and it is not limited to Western countries or industrial settings. For example, in an indoor air pollution intervention study in South Africa, even people in a control group that was not involved in the intervention showed positive effects in terms of use of fuel that is damaging to residents' lung, which the investigators attributed to the Hawthorne effect (Barnes, 2010).

Demand Characteristics—The tendency on the part of a research participant to act differently from normal after picking up clues as to the apparent purpose of the study.

One compelling example of a situation involving **demand characteristics** was provided by Orne and Scheibe (1962). These researchers told individual participants that they might experience sensory deprivation and negative psychological effects while sitting in a room. When the researchers included a "panic button," the participants tended to panic because they thought it would be an appropriate response in that situation. When there was no panic button, the participants experienced no particular adverse effects. The inference we can draw here is that when the participants concluded that a highly negative psychological condition would emerge, they complied with that expectation. When the expectation wasn't there, neither was the negative response.

More recently, Bryant, Mealey, Herzog, and Rychwalski (2001) discovered that people scored differently on the Rape Myth Acceptance Scale depending on whether a female surveyor was dressed conservatively versus provocatively. Such differences in responses might lead to very different conclusions that have nothing to do with a variable that the researchers are manipulating and everything to do with the attire of the person collecting the data.

Another source of bias associated with participants is **evaluation apprehension**. This bias arises because people think others are going to evaluate their behaviors. For example, people from China are more likely to generate less favorable self-descriptions when they believe others will be evaluating them than when they do not believe so Kim, Chiu, Peng, Cai, and Tov (2010).

> **Evaluation Apprehension**—The tendency to feel inadequate or to experience unease when one is being observed.

This evaluation apprehension is not always so benign. Researchers have shown that when people begin thinking about stereotypes applied to them, their behavior changes. Thus, women may perform less well on mathematics tests because women "aren't supposed" to be good at math (McGlone & Aronson, 2007; Spencer, Steele, & Quinn, 1999), African Americans may perform less well on academic tests because Blacks "aren't supposed" to be as strong academically as Whites (Steele & Aronson, 1995), and poor people "aren't supposed" to be as proficient as rich people (Croizet & Claire, 1998).

The effects of stereotyping hold true for people from different cultural backgrounds, including Italian (Muzzatti & Agnoli, 2007), German (Keller, 2007), French (Croizet & Claire, 1998), Chinese (Lee & Ottati, 1995), and Canadian (Walsh, Hickey, & Duffy, 1999). Fortunately, though, appropriate messages can mitigate them (McGlone & Aronson, 2007).

Surprisingly, even groups of people who are demonstrably proficient in an area can suffer from stereotype threat. Aronson et al. (1999) showed that math-proficient White males could be induced to perform more poorly than expected on a test of math skills if they were compared to a group that is expected to perform even better than they, namely, Asians.

As such, evaluation apprehension can exert notable effects on results in an experiment, making it seem that the IV has affected behavior when, in reality, a confounding variable has made the difference. This particular type of bias is likely to be more pronounced when the experimenter is examining participant (subject) variables, that is, the effects of predetermined characteristics like sex, race, age, and so on.

Comparisons between men and women, Black and White, young and old, rich and poor, and many other participant variables may result in distorted results because one group acts differently because they are "supposed to." Too many conclusions have probably been drawn about differences across groups because of effects related to evaluation apprehension in one form or another.

INTERACTION EFFECTS BETWEEN EXPERIMENTERS AND PARTICIPANTS

Research projects are social affairs. This may not be obvious at first glance, but whenever you get people together, they have social interactions of various kinds. However, when you are carrying out a research project, you don't want either experimenters or participants to communicate in ways that will compromise the study.

In a research setting, behaviors that we generally take for granted as normal (and maybe even desirable) become problematic. Consider the following situation: A college student agrees to participate in an experiment and, on arriving there, finds a very attractive experimenter. Isn't it reasonable to suppose that the student will act differently than if the experimenter weren't good looking? From the student's point of view, this is a great opportunity to show intelligence, motivation, creativity, humor, etc. In other words, the research project is a social affair.

Just as the experimenter and the participant bring their own individual predispositions to the lab, they bring their own interactive, social tendencies. Research results are affected not only by experimenter bias and participant bias, but also by interactions between experimenter and participant.

Biosocial Effect—The type of experimenter bias in which characteristics of the researcher like age, sex, or race affect the behavior of the participant.

Psychosocial Effect—The type of experimenter bias in which attitudes of the researcher affect the behavior of the participant.

If a participant responds to some "natural" characteristic of the researcher, we may have a distortion of experimental results due to a **biosocial effect**. For instance, if the experimenter seems too young to be credible, the participant may not take research seriously. Or if the participant is overweight, the experimenter may be abrupt and not be as patient in giving directions. Other examples of factors that could induce biosocial effects could include race, ethnicity, nationality, and religion. Obviously, these are not strictly biological characteristics, as the term "biosocial" implies. Nonetheless, these characteristics all pertain to what people may see as fundamental about another individual.

A different, but related, bias involves **psychosocial effects**. This type of bias involves psychological characteristics, like personality or mood. Researchers with different personality characteristics act differently toward participants. For instance, researchers high in the need for social approval smile more and act more friendly toward participants than those lower in this need (Rosnow & Rosenthal, 1997).

It is clear that the way an experimenter interacts with a participant can affect the outcome of a study (Rosenthal & Fode, 1966). For instance, Malmo, Boag, and Smith (1957, cited in Rosnow & Rosenthal, 1997) found that when an experimenter was having a bad day, participants' heart rates were higher compared to when the experimenter was having a good day.

Realism in Research

A potential weakness of the experimental approach is that it is usually a stripped-down version of reality. In an effort to create groups that are virtually identical except for differences on one dimension, scientists try to simplify the experimental setting so that anything that will get in the way of a clear conclusion is eliminated.

Mundane Realism—
The characteristic of a research setting such that it resembles the kind of situation that a participant would encounter in life.

When we use simple laboratory situations for our research, the result is often a reduction in **mundane realism**. When a situation has mundane realism, it resembles the normal environment you live in on an everyday basis. If you have ever volunteered to participate in a laboratory study, you probably might have seen pretty quickly that the environment was different from what you encounter normally.

The low level of mundane realism sometimes makes researchers wonder if their experimental results are applicable to normal human interaction. The simple version of reality in a laboratory can give us useful information about human behavior if the tasks of the participants have experimental realism. This type of realism relates to whether the participants engage in their tasks seriously.

An example of a series of studies that has little mundane realism is Stanley Milgram's obedience studies. He asked people to shock others if they made a mistake in a learning task in a laboratory. This is not something that most of us will ever do in our lives. As such, the mundane realism is fairly low. On the other hand, the research participants acted like they were very engaged in the task, showing nervousness and extreme discomfort in many cases. This behavior suggests a high level of experimental realism. When research shows good **experimental realism**, the research results may pertain to the real-world behaviors the researcher is investigating.

Experimental Realism—
The characteristic of a research setting such that the person participating in a study experiences the psychological state that the research is trying to induce, even if the research setting is artificial, like a laboratory.

The critical element regarding realism is that we want our research participants to be in the psychological state of interest to us. The nature of the setting, regardless of whether it is a laboratory, may not be relevant. We are more interested in whether the person is engaged in the task in the way that will provide insights into behaviors we are studying.

SUMMARY

The single most important advantage associated with experiments is that they allow you to determine the causes of behavior. Not only can you predict the behaviors, but you can also control them.

The basic idea behind the experiment is that you start with two groups that are equivalent and apply a treatment to one of them. If differences appear after you do that, you can assume that your treatment made a difference.

If life were this simple, we would not need to pay as close attention to the details of research as we must. Characteristics of experiments, participants, and the context of the research can all affect the outcome of a research project in subtle but important ways. For instance, extraneous variables that you don't know about can affect the DV, so you mistakenly think that your IV is responsible for differences across groups. One particular type of extraneous variable is the confounding variable, which affects at least one group in systematic ways.

It is also important to remember that experiments involve social interactions among experimenters and participants. These interactions can affect the outcome of research in predictable ways, although the problem is that researchers are often not aware of these effects in their own studies.

REVIEW QUESTIONS

Multiple Choice Questions

1. The research approach that involves changing the level, intensity, frequency, or duration of an independent variable is
   a. correlational.
   b. observational.
   c. experimental.
   d. validational.

2. Psychologists have speculated that having more acquaintances leads to better health. Research has supported this connection. Which principle of causation is met in this relation between acquaintances and health?
   a. internal validity rule.
   b. covariance rule.
   c. causal ambiguity rule.
   d. temporal precedence rule.

3. If we want to conclude that a given variable has a causal relation with a second variable, we have to be able to rule out other possible causal variables. The principle of causation involved here is the
   a. covariance rule.
   b. internal validity rule.
   c. causal ambiguity rule.
   d. temporal precedence rule.

4. In a research project, a group that experiences the manipulated independent variables is called the
   a. independent group.
   b. experimental group.
   c. control group.
   d. placebo group.

5. Researchers have discovered that children experiencing Attention Deficit Hyperactivity Disorder (ADHD) show improvements if they attend classes on involving behavioral and social skills, compared to a group of ADHD children who did not attend the classes. The group of children who attended the classes constitute the
   a. experimental group.
   b. independent group.
   c. control group.
   d. placebo group.

6. In medical research, groups sometimes undergo an experience that resembles the experimental manipulation but does not actually involve that manipulation. Such a group is called the
   a. independent group.
   b. experimental group.
   c. control group.
   d. placebo group.

7. Extraneous variables
   a. tend to be problems in single blind studies, but not double blind studies.
   b. tend to reduce the degree of external validity in a study.
   c. can be avoided through random sampling.
   d. can sometimes be dealt with by using control groups.

8. A group of researchers discovered that people who slept with night lights as children were more likely to be nearsighted than were children who did not have night lights. In the end, the night lights didn't seem to be the cause; rather parental nearsightedness was. Parental vision, which affected the DV, not the night lights, reflected the presence of
    a. a single blind design.
    b. a confound.
    c. lack of mundane realism.
    d. lack of experimental realism.

9. In a double blind study, an experimenter cannot influence participants' behaviors differently across groups. As such, we should expect that there will be little
    a. Hawthorne effect.
    b. external invalidity.
    c. placebo effect.
    d. experimenter bias.

10. If a researcher deceives a participant by telling the individual that a study is about one thing, but it is really about something else, the researcher is using
    a. a double blind study.
    b. a cover story.
    c. experimental realism.
    d. demand characteristics.

11. When a researcher sets up a study so that the participants do not know to what condition they have been assigned, we refer to this design as
    a. a blind study
    b. a cover story design.
    c. a control design.
    d. an externally valid design.

12. People often change their behavior when they know they are being observed in a scientific study, a phenomenon called
    a. mundane realism.
    b. experimental realism.
    c. the Hawthorne effect.
    d. external validation.

13. When psychologists Orne and Scheibe (1962) gave research participants a "panic button" in the event that they began to experience negative psychological effects while sitting in a room, the participants showed panic responses. When there was no mention of a panic button, the participants experienced no negative effects. Orne and Scheibe were documenting the existence of
    a. experimenter bias.
    b. mundane realism.
    c. demand characteristics.
    d. evaluation apprehension.

14. Participants sometimes act differently than normal in a research project because of the race or ethnicity of the experimenter. This change in behavior occurs because of what psychologists call
    a. psychosocial effects.
    b. biosocial effects.
    c. stereotype effects.
    d. experimenter bias effects.

15. Initial studies of fear of success included descriptions of fictitious characters with corresponding male and female names, like John and Joan, who were engaged in activities that could lead to success. The researchers did not realize that
    a. research participants tended to relate those names to actual people they knew.
    b. women were seen as being high in fear of success but were really high in expectation of failure.
    c. the names used as stimuli in the research were associated with different levels of achievement, with female names being associated with less success.
    d. over time, fear of success became less meaningful among men but not among women.

Essay Questions

16. Why is research involving already existing groups rather than randomly assigned groups prone to the effects of extraneous variables?
17. Explain how demand characteristics and evaluation apprehension affect participant behavior in research.

ANSWERS TO REVIEW QUESTIONS

Answers to Multiple Choice Questions

1.	c	6.	d	11.	a
2.	b	7.	d	12.	c
3.	b	8.	b	13.	c
4.	b	9.	d	14.	b
5.	a	10.	b	15.	c

Answers to Essay Questions

16. Why is research involving already existing groups rather than randomly assigned groups prone to the effects of extraneous variables?

    When you use existing or intact groups, you don't have a guarantee that they are equivalent; that is, if you were to measure them on the DV, they might differ from the start. If you didn't know about this difference, you would mistakenly attribute a difference at the end of the study to the IV.

    When groups are created by random assignment, there is less chance that the groups will differ systematically because differences that could be critical are spread out randomly across groups.

17. Explain how demand characteristics and evaluation apprehension affect participant behavior in research.

    With demand characteristics, the participants react to the perceived demands of the situation, that is, what they think the experimenter expects of them. As such, they don't act naturally. Instead, they respond to clues in the environment to direct their behaviors.

    Evaluation apprehension affects participants as they act differently because they know they are being observed. They may act in a particular way in order to look better in the eyes of the researcher, for instance.

EXPERIMENTS WITH ONE INDEPENDENT VARIABLE

LEARNING OBJECTIVES

After going through this chapter, you will be able to:

- Explain how experimental research can affect real-world decisions
- Identify and differentiate between independent and dependent variables
- Distinguish between qualitative and quantitative variables
- Explain the differences between different types of independent variables (IVs)
- Explain how experiments can lead to causal conclusions
- Identify statistical approaches to different research designs

KEY TERMS

CHAPTER PREVIEW

When you create experiments, you are trying to find the causes of behavior. In order to establish causation, you manipulate one variable to see its effect on another. Many of the concepts that psychologists deal with are complex and abstract; consequently, we are forced to create working definitions of variables that represent concepts that we cannot measure directly.

When you create a research project, there are many possible ways to set it up. You have to decide on which variables are relevant to your research question, then you have to narrow down the number of variables you will manipulate so that your methodology is manageable. There are always more variables that would be of interest than you could deal with in a single experiment.

Psychologists have devised many different ways to develop independent variables (IVs) and dependent variables (DVs). No matter how researchers define their variables, it is very important that the variables be objectively measurable. This allows others to understand how research has proceeded and how the methodology used by the investigators may have affected the outcome of the study.

Sometimes psychologists create simple studies with a single IV; most such studies in psychology have several comparison groups. In other cases, researchers manipulate more than one IV in a single experiment. The advantage of a multifactor study is that we can get a better look at the complex interplay of variables that affect behavior. After all, in our lives, most of what we do is a result of more than a single cause.

After we finish conducting an experiment, we complete data analysis that helps us understand our results. There are several standard statistical tests that we use, but data analysis is an evolving field and new techniques and approaches are emerging.

DETERMINING VARIABLES OF INTEREST

One of the first things that researchers learn is that there is no single way to define psychological concepts for the purpose of doing research. In addition, most of the time, there is no best way to set up a study to answer a research question. The way you set up your experiment is determined by many theoretical and practical considerations. Your choice of variables will reflect the specific question you want to address, the variables others have used, and the compromises you make between what you would like to do and what you actually can do.

As you will see, there are always many more variables that relate to a research question than you can possibly manipulate. On a practical level, if you want to manipulate many variables, it can mean that you need an unreasonably large sample size in order to carry out the study; or it can mean that a research session is too long and complicated to be realistic. In this section, we will consider the types of choices researchers have made in one particular area of psychology and the law, the accuracy of eyewitness testimony. The discussion here will illustrate how many different research variables you could consider; in your work, you have to limit your focus to only a few variables in a single study.

This area has generated considerable interest because of its importance in society. Before we outline the way researchers adopt independent and dependent variables, though, we will see how this type of research provides a good example of how societal influences can direct or retard the progress of research.

The Interaction of Society and Science

Alfred Binet, who achieved greatest recognition because of his work that led to intelligence testing, suggested over a century ago that we bring psychological science into the legal system. Unfortunately, his idea did not gain traction in his home country of France.

However, German psychologists dabbled in the area and, in the United States, the psychologist and German expatriate Hugo Münsterberg successfully advocated for research in psychology and the law. But when World War I broke out, the public was not favorably inclined toward Germans. Consequently, Münsterberg's credibility and influence in the United States diminished, and there was only a trickle of research for the next several decades.

It was not until Elizabeth Loftus's influential book, *Eyewitness Testimony* (Loftus, 1979), appeared that psychologists in significant numbers began to investigate the interface between psychology and the law. More recently, research has been stimulated as we have become aware of the fact that the majority of people who have been convicted of crimes but subsequently exonerated by DNA evidence were convicted on the basis of mistaken eyewitness identification (Wells, Memon, & Penrod, 2006). This interface of psychology and the law has been an important area in which experimental research has influenced the criminal justice system.

Variety of Research Variables

It would seem that people should be able to recognize somebody they saw commit a crime, but the data show that what people consider a straightforward task is actually quite difficult. In fact, in a high-stress situation, 50 percent of soldiers were unable to identify a person who had been interrogating them for 40 minutes (Morgan et al., 2004). Researchers have used different approaches to address the question of eyewitness behavior. The process of identification is complex; so is the research on the topic.

For example, psychologists have measured how confident people are in identifying a supposed perpetrator in a lineup. Wells et al. (2006) have noted that this is one of the "most researched questions in the study of eyewitnesses" (p. 65). This issue is critical because of the value that jurors place on confidence, a judgment accepted by the U.S. Supreme Court.

As it turns out, there is a significant, but imperfect, correlation between accuracy and confidence in judgment. That is, if you ask people how confident they are in their recognition of a supposed criminal, you can't always count on their accuracy. In order to understand the accuracy–confidence relationship better, you also have to know about other variables, like the similarity between the suspect and others in a lineup, the nature of viewing conditions, whether the eyewitness has been given feedback on correctness, and whether the eyewitness has been coerced into identifying a suspect.

Experimental participants who express high confidence tend to be more accurate in eyewitness identification. But even with the significant connection between confidence and accuracy, those with high accuracy may still be wrong a quarter of the time (Brewer, Keast, & Rishworth, 2002).

Researchers have also found that it makes a difference if people in a lineup appear all at once (as in most television shows) or sequentially (i.e., one at a time). Studies have shown the superiority of sequential lineups in reducing mistaken identifications (Steblay, Dysart, Fulero, & Lindsay, 2001), although sequential lineups may also lower correct identification of the target (Meissner, Tredoux, Parker, & MacLin, 2005).

In addition to measuring how confident experimental witnesses are, researchers have studied eyewitness accuracy by measuring another variable, response time to identify a suspect in a lineup. It turns out that people who make faster identifications tend to be more accurate than people who are slower (Dunning & Perretta, 2002). Unfortunately, what constitutes a fast or slow response changes in different viewing circumstances (Weber, Brewer, Wells, Semmler, & Keast, 2004). So theoretically, response latency could be useful in assessing the accuracy of eyewitness identification; practically, however, response latency may not be very useful at all.

As you can see, the experimental research on the accuracy of eyewitnesses involves a lot of intersecting variables. This brief review shows how one small area of research involves an enormous number of potential variables. If we are to understand the conditions in which we can trust eyewitness testimony, we will have to research many different variables. There are many other variables that were not mentioned here that are important. When psychologists investigate eyewitness behavior, they have to choose which variables to include in a given study and which to ignore.

Although it is true that psychologists know that eyewitness testimony is quite imperfect, many in criminal justice systems around the world (e.g., in the U.S., in China, and in Norway) do not know that eyewitnesses are often wrong, including judges, jurors, and lawyers (Magnussen, Melinder, Stridbeck, & Raja 2010; Wise, Gong, Safer, & Lee, 2010; Wise & Safer, 2010).

Nearly four decades ago, the U.S. Supreme Court made rulings on the use of eyewitness testimony that, at the time, were beneficial. Since then, however, additional research by psychologists has given us a better grasp of important cognitive and emotional factors that affect eyewitnesses. Researchers in this field have commented that it is time for the legal system to update its knowledge about eyewitness identification, given that misidentifications occur about 30% of the time (Wells, & Quinlivan, 2009).

Fortunately, with the help of psychological research, the effect of fallible eyewitnesses may be reduced. The Supreme Court of the state of New Jersey has ruled that judges must now tell jurors that factors like stress, the passage of time, and having to identify somebody of a different race can reduce accuracy in eyewitness identification (Weiser, 2012). This ruling is seen by some as a distinctly important because it involves the most complete examination scientific evidence related to eyewitness testimony.

In this chapter, we will be talking about research with a single IV, which is always a good place to start. But it does not take long before the issues become very complex and require multiple IVs. In the next chapter, you will see how researchers combine in a single study several IVs of the type discussed here.

INDEPENDENT AND DEPENDENT VARIABLES

The best way to begin your study of any psychological topic is to make sure you understand your concepts. Then you can come up with ways to measure them. After a while, these measurements that are critical to research are taken for granted, but they have to be developed.

Let's consider the way psychologists have measured depression in different projects associated with depression and memory. Investigators have regularly found that depressed people show poorer memory than others. As you have read, one way to assess depression is to use a score on the Beck Depression Inventory (BDI). You could define the amount of information in a person's memory simply as the number of words he or she recalls from a list of words. These two operational definitions are straightforward. However, if you want to assess a causal relationship between depression and memory, you cannot simply administer the BDI and see the relationship between the BDI score and a person's ability to recall a list of words. In this example, the BDI score and the number of words recalled may very well covary. Depressed people may remember less than nondepressed people. But it takes more than covarying (i.e., correlation) for us to conclude causation.

The second criterion for causation is temporal precedence; that is, the cause (depression) must precede the effect (memory). If you bring participants into your laboratory and measure their BDI score and then assess their memory, you can conclude that the depression score came first. This still isn't enough to determine cause and effect.

The third criterion stipulates that you have to be able to rule out other causal variables. In this instance, perhaps if a person has a very catastrophic experience, he or she might show signs of depression and also have poorer memory because the flashbacks of the experience constantly distract him or her from remembering. We can't rule out such an explanation.

An optimal strategy is to use an experimental approach, inducing depression in one group and leaving a second group unaffected, then assessing their memory. If you did this, you would be investigating two variables, (a) presence or absence of depression, the IV and (b) amount of material recalled, the DV.

> **Subject (Participant) Variable**—An independent variable that resembles a true IV but that is created on the basis of some preexisting characteristic of the participant, as in a quasi-experiment.

For this research involving depression, a true experimental manipulation would involve creating two groups by inducing different emotional states in them, then measuring the DV for each person. This design would make use of a true IV that is controlled by the experimenter. However, sometimes we can't actively manipulate a variable.

Subject (participant) variables like age, sex, political affiliation, and so on are beyond the control of the experimenter and are not true IVs. We cannot create women and men on the spot. A person's gender comes with

Manipulated Variable—
A true independent variable that is manipulated by an experimenter, with assignment of participants to groups according to some system rather than on the basis of preexisting characteristics like sex, age, etc.

Measured Variable—
A variable that is used to create groups to be compared, but assignment of participants to groups is on the basis of characteristics of the participants rather than according to a system created by the researcher.

Quasi-Experiment—A research project resembling a true experiment that involves comparison of groups that are not formed by random or systematic assignment by the investigator, but rather on the basis of participant characteristics.

Ex Post Facto Study—
A research project resembling a true experiment but using existing grouped data that did not involve random assignment of participants to conditions.

Independent Variable—
The variable that a researcher manipulates in a true experiment in order to see if changes in the variable lead to differences in an outcome behavior.

the person. You can measure the variable of gender; that is, you can determine if a person is a man or a woman, but you can't manipulate it.

Many researchers will treat existing depression, gender, and similar variables as true IVs for the purpose of designing research, but in reality when they study differences based on such variables, the research design is correlational, which does not permit us to conclude causation.

If a researcher manipulates the variable, like induced depression, the IV is a **manipulated variable**. On the other hand, if the value of the variable comes with the person, like gender, the IV is a **measured variable**. Manipulated variables lend themselves to cause and effect explanations; measured variables do not. Studies involving measured variables are often referred to as **quasi-experiments**; they look like experiments, but they really aren't. We'll cover quasi-experiments in detail in the next chapter.

Sometimes when researchers use existing data to create groups, like using psychiatric patients with high versus low BDI scores to create comparison groups, the approach is called an **ex post facto study**. The data may have been collected during diagnosis and not originally intended for research. It may resemble a true experiment because groups are created and compared, but it is also really correlational because variables have not actually been manipulated. Table 7.1 gives some examples of manipulated and measured variables.

Researchers rely on measured IVs because they have to. After all, you can't change a person's sex, age, political affiliation, and the like in your experiment. Sometimes, though, you can create a manipulated variable when you would normally expect a measured variable. As you have seen, depression, usually a measured variable, has been studied experimentally.

Types of Independent and Dependent Variables

Psychologists have shown considerable creativity in generating diverse IVs. The need for a vast array of IVs is clear when you think of all the different areas of research in psychology.

Researchers make their decisions about their IVs based on what others have already done and on current circumstances. When you make use of ideas of other researchers, you can save yourself a lot of effort in generating new variables. If a process worked for another researcher, it might very well work for you.

An **independent variable** is one that the experimenter manipulates in order to see if it has an effect on behavior. An IV must have at least two conditions or levels associated with it. In a true experiment, the researcher randomly assigns participants to the different groups, which generally leads to groups that are comparable at the beginning of the study. If the groups differ at the end, researchers conclude that the change associated with the IV made a difference.

TABLE 7.1   Examples of and Measured Manipulated Variables in Quasi-Experiments and True Experiments

Research Question	Independent and Dependent Variable
Measured Variables (Quasi-Experimental)	
Question: Do unhappy people differ from happy people in their responses to failures in completing tasks? (Lyubomirsky, Boehm, Kasri, & Zehm, 2011) **Results:** Unhappy people who perform poorly on tasks tend to dwell on their failures and perform less well on subsequent tasks than happy people do.	**IV:** Whether participants believed that they had performed well or poorly on a task. **DV:** Time to complete a later reading task, degree of concentration on a later task.
Question: Do depressed people from an Eastern culture show better specific autobiographical memory than depressed people from a Western culture? (Dritschel, Kao, Astell, Neufeind, & Lai, 2011) **Results:** Depressed people remembered fewer positive words than nondepressed people did.	**IV:** Country of participants (Taiwan or Great Britain). **DV:** Score on Autobiographical Memory Cueing Task.
Question: Do brain waves of women and men differ after sleep deprivation? (Armitage, Smith, C., Thompason, S., & Hoffman R., 2001) **Results:** Women showed more dramatic increases in slow waves after sleep deprivation.	**IV:** Participant's sex. **DV:** Incidence and amplitude of slow waves during sleep as measured with electroencephalograms (EEGs).
Manipulated Variables (Experimental)	
Question: Does exercise affect people's memories for the previous moods? (Anderson & Brice, 2011) **Results:** After exercising, participants' moods improved; in addition, after exercising, participants believed that their initial mood was better than it had actually been.	**IV:** Whether participants exercised (jogging for 10 minutes). **DV:** Mood as reported on the Incredibly Short Profile of Mood States.
Question: Does treating patients for pain before surgery affect pain and recovery after surgery? (Gottschalk et al., 1998) **Results:** Treating patients for pain before surgery begins led to less pain and quicker recovery after the surgery.	**IV:** Type of presurgical pain treatment (Epidural narcotic, local anesthesia, no presurgical pain medication). **DV:** Pain levels after surgery; activity level after surgery.
Question: Are people more accurate in identifying potential criminals in a lineup depending on whether all those in the lineup appear at the same time or one at a time? (Meissner, Tredoux, Parker, & MacLin, 2005) **Results:** Identification is more accurate when people see potential suspects one at a time.	**IV:** Nature of simulated lineup (simultaneous presentation of potential culprits versus sequential presentation). **DV:** Likelihood of identifying the actual culprit.

Dependent Variable— The outcome variable that a researcher measures.

The behavior that may differ as a function of the IV is called the **dependent variable**. That is, the value of the DV (i.e., the measurement that the researcher makes) depends on the nature of the IV.

Qualitative and Quantitative Independent Variables

There are different ways of considering IVs. One way is according to the type of measurement involved in measuring the IV. Another dimension of IVs is the nature of the experimental manipulation. We will consider these separately.

A **qualitative variable** involves variation on a nominal scale. That is, the change from one condition to another relies on a difference in categorization. In some cases, investigators use IVs whose groups are qualitatively, rather than quantitatively, different.

Qualitative Variable— A variable whose different values are based on qualitative differences (e.g., female and male) rather than on numerical differences.

For instance, Lang (1995) reported on the amount of time that people with phobias spent looking at different types of pictures. As you can see in Figure 7.1, these people spent little time looking at pictures of animals (the source of their phobias), preferring even negative stimuli (e.g., a mutilated face) to the pictures of the animals.

A second type of manipulation in an experiment can relate to **quantitative variables**. Quantitative variables change along a continuum and will differ in amount, intensity, frequency, or duration. One clever experiment using a quantitative variable that tells us something interesting and important about ourselves was performed by Ross, Lepper, and Hubbard (1975). They demonstrated how we can persist in believing things that, in some sense, we know are not true. They showed student participants pairs of fake suicide notes and told them that one was real; the participants were supposed to identify the real one. After going through 25 pairs

Quantitative Variable— A variable whose different values are based on numerical differences, like differences in amount, size, duration, etc.

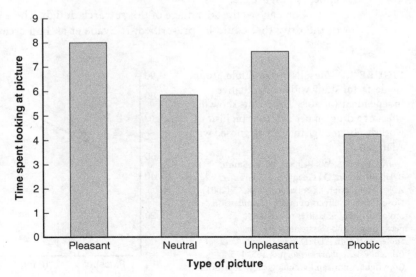

FIGURE 7.1 Amount of time participants with animal phobias spent looking at pictures. The data represent a qualitative dependent variable: type of picture.

Source: Lang, P. J. (1995). The emotion probe. *American Psychologist, 50*, 372–385. doi:10.1037/0003-066X.50.5.372. Copyright American Psychological Association. Used with permission.

of these notes, the researchers deceived the participants, telling them that they had either identified 24, 17, or 10 correctly. In this study, the IV was the number of correct guesses the participants were told they had made; it varied from high to medium to low. The experimenters had randomly assigned participants to one of the three groups in advance. The "24 correct" group was really no different from the "17 correct" or "10 correct" groups. This is a quantitative IV because the experimenters created three groups of participants who differed in a quantitative way—the number of correct responses they thought they had made.

The researchers then told the participants about the deception and that the feedback they were given was totally unrelated to their actual performance. The researchers then asked the participants to guess how many they really had gotten correct. The participants ignored the fact that the feedback on their performance was completely inaccurate, persisting in their belief that their actual accuracy matched the randomly assigned condition. That is, those who had thought they identified 24 of 25 correctly still thought they were above average, whereas those who thought they had identified only 10 of 25 still felt that they were below average. As the research showed, once people believe something about themselves, they become remarkably good at ignoring evidence to the contrary.

In this study, the IV had three levels, meaning three conditions, that differed numerically. One advantage of research with quantitative variables is that you can see whether more (or less) is better. You can also find out if there is a maximum effect when your manipulation occurs on a continuum. For instance, one example would be to see the effect of increasing dosage of a particular drug on people's or animals' behaviors. For instance, Evans et al. (2001) administered different amounts of the drug methylphenidate to students diagnosed with attention-deficit hyperactive disorder (ADHD) to get an idea of the dosage that would lead to optimal performance and behavior in school. These researchers found that a "more is better" approach is not necessarily optimal. In fact, a relatively low dose of the drug led to a very promising outcome, and improvements with higher dosages were not reliable across all students. The results of this single factor, multiple group design appear in Figure 7.2.

You can see the advantage of this research design. There are many possible dosages of the drug that could be prescribed. If Evans et al. had created a study with only two

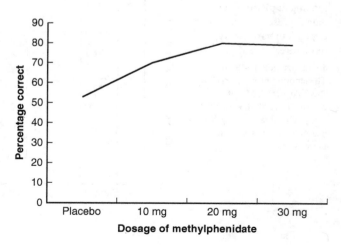

FIGURE 7.2 Results of a multiple-group, single-factor study with a quantitative independent variable. The results show the effect of a drug on performance on history worksheets among students diagnosed with ADHD.

Source: Evans, S. W., Pelham, W. E., Smith, B. H., Burkstein, O., Gnagy, E. M., Greiner, A. R., Altenderfer, L., & Baron-Myak, C. (2001). Dose-response effects of methylphenidate on ecological valid measures of academic performance and classroom behavior in adolescents with ADHD. *Experimental and Clinical Psychopharmacology, 9*, 163–175. Copyright American Psychological Association. Used with permission.

groups, it would have been impossible to get a good sense of how to use the drug most appropriately.

Some experiments lend themselves to qualitative variables, some to quantitative. You can also have a mixture of the two. Depending on the nature of your research question, you decide which approach to take. Table 7.2 presents some examples of qualitative and quantitative IVs and how they vary. As you can see in the table, researchers use qualitative variables like presence versus absence of a manipulation. For instance, Mennella and Gerrish (1998) wanted to find out whether the presence or absence of alcohol in breast milk made a difference in infants' sleep.

Why would anybody add alcohol to an infants' milk to see if it would sleep differently? Some people believe that alcohol enhances sleep. It would be worthwhile to find out if there is any benefit to an infant's being exposed to alcohol; unless there are clear positive effects that outweigh any negatives, we probably don't want to give an infant such a drug. As summarized in the Table 7.2, the benefit of alcohol is questionable indeed.

TABLE 7.2 **Examples of Qualitative and Quantitative Independent Variables and the Different Levels Used in Research Projects**

Research Question	Independent and Dependent Variable
Qualitative Independent Variable	
Question: Do infants sleep any differently when breast milk has alcohol in it? (Mennella & Gerrish, 1998)	**IV:** Presence or absence of alcohol in breast milk that had been expressed into a bottle.
Results: Babies exposed to alcohol sleep less and showed less movement (i.e., active sleep).	**DV:** Amount of time the babies slept; movement during sleep as recorded on a device that measured leg activity.
Question: Do bilingual people remember differently when asked questions in different languages? (Marian & Neisser, 2000)	**IV:** Language of stimulus words (Russian versus English).
Results: Russian–English bilinguals displayed better memory for events experienced while speaking Russian when quizzed in Russian; they remembered English-related events better when quizzed in English.	**DV:** Number of events remembered when prompted with a word either in Russian or in English.
Quantitative Independent Variable	
Question: Do jurors respond differently to strong evidence versus weak evidence? (Schul & Goren, 1997)	**IV:** Strength of evidence (based on witness's confidence, age of witness, and abnormality of defendant's actions).
Results: Strong evidence led to higher judgments of guilt unless participants were instructed to ignore it. When instructed to ignore strong evidence, participants did so.	**DV:** Judgment of guilt.
Question: Does caffeine affect blood pressure and heart rate in workers? (Lane, Phillips-Bute, & Pieper 1998)	**IV:** Dose of caffeine 50 milligrams–equal to about half a cup of coffee—versus 250 milligrams (equal to about two and a half cups of coffee).
Results: Higher levels of caffeine intake produced higher blood pressure and heart rate in workers.	**DV:** Blood pressure and heart rate as measured by a portable monitor.

You can also see how investigators use quantitative variables in Table 7.2. Schul and Goren (1997) varied the strength of evidence in a mock trial to see how participants would evaluate evidence that was supposedly strong or weak. Sometimes results can be surprising. In the mock trial, the pretend jurors were able to discount persuasive evidence of guilt when they were told to do so.

Independent Variables Created by Different Types of Manipulations

Another dimension on which we can identify IVs is according to how the IV is created. The IV can relate to the instructions that participants receive, the tasks they engage in, the situation, and the personal characteristics of the participant.

> **Task Variable**—An independent variable whose different conditions involve differences in a task performed by participants.

A **task variable** refers to an IV used to create groups that engage in somewhat different tasks or that are exposed to somewhat different stimuli. For instance, Sakaki, Gorlick, and Mather (2011) exposed their participants to pictures that were either negative (e.g., a snake), positive (e.g., appetizing food), or neutral (e.g., a woman talking on the phone). The participants' task was to answer one of three questions as quickly as they could. The questions focused on whether the picture involved a natural object, whether it depicted a common object, or whether it was large or small. As Figure 7.3 shows, when participants viewed negative pictures, it took them longer to answer the question than when the picture was either positive or neutral. The investigators found that simple judgments of size did not lead to different response times; they concluded that viewing negative pictures affects higher-order cognitive processes but not simple perceptual processes.

> **Instructional Variable**—An independent variable whose different conditions involve different instructions given by the researcher to participants.

With an **instructional variable**, the researchers provide participants in different groups with different directions. As you read above, Ross et al. (1975) discovered that people may not discount information that they learn to be false when they make subsequent decisions. McFarland, Cheam, and Buehler, R. (2007) found,

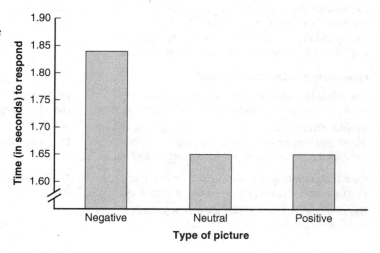

FIGURE 7.3 Time to respond to how common an object in a picture is as a function of type of picture. The independent variable in this example involves a task variable.

Source: Sakaki, M., Gorlick, M. A., & Mather, M. (2011). Differential interference effects of negative emotional states on subsequent semantic and perceptual processing. *Emotion, 11,* 1263–1278. doi:10.1037/a0026329. Copyright American Psychological Association. Adapted with permission.

however, that some types of wording will lead participants to reject incorrect information. After misleading participants, these investigators debriefed them either with a simple statement that the information was wrong or asked participants to engage in a task that made them think about the corrected information. When participants thought in some depth about the corrected information, it influenced later behavior, whereas if they received the simple statement, their behavior did not change. In this case, the IV was instructional because the participants in the different groups engaged in somewhat different tasks.

A **situational variable** involves changing the situation or context of the experiment for different groups. For instance, researchers conducted a study to find out whether inner city residents could be educated to engage in safer sexual practices (The NIMH Multisite HIV Prevention Trial, 1998). Participants either engaged in intensive, small group discussions of their sex lives and what they might want to change, or the participants listened to lectures and viewed a film on safe sex. All participants met twice a week for three weeks.

Situational Variable— An independent variable whose different conditions involve different environments or contexts for different participants.

In this experiment, the IV was situational: The participation involved different situations, the discussion versus the lecture. The outcome was that those people in the discussion groups experienced a lower incidence of sexually transmitted disease compared to the group that saw a film and listened to lectures.

A subject (participant) variable is used to compare people who differ on important characteristics at the beginning of a study. (Because the term *participant* sometimes replaces the term *subject* in psychological research with people, researchers also call these variables participant variables.) When you compare people on existing characteristics, this is not a true experimental manipulation; rather, it is quasi-experimental. Most researchers treat these subject variables as legitimate IVs, even though we know that we cannot attribute causation based on these IVs.

Cultural studies frequently report on subject variables. For example, de Fockert, Caparos, Linnell, and Davidoff (2011) compared a set of people from Western culture with rural participants from Northern Namibia in their responses to visual displays that had target stimuli that participants had to locate amid distracting symbols. The people from Northern Namibia were slower to respond than people from Western culture, but the Northern Namibians were less affected by the distracting stimuli.

In such research, you cannot assess the cause of any differences because, in addition to the difference in group membership, there are innumerable other differences across groups. It is important to recognize that the threat to internal validity is always present when you investigate people of different cultures. Your IV is only one of many possible sources of difference in behavior.

Similarly, researchers who have studied changes in the elderly have found a decreased sense of taste (Stevens, Cruz, Hoffman, & Patterson, 1995), but Schiffman (1997) suggested that it may be disease and medications that cause loss of taste abilities. When older adults are not on medications, she argued that their taste sensitivity doesn't decline. Age is another example of a subject variable that may speciously look like a causal variable. We are just too willing to believe that the elderly should be in a state of decline, so we attribute changes in taste sensitivity to age, ignoring other possibilities. This type of problem is always present with subject (participant) variables.

Types of Dependent Variables

Just as IVs can come in many varieties, so can DVs. DVs can be categorized as either qualitative or quantitative, for instance. They can also involve measures of amount, intensity, frequency, or duration.

When DVs are qualitative, researchers investigate whether a manipulation leads to different categorical outcomes. Suppose you were on a jury that had to decide on the guilt or innocence of a defendant. Your decision would depend on the nature of the evidence regarding guilt and innocence. It would involve a categorical outcome on a nominal scale; the defendant would fall into one of two categories: guilty or not guilty.

Psychologists have investigated the variables that influence jury responses. A typical approach is to present a fictitious trial transcript that varies in content to see if the change in content affects jury decisions on guilt and innocence.

On the other hand, quantitative DVs measure on an ordinal, interval, or ratio measurement scale. If participants in jury research assigned different monetary damages in a fictitious lawsuit based on different types of testimony, such a decision would involve a quantitative DV. Investigators using quantitative DVs are often interested in amount of change or direction of change in a score.

CONTROVERSY ON STUDYING RACE

Researchers have identified differences in pain responses in people of different races. One finding was that Blacks experience greater pain unpleasantness, emotional response to pain, and pain behavior than Whites, although pain intensity did not differ across groups (Riley et al., 2002). These types of comparisons will only be useful if the researchers are comparing groups whose members are meaningfully categorized. This same caution is true for the other behavioral differences that researchers have examined across racial and ethnic boundaries. There are several potential problems with research that investigates racial differences.

First, psychologists have increasingly questioned the categorization process. For instance, Helms, Jernigan, and Mascher (2005) pointed out that in much research, the investigators do not indicate the basis on which they included people in different groups. Operational definitions of the process of categorization are absent.

Second, investigators have convincingly argued that race is more a social than a biological phenomenon (Goodman, 2000). If this claim is valid, discussions based on race as a biological concept are bound to be invalid. Furthermore, genome research has shown remarkably little difference in genetic makeup across racial groups, with more variability within groups than across groups. In addition, Ossorio and Duster (2005) have pointed out that seemingly Black people can show genetic profiles resembling those typically occurring among Europeans, and seemingly White people can show genetic profiles associated with Africans. In light of this situation, Edwards, Fillingim, and Keefe (2001) have suggested that genetic research leads to the conclusion that race may be a meaningful construct only for discussion of behavioral and social issues, not biological or medical ones.

Third, there may be cultural differences in the ways that people within particular groups respond to pain. That is, those differences may be social rather than biological.

Fourth, social factors like discrimination and degree of access to health care may affect perceived pain. And factors like prolonged stress may affect a person's ability to cope with pain, leading to differences in responses to the pain.

Fifth, journal articles often do not mention the race and ethnicity of the experimenter. Research has revealed that the sex of the experimenter can affect pain responses (Levine & De Simone, 1991). It may be the case that the race or ethnicity of the experimenter may affect pain responses of patients and research participants.

These cautions are important because differences that appear with invalid grouping are, at best, hard to interpret. At worst, they may be entirely misleading. Given that a person may be assigned to a given category on one occasion and a different occasion on another is problematic (Helms et al., 2005). Even more distressing is the fact that racial categories are often based on what has been termed "folk taxonomies," that is, groupings based on social and stereotypical factors rather than scientific ones (Sternberg, Grigorenko, & Kidd, 2005).

Using Experiments to Determine Causation

The advantage of conducting a true experiment is that you can determine causation. For instance, several research projects have established the link between depression and poor memory. For example, Croll and Bryant (2000) found that women experiencing postnatal depression (i.e., depression after having given birth to a child) had poorer memories for events in their own lives and that it took them longer to retrieve memories compared to nondepressed women. In addition, adults over 50 years of age with unipolar major depression showed memory impairment that was unusual in a group that age (Lockwood, Alexopoulos, Kakuma, & Van Gorp, 2000). These studies are correlational, however, so they are not useful for finding causes.

It is not clear in advance that depression is causing the memory impairment. It could be that when people's memory begins to falter, they become depressed because of their memory difficulties. In order to experimentally explore this question of whether depression actually causes poorer memory, you have to define depression and develop some way to define thinking and problem solving. Then you have to induce depression in one group of people and not in another. Finally, you have to see whether the induced depression leads to worse cognitive processing.

Consider the research by Ellis, Thomas, and Rodriguez (1984). They induced depression in participants in one condition and did not alter the mood of people in a second group. Participants in the depressed group read a series of increasingly negative statements while the neutral participants read a series of very innocuous statements, the methodology devised by Velten (1968). In the Ellis and colleagues study, the participants with induced depression showed poorer recall of words (their DV) than those in a neutral mood. (This is a good illustration of a case in which the researchers decided to use another psychologist's methodology rather than creating their own.)

In this study, the researchers operationally defined depression as the state an individual was in after reading mood-depressing statements. They measured thinking in terms of the number of critical words the participants could recall. It is important in your research to make sure that you define your variables specifically in terms of how you measure or create them. Simply talking about "depression" or "thinking" is too vague.

Other researchers have defined thinking differently. For example, Bartolic and colleagues (1998) defined thinking, their DV, as the amount of brain activity, measured through electroencephalograms (EEGs), that took place when participants worked on a problem. Bartolic et al. also used Velten's methodology to induce depression in one group and to induce an elevated mood in a second group.

The research by Ellis et al. (1984) and Bartolic et al. (1998) led to the same general conclusion—that depression leads to changes in cognitive processing. Previous work had established a correlation between depression and poor memory, but the Ellis and colleagues experiments helped reinforce our confidence that the depression was causing poorer memory. The results from Bartolic et al. reinforced the idea that induced depression leads to similar brain activity as naturally occurring depression does.

Both of these experiments involved one IV and one DV. Ellis et al. (1984) studied the individual's mood (either depressed or not—IV) and degree of recall (number of words recalled—DV); Bartolic et al. (1998) investigated the individual's mood (depressed or elevated mood—IV) and cognitive activity (amount of EEG activity in different parts of the brain—DV). Their independent and dependent variables are clearly defined and obviously measurable. This makes it easier to understand and interpret their work.

Because these two studies used different methodologies but produced similar results, they have a good case for claiming good convergent validity in their discussion of the effect that depression has on thinking. Convergent validity is further established by the fact that the majority of published experimental research has shown the depression–memory link.

The issue is complex, though, and some research deviates. For instance, Hertel (1998) found that depression produced no worse memory than a nondepressed emotional state when participants had neutral thoughts, but people in the depressed state showed poorer memory when asked to focus their thoughts on themselves. Further, Kwiatkowski and Parkinson (1994) found that induced depression was associated with lower recall, but naturally occurring depression was not. The majority of research shows the depression–poor memory link, but investigators still have questions to answer.

CONTROVERSY ON STUDYING DEPRESSION EXPERIMENTALLY

In an experiment, the researcher creates a situation so that every participant in a given group is in the same psychological state with respect to the concept being studied.

If a scientist wants to see whether people in a depressed state act differently from those who aren't, the researcher depresses the people in the treatment group and compares them to people who have not been depressed by the experimenter.

This raises a dilemma and a question. First, is it acceptable to depress research participants to see if they behave differently from a control group? That is, is it ethical? As you already know, the ethical guidelines for research specify that a researcher should not put research participants at risk by exposing them to physical or emotional harm. You might argue that by inducing a state of depression, you could harm participants.

Second, if it is ethical to induce depression, how could you do it realistically? When people are depressed, it is often as a result of an accumulation of negative experiences. How could a researcher operationally define depression for the purposes of an experiment?

As it turns out, researchers have effectively used different means to induce depression in research participants without endangering them. For instance, Velten (1997) asked people to read statements that would depress their mood, like, "Every now and then I feel so tired and gloomy that I'd rather just sit than do anything." Others read statements like, "If your attitude is good, then things are good, and my attitude is good," which elevated their moods.

These statements had the desired effect, which was to induce different psychological states. The operational definition of depression here is the state a person is in after reading Velten's statements.

Is it fair to the participants, though? Was he exposing them to psychological or physical harm? Velten (and many other researchers using mood-changing manipulations) have asked this question and have used their expertise to anticipate the answer. Mood manipulations have weak and temporary, but consistent, effects. As a result, the researcher can induce a mood change that will not be very strong or last very long and that is easily reversed.

So it appears that we can safely and effectively induce a lowered mood. It is, fortunately, a pale copy of true depression, but we can use such changes in emotional states to study mental states related to depression. The good news is that such techniques are not harmful to participants when used carefully and can be used ethically to provide us with useful information about what happens when people are depressed.

Comparing Two Groups

If you have seen the movie *Legally Blonde*, you might recall a scene in which the attractive main character, Elle Woods, watches two women reject the advances of a male student. She then puts on an act in front of the other women to make them think that she finds him attractive. Afterward, those two women seem to find him more attractive. Is this purely fiction, or is there some reality to it?

Several researchers have carried out experiments to address this issue. Some of this research involves comparison of two groups. In a number of cases, the investigators have not studied people. Instead, they have observed the behaviors of birds and fish. This may sound like an odd strategy to learn about mating, but it has provided some insights into the way that organisms, including people, choose mates.

In many animal species, the female selects the mate with whom she will reproduce. According to evolutionary theory, she develops a strategy that helps her pick the mate with the best genes, presumably so that her offspring will have the greatest chance of survival. (Males of many species are generally less selective and will mate with as many females as possible.) One question that scientists have investigated is how those organisms choose one another for mating.

An interesting question in this area is to ask what causes a female fish to find a male fish attractive enough to want to mate with it. A number of investigators have researched this topic, with surprising results. For example, Hill and Ryan (2006) placed a female sailfin molly, a type of fish, in an environment in which she could choose to swim with either of two male mollies. The researchers recorded the amount of time the female spent with each male. They then let the female observe the less-preferred male fish interacting with another female sailfin molly. The next time she had the choice of which of the two fish to swim with, she spent more time with the formerly less-preferred fish, presumably because she had seen him with another female. That is, the researchers concluded, when the female saw a potential mate with another attractive female fish, that male became suddenly more attractive.

In this research, the investigators recorded the length of time that the female fish spent with the less-preferred male fish. Then they recorded the amount of time the female fish spent with that male after she had seen him with another female. In this case, the researchers defined the DV, attractiveness, as the amount of time the female spent with the male fish. Obviously, we can't directly assess what a fish thinks is attractive, but experts in this area agreed that the time spent with the male fish is a reasonable indicator of how attractive the female finds the male.

> **Repeated Measures Design**—A design in which a single participant is observed and measured on more than one level of an independent variable rather than measuring different individuals on each level of the independent variable.

In this example, the researchers used what is called a **repeated measures design**. They measured the DV twice for each fish—before the female saw the male fish with another female and again afterward—and looked for a change in the amount of time spent with the male. According to the logic of research, changes that occur after a treatment are likely to be due to that treatment. For this study, the researchers concluded that the female fish found the male fish more attractive because she had seen him with another female. (We will discuss the advantages of repeated measures designs more fully in the next chapter.)

This so-called mate copying behavior is not limited to fish. Researchers have found the same pattern with birds, too. In fact, even in bird species where birds are monogamous (i.e., two birds mate for life), there is a tendency among females to be attracted to males seen in the presence of other females (Swaddle, Cathey, Correll, & Hodkinson, 2005). In this research with birds, the DV was the amount of time the female bird spent in courtship display with the male.

Does the behavior of fish tell us anything about human behavior? Does it tell us anything about the behavior in *Legally Blonde*? It is a legitimate question to ask whether we can generalize from bird and fish behavior to human behavior. Referring to somebody as "bird brained" suggests that the person has a small brain and isn't very smart. When it comes to selecting mates, are humans any smarter than birds or fish?

Apparently, we may not be. A group of researchers (Jones, DeBruine, Little, Burriss, & Feinberg, 2007) showed women pairs of pictures; one picture was of a man paired with a second picture of a woman. The man's face was shown from the front; the woman's face was shown in profile, as if she were looking at the man. In one condition, the woman in the picture had a neutral expression; in a second condition, the woman was smiling. The question was whether the female participant would find the man more attractive, depending on the woman's expression in the picture. For this study, the researchers could not use the same DV as the investigators did with the fish and birds—that is, the time spent with the male. The human participants were only looking at pictures. (There are also ethical issues associated with fostering and observing reproductive behavior of people who participate in research.) So the investigators needed a different DV; they chose a common measurement, a score on a rating scale. The participants rated the man's attractiveness on an eight-point scale.

The participants were in one of two conditions. In one condition, the woman in the picture was smiling; in the second condition, the woman in the picture had a neutral expression. Thus, the IV here was type of facial expression of the woman in the picture; there were two groups for the IV, smiling face and neutral face.

The results showed a higher rating of attractiveness of men in the pictures when a woman appeared to be smiling at them. The researchers concluded that the IV (type of facial expression of the woman in the picture) affected the DV (the rating of the man's attractiveness). The investigators' interpretation of the results was that preferences for men were subject to social factors. The picture of a smiling woman next to a picture of a man increased the man's attractiveness for the same reason, the researchers concluded, that the attractiveness of male fish and birds increased—another female found him attractive, so he must have positive characteristics. Other research (Hazlett & Hoehn-Sarin, 2000) had revealed that women smile more when looking at pictures of attractive men. So when participants saw women smiling in the direction of a man's picture, the participants may have picked up cues about the man's suitability as a possible mate. In that research, the DV was the amount of movement of the muscles used in smiling; women smiled more when looking at pictures of men who were judged to be attractive.

Interestingly, when male participants rated the pictures of the men, the ratings were lower when the women was smiling. The researchers interpreted this to mean that the male participants unconsciously saw the man in the picture as competition.

In this study, the investigators used a slightly more complex design than described here, but one of their comparisons involved a simple comparison of two groups. As mentioned previously, most behavioral research involves more than a simple two-group comparison, but such comparisons can be a significant component of the results.

Generalizing Research Results

So can we conclude that the scene in *Legally Blonde* is more truth than fiction? Perhaps. We can recognize parallel behaviors across species, and we can identify behaviors caused by factors that we are unaware of. But we also need to recognize that there are limitations to the research cited here. One limitation here is that just because a woman sees a man as attractive, it does not necessarily follow that she will choose him as a reproductive mate. Second, there is a big difference between a female fish or bird's spending time with a male and providing a rating of attractiveness. Third, humans undoubtedly take into consideration many factors in deciding on a mate.

On the other hand, some preferences appear to be associated with biological factors that we cannot control and may not be aware of. For example, when women rated pictures of other women in one study, the ratings of the attractiveness of the women in the pictures depended on the estrogen levels of the female participants (Fisher, 2004). Women with high estrogen levels, reflecting maximal fertility, rated pictures of other women lower than did women with low estrogen levels.

What is clear here is that there are some parallels between the behavior of fish and birds and the behavior of humans. At the same time, we need to recognize that people make decisions based on more than attractiveness. Simply because attractiveness may change depending on the social context, it does not mean that people blindly follow hidden urges. Many other factors, including learned social norms, affect our behaviors.

The picture is complex, but sometimes simple experiments involving a comparison between two groups can provide insights into human behavior. Because our behaviors are not controlled by a single variable, though, we need to use caution in drawing conclusions based on a single experiment.

Comparing Multiple Groups

Sometimes a simple two-group experiment is too simple to answer a researcher's question. It may be necessary to create more than two groups in order to address an issue. Beins et al. (2007) conducted a follow-up study to previous research (Wimer & Beins, 2000). The earlier research involved presenting jokes to participants after they had learned to expect jokes that fell into one of the following categories: (a) horribly unfunny, (b) very unfunny, (c) very funny, and (d) hysterically funny. There was also a neutral category in which participants did not have any particular expectations.

In the earlier research, Wimer and Beins (2000) found that participants rated the jokes differently, depending on the message. When primed to expect mildly unfunny or mildly funny jokes, the participants gave lower and higher ratings, respectively. The neutral group was in the middle. The participants ignored the extreme messages entirely. (This earlier research was subsequently written for publication [Wimer & Beins, 2008].)

In the follow-up research, Beins et al. (2007) used cartoons rather than jokes and primed the participants to expect mildly funny or unfunny cartoons; there was also a group of participants who did not receive any message about how funny the cartoons were. So there were three groups to be compared. Figure 7.4 shows how the groups rated the cartoons. As you can see, there is a consistent increase toward more favorable ratings of jokes as you move from the prime to expect jokes that are not very funny, to the control group, to the prime about very funny jokes.

This humor research shows the advantage of having multiple groups. You can see how patterns emerge and gain a more complete understanding of what is going on in participants' heads. A simple, two-group study is useful, but a multiple-group study with one IV lets you expand the amount of information you get from your research.

FIGURE 7.4 Results of a multiple-group study in which the researchers compared the ratings of cartoons across three different conditions.

Copyright Bernard C. Beins, 2006. Used with permission.

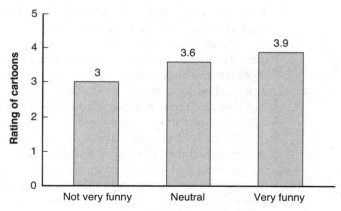

Data Analysis

Many tests are available for analysis of experimental data. When data are normally distributed, there are about equal sample sizes, and the variances of the different groups are equal, we typically use a group of tests referred to as parametric tests. When the data do not meet these criteria, we use nonparametric statistics.

The parametric tests predominate by a great margin. If you look at virtually any journal dealing with experimental methods in psychology, you will see great use of the Student's *t*-test, the analysis of variance (ANOVA), and Pearson's correlation, all of which are parametric. The tests are useful even when there are departures from the usual criteria for their use. You can see applications of the most commonly used tests in the statistics appendix.

Experiments with Two Groups

Student's *T*-Test—
A statistical test that compares two group means or compares a group mean to a population mean to assess whether the difference between means is reliable.

Researchers have traditionally used the **Student's *t*-test**, more often simply called the *t*-test, for comparing two groups. This test was invented in the early 1900s by William Gossett, who performed research for the Guinness Brewery. (The Guinness Brewery did not allow its employees to publish their work, so he published a paper about the statistic anonymously; he used the pseudonym *Student* in his article. This is why his test is called Student's *t*-test). At the time, it was the most advanced statistical technique available for experimental designs. We still use *t*-tests for such simple experiments, although it is acceptable to use the ANOVA (see below) to compare two groups.

There are three different *t*-tests, two of which are relevant here. The repeated measures *t*-test lets us compare two set of scores in which the scores are paired, as in a before-and-after design. The other relevant *t*-test is the independent groups *t*-test. It lets us compare scores in two groups when there is no connection between a score in the first group and any other score in the second group. When researchers randomly assign participants to different groups, this *t*-test is appropriate. (The third type of *t*-test is useful when a single group's mean is compared to a population mean. Researchers very rarely use this.)

Experiments with Multiple Groups

Analysis of Variance—
A statistical test that permits assessment of possible significant differences across multiple means.

When researchers use designs that call for multiple groups, the most commonly employed test is the **analysis of variance**, also known as the *F*-test. It was named after Ronald Fisher, who invented it. Recently, researchers have increased their use of regression analysis where they would formerly have used an ANOVA. In many cases, the two approaches give the same basic information.

The advantage of the ANOVA over the *t*-test is that the ANOVA permits comparison of multiple groups with a single test. It also keeps the probability of incorrectly rejecting the null hypothesis at the level the researcher sets, which is usually .05. That is, the ANOVA lets you compare multiple groups without increasing the chance that you mistakenly conclude there is a difference between means.

Planned Comparison—
A comparison of differences across levels of an independent variable when the researcher decides during the design of the study to make the comparison rather than waiting until after preliminary data analysis.

Post Hoc Comparison—
A comparison of differences across levels of an independent variable when the researcher decides to make the comparison after a preliminary data analysis.

If you compute an ANOVA and find that there is a significant difference between means, you don't know where the difference falls. For instance, in the research by Beins et al. (2007) in which there were three groups that received different messages about how funny a set jokes was, the significant F-value revealed that some of the groups differed from some others, but it didn't indicate which groups differed, only that there was a difference somewhere.

When you have multiple groups, you have options for comparing them after computing an ANOVA. When you know in advance which groups you want to compare, you conduct **planned comparisons**. When you look at your results and then decide to make a comparison between two groups, you use **post hoc comparisons**. There are different statistical assumptions associated with the two approaches. Without going into detail, it is enough at this point for you to know that the different statistics are designed to keep your Type I error rate from getting bigger than the .05 value you will probably use.

The philosophy underlying all of these tests is that your null hypothesis specifies that there is no difference between groups. The alternative hypothesis specifies that not all groups are equal. Supplemental tests can inform you about which groups differ if you conclude that not all are equal.

SUMMARY

In this chapter, you have seen how researchers create experiments. Psychologists recognize the importance of producing well-defined and objective definitions of the concepts we study. We have to develop concrete working definitions because many psychological topics involve very abstract ideas that are hard to study directly.

So in order to answer experimental questions, we set up one or more IVs to see how they affect a subsequent behavior, the DV. IVs can take many forms. The groups we study can differ quantitatively or qualitatively. Other types of IVs involve manipulations of situations, instructions, or tasks.

DVs are also quite diverse in different experiments. Most experiments involve manipulation of one to three IVs. It is not unusual for some experiments to have multiple DVs as well.

The advantage of comparing multiple groups at one time is that we can see how patterns emerge across several groups, particularly with quantitative variables. Furthermore, some questions are complicated enough that simply comparing two groups will not give us all the information we would like from a single study. So we add more groups to get a more complete picture of the behaviors that interest us.

After an experiment is complete, we analyze the results statistically to see if there are any significant effects. When researchers compare two groups, they typically use a Student's t-test, although there are some cases in which the ANOVA is appropriate. For experiments involving comparisons of more than two groups, researchers use the ANOVA. Finally, we have to decide what the results mean as we interpret the data and relate it to behavior.

REVIEW QUESTIONS

Multiple Choice Questions

1. The complex, abstract concepts that we cannot observe directly but that we study in psychology are
   a. manipulations.
   b. variables.
   c. main effects.
   d. constructs.

2. A group of psychologists studying humor reaction studied participants' enjoyment of jokes by recording how many times the participants grinned, smiled, and laughed. These measurements of grinning, smiling, and laughing to represent enjoyment involve
   a. manipulated variables.
   b. main effects of humor enjoyment.
   c. logistic analysis.
   d. an operational definition of humor appreciation.

3. When a researcher manipulates the environment to see if changes affect participants' behaviors, the behaviors that are measured for change are considered
   a. factorial variables.
   b. dependent variables.
   c. manipulated variables.
   d. repeated measures variables.

4. A variable that cannot be truly manipulated by a researcher, like sex or age of the participant, is called a
   a. dependent variable.
   b. qualitative variable.
   c. measured variable.
   d. situational variable.

5. When researchers use existing data to create groups for comparison, the approach is known as
   a. ex post facto.
   b. experimental.
   c. operational.
   d. quasi-experimental.

6. An independent variable whose groups differ on amount or frequency of some measurement is called
   a. task variable.
   b. quantitative variable.
   c. quasi-experimental variable.
   d. subject variable.

7. An independent variable
   a. has at most two levels.
   b. can have any number of levels.
   c. is never a manipulated variable.
   d. cannot be a qualitative variable.

8. Psychologists Marian and Neisser (2000) found that people fluent in both Russian and English had better memories for events experienced while speaking Russian if they were quizzed in Russian; they had better memories for events experienced while speaking English if they were quizzed in English. In this study, the independent variable was
   a. measured.
   b. instructional.

     c. qualitative.

     d. quasi-experimental.

9. When research participants listen to different types of instructions that might change their behavior regarding the dependent variable, we know that the independent variable is

     a. a situational variable.

     b. a subject variable.

     c. an instructional variable.

     d. a participant variable.

10. A study conducted by the National Institute of Mental Health revealed that when participants received a message about safe sex practices in a discussion format, they changed their sexual practices. In this study, the independent variable was

     a. a subject variable.

     b. a situational variable.

     c. an instructional variable.

     d. a measured variable.

11. Researchers who study differences in behaviors across races have discovered that

     a. differences in the sex of a researcher and a participant affect behavior more than differences in the race of the researcher and the participant.

     b. a person's social history, such a experiences of racism, may affect behavior, so differences in behaviors across races may not be due to race itself.

     c. racial categorization in older research was not objective, but new research has made categorization more accurate.

     d. genetic research has shown that racial categories are more useful for studying medical or biological phenomena and less useful for studying behaviors.

12. Researchers have wanted to set up studies to see if depression affects memory. To see if people who are depressed differ from those not depressed, researchers

     a. have induced mild states of depression in some participants but not others, then tested their memory.

     b. have typically given mild drugs to participants to simulate depression temporarily.

     c. have not discovered an effective way to induce, then remove, depression in research participants.

     d. cannot ethically induce a state that resembles depression.

13. Researchers who study depression experimentally have tried to induce mild states of depression in participants. This type of research

     a. has been considered unethical because of the possibility of psychological harm to participants.

     b. have been able to induce depression but have found it difficult to reverse the process.

     c. have found that some procedures seem to induce mild depression in a way that has construct validity.

     d. have found that experimental models of depression seldom match actual depression in useful ways.

14. The Student's *t*-test is typically used

     a. in comparing two groups to see if their means differ.

     b. when analyzing the results of a correlational design.

     c. as a follow-up to designs using case studies.

     d. in educational research.

15. Suppose you have conducted an analysis of variance in a design with multiple groups and obtained evidence of a significant difference among means. If you decided to investigate which means differed significantly, what test would you use?
    a. Multiple *t*-tests
    b. Planned comparisons
    c. Logistic regression
    d. Post hoc comparisons

Essay Questions

16. Why do we have to rely on operational definitions to study abstract hypothetical constructs?
17. How can a variable, like depression, be used either as an independent or as a dependent variable?
18. Identify and describe the four types of independent variables according to type of manipulation.

ANSWERS TO REVIEW QUESTIONS

Answers to Multiple Choice Questions

1. d	6. b	11. b
2. d	7. b	12. a
3. b	8. c	13. c
4. c	9. c	14. a
5. a	10. b	15. d

Answers to Essay Questions

16. Why do we have to rely on operational definitions to study abstract hypothetical constructs?

    Abstract hypothetical constructs are hard to characterize because they are not concrete. So we have to find out some objective way to measure them. Any measurement we choose is not going to be exactly the same as the underlying concept, but we need that measurement to represent the hard-to-define idea we want to deal with.

17. How can a variable, like depression, be used either as an independent or as a dependent variable?

    If an experimenter wanted to see if level of depression affected some behavior, the researcher would manipulate the depression level in participants to see if behavior changed. In this case, depression level would be the IV, the manipulated variable.

    If the experimenter wanted to see if some manipulation affected a person's level of depression, the researcher would manipulate an IV and see the result in terms of a person's depression level. In this case, depression would be a DV, or an outcome behavior.

18. Identify and describe the four types of independent variables according to type of manipulation.
    a. Task variable—The independent variable is set up so that participants in different conditions engage in different tasks.
    b. Instructional variable—The IV is set up so that participants in different conditions receive different instructions about what they are going to do.
    c. Situational variable—The IV is set up so that the context or setting of the experiment differs across groups.
    d. Subject variable—The IV is set up so that comparisons are made between two groups of people who differ in some preexisting way (e.g., sex, political affiliation, etc.)

■ ■ ■ ■ ■

CHAPTER EIGHT

EXPERIMENTS WITH MULTIPLE INDEPENDENT VARIABLES

CHAPTER OVERVIEW

LEARNING OBJECTIVES ■ **KEY TERMS** ■ **CHAPTER PREVIEW**

LEARNING OBJECTIVES

After going through this chapter, you will be able to:

- Identifying characteristics of factorial designs
- Describe the concept of main effects
- Describe the concept of interaction effects
- Illustrate patterns of results that indicate interaction and lack of interaction among variables
- Identify research designs in published studies

KEY TERMS

CHAPTER PREVIEW

Sometimes psychologists create simple studies with a single IV; most such studies in psychology have several comparison groups. In other cases, researchers manipulate more than one factor (i.e., more than one IV) in a single experiment. The advantage of a multi-factor study is that we can get a better look at the complex interplay of variables that affect behavior. After all, in our lives, most of what we do is a result of more than a single cause.

In this chapter, you will learn about experiments involving multiple IVs. The benefit of this approach is that we can examine individual IVs, but we can also see how different variables interact to produce unexpected results.

With these more complex designs, we use various statistical tests. The most common approach is the analysis of variance (ANOVA), which is sometimes supplemented by planned or post hoc comparisons. For studies with multiple DV, we typically use a multivariate ANOVA, followed by a standard ANOVA, called a univariate ANOVA.

RESEARCH WITH MULTIPLE INDEPENDENT VARIABLES

In the last chapter, you saw how researchers compare two or more groups using a single independent variable (IV). An expansion on the simplest design involves experiments that manipulate more than one IV. The advantage of this approach is that you can get a more detailed picture of behavior because you are observing more complex conditions.

Beyond multiple group studies, many experiments in psychology involve more than one factor, that is, more than just a single IV. One reason for using multiple IVs is that many psychological questions are too complicated to answer with a single independent variable. Another reason is that we often gain more than twice as much information from a two-factor study than we do from a single-factor study. And, even better, we may not have to expend twice as much energy and time when we use multiple IVs in a single study.

Factorial Design—
A design of a research study in which the investigator manipulates more than one independent variable in a single study, with each level of one IV crossed with each level of all other IVs.

When an experiment uses multiple IVs, if each level of one variable is crossed with every level of the other variables, the approach is referred to as a **factorial design.** If there are two variables, A and B, and if A has two levels (A_1 and A_2) and B has three levels (B_1, B_2, and B_3), we would have a factorial design if A_1 is paired with each of B_1, B_2, and B_3 and A_2 is paired with each of B_1, B_2, and B_3. Table 8.1 schematically illustrates a 2×3 design.

In theory, there is no limit to the number of factors you can study in an experiment. Three IVs is not unusual, and occasionally you will see four. Realistically, though, you won't encounter more than four except in extremely rare instances.

TABLE 8.1   Schematic Example of a Factorial Design Involving Two Independent Variables, A and B

Each level of an IV is paired with each level of the other IV. In this example, there are six conditions because the two levels of A are paired with the three levels of B, creating a 2×3 design. In factorial designs, the total number of conditions is equal to the number of levels of the variables multiplied together.

	B_1	B_2	B_3
A_1	A_1B_1	A_1B_2	A_1B_3
A_2	A_2B_1	A_2B_2	A_2B_3

To see how experimenters might create a study with multiple IVs, consider this situation: You hear somebody laugh, but you can't see him or her. What about the laughter would lead you to be more or less likely to want to meet that person?

Bachorowski and Owren (2001) played recorded laughter from either a woman or a man. This represents a qualitative variable because the voices differed by the category of the laugher—female or male. The researchers were not trying to assess the difference in behavior as a result of a numerical difference in the level of the IV, but rather on the basis of sex.

In this study, the participants provided a rating of their interest in meeting the person whose recorded laughter they had heard. The results showed that, on average, participants were about equally likely to want to meet women and men after hearing them laugh.

The researchers also manipulated a second qualitative IV in the experiment. This was whether the laugh was "voiced" like a real laugh; as the investigators explained, the voiced laughs were "harmonically rich" (p. 253). The second type of laugh was "unvoiced," including "grunt-, cackle-, and snortlike sounds" (p. 253). Participants were much more interested in meeting the people who had produced the voiced laughs.

In this study, there are two IVs; both are qualitative. One IV is gender of the laugher; it has two levels, female and male. The second IV is type of laugh, voiced and unvoiced. When you report your research, it will help your audience if you identify both the IV as a general concept and also the levels or conditions. The researchers here created qualitative IVs. The change from one group to another involves changing the quality of the stimulus, not a quantity.

Main Effect—In a factorial design, differences among groups for a single independent variable that are significant, temporarily ignoring all other independent variables.

MAIN EFFECTS

When we use factorial designs, we look at each IV individually. We temporarily isolate each IV and assess it as if it were the only one in the study. When we determine whether it has affected the DV, we are looking at a **main effect.** We monitor whether there is a significant main effect for each IV separately. So if the research design involves three IVs, we would test for three main effects.

Let's consider a study that links self-esteem, past experiences, and a concept called subjective distance. Ross and Wilson (2002) investigated how far in the past certain experiences felt depending on whether those experiences were positive or negative.

Specifically, Ross and Wilson randomly assigned students to a condition in which they were supposed to recall a college course in which they either performed well or poorly. The investigators also recorded the students' level of self-esteem as measured on a self-esteem inventory (Rosenberg, 1965) and how long ago the recalled course had taken place.

Consequently, we have three IVs of interest to us here. One IV is the Grade Condition, whether the student recalled a class that involved a good grade or a poor grade. This is a true manipulated IV because the researchers randomly assigned students to a group and told them to think of a class in which they did well or in which they did poorly.

The second IV is the students' self-esteem level, a measured variable rather than a true, manipulated IV. The third IV is how long ago the course in question had taken place, also a measured IV because the experimenters couldn't control how far in the past the course had occurred. Ross and Wilson included a fourth IV that isn't relevant to our discussion here. The DV we are interested in here is the subjective distance from the class in question. That is, how far in the past did that class seem to the participants?

Ross and Wilson discovered a significant main effect of time since the last class. More recent classes felt more recent. This offers no surprise. In fact, the researchers might have worried about their results if the students had consistently concluded that recent events seemed more remote than the remote events.

In addition, the investigators found a significant main effect of Grade Condition. Students who recalled classes in which they had earned poor grades tended to think of them as more remote; classes with good grades had the feel of being more recent. It's as if we keep good memories close and send bad memories to the attic. There was no main effect of self-esteem. That is, students with high and low self-esteem were comparable in their judgments of subjective distance.

In this discussion we can see that two IVs were related to students' feelings of how remote certain classes felt. Classes that students had completed in the most distant past felt remote, as we might expect. In addition, classes in which the student performed more poorly also seemed more remote. As such, there were two significant main effects—actual time since the class and the type of class the student recalled. On the other hand, students with high self-esteem made the same judgments of remoteness as did students with low self-esteem. This main effect—level of self-esteem—was not significant.

INTERACTIONS BETWEEN VARIABLES

Ross and Wilson's assessment of the main effects was interesting, but they also found some intriguing results when they examined the IVs together rather than in isolation. Remember that courses with good grades seemed closer. This was a significant main effect. Further, self-esteem was unrelated to subjective distance. However, these patterns weren't always present. Figure 8.1 illustrates the findings. High-grade courses were seen as being subjectively closer, but only for high self-esteem students. Students with low self-esteem tended to keep both successes and failures equally close, while high self-esteem students kept good memories close, shuffling less pleasant memories to a distance.

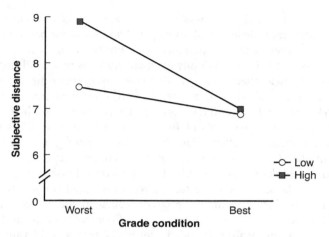

FIGURE 8.1   Subjective distance as affected by memory for a class resulting in a good or poor grade and student's self-esteem. The interaction suggests that high self-esteem students distance themselves from poor performance but not from good performance, whereas low self-esteem students react to good and poor performance comparably.

Source: Ross, M., & Wilson, A. E. (2002). It feels like yesterday: Self-esteem, valence of personal past experiences, and judgments of subjective distance. *Journal of Personality and Social Psychology, 82*(5), 792–803. doi:10.1037/0022-3514.82.5.792. Copyright American Psychological Association. Used with permission.

Interaction Effect—
In a factorial design, differences across groups of a single independent variable that are predictable only by knowing the level of another independent variable.

By looking at the effects of IVs together, you are examining **interactions.** In this study, Ross and Wilson found a significant interaction between grade condition and self-esteem. This means that in order to understand the effect of grade on subjective distance, you have to know whether the student showed low or high self-esteem.

Any time you need to know something about a second variable in order to understand the first variable, you have an interaction. Here we have to know about level of self-esteem in order to predict accurately whether students keep their negative experiences subjectively close or far.

Let's summarize what you need to do with a factorial study involving two IVs. When you study two variables in a single experiment, you assess the effect of the first variable on the DV—that is, the main effect associated with the first IV. You also assess the effect of the second variable on the DV, seeing if there is a main effect of the second IV. Further, you see if the two variables, considered together, produce a combination of effects that is not predictable from either one alone, that is, the interaction effect. Some researchers recommend investigating interactions first.

Interactions can be hard to understand because they reflect a level of complexity one step up from main effects. Interactions may reflect the fact that people may engage in different thought processes or behaviors when exposed to slightly different combinations of conditions.

With interactions you have to pay attention to more than one IV at a time. In addition, you have to pay attention to each level of each IV because data in a single cell may be responsible for a significant interaction. Because interactions are important and because they can be difficult to grasp, we will deal with different patterns of interactions in the discussion that follows.

What Do Interactions Mean?

Interactions reflect an element of complexity in behavior when we move from simple to more complicated investigations. In interpreting them, you need to ask yourself why a change in the level of one IV leads to a different change in behavior when paired with a second IV.

In our examples of interactions here, we are going to concentrate on two-way analyses—that is, designs that involve two independent variables. Such interactions are easier to conceptualize in two-dimensional graphs.

Some psychologists assert that, if there is a significant interaction, you should pay attention to the interaction effects first because the main effects, regardless of whether they are significant, might be irrelevant or they might not be particularly informative. This view has validity, but sometimes the main effects themselves can be important and interesting, even when there is an interaction.

As the number of IVs increases, the number of potential interactions to examine grows quite dramatically. If you have two IVs, there is a single possible interaction. If you have three IVs, there are four possible interactions. With four variables, there are six. The difficulties in interpretation often arise with the **higher order interactions,** that is, the interactions involving greater numbers of IVs. If you have a three-way interaction, it means that you need to look at every combination of three IVs combined. Gaining an understanding of what higher order interactions means can very difficult. You can see the number of interactions that are possible in different designs in Table 8.2. The rare five-variable design would require consideration of 26 potential interactions.

> **Higher Order Interaction**
> —An interaction in a factorial design that involves the joint effects of more than two independent variables.

TABLE 8.2   **The Number of Possible Main Effects and Interactions in Designs with 2, 3, and 4 Independent Variables**

Number of IVs	Two-way Interactions	Three-way Interactions	Four-way Interactions
2 (A, B)	1 A × B	—	—
3 (A, B, C)	3 A × B A × C B × C	1 A × B × C	—
4 (A, B, C, D)	6 A × B A × C A × D B × C B × D C × D	4 A × B × C A × B × D A × C × D B × C × D	1 A × B × C × D

Examining Main Effects and Interactions

We will discuss several patterns of results that lead to interaction effects; when we graph those results, each one will look slightly different. Graphs indicate whether an interaction might exist. As you can see in Figure 8.1, the lines in the graph are not parallel. In fact, they nearly intersect. When lines are parallel, there is no interaction. When lines are at an angle to one another, there may be an interaction. You need a statistical test to see whether the interaction is significant.

When interactions are present, it can mean that participants are engaged in different psychological processes in the different conditions. For instance, Fisher (2004) studied how women perceived attractiveness in other women. She presented female participants with pictures of women and of men, and the participants rated how attractive they found the person in each picture.

Fisher found a significant main effect of the sex of the person in the picture. The participants rated the women in the pictures as being more attractive, on average, than the men in the pictures. The ratings differed slightly depending on the estrogen level of the female participants, with lower ratings by women with high estrogen levels and higher ratings by women with low estrogen levels.

What is particularly interesting here is the interaction between sex of the person in the picture and the female participant's estrogen level. As you can see in Figure 8.2, women with high estrogen levels rated pictures of females as less attractive than did women with low estrogen levels. The participant's estrogen level had no relation to ratings of pictures of men. Fisher observed from these data that when women are at more fertile points in their ovulation cycles, they see other women as less attractive compared to when the participants are at less fertile points. In comparison, the rated attractiveness of men did not differ as a function of estrogen level.

These results reveal a clear interaction effect. If you want to know how much more attractive women rate a group of women in pictures than a group of men, you can't answer accurately without knowing about the estrogen level of the women doing the rating.

This research involves some important points. First, one of the variables, estrogen level, is a measured variable. Thus, we have to be cautious in talking about causation. Fisher

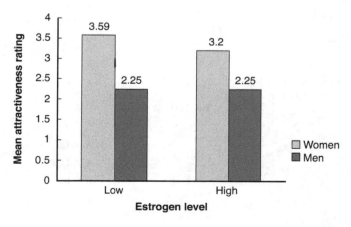

FIGURE 8.2 Illustration of an interaction in which the pattern of responses on the dependent variable for a given IV differs depending on the level of the second IV. In this study, women rated the attractiveness of females (white bars) and males (black bars) in pictures. The relative estrogen level was associated with different average ratings of women when estrogen levels differed.

Source: Fisher, M. L. (2004). Female intrasexual competition decreases female attractiveness. Proceedings of the Royal Society B, 271, S283–S285 by permission of the Royal Society.

pointed out that evolutionary theory predicts her results, so she appears confident in drawing a causal conclusion, even though this comparison did not involve a true IV.

A second important point is that Fisher did not measure estrogen levels directly. Rather, she asked the female participants to identify how many days it had been since menstruation. She classified women who were between 12 and 21 days since the beginning of menstruation as being high in estrogen (i.e., in the most fertile point of the ovulation cycle) and those outside that range as being low in estrogen. Thus, the operational definition of fertile or not fertile is based on the number of days since a woman's last period. As you may recall, we have to use operational definitions when we cannot measure a concept directly. The question always remains as to whether the operational definition is adequate for leading to valid conclusions. This operational definition is certainly not perfect, but it appears to be useful.

More recent research revealed supporting findings that women prefer sexier clothing when ovulating than when not ovulating. In this case, the investigators used a commercial product that measures luteinizing hormone, which signals the onset of ovulation (Durante, Griskevicius, Hill, Perilloux, & Li, 2011). The design involved two IVs, fertility status and number of items from which the women could select desired products. There was a main effect of fertility and no interaction between variables.

If Fisher had decided to conduct two separate studies, each with only one IV, she would have arrived at a less informative conclusion. If she had paid attention only to the first IV, estrogen level, she would have missed the interaction between estrogen level and sex of a person being evaluated. Similarly, if she had only looked at the sex of the person being rated, she would also have missed the importance of a woman's estrogen level. Only by looking at both the variables in combination could she see this interesting pattern emerging. The advantage of using a factorial design is that you can see how the variables work independently, but you can also see their combined effects.

Patterns of Interactions

When you assess your results, in some interactions, you might look individually at each level of an IV and see how the DV changes as you move across groups on the second IV. If the pattern changes differently for your different groups, there may be an interaction.

For example, researchers have discovered that when people intentionally suppress their emotions, there are negative outcomes, such as lowered mood states and low levels of life satisfaction. Most of the research has involved European American samples. So a group of investigators studied whether the consequences of emotional suppression are similar in non-Western populations (Soto, Perez, Kim, Lee, & Minnick, 2011). They compared a group of Hong Kong Chinese students and American students to see if such emotional suppression was associated with similar negative outcomes.

As you can see in Figure 8.3, the pattern of results differs for the two groups, revealing an interaction between emotion suppression and symptoms of depression. Emotion suppression had no effect on the symptoms of depression for students from Hong Kong, whereas it had a major impact for American students. This change across cultural groups reinforces the idea that you should not simply assume that what is true for one group holds true for another. And even within a single country, such as the United States, there may be differences across subgroups.

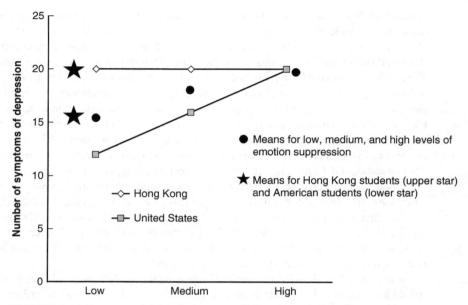

FIGURE 8.3   Symptoms of depression according to degree of emotion suppression.

Source: Soto, J. A., Perez, C. R., Kim, Y., Lee, E. A., & Minnick, M. R. (2011). Is expressive suppression always associated with poorer psychological functioning? A cross-cultural comparison between European Americans and Hong Kong Chinese. *Emotion, 11,* 1450–1455. doi:10.1037/a0023340. Copyright American Psychological Association. Reprinted with permission.

You can see an "It depends" statement about interactions here. Does emotion suppression lead to higher levels of negative symptoms? It depends on which group you examine. The answer is yes for American students but no for Hong Kong students.

In Figure 8.3, you can see the difference in number of symptoms for the two cultural groups. The Chinese students show a higher level of negative symptoms overall (represented by the stars), but as the interaction reveals, the increased level among those students is limited to certain conditions. Similarly, greater emotion suppression is associated with greater negative symptoms, but again only in certain conditions.

A final example of a different pattern of results that leads to an interaction occurs when there is no difference among most groups, but a single condition that departs from the rest. For example, in a study of prejudice against Black defendants in trials, Sommers and Ellsworth (2001) created fictitious trials in which they varied the cases in several ways. For our discussion, we are interested in two specific independent variables: race of the defendant (Black versus White) and type of trial (race is emphasized versus race is not emphasized in the trial summary).

The researchers asked the participants to recommend a sentence when the defendant was found guilty. As you can see in Figure 8.4, in three of four conditions, the jurors (who were White adults solicited for participation at an airport) recommended sentences of nearly equal length. The one exception involved the condition with Black defendants when the trial summary did not emphasize race.

(a)

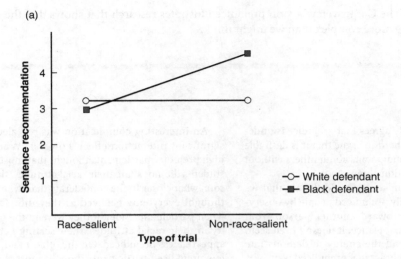

(b)

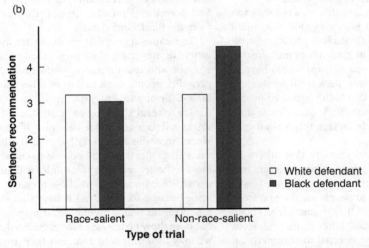

FIGURE 8.4   Interaction showing nearly equal responses for one group (White defendants) regardless of race salience, but a difference in the second condition (Black defendants). The line graph and the bar graph are based on the same data.

Source: Sommers, S. R., & Ellsworth, P. C. (2001). White juror bias: An investigation of prejudice against black defendants in the American courtroom. *Psychology, Public Policy, and Law, 7,* 201–229. Copyright American Psychological Association. Used with permission.

This is another instance in which a factorial design is critical. If race had been emphasized in a mock trial with the only comparison being sentences recommended for White versus Black defendants, there would have been no effect of the IV because the average sentence lengths for Black and for White defendants were about equal. Or if race had not been emphasized at all, it would have appeared that Black defendants received harsher sentences, which is not always the case.

The Controversy box on prejudice illustrates research that shows that the situation may be more complex than we might think.

■ ■ ■ ■ ■ ▬▬▬▬▬▬▬▬▬▬▬▬▬▬

CONTROVERSY:

On Prejudice

Just about everybody agrees that prejudice is undesirable. It would be hard to argue that it is desirable for people to make judgments about others without having any information about them.

Further, common sense would dictate that we could identify racially prejudiced people by observing their behavior toward another person from another group. At first glance, it doesn't even seem worthwhile to expend the energy to demonstrate that prejudiced people act in a prejudiced way.

As it turns out, though, this viewpoint is too simplistic. Sechrist and Stangor (2001) identified the prejudice level in their student participants, all of whom were White. The researchers then created a situation in which the participant would have to choose how far to sit from a Black confederate. You would probably predict that high prejudiced people would sit farther from the Black confederate than the low prejudiced people. In fact, this is what generally happened.

When the participants thought that others on their campus agreed with them in racial matters, low prejudiced people sat quite close to the confederate, whereas highly prejudiced people sat quite far from the confederate. That is, if they thought "everybody thinks like I do," the distance they chose to sit from the confederate strongly reflected their underlying attitude. There is no real surprise here.

An interesting complication was revealed by a significant interaction effect, however. When the high prejudice participants thought that most other students did not share their racial attitudes, they sat somewhat closer to the confederate than when they thought everybody believed as they did. That is, when participants thought they were in the minority in their racial attitudes, their seating behavior appeared less prejudiced. On the other hand, when low prejudiced participants thought most students had prejudicial racial attitudes, they sat farther from the Black confederate.

The data suggest that if people are aware that others do not share their prejudices, those people will act with less prejudice. Unfortunately, if low prejudice people think that most others are racially biased, the opposite may occur.

These results give us an indication of how we might reduce undesirable behavior. If we can convince those who are racially biased that others don't share their ideas, we may be able to change behaviors for the better; perhaps attitudes will follow. The worst situation will be to allow prejudice to continue because we let others believe that everybody around them is also prejudiced. It may be difficult, but if we show no tolerance for prejudiced attitudes, we may lead others to abandon their undesirable behaviors and maybe their attitudes.

IDENTIFYING RESEARCH DESIGNS

When you create an experiment, you need to specify very clearly your IVs and your DVs. Similarly, when you read about another study, you should identify each IV and DV. If you don't have a firm idea of what you are manipulating, you will have a hard time setting up your study; if you don't understand what somebody else did, you won't be able to understand and interpret those results.

In reading about the research of others, once you establish an IV, you should determine how many treatments were involved and the nature of the IV. For example, as you discovered in Table 7.1, Murray et al. (1999) wanted to know if people in a depressed state remembered more words from a list than nondepressed people. The IV here is Psychological State, and it has two levels, dysphoric (depressed) and euphoric (nondepressed). In that experiment, Psychological State was a manipulated variable because the researchers induced either a dysphoric or a euphoric state in participants randomly assigned to one of the two groups. The DV was the number of words remembered from a list. It was the only dependent measure involved.

However, their experiment involved a little more complexity. They also investigated whether the participants remembered different numbers of positive and negative words. Thus, they employed a second IV, Word Type; it had two levels, positive words and negative words.

Repeated Measures Design—A design in which a single participant is observed and measured on more than one level of an independent variable rather than measuring different individuals on each level of the independent variable.

All participants were exposed both to positive and to negative words during the learning phase of the study. This approach involves a **repeated measures design,** which means that participants are tested on all levels of at least one IV.

The design in the Murray et al. study is consequently called a 2 × 2 (which is read as "two by two") factorial design. Sometimes in journal articles, you will see such a design described as a "2 (Psychological State) × 2 (Word Type) factorial design with repeated measures on the second factor."

In a more general way of talking about a design, we would say that this experiment involved an A × B design. This tells us that there are two IVs, Variable A and Variable B. A and B are each associated with the number of conditions; in our example here, A = 2 and B = 2. So the A × B design in the Murray et al. study is a 2 × 2 design. A 2 × 2 design has four conditions because, as simple arithmetic tells you, 2 times 2 equals 4.

An example of a 2 × 3 design comes from the work of Budson et al. (2001); the design is outlined in Table 8.3. They compared Alzheimer's patients and healthy older adults on their ability to differentiate between pictures of nonsense shapes they either had or had not seen before. Some of the new shapes were very similar to the old ones, some of medium similarity, and some of low similarity.

Healthy adults were more easily fooled by new shapes that were similar to the old because they had been able to encode the previously seen shapes into memory. For the

TABLE 8.3   **An Example of a 2 (Type of Person) × 3 (Similarity of Image to Original) Factorial Design with Repeated Measures on the Second Factor. A 2 × 3 Design Implies That There Are Six Different Conditions**

	Low Similarity	Medium Similarity	High Similarity
Alzheimer's patient	Alzheimer's patient/Low similarity	Alzheimer's patient/Medium similarity	Alzheimer's patient/High similarity
Healthy elderly person	Healthy elderly person/Low similarity	Healthy elderly person/Medium similarity	Healthy elderly person/High similarity

Source: Budson, Daffner, Desikan, and Schacter (2001).

Alzheimer's patients, because their memories were generally poor, they were not fooled into thinking that they had seen a particular shape even if it was similar to ones they had actually seen because they didn't remember the similar ones to begin with.

The design was a 2 (Type of Person—Healthy versus Alzheimer's adult) $\times$ 3 (Similarity of Image—low, medium, or high) factorial design with repeated measures on the second factor. There were a total of 6 conditions (because $2 \times 3 = 6$). You can see the conditions in Table 8.3. Their dependent measure was the proportion of new images that the participants incorrectly identified as old.

DATA ANALYSIS

Many tests are available for analysis of experimental data. When data are normally distributed, when there are about equal sample sizes, and when the variances of the different groups are equal, we typically use a group of tests referred to as parametric tests. These include the Student's t-test, the ANOVA, and Pearson's correlation. When the data do not meet these criteria, we sometimes use nonparametric statistics.

The parametric tests predominate by a great margin. If you look at virtually any journal dealing with experimental methods in psychology, you will see great use of them. In reality, the tests are likely to lead to valid results even if deviations from normality and equal sample sizes aren't too great (Howell, 2007). Most researchers do not systematically test for departures from these criteria. You can see applications of the most commonly used tests in the statistics appendix.

■ ■ ■ ■ ■ ▬▬

CONTROVERSY:
Cell Phones and Driving

Cell phones are popular means of communication. By 2005, there were more cell phones in the United Kingdom than there were people (CIA–The World Factbook, 2007); in the United States there were 219 million cell phones for about 300 million people. Mobile phones allow people to be in contact virtually on demand, even when they are driving.

One important question that researchers have addressed is whether driving while talking on a cell phone is safe. Preliminary data using records from traffic accidents suggested that talking on a cell phone impairs people to the same degree as driving while drunk (Redelmeier & Tibshirani, 1997). Those data were archival, not experimental, though; they relied on cell phone records and reports of accidents while drivers were (or were not) talking on the phone, so it is not easy to spot cause-and-effect relations. In order to assess whether there is

a causal link between cell phone use and unsafe driving, investigators have created experiments that are useful for cause-and-effect explanations.

The research on the impact of cell phone use and driving has required varied approaches, each with its own strengths and weaknesses. For one thing, it would be unethical to create a situation in which a research participant was driving dangerously on roads and highways, so investigators have used laboratory-based driving simulators. One limitation of such studies is that participants know they are not on the road, so their driving behavior may not represent their behavior in a real-world situation. In this case, we hope that the experiments have experimental realism; that is, we hope that the participants are taking the research seriously and engaging in the same types of behaviors they normally do. With a driving simulator, there may actually be a high level of mundane realism as well, which is why psychologists use them to study behavior (e.g., Strayer, Drews, & Crouch, 2006).

On the other hand, some researchers have taken drivers on actual roads. For example, Harbluk, Noy, Trbovich, and Elizenman (2007) asked participants to drive on a busy four-lane city road while talking on a cell phone and engaging in easy and difficult tasks.

Based on the extensive research on this topic, the National Transport Safety Board has recommended completely banning cell phone use during driving.

Naturally, many people would be upset if they couldn't engage in such behavior while driving, but the data are quite clear in the message they convey. Interestingly, a psychology named Joseph Jastrow (1891) conducted research revealing that people cannot multitask, a finding repeating regularly since then (Beins, 2012).

Question for Discussion: If people were made aware of the research on cell phone use and driving, do you think they would reduce this behavior?

FACTORIAL DESIGNS

Data analysis in factorial designs typically involves the ANOVA. This statistic permits the researcher to compare each IV individually and the interaction between them.

Analysis of Variance (Omnibus *F*-Test)— A statistical analysis that permits simultaneous evaluation of differences among groups in research using multiple groups and multiple independent variables.

The first step for researchers typically involves what is called an omnibus *F*-test, commonly called **analysis of variance** (ANOVA). (There are related tests like the Multiple Analysis of Variance [MANOVA] and the Analysis of Covariance [ANCOVA], as well. They are variations on the ANOVA.) An omnibus *F*-test tells you whether the main effects are significant and whether any interactions are significant. After the omnibus *F*-test, researchers have several options. One is to discuss all main effects and interaction effects individually.

Planned Comparison— A comparison of differences across levels of an independent variable when the researcher decides during the design of the study to make the comparison rather than waiting until after preliminary data analysis.

Researchers also use **planned comparisons** when analyzing their results. This can involve using *t*-tests to see whether individual pairs of conditions differed from one another. If you decide before collecting any data to compare certain pairs of conditions, you should use planned comparisons. On the other hand, if you collect your data and conduct an ANOVA, then discover a potentially interesting comparison among groups, you should use **post hoc comparisons.**

Post Hoc Comparison —A comparison of differences across levels of an independent variable when the researcher decides to make the comparison after a preliminary data analysis.

You will probably be seeing greater use of confidence intervals and measures of effect size in the future. The most recent edition of the *Publication Manual of the American Psychological Association* specifies greater use of these statistics. You can refer to a statistics text for greater detail, but confidence intervals give you a sense of the range of scores that contains the true population mean from which your sample scores came, and measures of effect size inform you about whether your IV accounts for a small to a large amount of the difference across groups.

Illustration of a 2 × 3 Repeated Measures Design

To address the issue of cell phone use and the ability to attend to visual signals, Strayer and Johnston's (2001) participants either repeated words they heard on a cell phone or generated a word beginning with the same letter as a word they heard. In addition, the participants had to track (i.e., follow) a visual stimulus on a screen with a joystick and respond when they saw a specific target stimulus. This study involved two IVs. One IV was the difficulty of the tracking task, with two levels: easy and difficult. The second IV was the type of distracting task, with three levels: only the tracking task, repeating what the participant heard on the cell phone while tracking, and generating a word beginning with the letter of a word heard on the cell phone while tracking. In addition, every participant experienced the easy and difficult task and all three distraction conditions. Thus, the study involved a 2×3 design with repeated measures on both IVs.

In their two studies, Strayer and Johnston (2001) found that when participants were listening on the cell phone, they made twice as many errors as when not talking on the cell phone and took longer to react when they did spot a signal. In addition, when participants had to engage in a task requiring them to generate a word rather than just repeating a word they heard, they made more errors.

This study indicates that people who engage in tasks that involve some complexity, like coming up with a word beginning with a given letter, are less able to attend to stimuli around them. The word-generation task is somewhat similar to generating words in a conversation that requires some thought.

This study was a laboratory-based test of attention during a visual task; Strayer and Johnston were ultimately interested in how cell phone use affects driving, which is the focus of the next study we will discuss.

Illustration of a 2×2 Design with Repeated Measures on One Factor

In another experiment, Strayer, Drews, and Johnston (2003) used a driving simulator to represent real-world situations. There were two IVs in this study. Participants either drove without a cell phone or on a cell phone while engaged in a conversation with another person on a topic of interest to the participant. Each person drove with no cell phone in use half the time and with cell phone use in the other half. In addition, there were two traffic-density conditions, simulations of low traffic density and high traffic density; participants drove in only one of the two traffic-density conditions. Thus, this study involved a 2×2 design with repeated measures on one factor. The appropriate statistic here would be a 2×2 ANOVA.

Consistent with the earlier study by Strayer and Johnston (2001), the results of this experiment showed that cell phone use was detrimental to driving performance. Strayer and Johnston measured how long it took drivers to apply the brakes while talking on the cell phone, to release the brake pedal after using it, and to get back to normal driving speed after slowing down. All of these measurements showed poorer performance during cell phone use.

These studies were laboratory studies, so we can't be absolutely confident that it reflected real driving behavior. That is, it is always possible that the study results did not have external validity. Other researchers subsequently conducted studies to overcome this possible limitation.

Illustration of a 2 × 2 × 2 Design with Repeated Measures on All Factors

Some researchers actually took participants on the road to see the effects of cell phone use on driving (Recarte & Nunes, 2003). The participants drove about 186 miles (300 kilometers), a task that took about four hours.

At different points during the driving, participants had to learn some abstract information or some concrete information. At other points, they had to produce either abstract or concrete information. And during the trip, sometimes they had to engage in a detection task and sometimes there was no such detection task. The study involved a 2 × 2 × 2 design with repeated measures on all factors.

Their study involved numerous dependent variables. One DV was the extent to which drivers shifted their gaze during driving, that is, the extent to which they surveyed the road ahead of them. The analysis of the gazing behavior showed, among other things, that drivers narrowed their gaze when they had to generate complex responses. The data support the results generated by Strayer and Johnston (2001) in a nondriving, laboratory-based study. The data of Recarte and Nunes (2003) also support Strayer, Drews, and Johnston's (2003) results in a laboratory-based driving simulator.

One possible limitation to this real-road study was that the researchers could not control the driving situation. There were different drivers on the road for each participant, and the road conditions might have been slightly different. Other, hidden differences may also have been at work. The limitations may not be problematic, though, because other on-the-road research with cell phones led to the same results and conclusions (Harbluk et al., 2007).

Illustration of a One Variable Design with Repeated Measures on All Factors

Further research has suggested that driving while talking on a cell phone is about as dangerous as driving while drunk. Strayer, Drews, and Crouch (2006) looked at driving performance in a driving simulator when participants were in a control condition, while talking on a cell phone, and after having drunk a vodka–orange juice cocktail. In the alcohol condition, the blood alcohol level was 0.08 percent, which is a commonly used threshold for being labeled as driving while intoxicated.

Drunk drivers showed different patterns of disrupted driving (e.g., they were more aggressive in their behavior) than did cell-phone-using drivers (e.g., they were slower to respond). But both showed deteriorated abilities compared to the situation with no alcohol and no cell phones. This design involved repeated measures, so we can be assured that the participants in all conditions had the same level of competence at driving to begin with: They were the same people in each condition. The manipulation (cell phone, alcohol, neither cell phone nor alcohol) must have been responsible for differences in performance.

In this study, cell phone users showed the same deficiencies compared to non-users as in other studies. They were slower to brake, they applied more force to the brake when they did slow down, they showed longer following distances, took longer to resume normal speed after braking, and had more accidents. The researchers concluded that the relative danger each group poses is about the same. This conclusion based on experimental research is consistent with that generated a decade previously in archival research. Using a hands-free cell phone makes no difference (e.g., Redelmeier & Tibshirani, 1997).

It would be interesting to know if novice drivers are differentially affected by cell phone use compared to experienced drivers. It could be that, as people become better drivers (i.e., more experienced), they are able to drive well even if they talk on the phone.

Kass, Cole, and Stanny (2007) studied new drivers aged 14–16 and more experienced drivers aged 21–52. The investigators monitored performance in a driving simulator. The dependent variables included such behaviors as number of collisions, the number of pedestrians hit, speeding violations, stop signs missed, and center line crossings. Novice drivers made more overall errors than experienced drivers, but the difference between novice drivers with and without cell phones was similar to the difference between experienced drivers with and without cell phones. Thus, being an experienced driver did not mean that people were able to drive well while talking on the phone.

This study involved two comparison groups, novice and experienced drivers. It would have been impossible for the researchers to randomly assign people to conditions because the participants came to the study at a given age. So there could be important initial differences between the younger and the older people. It is not clear, though, why we would expect differences between the novices and experienced drivers that would influence the results; still, there might be differences that we don't know. The good news is that results make sense. You would expect novices to make more mistakes. And all the research suggests that everybody is hampered by cell phone use. So the possible limitations of this study are probably not troublesome.

THE CONCLUSION

The results of all the studies support the same conclusion: Talking on a cell phone while driving impairs a driver's ability. Each study had its own limitations, but other studies did not suffer from the same limitations. In the end, we have good convergent validity, with all the data pointing to the same conclusion.

One final situation in which cell phone use can be problematic involves pedestrians. That is, Hatfield and Murphy (2007) have demonstrated that pedestrians with cell phones engage in behaviors that may not be safe. These researchers monitored the behavior of people crossing streets while using or not using cell phones. The results were somewhat complicated, and there were differences in patterns of behaviors for women and for men, but the researchers found that using a cell phone while crossing a street is associated with unsafe behaviors, like not looking at traffic before venturing into a crossing and crossing more slowly compared to non-users.

Furthermore, Hyman, Boss, Wise, McKenzie, and Caggiano (2010) found that people using cell phones tend to walk more slowly than those not using cell phones and to walk a crooked path. In addition, 75 percent of such cell phone users failed to see a clown with a big red nose in a purple and yellow suit who was riding a unicycle around them. The results of these studies all point in the same direction: Cell phone use takes a lot of cognitive capacity, which means that people are less able to attend to the environment around them.

One embarrassing incident of texting and walking illustrates the problem. In January, 2011, a woman was walking through a mall as she used her cell phone to text. She fell into a pool of water as she texted because all of her attention was directed to texting rather to where she was walking (Why you should never walk and text, 2011. Retrieved from http://www.dailymail.co.uk/news/article-1347989/Girl-falls-mall-fountain-texting-Why-walk-text.html).

One conclusion is that some cell phone users may not be able to walk and talk at the same time.

SUMMARY

Behavior is complex, so studying behavior is complex. Experiments sometimes require more than one IV in order to provide answers to interesting research questions. Studies with multiple IVs are often referred to as having factorial designs. The advantage of factorial designs with multiple IVs is that a researcher can study behavior in greater detail and identify patterns of behavior that change when another variable is present.

When researchers create more complex designs, they investigate the effects of single IVs, just as researchers do in simple experiments. Each IV in a factorial study receives independent analysis. In addition, however, investigators assess what happens when they manipulate more than one variable in a single study. Sometimes variables interact to produce behaviors that are not predictable when the researcher examines them individually. These complex patterns are called interaction effects.

When you read about experiments or actually create your own, you need to identify your research design. You specify the number of IVs and the number of levels within each IV. Factorial designs are very common in psychological research, with most studies investigating the effects of two to four IVs.

The most common type of statistical analysis for factorial designs is the ANOVA. The ANOVA permits the researcher to assess the effect of each IV and of each combination of IVs. Psychologists also supplement the ANOVA with either planned comparisons or post hoc comparisons of individual conditions within the factorial design. In the future, statistical analysis is likely to include more systematic presentation of confidence intervals and effect sizes, and estimates of the probability that a result will be reproduced if an investigator replicates the study.

REVIEW QUESTIONS

Multiple Choice Questions

1. An advantage of a using multiple levels of an independent variable includes the fact that
   a. you generally can obtain more data from fewer participants.
   b. you can spot quantitative differences in behaviors more easily.
   c. you can treat a qualitative variable as if it were a quantitative variable.
   d. you can identify changes in patterns of responses across different amounts of an independent variable.

2. If a researcher reported that there was a significant difference between groups on one variable but not on a second variable, that researcher would be talking about
    a. main effects.
    b. interaction effects.
    c. measured effects.
    d. dependent effects.

3. In an experiment involving three independent variables, it is possible for the results to show
    a. more than three main effects.
    b. a factorial design.
    c. higher order interactions.
    d. extraneous variables.

4. Suppose you conducted a study using a factorial design and somebody asked you about the results for Variable A. If you replied that, to answer their question, they have to know which level of Variable B was involved, your experiment involved
    a. main effects.
    b. logistic analysis.
    c. measured variables.
    d. an interaction.

5. Budson et al. (2001) compared healthy adults and Alzheimer's patients regarding their memory. The people in the study were tested on their memory for nonsense shapes of three types: shapes they had seen, shapes they had not seen, and shapes that were similar to ones they had seen. This design involved
    a. planned comparisons.
    b. quantitative variables.
    c. repeated measures.
    d. situational variables.

6. The Student's *t*-test is typically used
    a. in comparing two groups to see if their means differ.
    b. when analyzing the results of a factorial design.
    c. as a follow-up to designs using logistic regression.
    d. in place of the correlation coefficient.

7. Suppose you have conducted an analysis of variance in a design with multiple groups and obtained evidence of a significant difference among means. If you decided to investigate which means differed significantly, you would use what test?
    a. Multiple *t*-tests
    b. Planned comparisons
    c. Logistic regression
    d. Post hoc comparisons

8. If your data analysis revealed that you have a significant interaction,
    a. your design involved a single-factor, multigroup design.
    b. you used a factorial design in your study.
    c. your design involved manipulated variables.
    d. your design involved only measured variables.

9. Strayer and Johnston (2001) created a study in which participants engaged in either an easy or a difficult task while trying to track a visual stimulus on a screen. In addition, there were three types of distracting tasks. The researchers measured how many errors the participants made in spotting visual stimuli. This research
    a. could not have involved a repeated measures design.
    b. involved five different conditions.

    c. involved only measured variables.

    d. used a 2 × 3 design

10. Strayer, Drews, and Johnston (2003) tested participants in a driving simulator while they either talked on a cell phone or did not. Afterward, participants received a surprise test of their memories for billboards that had appeared on their way. The design of this study

    a. was correlational.

    b. involved a 2 × 1 design.

    c. was a factorial design.

    d. could lead to analysis by a *t*-test.

11. Recarte and Nunes (2003) tested participants who drove for about four hours on a highway. During that time, the participants had to learn either abstract and concrete information, had to generate abstract and concrete information, and drove either with or without distraction. This design involved

    a. repeated measures on all factors.

    b. a correlational design.

    c. a partial factorial design.

    d. a main effect design but not an interaction design.

12. A study that compared novice drivers and experienced drivers with respect to the relative number of driving errors they made while using a cell phone or not using a cell phone resulted in the same amount of deterioration in both groups. This type of design

    a. is appropriate for analysis with a *t*-test.

    b. involved two manipulated variables.

    c. used a static group design.

    d. used a reduced factorial design.

Essay Questions

13. Traditionally, what statistical test has been used for a single-variable, two-group design? Why is it not appropriate for multiple groups or multiple variables?

14. In the Sommers and Ellsworth (2001) experiment on the effects of race on a trial verdict, explain how the interaction provided important information. Were the independent variables qualitative or quantitative? the dependent variables?

15. On a practical level, why wouldn't a researcher be likely to create an experiment with a 2 × 3 × 4 × 5 design?

ANSWERS TO REVIEW QUESTIONS

Answers to Multiple Choice Questions

1.	d	5.	c	9.	d
2.	a	6.	a	10.	d
3.	c	7.	d	11.	a
4.	d	8.	b	12.	c

Answers to Essay Questions

13. Traditionally, what statistical test has been used for a single-variable, two-group design? Why is it not appropriate for multiple groups or multiple variables?

    When there are multiple independent variables or more than two groups, you can use the analysis of variance. It has the advantage of being a single test that can let you compare all the groups at one time. In addition, an ANOVA can result in a lower rate of Type I errors.

14. In the Sommers and Ellsworth (2001) experiment on the effects of race on a trial verdict, explain how the interaction provided important information. Were the independent variables qualitative or quantitative? the dependent variables?

    In the Sommers and Ellison experiment, there was no difference in sentencing for Black defendants when a mock trial involved a specific statement about racial issues. On the other hand, when race was not mentioned, Black defendants received longer sentences than White defendants. If there had been only one variable, the investigators would not have seen the complex pattern of results.

    That is, if the researchers had only compared sentences of Black and White defendants in race-salient trials, they would have concluded that race was unimportant on sentence length. If the researchers had only compared sentences of Black and White defendants in non-race-salient trials, they would have concluded that race did make a difference. The truth is more complex: Race sometimes makes a difference, but sometimes it doesn't. You need a factorial design to see this complexity.

15. On a practical level, why wouldn't a researcher be likely to create an experiment with a $2 \times 3 \times 4 \times 5$ design?

    An experiment with this design would include 120 conditions. That would mean that, with a between-groups design, you would need 120 people to provide a single person in each condition, and you would never want a single person. If you wanted 10 people, which is still small, it would involve 1,200 people. If you used a repeated measures design, each person could in the extreme be involved with 120 conditions, which wouldn't be practical.

    In addition, it could be very difficult to interpret the interactions, especially if there were higher order interactions (e.g., three- or four-way interactions).

■ ■ ■ ■ ■

CHAPTER NINE

EXPANDING ON EXPERIMENTAL DESIGNS
Repeated Measures and Quasi-Experiments

CHAPTER OVERVIEW

LEARNING OBJECTIVES

After going through this chapter, you will be able to:

- Describe how repeated measures designs differ from independent groups designs
- Explain the advantages of repeated measures designs
- Describe situations in which repeated measures designs are not feasible

- Explain the different threats to internal validity
- Differentiate experimental designs from quasi-experimental designs
- Identify and describe the different types of quasi-experimental designs

KEY TERMS

CHAPTER PREVIEW

You already know the basic elements of experimental research. The ideas in this chapter will fill in some of the gaps when you need to expand on the basics of experimental design.

Throughout a research project you have to make many practical decisions about how you intend to carry out the project. One of the decisions includes whether you want to observe participants more than once, an approach called a repeated measures design. There are quite a few advantages to such a strategy: You are certain that participants are comparable across groups (because they are the same people being measured in different conditions), you can get a lot of information from a smaller number of participants, and you are more likely to detect small differences between groups.

Researchers frequently make use of repeated measures designs because they are very efficient and because the advantages often outweigh the disadvantages significantly. No method is without its disadvantages, though. For instance, in a repeated measures design, you have to worry that one treatment will have effects that persist, affecting later behaviors.

Another extension of the experimental design is the quasi-experiment. This approach involves comparing groups that may differ in critical ways at the outset of your study. For instance, if you compare women and men, you might conclude that they differ is a particular way, but you cannot conclude that your treatment caused a difference. The two groups may have come into your study already differing in important ways.

Although quasi-experiments resemble experimental designs, they lack random assignment of participants to groups. As a result, you can make meaningful and accurate descriptions and predictions, but it is hard to identify the cause of differences. Researchers have created quite a large number of different quasi-experimental designs that can lead to interesting and useful studies.

REPEATED MEASURES DESIGNS

Repeated Measures (Within-Subjects) Design—A research design in which the same individuals provide data in more than one group, essentially serving as their own control group.

Between-Groups Design—A research design in which a single individual does not provide data for more than one condition or group.

Setting up a research project is time consuming; carrying it out may be even more so. As a result, as an experimenter you want to maximize the amount of information you get from your work.

One obvious way to increase information is by manipulating more than one independent variable in a single study, that is, by using a factorial design. This approach might not save a lot of time or energy, though. You will have saved some time and effort in planning only one study, but you may need to test the same number of participants as if you had carried out two separate projects.

A different way to increase the economy of your work is to set up an experiment in which you test the same individuals in more than one condition in a single setting. When you collect data from the same people more than once in the same experiment, you are using a **repeated measures design**; this approach is also called a **within-subjects design**. It is called a within-subjects design because you are trying to find out if there are any differences in the way the participants within a single sample behave. You can contrast it with a **between-groups design** in which you test different participants in different groups. The goal is to see if there are any differences between groups.

ADVANTAGES OF REPEATED MEASURES DESIGNS

There are several advantages associated with repeated measures designs, some purely practical regarding carrying out your project and others statistical. There are also some limitations.

Increasing Efficiency in Data Collection

One advantage with a repeated measures design is that you might be able to increase the amount of data without a marked increase in time and effort. If your design involved three groups and you wanted to test 50 participants in each group, you would need a total of 150 participants. By using a repeated measures design, you could still test 50 but get the benefits of using 150 participants.

In some studies, you may gain a great deal of extra information with repeated measures. For instance, if you wanted to know whether people could remember a list of words better with fast versus slow presentation, you could use a repeated measures design, with each participant learning the words in each presentation condition. If the experiment takes 45 minutes for one condition, it might only take 15 more minutes to add the second condition. Thus, the experiment would be 33 percent longer, but you would get 100 percent more data. When there are small numbers of potential participants available, it can be very helpful to test them repeatedly.

If you added a second IV and tested the same participants on each level of that variable as well, you would still need only 50 participants, but the amount of data you collected could be much greater. Thus, you have effectively created two experiments with only a small increase in the amount of time you spend testing participants.

As you can see in Table 9.1, if you had a 2 × 3 design with no repeated measures, you would need to test many more people than if you use repeated measures. You could reduce

TABLE 9.1   Example of How Repeated Measures Leads to Greater Amounts of Data without Increases in the Number of Participants for a Hypothetical 2 × 3 Design

In this example, the researcher wants 50 data points in each of the six cells.

Number of Participants Required for Independent (Non-repeated) Measures. Participants experience only one of the six conditions.

Independent variable B	Independent Variable A		Total Number of Participants
	Group A_1	Group A_2	
Group B_1	50 different people	50 different people	100 for B_1
Group B_2	50 different people	50 different people	100 for B_2
Group B_3	50 different people	50 different people	100 for B_3
Total number of participants	150 for Group A_1	150 for Group A_2	300 participants

Number of Participants Required for Repeated Measures on Variable B. Participants experience B_1, B_2, and B_3, but only one of the groups for Variable A.

Independent variable B	Independent Variable A		Total Number of Participants
	Group A_1	Group A_2	
Group B_1	50	50	100 for B_1
Group B_2	50	50	100 for B_2
Group B_3	50	50	100 for B_3
Total number of participants	50 for Group A_1 because each person participates in B_1, B_2, and B_3	50 for Group A_2 because each person participates in B_1, B_2, and B_3	100 participants (The same 100 people are in B_1, B_2, and B_3)

Number of Participants Required for Repeated Measures on Variables A and B. Every participant experiences B_1, B_2, and B_3, and also A_1 and A_2. That is, each person is in all conditions.

Independent variable B	Independent Variable A		Total Number of Participants
	Group A_1	Group A_2	
Group B_1	50	50	50 for B_1 because the same people are in A_1 and A_2
Group B_2	50	50	50 for B_2 because the same people are in A_1 and A_2
Group B_3	50	50	50 for B_3 because the same people are in A_1 and A_2
Total number of participants	50 for Group A_1 because the same people are in B_1, B_2, and B_3	50 for Group A_2 because the same people are in B_1, B_2, and B_3	50 participants (The same 100 people are in B_1, B_2, and B_3; likewise, the same people are in A_1 and A_2)

the number of people you test from 300 to 50, which can be an immense saving of your time and a notable reduction in the number of people you have to recruit.

Increasing Validity of Data

A second advantage to using repeated measures is that you may have greater confidence in the validity of your data. Sometimes participants in different groups approach the same task very differently. Their behaviors may look as if the IV has made a difference when the participants' pre-existing perspectives are causing the changes. A repeated measures approach can remedy this problem.

One clever experiment reveals how this problem could occur. Birnbaum (1999) recruited participants via the Internet, asking them to serve in a "1-minute judgment" study. They were asked to "judge how large is the number 9" or "...the number 221." A rating of 1 reflected "very, very small," whereas a 10 reflected "very, very large."

Figure 9.1 reflects the participants' judgments. Surprisingly, the results showed that people believe that 9 is larger than 221. What is going on? Most likely, according to Birnbaum, people in the "Judge 9" Group were comparing 9 with single-digit numbers or with small numbers in general; in that context, 9 is pretty large. On the other hand, the participants in the "Judge 221" Group were comparing it with much larger numbers, so it seemed relatively small (Figure 9.2).

When you ask different people to provide ratings, you need to make sure that they are all using the same context. Thus, for this judgment task, you could provide an anchor for the participants; that is, you could say that for this judgment, 1 would be considered very, very small and 1,000 would be considered very, very large. Would this solve the problem? According to Birnbaum (1974), even when you do this, participants can rate smaller numbers as being bigger than larger ones. Participants rated 450 as larger than 550 when he provided anchors. Thus, when there are no objective guidelines for responses, it may be a good idea to include repeated measures in the research design. With repeated measures, it's the same person being measured in each condition, so changes in behavior are more

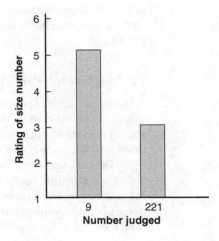

FIGURE 9.1 The surprising results of the study in which participants rated the size of "9" and "221" on a scale of 1 (*very, very small*) to 10 (*very, very large*). The study involved independent assignment to conditions rather than repeated measures. That is, different people judged the size of 9 and 221.

Source: Birnbaum, M. H. (1999). How to show that 9 > 221: Collect judgments in a between-subjects design. *Psychological Methods, 4*, 243–249. Copyright American Psychological Association. Adapted with permission.

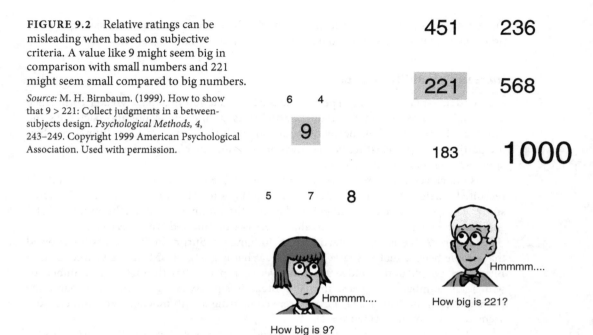

FIGURE 9.2 Relative ratings can be misleading when based on subjective criteria. A value like 9 might seem big in comparison with small numbers and 221 might seem small compared to big numbers.

Source: M. H. Birnbaum. (1999). How to show that 9 > 221: Collect judgments in a between-subjects design. *Psychological Methods, 4,* 243–249. Copyright 1999 American Psychological Association. Used with permission.

likely to be due to the IV than to differing perspectives. This problem of different contexts by raters occurs only for subjective judgments, not for objective measures, like grades or other concrete measurements.

Sometimes it makes the most sense to use repeated measures. For instance, Leirer, Yesavage, and Morrow (1991) investigated the effects of marijuana use in airline pilots over 48 hours. The researchers legally obtained marijuana and administered controlled doses to pilots who engaged in simulated flights. The investigators were interested in how long marijuana affected the pilots' performance and whether the pilots were aware of any effects of the marijuana on their behaviors. They discovered that most of the pilots experienced residual effects of marijuana after 24 hours, but they typically were not aware of the effects.

Finding Enough Participants

A third advantage of repeated measures designs is that if the group you wanted to test was rare, such as airline pilots or other highly trained experts in some field, you might not be able to find many such people. By using the repeated measures design, you can avoid the problem of running out of participants.

On the other hand, you may not have to worry about the availability of participants if they are plentiful, like students from large introductory psychology classes. If your testing sessions require a lot of time and effort, it may be better not to use a repeated measures design because your participants may be fatigued, bored, or otherwise worn out by the time they finish one condition and begin the next.

Reducing Error in Measurement

Another advantage with repeated measures designs is that, in general, your groups are equivalent at the outset because they are the same people in each group. The participants are serving as their own control group. Any characteristic that helps or hurts a person's performance is going to be the same across conditions. Further, you are increasing the number of data points in your analysis, which increases the power of your analysis, that is, the likelihood of rejecting the null hypothesis when you should (Vonesh, 1983).

A different design related to repeated measures involves matching participants in different groups. If you were going to investigate how long it takes for people to interact with a single stranger versus a group of strangers, you might initially measure your participants regarding their levels of introversion and extroversion. Then you could match two people on introversion–extroversion, assigning one to the "single stranger condition" and the other to the "multiple stranger conditions."

> **Natural Pairs**—A pairing of individuals, like twins, who are similar to one another in some way and are useful for comparison after being exposed to different levels of an independent variable.

In addition, researchers sometimes use **natural pairs** in a matched design. This could involve twins, siblings, or other pairs that share a variable that is important in the research. You can see how repeated measures and matching are conceptually related; the big difference is that in repeated measures, the participant is identical in all conditions whereas with matching, there is similarity across conditions, but the match is imperfect.

Matching is a less frequently used strategy in experimental, laboratory work. It is more likely in psychiatric or clinical research. In a psychiatric research project, Coverdale and Turbott (2000) assessed sexual and physical abuse among psychiatric patients compared to medical patients. They matched 158 psychiatric outpatients with 158 medical outpatients; the match was based on gender, age, and ethnicity.

The benefit of matching here is that if there are differences in rates of abuse associated with gender, age, and ethnicity, the researchers could be confident that these variables were equated across the two types of outpatient participants. These researchers discovered that the two groups did not differ in the incidence of childhood abuse, whereas as adults psychiatric patients were more susceptible to both physical and sexual abuse.

Laboratory researchers often stay away from matching because matching participants well can be difficult, especially if you want to use more than one variable. Consider the situation in which you have three variables you want to match, for example, age, years of education, and family income. If you are interested in creating two groups in which the first person in Group A is matched closely with the a person in Group B, you will find that it is easy to pair people initially, but the matches get worse as you continue because you lose some flexibility in later pairings.

You have two basic options when you have poor matches. One is to live with the best matches possible, even if they aren't very good. The problem here is that you lose the statistical advantages of matching. The second option is to discard matched pairs that are not good and to conduct your study with the pairs that remain. The drawback here is that you may end up with a small sample size that greatly reduces the chance that you will spot small but real differences across groups.

Because of these problems, psychologists do not use matching very frequently. Further, if you match your participants, you need to make sure that the matching variable is reliably associated with your dependent variable.

LIMITATIONS TO REPEATED MEASURES DESIGNS

Some research projects do not lend themselves to repeated measures designs and some variables make repeated measures impossible. If you conduct a study in which you compare people according to an existing personal characteristic, you will not be able to use repeated measurements. If you want to compare the study habits of high and low achieving students, it would be impossible to use repeated measures because each student would fall into only one of these categories.

Another consideration about testing the same person repeatedly is that, if you test participants over time, you have a big investment in each one. If they fail to return, you have committed time and effort that will not be repaid.

Possible, but Unlikely, Repeated Measures Designs

Other projects could conceivably be carried out using repeated measures, but it would not be a good idea. If you are planning a study on the acquisition of study skills with a new technique compared to a control group, it is pretty clear that you wouldn't want to use repeated measures. Once the students learned a skill in the experimental group, they would no longer be naive, so their performance in the control condition would have been influenced by the exposure to the experimental treatment.

Other research projects using repeated measures might be possible and would lead to valid results, but they would not be practical. For example, suppose you want to see whether young adults and older adults could complete a learning task with equal speed. This study might require many years with repeated measures because you would have to wait for participants to age.

You can see an example of this situation in research by May, Hasher, and Stoltzfus (1993). They investigated learning in people of different ages, using one set of young people and one set of old people. They could have waited for the young people to age for 50 years, but that isn't very reasonable. Unfortunately, one problem with studying groups of young and old people is that people growing up in different eras may simply be very different. This is particularly important in longitudinal studies (e.g., Schaie, 2000).

In addition, age may not be the best explanatory variable. For instance, May et al. (1993) found that when young and old people engaged in a learning task during their best time of the day (which tends to be in the morning for older people but later in the day for younger people), there was remarkably little difference in performance; and Ryan, Hatfield, and Hofstetter (2002) discovered that caffeine eliminates the decline in performance from morning to afternoon. Sometimes the obvious variable is not the only variable to consider.

Subject (Participant) Variables

In addition to age, there are other subject or participant variables that you will see frequently in psychological research. You generally can't use repeated measures when you examine pre-existing characteristics, such as sex, political affiliation (e.g., Democrat versus Republican), religious affiliation (Protestant, Catholic, Jewish, Muslim, etc.), and sexual

Order Effects—The result of multiple or repeated measurements of individuals in different experimental conditions such that a particular behavior changes depending on which condition it follows.

Sequence Effects—The result of multiple or repeated measurements of individuals in different experimental conditions such that they behave differently on later measurements as a result of having undergone the earlier measurements.

Transfer—A change in behavior in a repeated measures design that results from learning that takes place in an earlier condition.

Symmetric Transfer—A change in behavior in a repeated measures design that results from learning in an earlier condition, with the same degree of change in later behaviors, regardless of the order of conditions.

Asymmetric Transfer—A change in behavior in a repeated measures design that results from learning in an earlier condition, with differences in the amount of transfer in a later condition depending on which conditions occur first.

behavior (homosexual, heterosexual, bisexual, or none). You can't assign people to be Democrats, Protestants, etc. They are what they are.

Another case in which repeated measure would not be desirable is when the participants' behavior in one condition is essentially independent of their behavior in the other. As a general rule, if the correlation between participants' scores in two groups is less than about .25, repeated measures designs are not warranted (Vonesh, 1983).

Order and Sequence Effects

In within-subjects designs, confounds can result from either **order** or **sequence effects**. These effects are sometimes not distinguishable from one another in practice. There can be problems in repeated measures designs when different treatment sequences (e.g., A-B-C versus B-A-C) lead to different outcomes. If a particular treatment, no matter where in the sequence of treatments it occurs, affects performance in subsequent conditions, this would involve order effects.

For example, Löken, Evert, and Wessberg (2011) investigated the pleasantness of brush strokes on the palm of the hand and the arm depending on the rate of stroking. They found that ratings of pleasantness for the two sites differed when the palm was stimulated before the arm; participants thought that the stroking of the arm was more pleasant, but there was no such difference when the arm was stimulated first. There were clear order effects.

Order effects can occur when a person has the chance to evaluate a second stimulus after establishing the context with the first.

There are also potential sequence effects, which are progressive effects of testing when an individual is tested repeatedly. Fatigue that sets in after repeated testing is an example of an order effect.

When early behavior affects later behavior, it is called **transfer**; there are two types of transfer, **symmetric transfer** and **asymmetric transfer**. If people are tested twice (A-B), they may simply change after the first exposure. If the improvement in A when it occurs second equals the improvement in B when it occurs second, we have symmetric transfer. If A affects later performance on B, but B doesn't make a difference in later performance on A, we have asymmetric transfer. In the Löken et al. (2011) study mentioned above, there was asymmetric transfer.

Most psychological research on sequence effects has involved short-term effects in the laboratory. In reality, long-term sequence effects can also occur. In market research involving grocery store retailing, Paksoy, Wilkinson, and Mason (1985) suggested that researchers provide a "rest week" in their studies so that the effects of advertising and sales in week one of a study will not affect consumers' choices in week two, when a different IV is manipulated.

Counterbalancing—In a repeated measures design, the changing of the order of conditions across individuals to avoid contamination of data because of systematic sequence, order, or transfer effects.

Complete Counterbalancing—In a repeated measures design, the use of all possible orders of experimental conditions to avoid contamination of data because of systematic sequence, order, or transfer effects.

Partial Counterbalancing—In a repeated measures design, the use of a subset of all possible orders of experimental conditions to avoid contamination of data because of systematic sequence, order, or transfer effects.

Overcoming Sequence and Order Effects. When sequence effects are likely, researchers often use **counterbalancing** to avoid mistaking sequence or order effects for treatment effects. If you created a project with two conditions, A and B, you would want to test some participants in the AB order and other participants in the BA order. If you had three conditions, A, B, and C, you could order them ABC, ACB, BAC, BCA, CAB, and CBA if you wanted to use all possible orderings. This approach reflects **complete counterbalancing** because you use all possible orders.

As you add conditions, the number of orderings grows quickly and requires that you test a large number of participants. Thus, with three conditions, you have six orders; with four conditions, it grows to 24; with five, you have 120. Normally, you would test multiple participants in each order; so if you had four conditions (i.e., 24 orders) and if you wanted to include three participants per order, you would need to test 72 people. In addition, you would need a multiple of 24 participants (e.g., 48, 72, 96) in your study because there are 24 orders to repeat in each block.

Fortunately, there is no need to use complete counterbalancing. **Partial counterbalancing** can help keep experiments manageable. Only a subset of all orders is used.

DATA ANALYSIS WITH REPEATED MEASURES DESIGNS

When you create an experiment that uses repeated measures, you will be faced with choices about statistics that can become pretty complicated.

Many of the issues are beyond the scope of this book but you can see some common approaches to data analysis with repeated measures in the statistics appendix. Before you carry out a study with repeated measures, you should consult with somebody who knows the field. The last thing you want to do is to collect data that you won't be able to analyze properly. When investigators employ repeated measures designs, they often carry out data analyses that are not optimal, causing researchers either to miss differences between groups that are small, but real, or to conclude that there are differences when there aren't (Gaito, 1961; Pollatsek & Well, 1995; Reese, 1997).

A common statistical approach is to compare pretest and posttest scores with either a *t*-test or an analysis of variance (ANOVA), depending on how many groups and independent variables are involved. A closely related approach involves assessing change scores, which means subtracting a person's score at the end from the score at the beginning.

QUASI-EXPERIMENTAL DESIGNS

You have already had some exposure to quasi-experiments in the last chapter. Now you will learn about some of the specific issues associated with this approach.

In a quasi-experiment, researchers typically compare groups to see if they differ on a behavior of interest. That is, does this group of people differ from that group? Quasi-experiments can provide valuable information about group differences, but such designs are not ideal for assessing cause and effect. The researcher cannot randomly assign people to groups but can only assign participants to groups based on their pre-existing characteristics.

Questions that researchers address with quasi-experiments could include whether women and men differ in their behavior, whether young and old people are alike, whether beagles and German shepherds respond differently to children, etc. As you can imagine, there are many interesting questions that we can address with quasi-experiments. The fact that unites these examples is that participants and subjects belong in a category (female or male, young or old, beagles or German shepherds), and nothing that the researcher does is going to permit them to be placed in a different category. What differentiates a true experiment from a quasi-experiment is that, in true experiments, the researcher randomly assigns a participant to a given group. These independent variables are thus measured rather than manipulated variables.

Causation and Quasi-Experimental Designs

Quasi-experiments based on measured variables are really correlational in nature, so they do not allow you to identify causation. So if you compare female and male participants with respect to the way they act, you cannot conclude that any differences are due to sex. The problem is that from birth onward, parents (and everybody else) treat female and male babies differently. Through childhood and adolescence, and into adulthood, women and men experience the world around them in countlessly different ways.

We have different stereotypical images of women and men. These stereotypes may reveal a degree of truth, but we cannot tell why the differences emerge.

It is important to remember that sex can be a causal variable. For instance, the adult height of men and women is partially a function of their sex. (Multiple factors will influence any complex development, though, so there is more to your adult height than whether you are a woman or a man.) We have to remember that even though an independent variable in a quasi-experiment might be a causal variable, we just don't have enough information to conclude that.

In order to say that A causes B, three conditions must exist: A has to precede B, they have to covary (i.e., B must occur when A does), and A must be the most plausible cause of B with other potential causes ruled out. In a quasi-experiment, a failure to satisfy the last condition, ruling out alternate explanations, is the source of the problem.

Unfortunately, in a quasi-experiment we don't know when we have excluded all of the relevant variables, so we can't be completely confident in our conclusions. In general, you should be very cautious about making causal statements with quasi-experiments, just as you should be cautious with any correlational approach.

Combining Experimental and Quasi-Experimental Designs

Researchers quite commonly use a mixture of true and quasi-experiments because there are many interesting questions that can only be addressed with such a combination. For instance, it appears that highly neurotic people are more likely to associate sex with death than are less neurotic people (Goldenberg et al., 1999).

If you wanted to study the effect of neuroticism on reactions to different independent variables, you would have to use a quasi-experimental design because you cannot assign people to a level of neuroticism. They bring it with them on their own. You can manipulate other variables, though, and see how those variables affect people with different levels of neuroticism.

Goldenberg et al. discovered an interesting connection between a person's level of neuroticism and the individual's tendency to connect sex and death. To do so, they developed a mixture of true and quasi-experimental variables. You can see what happened regarding this sex, death, and neuroticism study in the Controversy box on sex and death.

- - - - - ▬▬

CONTROVERSY
On Sex and Death

Psychologists have speculated on the link between sex and death (e.g., Becker, 1973). Although the connection may not be obvious, it surfaces at times. For instance, as Goldenberg et al. (1999) point out, one term for orgasm in French is *le petite mort* (the little death, p. 1175).

The issue that these psychologists have dealt with is that thinking about the physical act of sex reminds people of their mortality. The result, according to Terror Management Theory (TMT), is that people seek to control their fear of death by changing the way they think about sex, removing it from the realm of death. One way to do this is to adopt a new view of sex as a more spiritual experience, not a death-related phenomenon.

Goldenberg et al. combined true and quasi-experimental variables to explore this question. They identified people who were high versus low in neuroticism, generating a quasi-experimental variable. The researchers then exposed these participants to questionnaires focused either on the sexual or the romantic aspects of sex, which was a true experimental manipulation. Thus, participants were either high or low in neuroticism and were primed either to the physical or to the romantic view of sex.

The researchers then gave the participants word stems (e.g., COFF__) and asked them to complete the word. The stems could be completed with death-related words (e.g., *coffin*) or non-death words (e.g., *coffee*).

Highly neurotic people were significantly more likely to complete the word stems with death-related words when they were exposed to the prime that focused on the physical aspects of sex; interestingly, these people were the least likely to generate death-related words when exposed to the romantic prime as shown in Figure 9.3.

In this mixture of a true and a quasi-experiment, Goldenberg et al. provide support for their hypothesis that for people who have anxieties toward both sex and death (i.e., highly neurotic people), thinking about the physical nature of sex makes them think of death.

In fact, even sex-themed humor primes high neuroticism participants to think of death (Dietz, Albowics, & Beins, 2011) and have the same effect as jokes explicitly about death (Beins, Doychak, Ferrante, Hirschman, Sherry, 2012).

We need to remember that it is not necessarily the neuroticism that makes people link sex and death. Whatever has made them neurotic may have also made them link sex and death. The connection is predictable, but we don't know exactly why it occurs.

As Goldenberg et al. have shown, though, the neurotic individuals can break this link by directing their attention to the romantic rather than to the physical nature of sexual behavior.

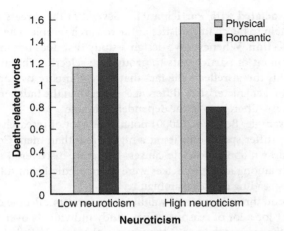

FIGURE 9.3 The relation between neuroticism and type of sex crime. According to Terror Management Theory, thoughts of sex are often linked with thoughts of death. People who are highly neurotic are more likely to think of the two together than are those with lower levels of neuroticism. That is, death-related words are more accessible to highly neurotic people after thinking of sex. The link can be broken, though, if the highly neurotic people are primed to change their thoughts of sex from physical to romantic.

Source: Goldenberg, J. L., McCoy, S. K., Pyszczynski, T., Greenberg, J., & Solomon, S. (2000). The body as a course of self-esteem: The effect of mortality salience on identification with one's body, interest in sex, and appearance monitoring. *Journal of Personality and Social Psychology, 79,* 118–130. Copyright American Psychological Association. Used with permission.

THREATS TO INTERNAL VALIDITY

The internal validity of a research project is critical to the level of confidence you have in your conclusions. The greater the internal validity, the more you can have faith that you know what factors cause an individual to act in a certain way.

The major threats to internal validity were initially elucidated by Campbell and Stanley (1966). Researchers now recognize that we have to take these potential problems very seriously. Such problems are common in applied research that takes place outside of the laboratory.

The reason that non-laboratory studies are more prone to these problems than other research is because we generally have less control over the research setting outside the lab. When we conduct theoretical or applied research in a laboratory, we can simplify the environment so that only a few easily identifiable differences exist between groups. If the groups then behave differently, we assume that a variable or a combination of variables that we manipulated had an effect.

If you create a study in a retail establishment, for instance, the company still wants to make money, so you have to work around the business that takes place. As such, you make compromises and conduct your study differently than if you could manipulate the situation to your liking.

Selection Threat— A threat to the internal validity of a study such that groups to be compared differ before being exposed to different experimental treatments, so any differences after treatment could be due to the initial differences rather than to the independent variable.

Maturation Threat— A threat to the internal validity of a study due to short- or long-term changes in a participant because of psychological changes like boredom, fatigue, etc. or because of physical maturation.

Attrition (Mortality) Threat—A threat to the internal validity of a study when participants drop out of a study, leading to a change in the nature of the sample.

History Threat—A threat to the internal validity of a study that results when some event outside the research project affects participants systematically.

Threats Associated with Participants.   Several of the threats to internal validity pertain to the characteristics of the research sample. The first threat involves **selection**. Whenever we design a study that does not involve random assignment of participants to group, the selection threat may be a problem. This threat reflects the fact that if we compare two groups with predetermined characteristics, differences other than the independent variable may cause differences in the dependent variable.

For example, Bell et al. (2000) noted that a lot of research has found that women suffer sports injuries at a higher rate than men. Conclusions have been drawn about possible causes. Bell et al. discovered that initial fitness levels among army inductees were more predictive of future injury than sex was, leading to causal ambiguity.

A second threat to internal validity is **maturation**. People change the way they act for a lot of reasons. If you study individuals over time, they may not be the same at the end as they were at the start. Their behavior with respect to your DV might change because of the changes in the participants, not because of your IV.

Maturation is more clearly a problem if you study children over time because they mature physically and psychologically in dramatic ways. But maturation can also come into play with adults. They may not change physically in obvious ways over a short period, but they can change psychologically. In this case, maturation does not only mean maturation of the kind from infancy to older childhood to adolescence; it means any physical or psychological changes, including fatigue, boredom, and having learned about the study, for example.

A third threat, **attrition** (also called subject mortality), can affect your results. If you test people over time, some may not return for later tests. You can't be sure that the people who drop out are like the ones that remain when it comes to your DV. For instance, if you are studying the development of skill over time, the participants who are progressing slowly may drop out, leaving you only with those people who are competent. Any conclusions you draw about your research will thus be based on a sample consisting of more proficient people.

The issue is not attrition in and of itself. Rather, problems arise because of nonrandom attrition. That is, the participants in one group who drop out may exhibit different characteristics from those who remain, so groups may look like they differ because of the IV; in reality, they may differ because of the effect of those who left the study.

A fourth threat to validity is **history**. Events during the course of a study may affect one group and not another. Even if you started with randomly assigned groups, this could happen. But if you are conducting a study with two different groups, like young people versus old people, one group may be affected by some event outside your research so their behaviors change. If you concluded that your IV is the reason for the differences across groups, you would be victimized by the history threat.

Instrumentation Threat—A threat to the internal validity of a study that results from changes in the way the dependent variable is measured, due to factors like poor calibration of mechanical equipment, or changes in the way researchers record subjective observations.

Testing Threat— A threat to the internal validity of a study that results when participants' behavior changes as a function of having been tested previously.

Statistical Regression Threat—A threat to the internal validity of a study that results when participants are categorized or selected for research participation on the basis of an initial observation that involves significant measurement error that is not likely to repeat itself on later measurements, giving the false impression that change is due to a treatment when it is really due to the difference in measurement error.

Threats Associated with Measurement.   A fifth threat to internal validity is **instrumentation**. This means that there is a problem in the way you measure your dependent variable over time. If you asked different questions to a group in the initial and final research sessions, your data would not be comparable because changing the questions might lead your participants to interpret them differently. Another situation in which instrumentation could be a problem would be if you used two different people to collect data at the beginning and at the end of the project; the second set of data collectors might introduce changes in the research environment, leading to changes in the way participants respond.

The instrumentation threat could also come into play if you were measuring behaviors with mechanical instruments. Sometimes these instruments need calibration or readjustment; if you don't do that, two measurements that should be the same could be different because of the machinery you are using.

A sixth threat to internal validity is **testing**. Sometimes, initial testing of your participants can sensitize them to the reasons for your research. As a result, they may act differently because they know too much about the nature of your research question, and it biases their responses.

A seventh threat to internal validity is **statistical regression**. A researcher might want to compare good and poor students who are admitted to a special program. In order to make the groups seem equivalent, the researcher might take the poorest students from the higher level group and the best students from the lower level group. This would mean that the two groups would seem equivalent to begin with.

Unfortunately, the better students who score low in their group may really be typical students who, for no systematic reason, scored poorly. Similarly, the poorer students at the top of their group may not be all that different from their peers; they just scored higher, also for unknown reasons.

So, in later testing, these better students' scores are likely to be closer to the mean of their group than they were on the initial testing. The poorer students' scores also go back where they belong, toward the low end of the scale.

This means that the average scores of the two groups would quite likely be different on the retest even if there were no independent variable at all. This phenomenon is sometimes called regression to the mean.

When researchers attempt to match participants in nonequivalent groups, there is a high likelihood of statistical regression. Consequently, if you are not going to randomly assign matched pairs to the different treatment conditions, you probably should not use matching as a strategy to equate groups because statistical regression can obscure the effects of your treatment.

These threats to internal validity, which are summarized in Table 9.2, reduce our confidence in the conclusions we draw about our results.

TABLE 9.2 Major Threats to the Internal Validity of a Research Project

Threat	Description
Selection	When participants are not randomly assigned to conditions, groups to be compared may differ before the experimental treatment is applied. Any difference between groups may be due to initial differences, not the treatment.
Maturation	In the short term, people become fatigued or bored, or they may learn how to perform better with practice on a task. So, behaviors may differ due to changes in psychological states. In the long term, people change physically and psychologically; such changes may affect behavior, not treatment.
Mortality (Attrition)	When researchers monitor participants over time, some participants may leave a study. If people with certain characteristics drop out, there may be a biasing effect so that the remaining sample contains people who are very different from the original sample. Differences in behaviors may not be due to the research variables.
History	An event may occur outside the study during the course of a research project that leads to a change in behavior. If one group is differentially affected, it may appear that a treatment was responsible for the differences between groups when, in fact, it was a particular event that influenced one of the groups.
Instrumentation	If the way a researcher measures the DV varies over time due to changes in equipment or to changes in subjective judgments by the researcher, differences in measurements may have nothing to do with the research variables.
Testing	When people go through a research protocol multiple times, they may change their behaviors because they are sensitized to the testing situation itself.
Statistical regression	When people exhibit extreme scores on an initial test, one of the reasons for the extreme score may be a random error. On a subsequent test, that random component of the score is no longer so prominent and the person's score regresses, that is, moves back toward the average of the group.

TYPES OF QUASI-EXPERIMENTAL DESIGNS

There are several quasi-experimental designs that psychologists regularly use. Some approaches resemble the typical experiment we have already discussed, with two or more groups being compared. Others depart from the typical model by incorporating measurements over a longer period of time than we generally see in an experiment.

Some researchers use quasi-experiments for laboratory studies, as we saw in the Goldenberg et al. (1999) study linking sex, neuroticism, and thoughts of death. But quasi-experiments are also frequently used in applied research outside the lab.

One-Group Pretest–Posttest Design—A quasi-experimental research design in which a single group is measured before a treatment is applied, then again afterward.

One-Group Pretest–Posttest Design

The simplest of the quasi-experimental designs is the **one-group pretest–posttest design**. As its name suggests, there is a single group of participants who are measured both before and after the application of a treatment. As you can see in the schematic outline below, it might be very easy to conduct this type of research.

Schematic Outline of a One-Group Pretest–Posttest Design

Single Group of Participants ⇒ Observation ⇒ Treatment ⇒ Observation

---

Commonly cited examples of this type of research include weight-loss programs and test preparation courses. In theory, there would be no problem with this kind of design if we could determine that nothing of interest happens in people's lives between observations other than the treatment. In reality, a lot happens between the "before" and the "after." What transpires in a person's life, not the treatment, may very well affect the measurements taken at the second observation.

Although there is no selection threat to internal validity here because there is no comparison across groups, the second observation could be affected by history, maturation, testing, and instrumentation.

Let's consider a weight-loss program. If researchers wanted to know if keeping a diary made a difference in weight loss, they could weigh a group of participants, ask them to keep a diary of food (and calories) consumed over eight weeks, then weigh them again after eight weeks. If the participants weighed significantly less at the end, it would be tempting to conclude that knowing how many calories you consumed made you more aware of your eating habits, so you cut down on your intake. Unfortunately, there could be a problem with history. If the research were done between mid-April and mid-June, the arrival of summer with its skimpy clothing might have motivated the people to lose weight; the diary may have been completely irrelevant.

This type of design is also prone to problems due to the threat of maturation. Between the start of the study and the final weigh-in, participants might become more motivated because they begin exercising and start to enjoy it.

The third threat in a one-group pretest–posttest design is testing. If an educator wanted to see if a test preparation course was effective in improving students' SAT scores, the researcher might see a gain in scores that was due to increases in familiarity with the test after taking it the first time. Sometimes the hardest part of a test is figuring out how to take it, not what the answers are. Continuing with the SAT example, if the students took a test at the end that just happened to be a little easier, they would score higher. The threat to internal validity here is called instrumentation, which means that changes in the measurement system are problematic.

We can also easily imagine the history threat. Perhaps students became more motivated by an inspiring teacher. The validity of the conclusions about test-preparation courses based on such a situation may be suspect.

It's important to remember that these threats are quite possible, but we don't know if problems are really present or not.

Could you actually demonstrate that nothing important outside your study happened? You probably couldn't, but you might be able to make a convincing argument that history was unlikely. The same is true for the other threats to validity. They could affect your final observations, but you might be able to persuade others that they weren't likely. The best strategy, though, is to create a design in which these problems are minimized.

Static-Group Comparison Designs

A somewhat more useful design expands on the one-group pretest–posttest design by adding a second group. This type of design, called the **static-group comparison design**, can be useful because it allows the researcher to assess different groups. Still, there is a selection threat in this design. The selection of participants is not randomized, so you don't know if your groups differed from the start.

> **Static-Group Comparison Design**—A quasi-experimental research design in which two groups that differ on some pre-existing dimension (i.e., participants are not randomly assigned to conditions) are compared.

An example of a static-group comparison design comes from a study that assessed the validity of a new test of mental functioning for people with visual impairments (Beauvais, Woods, Delaney, & Fein, 2004). The researchers studied three groups, adults with (a) visual impairment and normal mental functioning, (b) visual and neurological (i.e., mental) impairments, and (c) no impairment (the control group). When the investigators evaluated people in the three groups, the result showed that people with no impairment and those with only visual impairment scored comparably on the test, which is what you would expect because people with visual problems perform cognitively just like anyone else. But those with neurological and visual impairment scored more poorly.

Beauvais et al. (2004) concluded that the test was valid for discriminating between people with neurological problems and those without, as they had predicted. The limitation here is that participants were not randomly assigned to groups, so characteristics other than neurological impairment may have affected the test scores. There is no particular reason to believe that variables other than neurological impairment affect participants' performances, but it is always a possibility. That possibility is always present with static-group comparison designs.

You can see the schematic outline of the static-group comparison design below. The outline shows two groups, but you could include additional groups, as Beauvais et al. did.

> **Schematic Outline of a Static-Group Comparison Data**
>
> Nonrandom Placement in Group 1 ⇒ (Treatment ⇒) Observation
> Nonrandom Placement in Group 2 ⇒ (No Treatment ⇒) Observation

> **Nonequivalent Control Group Design**—A quasi-experimental research design in which two groups that differ on some pre-existing dimension (i.e., participants are not randomly assigned to conditions) are measured on a pretest, exposed to a treatment, and measured on a posttest.

Nonequivalent Control Group Designs

One way to compensate for the selection threat, at least in part, would be to collect data before applying an experimental treatment as well as after it. If you did this, you would be using a pretest–posttest design.

When you measure nonrandomly assigned participants on your dependent variable at the beginning of the study, apply the treatment, then measure them again, you are using a **nonequivalent control group design**. As the label suggests, your treatment and control groups may differ in important ways; that is, they are nonequivalent, even at the beginning of your study. But if you obtain a **baseline** measurement of each group, you can see if they differ at the start.

Schematic Outline of a Nonequivalent Control Group Design

Nonrandom Placement in Group 1 ⇒ Observation ⇒ Treatment ⇒ Observation
Nonrandom Placement in Group 2 ⇒ Observation ⇒ No Treatment ⇒ Observation

---

Baseline—A series of measurements recorded before a treatment is applied to see the normal course of behavior prior to an intervention.

For example, León, Brambila, de la Cruz, Colindres, Morales, and Vásquez (2005) tested use of approaches to offering family planning by counselors in Guatemala. The researchers created experimental groups in two areas of Guatemala with Mayan populations and Ladino populations, with corresponding control groups in two different areas. The investigators measured quality of care before and after counselors went through training in the new approach. Quality of care increased significantly, although the magnitude of improvement differed across groups. The difference across groups is likely due to factors external to the study, which is a problem for nonequivalent control group designs.

One of the reasons that the question of equivalence is so important is because when you measure people in existing categories over time, you don't know what change they would undergo over that period, even if you didn't apply a treatment.

If you look at Figures 9.4 and 9.5, you can see how you could be deceived regarding your results. In Figure 9.4, the results show that participants were measured twice. It appears that one group always scores higher than the other. However, if you had measured the participants earlier, you would have noted that the course of change of one group is markedly different from that of the other.

If this hypothetical study had included earlier measurements, a very different pattern of results would be apparent. Group A initially had higher scores that wouldn't be seen if only the last two measurements were made.

FIGURE 9.4 Illustration of possible result with a nonequivalent control group design. The inequality at the start and the different rate of change for the two groups leads to problems with interpretation of the results.

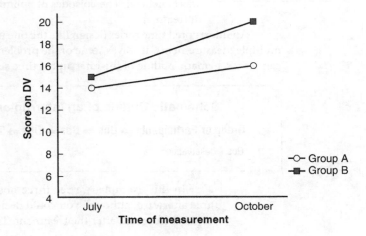

FIGURE 9.5   Illustration of possible pattern of results in a nonequivalent control group design. The final two measurements in this figure match those in Figure 9.3. If you only measured your participants in July and October (as in Figure 9.3), you would get a very different impression than if you assessed them in January and April as well. When you do not use random assignment of participants to groups, you cannot assume that they are equal to begin with; you also cannot assume that their patterns of change are going to be the same.

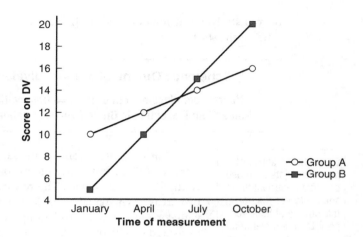

Interrupted Time Series Designs

In the one-group pretest–posttest design, one of the major problems is its simplicity. We measure participants only twice, but we don't know what has come before the first measurement nor what will follow the second one. We would be better off if we observed and measured the participants more than twice, which we do with an **interrupted time series design**.

Interrupted Time Series Design—A quasi-experimental research design in which a group is measured at different times, with a treatment applied at some point, resulting in baseline measurements and post-treatment measurements.

Simpson et al. (2006) used an interrupted time series design to study treatment for bulimia. They treated five women and one man who were experiencing eating disorders. Because of difficulties in the participants' abilities to travel to the therapist, each one experienced therapy via remote video sessions. The investigators assessed each participant multiple times prior to the start of the treatment, then again during the course of the therapy. Each person began treatment at a different point in time.

The researchers found that the intervention via videoconferencing was beneficial. The episodes of bulimic behavior diminished with the onset of treatment.

An interrupted time series design like the one used by Simpson et al. (2006) provides multiple measurements. It solves some of the problems of the pretest–posttest design. You can see a schematic outline of the interrupted time series design below.

Schematic Outline of an Interrupted Time Series Design*

Group or Participants ⇒ Obs ⇒ Obs ⇒ Obs ⇒ Treatment ⇒ Obs ⇒ Obs ⇒ Obs

*Obs = Observation

In this example, we see three observations before the treatment and three afterward, although you could decide to use different numbers of observations before and after the treatment. This type of design reduces the threats of maturation and testing. It is unlikely that you would be so unlucky in your research as to test your participants so that the only maturation occurs exactly when your treatment is in place.

In addition, when participants become sensitized because of an initial exposure to the measurement process, they are likely to be affected right away. As a result, in the schematic example, we would probably conclude that by the time they were observed and measured three times, any sensitization would have occurred. Again, you could be very unlucky and the testing effect might take hold only after your third observation, but this possibility is also pretty remote. If you thought it might happen, you could insert more observations prior to applying the treatment. Designs like this are useful because they allow researchers to establish a baseline of behavior against which behaviors after the treatment can be compared.

The threat that still exists is history. So you might be unlucky, seeing the effect of history just when your treatment goes into effect; it would be hard to spot.

Replicated Interrupted Time Series Design— A quasi-experimental research design in which different groups are measured in an interrupted time series design, with a treatment being applied at a different time for each group.

Replicated Interrupted Time Series Designs

If you added a control group to an interrupted time series design, you would have a more complicated methodology, but it would be associated with fewer threats to internal validity. The **replicated interrupted time series design** provides a control group and reduces the chance that your results will be affected by history. The schematic outline below is an extension to the simpler interrupted time series design.

Schematic Outline of a Replicated Interrupted Time Series Design*

Group 1 ⟹ Obs ⟹ Obs ⟹ Obs ⟹ Treatment ⟹ Obs ⟹ Obs v Obs
Group 2 ⟹ Obs ⟹ Obs ⟹ Treatment ⟹ Obs ⟹ Obs ⟹ Obs ⟹ Obs
Control Group ⟹ Obs ⟹ Obs ⟹ Obs ⟹ Obs ⟹ Obs ⟹ Obs

*Obs = Observation

There are different replicated designs. One approach is to apply the treatment at different times to the two groups. This will overcome many of our concerns about the history threat because a single historic episode is unlikely to affect the two groups at two different times. The selection threat is also reduced because we are observing the same people over time and can see a stable pattern of behaviors that is interrupted by the treatment.

A second design involves applying a treatment to one group but not to a control group. Here also the history threat is reduced. The reason we don't have to worry about it so much is that, if one occurs, it should happen to both groups, so its effects should be obvious.

This replicated interrupted time series design is not perfect, but even if the groups are not randomly assigned, the results are often amenable to a tentative causal analysis. For example, Hennigan et al. (1982) addressed an issue more than two decades ago that originated with the beginning of television broadcasting and continues today: Does television affect behavior in negative ways?

Although most people today grew up with television, it has not always existed. In fact, for some of us, radio was initially the dominant mass medium during childhood. In the early years of commercial television in the late 1940s, it was established in a number of cities in the United States, then Congress imposed a freeze that restricted its expansion. Because of the freeze, television became widespread in homes in some cities while others remained out of broadcasting range. Hennigan et al. used the results of this freeze to create an interrupted time series design. They looked at larceny rates (i.e., theft that does not involve violence or force) in cities before and after 50 percent of the homes in those cities had televisions.

The researchers reasoned that if television crime shows influenced actual crime, cities with early television stations should have an increase in larceny while the cities without television shouldn't. On the other hand, when the freeze on new stations was lifted, the cities that then gained television stations should show an increase in larceny, but the initial cities would not.

Figure 9.6 shows the results of the study. Crime was inching upward in the absence of television, but you can see that from 1949 to 1950, when television was introduced to the early cities, there was an increase in larceny in those cities. The areas without television did

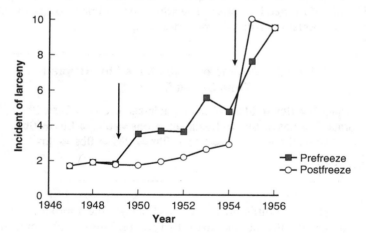

FIGURE 9.6   Introduction of television and incidence of larceny (cases per million population) in cities. Television became widespread by 1949 in the prefreeze cities; it was widespread in postfreeze cities around 1954. In each case, larceny increased following introduction of television. The arrows indicate the approximate time at which 50 percent of households in the two types of cities had televisions.

Source: Hennigan, K. M., Del Rosario, M. L., Heath, L., Cook, T. D., Wharton, J. D., & Calder, B. J. (1982). Impact of the introduction of television on crime in the United States: Empirical findings and theoretical implications. *Journal of Personality and Social Psychology, 42*, 461–577. Copyright American Psychological Association. Adapted with permission.

not show an upsurge. When the freeze set by Congress was lifted, the later cities showed an upsurge, whereas the initial cities did not. In 1946 and in 1956, the cities had comparable crime rates, which reassures us that the cities in the two conditions were roughly equivalent with respect to the DV of crime rate. They diverged when TV became prevalent in the different cities, then became similar again after they all had easy access to television.

Hennigan et al. concluded that television had a causal effect on the incidence of larceny. Television programs generally depicted middle- and upper-class individuals who owned desirable possessions. The investigators suggested that perhaps viewers were frustrated because their lives were more impoverished, so they pilfered items that they couldn't afford.

As you should recognize by now, though, this research was not experimental. The investigators did not randomly assign people to groups; rather, factors in everyday life that were beyond the control of the researchers determined a person's group.

One way to reduce the worries about the validity of the research findings is to use an experimental approach that will complement the nonexperimental research. Each approach will answer slightly different questions, but if the data point in the same direction, we will have convergent validity and can have faith in the overall validity of the research.

Since the Hennigan et al. study, the data have shown pretty clearly that exposure to violent media can increase aggressive tendencies (e.g., Report of the media, 2012). One such study involved participants who listened to music that either had or did not have violent lyrics (Anderson, Carnagey, & Eubanks, 2003). After hearing violent lyrics in an experiment, college students displayed higher levels of aggressive thought and more hostility compared to the students who heard nonviolent lyrics.

Researchers frequently use time-series designs for applied research where experiments are not practical or possible. It is typical to see these applications in studies of intervention programs, such as attempts to reduce the incidence of violence among adolescents at a runaway shelter (Nugent, Bruley, & Allen, 1998). This approach is also used in less traumatic circumstances, such as the effectiveness of psychological skills training in athletes (Brewer & Shillinglaw, 1992).

■ ■ ■ ■ ■

CONTROVERSY
On Using Laws To Change Behavior

Legislators create laws to change behaviors or to punish the people who engage in them. Laws are enacted all the time, but seldom repealed. When laws outlive their usefulness, people simply tend to ignore them. We all know of laws that are not enforced vigorously.

For example, drinking by people under 21 in the United States is illegal, but it is so widespread that we can only conclude that, as a society, we are not overly concerned with it. The public service campaigns to restrict young people's drinking might have an impact on some, but the drinking is still fairly widespread.

It might be illustrative to see if laws actually change what people do. Researchers have used time-series designs to find out.

Levitt and Leventhal (1986) studied whether the New York State bottle return bill has reduced the amount of litter in New York. This bill mandated that consumers pay a five cent deposit on beer and soda bottles and cans; the deposit is refunded when they return the container. Has it made a difference? This is an important question given that over a decade, if nothing were done to reduce litter, Americans could generate a billion tons; this litter would cost taxpayers a trillion dollars to clean up over the decade.

The researchers walked along highway entrance ramps and railroad tracks, counting the number of bottles and documenting the general level of litter. They chose sites in New York before and after the bottle bill passed and in New Jersey, which had no such law.

About a year after the bill became law, the researchers found that on the highway entrances there was significantly less litter in New York than in New Jersey for cans and bottles that were returnable in New York. The amount of nonreturnable litter (i.e., general garbage and trash) did not change. The picture was a little more complex on the railroad sites, but the law seemed to be effective as well. Thus, the bottle bill seemed to have changed behaviors; consumers didn't litter cans and bottles for which they paid a deposit. Unfortunately, other kinds of litter persisted.

On the west coast of the United States, a different set of researchers (Stolzenberg & D'Alessio, 1997) studied the effect of a very different California law using a time-series design. The California State Legislature passed a "Three Strikes and You're Out" law; this law mandates extended prison terms for repeat criminals. In one well-publicized example, a California man who had previously committed a felony received a mandatory prison sentence of 25 years to life after being convicted of stealing a slice of pizza from a group of children. (Fortunately, judges in California are now allowed discretion as to when they invoke this law, although the Supreme Court has ruled that people can be sentenced to lengthy prison terms for third offenses involving crimes like shoplifting.)

Stolzenberg and D'Alessio looked at the crime index for felonies and for petty theft from 1985 to 1994, when the law was passed, then monitored the crime rate for another year. California officials claimed that the law was successful; the felony crime rate was lower after the law was passed.

The researchers discovered, however, that for a year or so prior to the law, the crime rate had begun to decline. They concluded that the continued decline after the law took effect only reflected a trend that had begun well before the law was in existence.

More recently, sociologist Robert Nash Parker analyzed crime data in California and demonstrated that so-called "get tough" policies had nothing to do with the declining crime rates. States that don't have the "three-strikes" law have shown the same pattern of crime rates as California. Instead, he attributes the decline to less use of alcohol. His message is clear from part of the title of his research article: "Why California's three strikes is a complete failure" (Three-strikes law fails, 2012).

Stolzenberg and D'Alessio suggested that if other research supports their findings, it might be a good idea to repeal such three-strikes laws. For one thing, they are costly; it is expensive to incarcerate people. Another reason is that there may be other programs that actually will work for no greater cost. A third reason is that we may be wasting human talent and human lives by keeping people in prison for decades. The researchers are not proposing that criminals not be punished; they are saying that everybody in society will be better off when we have a logical criminal justice system.

This type of research can provide useful information for society. Well-designed investigations can tell us if we are making progress in dealing with societal issues and, if not, how we might be able to improve the situation.

SUMMARY

After reading this chapter, you should recognize the benefits of repeated measures designs. Psychologists rely on this approach because of its notable advantages. When you conduct research that involves repeated measures, you can have confidence that your groups are comparable from the start because each group has the same people. Thus, any differences that emerge are likely to be due to your treatments.

In addition, repeated measures designs are efficient, allowing researchers to double or triple (or more) the data they collect with minimal increases in costs. Further, if you are studying a relatively rare population, you can benefit by collecting all the data you can with your few participants. An added benefit is that your research design is more sensitive to small differences between groups. This means that if your treatment really has an effect, even if it is a small one, you are more likely to find a significant difference.

The drawback to repeated measures designs is that exposure to a treatment may have a long-lasting effect on the participant. In later observations, the person may be tired or bored, or the individual might perform better because he or she learned how to be more effective in the experimental task. These sequence effects can obscure a real difference or make a small difference look more important than it really is. Fortunately, there are ways to overcome these problems.

Another extension to the basic experimental design is the quasi-experiment. It is set up like an experiment, with different groups that are compared to see if they show the same behaviors. Quasi-experiments differ from true experiments in that quasi-experiments do not employ random assignment of participants to groups.

The participants differ on some characteristic to begin with, and it is this difference that leads them to be assigned to different groups. The problem here is that people in each group differ from the start, so if they differ at the end, your IV may have had an effect, but differences may have resulted from something other than your IV.

Researchers have devised quasi-experimental designs to overcome many of the problems that can affect the validity of the results. As we move from simple static-group comparison designs with one group to the replicated time-series design, we can gain confidence that the various threats to internal validity are unlikely.

With the sophistication of some of the quasi-experimental designs, we can begin to form tentative, causal conclusions. We should continue to show caution about deciding that our treatment actually causes some behavior, though, because quasi-experiments are really variants on correlational designs.

REVIEW QUESTIONS

Multiple Choice Questions

1. Another name for a repeated measures design is a
   a. within-subjects design.
   b. between-groups design.
   c. nonequivalent control group design.
   d. longitudinal design.
2. If you wanted to collect data from 50 participants and in each of three conditions, you wouldn't need to recruit 150 people if you used a
   a. nonequivalent control group design.
   b. replicated interrupted design.
   c. within-subjects design.
   d. between-subjects design.
3. If you are interested in studying how quickly people learn in early adulthood compared to old age, you would probably choose which design?
   a. Repeated measures design
   b. Between-groups design
   c. Interrupted time series design
   d. Partially counterbalanced design

4. Green and Vaid (1986) reported that when participants engage in two tasks at the same time, finger tapping and reading, it makes a difference if they start tapping with the left hand or the right hand. This is an example of a potential problem with
    a. order effects
    b. complete counterbalancing effects.
    c. partial counterbalancing effects.
    d. symmetric transfer effects.

5. When order effects occur in the same way regardless of whether the order is A-B or B-A, this is a case of
    a. incomplete counterbalancing.
    b. symmetric transfer.
    c. selection effect.
    d. latency effect.

6. Studies using a within-subjects design can analyze data on differences in performance at the start and end of the session through
    a. correlations.
    b. descriptive statistics.
    c. baseline analysis.
    d. change scores.

7. Goldenberg et al. (1999) discovered that highly neurotic people tend to associate sex with death. When they compared high and low neurotic people, they were using
    a. a time-series design.
    b. a quasi-experimental variable.
    c. a within-subjects design.
    d. asymmetric transfer.

8. Bell et al. (2000) found that people who are more physically fit suffer athletic injuries less often than people who are less fit. This threat to internal validity that keeps us from concluding that fitness is a causal variable is
    a. selection.
    b. maturation.
    c. statistical regression.
    d. history.

9. If research participants are assessed with a particular questionnaire early in a study, but the researchers change the questions for later assessment so participants can't simply repeat answers, what potential thread to internal validity would be at work here?
    a. instrumentation.
    b. testing.
    c. selection.
    d. history.

10. A study that looked at grades in a history class before and after students learned a memory technique would likely be a
    a. static-group comparison design.
    b. one-group pretest–posttest design.
    c. nonequivalent control group design.
    d. time series design.

11. If your research plan started with a static-group comparison design, then you added a pretest to the design, your new plan would involve a
    a. nonequivalent control group design.
    b. one-group pretest–posttest design.

    c. static-group comparison design.

    d. time series design.

12. If your research design involved collecting data on several different occasions before you applied your experimental treatment, followed by a series of additional measurements, you would be using

    a. a static-group comparison design.

    b. a one-group pretest–posttest design.

    c. an interrupted time series design.

    d. a nonequivalent control group design.

Essay Questions

13. Explain why repeated measures designs can be more useful than nonrepeated measures designs when participants provide subjective ratings. Why are objective measures less problematic in nonrepeated designs?

14. Why would counterbalancing help overcome problems of order effects?

15. What are the four threats to internal validity that are associated with participants?

ANSWERS TO REVIEW QUESTIONS

Answers to Multiple Choice Questions

1. a	5. b	9. a
2. c	6. d	10. b
3. b	7. b	11. a
4. a	8. a	12. c

Answers to Essay Questions

13. Explain why repeated measures designs can be more useful than nonrepeated measures designs when participants provide subjective ratings. Why are objective measures less problematic in nonrepeated designs?

    When participants engage in subjective ratings, as on a Likert-type scale, each person brings his or her own perspective to the judgment task. There is no guarantee that two different people will have the same subjective rating perspective. With objective measures, we rely less on personal perspectives and instead focus on more externally verifiable behaviors.

14. Why would counterbalancing help overcome problems of order effects?

    Counterbalancing helps overcome sequence and order effects by spreading the results of those effects across conditions. Thus, a participant who goes through condition A and then B might perform differently in B because of the experience with A. Another participant who goes through B and then A will have his or her performance affected in condition A rather than in B. Thus, order effects will be spread out over the different conditions.

15. What are the four threats to internal validity that are associated with participants?

    a. Selection—people in the groups to be compared differ from one another at the outset of the study.

    b. Maturation—people change over the course of a study either physically or psychologically.

    c. Attrition (Mortality)—different types of people may leave a study before it is completed.

    d. History—events not specifically associated with the treatment may affect the outcome for one group.

CHAPTER TEN

PRINCIPLES OF SURVEY RESEARCH

C H A P T E R   O V E R V I E W

LEARNING OBJECTIVES ■ KEY TERMS ■ CHAPTER PREVIEW

L E A R N I N G   O B J E C T I V E S

After going through this chapter, you will be able to:

- Describe the problems with early surveys of U.S. presidential elections in 1936 and 1948
- Explain the difference between a census and a sample
- Describe the degree of accuracy of national political polls
- Identify the ethical issues associated with survey research
- Describe the concept of the sampling frame
- Identify cultural issues associated with survey research
- Define and explain the difference between open-ended and closed-ended questions
- Explain the advantages and the disadvantages of open-ended and closed-ended questions
- Identify problematic issues associated with memories of past behaviors
- Identify problematic issues associated with surveys involving attitudes
- Identify strategies that will help avoid problems in creating memory questions in survey research
- Identify the methodological issues addressed in the survey research on adolescent smoking

238

- Describe the issues associated with survey research on sensitive issues
- Describe the two types of social desirability bias
- Explain strategies to overcome potential social desirability bias
- Differentiate the concepts of optimizing and satisficing in survey research
- Describe the problem of self-selected samples
- Identify four strategies for finding so-called hidden populations in survey research

---

KEY TERMS

Acquiescence, p. 253

Census, p. 240

Chain-referral methods, p. 256

Chronically accessible information, p. 247

Closed-ended question, p. 243

Hidden population, p. 256

Impression management, p. 251

Key informant sampling, p. 256

Nondifferentiation, p. 243

Open-ended question, p. 243

Optimizing, p. 253

Population, p. 240

Respondent-driven sampling, p. 257

Response bias, p. 250

Sampling frame, p. 242

Satisficing, p. 245

Self-deception positivity, p. 251

Self-selected samples, p. 255

Snowball sampling, p. 256

Social desirability bias, p. 251

Survey research, p. 239

Targeted sampling, p. 257

Telescoping, p. 246

Temporarily accessible information, p. 248

CHAPTER PREVIEW

Asking questions in survey research is an important aspect of research methodology. Surveys have become a fixture in modern life, with professional pollsters examining details of our lives and social scientists uncovering trends in attitudes and patterns of behavior. Most surveys rely on samples rather than on an exhaustive questioning of the entire population, which is a census.

Surveyors can choose from among different question types and content. The construction of the questions is probably the hardest part of a project because the form of a question influences responses, depending on the wording. In addition, respondents don't want to be seen in unfavorable light, so they may alter responses to make themselves look good and may tailor their answers to meet what they think are the expectations of the researcher. Fortunately, there are ways to avoid the obvious pitfalls in asking questions.

Finally, survey researchers prefer probability samples and are wary of self-selected convenience samples that do not represent the entire population. Researchers continue to develop new sampling strategies to overcome potential problems in current strategies.

SURVEYS: ANSWERING DIVERSE QUESTIONS

Survey Research—A research method in which an investigator asks questions of a respondent.

Beginning a little over half a century ago, investigators began developing the theory and techniques of **survey research.** Early in the 1900s, surveys took place that increased our information base on various topics, but by today's standards they were methodologically suspect. For instance, in 1936, the now defunct magazine *Literary Digest* inaccurately predicted that Franklin Roosevelt would lose the U.S. presidential election in a landslide. This may be the most famous error in the history of research. The problem was that the editors of that magazine used a sampling method that led to an unrepresentative picture of the voting population.

A little more than a decade later, a newspaper proclaimed that Thomas Dewey had defeated Harry Truman in the 1948 presidential election. The problem there was that in the forecasting, the newspaper also used a sampling technique that was prone to error in depicting the population as a whole and stopped polling two weeks prior to the election.

Today's researchers can also make mistakes, as they did in the 2000 presidential election when they declared that Al Gore won the state of Florida. In spite of this major mistake, current survey techniques provide very useful information most of the time. After all, in the 2000 presidential election, the pollsters called 49 of the 50 states correctly, a level of accuracy that is not unusual. Using samples to understand populations can lead to mistakes because we are using incomplete information to draw conclusions, but if researchers use proper techniques, the number of misjudgments and the magnitude of error are small.

Census versus Sample

> **Population**—A set consisting of every person or data point that would be of interest to a researcher.

> **Census**—Data collection that includes every member of a population of interest.

When researchers conduct survey research, they must decide whether to contact a sample (which is what we actually do) or everybody in the **population** of interest. Probably the most famous example of the latter is the census. The U.S. Constitution mandates a decennial **census,** that is, a complete counting of everybody living in the country every 10 years. The basic purpose of the census is to inform the Congress about how many people live in each state so there can be proportional representation in the House of Representatives. There are also other uses for the results, like figuring out where the population is growing so adequate highways can be built or where to build hospitals to meet the needs of an aging populace.

Although everybody agrees that the census is necessary, we must face the fact that it is very costly. The 2010 census had a price tag of about $13 billion, or about $42 to count each person (Costing the count, 2011), up from $7 billion, or about $25 per head, in 2000. Mailing a census form to every household in the country alone is an enormous expense; when people don't reply, a personal follow-up takes place, which is also expensive.

We also know that many people are missed in the census, particularly people who have no fixed address, people from countries where they may have had an appropriate fear of the government, and others. In addition, some people are counted twice, like those who own multiple homes. The process of counting every resident is not easy, cheap, or completely accurate. The census has never been perfect, beginning with the first one in 1790. Even with our increasing technical sophistication, the accuracy of the census is probably worse than it used to be.

Accuracy of Survey Results

How accurate are surveys that professional researchers conduct? When it comes to scientific research, we generally don't know. But we can look at the surveys whose accuracy has been assessed: polls for political elections. Researchers who are conducting scientific surveys often use the same methodologies that political pollsters do, so if the political surveys are accurate, it is likely that scientific surveys are, too.

So let's take a look at political surveys on a national level. There are about 100 million potential voters in the United States. It would make no sense to try to ask each of them about their views; it would take too long and cost too much money. If you wanted to characterize 100 million possible voters with reasonable accuracy, how many would you have to sample? Typically, political polls sample about 1,000 people; ranging from 700 or 800 to perhaps 1,500. These numbers reflect about .001 percent of the voting population.

How accurate are these polls? After every election, the vote count provides a test. In the 2008 U.S. presidential election, the predictions of percentage vote for the winner in eight major final pre-election polls differed from the actual vote by an average of less than 1 percent (Election results, 2010; FiveThirtyEight, 2008), a figure similar to those in 2000 and 2004 (Election polls, 2010; High accuracy found, 2001). Polls for the 2004 election were the most accurate to that time (Traugott, 2005), and those for the most recent election seem just as accurate. The polls are not error-free, but they are pretty impressive, especially when you consider the modest sample sizes.

When you sample a subset of the population, you can count on getting some differences between your sample and the population. If you have a small sample, a few unusual people can distort your results; if you have a large sample, those same unusual people don't make much of a difference.

This means that you can get a pretty good picture of your population by sampling a relatively small number of people. As you increase your sample size, the accuracy of your information grows, but for a population as large as 100 million voters, once you reach a sample size of about 1,000, your accuracy doesn't grow very much for each new person you sample. As a result, it doesn't pay to increase your sample size above a certain point if you are not going to increase the sample greatly.

If the population from which you want to sample is relatively small, you might need a larger proportion in order to end up with accurate results, but the actual number will not be all that large.

ETHICS IN SURVEY RESEARCH

All research carries the requirement of ethical behavior on the part of the investigator. With regard to survey research, we have to pay attention to two critical, related considerations—anonymity and confidentiality. It is standard practice to completely guarantee both the anonymity and the confidentiality of responses.

If a researcher is tracking whether people have responded and wants to send a reminder to those who have not completed a survey, some kind of identification is necessary. In the rare event that an investigator needs to identify respondents, the data cannot be anonymous.

When researchers cannot guarantee anonymity, they can at least assure respondents that participation will be kept confidential. Confidentiality means that nobody will be able to connect a given person with participation in a study. This is typically assured by reporting the data only in aggregate, that is, in a summarized form so that nobody can tell who responded in one way or another. For surveys that ask sensitive questions, you must provide such assurances because your respondents will either decline to respond or will not tell the whole truth.

The situation is complex because, with sensitive questions, anonymity may be a critical issue. For example, when Lavender and Anderson (2009) studied behaviors associated with eating disorders (extreme dieting, purging, investment in body weight and shape, fear of weight gain, and the belief that others worry about their weight), they discovered that their respondents reported a higher incidence of problematic behaviors when the respondents were more confident that their responses were truly anonymous. The effect was more pronounced with questions associated with more undesirable behaviors, suggesting that the quality of data may be lower when respondents are responding to very sensitive questions and are not completely sure that their responses are anonymous.

Ironically, if you make a big point of assuring confidentiality and anonymity, it may arouse suspicions in those you survey (Singer, Von Thurn, & Miller, 1995). In a situation involving mundane questions, it might be more reasonable to play down the confidentiality and anonymity aspects because they may distract a participant from the real purpose of the study.

SELECTING YOUR METHODOLOGY

Most research projects begin with a general question that needs an answer. After that, practical issues arise. In the case of surveys, the critical issues include identifying the sampling frame. The **sampling frame** is the entire list of people from which the sample is drawn. In psychological research, we seldom have a list of all possible respondents; in fact, we usually do not even have any way to detail the population of interest to us. Nonetheless, any survey research that we conduct should begin with an identification of the source of our respondents that will lead to our actual sample.

> **Sampling Frame**—A subset of a population from which a sample is actually selected.

We decide the specific means of constituting a sample. This step is critical if we are interested in drawing conclusions that generalize beyond our sampling frame. Researchers who conduct surveys prefer to use probability samples. If the process is done properly, researchers can be confident that the sample is likely to represent the entire population.

Researchers also spend considerable time developing the questions. Creating survey questions seems as if it should be easy but is probably the most difficult part of survey research and requires the greatest creativity and insight. And it takes on even greater importance when the sampling frame contains people of diverse backgrounds. For example, investigators studied the effect of wording of questions on the Center for Epidemiologic Studies Depression Scale (CES-D) and found notable differences among Mexican Americans, Black Americans, and White Americans due simply to differences in the way the items are structured. Mexican Americans were more likely to endorse a greater number of depressive items compared to White and Black Americans (Kim, Chiriboga, & Jang, 2009).

And as Chen (2008) noted, there are four general issues associated with making comparisons across cultures, including problems with translation from one language to another, the possibility that an item does not really measure the same construct in different cultures, varying response styles across cultures, and issues of social desirability. Oyserman, Coon, and Kemmelmeier (2002) pointed out, for instance, that people from cultures that are high in both collectivistic and individualistic tendencies often use more extreme ratings on a Likert-type scale than do people from cultures low in those tendencies.

In addition, some groups that are known to value relationships and sincerity tend to show acquiescence in their responses. Such groups include Hispanics and African Americans. On the other hand, Anglo Americans have a predisposition to select extreme responses on rating scales, whereas people from East Asian countries are more likely to use the middle of a scale. These patterns can complicate interpreting results because other tendencies further confuse the picture. For example, Mexicans are likely to systematically choose extreme responses on a scale, particularly when responding in Spanish (Chen, Lee, & Stevenson, 1995; Davis, Resnicow, & Couper, 2011). Another issue that surveyors face is **nondifferentiation,** which involves a response tendency to assign the same rating to different questions, regardless of their content. There is no evidence that this behavior is cultural; rather it involves individual differences across respondents.

> **Nondifferentiation**—The tendency of respondents to give the same answer to questions, regardless of content.

Further complicating the picture is that people may respond to items differently depending on their degree of acculturation into a new culture. In assessing depression, Chiriboga, Jang, Banks, and Kim (2007) reported that elderly Mexican Americans showed different patterns of responses depending on the degree to which they were proficient in English, the language in which they were tested. In such groups, it is likely that language skills will affect most research results involving verbal responses.

Another important issue that has gained importance in the past decade is the use of computers to collect self-report data. Switching from paper and pencil to a computer might seem like a minor issue, but there is no guarantee that people will respond the same way for both. (You can refer to Chapter 6 for guidance regarding online data collection.)

Fortunately, for many measurements, respondents have shown comparable behavior (e.g., Vispoel, 2000) although there can be some differences. For instance, Heerwegh (2009) found that nonresponse to items was greater for Web-based surveys, but social desirability bias was less, although the differences were quite small. Further, having multiple items on a screen shortens the length of the interview, but respondents may have a less positive response to the session than with fewer items per screen (Toepoel, Das, & Van Soest, 2009).

Any time you change methodologies, you don't know if the new and the old means will result in the same outcome until you research the question. There seems to be reason to be optimistic that computerized data collection will lead to results that are as valid as those in traditional methods.

One practical example of the difficulty in answering even a simple question involves the determination of how many adolescents in the United States smoke. A generally accepted answer based on survey research is about 4 million, but this number can be deceiving because the definition of "smoking" makes a big difference in the number that you accept as valid. The Controversy box on adolescent smoking at the end of this section illustrates this problem.

> **Open-Ended Question**—In survey research, a question that respondents answer using their own words, unconstrained by choices provided by the researcher.

Question Types

In terms of question and response structure, there are two main types of survey items: **open-ended questions,** which allow respondents to generate an answer without limitations regarding length or content, and **closed-ended questions,** which require respondents to select from a set of answers already provided. Each type has its own advantages and disadvantages. Table 10.1 shows how a researcher might develop different types of questions to investigate a topic.

> **Closed-Ended Question**—In survey research, a question that contains a set of answers that a respondent chooses.

TABLE 10.1   Examples of Questions in Open-versus Closed-Ended Formats That Relate to the Same General Topic, Alcohol Consumption

Open-Ended Question:

Describe the situations in which you consume alcoholic beverages and what you drink. (Note: You would only ask this question after you have established that the individual does consume alcohol.)

Closed-Ended Questions:

1. On how many days per week do you consume alcohol?

   ☐ None

   ☐ 1–2 times per week

   ☐ 3–4 times per week

   ☐ 5 or more times per week

2. When you drink alcoholic beverages, what do you drink most frequently?

   ☐ I do not drink alcoholic beverages

   ☐ Beer

   ☐ Wine

   ☐ Liquor (Gin, Vodka, Scotch, Bourbon)

3. Which of the following statements describes the most likely situation when you drink alcoholic beverages?

   ☐ I do not drink alcoholic beverages

   ☐ I am alone

   ☐ I am with one other person

   ☐ I am in a small group (2–5 people)

   ☐ I am in a larger group (6 or more people)

4. Do you think today it is easier, no different, or harder for teenagers to obtain alcohol compared to 10 years ago?

   ☐ Easier

   ☐ No different

   ☐ Harder

5. The minimum legal age for drinking alcoholic beverages in the United States is 21 years. Do you agree with the statement, "The minimum legal age for drinking should remain at 21 years"?

   ☐ Strongly agree

   ☐ Agree

   ☐ Disagree

   ☐ Strongly disagree

   ☐ No opinion

If you attempted to answer an open-ended question about drinking alcohol, you could discuss many different aspects of drinking behavior. You would determine what you thought was important and what was irrelevant, then respond accordingly. The advantage of such questions is that they provide a rich body of information. The disadvantage is that they can be harder to categorize, sort, and summarize because the responses can go in any direction the respondent wants to take them.

On the other hand, researchers can use closed-ended questions. These items do not permit free responding. There is a set of responses from which to choose, such as *yes–no or strongly agree/somewhat agree/somewhat disagree/strongly disagree*. The information provided by such questions is not as rich as with open-ended questions, but they are much easier to score and summarize. Further, with closed-ended questions, the investigator can make sure that the respondent has the chance to answer questions of critical importance to the research project. For example, if the investigator wants to know whether teenagers drink alone or with others, the closed-ended question may provide that information from every respondent. Few people may address that issue in the open-ended question. Interestingly, it appears to be fairly easy to get respondents to generate more complete answers. Smyth, Dillman, Christian, and McBride (2009) found that simply increasing the size of boxes provided for answers and telling people they can exceed the initial size of Web-based response boxes led to longer responses, particularly for people with low motivation levels.

Although research has shown that both types of question format lead to answers of comparable validity, since the 1940s, researchers have preferred closed-ended questions because such a format lends itself to easier scoring.

> **Satisficing**—The tendency of respondents to be satisfied with the first acceptable response to a question or on a task, even if it is not the best response.

However, evaluation of closed-ended questions has revealed some of their limitations. For instance, if people can choose from among answers prepared by the surveyor or can generate their own, they will often pick one of the surveyor's responses, even if they can provide their own, better answer (Krosnick, 1999). One reason is that people generally don't want to work any harder than they have to. This phenomenon of selecting the first acceptable answer, even if it is not the best, is called **satisficing**.

Question Content

A key difference among questions involves what the researcher is trying to measure. In general, we can divide the purpose of the questions into three domains: measures of memory and behavior, measures of attitude and opinion, and demographics.

Memory Questions. Most of the time in our lives, when we converse with people, we assume that they are telling us the truth. This is usually a reasonable assumption. The same is probably true regarding answers on a questionnaire. At the same time, we all know that we do not always tell the whole truth, and sometimes we lie outright. This pattern is also true for responses to surveys.

People may not be lying when they misreport their behaviors. They may not know the answer to a question, but they give it their best guess (maybe a bad one), trying to be helpful. When you want people to tell you how often they have engaged in mundane behaviors that don't stand out in memory, they are prone to significant error (Rockwood, Sangster, & Dillman, 1997). For example, for many students, it would be difficult to answer precisely the question, "How often in the past two months have you eaten pizza?" The episodes individually do not stand out in memory because they are so normal. Thus, it may be difficult to come up with an accurate response.

Sometimes researchers ask respondents to answer questions that require the person to remember something. For instance, Kleck and Gertz (1995) wanted to know the extent to which people report having protected themselves with handguns against burglars. Their analysis revealed 2.5 million instances of such protection, implying that handguns in such situations exert a positive effect. Hemenway (1997) argued that the problem with Kleck and Gertz's data is that more people claim to have protected themselves with guns during burglaries than were actually burglarized.

Hemenway argued that whenever you ask a sample to remember relatively rare events of any kind, a small increase in false positives (i.e., saying something happened when it did not) leads to an inappropriately large estimate when you generalize to the population.

Hemenway's point about the reporting of rare events was reinforced by further research. Cook and Ludwig (1998) noted that reports of defensive gun use (DGU) in studies with relatively small samples suggest greater rates of DGU than are likely to be true. This doesn't mean that there is not significant defensive gun use, only that we may not know how often it occurs. Considering less controversial topics, Wentland and Smith (1993) noted that people have trouble with remembering if they have a library card.

We can identify four particularly troublesome problems associated with memory questions. First, people use different strategies to recall events from the recent past and distant past in some cases. When Winkielman, Knäuper, and Schwarz (1998) inquired of people how often they have been angry in the last week versus in the last year, the respondents interpreted the meaning of the question differently. In the "last week" group, participants decided that the surveyor wanted a report of minor irritations, whereas the "last year" group focused on major irritations.

> **Telescoping**—A phenomenon of memory in which events that occurred in the distant past are remembered as having occurred more recently than they actually did.

A second source of problems is that, when a question involves a time span (e.g., "How many times in the last year have you…"), people may engage in a memory phenomenon called **telescoping.** When you look through a telescope, distant objects do not seem as far away as they really are; similarly, when people try to remember events from the past, things that happened a long time ago tend to be remembered as having happened more recently than they actually did.

A third difficulty is that the nature of previous questions affects the responses to later ones. People want to appear consistent in their responses, so they may use previous answers to help them form responses to new questions. Todorov (2000) discovered that people reported different levels of vision problems in a health survey depending on what questions had been asked just before a critical question.

A fourth concern involves the nature of alternatives presented in a closed-ended question. Schwarz (1999) and others have reported that the scale of alternatives can make a big difference in a person's response.

For example, Schwarz, Hippler, Deutsch, and Strack (1985) asked people how much television the average German citizen watched daily. Respondents saw one of two scales for their response, such as the kind in Figure 10.1. Over a third of those who answered using the high-frequency scale estimated more than two and a half hours a day. Less than half that number using the low-frequency scale responded as such.

How much television does the average viewer watch per day?

0 to 0.5 hr	5 to 1.0 hr	1 to 1.5 hr	1.5 to 2 hr	2 to 2.5 hr	More than 2.5 hr
○	○	○	○	○	○

How much television does the average viewer watch per day?

Up to 2.5 hr	2.5 to 3 hr	3 to 3.5 hr	3.5 to 4 hr	4 to 4.5 hr	More than 4.5 hr
○	○	○	○	○	○

FIGURE 10.1 Illustration of scales that lead to different answers. When the range of options includes smaller values, people reply that the typical person watches less television than when the range of options includes larger values.

Why would there be such a discrepancy? Respondents get information about the survey from its format. So the way the questions are worded and their visual appearance clue respondents to "appropriate" answers (Christian, Parsons, & Dillman, 2009). People responding to the low-frequency scale expressed a belief that the typical person watched 2.7 hours of television a day, whereas those responding on the high-frequency scale suggested that the typical person watched 3.2 hours. Given that people's memories are pretty fragile, the nature of the scale could influence responses notably.

Table 10.2 provides some guidelines about asking questions when you want people to recall something. You will notice that some of the points seem to contradict one another. For example, one element says to ask for specific information and another says not to. When you are preparing survey questions, you need to make decisions about each question in the context in which it is asked. Sometimes you will want to ask specific questions, sometimes you will not.

Attitude Questions. People have attitudes on many different issues and they are often willing to share them. But asking about attitudes is difficult. There are seven major concerns that researchers have to ponder.

One prime concern with questions about attitudes, just as with memory questions, is the wording of the item. For example, emotionally laden terms can result in answers that are more likely to be responses to the wording than to the meaning of the question. For instance, a question that refers to sexual material as "hard-core pornography" is likely to elicit negative responses because of the attitude to the words, even if those words do not describe that sexual material very well.

Professional researchers are likely to be sensitive to the biasing factor of the words they use, but sometimes the effects are subtle. Rasinski (1989) pointed out that people voiced less support for "welfare" for the poor than they did for "assistance to the poor."

A second variable that can affect responses is the order of the questions. Memories and feelings about a topic that always surface when a respondent addresses some topic are **chronically accessible.** This means that respondents call some information to mind very readily; this information will affect

> **Chronically Accessible Information**—Memories that are available for retrieval at any time.

TABLE 10.2   Elements for Constructing Survey Questions Involving Respondents' Memory

Guideline	Comment
Do not ask for details of mundane activities that are beyond a person's ability to remember (e.g., "How many people are usually in the library when you study there?").	Some people are better at remembering details than others are; asking for too much recall of detail may lead some groups to produce low-quality data based on faulty estimates.
If possible when you ask people how frequently they have engaged in a behavior, request the respondent to provide as specific a number as possible.	If you give respondents a series of alternatives to choose from, the scale you use will influence the answer to this question and possibly to others.
If you need to ask about specific periods of time, make sure that the respondent can accurately gauge behaviors in the time frame you specify.	People are better at the recent past than the distant past. Further, respondents are more accurate for behaviors they engage in on a regular schedule.
Avoid questions that have vague quantifiers (e.g., "rarely" or "sometimes"); instead, use more specific quantifiers (e.g., "twice a week").	Vague quantifiers like "frequently" differ depending on the person and on the event being judged. For example, "frequent headaches" means something different than "frequent brushing of teeth."
Avoid questions that require overspecific quantifiers (e.g., "How many times have you eaten at a restaurant in the past year?"); instead give ranges (e.g., "0–1 times," "2–3 times," etc.).	When people engage in commonplace activities on an irregular basis, precise estimates are little more than guesses.
Do not ask questions using words that might distract the respondent (e.g., offensive or inflammatory words).	Respondents may use negative or emotionally charged words as a clue to how often they should report a behavior, trying to avoid a negative evaluation of such behavior.

Temporarily Accessible Information—Memories that are available for retrieval only when cued by exposure to information that cues those memories.

their responses. Other memories and feelings might be **temporarily accessible.** This information also affects responses, but only if it has been recently brought into awareness, as by an earlier question on the survey.

Such accessibility may explain why, in nationwide polls, people generally claim that their own school systems are doing a good job, but that the nation's schools as a whole are not doing well (e.g., Satisfaction with local schools, 2005). When events in educational settings are especially troubling, news reports highlight the problem. So people compare their own schools with the negative reports elsewhere and conclude that their own system is just fine.

A third feature that guides participants' responses is their perceptions of the purpose of the interview or questionnaire. In one study, participants completed a questionnaire that had printed on the top "Institute for Social Research," whereas others saw "Institute for Personality Research." The responses of the two groups differed, with the first group concentrating on social variables in their answers and the second group concentrating on personality issues (Norenzayan & Schwarz, 1999).

A fourth possible variable influencing the expression of attitudes is the sensitivity of the issue being investigated. People may be reluctant to admit to drunken driving, illegal drug use, some sexual behaviors, and other such issues. There are two likely sources of invalidity for analysis of responses to these items. One source is nonresponse. That is, people simply ignore the question. The problem is that if too many people fail to answer the item, you may have problems with the representativeness of the answers you actually get. A second likely source of invalidity is simple lying.

A fifth factor that may come into play in personal interviews is the nature of the person doing the questioning. For example, Finkel, Guterbok, and Borg (1991) discovered that White respondents were more likely to express support for a Black candidate when an interviewer was Black rather than White, even when the interview was over the telephone.

In considering a sixth possible source of problems with the quality of data, it is important to distinguish between attitudes and opinions that people already have, as opposed to attitudes that they create when a researcher asks them a question. Some people might not actually have an opinion on some topic until the surveyor asks them about it. They then construct one. Sometimes people even report attitudes on fictional topics because they might feel foolish about saying they don't know about a topic. Another reason for making up an opinion is that respondents assume that the surveyor is asking a reasonable question, so they draw from their knowledge of apparently related topics and give an answer that would be consistent with their attitudes in general (Schwarz, 1999).

A seventh concern about obtaining high-quality data with attitudinal questions is that people may hold a positive or a negative attitude about some topic, but it is not always clear how deeply they hold that attitude. People may have their beliefs, but commitment to act on them is another matter. These seven concerns are summarized in Table 10.3.

TABLE 10.3 Seven Major Concerns About Surveys That Investigate Respondents' Attitudes

Concern	Reason for Concern
Wording of the question	Wording that predisposes a respondent to answer in a particular way (e.g., an item that is emotionally loaded) does not give valid information about an attitude because the person is responding on the basis of wording.
Order of the question	Early questions may prime a respondent to think about issues in a given way or may bring information into memory so that it affects responses to a later question.
Perceived purpose of the survey	Respondents may interpret the meaning of questions differently, depending on what they believe is the underlying purpose of the survey.
Sensitivity of the issue being investigated	People may alter their responses or simply lie when asked about issues that might be embarrassing or otherwise make the respondent uncomfortable. Respondents may also omit answers to such questions.
The nature of the surveyor	People may respond more frankly to a researcher who is similar to them, particularly when the survey involves sensitive issues.
Respondents may not have pre-existing attitudes about a topic	Sometimes people are not aware of the issues being surveyed, so they don't have attitudes about them. They may make up their attitudes on the spot, sometimes on the basis of previous questions and their responses to them.
Surveys may not reveal the intensity with which a respondent holds an attitude	We can identify the extent of agreement with an issue, but we don't know the depth of feeling or commitment associated with that issue.

RESPONSE BIAS

Sometimes respondents show certain patterns in their answers, regardless of the content of the question. One person may be likely to agree with questions most of the time; another person might be likely to disagree most of the time. When people engage in such patterns of behavior, they are showing **response bias.** Sometimes such answering is culturally based; sometimes it is related to evaluation apprehension; sometimes it involves individual differences.

> **Response Bias—A** tendency of a respondent to answer in predictable ways, independent of the question content, such as always agreeing with a statement or always providing high or low ratings on a Likert scale.

Researchers are now developing models that are helping us understand the nature of people's response tendencies. For example, Shulruf, Hattie, and Dixon (2008) created a five-stage model of how people comprehend and respond to survey questions. In this model, respondents are seen as progressing through the following steps: (a) understanding the question, (b) establishing the context, (c) retrieving available information about related behaviors, (d) integrating information and assessing impression management, and (e) evaluating all the information and aligning it with the available range of responses.

As you can see, the process of answering a question may take considerable mental processing. A person needs to understand the question itself, figure out how it relates to the current situation, and then decide what to reveal to the researcher. A respondent could provide data of low quality if there is a problem in any of the stages.

Shulruf et al. (2008) described the various stages of the process during which response biases may arise. You will read about these response biases shortly. They speculated that social desirability biases arise in stages 3 and 4 and that acquiescence appears in stage 5. The tendency to respond either with extreme or with neutral values on a scale also arises in stage 5. The decision to choose an easy answer (as opposed to one that requires some thought) might be associated with stage 1.

Studying Sensitive Issues

Sometimes the best way to get information from people is simply to ask them. Surprisingly, many people are willing to give researchers reports of intimate details of their lives. (In fact, some people are willing to do it on national television.) However, professional researchers are more interested in good data than in good television drama. One approach is simply to guarantee anonymity to respondents. In many cases, this promise will suffice; naturally, it relies on trust between the researcher and the respondent.

Researchers have documented the fact that, in some cases, it does not make much of a difference whether people complete questionnaires anonymously. Clients at a substance abuse clinic responded to questions about their satisfaction and their motivation related to the treatment program. The clients generated the same patterns of response across three administrations of the same questionnaire; one administration was anonymous, whereas for the other two, the clients gave the survey directly to a therapist (Leonhard et al., 1997).

Are Telephone Surveys Appropriate for Sensitive Issues?   Researchers are appropriately concerned that telephone interviews may not generate high-quality data. However, studies show that telephone surveys can be highly effective when done properly. Johnson and colleagues (2000) found that when respondents think that an interviewer is different from them, they are less forthcoming in reporting drug use in a telephone survey. A respondent talking to somebody of the same relative age, gender, race, and educational level may be more likely to report sensitive behaviors than when the interviewer is seen as different.

In a comparison of telephone and other survey techniques, McAuliffe et al. (1998) reported that researchers can get very high-quality data with telephone surveys, even when the topic involves an issue like substance abuse, and suggested that telephone surveys can be as useful as any other mode.

A more recent issue has focused on the quality of data collected via the Internet. Fortunately, researchers have found fairly regularly that computer-based data collection is as good as in-person data collection. For example, in research on sexual behavior and drug use, the results on in-person surveys were comparable to those on the Internet (McMorris, Petrie, Catalano, Fleming, Haggerty, & Abbott, 2009). In other research on such issues as birth control use, Internet surveys provided the same quality of data as traditional paper-and-pencil surveys (Uriell & Dudley, 2009).

Social Desirability

Social Desirability Bias—The tendency of respondents to answer questions in ways that generate a positive impression of themselves.

In an attempt to look good (or to avoid looking bad), people do not always tell the truth. Researchers have written extensively about this problem, referred to as **social desirability bias.** It can take two forms. One is **impression management,** which involves active deception by respondents to keep the researcher from forming a negative impression of them. A second component of social desirability bias is **self-deception positivity,** which occurs when people do not consciously give inappropriate responses but, rather, give a generally honest but overly positive self-report.

Impression Management—A form of social desirability bias in which respondents actively deceive a researcher in order to generate a positive impression of themselves in the researcher's eyes.

One domain that has received considerable attention regarding social desirability bias is self-concept and its relation to sex differences. The stereotypical belief is that women are more likely to excel in verbal and artistic areas, whereas men are more proficient in math and physical domains. In some research, female and male students report such differences in expertise on questionnaires even when performance is comparable across groups. The gender differences in beliefs seemed to occur because of impression management, the intentional form of social desirability bias, suggesting that differences in self-concept across sexes may occur because of a desire to report conformity to the stereotype (Vispoel & Forte Fast, 2000).

Self-Deception Positivity—A form of social desirability bias in which respondents provide generally honest, but overly optimistic, information about themselves that generates a positive impression of them.

Researchers have found socially desirable responses to be problematic in a number of different domains, including marketing (King & Bruner, 2000), self-concept (Vispoel & Forte Fast, 2000), sexual behavior (Meston, Heiman, Trapnell, & Paulhus, 1998), mathematics ability (Zettle & Houghton, 1998), attendance at religious services (Presser & Stinson, 1998), and personality reports (Francis & Jackson, 1998).

How can you deal with social desirability bias? Enlightening respondents about the existence of such response biases can help (Hong & Chiu, 1991). Another strategy is to create forced-choice questions so that

TABLE 10.4   **Representing Both Sides of an Issue in a Potential Survey Question and How to Reduce the Likelihood of Response Bias to It.**

Poor Item: **To what extent do you agree that the Statistics course should be eliminated as a required course for a Psychology major?**

_____ Strongly agree

_____ Somewhat agree

_____ Somewhat disagree

_____ Strongly disagree

Problem: Only one side of the issue (i.e., eliminating Statistics) is represented. A respondent might think that the interviewer is stating his or her own opinion and might consequently give an "agree" reply, acquiescing with the interviewer.

Better Item: **Do you think that the Statistics course should be eliminated as part of the Psychology major or do you think that the Statistics course should be kept as part of the Psychology major?**

_____ Eliminate the Statistics course

_____ Keep the Statistics course

_____ No opinion

Note: The "No opinion" option should be at the end rather than between the other two options so that the respondent does not confuse it with a neutral response.

respondents must select from among a number of equally attractive or unattractive choices (Ray, 1990). Another approach to reducing social desirability bias is to give both sides of an attitude in the question stem. Table 10.4 gives an example of how to present both sides of an issue in the question.

Finally, some researchers (e.g., Krosnick, 1999) believe that social desirability may not occur to the extent that other researchers claim. For instance, when people complete surveys on voting behavior, the percentage of respondents who report voting in the most recent election exceeds the proportion of the population that actually did. Researchers have interpreted this discrepancy to reflect social desirability bias by participants.

Newer research, however, suggests two alternate interpretations. First, people who vote are more likely to respond to surveys than those who don't vote. So the discrepancy in percentages who say they voted and who actually did may reflect a bias in the survey sample, not social desirability bias. A second interpretation is that people with a habit of voting and who did not vote in the most recent election may think (erroneously), "I always vote, so I must have voted in the most recent election." This type of response indicates a memory problem, not a social desirability bias.

Acquiescence

When somebody asks you, "How are you?" your tendency is probably to respond that you are fine. Usually, they are really only extending a greeting and don't expect (or even want) a litany of your woes.

Acquiescence—In survey research, the tendency to agree with the assertion of a question, regardless of its content.

A related dynamic can occur with surveys. Sometimes it is just easier to respond "yes" or to agree with a question. So that's what respondents may do, engaging in **acquiescence,** the tendency to agree with the assertion of a question, regardless of what it is. When the same question appears in two forms on a survey (e.g., "I enjoy socializing" and "I don't enjoy socializing"), respondents often agree with both, even though the people are directly contradicting themselves (Krosnick, 1999).

Krosnick (1999) described several explanations for people's tendency to acquiesce. One reason has to do with personality characteristics. Some people's personalities simply predispose them to want to agree with an assertion. Another explanation is that respondents often view surveyors as having higher status, so they feel compelled to agree with an assertion that the surveyor presents because we are "supposed to" agree with our superiors. As noted before, cultural factors can also play a role. Acquiescence can also be explained through the concept of satisficing, which we encounter below.

Satisficing versus Optimizing

Optimizing—The tendency of respondents to search for the best response to a question.

In survey research, participants often spend time deciding on responses to a question. When they try to generate the best answers, they are engaging in **optimizing.** With memory questions, an attempt to optimize can involve trying to balance two conflicting concepts. Respondents want to provide good information and they want to give the most precise answer they can. There is a trade-off here, however. Attempts at greater precision may actually be associated with less accuracy because people may start filling in details erroneously when trying to be too specific (Ackerman & Goldsmith, 2008). That is, people are working very hard and end up trying to provide details that are beyond what they can realistically give.

On the other hand, sometimes people are responding to a difficult question. They might spend a few moments trying to conjure up the answer and as soon as they identify a possibility, they go for that answer without considering other possibilities, a process called satisficing, which means that accepting the first answer acceptable to them, even if it wasn't the best answer.

Suppose you are taking a test and you encounter a difficult question. You might spend a few moments trying to conjure up the answer and as soon as you identify a possibility, you go for that answer without considering other possibilities. If you have ever done this, you have engaged in satisficing, which means that you adopted the first acceptable answer, even if it wasn't the best answer.

This tactic occurs regularly when people answer survey questions. Obviously, what works for the respondent can be a problem for the researcher.

According to Krosnick (1999), satisficing is likely to occur for any of three general reasons: (a) high task difficulty, (b) lower respondent ability, and (c) low respondent motivation. Optimizing is the complement to satisficing. When a respondent optimizes, the person works to generate the best possible answer.

Why would a survey question pose difficulties? Understanding a question and responding to it is actually a complex process. First, respondents must work to understand the point of the question.

Second, respondents have to search through memory to find relevant information. We know that the context in which a question is asked affects a person's response. Regarding surveys, it may be hard for somebody to remember events being probed in the context of the research setting because those events are neither chronically nor temporarily accessible.

A third task required of a respondent for generating good answers to survey questions is organizing everything that has been recalled.

Finally, in order to generate a high-quality response to a question, a person must choose from among the alternatives presented on a questionnaire. When people listen to an interviewer give a series of alternatives, there can be a tendency to select the later alternatives because they are easier to remember. When a questionnaire is on paper, there is a tendency for a respondent to pay more attention to the first alternatives (Krosnick, 1999).

If a person's cognitive processes fail at any step in this chain of events, a respondent will provide lower-quality information.

A related factor that leads to satisficing is the participant's level of ability. Researchers have discovered that respondents with lower ability levels tend to satisfice because they are unable to generate high-quality responses. Further, after the participant has answered a few questions, the motivation to respond may decrease. You may have participated in a psychology experiment as part of a course or for extra credit. Many students in such situations are in a hurry to complete this activity, so they are often less motivated to spend time on a response or to think deeply about a question. Many people have the same experience, engaging in satisficing as a result.

Minimizing the Occurrence of Satisficing

There will probably always be tension between the desires of the respondent and the needs of the researcher. If you conduct survey research, you will want to encourage people to optimize. How can you do this?

One way to minimize the possibility of satisficing is to create survey questions that are easily understood. In addition, when you ask people to remember events, it may help to ask several related questions so the information is more accessible. People may generate more accurate responses when the surveyor encourages them to remember events related to or close in time to the critical event, rendering obscure memories temporarily accessible.

Some researchers have suggested that you can reduce the probability of acquiescence and satisficing by not giving respondents a "No opinion" option (O'Muircheartaigh, Krosnick, & Helic, 2000). The logic is that if you want participants to think about their responses and give high-quality answers, you should not allow them to say "No opinion." Other investigators have suggested just the opposite, that allowing a "No opinion" option leads to more valid data (Krosnick et al., 2002).

As you can see, it isn't clear whether it is a good idea to give people a choice to say they have no opinion or are neutral about an issue. Sometimes people really are neutral, but sometimes they take the "No opinion" option as an opportunity not to think about an issue. The research against including the "No opinion" option indicates that people may use that option inappropriately when they are low in cognitive skills and motivation (Krosnick et al., 2002); that is, they may be satisficing.

■ ■ ■ ■ ■

CONTROVERSY:
Adolescent Smoking

The U.S. government regularly conducts surveys on health-related matters. The National Household Survey on Drug Abuse specifically investigates the use of various legal and illegal drugs. Based on the results of such surveys, various prominent people (e.g., then-President Bill Clinton) have publicly stated that 4 million adolescents (aged 12–17) smoke (Kovar, 2000).

This figure may be alarming and, if true, signals potentially serious health issues. In order to figure out what to do about such apparently prevalent smoking behavior, we need to understand what the data really signify. What constitutes an "adolescent"? What do we mean when we say that a person is a "smoker"?

An adolescent is somebody from age 12 to 17. A 12-year-old is very different from a 17-year-old on many dimensions. As it turns out, very few 12-year-olds smoke, so to believe that 12-year-olds are being lured into smoking is not accurate. Most of the smoking occurs toward the top of the age range.

When it came to defining a smoker in the survey, anybody who had had even one puff within the past 30 days was considered a smoker. One puff on one day is very different from a pack-a-day smoker.

About 25 percent of the adolescent smokers were heavy smokers. The survey defined "heavy" as indicating that the person smoked 10 cigarettes or more a day for over 20 days in the past month.

Of the middle group of smokers (41 percent of adolescents), most used 1–5 cigarettes on the days when they smoked, and they smoked relatively infrequently. The results also revealed that 31 percent of the "smokers" had less than one cigarette when they did smoke.

What do these data tell us? The sad news is that the heavy smokers are probably already addicted in adolescence; many report smoking more than they really want to. The better news is that about 2 in 5 of these teen smokers have had less than half a pack of cigarettes in their entire lifetime and are unlikely to become addicted.

Knowing the complete picture, which means understanding the definitions used in the survey, will allow us to generate public health policies that do what we want them to.

Question for Discussion: Why does knowing the details of this research lead to more useful information?

Finally, if you can keep your respondents motivated, such as by establishing a positive atmosphere and by making sure they know that their answers are important, you may be able to decrease satisficing.

Self-Selected Samples—In survey research, a nonrandom, biased sampling technique in which people choose to participate in the research rather than being selected by the investigator.

SAMPLING ISSUES

Most psychological research involves students, groups of people who are easily available, which is why this approach involves what is called a convenience sample, as you learned in Chapter 5.

However, there are also drawbacks with this approach. If you are interested in claiming that your research results are typical of people, you have to make sure that the people you study are typical of people in general.

Popular surveys rely on **self-selected samples.** These are groups of people who volunteer to participate without having been contacted by the researchers. They may see a notice on the Internet, for example, and decide it would be interesting to participate. Or they may be willing to call a 900-number, which costs them money, in order to express their opinion. Or they may respond to a talk show host. The types of people who engage in this responding are different from the population as a whole. In fact, professional researchers regard such polls as entirely nonscientific and therefore useless in telling us what the population thinks about a topic. Some investigators refer to such polls by the derogatory acronym SLOP (i.e., Self-Selected Opinion Poll; Horvitz et al., 1995).

Finding Hidden Populations

In survey research, some groups of people are difficult to study because they don't want to be found. Such groups are referred to as **hidden populations.** Two characteristics typify hidden populations: First, it is impossible to establish who constitutes the population and, second, there are strong privacy issues associated with the groups (Heckathorn, 1997).

If we want to find out about such groups, we can't use probability samples because probability samples require that we be able to identify the entire pool of possible respondents. So researchers have to make compromises in collecting data. Researchers studying hidden populations have turned to a class of techniques called **chain-referral methods.**

One chain-referral method for contacting respondents involves **snowball sampling,** which relies on the fact that an individual from a hidden population is likely to know others from that group. The volunteer identifies a certain number of people that the researcher will contact; the researcher will then ask each of these second-stage individuals to provide the names of yet others. The process continues through as many stages as the researchers determine desirable. Kaplan, Korf, and Sterk (1987) studied heroin use among addicts in the Netherlands. They identified a single user and asked for names of others who fit their target categories, either prostitutes or foreigners. These referrals then identified others, and so on.

Snowball samples often contain quite cooperative volunteers who have a large social network. They are a variation on convenience samples, so it is not always clear to whom the researchers can generalize their findings.

A second approach to contacting respondents from hidden populations is to use **key informant sampling.** This technique relies on information from knowledgeable individuals rather than from members of the target population itself.

For example, a researcher might contact social workers to get information about patterns of sexual behavior in the population the social workers serves. Key informant sampling may reduce the respondent's reluctance to report unusual behaviors, but it may introduce the biases of that individual and is based on the limited number of people the social worker sees.

Hidden Population— Population of interest that are hard to study because the people in those groups are engaged in activities that may be embarrassing or illegal (e.g., drug users), so they do not want to be recognized as members of that population.

Chain-Referral Methods— A set of sampling techniques that relies on people who know about a population or are members of that population to gain access to information about the group.

Snowball Sampling— A chain-referral sampling technique in which one person from a population of interest identifies another person from that population to a researcher who contacts that second person, then that new individual refers yet another person, for as many stages as desired by the researcher.

Key Informant Sampling— A sampling technique that relies on getting information from people who know about a population of interest rather than from members of that population themselves.

Targeted Sampling— A sampling technique that relies on finding locations that attract members of the population of interest and getting information from these people at such locations.

Respondent-Driven Sampling—A sampling technique in which a researcher uses a member of the population of interest to actively recruit others, often with some incentive like money for engaging in this recruiting.

A third approach is **targeted sampling.** With this technique, researchers work in advance to identify their population as well as possible, then to find out the different places that attract the widest range of people from that population. The results will only be as good as the researcher's knowledge of where to find members of the target population.

Heckathorn (1997) has developed a new approach called **respondent-driven sampling.** In this approach, researchers use two types of incentives to attract participants. Primary incentives are offered to individuals; one such incentive may be money. The difference between this technique and other chain-referral methods involves the presence of secondary reward for getting others to join. When a participant identifies a potential candidate for the research, that participant uses peer pressure and social approval to induce a new person to join the project. That is, the researcher doesn't actively recruit the next person; that task is performed by the first participant.

Your choice of which chain-referral methods to use depends on the practical issues involved in your particular study. If the population is very closed, you may need to use respondent-driven samples, as Heckathorn did with the heroin users he studied. On the other hand, if the population is only somewhat hidden, snowball sampling might be adequate. For example, Frank and Snijders (1994) were able to use snowball sampling in their study of heroin use in the Netherlands because heroin use is more open there.

SUMMARY

Professional surveyors and pollsters have developed techniques that allow researchers to use small samples to make accurate predictions and descriptions of a larger population. As a result, the more economic practice of sampling typically means that researchers don't need a census.

The most common technique in scientific survey research is the telephone survey. For most questions, people who are available over phone adequately represent the entire population. Researchers who use probability sampling can generate a good picture of the population with a relatively small set of responses.

Researchers also have to painstakingly create survey questions that lead to valid responses. This is often the most difficult part of conducting good survey research. Whether you are asking for attitudes or for people to remember past behaviors, subtle differences in the way questions are worded and presented can make a notable difference in the responses that a person makes.

Sometimes different respondents interpret the same question in different ways. They may also show response biases that will either make them look better or make it easier for them to complete a questionnaire without really thinking about the issues at hand. Researchers must work hard to overcome these tendencies on the part of respondents.

Finally, some populations don't want to be found, like those involved in criminal activity or other undesirable or embarrassing behaviors. Investigators have developed techniques designed to make contact with these hidden populations. The samples may not be probability samples, but they often provide useful information.

REVIEW QUESTIONS

Multiple Choice Questions

1. Psychologists typically do not use a census in their research because
   a. a census often leads to telescoping of responses.
   b. census responses often result in nondifferentiation.
   c. respondent-driven sampling leads to better generalization.
   d. a census is generally too costly.

2. Researchers have greatest confidence in being able to generalize the results of research based on
   a. sampling frames.
   b. surveys.
   c. probability samples.
   d. randomly selected questions.

3. On the U.S. census that everybody has to complete, people identify their racial/ethnic status by selecting from among options provided on the form. This type of a question is
   a. a closed-ended question.
   b. almost always responded to accurately.
   c. part of the sampling frame.
   d. used because respondents are from a self-selected sample.

4. Researchers may avoid open-ended items on questionnaires because such items
   a. are not very scientific.
   b. permit too limited a range of responses.
   c. can result in responses that are difficult to code and categorize.
   d. generally provide details about behaviors but not the context in which they occur.

5. One of the difficulties surveying people about rare events is that
   a. those events are likely to involve sensitive issues that people are reluctant to discuss.
   b. a small increase in the rate of false positives leads to a very large, inaccurate estimate when generalized to the population.
   c. people have very different attitudes about rare events, so accurate responses are difficult to get.
   d. people are likely to show high levels of acquiescence about such items.

6. By the time a person is near the end of a questionnaire, the responses
   a. have probably shifted from optimizing to acquiescence.
   b. will no longer show telescoping.
   c. will be affected by how the respondent answered earlier questions.
   d. will show high levels of self-deception positivity.

7. When people are able to retrieve information from memory only after being primed by an earlier question on the topic, we say that the memory is
   a. targeted.
   b. nondifferentiated.
   c. temporarily accessible.
   d. respondent-driven.

8. When respondents make up an attitude on the spot while answering a question,
   a. the researcher can find out by asking the respondent to answer the question again.
   b. the respondents answer more slowly than when they have a pre-existing attitude.
   c. they usually claim to hold that attitude firmly and deeply.
   d. they may engage in impression management tactics.

9. Sometimes, respondents engage in active deception to keep the researcher from forming a negative image of the respondent. This behavior is called
   a. self-deception positivity.
   b. impression management.
   c. acquiescence.
   d. satisficing.
10. Research has revealed that we can reduce social desirability bias by
    a. telling respondents that we will be able to detect false responses on their part.
    b. avoiding forced choice responses and creating open-ended questions instead.
    c. educating respondents about this type of bias.
    d. presenting only one side of an issue in a given question so respondents cannot focus on only the positive response.
11. When a person responds the same way to just about every item on a rating scale, this respondent is engaging in
    a. nondifferentiation.
    b. telescoping.
    c. acquiescence.
    d. satisficing.
12. It could be useful to know about undocumented workers and how they live, but such people are reluctant to participate in anything they think might be associated with the government. These immigrants constitute a
    a. sampling frame.
    b. chronically inaccessible, self-selected sample.
    c. hidden population.
    d. nondifferentiated sample.
13. Researchers sometimes use a member of a hidden population to provide names of other members of that population to recruit participants in research. The resulting sample would involve
    a. chain-referral method.
    b. sampling frame.
    c. probability sample.
    d. self-selected sampling.
14. When researchers try to contact members of hidden populations by finding out where such people congregate, the sampling technique they are using is
    a. key informant sampling.
    b. snowball sampling.
    c. targeted sampling.
    d. probability sampling.

Essay Questions

15. Why do open-ended questions provide more information to survey researchers than closed-ended questions? What drawbacks are associated with open-ended questions?
16. Identify the seven major problems associated with survey questions about attitudes.
17. Why does the research on how many adolescents smoke reflect the difficulty in creating good survey research?
18. What two characteristics typify hidden populations?

ANSWERS TO REVIEW QUESTIONS

Answers to Multiple Choice Questions

1. d	6. c	11. a
2. c	7. c	12. c
3. a	8. b	13. a
4. c	9. b	14. c
5. b	10. c	

Answers to Essay Questions

15. Why do open-ended questions provide more information to survey researchers than closed-ended questions? What drawbacks are associated with open-ended questions?

    Suggested points:

    Open-ended questions allow a respondent to provide the best answer to a question, whereas closed-ended questions force the respondent to choose from a selected set. The open-ended questions may lead to answers that the researcher doesn't anticipate, which could be positive, leading to more valid answers; such answers could be problematic, though, because they are hard to code and summarize when respondents take very different paths to their answers.

16. Identify the seven major problems associated with survey questions about attitudes.
    a. The wording of a question can lead a respondent in a particular direction, especially with emotionally sensitive topics.
    b. Previous questions have an effect on what kind of information people have in mind when they respond to a later item.
    c. The respondents' beliefs about what the interview is supposed to be about will lead them to tailor their responses so as to be more helpful to the surveyor.
    d. The sensitivity of an issue is critical to whether and how people respond.
    e. The characteristics of the person doing the interview can be important; respondents are more forthcoming with people who are similar to them.
    f. It is hard to distinguish between responses based on an existing attitude and attitudes that the respondent has just made up.
    g. It is hard to differentiate between attitudes that are deeply and shallowly held.

17. Why does the research on how many adolescents smoke reflect the difficulty in creating good survey research?

    The research on adolescent smoking is difficult because adolescence spans the ages of 12–17 years. The younger adolescents are different in physical, psychological, and others ways from the older ones. The younger adolescents were quite unlikely to smoke anything at all. So categorizing all adolescents together may distort the results.

    In addition, defining what it means to smoke is hard. If an adolescent had had even a puff of a cigarette, it was considered smoking and would be categorized (for some data analysis) the same way as a pack-a-day smoker. Most of the infrequent smokers had less than one cigarette a day when they smoked.

    Depending on how you define adolescents and how you categorize them and depending on how you define smoking can lead to different pictures of who smokes and how much.

18. What two characteristics typify hidden populations?
    a. It is impossible to establish exactly who constitutes the population.
    b. There are privacy issues associated with the population.

CHAPTER ELEVEN

CORRELATIONAL RESEARCH

CHAPTER OVERVIEW

LEARNING OBJECTIVES ■ KEY TERMS ■ CHAPTER PREVIEW

LEARNING OBJECTIVES

After going through this chapter, you will be able to:

- Differentiate between relationship studies and prediction studies
- Explain the difference between correlational design and correlational analysis
- Describe the concept of positive correlation and negative correlation
- Identify the factors that can affect the size of a correlation coefficient
- Identify the traditional correlational tests
- Explain how researchers use regression analysis in research

KEY TERMS

CHAPTER PREVIEW

Psychologists use correlational studies to investigate the relationships among variables when there is a lot of complexity in the behavior and when experimental approaches are not feasible. Correlational studies permit us to find relationships and to make accurate predictions about behavior.

There are different correlational approaches. The simplest involves bivariate relationships between two variables. Researchers typically employ the standard, well-known Pearson product–moment correlation in such circumstances, although we also use several other correlational tests associated with it.

When we want to see how variables interconnect, we rely on more complex approaches. Multivariate tests, which involve at least three variables, allow us to see a more complex picture of behavior. Some of the newer multivariate correlational approaches actually move us in the direction of making tentative statements about causation.

These varied approaches are useful, but we must use them appropriately for arriving at helpful descriptions of behavior. Many of the multivariate models of behavior are quite complex, so it is important to know how to use them and to be able to identify their limitations.

In this chapter, you will encounter the critical aspects of different correlational approaches so you can understand how we employ them in research.

CORRELATIONAL STUDIES

Psychologists, like most scientists, search for causes. We want to know why people act as they do, although this can be an elusive goal. In some cases, we are not able to identify what variables affect behavior directly, but we can find patterns and relationships that make behavior predictable. **Correlational studies** tell us which variables and behaviors are related. In a correlational study, we take what nature gives us and see how things interconnect.

Correlational Study—
An approach to research that involves measuring different variables to see whether there is a predictable relationship among the variables.

Finding Relationships

During college years, students often form relationships that last a lifetime. Researchers have assessed the degree to which long-term couples show similar personality traits; they have found that couples share personality characteristics degree of like openness and agreeableness. Such studies are correlational in approach. The investigators do not manipulate any variables and don't try to assess any causal relations. Rather, they are interested simply in finding stable patterns in the data.

The data suggest that comparability of personalities is due to assortative mating, that is, due to choices of partners on the basis of personality characteristics; similarities among spouses exist from the start and are not a function of growing similarity over time (Caspi, Herbener, & Ozer, 1992; Mascie-Taylor, 1989). In fact, Caspi et al. (1992) compared correlations when the couples became engaged to be married and 20 years later. The correlations were remarkably consistent over that time, as you can see in Table 11.1.

McCrae et al. (2008) further studied the relations between personalities in married couples in greater depth, focusing on the elements of the Big Five personality theory. They correlated self-ratings of husbands and wives in four cultures (American, Dutch, Czech, and Russian) and ratings of husbands and wives of their spouses.

The correlations of personality traits of McCrae et al. (2008) were generally not as large as the attitudinal correlations of Caspi et al. (1992), but many were significant. As other investigators have found, the personality traits showing the greatest correlations were openness to experience and agreeableness. When McCrae et al. separated the correlations into younger and older Dutch couples, they found similar correlations, suggesting that similarity among spouses does not develop over time; it is there from the start.

TABLE 11.1 **Couple Correlations for Values and Attitudes at the Time of Engagement (Time 1) and 20 Years Later (Time 2)**

Measure	Time 1 (Engagement)	Time 2 (20 years later)
Study of values[a]		
Theoretical	.27***	.27***
Economic	.27***	.36***
Aesthetic	.38***	.36***
Political	.34***	.38***
Religious	.52***	.58***
Attitude toward marriage[b]		
Daily activities	.22**	.25***
Companionship	.16*	.23**
Premarital sex	.24**	.25***
Fidelity	.21**	.22**

[a] $n = 165$ couples. [b] $n = 161$ couples.

*$p < .05$, **$p < .01$, ***$p < .001$

Source: Caspi, A., Herbener, E. S., & Ozer, D. J. (1992). Shared experiences and the similarity of personalities: A longitudinal study of married couples. *Journal of Personality and Social Psychology, 62*, 281–291. doi:10.1037/0022-3514.62.2.281. Copyright American Psychological Association. Reprinted with permission.

Naturally, these couples were successful in that their marriages had lasted a long time. It is not clear that divorced or separated couples would show similar personality patterns, but that is an interesting research question in itself.

Some research does not have such far-reaching implications. For instance, it is no secret that many students don't like to take classes that meet early in the morning. And many professors only like to meet early in the morning. This unfortunate mix of preferences suggests that either students or professors will not be working at their best times. Investigators have used a correlational approach to see if grades are correlated with the construct of *morningness* (Guthrie, Ash, & Bendapudi, 1995). It appears that the more oriented toward morning a student is, the higher his or her overall GPA tends to be. This is an example of a correlational study designed to find out if there is a relation between variables. The correlation is not great, but it is reliable.

Let's briefly go over the concept of correlations. We can make predictions about students' grades based on multiple variables: the amount of time they study, the percentage of time they go to class, the amount of time required for family activities, how many hours a week they work, how much partying they do, and on and on indefinitely. These variables might be associated with better or worse grades. Hypothetically, if we knew about all possible sources associated with grades, we could identify the relation each one had with grades. Each variable would provide some amount of information. Ultimately, we could predict grades perfectly, accounting for 100 percent of the difference among students.

How did Guthrie et al. discover this relationship? They conducted a relationship study in which they looked at the associations among variables like GPA, when students tended to study, and other factors. They assessed morningness by means of a simple 13-item scale devised by Smith, Reilly, and Midkiff (1989). Then they computed the correlation coefficients among variables.

With respect to the study of married couples, the correlations between wife and husband personality traits were reliable, but not large. This result means that you can count on similarity of personalities, but such similarities predict only a small amount of the personality patterns. There are many other factors that undoubtedly relate to similarities in personality among married couples.

This kind of relationship study is useful for preliminary investigations in which a researcher does not yet know if variables are related to one another. There are two important points to remember when considering relationship studies. The first is that your variables have to have construct validity. That is, they have to relate meaningfully to what you are measuring. In the case of the morningness study, you would need to have a good measure of morningness. Guthrie et al. used a scale validated by other researchers.

The second thing to remember is that if you compute correlation coefficients on a lot of different variables, you will get some significant relationships that are meaningless. Five percent of the time, variables with no actual underlying relationship will appear significant. So if you are going to compute multiple correlations, you should remember that some of them will be significant when they don't mean anything.

In general, it is not a wise idea to compute correlations just to compute them; you should look for associations between variables when you expect there to be a relation, not just throw variables together and see what happens.

Making Predictions

When you find relationships between variables, sometimes you can go a step further and make predictions regarding the variables and behaviors of interest to you. Colleges and universities do this each year when they decide which students to accept. A project designed to predict some outcome variable in correlational research is called a **prediction study**.

> **Prediction Study**—A correlational study in which the goal is to predict the value of one variable given the level of another variable, with the predictor variable often occurring before the criterion variable rather than simultaneously.

Many variables may help predict student success in college, including SAT scores and high school grades. In prediction studies, the outcome that interests us is the **criterion variable**, which we want to predict. The variable that we use to make the prediction is called the **predictor variable**. As such, SAT scores are one of the predictor variables that colleges use, while first-year GPA is the criterion variable. SAT scores are moderately correlated to first-year GPA. About 25 percent of the difference from one person to the next is predictable on the basis of GPA. This is not too bad when you consider all the factors related to student achievement in college.

> **Criterion Variable**—In a prediction study, the variable that an investigator is trying to predict.

The remaining 75 percent of the difference across students might be predictable based on as-yet unknown factors. Thus, when applicants complain that others with lower SAT scores have been admitted to a college and that they haven't, it is appropriate to keep in perspective that variables other than SAT scores predict more of the variability among students than the standardized test does.

> **Predictor Variable**—In a prediction study, the variable that an investigator is using to predict another variable.

If making such predictions were easy, admissions officers would have little difficulty deciding which students to admit. And the outcome would be that each student who enrolled would succeed, whereas each student who did not gain admission would not have succeeded. This is far from the truth. SAT scores may be one predictor of future performance, but an imperfect and incomplete predictor.

CONTROVERSY:
The Media and Violence

A persistent societal question is the effect of media violence on behavior. Do people who see violence enacted on television, in the movies, or in video games become violent and aggressive in their own lives?

Researchers in this area have concluded that there is a causal link: Exposure to violence leads to violent behavior (Carnagey, Anderson, & Bartholow, 2007). Over the past decades, investigators have accumulated evidence addressing this question. For instance, the introduction of television, with its violence, was associated with an increase in burglaries in the 1950s in a large number of cities in the United States (Hennigan et al., 1982). Exposure to realistic crime programs among adolescents in the United States can be associated with risk taking, including vandalism and trespassing (Kremar & Greene, 2000). In India, attitudes toward violence changed after exposure to violent television programs (Varma, 2000).

The problem with many such studies is that they don't really inform us about the causes of violent behavior. The research is usually correlational. With respect to specific types of violence (i.e., homicides), other variables like divorce rates and other social factors (Jensen, 2001) may be better predictors than media violence.

This question of causation is fundamental to psychologists who study complex behavior. How do we handle the dilemma of relying on correlational data when we want to determine causation?

Researchers use different types of studies to paint a complete picture of the situation. Substantial correlational research has revealed a clear link between media violence and actual violence. In addition, experiments have consistently demonstrated a causal link between exposure to violence and self-reports of aggression and hostility (e.g., Scharrer, 2001), even though this research doesn't deal with actual violence. And the evidence keeps increasing. For example, Anderson, Gentile, and Buckley (2007) showed that exposure to a violent video game increased the level of aggressive behavior among children and college students. Future directions in this experimental research could include an examination of physiological effects of exposure to violence in the growing area of social neuroscience (Carnagey, Anderson, & Bartholow, 2007).

The picture is not perfect, but we can draw conclusions based on the best evidence available. The overall analysis of correlational and experimental research affirms that the causal link between media violence and aggressiveness is nearly as strong as the link between smoking and cancer, and stronger than the connection between condom use (or non-use) and AIDS transmission, exposure to lead and lower IQ scores, and homework and academic achievement. The connection is apparent both in correlational and in experimental research (Anderson & Bushman, 2001; Bushman & Anderson, 2001).

Interestingly, over the last quarter century, as the science has become clearer, the news media have ignored the research. News outlets are less likely to report the strength of the connection between media violence and actual violence than before (Bushman & Anderson, 2001).

Question for Discussion: How can correlational and experimental approaches each help overcome the limitations of the other approach?

USING THE CORRELATIONAL APPROACH

> **Correlational Analysis**—A statistical approach used in research that uses any of a variety of correlational tests, regardless of whether the research is a correlational study or not.

It is important to distinguish between correlational studies and correlational analyses. A correlational study relies on making measurements without controlling or trying to manipulate variables. The purpose is to identify connections among variables. On the other hand, **correlational analysis** involves your statistical approach and says nothing about your methodology.

Correlational Studies

> **Third Variable Problem**—In correlational studies, the problem in assessing cause and effect due to the fact that when two variables are correlated, an outside (or third) variable is responsible for any causation.

When you perform a correlational study, you can logically conclude that variables are associated, but not that one causes another. Keep in mind that there may really be a causal connection; the problem is that correlational studies don't give you enough information to let you know. There may be a third factor that is really the cause; psychologists refer to this as the **third variable problem**.

Another problem with assessing causation with correlational data is that you don't know which way the causation proceeds. This problem is one

Directionality Problem—In correlational studies, the problem in assessing cause and effect when two variables are correlated when a researcher does not know which of two variables has a causal effect on the other.

of **directionality**. Logically, in a correlational analysis A could cause B or B could cause A. Consider the morningness scale (Guthrie et al., 1995). It could be that students do well in early classes because they are morning people, as indicated on their responses to the scale. On the other hand, they might conclude that they are morning people because they do well in early classes.

It is important not to fall for an apparent cause–effect relationship that is not valid. One area of research that has been prone to criticism that causal relationships are not real is whether watching violence on television leads to violent behavior. Seeing violence could lead to violence. However, you could argue that people prone to violence like to watch violence on television. There is a real possibility of a problem with directionality.

In the Controversy box on the media and violence, you have seen the current scientific status of the argument. A great many media researchers have concluded that there is a causal relationship here: Media violence leads to violent behavior.

Correlational Analysis

Correlational analyses are not the same as correlational studies. A correlational analysis uses correlations as a statistical approach, but if the research design is experimental, we can still draw causal conclusions. This is easy to grasp by considering a hypothetical two-group study. If we create two groups, randomly assign participants to them to generate equivalent groups, and apply a treatment to only one of the two groups, we have a basic experiment. If the two groups differ at the end, we assume the treatment made the difference.

Positive (Direct) Correlation—A relation between two variables such that when the value of one variable increases, so does the value of the second variable, and when the value of one variable decreases, so does the value of the second.

The normal approach to data analysis with such a design is to compute a t-test, which lets us know if two groups differ reliably. However, we could legitimately compute a correlation coefficient. It would tell us exactly what the t-test does. If you look at Table 11.2, you can see how comparable the two tests are.

It is important to remember that the research design, not the statistical test, determines the type of conclusion you can draw. If you employ a correlational study, no matter what statistical test you compute, it does not allow you to assess causation; similarly, if you use an experimental approach, doing a correlational analysis does not keep you from drawing causal conclusions.

Negative (Indirect) Correlation—A relation between variables such that when the value of one variable increases, the value of the second variable decreases.

Positive and Negative Correlations

Correlations can be either **positive** (direct), **negative** (indirect), or nonexistent. Perfect positive correlations have a value of $+1.00$; perfect negative correlations, -1.00. Sometimes correlations are so close to zero that we conclude that two variables have no bearing on one another. For instance, Lang and Heckhausen (2001) discovered that life satisfaction and age are not

TABLE 11.2   Illustration of How Correlational and Experimental Analyses Lead to the Same Conclusions

Suppose you have two groups with 10 participants in each. Let's label them simply Group 1 and Group 2. If you compute a t-test for independent groups, you get: $t(18) = -3.55$, $p = .002$

Group 1	6	8	7	5	6	9	7	4	8	9
Group 2	5	6	3	7	2	3	1	5	4	5

You can rearrange the data, as follows, showing each score next to its appropriate group:

6	8	7	5	6	9	7	4	8	9	5	6	3	7	2	3	1	5	4	5
1	1	1	1	1	1	1	1	1	1	2	2	2	2	2	2	2	2	2	2

Now we can compute the familiar Pearson product–moment correlation coefficient on the two variables, Group and Score. (When one variable is ordinal, interval, or ratio, and the second variable is dichotomous [i.e., it can take one of two values], the Pearson r is called a point-biserial correlation.) When we do this, we get: $r(18) = -.642$, $p = .002$. The next step in a correlational analysis is to see if the correlation is significant, for which we use a t-test with the following formula:

$$t = \frac{r\sqrt{N - 2}}{\sqrt{1 - r^2}}$$

$$t - \frac{(-.642)(4.243)}{.767} = -3.55$$

If you notice, the value of t here is the same as when you completed your t-test. The analyses from the correlational and experimental approaches provide the same information.

---

correlated. The value of their correlation coefficient was .05. This value is so close to zero that, among their participants who ranged in age from 20 to around 70, knowing their age doesn't help you predict how satisfied they are with their lives. (This may surprise students who are 20, but it won't surprise students who are 40 or older.)

A positive or direct correlation implies that when the value of one of the two variables being correlated gets larger, so does the other. According to another analysis by Lang and Heckhausen (2001), perceived control over life is positively correlated with life satisfaction. This means that, in general, the more control people felt in their lives, the more satisfied they were. You can't conclude here that perceived control leads to greater satisfaction, though, because satisfaction in life may lead to a feeling of control. You don't know the direction of causation.

A negative or indirect correlation arises when the value of one of the two variables being correlated gets larger, the value of the other variable gets smaller. Lang and Heckhausen observed a negative correlation between the number of negative events in people's lives (like losing something or having a small accident) and their perception of control. When people experience many negative events, they are likely to feel lower levels of control.

Strength of Association

The strength of the association between variables is reflected in the absolute value of the correlation coefficient. Consequently, coefficients of –.50 and +.50 reflect equally strong correlations. Further, a correlation of –.80 reveals a stronger association than does a correlation of +.50 because the absolute value of this negative correlation is .80, which is larger than .50.

Scatter Diagram—A graphical representation showing the relationship between two quantitative variables, with one variable represented on the horizontal (X) axis and the other on the vertical (Y) axis.

You can change a negative correlation into a positive correlation simply by changing the scale on which you measure one of the variables. Considering the relation between the amount of time you spend studying for a test and your score on the test, we would expect a positive correlation. You could create a negative correlation by changing one variable to the number wrong on the test instead of the number right. The absolute value of the correlation coefficients would be the same, but the sign would change. You would have the same predictability associated with each one. In Figure 11.1, you can see graphically what happens.

If you create a **scatter diagram** to represent the relation between two variables, as the correlation coefficient approaches 1.0 or to –1.0, the points in the graph appear to form a straight line. As the correlation heads toward zero, the pattern becomes rounder until, when $r = 0$, the display of data points is nearly circular. These relationships are demonstrated in Figure 11.2. When r is close to 1.0 or –1.0, the value of Y is clearly predictable from the value of X.

Linear Relationship—A relationship between two variables that can be represented graphically as a straight line, with the increase in value of one unit on the first variable being systematically associated with a constant increase or decrease on the second variable.

Factors Affecting the Size of a Correlation Coefficient

We use correlation coefficients to see if two variables are associated. Sometimes the correlational tests we typically use can lead us to believe that variables are unrelated. However, there can be cases in which two variables are correlated in reality, but a statistical analysis doesn't reveal it.

Nonlinear Relationship—A relationship between two variables that can be represented graphically as a curved line, reflecting the fact that a change in value of one unit on the first variable is associated with different amounts of change on the second variable, depending on the value of the first.

Nonlinearity.   The typical correlations we use work best when the data show a **linear relationship**, that is, when a particular amount of change in the value of X is associated with a stable amount of change in the value of Y, no matter where on the X-axis the change occurs. Figure 11.3a shows a simple example of how the same change in X is associated with a different amount of change in Y, depending on the values of X. In Figure 11.3a, for lower values of X, a change of one unit on X is related to a small change in Y; for higher values of X, the same change is associated with large changes in Y. This pattern of change reflects a **nonlinear relationship**.

(a) $r = .58$

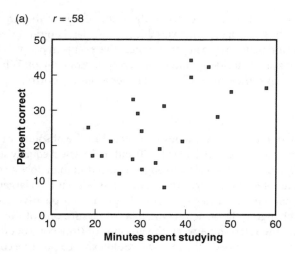

(b) $r = -.58$

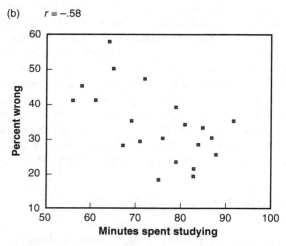

FIGURE 11.1   Hypothetical example illustrating how a single data set can lead to a negative or to a positive correlation, depending on how the variable is defined: (a) shows that more studying is associated with a higher number correct, (b) shows that more studying is associated with fewer errors. Both correlations are legitimate and provide the same information. The only change is in the way information is labeled on the Y-axis. In both cases, the strength of the correlation is the same.

For example, LaHuis, Nicholas, and Avis (2005) measured speed and accuracy of job-related tasks of clerical workers along with their conscientiousness as measured on a 17-item inventory. The results indicated a nonlinear relation between job performance and conscientiousness. At low levels of conscientiousness, workers showed relatively poor performance; as conscientiousness increased, so did performance. But after a point, performance stopped increasing even when conscientiousness rose. The performance measures just leveled off.

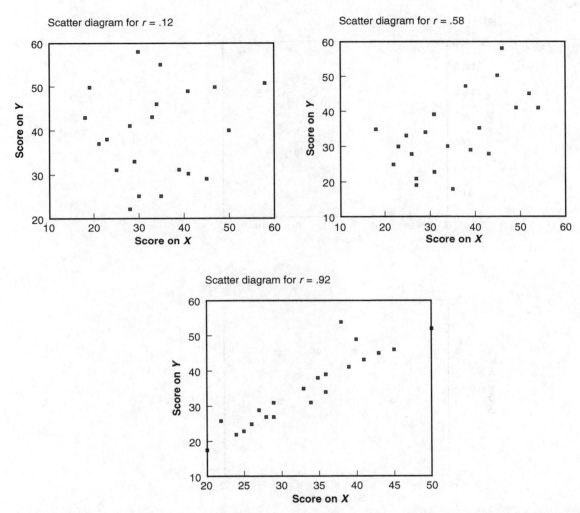

FIGURE 11.2 Scatter diagrams for different values of the Pearson product–moment correlation coefficient. Notice that with higher correlations, the scores tend to resemble a straight line where Y values rise predictably with X values. When the correlation decreases, the scores tend to become more scattershot and Y scores no longer change as predictably with X values. As the correlation coefficient approaches zero, meaningful predictability vanishes.

Pearson Product–Moment Correlation—A bivariate, correlational measure that indicates the degree to which two quantitative variables are related.

This nonlinear relation provides a good example of how a nonlinear pattern can obscure a real relation between variables. LaHuis et al. (2005) reported that the linear relation was nonsignificant. If they had computed only a **Pearson product–moment correlation**, which is only useful with linear relations, they would have concluded that conscientiousness was not related to job performance when, in fact, there is a predictable and reliable association between the two variables, as shown in Figure 11.3b.

(a)

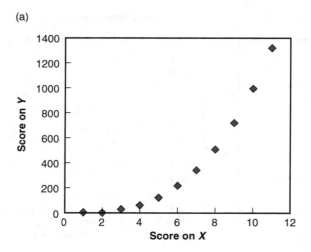

(b)

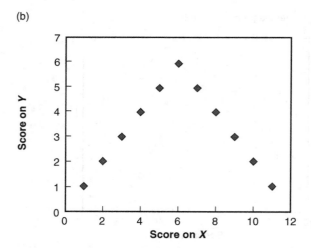

FIGURE 11.3   Examples of nonlinear relationships that obscure the strength of the association between two variables. In (a) we have a perfect nonlinear relationship, but the Pearson correlation coefficient is less than 1.0 ($r = .92$). A change in X from 1 to 4 is associated with a change in Y of 63, whereas the same size change on X from 8 to 11 is associated with a change of 819. This reflects one of many types of nonlinear relationships; you can see how the line curves. In (b) the relationship is again perfectly predictable, but the Pearson r is 0 because the it is maximally useful for linear relationships.

If you collect data that are nonlinear, the frequently used Pearson r may still result in a significant correlation, but it will suggest a less predictable relationship than actually exists.

Restrictions in Range.   Sometimes there may be a legitimate relationship between two variables, but you may compute a lower correlation coefficient in your sample than you

Restricted Range Problem—In a correlational analysis, the failure to spot a real relationship between variables because the range of cores on at least one of the variables obscures that relationship.

would have if you had access to the entire population. The problem may be with a **restricted range**.

Take a look at Figure 11.4, which represents a hypothetical population. You can see a clear, but imperfect, relation between X and Y. A problem can arise if you sample from the middle range of scores and neglect extreme scores. For instance, if you plotted the association between SAT scores and school grades for the entire population, you would see a clear pattern.

(a)

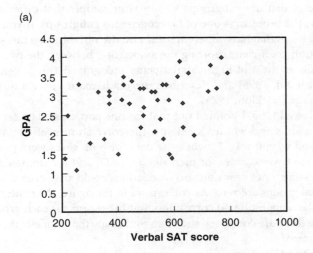

(b)

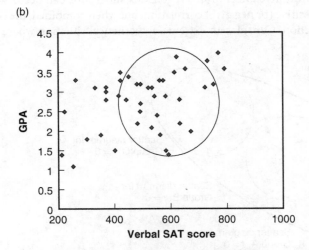

FIGURE 11.4 Fictitious example of the relation between SAT scores and GPA and how the correlation coefficient is affected by a restricted range. This scatter diagram in (a) depicts a correlation with $r = .45$ for this population. If there is a restricted range of SAT scores, which would not be uncommon at many schools, the trend toward higher GPAs as SAT scores are larger tends to disappear. The correlation coefficient for (b) is .29, which would not be significant in this example.

If you sampled from a group of typical students, though, you would probably not find many with extremely low SAT scores or with extremely high SAT scores. So you are stuck with the middle group of people, which is most of us.

The population pattern shows a trend, but the sample inside the circle shows what would happen with a restricted range of SAT scores. One of the problems is that if you wind up with a small correlation coefficient, you can't tell whether there is no relation between variables or whether you have a restricted range problem.

Heterogeneous Subgroups.   A third problem that affects the size of the correlation coefficient is the presence of distinct subgroups within your sample that differ from one

> **Heterogeneous Subgroup Problem**—In a correlational analysis, the appearance of a positive correlation in an overall data set and a negative correlation in subgroups or vice versa.

another; the problem is one of **heterogeneous subgroups**. If you are measuring groups that have different means on the variables you measure, your correlation coefficient showing the association between the two variables could be artificially high. Statisticians recognized this a century ago (e.g., Pearson, 1896) and described the mathematics over a quarter of a century ago (Sockloff, 1975).

Howell (2007) pointed out that for one particular data set that correlated men's and women's heights, the correlation coefficient between height and weight was .78 when the data for both sexes were pooled. The correlation between these two variables for men alone was .60 and for women alone was .39 (p. 265). Figure 11.5 illustrates how nonzero correlations could arise even when correlations within individual groups are zero. As you can see in the figure, the scatter diagram for each group is circular, suggesting no correlation. But the means for each group differ, so the pattern when the three are combined shows an oval shape that suggests that the correlation is greater than zero.

Another counterintuitive effect of heterogeneous subgroups can occur when individual groups have a positive (or negative) correlation, but when combined, the correlation is in the opposite direction. Consider an extreme, hypothetical situation where you want

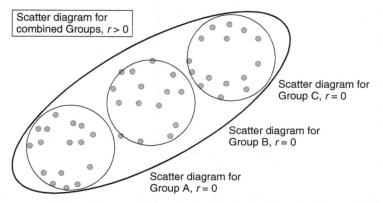

FIGURE 11.5   Illustration of how combining with different average scores can lead to an increase in values of the correlation coefficient because it is oval shaped, even though the groups providing the data each show correlations of zero.

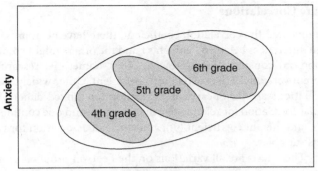

FIGURE 11.6 Example of the effect of heterogeneous subgroups on the correlation coefficient. Each subgroup in the fictitious example shows less anxiety as the school year progresses, which could lead to negative correlations within each grade, while the overall correlation would be positive.

to find out if the anxiety among elementary school children changes as reading proficiency increases. Suppose that, as reading skills improve, children do become more comfortable and less anxious. But suppose also that, as children get older, their anxiety levels start out higher early in the school year, then decrease.

You might end up with the pattern shown in Figure 11.6. When all the data are combined, the overall pattern seems to indicate a positive correlation, whereas each individual group shows a negative correlation. This reversal of the sign of the correlation is likely to be fairly rare, but combining heterogeneous subgroups can have an impact on your correlation coefficients.

TRADITIONAL CORRELATIONAL TESTS

The first correlation coefficients were invented about a century ago; we now call them bivariate correlations. They involved two (bi-)variables. The most common such test is the Pearson *r*.

Generally, when we talk about finding relations among variables, if the data are dichotomous (i.e., they can take only two values, like 0 or 1 or female and male), we talk about tests of association. When the data fall on a continuum, we refer to tests of correlational measures. This semantic difference gives us information about the nature of our data, but the underlying mathematics are often identical.

The Pearson Product–Moment Correlation

The Pearson *r* is useful for assessing the degree to which scores on two different variables show a linear relation. For example, there is a linear relation between frequency of parents spanking their children and children's antisocial behavior; more spanking is associated with higher rates of antisocial behavior (Straus, Sugarman, & Giles-Sims, 1997). This result means that there is a predictable relationship between the variables. Remember, though, that the relationship here is correlational, so we cannot determine causation.

Alternate Bivariate Correlations

Since Karl Pearson invented the correlation coefficient, there have been important extensions to it. The main differences between Pearson's *r* and the others might come in applications that are beyond our considerations (Howell, 2007). Sometimes researchers choose

Bivariate Correlation— A correlational analysis relating only two variables.

different versions of the correlation coefficient. Other widely used **bivariate correlations** are the Spearman correlation for ranked data (r_s), the pointbiserial correlation for relating one dichotomous and one continuous variable (r_{pb}), and the phi coefficient (Φ), a measure of association for two dichotomous variables.

These tests are all variations on the Pearson product–moment correlation, for which you can use the Pearson formula. There are other formulas that researchers sometimes use, but they are merely algebraic manipulations of the standard formula.

The formula typically used for the Spearman correlation will result in the same numerical value as the Pearson formula. The Pearson formula is actually more generally useful because scores with tied ranks make the Spearman formula inaccurate, whereas the Pearson formula is still applicable (Howell, 2007).

Linear Regression

One statistical approach that has been around for quite a long time because its computations are relatively straightforward is multiple regression. If you can remember back to your high school algebra class, you may recall the formula for a straight line, $Y = a + bX$, where a is the Y-intercept and b is the slope. That simple formula lets you plot a straight line on a graph such that for every increase of 1 unit on X, you get a particular increase on the Y variable. So if b = 2, every increase in X leads to an increase of 2 on Y.

You can see an example in Figure 11.7. If you bought 5 lottery tickets at $1.00 each, the cost is predictable. In linear regression analysis, we use the concept of predicting Y

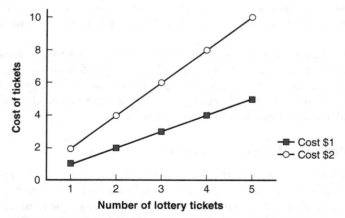

FIGURE 11.7 Simple example to illustrate $Y = a + bX$, with the Y-intercept = 0 and the slope (b) changing from 1 to 2. When b increases, the slope of the line does, too. This means that when b increases, every change in X means a big change in Y.

from X, but it gets more complicated than buying lottery tickets because human behavior is never this simple.

For example, Benfante and Beins (2007) measured the sense of humor of participants using the Multidimensional Sense of Humor Scale (MSHS, Thorson & Powell, 1993) and asked the participants to rate the funniness of a set of jokes on a scale of 1 (*not very funny*) to 7 (*very funny*). One question is whether knowing the level of a person's sense of humor would let us predict their average rating of the jokes. This research questions lends itself to regression analysis. The general formula for linear relationships is

Average Rating = Constant + Slope × Sense of Humor Score

The value of the slope was 0.76; the value of the Y-intercept (the constant) was 1.84. Analysis of the data indicated that the score on the MSHS was correlated with joke ratings. The value of the correlation coefficient was .29, which signals a reliable but not a perfect correlation: The better the sense of humor, the higher a person rated the jokes.

The regression analysis led to the following equation that we can use to predict joke ratings. If somebody's sense of humor score on a scale of 1–5 was a 4.0, the best prediction of the participant's average joke rating based on the data is as follows:

Average Rating = 1.84 + . 76 × Sense of Humor Score
Average Rating = 1.84 + (.76 × 4.0)
Average Rating = 1.84 + 3.04
Average Rating = 4.88

Thus, for the set of jokes used in the study, if we knew that a person's sense of humor score was 4, that person is likely to have rated the jokes, on average, with a score of 4.88.

The predictions are not perfect because the correlation between MSHS score and average joke rating is not perfect. Still, the prediction would be better than just guessing that the person's rating would be at the average for the group, which would be a reasonable guess because most people are somewhere around the average. If the correlation were not significant, your best prediction of the participant's rating of the jokes would have been the mean rating of all participants, which was 4.29. As you can see, there is a noticeable discrepancy between a prediction based on the mean and the prediction based on regression analysis. The stronger the association between variables, the better the prediction.

Zero-Order Correlation—A correlational analysis involving two variables.	**CORRELATIONS WITH MULTIPLE VARIABLES**

CORRELATIONS WITH MULTIPLE VARIABLES

Zero-Order Correlation—A correlational analysis involving two variables.

As a first step in finding out how variables relate to one another, the bivariate correlations we've encountered are quite helpful. At some point, though, we are likely to decide that behavior is too simple to be handled by two variables. So we begin to assemble the puzzle of behavior using many pieces (i.e., variables) and we move from the bivariate, or **zero-order correlations**, to **higher-order correlations** that relate multiple variables simultaneously.

Higher-Order Correlation—A correlational analysis involving more than two variables.

Fortunately, we have quite a number of useful statistical tools to help us begin to fathom the interrelationships among sets of variables. Many of these tools have been around for decades, but it hasn't been until computers have eased the tedium of calculation that psychologists have adopted them.

Multivariate Statistics— Statistical approaches that can accommodate simultaneous analysis of multiple variables.

Today, **multivariate statistics** are a common tool in correlational research. The critical component in using them is no longer accuracy in computation because computerized statistical packages have eliminated that problem. Now we have to worry about using these statistics appropriately and interpreting them meaningfully.

Multiple Regression—A correlational technique that employs more than one predictor variable to estimate the value of a criterion variable.

Multiple Regression

In **multiple regression**, we use more than one predictor variable to estimate the outcome. Your equation for two predictor variables would be as follows:

$$Y = \text{Constant} + (\text{Slope}_1 \times \text{Score}_1) + (\text{Slope}_2 \times \text{Score}_2),$$

which tells you that the Y score you are trying to predict, the criterion variable, will be a function of the score on the first predictor variable, Score_1, and the slope associated with it, plus the score on the second predictor variable, Score_2, times its slope. The formula may look intimidating, but the logic is the same as for the simple, one-variable equation: Given the value of your X variables, you can generate a prediction of Y.

In the humor study by Benfante and Beins (2007), they wanted to know if they could predict how funny people thought they were based on how extraverted the participants were and how the participants rated the jokes. That is, do people who score high on a scale of extraversion think they are funnier than people who score low? And do people who rate jokes as being very funny rate themselves as funnier than those who rate jokes lower?

These questions lend themselves to multiple regression analysis. In this case, the participants' score on an extraversion scale and their average joke ratings were the two predictor variables; their self-rating of how funny they were on a scale of 1 (*I'm not very funny*) to 10 (*I'm very funny*) was the criterion variable that the researchers were trying to predict.

The data revealed that both of these predictor variables were useful in estimating the participants' self-ratings as to how funny they thought they were. That is, both variables predicted significantly how funny people thought they were.

The values of the Y-intercept and the slopes for the two variables appear in Table 11.3. The regression equation for a participant whose extraversion score is low (2) and whose self-rating of funniness is low (3) is as follows:

$$\text{Self-Rating of Funniness} = \text{Constant} + (\text{Slope}_{\text{extraversion}} \times \text{Extraversion Score}) + (\text{Slope}_{\text{ratings}} \times \text{Mean Joke Rating})$$
$$\text{Self-Rating of Funniness} = 3.48 + (0.35 \times 2) + (0.52 \times 3)$$
$$\text{Self-Rating of Funniness} = 3.48 + 0.70 + 1.56$$
$$\text{Self-Rating of Funniness} = 5.74$$

TABLE 11.3   The Values of the Constant (The Y-intercept) and the Slopes in the Regression Analysis Designed to Predict People's Self-Ratings about How Funny They Think They Are on a Scale of 1 (*I'm Not Very Funny*) to 10 (*I'm Very Funny*)

	Coefficient
Constant (Y-intercept)	3.483
Extraversion	0.521
Ratings of jokes	0.348

Based on Their Extraversion Scores and the Ratings They Gave to a Set of Jokes (Benfante & Beins, 2007).

Thus, our best prediction of a person's self-rating of funniness in this case would be 5.74. If these variables were not significant predictors of the self-rating, our best prediction would be the mean of the entire group, which is 6.85. Again, the prediction will not be perfect because the correlations are not perfect; but knowledge of how people rate jokes and how extraverted they are can help us predict how funny they feel they are.

Multiple regression research has shed light on a topic that has emerged lately, the role of fathering in children's development. For over a century, most research has focused on the role of the mother, but we now know that the father–child relationship has implications for development of the child's social competence, cognitive development, and life satisfaction. Cruz et al. (2011) studied Mexican American families to see which of four factors predicted children's perceptions of paternal warmth and interaction: positive parenting (e.g., educational involvement), cultural values (e.g., the importance of self-reliance as an American value and respect as a Mexican value), language use (Spanish versus English), and positive machismo (e.g., *A man's #1 priority is his family*). The variables that predicted children's perceptions of their fathers' warmth in the multiple regression analysis were positive machismo and the father's education. Cruz et al. noted that these results have potential implications for clinical treatment; paternal involvement may be an important aspect of psychosocial interventions.

AN APPLICATION OF MULTIPLE REGRESSION: THE MENTAL HEALTH OF COLLEGE STUDENTS

College students generally show good mental health. The suicide rates of college students, for example, are consistently lower than those of the general population of the same age. Still, there are high rates of suicidal ideation among young people, with 30–40 percent of high school and college students seriously thinking about it (Gutierrez et al., 2000). Men are more prone to suicide than women, even though women report more symptoms on inventories related to suicide proneness (Klibert, Langhinrichsen-Rohling, Luna, & Robichaux, 2011)

In the past, institutions have sometimes taken the action of sending the students home for help. Recently, schools have tried to take a more proactive role, working to prevent the situation from deteriorating to the point of tragedy. We can use the information that psychologists have provided. Often their research involves complex, correlational analyses because life and death are very complex matters. There aren't going to be simple answers because the problem isn't simple.

Factors associated with suicide proneness include procrastination and achievement motivation. There is a positive correlation between procrastination and suicide proneness and a negative correlation between achievement motivation and suicide proneness. So could these factors be useful in predicting what students are at risk? Unfortunately, although these correlations appear to be reliable, the predictive ability of these variables is very low (Klibert et al., 2011).

Fortunately, other researchers (e.g., Gutierrez et al., 2000) have developed a more predictive model capable of predicting suicidal ideation. Using the multivariate approach called factor analysis, they identified two factors associated with risk assessment among students. One factor was associated with negative themes, like repulsion by life, hopelessness, low survival and coping beliefs, and negative self-evaluation. Higher levels on these dimensions were associated with greater thought of suicide. A second factor was associated with less suicide risk. This factor included such protective variables as fear of social disapproval, fear of suicide, and a sense of responsibility to one's family.

Based on these results, a therapist or counselor might be able to spot potential problems before they get out of hand. But this strategy relies on students seeking help in the first place. Fortunately, psychologists have also identified variables correlated with student attitudes toward seeking psychological help.

Komiya, Good, and Sherrod (2000) used multiple regression to identify important variables associated with seeking help, which include gender, the stigma associated with seeking help, emotional openness, and severity of symptoms. Women were more likely to seek help; part of this tendency is that women are often more emotionally open. As symptoms grow more severe, students are more likely to see a therapist or counselor. Finally, students are more likely to get help if there is less stigma associated with therapy.

The issue of stigma being associated with mental health counseling is potentially important. According to Kim, Kim, and Park (2011), Asian women are reluctant to seek psychological treatment, so interventions that reduce depression and provide social support can be crucial in reducing symptoms of depression, which are associated with suicidal thought. In an intervention designed to provide such support, symptoms of depression and incidence of suicidal thought diminished significantly among female Korean college students.

These results can suggest options for increasing student use of counseling centers. Psychological research can be an important component in identifying ways to maximize student use of mental health resources.

SUMMARY

We have seen how psychologists use correlational approaches to study complex behavioral patterns. Experimental approaches are useful and often preferred, but correlational studies may actually provide a better means of understanding complex aspects of behavior.

By using correlational approaches, we can see how different behaviors interrelate and we can often apply this knowledge to predicting behavior. When we recognize the power (and limitations) of the approaches, we can begin to understand the complex interconnections among variables that we may miss in simplified experimental settings.

Researchers use correlational approaches to spot associations among variables and to make predictions about behavior. The reason that we cannot use such analyses to be certain about causation is that there may be other variables influencing the ones we are investigating and that if there is a causal relationship, we don't always know which variable is the cause and which is the effect.

The first correlation coefficient was invented about a century ago. Afterward, different correlational statistics flourished and newer approaches have emerged. One of the commonly used approaches includes multiple regression, which allows us to make better predictions about behavior based on more information, that is, based on more variables. When used appropriately, these techniques provide us with power tools for understanding and predicting behavior.

REVIEW QUESTIONS

Multiple Choice Questions

1. When Guthrie, Ash, and Bendapudi (1995) investigated whether students' grades and their tendency to be morning or evening people are associated, these investigators conducted
   a. a prediction study.
   b. a relationship study.
   c. confirmatory factor analysis.
   d. multiple regression.

2. If you were studying 10 variables to see whether they were correlated and if you computed all possible correlation coefficients,
   a. five percent of your correlations would be significant but actually meaningless.
   b. you would want to pay attention to higher-order correlations more than to zero-order correlations.
   c. by choosing the proper variables, you could begin to identify causal relationships.
   d. your best approach to examining the correlations would be to create a third variable problem.

3. A clinician might want to know whether a psychological inventory would predict future levels of depression in clients. Those future levels of depression would constitute a
   a. predictor variable.
   b. criterion variable.
   c. confirmatory variable.
   d. manipulated variable.

4. Psychologists have discovered that people high in neuroticism associated sex with death more than people low in neuroticism do. We can't conclude that neuroticism causes people to associate sex with death because the outside variables that lead to neuroticism could also lead to thoughts of sex and death. This illustrates the
   a. directionality problem.
   b. third variable problem.
   c. restricted range problem.
   d. latent variable problem.

5. When two variables are related in such a way that when one increases, so does the other, you can conclude that
   a. there is no problem with directionality.
   b. factor analysis is inappropriate.

c. the relation between variables is positive.

d. there are no latent variables affecting the relationship.

6. If a researcher wanted to know whether certain behaviors are associated with income, he or she might be reluctant to travel to a poor part of town that has a high crime rate. As a result, the data would not include very low values of income levels and the correlation coefficient would be lower than if such data were included. The potential problem in this case is

a. heterogeneous subgroups.

b. nonlinear relationships.

c. the presence of latent variables.

d. a restricted range.

7. The Pearson product–moment correlation and the Spearman correlation both involve

a. higher-order correlations.

b. multiple regression.

c. bivariate correlations.

d. nonlinear correlations.

8. When you try to predict the value of an outcome variable from several variables, you are likely to be using

a. multiple regression.

b. the Pearson product–moment correlation.

c. the analysis of variance.

d. heterogeneous subgroups.

9. In correlational modeling, a researcher selects a set of variables to predict some behavior. The results from that set of variables may not be the same as when a different set of variables had been used. This limitation reflects a problem with

a. zero-order correlations.

b. restricted range.

c. directionality.

d. generalizability.

10. The research showing that people who watch violent television and movies also engage in more aggressive behavior involves

a. confirmation bias.

b. unstable predictor variables.

c. correlational studies.

d. heterogeneous subgroups.

Essay Questions

11. What is the difference between a relationship study and a prediction study? Which one is likely to be more preliminary? Why?

12. Why is it important to recognize if your variables are related in a nonlinear way?

ANSWERS TO REVIEW QUESTIONS

Answers to Multiple Choice Questions

1. b	5. c	9. d
2. a	6. d	10. c
3. b	7. c	
4. b	8. a	

Answers to Essay Questions

11. What is the difference between a relationship study and a prediction study? Which one is likely to be more preliminary? Why?

A relationship study involves establishing which variables are reliably related to one another. A prediction study involves using a predictor variable to predict a criterion variable.

A relationship study might precede a prediction study because we need to understand which variables are related before we can make useful predictions based on those relationships.

12. Why is it important to recognize if your variables are related in a nonlinear way?

If your variables are nonlinearly related, you should be cautious about using the standard Pearson correlation. You might need to test for nonlinearity and use a different correlational approach to identify whether the relation between variables is reliable.

····· ──────────────────────────

CHAPTER TWELVE

STUDYING PATTERNS IN THE NATURAL WORLD

Observational Approaches

CHAPTER OVERVIEW

LEARNING OBJECTIVES ■ **KEY TERMS** ■ **CHAPTER PREVIEW**

LEARNING OBJECTIVES

After going through this chapter, you will be able to:

- Distinguish the characteristics of systematic observation and casual observation
- Explain how particularistic and universalistic research differ
- Describe the concepts of anthropomorphism and theromorphism
- Identify the different strategies researchers use in naturalistic observation
- Identify issues that are important for sampling behavior in naturalistic observation
- Explain how an ethological approach can be useful in clinical psychological research
- Identify the ethical issues associated with observational research

KEY TERMS

CHAPTER PREVIEW

One of the most pronounced differences between the way scientists study the world and the way that most people observe their world involves the degree to which the observations are systematic and focused. Most of the time, people (including scientists who are "off duty") manage to ignore most of the things that go on around them. If something catches our eye or attracts some interest, we pay attention to it. Otherwise, we ignore it.

In scientific research, we observe certain behaviors or events with meticulous care, trying not to miss occurrences that are critical to our research topic. Depending on the research, a scientist will pay attention to one set of behaviors and ignore others.

In this chapter, you will see how scientists set up the strategies of their research and collect data in the natural world. The approaches discussed here rely on phenomena that exist regardless of whether a researcher studies it. For example, a soccer game will take place whether a scientist decides to investigate the degree to which players are prone to break the rules under certain conditions. Given that the activity to be observed will take place, it is the observer's responsibility to identify which behaviors to attend to and to define them appropriately.

In addition, researchers have to consider issues of sampling. With observational studies, the question of sampling refers to when, where, and how to select the events to be recorded, not only whom to study. There are several strategies that researchers use in setting up their procedures. Very often there is a trade-off between what is practical and what is ideal. Observational techniques may require extensive time commitments that involve resources in excess of what the researcher can devote to the project. Thus, compromises have to be made that will make the research possible without affecting too greatly the validity of the data.

Another important element in planning observational research is that of ethics. Is it appropriate to observe people without getting their consent or debriefing them? There are some circumstances where these ethical issues pose no problems, but in other conditions, there are notable ethical considerations.

Observational approaches have a distinct set of advantages and disadvantages, just like any other scientific method. Researchers still have to pay attention to issues of reliability and validity, because when the researchers interpret the data to find out what they mean, the conclusions are meaningless if the data are not reliable and valid. There are also some very practical questions that investigators have to address in setting up their research.

OBSERVATIONAL APPROACHES

Researchers can search for patterns of behavior and relationships among behaviors by directly recording how human and nonhuman animals behave in their natural environments. This approach is called **observational research.** Scientists who make use of observational approaches do not typically create experimental situations to study; in many cases, they try their best to remain completely unnoticed by those they study. Observational researchers try to record behaviors as accurately as they can, noting the context in which those behaviors occur. Observational research seems as if it would be easy to conduct, but there are many pitfalls to avoid.

> **Observational Research**—A methodology in which investigators are trained to record human or nonhuman behavior exactly as it occurs, attempting to avoid interpretation or subjective evaluation.

In this chapter, we will cover various aspects of observational research. Psychologists do not use observational research as extensively as some other behavioral scientists like sociologists and anthropologists. Nonetheless, these methods can provide a wealth of information about human behavior and attitudes.

SCIENTIFIC VERSUS CASUAL OBSERVATION

In everyday life, we observe behavior and make predictions all the time. For instance, if you are driving your car on the highway, you monitor the way others are driving, anticipating what they are likely to do. Such casual observation is very important. But it differs from scientific observation. In research we engage in systematic observation. This means that we make note of behavior exactly how and when it occurs, without trying to interpret it. **Systematic observation** generally takes place in the preliminary stages of research, before the investigators develop hypotheses.

> **Systematic Observation**—A form of observational research in which an investigator records behavior as it naturally occurs, attempting to note every behavior exactly as it emerges, often in a laboratory as an initial stage of research and prior to the development of hypotheses.

It is impossible to record accurately every behavior a person or animal engages in, so observational researchers limit themselves to certain behaviors that are important in the current research project. Think of the behavior of referees in soccer (or any other sporting event). In a very real sense, they are acting like scientists who are engaged in systematic observation. While on the field, they watch for certain patterns of behavior on the part of the players; in this example, the officials focus on behaviors that relate to the rules of the game. Referees do not take detailed notes as scientists do, but keep track of important behaviors just as scientists do.

On the other hand, parents are likely to observe their own children in great detail, ignoring other occurrences on the field. Parents are notorious for showing low levels of objectivity: Any contact with their children should be called fouls, whereas their children seldom violate the rules.

Sports officials are supposed to maintain objectivity, just as scientists are. The events that occur are what they are; neither scientists nor referees are supposed to inject their own values or desires into their work. However, scientists and referees do bring their own biases into their work. After all, they are human like the rest of us. The unfortunate outcome can be either poor science or poor sport. The advantage in science is that other researchers may try to replicate the findings; therefore, invalid scientific findings can ultimately be corrected.

STUDYING NATURAL BEHAVIORS

The term natural behavior in research refers to behaviors that psychologists, sociologists, anthropologists, and others study in a natural setting as opposed to in a laboratory. Scientists call such research **naturalistic observation.** In many cases, those being observed are unaware that a researcher is recording behaviors.

> **Naturalistic Observation**—A form of observational research involving the recording of behavior as it naturally occurs, without any attempt at intervention, often without the knowledge of those being observed.

Naturalistic observation can be useful in research in cases where cultural differences might affect results. For example, Rai and Fiske (2010) noted that in some cultures, people may take offense when asked about personal issues. When cultural differences may affect research outcomes, naturalistic observation may be a good alternative and may avoid response biases on the part of those being studied.

For investigators who have a specific, practical goal in their research, like solving a problem of communication among coworkers, the naturalistic approach might work best. Researchers refer to this type of research as **particularistic** because it addresses a particular or specific question that might be limited to a single setting.

> **Particularistic Research**—Investigation taking place at a specific time and place that focuses on a single question and that is not oriented toward general questions.

Just because the research is naturalistic, we can't assume that it provides us with a high degree of external validity. If you conduct an observational study on your campus of whether men hold doors open for women more than vice versa, the results may or may not apply to any other campus, to older populations, to people in other parts of the country, or to any other groups. You have a particular result in a natural setting, but you don't know if the same thing would happen with other people elsewhere.

When the investigators are more interested in addressing general principles, like the conditions that lead people to engage in helping behavior, it is easier to test hypotheses in a controlled environment. We refer to the research goal here as **universalistic,** meaning that we don't intend to limit our conclusions to what happens in the simple laboratory setting. Rather, it will have more general, theoretical implications.

> **Universalistic Research**—Investigation whose goal is to address a general question that extends beyond the specific time and place where the research itself occurs.

Observational techniques constitute a small, but important, domain in psychology. You are likely to encounter it in three particular types of research, involving the study of children, psychiatric populations, and nonhumans. In many cases, observational research is not experimental; that is, researchers don't generally manipulate anything in the environment. Rather, they observe an organism as it behaves in a particular environment.

Studying Complex Human Behavior

People are complex; so are our behaviors. When psychologists use laboratory studies to investigate behaviors, the research generally involves relatively simple observations and measurements. For instance, how long does it take to solve a problem, how much money would a mock jury award a plaintiff in a trial, how long will an animal persist in a nonrewarded behavior, or can people be primed to conform to a group's views? Each of these topics may involve complex behavior, but the measurements that researchers make are pretty simple: number of seconds to solve the problem, a dollar amount given to a plaintiff, number of nonreinforced bar presses, and the percentage of the time a person agrees with a group.

The value of laboratory studies is that they can remove many of the effects of factors that are not of interest to the researcher. What remains is a simplified version of reality that allows complex behavior to be broken into individual elements.

Observational research, on the other hand, involves behavior in its complexity. One disadvantage is that the researcher cannot always tell what causes the behavior to occur because so many things are happening at the same time; the advantage is that the researcher can determine realistically what behaviors occur in a given situation because they indeed naturally happened.

For example, Snowden and Christian (1999) wanted to find out how parents of gifted students fostered their children's development. The researchers asked the parents to complete a questionnaire, then followed up with a visit to their home for purposes of an interview and naturalistic observation. During the observation and interview, the researchers discovered (among other things) that the parents were affectionate, allowed the children freedom of self-expression, and provided materials for creativity.

An important component of the research was finding out how the parents and children really interacted. The only way to do this is to observe directly. As you already know, a household with children is a busy, complex environment, with a lot happening that is out of control of the researchers. Consequently, the investigators could identify what factors in the household might be involved in fostering the children's intellectual growth, but it is impossible to say which specific factors or combination of factors may be critical.

Schools provide a natural environment for observation. Increasing numbers of children are enrolled in preschools because parents have jobs that prevent them from caring for their children during daytime hours. Thus, with children in the preschools and parents who may not have a lot of time to take the children to a psychologist or psychiatrist, it can make sense for the professional to observe the child in the preschool itself. Further, this setting is a more natural environment than a clinic or office, so the assessment and evaluation can be based on more valid observations. Finally, the preschool setting may be the cause, in part, of problems that develop. When these reasons are combined with the fact that it is easier to discuss the problems with teachers on site, we can see that naturalistic observation may be an effective means to document difficulties among preschoolers (Kaplan, 1999).

Ethology

Most of our discussion of observational research will involve studies of human behavior. However, there are various traditions in studying natural behavior in nonhuman animals. For instance, **ethologists,** scientists who investigate broad or general patterns of behavior of organisms in a natural environment often study nonhumans, although their techniques are appropriate for the study of human behavior as well.

Ethologist—A researcher who studies behavior, usually of animals, in their natural environment.

As you saw in Chapter 2, there are ethical arguments concerning research with animals that need consideration prior to beginning an investigation. Researchers who think that animal research is appropriate are also required to keep ethical and legal considerations in mind in planning their work with captive animals.

Ethological studies of people can be very instructive as well. For instance, investigators (Troisi, 2002; Brüne, Sonntag, Abdel-Hamid, Lehmkämper, Juckel, & Troisi, 2008) have commented that ethological approaches are useful in detecting stress in clinical populations and that nonverbal behaviors can differentiate schizophrenic and nonschizophrenic individuals. Knowledge of culture-specific verbal behavior is additional helpful in distinguishing the clinical and nonclinical populations. Troisi (1999) pointed out that although people with schizophrenia show poorer prognosis for recovery than most psychiatric disorders, there are wide individual differences in recovery. Troisi speculated that ethological approaches could help identify early in treatment those patients who are less or more likely to recover normal behavior. Based on the ethological data, Troisi and colleagues (1991) reported that schizophrenic patients who made less eye contact with an interviewer and who closed their eyes more had poorer prognoses than other patients. Not only is this type of research useful in predicting treatment outcomes, but it can also shed light on particular behaviors, like disturbed social behavior.

Describing the Behavior of Nonhuman Animals

Depending on what kind of animal a researcher investigates, we see differences in terminology in the descriptions and interpretations of the results. When an investigator studies nonhuman animals, explanations of how the animals act in the presence of others might invoke the idea of territoriality. For instance, birds that alight on railings or power lines tend to maintain a "comfortable" distance between themselves and their neighbors. When the distance between two birds becomes small, they begin to peck at one another, gradually separating to an acceptable distance (Dixon, 1998). Imagine two children in a car who are taking a long trip. They show the same "pecking" behavior with one another.

When the investigator studies people in this kind of situation, results are likely to be characterized in terms of an individual's personal space or comfort zone. Researchers tend to describe the behavior of animals, but to discuss the motives and thoughts of people.

Even though researchers may be studying the same underlying phenomenon, they often use different terms that reflect the history and traditions of the field. When research involves nonhuman animals, we tend to avoid developing explanations that make use of internal, mental processes. Thus, many investigators who study animal behavior may give a description of how an animal responds to the presence of another, but you will seldom see a statement that the animal is "uncomfortable." Discomfort is a human feeling that we can describe because we have language; we can't tell if an animal is experiencing the same emotion that we would in a similar situation.

Part of the reason for this tendency is that psychologists began studying animal behavior in great depth when behavioral theory dominated. Behaviorists were loath to invoke mental concepts for human or nonhuman behavior. Behaviorists studied behavior, not thought processes that were unobservable and therefore not thought to be scientific.

Another reason for a cautious approach in describing animal behavior is that, prior to the behaviorists, scientists would too freely attribute human emotions to nonhuman animals. Such attribution is called **anthropomorphism.** If you were to say that your dog runs to you when you get

---

Anthropomorphism— The attribution of human characteristic to nonhuman animals, such as an animal being called lonely.

Theromorphism—The attempt to understand the behavior of nonhuman animals by speculating about the behavior within the context of the animal's perspectives.

Evolutionary Psychology—A relatively recent branch of psychology whose focus is human behavior from the perspective of its evolutionary development.

home because it likes you, you would be anthropomorphizing. That is, you would be attributing a human emotion to a nonhuman animal. Researchers often prefer **theromorphism,** which focuses more on the animal's perceptions and behaviors than on the way a human would respond.

The distinction between anthropomorphism and theromorphism is an interesting one because it can dramatically affect the way we view behaviors.

Ethological approaches can be useful in comparing behaviors across species. In fact, ethologists have a long tradition of such comparative research. Currently, the domain of **evolutionary psychology** attempts to provide an overriding theoretical approach to explaining the behaviors of people with an evolutionary focus. This approach may also be useful in understanding the interrelatedness of behaviors of different species.

Although virtually all scientists recognize the explanatory power of the theory of evolution in biological sciences, the field of evolutionary psychology is still controversial; we do not know how useful it will ultimately be in explaining human behavior. At the same time, that is what science is all about. Hypotheses are generated and tested. If the results of research support the hypothesis and the theory, we increase our confidence in the explanatory power of the theory, at least until a better set of explanations comes along.

APPROACHES TO OBSERVATIONAL RESEARCH

As with any research project, observational investigators have to make some very practical decisions. These decisions are important because they can affect the outcome and conclusions of the research. Some decisions revolve around how to collect observational data. Some techniques require that the observer record behaviors simply and descriptively. Other approaches lead to categorization and summarizing behaviors that occur.

Five Practical Steps in Observational Research

Observational strategies differ from laboratory approaches in a number of ways. One commonality is that you have to make decisions about exactly how you want to carry out your study. Some decisions are similar to those in laboratory studies, but there are some unique determinations as well.

First, you need to find out what others have already done that relates to your project. Replication is useful, but you don't really want to devote a lot of time and energy to research that only repeats what others have done.

Second, you should develop and employ specific methods that experts in the area will recognize as valid. This means you should develop ways to measure the hypothetical constructs of interest to you. If published research has provided you with tools, make use of them. For instance, Troisi's (1999) Ethological Coding System for Interviews (ECSI) could give you the means for documenting behaviors when people talk. The ECSI was developed for Troisi's work with psychiatric populations, but you could adapt it to your own nonpsychiatric population.

Third, you must determine the details of your observations. You have to identify the settings in which you will observe behaviors. This will involve the location or locations where you will collect data, the times of day and days of the week you will do it, and the duration of data collection.

Sometimes these decisions may be nearly fixed. For instance, if you are going to set up a videotape recorder and complex instrumentation, you may have to determine which location you want to use and stay there. Similarly, if you are going to monitor behaviors in places where you have limited access, you will be constrained by the realities of the situation.

A fourth step is to determine your sampling strategy. In most psychological research, sampling is largely concerned with the participants who provide the data. In observational studies, you also have to consider what events you are going to code and what your strategy will be during observation.

Continuous Real-time Measurement—The measurement of the duration of behaviors as they occur.

For instance, with respect to temporal aspects of collecting data, you may engage in **continuous real-time measurement, time-point sampling, or time-interval sampling.** Continuous real-time measurement involves monitoring how long behaviors of interest last. Each time the observed person engages in the behavior being studied, the researcher records how long the behavior persists over the course of the recording session. On the other hand, in time-point sampling, observers determine points in time when they look to see whether a behavior is or is not occurring. In time-interval sampling, the observer notes whether a behavior has occurred within a predetermined interval.

Time-point Sampling— The measurement of the occurrence of a behavior by selecting specific points in time and recording whether the behavior is occurring at that instant.

The fifth step is to train the observers so that data collection is reliable. Because observational research often takes place in the field, there are going to be a lot of distractions; it will help for observers to know exactly what they are supposed to pay attention to. Further, the observers must follow a strict protocol in observing, judging, and recording relevant behaviors. If all the observers are not doing the same thing, reliability and validity will suffer.

Time-interval Sampling—The measurement of behavior by noting whether it has occurred within a specified time interval or intervals.

By following these steps, you will be able to create a study that will result in high-quality data. The effect will be that you will have more useful information about behavior in natural settings.

Approaches to Measurement

When you observe behavior as it naturally unfolds, you have to make decisions about what to record. If you are using the traditional approach of watching and recording in a notebook, it will be impossible in most situations to identify every behavior your subject engages in. There will be large and small movements, changes in facial expressions, vocalizations, and so on. They are so numerous and varied that you won't be able to keep track of them all accurately.

In the past several decades, researchers have made increasing use of videotaping (e.g., Pepler & Craig, 1995) or audiotaping (e.g., Mehl, 2006; Tapper & Boulton, 2002) to capture behaviors. This technology allows the investigator to review the behaviors as many times as necessary to provide a complete description of what is happening. Even this approach will not solve all observational problems because the camera angle emphasizes some behaviors but misses others.

As an example, you only need to watch replays of a major college or professional football game. All too often, even with the multiple camera angles they employ, it isn't entirely clear what happened in a play. The advantages of videotaping and audiotaping are that they can reduce (but not eliminate) the ambiguity of observation and can preserve a record of the behavior permanently.

Other decisions in measurement involve the nature and frequency of observations. For instance Paolisso and Hames (2010) have noted that periodic, instantaneous sampling of behaviors is useful for detecting a variety of behaviors, but not how often they occur or how long they last. In contrast, a self-reported diary, while not involving real-time data collection is more useful for identifying average or typical behaviors during a person's day. Depending on the nature of your research question, you have to decide which approach suits your needs.

As you've already read, psychologists do not use observational research extensively; most of the time, this approach involves either nonhuman animals (e.g., a study of livestock movement using GPS tracking; Perotto-Baldivieso, Cooper, Cibils, Figueroa-Pagán, Udaeta, & Black-Rubio, 2012) or applied research with people (e.g., Brüne et al, 2008). Still, if you are planning observational research, you can find examples in the research literature to guide you.

SAMPLING ISSUES IN OBSERVATIONAL RESEARCH

In observational research, the question of sampling can be quite complex. The investigator needs to worry about samples of people, of behaviors, and of times during which behaviors are sampled.

Most research does not use random sampling either of people or of behaviors. That is, we decide what materials the participants will see and we collect convenience samples of college students or laboratory rats, then we observe behaviors that are convenient for one reason or another (e.g., others used them in their research). For example, Jenni (1976) and Jenni and Jenni (1976) studied differences in the way female and male students carry their books on campus. This behavior is one of many behaviors that the investigators could have investigated.

Number of Sampling Blocks

Moore (1998) provided a good example of how much data is needed to represent behavior accurately, at least in the observation of problem students in school. He observed three students continuously through the day on 20 different days, collecting data in 8-minute blocks. He monitored several target behaviors: on/off task, isolating self, verbal refusal, daydreaming, inappropriate verbalization, noncompliance, disruptive behavior, and aggression.

He then investigated what the results would have been like with smaller amounts of sampling. Using the data he had collected, he took randomly selected groups of 4, 8, 12, 16, 20, and 30 blocks from the population of forty-eight 8-minute blocks and compared the subsamples to the entire set of 48 blocks. This process simulated a large number of studies with 4, 8, etc. observation periods.

When he used relatively few (4 or 8) observations, he found notable discrepancies between the samples and the criterion. Keep in mind that a researcher who used eight 8-minute blocks would devote over an hour's worth of time to the task. Moore studied three students with four independent observers during actual observations. If a researcher observed three children, the time commitment would be over three hours. Multiply this by the number of different observers used. In Moore's study, the observation time rose to over 12 hours.

What happens with twelve 8-minute blocks? Such a study would involve over four and a half hours of data collection per observer on three students. This is a lot of time and energy to expend gathering questionable data. According to Moore, the quality of the data even at 12 observation periods is still suspicious. Figure 12.1 shows the degree of difference between the smaller samples and the criterion value based on forty-eight 8-minute blocks. The dependent measure is the number of times that the students engaged in group activity.

As you can see in the figure, the deviations are striking. If this study had been done with only four 8-minute observation periods, then, according to the data collected by the investigators, the researchers would, on average, be wrong in their estimate of group activity by 50 percent.

How long do researchers actually observe behavior in their studies? According to the data by Odom and Ogawa (1992), researchers collected data over a wide range of periods, but sometimes as little as six minutes. The implication of such a small observation period is that we may not be able to place much faith in the data generated. Moore (1998) pointed

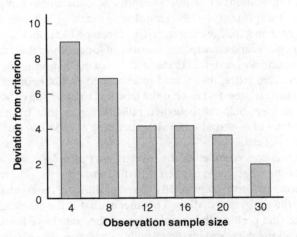

FIGURE 12.1 The degree to which samples showed deviations from the number of instances of actual group activity. The estimates of group activity deviated from a valid criterion of about 17, with greater error associated with fewer observations sampled. With only four observation periods, the estimate of the amount of group activity was off by about 50 percent; with 30 observations, the error fell to about 13 percent. The greater the number of 8-minute blocks sampled, the more accurate the estimate of activity.

Source: Moore, S. R. (1998). Effects of sample size on the representativeness of observational data used in evaluation. *Education and Treatment of Children, 21,* 209–226.

out that if researchers are interested in studying changes in behavior over time, small numbers of sampling blocks may provide inaccurate baseline data and follow-up data. The result would be an undesirably low level of both reliability and validity.

This is why some researchers spend extensive periods of time observing behaviors. For instance, Troisi spent 263 hours observing grooming behavior in female monkeys. They found that the monkeys tended to spend time grooming other monkeys that were aggressive toward them. Without this sizable expenditure of time, the actual patterns of behavior might not be clear.

Methods of Sampling Events During Observation

The goal of making observations is to understand behavior beyond the time of data collection. We hope that our sample of observed behaviors is representative of the larger population. One way to increase the likelihood that the behaviors we sample are representative of the population is to use random sampling of behaviors. In the case of observational research, the population is the entire set of behaviors of interest. Random sampling of behaviors is as important as random sampling of people.

One implication of random sampling of behaviors is that the researchers need to be able to monitor them at any time, in any place, and under any conditions (Peregrine, Drews, North, & Slupe, 1993). This is an unlikely combination. Researchers have personal lives and don't want to be in the field all the time; those who are observed are unwilling to let researchers invade their privacy.

In order to see the implications of various random and nonrandom sampling techniques on research results, Peregrine et al. (1993) monitored touching behavior of children in a child development center on a college campus. They videotaped 32 hours of interaction, recorded the action taking place, and counted the number of touches and their duration.

Every time they rewound and reviewed the tape, it increased their time commitment. If they had to watch each event twice, they would have needed 64 hours of viewing time to code the data, plus the time to stop and rewind the tape and to enter the data. Two coders watched all the tapes so they could estimate their reliability in coding. In the end, they divided the tape into 32 hours of 3-second intervals, generating over 38,000 time intervals, each one with several pieces of data.

Once this gigantic task was completed, the investigators sampled from among the 3-second intervals, simulating what would happen with different observational techniques.

When the researchers randomly sampled 10 percent of the data, the results were very similar to the data from the entire population. This means that if the investigators randomly sampled 3,800 3-second periods, they would capture the same basic information as they had when they used all the data. Systematic sampling of 10 percent also worked well. For this, they sampled every 10th time interval.

They concluded that if they were interested in touching behavior within a child development center, they could sample 3,800 random 3-second intervals and end up with a representative sample. It would not be representative of touching behavior in different settings, though.

Peregrine et al. also looked at what would happen if they restricted their observations to a single type of activity, like playing with blocks. The result was that their estimates of touching behavior were higher than had actually occurred through the entire set of 3-second intervals. As they pointed out, playing with blocks involves reaching for them, which might result in greater accidental or cooperative touching than other behaviors.

The implication here is that if researchers select some activity and monitor behavior only during that activity, they might end up with a distorted picture of what happens in general; their results might pertain only to the particular event they sampled. Suppose, for example, that instead of choosing to observe while the children were playing with blocks, they observed during a reading period. The point is that you have to sample across a variety of behaviors if you want to make general statements about what people do in a variety of situations.

They also employed a third sampling technique, **cluster sampling of behaviors.** In cluster sampling, researchers pick a start time and watch for some predetermined time period. So instead of 3-second intervals, the researchers investigated what would happen if they observed behavior during fewer, but longer, time intervals.

> **Cluster Sampling of Behaviors**—In naturalistic observation, the recording of behaviors in specified, extended time periods, a method that can lead to biased estimates of how often particular behaviors occur over the long run.

They found out that cluster sampling is a poor way to collect data. The results from 15-, 30-, and 60-minute clusters were unlike that from the entire population of 3-second intervals. In fact, Peregrine et al. discovered that in order to generate valid data, they needed to sample 57 percent of the entire 32 hours. This is more than a fivefold increase over the 10 percent needed for random sampling. The researchers noted that the effect of using long clusters is to increase the variability of the measurements, so it is possible that estimates of the occurrence of a given behavior will be either very high or very low.

We can see that random sampling is the most efficient way to collect valid data. The drawback is that sometimes it is difficult to do. The trade-off is time and energy versus quality of the data. As such, you have to decide on the best compromise for your own research.

Estimating the Frequency and Duration of Behaviors

When you observe behavior naturalistically, you could be overwhelmed with choices about what behaviors to study and how to study them. For example, Zinner, Hindahl, and Schwibbe (1997) studied observed behaviors in a group of baboons (*Papio hamadryas*). The researchers recorded frequency and duration of locomotion (moving about), grooming, approaches to another baboon, and threats.

> **One/Zero Sampling**— In naturalistic observation, the recording of whether a behavior occurs (earning a score of one) or not (earning a score of zero), a technique that tends to overestimate the amount of time a behavior is exhibited but underestimates the frequency of its occurrence.

The researchers engaged in an enormous initial data collection task. Their database consisted of 324 videos of 45 minutes of continuously videotaped activity in several different settings. They counted how often the target behaviors occurred and for how long.

One technique they investigated was **one/zero sampling,** which is used with time sampling. It involves recording whether a target behavior occurs at all in an interval. If it appears, the interval gets a score of 1; otherwise, the score for that interval is 0. Zinner et al. reported that one/zero sampling tends to overestimate the amount of time an animal engages in a behavior and underestimates how frequently it occurs. Still, they noted that one/zero sampling can be an effective strategy for short intervals; its reliability decreases as the sampling interval increases.

ETHOLOGICAL OBSERVATIONS IN CLINICAL RESEARCH

Ethological research tends not to involve real-life applications, although some interesting research by Troisi and colleagues (1999, 2007) reveals how this approach can be used to study human behavior. In different studies, he recorded behaviors of schizophrenics during an interview using structured observations. He employed the ECSI, a 37-item list of definitions of behavior for analyzing the data after interviews. Table 12.1 shows some of the behaviors and how they were defined. You can see that the definitions vary in detail. For example, the definition of a laugh allowed him to differentiate among different facial expressions, like grins, smiles, and so forth.

Could you differentiate in recording a smile versus a grin? Although in everyday life we can do it, it is not easy to come up with a formal definition of each one that will fit all people and that will result in reliable and valid coding. Troisi et al. (2007) found that non-verbal behaviors like facial expressions were good predictors of social disabilities among people with schizophrenia. Beyond this, Troisi, Spalletta, and Pasini (1998) concluded on the basis of ethological coding that schizophrenics tend to show less friendliness and less gesturing than a control group. They also pointed out that some schizophrenics had ethological profiles that were essentially the same as those of people in the control group, which is typical of research on schizophrenia. Interestingly, this type of behavior coding could

TABLE 12.1   Examples of Definitions from the Ethological Coding System for Interviews (ECSI)

Specific definitions are critical in allowing observers to record and code data reliably and accurately, especially when there are behaviors that can be closely related to one another, like a laugh and a grin. The ECSI has 37 defined behaviors that measure affiliation, submission, prosocial behavior, flight, assertion, displacement, and relaxation.

Behavior	Definition
Facial expressions	
Smile	The lip corners are drawn back and up.
Laugh	The mouth corners are drawn up and out, remaining pointed, the lips parting to reveal some of the upper and lower teeth.
Head movements	
Look at/look away	Looking at the interviewer/Looking away from the interviewer.
Bob/thrust	A sharp upward movement of the head, rather like an inverted nod/A sharp forward movement of the head toward the interviewer.
Other movements	
Shrug	The shoulders are raised and dropped again.
Wrinkle	A wrinkling of the skin on the bridge of the nose.
Groom	The fingers are passed through the hair in a combing movement.
Yawn	The mouth opens wide, round and fairly slowly, closing more swiftly. Mouth movement is accompanied by a deep breath and often closing of the eyes and lowering of the brows.

Source: Troisi (1999).

have practical implications for people prior to the onset of schizophrenia. Troisi et al.'s (1998) results are consistent with earlier research findings that preschizophrenic children showed some of the same abnormal patterns of facial expression that occur after schizophrenic symptoms appear (Walker, Grimes, Davis, & Smith, 1993).

Psychiatric researchers typically do not employ ethological methods. Instead, they use randomized clinical trials (RCTs) and rating scales to study their patients. This typical approach often involves creating two or more groups that receive different treatments and perhaps a placebo; the investigator usually records changes in behavior or degree of improvement in people exposed to different treatments. The RCTs and rating scales are simply more efficient, taking perhaps 10 percent of the time that ethological approaches would require (Troisi & Moles, 1999). Investigators have to balance the extra time and money that ethological approaches require against the added information that is gained. As Troisi and Moles demonstrated, though, ethological approaches provide information that RCTs and clinical rating scales do not.

For instance, gender differences among depressed patients are clear with the ethological approach. Troisi and Moles (1999) found that their depressed female participants showed greater hostility as reflected in the ethological profiles. This leads to the hypothesis that women would be less likely to respond to antidepressant medications than men are. In fact, research has revealed this to be true (e.g., Overall, Hollister, Johnson, & Pennington, 1966). This type of research is important because we know that hostile people are less likely to respond to psychotropic medication than are others.

Further support for the use of ethological methods is shown by the fact that depressed patients had higher levels of assertion during psychiatric interviews than controls did. In addition, women showed greater levels of assertion than men, particularly when depressed women and men were compared. The pattern appears in Figure 12.2.

Troisi and Moles (1999) suggested that interpersonal factors underlie women's depressions more so than men's and that it is important for therapists to be aware of this fact if therapy is to be successful. Ethological studies will reveal such patterns, they argued. RCTs and simpler clinical rating scales will not.

THE HUMAN SIDE OF OBSERVATIONAL RESEARCH

As with any method, there are details that we have to consider when planning observational studies. The issues include the setting in which we will observe the behaviors, the means of recording behavior, and how long we will observe and how we sample the events. We also have to consider the ethics of observing behavior, the investigators' relationships with those being observed, and how personal and social issues affect both the researcher and the subject.

Ethics

Any time you study people, you may have an impact on them. In a controlled, laboratory study you are sure that participants know what is going on because you provide them with sufficient information in advance to decide if they want to participate, then you debrief them at the end. At the conclusion of an experimental session, you can be confident that they know as much as they should know and that you have answered all of their questions.

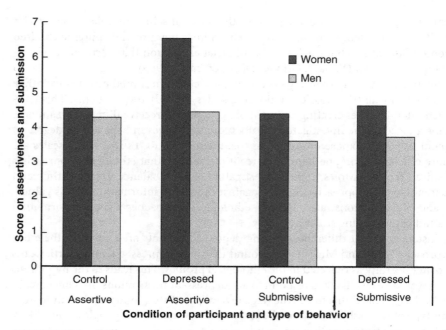

FIGURE 12.2   Differences in level of assertion and submission by depressed men and women compared to controls. The data were collected using an ethological approach that allows coding of behaviors that are not easily obtained with rating scales. This type of information can be important because patients with interpersonally based depression, which will have a large component related to assertion and submission, are less likely to respond to medical intervention than are others.

Source: Troisi and Moles (1999).

Observational studies are somewhat different. The people being monitored do not necessarily know that they are the subjects of study. In most cases, they neither give informed consent nor receive a debriefing.

In the abstract, the ethical issues of observational research are very clear and straightforward. In general, researchers (and the federal officials who issue governmental guidelines) agree that there is no problem in observing public behavior when the researcher doesn't manipulate any variables or intervene in the situation.

So if you are going to observe people's behaviors as they walk down the street or in any public setting, you don't need their permission. If you intend to manipulate any variables or intervene in the situation, though, the situation changes. At this point, you are not merely an observer of public behavior. You are a researcher who is changing the course of people's behavior, even if in an apparently trivial way. As such, you should seek approval from your Institutional Review Board (IRB).

Another important issue is defining what constitutes public behavior. A commonsense rule can sometimes be all we need. For example, we would probably get no disagreement if we concluded that any behavior in a public park, on a public beach, or at a sporting event is public behavior. We would also be likely to get little argument if we were to maintain that when people engage in sexual behavior in their homes, they can expect to be left unobserved.

The problem, of course, is that life doesn't involve only clear-cut cases. Ambiguity is all too predictable in our lives. One notorious example of research that has generated serious controversy involved an investigator who studied men who engaged in sexual activity (which you could consider private behavior) in a men's restroom in a public park (which might make it public, at least to men). Humphreys (1975) studied the behavior of men who engaged in anonymous sex in a generally public area. The ethical status is complicated (Reynolds, 1982).

You might not want to conduct such research yourself, but that is not the issue here. Our personal sensibilities differ, so what one person thinks is unsavory, another might not object to. The critical issue is whether research like that of Humphreys is within ethical boundaries. Such a proposal would probably not be approved by any IRB now; at the time the research took place, in the late 1960s, IRB approval was not mandated; in fact, there were no IRBs at all. In the Controversy box on public versus private sex, you will see some of the issues associated with the ethics of this research.

In discussing controversies like this, you should remember that most psychological research is completely within the boundaries of ethical guidelines. Sometimes extreme cases can illustrate the issues that we have to deal with, but these extreme cases are just that—extreme. They don't resemble the kind of research that the overwhelming majority of scientists engage in. The point to consider here is that we ultimately want to treat people with respect. By discussing cases that are potentially troublesome, we can get a sense of how our own research should proceed.

Participant–Observer Interactions

An ethical issue that is closely allied to practical issues is the extent to which an observer interacts with those being watched. In the classical observational study, researchers are removed from the subjects of their study.

For instance, a quarter of a century ago, a researcher used a noninteractive approach to see how students carried their books (Jenni, 1976). She observed 2,626 people in the United States, Canada, and Central America and found that girls and women carried books with their arms wrapped around the books and held near their chest; boys and men held the books on their hips. She attributed the differences to psychological, social, and biological factors.

The investigator had no need to interact with a student; she merely noted how the students carried their books. The situation involved public areas and public behaviors; there would be no particular ethical issues with this research. But sometimes we can't get the type of information we want by using simple, remote observation. It can be helpful to be part of a group in order to see how it functions. This raises ethical questions. If you joined a group in order to study them, you would be creating relationships with the group members. We could argue that you are deceiving them. Further, we could argue that you are invading their privacy. You might be putting them at risk of psychological harm if they discover your true purposes after they form a close friendship with you. Is it ethical to establish such a relationship with people simply to be able to study them?

We can depict observational research according to whether the investigator interacts with the group and whether the subjects know they are being observed. Table 12.2 indicates some of the ethical issues associated with the different approaches.

TABLE 12.2   Relationship Between Observer and Participant in Observational Research

There are different ethical considerations associated with each approach.

	Researcher Interacts with People Being Observed	**Researcher Does Not Interact with People Being Observed**
People know they are being observed	Ethical considerations are minimal as long as those being observed are aware of the nature of the research.	Ethical considerations may be minimal if behavior is public. If behaviors are normally considered private, however, there may be ethical issues associated with this research, depending on whether those being observed consent to such observation.
People don't know they are being observed	The researcher might be invading the privacy of the group, deceiving them, and putting them as psychological risk if they discover that a friendship has been based on such deception. The researcher may need to seek IRB approval before undertaking this research.	Ethical considerations may be minimal if behavior is public. Because people don't know they are being observed, they may engage in private behaviors, raising potential ethical issues.

Subject Reactivity

When we are aware that others are watching us, we often act differently than when we are confident of being unobserved. When people know that a researcher is investigating them,

> **Subject Reactivity**—The tendency of people being observed to act differently than normal as a result of their awareness of being monitored.

the problem of subject reactivity arises. With **subject reactivity,** people act in unusual ways, so the researcher may not be getting a realistic depiction of the way behavior unfolds.

Psychologists who study behavior in laboratories are aware that participants can purposefully change their behaviors, but in the lab, we can control the environment so as to minimize the effects of reactivity. Because observational research does not involve manipulation or intervention most of the time, we can't control reactivity as well. This is why investigators like to keep subjects unaware that they are being observed.

When people know that researchers are monitoring their behaviors, it sometimes does not affect their activities. For example, Jacob et al. (1994) monitored two types of families, distressed and nondistressed. In the distressed families, the father was diagnosed either as alcoholic or as depressed; in the nondistressed families, there were no major psychiatric problems among the parents. The researchers arranged the methodology so that the families did not always know whether their behaviors were being recorded. They discovered little reactivity in either type of family. Why would the families not change their behaviors, given that we know that reactivity is a potentially major problem in observational studies? According to Jacob et al., there are three possible reasons.

First, families have developed routine ways of interaction; it may be hard for them to reliably change the dynamics of their interactions. Second, because families are routinely very busy, they may not have the luxury of trying to figure out how to change their behaviors during monitoring. Third, there may be little motivation for them to change their behaviors. After all, the families have limited interaction with the researchers and no deep, personal relationships with them. So there is little reason for the family to invest energy in changing their behaviors for a group of strangers.

We can't count on such natural behavior, though. As Pepler and Craig (1995) have pointed out, when children move into adolescence, aggressive behaviors may change when the children know they are being observed. Pepler and Craig videotaped and audiotaped children on a playground. The video was remote, but the children wore wireless microphones. The younger children seemed to act naturally during the monitoring.

Observer Effects

There are two noteworthy observer effects that can occur in naturalistic observation. When people have to monitor behavior and make decisions about it, there is ample opportunity for the individual to selectively observe or remember some behaviors and to ignore others. This may not represent a lack of integrity by the researcher, just an unwitting human tendency. Still, it is a real research dilemma.

Observer Bias—The tendency on the part of observers to bring their biases and predispositions to the recording of data, a process that may be unintentional.

One problem involves **observer bias.** Just like the rest of us, observers have their own points of view that can affect the way they observe and record information. We all know that any given behavior could be interpreted in very different ways. As objective as observers try to be, we know that people are going to insert their predispositions into everything they do. One way to reduce the effects of observer bias is to create a **behavior checklist** with objective definitions of behaviors to be coded. When Troisi (1999) observed the behaviors of schizophrenics, he used a checklist that would enhance the reliability of measurements. Some of the behaviors he studied are shown in Table 12.1. With explicit definitions on such a checklist, researchers have little latitude for letting their predispositions interfere with the data collection.

Behavior Checklist—A list of behaviors to be recorded in naturalistic observation.

Observer Drift—The tendency on the part of an observer to change criteria for recording behaviors over time.

The second problem is **observer drift,** in which the coding scheme used by an observer changes over time. This is similar to the threat to validity called instrumentation that you encountered with regard to quasi-experimental designs. Basically, the criteria used by the observer change from the beginning to the end of data collection.

Interobserver (Interrater) Reliability—The degree to which two or more observers agree in their coding and scoring of behaviors they are observing and recording.

One of the ways that we try to avoid a lowering of the reliability of our observations is to use multiple observers. We assess the reliability of their measurements to see if they are doing the same thing in their coding by assessing **interobserver reliability** (also called **interrater reliability**), the extent to which they agree in their coding. Unfortunately, at times two (or more) observers may begin to code in the same idiosyncratic way. They unknowingly change their way of looking at things so that they are engaged in the same inappropriate coding patterns. If we compared two observers whose coding strategies had drifted, we would find that, although they tended to agree with each other, their data would not be consistent with that of other observers.

We can minimize the effects of observer drift by taking these steps:

- objective criteria.
- training of observers.
- observers.
- at interobserver reliability.
- pair so the same people don't always collect data together.

CONTROVERSY:
Public versus Private Sex

Normally, we think of sexual behavior as being an intimate and private affair. This feature makes sex difficult to study, especially when the sexual activity is relatively unusual. In spite of this limitation, one particular researcher (Humphreys, 1975) managed such research. It was a highly controversial study of sexual behavior that generated a great deal of debate regarding its ethics.

Humphreys wanted to find out how men who engaged in anonymous homosexual behavior differed from men who were not known to have done so. He went to a certain restroom in a public park where men would go to engage in anonymous homosexual sex. His role was to act as a lookout in case the police or rowdy teenagers approached. While acting as the lookout, he recorded the nature of the sexual activity.

After they had finished, he noted their license plate numbers, then went to the police and, using a cover story, obtained their names and addresses. Eighteen months later, he went to their homes to interview them, surveying them regarding other topics.

Is this research ethical? Should he have been watching them engage in sexual activity? You could argue that he invaded their privacy, he lied to the police, and he helped them engage in illegal activities. If he had ever had to turn his records over to the police and the men's names became public, they might have been put at risk for psychological harm (embarrassment and ostracism) or physical harm (legal prosecution).

Consider this, though. You could argue that he wasn't deceiving them because he agreed to act as a lookout, and he did. (He actually got arrested a couple of times while doing it.) You could also maintain that he didn't invade their privacy. After all, they were engaging in behavior with a total stranger that they would never again see and were doing it in a public facility in front of a lookout.

What about the possible physical or psychological risk? Humphreys took great pains to keep his records out of the hands of others. He rented a safe deposit box in another state that would have been inaccessible to police in just about any foreseeable case. In reality, there was little chance of harm befalling the men due to his research.

Finally, what did he find? Humphreys discovered that the men who engaged in this behavior did not differ in any systematic way from men who were not known to have done it. That is, there was remarkably little difference between "them" and "us."

Question for Discussion: Is it possible to argue that the benefits of this research outweigh its ethical problems?

DATA ANALYSIS IN OBSERVATIONAL RESEARCH

Data analysis in observational research spans the range from simple descriptions of behavior to complex statistical analysis. In a naturalistic observation study of children on a playground at school, Pepler and Craig (1995) relied on simple Pearson product–moment correlations, whereas in an ethological comparison of differences in schizophrenics and controls, Troisi et al. (1998) conducted analyses of variance. Some researchers prefer to use qualitative descriptions instead of or in addition to quantitative analysis (e.g., Henwood, 1996; Krahn & Putnam, 2003).

You can find about as many different statistical approaches in observational studies as you will in any other form of research. Because there is no control of variables, though, the research is correlational.

SUMMARY

Observational research provides us with interesting ways to understand behavior. In the most basic form, a researcher simply monitors and records the behaviors of interest. It is a good way to study human and nonhuman activity as it naturally unfolds. Although observational studies are conceptually fairly simple, they actually require attention to a considerable number of details. In order to guarantee reliability and validity, researchers have to develop very specific definitions of variables and to define precisely those conditions in which the behaviors will be observed.

Depending on the nature of the research, observations can be structured or unstructured. Structured observations entail paying attention only to a very restricted set of behaviors; unstructured observations are wider in scope. The investigators need to decide who they will observe, for how long, whether they want to count the number of behaviors or the duration of those behaviors (or both), and the time and location of observation. All of these factors can play critical roles in the results of the research.

Most (but not all) observational studies are field studies because laboratory environments are generally too simple to capture complex behaviors and complex interaction. So when researchers begin their planning, they need to consider the ethical issues associated with observing people who may not know they are under scrutiny. The problems don't disappear if you tell people they are being observed because the subjects of your study may begin to act differently when they know you are watching. We need to take great care so that personal characteristics of the subjects and the observers don't produce misleading results.

REVIEW QUESTIONS

Multiple Choice Questions

1. The study of the behavior of human and nonhuman animals in the natural environment, without any manipulation of variables, is called
    a. subjective research.
    b. anthropometric research.
    c. observational research.
    d. quasi-experimental research.

2. When researchers do not know exactly what behaviors to expect in their observational research, they can set up an artificial situation in a lab and observe behaviors in a preliminary study. Based on the preliminary data, the researchers can then generate hypotheses about behavior in the actual study. The preliminary study would involve
   a. systematic observation.
   b. variable research.
   c. anthropomorphic research.
   d. quasi-experimental research.

3. If researchers wanted to study how long museum visitors looked at various displays in order to learn more about how to set up the displays, the investigators could monitor the behaviors of the visitors. Such research would be called
   a. universalistic.
   b. continuous.
   c. reactive.
   d. particularistic.

4. The researcher Jane Goodall observed the behaviors and social structures of chimpanzees in the wild for many years. Her research could be classified as
   a. experimental.
   b. a case study.
   c. systematic observation.
   d. ethological.

5. The relatively new area of psychology that focuses on human behavior by focusing on the development of our species is called
   a. evolutionary psychology.
   b. anthropomorphism.
   c. theromorphism.
   d. universalism.

6. If a researcher monitored how long a person kept smiling or laughing after seeing a person slip on a banana peel, the data collection would involve
   a. time-point sampling.
   b. time-interval sampling.
   c. continuous real-time sampling.
   d. cluster sampling.

7. If a researcher observes whether a behavior of interest occurs during short, randomly selected intervals, the approach to data collection is
   a. continuous real-time sampling.
   b. time-interval sampling.
   c. cluster sampling.
   d. time-point sampling.

8. One way to increase the likelihood that behaviors of interest in observational research are representative of behaviors in general is to
   a. observe a few behaviors at great length.
   b. take a random sample of behaviors at different times and places.
   c. use universalistic research techniques.
   d. create a comprehensive behavior checklist for observers to use.

9. In observational research, using a small number of long observation times rather multiple, short intervals is called
   a. cluster sampling.
   b. one/zero sampling.
   c. time-point sampling.
   d. time-interval sampling.

10. In naturalistic observation, the practice of dichotomous recording whether a behavior occurs or not constitutes
    a. cluster sampling.
    b. one/zero sampling.
    c. continuous real-time sampling.
    d. time-interval sampling

11. Walker et al.'s (1993) research with ethological coding among children
    a. revealed that preschizophrenic children showed some of the same abnormal patterns of facial expression that occur after schizophrenic symptoms appear.
    b. led to the finding that schizophrenics seldom had ethological profiles that resembled those of people in a control group.
    c. showed that behaviors that were similar, like smiling versus grinning, were hard to differentiate reliably.
    d. led to extensive use of ethological approaches in clinical research.

12. If people are observed by a researcher who has joined their organization in order to be able to study them, the researcher must
    a. consider the possibility that there may be an invasion of privacy even if the people engage in lawful public behavior.
    b. get informed consent for studying any behavior members engage in while part of the group.
    c. get approval from an Institutional Review Board even if the people in the group know they are being observed.
    d. consider whether deceiving participants about his or her membership in the group might put group members at risk if they discovered that a friendship has been based on deception.

13. The tendency of researchers to bring their biases and predispositions to the recording of data is called
    a. reactivity.
    b. observer drift.
    c. lack of interrater reliability.
    d. observer bias.

14. When two different researchers code the same behavior in the same setting, they
    a. can assess interobserver reliability.
    b. can rely on subjective criteria for coding.
    c. may eliminate systematic training of observers.
    d. reduce the likelihood of subject reactivity.

15. Some researchers previously labeled aggressive sex on the part of a male animal rape. This type of labeling reflects
    a. theromorphism.
    b. observer bias.
    c. subject reactivity.
    d. anthropomorphism.

Essay Questions

16. Identify the advantages of conducting on-site observations of children in schools when those children have behavior problems.
    What crucial decisions are associated with sampling in observational research?
17. What crucial decisions are associated with sampling in observational research?
18. How do ethological and randomized clinical trials differ in the study of psychiatric patients? What are the advantages and disadvantages of each?

ANSWERS TO REVIEW QUESTIONS

Answers to Multiple Choice Questions

1. c	6. c	11. a
2. a	7. b	12. d
3. d	8. b	13. d
4. d	9. a	14. a
5. a	10. b	15. d

Answers to Essay Questions

16. Identify the advantages of conducting on-site observations of children in schools when those children have behavior problems.

    Because of hectic parental schedules, it may be difficult for them to arrange appointments with a clinician. Observation in the school may be more convenient. In addition, the setting is a natural one for a child, so observations can take place in a place that is normal for the child. The clinician is also able to observe more complex interactions that are apparent in an office visit. Finally, the school may be part of the problem; observing behavior in that setting may give a clue to the source of the difficulty.

17. What crucial decisions are associated with sampling in observational research?

    Sampling in observational research involves three different elements. First, who will be observed? The nature of the population needs to be determined. Second, what specific behaviors will be the focus of observations? Third, what kind of temporal sampling will be done: continuous, intermittent, time of day, etc.

18. How do ethological and randomized clinical trials differ in the study of psychiatric patients? What are the advantages and disadvantages of each?

    A randomized clinical trial typically involves creating two or more groups that receive different treatments, either qualitatively different therapies or different dosages of a medication. One group usually involves the accepted treatment for the problem being studied. The dependent measure typically includes relatively simple measurements, such as numbers on a rating scale and degree of improvement in behavior.

    An ethological approach would involve studying a more extensive set of behaviors that are more "natural," that is, that the participants are likely to show in everyday behavior.

    A RCT usually requires a smaller commitment of time by the researcher. On the other hand, the ethological approach provides a richer data set involving naturally occurring behaviors.

■ ■ ■ ■ ■

CHAPTER THIRTEEN

RESEARCH IN DEPTH
Longitudinal and Single-Case Studies

CHAPTER OVERVIEW

LEARNING OBJECTIVES ■ KEY TERMS ■ CHAPTER PREVIEW

LEARNING OBJECTIVES

After going through this chapter, you will be able to:

- Identify the three possible reasons that people change psychologically over time
- Differentiate between longitudinal and cross-sectional research
- Describe the concept of cohort effects
- Differentiate trend studies, cohort studies, cohort-sequential studies, and panel studies
- Differentiate prospective and retrospective research designs in longitudinal research
- Describe how attrition can affect the outcome of longitudinal research
- Describe and differentiate withdrawal design, ABAB design, multiple baseline design, and single-subject randomized control trial

- Identify the strengths and weaknesses of single-participant designs
- Identify four common misconceptions among researchers about single-participant experiments
- Differentiate case studies and single-participant experiments
- Identify the strength and weaknesses of case study designs

KEY TERMS

ABA design, p. 324
ABAB design, p. 325
Case study, p. 328
Cohort effects, p. 310
Cohort sequential design, p. 314
Cohort study, p. 314

Cross-sectional research, p. 310
Gerontologist, p. 309
Longitudinal research, p. 309
N of 1 randomized clinical trial (RCT), p. 325

Panel study, p. 315
Prospective study, p. 319
Retrospective study, p. 318
Trend studies, p. 311
Withdrawal design, p. 324

CHAPTER PREVIEW

In this chapter we will cover some techniques that deal with different types of research questions than we have encountered previously. The approaches here are typically employed by researchers with questions that involve in-depth study of people.

Each of these domains has developed its own traditions that sometimes differ from the ones we have already covered. This research may also answer different types of questions. Both of them have added to our understanding of behavior.

Psychologists who study development across time make use of longitudinal research. In this field, we have to deal with change over a long period, sometimes years and decades. As a result, there are special considerations to ponder. When our studies are temporally compact and can be created and completed within a matter of weeks, we think differently from when our studies will not be over for a very long time.

A second specialized research design involves single-participant research. In applied fields, particularly in psychotherapeutic settings, and in theoretical work, we may be interested in studying a single individual in depth. We can do so in a quantitative way, with N of 1 randomized clinical trials (RCT) and experimental analysis of behavior that often entails animal research. We can also use the relatively rare case study approach that tends to be more qualitative.

LONGITUDINAL RESEARCH

If you observe people long enough, you will see that they change in predictable ways. Sometimes the changes take place fairly quickly. Infants one year old are very different than they were even a month or two before. College students become much more sophisticated thinkers between the start of their college careers and their graduation. More mature adults show consistent developmental changes as they progress from being the "young-old," the "old," and finally, the "old-old."

Longitudinal Research—A design in which an investigator studies the same people or the same population (but different individuals) over time, sometimes across decades.

Gerontologist—A scientist who studies the psychological, social, and biological aspects of aging.

Psychologists have developed techniques to study people at different stages in their lives. One such approach is called longitudinal research. In psychology, **longitudinal research** refers to the study of individuals over time, often using repeated measurements. It is similar in many ways to the other methods you know about, but there are also some elements that are unique because of the time span of such projects.

Within psychology, developmental psychologists make greatest use of longitudinal research. A developmental psychologist, or developmentalist, is interested in the nature and causes of change. Developmentalists may specialize in a particular part of the lifespan, including infant years, adolescence, early adulthood, or old age. Just as psychologists who study children may limit their focus to infancy, the toddler period, or some other pre-adolescent time, psychologists specializing in the elderly (who may be called **gerontologists**) sometimes focus on one of the specific categories of old age.

Common Themes in Longitudinal Research

When researchers study change over either a short or a long time span, they investigate the psychological and physiological causes of development. We can conveniently categorize the sources of difference among people into three general groups. First, some researchers may focus on genetic differences that underlie behavior. Scientists recognize that genetic factors can affect behaviors that psychologists study, but the extent to which genes control behavior is overwhelmed by other factors. Genetic factors may explain up to 25 percent of the variability in cognitive ability across different people, but much less for personality characteristics (Schaie, 2000). These figures suggest that the vast majority of individual differences arise from causes other than genetics.

A second potential cause for individual differences is environmental. Thus, a person's education, family structure, socialization, and access to good nutrition and health care have an effect on behavior and attitudes. Not surprisingly, these situational factors are important for the emergence of most of the variability in behavior. Another environmental (i.e., social) aspect of change involves cohort effects, that is, the effects of one's peers, that begin to exert pronounced consequences beginning with school years, but less so during infancy and toddlerhood.

Research on environmental causes of change is complex because it is virtually impossible to identify all of the individual factors that affect even the simplest of behaviors. Further, almost all longitudinal research is descriptive, not experimental. That is, the investigators do not manipulate independent variables in a controlled setting. Rather, they follow the course of a person's life over some time span and try to isolate important variables associated with behavior. This correlational approach allows us to spot relationships among variables, but not causes.

A third domain involves the interaction between genetics and environment. The reason for complexity here is that we still have a very incomplete knowledge base related to how genes and the environment interact for different people. For some behaviors, we will probably ultimately conclude that a complete understanding requires knowledge both of genetic and of environmental factors, particularly for some psychological disorders.

Many of the underlying research concerns are similar, regardless of time of life studied. We have to pay attention to the sample and whether it represents the population we are interested in. We also have to minimize the threats to internal and external validity. In this section, you will see how psychologists plan longitudinal research so that it is maximally informative.

Cross-Sectional versus Longitudinal Research

When we discuss contemporary research, it is easy to assume that psychologists have always used the methods we now use. In reality, research strategies have to be invented. Normally, we persist in using the approach with which we are most comfortable. It is likely to be the approach that our peers and contemporaries use. That is why so many research reports describe similar methods.

On the other hand, when we become aware of the limitations of the dominant strategies, we work to overcome them. It isn't always clear how to fix the problems. It takes a lot of thought and testing to determine how to replace a current method with a valid new approach. When somebody develops a new strategy, it might be "obvious" that it is appropriate, but until we create a new blueprint, it really isn't all that obvious.

Psychologists who study developmental processes have developed increasingly useful strategies. Initially, the approach to developmental questions, particularly for studying aging, did not include longitudinal research. Instead researchers used **cross-sectional research** (Schaie, 2000). From the beginning of the 1900s and for the subsequent several decades, if investigators wanted to know how younger and older adults differed in their intellectual functioning, they would locate two samples, one younger and one older, and assess differences in their abilities.

Although cross-sectional studies dominated, not all psychologists used them exclusively. Lewis Terman's longitudinal study of gifted people from childhood into old age is a case in point. The research began in the 1920s, when cross-sectional studies were the norm. (The vast majority of experimental research still employs cross-sectional research.)

Cross-Sectional Research—A design in which an investigator studies groups differing on some characteristic (e.g., age) at the same time, in contrast to a longitudinal approach that studies the same individuals over time.

Although a cross-sectional plan seemed like a reasonable approach for the first three decades of the twentieth century, after a while some cracks appeared in the foundation. For instance, researchers discovered that they could not replicate the well-documented decline in cognitive functioning across the lifespan that early cross-sectional studies reported (e.g., Jones & Contrad, 1933). Gradually through the 1930s, longitudinal studies became more common.

Researchers began to realize that in a nonequivalent groups design that investigates groups of people who grew up in different eras, the participants differed in more than just age. They experienced life from a different viewpoint, and may have had different opportunities for education and health care. Any of these factors (or countless others) could affect mental abilities; age might be important but it might also be irrelevant.

Cohort Effects—Differences across age groups having to do with characteristics of the era in which a person grew up rather than to age effects specifically.

Differences between groups that result from participants having had quite different life experiences are called **cohort effects**. A cohort is a population whose members have some specific characteristic in common, like a birth cohort, a group of people born about the same time. A cohort doesn't have to rely on age; studying psychology majors as compared to other majors will also involve cohorts.

Once researchers accepted the notion of studying the same people over time, investigators often used two-point studies, with researchers observing their participants twice. Such studies were useful, but they were not perfect. One of the problems with two-point studies is statistical regression, sometimes called regression to the mean. It refers to the fact that when people are measured and show extreme scores, they often have less extreme scores the next time. In many cases, the extreme scores included a large amount of measurement error that is unlikely to occur in subsequent measurements. So when changes in scores occur, the result might be meaningless in a developmental sense.

Further, some variables that researchers measure show different results in cross-sectional and longitudinal studies, with longitudinal studies sometimes failing to replicate cross-sectional studies and sometimes showing greater differences (Schaie, 1992).

The methodological innovation that has allowed greater understanding of the developmental process is the longitudinal approach. Once psychologists recognized the realities of cohort effects, they began to study the same individuals across time. This strategy removes some of the difficulties associated with cross-sectional research.

VARIETIES OF LONGITUDINAL RESEARCH

Researchers generally categorize longitudinal research according to the way participants are selected for a study. In some longitudinal research, the measurements at each time interval involve the same people. In other designs, the measurements include different people across time. Psychological research is more likely to include the same people in each observation frame. Other research may sample from a population without concerns as to whether the same individuals are included. Such studies often involve large, perhaps national, samples.

Another way to categorize psychological studies may involve questionnaires or direct observation of behaviors and frequently involve panel studies, which are described below. Sociologists and medical researchers are often more likely to make use of trend and cohort studies, which are often much larger in scope than those done by psychologists who have direct contact with participants.

Trend Studies

Trend Studies—A variety of longitudinal research in which an investigator samples randomly from a generally defined population over time, with different individuals constituting each sample.

When investigators assess a general population across time, they sometimes sample randomly at each data-collection point. Depending on the nature of the study, this approach can result in a completely different sample each time. This total replacement of participants is characteristic of **trend studies**.

One example of a trend study involves the prevalence of suicidal thoughts in young people. Late adolescence and young adulthood seem like precarious times for youth in the United States. One manifestation of the problem is suicides on college campuses. Such tragedies are in the news all too frequently.

One report noted that six students at New York University had committed suicide within a one-year period (Caruso, 2004). For more on suicide, visit http://www.suicide.org/joann-mitchell-levy-nyu-suicides.html. In other well-publicized news, three Massachusetts students (at MIT, Harvard, and the University of Massachusetts at Amherst) died during a single week in 1998 amid suspicion that the deaths were suicides, according to a story in the *Christian Science Monitor* (April 7, 1998). MIT and Harvard lead the nation in student suicides, as noted in the University of Illinois's Daily *Illini* (February 14, 2001). As of several years ago, Penn State suffered an average of two student suicides a year, according to its online student newspaper, *The Digital Collegian* (July 24, 1997). When such deaths occur, college administrators and faculty ponder what they can do to keep students from feeling the despair that leads them to take their lives.

How to establish programs for prevention is not an easy task because the incidence of suicide attempts differs across groups. For instance, among American Indians, about 20 percent of deaths among adolescents aged 15–19 are due to suicide, whereas it is significantly lower among Asian Americans (Goldston et al., 2008). And just as the incidence of suicide attempts differs across ethnic groups, as you can see in Figure 13.1, so do the factors associated with vulnerability to or protection from suicide.

The effects of culture are not surprising, given that other researchers have documented different patterns in a wide variety of European countries (da Veiga & Saraiva, 2003). For these countries, the patterns over time tend to be stable, suggesting that the structure of the cultures may be responsible.

Any suicide is a calamity for the friends and family of the victim, but we don't know whether suicide rates are going up or down, or staying the same. Colleges only began keeping track of suicides in 1990. Ironically, given the media attention when suicides occur on campuses, the suicide rate among students is half the rate of others the same age. Over the past decades, suicides among the young have increased dramatically, though.

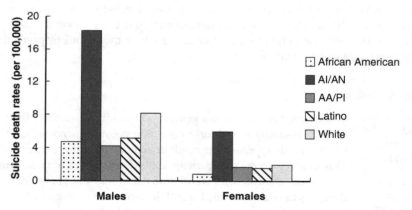

FIGURE 13.1   Incidence of suicide deaths in different ethnic groups in the United States.
Source: Goldston et al. (2008). Copyright American Psychological Association. Reprinted with permission.

We can figure the suicide rate among students, but how many students actually think about suicide? Fortunately, researchers in Vermont, in an attempt to anticipate and prevent problems in that state, have collected data from middle- and high-school students over time that may shed light on the question. This data set can form a trend study sampled from the state's population of high-school students every two years since the mid-1990s.

The percentage of students who have had suicidal ideation (i.e., thoughts of suicide) in the 12 months prior to the survey was alarmingly high, 28 percent, in 1995; furthermore, among girls, 30 percent seriously thought of suicide in 1997. Figure 13.2 shows the extent to which students made plans, attempted suicide, and required medical attention. Fortunately, even though a large percentage of students thought about suicide, many fewer youths made plans or attempted suicide (Vermont Youth Risk Behavior Survey: Statewide Report, 1995, 1997, 1999, 2001, 2003, 2005, 2009) and the incidence has declined since 1995.

The results of this trend study suggested that we cannot ignore the problems of the young. In fact, David Satcher, former Surgeon General of the United States, has declared that suicide is a public health crisis. College officials have begun to pay significant attention to ways of preventing student deaths.

Another type of trend study might, in repeated assessments, include some of the same participants. If we were interested in the extent to which 8th-grade teachers include novels in their reading assignments, we could sample from that population of teachers periodically. Some teachers might appear in both samples. As long as the sample is large, though, the instances of such overlap will be minimal. In any case, if the sampling is random, we will likely generate a representative sample each time, regardless of the degree of overlap among participants.

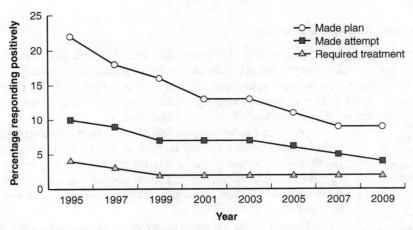

FIGURE 13.2 Incidence of suicide ideation and attempts among students in Vermont. Thoughts of suicide occurred to up to 25 percent of students, while decreasing numbers actually made a plan, attempted suicide, and required medical attention after an attempt.

Note: Made plan = Actually made a plan to commit suicide; Attempted = Carried out a suicide attempt; Medical = Carried out an attempt that required medical intervention.

Trend studies typically involve applied research. They may be associated with long-term changes associated with critical societal issues, like suicide.

Cohort Studies

Cohort Study—A variety of longitudinal research in which an investigator samples randomly from a population selected because of a specific characteristic, often age.

When researchers study a specific, well-defined population over time but sample different people at each data-collection point, they are using a **cohort study**. (Trend studies examine more general populations.)

One of the most well-known cohort studies is the Nurses Health Study, which began in 1976. It involves about 122,000 nurses from the original cohort, followed by a new generation of nurses in 1989. (This research design is known in the medical field as an observational epidemiology study.) The project began in order to study the long-term effects of using oral contraceptives. Every two years, cohort members receive a survey with questions about health-related topics. At the request of the participants, the investigators began adding questions on a variety of topics, like smoking, nutrition, and quality of life issues. The researchers even collected toenail clippings so they could identify minerals in food that the participants ate.

Psychologists do not use trend studies or cohort studies very extensively. These approaches are more within the province of medical research. Psychologists can benefit from the data, though. It is not unusual for researchers to make their large data sets available to others. Thus, when there is a large database that extends across years or decades, psychologists can identify questions of interest and see how respondents have answered. For instance, the Nurses Health Study includes quality of life information that might help us answer behavioral and attitudinal questions.

Cohort Sequential Studies

If you wanted to compare people of different ages, you could use a cross-sectional design wherein you select samples of such individuals and investigate differences that might exist between them. The problem in interpretation, as mentioned before, is that the people have different life experiences because of the particular environment in which they grew up. You may not be able to attribute differences to age alone.

Cohort Sequential Design—A variety of longitudinal research in which an investigator repeatedly measures a cohort group (e.g., people 60 years of age) over time, adding a new cohort (e.g., new 60-year-olds) in each wave in order to differentiate between cohort effects and age effects.

One solution to this problem is the **cohort sequential design**. This technique involves measuring samples of people at a selected age and testing them on a regular basis. In this approach, you study people of a given age, for example, 60 years old, then study them at some later point, like when they are 67. During the second test, you could also investigate a new group of 60-year-olds.

This gives you the opportunity to test 60-year-olds from slightly different eras to see if there is something special about being 60. You can also see how people change over time. The cohort sequential design mixes the cross-sectional approach with the longitudinal. The strength of the cohort sequential design is that it can help you spot changes due to age as well as to differences in the environment in which people develop.

A classic example of this research began in the 1950s by Warner Schaie. He selected a group of elderly people and tested them on their cognitive ability every seven years. At the second testing phase, he assessed the original group but also included a new group of people that he tested every seven years. This second group was as old when tested as the first group was at its initial testing. Then, at the third testing phase, he included a new group that was as old as his first group at their initial testing. So he started with a group of 60-year-olds. Seven years later, he tested these people who were now 67 and began assessment of a new group of 60-year-olds. After another seven years, he brought in a new group of 60-year-olds to compare with the second group, now aged 67, and the first group, now aged 74.

Over four decades, he tested different groups at the same age in their lives but who grew up in different times. He was able to spot changes in their behavior as they aged and was also able to look for differences that might be attributable to cohort effects.

People performed very differently depending on when they were born. Earlier birth dates were associated with poorer performance for the same age. When people born in 1896 were tested at age 60, their performance was clearly lower than the cohorts from all other birth years when those cohorts were tested at age 60. In fact, with each successive cohort, performance at age 60 was higher than that of the previous cohort.

Thus, there is nothing special about the absolute test scores at age 60 (or at any other age); it is more reasonable to believe that having been born later led to different experiences, perhaps involving education, nutrition, health care, etc. that would be important in development and maintenance of their cognitive skill.

Bray, Adams, Getz, and Baer (2001) used this design to study alcohol use in children over a three-year period. In the first year, one cohort was in the 6th grade, the second cohort was in the 7th grade, and the third cohort was in the 8th grade. In the second year, the previous 6th graders were now in the 7th grade, so their alcohol use could be compared with that of the children who had been in the 7th grade the year before (and who were now in the 8th grade). In the third year, the original 6th graders were in the 8th grade, so their drinking could be compared to those children who were in the 8th grade in the first year of the study. Their results appear in Figure 13.3. Although the research lasted three years, the investigators ended up with data on children as young as 6th grade and as old as 10th grade, a five-year span. You can see the similarities in patterns of data for the different cohorts.

Other researchers have also used this approach to study alcohol use in children. For example, Duncan, Duncan, and Strycker (2005) have studied alcohol use even in younger children (i.e., 4th graders). Some children that young had already begun drinking.

Panel Studies

Panel Study—A variety of longitudinal research in which an investigator studies the same individuals over time.

Another general category of longitudinal studies is the **panel study**. In this design, the same participants are followed throughout the course of the study. The most famous study of people throughout their lifespan was initiated by Lewis Terman in the 1920s. When he began, he didn't suspect that it would become a lifelong enterprise for him. At his death in 1956, the research was still going strong. In fact, his successors have kept it alive into its ninth decade.

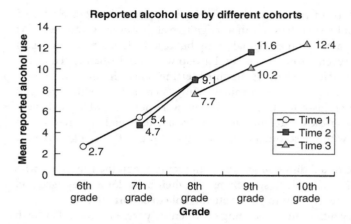

FIGURE 13.3   Example of a cohort-sequential analysis of alcohol use by children. The researchers studied children for the same three-year period. One cohort was in the 6th grade at the start of the research, the second cohort was in the 7th grade, and the third cohort was in the 8th grade. The results reflect an increase in alcohol use as the children get older, with similar but not identical patterns across the three years.

Source: Bray, J. H., Adams, G. J., Getz, J. G., and Baer, P. E. (2001). Developmental, family, and ethnic influences on adolescent alcohol usage: A growth curve approach. *Journal of Family Psychology*, 15, 301–314. Copyright 2001 by the American Psychological Association. Adapted with permission.

Terman was born in Indiana in 1877 but moved to Los Angeles after contracting tuberculosis. (Ironically, the relocation was for the clean air that he could expect in Los Angeles at that time.) While teaching there, he identified 1,528 children with IQ scores over 135 and compared them to a comparable group of unselected children, a typical cross-sectional approach. Many writers have detailed the research (e.g., Holahan & Sears, 1995) but, in essence, the gifted children and adolescents matured into adults who tended to be happy, healthy, successful, and productive.

A more typical (i.e., shorter) example of a longitudinal study involved a project that studied a group of Chinese immigrant children in the United States who acted as so-called *language brokers*, that is, who acted as translators for their parents who did not speak English very well or at all (Wu & Kim, 2009). The investigators wanted to know whether the children found translating for parents a positive experience or a burden. They administered questionnaires to the children at two points four years apart. Not surprisingly, the results were complicated, but Wu and Kim found that when the adolescent children were more Chinese in their cultural orientation, they were more positive about their language brokering; in contrast, when they were more Westernized in their cultural orientation, they felt that language brokering was a burden. In addition, the children's attitudes toward mothers and fathers differed in the second testing, partially as a function of cultural orientation and relationship with the mother at the first time of testing. By knowing about the children's attitudes early in the study, the researchers were better able to understand the changing dynamics of the adolescents' relationships with their parents in this regard.

CONTROVERSY:
On Student Achievement

Are students getting proficient than they were in previous generations? Each generation of parents seems to be worried that their children are not learning as much in school as they did when they were students. It doesn't matter that the parents of the current group of parents had the same worry, as did each previous generation before them. It is an empirical question as to whether current students are less capable than previous students; that is, we can use data to answer the question.

The National Assessment of Educational Progress (NAEP) project is an example of a trend study. Since 1971, students at grades 4, 8, and 12 have been tested in a variety of subject areas, such as reading, mathematics, and science. The results are often called the "nation's report card."

In Figure 13.4, you can see how 4th and 8th graders have changed over the past two decades in math. As you can see, the news is pretty good—performance has gone up on average for the two groups. In fact,

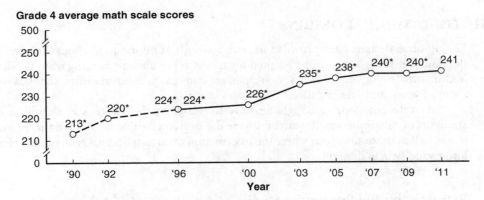

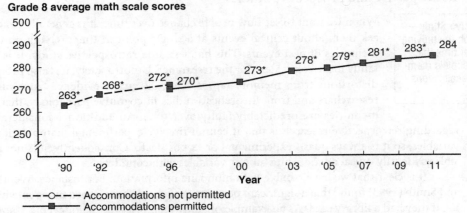

FIGURE 13.4 Changes in math scores of students in grades 4 and 8 on the National Assessment of Educational Progress between 1990 and 2011.

Source: National Assessment of Educational Progress: Findings in Brief—Reading and Mathematics 2011 (2011).

since 1973, math scores have increased fairly consistently (Rampey, Dion, & Donahue, 2009). In reading, students in grade 8 have shown an improvement, but not those in grade 4. But at least the 4th graders have held steady and even risen a little, although the change was not significant.

At each NAEP testing, there will be a different set of students because when the test is administered every two or three years, the students in the 12th grade will have changed. The samples used in NAEP can be considered to involve different cohorts in one sense because the actual participants differ each time, but they involve the same cohort in the sense that they sample 12th graders each time. (The unfortunate student who is in the 12th grade for three years and is selected to participate in two tests is rare and unlikely to be sampled more than once.)

What do these numbers say about the current generation of students? Should we believe the comments people make about how deficient students are today? The answer is that, although the situation in some schools, some neighborhoods, and some states is in dire need of remedy, the picture is not all that bleak. There is certainly room for improvement, but it appears that we are no worse off now than we were in the 1970s.

ISSUES IN LONGITUDINAL DESIGNS

Longitudinal designs have provided us with a wealth of information about the ways we develop over time. They can be adapted for use with populations ranging from neonates and infants to the very old. If you are patient enough, you can monitor changes over months, years, and even decades.

As with any design, though, we have to recognize the weaknesses as well as the strengths of this approach. Researchers have discovered effective uses of long-term studies, as well as those situations where the information from longitudinal research may have lower validity than desirable.

Retrospective and Prospective Studies

Retrospective Study—
An approach to studying change over time that relies on people's memories and recollections of the past.

When we want to see how people change over time, it is generally easier to ask them about critical events at a single point in time, relying on their memories of past events. This happens in a **retrospective study**. It is certainly more convenient for the researcher. Unfortunately, it is also prone to distortions from memory lapses. There is ample evidence from survey researchers and from theoretical studies in cognitive psychology, that our memories are predictably faulty over time. An additional consideration regarding retrospective research is that it cannot involve experimental manipulation of variables, so it is always quasi- experimental or ex post facto. Consequently, it is not possible to identify causal relationships among variables with confidence.

It is clear that we have trouble with mundane information. For instance, Wentland and Smith (1993) found that a significant percentage of people have a hard time remembering if they had a library card. As an example of faulty memories for major events, Cannell, Fisher, and Bakker (1965, cited in Judd, Smith, & Kidder, 1991) demonstrated that people erred in determining how many times they had been hospitalized in the past year.

We are also likely to reconstruct details of the past, in effect creating memories that fit the overall structure of what we are trying to recall. We don't do this intentionally, but it happens just the same. In longitudinal research, we shouldn't expect people to show high levels of mnemonic accuracy for remote events, even for significant events. This is particularly true when we ask children about their behavior. Furthermore, asking their parents does not lead to greater accuracy.

Prospective Study—An approach to studying change over time that identifies research participants at the beginning of the project who are followed throughout the course of the research.

The alternative to a retrospective study is a **prospective study**. In this approach, researchers identify the participants they want to observe and follow them forward in time. Sometimes this is relatively easy, as in Bond et al.'s (2001) study of bullying behavior. They identified their population, created a sample, and questioned them while the events of interest were likely to be fresh in memory.

Other prospective studies rely on some event whose impact the researchers want to assess. Researchers sometimes initiate research when something of interest happens in society. For instance, Hurricane Andrew hit Florida in 1992, causing massive damage and suffering. A team of psychologists used that event to study the course of posttraumatic stress in children.

La Greca, Silverman, Vernberg, and Prinstein (1996) studied 442 elementary-school children after the hurricane. The investigators administered the Posttraumatic Stress Disorder Reaction Index for Children (RI), the Hurricane-Related Traumatic Experiences (HURTE) measure, the Social Support Scale for Children (SSSC), the Kidcope survey, and the Life Event Schedule (LES). Measurements were obtained three, seven, and 10 months after the hurricane. They found that 12 percent of the children experienced severe to very severe levels of posttraumatic stress disorder (PTSD) at 10 months.

You can see that it would be nearly impossible to obtain valid data with a retrospective study of the effects of the hurricane. You can't go back in time to administer the RI (or any of the other scales). It is also unreasonable to think that the children could reconstruct their reactions from seven or 10 months previously. In order to know how feelings and emotions change over time, the only viable approach is prospective.

As in the latter example, the decision to use a prospective or a retrospective design is sometimes not under the control of the researcher. Prospective research is possible when the investigators identify a question and have a group that they can follow into the future. Retrospective research is called for when the answer to a research question lies, at least in part, in what has already happened.

Attrition

The single largest methodological concern in longitudinal studies is the fact that some people will stop participating. In and of itself, the loss of data reduces the amount of information that you have for drawing conclusions, but if your sample is sufficiently large to begin with, the loss of a small amount of data may not be problematic. The study of bullying by Bond et al. (2001) began with 2,680 students, but by the end of their data collection, only 2,365 remained. Still, that is a significant sample; the loss of over 300 participants is notable but may not affect the power of statistical analysis.

The biggest issue associated with this loss of participants, known as attrition, is that you don't always know whether those who disappear differ from those who remain. (If this phenomenon sounds familiar, it is because you encountered it in the context of experimental research, where it is sometimes called subject or participant mortality.) Bond et al. (2001) reported that the attrition rate in their bullying study was higher for boys than for girls. They also noted in their results that boys showed a lower incidence of depression associated with bullying in boys. Could it be that a significant proportion of the boys who left the study experienced depression from bullying?

Further, attrition was greater for students with single-parent families. Is it possible, or even likely, that students in such circumstances are more susceptible to depression? Without being able to ask them, we don't know. Thus, the conclusion by the researchers that boys experience less depression may have been biased to reflect the remaining participants, who could very well differ from those who departed.

Sometimes it is hard to anticipate whether attrition will affect outcomes, but the concern is real. For example, McCoy et al. (2009) reported that in a year-long study of alcohol use among college freshmen, the students who dropped out of the study were systematically different from those who remained. The students who left the study reported heavier drinking, more drunkenness, getting into a greater number of fights, and higher levels of smoking than those who participated in the study to the end. Previous work revealed that heavier drinkers had lower high school GPAs, which may also be related to the research findings (Paschall & Freisthler, 2003).

The nature of the samples is extremely important in this kind of research because of the different patterns of alcohol use by students of different ethnicity and race. For example, Paschall, Bersamin, and Flewelling (2005) reported that White students showed a much higher incidence of heavy drinking (44.9 percent of those responding) than did Hispanic students (30.0 percent), Asian students (22.4 percent), and Black students (under 14.1 percent). The incidence of attrition is also of interest; in the Paschall et al. study, the attrition rate was higher among Black students than for other groups and that nondrinkers were more likely to leave the study than were drinkers.

In a study of nonstudents, Hayslip, McCoy-Roberts, and Pavur (1998–1999) investigated in a three-year study how well adults cope after the death of a loved one. They reported, first of all, that attrition at six months was associated with an active decision by the respondent to leave the study whereas at three years, the researchers had simply lost track of the individuals, some of whom might have participated if found.

The investigators also discovered that attrition did not seem to affect the nature of the results of their research on the effects of the death of a spouse. The results and conclusions would have been pretty much the same whether or not those who left had been included.

On the other hand, Hayslip et al. (1998–1999) noted that those who had suffered a nonconjugal loss (i.e., somebody other than a husband or wife) and who dropped out were younger, less active in their coping, were in better health, and were less lonely at the beginning of the study. The researchers pointed out poorer psychological recovery after the death of a spouse or other loved one is associated with younger age, poorer health, and more loneliness. Given that nonconjugal dropouts were younger, they might be expected to show poorer outcomes. Their attrition might affect conclusions greatly because those remaining in the sample were the types of people you would expect to do well. Thus, typical outcomes would appear rosier because of those who had left and were not included in the data.

Dropouts were also in better health and less lonely, factors associated with better psychological outcomes. If your study experienced attrition by those who were healthy and not lonely, you would lose people who typically recover well. As a result, your sample would look bleak, not because people can't recover from bereavement, but because the people who agree to be studied are likely to have worse outcomes than those who leave.

Hayslip et al. (1998–1999) concluded that we need to be very sensitive to the nature of those who leave longitudinal projects. There is a realistic chance that dropouts lead to biased results, therefore less valid conclusions. Given the potential importance of attrition, it is common for researchers to report the degree of attrition in their reports. This information can help readers gain a sense of how confident they should be in the results. The reality of longitudinal research is that you can count on losing people. An important question is whether those who leave a study differ in relevant ways from those who remain.

When La Greca and her colleagues (1996) studied students over 10 months who suffered through Hurricane Andrew, they recorded the dropouts, documented the reasons for the attrition, and formally compared participants and nonparticipants. Figure 13.5 displays the percentage of the initial 568 students in the Hurricane Andrew study who departed and the general reason for having done so. As you can see, over 8 percent had departed by seven months and a total of about 22 percent by 10 months. These attrition figures are not unusual for such research.

Fortunately, La Greca et al. discovered that those who dropped out did not differ from those who remained in terms of grade, gender, ethnicity, or initial symptoms of

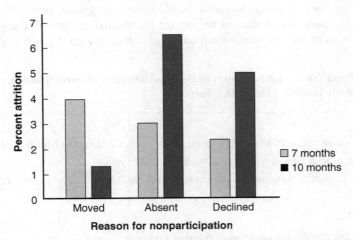

FIGURE 13.5 Reason for nonparticipation in the Hurricane Andrew study of posttraumatic stress disorder (PTSD). The researchers documented the reasons for nonparticipation and compared those who left the study with those who remained. Of the initial 568 elementary-school students, just over 22 percent dropped out of the study for reasons that were sometimes clear (e.g., they had moved) or vague (e.g., they simply declined). Those who participated did not differ from those who dropped out.

Sources: La Greca et al. (1996). Copyright American Psychological Association. Reprinted with permission.

PTSD. It is likely that the students who participated throughout the study were representative of the entire set of 568 who began the project.

Even though the research by Le Greca et al. did not seem affected by attrition, it remains a serious issue. In a study of attrition during treatment after Hurricane Katrina in 2005, Wang et al. (2007) found that 49 percent of those who had serious mental health issues dropped out of treatment. The risk factors for attrition included being of minority ethnicity and never having been married. If these patterns hold for research, the representativeness of a final sample might be questionable.

We have found ways to reduce the attrition rates, although they are not without cost. The tactics involve a commitment of time and expense on the researcher's part.

For example, Wutzke, Conigrave, Kogler, Saunders, and Hall (2000) studied a group of 554 Australians who engaged in heavy drinking. The project extended for 10 years, a period of time that generally leads to notable attrition among highly educated and cooperative participants, and extremely high levels among people with substance abuse problems. At the end of their 10 years, Wutzke et al. randomly sampled and reviewed 20 percent ($n = 109$) of the records to see how well contact had been maintained. Surprisingly, 72.5 percent of the 109 people had been successfully located for the study; over 78 percent of the total group of 554 had been located.

The researchers had prepared well and worked diligently throughout the study to keep in touch with the participants. They enhanced their success by taking a number of steps as they initiated their project and as they conducted it. Table 13.1 presents their strategies to avoid losing track of people and maintaining the participants' motivation to continue in the project. Some of these steps are seemingly obvious, like getting participants' full names and people related to them; others are less obvious, like maintaining participants' motivation by sending birthday cards. As obvious as they might be, researchers have not always carried them out. These steps are very relevant for studies of a large and heterogeneous population.

TABLE 13.1   Steps Taken By Researchers to Decrease Attrition of Participants in a Longitudinal Study Involving Heavy Drinkers

---

Preparation

- Ensuring that dates of birth and middle names were collected (to make later tracing easier)
- Identifying a contact person who lived at a different address
- Maintaining contact throughout the project with such mailings as birthday cards or regular newsletters

Persistence

- Beginning a trace of the person as soon as contact is lost
- Making multiple phone calls to set up appointments for interviews
- Showing willingness to conduct interviews at times and locations convenient for the respondent
- Providing incentives to offset the inconvenience of participation

---

Source: Wutzke et al. (2000).

Finally, when you are studying older people, an additional reason for attrition is likely, namely, the death of the participant. In the study begun by Terman in 1921, there has been considerable attrition, as you might expect. However, in the 35th year of the study (1955), over 88 percent of the women and over 87 percent of the men remained in the project.

When Terman died in 1956, the attrition rate increased, possibly because the participants had felt a very strong personal connection with him. Between 1955 and 1960, the number who actively declined to participate exceeded the total attrition since 1921 (Holahan & Sears, 1995). Since 1972, attrition has been more likely due to death than to a choice to drop out. Remarkably, only 8 percent of the women and 6 percent of the men have been "lost," the researchers' term for loss of contact because they can't find the person.

It is ironic that the exceedingly low attrition in the Terman study is fairly unimportant in some ways. The sample he chose in 1921 wasn't representative either of the population generally or of gifted children specifically. As a result, we don't know exactly to whom we can generalize the results of the research.

SINGLE-SUBJECT EXPERIMENTATION

In the past century, psychologists have developed the tradition of conducting studies with groups of participants, ignoring the behavior of single individuals. As a discipline, psychology was not always oriented toward this approach. In the early years of psychology, researchers often studied a single person intensively.

Experimentalists and clinicians shared this methodology. Freud used single-participant studies in his clinical work, as did John Watson (e.g., Little Albert) in his research on learning. Then in the early decades of the twentieth century, experimental psychologists gravitated toward the study of groups. Single-subject experimental research did not return until the middle of the century. When it was resurrected, researchers often conducted long-term studies of single subjects, often rats and pigeons. The research reports were largely devoid of statistical analysis; visual displays of data replaced statistics. The behaviorists who resurrected single-subject research believed that enough data over many experimental trials would reveal important patterns of behavior, so statistical treatment wasn't necessary. Today, single-subject studies with people tend to involve those with psychological problems.

Experimental Analysis of Behavior

The experimental analysis of behavior reflects a unique tradition in research. It arose from the behaviorist tradition and had significant focus on the study of reinforcement contingencies. Because one of the major tenets of behaviorism was that we can discover general principles and laws of behavior, researchers believed that studies with large numbers of subjects were not only unnecessary, but also undesirable. By using many subjects and averaging the data on their performance, the behaviorists thought that we would lose sight of critical individual details.

Consequently, the tradition of using one or a few subjects emerged. Psychologists who engage in the experimental analysis of behavior often still rely on single subjects or perhaps small groups and may rely on visual presentation of results rather than on complex statistical analysis. These researchers are not immune to psychological culture, though, so even these psychologists have altered their traditions somewhat, using some statistical analysis to help them understand their research results.

Within the realm of experimental analysis of behavior, two distinct paths have developed. Some experimenters rely on studies of animal behavior; their work is largely theoretical. When researchers use experimental analysis of behavior with people, their projects sometimes focus on theory, but sometimes the projects involve applications. Their investigations often involve people in clinical settings and tend to be less theoretical, although clearly based on behavioral theory. The experimental analysis of behavior is likely to be highly objective and quantitative.

METHODS OF SINGLE-CASE DESIGNS

Studies with single individuals, whether human or nonhuman, do not differ in concept from many of the other approaches we have already covered. The biggest difference involves the number of people or animals tested, not necessarily the methodology. In fact, this difference in the number of participants is not necessary; single-case research can involve multiple cases. The researchers are likely to report on them individually, though. Case studies can involve controlled observations, like experiments. They can also rely on questionnaires and naturalistic observation.

Another difference between single-case analyses and group analyses is that single-case research involves continuous monitoring of behavior over time. In this sense it resembles time-series or longitudinal designs more than the typical cross-sectional design.

Withdrawal Designs

Withdrawal Design— A research method in which an investigator observes a baseline of behavior, applies a treatment, and assesses any behavioral change, then removes or withdraws the treatment to see the degree to which the behavior reverts to baseline levels.

ABA Design—A type of withdrawal design in which a treatment is applied only once, then withdrawn.

Single-case research can take many different forms. The general process involves assessing the behavior or behaviors of interest to monitor the baseline rate of the behaviors. Then a treatment begins. After that, different designs lead to different steps.

One design, the **withdrawal design**, entails a baseline phase, a treatment phase, then a return to a baseline phase. It is represented as an **ABA design** because researchers refer to the baseline period with the letter A and the treatment with the letter B. If treatment is effective, a simple withdrawal design should document that there is movement toward the desired outcome during the treatment phase. In medical or psychiatric research that assesses whether a drug stabilizes a person's condition, a return of the symptoms to the original level when the treatment is withdrawn may be entirely predictable, even desirable for assessing the effectiveness of a treatment. This design is most useful when researchers expect that after a treatment is removed, the original pattern of behavior will recur. In such a case, the ABA design permits the researchers to identify cause and effect relationships.

A return to baseline in such a medical study would indicate that the medication is working as it should. If the condition did not return to baseline levels when the medication was removed, the investigator might not be sure that the medication made a difference. Some alternate explanation might be better.

In much psychological research, it isn't clear what will happen in the second base-line phase. After a behavioral treatment phase ends, we hope that the desired behavior change is going to persist. So in the second baseline phase, we hope there isn't a return to the first level. In some cases, though, research has shown that people's fear responses may return when the person is exposed to the fear-producing context and even to new contexts (Neumann & Kitlertsirivatana, 2010).

> **ABAB Design**—A type of withdrawal design that uses a baseline period followed by application of a treatment, the withdrawal of the treatment (as in an ABA design), and reapplication of the treatment.

In order to strengthen the internal validity of single-case research, investigators sometimes withdraw a treatment to see if a person's condition worsens, then they introduce a second baseline phase, followed by a reintroduction of the treatment, creating an **ABAB design**.

The basic ABAB design has many variations. Sometimes researchers want to assess different treatments, so after baseline phases, they introduce different treatments. If there are two different treatments, we represent the design as AB_1AB_2.

Single-Subject Randomized Controlled Trials

In medical or clinical research, large-scale studies may not be feasible. When an investigator wants to assess treatment with a single person, one option is the *N* **of 1 Randomized Clinical Trial (RCT)**. In this approach, the researcher studies the effect of treatment on a single individual by exposing the individual to a treatment and a placebo in random order over time (e.g., ABBABAABBAB). Both the clinician and the patient are blind as to the treatment at any given time. Because neither the clinician nor the patient is aware of whether a treatment or a placebo phase is underway, there won't be any experimenter effects or demand characteristics. Any changes in the patient are likely to be due to the effectiveness of the treatment rather than to some extraneous variable.

> *N* **of 1 Randomized Clinical Trial**—A research design involving the study of a single person over multiple trials, with trials involving application of the treatment and trials with no application of the treatment occurring in random order.

This approach makes sense only when several criteria are met. First, the patient's problem must be chronic but relatively stable. If the symptoms are too variable or time-limited, it is difficult to attribute any changes to the treatment. Second, the treatment (usually a drug in this kind of study) should have a rapid effect and also a rapid cessation of effect. This criterion is important because the researcher doesn't want to have carryover effects that can interfere with conclusions about the effectiveness of the different approaches. Finally, there needs to be a clear and objective outcome that can be measured reliably (Cook, 1996).

Strengths of Single-Participant Designs

Just like any other method of research, single-case studies help fill in the gap in our knowledge of behavior. These approaches have some notable strengths. First, one of the most pronounced advantages is the amount of detail reported about a person. Entire books can be (and have been) written about exceptional people.

These designs are time and labor intensive; you can easily see why an investigator might limit the research to a single person. The amount of detail to sort through would be overwhelming if the researcher studied many people. The researcher would also have a harder time sorting out the relevant detail from the irrelevant if multiple people were involved.

Second, case studies and single-case experiments are also useful when we want to investigate rare phenomena. Researchers may not be able to locate a large group of individuals if the phenomena of interest seldom occur.

A third strength of single-case studies relates to creating and evaluating research hypotheses. We can use the results of single-participant studies to generate hypotheses that can be tested with larger numbers of people. Single-case studies can also test hypotheses based on existing theory.

A further advantage of single-case studies is that they provide help in developing and assessing therapeutic or intervention techniques. The causes of psychological difficulties in clients and patients may be unique to each person. As a result, using large numbers of research participants may actually obscure the effectiveness of a therapeutic technique that might be helpful for a particular person.

Whenever we want to know about behaviors that are particular to a single person, single-case designs can be highly beneficial. In addition to the realm of clinical psychology, single-case research can be important in areas like sports psychology (Hrycaiko & Martin, 1999). In clinical psychology, the aim is to improve a person's psychological state; in sports psychology, the goal is to enhance performance. In both cases, there are likely to be individual characteristics that are critical to change; group research would probably not be optimal in either field.

Weaknesses of Single-Participant Designs

Probably the biggest limitation of single-subject studies involves the question of external validity. In one sense, they have a high degree of external validity; case studies typically do not use controlled, laboratory manipulations as experiments do. There is generally nothing artificial about them. Thus, the studies tell us about a person in his or her natural environment.

Another component of external validity is relevant here, though. We cannot be sure that conclusions based on a single person will generalize to anybody else. In fact, because this research often involves rare phenomena, it is not clear that there are many others to whom we would be able to generalize. The results might pertain to only one person.

In addition to questions of external validity, we are also faced with potential problems with internal validity. Causal conclusions about the person's behaviors are risky if there is no controlled manipulation of variables in the research.

Misunderstandings about Single-Case Research

Single-case research is fairly rare in psychological and psychiatric research. There are several possible reasons.

First, the tradition in psychology is cross-sectional research involving comparisons between groups. Most training in graduate programs therefore focuses on research with groups rather than with individuals. For many researchers, single-case studies don't look like normal, psychological research, and the psychologists may not be well versed in the details of single-case approaches.

Second, researchers may confuse the relative subjectivity of some case-study approaches and the relative objectivity of single-subject experiments that are highly controlled. Furthermore, most psychologists and other researchers have little training in qualitative approaches. A qualitative study can provide a lot of information about behavior, but it is likely to be different information from that produced in a quantitative study. In other words, psychologists like research involving numbers and quantitative analysis.

Third, some researchers believe that the levels of internal and external validity are low in single-participant research. There is some truth to this claim, but the same can be said for cross-sectional designs. Most behavioral research involves convenience samples, so concerns about generalizability (i.e., external validity) exist for all types of data collection. Further, given that much experimentation occurs in laboratories, the question of external validity arises again. The issue of internal validity may be notable in case studies, but is less relevant for N of 1 RCT studies. Experiments with a single case may have levels of internal validity that are as high as in cross-sectional research.

Fourth, some researchers claim that the data analysis in single-case research is too subjective. It is true that there will be some subjectivity when an investigator works with subjective phenomena, like emotional states. But this is no different than with cross-sectional research. For researchers interested in the experimental analysis of behavior, they may avoid statistical analyses, but when the data are objective and when objective criteria for drawing conclusions are set ahead of time, data analysis is simply different, not necessarily less valid.

CASE STUDIES

Case studies are investigations that focus on a single individual (occasionally a few people) in great detail. Historically, case studies did not include controlled observations, and took place in the context of psychotherapy (Kazdin, 1998). In contemporary applications, though, investigators make use of interventions and control (e.g., Cytowic, 1993; Mills, Boteler, & Oliver, 1999).

This approach to research is often seen as having more problems than other techniques. In fact, even though a new journal has appeared that deals only with case studies, some journals do not accept them as research papers. In other journals, case studies are for teaching purposes rather than research questions (Gawrylewski, 2007a). Questions of causation, generalizability, and interpretation biases are among the most notable concerns. In addition, in the psychological and medical literature, case studies play a small role in research.

In case studies, it is hard to see what factors lead to certain behaviors and which are merely correlated with those behaviors. In essence, there is the problem of too many rival hypotheses and no way to see which ones are best. A second caution about case studies concerns whether we can generalize from a particular patient or client to others.

An additional concern about case studies in general is interpretive. That is, what does the information mean? It is possible for researchers to ignore viable explanations for behaviors because those explanations do not fit with their theoretical position. This is not an attempt to deceive. Rather, it is a natural inclination on our part to accept information that supports what we believe and to ignore information that doesn't. The problem is exacerbated by the fact that studies of a single person often rely on clinical judgment and subjectivity that another person may not be able to replicate objectively.

Because of these problems, case studies are fairly rare in the research literature. At the same time, it is easy to see why clinicians use this approach. People with ailments that are interesting (in the research sense) are likely to be rare, at least when they first appear. As a case in point, AIDS was initially a puzzle to the medical community; young, healthy people were contracting unusual, fatal diseases for no apparent reason. Initial research could only involve case studies because there were so few instances.

When the numbers began to grow, preliminary studies showed patterns. Initially, physicians thought that the disease was limited to gay men, which accounts for its initial label, Gay Related Immune Deficiency (GRID). Without continued research with larger numbers of people, it would have been impossible to understand the nature of what was ultimately renamed AIDS. But the initial case studies provided critical clues to the disease.

Within psychology, case studies can give us a lot of compelling information about individual people. The clinical researcher can then try to understand an individual's behavior by fitting a large number of puzzle pieces together. For example, how would you react if somebody told you that he knew that the food being cooked for dinner wasn't done yet because "there aren't enough points on the chicken?" Is this the utterance of a delusional person? What do "points" have to do with how well done a chicken is? You can see how an interesting **case study** shed light on the perceptions of the man for whom flavors had shapes (Cytowic, 1993), shapes that were as real to him as the flavor of chicken is to us.

Case Study—A research design involving the in-depth study of one or a few people, historically with no manipulation of variables, although such manipulations can occur in contemporary designs.

Researchers have estimated that as few as one person in about 100,000 has such experiences, known as synesthesia (Cytowic, 1997), although some have produced higher estimates of one person in 2,000 (Baron-Cohen, Burt, Smith-Laittan, Harrison, & Bolton, 1996). Obviously, if you wanted to study synesthesia, you would have a hard time finding a group to study. Case studies or single-case experiments make the most sense. You can see in the next section how Cytowic used a case study to investigate a synesthete he met.

A CASE STUDY WITH EXPERIMENTAL MANIPULATIONS: TASTING POINTED CHICKENS AND SEEING COLORED NUMBERS

When somebody scratches his or her fingernails on a blackboard, the sound can send shudders down our spines, even though we have not been touched. This effect is an analogue to that of people who experience synesthesia, or the mixing of different sensory modalities. This mixing is so bizarre from our perspectives that descriptions sound like they are coming from delusional people.

Should we believe people who claim that the sound of a pager causes them to see "blinding red jaggers" or that the poison strychnine and angel food cake have the same "pink smell" (Cytowic, 1993, p. 48). Or that the number 257 induces "a swirl that consists of yellowish orange as the dominant color, green as the next most dominant, and lastly there is a small amount of pink" (Mills, Boteler, & Oliver, 1999, p. 183)?

Synesthesia can take many different forms. In the case of the man Cytowic studied, flavors had shapes. The most famous synesthete in the psychological literature experienced shapes and colors when he heard words; for him, a particular tone looked like fireworks tinged with a pink-red hue, an unpleasant taste, and was rough enough to hurt your hand (Luria, 1968).

In another documented case, the synesthete converted visually presented numbers to colors, but also experienced synesthesia to spoken numbers, music, voices, emotions, smells, and foods (Mills et al., 1999). When she saw a written number, she perceived different colors in front of her eyes. For example, a 1 was White, 2 was yellowish orange, 5 was kelly green, and 7 was pink. Each of the single digits had its own, consistent color. Multiple-digit numbers combined colors, with the color associated with the first digit predominating.

Synesthetes respond to the world in ways that are very consistent for them, even if they are strange to us. This is an ideal situation for a case study. Cytowic (1993) met a synesthete, Michael, and spent an extended period studying his perceptions. Cytowic became aware of how special this person was when the synesthete didn't want to serve the chicken he was cooking yet because it was "round," without enough "points." He also reported being able to smell a tree that nobody else could, and it wasn't because their noses were stuffed. He was able to look at a tree and smell it because his brain processed its visual components and sent information to the part of his brain that dealt with smell.

Over the course of two years, Cytowic exposed Michael to different manipulations to see how he reacted. During the development of the case study, Michael reported that quinine, a bitter liquid, felt like polished wood, whereas another liquid had "the springy consistency of a mushroom, almost round,...but I feel bumps and can stick my fingers into little holes in the surface" (Cytowic, 1993, p. 64).

The functioning of the brain is complex in synesthesia, as it is for everything else, but Cytowic used the results of his study with Michael to discover some important elements of the phenomenon. He presented various liquids to see what shapes and colors they generated. He also investigated the effects of amphetamines and alcohol on synesthesia; amphetamines blocked synesthesia, whereas alcohol enhanced it. Cytowic also injected radioactive gas to identify the parts of the brain involved in synesthesia; he found that during synesthesia, there was minimal blood flow to Michael's cortex. At the same time, blood flow to the emotional center of the brain, the limbic system, increased greatly.

Cytowic provided an extended case study of the experiences of the synesthete and wound up with a description not only of Michael's feelings and perceptions but also of patterns of brain activity. Such research is only possible in single-subject research.

SUMMARY

Psychologists have created specialized approaches to research to answer questions about behavior when traditional experiments may not suffice. Developmental psychologists use longitudinal approaches to study how people change over time. Some longitudinal research in psychology has continued for over 80 years. With research like this, the investigators have to contend with considerably different issues than they do in typical, short-term cross-sectional experiments. Psychologists have developed a variety of methods to maximize the validity of the information obtained in these long-range projects.

Longitudinal projects often involve studying the same people over time. For example, Terman's multi-decade study followed a set of people identified in childhood as gifted throughout their lives. Sometimes, researchers investigate groups whose members change over time. The National Assessment of Educational Progress studies 12th graders across time, so there is a new group of students for each phase of the research. Other research follows the same people over time, but also brings new people into the study at regular intervals.

Sometimes researchers study the same individual over time, concentrating on one person (or a few) rather than on a group. Like longitudinal studies, single-case studies involve observing the same person over time, with multiple repeated measures. Depending on the specific research question, investigators might introduce a treatment, then withdraw it, sometimes multiple times. Psychologists are often not well trained in the use of single-case designs, one of the reasons that this approach is relatively rare in psychology.

REVIEW QUESTIONS

Multiple Choice Questions

1. Lewis Terman's study of gifted children that continued to follow them through adulthood and into old age constitutes
    a. multiple baseline research.
    b. cross-sectional research.
    c. trend research.
    d. longitudinal research.
2. A researcher who wants to know if elderly people are more health conscious than younger people could study a group of elderly people and a group of young people to assess any differences. Such an approach would involve
    a. multiple baseline research.
    b. b cohort research.
    c. longitudinal research.
    d. cross-sectional research.
3. To avoid cohort effects, researchers can
    a. conduct cross-sectional studies.
    b. use multiple baseline studies.
    c. make use of panel studies.
    d. conduct retrospective studies.
4. To find out if using night lights affected the development of nearsightedness, a group of researchers asked parents whether their teen-aged children had slept with night lights on as infants. This research illustrates a
    a. retrospective design.
    b. cohort design.
    c. cross-sectional design.
    d. longitudinal design.
5. The single largest methodological concern in longitudinal studies is
    a. cohort effects.
    b. attrition.

    c. trend effects.

    d. retrospective errors.

6. Wutzke et al. (2000) studied ways to reduce attrition in longitudinal research on heavy drinkers. They found that they could reduce attrition by

    a. promising the participants total confidentiality and anonymity in their participation.

    b. increasing internal motivation rather than relying on incentives to the participants.

    c. maintaining a strict policy of participation in order to establish routines for participation.

    d. maintaining contact throughout the project by sending birthday cards or regular newsletters.

7. Studies in the experimental analysis of behavior rely on

    a. case studies.

    b. cohort-sequential studies.

    c. trend studies.

    d. single-subject studies.

8. An ABA design would not be useful in research if

    a. a treatment had a permanent effect.

    b. a researcher expected a high level of attrition.

    c. the research is prospective.

    d. participants form a cohort.

9. Single-subject research that involves a series of measurements of a dependent variable during periods when a treatment is applied and also when the treatment is not given could be classified as

    a. an N of 1 randomized clinical trial.

    b. a multiple baseline design.

    c. a trend study.

    d. a panel study.

10. The most notable weakness of single-subject designs is

    a. they are not useful for generating hypotheses that can be tested with larger groups.

    b. they are not helpful in studying rare phenomena.

    c. the results from such designs may not be generalizable to others.

    d. they are susceptible to cohort effects.

11. The state of Vermont tried to anticipate the degree to which middle- and high-school students contemplated suicide. The state collected data from students in 1993, 1995, and 1997. This approach reflects

    a. a cohort study.

    b. a trend study.

    c. a cross-sectional study.

    d. a retrospective study.

Essay Questions

12. What are the advantages of longitudinal designs and cross-sectional designs?

13. How does a panel study differ from a trend study? What are the advantages of each?

14. In the Bond, Carlin, Thomas, Rubin, and Patton (2001) study on bullying in schools and depression, why could attrition have influenced their results?

15. Why might an ABA design not be appropriate for behavioral (as opposed to drug) treatment for depression?

16. What are the advantages of single-case research?

ANSWERS TO REVIEW QUESTIONS

Answers to Multiple Choice Questions

1. d	5. b	9. a
2. d	6. d	10. c
3. c	7. d	11. b
4. a	8. a	

Answers to Essay Questions

12. What are the advantages of longitudinal designs and cross-sectional designs?

Longitudinal designs permit the study of change in an individual over time, avoiding cohort effects that could confuse change over time in a person with change due to different environments. Cross-sectional designs are quicker to complete, allowing assessment of different populations in a short time period.

13. How does a panel study differ from a trend study? What are the advantages of each?

A panel study typically involves the study of the same people in successive waves of data collection. A trend study involves studying the same population over time, but not necessarily the same people.

The advantages of panel studies include the fact that you are studying the same people, so the nature of the sample doesn't change.

The advantages of trend studies include the fact that you don't have to worry about keeping track of the same people or about attrition because you sample from the population at each measurement.

14. In the Bond, Carlin, Thomas, Rubin, and Patton (2001) study on bullying in schools and depression, why could attrition have influenced their results?

In the Bond et al. study, they found that boys showed less depression as a result of bullying. However, the attrition rate for boys was larger than for girls. This might mean that boys who were affected by the bullying by becoming depressed may have dropped out of the study, whereas boys not so affected did not drop out. It would have distorted the effect of bullying on boys.

Further, there was more attrition for students from single-parent families. Perhaps people in such families are differentially susceptible to depression than are students from two-parent (or other) families.

15. Why might an ABA design not be appropriate for behavioral (as opposed to drug) treatment for depression?

An ABA design presupposes that at the second baseline phase (i.e., the second *A* phase), the individual's behavior will return to the way it was before the treatment. In behavioral treatment for depression, if therapy is successful, the person will not return to his or her original depressed state. Thus, an ABA design will not be appropriate.

16. What are the advantages of single-case research?

The advantages of single-case research are as follows:

a. Single-case research provides a wealth of detail, much more than for a group design, where in-depth information would be too much to evaluate.
b. Single-case research is also good for studying rare phenomena.
c. Single-case research can be used for creating and testing research hypotheses.
d. Single-case research is useful for studying clinical interventions on single people whose specific symptoms are unique.

CHAPTER FOURTEEN

PEOPLE ARE DIFFERENT
Considering Cultural and Individual Differences in Research

CHAPTER OVERVIEW

LEARNING OBJECTIVES ■ KEY TERMS ■ CHAPTER PREVIEW

LEARNING OBJECTIVES

After going through this chapter, you will be able to:

- Explain how different cultural perspectives affect the research process
- Distinguish between the concepts of race and ethnicity
- Understand the difficulties in categorizing people according to culture and background
- Describe why psychologists generally do not regard race as a biological construct
- Explain the effect of culture on mental health research
- Explain the difficulty in studying gender and sex differences

KEY TERMS

Absolutism, p. 341
Back translation,
     p. 353
Content validity,
     p. 352

Culture, p. 335
Emic, p. 341
Ethnicity,
     p. 336
Etic, p. 341

Interpretation
     paradox, p. 342
One-drop rule
     (hypodescent),
     p. 344

Race, p. 336
Relativism,
     p. 341
Universalism,
     p. 341

CHAPTER PREVIEW

Most psychologists would agree that our attitudes and beliefs affect the way we make judgments. When we draw a conclusion about somebody's behavior, our judgments may reflect us as much as the people we observe. That is, we see others in a particular way because of who we are. If we share the same culture as those we study, we may be able to gain insights into why they act as they do. On the other hand, when we observe behaviors of those in other cultures, we may not understand what motivates them.

Understanding the effects of culture on behavior requires detailed knowledge of the person being observed as well as that person's culture, which is not easy. The issues we have to consider are complex. For instance, how do culture, ethnicity, and race affect behavior? The answer is certainly complex. Even though most people firmly believe that there are several easily definable races of people, many scientists have come to the conclusion that the concept of race is a social construction, not a biological fact. According to a great number of anthropologists, sociologists, psychologists, biologists, and geneticists, race is not a particularly useful biological concept. Yet many people believe that it exists.

Even though a concept like race may be scientifically invalid, we can still identify behaviors associated with culture or ethnicity, although there are pitfalls we need to avoid. Research participants are often assigned to categories in simplistic and contradictory ways from one study to another. Fortunately, more researchers are coming to the realization that we need to have good cross-cultural knowledge if we are going to understand people.

Finally, studying differences between women and men poses problems in research. Sometimes, investigators find ways to reinforce pre-existing beliefs by failing to acknowledge what might be considered cultural differences between the sexes. The researchers may believe in myths that are not true, so their research may be flawed.

Throughout this chapter, your beliefs will be challenged, and you will have to deal with controversies that, ultimately, may make you view people differently and change the way you think about studying them.

DIFFERENT CULTURAL PERSPECTIVES

It would be a mistake to assume that all people think as we do. As a result, we should be cautious in interpreting why people act as they do when these people come from a culture that is different from ours.

For example, Stiles, Gibbons, and Schnellman (1990) asked Mexican and American adolescents to characterize members of the opposite sex. Mexican adolescents relied on stereotypes and talked about internal characteristics. American adolescents were more likely to use physical and sexual descriptors. In addition, the girls who participated in the study tended to make different drawings, depending on their culture. Mexican girls depicted men helping them more than American girls did. If we wanted to study attitudes of Mexican and of American adolescents, we might have a hard time comparing their responses because they would be using different worldviews to generate their responses.

Beyond this, Cohen and Gunz (2002) have documented that people born in Western and Eastern countries have quite different memories of events in their lives. Those from Asia tended to remember events in the first person (e.g., "I did this") when the memories did not involve their being at the center of attention; when they were the center of attention, their memories were in the third person (e.g., "he did this"). People born in the Western world showed memories that were just the opposite, with the center of attention being associated with the first person. The researchers concluded that the differential perspectives on the world actually dictated the way information is processed and the form of subsequent memory.

If the investigators are correct, we can expect people from different cultures to think about things very differently, so if we give them the same task to complete, they may be engaged in quite different mental processes. As such, comparisons about performance may be difficult.

What Is Culture?

Culture—The customs, behaviors, attitudes, and values (psychological culture) and the objects and implements (physical culture) that can be used to identify and characterize a population.

Sometimes we think that we understand a concept, but when we try to express our ideas in words, it is very difficult. **Culture** is one such concept. We all know people who act differently than we do because of cultural differences. If somebody asked you to identify differences between your culture and that of another person, you would probably discuss differences in religious beliefs, eating habits, clothing, etc. This is typically what we mean by "culture" (Matsumoto, 1994). At the same time, we have only identified some of the signs associated with cultural differences; we haven't defined culture itself.

Throughout this chapter it will become apparent that our concepts of culture, ethnicity, and race are quite vague and subjective. Unfortunately, the research literature is at times just as confusing. Different investigators use the same term but define it in diverse ways.

Culture.   We can identify two distinct components of culture. Physical culture relates to objects like tools and buildings. Subjective culture, which is of interest to psychologists, refers to such things as familial patterns, language habits, attire, and a wide range of other characteristics that pass from one generation to the next (Betancourt & Lôpez, 1993; Matsumoto, 1994).

Other psychologists have defined culture somewhat differently from Matsumoto (1994), involving the notion that culture is not something "out there," but rather that it is a cognitive response a person makes on the basis of his or her interactions with others (Segall, Lonner, & Berry, 1998). For example, it seems unlikely that Americans are overtly conscious of being Americans on a daily basis; this categorization makes sense only when they want to make some contrast. In their communities, they are simply who they are. Similarly, think about Mexican citizens. People living in Mexico City feel no need to identify themselves as Mexicans or as Hispanics because on a daily basis, it is not a relevant consideration. On the other hand, when people live in a country different from that of their birth, they would likely describe themselves according to place of birth because that information might be relevant to understanding their behavior and because it draws a contrast between them and others.

> **Race**—A controversial concept with very limited construct validity about classification of people based on real or imagined biological traits, most often centering on skin color.

> **Ethnicity**—A concept related to a person's identification with a particular group of people, often based on ancestry, country of origin, or religion.

Race and Ethnicity.   Race and **ethnicity** are also difficult concepts. When discussing race, researchers (and people in general) often think of biological characteristics. People who make distinctions this way hope to use an objective, biological means to categorize people.

On the other hand, ethnicity is often thought of as a more subjective concept. A person's ethnicity is associated with affiliation. That is, to what group do people think they belong or what group has affected the way an individual thinks and acts?

It doesn't help researchers that the concept of ethnicity itself is somewhat unclear. For instance, Phinney (1996) noted that "ethnicity is most often thought of as culture.... To understand the psychological implications of ethnicity, it is essential to identify the specific cultural characteristics associated with an ethnic group and with the outcomes of interest such as educational achievement or mental health" (p. 920). She pointed out that the cultural characteristics (e.g., attitudes and behaviors) are often used to explain ethnic differences.

Matsumoto (1993) depicted ethnicity differently, suggesting that ethnicity "is defined most often by biological determinants; culture, however, must be defined by sociopsychological factors.... Defined in this way, the parameters of culture are 'soft,' and perhaps more difficult to distinguish, than the parameters of ethnicity, which are set in biology and morphological differences" (p. 120). An additional argument is that race is a category imposed by a dominant group, whereas ethnicity is an affiliation that people choose (Markus, 2008).

Complicating all these issues is the fact that in research, people often use culture interchangeably with race, ethnicity, and nationality (Betancourt & Lôpez, 1993). In many studies, people must often indicate race by selecting categories that really encompass ethnicity or nationality, not race. Latinos, for instance, can be White, Black, Asian, American Indian, or any combination thereof. It is pretty clear that researchers have not yet solved even the issues of defining terms, much less behaviors associated with cultural differences.

Finally, before we make sweeping claims about people based on nationality, it would be important to keep in mind that there seems to be no convincing evidence that people within a given nation show marked similarities with respect to personality. McCrae and Terracciano (2006) addressed the question of whether there really are national characteristics. Their data led to the conclusion that "people everywhere find it easy to develop stereotyped ideas of whole nations and agree well enough with each other to believe their views are consensually validated. But while there is some consensus, there is no accuracy. National-character stereotypes are apparently not even exaggerations of real differences: They are fictions" (p. 160).

DEFINING AN INDIVIDUAL'S CULTURE, ETHNICITY, AND RACE

Scientific designations should be based on valid, objective, and stable scientific criteria. The categories researchers use often reflect social and political conditions. For example, in record keeping, the Census Bureau is not trying to be scientific; it is trying to describe the population of the United States. Still, scientific research relies on Census Bureau categories. Berreby (2000) has pointed out that the utility of racial classifications depends in part on how well people define the categories they use.

Further, Rodriguez (2000) pointed out that the concept of race or ethnicity may not help us understand behavior because an individual may fall into different categories, depending on who is doing the assessment. For instance, when the U.S. government collects data on an individual, the Bureau of the Census does not regard Hispanics as constituting a race, whereas federal agencies that deal with civic rights issues do have a separate racial category for Hispanics. Suppose you wanted to carry out a research project to see if people in different racial categories achieve different educational levels. Would your data include a racial category for Hispanics? With governmental categories, you could argue either way, if you consider that the government has sanctioned both approaches. This duality is problematic for scientific research, which relies on objective and stable measurements and classifications.

Another concern in categorizing research participants is that a researcher may use terms that are clear in the context of an investigation but that might be unclear to others. For instance, Selten et al. (2001) examined psychotic disorders among Turkish, Moroccan, and Hindustani people who had migrated to the Netherlands. But Bhui and Bhugra (2001) pointed out that the terms *Turkish* and *Moroccan* reflect place of birth, whereas *Hindustani* refers to religion. Such a mixture of categories can cause confusion in cross-cultural comparisons. Suppose a Turk was a Hindu. Into what category would he or she fall?

Further, how a person identifies with a given ethnic group can change, depending on the particular context and the degree of the person's acculturation and may very well change over the course of the person's life. For instance, Benet-Martinez, Leu, Lee, and Morris (2002) discovered that Chinese Americans switch their cultural perspective from Chinese to American in different ways, depending on whether they viewed Chinese and American cultures as consistent or contradictory with one another.

As a result, studying the effect of ethnicity is very difficult: It is hard to define ethnicity precisely and an individual's commitment to a given ethnic group will vary according to the present circumstances.

Criteria for Inclusion in a Group

The criteria for inclusion in a group change over time. For instance, over the years the United States census has classified people into ethnic groups on the basis of what language they spoke, then their last name, then their place of origin, and now, through self-identification.

Asking people to place themselves into categories can itself lead to problems. Self-categorization changes depending on whether people are given a list of groups from which they must choose or can identify their preferred group affiliation on their own. The self-selection also depends on perceived advantages associated with being considered as a member of one group or another (Panter, Daye, Allen, Wightman, & Deo, 2009).

Clearly, people classify themselves differently depending on what is at stake (e.g., Panter et al., 2009; Phinney, 1996). For example, Phinney (1996) cited research in which 259 university students self-identified as American Indian or Alaska Native. Only 52 could provide confirmation that they belonged in those categories. If tuition aid depends on ethnic status, people might classify themselves differently. Research often relies on data resulting from these self-classifications.

In addition, as Phinney (1996) pointed out, when we try to categorize people according to ethnicity, the labels we create are not particularly useful when people come from mixed backgrounds. Beyond that, Phinney noted that "a common practice is to interpret empirical results or clinical observations in terms of cultural characteristics that are assumed to exist but that are not directly assessed" (p. 921). That is, researchers make assumptions about behaviors of the groups they are studying, but the researchers often do not check to make sure that their assumptions are valid. According to Phinney, when investigators have taken the time to look at supposedly relevant cultural characteristics, the results have often shown that researchers' assumptions are misguided.

As an example of a difficulty in categorization, consider the Chinese, a group that has recently been studied extensively in cross-cultural psychology. Chang (2000) noted that the Chinese are not easy to characterize because being *Chinese* can mean an enormous number of things. For one thing, there is no single "race" because of the genetic and anthropological variability among the Chinese, who can count over 50 ethnic minorities encompassed under the overarching term "Chinese." In addition, the diversity in language is so great that you could find two languages labeled "Chinese" that are as different from one another as German is from French. Another consideration is that people from urban and rural areas can have very different cultures, as can people who are either literate or illiterate.

Researchers studying Chinese people living outside China sometimes use the family name as an indicator of being Chinese. This is a problematic strategy. Chang pointed out that the name Lee can be Chinese and has been used to signify Chinese ethnicity even though Lee is also a Korean and a Vietnamese name. Lee can also be a Western name—there is no evidence that the Confederate General Robert E. Lee was Chinese. Further, the most common Chinese surname, Chang, is also a Korean name.

Sometimes, researchers are even broader in their categorization schemes. Cohen and Gunz (2002), in studying the difference between Eastern and Western thought, simply included a participant in the Eastern category if he or she had been born in Asia. The range of ethnicity across groups is vast. Participants in the Asian group were probably as different from one another as they were from the participants who grew up in North America. In other research, Kim, Atkinson, and Yang (1999) put into one category Asian Indians, Cambodians, Filipinos, Hmong, Japanese, Koreans, and others. This represents a stereotype that all people from Eastern cultures share significant attitudes and behaviors and that they all differ from people in the West.

To add to the confusion, Kim et al. (1999) have suggested that as people from Asian countries become acculturated to the United States, their behaviors change more quickly than their attitudes, which may not change even across generations. So in one sense, they are attitudinally still members of an ethnic group but behaviorally they are not. When we describe people within some arbitrarily determined category, we may be talking about very different types of people as though they were the same, and we may incorrectly decide that a single person is more consistently ethnic than he or she really is.

Because of these complex issues, some psychologists have argued that because of the methodological and conceptual problems associated with categorizing people, it is not useful to regard people from a given category as constituting an intact group. This issue looms large because research often do not use empirical assessments to verify that people in a given group actually share important behaviors and attitudes other than race (Helms, Jernigan, & Mascher, 2005). With respect to health-related research, Shields et al. (2005) suggested that researchers report the ethnic and racial makeup of their samples but not use the categories as variables in statistical analysis.

Social Issues and Cultural Research

The way we categorize people has implications for the way we think of social issues. As you can see in Figure 14.1, the National Center for Educational Statistics reported that high school dropout rates for Hispanics are very high (Chapman, Laird, Ifill, & KewalRamani, 2011; Kaufman, Kwon, Klein, & Chapman, 2000). What should we conclude from the fact that Hispanics are several times as likely to drop out of high school as Americans of Asian descent? This question is too simplistic because dropout rates for Hispanics drop by two thirds for families who have been in the United States for two generations or more. As such, ethnic categories are less important than degree of acculturation.

Rather than concentrating on ethnicity, it might make more sense to talk about other variables, like the number of years people have lived in a given culture, socioeconomic status, fluency in English, nature of one's peers, and so forth (Chiriboga, Jang, Banks, & Kim, 2007; Watkins, Mortazavi, & Trofimova, 2000).

Yee, Fairchild, Weizmann, and Wyatt (1993) summarized the problems nicely: They noted that psychologists themselves use common stereotypes and rely on self-identification.

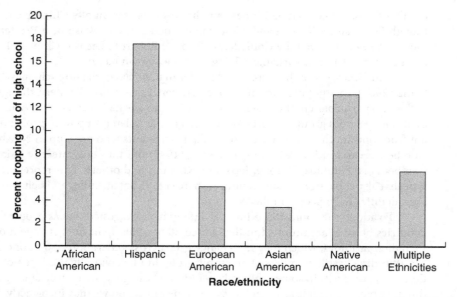

FIGURE 14.1   High school dropout rates according to ethnicity/race in the United States. *Source:* Laird et al. (2007).

The use of stereotypes suffers from four notable problems: It (a) neglects important differences among people in the same group, (b) assumes with no proof that behaviors that differ across groups are based on racial or cultural differences, (c) inappropriately depicts race and other variables as being related, and (d) relies on ideas for which there is no scientific consensus.

CROSS-CULTURAL CONCEPTS IN PSYCHOLOGY

Historically, psychologists have not concerned themselves with cultural differences. From the first decades of the 1900s and into the 1960s, most psychologists were behaviorists who thought that organisms were similarly affected by reinforcement contingencies—how often they were rewarded or punished. As a result, it didn't make much difference to psychologists whether they studied rats, pigeons, or people from any background. The causes of behavior were seen as the same universally.

Are Psychological Constructs Universal?

Early cross-cultural researchers imposed their own cultural viewpoints on the behaviors of the people they studied, which meant that they failed to understand the subtleties of other cultures. Such an approach could probably be forgiven because the researchers were opening up a new field of study and knew much less than they thought they did or needed to know for complete understanding of the people they researched. Still, after a while, it became clear that things were not as simple as people had hoped.

Etic—A research finding that appears to be universally true across cultures.

Emic—A research finding that is valid only within a given culture.

One of the distinctions that resulted from critical analysis of the research was between an **etic** and an **emic**. An etic refers to findings that result from studies across cultures and that may hold true cross-culturally. Thus, many people might regard the taboo against incest or cannibalism as an etic. On the other hand, an emic refers to a finding that is particular to a single culture that is being studied and understood in local terms. Although these two terms are gaining wider recognition in psychology, they are still controversial because the distinction between etic and emic perspectives are not always clear (Lonner, 1999).

The case of anorexia and bulimia is instructive here. Smith, Spillane, and Annus (2006) have argued that anorexia appears consistently across cultures, but that bulimia is a phenomenon of Western culture. Thus, two conditions that many people regard as having overlap in causes may show very different cultural manifestations.

In the study of different cultures, Berry, Poortinga, Segall, and Dasen (1992, cited in Segall et al., 1998) identified three orientations in cross-cultural psychology: absolutism, relativism, and universalism.

Absolutism—In discussions of cultural research, the concept that maintains that behavioral phenomena can be viewed from the same perspective, regardless of the culture in which they appear.

The first orientation, **absolutism**, assumes that behavioral phenomena are basically the same, regardless of cultures. In this view, depression will be depression; it does not differ from one locale to another. Should we believe this? Price and Crapo (1999) illustrate the difficulty with accepting the concept of depression as a single, unvarying construct across cultures. For example, the Hopi do not have a single category that corresponds to the Western view of depression; they have five different categories. For them *depression*, as most of us view it, would be too broad a label to be therapeutically useful. Further, the hopelessness of major depression would be accepted by some Buddhists as simply being "a good Buddhist" (p. 126). In a Buddhist culture, it would make no sense to describe symptoms of depression (as we know them) as a pathological condition because Buddhists believe that hopelessness is part of the world and that salvation arises, in part, in recognition of this hopelessness.

Relativism—In discussions of cultural research, the concept that maintains that behavioral phenomena can be understood only within the context of the culture in which they occur.

A second orientation is **relativism**. A relativistic approach stands in contrast to absolutism in that relativists make no attempts to relate psychological constructs across cultures. A researcher with this orientation would undertake only emic research, believing that the phenomena of any culture stands independently from those in any other. According to Segall et al. (1998), few psychologists favor the extreme of either absolutism or relativism. Most fall between these two poles.

Universalism—A moderating view in cultural research that maintains that behavioral phenomena may be based on invariant psychological processes but that each culture will induce different manifestations of those underlying processes.

The final orientation is **universalism**. This approach strikes a balance between absolutism and relativism, accepting the idea that there may be universal psychological processes, but that they manifest differently, depending on the particular culture. For example, Segall, Campbell, and Herskovits (1966) found that susceptibility to perceptual illusions was widespread and suggested universal, underlying cognitive processes. At the same time, reactions differed depending on a person's life experience.

According to the absolutist viewpoint, if perceptual illusions are caused by universal sensory processes, we should all experience illusions the same way. But that usually doesn't happen. According to the relativist viewpoint, there could be little or no similarity in perceptions across cultures because perception in this orientation arises only from experience. That, too, doesn't seem very common. According to the universalist perspective, the same internal processes take place but lead to different interpretations because of experience. The truth is likely to fall somewhere between the extreme viewpoints.

Although scientists hope for psychological constructs that are valid across cultures, careful examination of behaviors so far leads us to be careful to avoid falling prey to our own cultural biases. In the Controversy box on neurological diagnosis, we see that something as objective as medical diagnosis is susceptible to cultural influences. The case study provided by Klawans (2000) provides an illustration of cultural problems in diagnosing brain damage. The patient and the physician came from different backgrounds and had radically different points of view, which could pose challenges for adequate diagnosis and treatment.

Issues in Cross-Cultural Research

When researchers pursue cross-cultural research, they can fall prey to certain problems in interpreting their data. Van de Vijver and Leung (2000) have identified four major concerns in research on people from different cultural groups.

1. First, although some behavioral differences across cultures reflect important cross-cultural differences in thought and behavior, some differences in behavior are quite superficial and do not relate to important, underlying psychological processes.
2. Second, sometimes psychological tests legitimately generate different patterns of scores across cultures. There is often a tendency to treat them as artifacts of measurement error, that is, to see the test as deficient rather than as identifying true differences between groups. In other words, when we indeed find cultural differences, it might be tempting to ignore them rather than share unpopular results.
3. Third, researchers are prone to overgeneralization from their results. That is, differences due to small sample biases or poor measurement instruments may lead researchers to make more of their data than they should.
4. Fourth, differences across groups may reflect lack of equivalence across samples. The differences could occur because the samples contain different types of people who differ in critical ways, not because the cultures differ.

> **Interpretation Paradox—**
> In cultural research, the fact that large differences between groups are easy to spot but hard to understand because there are so many factors that could be responsible, whereas small differences are harder to spot but easier to explain.

These difficulties imply what van de Vijver and Leung (2000) call the **interpretation paradox** of cross-cultural research. Large differences between very diverse cultures are easy to obtain but hard to interpret because the reasons for the differences may be caused by any of a number of multiple factors. On the other hand, small differences between people of similar cultures may be hard to spot, but when observed, are easy to interpret because the groups being assessed share many features, so the reasons for differences stand out and are easy to identify.

CONTROVERSY:
Does Culture Make a Difference in Neurological Diagnosis?

Diagnosing a medical or psychiatric condition resembles the formal research process quite closely. Physicians initially ask enough questions to allow them to form hypotheses about a problem. They then make observations and draw conclusions. If they still don't have enough information to identify the source of a patient's problems, they generate more hypotheses and ask more questions. Finally, the physician comes to a conclusion and treats the patient. In many cases, the ultimate diagnoses are correct, but sometimes they are wrong. This is exactly what happens in research. With luck, we are right most of the time, but research and diagnosing are complicated enough that sometimes we are wrong.

The neurologist Harold Klawans (2000) described a case from the 1970s in which a patient with neurological problems was initially misdiagnosed because of cultural factors. The patient, who had suffered repeated blackouts due to carbon monoxide poisoning in the workplace, was brought to a Chicago hospital.

As part of the diagnostic process, an attending neurologist asked the patient who the mayor of Chicago was. He responded correctly, but was unable to identify any other, previous mayors, asking if there ever had been any other mayors. He was also unable to name the current president or any previous presidents. The patient did not know that President John Kennedy had been assassinated, and had no knowledge of the Vietnam War, which was a very controversial aspect of American culture at the time. This patient was an American who had lived through all of these events, so it was very strange for him not to have such fundamental cultural knowledge.

The neurologist finally asked the patient to identify which of four objects was different from the others: hammer, wood, chisel, and wrench. The patient replied that none of them was different; they were all the same. At that point, the doctor concluded that the patient had suffered severe brain damage.

As Klawans discovered through further questioning, though, the patient's memory for some things (like baseball) going back 40 years was very acute. The trouble with the initial diagnosis was that the first doctor had not taken culture into account. The patient, who had grown up in Mississippi in the 1930s, had gone to school for two years and had never learned to read. As a result, the patient's memories rested on what he had experienced directly. He didn't watch the news on television, so it is no surprise that he didn't know about the president, about the Vietnam War, or about politics. None of these things had ever entered his world.

Klawans stated that people who don't read don't classify objects the way that literate people do. The task of categorizing the hammer, wood, chisel, and wrench is a foreign concept to them. It is only relevant to those of us who use written words to designate objects. The ability to read brings a set of skills that we take for granted, like classifying, but that ability is very closely bound to literacy.

If the patient hadn't experienced it himself, he didn't have a memory for an event. Imagine for yourself how much you would know about world events if you didn't read about them or see them on the news. His concept of the world was very different from that of the first doctor. In the end, it was clear that the patient's mental faculties were as sharp as anyone else's. Had Klawans not been attuned to this cultural difference, the patient might have been diagnosed with severe brain damage.

IS THERE A BIOLOGICAL BASIS FOR RACE?

Psychologists in the United States have studied one particular ethnic group to a great extent, Blacks or African Americans. Very often, the research does not appear to center around culture or ethnicity. Rather, investigators cast their studies in terms of race.

One-Drop Rule (Hypodescent)—One means by which a person is racially categorized as a member of a low status group such that if he or she has "one drop" of blood from a given group (i.e., any ancestor, no matter how remote, from that group), the individual is automatically classified as being from that group, used specifically with people of African descent who live in the United States.

You probably imagine a person's race as something that is clearly defined; many people do. The problem lies in the process we use to classify a person. In the United States, we have had a tradition of calling a person "Black" or African American if the person has any African ancestry, no matter how remote or how little. This pattern is known colloquially as the **one-drop rule**, also known as hypodescent. A person is Black if he or she has "one drop of Black blood." In Brazil, a person with any Caucasoid features is regarded as "White" (Zuckerman, 1990). The validity of such racial categorization is suspect if a person's race changes simply because he or she enters a different country.

Psychologists continue to use race as a conceptual category in research, despite good arguments for not doing so (e.g., Helms, Jernigan, & Mascher, 2005). For instance, racial categories can reflect researchers' beliefs more than actual characteristics of participants. In addition, in many studies, researchers do not report the operational definitions of race by which they categorize participants. As Helms et al. reported, researchers sometimes classify people of Asian descent as minorities and sometimes as "White," even in the same study. Liang, Li, and Kim (2004) suggested that this multiple categorization occurs in everyday life and may cause stress, independent of the supposed racial category.

The Criteria for Race

Race is clearly a strange concept scientifically. Why does a single ancestor determine race when there are so many ancestors who are ignored? And why does a single Black ancestor make a person Black, when a single White ancestor does not make a person White? The concept of race in scientific research is troublesome; race-determining characteristics fall on a continuum, but people create all-or-none categories. Whenever you have a continuum, but you try to make discrete categories, you have to make a decision as to where to put the cutoff for inclusion into different categories. Such decisions are arbitrary, and another person could make a different decision that has as much validity (or lack thereof) as yours.

The use of the concept of race, even among the educated, has sometimes been very loose. For instance, *The Mother's Encyclopedia* (1942) discussed rheumatic fever, asserting that "some races who live in New York are especially prone to it, particularly Italians and Jewish people" (p. 1028). Further, in the United States, there used to be a greater belief in the nature of the continuum regarding Black and White, even if there was no real scientific basis for it. Historically, an individual with one Black grandparent was classified as a quadroon; a person with one Black great-grandparent was listed as an octoroon. These "races" were considered as real as any others.

A great many scientists have concurred that race is a social construction, not a natural phenomenon. Anthropologists and some biologists seem to have caught on to this idea some time ago, but some social and behavioral scientists have been slower to adopt this conclusion.

The problem with race as a construct that might help us understand behavior is that individual differences within races overwhelm the biological differences between races. In other words, if you look at the variability between any two people in the same culture, they show much more variability in genetic makeup than do two "average" people with ancestors on different continents.

At the phenotypical level, race is often defined in terms of features like skin color, but also hair type, eye color, and facial features. These turn out to be unreliable markers for race; in fact, they are not correlated with one another, meaning that just because a person shows one "racial" characteristic, it doesn't mean that he or she will show the others (Zuckerman, 1990). In addition, there are people in the so-called Negroid groups who are lighter in skin color than others in the so-called Caucasoid groups.

As you will see in the Controversy box on racial categories, scientists have identified a number of different problems associated with the use of racial categories in scientific research. There will undoubtedly be continued debate about the topic of race because of its importance as a social concept.

Current Biological Insights Regarding Race

Scientists working on the Human Genome Project, which is an attempt to identify the genetic makeup of human beings, has brought attention to this issue. According to Harold Freeman of North General Hospital in Manhattan, the percentage of genes that reflect differences in external appearances associated with race is about 0.01 percent (Angier, 2000).

Since the emergence of humans in present form, there have been about 7,000 generations. This is not a sufficiently large number to lead to clear differentiation of one group from another, according to geneticists. Further, there has always been mixing of genes of various groups when they come in contact with one another, intermarry, and reproduce. Biological variables may differentiate groups in a general way, but these variables are not, in and of themselves, markers for race because a person from any group could show them. "For instance, Afro-Americans [sic] are at a higher risk [for essential hypertension] than Anglo-Americans. From our perspective, what is of scientific interest is not the race of these individuals, but the relationship between the identified biological factors...and hypertension" (Betancourt & Lôpez, 1993, p. 631). The biological factors contribute causally to the hypertension; race is a correlational variable.

Still, some psychologists argue that real racial differences exist. They cite the notion that brain sizes, on average, are largest in Asians, middle-sized in Whites, and smallest in Blacks, a pattern that reflects trends in IQ scores. That is, the claim is that IQ score and brain size are positively correlated. At the same time, Peters (1993) noted that in studies of brain size and IQ, measurement error as small as one millimeter could account for the observed difference across races.

Current Controversies

Modern psychologists (e.g., Cernovsky, 2000) have countered the argument about brain size and intelligence with the fact that mean brain size of groups living near the equator is less than that of groups nearer the poles, so that brain size is correlated with geography of one's ancestors and not much else. Besides, women's brains are smaller than men's, even after body size is taken into consideration. There is no evidence that women are less intelligent than men.

Another problem arises when we equate a score on a standardized test with intelligence. An IQ score is just that, a test score. It relates to behaviors that the test makers regard as important, like how well you do in school. It is true that your grades in school will correlate pretty well with your IQ score, but much of that may be due to the fact that IQ scores are based, to a degree, on tasks that are valued in educational settings. Thus, it is no surprise that people who score low on intelligence tests do not do well in school.

Flynn (1999) has refuted a number of arguments that relate IQ and race, concluding that environmental differences explain differences in scores on IQ tests and that genetic (i.e., racial) interpretations, when investigated empirically, lead to conclusions that simply do not make sense. In fact, he has documented and discussed the regular increase in IQ scores across many countries over the past several decades that have emerged in too short a time to be genetically mediated (e.g., Flynn, 1999). There is good reason to believe that the causes are environmental, such as improved nutrition for pregnant women (Lynn, 2009) and increased access to education with better pedagogical practices (Blair, Gamson, Thorne, & Baker, 2005). Further, the Flynn effect may have disappeared or reversed itself in some countries (Shayer & Ginsburg, 2009; Teasdale & Owen, 2005), while progressing in other, such as Estonia (Must, teNijenhuis, Must, & van Vianen, 2009), again within a time frame too rapid to be genetically based.

The controversy will undoubtedly persist for a long time because the issues remain socially controversial and complex and the arguments multifaceted.

- - - - -

CONTROVERSY:
Skull Size, Intelligence, and a Charge of Scientific Misconduct

The history of the United States is not positive when viewed in the light of racial issues. People from Africa or African backgrounds were enslaved, and the impact is still felt today. With this accurate perspective in mind, the late paleontologist Stephen Jay Gould analyzed the nineteenth-century research of Samuel George Morton, who had measured the cranial capacity of skulls of people from diverse races and ethnicities.

According to Gould (1981), Morton may have been predisposed to believe that Caucasian skulls were larger because they had bigger brains that were associated with greater levels of intelligence compared to other groups. Gould examined Morton's data and concluded that Morton's biases led to the conclusion that Caucasian brains were indeed larger than those of other groups. Morton found that Whites had the largest brains, Indians were in the middle, and Blacks were on the bottom. Gould maintained that Morton's sample of skulls was poor and included a large number of Peruvian Inca skulls; these people were small of stature. He had very few Iroquois Indians, whose skulls were large. As a result, the mean skull size of Indians was artificially low.

Gould's analysis has been widely regarded for over 30 years as evidence of misconduct by Morton. Recently, though, a team of researchers remeasured skulls that Morton had used in his research and concluded that Gould's analysis was erroneous (Lewis et al., 2011). These investigators discovered that Gould's reanalysis of Morton's data, which did not include remeasuring the skulls, was problematic. They concluded that Morton's procedures were sound and that his measurements were not biased. They also suggested that there is no clear evidence that Morton associated brain size with intelligence to begin with.

Unfortunately, Gould has died, so we do not know how he would have responded. But as Lewis et al. (2011) noted, there would have been an interesting debate on the matter.

Questions for Discussion: Even when researchers are trying to act in good faith in their research, is it possible that their biases might still influence their results? Their conclusions? How might this happen?

Could historical mistakes concerning the relationship between race and the measurement of IQ recur today? How?

CONTROVERSY:
Are There Really Different Races?

How many races are there? Many people in the United States would list White, Black, Hispanic, Native American, and Asian, believing that these categories are valid, discrete groupings. That is, you are White or you are not; you are Black or you are not; etc. Everybody falls into one and only one category.

The truth is not so simple. In reality, there do not seem to be biologically based markers that separate people conveniently and reliably. For example, skin color, which many people use to define inclusion in a racial category, is inconsistent. There are Black people who are lighter than White people. Similarly, people of Asian descent span many different skin colors. The same is true for Native Americans and Hispanics. Skin lightness or darkness may be the most obvious trait that people rely on, but any characteristic you select has the same weaknesses.

People are very hard to classify precisely and objectively. One reason is that the differences among people are usually on a continuum. One person has more or less of this or that trait. When you have such continua, any point on the continuum that you use to create categories is going to be arbitrary; another person can justify using a different point.

Once scientists decided that racial differences were interesting, there were always problems defining race. In the 1920s, scientists agreed that there were three European races; in the 1930s, they changed it to 10 European races. At the same time, there was a single African-based racial category. Africa is a big continent (over 11 million square miles); Europe is a small continent (about 4 million square miles). Not surprisingly, Africans show much greater genetic diversity than Europeans do. Why then was there only one African race? The categorization process was based on socially derived beliefs, not scientific measurement.

In addition, if you look at a map, it is not clear where Europe ends and Asia begins. The boundary is arbitrary. Further, if you look at a map, you will see that the line that divides Asia and Africa is also arbitrary. So is the distinction between Asian and African people. By the same token, why should we have any faith that the distinction between Europeans and Asians is real? It is too easy to form stereotypes and consider them to be objective, reliable, and valid. But assigning people to different racial categories based on an arbitrary boundary is questionable. In some ways, it would be similar to identifying people from Ohio and Michigan as being from different races based on an arbitrary politically drawn line.

In terms of psychological research, we see again and again that behaviors and characteristics attributed to race generally have their causes in social or environmental factors. When researchers account for these factors, the effect of "race" generally diminishes or vanishes.

If a fine analysis eliminates effects of "race" on behavior in most of situations that have been studied, a critical thinker might conclude that the remaining differences could well be due to factors that researchers have not yet identified.

Nobody has yet identified scientifically reliable and valid definitions of race based on biology or genetics. As Yee et al. (1993) and others have pointed out, even in scientific research, depictions of race are generally made from a layperson's point of view, with no real scientific backing. Finally, it seems reasonable to believe that when one argument after another falls, it becomes more parsimonious to believe that racial factors per se are irrelevant and that social and economic factors create differences between groups.

PRACTICAL ISSUES IN CULTURAL RESEARCH

Sue (1999) has pointed out some of the major issues in carrying out cross-cultural research. One of them is that many researchers may have difficulty finding participants from different cultural groups. Just like students who have little time for anything other than home life, school work, and extracurricular activities, researchers have limited amounts of time.

The result is that when they plan their own research, they make use of student partic-ipants because of availability; it doesn't hurt that the students are also willing, bright, and motivated. The people who volunteer for research are different from people in general and in many colleges may not show much cultural diversity. And even when there is diversity, research samples may include mostly students. The truth is that it would take a consider-able amount of time, money, and energy to find the diverse samples that are desirable. Given the practical considerations, researchers generally feel that they have to live with the samples they can access, even if it limits how well their results apply to different groups.

Lack of Appropriate Training among Researchers

In addition to having access to fairly homogeneous samples, researchers may simply not have the knowledge or training needed to conduct high quality, cross-cultural research. Fortunately, the Council of National Psychological Associations for the Advancement of Ethnic Minority Interests has developed guidelines published by the American Psychological Association for research with ethnic minority communities (Council of National Associations, 2000). Some of their major points appear in Table 14.1.

These considerations are important in any research project. They just happen to be particularly relevant to research with ethnic minorities. If you keep these points in mind, any research with any population will be better.

TABLE 14.1   Important Considerations Regarding Research with People of Ethnic Groups

Personal Characteristics	Develop awareness of the culture of the group you study
	Become aware of the effects of the culture and oppression and discrimination
	Recognize multiple linguistic and communication styles
	Recognize the heterogeneity that exists within any simple ethnic label
	Identify the degree to which an individual is acculturated.
Research Considerations	Recognize cultural assumptions and biases in creating methods and materials
	Make sure all measurement instruments make sense from the cultural viewpoint of the group you study
	Use measurement instruments that are appropriately normed and that have established reliability and validity
	Determine if the research is culturally relevant to the group you study
	Establish appropriate comparison (control) groups
	Use adequately translated materials to maximize effectiveness of communication
	Conduct a cost/benefit analysis to make sure the research is worth doing
Outcomes	Interpret results within the appropriate cultural context
	Consider alternate explanations
	Remember that difference does not mean deviance
	Request help from community members in interpreting your research results
	Increase mainstream outlets for minority research
	Recognize the existence of confounding variables like educational level and socioeconomic status

Source: Council of National Psychological Associations (1999).

WHY THE CONCEPTS OF CULTURE AND ETHNICITY ARE ESSENTIAL IN RESEARCH

After the long discussion about the controversial concepts of race and ethnicity, you may wonder why we should consider it in our research. The reason is that various groups of people differ from one another in many ways. These groups just don't differ in the simplistic ways we normally think. We need to identify what differences appear across groups, as well as what differences occur within groups. We also need to identify factors that cause those differences because group affiliation alone may not be the only, or the most important, reason.

Differences Due to Language and Thought Processes

The importance of culture on psychological processes stands out clearly in a body of research associated with the way people recognize emotions on the faces of people in photographs. For example, Matsumoto, Anguas-Wong, and Martinez (2008) tested native Spanish speakers who were proficient in English either in Spanish or in English. Participants saw photographs and attempted to identify the emotion of the person depicted and to rate the intensity of the emotion. The participants were better at recognizing emotions when tested in English, even though their native language was Spanish. On the other hand, they rated the intensity of the emotions higher when doing it in Spanish. In earlier research, Matsumoto and Assar (1992) tested students in India who were bilingual in English and in Hindi. The students recognized emotions more accurately when they used English than Hindi. According to Matsumoto and Assar, people who speak English come from cultures in which people are used to talking openly about emotions. This cultural effect may lead English speakers to greater recognition and accurate judgment of emotions.

Further support for the importance of language in thought came from research by Marian and Neisser (2000), who demonstrated that bilingual people have easier access to memories when they try to recall those memories using the language they would have used when they initially experienced the event.

Language involves more than different word use. In fact, Ball, Giles, and Hewstone (1984) suggested that in order to learn a second language, you must also learn the culture of that language. You won't understand the language completely unless you know its context. The research by Matsumoto and colleagues reveals that culture may affect the way people think about or express their ideas. If you were conducting research that involved only speakers of English (which is true for the vast majority of psychological research), your conclusions about how people respond to the world around them will be very limited.

Language may also influence thought in other ways. Hedden et al. (2002) noted that Chinese speakers have an advantage over English speakers in some numerical tasks because the Chinese words representing numbers are shorter, thus easier to remember. They found no such advantage on a visuo-spatial task involving completing visual patterns. Thus, language may affect not only what you think but also how you think. Cross-cultural research needs to take such differences into account.

Differences in Simple and Complex Behaviors

Even simple responses may differ as a function of culture. When Chinese and American students indicated how often they engaged in certain behaviors, the Chinese participants may have had better memories than American students (Ji, Schwarz, & Nisbett, 2000). The researchers concluded that, as members of a collectivist society, the Chinese are expected to monitor their own behaviors closely. The Americans, on the other hand, did not seem to have as reliable a memory for their behaviors and had to estimate them. Thus, even a simple memory task may lead to fundamentally different ways of responding, depending on your culture.

Not surprisingly, differences in behaviors also occur in more complex situations. For instance, people in China seem to have a different approach to problem solving than people in the Western world. Peng and Nisbett (1999) studied Chinese students and American students in several experiments to see how they responded to contradictory statements in decision making. Chinese students were generally more comfortable accepting two contradictory statements as involving partial truths; American students were more likely to look for a single, logical truth.

These differences reflect fundamentally different views of the world. If you look at the psychological literature in problem solving, you find that there is remarkably little non-Western thought. In problem solving, the emphasis in most research is on logic and rationality that arrives at a single, logically coherent response. Before we claim that such approaches are a good general characterization of problem solving, we should remember that perhaps a billion people (or more) in this world would disagree with our representation of thought and decision-making.

It is important to remember that the modes of thought favored in the East and in the West are both useful and valid, but both are incomplete. As Peng and Nisbett (1999) pointed out, the world is complex and contradictory. Thus, we may have to accommodate our thoughts to accept potential contradictions and incomplete knowledge. At the same time, a non-dialectical or Western approach is useful for identifying when a particular argument is better supported by data and for generating useful counterarguments to rebut a possibly flawed argument.

If we want to generate a complete description of the way people think and solve problems, we cannot ignore the fact that our approach to problem solving reflects ways that we are comfortable with, but they are not the only ways that are valid. Knowing about culture helps us know about thought. Ignoring the effects of culture will mean that we have incomplete knowledge about thought and behavior.

Is Culture-Free Theory Really Free of Culture?

The importance of understanding cultural effects on behavior emerges when we look at the studies of how babies attach themselves to parents. Rothbaum, Weisz, Pott, Kiyake, and Morelli (2000) described the general tenets of attachment theory and assessed whether the theory is more culturally relevant in the Western hemisphere than elsewhere. This is an important discussion because many psychologists view attachment theory as evolutionarily based, thus free of cultural biases.

Three of the important tenets of attachment are as follows: First, there is a connection between maternal sensitivity and security of attachment. Second, secure children are more socially and emotionally competent than insecure children. Third, infants who show higher levels of adaptation are more likely to explore when they feel secure. These notions seem pretty straightforward. The research on attachment has typically involved middle-class American children. If attachment were strictly a part of evolutionary development, this would not be a problem. However, cultural differences may be important in the behaviors, and the very basis of the theory may be biased toward Western perspectives (Keller, 2007).

As Rothbaum et al. (2000) note, when parents or teachers identify potentially problematic behavior, the Japanese may identify one set of behaviors as appropriate and a different set as troublesome. The Americans could reverse the pattern. Rothbaum et al. maintain that in order to understand the nature of children's attachment, we have to understand the culture because attachment theory is not as culture-free as psychologists have traditionally believed.

These researchers may raise valid points, but not all psychologists agree. For instance, Chao (2001) suggested that Rothbaum didn't define the term *culture* adequately, equating it with nations. Van Ijzendoorn and Sagi (2001) and Chao also argued that there is too much variability within Japanese and within American cultures for easy generalizations about Japanese people and American people. The disagreements aren't reconciled easily because of the difficulties associated with cultural research.

Similarities and Differences within the Same Culture

People who grow up in the same culture share attitudes, values, and behaviors, but such people are not merely clones of one another. Part of the problem is that people in a group may show similarities on one dimension but not on another. Matsumoto (1993) investigated differences in emotion among Americans of various ethnic groups.

He asked his research participants to identify the emotion displayed in facial photographs and rate its intensity. They also indicated how appropriate a display of the emotion was. He discovered that some differences existed among Asian Americans, Blacks, Hispanics, and Whites, but the differences were inconsistent. Sometimes the different groups rated emotions in the pictures the same, but sometimes not. For example, Americans of Asian ancestry looked at a given picture and saw less anger than an American of African ancestry. But the Asian Americans saw an equal amount of sadness as African Americans. In addition, African Americans saw more intense emotions generally in pictures of White people than did Asian, Hispanic, or White Americans.

This pattern of findings suggests that if we are studying emotions, we could sometimes treat all Americans as more or less similar (e.g., for happiness and sadness), but not all the time (e.g., for fear). Simple research like this can reflect the complexity of cross-cultural studies.

Finally, researchers who assume that people within a given nation share stereotypical traits may be making a significant mistake. As noted before, McCrae and Terraccianno (2006) have demonstrated that there is no empirical support for a so-called national culture.

CULTURAL FACTORS IN MENTAL HEALTH RESEARCH

Psychologists continue to make progress in mental health research, documenting the effectiveness of various therapies for different problems and identifying variables associated with normal and abnormal behavior. As we have recognized the diversified culture in the United States, we have begun to pay attention to the different needs of people of varying backgrounds, although we still know much less than we need to know.

One type of research that clinical psychologists conduct involves assessing the validity of psychological tests across cultural boundaries. If we cannot translate tests into different languages to convey the same ideas as they do in English, we cannot be confident that test results signify the same psychological processes. A poorly translated test will not assess the same thing in both languages. Problems also occur when clinicians try to use a test with minority or immigrant populations when that test is created for and standardized on a White population born in the United States and raised to speak English. In either case, the scores might mean different things.

Chen (2008) has identified four major issues associated with testing people from different cultures. They include issues of (a) translation: Do questions in different languages actually ask the same thing? (b) construct invariance: Are the concepts the same across cultures? (c) response styles: Do people in different cultures tend to show the same response patterns? and (d) social desirability: Are there differences in impression management across cultures? Some of these concerns were raised in the context of survey research but are worth mentioning again. Examples of some of the problems appear below.

Content Validity

The process of ensuring that psychological tests serve diverse populations is difficult (Rogler, 1999). Diagnostic and research instruments need to make sense from the viewpoint of those who use them; that is, the tests must show, among other things, **content validity**. The questions should, in expert judgment, relate to what the test assesses. When psychologists create tests, they have to decide what questions to ask. This is where their expert judgment comes in. The problem is that potential patients or clients may not share the same culture as the psychologist, so the patient or client may be answering a different question than the clinician is asking.

> **Content Validity**—The degree to which the material contained in a test relates to the concept being assessed.

Rogler (1999) illustrated this point through a particular question on the Diagnostic Interview Schedule (DIS), which he noted is the most influential test in psychiatric epidemiology. The question asks, "Do you often worry a lot about having clean clothes?" This question might be useful in identifying whether people are overly distressed about unreasonable things. The problem with this question is that it assumes that the person answering it has access to running water. If you have all the water you need, then worrying about clean clothes might be a sign of psychological distress. On the other hand, if you do not have access to running water, laundry facilities, and so forth, such a worry becomes a reasonable preoccupation.

As it turns out, many Plains Indians in the United States do not have access to running water. As such, to respond that they do not worry about clean clothes would probably be more indicative of a problem than if they replied that they do worry. From this point of view, we can see that what might be an appropriate question on the DIS for many would be entirely inappropriate for others.

Translation Problems

If questions pose difficulties within the same language, imagine what problems arise if we try to translate the test into a different language for use by people whose cultural outlook does not match ours. Rogler (1999) provided another example from the DIS to illustrate the dilemma of creating a faithful translation of a test item into a different language.

He identified the question that reads, "I felt I could not shake off the blues even with help from my family or friends." In trying to translate this apparently simple and straight-forward item into Spanish, he encountered great difficulty. In translation, an individual tries to stay as close to the original wording as possible, but there were no suitable Spanish equivalents. One problem here is that in English, "the blues" has a particular meaning that does not survive in a translation to the Spanish word *azul*, the color blue. Rogler also noted that in the United States, we often think that it would be possible, by force of will, to "shake off" an unwanted mood. Is this concept shared by Spanish speakers? If so, what Spanish verb would be appropriate? He wondered whether the word *sacudir* would be a good translation. It means to shake off vigorously like a dog shakes water off its body. He decided that sacudir would not be appropriate.

After considerable contemplation, he translated the item by rewording the original English sentence to read "I could not get over feeling sad even with help from my family or friends." He then found it easier to prepare a Spanish version. Normally, a translator tries not to deviate from the original form of an item, but in this case, there was probably no alternative if the translation was to be meaningful. Table 14.2 provides other examples that Rogler generated to illustrate the cultural biases of the DIS.

Back Translation—In cross-cultural research, the process by which comparable testing instruments are developed, by translating from an original language to a second language, then back to the first to ensure that the original version and the translation back into that language produce comparable meanings.

One useful technique for ensuring comparability of items across languages is **back translation** (Banville, Desrosiers, & Genet-Volet, 2000). In this process, an item is translated from one language to a second. Then a blind translator converts it back to the first language. For example, an item might start in English, be translated into Spanish, then back again into English. If the original version in the first language is equivalent in meaning to the version that has been translated out of, then back into, English, the item is likely to capture the same concepts in both languages.

Cross-Cultural Norms

Relatively few distress inventories have received scrutiny on a cross-cultural basis; none have involved norms with college students (Cepeda-Benito & Gleaves, 2000). Ironically, although college students form the typical research participant in psychology, the clinical literature seems to underrepresent them.

When researchers have investigated cross-cultural equivalence of inventories, they have revealed a complex picture. For instance, the complete version of the Center for

TABLE 14.2   Examples Reflecting a Strong Effect of Culture That May Cause Problems Across Cultures

Example	Reason for the Problem
In assessing dissociation, the Dissociative Experience Scale asks about the following: "Some people have the experience of driving a car and suddenly realizing that they don't remember what has happened during all or part of the trip."	The question assumes that the person taking the test takes long car trips. This kind of factual assumption is a problem because people living in the inner city rarely, if ever, drive in places that do not have heavy traffic. As such, an answer to the question will not provide useful information.
Translation of the Clinical Analysis Questionnaire into Spanish.	Thirty-six percent of test items contained grammatical errors and involved direct translation of colloquialisms that made no sense in Spanish. With these translation problems, we could conclude that the questions in the different languages did not have the same meaning.
How does schizophrenia affect decision-making among married couples in San Juan, Puerto Rico?	Among the people studied, decision-making was not a critical aspect of familial interactions, as it is in the United States. In Puerto Rico, the corresponding dimension was how "men's work" and "women's work" was divided. Knowing about decision-making would not help in understanding problems or devising treatments.
Description of symptoms of bipolar disorder in the Amish.	The typical examples that clinicians look for include buying sprees, sexual promiscuity, and reckless driving, which are not applicable to the Amish. Instead, relevant symptoms involve behaviors like excessive use of public telephones, treating livestock too roughly, or giving gifts during the wrong season of the year.

Source: Rogler (1999)

Epidemiologic Studies–Depression scale seems valid for Americans of African, European, and Mexican descent (Aneschensel, Clark, & Frerichs, 1983), although the short version produces differences between Americans of African and European descent (Tran, 1997, cited in Cepeda-Benito & Gleaves, 2000).

In one study, Cepeda-Benito and Gleaves (2000) investigated the generalizability of the Hopkins Symptom Checklist-21 (HSCL-21) across Blacks, Hispanics, and Whites. This test is a short, 21-item version of a longer, 57-item inventory designed to measure distress. The HSCL-21 shows validity across a wide array of cultural groups, including Italian, Vietnamese, Latino, and European Americans. Cepeda-Benito and Gleaves investigated whether college students of differing backgrounds responded uniquely to it.

They discovered that the HSCL-21 would be an appropriate test of Black, Hispanic, and White college students. Given that other research revealed good construct validity of the inventory, one might have a degree of confidence that a clinician might use this test appropriately with students of many ethnic groups.

Cepeda-Benito and Gleaves (2000) were appropriately cautious in stating that their participants may not be representative of other ethnic college populations. Also, it is true that not every American ethnic group was represented in the research, but its generality across the three disparate groups tested provided cautious optimism. Unfortunately, the number of psychological tests that have been normed for varied groups is still uncomfortably small.

Cross-Cultural Diagnoses

One consequence of the lack of information on the validity of psychological tests for minority populations is that the tests might lead to diagnoses that are based more on ethnicity than on problematic behavior. As Iwamasa, Larrabee, and Merritt (2000) have shown, people may be predisposed to classify individuals of different ethnic groups in predetermined ways.

Iwamasa et al. (2000) identified the criteria for personality disorders listed in the *Diagnostic and Statistical Manual* (DSM; American Psychiatric Association, 1987). In clinical work, mental health workers observe an individual and make note of behaviors that occur. If a person shows a certain, well-specified group of behaviors, he or she may be diagnosed with a particular personality disorder as a result. In Iwamasa et al.'s study, the researchers asked their participants to sort these diagnostic criteria in three different ways: according to their presence in men versus women, by ethnicity, and by self (i.e., is this characteristic of you?). Some of the statements that the participants rated appear in Table 14.3. The participants did not know that they were dealing with clinical diagnostic criteria. Rather, they simply identified their stereotypes of the "normal" behaviors of people of different types.

The results suggest that strong cultural effects could occur in diagnosing personality disorders. The college students' beliefs about normal characteristics of Blacks are the same as the criteria used by psychologists and psychiatrists to diagnose antisocial and paranoid personality disorders. Similarly, the students' depiction of the typical behavior of Asian Americans reflects what clinicians look for in people who are schizoid. According to the research results, people of European descent showed a wide range of behaviors associated with different pathologies.

TABLE 14.3 Examples of Descriptions from DSM-III-R That Participants Rated as Typical in Men versus Women, in Different Ethnic Groups, and of the Participants Themselves

Examples of Description	Personality Disorder with Which the Description Is Associated	Group in Which the "Symptoms" Are Considered Typical
Has no regard for the truth	Antisocial	African American
Has never sustained a totally monogamous relationship for more than one year		
Is easily hurt by criticism or disapproval	Avoidant	European American
Fears being embarrassed by blushing, crying, or showing signs of anxiety in front of other people		
Inappropriate, intense anger or lack of control of anger, for example, frequent displays of temper, constant anger, recurrent physical fights	Borderline	European American
Chronic feelings of emptiness or boredom		

(continued)

TABLE 14.3 **(Continued)**

Examples of Description	Personality Disorder with Which the Description Is Associated	Group in Which the "Symptoms" Are Considered Typical
Feels devastated or helpless when close relationships end	Dependent	European American
Allows others to make most of his or her important decisions, for example, where to live, what job to take		
Is overly concerned with physical attractiveness	Histrionic	European American
Is uncomfortable in situations in which he or she is not the center of attention		
Reacts to criticism with feelings of rage, shame, or humiliation (even if not expressed)	Narcissistic	European American
Believes that his or her problems are unique and can be understood only by other special people		
Perfectionism that interferes with task completion, for example, inability to complete a project because own overly strict standards are not met	Obsessive-Compulsive	European American
Inability to discard worn-out or worthless objects even when they have no sentimental value		
Expects, without sufficient basis, to be exploited or harmed by others	Paranoid	African American
Bears grudges or is unforgiving of insults or slights		
Neither desires nor enjoys close relationships, including being part of a family	Schizoid	Asian American
Is indifferent to the praise and criticism of others		
Odd or eccentric behavior or appearance	Schizotypal	Native American
Inappropriate or constricted affect, for example, silly, aloof, rarely reciprocates gestures or facial expressions, such as smiles or nods		

Source: Iwamasa et al. (2000).

These results suggested that when people think of the behavior of Blacks, Whites, Asian Americans, and Native Americans, those behaviors are the same ones used by mental health practitioners to diagnose psychological disorders. The problem is not with Americans of various heritages. The problem is with people's biases and assumptions. If a psychiatrist or clinical psychologist used implicit stereotypes in dealing with different types of patients or clients, it could lead to differential diagnoses for what might be normal behavior.

Iwamasa et al. studied undergraduate volunteers, not clinicians. In addition, the undergraduates did not assign the diagnostic criteria in the same way that clinicians do. Would the results generalize to clinical psychologists and psychiatrists? Given that mental health workers are members of society, with the same biases, we might suspect so, although we don't know. Only when research takes place in a clinical setting will we know how cultural biases affect the ways that practitioners diagnose people. Until this research is conducted, we need to be skeptical that the best decisions are being made.

SEX AND GENDER: DO MEN AND WOMEN COME FROM DIFFERENT CULTURES?

Much has been made of the behavioral differences between men and women. Is it really true that men are from Mars and women are from Venus (Gray, 1992)? The short answer is that men and women may differ in some ways, but there are more similarities than differences (e.g., Eagly, 2009; Hyde, 2005)

If we regard culture the way that Matsumoto (1994) defined it, as "the set of attitudes, values, beliefs, and behaviors, shared by a group of people, communicated from one generation to the next via language or some other means of communication" (p. 4), we might very well argue that men and women are culturally different in some important ways. In addition, people stereotype men and women differently, just as people stereotype Whites and Blacks differently.

Iwamasa et al.'s (2000) research on the perception of stereotypically female or male behaviors also shed light on the fact that people have certain expectations about behaviors across the sexes. The investigators found that normal but stereotypically female behavior was associated with certain disorders (e.g., avoidant personality, paranoia) and normal but stereotypically male behavior with others (antisocial personality, schizoid personality).

In the realm of everyday behavior, people often make a big issue of the differences between women and men in math test scores, which are small when they exist at all. Although we don't understand all the factors associated with any differences, there are enough ambiguities that we should be skeptical of biological explanations. Some important issues about gender differences appear in the Controversy box on whether men are better than women at math.

Stereotypes and Gender-Related Performance

Could stereotypes of women negatively affect their performance in the same way that stereotypes affect the performance of African Americans and Asian Americans (Cheryan & Bodenhausen, 2000; Steele & Aronson, 1995)? According to Inzlicht and Ben-Zeev (2000), when women attempt to solve difficult math problems in the presence of men, they are less successful than when they are in the presence of other women only. These researchers suggest that, in the presence of men, women act out the stereotype of poorer female performance in mathematics, although other investigators have found that stereotype threat occurs mainly in conjunction with anxiety (Delgado & Prieto, 2008).

Moving back to the question of possible cultural differences between men and women, it seems that some psychologists might be comfortable with the idea. Women see themselves as different from men in some respects; men see themselves as different from women in some respects. Knowing what you do about our culture, do you think that these perceived differences revolve around attitudes, beliefs, and behaviors that are passed from one generation to another? If so, they fit generally accepted definitions of cultural differences.

CONTROVERSY:
Are Men Better than Women at Mathematics?

It is a very widely held belief that women have better verbal abilities than men. Conversely, many people believe that men show better mathematical abilities than women do. In fact, among the general public, you don't hear much argument about it. Just take a look at high school math courses: Boys like them and are more likely to enroll in them. On the other hand, girls like poetry and literature and are more willing to enroll in them. Given that most people will gravitate toward things they do better in, doesn't this say something about the relative abilities of boys and girls in math and English?

The patterns of enrollment in math and English definitely give us important information, but not necessarily the information we think. Maybe ability doesn't have as much to do with enrollment and success in classes as other factors like encouragement and discouragement. Consider the fact that, at one point, talking Barbie dolls complained how hard mathematics is. Is there a message here? Perhaps years of emphasizing that girls don't like math but boys do, and that boys don't like English but girls do takes its toll.

As Caplan and Caplan (1999) have noted, the popular media have reported about male superiority in mathematics. Should we believe these accounts of sex differences in mathematical abilities?

Two decades ago, Benbow and Stanley (1980, 1983) claimed that hormonal differences in math performance may have been responsible for the differences between men and women. As Caplan and Caplan pointed out, however, nobody bothered to measure hormonal levels of the men or women in the research. Thus, the argument that hormones affect performance goes something like this: Men have higher testosterone levels than women. The men scored higher than the women. Thus, higher testosterone levels lead to higher

math scores. Logically, you cannot use two true, but unrelated, statements to prove an argument. There doesn't seem to be any reliable evidence that testosterone levels bear any relationship to math ability.

According to Caplan and Caplan, people are predisposed to believe in male superiority in math. As such, they are likely to accept plausible sounding arguments ("the difference is hormonal") even though those arguments are not based on research. When people are predisposed to believe in this difference between the sexes, they tend to ignore potentially potent factors like parents' and teachers' expectations, and responses to society's stereotypes.

We also have to take into consideration the dynamics of the testing situation. As Inzlicht and Ben-Zeev (2000) have shown, the context in which women take tests can influence their performance. Women doing math in the presence of men didn't perform as well as when they were in a single-sex environment. Another point to remember is that research has consistently documented female strengths in quantitative courses (e.g., Schram, 1996). Before we accept facile explanations based on questionable theory, we should rely on well-documented information and explanations that research has provided.

Finally, how do we explain the fact that recent research has revealed that the gap in women's and men's scores is narrowing. Are women becoming more masculine? Are men becoming more feminine? Are men's and women's hormonal levels changing? These are generally unlikely explanations. Greater emphasis on female success in math courses, increased encouragement to take math courses, higher motivation levels, and the nature of the testing situation are probably better explanations.

SUMMARY

In order to understand why people act as they do, we need to understand the cultural context in which those behaviors occur. The effects of culture, race, and ethnicity all surface in our behaviors. The problem that researchers face in considering these contextual questions is that the terms people use every day and even in scientific research are often quite vague. One researcher may refer to ethnicity in describing a behavior, whereas a different researcher may refer to culture in describing the same thing. Because of the problems with definitions, the conclusions that people draw about causes of behavior are sometimes suspect.

One persistent controversy in this area involves the questionable concept of race. There are quite a number of supposed racial categories. The problem is that these categories aren't scientifically defensible. The recent work in genetics indicates that genes are not going to be a useful way of defining races. Still, some scientists maintain that racial categories are useful in their research, even if they cannot define the concept very well.

Because of the complexities of culture, race, and ethnicity, scientific researchers have to work hard to understand the relationship between these constructs and people's behaviors. Research across cultures can be difficult because cultural factors may cause people to understand even simple situations differently. Judgments made by two people from the same cultural background may differ greatly; judgments across cultural boundaries may be nearly impossible to understand without research into those factors. Within the United States, differences between men and women have provided a good deal of controversy, with many questions yet unanswered.

REVIEW QUESTIONS

Multiple Choice Questions

1. The customs, values, and attitudes that can be used to characterize and identify a population refer to
   a. an etic.
   b. an emic.
   c. culture.
   d. relativism.
2. The notion that a person identifies with a particular group of people based on ancestry, religion, or country of origin involves the concept of
   a. ethnicity.
   b. race.
   c. physical culture.
   d. psychological culture.
3. When researchers try to study potential differences across racial and ethnic groups, the categories they use
   a. now rely on well-specified biological and genetic differences.
   b. generally overlap with religious categories, making comparisons difficult.
   c. are unchanging for a single individual over that person's lifespan.
   d. often rely on governmental rather than scientific criteria.

4. When researchers study differences between Hispanic and Anglo residents of the United States,
   a. the research shows few reliable differences between the groups.
   b. the research relies on categories recognized by behavioral scientists.
   c. the research often ignores the differences among people within each group itself.
   d. the research typically uses categorization data from several decades ago, so the results are questionable.

5. The virtually universal taboo against cannibalism would be regarded by researchers as
   a. a universal construct.
   b. a hypothetical construct.
   c. an etic.
   d. an emic.

6. The concept that internal, psychological processes may be universal but that they are expressed differently across cultures is associated with
   a. absolutism.
   b. etics.
   c. universalism.
   d. ethnic constructs.

7. The concept of race is controversial scientifically because
   a. the social history of the races has always been troublesome.
   b. the genetic differences between some races is larger than it is between other races.
   c. depending on the categorization process used, an individual could be placed in different racial categories.
   d. scientists have not been able to determine exactly where the different races fall on the racial continuum.

8. According to the Council of National Psychological Associations, investigators conducting cultural research should note that
   a. the differences across cultural groups are usually much larger than the differences within groups.
   b. developing test norms for a new culture is often costly and is not worth the cost most of the time because the norms change slowly.
   c. understanding the degree of acculturation of participants is critical to interpreting results.
   d. it is most useful to develop a single interpretation of research results and to avoid the complication of seeking alternate explanations.

9. Matsumoto and Assar (1992) tested participants who spoke English and Hindi on their abilities to recognize emotions of people in photographs. They concluded that
   a. the participants were engaged in the same types of mental processing regardless of language.
   b. the participants' thought processes were more conducive to thinking about emotions when they spoke English.
   c. speakers of English had less willingness to deal with the emotions depicted in the photographs.
   d. the same ideas and emotions are expressed easily in either language.

10. If American research participants were asked to identify the emotion in a facial photograph and rate its intensity, the results might be hard to interpret because
    a. there is little agreement on what behaviors are associated with different emotions.
    b. Americans of different cultural backgrounds show similar responses to some emotions but different responses to others.

    c. people often label the emotion depicted in a photograph very differently and with little consistency.

    d. people from different parts of the country label emotions in consistently different ways.

11. When a test is successfully back translated, it
   a. can be retranslated into virtually any new language.
   b. retains the same meaning in the initial language and the language into which it is translated.
   c. will have validity with respect to cross-cultural norms.
   d. cannot be forward translated afterward.

12. Iwamasa et al. (2000) studied differences in stereotypical female and male behaviors and found that
   a. there are really few consistent differences in behaviors across genders, even though many people perceive differences.
   b. the differences in math and verbal performances between women and men are consistently large.
   c. the stereotypes about male and female differences are true for most high school and college students.
   d. stereotypically female behaviors were associated with certain disorders and stereotypically male behaviors were associated with other disorders.

13. In the discussions of female–male differences in math ability, researchers
   a. have tended not to publish the studies showing female superiority.
   b. measured hormonal differences between women and men and found that the hormones played a part in the higher scores of men.
   c. discovered that if women are tested with men, the women use the situation competitively to raise their math performance.
   d. have reported that the differences between sexes is, on average, small and is getting smaller.

Essay Questions

14. Why is it so hard to distinguish among the effects of culture, race, and ethnicity in our research?
15. Why should we differentiate between etics and emics in our explanations of behavior?
16. Why are culture, race, and ethnicity hypothetical constructs? In what sense are they useful and in what sense are they limited?
17. What are some difficulties that scientists have had in categorizing people by race and in defining race?
18. Why is content validity a critical concept to consider in conducting research on tests administered by mental health workers when working with people from different backgrounds and cultures?

ANSWERS TO REVIEW QUESTIONS

Answers to Multiple Choice Questions

1. c	6. c	11. b
2. a	7. c	12. d
3. d	8. c	13. d
4. c	9. b	
5. c	10. b	

Answers to Essay Questions

14. Why is it so hard to distinguish among the effects of culture, race, and ethnicity in our research?

People, including psychologists, use the terms *culture*, *race*, and *ethnicity* very imprecisely. One researcher might refer to a person's culture but a second researcher might refer to race or ethnicity in explaining the same behaviors; the researchers might mean the same thing, but they use different terms to refer to the same thing. Or they might really mean different things when they use the terms differently. Unfortunately, there is no consistent agreement about what the terms mean. In addition, the concept of race is problematic because there are not characteristics that we can use to reliably categorize people racially; there will always be confusion because some people resist easy categorization. Many scientists regard race as a social construction rather than as a biological fact.

It is important to distinguish between them because they can refer to useful constructs. For instance, ethnicity is often associated with affiliation (e.g., who do you think you belong with), whereas culture pertains to the objects we use (physical culture) or to behaviors (subjective culture).

15. Why should we differentiate between etics and emics in our explanations of behavior?

Etics are research results that hold true across cultures; emics are research results pertaining to a single culture. It is important to differentiate between them because we need to pay attention to the fact that behaviors in different societies may have very different causes and explanations.

16. Why are culture, race, and ethnicity hypothetical constructs? In what sense are they useful and in what sense are they limited?

Culture, race, and ethnicity are hypothetical constructs because they are concepts that psychologists have constructed to help explain and understand behavior. They are hypothetical because we hypothesize that they exist and that they are going to be useful, explanatory concepts.

Sometimes these constructs are helpful because, when measured appropriately, they might be helpful in our understanding of why people in some groups act one way, whereas people in another group act differently. Not everybody in a group acts and thinks the same way, but the hypothetical constructs of culture and ethnicity can give some insights into group processes.

On the other hand, none of these concepts can be precisely defined and measured, which is why we rely on external markers (e.g., skin color) to represent them. These external markers may not really be very helpful in understanding behavior because they are only imperfectly correlated with thought and behavior. People within a given group differ from one another in many ways, so trying to figure out how a single person thinks is not feasible.

17. What are some difficulties that scientists have had in categorizing people by race and in defining race?
    a. Skin color has often been a means by which people are racially categorized. This is unreliable because sometimes people with darker skin will be considered "White" while people with lighter skin will be considered "Black."
    b. Race is seen as involving discrete, mutually exclusive categories; a person falls in one and only one category. In reality, the characteristics associated with the categories fall on a continuum, so the cutoff points are arbitrary.
    c. Scientists have not reached consensus about what racial categories there might actually be. There is no set number of racial categories that scientists agree on.
    d. Geographical criteria for race is unreliable because there are many people whose birthplace is not a reliable indicator of their ancestry, which is likely to be mixed in any case.
    e. When scientists did create racial categories, they were based on subjective, nonscientific criteria.

18. Why is content validity a critical concept to consider in conducting research on tests administered by mental health workers when working with people from different backgrounds and cultures?

Content validity relates to the questions that clinicians ask when working with a client. In order to draw good conclusions, the clinician must ask appropriate questions. What will be appropriate in one setting or with one group may not be useful in another context.

People with different lifestyles may not share the same perspective, so a simple question might indicate something quite different across groups. Similarly, a certain behavior will reflect normal functioning in one culture, abnormal functioning in a second, and be completely irrelevant in a third. The potential problems are compounded when a clinician wants to translate a question into a different language; there may not be corresponding ideas in different languages.

In order for test items to be valid for different groups, the concepts have to address the appropriate ideas using appropriate words. Without content validity, answers to individual questions on a test may mislead a clinician entirely.

WRITING A RESEARCH REPORT

Most research reports in psychology appearing in journals have a standard format, which is specified in the *Publication Manual of the American Psychological Association* (6th ed.). The use of a consistent style makes it easier for readers to locate critical information. In addition, once writers learn the basics of APA style, it can be easier to write up a report because it is clear where to put various kinds of information.

In general, APA-style papers have the following components in this order:

- Title Page
- Abstract
- Introduction
- Methods
- Results

- Discussion
- References
- Tables
- Figures

Occasionally, there are deviations from this listing. For instance, if a manuscript reports on two or more studies, the author might combine the Results and Discussion section for each study rather than creating two sections. Then there might be a General Discussion after the final study. Following APA style isn't difficult, but you have to pay attention to the details.

As with any writing you do, it is important to communicate well. The former editor of the journal *Teaching of Psychology*, Charles Brewer, has commented that writers should strive for "clarity, conciseness, and felicity of expression." This means that you should be clear in making your points; you should use economy in your writing, keeping it as short as you can while still getting your message across; and you should write so that your readers don't have to fight their way through a tangled thicket of words to get your point.

This appendix is designed to help you learn appropriate formatting so your reader knows where to find information. It will also be somewhat useful in giving you guidance on writing style. Remember that this guide to APA style only highlights the material in the *Publication Manual of the American Psychological Association*. The information here will be useful for creating a basic APA-formatted manuscript. There are many other details in the *Publication Manual* itself.

FORMATTING YOUR MANUSCRIPT

There are a few general considerations involved in formatting an APA-style manuscript. To begin with, you should set your margins at one inch on the top, bottom, and sides. Then leave them that way. In addition, everything in the manuscript should be double spaced. Set your word processor's line spacing at double spaced. Then leave it that way.

Another aspect of APA style is that every page should be numbered in the upper right-hand corner, next to the short title. The best way to display the header and to paginate appropriately is with your word processor's function for creating a page header. By using the header function, you guarantee that this information appears where it needs to on every page. If you type in the header and the page number manually, any time you add or eliminate material in your manuscript, the header and page number will wind up in the wrong place.

When you are typing your manuscript, you will create several different sections (e.g., Introduction, Methods, Results, Discussion). For most of these sections, you do not begin a new section on a new page. As a rule, just continue to type, using normal double spacing between lines. There are some exceptions to this; they are explained below.

In addition, you have to create headings for each section. There are different levels of headings, depending on the complexity of your manuscript. For most single-study manuscripts, you will use two different types of headings.

When you finish typing the main body of the manuscript and the references, you then add any tables that you want to include. The tables do not appear on the pages with the normal text. They are put at the end, right after the references. Each table goes on a separate page. If you have created figures, place each one on its own page with a figure caption on that page. (In previous editions of the APA manual, the figure captions went on a separate page; this is no longer the case.) Graphs, charts, and pictures are all classified as figures.

The general points in this section appear in Figure A-1. Remember that this is a primer on APA style. There are other guidelines that are relevant to more complex manuscripts than you are likely to produce. You can refer to the *Publication Manual* for those details. You can also learn from reading and referring to journal articles that have been published.

TITLE PAGE

The title page is pretty simple to construct, but it is important to include all the information that is required. You can see the general format in Figure A-2. There are three main components of the title page: the running head, and the title, and the author information.

Running Head

The running head consists of a shortened version of the paper's title. The running head helps others keep your manuscript together and in the right order if printed pages become separated. If the title of your paper is "Study habits of college students over four years,"

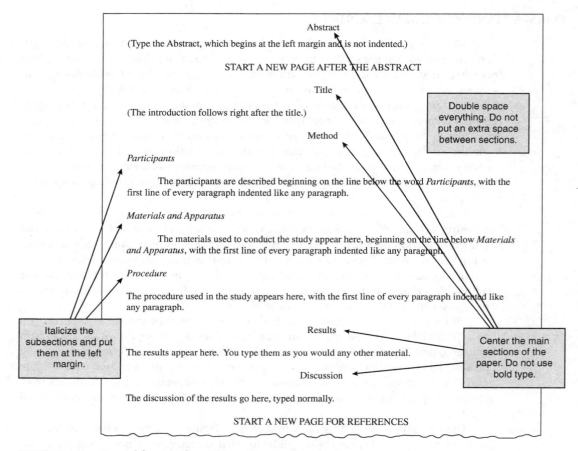

FIGURE A-1   General format of an APA-style research report.

the running head would be something like *STUDENT STUDY HABITS* (typed in all capital letters). (You should not italicize it. The examples in this appendix appear in italics so you can see them, but you rarely use italics in a research report.)

The running head appears on every page of the manuscript, so it is best to use your Header/Footer capability on your word processor to create it. In this way, your computer will make sure that the pages are numbered correctly and that the running head is in place, even if you revise your paper, adding or eliminating material.

The words "RUNNING HEAD" appear only on the title page. On all other pages, only the actual running head appears. The running head is like an abbreviated title. It should explain the general nature of your project. It is limited to a maximum of 50 characters (i.e., letters and spaces). Your full title may be longer than 50 characters, so the running head

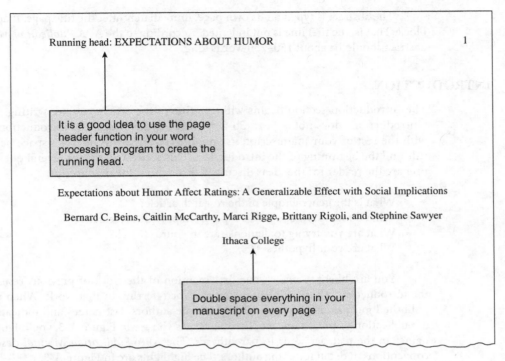

Running head: EXPECTATIONS ABOUT HUMOR   1

It is a good idea to use the page header function in your word processing program to create the running head.

Expectations about Humor Affect Ratings: A Generalizable Effect with Social Implications

Bernard C. Beins, Caitlin McCarthy, Marci Rigge, Brittany Rigoli, and Stephine Sawyer

Ithaca College

Double space everything in your manuscript on every page

FIGURE A-2   Format of a title page in APA style.

needs to be a shorter version of the title. If you title is fewer than 50 characters, you can use the full title of your paper as the running head.

Title and Author Information

The title of the paper should clue the reader into the nature of your project. The recommended length is 10–12 words. Your name and your affiliation, which will be your school (unless your instructor tells you otherwise for a class paper), appear just below the title of the paper. They let the reader know who you are and where you come from. In a manuscript submitted to a journal, you would include an author note on the title page; this feature is not usually required in a paper for a course.

ABSTRACT

The abstract is a brief description of the purpose of the project, what methods the author used to address the issues of interest, the results of data collection, and the conclusions and interpretations the author drew. This section gives the reader a general sense of the paper so he or she can decide whether to read the entire paper.

The abstract is typed on its own page, immediately after the title page. It appears as a block. That is, the first line is not indented. According to the APA *Publication Manual*, the abstract should be about 150–250 words long.

INTRODUCTION

The Introduction section begins with the title of the article you are writing. The word "Introduction" does not appear. So type the title, then begin the introduction itself. As with the rest of your manuscript, use double spacing, with no extra space between the title and the beginning of the introduction. This section addresses several questions that prepare the reader for the ideas discussed throughout the manuscript:

- What is the general topic of the research article?
- What do we know about this topic from previous research?
- What are you trying to demonstrate in your research?
- What are your hypotheses?

You are likely to make your first mention of the work of previous researchers in the introduction. There is a general format for referring to that work. When you cite a published journal article, you typically use the authors' last names and indicate the year of publication or presentation of their work. As you see in Figure A-3, you might mention names in the text per se or in parentheses. The APA *Publication Manual* describes the conventions in detail for citing authors. The highlights are in Figure A-3.

METHOD

This section of the manuscript contains several subparts. Each one is pretty much self-contained. The purpose of the Method section is to let the reader know how you actually carried out your project. There should be enough detail so another person could read your words and reproduce your study in nearly identical form. You should present only those details that would be relevant to the purpose and outcome of the study. The different segments of the Method section describe who took part, what materials and implements were important in carrying out the study, and the procedure used to complete the research.

Participants

In this subsection, you tell the reader who participated in the study, how many people (or rats, mice, pigeons, etc.) were involved, and the demographics of your sample (e.g., age, ethnicity, educational level, etc., as appropriate). The information readers need to know about your participants includes the following:

- How many humans or nonhumans were studied?
- If there were nonhuman animals, what kind were they?
- If there were people, what were their characteristics (e.g., average and range of age, gender, race or ethnicity, were they volunteers or were they paid, etc.)?

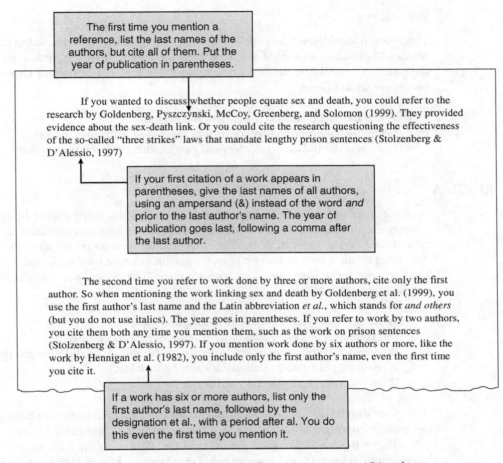

The first time you mention a reference, list the last names of the authors, but cite all of them. Put the year of publication in parentheses.

If you wanted to discuss whether people equate sex and death, you could refer to the research by Goldenberg, Pyszczynski, McCoy, Greenberg, and Solomon (1999). They provided evidence about the sex-death link. Or you could cite the research questioning the effectiveness of the so-called "three strikes" laws that mandate lengthy prison sentences (Stolzenberg & D'Alessio, 1997)

If your first citation of a work appears in parentheses, give the last names of all authors, using an ampersand (&) instead of the word *and* prior to the last author's name. The year of publication goes last, following a comma after the last author.

The second time you refer to work done by three or more authors, cite only the first author. So when mentioning the work linking sex and death by Goldenberg et al. (1999), you use the first author's last name and the Latin abbreviation *et al.*, which stands for *and others* (but you do not use italics). The year goes in parentheses. If you refer to work by two authors, you cite them both any time you mention them, such as the work on prison sentences (Stolzenberg & D'Alessio, 1997). If you mention work done by six authors or more, like the work by Hennigan et al. (1982), you include only the first author's name, even the first time you cite it.

If a work has six or more authors, list only the first author's last name, followed by the designation et al., with a period after al. You do this even the first time you mention it.

FIGURE A-3   Reference formats for citing work in a manuscript in APA style.

Apparatus and Materials

The basic issues in this subsection involve what you needed to carry out your study. Sometimes you have used machines, computers, or other instrumentation. Much psychological research also requires materials that participants read, learn, memorize, and so on. When you have created your own apparatus, you should describe it in great detail. If you used commercially available apparatus, you can simply mention the type of apparatus (with make and model), the company that provided it, and any other relevant details that would be useful for somebody who might want to replicate or simply understand your approach. Important information about materials and apparatus include:

- How many and what kind of stimuli, questions, etc., were used?
- What instrumentation, if any, was used to present material to participants and to record their responses?

Procedure

This subsection addresses the issue of what the participants actually did during the research session. The details here should give a complete account of what your participants did from the time the study began until the debriefing was done. The important elements of the procedure are as follows:

- When the participants arrived, what did they do?
- What did the experimenters do as they interacted with participants?
- In what order did experimenters and participants carry out their tasks?

RESULTS

In this section, you give a verbal description of your results, accompanied by appropriate quantitative information (e.g., means and standard deviations, statistical analyses). It is often difficult for a reader to understand your results if you simply list all of them without describing them. A long series of means, for instance, can be hard for a reader to comprehend without some narrative to accompany them. The critical questions in the Results section include the following:

- What were patterns of behaviors among participants?
- Did responses and behaviors differ when groups were compared?
- What types of responses or reactions are predictable in the different groups?
- Were there predictable relationships among variables?
- What were the results of any statistical tests?

Your Results section can also include tables and figures. Sometimes a table or a figure can present important information much more simply than you can describe it in words. When that is the case, make good use of tables and figures. At the same time, try to avoid using tables and figures that do present only a small amount of useful information. You probably don't want to use a graph, for example, if you have only two data points to compare.

In detailing your results, make sure that you give enough of a verbal description so the reader has a good idea of what you found. If you present only numerical information, the reader may have difficulty understanding which results were most important and how they related to one another.

Tables

Tables can present data very effectively and efficiently. They are relatively easy to create with the Tables function in your word processing program. Figure A-4 outlines some of the main considerations in the use of a table.

At times, tables can get quite complex, especially when there are many groups being compared or when researchers use complex statistical analyses. The basic format is pretty simple, though. The table consists of a label that gives enough information to the readers so they don't have to refer back to the text to comprehend the contents of the table. The table also contains data, often organized by conditions or groups. Sometimes, mean

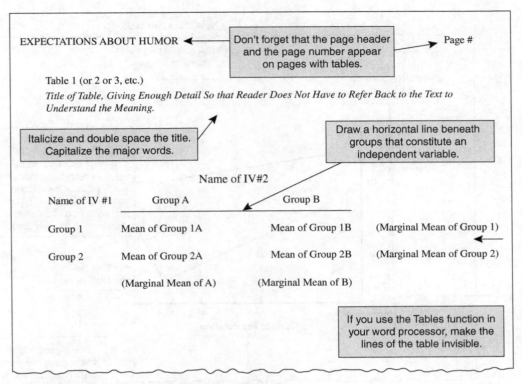

FIGURE A-4 Example of a results table in APA style.

values appear in the margins of the tables, the so-called marginal means. In some cases, tables may not contain numbers, but only words and text. This type of table follows the same general principles as numeric tables.

Figures

Graphs and charts used to be difficult to construct when an author had to draw them by hand. Currently, however, data analysis software and spreadsheets permit easy construction of graphs. It is important to remember that when you use graphic presentations, you should make sure that they convey the information you want in a manner that is easy for the reader to comprehend. It takes some practice in creating effective visual presentations; you can learn how to construct them by looking at published figures to see which ones are effective and which ones are not.

The main types of figures used in research articles are line graphs, bar graphs, and scatter diagrams. Line graphs show the relation between two quantitative variables. Bar graphs are often used to represent relations among categorical variables. Scatter diagrams usually reflect correlational analyses. Figures A-5 and Figure A-6 provide examples of line graphs that look slightly different, but that convey the same information. The two graphs show that the depiction can look different depending on which independent variable you put on the X-axis and which variable you place in the graph.

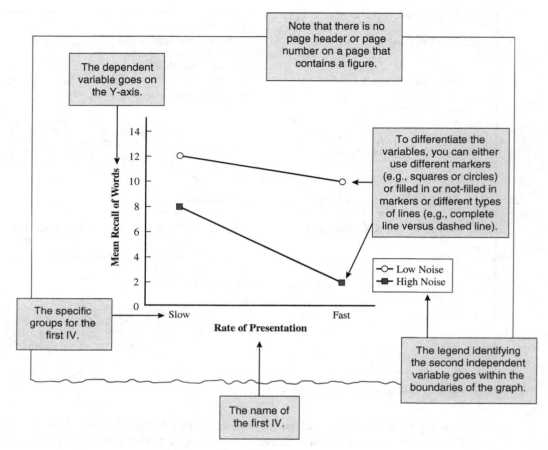

FIGURE A-5   Example of a line graph in APA style.

You can represent your data in bar graphs. Typically, bar graphs represent categorical data, but the example in Figure A-7 is based on the same continuous data we've been working with in these examples. You can see that the visual representation of the bar graph shows the same pattern that you saw in Figure A-5.

If you have completed a correlational analysis, you might want to present a scatter diagram that reveals the relation between two variables. The basic format of this type of figure is the same as for line graphs and bar graphs. The type of information in a scatter diagram is different in an important way, though. Unlike line and bar graphs, which present data at the level of groups, a scatter diagram includes data points from each individual on two variables being measured.

Statistical Results

The statistics that you are most likely to use in your research report are the analysis of variance, the Student's t-test, the Pearson product–moment correlation, and the Chi-Square

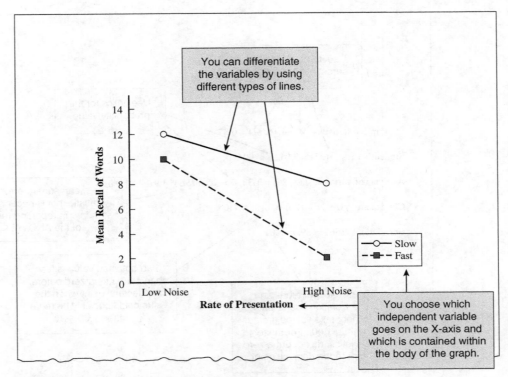

FIGURE A-6 Example of a line graph in APA style (version 2).

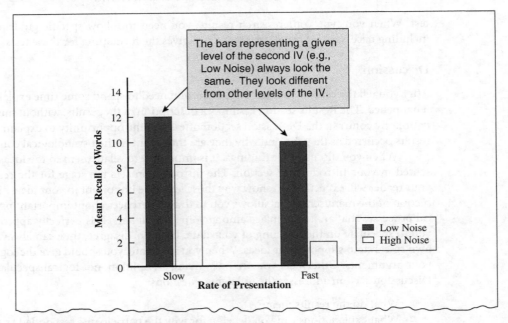

FIGURE A-7 Example of a bar graph in APA style.

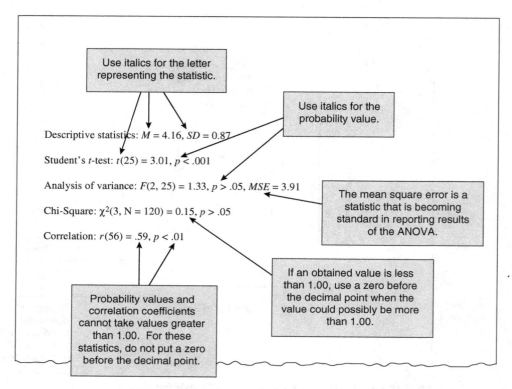

Use italics for the letter representing the statistic.

Use italics for the probability value.

Descriptive statistics: $M = 4.16$, $SD = 0.87$

Student's t-test: $t(25) = 3.01$, $p < .001$

Analysis of variance: $F(2, 25) = 1.33$, $p > .05$, $MSE = 3.91$

Chi-Square: $\chi^2(3, N = 120) = 0.15$, $p > .05$

Correlation: $r(56) = .59$, $p < .01$

The mean square error is a statistic that is becoming standard in reporting results of the ANOVA.

If an obtained value is less than 1.00, use a zero before the decimal point when the value could possibly be more than 1.00.

Probability values and correlation coefficients cannot take values greater than 1.00. For these statistics, do not put a zero before the decimal point.

FIGURE A-8   Format for presenting statistical results in APA style.

test. When you type your research results, you need to follow specific guidelines about including necessary information. Figure A-8 gives the formatting for these tests.

Discussion

After you tell the reader what has happened, you need to spend some time explaining why it happened. The Results section is simply a description of the results, without much explanation. By contrast, the Discussion section offers you the opportunity to explain why your results occurred as they did and why they are important to the psychological community.

When you discuss your findings, it is important to relate them to the ideas you presented in your Introduction section. The introduction sets the stage for the research, so your reader will expect you to show why those ideas are important to your ideas. This is the section of the manuscript that allows you to draw inferences about important psychological processes that are taking place among your participants. It is perfectly appropriate for you to speculate on the meaning of your data. If others disagree, they can always do their own research to support their ideas. When you speculate, you should give the logic behind your arguments. Otherwise, you are only giving an opinion, not logical speculation. The Discussion section addresses the following questions:

- What do the results mean?
- What explanations can you develop for why the participants responded as they did?

- What psychological processes help you explain participants' responses?
- What questions have not been answered fully?
- How can your results relate to the research cited in the introduction?
- How do your results relate to other kinds of research?

Did any new ideas emerge that you could evaluate in a subsequent experiment?

References

The Reference section includes the full citation for any work that you referred to in your writing. This section is only for works cited in your paper; it is not a general bibliography related to your topic. The rule is that if something was referred to in the manuscript, it belongs here; if a work was not mentioned in your writing, it does not appear here.

The reference section is actually fairly easy to create because you know exactly what the section must contain. The only difficulty is making sure that you use the correct format in the citation. You may be familiar with styles other than APA's, like MLA (from the Modern Language Association) or the Chicago style. They are considerably different from APA style. Fortunately, in your manuscripts, you are likely to use only a few of the many types of sources available, so it is easy to become familiar with the rules for citing references. Examples appear in Figures A-9 through A-12.

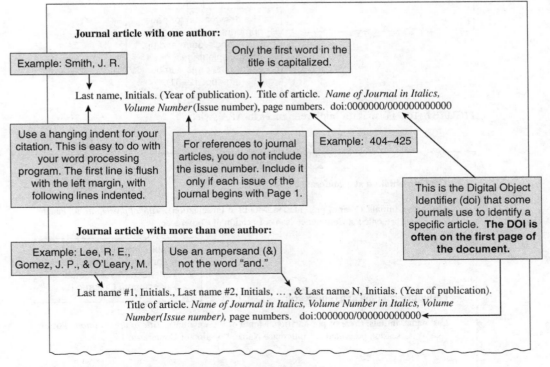

FIGURE A-9 Format for journal article references in APA style.

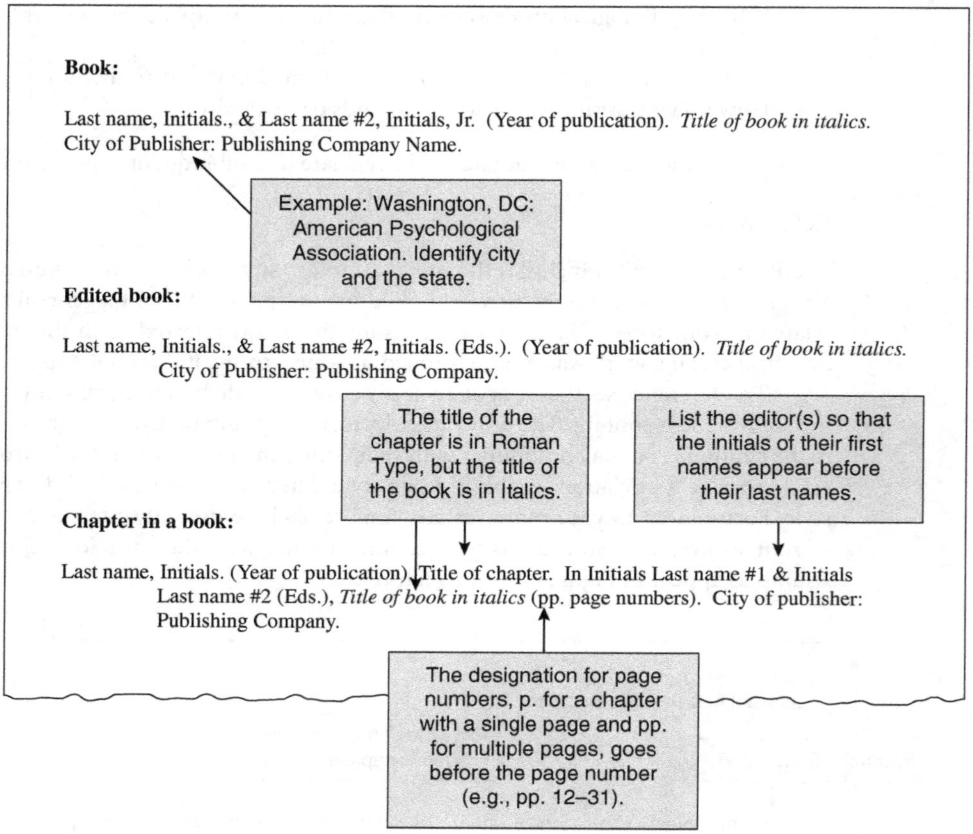

Book:

Last name, Initials., & Last name #2, Initials, Jr. (Year of publication). *Title of book in italics.*
City of Publisher: Publishing Company Name.

> Example: Washington, DC:
> American Psychological
> Association. Identify city
> and the state.

Edited book:

Last name, Initials., & Last name #2, Initials. (Eds.). (Year of publication). *Title of book in italics.*
City of Publisher: Publishing Company.

> The title of the
> chapter is in Roman
> Type, but the title of
> the book is in Italics.

> List the editor(s) so that
> the initials of their first
> names appear before
> their last names.

Chapter in a book:

Last name, Initials. (Year of publication). Title of chapter. In Initials Last name #1 & Initials
Last name #2 (Eds.), *Title of book in italics* (pp. page numbers). City of publisher:
Publishing Company.

> The designation for page
> numbers, p. for a chapter
> with a single page and pp.
> for multiple pages, goes
> before the page number
> (e.g., pp. 12–31).

FIGURE A-10   Format for book references in APA style.

> Example: 2002, August

Oral presentation at a conference:

Last name, Initials. (Year of presentation, Month of Presentation). *Title of presentation.* Paper
presented at Conference Name, Location of Conference.

> Example: Paper presented at
> the annual convention of the
> American Psychological
> Association, Chicago IL.

Poster presentation at a conference:

Last name, Initials. (Year of presentation, Month of Presentation). *Title of presentation.* Poster
session presented at Conference Name, Location of Conference.

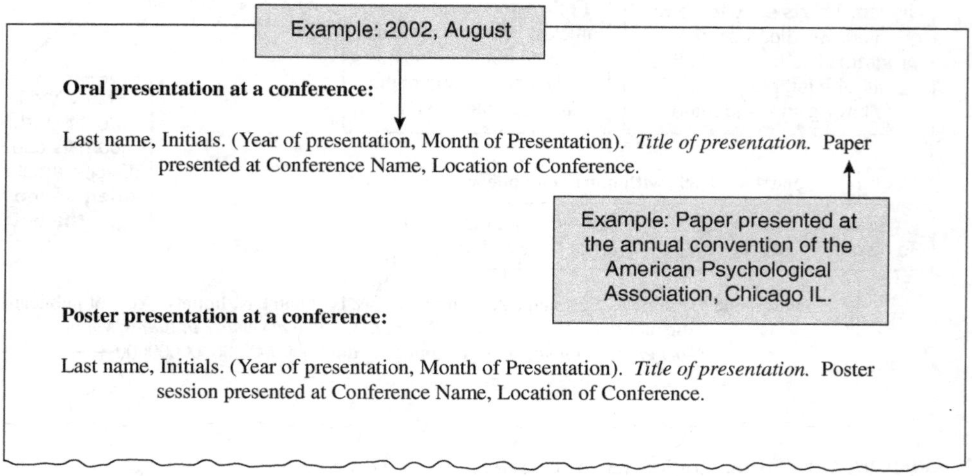

FIGURE A-11   Format for oral and poster presentation references in APA style.

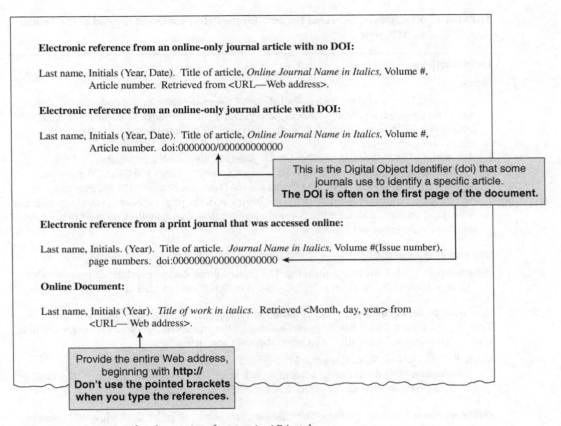

Electronic reference from an online-only journal article with no DOI:

Last name, Initials (Year, Date). Title of article, *Online Journal Name in Italics,* Volume #,
    Article number. Retrieved from <URL—Web address>.

Electronic reference from an online-only journal article with DOI:

Last name, Initials (Year, Date). Title of article, *Online Journal Name in Italics,* Volume #,
    Article number. doi:0000000/000000000000

> This is the Digital Object Identifier (doi) that some journals use to identify a specific article. **The DOI is often on the first page of the document.**

Electronic reference from a print journal that was accessed online:

Last name, Initials. (Year). Title of article. *Journal Name in Italics,* Volume #(Issue number),
    page numbers. doi:0000000/000000000000

Online Document:

Last name, Initials (Year). *Title of work in italics.* Retrieved <Month, day, year> from
    <URL— Web address>.

> Provide the entire Web address, beginning with **http://** **Don't use the pointed brackets when you type the references.**

FIGURE A-12   Format for electronic references in APA style.

The most common sources are journal articles, books and book chapters, presentations at conferences, and electronic resources. You can see how to format them in Figures A-9 through A-12. Specific examples appear in Table A-1. Each of these can come in several different varieties, so you will have to make sure that you are following the APA guidelines exactly. For details on the less common types of references, you can consult the *Publication Manual of the American Psychological Association.* There are also numerous Web sites that provide help. The technical information about the citations tells the reader:

- What research was cited in the report (e.g., work published in journals or other written sources, research presentations, personal communications)?
- Where was the information made public?

TABLE A-1 Examples of Reference Formats for the Reference List at the End of the Article in APA style.

Journal articles:

Notes:

1. Most journal articles now have a so-called *digital object identifier*, or *doi* designation. If there is no doi for a journal article, the citation simply ends right after the page numbers of the article. If there is a doi, it comes immediately after the period following the page numbers of the journal article.
2. You do not include the issue number for the journal, only the volume number, if the journal has continuous pagination. If the first issue of a volume has pages 1 to 64 and the second begins with page 65, you don't need to include the issue number, only the page numbers of the article. On the other hand, if each issue begins with the page number 1, you do include the issue number. Almost all scientific journals have continuous pagination, so most of the time you don't include the issue number.

One author of an article:

Heitzmann, D. (2011). Recalling our roots: The joy of college student psychotherapy. *Journal of College Student Psychotherapy, 25,* 103–104. doi:10.1080/87568225.2011.556924

Two to six authors of an article: (All authors' names appear, with a comma after each one, including the author whose name appears just before the ampersand [&] when there are multiple authors. The citation ends with the page numbers of the article.)

Mitchell, S. L., Darrow, S. A., Haggerty, M., Neill, T., Carvalho, A., & Uschold, C. (2012). Curriculum infusion as college student mental health promotion strategy. *Journal of College Student Psychotherapy, 26,* 22–38. doi:10.1080/87568225.2012.633038

Article with more than six authors: The following article had 48 authors, which would take too much space in the reference section. So you cite only the first six, then type three ellipsis points (…), an ampersand (&), and the final author. There should be commas after all authors' names except the final author:

Löckenhoff, C. E., De Fruyt, F., Terracciano, A., McCrae, R. R., De Bolle, M., Costa, P. R., &… Yik, M. (2009). Perceptions of aging across 26 cultures and their culture-level associates. *Psychology and Aging, 24,* 941–954. doi:10.1037/a0016901

Reference in Internet-only journal article:

Katz, J., Tirone, V., & van der Kloet, E. (2012). Moving in and hooking up: Women's and men's casual sexual experiences during the first two months of college. *Electronic Journal of Human Sexuality, 12.* Retrieved from http://www.ejhs.org/volume15/Hookingup.html

Reference to an article published online in advance of the print journal:

Swanson, H. L. (2011, August 22). Working memory, attention, and mathematical problem solving: A longitudinal study of elementary school children. *Journal of Educational Psychology.* Advance online publication. doi:10.1037/a0025114

TABLE A-1   (Continued)

Book:

Cytowic, R. E. (1993). *The man who tasted shapes*. New York, NY: G. P. Putnam & Son.

Edited book:

Davis, S. F., & Buskist, W. (Eds.) (2002). *The teaching of psychology: Essays in honor of Wilbert J. McKeachie and Charles L. Brewer*. Mahwah, NJ: Erlbaum.

Chapter in an edited book:

Gardner, H., Krechevsky, M., Sternberg, R. J., & Okagaki, L. (1994). Intelligence in context: Enhancing students' practical intelligence for school. In K. McGilly (Ed.), *Classroom lessons: Integrating cognitive theory and classroom practice* (pp. 105, 127). Cambridge, MA: MIT Press.

Ball, P., Giles, H., & Hewstone, M. (1984). Second language acquisition: The intergroup theory with catastrophic dimensions. In H. Tajfel (Ed.), *The social dimension* (Vol. 2, pp. 668, 694). Cambridge, UK: Cambridge University Press.

Online document:

Lloyd, M.A. (2001, January 20). Marky Lloyd's careers in psychology page. Retrieved April 2, 2012 from http://www.psywww.com/careers/index.htm.

Oral presentation at a conference:

Loftus, E. F. (2003, January). *Illusions of memory*. Presented at the National Institute on the Teaching of Psychology. St. Petersburg Beach, FL.

Paper session at a conference:

Freedner, E., Wright, F., & Beins, B. C. (2007 April). *How expectation affects humor appreciation*. Paper presentation at the University of Scranton Psychology Conference, Scranton, PA.

Poster session at a conference:

Doychak, K., Herschman, C., Ferrante, P., & Beins, B. C. (2012, March). *Sense of humor: Are we all above average?* Poster session at the annual convention of the Eastern Psychological Association, Pittsburgh, PA.

WRITING STYLE

As the *Publication Manual of the American Psychological Association* points out, scientific writing is different from fiction or other creative writing. Scientific writing benefits from clear and direct communication, whereas creative writing benefits from the creation of ambiguity, abrupt changes in perspective, and other literary devices. When you write a research report, you should concentrate on making your point clearly, avoiding prose that doesn't contribute to the logic of your arguments.

This section presents some common problems in writing that you should note. Much of your writing to this point has probably been more literary than scientific, so you might have to unlearn some habits that you have developed.

Precision of Expression

When you write, avoid using more words than you need and avoid words that are more technical than necessary. Sometimes communication is better when you use a technical term because it has a specific meaning that the term transmits very efficiently. On the other hand, when you use complex wording to describe a simple situation, the reader can get confused. Using impressive terminology may not help you get your point across.

Just as you should avoid being too technical, you have to make sure that you are not too informal in your language. If an experiment has some methodological flaws, for example, and the results might be confounded, you should not make vague statements like *The methodological flaws skewed the results* because the word *skew* could mean just about anything. You would want to be more specific, suggesting that *The methodological flaws led to higher mean scores in Groups A and B*, or something equally explanatory. Or if your participants engaged in a behavior in some circumstances, you should specify how often the behavior occurred; ill-defined statements like *most of the time* do not communicate as precisely as you want in a research report.

Another grammatical feature that leads to problems is the use of passive-voice verbs (e.g., *they were asked to move* instead of *I asked them to move*). For one thing, such verbs make for dull prose. Another problem is that passive-voice verbs lead to lack of clarity. That is, to say that *The participants were given the materials* means that you are not telling your reader who did the giving. When you use passive-voice verbs, the actor is often hidden. In some cases, it is important to know who completed the action. In virtually all cases, active-voice verbs make your prose more interesting.

Avoiding Biased Language

When you describe or refer to people in your writing, use language that gets your point across but also shows sensitivity to the individuals and groups to which you refer. For example, sexist language can be problematic. If you make a statement that *The pioneers, their wives, and their children who settled the western states experienced hardships we cannot even imagine*, you are showing bias in your language. The implication is that the men were the pioneers, whereas the women and children were not.

Another type of bias that we see less than we used to regarding the sexes is the use of the word *man* to refer to people in general. The convention of using *man* to refer to people also led to the use of male pronouns (i.e., *his, him*) when the meaning supposedly included women. This change has led to the use of plural pronouns in referring to a single person (e.g., *A student can be rude when they use their cell phones in class*). Although this has gained acceptance in speech, it is not appropriate in formal writing because if you use a pronoun to refer to a *student*, the pronoun must be singular. One solution is to use plural nouns (e.g., *student*) so the use of plural pronouns is grammatically consistent. The use of *he or she, his or her*, or other double pronouns can also solve the problem if you use a singular noun.

A further issue regarding pronouns involves the use of first-person pronouns (e.g., *I* or *we*). Many students have learned to avoid using the personal pronoun *I*. Teachers have said to use passive-voice verbs or to use *we* in their writing when they mean only a single person, that is, themselves. According to APA style, it is appropriate to use *I* when referring to yourself). Using *I* also avoids the use of passive-voice verbs, which you should keep to an absolute minimum.

Another issue involves sensitivity to diverse groups, particularly with respect to the labeling of those groups. It is impossible to state a set of unchanging rules because the terms we use to denote people in various groups change. It may not be possible to satisfy everybody in every group, but you should be aware of the terms that any particular time are appropriate for describing them. Incidentally, if you use the words *Black* and *White* as racial or ethnic terms, these words should be capitalized.

Recently, authorities on writing have concluded that it is not appropriate to refer to people as though a single characteristic defined them completely. For example, in discussing people with handicaps, you should avoid calling them *the handicapped* because such a term implies that the handicap is perhaps their most significant characteristic. Noting that they are either *handicapped people* or *people with handicaps* highlights the fact that they are, first and foremost, people. For a task as difficult as writing well, these few rules will not suffice by themselves. But they provide a good start.

The following section presents a brief example of an APA-style paper based on research conducted by students and presented at the annual convention of the New England Psychological Association in 2007.

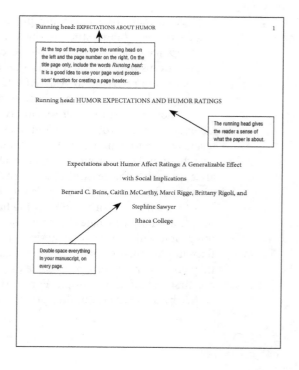

Running head: EXPECTATIONS ABOUT HUMOR   1

At the top of the page, type the running head on the left and the page number on the right. On the title page only, include the words *Running head:* It is a good idea to use your page word processors' function for creating a page header.

Running head: HUMOR EXPECTATIONS AND HUMOR RATINGS

The running head gives the reader a sense of what the paper is about.

Expectations about Humor Affect Ratings: A Generalizable Effect

with Social Implications

Bernard C. Beins, Caitlin McCarthy, Marci Rigge, Brittany Rigoli, and

Stephine Sawyer

Ithaca College

Double space everything in your manuscript, on every page.

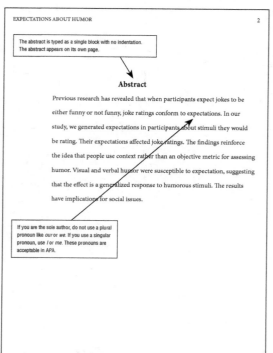

The abstract is typed as a single block with no indentation. The abstract appears on its own page.

Abstract

Previous research has revealed that when participants expect jokes to be either funny or not funny, joke ratings conform to expectations. In our study, we generated expectations in participants about stimuli they would be rating. Their expectations affected joke ratings. The findings reinforce the idea that people use context rather than an objective metric for assessing humor. Visual and verbal humor were susceptible to expectation, suggesting that the effect is a generalized response to humorous stimuli. The results have implications for social issues.

If you are the sole author, do not use a plural pronoun like *our* or *we*. If you use a singular pronoun, use *I* or *me*. These pronouns are acceptable in APA.

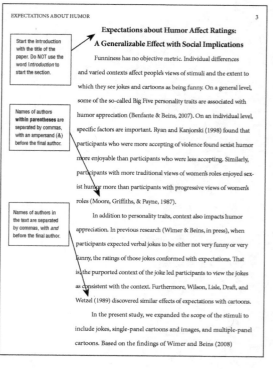

Expectations about Humor Affect Ratings:
A Generalizable Effect with Social Implications

Start the introduction with the title of the paper. Do NOT use the word *Introduction* to start the section.

Funniness has no objective metric. Individual differences and varied contexts affect people's views of stimuli and the extent to which they see jokes and cartoons as being funny. On a general level, some of the so-called Big Five personality traits are associated with humor appreciation (Benfante & Beins, 2007). On an individual level, specific factors are important. Ryan and Kanjorski (1998) found that participants who were more accepting of violence found sexist humor more enjoyable than participants who were less accepting. Similarly, participants with more traditional views of women's roles enjoyed sexist humor more than participants with progressive views of women's roles (Moore, Griffiths, & Payne, 1987).

Names of authors within parentheses are separated by commas, with an ampersand (&) before the final author.

Names of authors in the text are separated by commas, with *and* before the final author.

In addition to personality traits, context also impacts humor appreciation. In previous research (Wimer & Beins, in press), when participants expected verbal jokes to be either not very funny or very funny, the ratings of those jokes conformed with expectations. That is, the purported context of the joke led participants to view the jokes as consistent with the context. Furthermore, Wilson, Lisle, Draft, and Wetzel (1989) discovered similar effects of expectations with cartoons.

In the present study, we expanded the scope of the stimuli to include jokes, single-panel cartoons and images, and multiple-panel cartoons. Based on the findings of Wimer and Beins (2008)

> The first time you refer to a study with multiple authors, use all their names if there are five or fewer authors. After that, if there are two authors, always use both their names. With three or more authors, just use the first author's name followed by "et al." If there are six or more authors, just cite the first author followed by *i.e,* even the first time you cite it.

with jokes and of Wilson et al. (1989) with cartoons, we hypothesize that participants will conform to expectations in their ratings of the stimuli.

It is an open question at this point whether participants will react to the varying types of stimuli in the same way. Single-panel stimuli have greater immediacy than do jokes that require reading from start to finish. Multiple-panel cartoons may be midway between the other two types of stimuli with regard to how much cognitive processing must take place prior to getting the point of the humor. If participants develop an overall mindset based on their expectations, they may show the same pattern of rating for all types of humor, regardless of cognitive effort required for understanding it. On the other hand, if the pattern of elevated or depressed ratings emerges after complete processing of a stimulus, the single-panel cartoons may show less effect of expectation.

> In a paper reporting a single study, two levels of headings are usually sufficient. The major headings are centered. The minor headings are on the left margin and are in bold.

Method

Participants

> Do not start sentences with numerals. If you have to start a sentence numerically, write out the number. Generally, try to put the number somewhere within the sentence.

We recruited 94 participants from psychology classes. They volunteered in exchange for extra credit in those classes. Participants were predominantly white (84%), but also included students from various other groups, including Asian (9.6%), Hispanic (3.2%), and Black (1.1%). Some students chose the "Other" category (2.1%). The mean age was 19.13 years (*SD* = 1.12).

Materials and Apparatus

The stimuli included 30 stimuli: 10 jokes, 10 single-panel images or cartoons, and 10 multiple-panel cartoons. We found them on various sites on the internet. The stimuli were in randomized blocks of three such that each block had one stimulus of each type. Participants viewed the stimuli as we projected them onto a screen using PowerPoint.

> When you use rating scales, put the verbal anchors within parentheses, in italics.

Procedure

After completing informed consent forms, the participants learned that previous participants had rated the stimuli and that we wanted to get their ratings. In one group, participants heard, embedded in the general directions, that previous participants had rated the jokes as not very funny. A second group learned that participants had rated the stimuli as very funny. In a control group, they only learned that others had already rated the stimuli. Participants rated the stimuli on a scale of 1 (*Not very funny*) to 7 (*Very funny*).

> When presenting statistics, if it uses a Roman letter (e.g., *M* for the mean, *F* for the results of an analysis of variance, or *p* for a probability value), italicize the letter.

Results

As hypothesized, participants conformed to the message they had received about whether the jokes were funny. Participants in the Very Funny group produced the lowest mean ratings (*M* = 2.88, *SD* = 0.876), followed by Control participants (*M* = 3.54, *SD* = 0.993), and Not Very Funny participants (*M* = 2.90, *SD* = 0.917).

> When presenting statistics, if it uses a Greek letter, do not italicize the letter.

The mean for the Not Very Funny condition was significantly lower than the other two, which did not differ significantly, $F(2, 91) = 11.263$, $p < .001$, $\eta^2 = .198$. The results appear in Figure 1.

The type of stimulus was significant. Participants rated jokes as funniest (*M* = 3.79, *SD* = 1.02), followed by single-panel stimuli (*M* = 3.52, *SD* = 1.04), and multiple-panel cartoons (*M* = 3.04, *SD* = 0.98). All three differed significantly, $F(2, 182) = 40.123$, $p < .001$, $\eta^2 = .306$. The interaction between variables was not significant, $F(4, 182) = 0.141$, $p = .967$.

> If you create a figure or a table, make sure you refer to it in the text.

The results reveal that the effects of priming were the same for a given expectation, regardless of type of stimulus. It made no difference regarding ratings whether the participant was assessing a text-based joke, a single-panel cartoon, or a multi-panel cartoon. These results appear in Table 1.

Discussion

Once again, the results indicate that people are susceptible to context when they respond to humor. The same stimulus can be seen as very funny or not very funny, depending on the setup. And the effect seems generalizable: The same effect emerges, regardless of stimulus type.

This susceptibility to a message has implications for the use of humor in everyday life. When the radio personality Don Imus made

racially offensive comments on his program, he intended it to be embedded in a humorous context. That is, he was saying, "This is funny," with the expectation that the audience would find it so.

As it turned out, although a message can sway people in a particular direction, people will reject improbable messages about humor (Wimer & Beins, 2008). Furthermore, individual characteristics of a (large) subset of listeners may lead them to find an attempt at humor to be offensive (e.g., Moore et al., 1987; Ryan & Kanjorski, 1998).

> In the Discussion section, it is a good idea to talk about the research you mentioned in your introduction.

Interestingly, even though people find some humor to be offensive, they may also find it funny (Beins et al., 2005) and may be inclined to repeat it even when they find it offensive (Ryan & Kanjorski, 1998). So for situations like those of Don Imus, he may encounter contradictory responses: Some people may find his statements funny because of expectations, but they may also find them offensive. Those who experience extreme reactions and outrage are probably not likely to find the attempt at humor actually to be funny. But the dynamics of who will find something funny are complicated enough that a potentially offensive statement will lead to a variety of reactions. And, as Wimer & Beins (2008) showed, if the humor is outrageous enough, people will cease to accept the message that it is funny.

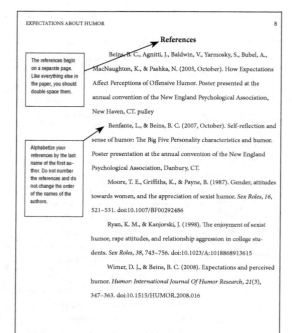

References

The references begin on a separate page. Like everything else in the paper, you should double space them.

Beins, B. C., Agnitti, J., Baldwin, V., Yarmosky, S., Bubel, A., MacNaughton, K., & Pashka, N. (2005, October). How Expectations Affect Perceptions of Offensive Humor. Poster presented at the annual convention of the New England Psychological Association, New Haven, CT. pulley

Alphabetize your references by the last name of the first author. Do not number the references and do not change the order of the names of the authors.

Benfante, L., & Beins, B. C. (2007, October). Self-reflection and sense of humor: The Big Five Personality characteristics and humor. Poster presentation at the annual convention of the New England Psychological Association, Danbury, CT.

Moore, T. E., Griffiths, K., & Payne, B. (1987). Gender, attitudes towards women, and the appreciation of sexist humor. *Sex Roles, 16*, 521–531. doi:10.1007/BF00292486

Ryan, K. M., & Kanjorski, J. (1998). The enjoyment of sexist humor, rape attitudes, and relationship aggression in college students. *Sex Roles, 38*, 743–756. doi:10.1023/A:1018868913615

Wimer, D. J., & Beins, B. C. (2008). Expectations and perceived humor. *Humor: International Journal Of Humor Research, 21*(3), 347–363. doi:10.1515/HUMOR.2008.016

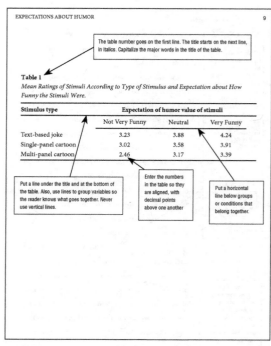

The table number goes on the first line. The title starts on the next line, in italics. Capitalize the major words in the title of the table.

Table 1
Mean Ratings of Stimuli According to Type of Stimulus and Expectation about How Funny the Stimuli Were.

Stimulus type	Expectation of humor value of stimuli		
	Not Very Funny	Neutral	Very Funny
Text-based joke	3.23	3.88	4.24
Single-panel cartoon	3.02	3.58	3.91
Multi-panel cartoon	2.46	3.17	3.39

Put a line under the title and at the bottom of the table. Also, use lines to group variables so the reader knows what goes together. Never use vertical lines.

Enter the numbers in the table so they are aligned, with decimal points above one another.

Put a horizontal line below groups or conditions that belong together.

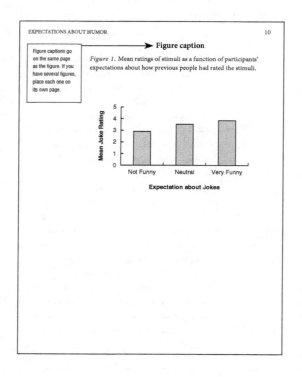

Figure caption

Figure captions go on the same page as the figure. If you have several figures, place each one on its own page.

Figure 1. Mean ratings of stimuli as a function of participants' expectations about how previous people had rated the stimuli.

STATISTICS REVIEW

INTRODUCTION

In this appendix, you can review basics of how psychologists use statistics. The most common approaches include the *t*-test, analysis of variance (ANOVA) and its related tests, and correlational tests. If you are interested in exploring different approaches or the theory that underlies statistical usage, you should consult a statistics textbook.

You should develop your statistical plan during the design of your research. There are few things as frustrating as finding out after completing a lengthy study that your design is not amenable to statistical analysis. You have results but you can't analyze them; as a result, you won't have as good a grasp of the question you are investigating as you would like.

You may discover that, after you design your research, you have to make changes because your initial design does not lend itself to easy analysis. What it comes down to is that you have to know what kinds of questions your methodology permits and what statistical tests will help you answer them.

THE USE OF STATISTICS

A century ago, psychologists used descriptive statistics like correlations, means, and standard deviations. An advanced test was the *z*-test, which let investigators understand probability analysis. Most of the statistical tests that we take for granted had yet to be invented.

At the end of the nineteenth century, Karl Pearson invented the correlation coefficient as we know it after Francis Galton proposed the initial concept. In the first decade of the twentieth century, William F. Gossett invented the *t*-test. By the 1930s, Ronald Fisher (1932, 1935) devised the ANOVA; the *F*-value of the ANOVA stands for Fisher.

Fisher is responsible for the use of the null hypothesis testing that dominates psychology today. He argued that a null hypothesis of equality between means could never be proven, but it could be disproven. So he argued that we should set up a test to see if the null hypothesis is universally true; if the difference across groups was large enough, we could use that fact as a demonstration that the null hypothesis of no difference was false. The only option left is to accept the idea that the groups were not universally equal.

Through manipulation of variables, Fisher showed us how we can reliably demonstrate that scores in different groups vary. Differences were said to be significant, which doesn't necessarily mean important. It just means that we can expect them to occur reliably. Significant as used by statisticians doesn't mean the same thing as significant in everyday language.

With the advent of these ideas, the way was paved for refinement of statistical approaches. By the middle of the twentieth century, the statistics most commonly used today were becoming increasingly well known.

When computers made complex data analysis feasible, the highly complex statistical designs of today became practical. Theoretical and applied statisticians continue to work on new approaches, most of which have their theoretical basis in the initial work of Fisher and Pearson.

COMMON STATISTICS

As you read research reports, you will see that certain statistics appear repeatedly. These include the ANOVA, *t*-tests, correlations, and regressions. This set constitutes most of the tests known as **parametric statistics**. When you use these tests, you generally want to have equal sample sizes, equal variances, and normally distributed scores.

> **Parametric Statistics—** Statistical tests whose use assumes certain underlying characteristics of the distribution of data such as normality and equal variances across groups.

With equal samples sizes and variances and with normally distributed scores, the answers we arrive at will be statistically sound. Our decisions about whether to reject the null hypothesis will be relatively free of Type I and Type II errors. The tests are robust, though, in that they withstand some notable departures from these assumptions. For instance, as long as the number of data points in any cell is not more than about twice as large as the smallest, the use of these tests will lead to decent conclusions. Similarly, as long as the ratio of the largest variance to the smallest is not more than about four or five, we can have confidence in our conclusions. If the distribution of scores is not normal, the tests can still be remarkably useful (Howell, 2007). Problems arise if we begin to violate all of the requirements. Sometimes we will need to select different tests of the null hypothesis that do not have these requirements.

Even so, some psychologists have criticized the use of tests of the null hypothesis altogether (e.g., Falk, 1986; Falk & Greenbaum, 1995; Wilcox, 1998), although you can still find cogent arguments in its favor (Frick, 1996).

Recently, the American Psychological Association created a task force to investigate the use of statistics and to provide guidance for researchers. The task force concluded that null hypothesis testing was appropriate for answering some questions, but that the standard parametric statistics should be supplemented with other information.

An important point raised by the task force is that we should rely on the simplest statistical test that will allow us to answer our questions. Complex analyses might needlessly obscure the concepts we are dealing with. That being said, we need to realize that there is sometimes a need for very complex statistical analyses because the psychological questions we ask are often complex.

In this appendix, you can review basics of how psychologists use statistics. The most common approaches include the t-test, ANOVA and its related tests, and correlational tests. If you are interested in exploring different approaches or the theory that underlies statistical usage, you should consult a statistics textbook.

Effect Size

Researchers are increasingly reporting a statistic that gives an assessment of how powerful the independent variable is in its effects on the dependent variable. That is, how much of the difference in scores across groups is due to the effect of the IV and how much is due to the effect of random variation and measurement error. Such an analysis involves a concept called effect size. For the t-test, the statistic that gives information on effect size is d. It is simple to compute. By convention, psychologists regard values of d around .20 as small, around .50 as moderate, and around .80 as large. The effect size represented in this example would be considered quite large.

When we use ANOVA, we often use different measures of effect size, notably eta-squared (η^2) and omega-squared (ω^2). We will use eta-squared for our worked examples. The values for small to large effect size have not been standardized in complex, factorial designs.

Confidence Intervals

When we conduct statistical analyses, the results are based on samples that we hope will represent the population. Unfortunately, it is virtually always the case that the mean value of a sample will differ from that of the population, even if only by a small amount. As a result, we often include in our data analysis a statement of a confidence interval, which is the range of values that has a certain likelihood of containing the population mean.

If we speak of a 95 percent confidence interval, we can identify the range of scores in which we are 95 percent confident that we would find the population mean. (It is possible to compute a confidence interval for any statistical parameter, but psychologists typically limit this analysis to means or differences between means.) A large confidence interval indicates uncertainty because it says that the true value of the population mean could be anywhere within a large span.

Our estimates are generally closer to the population mean when we use large samples. When sample sizes are small, one or two extreme data points can affect the size of the mean greatly. Consequently, your measurements can easily be affected by outliers. As a result, with small samples there will be greater uncertainty about whether your sample mean is a good estimate of the population mean; this is reflected in the large confidence interval.

Conversely, a few aberrant data points will not affect the mean of large samples, so your sample mean is not likely to be affected by outliers, and your estimate of the population mean is likely to be near the actual value. Thus, confidence intervals are smaller for large samples.

To compute a 95 percent confidence interval for estimating the population mean, you can use the following formula:

$$\mu = Mean \pm t_{.05/2}(s/\sqrt{n})$$

where you insert the mean of your sample (*Mean*), the critical value of the two-tailed *t* statistic ($t_{.05}$) that is appropriate for your sample size (df = 24), the standard deviation of the sample (*s*), and the square root of the sample size (*n*).

If you recorded data for 25 participants, and the mean and standard deviation were 50 and 10, respectively, you would compute your confidence interval as follows:

$$\mu = 50 \pm 2.064(10/\sqrt{25}) = 50 \pm 2.064(2) = 50 \pm 4.128$$
$$= 50 + 4.128 = 54.128$$
$$= 50 - 4.128 = 45.872$$

So the 95 percent confidence interval would be 45.872 to 54.128.

Steps for calculating the confidence intervals for individual tests appear below.

Power

When we analyze our data for statistical significance, our decision can go in one of two directions. We could reject the null hypothesis and claim that we have discovered a reliable relation among or difference between variables. Or we could decide that we do not have enough evidence to support such a claim.

It can be helpful to determine how likely we are to correctly reject the null hypothesis, when it is false. This probability is known as power. The power of our statistical analysis, that is, the probability of rejecting the null hypothesis when we should, depends on several factors.

One factor is the alpha level we use. Typically, we are satisfied with the knowledge that we will wrongly reject the null hypothesis only 5 percent of the time, which is the alpha value we choose. If we choose a larger value of alpha, say 10 percent, we are more likely to say that an effect is significant because we are setting a looser criterion. We will appropriately reject the null hypothesis more often, thereby avoiding a Type I error. But we will also be more likely to reject the null hypothesis when we should not, committing a Type II error. With a larger alpha, we are simply more willing to reject the null hypothesis, regardless of whether it is true.

Conversely, we can set a tighter criterion, perhaps with alpha at 1 percent. We will be less likely to reject the null hypothesis, whether or not we should. When we use a loose criterion for rejecting the null hypothesis, our power increases because we are simply more likely to conclude that there is an effect. The price we pay is that we are more likely to reject the null when we should not.

A second factor affecting power is effect size. If we are comparing the means of two groups that come from very different populations, we are likely to see a large effect size.

On the other hand, if the means come from two similar populations, the difference between the means of our samples will likely be small, reflecting the small effect size.

A third factor related to power is sample size. The larger the sample size, the more likely we are to spot an effect, even if it is a small one. Thus, small differences of a few points in SAT scores from one year to the next are likely to be significant because of the very large national samples. If you are conducting research and have reason to believe that your samples are really different but that the differences are not large, you will be less likely to spot the difference with small samples. Choosing large samples helps you spot small differences that are reliable.

It is possible to conduct a power analysis in advance of your research to see how large a sample you need to have high confidence that you will be able to spot differences that may be large or small. Some statistics packages, like SPSS, include a statement of retrospective power based on data already corrected; this statistic is useful for planning future studies but, as Howell (2007) has noted, not for explaining the outcome of a study you may have just conducted. He provides an accessible discussion of the computations of power.

INDEPENDENT GROUPS *T*-TEST

The independent groups *t*-test compares two samples to see if they differ from one another reliably. That is, is the difference between the two groups large enough to convince us that if we repeated our data collection, we would end up with similar results the second time.

Independent Groups *T*-Test—Statistical test used to assess whether the means differ across two groups with different participants in each group.

You can also use the ANOVA to compare two groups. Your decision to reject or not to reject the null hypothesis will be the same regardless of whether you use a *t*-test or the ANOVA because the *t*-test is algebraically related to the ANOVA comparing two independent groups. Historically, we have used the *t*-test for two groups; this tradition continues for studies with a single IV and only two groups to compare.

The formula for the **independent groups *t*-test** appears below. When the two groups show unequal variances, you should consult a statistics text for guidance.

$$t = \frac{M_A - M_B}{\sqrt{s_p^2 \left[\frac{1}{N_A} + \frac{1}{N_B} \right]}}$$

where M = means of groups A and B

N = number of observations in groups A and B

s^2 = the pooled variance given in the equation below

$$s_p^2 = \frac{(N_A - 1)s_A^2 + (N_B - 1)s_B^2}{N_A + N_B - 2}$$

where s^2 = variance of the group based on the unbiased estimate of the population variance.

Worked Example for Independent Groups *t*-Test

Participants are tested either in Condition A or Condition B	A	B	
Data for groups A and B	6	4	$t = [(1) - (2)]/ (10)$
	5	8	$= (6.3 - 3.7) / 0.80$
	8	3	$= 2.6 / 0.80$
	3	3	$= 3.24$
	6	5	
	7	3	
	7	4	
	6	2	
	9	3	
		2	
Mean	(1) 6.3	(2) 3.7	
Standard deviation	1.73	1.77	
Standard deviation squared (Variance)	(3) 3.00	(4) 3.12	
N	(5) 9	(6) 10	
Pooled variance			$[(5) * (3) + (6) * (4)]/[(7) + (8)]$
			$[(8 * 3.00) + (9 * 3.12)] / 17$
			$= (23.92 + 28.17) / 17$
			$= (9)\ 3.06$
Standard error of the difference			$= (10)\ \sqrt{\dfrac{(9)}{(5)} + \dfrac{(9)}{(6)}} = \sqrt{0.6470}$
			$= 0.80$
Degrees of freedom	(7) 8	(8) 9	$(5) + (6) = 17$
Critical *t*-value ($\alpha = .05$, two tails)			2.11
Decision			**Reject the null hypothesis. The obtained value of *t* is greater than the critical value. Do not conclude that the two groups are significantly different.**

In the example above, there are two groups, one having 9 data points, the other having 10. After finding the means and standard deviations for each group separately, it is easy to enter the values into the formula and compute your value of *t*. You then compare your obtained value with the critical value from the table of *t* values. If your obtained value is greater than the critical value in the table, reject the null hypothesis. If your obtained value is less than the critical value in the table, do not reject the null hypothesis.

Supplemental Analyses: Effect size:

$$d = \frac{Mean_A - Mean_B}{s},$$

$$s = \sqrt{s_A^2 + s_B^2} = \sqrt{3.00 + 3.12} = \sqrt{6.12} = 2.47$$

$$d = \frac{6.3 - 3.7}{2.47} = \frac{2.6}{2.47} = 1.05$$

Confidence Interval.   To compute the confidence interval to estimate how far apart two population means are, you can use the formula below:

$$CI_{.95} = Mean_1 - Mean_2 \pm t_{.05/2}(s_p^2)$$
$$= 2.6 \pm 2.11(1.3229)$$
$$= 2.6 \pm 2.79$$
$$= -0.19 \text{ to } 5.39$$

Thus, the confidence interval is –0.19 to 5.39. When the t value is not significant, the confidence interval contains zero, which is true for this example.

MATCHED SAMPLES/REPEATED MEASURES T-TEST

When you have two groups of scores that are paired, you use a different formula for the t-test. You use this version of t when a score in one group is paired for a specific reason with a score in the second group. For instance, if you administer a memory test to a person working alone, then a similar test when that person is in a group, you can compare the individual's score in the two conditions. It makes sense to pair the two scores because they came from the same person.

When you test the same person on two different occasions, that participant is likely to score similarly each time. When you have paired scores that are likely to be correlated, it makes sense to use this version of t because there is a better chance of detecting small differences between conditions.

> **Is the "Paired T-Test"?**
> **Pairs**—Statistical test use to assess whether the means differ across two conditions when the measurements in those conditions are paired, often because the same people are measured in the two conditions.

$$t = \frac{\overline{D}}{\frac{S_{\overline{D}}}{\sqrt{N}}}$$

D = Mean of the difference scores
S = Standard deviation of the difference scores
N = Number of **pairs** of scores (not the total number of scores)

Worked Example of a Matched Samples/Repeated Measures *t*-Test

Participants are tested in both conditions		A	B	Difference Score	
	Participant 1	11	9	2	t = (1) / [(2) / (3)]
	Participant 2	9	4	5	t = 3.2/[2.39/2.24]
	Participant 3	12	12	0	= 2.99
	Participant 4	5	2	3	
	Participant 5	17	11	6	
Mean				**(1)** 3.2	
Standard deviation				**(2)** 2.39	
N				5	
Square root of N				**(3)** 2.24	
Standard error					= 2.39/2.24
					= 1.07
Degrees of freedom					= # Pairs – 1
					= 4
Critical *t*-value (α =.05, two tails)					2.776
Decision					**Reject the null hypothesis. The obtained value of *t* is greater than the critical value. Conclude that the two groups are significantly different.**

How to Designate the *t*-value: $t(4) = 2.776, p < .05$

Supplemental Analyses: **Effect size.** Computing the effect size here is fairly simple.

$$d = \frac{\overline{D}}{S} = 3.2 / 2.39 = 1.33$$

where *d* reflects the effect size, $\overline{D}$ is the mean difference between the matched pairs, and *S* reflects the standard deviation of the difference scores.

ANALYSIS OF VARIANCE

The analysis of variance permits us to test for differences among multiple groups at the same time. Unlike the *t*-test, which is limited to comparisons of two groups at a time, the ANOVA can assess as many groups as you care to compare. (If you have only two groups, the ANOVA is perfectly applicable, although traditionally researchers have used the *t*-test.)

The advantage of the ANOVA is that you can be confident that the number of Type I errors that occur is at the level that you set. These errors arise when you conclude that there is a difference between groups that really occurred by chance, not because of the effect of your independent variable. In most cases, researchers want to keep Type I errors at no more than 5 percent. If you used multiple t-tests, as the number of comparisons you make increased, so would the likelihood that you would conclude that there was a reliable difference that would actually be due to chance.

An additional strength of the ANOVA is that we can make comparisons involving more than one independent variable. When an analysis involves a single IV, we call the test a One-Way ANOVA; if there are two IVs, we have a Two-Way ANOVA; and so on. For tests involving two or more IVs, we often refer to the design as factorial ANOVAs. Factorial ANOVAs let us see if there are main effects for each IV separately and if there are interaction effects among variables.

The underlying concept is the same for them all. We identify the magnitude of the differences among groups that are due to treatment effects, that is, to the IV; then we assess the size of the differences due to error. Finally, we see how large the treatment effect is compared to the error effect. If the treatment effect is big enough relative to the error effect, we conclude that the IV had a reliable effect on the behavior we are assessing.

As with t-tests, we can perform ANOVAs for data sets involving either independent groups or repeated measures groups. In this section, you will see how to compute One-Way ANOVAs involving both independent groups and repeated measures. You will also see how to compute a Two-Way ANOVA involving independent groups. For analysis of Two-Way or higher ANOVAs with repeated measures, you should consult a higher level statistics text. In general, you would carry out such tests via computer because the amount of calculation is extensive, particularly with repeated measures designs.

ONE-WAY INDEPENDENT GROUPS ANALYSIS OF VARIANCE

When you have multiple groups in which the data are unrelated across groups, you have an independent groups design. This means that there is no particular reason to pair a score in one group with any specific score in another group. When you have different people in each group rather than repeating measurements of the same people participating in different groups, you are using an independent groups design.

Worked Example of One-Way Independent Groups ANOVA

Group 1		Sum of Scores ΣX	Sum of Squared Scores ΣX^2	Sum of Scores Squared $(\Sigma X)^2$	N_1
X	X^2	35	315	$35^2 = 1225$	4
7	49				
9	81				
8	64				
11	121				

(*continued*)

Worked Example of One-Way Independent Groups ANOVA (Continued)

Group 2		Sum of Scores ΣX	Sum of Squared	Sum of Scores	N_2
X	X^2	$8 + 10 + 11 + 11$	Scores ΣX^2	Squared $(\Sigma X)^2$	4
8	64	40	$64 + 100 + 100 + 121$	$40^2 = 1600$	
10	100		406		
11	121				
11	121				

Group 3		Sum of Scores ΣX	Sum of Squared	Sum of Scores	N_3
X	X^2	$11 + 10 + 11 + 12$	Scores ΣX^2	Squared $(\Sigma X)^2$	4
11	121	44	$121 + 100 + 121 + 144$	$44^2 = 1936$	
10	100		486		
11	121				
12	144				

Totals	Sum of Scores ΣX_{TOTAL}	Sum of Squared Scores ΣX^2_{TOTAL}	Sum of Scores Squared $(\Sigma X)^2_{TOTAL}$	N_{TOTAL} 12
	115	1139	4497	12

Computing Sums of Squares

$$SS_{TOTAL} = \sum X_1^2 + \sum X_2^2 + \sum X_3^2 - \frac{\left(\sum X_1 + \sum X_1 + \sum X_1 \right)^2}{N_{TOTAL}}$$

$$SS_{TOTAL} = 315 + 406 + 486 - \frac{(31 + 40 + 44)^2}{12} \quad \text{Total Sum of Squares (SS}_{TOTAL})$$

$$= 1207 - (119^2/12)$$
$$= 1207 - (14161/12)$$
$$= 1207 - 1180.08$$
$$= 26.92$$

Treatment Sum of Squares (SS$_{TREATMENT}$) [also called Between Groups Sum of Squares]

$$SS_{TREATMENT} = \frac{\left(\sum X_1 \right)^2}{N_1} + \frac{\left(\sum X_2 \right)^2}{N_2} + \frac{\left(\sum X_3 \right)^2}{N_3} - \frac{\left(\sum X_1 + \sum X_2 + \sum X_3 \right)^2}{N_{TOTAL}}$$

Error Sum of Squares (SS$_{ERROR}$) [also called Within Groups Sum of Squares]

$$SS_{ERROR} = SS_{TOTAL} - SS_{TREATMENT}$$
$$SS_{ERROR} = 26.92 - 10.17$$
$$= 16.75$$

Computing Degrees of Freedom

$$df_{TOTAL} = (N_{TOTAL} - 1) = (12 - 1) = 11$$
$$df_{TREATMENT} = (\# \; Groups - 1) = (3 - 1) = 2$$
$$df_{ERROR} = df_{TOTAL} - df_{TREATMENT} = 11 - 2 = 9$$

Computing Mean Squares

$$MS_{TREATMENT} = \frac{SS_{TREATMENT}}{df_{TREATMENT}}$$
$$= 10.17/2$$
$$= 5.08$$

$$MS_{ERROR} = \frac{SS_{ERROR}}{df_{ERROR}}$$
$$= \frac{16.75}{9}$$
$$= 1.86$$

ANOVA Summary Table

Source of Variation	Sum of Squares	Degrees of Freedom	Mean Square	F	Prob.	Effect Size
TREATMENT (Between Groups)	10.17	2	5.08	2.73	>.05	.38
ERROR (Within Groups)	20.75	9	1.86			
TOTAL	26.92	11				

$$\eta^2 = \frac{SS_{TREATMENT}}{SS_{TOTAL}}$$
$$= \frac{10.17}{26.92} = .38$$

How to designate the F-value: $F(2,9) = 1.34, p > .05$

Decision: Look up the critical value in the F-Table for 2 and 9 degrees of freedom. For an alpha value (Type I error rate) of 5 percent, the critical value is 4.26.

In order to conclude that there are differences across groups, we need a computed value of F equal to or greater than 4.26. Our computed value is smaller than that, 2.73. Thus, we can conclude that the groups differ from one another for unknown reasons, not because of the effects of the independent variable. If the computed F-value is less than one, the F will never be significant.

Supplemental Analysis: **Effect size:** In recent years, investigators have started reporting effect sizes. An effect size indicates the strength of the relationship you are assessing.

A statistically significant effect can be small; likewise, a nonsignificant effect can be large. Effect sizes tell you the relative magnitude of strength of your independent variable on the dependent variable. According to the conventions adopted by psychologists, an effect size of about .20 is considered small; an effect size of about .50 is moderate; and an effect size around .80 is large.

In general, a measure of effect size reflects how much of the variability in scores is due to your manipulation. Powerful IVs lead to large effect sizes; manipulations that are weak lead to small effect sizes. It is important to remember that a small effect size can be very real and can be very important.

One statistic that researchers use to assess effect sizes is eta-squared (η^2). It is useful when you are interested in describing the effect sizes for your own research project. If you want to generalize beyond your own data, other statistics are preferred (Howell, 2007).

An additional, supplemental approach involves determining which groups differ from one another when you are comparing multiple conditions. In this example, we have three groups. If there is a significant difference between some of the groups, based on the ANOVA alone, we don't know which groups differ from one another. Groups 1 and 2 might differ from one another, but Groups 2 and 3 might not. We also don't know if Groups 1 and 3 differ.

Several different statistical tests exist that let us determine which groups differ from one another. Because the details differ in their application, if you are interested in using such tests after computing a *F*-value, you should consult a statistics book or make use of appropriate options in a computerized statistical package.

Confidence Intervals. After an ANOVA, we can compute pairwise confidence intervals. That is, we can establish confidence intervals for any two groups that will estimate how far the population means for the two groups are from one another. Psychologists rarely perform the computations to assess differences across multiple pairs of means.

FACTORIAL ANALYSIS OF VARIANCE

When we manipulate more than one independent variable in an experiment, we can assess the effects of the IVs through a factorial ANOVA. This statistical approach allows us to see whether the main effects are significant; in addition, we can investigate whether the two variables interact in ways that are not predictable from either independent variable alone.

The computations for a factorial ANOVA aren't difficult, but they can be tedious with a large data set. Researchers invariably use computerized statistical packages for analyzing the results of factorial designs. The example here involves very small data sets for convenience. In actual research, it is unlikely that an investigator would carry out such a small-scale study.

This statistical analysis involves computation of the same sums of squares as the other ANOVAs, with the addition of a new term, the interaction effect. The nature of the computations is similar, though. This example involves an independent groups design; the calculations for a repeated measures design are more involved. If you plan a study with repeated measures, you should refer to a statistics book because additional statistical issues complicate the analysis.

Worked example of a factorial ANOVA

This example involves a 2×3 design, which means that there are two IVs. Variable A has two levels, while Variable B has three. There is no limit to the number of levels that an IV can take, nor is there a limit to the number if IVs allowed.

The analysis will involve seeing whether the main effects for the two variables are significant and whether the interaction is significant.

	A_1B_1	$A_1B_1^2$	A_2B_1	$A_2B_1^2$	A_3B_1	$A_3B_1^2$	
B1	4	16	6	36	9	81	
	5	25	7	49	8	64	
	5	25	6	36	7	49	
	7	49	8	64	8	64	

$\Sigma A_1B_1 = 21$	$\Sigma A_2B_1 = 27$	$\Sigma A_3B_1 = 32$	$\Sigma B_1 = 80$
$(\Sigma A_1B_1)^2 = 441$	$(\Sigma A_1B_1)^2 = 729$	$(\Sigma A_1B_1)^2 = 1024$	$(\Sigma B_1)^2 = 6400$
$\Sigma A_1B_1^2 = 115$	$\Sigma A_2B_1^2 = 185$	$\Sigma A_3B_1^2 = 258$	$\Sigma B_1^2 = 2194$
$N_{A1-B1} = 4$	$N_{A2-B1} = 4$	$N_{A3-B1} = 4$	$N_{B1} = 12$

	A_1B_2	$A_1B_2^2$	A_2B_2	$A_2B_2^2$	A_3B_2	$A_3B_2^2$	
B2	5	25	4	16	3	9	
	4	16	7	49	2	4	
	3	9	6	36	4	16	
	7	49	8	64	2	4	

$\Sigma A_1B_2 = 19$	$\Sigma A_2B_2 = 25$	$\Sigma A_3B_2 = 11$	$\Sigma B_2 = 55$
$(\Sigma A_1B_1)^2 = 361$	$(\Sigma A_1B_1)^2 = 289$	$(\Sigma A_1B_1)^2 = 121$	$(\Sigma B_2)^2 = 3025$
$\Sigma A_1B_2^2 = 99$	$\Sigma A_2B_2^2 = 165$	$\Sigma A_3B_2^2 = 33$	$\Sigma B_2^2 = 771$
$N_{A1-B2} = 4$	$N_{A2-B2} = 4$	$N_{A3-B2} = 4$	$N_{B2} = 12$

$\Sigma A_1 = 40$	$\Sigma A_2 = 52$	$\Sigma A_3 = 43$
$(\Sigma A_1B_1)^2 = 1600$	$(\Sigma A_1B_1)^2 = 1936$	$(\Sigma A_1B_1)^2 = 1849$
$\Sigma A_1^2 = 802$	$\Sigma A_2^2 = 1018$	$\Sigma A_3^2 = 291$
$N_{A1} = 8$	$N_{A2} = 8$	$N_{A3} = 8$

$\Sigma X_{TOTAL} = 135$

$(\Sigma X_{TOTAL})^2 = 18225$

$\Sigma X^2_{TOTAL} = 1475$

$N_{TOTAL} = 24$

Calculate Sums of Squares:

Total Sum of Squares:

$$SS_{TOTAL} = \sum X_{TOTAL}^2 - \frac{\left(\sum X_{TOTAL}\right)^2}{N_{TOTAL}}$$

$$= 855 - \frac{(135)^2}{24} = 855 - \frac{18225}{24}$$

$$= 855 - 759.38$$

$$= 95.63$$

Variable A Sum of Squares (SS_A):

$$SS_A = \frac{\left(\sum A_1\right)^2}{N_{A_1}} + \frac{\left(\sum A_2\right)^2}{N_{A_2}} + \frac{\left(\sum A_3\right)^2}{N_{A_3}} - \frac{\left(\sum X_{TOTAL}\right)^2}{N_{TOTAL}}$$

$$= \frac{(40)^2}{8} + \frac{(52)^2}{8} + \frac{(43)^2}{8} - \frac{(135)^2}{24}$$

$$= \frac{1600}{8} + \frac{2704}{8} + \frac{1849}{8} - 759.38$$

$$= 200 + 338 + 231.13 - 759.38$$

$$= 9.75$$

Variable B Sum of Squares (SS_B):

$$SS_B = \frac{\left(\sum B_1\right)^2}{N_{B_1}} + \frac{\left(\sum B_2\right)^2}{N_{B_2}} - \frac{\left(\sum X_{TOTAL}\right)^2}{N_{TOTAL}}$$

$$= \frac{(80)^2}{12} + \frac{(55)^2}{12} - \frac{(135)^2}{24}$$

$$= \frac{6400}{12} + \frac{3025}{12} - 759.38$$

$$= 533.33 + 252.08 - 759.38$$

$$= 26.03$$

Interaction Sum of Squares ($SS_{A \times B}$):

$$SS_{A \times B} = \frac{\left(\sum X_{A_1 B_1}\right)^2}{N_{A_1 B_1}} + \frac{\left(\sum X_{A_2 B_1}\right)^2}{N_{A_2 B_1}} + \frac{\left(\sum X_{A_3 B_1}\right)^2}{N_{A_3 B_1}} + \frac{\left(\sum X_{A_1 B_2}\right)^2}{N_{A_1 B_2}} + \frac{\left(\sum X_{A_2 B_2}\right)^2}{N_{A_2 B_2}} + \frac{\left(\sum X_{A_3 B_2}\right)^2}{N_{A_3 B_2}}$$

$$- \frac{\left(\sum X_{TOTAL}\right)^2}{N_{TOTAL}} - SS_A - SS_B$$

$$= \frac{(21)^2}{4} + \frac{(27)^2}{4} + \frac{(32)^2}{4} + \frac{(19)^2}{4} + \frac{(25)^2}{4} + \frac{(11)^2}{4} - 759.38 - 9.75 - 26.03$$

$$= 30.09$$

Error Sum of Squares (SS_{ERROR})

$$SS_{ERROR} = SS_{ERROR} - SS_A - SS_B - SS_{A \times B}$$
$$= 95.63 - 9.75 - 26.03 - 30.09$$
$$= 29.76$$

Calculating Degrees of Freedom:

$$df_{TOTAL} = N_{TOTAL} - 1 = 24 - 1 = 23$$
$$df_A = \#\ Groups_A - 1 = 3 - 1 = 2$$
$$df_B = \#\ Groups_B - 1 = 2 - 1 = 1$$
$$df_{A \times B} = (df_A)(df_B) = (2)(1) = 2$$
$$df_{ERROR} = df_{TOTAL} - dfA - dfB - df_{A \times B} = 23 - 2 - 1 - 2 = 18$$

Calculating Mean Squares

$$MS_A = SS_A/df_A = 9.75/2 = 4.88$$
$$MS_B = SS_B/df_B = 26.03/1 = 26.03$$
$$MS_{A \times B} = SS_{A \times B}/df_{A \times B} = 30.09/2 = 15.04$$
$$MS_{ERROR} = SS_{ERROR}/df_{ERROR} = 29.76/18 = 1.65$$

Calculating F-values:

$$F_A = \frac{MS_A}{MS_{ERROR}} = \frac{4.88}{1.65} = 2.96$$

$$F_B = \frac{MS_B}{MS_{ERROR}} = \frac{26.03}{1.65} = 15.78$$

$$F_{A \times B} = \frac{MS_{A \times B}}{MS_{ERROR}} = \frac{15.04}{1.65} = 9.12$$

ANOVA Summary Table

Source of Variation	Sum of Squares	Degrees of Freedom	Mean Square	F	Effect Size
Variable A	9.75	2	4.88	2.96	.25
Variable B	26.03	1	26.03	15.78	.47
Interaction of A × B	30.09	2	15.04	9.12	.50
Error	29.76	18	1.65		
Total	95.63	23			

How to Designate the F-values:

> *Variable A:* $F(2,18) = 2.96, p > .05$
> *Variable B:* $F(1,18) = 15.78, p < .01$
> *Interaction Effect:* $F(2,18) = 9.12, p < .01$

Decision: *Main effect of Variable A*: To find the critical F-value for a 5 percent error rate, look in the appropriate table of F-values for 2 and 18 degrees of freedom. This critical value in the table is 3.55. Our computed value, 2.96, is smaller than the critical value. The difference among groups is not significant, so we conclude that any differences are attributable to measurement error, not the effects of Variable A.

Main effect of Variable B: To find the critical F-value for a 5 percent error rate, look in the F table for 1 and 18 degrees of freedom. The critical value in the table is 4.41. Our computed value, 15.78, is larger than the critical value. So we conclude that the difference among groups is attributable to the effect of Variable B.

Interaction between Variable A and Variable B: To find the critical F-value for a 5 percent error rate, look in the F table for 2 and 18 degrees of freedom. The critical value in the table is 3.55. Our computed value, 9.12, is larger than the critical value. So we conclude that the pattern of scores on B changes depending on which group on Variable A you are considering. Figure B-1 shows how the values of B change depending on which level of A is under consideration.

The significant main effect of Variable B may be due largely to the fact that one group, A_3B_2, has caused the overall average of Variable B to drop greatly. You should be cautious about asserting that B_1 and B_2 really are all that different. Without the effect of the single, low group, B_1 and B_2 are not all that different.

Supplementary Analysis: You can assess effect size here with eta-squared (η^2). You find the effect size for each main effect and for the interaction.

There is an important computational difference in computing effect size for a factorial design compared to a one-way design. For a one-way ANOVA, you divided $SS_{TREATMENT}$ by SS_{TOTAL}. To compute eta-squared for a factorial design, you divide the $SS_{TREATMENT}$ term by the ($SS_{TREATMENT} + SS_{ERROR}$).

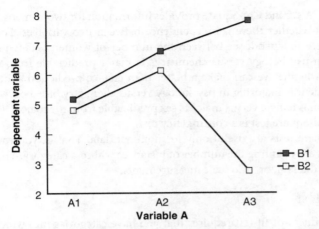

FIGURE B-1   Illustration of interaction of Variables A and B. The pattern of results for Variable B differs depending on which level of Variable A is under consideration.

$$\eta^2 = \frac{SS_{TREATMENT}}{SS_{TREATMENT} + SS_{ERROR}}$$

$$\eta_A^2 = \frac{9.75}{(9.75 + 29.75)} = .25$$

$$\eta_B^2 = \frac{26.03}{(26.03 + 29.75)} = .47$$

$$\eta_{A \times B}^2 = \frac{30.08}{(30.08 + 29.75)} = .50$$

As these values are interpreted by researchers, the effect size for Variable A is small, whereas the effect sizes for Variable B and the interaction are moderate.

An additional supplemental analysis investigates where differences lie among multiple groups. When you employ an independent variable that has more than two levels, it is not immediately clear which groups differ significantly when you obtain a significant F-value. In this example, there is no main effect of Variable A. If there were, you would conduct a post hoc analysis to see which of the groups, when paired, differed significantly. You can consult a statistics book for details on the different tests you could use.

CHI-SQUARE

Goodness-of-fit Test—
Statistical test that assesses whether observed data fit a theoretical or a predicted pattern.

There are two commonly used Chi-Square tests. (*Chi* sounds like *sky* with the *s* missing.) One provides information about whether the number of observations that you obtain in different categories matches your predictions. This is the **goodness-of-fit test**. Is there a good fit between what you expect and what you get? We use this test when we have one-dimensional tables.

Contingency Test—
Statistical test that assesses whether values on a second variable are contingent on or predictable from values on a first variable.

A second Chi-Square provides information for two-dimensional tables about whether there is independence between two variables. For instance, is there independence between the number of women versus men majoring in psychology versus chemistry? Is major predictable from sex, which asks whether we can make a better than chance prediction about whether a student is majoring in psychology versus chemistry based on whether the person is female versus male? Is sex predictable from the major? This variety of Chi-Square test is a **contingency test**.

These Chi-Square tests are useful only for nominal data. That is, you can only use these tests when you are counting the number of instances within a category. You can't use the tests for ordinal, interval, or ratio scale measurements.

Goodness-of-Fit Test

The Chi-Square goodness-of-fit test requires that you have categories into which individual observations fall. That is, you make a single observation and record that observation as belonging with category A, B, C, ...You repeat this for each observation. In order for Chi-Square to provide valid information, each observation must be independent of the others. You can't measure people repeatedly because one person's behavior at two different times may be highly related.

The idea of the Chi-Square test is to find out whether expected counts in each category match what you actually observe. In most psychological research, our null hypothesis specifies that there be equal numbers of observations in each category. You would depart from this strategy if you have specific expectations.

$$\chi^2 = \frac{\sum (O - E)^2}{E}$$

where O = Number of observations and E = Expected number of observations.

Suppose you wanted to know if students had preferences for class times during the day. You could categorize the classes as early morning, late morning, early afternoon, and late afternoon. If you asked a randomly selected group of students to state a preference, you could tally them and compute a value of Chi-Square to test whether all times are seen as equally desirable. For the fictitious data set below, you could answer this question.

	8 a.m. or 9 a.m.	11 a.m. or noon	1 p.m. or 2 p.m.	3 p.m. or 4 p.m.	Total
Observed values	8	28	22	15	73
Expected values	*18.25*	*18.25*	*18.25*	*18.25*	

Computing Expected Values: In this case, our assumption is that students don't have preferences for particular times of the day. Although in reality it is probably safe to assume that students wouldn't want early morning classes, we don't have good information about what percentage of students would prefer each category. So our null hypothesis at this point is that all times are equally desirable.

There are 73 observations in our sample. If we assume equal representation in each of the 4 time slots, we would compute the expected values as the total number of observations divided by the number of categories: 73/4 = 18.25. Using the formula for Chi-Square given above, we can compute our statistic.

$$\chi^2 = \sum \frac{(Observed - Expected)^2}{Expected}$$

$$= \frac{(8 - 18.25)^2}{18.25} + \frac{(28 - 18.25)^2}{18.25} + \frac{(22 - 18.25)^2}{18.25} + \frac{(15 - 18.25)^2}{18.25}$$

$$= \frac{(-10.25)^2}{18.25} + \frac{(9.75)^2}{18.25} + \frac{(3.75)^2}{18.25} + \frac{(-3.25)^2}{18.25}$$

$$= \frac{105.06}{18.25} + \frac{95.06}{18.25} + \frac{14.06}{18.25} + \frac{10.56}{18.25}$$

$$= 5.76 + 5.21 + 0.77 + 0.58$$

$$= 12.32$$

Calculating Degrees of Freedom: For a Chi-Square goodness-of-fit test, the degrees of freedom is the number of categories minus one. There are four categories in this example, so the degrees of freedom is (4 − 1) = 3.

The Decision: To find the critical value of Chi-Square in the table for a Type I error rate of 5 percent, we use 3 degrees of freedom and the column labeled .05. The critical value is 7.815. Our computed value is larger than the critical value in the table, so we reject the null hypothesis and conclude that students do not prefer all times of the day for their classes. According to these fictitious data, we would conclude that students prefer middle of the day to early or late.

Test of Independence

The Chi-Square test of independence, like the goodness-of-fit test, involves whether we can make accurate predictions about the number of observed events when we have two (or more) variables from which we make the predictions.

Jenni and Jenni (1976) observed college students carrying their books on campus and noted how the students held them. One category of carrying them was across the front of the body with one or both arms wrapped around the books; a second category was for the books to be held more toward the side, pinched from above or supported from below by the hand and/or arm. The researchers investigated whether book carrying was associated with sex.

They observed several hundred college students. If you conducted this study in 1976 with a smaller number of students, you might have obtained the fictitious data below, which you could analyze with a Chi-Square test of independence. There are two variables: sex of the student and category of carrying. The question is whether you can predict the sex of the carriers by knowing how they carry the books or, alternatively, whether you can predict how people will carry their books, given that you know their sex.

Observed Values	Female Observed	Expected	Male Observed	Expected	(Total)
Front	21	12	3	14	(24)
Side	5	14	23	12	(28)
(Total)	(26)		(26)		(52)

Computing Expected Values: For this 2×2 design, you need to compute expected values for each of the four conditions. As a rule of thumb, you should avoid computing Chi-Square values when a large percentage of your expected values are smaller than 5. It is probably not problematic as long as the number of such expectations is under 20 percent of the total number of cells (Howell, 2007). As you can see in this example, one of the cells has fewer than 5 observations, but the expected value is greater than 5. It is the expected value that is important to consider, not the observed value.

The expected value is computed by multiplying the row total for each cell times the column total for that cell, then dividing by the total number of observations. You do this for each cell. In the present example, you find the expected value for each of the four cells.

Once you have the set of observed and expected values, you can compute the value of Chi-Square, based on the formula above.

$$Expected = \frac{(Total_{Row}) \times (Total_{Column})}{N_{Total}}$$

$$Expected_{Female-Front} = \frac{24 \times 26}{52} = \frac{624}{52} = 12$$

$$Expected_{Female-Side} = \frac{28 \times 26}{52} = \frac{728}{52} = 14$$

$$Expected_{Male-Front} = \frac{24 \times 26}{52} = \frac{624}{52} = 12$$

$$\chi^2 = \sum \frac{(Observed - Expected)^2}{Expected}$$

$$= \frac{(21 - 12)^2}{12} + \frac{(5 - 14)^2}{14} + \frac{(3 - 14)^2}{14} + \frac{(23 - 12)^2}{12}$$

$$= \frac{9^2}{12} + \frac{(-9)^2}{14} + \frac{(-11)^2}{14} + \frac{11^2}{12}$$

$$= \frac{81}{12} + \frac{81}{14} + \frac{121}{14} + \frac{121}{12}$$

$$= 6.75 + 5.79 + 8.64 + 10.08$$

$$= 31.26$$

Calculating Degrees of Freedom: Degrees of freedom for this Chi-Square test equals the number of rows minus one times the number of columns minus one, or $(R - 1)(C - 1)$.

There are two rows and there are two columns in this design, so $(R - 1)(C - 1) = (2 - 1)(2 - 1) = (1)(1) = 1$.

The Decision: When there is one degree of freedom and when you want your Type I error rate to be 5 percent, you look for the critical value in the Chi-Square table for the probability of .05 and 1 degree of freedom. The critical value is 3.841.

The value we computed is 31.26, which exceeds the critical value needed for significance. Thus, we can conclude that there is a great deal of predictability regarding sex of students and the manner in which they carry their books.

This research took place over a quarter of a century ago. Virtually nobody had backpacks then. It would be interesting to see if the effect replicated today, with different means of conveying books from place to place and different types of students. Have women and men changed?

CORRELATIONAL ANALYSES

There are quite a few correlational analyses that researchers use to assess the relations among variables. The most common correlational analysis is the Pearson product–moment correlation. It provides information as to whether a linear relation exists between two variables. Curvilinear relations require more advanced statistics.

A second correlational approach is regression analysis, which allows us to identify the pattern of changes in scores and to make predictions of a criterion variable based on a single predictor variable. The linear regression analysis we will see here is based on the Pearson correlation for linear relationships.

Pearson Product–Moment Correlation

The Pearson product–moment correlation is the most widely used correlation coefficient. In fact, some of the other correlations and tests of associations are merely algebraic manipulations of the Pearson r.

The formula for the Pearson product–moment correlation appears below. There are several different ways to represent the formula. They will produce the same result, but this formula is fairly easy to use.

$$r = \frac{N\left(\sum AB\right) - \left(\sum A\right)\left(\sum B\right)}{\sqrt{\left[N\left(\sum A^2\right) - \left(\sum A\right)^2\right]\left[N\left(\sum B^2\right) - \left(\sum B\right)^2\right]}}$$

N = Number of pairs
$\sum AB$ = Summed cross-product for each pair
$\sum A$ = Sum of scores in Group A
$\sum B$ = Sum of scores in Group B

In the worked example below, the obtained correlation coefficient is negative, which reflects the fact that scores in A that are high tend to be paired with scores in B that are low and vice versa. With a two-tailed, nondirectional test, the absolute value of r is compared with the critical value from the table.

Worked Example of Pearson Product–Moment Correlation

	A	A^2	B	B^2	Cross-Product of A * B
	1	1	4	16	4
	3	9	8	64	24
	6	36	6	36	36
	7	49	2	4	14
	7	49	3	9	21
	8	64	2	4	16
	9	81	1	1	9

Number of observations (1) 7 (1) 7

Sum of cross-products (2) 124

Sum of scores in group (3) 41 (4) 26

Square of sum of scores (5) 1681 (6) 676

Sum of scores squared (7) 289 (8) 134
in group

Value of r

$$r = \frac{[(1)(2) - (3)(4)]}{\text{SQRT}\{[(1)(7) - (5)][(1)(8) - (6)]\}}}$$

$$= \frac{(7)(124) - (41)(26)}{\text{SQRT}\{[7(289) - 1681][7(134) - 676]\}}$$

$$r = \frac{868 - 1066}{\text{SQRT}[(342)(262)]} = \frac{-198}{299.34}$$

$$= -.66$$

Note: SQRT = Square Root

Degrees of freedom

Pairs – 2 = 5

Critical value (α =.05,
two tails) from table
of critical r values

.7545

Decision

Do not reject the null hypothesis. The computed value is less than the critical value. There is not enough evidence to conclude that there is a relationship between a person's score in condition X and that person's score in condition Y.

How to designate *r* values: $r(5) = .75, p < .05$

Other Correlation Coefficients:

The Pearson product–moment correlation is the most commonly used bivariate correlation (i.e., a correlation with two variables). There are other, specialized correlation coefficients that are related to the Pearson *r*. The most common of these are the point-biserial correlation, the Spearman correlation for ranks, and the phi coefficient.

Researchers use the point-biserial correlation with bivariate analyses involving one continuous variable and one dichotomous variable that can take only two values (e.g., male or female). In the past, authors have presented a specialized formula for computing the point-biserial correlation. In fact, there is no need for a special formula because we can use the formula for the Pearson *r* to obtain the point-biserial correlation coefficient.

To compute a point-biserial correlation, you simply number your dichotomous variable with any two numbers. (Usually we use 0 and 1 or 1 and 2, but the result will be the same no matter what numbers you use.) Then you compute the Pearson *r* using your two numbers paired with your continuous variable. So to investigate the relation between one's sex and one's grade point average, for example, you could code women as zero and men as one. Then you would calculate the correlation coefficient where each woman, scored as zero, would be paired with her GPA and each man, scored as one, would be paired with his GPA. And you would calculate the Pearson *r*. You can test the correlation for significance the same way you would for the standard Pearson *r*, with a *t*-test.

A second correlation related to the Pearson *r* is the Spearman correlation for ranks. This correlation involves one variable that is continuous and the other ranked. As with the point-biserial correlation, one can simply use the formula for the Pearson *r* to compute the Spearman *r*. Authors have presented an alternate formula for the Spearman *r*, but that formula results in the same coefficient as the standard Pearson *r* when there are no tied ranks. When there are tied ranks, the alternate formula is inaccurate if you do not apply a correction factor (Howell, 2007).

After your computation, you can test the correlation for significance. As with the Pearson *r*, you test for significance using a *t*-test.

Finally, when the data involve two dichotomous variables, researchers sometimes use the phi coefficient (Φ). For instance, if you wanted to see whether voting (or not voting) is related to gender, you could use two dichotomous variables, male–female and voted–did not vote.

You could code women as zero and men as one; you could also code not voting as zero and voting as one. So a woman who voted would have scores of 0, 1; a man who did not vote would have 1, 0. After coding the sex and voting pattern appropriately, you would have a series of paired scores consisting of some combination of one and zero. At this juncture, you can simply compute the standard Pearson *r*, as you would with the point-biserial and ranked data.

Testing the significance of Φ is a little different than for the other tests. In this case, you compute a value of Chi-Square (χ^2). We will use a different version of the formula for Φ than we did for the Pearson *r*; the two equations lead to the same outcome. Because of the difference in testing for significance, however, we will work through an example.

Coding of Sex: Women = 0; Men = 1
Coding of Vote: Did not vote = 0; Voted = 1

| Sex: | 0 | 0 | 0 | 0 | 0 | 0 | 0 | 0 | 0 | 0 | 0 | 0 | 1 | 1 | 1 | 1 | 1 | 1 | 1 | 1 |
| Vote?: | 1 | 1 | 0 | 0 | 0 | 1 | 0 | 1 | 1 | 1 | 1 | 1 | 1 | 1 | 0 | 1 | 1 | 0 | 0 | 1 |

$$COVxy = \frac{\sum XY - \frac{\sum X \sum Y}{N}}{N-1} = \frac{5 - \frac{(8)(13)}{20}}{19} = -0.2/19 = -0.0105$$

$Sx = 0.5026$
$Sy = 0.4894$

$$\Phi = r = \frac{COV_{xy}}{(s_x)(s_y)} = \frac{-0.0105}{(.5026)(.4894)} = .0432$$

In order to test for significance, we use χ^2 instead of t. The computation is simple.

$$\chi^2 = N\Phi^2 = 20(.0432^2) = 0.0373$$

In this test, there is one degree of freedom, so the critical value of χ^2 is 3.84. Our computed value is less than the critical value, so we declare that the value of Φ is nonsignificant. There is no relation between one's sex and whether one votes, according to these data. Incidentally, women typically do vote in higher percentages than men, with percentages generally in accord with what we see in this data set. But with the small sample size, the effect is not significant because the power is very small.

Supplementary Analysis: After computing a correlation coefficient, we can assess the size of the effect, just as we could do so for a test of differences between means. This analysis of effect size is generally done only for the Pearson r with two sets of continuous variables, not with the point-biserial or Spearman correlation for ranks, nor with Φ. The computation is extremely simple. All we need to do is to square the value of the correlation coefficient:

$$r^2 = (.66)^2 = .4356$$

This value represents the amount of variability in one factor that is predicted by the other factor. Thus, we can say that about 44 percent of the differences in Y scores is predictable from knowing the X scores. The other 56 percent is explainable from unknown causes. As the value of the correlation coefficient approaches 1.00, so does the value of r-squared. If variables were perfectly correlated, our predictions would be perfect. Behavior is so complex, though, that we might be satisfied with predicting 10 percent of the variability or less.

Linear Regression Analysis

In many cases, researchers who conduct correlational analyses also generate predictions of a criterion variable (sometimes the dependent variable) given a particular value of the predictor variable (sometimes the independent variable). The terms independent and dependent variable are more likely to be used when the research is experimental but uses regression analysis.

The simplest of these involves linear regression on one variable. One predictor variable is used to estimate a criterion variable. For more advanced regression analysis, such as that using multiple predictor variables or nonlinear regression, you should consult a statistics book. We will use the values for the correlation example to generate the regression line that we use to make predictions about the Y value, the criterion, based on the X value, the predictor.

In predicting a value of the DV, we use the formula for a straight line:

$$Y = a + bX,$$

where

a = the Y-intercept,
b = the slope of the line,
X = the value of the predictor variable, and
Y = the value of the criterion variable.

After completing a correlational analysis, we compute values of a and b based on statistical values from the correlation computations.

Calculating the slope (b):

$$b = r \frac{S_{criterion}}{S_{predictor}} = -.66\left(\frac{2.50}{2.85}\right) = (-.66)(.88) = -.58$$

The negative value of the correlation coefficient means that as the value of the predictor value increases, the value of the criterion variable decreases. The value of –.58 for the slope means that as the value of the predictor variable (usually the X value) increases by a value of one, the value of the criterion (usually the Y value) decreases by 0.58.

Calculating the Y-intercept:

$$a = Mean_{criterion} - b(Mean_{predictor})$$
$$= 3.71 - (-.58)(5.86) = 3.71 - (-3.40) = 7.11$$

According to this analysis, if the value of X is zero, the value of Y should be around 7.11. As the value of the predictor variable increases, our prediction of the value of the criterion variable will decrease because the slope is negative. So, as the value of X goes from zero to larger numbers, the value of Y will diminish.

Estimating a value of Y based on X:

If the predictor value, X, is 7, what is our best prediction of the criterion variable, Y?

$$Y = a + bX$$
$$Y = 7.11 + (-.58)X$$
$$= 7.11 + (-.58)7 = 7.11 + (-4.06) = 7.11 - 4.06 = 3.05$$

If the value of X is 7, our best prediction for the value of Y is 3.05, which is reasonably consistent with the data set, as you can see in Figure B-2. The higher the value of the correlation coefficient, the better your prediction will be.

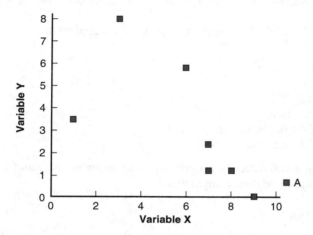

FIGURE B-2   Scatterplot for correlation and regression data. The downward trend of the data when X increases reveals a negative correlation.

STATISTICAL TABLES

TABLE C.1   Significance values for the *t* distribution.

Computed values of t are significant if they are larger than the critical value in the table.

α LEVELS FOR DIRECTIONAL (ONE-TAILED) TESTS

	.05	.025	.01	.005	.0005

α LEVELS FOR NONDIRECTIONAL (TWO-TAILED) TESTS

df	.10	.05	.02	.01	.001
1	6.314	12.706	31.821	63.657	636.619
2	2.920	4.303	6.965	9.925	31.598
3	2.353	3.182	4.541	5.841	12.924
4	2.132	2.776	3.747	4.604	8.610
5	2.015	2.571	3.365	4.032	6.869
6	1.943	2.447	3.143	3.707	5.959
7	1.895	2.365	2.998	3.499	5.408
8	1.860	2.306	2.896	3.355	5.041
9	1.833	2.262	2.821	3.250	4.781
10	1.812	2.228	2.764	3.169	4.587
11	1.796	2.201	2.718	3.106	4.437
12	1.782	2.179	2.681	3.055	4.318
13	1.771	2.160	2.650	3.012	4.221
14	1.761	2.145	2.624	2.977	4.140
15	1.753	2.131	2.602	2.947	4.073
16	1.746	2.120	2.583	2.921	4.015
17	1.740	2.110	2.567	2.898	3.965
18	1.734	2.101	2.552	2.878	3.922
19	1.729	2.093	2.539	2.861	3.883
20	1.725	2.086	2.528	2.845	3.850
21	1.721	2.080	2.518	2.831	3.819
22	1.717	2.074	2.508	2.819	3.792
23	1.714	2.069	2.500	2.807	3.767
24	1.711	2.064	2.492	2.797	3.745
25	1.708	2.060	2.485	2.787	3.725
26	1.706	2.056	2.479	2.779	3.707
27	1.703	2.052	2.473	2.771	3.690
28	1.701	2.048	2.467	2.763	3.674
29	1.699	2.045	2.462	2.756	3.659
30	1.697	2.042	2.457	2.750	3.646
40	1.684	2.021	2.423	2.704	3.551
60	1.671	2.000	2.390	2.660	3.460
120	1.658	1.980	2.358	2.617	3.373
∞	1.645	1.960	2.326	2.576	3.291

© R. A. Fisher and F. Yates (2007) *Statistical Tables for Biological, Agricultural and Medical Research,* reprinted by permission of Pearson Education Limited. Adapted from Table III. Adapted from Table 3.

TABLE C.2   Significance values for the analysis of variance (F test).

Degrees of freedom for treatments ($df_{between}$) appear in the left column. Degrees of freedom for the error term (df_{within} or df_{error}) are across the top. Computed values of F are significant if they are larger than the critical value in the table.

Values for α = .05 are in normal Roman type

Values for α = .01 are in bold type

Values for α = 0.001 are in italics

DF FOR THE NUMERATOR
(DF$_{BETWEEN}$ OR DF$_{TREATMENT}$)

		1	2	3	4	5	6	8	12	24

DF FOR THE DENOMINATOR
(DF$_{WITHIN}$ OR DF$_{ERROR}$)

		1	2	3	4	5	6	8	12	24
1	α = .05	161.4	199.5	215.7	224.6	230.2	234.0	238.9	243.9	249.0
	α = .01	**4052**	**4999**	**5403**	**5625**	**5764**	**5859**	**5982**	**6106**	**6234**
	α = .001	*405284*	*500000*	*540379*	*562500*	*576405*	*585937*	*598144*	*610667*	*623497*
2	α = .05	18.51	19.00	19.16	19.25	19.30	19.33	19.37	19.41	19.45
	α = .01	**98.50**	**99.00**	**99.17**	**99.25**	**99.30**	**99.33**	**99.37**	**99.42**	**99.46**
	α = .001	*998.5*	*999.0*	*999.2*	*999.2*	*999.3*	*999.3*	*999.4*	*999.4*	*999.5*
3	α = .05	10.13	9.55	9.28	6.12	9.01	8.94	8.84	8.74	8.64
	α = .01	**34.12**	**30.82**	**29.46**	**28.71**	**28.24**	**27.91**	**27.49**	**27.05**	**26.60**
	α = .001	*167.0*	*148.5*	*141.2*	*137.1*	*134.6*	*132.8*	*130.6*	*128.3*	*125.9*
4	α = .05	7.71	6.94	6.59	6.39	6.26	6.16	6.04	5.91	5.77
	α = .01	**21.20**	**18.00**	**16.69**	**15.98**	**15.52**	**15.21**	**14.80**	**14.37**	**13.93**
	α = .001	*74.14*	*61.25*	*56.18*	*53.44*	*51.71*	*50.53*	*49.00*	*47.41*	*45.77*
5	α = .05	6.61	5.79	5.41	5.19	5.05	4.95	4.82	4.68	4.53
	α = .01	**16.26**	**13.27**	**12.06**	**11.39**	**10.97**	**10.67**	**10.29**	**9.89**	**9.47**
	α = .001	*47.18*	*37.12*	*33.20*	*31.09*	*29.75*	*28.84*	*27.64*	*26.42*	*25.14*
6	α = .05	5.99	5.14	4.76	4.53	4.39	4.28	4.15	4.00	3.84
	α = .01	**13.74**	**10.92**	**9.78**	**9.15**	**8.75**	**8.47**	**8.10**	**7.72**	**7.31**
	α = .001	*35.51*	*27.00*	*23.70*	*21.92*	*20.81*	*20.03*	*19.03*	*17.99*	*16.89*
7	α = .05	5.59	4.74	4.35	4.12	3.97	3.87	3.73	3.57	3.41
	α = .01	**12.25**	**9.55**	**8.45**	**7.85**	**7.46**	**7.19**	**6.84**	**6.47**	**6.07**
	α = .001	*29.25*	*21.69*	*18.77*	*17.19*	*16.21*	*15.52*	*14.63*	*13.71*	*12.73*
8	α = .05	5.32	4.46	4.07	3.84	3.69	3.58	3.44	3.28	3.12
	α = .01	**11.26**	**8.65**	**7.59**	**7.01**	**6.63**	**6.37**	**6.03**	**5.67**	**5.28**
	α = .001	*25.42*	*18.49*	*15.83*	*14.39*	*13.49*	*12.86*	*12.04*	*11.19*	*10.30*
9	α = .05	5.12	4.26	3.86	3.63	3.48	3.37	3.23	3.07	2.90
	α = .01	**10.56**	**8.02**	**6.99**	**6.42**	**6.06**	**5.80**	**5.47**	**5.11**	**4.73**
	α = .001	*22.86*	*16.39*	*13.90*	*12.56*	*11.71*	*11.13*	*10.37*	*9.57*	*8.72*
10	α = .05	4.96	4.10	3.71	3.48	3.33	3.22	3.07	2.91	2.74
	α = .01	**10.04**	**7.56**	**6.55**	**5.99**	**5.64**	**5.39**	**5.06**	**4.71**	**4.33**
	α = .001	*21.04*	*14.91*	*12.55*	*11.28*	*10.48*	*9.92*	*9.20*	*8.45*	*7.64*

(continued)

TABLE C.2   Continued

DF FOR THE NUMERATOR
(DF_BETWEEN OR DF_TREATMENT)

		1	2	3	4	5	6	8	12	24

DF FOR THE DENOMINATOR
(DF_WITHIN OR DF_ERROR)

		1	2	3	4	5	6	8	12	24
11	α = .05	4.84	3.98	3.59	3.36	3.20	3.09	2.95	2.79	2.61
	α = .01	**9.65**	**7.20**	**6.22**	**5.67**	**5.32**	**5.07**	**4.74**	**4.40**	**4.02**
	α = .001	*19.69*	*13.81*	*11.56*	*10.35*	*9.58*	*9.05*	*8.35*	*7.63*	*6.85*
12	α = .05	4.75	3.88	3.49	3.26	3.11	3.00	2.85	2.69	2.50
	α = .01	**9.33**	**6.93**	**5.95**	**5.41**	**5.06**	**4.82**	**4.50**	**4.16**	**3.78**
	α = .001	*18.64*	*12.97*	*10.80*	*9.63*	*8.89*	*8.38*	*7.71*	*7.00*	*6.25*
13	α = .05	4.67	3.80	3.41	3.18	3.02	2.92	2.77	2.60	2.42
	α = .01	**9.07**	**6.70**	**5.74**	**5.20**	**4.86**	**4.62**	**4.30**	**3.96**	**3.59**
	α = .001	*17.81*	*12.31*	*10.21*	*9.07*	*8.35*	*7.86*	*7.21*	*6.52*	*5.78*
14	α = 5	4.60	3.74	3.34	3.11	2.96	2.85	2.70	2.53	2.35
	α = .01	**8.86**	**6.51**	**5.56**	**5.03**	**4.69**	**4.46**	**4.14**	**3.80**	**3.43**
	α = .001	*17.14*	*11.78*	*9.73*	*8.62*	*7.92*	*7.43*	*6.80*	*6.13*	*5.41*
15	α = .05	4.54	3.68	3.26	3.06	2.90	2.79	2.64	2.48	2.29
	α = .01	**8.68**	**6.36**	**5.42**	**4.89**	**4.56**	**4.32**	**4.00**	**3.67**	**3.29**
	α = .001	*16.59*	*11.34*	*9.34*	*8.25*	*7.57*	*7.09*	*6.47*	*5.81*	*5.10*
16	α = .05	4.49	3.63	3.24	3.01	2.85	2.74	2.59	2.42	2.24
	α = .01	**8.53**	**6.23**	**5.29**	**4.77**	**4.44**	**4.20**	**3.89**	**3.55**	**3.18**
	α = .001	*16.12*	*10.97*	*9.00*	*7.94*	*7.27*	*6.81*	*6.19*	*5.55*	*4.85*
17	α = .05	4.45	3.59	3.20	2.96	2.81	2.70	2.55	2.38	2.19
	α = .01	**8.40**	**6.11**	**5.18**	**4.67**	**4.34**	**4.10**	**3.79**	**3.45**	**3.08**
	α = .001	*15.72*	*10.66*	*8.73*	*7.68*	*7.02*	*6.56*	*5.96*	*5.32*	*4.63*
18	α = .05	4.41	3.55	3.16	2.93	2.77	2.66	2.51	2.34	2.15
	α = .01	**8.28**	**6.01**	**5.09**	**4.58**	**4.25**	**4.01**	**3.71**	**3.37**	**3.00**
	α = .001	*15.38*	*10.39*	*8.49*	*7.46*	*6.81*	*6.35*	*5.76*	*5.13*	*4.45*
19	α = .05	4.38	3.52	3.13	2.90	2.74	2.63	2.48	2.31	2.11
	α = .01	**8.18**	**5.93**	**5.01**	**4.50**	**4.17**	**3.94**	**3.63**	**3.30**	**2.92**
	α = .001	*15.08*	*10.16*	*8.28*	*7.26*	*6.62*	*6.18*	*5.59*	*4.97*	*4.29*
20	α = .05	4.35	3.49	3.10	2.87	2.71	2.60	2.45	2.28	2.08
	α = .01	**8.10**	**5.85**	**4.94**	**4.43**	**4.10**	**3.87**	**3.56**	**3.23**	**2.86**
	α = .001	*14.82*	*9.95*	*8.10*	*7.10*	*6.46*	*6.02*	*5.44*	*4.82*	*4.15*
21	α = .05	4.32	3.47	3.07	2.84	2.68	2.57	2.42	2.25	2.05
	α = .01	**8.02**	**5.78**	**4.87**	**4.37**	**4.04**	**3.81**	**3.51**	**3.17**	**2.80**
	α = .001	*14.59*	*9.77*	*7.94*	*6.95*	*6.32*	*5.88*	*5.31*	*4.70*	*4.03*
22	α = .05	4.30	3.44	3.05	2.82	2.66	2.55	2.40	2.23	2.03
	α = .01	**7.94**	**5.72**	**4.82**	**4.31**	**3.99**	**3.76**	**3.45**	**3.12**	**2.75**
	α = .001	*14.38*	*9.61*	*7.80*	*6.81*	*6.19*	*5.76*	*5.19*	*4.58*	*3.92*

TABLE C.2   Continued

DF FOR THE NUMERATOR
(DF$_{BETWEEN}$ OR DF$_{TREATMENT}$

		1	2	3	4	5	6	8	12	24

DF FOR THE DENOMINATOR
(DF$_{WITHIN}$ OR DF$_{ERROR}$)

		1	2	3	4	5	6	8	12	24
23	$\alpha = .05$	4.28	3.42	3.03	2.80	2.64	2.53	2.38	2.20	2.00
	$\alpha = .01$	**7.88**	**5.66**	**4.76**	**4.26**	**3.94**	**3.71**	**3.41**	**3.07**	**2.70**
	$\alpha = .001$	*14.19*	*9.47*	*7.67*	*6.69*	*6.08*	*5.65*	*5.09*	*4.48*	*3.82*
24	$\alpha = .05$	4.26	3.40	3.01	2.78	2.62	2.51	2.36	2.18	1.98
	$\alpha = .01$	**7.82**	**5.61**	**4.72**	**4.22**	**3.90**	**3.67**	**3.36**	**3.03**	**2.66**
	$\alpha = .001$	*14.03*	*9.34*	*7.55*	*6.59*	*5.98*	*5.55*	*4.99*	*4.39*	*3.74*
25	$\alpha = .05$	4.24	3.38	2.99	2.76	2.60	2.49	2.34	2.16	1.96
	$\alpha = .01$	**7.77**	**5.57**	**4.68**	**4.18**	**3.86**	**3.63**	**3.32**	**2.99**	**2.62**
	$\alpha = .001$	*13.88*	*9.22*	*7.45*	*6.49*	*5.88*	*5.46*	*4.91*	*4.31*	*3.66*
26	$\alpha = .05$	4.22	3.37	2.98	2.74	2.59	2.47	2.32	2.15	1.95
	$\alpha = .01$	**7.72**	**5.53**	**4.64**	**4.14**	**3.82**	**3.59**	**3.29**	**2.96**	**2.58**
	$\alpha = .001$	*13.74*	*9.12*	*7.36*	*6.41*	*5.80*	*5.38*	*4.83*	*4.24*	*3.59*
27	$\alpha = .05$	4.21	3.35	2.96	2.73	2.57	2.46	2.30	2.13	1.93
	$\alpha = .01$	**7.68**	**5.49**	**4.60**	**4.11**	**3.78**	**3.56**	**3.26**	**2.93**	**2.55**
	$\alpha = .001$	*13.61*	*9.02*	*7.27*	*6.33*	*5.73*	*5.31*	*4.76*	*4.17*	*3.52*
28	$\alpha = .05$	4.20	3.34	2.95	2.71	2.56	2.44	2.29	2.12	1.91
	$\alpha = .01$	**7.64**	**5.45**	**4.57**	**4.07**	**3.75**	**3.53**	**3.23**	**2.90**	**2.52**
	$\alpha = .001$	*13.50*	*8.93*	*7.19*	*6.25*	*5.66*	*5.24*	*4.69*	*4.11*	*3.46*
29	$\alpha = .05$	4.18	3.33	2.93	2.70	2.54	2.43	2.28	2.10	1.90
	$\alpha = .01$	**7.60**	**5.42**	**4.54**	**4.04**	**3.73**	**3.50**	**3.20**	**2.87**	**2.49**
	$\alpha = .001$	*13.39*	*8.85*	*7.12*	*6.19*	*5.59*	*5.18*	*4.64*	*4.05*	*3.41*
30	$\alpha = .05$	4.17	3.32	2.92	2.69	2.53	2.42	2.27	2.09	1.89
	$\alpha = .01$	**7.56**	**5.39**	**4.51**	**4.02**	**3.70**	**3.47**	**3.17**	**2.84**	**2.47**
	$\alpha = .001$	*13.29*	*8.77*	*7.05*	*6.12*	*5.53*	*5.12*	*4.58*	*4.00*	*3.36*
40	$\alpha = .05$	4.08	3.23	2.84	2.61	2.45	2.34	2.18	2.00	1.79
	$\alpha = .01$	**7.31**	**5.18**	**4.31**	**3.83**	**3.51**	**3.29**	**2.99**	**2.66**	**2.29**
	$\alpha = .001$	*12.61*	*8.25*	*6.60*	*5.70*	*5.13*	*4.73*	*4.21*	*3.64*	*3.01*
60	$\alpha = .05$	4.00	3.15	2.76	2.52	2.37	2.25	2.10	1.92	1.70
	$\alpha = .01$	**7.08**	**4.98**	**4.13**	**3.65**	**3.34**	**3.12**	**2.82**	**2.50**	**2.12**
	$\alpha = .001$	*11.97*	*7.76*	*6.17*	*5.31*	*4.76*	*4.37*	*3.87*	*3.31*	*2.69*
120	$\alpha = .05$	3.92	3.07	2.68	2.45	2.29	2.17	2.02	1.83	1.61
	$\alpha = .01$	**6.85**	**4.79**	**3.95**	**3.48**	**3.17**	**2.66**	**2.34**	**1.95**	
	$\alpha = .001$	*11.38*	*7.32*	*5.79*	*4.95*	*4.42*	*4.04*	*3.55*	*3.02*	*2.40*
$\times$	$\alpha = .05$	3.84	2.99	2.60	2.37	2.21	2.10	1.94	1.75	1.52
	$\alpha = .01$	**6.64**	**4.60**	**3.78**	**3.32**	**3.02**	**2.80**	**2.51**	**2.18**	**1.79**
	$\alpha = .001$	*10.83*	*6.91*	*5.42*	*4.62*	*4.10*	*3.74*	*3.27*	*2.74*	*2.13*

TABLE C.3 Significance values for the Pearson product–moment correlation (*r*).

Computed values of *r* are significant if they are larger than the value in the table.

α LEVELS FOR DIRECTIONAL (ONE-TAILED) TESTS

	.05	.025	.01	.005	.0005

α LEVELS FOR NONDIRECTIONAL (TWO-TAILED) TESTS

df (# pairs - 2)	.1	.05	.02	.01	.001
1	.9877	.9969	.9995	.9999	.9999988
2	.9000	.9500	.9800	.9900	.9990
3	.8054	.8783	.9343	.9587	.9912
4	.7293	.8114	.8822	.9172	.9741
5	.6694	.7545	.8329	.8745	.9507
6	.6215	.7067	.7887	.8343	.9249
7	.5822	.6664	.7498	.7977	.8982
8	.5494	.6319	.7155	.7646	.8721
9	.5214	.6021	.6851	.7348	.8471
10	.4973	.5760	.6581	.7079	.8233
11	.4762	.5529	.6339	.6835	.8010
12	.4575	.5324	.6120	.6614	.7800
13	.4409	.5139	.5923	.6411	.7603
14	.4259	.4973	.5742	.6226	.7420
15	.4124	.4821	.5577	.6055	.7246
16	.4000	.4683	.5425	.5897	.7084
17	.3887	.4555	.5285	.5751	.6932
18	.3783	.4438	.5155	.5614	.6787
19	.3687	.4329	.5043	.5487	.6652
20	.3598	.4227	.4921	.5368	.6524
25	.3233	.3809	.4451	.4869	.5974
30	.2960	.3494	.4093	.4487	.5541
35	.2746	.3246	.3810	.4182	.5189
40	.2573	.3044	.3578	.3932	.4896
45	.2428	.2875	.3384	.3721	.4648
50	.2306	.2732	.3218	.3541	.4433
60	.2108	.2500	.2948	.3248	.4078
70	.1954	.2319	.2737	.3017	.3799
80	.1829	.2172	.2565	.2830	.3568
90	.1726	.2050	.2422	.2673	.3375
100	.1638	.1946	.2301	.2540	.3211

TABLE C.4   Significance values for chi-square ($\chi 2$).

Computed values of χ^2 are significant if they are larger than the value in the table.

df	.10	.05	.01	.001
		α LEVELS		
1	2.706	3.841	6.635	10.827
2	4.605	5.991	9.210	13.815
3	6.251	7.815	11.345	16.266
4	7.779	9.488	13.277	18.467
5	9.236	11.070	15.086	20.515
6	10.645	12.592	16.812	22.457
7	12.017	14.067	18.475	24.322
8	13.362	15.507	20.090	26.125
9	14.684	16.919	21.666	27.877
10	15.987	18.307	23.209	29.588
11	17.275	19.675	24.725	31.264
12	18.549	21.026	26.217	32.909
13	19.812	22.362	27.688	34.528
14	21.064	23.685	29.141	36.123
15	22.307	24.996	30.578	37.697
16	23.542	26.296	32.000	39.252
17	24.769	27.587	33.409	40.790
18	25.989	28.869	34.805	42.312
19	27.204	30.144	36.191	43.280
20	28.412	31.410	37.566	45.315
21	29.615	32.671	38.932	46.797
22	30.813	33.924	40.289	48.268
23	32.007	35.172	41.638	49.728
24	33.196	36.415	42.980	51.179
25	34.382	37.652	44.314	52.620
26	35.563	38.885	45.642	54.052
27	36.741	40.133	46.963	55.476
28	37.916	41.337	48.278	56.893
29	39.087	42.557	49.588	58.302
30	40.256	43.773	50.892	59.703

TABLE C.5   One thousand random numbers.

10801	69621	92008	13317	76917	21943	73624	80445	29832	36976
74959	65233	71968	87168	49732	01869	62348	31099	27069	48371
04613	70583	61117	90612	27112	01158	40970	13707	57074	68148
43119	10341	52504	17521	91658	65932	27217	27220	36299	18907
05196	58937	49852	05962	21349	22112	96044	51822	80307	48511
91846	14339	69334	41114	74998	67265	24494	94609	07506	41925
32611	04453	39706	93180	28343	65808	56739	35441	06383	48345
31612	64859	57247	48883	88849	12957	96368	59157	01457	32286
06811	56453	31190	40241	93777	05674	14878	98541	19978	62941
49156	18317	52290	57437	34766	15564	27358	88676	90462	01447
85083	29866	24889	75946	83452	05025	45481	38172	06556	95725
92686	83627	63324	76877	42736	18599	10076	18987	46692	83214
04153	87384	98578	37405	71255	76724	34331	18744	49206	88389
36264	00862	77603	18063	85971	93189	78687	87926	09703	18024
93188	81477	60543	71093	49282	95305	85972	18871	55505	67354
81856	61512	41926	55090	80158	50833	24492	84373	91432	73511
60993	75429	71568	64945	59296	65966	69284	44770	56988	42531
48760	55612	43419	41346	72776	03145	51665	93169	46002	12986
05686	49443	41186	29474	02306	80764	14764	71099	10101	99774
71131	17438	61830	52767	85360	99494	90297	05596	74534	35407

REFERENCES

Abreu, J. M., & Gabarain, G. (2000). Social desirability and Mexican American counselor preferences: Statistical control for a potential confound. *Journal of Counseling Psychology, 47,* 165–176.

ACHRE Report. (n.d.). Retrieved March 19, 2008, from www.hss.energy.gov/healthsafety/ohre/roadmap/achre/chap7_2.html

Ackerman, R., & Goldsmith, M. (2008). Control over grain size in memory reporting—with and without satisficing knowledge. *Journal of Experimental Psychology: Learning, Memory, and Cognition, 34,* 1224–1245. doi:10.1037/a0012938

Adair, J. G. (1984). The Hawthorne effect: A reconsideration of the methodological artifact. *Journal of Applied Psychology, 69,* 334–345.

Adair, J. G., Dushenko, T. W., & Lindsay, R. C. L. (1985). Ethical regulations and their impact on research practice. *American Psychologist, 40,* 59–72.

Alcock, J. (2011, January 6). Back from the future: Parapsychology and the Bem affair. *Skeptical Inquirer.* Retrieved from http://www.csicop.org/specialarticles/show/back_from_the_future

Altevogt, B. M., Pankevich, D. E., Shelton-Davenport, M. K., & Kahn, J. P. (Eds.) (2011). *Chimpanzees in biomedical and behavioral research.* Washington, DC: National Academies Press.

Al-Turkait, F. A., & Ohaeri, J. U. (2010). Dimensional and hierarchical models of depression using the Beck Depression Inventory-II in an Arab college student sample. *BMC Psychiatry, 10* [Electronic version]. doi:10.1186/1471-244X-10-60

American College Health Association-National College Health Assessment Spring 2008 Reference Group Data Report (Abridged) (2009). *Journal of American College Health, 57,* 477–488. doi:10.3200/JACH.57.5

American Psychiatric Association. (1987). *Diagnostic and statistical manual of mental disorders* (3rd ed., revised). Washington, DC: Author.

American Psychological Association. (1994). *Publication manual of the American Psychological Association* (4th ed.). Washington, DC: Author.

American Psychological Association. (2002). Ethical principles of psychologists and code of conduct. *American Psychologist, 57,* 1060–1073.

American Psychological Association. (2010). *Publication manual of the American Psychological Association* (6th ed.). Washington, DC: Author.

Americans felt uneasy toward Arabs even before September 11. (2001). Retrieved September 29, 2001, from http://www.gallup.com/poll/releases/pr010928.asp

Anderson, C. A., & Bushman, B. J. (2001). Effects of violent video games on aggressive behavior, aggressive cognition, aggressive affect, physiological arousal, and prosocial behavior: A meta-analytic review of the scientific literature. *Psychological Science, 12,* 353–359.

Anderson, C. A., Carnagey, N. L., & Eubanks, J. (2003). Exposure to violent media: The effects of songs with violent lyrics on aggressive thoughts and feelings. *Journal of Personality and Social Psychology, 84,* 960–971.

Anderson, C. A., Gentile, D. A., & Buckley, K. E. (2007). Violent video game effects on children and adolescents: Theory, research, and public policy. New York: Oxford University Press.

Anderson, J., & Fienberg, S. E. (2000). Census 2000 controversies. *Chance, 13*(4), 22–30.

Anderson, K. C., & Insel, T. R. (2006). The promise of extinction research for the prevention and treatment of anxiety disorders. *Biological Psychiatry, 60,* 319–321.

Anderson, R. J., & Brice, S. (2011). The mood-enhancing benefits of exercise: Memory biases augment the effect. *Psychology of Sport and Exercise, 12,* 79–82. doi:10.1016/j.psychsport.2010.08.003

André, N., & Metzler, J. N. (2011). Gender differences in fear of success: A preliminary validation of the Performance Success Threat Appraisal Inventory. *Psychology of Sport and Exercise, 12,* 415-422. doi:10.1016/j.psychsport.2011.02.006

Aneschensel, C. S., Clark, V. A., & Frerichs, R. R. (1983). Race, ethnicity, and depression: A confirmatory analysis. *Journal of Personality and Social Psychology, 44,* 385–398.

Angier, N. (2000, August 22). Do races differ? Not really, DNA shows. *New York Times* on the Web [http://www.nytimes.com/library/national/science/082200sci-genetics-race.html]. Retrieved August 22, 2000.

Anorexia may not have cultural roots. (2001). Retrieved April 28, 1998, from http://www.intelihealth.com

Armitage, R., Smith, C., Thompason, S., & Hoffman, R. (2001). Sex differences in slow-wave activity in response to sleep deprivation. *Sleep Research Online, 4,* 33–41. Retrieved from, http://www.sro.org/2001/Armitage/33/

Aronson, J., Lustina, M. J., Good, C., Keough, K., Steele, C. M., & Brown, J. (1999). When white men can't do math: Necessary and sufficient factors in stereotype threat. *Journal of Experimental Social Psychology, 35,* 29–46.

Ashcraft, M. H., & Krause, J. A. (2007). Social and behavioral researchers' experiences with their IRBs. *Ethics & Behavior, 17,* 1–17.

419

Austad, S. N. (2002). A mouse's tale. *Natural History,* *111*(3), 64–70.

Austin, E. J. (2010). Measurement of ability emotional intelligence: Results for two new tests. *British Journal of Psychology, 101,* 563-578. doi:10.1348/000712609X474370

Avoiding plagiarism, self-plagiarism, and other questionable writing practices: A guide to ethical writing. (2009). Office of Research Integrity. Retrieved December 11, 2009, from http://ori.dhhs.gov/education/products/plagiarism

Azar, B. (2000a, April). Online experiments: Ethically fair or foul? *Monitor on Psychology, 31,* 50–52.

Azar, B. (2000b, April). A web of research. *Monitor on Psychology, 31,* 42–44.

Babbie, E. (1995). *The practice of social research* (7th ed.). Belmont, CA: Wadsworth.

Bachorowski, J-A., & Owren, M. J. (2001). Not all laughs are alike: Voiced but not unvoiced laughter readily elicits positive affect. *Psychological Science, 12,* 252–257.

Baker, J. P. (2008). Mercury, vaccines, and autism: One controversy, three histories. *American Journal of Public Health, 98,* 244–253. doi:10.2105/AJPH.2007.113159

Ball, P., Giles, H., & Hewstone, M. (1984). Second language acquisition: The intergroup theory with catastrophic dimensions. In H. Tajfel (Ed.), *The social dimension* (Vol. 2, pp. 668–694). Cambridge, UK: Cambridge University Press.

Banville, D., Desrosiers, P., & Genet-Volet, G. (2000). Translating questionnaires and inventories using a cross-cultural translation technique. *Journal of Teaching in Physical Education, 19,* 374–387.

Barchard, K. A., & Williams, J. (2008). Practical advice for conducting ethical online experiments and questionnaires for United States psychologists. *Behavior Research Methods, 40,* 1111–1128. doi:10.3758/BRM.40.4.1111

Barnes, B. R. (2010). The Hawthorne Effect in community trials in developing countries. *International Journal Of Social Research Methodology: Theory & Practice, 13*(4), 357–370. doi:10.1080/13645570903269096

Barnett, W. S. (1998). Long-term cognitive and academic effects of early childhood education of children in poverty. *Preventive Medicine: An International Devoted to Practice & Theory, 27,* 204–207.

Baron-Cohen, S., Burt, L., Smith-Laittan, F., Harrison, J., & Bolton, P. (1996). Synaesthesia: Prevalence and familiarity. *Perception, 25,* 1073–1079.

Barreto, R. E., Volpato, G. L., & Pottinger, T. G. (2006). The effect of elevated blood cortisol levels on the extinction of a conditioned stress response in rainbow trout. *Hormones and Behavior, 50,* 484–488. doi:10.1016/j.yhbeh.2006.06.017

Bartels, M., van Weegen, F. I., van Beijsterveldt, C. M., Carlier, M., Polderman, T. C., Hoekstra, R. A., & Boomsma, D. I. (2012). The five factor model of personality and intelligence: A twin study on the relationship between the two constructs. *Personality and Individual Differences, 53,* 368–373. doi:10.1016/j.paid.2012.02.007

Bartolic, E. I., Basso, M. R., Schefft, B. K., Glauser, T. T., & Titanic-Schefft, M. M. (1999). Effects of experimentally-induced emotional states on frontal lobe cognitive task performance. *Neuropsychologia, 37,* 677–683. doi:10.1016/S0028-3932(98)00123-7

Basha, S. A., & Ushasree, S. (1998). Fear of success across life span. *Journal of Personality & Clinical Studies, 14,* 63–67.

Batson, C. D., Duncan, B., Ackerman, P., Buckley, T., & Birch, K. (1981). Is empathetic emotion a source of altruistic motivation? *Journal of Personality and Social Psychology, 40,* 290–302.

Baumrind, D. (1964). Some thoughts on ethics of research: After reading Milgram's "Behavioral study of obedience." *American Psychologist, 19,* 421–423.

Beach, F. A. (1950). The Snark was a Boojum. *American Psychologist, 5,* 115–124.

Beauvais, J. E., Woods, S. P., Delaney, R. C., & Fein, D. (2004). Development of a tactile Wisconsin card sorting test. *Rehabilitation Psychology, 49,* 282–287.

Becker, E. (1973). *The denial of death.* New York: Free Press.

Beins, B. C. (2010, August). Students and psychological research: Fostering scientific literacy. In B. C. Beins (Chair), *Psychology, psychology students, and scientific literacy—implications for teaching.* Symposium presented at the annual convention of the American Psychological Association, San Diego, CA.

Beins, B. C. (2012, August). Why Joseph Jastrow Would Not Have Texted While Driving. In B. C. Beins (Chair), *History and undergraduate psychology: Integrating the past in the contemporary curriculum.* Symposium presented at the annual convention of the American Psychological Association, Orlando, FL.

Beins, B. C., & Beins, A. M. (2012). *Effective writing in psychology: Posters, papers, and presentations* (2nd ed.). Boston, MA: Wiley-Blackwell.

Beins, B. C., Doychak, K., Ferrante, P., Herschman, C., & Sherry, S. (2012). *Jokes and Terror Management Theory: Humor May Not Help Manage Terror.* Presented at the annual convention of the New England Psychological Association, Worcester, MA.

Beins, B. C., McCarthy, C., Rigge, M., Rigoli, B., & Sawyer, S. (2007, October). Expectations about humor affect ratings: A generalizable effect with social implications. Poster presentation at the annual convention of the New England Psychological Association, Danbury, CT.

Bell, N. S., Mangione, T. W., Hemenway, D., Amoroso, P. J., & Jones, B. H. (2000). High injury rates among female Army trainees: A function of gender? *The American Journal of Preventive Medicine, 18* (3 Supplement 1), 141–146.

Bem, D. J. (2011). Feeling the future: Experimental evidence for anomalous retroactive influences on cognition and affect. *Journal of Personality and Social Psychology, 100,* 407–425. doi:10.1037/a0021524

Benbow, C. P., & Stanley, J. C. (1980). Sex differences in mathematical ability: Fact or artifact? *Science, 10,* 1262–1264.

Benbow, C. P., & Stanley, J. C. (1983). Sex differences in mathematical reasoning ability: More facts. *Science, 222,* 1029–1030.

Benet-Martínez, V., Leu, J., Lee, F., & Morris, M. W. (2002). Negotiating biculturalism: Cultural frame switching in biculturals with oppositional versus compatible cultural identities. *Journal of Cross-Cultural Psychology, 33,* 492–516.

Benfante, L., & Beins, B. C. (2007, October). Self-reflection and sense of humor: The big five personality characteristics and humor. Poster presentation at the annual convention of the New England Psychological Association, Danbury, CT.

Benton, S. A., Robertson, J. M., Tseng, W., Newton, F. B., & Benton, S. L. (2003). Changes in counseling center client problems across 13 years. *Professional Psychology: Research and Practice, 34,* 66–72. doi:10.1037/0735-7028.34.1.66

Berkowitz, L. (1992). Some thoughts about conservative evaluations of replications. *Personality & Social Psychology Bulletin, 18,* 319–324.

Berreby, D. (2000). Race counts. [Review of Changing race: Latinos, the census and the history of ethnicity in the United States.] *The Sciences, 40,* 38–43.

Berry, J. W., Poortinga, Y. H., Segall, M. H., & Dasen, P. R. (1992). *Cross-cultural psychology: Research and applications.* New York: Cambridge University Press.

Bersamin, M., Paschall, M. J., & Flewelling, R. L. (2005). Ethnic differences in relationships between risk factors and adolescent binge drinking: A national study. *Prevention Science, 6,* 127–137. doi:10.1007/s11121-005-3411-6

Betancourt, H., & López, S. R. (1993). The study of culture, ethnicity, and race in American psychology. *American Psychologist, 48,* 629–637.

Bhui, K., & Bhugra, D. (2001). Methodological rigour in cross-cultural research. *British Journal of Psychiatry, 179,* 269.

Bhutta, Z. A. (2002) Ethics in international health research: A perspective from the developing world. *Bulletin of the World Health Organization, 80,* 114–120.

Birnbaum, M. H. (1974). Using contextual effects to derive psychophysical scales. *Perception and Psychophysics, 15,* 89–96.

Birnbaum, M. H. (1999). How to show that 9 > 221: Collect judgments in a between-subjects design. *Psychological Methods, 4,* 243–249.

Blair, C., Gamson, D., Thorne, S., & Baker, D. (2005). Rising mean IQ: Cognitive demand of mathematics education for young children, population exposure to formal schooling, and the neurobiology of the

prefrontal cortex. *Intelligence, 33,* 93–106. doi:10.1016/j.intell.2004.07.008

Bleiberg, J., Garmoe, W., Cederquist, J., Reeves, D., & Lux, W. (1993). Effects of dexedrine on performance consistency following brain injury: A double-blind placebo crossover case study. *Neuropsychiatry, Neuropsychology, and Behavioral Neurology, 6,* 245–248.

Boettger, M., Schwier, C., & Bär, K. (2011). Sad mood increases pain sensitivity upon thermal grill illusion stimulation: Implications for central pain processing. *Pain, 152,* 123–130. doi:10.1016/j.pain.2010.10.003

Bond, L., Carlin, J. B., Thomas, L., Rubin, K., & Patton, G. (2001). Does bullying cause emotional problems? A prospective study of young teenagers. *BMJ: British Medical Journal, 323,* 480–484. doi:10.1136/bmj.323.7311.480

Bosworth, H. B., & Schaie, K. W. (1999). Survival effects in cognitive function, cognitive style, and sociodemographic variables in the Seattle Longitudinal Study. *Experimental Aging Research, 25,* 121–139.

Bowman, L. L., & Anthonysamy, A. (2006). Malaysian and American students' perceptions of research ethics. *College Student Journal, 40,* 11–24.

Boyack, K.W., Klavans, R., & Börner, K. (2005). Mapping the backbone of science. *Scientometrics, 64,* 351–374.

Bramel, D., & Friend, R. (1981). Hawthorne, the myth of the docile worker, and class bias in psychology. *American Psychologist, 36,* 867–878.

Bray, J. H., Adams, G. J., Getz, J. G., & Baer, P. E. (2001). Developmental, family, and ethnic in influences on adolescent alcohol usage: A growth curve approach. *Journal of Family Psychology, 15,* 301–314.

Brewer, B. W., & Shillinglaw, R. (1992). Evaluation of a psychological skills training workshop for male intercollegiate lacrosse players. *Sport Psychologist, 6,* 139–147.

Brewer, N., Keast, A., & Rishworth, A. (2002). The confidence-accuracy relationship in eyewitness identification: The effects of reflection and disconfirmation on correlation and calibration. *Journal of Experimental Psychology: Applied, 8,* 46–58.

Bröder, A. (1998). Deception can be acceptable. *American Psychologist, 53,* 805–806.

Broman, C. L. (2005). Stress, race, and substance use in college. *College Student Journal, 39,* 340–352.

Brüne, M., Sonntag, C., Abdel-Hamid, M., Lehmkämper, C., Juckel, G., & Troisi, A. (2008). Nonverbal behavior during standardized interviews in patients with schizophrenia spectrum disorders. *Journal of Nervous and Mental Disease, 196,* 282–288. doi:10.1097/NMD.0b013e31816a4922

Bryant, J. A., Mealey, L., Herzog, E. A., & Rychwalski, W. L. (2001). Paradoxical effect of surveyor's conservative versus provocative clothing on rape myth acceptance of males and females. *Journal of Psychology & Human Sexuality, 13,* 55–66. doi:10.1300/J056v13n01_03

Budson, A. E., Desikan, R., Daffner, K. R., & Schacter, D. L. (2001). Perceptual false recognition in Alzheimer's disease. *Neuropsychology, 15,* 230–243. doi:10.1037/0894-4105.15.2.230

Bull, R., & Stevens, J. (1980). Effect of unsightly teeth on helping behavior. *Perceptual and Motor Skills, 51,* 438.

Burger, J. M. (2009). Replicating Milgram: Would people still obey today? *American Psychologist, 64,* 1–11.

Burtt, H. E. (1920). Sex differences in the effect of discussion. *Journal of Experimental Psychology, 3,* 390–395.

Bushman, B. J., & Anderson, C. A. (2001). Media violence and the American public: Scientific facts versus media misinformation. *American Psychologist, 56,* 477–489.

Cai, W-H., Blundell, J., Han, J., Greene, R. W., & Powell, C. M. (2006). Postreactivation glucocorticoids impair recall of established fear memory. *Journal of Neuroscience, 26,* 9560–9566.

Campbell, D. T., & Stanley, J. C. (1966). *Experimental and quasi-experimental designs for research.* Chicago, IL: Rand McNally.

Campbell, F. A., Pungello, E. P., Burchinal, M., Kainz, K., Pan, Y., Wasik, B. H., et al. (2012). Adult outcomes as a function of an early childhood educational program: An Abecedarian Project follow-up. *Developmental Psychology.* Advance online publication. doi: 10.1037/a0026644

Campos, R. C., & Gonçalves, B. (2011). The Portuguese version of the Beck Depression Inventory-II (BDI-II): Preliminary psychometric data with two nonclinical samples. *European Journal of Psychological Assessment, 27*(4), 258–264. doi:10.1027/1015-5759/a000072

Caplan, P. J., & Caplan, J. B. (1999). Thinking critically about research on sex and gender (2nd ed.). New York: Longman.

Carey, B. (2011, November 2). Fraud case seen as red flag for psychology research. Retrieved from http://www.nytimes.com/2011/11/03/health/research/noted-dutch-psychologist-stapel-accused-of-research-fraud.html

Carnagey, N. L., Anderson, C. A., & Bartholow, B. D. (2007). Media violence and social neuroscience: New questions and new opportunities. *Current Directions in Psychological Science, 16,* 178–182.

Carr, S. C., Munro, D., & Bishop, G. D. (1995). Attitude assessment in non-Western countries: Critical modifications to Likert scaling. *Psychologia, 39,* 55–59.

Carstens, C. B., Haskins, E., & Hounshell, G. W. (1995). Listening to Mozart may not enhance performance on the revised Minnesota paper form board test. *Psychological Reports, 77,* 111–114.

Caruso, K. (2004, September 6). Joann Mitchell Levy, sixth NYU student to die by suicide in the past year. Retrieved August 3, 2007, from http://www.suicide.org/joann-mitchell-levy-nyu-suicides.html

Case summaries. (2004). Office of Research Integrity Newsletter, *12*(4), 5–7. Retrieved June 1, 2007, from http://ori.dhhs.gov/documents/newsletters/vol12_no2.pdf

Caspi, A., Herbener, E. S., & Ozer, D. J. (1992). Shared experiences and the similarity of personalities: A longitudinal study of married couples. *Journal of Personality and Social Psychology, 62,* 281–291. doi:10.1037/0022-3514.62.2.281

Ceci, S. J., & Bruck, M. (2009). Do IRBs pass the minimal harm test? *Perspectives in Psychological Science, 4,* 28–29.

Cepeda-Benito, A., & Gleaves, D. H. (2000). Cross-ethnic equivalence of the Hopkins Symptom Checklist-21 in European American, African American, and Latino college students. *Cultural Diversity and Ethnic Minority Psychology, 6,* 297–308.

Cernovsky, Z. Z. (2000). On the similarities of American blacks and whites. In B. Slife (Ed.), *Taking sides: Clashing views on controversial psychological issues* (pp. 184–187). Guilford, CT: Dushkin/McGraw Hill.

Chabris, C. F., Steele, K. M., Bella, S. D., Peretz, I., Dunlop, T., Dawe, L. A., et al. (1999). Prelude or requiem for the "Mozart effect"? *Nature, 400,* 826–828.

Chang, W. C. (2000). In search of the Chinese in all the wrong places! *Journal of Psychology in Chinese Societies, 1,* 125–142.

Chao, R. (2001). Integrating culture and attachment. *American Psychologist, 56,* 822–823.

Charges of fake research hit new high. (2005, July 10). Retrieved from http://www.msnbc.msn.com/id/8474936/ns/health-health_care/t/charges-fake-research-hit-new-high/

Charges of fake research hit new high. (2005, July 10). Retrieved June 1, 2007, from http://www.msnbc.msn.com/id/8474936

Chen, C., Lee, S-Y., & Stevenson, H. W. (1995). Response style and cross-cultural comparisons of rating scales among East Asian and North American students. *Psychological Science, 6,* 170–175.

Chen, F. (2008).What happens if we compare chopsticks with forks? The impact of making inappropriate comparisons in cross-cultural research. *Journal of Personality and Social Psychology, 95,* 1005–1018. doi:10.1037/a0013193

Cheryan, S., & Bodenhausen, G. V. (2000). When positive stereotypes threaten intellectual performance: The psychological hazards of "model minority" status. *Psychological Science, 11,* 399–402.

Chilcot, J., Norton, S., Wellsted, D., Almond, M., Davenport, A., & Farrington, K. (2011). A confirmatory factor analysis of the Beck Depression Inventory-II in end-stage renal disease patients. *Journal of Psychosomatic Research, 71,* 148–153. doi:10.1016/j.jpsychores.2011.02.006

Chiriboga, D. A., Jang, Y., Banks, S., & Kim, G. (2007). Acculturation and its effect on depressive symptom

423

structure in a sample of Mexican American elders. *Hispanic Journal of Behavioral Sciences, 29*(1), 83–100. doi:10.1177/0739986306295875

Cho, H., & LaRose, R. (1999). Privacy issues in internet surveys. *Social Science Computer Review, 17*, 421–434.

Christakis, D. A. (2009). The effects of infant media usage: What do we know and what should we learn? *Acta Paediatrica, 98*, 8–16. doi:10.1111/j.1651-2227.2008.01027.x

Christensen, L. (1988). Deception in psychological research: When is its use justified? *Personality and Social Psychology Bulletin, 14*, 664–675.

Christian, L., Parsons, N. L., & Dillman, D. A. (2009). Designing scalar questions for Web surveys. *Sociological Methods & Research, 37*, 393–425. doi:10.1177/0049124108330004

Cialdini, R. B. (1980). Full-cycle social psychology. *Applied Social Psychology Annual, 1*, 21–47.

Cialdini, R. B., Darby, B. L., & Vincent, J. E. (1973). Transgression and altruism: A case for hedonism. *Journal of Experimental Social Psychology, 9*, 502–516. doi:10.1016/0022-1031(73)90031-0

CIA–The world factbook–United Kingdom. (2007). Retrieved July 11, 2007, from https://www.cia.gov/library/publications/the-world-factbook/geos/uk.html

Clark, D. M., & Teasdale, J. D. (1985). Constraints on the effects of mood on memory. *Journal of Personality and Social Psychology, 52*, 749–758.

Clark, M., Rogers, M., Foster, A., Dvorchak, F., Saadeh, F., Weaver, J., & Mor, V. (2011). A randomized trial of the impact of survey design characteristics on response rates among nursing home providers. *Evaluation & the Health Professions, 34*(4), 464–486. doi:10.1177/0163278710397791

Clawson, R. A., & Trice, R. (2000). Poverty as we know it: Media portrayals of the poor. *Public Opinion Quarterly, 64*, 53–64.

Cohen, D., & Gunz, A. (2002). As seen by the other…: Perspectives on the self in the memories and emotional perceptions of Easterners and Westerners. *Psychological Science, 13*, 55–59.

Cohen, S., Alper, C. M., Doyle, W. J., Treanor, J. J., & Turner, R. B. (2006). Positive emotional style predicts resistance to illness after experimental exposure to rhinovirus or influenza A virus. *Psychosomatic Medicine, 68*, 809–915.

Cohen, S., Tyrrell, D. A., & Smith, A. P. (1991). Psychological stress and susceptibility to the common cold. *New England Journal of Medicine, 325*, 606–612.

Coile, D. C., & Miller, N. E. (1984). How radical animal activists try to mislead humane people. *American Psychologist, 39*, 700–701.

Consumers in the 18-to-24 age segment view cell phones as multi-functional accessories: Crave advanced features and personalization options. (2007, January 22).

Retrieved July 24, 2007, from http://www.comscore.com/press/release.asp?press=1184

Cook, D. J. (1996). Randomized trials in single subjects: The N of 1 study. *Psychopharmacology Bulletin, 32*, 363–367.

Cook, P. J., & Ludwig, J. (1998). Defensive gun uses: New evidence from a national survey. *Journal of Quantitative Criminology, 14*, 111–131.

Costing the count. (2011, June 2). *The Economist.* Retrieved from http://www.economist.com/node/18772674?story_id=18772674&CFID=165420949&CFTOKEN=32425086

Council of National Psychological Associations for the Advancement of Ethnic Minority Interests. (2000). Guidelines for research in ethnic minority communities. Washington, DC: American Psychological Association.

Couper, M. P., Kapteyn, A., Schonlau, M., & Winter, J. (2007). Noncoverage and nonresponse in an Internet survey. *Social Science Research, 36*, 131–148.

Coverdale, J. H., & Turbott, S. H. (2000). Sexual and physical abuse of chronically ill psychiatric outpatients compared with a matched sample of medical outpatients. *Journal of Nervous and Mental Disease, 188*, 440–445.

Cox, C. R., & LeBoeuf, B. J. (1977). Female incitation of male competition: A mechanism in sexual selection. *American Naturalist, 111*, 317–335.

Cranford, J. A., McCabe, S. E., Boyd, C. J., Slayden, J., Reed, M. B., Ketchie, J. M., et al. (2008). Reasons for nonresponse in a web-based survey of alcohol involvement among first-year college students. *Addictive Behaviors, 33*, 206–210. doi:10.1016/j.addbeh.2007.07.008

Crocker, P. R. E. (1993). Sport and exercise psychology and research with individuals with physical disabilities: Using theory to advance knowledge. *Adapted Physical Activity Quarterly, 10*, 324–335.

Croizet, J-C., & Claire, T. (1998). Extending the concept of stereotype and threat to social class: The intellectual underperformance of students from low socioeconomic backgrounds. *Personality & Social Psychology Bulletin, 24*, 588–594.

Croll, S., & Bryant, R. A. (2000). Autobiographical memory in postnatal depression. *Cognitive Therapy and Research, 24*, 419–426.

Cruz, R. A., King, K. M., Widaman, K. F., Leu, J., Cauce, A., & Conger, R. D. (2011). Cultural influences on positive father involvement in two-parent Mexican-origin families. *Journal of Family Psychology, 25*, 731–740. doi:10.1037/a0025128

Cunningham, S. (1984). Genovese: 20 years later, few heed a stranger's cries. *Social Action and the Law, 10*, 24–25.

Cytowic, R. E. (1993). *The man who tasted shapes.* New York: G. P. Putnam & Son.

Cytowic, R. E. (1997). Synaesthesia: Phenomenology and neuropsychology–A review of current knowledge.

In S. Baron-Cohen & J. E. Harrison (Eds.), *Synaesthesia: Classic and contemporary readings.* Cambridge, MA: Blackwell.

Darley, J. M., & Latané, B. (1968).Bystander intervention in emergencies: Diffusion of responsibility. *Journal of Personality and Social Psychology, 8,* 377–383.

da Veiga, F., & Saraiva, C. (2003). Age patterns of suicide: Identification and characterization of European clusters and trends. *Crisis: Journal of Crisis Intervention and Suicide Prevention, 24,* 56–67. doi:10.1027//0227-5910.24.2.56

Davies, M., Stankov, L., & Roberts, R. D. (1998). Emotional intelligence: In search of an elusive construct. *Journal of Personality and Social Psychology, 75,* 989–1015.

Davis, R. E., Resnicow, K., & Couper, M. P. (2011). Survey response styles, acculturation, and culture among a sample of Mexican American adults. *Journal of Cross-Cultural Psychology, 42,* 1219–1236.

Dawes, S. E., Suarez, P. P., Vaida, F. F., Marcotte, T. D., Atkinson, J. H., Grant, I. I., et al. (2010). Demographic influences and suggested cut-scores for the Beck Depression Inventory in a non-clinical Spanish speaking population from the US-Mexico border region. *International Journal of Culture and Mental Health, 3,* 34–42. doi:10.1080/17542860903533640

DeAndrea, D. C., Shaw, A. S., & Levine, T. R. (2010). Online language: The role of culture in self-expression and self-construal on Facebook. *Journal of Language and Social Psychology, 29*(4), 425–442. doi:10.1177/0261927X10377989

Deci, E. L., & Ryan, R. M. (1985).*Intrinsic motivation and self-determination in human behavior.* New York: Plenum.

Deese, J., & Hulse, S. H. (1967). The psychology of learning (3rd ed.). New York: McGraw-Hill.

de Fockert, J. W., Caparos, S., Linnell, K. J., & Davidoff, J. (2011). Reduced distractibility in a remote culture. *Plos ONE, 6*(10). doi:10.1371/journal.pone.0026337

Delgado, A. R., & Prieto, G. (2008). Stereotype threat as validity threat: The anxiety-sex-threat interaction. *Intelligence, 36,* 635–640. doi:10.1016/j.intell.2008.01.008

Demographics of internet users. (2007). Pew Internet & American Life Project, February 15–March 7, 2007 Tracking Survey. Retrieved July 17, 2007, from http://www.pewinternet.org/trends/User_Demo_6.15.07.htm

Demographics of internet users. (2009). Pew Internet and American Life Project. Retrieved December 17, 2009, from www.pewinternet.org/Trend-Data/Whos-Online.aspx

Diener, E., Matthews, R., & Smith, R. E. (1972). Leakage of experimental information to potential future subjects by debriefed subjects. *Journal of Experimental Research in Personality, 6,* 264–267.

Dietz, A., Albowicz, C., & Beins, B. C. (2011, October). *Neuroticism and sex-related jokes: Sex primes mortality salience.* Poster presentation at the annual convention of the New England Psychological Association, Fairfield, CT.

Dillman, D. A. (2000). *Mail and internet surveys: The tailored design method.* New York: Wiley.

Dillman, D. A., Phelps, G., Tortora, R., Swift, K., Kohrell, J., Berck, J., Messer, B. L. (2009). Response rate and measurement differences in mixed-mode surveys using mail, telephone, interactive voice response (IVR) and the Internet. *Social Science Research, 38,* 1–18. doi:10.1016/j.ssresearch.2008.03.007

Dixon, A. K. (1998). Ethological strategies for defence in animals and humans: Their role in some psychiatric disorders. *British Journal of Medical Psychology, 71,* 417–445.

Dixon, W. A., & Reid, J. K. (2000). Positive life events as a moderator of stress-related depressive symptoms. *Journal of Counseling & Development, 78,* 343–347.

Dozois, D. J. A., Dobson, K. S., & Ahnberg, J. L. (1998). A psychometric evaluation of the Beck Depression Inventory–II. *Psychological Assessment, 10,* 83–89.

Dritschel, B., Kao, C., Astell, A., Neufeind, J., & Lai, T. (2011). How are depression and autobiographical memory retrieval related to culture? *Journal of Abnormal Psychology, 120,* 969–974. doi:10.1037/a0025293

Dubowitz, G. (1998). Effect of temazepam on oxygen saturation and sleep quality at high altitude: Randomised placebo controlled crossover trial. *British Medical Journal, 316,* 587–589.

Duncan, S. C., Duncan, T. E., & Strycker, L. A. (2006). Alcohol use from ages 9 to 16: A cohort-sequential latent growth model. *Drug and Alcohol Dependence, 81,* 71–81.

Dunning, D., & Perretta, S. (2002). Automaticity and eyewitness accuracy: A 10–12 second rule for distinguishing accurate from inaccurate positive identifications. *Journal of Applied Psychology, 87,* 951–962.

Durante, K. M., Griskevicius, V., Hill, S. E., Perilloux, C., & Li, N. P. (2011). Ovulation, female competition, and product choice: Hormonal influences on consumer behavior. *Journal of Consumer Research, 37,* 921–934. doi:10.1086/656575

Eagles, J. M., Andrew, J. E., Johnston, M. I., Easton, E. A., & Millar, H. R. (2001). Season of birth in females with anorexia nervosa in Northeast Scotland. *International Journal of Eating Disorders, 30,* 167–175.

Eagly, A. H. (2009). The his and hers of prosocial behavior: An examination of the social psychology of gender. *American Psychologist, 64,* 644–658. doi:10.1037/0003-066X.64.8.644

Edwards, C. L., Fillingim, R. B., & Keefe, F. (2001). Race, ethnicity and pain. *Pain, 94,* 133–137.

Eichenwald, K., & Kolata, G. (1999, May 16). Drug trials hide conflicts for doctors. *New York Times.* Retrieved from http://www.nytimes.com/library/politics/051699drug-trials.html

Ellis, H. C., Thomas, R. L., & Rodriguez, I. A. (1984). Emotional mood states and memory: Elaborative encoding, semantic processing, and cognitive effort. *Journal of Experimental Psychology: Learning, Memory, and Cognition, 10*, 470–482.

Elms, A. C. (2009). Obedience lite. *American Psychologist, 64*, 32–36.

Engelhardt, C. R., Bartholow, B. D., Kerr, G. T., & Bushman, B. J. (2011). This is your brain on violent video games: Neural desensitization to violence predicts increased aggression following violent video game exposure. *Journal of Experimental Social Psychology, 47*, 1033–1036. doi:10.1016/j.jesp.2011.03.027

Ethical principles of psychologists and code of conduct. (2002). Retrieved from www.apa.org/ETHICS/code2002.html

Evans, S. W., Pelham, W. E., Smith, B. H., Burkstein, O., Gnagy, E. M., Greiner, A. R., et al. (2001). Dose-response effects of methylphenidate on ecological valid measures of academic performance and classroom behavior in adolescents with ADHD. *Experimental and Clinical Psychopharmacology, 9*, 163–175.

Fairburn, C. G., Welch, S. L., Norman, P. A., O'Connor, B. A., & Doll, H. A. (1996). Bias and bulimia nervosa: How typical are clinical cases? *American Journal of Psychiatry, 153*, 386–391.

Falk, R. (1986). Misconceptions of statistical significance. *Journal of Structural Learning, 9*, 83–96.

Falk, R., & Greenbaum, C. W. (1995). Significance tests die hard: The amazing persistence of a probabilistic misconception. *Theory & Psychology, 5*, 75–98.

Fanelli, D., Innogen, & ISSTI. (2009). How many scientists fabricate and falsify research? *Office of Research Integrity Newsletter, 17*(4), 11. Retrieved from http://ori.dhhs.gov/documents/newsletters/vol17_no4.pdf

Farley, P. (2003, January 21). Young scientist's paper gets him in hot water with colleagues. Retrieved January 23, 2003, from http://www.boston.com

Fausto-Sterling, A. (1993). The five sexes: Why male and female are not enough. *The Sciences, 33*(2), 20–25.

Felmingham, K., Kemp, A., Williams, L., Das, P., Hughes, G., Peduto, A., et al. (2007). Changes in anterior cingulate and amygdala after cognitive behavior therapy of posttraumatic stress disorder. *Psychological Science, 18*, 127–129.

Fernandez, E., & Sheffield, J. (1996). Relative contributions of life events versus daily hassles to the frequency and intensity of headaches. *Headache, 36*, 595–602.

Finkel, S. E., Guterbok, T. M., & Borg, M. J. (1991). Race of interviewer effects in a preelection Poll: Virginia 1989. *Public Opinion Quarterly, 55*, 313–330.

Fisher, C. (2005). Deception research involving children: Ethical practices and paradoxes. *Ethics & Behavior, 15*, 271–287.

Fisher, C. B., & Fyrberg, D. (1994). Participant partners: College students weigh the costs and benefits of deceptive research. *American Psychologist, 49*, 417–427.

Fisher, M. L. (2004). Female intrasexual competition decreases female facial attractiveness. *Proceedings of the Royal Society B, 271*, S283–S285. doi:10.1098./rsbl.2004.0160

Fisher, R. A. (1932). *Statistical methods for research workers* (4th ed.). Edinburgh, Scotland: Oliver & Boyd.

Fisher, R. A. (1935). *The design of experiments*. Edinburgh, Scotland: Oliver & Boyd.

Flynn, J. R. (1999). Searching for justice: The discovery of IQ gains over time. *American Psychologist, 54*, 5–20.

Fombonne, R. (2001). Is there an epidemic of autism? *Pediatrics, 107*, 411–412. doi: 10.1542/peds.107.2.411

Francis, L. J., & Jackson, C. J. (1998). The social desirability of toughmindedness: A study among undergraduates. *Irish Journal of Psychology, 19*, 400–403.

Frank, O., & Snijders, T. (1994). Estimating the size of hidden populations using snowball sampling. *Journal of Official Statistics, 10*, 53–67.

French, S., & Joseph, S. (1999). Religiosity and its association with happiness, purpose in life, and self-actualisation. *Mental Health, Religion & Culture, 2*, 117–120. doi:10.1080/13674679908406340

French, S., & Stephen, J. (1999). Religiosity and its association with happiness, purpose in life, and self-actualisation. *Mental Health, Religion & Culture, 2*, 117–120.

Frick, R. W. (1996). The appropriate use of null hypothesis testing. *Psychological Methods, 1*, 379–390.

Friman, P. C., Allen, K. D., Kerwin, M. L. E., & Larzelere, R. (2000). Questionable validity, not vitality. *American Psychologist, 55*, 274–275. doi:10.1037/0003-066X.55.2.274

Fukuda, E., Saklofske, D. H., Tamaoka, K., & Lim, H. (2012). Factor structure of the Korean version of Wong and Law's Emotional Intelligence Scale. *Assessment, 19*, 3–7. doi:10.1177/1073191111428863

Gadzella, B. M., Masten, W. G., & Stacks, J. (1998). Students' stress and their learning strategies, test anxiety, and attributions. *College Student Journal, 32*, 416–422.

Gaito, J. (1961). Repeated measurements designs and counterbalancing. *Psychological Bulletin, 58*, 46–54.

Gaito, J. (1980). Measurement scales and statistics: Resurgence of an old misconception. *Psychological Bulletin, 87*, 564–567.

Gao, Z., & Zhang, T. (2011). Development and application of Fear of Success Questionnaire. *Chinese Journal of Clinical Psychology, 19*, 602–605. Retrieved from PsycINFO on September 3, 2012.

Gardner, H. (1999). *Intelligence reframed: Multiple intelligences for the 21st century*. New York: Basicbooks.

Gardner, H., Krechevsky, M., Sternberg, R. J., & Okagaki, L. (1994). Intelligence in context: Enhancing students' practical intelligence for school. In K. McGilly (Ed.), *Classroom lessons: Integrating cognitive theory and classroom practice* (pp. 105–127). Cambridge: MIT Press.

Gawrylewski, A. (2007a). Case reports: Essential or irrelevant? *The Scientist.* Retrieved May 14, 2007, from http://www.the-scientist.com/news/home/53192

Gawrylewski, A. (2007b). The trouble with animal models. *The Scientist.* Retrieved August 10, 2007, from http://www.the-scientist.com/article/home/53306

Gehrick, J-G., & Shapiro, D. (2000). Reduced facial expression and social context in major depression: Discrepancies between facial muscle activity and self-reported emotion. *Psychiatry Research, 95,* 157–167.

Geier, A. B., Rozin, P., & Doros, G. (2006). Unit bias: A new heuristic that helps explain the effect of portion size on food intake. *Psychological Science, 17,* 521–525. doi:10.1111/j.1467-9280.2006.01738.x

Gendall, P., Hoek, J., & Brennan, M. (1998). The tea bag experiment: More evidence on incentives in mail surveys. *Journal of the Market Research Society, 40,* 347–351.

Geurts, H. M., Luman, M., & van Meel, C. S. (2008). What's in a game: The effect of social motivation on interference control in boys with ADHD and autism spectrum disorders. *Journal of Child Psychology and Psychiatry, 49,* 848–857. doi:10.1111/j.1469-7610.2008.01916.x

Ghose, T. (2012, January). More retractions, not dishonesty. Retrieved from http://the-scientist.com/2012/01/12/more-retractions-not-dishonesty/

Gigliotti, L. M. (2011). Comparison of an Internet versus mail survey: A case study. *Human Dimensions of Wildlife, 16*(1), 55–62. doi:10.1080/10871209.2011.535241

Gladwell, M. (2002, March 13). John Rock's error. *The New Yorker,* 52–63.

Glaze, J. A. (1928). The association value of nonsense syllables. *Journal of Genetic Psychology, 35,* 255–269.

Gloria, A. M., Castellanos, J., Kanagui-Muñoz, M., & Rico, M. A. (2012). Assessing Latina/o undergraduates' depressive symptomatology: Comparisons of the Beck Depression Inventory-II, the Center for Epidemiological Studies-Depression Scale, and the Self-Report Depression Scale. *Hispanic Journal of Behavioral Sciences, 34,* 160–181. doi:10.1177/0739986311428893

Glueck, W. F., & Jauch, L. R. (1975). Sources of ideas among productive scholars: Implications for administrators. *Journal of Higher Education, 46,* 103–114.

Goldenberg, J. L., Pyszczynski, T., McCoy, S. K., Greenberg, J., & Solomon, S. (1999). Death, sex, love, and neuroticism: Why is sex such a problem? *Journal of Personality and Social Psychology, 77,* 1173–1187.

Goldston, D. B., Molock, S., Whitbeck, L. B., Murakami, J. L., Zayas, L. H., & Hall, G. (2008). Cultural considerations in adolescent suicide prevention and psychosocial treatment. *American Psychologist, 63,* 14–31. doi:10.1037/0003-066X.63.1.14

Goleman, D. (1996). *Emotional intelligence.* New York: Bantam Books.

Goodman, A. H. (2000). Why genes don't count (for racial differences in health). *American Journal of Public Health, 90,* 1699–1702.

Goodman-Delahunty, J. (1998). Approaches to gender and the law: Research and applications. *Law and Human Behavior, 22,* 129–143.

Gorenstein, C., Andrade, L., Filho, A. H. G. V., Tung, T., & Artes, R. (1999). Pschometric properties of the Portuguese version of the Beck Depression Inventory on Brazilian college students. *Journal of Clinical Psychology, 55,* 553–602.

Gosling, S. D., Vazire, S., Srivastava, S., & John, O. P. (2004). Should we trust web-based studies? A comparative analysis of six preconceptions about internet questionnaires. *American Psychologist, 59,* 93–104.

Gottschalk, A., Smith, D. S., Jobes, D. R., Kennedy, S. K., Lally, S. E., Noble, V. E., et al. (1998). Preemptive epidural analgesia and recovery from radical prostatectomy: A randomized controlled trial. *Journal of the American Medical Association, 279,* 1076–1082.

Gould, S. J. (1981). *The mismeasure of man.* New York: W. W. Norton.

Graham, J. M. (2011). Measuring love in romantic relationships: A meta-analysis. *Journal of Social and Personal Relationships, 28*(6), 748–771. doi:10.1177/0265407510389126

Gray, J. (1992). *Menare from Mars, women are from Venus: A practical guide for improving communication and getting what you want in your relationships.* New York: HarperCollins.

Green, A., & Vaid, J. (1986). Methodological issues in the use of the concurrent activities paradigm. *Brain and Cognition, 5,* 465–476.

Green, C. W., & Reid, D. H. (1999). A behavioral approach to identifying sources of happiness and unhappiness among individuals with profound multiple disabilities. *Behavior Modification, 23,* 280–293.

Gruder, C. L., Stumpfhauser, A., & Wyer, R. S. (1977). Improvement in experimental performance as a result of debriefing about deception. *Personality and Social Psychology Bulletin, 3,* 434–437.

Guerra, P., Campagnoli, R. R., Vico, C., Volchan, E., Anllo-Vento, L., & Vila, J. (2011). Filial versus romantic love: Contributions from peripheral and central electrophysiology. *Biological Psychology, 88,* 196–203. doi:10.1016/j.biopsycho.2011.08.002

Gunewardene, A., Huon, G. F., & Zheng, R. (2001). Exposure to westernization and dieting: A cross-cultural study. *International Journal of Eating Disorders, 29,* 289–293.

Gunnell, D., Rogers, J., & Dieppe, P. (2001). Height and health: Predicting longevity from bone length in archaeological remains. *Journal of Epidemiology and Community Health, 55,* 505–507.

Guthrie, J. P., Ash, R. A., & Bendapudi, V. (1995). *Journal of Applied Psychology, 80*, 186–190.

Gutierrez, P. M., Osman, A., Kopper, B. A., Barrios, F. X., & Bagge, C. L. (2000). Suicide risk assessment in a college student population. *Journal of Counseling Psychology, 47*, 403–413.

Gwiazda, J., Ong, E., Held, R., & Thorn, F. (2000). Vision: Myopia and ambient night-time lighting. *Nature, 404*, 144.

Hahn, P. W., & Clayton, S. D. (1996). The effects of attorney presentation style, attorney gender, and juror gender on juror decisions. *Law and Human Behavior, 20*, 533–554.

Hall, M. E., MacDonald, S., & Young, G. C. (1992). The effectiveness of directed multisensory stimulation versus non-directed stimulation in comatose CHI patients: Pilot study of a single subject design. *Brain Injury, 6*, 435–445.

Halvari, H., & Kjormo, O. (2000). A structural model of achievement motives, performance approach and avoidance goals and performance among Norwegian Olympic athletes. *Perceptual & Motor Skills, 89*, 997–1022.

Handling misconduct: Case summaries. (2009). Office of Research Integrity. Retrieved December 11, 2009, from http://ori.hhs.gov/misconduct/cases/

Harbluk, J. L., Noy, Y. I., Trbovich, P. L., & Elizenman, M. (2007). An on-road assessment of cognitive distraction: Impacts on drivers' visual behavior and braking performance. *Accident Analysis and Prevention, 39*, 372–379.

Harris, B. (1980). The FBI's files on APA and SPSSI: Description and implications. *American Psychologist, 35*, 1141–1144.

Harris, G., & Roberts, J. (2007, June 3). After sanctions, doctors get drug company pay. *The New York Times* [Electronic version]. Retrieved October 5, 2007, from http://www.nytimes.com/2007/06/03/health/03docs.html

Harrowing, J. N., Mill, J. J., Spiers, J. J., Kulig, J. J., & Kipp, W. W. (2010). Culture, context and community: Ethical considerations for global nursing research. *International Nursing Review, 57*, 70–77. doi:10.1111/j.1466-7657.2009.00766.x

Hashemi, L., & Webster, B. S. (1998). Non-fatal workplace violence workers' compensation claims (1993–1996). *Journal of Occupational and Environmental Medicine, 40*, 561–567.

Hatfield, J., & Murphy, S. (2007). The effects of mobile phone use on pedestrian crossing behaviour at signalised and unsignalised intersections. *Accident Analysis and Prevention, 39*, 197–205.

Hay, C. A., & Bakken, L. (1991). Gifted sixth-grade girls: Similarities and differences in attitudes among gifted girls, non-gifted peers, and their mothers. *Roeper Review, 13*, 158–160.

Hayslip, B., McCoy-Roberts, L., & Pavur, R. (1998). Selective attrition effects in bereavement research: A three-year longitudinal analysis. *Omega, 38*, 21–35.

Hazlett, R. L., & Hoehn-Saric, R. (2000). Effects of perceived physical attractiveness on females' facial displays and affect. *Evolution and Human Behavior, 21*, 49–57.

Headden, S. (1997, December 8). The junk mail deluge. *U.S. News & World Report*, 42–48.

Heaven, P. L., & Ciarrochi, J. (2012). When IQ is not everything: Intelligence, personality and academic performance at school. *Personality and Individual Differences, 53*, 518–522. doi:10.1016 /j.paid.2012.04.024

Heckathorn, D. D. (1997). Respondent-driven sampling: A new approach to the study of hidden populations. *Social Problems, 44*, 174–199.

Hedden, T., Park, D. C., Nisbett, R., Ji, L. J., Jing, Q., & Jiao, S. (2002). Cultural variation in verbal versus spatial neuropsychological function across the lifespan. *Neuropsychology, 16*, 65–73.

Heerwegh, D. (2009). Mode differences between face-to-face and web surveys: An experimental investigation of data quality and social desirability effects. *International Journal of Public Opinion Research, 21*, 111–121. doi:10.1093/ijpor/edn054

Helms, J. E., Jernigan, M., & Mascher, J. (2005). The meaning of race in psychology and how to change it: A methodological perspective. *American Psychologist, 60*, 27–36.

Hemenway, D. (1997). The myth of millions of annual self-defense gun uses: A case study of survey overestimates of rare events. *Chance, 10*, 6–10.

Hennigan, K. M., Del Rosario, M. L., Heath, L., Cook, T. D., Wharton, J. D., & Calder, B. J. (1982). Impact of the introduction of television on crime in the United States: Empirical findings and theoretical implications. *Journal of Personality and Social Psychology, 42*, 461–577.

Henwood, K. L. (1996). Qualitative inquiry: Perspectives, methods and psychology. In J. T. E. Richardson (Ed.), *Handbook of qualitative research methods for psychology and the social sciences* (pp. 25–40). Malden, MA: BPS Blackwell.

Heron, J., Golding, J., & ALSPAC Study Team. (2004). Thimerosal exposure in infants and developmental disorders: A prospective cohort study in the United Kingdom does not support a causal association. *Pediatrics, 114*, 577–583. doi: 10.1542/peds.2003-1176-L

Hertel, P. T. (1998). Relation between rumination and impaired memory in dysphoric moods. *Journal of Abnormal Psychology, 107*, 166–172.

Hertz-Picciotto, I., Green, P. G., Delwiche, L., Hansen, R., Walker, C., & Pessah, I. N. (2009). Blood mercury concentrations in CHARGE study: Children with and without autism. *Environmental Health Perspectives*.

Retrieved December 10, 2009, from http://ehp.niehs.nih.gov/members/2009/0900736/0900736.pdfdoi:10.1289/ehp.0900736

Heuer, H., Spijkers, W., Kiesswetter, E., & Schmidtke, V. (1998). Effects of sleep loss, time of day, and extended mental work on implicit and explicit learning of sequences. *Journal of Experimental Psychology: Applied, 4,* 139–162.

High accuracy found in 2000 elections. (2001, January 4). *St. Petersburg Times,* 3A.

Hill, S. E., & Ryan, M. J. (2006). The role of model female quality in the mate choice copying behaviour of sailfin mollies. *Biology Letters, 2,* 203–205.

Hilts, P. J., & Stolberg, S. G. (1999, May 13). Ethical lapses at Duke halt dozens of human experiments. *New York Times.* Retrieved May 13, 1999, from http://www.nytimes.com/yr/mo/day/news/national/science/sci-duke-research.html

Hoekstra-Weebers, J. E. H. M., Jaspers, J. P. C., Kamps, W. A., & Klip, E. C. (2001). Psychological adaptation and social support of parents of pediatric cancer patients: A prospective longitudinal study. *Journal of Pediatric Psychology, 26,* 225–235.

Holahan, C. K., & Sears, R. R. (1995). *The gifted group in later maturity.* Stanford, CA: Stanford University Press.

Holmes, J. D., Beins, B. C., & Lynn, A. (2007, June). Student views of psychology as a science: Findings and implications. Presented at the Eastern Conference on the Teaching of Psychology, Staunton, VA.

Holmes, T. H., & Rahe, R. H. (1967). The Social Readjustment Rating Scale. *Journal of Psychosomatic Research, 11,* 213–218.

Hong, Y., & Chiu, C. (1991). Reduction of socially desirable responses in attitude assessment through the enlightenment effect. *Journal of Social Psychology, 131,* 585–587.

Horvitz, D., Koshland, D., Rubin, D., Gollin, A., Sawyer, T., & Tanbur, J. M. (1995). Pseudo-opinion polls: SLOP or useful data? *Chance, 8,* 16–25.

Howell, D. C. (2007). Statistical methods for psychology (6th ed.). Belmont, CA: Wadsworth.

Hrycaiko, D., & Martin, G. L. (1999). Applied research studies with single-subject designs: Why so few? *Journal of Applied Sport Psychology, 8,* 183–199.

Humphreys, K. (2009). Responding to the psychological impact of war on the Iraqi people and U.S. veterans: Mixing icing, praying for cake. *American Psychologist, 64,* 712–723. doi:10.1037/0003-066X.64.8.712

Humphreys, L. (1975). *Tearoom trade: Impersonal sex in public places* (2nd ed.). Chicago, IL: Aldine.

Hyde, J. (2005). The Gender Similarities Hypothesis. *American Psychologist, 60,* 581–592. doi:10.1037/0003-066X.60.6.581

Hyman, I. R., Boss, S., Wise, B. M., McKenzie, K. E., & Caggiano, J. M. (2010). Did you see the unicycling clown? Inattentional blindness while walking and talking on a cell phone. *Applied Cognitive Psychology, 24,* 597–607. doi:10.1002/acp.1638

Ideland, M. (2009). Different views on ethics: How animal ethics is situated in a committee culture. *Journal of Medical Ethics, 35,* 258–261. doi:10.1136/jme.2008.026989

Imrie, R., & Ramey, D. W. (2000). The evidence for evidence-based medicine. *Complementary Therapies in Medicine, 8,* 123–126.

Inzlicht, M., & Ben-Zeev, T. (2000). A threatening intellectual environment: Why females are susceptible to experiencing problem-solving deficits in the presence of males. *Psychological Science, 11,* 365–371.

Ioannidis, J. P. A. (2005). Why most published research findings are false. *PLoS Med, 2:* e124. doi:10.1371/journal.pmed.0020124

Iwamasa, G. Y., Larrabee, A. L., & Merritt, R. D. (2000). Are personality disorder criteria ethnically biased? A card-sort analysis. *Cultural Diversity and Ethnic Minority Psychology, 6,* 284–296.

Izawa, M. R., French, M. D., & Hedge, A. (2011). Shining new light on the Hawthorne illumination experiments. *Human Factors, 53,* 528–547. doi:10.1177/0018720811417968

Jacob, T., Tennenbaum, D., Seilhamer, R. A., Bargiel, K., & Sharon, T. (1994). Reactivity effects during naturalistic observation of distressed and nondistressed families. *Journal of Family Psychology, 8,* 354–363.

Jastrow, J. (1891). Studies from the laboratory of experimental psychology of the University of Wisconsin. *American Journal of Psychology, 4,* 198–223. doi:10.2307/1411267

Jenni, D. A., & Jenni, M. A. (1976). Carrying behavior in humans: Analysis of sex differences. *Science, 194,* 859–860.

Jenni, M. A. (1976). Sex differences in carrying behavior. *Perceptual and Motor Skills, 43,* 323–330.

Jennings, C. (2000, May/June). [Letter to the editor.] *The Sciences, 40,* 3, 5.

Jensen, G. F. (2001). The invention of television as a cause of homicide: The reification of a spurious relationship. *Homicide Studies, 5,* 114–130.

Ji, L.J., Schwarz, N., & Nisbett, R. E. (2000). Culture, autobiographical memory, and behavioral frequency reports: Measurement issues in cross-cultural studies. *Personality and Social Psychology Bulletin, 26,* 585–593.

Ji, L., Zhang, Z., & Nisbett, R. E. (2004). Is it culture or is it language? Examination of language effects in cross-cultural research on categorization. *Journal of Personality and Social Psychology, 87,* 57–65. doi:10.1037/0022-3514.87.1.57

Ji, Y., Hwangbo, H., Yi, J., Rau, P., Fang, X., & Ling, C. (2010). The influence of cultural differences on the use of social network services and the formation of social capital. *International Journal of Human-Computer Interaction, 26*(11–12), 1100–1121. doi:10.1080/10447318.2010.516727

Jin, L. (2011). Improving response rates in web surveys with default setting: The effects of default on web survey participation and permission. *International Journal of Market Research, 53*, 75–94. doi:10.2501

Johnson, T. P., Fendrich, M., Shaligram, C., Garcy, A., & Gillespie, S. (2000). An evaluation of the effects of interviewer characteristics in an RDD telephone survey of drug use. *Journal of Drug Issues, 30*, 77–102.

Jones, B. C., DeBruine, L. M., Little, A. C., Burriss, R. P., & Feinberg, D. R. (2007). Social transmission of face preferences among humans. *Proceedings of the Royal Society B, 274*, 899–903.

Jones, H. E., & Contrad, H. S. (1933). The growth and decline of intelligence: A study of a homogeneous group between the ages of ten and sixty. *Genetic Psychology Monographs, 13*, 223–298.

Judd, C. M., Smith, E. R., & Kidder, L. H. (1991). *Research methods in social relations*. Fort Worth, TX: Holt, Rinehart, & Winston.

Juhnke, R., Barmann, B., Cunningham, M., & Smith, E. (1987). Effects of attractiveness and nature of request on helping behavior. *Journal of Social Psychology, 127*, 317–322.

Kaneto, H. (1997). Learning/memory processes under stress conditions. *Behavioural Brain Research, 83*, 71–74.

Kaplan, C. D., Korf, D., & Sterk, C. (1987). Temporal and social contexts of heroin-using populations: An illustration of the snowball sampling technique. *Journal of Nervous and Mental Disease, 175*, 566–574.

Kaplan, M. D. (1999). Developmental and psychiatric evaluation in the preschool context. *Child and Adolescent Psychiatric Clinics of North America, 8*, 379–393.

Kasof, J. (1993). Sex bias in the naming of the stimulus person. *Psychological Bulletin, 113*, 140–163.

Kass, S. J., Cole, K. S., & Stanny, C. J. (2007). Effects of distraction and experience on situation awareness and simulated driving. *Transportation Research Part F, 10*, 321–329.

Katsev, R., Edelsack, L., Steinmetz, G., Walker, T., & Wright, R. (1978). The effect of reprimanding transgression on subsequent helping behavior: Two field experiments. *Personality and Social Psychology Bulletin, 4*, 326–329.

Kaufman, P., Kwon, J. Y., Klein, S., & Chapman, C. D. (2000). *Dropout rates in the United States: 1999*. Washington, DC: National Center for Educational Statistics.

Kaur, M., Liguori, A., Lang, W., Rapp, S. R., Fleischer, A. B., & Feldman, S. R. (2006). Induction of withdrawal-like symptoms in a small randomized, controlled trial of opioid blockade in frequent tanners. *Journal of the American Academy of Dermatology, 54*, 709–711.

Kazdin, A. E. (1998). *Research design in clinical psychology* (3rd ed.). Boston, MA: Allyn and Bacon.

Keith-Spiegel, P., & Koocher, G. P. (2005). The IRB paradox: Could the protectors also encourage deceit? *Ethics & Behavior, 15*, 339–349.

Keller, J. (2007). Stereotype threat in classroom settings: The interactive effect of domain identification, task difficulty and stereotype threat on female students' maths performance. *British Journal of Educational Psychology, 77*, 323–338.

Kellett, S., & Beall, N. (1997). The treatment of chronic post-traumatic nightmares using psychodynamic-interpersonal psychotherapy: A single-case study. *British Journal of Medical Psychology, 70*, 35–49.

Kennedy, D., & Norman, C. (2005, July 1). What we don't know. *Science, 309*, 75.

Kiecker, P., & Nelson, J. E. (1996). Do interviewers follow telephone survey instructions? *Journal of the Market Research Society, 38*, 161–176.

Kim, B. S. K., Atkinson, D. R., & Yang, P. H. (1999). The Asian Values Scale: Development, factor analysis, validation, and reliability. *Journal of Counseling Psychology, 46*, 342–352.

Kim, G., Chiriboga, D. A., & Jang, Y. (2009).Cultural equivalence in depressive symptoms in older White, Black, and Mexican-American adults. *Journal of the American Geriatrics Society, 57*, 790–796. doi:10.1111/j.1532-5415.2009.02188.x

Kim, G., Kim, K., & Park, H. (2011). Outcomes of a program to reduce depression. *Western Journal of Nursing Research, 33*, 560–576. doi:10.1177/0193945910386249

Kim, Y., Chiu, C., Peng, S., Cai, H., & Tov, W. (2010). Explaining east-west differences in the likelihood of making favorable self-evaluations: The role of evaluation apprehension and directness of expression. *Journal of Cross-Cultural Psychology, 41*, 62–75. doi:10.1177/0022022109348921

King, M. F., & Bruner, G. C. (2000). Social desirability bias: A neglected aspect of validity testing. *Psychology and Marketing, 17*, 79–103.

Klawans, H. (2000). *Defending the cavewoman and other tales of evolutionary neurology*. New York: W. W. Norton.

Kleck, G., & Gertz, M. (1995).Armed Resistance to Crime: Prevalence and Nature of Self-Defense with a Gun. *Journal of Criminal Law and Criminology, 86*, 150–187.

Klibert, J., Langhinrichsen-Rohling, J., Luna, A., & Robichaux, M. (2011). Suicide proneness in college students: Relationships with gender, procrastination, and achievement motivation. *Death Studies, 35*, 625–645. doi:10.1080/07481187.2011.553311

Komiya, N., Good, G. E., & Sherrod, N. B. (2000). Emotional openness as a predictor of college students' attitudes toward seeking psychological help. *Journal of Counseling Psychology, 47*, 138–143.

Korn, J. H. (1998). The reality of deception. *American Psychologist, 53*, 805.

Kourosh, A. S., Harrington, C. R., & Adinoff, B. (2010). Tanning as a behavioral addiction. *The American Journal of Drug and Alcohol Abuse, 36*, 284–290. doi:10.3109/00952990.2010.491883

Kovar, M. G. (2000). Four million adolescents smoke: Or do they? *Chance, 13*, 10–14.

Kozulin, A. (1999). Profiles of immigrant students' cognitive performance on Raven's Progressive Matrices. *Perceptual & Motor Skills, 87,* 1311–1314.

Krahn, G. L., & Putnam, M. (2003). Qualitative methods in psychological research. In M. C. Roberts & S. S. Ilardi (Eds.), *Handbook of research methods in clinical psychology* (pp. 176–195). Malden, MA: Blackwell.

Krantz, J. H., & Dalal, R. (2000). Validity of Web-based psychological research. In M. H. Birnbaum (Ed.), *Psychological experiments on the Internet* (pp. 35–60). San Diego, CA: Academic Press.

Kraut, A. G. (2012, January). Despite occasional scandals, science can police itself. *Observer, 25*(1), 11, 22.

Kremar, M., & Greene, K. (2000). Connections between violent television exposure and adolescent risk taking. *Media Violence, 2,* 195–217.

Krishnan, A., & Sweeney, C. J. (1998). Gender differences in fear of success imagery and other achievement-related background variables among medical students. *Sex Roles, 39,* 299–310.

Krosnick, J. A. (1999). Survey research. *Annual Review of Psychology, 50,* 537–567.

Krosnick, J. A., Holbrook, A. L., Sberent, M. K., Carson, R. T., Hanemann, W. M., Kopp, R. J., et al. (2002). The impact of "no opinion" response options on data quality: Non-attitude reduction or an invitation to satisfice. *Public Opinion Quarterly, 66,* 371–403.

Kumari, R. (1995). Relation of sex role attitudes and self-esteem to fear of success among college women. *Psychological Studies, 40,* 82–86.

Kun, B., Urbán, R., Paksi, B., Csóbor, L., Oláh, A., & Demetrovics, Z. (2012). Psychometric characteristics of the Emotional Quotient Inventory, Youth Version, Short Form, in Hungarian high school students. *Psychological Assessment, 24,* 518–523. doi:10.1037/a0026013

Kwiatkowski, S. J., & Parkinson, S. R. (1994). Depression, elaboration, and mood congruence: Differences between natural and induced mood. *Memory & Cognition, 22,* 225–233.

La Greca, A. M., & Silverman, W. K. (2009). Treatment and prevention of posttraumatic stress reactions in children and adolescents exposed to disasters and terrorism: What is the evidence? *Child Development Perspectives, 3,* 4–10. doi:10.1111/j.1750-8606.2008.00069.x

LaGreca, A. M., Silverman, W. K., Vernberg, E. M., & Prinstein, M. J. (1996). Symptoms of posttraumatic stress in children after Hurricane Andrew: A prospective study. *Journal of Counseling and Clinical Psychology, 64,* 712–723.

LaHuis, D. M., Nicholas, R., & Avis, J. M. (2005). Investigating nonlinear conscientiousness-job performance relations for clerical employees. *Human Performance, 18,* 199–212.

Laidler, J. R. (2004). The "Refrigerator Mother" hypothesis of autism. Retrieved December 10, 2009, from www.autism-watch.org/causes/rm.shtml

Lane, J. D., Phillips-Bute, B. G., & Pieper, C. F. (1998). Caffeine raises blood pressure at work. *Psychosomatic Medicine, 60,* 327–330.

Lang, F. R., & Heckhausen, J. (2001). Perceived control over development and subjective well-being: Differential benefits across adulthood. *Journal of Personality and Social Psychology, 81,* 509–523.

Lang, P. J. (1995). The emotion probe. *American Psychologist, 50,* 372–385. doi:10.1037/0003-066X.50.5.372

Latané, B., & Darley, J. M. (1970). *The unresponsive bystander: Why doesn't he help?* New York: Appleton-Century-Crofts.

LatanŽ, B., & Darley, J. M. (1970). *The unresponsive bystander: Why doesn't he help?* New York: Appleton-Century-Crofts.

Lavender, J. M., & Anderson, D. A. (2009). Effect of perceived anonymity in assessments of eating disordered behaviors and attitudes. *International Journal of Eating Disorders, 42,* 546–551. doi:10.1002/eat.20645

Lavender, J. M., & Anderson, D. A. (2010). Contribution of emotion regulation difficulties to disordered eating and body dissatisfaction in college men. *International Journal of Eating Disorders, 43,* 352–357.

Lawson, C. (1995). Research participation as a contract. *Ethics and Behavior, 5,* 205–215.

LeBel, E. P., & Peters, K. R. (2011). Fearing the future of empirical psychology: Bem's (2011) evidence of psi as a case study of deficiencies in modal research practice. *Review of General Psychology, 15,* 371–379. doi:10.1037/a0025172

Lee, Y.-T., & Ottati, V. (1995). Perceived in-group homogeneity as a function of group membership salience and stereotype threat. *Personality & Social Psychology Bulletin, 21,* 610–619.

Lehman, D. R., Lempert, R. O., & Nisbett, R. E. (1988). The effects of graduate training on reasoning: Formal discipline and thinking about everyday-life events. *American Psychologist, 43,* 431–442.

Leirer, V. O., Yesavage, J. A., & Morrow, D. G. (1991). Marijuana carry-over effects on aircraft pilot performance. *Aviation, Space, and Environmental Medicine, 62,* 221–227.

León, F. R., Brambila, C., de la Cruz, M., Colindres, J., Morales, C., & Vásquez, B. (2005). Providers' Compliance with the Balanced Counseling Strategy in Guatemala. *Studies in Family Planning, 36,* 117–126.

Leonhard, C., Gastfriend, D. R., Tuffy, L. J., Neill, J., & Plough, A. (1997). The effect of anonymous vs. nonanonymous rating conditions on patient satisfaction and motivation ratings in a population of substance abuse patients. *Alcoholism: Clinical and Experimental Research, 21,* 627–630.

LeSage, J. (2011). Do what the neighbors do: Reopening businesses after Hurricane Katrina. *Significance, 8,* 160–163.

Levine, F. M., & De Simone, L. L. (1991). The effects of experimenter gender on pain report in male and female subjects. *Pain, 44,* 69–72.

Levitt, L., & Leventhal, G. (1986). Litter reduction: How effective is the New York State bottle bill? *Environment and Behavior, 18,* 467–479.

Lewis, C. A., McCollam, P., & Joseph, S. (2000). Convergent validity of the Depression-Happiness Scale with the Bradburn Affect Balance Scale. *Social Behavior & Personality, 28,* 579–584.

Lewis, J. E., DeGusta, D., Meyer, M. R., Monge, J. M., Mann, A. E., & Holloway, R. L. (2011). The mismeasure of science: Stephen Jay Gould versus Samuel George Morton on skulls and bias. *Plos Biology, 9*(6), e1001071, doi:10.1371/journal.pbio.1001071

Liang, C. T. H., Li, L. C., & Kim, B. S. K. (2004). The Asian American Racism-Related Stress Inventory: Development, factor analysis, reliability, and validity. *Journal of Counseling Psychology, 51,* 103–114.

Lifton, R. J. (1986). *The Nazi doctors: Medical killing and the psychology of genocide.* New York: Basic Books.

Liston, C., & Kagan, J. (2002). Memory enhancement in early childhood. *Nature, 419,* 896.

Lockwood, K. A., Alexopoulos, G. S., Kakuma, T., & Van Gorp, W. G. (2000). Subtypes of cognitive impairment in depressed older adults. *American Journal of Geriatric Psychiatry, 8,* 201–208.

Loftus, E. F. (1975). Leading questions and the eyewitness report. *Cognitive Psychology, 7,* 560–572.

Loftus, E. F. (1979). Eyewitness testimony. Cambridge, MA: Harvard University Press.

Loftus, E. F. (1997). Memories for a past that never was. *Current Directions in Psychological Science, 6,* 60–65.

Loftus, E. F. (2003, January). Illusions of memory. Presented at the National Institute on the Teaching of Psychology. St. Petersburg Beach, FL.

Loftus, E. F., & Marburger, W. (1983). Since the eruption of Mount St. Helens, has anyone beaten you up? Improving the accuracy of retrospective reports with landmark events. *Memory and Cognition, 11,* 114–120.

Löken, L. S., Evert, M., & Wessberg, J. (2011). Pleasantness of touch in human glabrous and hairy skin: Order effects on affective ratings. *Brain Research, 141,* 79–15. doi:10.1016/j.brainres.2011.08.011

Lonner, W. J. (1999). Helfrich's "principle of triarchic resonance": A commentary on yet another perspective on the ongoing and tenacious etic–emic debate. *Culture & Psychology, 5,* 173–181.

López-Muñoz, F., & Álamo, C. (2009). Psychotropic drugs research in Nazi Germany: The triumph of de principle of malfeasance. *ActaNeuropsychiatrica, 21*(2), 50–53. doi:10.1111/j.1601-5215.2008.00338.x

Lord, F. M. (1953). On the statistical treatment of football numbers. *American Psychologist, 8,* 750–751.

Lück, H. E. (2009). Der Hawthorne-effekt—Ein effekt für viele gelegenheiten?. *Gruppendynamik und Organisationsberatung, 40,* 102–114. doi:10.1007/s11612-009-0055-1

Luria, A. R. (1968). *The mind of a mnemonist.* New York: Basic Books.

Lynn, R. (2009). What has caused the Flynn effect? Secular increases in the Development Quotients of infants. *Intelligence, 37,* 16–24. doi:10.1016/j.intell.2008.07.008

Lyubomirsky, S., Boehm, J. K., Kasri, F., & Zehm, K. (2011). The cognitive and hedonic costs of dwelling on achievement-related negative experiences: Implications for enduring happiness and unhappiness. *Emotion, 11,* 1152–1167. doi:10.1037/a0025479

MacCann, C. (2010). Further examination of emotional intelligence as a standard intelligence: A latent variable analysis of fluid intelligence, crystallized intelligence, and emotional intelligence. *Personality and Individual Differences, 49,* 490-496. doi:10.1016/j.paid. 2010.05.010

MacGeorge, E. L., Samter, W., Feng, B., Gillihan, S. J., & Graves, A. R. (2004). Stress, social support, and health among college students after September 11, 2001. *Journal of College Student Development, 45,* 655–670.

Magnussen, S., Melinder, A., Stridbeck, U., & Raja, A. Q. (2010). Beliefs about factors affecting the reliability of eyewitness testimony: A comparison of judges, jurors and the general public. *Applied Cognitive Psychology, 24,* 122–133. doi:10.1002/acp.1550

Mandal, E. (2007). Gender, Machiavellianism, study major, and fear of success. *Polish Psychological Bulletin, 38,* 40–49.

Manning, R., Levine, M., & Collins, A. (2007). The Kitty Genovese murder and the social psychology of helping: The parable of the 38 witnesses. *American Psychologist, 62,* 555–562. doi:10.1037/0003–066X.62.6.555

Manucia, G. K., Baumann, D. J., & Cialdini, R. B. (1984). Mood influences on helping: Direct effects or side effects? *Journal of Personality and Social Psychology, 46,* 357–364.

Marans, D. G. (1988). Addressing researcher practitioner and subject needs: A debriefing-disclosure procedure. *American Psychologist, 43,* 826–828.

Marian, V., & Neisser, U. (2000). Language-dependent recall of autobiographical memories. *Journal of Experimental Psychology: General, 129,* 361–368.

Markus, H. (2008). Pride, prejudice, and ambivalence: Toward a unified theory of race and ethnicity. *American Psychologist, 63,* 651–670. doi:10.1037/0003-066X.63.8.651

Martin, G. N. (2000). There's more neuroscience. *American Psychologist, 55,* 275–276. doi:10.1037/0003-066X.55.2.275

Martin, P. R., & Petry, N. M. (2005). Are Non-substance-related Addictions Really Addictions? *The American Journal on Addictions, 14,* 1–7. doi:10.1080/10550490590899808

Martinez-Ebers, V. (1997). Using monetary incentives with hard-to-reach populations in panel surveys. *International Journal of Public Opinion Research, 9,* 77–86.

Martinsen, E. W., Friis, S., & Hoffart, A. (1995). Assessment of depression: Comparison between Beck Depression Inventory and subscales of Comprehensive

Psychopathological Rating Scale. *ActaPsychiatricaScandinavica, 92,* 460–463.

Martinson, B. C., Anderson, M. S., & de Vries, R. (2005). Scientists behaving badly. *Nature, 435,* 737–738.

Mascie-Taylor, C. G. (1989). Spouse similarity for IQ and personality and convergence. *Behavior Genetics, 19,* 223–227. doi:10.1007/BF01065906

Matsumoto, D. (1993). Ethnic differences in affect intensity, emotion judgments, display rule attitudes, and self-reported emotional expression in an American sample. *Motivation and Emotion, 17,* 107–123.

Matsumoto, D. (1994). *Cultural influences on research methods and statistics.* Pacific Grove, CA: Brooks/Cole.

Matsumoto, D., Anguas-Wong, A., & Martinez, E. (2008). Priming effects of language on emotion judgments in Spanish-English bilinguals. *Journal of Cross-Cultural Psychology, 33,* 335–342. doi:10.1177/0022022108315489

Matsumoto, D., & Assar, M. (1992). The effects of language on judgments of universal facial expressions of emotion. *Journal of Nonverbal Behavior, 16,* 85–99.

Matsumoto, D., & Yoo, S. H. (2006). Toward a new generation of cross-cultural research. *Perspectives on Psychological Science, 1,* 234–250.

Matthews, G. A., & Dickinson, A. M. (2000). Effects of alternative activities on time allocated to task performance under different percentages of incentive pay. *Journal of Organizational Behavior Management, 20,* 3–27.

May, C. P., Hasher, L., & Stoltzfus, E. R. (1993). Optimal time of day and the magnitude of age differences in memory. *Psychological Science, 4,* 326–330.

Mayer, J. D., Salovey, P., Caruso, D. R., & Sitarenios, G. (2001). Emotional intelligence as a standard intelligence. *Emotion, 1,* 232–242.

Mazzoni, G. L., & Loftus, E. F. (1998). Dream interpretation can change beliefs about the past. *Psychotherapy: Theory, Research, Practice, Training, 35,* 177–187. doi:10.1037/h0087809

McAuliffe, W. E., Geller, S., LaBrie, R., Paletz, S., & Fournier, E. (1998). Are telephone surveys suitable for studying substance abuse? Cost, administration, cover and response rate issues. *Journal of Drug Issues, 28,* 455–481.

McCabe, S. E. (2004). Comparison of web and mail surveys in collecting illicit drug use data: A randomized experiment. *Journal of Drug Education, 34,* 61–72. doi:10.2190/4HEY-VWXL-DVR3-HAKV

McCallum, R. C., & Austin, J. T. (2000). Applications of structural equation modeling in psychological research. *Annual Review of Psychology, 51,* 201–226.

McClung, H. J., Murray, R. D., & Heitlinger, L. A. (1998). The internet as a course for current patient information. *Pediatrics, 101,* e2 [online].

McCoy, T. P., Ip, E. H., Blocker, J. N., Champion, H., Rhodes, S. D., Wagoner, K. G., & Wolfson, M. (2009).

Attrition bias in a U.S. Internet Survey of alcohol use among college freshmen. *Journal of Studies on Alcohol and Drugs, 70,* 606–614.

McCrae, R. R., Martin, T. A., Hrebícková, M., Urbánek, T., Willemsen, G., & Costa, P. T., Jr. (2008). Personality trait similarity between spouses in four cultures. *Journal of Personality, 76,* 1137–1163. doi:10.1111/j.1467-6494.2008.00517.x

McCrae, R. R., & Terracciano, A. (2006).National character and personality. *Current Directions in Psychological Science, 15,* 156–161. doi:10.1111/j.1467-8721.2006.00427.x

McCree-Hale, R., De La Cruz, N. G., & Montgomery, A. (2010). Using downloadable songs from Apple iTunes as a novel incentive for college students participating in a web-based follow-up survey. *American Journal of Health Promotion, 25,* 119–121.

McFarland, C., Cheam, A., & Buehler, R. (2007). The perseverance effect in the debriefing paradigm: Replication and extension. *Journal of Experimental Social Psychology, 43,* 233–240. doi:10.1016/j.jesp.2006.01.010

McGlone, M. S., & Aronson, J. (2007). Forewarning and forearming stereotype-threatened students. *Communication Education, 56,* 119–133.

McGuire, W. J. (1983). A contextualist theory of knowledge: Its implications for innovation and reform in psychological research. In L. Berkowitz (Ed.), *Advances in Experimental Social Psychology* (Vol 16, pp. 1–47). Orlando, FL: Academic Press.

Mcintosh, S., Sierra, E., Dozier, A., Diaz, S., Quiñones, Z., Primack, A., et al. (2008). Ethical review issues in collaborative research between us and low—middle income country partners: A case example. *Bioethics, 22*(8), 414–422. doi:10.1111/j.1467-8519.2008.00662.x

McMorris, B. J., Petrie, R. S., Catalano, R. F., Fleming, C. B., Haggerty, K. P., & Abbott, R. D. (2009). Use of web and in-person survey modes to gather data from young adults on sex and drug use: An evaluation of cost, time, and survey error based on a randomized mixed-mode design. *Evaluation Review, 33,* 138–158. doi:10.1177/0193841X08326463

Medin, D., Bennis, W., & Chandler, M. (2010). Culture and the home-field disadvantage. *Perspectives on Psychological Science, 5,* 708–713. doi:10.1177/1745691610388772

Mehl, M. R. (2006). The lay assessment of subclinical depression in daily life. *Psychological Assessment, 18,* 340–345.

Meissner, C. A., Tredoux, C. G., Parker, J. F., & MacLin, O. H. (2005). Eyewitness decisions in simultaneous and sequential lineups: A dual-process signal detection theory analysis. *Memory & Cognition, 33,* 783–792.

Melnik, T. A., Baker, C. T., Adams, M. L., O'Dowd, K., Mokdad, A. H., Brown, D. W., et al. (2002). Psychological and emotional effects of the September 11 attacks on the World Trade Center—Connecticut,

New Jersey, and New York, 2001. *Mortality and Morbidity Weekly Report, 51*, 784–786.

Mendoza, M. (2005). Allegations of fake research hit new high. *Yahoo News.* Retrieved July 12, 2005, from http://www.news.yahoo.com

Mennella, J. A., & Gerrish, C. J. (1998). Effects of exposure to alcohol in mother's milk on infant sleep. *Pediatrics (online), 101*, e2.

Meston, C. M., Heiman, J. R., Trapnell, P. D., & Paulhus, D. L. (1998). Socially desirable responding and sexuality self-reports. *Journal of Sex Research, 35*, 148–157.

Milgram, S. (1963). Behavioral study of obedience. *Journal of Abnormal and Social Psychology, 67*, 371–378.

Milgram, S. (1964). Issues in the study of obedience: A reply to Baumrind. *American Psychologist, 19*, 848–852.

Milgram, S. (1974). *Obedience to authority: An experimental view.* New York: Harper & Row.

Miller, A. G. (2009). Reflections on "Replicating Milgram" (Burger, 2009). *American Psychologist, 64*, 20–27.

Miller, J. D. (2007a, February). The public understanding of science in Europe and the United States. Presented at the annual meeting of the American Association for the Advancement of Science, San Francisco, CA.

Miller, J. D. (2007b, February). Civic scientific literacy across the life cycle. Presented at the annual meeting of the American Association for the Advancement of Science, San Francisco, CA.

Miller, M. A., & Rahe, R. H. (1997). Life changes scaling for the 1990s. *Journal of Psychosomatic Research, 43*, 279–292.

Miller, N. (1985). The value of behavioral research on animals. *American Psychologist, 40*, 423–440.

Miller, R. S. (1995). On the nature of embarrassability: Shyness, social evaluation, and social skill. *Journal of Personality, 63*, 315–339.

Mills, C. G., Boteler, E. H., & Oliver, G. K. (1999). Digit synaesthesia: A case study using a stroop-type test. *Cognitive Neuropsychology, 16*, 181–191.

Miracle, A. D., Brace, M. F., Huyck, K. D., Singler, S. A., & Wellman, C. L. (2006). Chronic stress impairs recall of extinction of conditioned fear. *Neurobiology of Learning and Memory, 85*, 213–218.

Miskimen, T., Marin, H., & Escobar, J. (2003). Psychopharmacological research ethics: Special issues affecting U.S. ethnic minorities. *Psychopharmacology, 171*(1), 98–104. doi:10.1007/s00213-003-1630-8

Mobile web audience already one-fifth the size of PC-based internet audience in the U.K. (2007, May 14). Retrieved July 24, 2007, from http://www.comscore.com/press/release.asp?press=1432

Modern Language Association of America. (1995). MLA handbook for writers of research papers (4th ed.). New York: Author.

Mohr, D. C., Goodkin, D. E., Bacchetti, P., Boudewyn, A. C., Huang, L., Marrietta, P., et al. (2000). Psychological stress and the subsequent appearance of new brain MRI lesions in MS. *Neurology, 55*, 55–61.

Möller, F. R. (2000, May/June). [Letter to the editor.] *The Sciences, 40*, 5.

Möller, I., Krahé, B., Busching, R., & Krause, C. (2012). Efficacy of an intervention to reduce the use of media violence and aggression: An experimental evaluation with adolescents in Germany. *Journal of Youth and Adolescence, 41*, 105–120. doi:10.1007/s10964-011-9654-6

Mook, D. G. (1983). In defense of external invalidity. *American Psychologist, 38*, 379–387.

Moonsinghe, R., Khoury, M. J., & Janssens, A. C. J. W. (2007). Most published research findings are false—but a little replication goes a long way. *PLoS Medicine, 4*, e28, 218–221.

Moore, D. W. (2005) Three in four Americans believe in paranormal. *Gallup News Service.* Retrieved May 17, 2007, from http://home.sandiego.edu/~baber/logic/gallup.html

Moore, S. R. (1998). Effects of sample size on the representativeness of observational data used in evaluation. *Education and Treatment of Children, 21*, 209–226.

Morgan, C. A., Hazlett, G., Doran, A., Garrett, S., Hoyt, G., Thomas P., et al. (2004). Accuracy of eyewitness memory for persons encountered during exposure to highly intense stress. *International Journal of Law and Psychiatry, 27*, 265–279.

Morris, J. S., Scott, S. K., & Dolan, R. J. (1999). Saying it with feeling: Neural responses to emotional vocalizations. *Neuropsychologia, 37*, 1155–1163.

Müller, F. R. (2000, May/June). [Letter to the editor.] *The Sciences, 40*, 5.

Münsterberg, H. (1914). *Psychology and social sanity.* New York: Doubleday, Page, & Co.

Murray, L. A., Whitehouse, W. G., & Alloy, L. B. (1999). Mood congruence and depressive deficits in memory: A forced-recall analysis. *Memory, 7*, 175–196. doi:10.1080/741944068

Must, O., teNijenhuis, J., Must, A., & van Vianen, A. M. (2009). Comparability of IQ scores over time. *Intelligence, 37*, 25–33. doi:10.1016/j.intell.2008.05.002

Muzzatti, B., & Agnoli, F. (2007). Gender and mathematics: Attitudes and stereotype threat susceptibility in Italian children. *Developmental Psychology, 43*, 747–759.

Nadkarni, A., & Hofmann, S. G. (2012). Why do people use Facebook? *Personality and Individual Differences, 52*(3), 243–249. doi:10.1016/j.paid.2011.11.007

National Academy of Sciences and Institute of Medicine. (2008). *Science, Evolution, and Creationism.* Washington, DC: The National Academies Press.

National Assessment of Educational Progress: Findings in Brief—Reading and Mathematics 2011. (2011). Retrieved from http://nces.ed.gov/nationsreportcard/pdf/main2011/2012459.pdf

Neumann, D. L., & Kitlertsirivatana, E. (2010). Exposure to a novel context after extinction causes a renewal of extinguished conditioned responses: Implications for the treatment of fear. *Behaviour Research and Therapy, 48*, 565–570.

Newman, J., Rosenbach, J. H., Burns, K. L., Latimer, B. C., Matocha, H. R., & Vogt, E. E. (1995). An experimental test of "the Mozart effect." Does listening to his music improve spatial ability? *Perceptual and Motor Skills, 81*, 1379–1387.

Nisbet, M. (1998). New poll points to increases in paranormal belief. *Skeptical Inquirer, 22*(5), 9.

Nisbett, R. E., Peng, K., Choi, I., & Norenzayan, A. (2001). Culture and systems of thought: Holistic versus analytic cognition. *Psychological Review, 108*, 291–310. doi:10.1037/0033-295X.108.2.291

Norenzayan, A., & Schwarz, N. (1999). Telling what they want to know: Participants tailor causal attributions to researchers' interests. *European Journal of Social Psychology, 29*, 1011–1020.

North, C. S., Nixon, S. J., Shariat, S., Mallonee, S., McMillen, J. C., Spitznagel, E. L., & Smith, E. M. (1999). Psychiatric disorders among survivors of the Oklahoma City bombing. *Journal of the American Medical Association, 282*, 755–762.

Novotney, A. (2012, February). R U friends 4 real? *Monitor on Psychology, 43*(2), 62.

Nugent, W. R., Bruley, C., & Allen, P. (1998). The effects of aggression replacement training on antisocial behavior in a runaway shelter. *Research on Social Work Practice, 8*, 637–656.

O'Muircheartaigh, C., Krosnick, J. A., & Helic, A. (2000). Middle alternatives, acquiesence, and the quality of questionnaire data. Working paper, Harris School, University of Chicago.

Odom, S. L., & Ogawa, I. (1992). Direct observation of young children's social interactions with peers: A review of methodology. *Behavioral Assessment, 14*, 407–441.

Office of Research Integrity Annual Report 2008. (2009). Retrieved from http://ori.hhs.gov/documents/annual_reports/ori_annual_report_2008.pdf

Olkin, I. (1992). Reconcilable differences: Gleaning insight from conflicting scientific studies. *The Sciences, 32*, 30–36.

Olmstead, D. (2009, July 27). Olmsted on autism: Mercury mayhem. *Age of Autism.* Retrieved July 25, 2012 from http://www.ageofautism.com/2009/07/olmsted-on-autism-mercury-mayhem.html

Omer, S. B., Salmon, D. A., Orenstein, W. A., deHart, M. P., & Halsey, N. (2009). Vaccine refusal, mandatory immunization, and the risks of vaccine-preventable diseases. *New England Journal of Medicine, 360*, 1981–1988. Retrieved from http://content.nejm.org/cgi/reprint/360/19/1981.pdf

Orne, M. T. (1962). On the social psychology of the psychological experiment: With particular reference to demand characteristics and their implications. *American Psychologist, 17*, 776–783.

Orne, M. T., & Scheibe, K. T. (1962). The contribution of nondeprivation factors in the production of sensory deprivation effects. *Journal of Abnormal and Social Psychology, 68*, 3–12.

Ornstein, R., & Sobel, D. (1987). *The healing brain.* New York: Simon and Schuster.

Ortigue, S., Bianchi-Demicheli, F., Patel, N., Frum, C., & Lewis, J. W. (2010). Neuroimaging of love: fMRI meta-analysis evidence toward new perspectives in sexual medicine. *Journal of Sexual Medicine, 7*(11), 3541–3552. doi:10.1111/j.1743-6109.2010.01999.x

Ortmann, A., & Hertwig, R. (1997). Is deception acceptable? *American Psychologist, 52*, 746–747.

Osofsky, H. J., Osofsky, J. D., Kronenberg, M., Brennan, A., & Hansel, T. (2009). Posttraumatic stress symptoms in children after Hurricane Katrina: Predicting the need for mental health services. *American Journal of Orthopsychiatry, 79*, 212–220. doi:10.1037/a0016179

Ossorio, P., & Duster, T. (2005). Race and genetics: Controversies in biomedical, behavioral, and forensic sciences. *American Psychologist, 60*, 115–128.

Overall, J. E., Hollister, L. E., Johnson, M., & Pennington, V. (1966). Nosology of depression and differential response to drugs. *Journal of the American Medical Association, 195*, 946–948.

Oyserman, D., Coon, H. M., & Kemmelmeier, M. (2002). Rethinking individualism and collectivism: Evaluation of theoretical assumptions and meta-analyses. *Psychological Bulletin, 128*, 3–72. doi:10.1037/0033-2909.128.1.3

Paasche-Orlow, M. K., Taylor, A. A., & Barncati, F. L. (2003). Readability standards for informed-consent forms as compared with actual readability. *New England Journal of Medicine, 348*, 721–726.

Paksoy, C., Wilkinson, J. B., & Mason, J. B. (1985). Learning and carryover effects in retail experimentation. *Journal of the Market Research Society, 27*, 109–129.

Panter, A. T., Daye, C. E., Allen, W. R., Wightman, L. F., & Deo, M. E. (2009). It matters how and when you ask: Self-reported race/ethnicity of incoming law students. *Cultural Diversity and Ethnic Minority Psychology, 15*, 51–66. doi:10.1037/a0013377

Paolisso, M., & Hames, R. (2010). Time diary versus instantaneous sampling: A comparison of two behavioral research methods. *Field Methods, 22*, 357–377. doi:10.1177/1525822X10379200

Park, R. L. (2003). The seven warning signs of bogus science. *Chronicle of Higher Education, 49*(21), B20. Retrieved March 3, 2003, from http://www.chronicle.com/free/v49/i21/21b02001.htm

Paschall, M. J., & Freisthler, B. (2003). Does heavy drinking affect academic performance in college? Findings from a prospective study of high achievers. *Journal of Studies on Alcohol, 64*, 515–519.

Patterson, A. L., Morasco, B. J., Fuller, B. E., Indest, D. W., Loftis, J. M., & Hauser, P. (2011). Screening for depression in patients with hepatitis C using the beck depression inventory-II: Do somatic symptoms compromise validity? *General Hospital Psychiatry, 33*(4), 354–362. doi:10.1016/j.genhosppsych.2011.04.005

Pearson, K. (1896). Mathematical contributions to the theory of evolution. III. Regression, heredity and panmixia. *Philosophical Transactions of the Royal Society (Series A), 187*, 253–318. Retrieved July 31, 2007, from http://links.jstor.org/sici?sici=02643952%281896%29187%3C253%3AMCTTTO%3E2.0.CO%3B2-%23

Peirce. C. S. (1877). The fixation of belief. *Popular Science Monthly, 12*, 1–15. Retrieved from www.peirce.org/writings/p107.html

Peng, K., & Nisbett, R. E. (1999). Culture, dialectics, and reasoning about contradiction. *American Psychologist, 54*, 741–754.

Pepler, D. J., & Craig, W. M. (1995). A peek behind the fence: Naturalistic observations of aggressive children with remote audiovisual recording. *Developmental Psychology, 31*, 548–553.

Perceptions of foreign countries. Retrieved September 29, 2001, from http://www.gallup.com/poll/releases/pr010928.asp.

Peregrine, P. N., Drews, D. R., North, M., & Slupe, A. (1993). Sampling techniques and sampling error in naturalistic observation: An empirical evaluation with implications for cross-cultural research. *Cross-Cultural Research, 27*, 232–246.

Perotto-Baldivieso, H., Cooper, S., Cibils, A., Figueroa-Pagán, M., Udaeta, K., & Black-Rubio, C. (2012). Detecting autocorrelation problems from GPS collar data in livestock studies. *Applied Animal Behaviour Science, 136*, 117–125. doi:10.1016/j.applanim.2011.11.009

Peters, M. (1993). Still no convincing evidence of a relation between brain size and intelligence in humans. *Canadian Journal of Experimental Psychology, 47*, 751–756.

Peytchev, A., Carley-Baxter, L. R., & Black, M. C. (2011). Multiple sources of nonobservation error in telephone surveys: Coverage and nonresponse. *Sociological Methods & Research, 40*(1), 138–168. doi:10.1177/0049124110392547

Phillips, D. P., Christenfeld, N., & Ryan, N. M. (1999). An increase in the number of deaths in the United States in the first week of the month–An association with substance abuse and other causes of death. *New England Journal of Medicine, 341*, 93–98.

Phinney, J. S. (1996). When we talk about American ethnic groups, what do we mean? *American Psychologist, 51*, 918–927.

Plous, S. (1996a). Attitudes toward the use of animals in psychological research and education. *American Psychologist, 51*, 1167–1180.

Plous, S. (1996b). Attitudes toward the use of animals in psychological research and education: Results from a national survey of psychology majors. *Psychological Science, 7*, 352–358.

Pollatsek, A., & Well, A. D. (1995). On the use of counterbalanced designs in cognitive research: A suggestion for

a better and more powerful analysis. *Journal of Experimental Psychology: Learning, Memory, and Cognition, 21*, 785–794.

Powell, M. C., & Fazio, R. H. (1984).Attitude accessibility as a function of repeated attitudinal expression. *Personality and Social Psychology Bulletin, 10*, 139–148.

Presser, S., & Stinson, L. (1998). Data collection mode and social desirability bias in self-reported religious attendance. *American Sociological Review, 63*, 137–145.

Price, W. F., & Crapo, R. H. (1999). *Cross-cultural perspectives in introductory psychology* (3rd ed.). Pacific Grove, CA: Brooks/Cole Wadsworth.

Quinn, G. E., Shin, C. H., Maguire, M. G., & Stone, R. A. (1999). Myopia and ambient lighting at night. *Nature, 399*, 113–114.

Quinn, R. P., Gutek, B. A., & Walsh, J. T. (1980). Telephone interviewing: A reappraisal and a field experiment. *Basic and Applied Social Psychology, 1*, 127–153.

Quraishi, M. (2008).Researching Muslim prisoners. *International Journal of Social Research Methodology: Theory & Practice, 11*, 453–467. doi:10.1080/13645570701622199

Radford, B. (1998). Survey finds 70% of women, 48% of men believe in paranormal. *Skeptical Inquirer, 22*(2), 8.

Radner, D., & Radner, M. (1982). *Science and unreason.* Belmont, CA: Wadsworth.

Rai, T. S., & Fiske, A. (2010). ODD (observation- and description-deprived) psychological research. *Behavioral and Brain Sciences, 33*, 106–107. doi:10.1017/S0140525X10000221

Ramírez-Esparza, N., Mehl, M. R., Álvarez-Bermúdez, J., & Pennebaker, J. W. (2009). Are Mexicans more or less sociable than Americans? Insights from a naturalistic observation study. *Journal of Research in Personality, 43*, 1–7. doi:10.1016/j.jrp.2008.09.002

Rampey, B. D., Dion, G. S., & Donahue, P. L. (2009).*The nation's report card: trends in academic progress in reading and mathematics 2008.* Retrieved from http://nces.ed.gov/nationsreportcard/pubs/main2008/2009479.asp

Rasinski, K. A. (1989). The effect of question wording on public support for government spending. *Public Opinion Quarterly, 53*, 388–394.

Rauch, S. L., Shin, L. M., & Phelps, E. A. (2006). Neurocircuitry models of posttraumatic stress disorder and extinction: Human neuroimaging research—past, present, and future. *Biological Psychiatry, 60*, 376–382.

Rauscher, F. H., Shaw, G. L., & Ky, K. N. (1993). Music and spatial task performance. *Nature, 365*, 611.

Rauscher, F. H., Shaw, G. L., & Ky, K. N. (1995). Listening to Mozart enhances spatial-temporal reasoning: Towards a neurophysiological basis. *Neuroscience Letters, 185*, 44–47.

Rauscher, F. H., Shaw, G. L., Gordon, L. (1998). Key components of the Mozart effect. *Perceptual and Motor Skills, 86*, 835–841.

Ray, J. J. (1990). Acquiescence and problems with forced-choice scales. *Journal of Social Psychology, 130*, 397–399.

Recarte, M. A., & Nunes, L. M. (2000). Effects of verbal and spatial-imagery tasks on eye fixations while driving. *Journal of Experimental Psychology: Applied, 6,* 31–43.

Recarte, M. A., & Nunes, L. M. (2003). Mental workload while driving: Effects on visual search, discrimination, and decision making. *Journal of Experimental Psychology: Applied, 9,* 119–137.

Redelmeier, D. A., & Tibshirani, R. J. (1997). Association between cellular-telephone calls and motor vehicle collisions. *New England Journal of Medicine, 336,* 453–458.

Reese, H. W. (1997). Counterbalancing and other uses of repeated-measures Latin-square designs: Analysis and interpretation. *Journal of Experimental Child Psychology, 64,* 137–158.

Renner, M. J., Mackin, R. S. (1998) A life stress instrument for classroom use. *Teaching of Psychology, 25,* 46–48.

Report of the Media Violence Commission (2012). *Aggressive Behavior, 38,* 335–341. doi:10.1002/ab21443

Research Ethics and the Medical Profession. (1996). Report of the Advisory Committee on Human Radiation Experiments. *Journal of the American Medical Association, 276,* 403–409.

Reynolds, P. D. (1982). *Ethics and social science research.* Englewood Cliffs, NJ: Prentice-Hall.

Richter, P., Joachim, W., & Bastine, R. (1994). Psychometrischeeigenschaften des Beck Depressioninventars (BDI): EinÜberblick. *ZeitschriftfürKlinischePsychologie: Forschung und Praxis, 23,* 3–19.

Rieps, U-D. (2010). Design and formatting in internet-based research. In S. D. Gosling & J. A. Johnson (Eds.), *Advanced methods for conducting online behavioral research* (pp. 29–43). Washington, DC: American Psychological Association.

Riley, J. L., Wade, J. B., Myers, C. D., Sheffield, D., Papas, R. K., & Price, D. D. (2002). Racial/ethnic differences in the experience of pain. *Pain, 100,* 291–298.

Ring, K., Wallston, K., & Corey, M. (1970). Mode of debriefing as a factor affecting subjective reaction to a Milgram-type obedience experiment: An ethical inquiry. *Representative Research in Social Psychology, 1,* 67–88.

Ritchie, S. J., Wiseman, R., & French, C. C. (2012) Failing the future: Three unsuccessful attempts to replicate Bem's "retroactive facilitation of recall" effect. *PLoS ONE 7:* e33423. doi:10.1371/journal.pone.0033423 3

Roberts, R. D., Zeidner, M., & Matthews, G. (2001). Does emotional intelligence meet traditional standards for an intelligence? Some new data and conclusions. *Emotion, 1,* 196–231.

Robins, R. W., & Gosling, S. D., & Craik, K. H. (1999). An empirical analysis of trends in psychology. *American Psychologist, 54,* 117–128.

Rockwood, T. H., Sangster, R. L., & Dillman, D. A. (1997). The effect of response categories on survey questionnaires: Context and mode effects. *Sociological Methods and Research, 26,* 118–140.

Rodriguez, C. E. (2000). *Changing race: Latinos, the census and the history of ethnicity in the United States.* New York: New York University Press.

Rogler, L. H. (1999). Methodological sources of cultural insensitivity in mental health research. *American Psychologist, 54,* 424–433.

Rosenberg, M. (1965). *Society and the adolescent self-image.* Princeton, NJ: Princeton University Press.

Rosenthal, R. (1979). The "file drawer problem" and tolerance for null results. *Psychological Bulletin, 86,* 638–641.

Rosenthal, R., & Fode, K. L. (1966). Three experiments in experimenter bias. *Psychological Reports, 12,* 491–511.

Rosenthal, R., & Rosnow, R. L. (1975). *The volunteer subject.* New York: Wiley.

Rosnow, R. L., & Rosenthal, R. (1997). *People studying people: Artifacts and ethics in behavioral research.* New York: W. H. Freeman.

Ross, L. M., Hall, B. A., & Heater, S. L. (1998). Why are occupational therapists not doing more replication research? *American Journal of Occupational Therapy, 52,* 234–235.

Ross, L., Lepper, M. R., & Hubbard, M. (1975). Perseverance in self-perception and social perception: Biased attribution processes in the debriefing paradigm. *Journal of Personality and Social Psychology, 32,* 880–892.

Ross, M., & Wilson, A. E. (2002). It feels like yesterday: Self-esteem, valence of personal past experiences, and judgments of subjective distance. *Journal of Personality and Social Psychology, 82,* 792–803.

Rothbaum, F., Weisz, J., Pott, M., Kiyake, K., & Morelli, G. (2000). Attachment and culture: Security in the United States and Japan. *American Psychologist, 55,* 1093–1104.

Rothman, D. J. (1994, January 9). Government guinea pigs. *New York Times,* Section 4, 23.

Rowe, R. M., & McKenna, F. P. (2001). Skilled anticipation in real-world tasks: Measurement of attentional demands in the domain of tennis. *Journal of Experimental Psychology: Applied, 7,* 60–67.

Rozin, P. (2006). Domain denigration and process preference in academic psychology. *Perspectives on Psychological Science, 1,* 365–376. doi:10.1111/j.1745-6916.2006.00021.x

Rozin, P. (2007). Exploring the landscape of modern academic psychology: Finding and filling the holes. *American Psychologist, 62,* 754–766. doi:10.1037/0003-066X.62.8.754

Rubin, Z. (1970). Measurement of romantic love. *Journal of Personality and Social Psychology, 16,* 265–273. doi:10.1037/h0029841

Rubin, Z. (1985). Deceiving ourselves about deception: Comment on Smith and Richardson's "Amelioration of deception and harm in psychological research." *Journal of Personality and Social Psychology, 48,* 252–253.

Ryan, L., Hatfield, C., & Hofstetter, M. (2002). Caffeine reduces time-of-day effects on memory performance in older adults. *Psychological Science, 13,* 68–71.

Ryckman, R. M., Thornton, B., & Gold, J. A. (2009). Assessing competition avoidance as a basic personality dimension. *Journal of Psychology: Interdisciplinary and Applied, 143,* 175–192. doi:10.3200/JRLP.143.2. 175–192

Sakaki, M., Gorlick, M. A., & Mather, M. (2011). Differential interference effects of negative emotional states on subsequent semantic and perceptual processing. *Emotion, 11,* 1263–1278. doi:10.1037/a0026329

Sambraus, H. H. (1998). Applied ethology—Its task and limits in veterinary practice. *Applied Animal Behaviour Science, 59,* 39–48.

Sample, I. (2012, January 5). Andrew Wakefield sues BMJ for claiming MMR study was fraudulent. *The Guardian.* Retrieved January 31, 2012, from http://www.guardian.co.uk/society/2012/jan/05/andrew-wakefield-sues-bmj-mmr

Satisfaction with local schools. (2005). Survey Research Unit School of Public Affairs Baruch College/ CUNY. Retrieved February 9, 2007, from http://etownpanel.com/results.htm

Saw, S-M., Wu, H-M., Hong, C-Y., Chua, W-H., Chia, K-S., & Tan, D. (2001). Myopia and night lighting in children in Singapore. *British Journal of Ophthalmology, 85,* 527–528.

Schaie, K. W. (1992). The impact of methodological changes in gerontology. *International Journal of Aging and Human Development, 35,* 19–29.

Schaie, K. W. (2000). The impact of longitudinal studies on understanding development from young adulthood to old age. *International Journal of Behavioral Development, 24,* 257–266.

Scharrer, E. (2001). Men, muscles, and machismo: The relationship between television violence exposure and aggression and hostility in the presence of hypermasculinity. *Media Psychology, 3,* 159–188.

Schechter, R., & Grether, J. K. (2008).Continuing increases in autism reported to California's developmental services system: Mercury in retrograde. *Archives of General Psychiatry, 65,* 19–24. doi:10.1001/archgenpsychiatry.2007.1

Schiffman, S. S. (1997). Taste and smell losses in normal aging and disease. *Journal of the American Medical Association, 278,* 1357–1362.

Schillewaert, N., Langerak, F., & Duhamel, T. (1998). Non-probability sampling for WWW surveys: A comparison of methods. *Journal of the Market Research Society, 40,* 307–322.

Schneiderman, I., Zilberstein-Kra, Y., Leckman, J. F., & Feldman, R. (2011). Love alters autonomic reactivity to emotions. *Emotion, 11,* 1314–1321. doi:10.1037/a0024090

Scholer, S. J., Hickson, G. B., & Mitchel, E. F., & Ray, W. A. (1998). Predictors of mortality from fires in young children. *Pediatrics, 101,* e12. [online].

Schram, C. M. (1996). A meta-analysis of gender differences in applied statistics achievement. *Journal of Educational and Behavioral Statistics, 21,* 55–70.

Schul, Y., & Goren, H. (1997). When strong evidence has less impact than weak evidence: Bias, adjustment, and instructions to ignore. *Social Cognition, 15,* 133–155.

Schuller, R. A., & Cripps, J. (1998). Expert evidence pertaining to battered women: The impact of gender of expert and timing of testimony. *Law and Human Behavior, 22,* 17–31.

Schulz, D., Buddenberg, T., & Huston, J. P. (2007). Extinction-induced "despair" in the water maze, exploratory behavior and fear: Effects of chronic antidepressant treatment. *Neurobiology of Learning and Memory, 87,* 624–634.

Schwarz, N. (1999). Self-reports: How the questions shape the answers. *American Psychologist, 54,* 93–105.

Schwarz, N., Hippler, H. J., Deutsch, B., & Strack, F. (1985). Response categories: Effects on behavioral reports and comparative judgments. *Public Opinion Quarterly, 49,* 388–395.

Scientists should adopt codes of ethics, scientist-bioethicist says. (2007, February 5). Retrieved May 31, 2007, from http://www.sciencedaily.com/releases/2007/02/070201144615.htm

Scriven, M., & Paul, R. (2007). Defining critical thinking. Retrieved March 19, 2008, from http://www.criticalthinking.org/aboutCT/define_critical_thinking.cfm

Sechrist, G. B., & Stangor, C. (2001). Perceived consensus influences intergroup behavior and stereotype accessibility. *Journal of Personality & Social Psychology, 80,* 645–654.

Segall, M. H., Campbell, D. T., & Herskovits, M. J. (1966). *The influence of culture on visual perception.* Indianapolis, IN: Bobbs-Merrill.

Segall, M. H., Lonner, W. J., & Berry, J. W. (1998). Cross-cultural psychology as a scholarly discipline: On the flowering of culture in behavioral research. *American Psychologist, 53,* 1101–1110.

Seiffge-Krenke, I., Bosma, H., Chau, C., Çok, F., Gillespie, C., Loncaric, D., et al. (2010). All they need is love? Placing romantic stress in the context of other stressors: A 17-nation study. *International Journal of Behavioral Development, 3,* 106–112. doi:10.1177/0165025409360290

Selten, J.-P., Veen, N., Feller, W., Blom, J. D., Schols, D., Camoeni`, W., et al. (2001). Incidence of psychotic disorders in immigrant groups to the Netherlands. *British Journal of Psychiatry, 178,* 367–372.

Shannon, E. R., Neibling, B. C., & Heckert, T. M. (1999). Sources of stress among college students. *College Student Journal, 33,* 312–317.

Sharma, A., Prabha, C., & Malhotra, D. (2009). Perceived sex role and fear of success in depression of working women. *Journal Of The Indian Academy Of Applied Psychology, 35*(2), 251–256. Retrieved from PsycINFO September 3, 2012.

Shayer, M., & Ginsburg, D. (2009).Thirty years on—a large anti-Flynn effect? (II): 13-and 14-year-olds. Piagetian tests of formal operations norms 1976-2006/7.

British Journal of Educational Psychology, 79, 409–418. doi:10.1348/978185408X383123

Sher, K. J., Wood, M. D., Wood, P. K., & Raskin, G. (1996). Alcohol outcome expectancies and alcohol use: A latent variable cross-lagged panel study. *Journal of Abnormal Psychology, 105,* 561–574.

Shields, A. E., Fortun, M., Hammonds, E. M., King, P. A., Lerman, C., Rapp, R., & Sullivan, P. F. (2005). The use of race variables in genetic studies of complex traits and the goal of reducing health disparities: A transdisciplinary perspective. *American Psychologist, 60,* 77–103. doi:10.1037/0003-066X.60.1.77

Shih, T-H., & Fan, X. (2008).Comparing response rates from Web and mail surveys: A meta-analysis. *Field Methods, 20,* 249–271. doi:10.1177/1525822X08317085

Shulruf, B., Hattie, J., & Dixon, R. (2008). Factors affecting responses to Likert type questionnaires: Introduction of the ImpExp, a new comprehensive model. *Social Psychology of Education, 11,* 59–78. doi:10.1007/s11218-007-9035-x

Simonsohn, U. (2011). Lessons from an "oops" at Consumer Reports: Consumers follow experts and ignore invalid information. *Journal of Marketing Research, 48,* 1–12. doi:10.1509/jmkr.48.1.1

Simpson, S., Bell, L., Britton, P., Mitchell, M., Morrow, M., Johnston, A. L., & Brebner, J. (2006). Does video therapy work? A single case series of bulimic disorders. *European Eating Disorders Review, 14,* 226–241.

Sinclair, R. C., Moore, S. E., Mark, M. M., Soldat, A. S., & Lavis, C. A. (2010). Incidental moods, source likeability, and persuasion: Liking motivates message elaboration in happy people. *Cognition and Emotion, 24,* 940–961.

Singer, B., & Benassi, V. A. (1981, Winter). Fooling some of the people all of the time. *Skeptical Inquirer, 5,* 17–24.

Singer, E., Von Thurn, D. R., & Miller, E. R. (1995). Confidentiality assurances and survey response: A review of the experimental literature. *Public Opinion Quarterly, 59,* 266–277.

Singh, S. (1999). *The code book: The evolution of secrecy from Mary Queen of Scots to quantum cryptography.* New York: Doubleday.

Smith, C. S., Reilly, C., & Midkiff, K. (1989). Evaluation of three circadian rhythm questionnaires with suggestions for an improved measure of morningness. *Journal of Applied Psychology, 74,* 728–739.

Smith, G. T., Spillane, N. S., & Annus, A. M. (2006). Implications of an emerging integration of universal and culturally specific psychologies. *Perspectives on Psychological Science, 1,* 211–233. doi:10.1111/j.1745-6916.2006.00013.x

Smith, J. A. (1997). Developing theory from case studies: Self-reconstruction and the transition to motherhood. In N. Hayes (Ed.), *Doing qualitative analysis in psychology.* Hove, East Sussex, UK: Psychology Press.

Smyth, J. D., Dillman, D. A., Christian, L., & McBride, M. (2009). Open-ended questions in web surveys: Can increasing the size of answer boxes and providing extra verbal instructions improve response quality? *Public Opinion Quarterly, 73,* 325–337. doi:10.1093/poq/nfp029

Snowden, P. L., & Christian, L. G. (1999). Parenting the young gifted child: Supportive behaviors. *Roeper Review, 21,* 221.

Sockloff, A. L. (1975). Behavior of the product-moment correlation coefficient when two heterogeneous subgroups are pooled. *Educational and Psychological Measurement, 35,* 267–276.

Soliday, E., & Stanton, A. L. (1995). Deceived versus nondeceived participants' perceptions of scientific and applied psychology. *Ethics and Behavior, 5,* 87–104.

Sommers, S. R., & Ellsworth, P. C. (2001). White juror bias: An investigation of prejudice against black defendants in the American courtroom. *Psychology, Public Policy, and Law, 7,* 201–229.

Soto, J. A., Perez, C. R., Kim, Y., Lee, E. A., & Minnick, M. R. (2011). Is expressive suppression always associated with poorer psychological functioning? A cross-cultural comparison between European Americans and Hong Kong Chinese. *Emotion, 11,* 1450–1455. doi:10.1037/a0023340

Spear, J. H. (2007). Prominent schools or other active specialties?A fresh look at some trends in psychology. *Review of General Psychology, 11,* 363–380. doi:10.1037/1089-2680.11.4.363

Spencer, S. J., Steele, C. M., & Quinn, D. M. (1999). Stereotype threat and women's math performance. *Journal of Experimental Social Psychology, 35,* 4–28.

Stapel, D. A., & Lindenberg, S. (2011). Coping with chaos: How disordered contexts promote stereotyping and discrimination. *Science, 332,* 251–253. doi:10.1126/science.1201068

Steblay, N. M., Dysart, J., Fulero, S., & Lindsay, R. C. L. (2001). Eyewitness accuracy rates in sequential and simultaneous lineup presentations: A meta-analytic comparison. *Law and Human Behavior, 25,* 459–474.

Steele, C. M., & Aronson, J. (1995). Stereotype threat and the intellectual test performance of African Americans. *Journal of Personality and Social Psychology, 69,* 797–811.

Steele, K. M., Bass, K. E., & Crook, M. D. (1999). The mystery of the Mozart effect: Failure to replicate. *Psychological Science, 10,* 366–369

Steer, R. A., Rissmiller, D. J., & Beck, A. T. (2000). Use of Beck Depression Inventory-II with depressed geriatric inpatients. *Behaviour Research & Therapy, 38,* 311–318.

Steer, R. A., Rissmiller, D. J., Ranieri, W. F., & Beck, A. T. (1994). Use of the computer-administered Beck Depression Inventory and Hopelessness Scale with psychiatric inpatients. *Computers in Human Behavior, 10,* 223–229.

Steinberg, N., Tooney, N., Sutton, C., & Denmark, F. (2000, May/June). [Letter to the editor.] *The Sciences, 40,* 3.

Sternberg, R. J. (1985). *Beyond IQ: A triarchic theory of human intelligence*. New York: Cambridge University Press.

Sternberg, R. J. (1999). A triarchic approach to the understanding and assessment of intelligence in multicultural populations. *Journal of School Psychology, 37*, 145–159.

Sternberg, R. J., Grigorenko, E. L., & Kidd, K. K. (2005). Intelligence, race, and genetics. *American Psychologist, 60*, 46–59.

Stevens, J. C., Cruz, L. A., Hoffman, J. M., & Patterson, M. Q. (1995). Taste sensitivity and aging: High incidence of decline revealed by repeated threshold measures. *Chemical Senses, 20*, 451–459.

Stevens, S. S. (1946). On the theory of scales of measurement, *Science, 103*, 677–680.

Stevens, S. S. (1951). Mathematics, measurement, and psychophysics. In S. S. Stevens (Ed.), *Handbook of experimental psychology*. New York: Wiley.

Stiles, D. A., Gibbons, J. L., & Schnellman, J. D. (1990). Opposite-sex ideal in the U.S.A. and Mexico as perceived by young adolescents. *Journal of Cross-Cultural Psychology, 21*, 180–199.

Stokes, S. J., & Bikman, L. (1974).The effect of the physical attractiveness and role of the helper on help seeking. *Journal of Applied Social Psychology, 4*, 286–294.

Stolzenberg, L., & D'Alessio, S. J. (1997). "Three strikes and you're out": The impact of California's new mandatory sentencing law on serious crime rates. *Crime and Delinquency, 43*, 457–469.

Straus, M. A., Sugarman, D. B., & Giles-Sims, J. (1997). Spanking by parents and subsequent antisocial behavior of children. *Archives of Pediatrics and Adolescent Medicine, 151*, 761–767.

Strayer, D. L., & Johnston, W. A. (2001). Driven to distraction: Dual-task studies of simulated driving and conversing on a cellular telephone. *Psychological Science, 12*, 462–466

Strayer, D. L., Drews, F. A., & Crouch, D. J. (2006). A comparison of the cell phone driver and the drunk driver. *Human Factors, 48*, 381–391.

Strayer, D. L., Drews, F. A., & Johnston, W. A. (2003). Cell phone-induced failures of visual attention during simulated driving. *Journal of Experimental Psychology: Applied, 9*, 23–32.

Strober, M., Freeman, R., Lampter, C., Diamond, J., & Kaye, W. (2001). Males with anorexia nervosa: A controlled study of eating disorders in first-degree relatives. *International Journal of Eating Disorders, 29*, 263–269.

Strohmetz, D. B., & Moore, M. P. (2003, March). Impact of a tattoo on a helping request. Poster presented at the annual convention of the Eastern Psychological Association, Baltimore, MD.

Sue, S. (1999). Science, ethnicity, and bias: Where have we gone wrong? *American Psychologist, 54*, 1070–1077.

Sundblom, D. M., Haikonen, S., Niemi-Pynttaeri, J., & Tigerstedt, I. (1994). Effect of spiritual healing on chronic idiopathic pain: A medical and psychological study. *Clinical Journal of Pain, 10*, 296–302.

Swaddle, J. P., Cathey, M. G., Correll, M., & Hodkinson, B. P. (2005). Socially transmitted mate preferences in a monogamous bird: A non-genetic mechanism of sexual selection. *Proceedings of the Royal Society B, 272*, 1053–1058.

Swami, V., Stieger, S., Pietschnig, J., Nader, I. W., & Voracek, M. (2011). Using more than 10% of our brains: Examining belief in science-related myths from an individual differences perspective. *Learning and Individual Differences*. Advance online publication. doi:10.1016/j.lindif.2011.12.005

Takooshian, H., & O'Connor, P. J. (1984). When apathy leads to tragedy: Two Fordham professors examine "Bad Samaritanism." *Social Action and the Law, 10*, 26–27.

Tang-Martínez, Z., & Mechanic, M. (2000, May/June). [Letter to the editor.] *The Sciences, 40*, 5–6.

Tapper, K., & Boulton, M. J. (2002). Studying aggression in school children: The use of a wireless microphone and micro-video camera. *Aggressive Behavior, 28*, 356–365.

Taylor, S. J., & Bogdan, R. (1998). *Introduction to qualitative research methods*. New York: Wiley.

Teasdale, T. W., & Owen, D. R. (2005). A long-term rise and recent decline in intelligence test performance: The Flynn Effect in reverse. *Personality and Individual Differences, 39*, 837–843. doi:10.1016/j.paid.2005.01.029

Teeter, P. A., & Smith, P. L. (1989). Cognitive processing strategies for normal and LD children: A comparison of the K-ABC and microcomputer experiments. *Archives of Clinical Neuropsychology, 4*, 45–61.

The Mother's Encyclopedia. (1942). Vol. 5, New York: The Parents' Institute.

The NIMH Multisite HIV Prevention Trial: Reducing HIV sexual risk behavior. (1998). *Science, 280*, 1889–1894.

The score: Teens highly engaged online. (2006, March 16). Retrieved July 27, 2007, from http://www. imediaconnection.com/content/8691.asp

Thompson, J. K., & Heinberg, L. J. (1999). The media's influence on body image disturbance and eating disorders: We've reviled them, now can we rehabilitate them? *Journal of Social Issues, 55*, 339–353.

Thompson, J. K., & Stice, E. (2001). Thin-ideal internalization: Mounting evidence for a new risk factor for body-image disturbance and eating pathology. *Current Directions in Psychological Science, 10*, 181–183.

Thompson, W. F., Schellenberg, E. G., & Husain, G. (2001). Arousal, mood, and the Mozart effect. *Psychological Science, 12*, 248–251.

Thornhill, R., & Palmer, C. T. (2000). Why men rape. *The Sciences, 40*, 30–36.

Thorson, J. A., & Powell, F. C. (1993). Development and validation of a multidimensional sense of humor scale. *Journal of Clinical Psychology, 49*, 13–23.

Three strikes law fails to reduce crime. (2012, February 28). *Physorg.com.* Retrieved March 14, 2012, from http://www.physorg.com/news/2012-02-three-strikes-law-crime.html

Todorov, A. (2000). Context effects in national health surveys: Effects of preceding questions on reporting serous difficulty seeing and legal blindness. *Public Opinion Quarterly, 64,* 65–76.

Toepoel, V., & Dillman, D. A. (2011). Words, numbers, and visual heuristics in web surveys: Is there a hierarchy of importance? *Social Science Computer Review, 29,* 193–207. doi:10.1177/0894439310370070

Toepoel, V., Vis, C., Das, M., & van Soest, A. (2009). Design of Web questionnaires: An information-processing perspective for the effect of response categories. *Sociological Methods & Research, 37,* 371–392. doi:10.1177/0049124108327123

Traugott, M. W. (2005). The accuracy of the national preelection -olls in the 2004 presidential election. *Public Opinion Quarterly, 69,* 642–654. doi: 10.1093/poq/nfi061

Troisi, A. (1999). Ethological research in clinical psychiatry: The study of nonverbal behavior during interviews. *Neuroscience and Biobehavioral Reviews, 23,* 905–913.

Troisi, A. (2002). Displacement activities as a behavioral measure of stress in nonhuman primates and human subjects. Stress: *The International Journal on the Biology of Stress, 5,* 47–54. doi:10.1080/102538902900012378

Troisi, A., & Moles, A. (1999). Gender differences in depression: An ethological study of noverbal behavior during interviews. *Journal of Psychiatric Research, 33,* 243–350. doi:10.1016/S0022-3956(98)00064-8

Troisi, A., Pasini, A., Bersani, G., Di Mauro, M., & Ciani, N. (1991). Negative symptoms and visual behavior in DSM-III-R prognostic subtypes of schizophreniform disorder. *ActaPsychiatria Scandinavia, 83,* 391–394.

Troisi, A., Pompili, E., Binello, L., & Sterpone, A. (2007). Facial expressivity during the clinical interview as a predictor functional disability in schizophrenia: A pilot study. *Progress in Neuro-Psychopharmacology & Biological Psychiatry, 31,* 475–481.

Troisi, A., Spalletta, G., & Pasini, A. (1998). Non-verbal behavior deficits in schizophrenia: An ethological study of drug-free patients. *ActaPsychiatricaScandinavica, 97,* 109–115.

Trope, Y., & Fishbach, A. (2000). Counteractive self-control in overcoming temptation. *Journal of Personality and Social Psychology, 79,* 493–506.

Tsouderos, T., & Callahan, P. (2009, November 22). Risky alternative therapies for autism have little basis in science. Retrieved July 25, 2012 from http://www.chicagotribune.com/health/chi-autism-treatments-nov22,0,7095563,full.story

Underwood, B. J., & Freund, J. S. (1970). Word frequency and short-term recognition memory. *American Journal of Psychology, 83,* 343–351.

Unsworth, S. J., Levin, W., Bang, M., Washinawatok, K., Waxman, S. R., & Medin, D. L. (2012). Cultural differences in children's ecological reasoning and psychological closeness to nature: Evidence from Menominee and European American children. *Journal of Cognition and Culture, 12,* 17–29. doi:10.1163/156853712X633901

Uriell, Z. A., & Dudley, C. M. (2009). Sensitive topics: Are there modal differences? *Computers in Human Behavior, 25,* 76–87. doi:10.1016/j.chb.2008.06.007

Vadillo, M. A., Bárcena, R., & Matute, H. (2006). The internet as a research tool in the study of associative learning: An example from overshadowing [Electronic Version]. *Behavioural Processes, 73,* 36–40.

van de Vijver, F. R., & Leung, K. (2000). Methodological issues in psychological research on culture. *Journal of Cross-Cultural Psychology, 31,* 33–51. doi:10.1177/0022022100031001004

van IJzendoorn, M. H., & Sagi, A. (2001). Cultural blindness or selective inattention? *American Psychologist, 56,* 824–825. doi:10.1037/0003-066X.56.10.824

Varma, A. (2000). Impact of watching international television programs on adolescents in India. *Journal of Comparative Family Studies, 31,* 117–126.

Varvel, S. A., Wise, L. E., Niyuhire, F., Cravatt, B. F., & Lichtman, A. H. (2007). Inhibition of fatty-acid amide hydrolase accelerates acquisition and extinction rates in a spatial memory task. *Neuropsychopharmacology, 32,* 1032–1041.

Vasalou, A., Joinson, A. N., & Courvoisier, D. (2010). Cultural differences, experience with social networks and the nature of "true commitment" in facebook. *International Journal of Human-Computer Studies,* doi:10.1016/j.ijhcs.2010.06.002

Vasquez, D. (2009, April 7). All wired up but not so happy about it. Retrieved from http://www.medialifemagazine.com:8080/artman2/publish/New_media_23/All_wired_up_but_not_so_happy_about_it.asp

Velleman, P. F., & Wilkinson, L. (1993). Nominal, ordinal, interval, and ratio typologies are misleading. *American Statistician, 47,* 65–72.

Velten, E. (1968). A laboratory task for induction of mood states. *Behaviour Research and Therapy, 6,* 473–482.

Velten, E., Jr. (1997). A laboratory task for induction of mood states. In S. Rachman (Ed.), *Best of behavior research and therapy* (pp. 73–82). New York: Pergamon/Elsevier Science.

Vermont youth risk behavior survey. (1995). Retrieved from http://healthvermont.gov/pubs/yrbs/yrbs_1995.pdf

Vermont Youth Risk Behavior Survey: Statewide Report. (1997). Retrieved August 3, 2007, from http://healthvermont.gov/pubs/yrbs/yrbs_1997.pdf

The 1999 Vermont youth risk behavior survey. (1999). Retrieved from http://healthvermont.gov/pubs/yrbs/YRBSST991.PDF

Vermont Youth Risk Behavior Survey: Statewide Report. (2001). Retrieved August 3, 2007, from http://healthvermont.gov/pubs/yrbs/yrbs_2001.pdf

Vermont Youth Risk Behavior Survey: Statewide Report. (2003). Retrieved August 24, 2012, from http://healthvermont.gov/adap/clearinghouse/yrbs_2003_report.pdf

Vermont youth risk behavior survey. (2005). Retrieved from http://healthvermont.gov/pubs/yrbs2005/2005yrbs.aspx

Vermont youth risk behavior survey. (2009). Retrieved from http://healthvermont.gov/pubs/yrbs2009/2009YouthRiskBehaviorSurvey.asp

Villiger, C., Niggli, A., Wandeler, C., & Kutzelmann, S. (2012). Does family make a difference? Mid-term effects of a school/home-based intervention program to enhance reading motivation. *Learning and Instruction, 22,* 79–91. doi:10.1016/j.learninstruc.2011.07.001

Vink, T., Hinney, A., Van Elburg, A. A., Van Goozen, S. H. M., Sandkuijl, L. A., Sinke, R. J., et al. (2001). Association between an agouti-related protein gene polymorphism and anorexia nervosa. *Molecular Psychiatry, 6,* 325–328.

Vispoel, W. P. (2000). Computerized versus paper-and-pencil assessment of self-concept: Score comparability and respondent preferences. *Measurement and Evaluation in Counseling and Development, 33,* 130–143.

Vispoel, W. P., & Forte Fast, E. E. (2000). Response biases and their relation to sex differences in multiple domains of self-concept. *Applied Measurement in Education, 13,* 79–97.

Vonesh, E. F. (1983). Efficiency of repeated measures design versus completely randomized designs based on multiple comparisons. *Communications in Statistics–Theory and Methods, 12,* 289–302.

Wadman, M. (2005). One in three scientists confesses to having sinned. *Nature, 435,* 718–719.

Wagle, A. C., Ho, L. W., Wagle, S. A., & Berrios, G. E. (2000). Psychometric behaviour of BDI in Alzheimer's disease patients with depression. *International Journal of Geriatric Psychiatry, 15,* 63–69.

Wainer, H. (1999). The most dangerous profession: A note on nonsampling error. *Psychological Methods, 4,* 250–256.

Waldo, C. R., Berdahl, J. L., & Fitzgerald, L. F. (1998). Are men sexually harassed? If so, by whom? *Law and Human Behavior, 22,* 59–79.

Walker, E. F., Grimes, K. E., Davis, D. M., & Smith, A. J. (1993). Childhood precursors of schizophrenia: Facial expression of emotion. *American Journal of Psychiatry, 150,* 1654–1660.

Wallace, W. P., Sawyer, T. J., & Robertson, L. C. (1979). Distractors in recall, distractor-free recognition, and the word-frequency effect. *American Journal of Psychology. 91,* 295–304.

Waller, G., Meyer, C., & van Hanswijck de Jonge, L. (2001). Early environmental influences on restrictive pathology among nonclinical females: The role of temperature at birth. *International Journal of Eating Disorders, 30,* 24–208.

Walsh, M., Hickey, C., & Duffy, J. (1999). Influence of item content and stereotype situation on gender differences in mathematical problem solving. *Sex Roles, 41,* 219–240.

Walsh, W. B. (1976). Disclosure of deception by debriefed subjects: Another look. *Psychological Reports, 38,* 783–786.

Wang, P. S., Gruber, M. J., Powers, R. E., Schoenbaum, M., Speier, A. H., Wells, K. B., & Kessler, R. C. (2007). Mental health service use among Hurricane Katrina survivors in the eight months after the disaster. *Psychiatric Services, 58,* 1403–1411.

Wann, D. L., & Wilson, A. M. (1999). Relationship between aesthetic motivation and preferences for aggressive and nonaggressive sports. *Perceptual & Motor Skills, 89,* 931–934.

Watkins, D., Mortazavi, S., & Trofimova, I. (2000). Independent and interdependent conceptions of self: An investigation of age, gender, and culture differences in importance and satisfaction ratings. *Cross-Cultural Research: The Journal of Comparative Social Science, 34,* 113–134.

Weber, N., Brewer, N., Wells, G. L., Semmler, C., & Keast, A. (2004). Eyewitness identification accuracy and response latency: The unruly 10–12 second rule. *Journal of Experimental Psychology: Applied, 10,* 139–147.

Weiser, B. (2012, July 19). New Jersey Court Issues Guidance for Juries About Reliability of Eyewitnesses. *New York Times.* Retrieved from http://www.nytimes.com/2012/07/20/nyregion/judges-must-warn-new-jersey-jurors-about-eyewitnesses-reliability.html

Wells, G. L., Memon, A., & Penrod, S. D. (2006). Eyewitness evidence: Improving its probative value. *Psychological Science in the Public Interest, 7,* 45–75.

Wells, G. L., & Quinlivan, D. S. (2009). Suggestive eyewitness identification procedures and the Supreme Court's reliability test in light of eyewitness science: 30 years later. *Law and Human Behavior, 33,* 1–24. doi:10.1007/s10979-008-9130-3

Wentland, E. J., & Smith, K. W. (1993). *Survey responses: An evaluation of their validity.* Boston, MA: Academic Press.

Westen, D. (1998). The scientific legacy of Sigmund Freud: Toward a psychodynamically informed psychological science. *Psychological Bulletin, 124,* 333–371.

What is plagiarism? (2010). Retrieved December 11, 2009, from http://wps.prenhall.com/hss_understand_plagiarism_1/0,6622,427065-,00.html

Why you should never walk and text: Distracted woman falls into shopping mall water fountain. (2011, January 18).

Mail Online. Retrieved from http://www.dailymail. co.uk/news/article-1347989/Girl-falls-mall-fountain-texting-Why-walk-text.html

Wigfield, A., & Guthrie, J. T. (1997). Relations of children's motivation for reading to the amount and breadth or their reading. *Journal of Educational Psychology, 89,* 420–432. doi:10.1037/0022-0663.89.3.420

Wilcox, R. R. (1998). How many discoveries have been lost by ignoring modern statistical methods? *American Psychologist, 53,* 300–314.

Wilkinson, L., & the Task Force on Statistical Inference. (1999). Statistical methods in psychology journals: Guidelines and explanations. *American Psychologist, 54,* 594–604.

Willimack, D. K., Schuman, H., Pennell, B-E., & Lepkowski, J. M. (1995). Effects of a prepaid nonmonetary incentive on response rates and response quality in a face-to-face survey. *Public Opinion Quarterly, 59,* 78–92.

Wilson, D. W. (1978). Helping behavior and physical attractiveness. *Journal of Social Psychology, 104,* 313–314.

Wimer, D. J., & Beins, B. C. (2000, August). Is this joke funny? Only if we say it is. Presented at the annual convention of the American Psychological Association. Washington, DC.

Wimer, D. J., & Beins, B. C. (2008). Expectations and perceived humor. *Humor: International Journal of Humor Studies, 21,* 347–363. doi:10.1515/HUMOR.2008.016

Winkielman, P., Knäuper, B., & Schwarz, N. (1998). Looking back at anger: Reference periods change the interpretation of (emotion) frequency questions. *Journal of Personality and Social Psychology, 75,* 719–728.

Wise, R. A., Gong, X., Safer, M. A., & Lee, Y. (2010). A comparison of Chinese judges' and US judges' knowledge and beliefs about eyewitness testimony. *Psychology, Crime & Law, 16,* 695–713.

Wise, R. A., & Safer, M. A. (2010). A comparison of what U.S. judges and students know and believe about eyewitness testimony. *Journal of Applied Social Psychology, 40,* 1400–1422. doi:10.1111/j.1559-1816. 2010.00623.x

Wrzesniewski, A., McCauley, C. R., Rozin, P., & Schwartz, B. (1997). Jobs, careers and callings: A tripartite categorization of people's relations to their work. *Journal of Research in Personality, 31,* 21–33. doi:10.1006/jrpe.1997.2162

Wu, N. H., & Kim, S. (2009). Chinese American adolescents' perceptions of the language brokering experience as a sense of burden and sense of efficacy. *Journal of Youth and Adolescence, 38,* 703–718. doi:10.1007/s10964-008-9379-3

Wutzke, S. E., Conigrave, K. M., Kogler, B. E., Saunders, J. B., & Hall, W. D. (2000). Longitudinal research: Methods for maximizing subject follow-up. *Drug and Alcohol Review, 19,* 159–163.

Yee, A. H., Fairchild, H. H., Weizmann, F., & Wyatt, G. E. (1993). Addressing psychology's problem with race. *American Psychologist, 48,* 1132–1140.

Yetter, G., & Capaccioli, K. (2010). Differences in responses to Web and paper surveys among school professionals. *Behavior Research Methods, 42,* 266–272. doi:10.3758/BRM.42.1.266

Yick, A. G. (2007). Role of culture and context: Ethical issues in research with Asian Americans and immigrants in intimate violence. *Journal of Family Violence, 22*(5), 277–285. doi:10.1007/s10896-007-9079-x

York, J., Nicholson, T., Minors, P., & Duncan, D. F. (1998). Stressful life events and loss of hair among adult women: A case-control study. *Psychological Reports, 82,* 1044–1046.

Zadnik, K., Jones, L. A., Irvin, B. C., Kleinstein, R. N., Manny, R. E., Shin, J. A., & Mutti, D. O. (2000). Vision: Myopia and ambient night-time lighting. *Nature, 404,* 143–144.

Zajonc, R. B. (1965). Social facilitation, *Science, 149,* 269–274.

Zeller, S., Lazovich, D., Forster, J., & Widome, R. (2006). Do adolescent indoor tanners exhibit dependency? *Journal of the American Academy of Dermatology, 54,* 589–596.

Zettle, R. D., & Houghton, L. L. (1998). The relationship between mathematics and social desirability as a function of gender. *College Student Journal, 32,* 81–86.

Zielinska, E. (2012, January 9). Wakefield sues for libel in Texas. *The New Scientist.* Retrieved January 31, 2012, from http://the-scientist.com/2012/01/09/wakefield-sues-for-libel-in-texas/

Zimbardo, P. G. (1973). On the ethics of intervention in human psychological research: With special reference to the Stanford prison experiment. *Cognition, 2,* 243–256.

Zimmerman, F. J., Christakis, D. A., & Meltzoff, A. N. (2007). Associations between media viewing and language development in children under age 2 years. *Journal of Pediatrics, 151,* 364–368. doi:10.1016/j.jpeds.2007.04.071

Zinner, D., Hindahl, J., & Schwibbe, M. (1997). Effects of temporal sampling patterns of all-occurrence recording in behavioural studies: Many short sampling periods are better than a few long ones. *Ethology, 103,* 236–246.

Zuckerman, M. (1990). Some dubious premises in research and theory on racial differences. *American Psychologist, 45,* 1297–1303.

Zusne, L., & Jones, W. H. (1989). *Anomalistic psychology: A study of magical thinking* (2nd ed.). Hillsdale, NJ: Erlbaum.

SUBJECT INDEX